Lecture Notes in Artificial Intelligence   11224

Subseries of Lecture Notes in Computer Science

More information about this series at http://www.springer.com/series/1244

Tim Miller · Nir Oren
Yuko Sakurai · Itsuki Noda
Bastin Tony Roy Savarimuthu
Tran Cao Son (Eds.)

PRIMA 2018: Principles and Practice of Multi-Agent Systems

21st International Conference
Tokyo, Japan, October 29 – November 2, 2018
Proceedings

 Springer

Editors
Tim Miller ⓘ
School of Computing and Information
Systems
University of Melbourne
Melbourne, Australia

Nir Oren ⓘ
Department of Computer Science
University of Aberdeen
Aberdeen, UK

Yuko Sakurai ⓘ
Artificial Intelligence Research Center
(AIRC)
National Institute of Advanced Industrial
Science and Technology (AIST)
Tokyo, Japan

Itsuki Noda ⓘ
Artificial Intelligence Research Center
(AIRC)
National Institute of Advanced Industrial
Science and Technology (AIST)
Tsukuba, Japan

Bastin Tony Roy Savarimuthu
University of Otago
Dunedin, New Zealand

Tran Cao Son
Computer Science Department
New Mexico State University
Las Cruces, USA

ISSN 0302-9743   ISSN 1611-3349   (electronic)
Lecture Notes in Artificial Intelligence
ISBN 978-3-030-03097-1   ISBN 978-3-030-03098-8   (eBook)
https://doi.org/10.1007/978-3-030-03098-8

Library of Congress Control Number: 2018958774

LNCS Sublibrary: SL7 – Artificial Intelligence

This Springer imprint is published by the registered company Springer Nature Switzerland AG
The registered company address is: Gewerbestrasse 11, 6330 Cham, Switzerland

Preface

Welcome to the proceedings of the 21st International Conference on Principles and Practice of Multi-Agent Systems (PRIMA 2018) held in Tokyo, Japan, from October 29 to November 2.

Originally started as a regional (Asia-Pacific) workshop in 1998, PRIMA has become one of the leading and most influential scientific conferences for research on multi-agent systems. Each year since 2009, PRIMA has brought together active researchers, developers, and practitioners from both academia and industry to showcase, share, and promote research in several domains, ranging from foundations of agent theory and engineering aspects of agent systems, to emerging interdisciplinary areas of agent-based research. PRIMA's previous editions were held in Nagoya, Japan (2009), Kolkata, India (2010), Wollongong, Australia (2011), Kuching, Malaysia (2012), Dunedin, New Zealand (2013), Gold Coast, Australia (2014), Bertinoro, Italy (2015), Phuket, Thailand (2016), and Nice, France (2017).

This year, we received 95 full paper submissions and eight short paper submissions from 24 countries, including seven papers submitted to the social science track, chaired by Michael Mäs. Each submission was carefully reviewed by three members of the Program Committee (PC) composed of 94 prominent world-class researchers. In addition, seven sub-reviewers were called upon to review submissions. The PC and senior PC (SPC) included researchers from 23 countries. The review period was followed by PC discussions moderated by SPC members. The PRIMA SPC has been part of the PRIMA reviewing scheme since 2010, and this year it included 17 members. At the end of the reviewing process, in addition to the technical reviews, authors received a summary meta-review by an SPC member.

PRIMA 2018 accepted 27 full papers (an acceptance rate of 28%) and 31 submissions were selected to appear as short papers. Two papers were accepted to be presented in the social science track. In total, 27 full papers and 30 short papers are included in the present proceedings. Papers accepted into the social science track were fast-tracked into the *Journal of Artificial Societies and Social Simulation*, and are not included in the present proceedings. In addition to the paper presentations and poster sessions, the conference also included four keynote talks: Prof. Manuela M. Veloso, Prof. Michael Luck, President Hideyuki Nakashima, and Associate Prof. Fujio Toriumi.

We would like to thank all individuals, institutions, and sponsors that supported PRIMA 2018. Mainly we thank the authors for submitting high-quality research papers, confirming PRIMA's reputation as a leading international conference in multi-agent systems. We are indebted to our PC and SPC members and additional reviewers for spending their valuable time by providing careful reviews and recommendations on the submissions, and for taking part in follow-up discussions. We thank the journal of *Autonomous Agents and Multi-Agent Systems* for agreeing to fast track selected papers. We also thank EasyChair for the use of their conference management system. Finally, we are very grateful to the sponsors who supported PRIMA financially, making the conference accessible to a larger number of delegates.

September 2018

Tim Miller
Nir Oren
Yuko Sakurai
Itsuki Noda
Bastin Tony Roy Savarimuthu
Tran Cao Son

Organization

General Chairs

Itsuki Noda	National Institute of Advanced Industrial Science and Technology, Japan
Bastin Tony Roy Savarimuthu	University of Otago, New Zealand
Tran Cao Son	New Mexico State University, USA

Program Chairs

Nir Oren	University of Aberdeen, UK
Tim Miller	University of Melbourne, Australia
Yuko Sakurai	National Institute of Advanced Industrial Science and Technology, Japan

Social Science Track Chair

Michael Mäs	University of Groningen, The Netherlands

Finance Chair

Taiki Todo	Kyushu University, Japan

Web Chair

Yuu Nakajima	Toho University, Japan

Publicity Chairs

Koichi Moriyama	Nagoya Institute of Technology, Japan
Quan Bai	Auckland University of Technology, New Zealand

Social Events Chair

Yuichi Sei	The University of Elecro-Communications, Japan

Sponsorships Chair

Fujio Toriumi	The University of Tokyo, Japan

Workshop Chairs

Kiyoshi Izumi	The University of Tokyo, Japan
Jiamou Liu	Auckland University, New Zealand
Hiroki Sakaji	The University of Tokyo, Japan
Takashi Shimada	The University of Tokyo, Japan
Hiroyasu Matsushima	The University of Tokyo, Japan

PRIMA Steering Committee

Aditya Ghose (Chair)	University of Wollongong, Australia
Takayuki Ito (Deputy Chair)	Nagoya Institute of Technology, Japan
Makoto Yokoo (Past Chair and Ex Officio Member)	Kyushu University, Japan
Abdul Sattar (Treasurer)	Griffith University, Australia
Guido Governatori	NICTA, Australia
Sandip Sen	University of Tulsa, USA
Toshiharu Sugawara	Waseda University, Japan
Iyad Rahwan	Masdar Institute of Science and Technology, United Arab Emirates
Wayne Wobcke	University of New South Wales, Australia
Frank Dignum	Utrecht University, The Netherlands
Martin Purvis	University of Otago, New Zealand
Guido Boella	University of Turin, Italy
Edith Elkind	University of Oxford, UK
Bastin Tony Roy Savarimuthu	University of Otago, New Zealand
Hoa Dam	University of Wollongong, Australia
Jeremy Pitt	Imperial College, UK
Yang Xu	University of Electronic Science and Technology, China
Jane Hsu	National Taiwan University, Taiwan
Andrea Omicini	University of Bologna, Italy
Qingliang Chen	Jinan University, Guangzhou, China
Paolo Torroni	University of Bologna, Italy
Serena Villata	Inria Sophia Antipolis, France
Katsutoshi Hirayama	Kobe University, Japan
Matteo Baldoni	University of Turin, Italy
Amit K. Chopra	Lancaster University, UK
Tran Cao Son	New Mexico State University, USA
Michael Mäs	University of Groningen, The Netherlands

Senior Program Committee

Bo An	Nanyang Technological University, Singapore
Matteo Baldoni	University of Turin, Italy
Rafael H. Bordini	PUCRS, Brazil
Amit Chopra	Lancaster University, UK
Mehdi Dastani	Utrecht University, The Netherlands
Paul Davidsson	Malmö University, Sweden
Yves Demazeau	CNRS, LIG, France
Sylvie Doutre	University of Toulouse 1, IRIT, France
Rino Falcone	Institute of Cognitive Sciences and Technologies-CNR, Italy
Nathan Griffiths	The University of Warwick, UK
Mingyu Guo	The University of Adelaide, Australia
Katsutoshi Hirayama	Kobe University, Japan
Michael Mäs	University of Groningen, The Netherlands
Toshiharu Sugawara	Waseda University, Japan
Paolo Torroni	University of Bologna, Italy
Makoto Yokoo	Kyushu University, Japan
Dengji Zhao	Shanghai Tech University, China

Program Committee

Yoosef Abushark	King Abdulaziz University, Saudi Arabia
Quan Bai	Auckland University of Technology, New Zealand
Stefano Balietti	Microsoft, USA
Nathanaël Barrot	Riken AIP, Kyushu University, Japan
Michelle Blom	The University of Melbourne, Australia
Olivier Boissier	Mines Saint-Etienne, Institut Henri Fayol, France
Qingliang Chen	Jinan University, China
Stefania Costantini	University of L'Aquila, Italy
Madalina Croitoru	LIRMM, University of Montpellier II, France
Célia Da Costa Pereira	Université Nice Sophia Anipolis, France
Dave De Jonge	Western Sydney University, Australia
Emir Demirović	The University of Melbourne, Australia
Nirmit Desai	IBM, USA
Paolo Felli	University of Nottingham, UK
Nicoletta Fornara	Università della Svizzera Italiana, Italy
Katsuhide Fujita	Tokyo University of Agriculture and Technology, Japan
Naoki Fukuta	Shizuoka University, Japan
The Anh Han	Teesside Univeresity, UK
Daisuke Hatano	RIKEN AIP, Japan
Hiromitsu Hattori	Ritsumeikan University, Japan
Andreas Herzig	CNRS, IRIT, University of Toulouse, France
Koen Hindriks	Delft University of Technology, The Netherlands
Reiko Hishiyama	Waseda University, Japan

Alice Toniolo	University of St. Andrews, UK
Hideaki Uchida	The University of Tokyo, Japan
Suguru Ueda	Saga University, Japan
Leon van der Torre	University of Luxembourg, Luxembourg
Wamberto Vasconcelos	University of Aberdeen, UK
Mor Vered	Bar-Ilan University, Israel
Serena Villata	CNRS, Laboratoire d'Informatique, Signaux et Systèmes de Sophia-Antipolis, France
Matt Webster	University of Liverpool, UK
Brendon J. Woodford	University of Otago, New Zealand
Nitin Yadav	The University of Melbourne, Australia
Shohei Yamane	Fujitsu Laboratories Ltd., Japan
William Yeoh	Washington University in St. Louis, USA
Thomas Ågotnes	University of Bergen, Norway

Additional Reviewers

Martin Berger
Giovanni Ciatto
Christopher-Eyk Hrabia
Yuxuan Hu

Jeehang Lee
Christian Rakow
Shiqing Wu

Contents

Economic Paradigms

Engineering Multi-agent Systems and Human-Agent Interaction

Logic and Reasoning

Short Papers

Agent-Based Modeling and Simulation

Modeling a Real-Case Situation of Egress Using BDI Agents with Emotions and Social Skills

Marion Valette[1,3], Benoit Gaudou[2,4(✉)], Dominique Longin[1],
and Patrick Taillandier[3]

[1] CNRS-IRIT, Paul Sabatier University, Toulouse, France
[2] University Toulouse 1 Capitole, UMR 5505 IRIT, CNRS, Toulouse, France
benoit.gaudou@ut-capitole.fr
[3] MIAT, INRA, Toulouse, France
[4] Sorbonne University, IRD, UMMISCO, 93143 Bondy, France

Abstract. To be realistic, evacuation simulations have to consider several aspects of the human psychology that affect their decision-making process. Among them we find social relationships and emotions like fear. The former has been proven to have a great influence on the outcomes of simulations as they modify the behaviour of agents to make them escape in groups. This phenomenon strongly affects the efficiency of the evacuation. The latter impacts the ways the people will try to escape, leading to adaptation and unplanned behaviour. This paper presents an evacuation model that includes cognition with a BDI architecture to represent the way agents do complex reasoning, social relationships and a modelling of fear. The model is applied to simulate the fire of the Rhode Island Station Nightclub in 2003. We shows that after calibration, the model enables to reproduce in a credible way the real event.

Keywords: BDI · Egress · Simulation · Social relationships
Emotions.

1 Introduction

In the domain of evacuation studies, it is almost impossible to make real-scale experiments. Indeed, the behaviour of the people involved in fire drills is different from the one they would have in real egress, as their physical integrity is not actually threatened. Besides, it is forbidden by ethics to perform experiments with humans without telling them what they participate in. This is why simulations are needed to help design better security policies. But in order to be used as scientific or decision-support tools, simulations involving humans have to be realist in terms of human evacuation behaviors and therefore consider and implement many aspects of their cognition, and in particular the factors that influence their decision-making process in emergency situation.

© Springer Nature Switzerland AG 2018
T. Miller et al. (Eds.): PRIMA 2018, LNAI 11224, pp. 3–18, 2018.
https://doi.org/10.1007/978-3-030-03098-8_1

This article introduces a model including cognition with a BDI architecture, social relationships and emotions and studies the relationships and interactions between them. This model, that is highly modular, enables to separately and simultaneously use these different aspects in order to control the complexity of the model. It uses the BDI (for Belief, Desire, Intention) [10,15] paradigm to model the cognition of agents and takes into account the social relationships between people and their emotions, particularly fear. The first level of social relationship taken into account by an agent is the group of close relationships: friends will first try to gather before evacuating together (one of the individuals becoming the leader and the other ones following him/her). The second level is related to gregarious and imitation behavior: in some specific situations, individuals can follow a crowd of unrelated people. In addition, the model allows the agents to adapt to the situation, for example by exiting in some extreme situations through windows instead of using the doors initially recognized as exits.

The model was implemented with the GAMA platform [12]. This open-source platform, which is dedicated to the development of simulation of agent-based models, allows to easily integrate spatial data such as building plans. In addition, it provides modelers with numerous primitive dedicated to agent movement, which greatly eases the development of pedestrian models. At last, it integrates a BDI architecture that includes several modules dedicated to social relationships, emotions and norms [6].

In order to illustrate how the model enables to reproduce in a credible way egress situation, we propose in this paper an application for the classic case-study of the evacuation of the Station Night club.

The paper is structured as follows. In Sect. 2, we further discuss the importance of the three aspects cited above. Section 3 describes the case study that is used to illustrate the model. In Sect. 4, we depict the model using the ODD protocol. Afterwards, in Sect. 5, the results of the simulation for the case study are presented. In Sect. 6, some scenarios are tested to show the influence of a few parameters.

2   State of the Art

Multiple simulations of emergency situations already exist. But places like office buildings and railway stations, whose evacuation has been largely studied, are mostly occupied by business people, who are familiar with the environment and disconnected from one another [18,24]. Some models only consider crowds without making any distinctions between agents, using for example model based on forces [20] or cellular automaton [4].

Buildings like airports [22] or nightclub in contrast bring together people who have no or little knowledge of their surroundings, and often who have strong social relationships. Therefore simulations of such places need to consider more aspects than just the individual movement of each person. Many models [9,11] have shown the importance of taking into account the social relationships that exist in groups, in particular in egress situations, as they have a great influence on the death toll and duration of the evacuation. People indeed tend to escape in groups, so they must look for their friends and relatives before reaching an exit, which considerably increases the evacuation time.

In addition, as it is recognized to be a key factor in egress situation, some focus on complex representations of emotions, for example based on the Orthony, Clore and Collins' theory [2,16,17]. But few models include all three aspects (differentiation of persons, social relationships and emotions) and thus the way they interact to drive the agent behavior.

Finally, to obtain realistic simulations, the complexity of human behaviour needs to be captured. Therefore cognition has to be implemented. For this purpose, different architectures such as the ones listed in [5] have been theorized and developed. The BDI architecture [7] has proven itself to be well adapted to model humans [1,3], as it is close to folk psychology and natural language. Several works such as [19] have already used this architecture to model the crowds during emergency evacuation, but without considering all the aspect mentioned above.

3   Case-Study: The Station Night Club Evacuation

The case-study we propose to use as a base to present our model concerns the fire of the Station Night club, located in Rhode Island (U.S.A), which burned on February 20, 2003 (see Fig. 1). This case study is that it has been studied extensively in the past and there is a lot of information on it allowing to validate the model proposed. The fire was triggered by the ignition of polyurethane foam on the walls and ceiling by pyrotechnics. The ignition points were located on the raised platform on the east side of the building (see Fig. 1). It spread rapidly, whereas a dense black toxic smoke filled the whole club. In less than 3 min, the flames were all over the place. The building was mainly made of wood and had no sprinklers. That night, the building hosted about 465 persons, more than the authorized limit, which led, despite a rapid intervention of the firemen, to a heavy human toll, with 100 deceased persons and 230 injured. People started to evacuate approximately 20 seconds after ignition, and most persons escaped during the first 150 seconds. There were four exits: the front door entrance or main entrance, the main bar exit, the kitchen exit, and the platform exit.

The platform exit was blocked by the staff who reserved it for the musicians and professionals. Besides, it became fast unreachable because of the spreading of the fire, which explains the low number of people who escaped through it. The kitchen door was also badly indicated and visible. The two remaining exits were fast blocked by the crowd, so some people started to look for alternatives, and broke the windows situated on the northern wall. About one third of the evacuees used that way to escape, one third went through the main entrance, and the last third split into the three other doors. The actual figures are summarized in Table 1. All real data come from El-Tawil *et al.* [11].

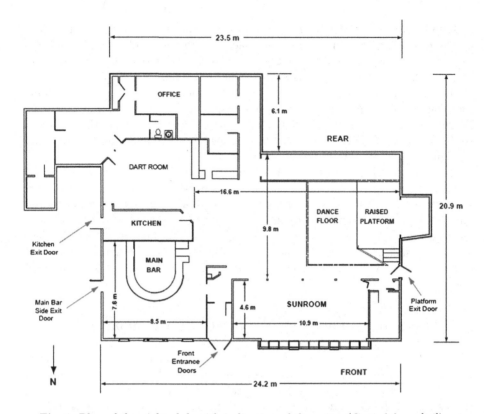

Fig. 1. Plan of the night club with indication of the exits (Copied from [14])

Table 1. Distribution of the people having evacuated through each exits

Main	Bar	Kitchen	Platform	Windows
128	78	17	24	105

4   Description of the Model

In the following, we describe the model using the ODD (Overview, Design concepts, and Details) protocol [13]. This is a standard protocol designed to describe individual-based and agent-based models, in order to make them more understandable.

4.1   Purpose of the Model

The purpose of this model is to simulate the evacuation of a building, in particular night-clubs, in order to evaluate the influence of emotions and social relationships [6,8] on the efficiency of the evacuation.

4.2   Entities, State Variables and Scales

This model includes several types of entities. Their most important variables and actions are presented in the class diagram shown in Fig. 2.

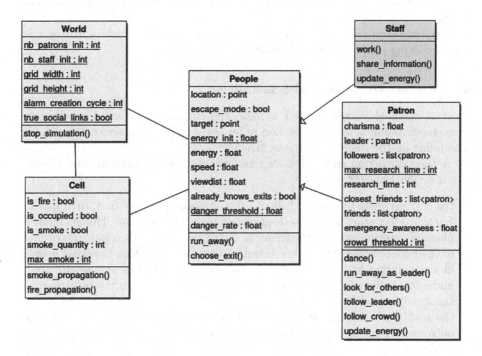

Fig. 2. Class diagram of the model

The key entities represent people agents. The People species contains all the attributes (target destination, speed, a set of known exits) and action (choose an exit and run away) related to the individual evacuation. It also includes the management of people emotions with *danger_rate*, which represents the fear emotion intensity, and *danger_threshold* attributes. The People species is specialized in two sub-types of agent: Staff and Patron.

Staff main objective is to help Patrons to evacuate the building by sharing information about exits. Patron agents add mainly the social components to the People agents: it adds the lists of close friends and of possible followers, a charisma value, used to determine the leader in a group of close friends, the maximum search time before leaving the place without the missing friends, a crowd threshold, used to determine when a patron stops to follow its leader to follow the patrons around him, and an emergency awareness, which characterizes the response time of an agent when it perceives the danger. In the following, unless specified, the term group refers to friends spatially close, when the expression friend group or social group refer to the whole social group of the agents, which can be physically divided. As far as actions are concerned, it introduces the capability to look for others or follow leaders.

Finally the building is discretized using a grid of Cells. These Cell agents are used to diffuse the fire and smoke. They are also used to help the computation of the shortest path to the exit chosen by each agent who is running away from the fire.

One time step represents one second, and the simulation lasts until there is no more living people inside the building.

4.3   Process Overview and Scheduling

As it is classical in agent-based models, the simulation is based on discrete time steps. As far as agent activation order is concerned, we rely on the default scheduling on the model underlying GAMA.

Actions during an simulation step are executed in the following order (each one is detailed in Sect. 4.7):

- the patrons are activated in their order of creation (patron 0 first, then patron 1, *etc.*). They start by the perceptions of their environment. This includes a phase of determination of the leader of each group. Then, they move according to their goals, which depend on their social relationships with the other people in the building and on personal characteristics. Their fear is modeled by a numerical value (danger rate) and a threshold, above which the behaviour of the agent is modified (valid also for the staff);
- the staff is activated, they perceive their environment. Then they help the patrons near them. If there is nobody or if their danger rate is too high, they run away;
- Every two time steps, the grid propagates the fire to the four neighbors of each cell in fire and at every iteration, it propagates the smoke to the eight neighbors of cells whose smoke density is greater than a given threshold. Here the cells are activated in a random order.

4.4   Design Concepts

Basic Principles. This model uses the BDI paradigm [10,15] to implement cognitive agents [23]. It relies on the BDI architecture implemented in GAMA, described in details in [8,21]. It is based on three sets: the belief base (what the agent believes to be true), the desire base (what it wants), and the intention base (what it is doing).

In our model, the beliefs are only used to model the knowledge about the exits. Each agent has the beliefs of the location of each exit it knows. The BDI architecture provides primitives to automatically create beliefs or desires from perceptions. When an agent perceives an exit by walking near it, this one is added to its belief base.

The desires of an agent depend on its species (patron or staff), its social relationships, or if it is a leader or not, *etc.* Each desire has a priority. The choice of an intention to fulfill among the existing desires is driven by theses priorities: when the agent has no intention, the desire with the highest priority becomes the intention. The agent will then execute the plan corresponding to its intention. If a new desire with higher priority arises, it can drop its intention to consider a new one.

To fulfill its intentions, the agent has a set of plans that will be executed if the activation condition (expressed in terms of intention) is fulfilled. In our model, the people agents have two plan: running away and choosing an exit. Patron agents have three additional plans: looking for their friends, following the leader, and following the crowd. At last staff agents have all the people agent plans and the plan to share information. All the plans are described in Sect. 4.7).

This architecture has the advantage to help the design of modular agents internal structure, separating clearly the perception and the actions, executed in plans. These two components are coupled through the various mental states of the agent.

Adaptation. The patrons have a danger rate, which allows them to change their behaviors when the close environment is changing. For example, when their danger rate becomes too high, they can change their target, and if it was an exit, it is no longer considered as a possible way out. They can also decide to break a window to go out quicker. This is a way to get out that was not planned at the origin for them.

Sensing. All agents have a view distance, within which they can perceive several things like the fire and the exits. Furthermore, each species of agents has specific perceptions. The staff can perceive the patrons to inform them of the exits. The patrons can perceive their friends and the patrons who are heading to a window. This perception can be interpreted as a capacity to imitate the behaviour of others. After this perception, the agent can indeed change its target to go to the window too. Moreover, the agents can hear the alarm.

Interaction. Two agents cannot be on the same cell, thus the movement of an agent will be impacted by the other agents. In addition, the patrons in a group interact via a leader/follower relationship, that is, a patron follows its leader but have no interaction with the other members of its group. Furthermore, the staff shares information about the exits with the patrons, to do so they give them the location of the exits. They also interact in order to tell others that they have to flee if they are not already aware of that.

Stochasticity. During the initialization, people are placed randomly in the available space. Their initial value of speed is randomly chosen between two realistic bounds, when their initial value of energy, their emergency awareness and their charisma are chosen between two arbitrary limits. Their danger threshold, maximum search time and crowd threshold are chosen in a range of values defined around the related global parameter[1].

During the simulation, the targets of patrons who are looking for their friends are random. In the case where the agent who wants to run away is stuck or in too much danger, the exit it will go to is randomly chosen among its known exits.

The cells of the grid are activated in a random order to simulate a more realistic propagation of the smoke and fire.

Observation. The model is observed through a 3D representation (see Fig. 3) of the building with visuals of the patrons, staff, fire, smoke. It is also possible to at every time step different information about the agents like their danger rate, *etc.*. There are also monitors which shows the number of dead, injured and safe and sound people, and the number of people who went out through each door.

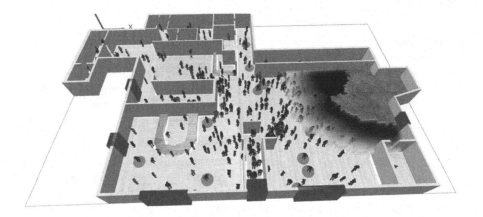

Fig. 3. 3D visualization of the simulation

4.5   Initialization

At the beginning of the simulation, all agents and variables are created and initialized. First the geometries (walls, bars, and exits) are built from shape file input data, then the grid is created. The initial number of patrons is created, the socials links are determined, based on real data [11], with the following rules: one agent can be a member of only one group of friends, and these friends are randomly selected among a list. This list is composed of all the persons close to the agent and of a few persons spatially further. At last, the staff is created, with one person located near the exit next to the raised platform (where the fire starts) to prevent patrons from using this door. At that moment, each patron is its own leader.

---

[1] These parameter values are computed in the calibration presented in Sect. 5.

The clients are in majority placed randomly in the dance floor, while the rest and the staff are randomly placed in the building. The staff knows all exits, while only a third of the patrons have already been there before and know three exits (the main one, the one near the main bar and the one near the raised platform). All other patrons only know the main entrance.

4.6   Input Data

The model uses *shape files*[2] to design the walls, bars, and exits. The model users have also to provide information about the human agents, such as their number and the distribution of the size of the social groups.

4.7   Sub-models

Smoke and Fire Spread. As the main goal of the model is to evaluate the impact of social behaviors on evacuation, we chose for this first version of the model to use simple smoke and fire diffusion models, but we plan to integrate more realistic models in the further.

Thus, in our model, every two time steps, each cell in fire propagates it to its four closest neighbours. The cells are activated in a random order to ensure a little bit of realism in the propagation. The Fig. 4 explains the beginning of this process. The number in each cell refers to the activation order, the cells in red are in fire.

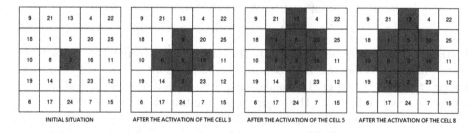

Fig. 4. Propagation of the fire

With regard to the smoke, the propagation principle is slightly different. Each cell has a smoke density, that can vary between 0 and a maximum quantity (here 100). At the beginning of the fire, we set the smoke density of the cells in fire and their neighbours to the maximum. To be able to propagate the fire, a cell has to have a density strictly greater than 1. Then the smoke propagates with the same pattern as the fire, except for the fact that it spreads to the eight neighbours. Each time the smoke propagates to a cell, its smoke density is increased by one.

---

[2] A shape file is a file format for geographical information systems, it contains all the information linked to the geometry of the described objects.

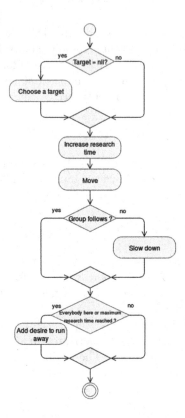

Fig. 5. Looking for others

Search. As soon as a patrons detects the danger, by perceiving the fire or the alarm, it starts to look for its group of friends. Since all patrons are their own leader at the beginning of the simulations, they all do the following: as long as the group is not complete or the maximum search time has not been reached, the leader looks for its friends. They remember where they have seen their friends for the last time, so their first targets are those locations. If during their moves, friends find each other, a leader is determined from their charisma, except in the case where a friend alone finds a group already formed, here the leader of the group stays leader (cf. Fig. 5).

Evacuation.

Run Away. Leaders and persons alone who want to run away first choose a target. To this end, if they are not in danger, they choose the closest exit among their known doors. Otherwise they choose a random one. They can choose a new target if the danger becomes too important. If their danger rate is higher than their respective thresholds or if at least one of the windows is broken, they can choose to exit through the window. Then they move towards that target, and when they reach it, they are removed from the simulation.

Follow Leader. The others patrons follow their leader when it looks for others or toward an exit. Therefore, they move on a cell near the one of the leader. If their leader dies, they have the desire to keep looking for other friends.

Follow the Crowd. When a follower is too far from its leader, and surrounded by more people than its crowd threshold patrons, it begins to follow them. That means that its heading is the mean of the heading of the costumers around him. If the number of patrons near him becomes less than the half of the threshold, the agent changes its intention to look for others.

Updates of Attributes.

Speed. The speed is updated according to the level of energy of the agent through the following formula:

$$speed = \begin{cases} speed\_init & \text{if } energy > 0.8 * energy\_init \\ speed\_init * \frac{energy}{0.8 * energy\_init} & \text{else} \end{cases}$$

In addition, for the leader, it also depends on whether the others are following it or not. If the group that follows the leader is not physically close enough to it, the speed of the leader will correspond to the minimum between the value computed from the previous formula and the min of the follower speeds divided by two.

Danger rate. The danger rate is computed from the mean of smoke density (normalized by the maximum quantity) in the cells visible for the agent (VC) with the following formula:

$$danger\_rate = \frac{energy\_init}{energy} * \frac{\sum_{c \in VC} \frac{smoke\_quantity_c}{max\_smoke}}{\#(VC)}$$

where $smoke\_quantity_c$ is the smoke quantity of the visible cell c. Thus, it increases when the agent looses energy and is surrounded by a high quantity of smoke.

Energy. Each agent who is located on a cell on fire looses 2 points of energy. If it is on a cell c with smoke, it looses $1.5 * \frac{smoke\_quantity_c}{max\_smoke}$ points of energy. These numerical values are a simplification of the rules described in [11].

Share Information. The staff can inform the clients near them about all the exits of the building. Moreover, if the patron knows the exit near the stage, they forbid him to use it, as it is considered to be reserved for the musicians and staff.

5   Results

The model was applied to the case study of the Rhode Island Station Nightclub. For that, we digitized the nightclub plan as shapefiles. We used the data provided by [11] to initialize the human agents and the real values for the time of the alarm triggering (30 s) and the initial number of staff members (10) parameters.

To make the model closer to the reality, we calibrated it using a genetic algorithm. Three parameters were concerned by this calibration: the fear threshold, the crowd threshold (the limit of people around a follower which makes him start to follow the crowd instead of its leader) and the maximum search time (in seconds). These parameters are used to initialize the related attributes for each agent: the value of their attribute corresponds to a random value choice around the parameter value. We run 4 replications for each parameter value set. The final parameter set is given in Table 2. The fitness function used for the calibration was computed from following indicators: the numbers of deceased people, of injured people, of safe and sound people, and the numbers of people who exited through each exit, including the windows.

Table 2. Parameters of the base case

	Danger threshold	Crowd threshold	Maximum search time
Minimum	0.3	15	10
Maximum	0.6	35	15

Table 3 shows the results obtained with this parameter sets. The results are close to the real ones. However, as shown by the high value of the standard deviation, the simulation results vary a lot from one to another.

Table 3. Comparison between reality and simulations (mean on 1120 runs)

		Deceased	Injured	Main exit	Windows
Reality		100	230	128	105
Simulation	Mean	121	202	161	112
	Std	22	17	49	51

6   Scenario

We first tested two scenarios to show the influence of the emotions and of social relationships, before testing the impact of the number of staff members and of the environment awareness.

6.1   Scenario 1: Influence of Emotions

As a first experiment, named Scenario 1, we remove the fear from the simulation. We observe more deceased people, which can be explained by the fact that they tend, without the effect of the fear, to stay longer in the toxic smoke. Furthermore, as the decision to escape through a window is triggered by fear, the number of people exiting this way falls to zero. More people used the main entrance and the others values do not significantly change (see Table 4 where the results of the Scenario 1 are compared to the Base Case, corresponding to the results after the calibration).

Table 4. Comparison between the calibrated results (Base Case) and the results of the Scenario 1, where emotions do not have any effect on the behaviour (in number of people, mean over 764 runs for the tested case)

	Deceased	Safe	Injured	Main exit	Windows
Base case	121	132	202	161	112
Scenario 1	158	133	164	230	0

6.2   Scenario 2: Influence of Social Relationships

In a second experiment, called scenario 2, we tested the influence of social relationships by removing them. We obtain the results summed up in Table 5. The result shows that the number of casualties has drastically diminished, since the patrons go right away to the exits. They tend to exit more by the main entrance and the windows as they are the closest from the dance floor.

Table 5. Comparison between the calibrated results (Base Case) and the results of the Scenario 2, where Patrons do not have any social relationships (in number of people, mean over 596 runs for the tested case)

	Deceased	Safe	Injured	Main exit	Windows
Base case	121	132	202	161	112
Scenario 2	28	234	193	208	181

6.3   Scenario 3: Adding Staff

We progressively increase the staff member number to see if they can help to decrease the casualties by giving information about unsaturated exits. Therefore we run the simulations with respectively 10 (normal case), 30 and 50 staff members. As this makes the total number of persons in the club vary, the results are the proportion (in percentage) of persons deceased, injured, safe and sound and through each exit. Table 6 shows that the proportions of people who escape safely increases as the proportion of injured people decreases. But as the standard deviations for those results are respectively around 25 (deceased), 18 (safe) and 18 (injured), the observed variations are too small to be significant. Fewer people leave through the main exit and more through the kitchen and bar ones, as more people know them thanks to the staff. Consequently, the proportion of people who go out through the windows decreases.

Table 6. Proportions' evolution with the number of staff members (in percentage)

Staff members	Deceased	Safe	Injured	Bar exit	Main exit	Windows
10	26.6	29.0	44.4	8.7	35.5	24.7
30	27.0	30.1	42.9	10.8	33.5	23.4
50	27.1	31.1	41.8	12.5	32.9	22.0

6.4   Scenario 4: More Environment Awareness

We carried out a last experiment to evaluate the sensibility of the simulation results to the variation of the awareness parameter around the solution found though calibration. This corresponds to evaluate the impact of providing more information to the patrons about the club. We ran simulations with respectively 33% of people who knows several exits (normal case, obtained after calibration), 66% and 100%. Table 7 shows that the number (or proportion as the initial number of persons inside is constant) of injured costumers remains constant, whereas the number of deceased people increases slightly. The numbers of people exiting through the kitchen's and scene's exits raise and the one through the bar's and main exit fall. Regarding the windows, the numbers are roughly constant.

Table 7. Proportions' evolution with environment awareness (in percentage)

Awareness	Deceased	Injured	Bar exit	Kitchen exit	Main exit	Windows
33%	26.6	44.4	8.7	4.2	35.5	24.7
66%	27.6	44.6	6.2	6.2	34.8	24.6
100%	28.6	44.7	3.6	8.2	33.4	25.6

As the variations are really small, we can conclude that the awareness does not have influence on the simulation, around the solution found by the calibration.

7   Conclusion

In this paper, we described an evacuation model which includes three main features: a BDI architecture, social relationships and emotions, implemented with the GAMA agent-based modeling and simulation platform. The model has been apply to reproduce the event that occurred at the Station Nightclub. After calibration, the model has allowed to reflect the reality of the case study, which allowed us to test different scenarios. These experiments showed the importance of taking into account the emotions and social relationships in that type of model as they profoundly influence the outcomes of the simulation.

With this model, we are facing a classical issue when we want to reproduce some extreme event: we only have a single data set to calibrate on, which can restrict the generic aspect of the model and produce simulation results with a large variability. Future search will thus invest new methods of calibration dedicated to this issue.

To improve the credibility of the model, we plan as well to integrate in the further more realist models of fire and smoke propagation. To this purpose, we are currently working on a module dedicated to the importation of 3D BIM (Building Information Modeling) data-models. These data-models are nowadays a standard for describing buildings in civil engineering and architecture, and will allow us to directly reuse realist fire and smoke propagation models.

Acknowledgment. This work is supported by the ANR ACTEUR project.

References

1. Adam, C., Gaudou, B.: BDI agents in social simulations: a survey. Knowl. Eng. Rev. **31**(3), 207–238 (2016)
2. Adam, C., Herzig, A., Longin, D.: A logical formalization of the OCC theory of emotions. Synthese **168**(2), 201–248 (2009)
3. Adam, C., Taillandier, P., Dugdale, J.: Comparing agent architectures in social simulation: BDI agents versus finite-state machines. In: HICSS (2017)
4. Alizadeh, R.: A dynamic cellular automaton model for evacuation process with obstacles. Saf. Sci. **49**(2), 315–323 (2011)
5. Balke, T., Gilbert, N.: How do agents make decisions? A survey. J. Artif. Soc. Soc. Simul. **17**(4), 13 (2014)
6. Bourgais, M., Taillandier, P., Vercouter, L.: Enhancing the behavior of agents in social simulations with emotions and social relations. In: Dimuro, G.P., Antunes, L. (eds.) MABS 2017. LNCS (LNAI), vol. 10798, pp. 89–104. Springer, Cham (2018). https://doi.org/10.1007/978-3-319-91587-6_7
7. Bratman, M.: Intention, Plans, and Practical Reason. Center for the Study of Language and Information (1987)
8. Caillou, P., Gaudou, B., Grignard, A., Truong, C.Q., Taillandier, P.: A simple-to-use BDI architecture for agent-based modeling and simulation. In: Jager, W., Verbrugge, R., Flache, A., de Roo, G., Hoogduin, L., Hemelrijk, C. (eds.) Advances in Social Simulation 2015. AISC, vol. 528, pp. 15–28. Springer, Cham (2017). https://doi.org/10.1007/978-3-319-47253-9_2

9. Chu, M.L., Parigi, P., Law, K.H., Latombe, J.-C.: Simulating individual, group, and crowd behaviors in building egress. Simulation **91**(9), 825–845 (2015)
10. Cohen, P.R., Levesque, H.J.: Intention is choice with commitment. Artif. Intell. J. **42**(2–3), 213–261 (1990)
11. El-Tawil, S., Fang, J., Aguirre, B., Best, E.: A computational study of the station nightclub fire accounting for social relationships. JASSS **20**(4), 10 (2017)
12. Grignard, A., Taillandier, P., Gaudou, B., Vo, D.A., Huynh, N.Q., Drogoul, A.: GAMA 1.6: advancing the art of complex agent-based modeling and simulation. In: Boella, G., Elkind, E., Savarimuthu, B.T.R., Dignum, F., Purvis, M.K. (eds.) PRIMA 2013. LNCS (LNAI), vol. 8291, pp. 117–131. Springer, Heidelberg (2013). https://doi.org/10.1007/978-3-642-44927-7_9
13. Grimm, V., Berger, U., DeAngelis, D.L., Polhill, J.G., Giske, J., Railsback, S.F.: The ODD protocol: a review and first update. Ecol. Model. **221**(23), 2760–2768 (2010)
14. Grosshandler, W.L., Bryner, N., Madrzykowski, D., Kuntz, K.: Report of the technical investigation of the station nightclub fire. Technical report 2, National Construction Safety Team Act Reports (NIST NCSTAR) (2005)
15. Herzig, A., Longin, D.: C&L intention revisited. In: Dubois, D., Welty, C., Williams, M.-A., (eds.) KR 2004, Whistler, Canada, 2–5 June, pp. 527–535. AAAI Press (2004)
16. Lorini, E., Longin, D., Mayor, E.: A logical analysis of responsibility attribution: emotions, individuals and collectives. J. Log. Comput. **24**(6), 1313–1339 (2014)
17. Ortony, A., Clore, G.L., Collins, A.: The Cognitive Structure of Emotions. Cambridge University Press, Cambridge (1990)
18. Shen, T.-S.: ESM: a building evacuation simulation model. Build. Environ. **40**(5), 671–680 (2005)
19. Shendarkar, A., Vasudevan, K., Lee, S., Son, Y.-J.: Crowd simulation for emergency response using BDI agents based on immersive virtual reality. Simul. Model. Pract. Theory **16**(9), 1415–1429 (2008)
20. Song, W., Xuan, X., Wang, B.-H., Ni, S.: Simulation of evacuation processes using a multi-grid model for pedestrian dynamics. Phys. A: Stat. Mech. Its Appl. **363**(2), 492–500 (2006)
21. Taillandier, P., Bourgais, M., Caillou, P., Adam, C., Gaudou, B.: A BDI agent architecture for the GAMA modeling and simulation platform. In: Nardin, L.G., Antunes, L. (eds.) MABS 2016. LNCS (LNAI), vol. 10399, pp. 3–23. Springer, Cham (2017). https://doi.org/10.1007/978-3-319-67477-3_1
22. Tsai, J., et al.: ESCAPES: evacuation simulation with children, authorities, parents, emotions, and social comparison. In: AAMAS, Richland, SC, pp. 457–464 (2011)
23. Wooldridge, M.: Reasoning about Rational Agents. MIT Press, Cambridge (2000)
24. Yuan, J.P., Fang, Z., Wang, Y.C., Lo, S.M., Wang, P.: Integrated network approach of evacuation simulation for large complex buildings. Fire Saf. J. **44**(2), 266–275 (2009)

Discovering Emergent Agent Behaviour with Evolutionary Finite State Machines

Martin Masek[1], Chiou Peng Lam[1], Lyndon Benke[2]([⊠]), Luke Kelly[1], and Michael Papasimeon[2]([⊠])

[1] School of Science, Edith Cowan University, Perth, Australia
[2] Defence Science and Technology Group, Melbourne, Australia
{lyndon.benke,michael.papasimeon}@dst.defence.gov.au

Abstract. In this paper we introduce a novel approach to discovering emergent behaviour in multiagent simulations, using evolutionary finite state machines to model intelligent agents in an adversarial two-player game. Agent behaviour is modelled as a finite set of predetermined states. The logic that leads to transitions between states is evolved to maximise fitness, which is determined through execution in a constructive simulation environment. The resultant evolved finite state machine (E-FSM) is evaluated for two finite state machine implementations, one with states specifically designed to perform a known behaviour and the other with states consisting of generic actions. Our experiments demonstrate that this approach can discover complex emergent behaviours from simple, generic actions, and use these behaviours to achieve a position of tactical superiority in the domain of air combat simulation.

Keywords: Emergent behavior · Evolutionary algorithms
Multiagent simulation · Air combat simulation

1 Introduction

Increasingly, the military uses simulations for defence applications, such as training, concept development and experimentation, and as an alternative to live training exercises which involve expensive aircraft and require the presence of highly trained pilots. These simulations have incorporated intelligent agents to model individual and team decision-making, for a variety of reasons including the development and assessment of tactics for air combat [2]. A typical agent has a role, such as ally or adversary, and its behaviour is traditionally scripted by hand mapping observations to actions.

The process of scripting these behaviour models for specific simulation environments is labour intensive, costly, requires domain expertise, and may require the use of dedicated agent behaviour authoring tools. Any subsequent variations to the agent behaviour require manual modifications to the existing model. In

---

This work was supported by the Australian Defence Science and Technology Group.

T. Miller et al. (Eds.): PRIMA 2018, LNAI 11224, pp. 19–34, 2018.
https://doi.org/10.1007/978-3-030-03098-8_2

addition, these scripted behaviour models are limited in their ability to discover novel behaviours.

Adaptive machine learning systems have been employed as an alternative to human test pilots and live training exercises [13]. Smith et al. [13] argued that this approach has numerous advantages, namely, a distilled analytical model that captures combat simulation, eliminates bias from the pilots' previous experiences, and does not have the constraints typically associated with real-time simulations.

Technological advances for fighter aircraft, such as stealth, advanced avionics and weapons, electronic warfare, and increased networking capabilities, require sophisticated tactics to be exploited effectively. As a result, there is a need for new techniques to adequately explore fighter combat behaviour. Artificial intelligence techniques, such as automated planning [8,9] and differential game theory [7], have been employed to automate the discovery of new tactical behaviours by optimising action selection in a close range two player air combat scenario.

In this paper, we demonstrate that the integration of evolutionary algorithms with finite state machines provides a viable approach to tactical behaviour discovery. The approach involves the evolution of a behavioural model in the form of a finite state machine (FSM) using genetic algorithms, to produce an Evolved Finite State Machine (E-FSM) that can automate the generation of complex tactical behaviours in multiagent simulations.

The contributions are (1) a generalisable evolutionary approach to evolving finite state machine transitions in multiagent simulations, and (2) the development of a chromosome representation for evolving rules for transitions of finite state machines.

The paper is structured as follows: A discussion of related works is first presented in Sect. 2. Section 3 describes the air combat problem, namely the stern conversion manoeuvre, and the corresponding stern conversion agent controller used in this study. Our evolutionary approach is outlined in Sect. 4, followed descriptions of the sets of experiments and associated results and discussion in Sect. 5. Lastly, conclusions and future works are presented in Sect. 6.

2   Related Work

Existing research has explored the use of machine learning to automatically generate behaviour models incorporating techniques such as evolutionary algorithms and dynamic scripting, in conjunction with employing FSMs or behaviour trees as models for capturing agent behaviour.

The Smart Bandits project [11] employed machine learning techniques to generate FSM-based behaviour models that can be used for air-to-air tactic training. While Smart Bandits provides no adaptive capabilities, Toubman et al. [14] incorporated dynamic scripting in their approach for developing adaptive FSMs that can be used against opponents in air combat.

Revello [10] presented a GA-based approach for generating war game strategies whereby the various ship groups demonstrated emergent behaviours, moving in a coordinated fashion even though there was no exchange of information in terms of their respective movements.

Smith et al. [13] evolved a learning classifier system that produced novel one-vs-one WVR manoeuvres in the role of a fighter pilot using the AASPEM system as the simulator environment. The GA population consists a set of classifiers and through an iterative process of fitness evaluation of the classifiers, selection and genetic operations, produced several novel strategies that were subsequently evaluated and approved by test fighter pilots.

Other researchers such as Mulgund et al. [5] and Keshi et al. [4] have applied genetic algorithms to optimise tactical parameters in BVR involving scenarios of many-vs-many using hierarchical encoding involving binary codes for chromosome representation. Yao et al. [15] described an approach where air combat manoeuvres are represented using behaviour trees and through grammatical evolution, generates adaptive human behaviour models for BVR engagements.

While Toubman et al. [14] and others have applied evolutionary algorithms to FSM behaviour models, those approaches relied on hand-authored tactical behaviours. The approach presented here obviates the need for problem-specific tactics, by evolving transitions between generic agent actions using kinematic properties of the entities. This enables the emergence of complex behaviours without predisposing the system towards known solutions. Unlike the approach taken by researchers such as Smith et al. [13], by incorporating an FSM our approach produces human-readable tactics, and allows the modelling of agent behaviours with higher levels of complexity if required, enabling the discovery of emergent behaviours for problem scenarios with different levels of abstraction.

3   Problem Description

The problem used to evaluate our approach is that of an aircraft that aims to manoeuvre into a particular position of tactical superiority with respect to a single adversary aircraft. This position is defined as being behind the adversary and following it. In this position, the aircraft can fire on its adversary, whilst being out of range of the adversary's weapons.

The classical scenario that models this is the stern conversion intercept (described by Shaw [12]), a two-player scenario where the aircraft are within visual range and initially flying towards each other (Fig. 1). Execution of the manoeuvre as described relies on a number of tactical parameters, which are dependent on the manoeuvring capabilities of the aircraft.

An implementation of the stern conversion manoeuvre as a finite state machine is shown in Fig. 2, where each state represents the execution logic of a single section or subtask of the manoeuvre. The transitions between the states, based on various conditions defined by Shaw [12], result in a sequence that realises the complex behaviour. A description of the states is given in Table 1.

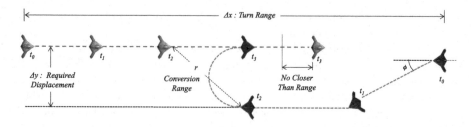

Fig. 1. The sequence of subtasks and tactical parameters required to execute the classical stern conversion manoeuvre.

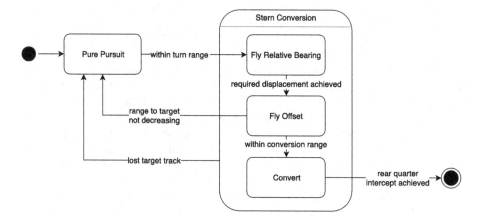

Fig. 2. FSM implementing the Shaw stern conversion manoeuvre.

4   Proposed Approach

4.1   A Flexible FSM Model

Our approach to the exploration of air combat strategies employs a flexible FSM model, where a set of states is provided as input and an evolutionary algorithm is used to determine appropriate transition conditions so that the FSM can act as an agent controller that achieves a particular goal. The transition conditions in our approach are based on the kinematic properties of an aircraft and a measure of goal achievement for the evolutionary algorithm is obtained through agent-based simulation.

A generic FSM controller, employing n states, is shown in Fig. 3. From each state it is possible to transition into any other state, depending on a set of conditions. Each state corresponds to an action that is performed in that state, such as flying an aircraft in a particular manner, and a set of conditions that are constantly checked while in that state to determine if the FSM should transition to another state.

The functional logic of the generic FSM is provided in Algorithm 1, where the FSM starts in State 1. In the case where transition conditions for moving

Table 1. States and transitions for the FSM stern conversion agent

State	Action	Transitions
(a) Pure pursuit	Point aircraft at and fly directly towards red aircraft	If distance to red aircraft less than **turn range** and red aligned with blue, transition to (b)
(b) Fly relative bearing	Turn by **turn angle** and fly straight on that bearing	If lateral separation between red and blue greater than **required displacement** transition to (c)
(c) Fly offset	Fly parallel to heading of red aircraft	If distance between red and blue less than **conversion range** transition to (d). If distance between red and blue not decreasing transition to (a)
(d) Convert	Turn to match red heading. Approach no closer than **no closer range**	If the rear quarter intercept criteria have been met then the maneuver reaches the end/final state as it has been successfully executed

into more than one state become valid, the next state is chosen probabilistically. In its simplest form, the choice of valid transition can be random, as was done in our experiments, or each transition can be assigned its own probability.

The key difference between the approach taken here is and a regular finite state machine is that in this case we only assume what states the pilot agent can be in. We don't make any assumptions about the transition events or the transition probabilities between states. Rather, the transitions between the predetermined states are evolved and hence generated dynamically. This allows for the possibility of new tactical behaviour to emerge and to be potentially discovered.

Algorithm 1. Functional logic for the generic FSM agent controller.

```
currentState = State1; nextPossibleStatesList = empty;
loop
    performAction(currentState);
    for nextStateToCheck ← 1 to n do
        if transitionConditionsSatisfied(currentState, nextStateToCheck) then
            append nextStateToCheck to nextPossibleStatesList;
        end
    end
    if nextPossibleStatesList not empty then
        currentState = randomChoice(nextPossibleStatesList);
        nextPossibleStatesList = empty;
    end
end
```

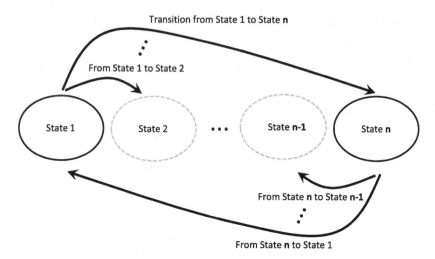

Fig. 3. A generic n-state finite state machine where each state corresponds to some action taken by the agent. From each state, a transition can occur to any other state. The conditions that would lead to state transitions are evolved in our approach to suit a particular task.

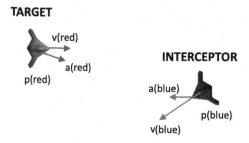

Fig. 4. Kinematic properties of the Red and Blue aircraft; each has a position (p), velocity vector (v) and acceleration vector (a). (Color figure online)

4.2　Kinematic Transition Model

We base the transition conditions for the air combat domain on the kinematic properties of the aircraft taking part in the scenario: position ($\mathbf{p}$), velocity ($\mathbf{v}$) and acceleration ($\mathbf{a}$). For the case of two aircraft (denoted Blue and Red), these parameters are shown in Fig. 4. Each kinematic parameter is a vector quantity with three Cartesian components, along the x, y and z axes.

　　The kinematic properties are transformed from values with reference to a fixed world coordinate system, to a coordinate system relative to the aircraft controlled by the FSM. This ensures that the transition parameters are rotation and translation invariant (i.e. not specific to a particular position and orientation in the world), and is obtained by calculating the difference vectors for each parameter:

$$\boldsymbol{\Delta p} = (\Delta p_x, \Delta p_y, \Delta p_z) = (p_{xRed} - p_{xBlue}, p_{yRed} - p_{yBlue}, p_{zRed} - p_{zBlue})$$
$$\boldsymbol{\Delta v} = (\Delta v_x, \Delta v_y, \Delta v_z) = (v_{xRed} - v_{xBlue}, v_{yRed} - v_{yBlue}, v_{zRed} - v_{zBlue})$$
$$\boldsymbol{\Delta a} = (\Delta a_x, \Delta a_y, \Delta a_z) = (a_{xRed} - a_{xBlue}, a_{yRed} - a_{yBlue}, a_{zRed} - a_{zBlue})$$

where $\boldsymbol{\Delta p}$ is the distance vector between the two aircraft, and $\boldsymbol{\Delta v}$ and $\boldsymbol{\Delta a}$ are the difference vectors between the velocity and acceleration vectors. The three vectors are then rotated to compensate for the heading direction of the blue aircraft. After transformation the values correspond to the position, velocity and acceleration of the red aircraft as they would be perceived by the pilot of the blue aircraft. The values of these transformed kinematic parameters can then be used to determine whether a transition should take place.

A wide number of algorithmic approaches can be employed to implement the transition conditions. We employ a simple model, checking that $\boldsymbol{\Delta p}$, $\boldsymbol{\Delta v}$ and $\boldsymbol{\Delta a}$ are within a certain range of values. The minimum and maximum bounds on the transition condition ranges are represented by a set of constants, determined through an evolutionary approach (described in Sect. 4.3). Evaluation for the transition from a particular state i to another state j requires 18 constants since there are three kinematic parameters ($\boldsymbol{\Delta p}$, $\boldsymbol{\Delta v}$ and $\boldsymbol{\Delta a}$), each of these has three Cartesian components (x, y and z), and each of these has both a lower and upper bound. For an FSM with n states, in each state a total of $n - 1$ transitions need to be checked, thus $18 \times (n - 1)$ boundary checks, making the computational complexity of the FSM transition model $O(n)$. The storage complexity is $O(n^2)$ as the total number of constants to be stored is:

$$n_{constants} = 18 \times (n_{states} - 1) \times n_{states} \tag{1}$$

These constants are denoted by $A_{ij}, B_{ij}, C_{ij}, D_{ij} \cdots R_{ij}$. To determine if a transition from current state i to next state j can be taken, the current $\boldsymbol{\Delta p}$, $\boldsymbol{\Delta v}$ and $\boldsymbol{\Delta a}$ is evaluated against the bounds, as shown in Table 2.

Table 2. An example of the transition logic conditions that must all be satisfied for a change of state from state i to state j. The 18 transition parameters (A to R) act as thresholds for the relative position ($\boldsymbol{\Delta p}$), velocity ($\boldsymbol{\Delta v}$) and acceleration ($\boldsymbol{\Delta a}$) in each transition.

Relative position	Relative velocity	Relative acceleration
$A_{ij} < \Delta p_x < B_{ij}$	$G_{ij} < \Delta v_x < H_{ij}$	$M_{ij} < \Delta a_x < N_{ij}$
$C_{ij} < \Delta p_y < D_{ij}$	$I_{ij} < \Delta v_y < J_{ij}$	$O_{ij} < \Delta a_y < P_{ij}$
$E_{ij} < \Delta p_z < F_{ij}$	$K_{ij} < \Delta v_z < L_{ij}$	$Q_{ij} < \Delta a_z < R_{ij}$

4.3 Genetic-Based Approach to Transition Evolution

Our evolutionary approach to determining the optimal boundaries for transition conditions is based on the genetic algorithm (GA), originally developed by Holland (1992) [3]. The GA takes an initial set of candidate solutions to the problem, called the *population*. For the purposes of the algorithm, individuals are encoded as a set of attributes, the *gene*, with the set of genes called a *chromosome*.

In our approach, the boundary constants each form a gene, with the complete set of constants forming the chromosome. Thus for an FSM with n states, given Eq. 1, there are $18 \times (n - 1) \times n$ genes in each chromosome. The chromosome representation is shown in Fig. 5, with the constants laid out sequentially. For the purposes of the GA, each constant is stored as a real number, normalised to be in the range [0.0–1.0]. The values are mapped during execution to an actual range for the kinematic parameters by considering their physical bounds, based on mission parameters and aircraft capabilities.

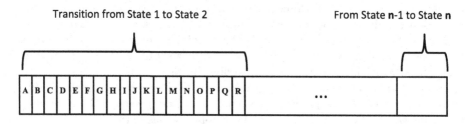

Fig. 5. Chromosome representation for evolving FSM transitions.

5   Evaluation

5.1   Experimental Results

The evolved finite state machine (E-FSM) approach described in Sect. 4 was evaluated for two FSM implementations (described below), one with states specifically designed to perform a known behaviour, and the other with states consisting of generic actions utilised by Park et al. [7]. The scenario used for our experiments is a two player close-range air combat engagement, as per the initial conditions for Shaw's stern conversion scenario described in Sect. 3.

Each implementation of the E-FSM approach is evolved against a set of four opponent models, described in Table 3. The range of permitted transition boundary parameter values is given in Table 4, chosen based on the scenario scale and aircraft characteristics to speed up convergence by avoiding values that in practice could not be reached. Each experiment was repeated 30 times with different initial populations, to examine the range of solutions produced by the non-deterministic evolution process.

Genetic Algorithm Parameters. The population is initialised by generating a set of individuals such that each gene that corresponds to a minimum bound has its value set to a random number in the range of [0, 0.5], while each gene

Table 3. Description of the four opponent models used to evaluate each implementation of the E-FSM approach.

Opponent	Behaviour description
Straight Line	Non-reactive; flies in a straight line as per the red target aircraft in Shaw's stern conversion (Fig. 1)
Pure Pursuit	Pursues the blue fighter using the *pure pursuit* behaviour described in Table 1(a)
Shaw	Attempts the classical stern conversion manoeuvre using the stern conversion specific FSM described in Table 1, with hand-selected transition parameters
Evolved Shaw	Attempts the stern conversion manoeuvre using the stern conversion specific FSM described in Table 1, with transition parameters evolved against a straight line agent

Table 4. Kinematic parameter ranges used to reduce experimental run time.

Kinematic parameter	Encoded range	Actual range
Δp	$[0,1]$	$[-48152, 48152]$ m
Δv	$[0,1]$	$[-1000, 1000]$ ms^{-1}
Δa	$[0,1]$	$[-100, 100]$ ms^{-2}

that corresponds to a maximum bound has its gene value initialised to a random number in the range $[0.5, 1]$.

Evolution proceeds for a pre-determined number of generations, each of which involves comparing the performance of individuals in the candidate population through 5 runs in a constructive simulation environment, with a maximum simulation run-time of 250 s.

The population is updated after each generation by copying a number of individuals, selected using Stochastic Universal Sampling [1], and the single most fit candidate (the *elite*), into the next generation. Selected individuals are combined using single point crossover and two point crossover [3]. Mutation is controlled using the Gaussian mutation operator, as it is flexible enough to allow for both fine tuning of solutions and searching of the domain. The value for a mutated gene is calculated using the equation $x = x + \mathcal{N}(0,1)$ where $\mathcal{N}(0,1)$ is the Gaussian Normal distribution with a mean of 0 and a standard deviation of 1. The probability as to whether a gene undergoes mutation is associated with the mutation probability, p_m, and this has been assigned a value of 0.1, based on initial experimental results.

Experiments are terminated when either of the following conditions are met: the number of generations reaches a pre-defined maximum number, or there has been no improvement in the fitness value in the population for N consecutive generations.

Fitness Evaluation. In this study, the fitness of an individual is calculated from the output of a set of runs in the constructive air combat simulator ACE Zero [6]. We base our success measure for blue on the achievement of a position of superiority, defined as being behind the red agent and following it. We consider the blue aircraft to have succeeded if during the simulation run the following criteria have been met (illustrated in Fig. 6):

1. Target aircraft is within 30° of attacking aircraft nose ($\phi_1 < 30$)
2. Attacking aircraft is within 30° of threat aircraft tail ($\phi_2 < 30$)
3. Range to the target aircraft is between 500 and 3000 feet ($500 < r < 3000$)
4. Separation in altitude is less than 500 feet ($\Delta a < 500$)
5. Difference in velocity is less than 100 knots ($\Delta v < 100$)

To calculate the fitness of a blue aircraft in a particular simulation run, we initialise its fitness to 0 at the start of the simulation, then check each of the six conditions at intervals of 1 s of simulated time. For each condition that is true at the particular point in time we add 1 to the fitness. Thus, the more conditions that are true at a particular time, the higher the fitness for that time interval. Fitness is summed across time intervals, so that a higher fitness results the longer a condition is true.

While more criteria could be considered, for example that the above criteria be met continuously for a long enough duration to launch a weapon, through our experiments we confirmed that the above five criteria were sufficient to produce valid solutions.

One simulation run results in a single fitness score. Due to the non-determinism that is present when multiple transition conditions are satisfied, we take the average fitness of five simulation runs and associate that with the individual.

Problem-Specific E-FSM Results. The problem-specific E-FSM has states hand-coded to enact the stern conversion manoeuvre as described by Shaw [12] (Fig. 2), with the original tactical-parameter-based transitions replaced by the flexible kinematics-based model described in Sect. 4. This FSM has 4 states, resulting in a chromosome with 216 genes as per Eq. 1. An initial population of 50 individuals is evolved through a maximum of 300 generations, and the individual with the highest fitness after termination is selected for examination.

Figure 7 illustrates exemplary results for each of the opponent types described in Table 3. Against the Straight Line opponent, the evolved problem-specific FSM found the classical stern conversion sequence (that is, the states in Table 1 executed in order), despite having no knowledge of the tactical parameters traditionally used to execute the state transitions. Against the Pure Pursuit opponent, the agent learned to stay in the Pure Pursuit state. In the case of the Shaw opponent, a hand-optimised stern conversion FSM, the problem-specific E-FSM learned a novel tactic, waiting for its opponent to turn away before turning to follow it as it passed. Against the more adept Evolved Shaw opponent, which had itself been evolved against a Straight Line agent, the E-FSM learned to

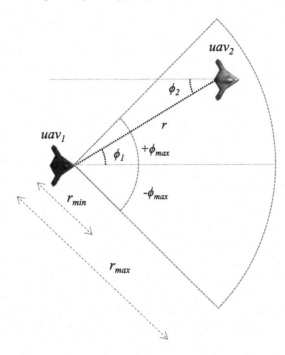

Fig. 6. Illustration of the criteria used to evaluate the fitness of an individual. Blue is in a position of superiority, corresponding to a high fitness score.

counteract the behaviour of its opponent to complete the manoeuvre behind it. In all cases, the evolutionary approach successfully found effective behaviours to achieve a position of tactical superiority.

Generic E-FSM Results. The generic E-FSM has states based on generic aircraft manoeuvre actions, taken from Park [7] (illustrated in Fig. 8). In previous versions of the evolutionary finite machine, the states represented either high level or intermediate level goals or maneuvers that the pilot agent was trying to achieve (such as flying an offset maneuver). In this iteration described here, break the maneuvers down even further into low level actions such as flying left and up, level flight and right and down. These represent some of the lowest level actions a pilot can take to control an aircraft. By assembling a sequence of these low level aircraft control actions, a pilot can assemble a different higher level maneuvers that will enable it to undertake to model basic fighter combat. Through the evolution of the transitions between these low level actions–states we can generate air combat behaviour against a maneuvering opponent without the constraints of a pre-determined tactic such as that descrbed by Shaw [12].

Due to the generic E-FSM having 7 states, it results in a chromosome with 756 genes as per Eq. 1. As the chromosome size is much larger than for the problem-specific E-FSM, resulting in a larger search space, more extensive exploration

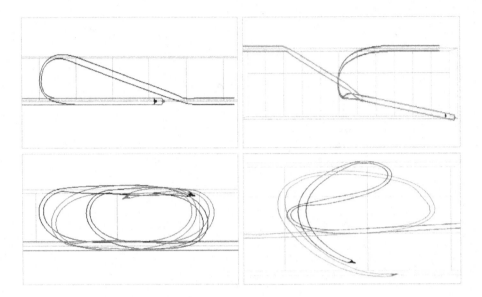

Fig. 7. Example traces for the problem-specific E-FSM against red opponents (clockwise from top left): Straight Line, Shaw, Evolved Shaw, Pure Pursuit. (Color figure online)

was enabled through a larger population of 100, and by increasing the maximum number of generations to 1000. The large size of the chromosome also led us to lower mutation probability to 0.001 and use two-point crossover to prevent excessive modification between generations.

Figure 9 illustrates exemplary results for each of the opponent types described in Table 3. Against the Straight Line opponent, the generic E-FSM found an effective set of transitions between the generic manoeuvre states to approximate the classical stern conversion sequence, although with a lower average fitness score than the problem-specific E-FSM (which has states specifically designed for this opponent). Against the Pure Pursuit opponent, the agent learned a behaviour that approximated the hand-coded pure pursuit behaviour of the problem-specific FSM, continually transitioning between basic manoeuvres to follow its opponent. The pursuit behaviour discovered by the generic E-FSM achieved a higher fitness than the hand-coded Pure Pursuit state, suggesting that the agent had found a superior tactic (most likely the more efficient lead pursuit). In the case of the Shaw opponent, the generic E-FSM learned a similar strategy to the problem-specific E-FSM, waiting for its opponent to turn away before turning to follow it. Against the more adept Evolved Shaw opponent, the generic E-FSM achieved significantly improved performance over the problem-specific E-FSM, discovering a novel tactic (drawing its opponent into a turn before looping around behind it) that was not found when the hand-coded, stern conversion specific states were used. In all cases apart from the straight line opponent, the generic E-FSM attained significantly higher fitness scores than the problem-specific E-FSM.

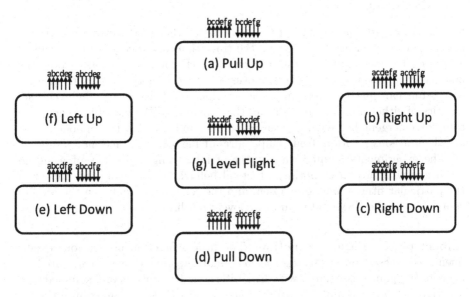

Fig. 8. Representation of the states in the Generic E-FSM, where each state represents a low level aircraft control. The arrows above each state indicate that the E-FSM can evolve to transition to any possible state.

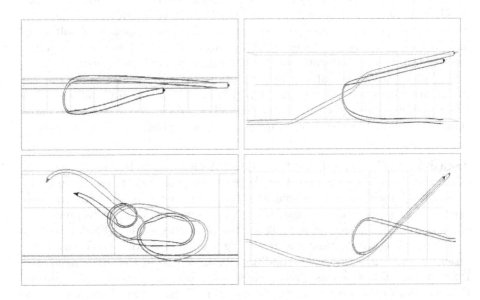

Fig. 9. Example traces for the generic E-FSM against red opponents (clockwise from top left): Straight Line, Shaw, Evolved Shaw, Pure Pursuit. (Color figure online)

5.2   Discussion

In comparison to traditional approaches such as the hand-coded state transition logic described in Sect. 3, where the transitions are specific to the problem and must be determined by the analyst for each combination of aircraft, the kinematic approach was able to discover a sequence of transitions to enact a successful rear-quarter intercept without prior knowledge of the flight characteristics of either aircraft. In addition, the generic E-FSM was able to generate complex emergent behaviours, such as pursuit and drawing the opponent into an advantageous position, from simple aircraft flight control actions.

The experiments highlight a number of interesting properties of using an evolutionary approach to optimise tactical behaviour, primarily the impact of the particular fitness function chosen, and the relationship between the level of complexity of the FSM states and the novelty of discovered behaviours.

Impact of the Fitness Function. The fitness function used in our experiments was based purely on the desired final outcome (Fig. 6), calculated by aggregating points associated with five criteria at 1 s intervals and summed over a period of 250 s of simulation time. Since the objective is to maximise the fitness function, the evolved model is naturally biased towards solutions that avoid any intermediate manoeuvres that reduce fitness, although these may subsequently be helpful in better achieving the final goal. For example, when evolving the problem-specific E-FSM against a straight line opponent, the classical stern conversion manoeuvre (Fig. 1) achieves a rear-quarter intercept faster than the greedy behaviour of remaining in the Pure Pursuit state. However, the stern conversion manoeuvre begins with a turn away from the opponent, resulting in an initial loss of fitness. In comparison, a solution where the blue aircraft points continuously at its opponent over the same time period (pure pursuit) will be ranked higher in fitness initially, despite ultimately taking longer to achieve the rear-quarter intercept. As a result, it is important to develop the fitness function carefully to avoid biasing discovered behaviours in this way, and to allow sufficient evolution time for manoeuvres with lower initial fitness to be found.

Transitional Complexity of Solutions. A factor in finding an effective set of transition conditions for the FSM is the number of transitions that need to be made to reach an optimal solution. The evolutionary process favours solutions with lower transitional complexity. For example, performing the prescribed stern conversion manoeuvre depends on the problem-specific E-FSM executing four states at the right time and in the right order, requiring the correct evolution of up to 216 transition condition parameters. On the other hand, the Pure Pursuit state provides a relatively strong solution on its own. This means that solutions that involve staying in the Pure Pursuit state have a very low transitional complexity, and require the correct optimisation of fewer transition condition parameters (none if the FSM starts in the Pure Pursuit state). As a result, sufficient exploration should be enabled during evolution to search the solution space, so that more complex manoeuvres can be found. The more complex a manoeuvre, in terms of the number and sequence of transitions that need to occur, the longer it can be expected to take to evolve.

State Complexity and Solution Novelty. It is observed from the experimental results that, when implementing the E-FSM approach, the use of more complex, problem-specific states predisposes the evolutionary search toward known solutions, while the use of simpler states produces more novel solutions (although at a computational cost). While the problem-specific E-FSM often converged to a solution within 20 generations, it did so in many cases by settling quickly on a sub-optimal solution, such as staying in the Pure Pursuit state (which is able to achieve the final goal on its own). In contrast, the states of the generic E-FSM correspond to simple directional changes for the aircraft, so evolving a novel sequence of state transitions is the only way to achieve the target goal without an initial workable solution.

6   Conclusion

We have demonstrated an effective approach to discovering emergent tactical behaviours, using the combination of evolutionary algorithms with finite state machines in the context of adversarial air combat. The incorporation of FSMs produces human-readable tactics, and enables the modelling of agent behaviour at varying levels of complexity, avoiding the predisposition towards known solutions that results from hand-coding behaviours, while enabling the modelling of actions at higher levels of abstraction as required.

It was found that there is a strong relationship between the complexity of the FSM states, the time taken to find an effective solution, and the novelty of discovered behaviours. For example, a generic FSM, with simple states representing low-level aircraft directional changes, took many more generations to find an optimal solution than a problem-specific FSM, whose more complex states were hand-coded for the specific scenario. However, the generic FSM achieved superior performance when evolved against reactive opponents, and discovered novel tactics that were not seen when using problem-specific states.

Future work will involve scaling the approach presented here to more complex scenarios involving teams of agents employing beyond visual range sensors and weapons (requiring more sophisticated transition conditions than the kinematic parameters used to determine state transitions in this study), and the integration of co-evolutionary methods.

References

1. Baker, J.E.: Reducing bias and inefficiency in the selection algorithm. In: Proceedings of the Second International Conference on Genetic Algorithms, vol. 206, pp. 14–21 (1987)

2. Heinze, C., Papasimeon, M., Goss, S., Cross, M., Connell, R.: Simulating fighter pilots, Birkhuser, Basel, pp. 113–130, November 2008. https://doi.org/10.1007/978-3-7643-8571-2_7
3. Holland, J.H.: Adaptation in Natural and Artificial Systems: An Introductory Analysis with Applications to Biology, Control, and Artificial Intelligence. MIT Press, Cambridge (1992)
4. Keshi, Z., Zhengping, W.: On optimizing large-scale air-combat formation with simulated-annealing GA (genetic algorithm). In: 24th International Congress of the Aeronautical Sciences (2004)
5. Mulgund, S., Harper, K., Krishnakumar, K., Zacharias, G.: Air combat tactics optimization using stochastic genetic algorithms. In: 1998 IEEE International Conference on Systems, Man, and Cybernetics, vol. 4, pp. 3136–3141. IEEE (1998)
6. Papasimeon, M., Benke, L., Brain, R., Finkelstein, L.: Multiagent simulation of adversarial socio-technical systems. Presented at the Industrial Track, 2018 International Conference on Autonomous Agents and Multi-Agent Systems (AAMAS 2018) (2018)
7. Park, H., Lee, B.Y., Tahk, M.J., Yoo, D.W.: Differential game based air combat maneuver generation using scoring function matrix. Int. J. Aeronaut. Space Sci. 17(2), 204–213 (2016)
8. Ramirez, M., Papasimeon, M., Benke, L., Lipovetzky, N., Miller, T., Pearce, A.R.: Real-time UAV maneuvering via automated planning in simulations. In: International Joint Conferences on Artificial Intelligence Organization, pp. 5243–5245, August 2017. https://doi.org/10.24963/ijcai.2017/778, https://www.ijcai.org/proceedings/2017/778
9. Ramirez, M., et al.: Integrated hybrid planning and programmed control for real-time UAV maneuvering. In: Proceedings of the Seventeenth International Conference on Autonomous Agents and Multiagent Systems, AAMAS 2018, July 2018
10. Revello, T.E., McCartney, R.: Generating war game strategies using a genetic algorithm. In: Proceedings of the 2002 Congress on Evolutionary Computation CEC 2002, vol. 2, pp. 1086–1091. IEEE (2002)
11. Roessingh, J., et al.: Modelling CGFs for tactical air-to-air combat training motivation-based behaviour and machine learning in a common architecture. Technical report, National Aerospace Laboratory NLR (2011)
12. Shaw, R.L.: Fighter Combat. Naval Institute Press, Annapolis (1985)
13. Smith, R., Dike, B., Ravichandran, B., El-Fallah, A., Mehra, K.: Discovering novel fighter combat maneuvers: simulating test pilot creativity. In: Creative Evolutionary Systems, pp. 467-VIII. Elsevier (2002)
14. Toubman, A., Roessingh, J.J., Spronck, P., Plaat, A., van den Herik, H.J.: Rapid adaptation of air combat behaviour. In: ECAI. Frontiers in Artificial Intelligence and Applications, vol. 285, pp. 1791–1796. IOS Press (2016)
15. Yao, J., Huang, Q., Wang, W.: Adaptive human behavior modeling for air combat simulation. In: 2015 IEEE/ACM 19th International Symposium on Distributed Simulation and Real Time Applications (DS-RT), pp. 100–103. IEEE (2015)

Realization of Two Types
of Compact City
- Street Activeness and Tramway -

Hideyuki Nagai[1(✉)] and Setsuya Kurahashi[2]

[1] Department of Risk Engineering, Graduate School of Systems and Information
Engineering, University of Tsukuba, Tokyo, Japan
s1530156@u.tsukuba.ac.jp
[2] Graduate School of System Management, University of Tsukuba, Tokyo, Japan
kurahashi.setsuya.gf@u.tsukuba.ac.jp

Abstract. The purpose of this research is to verify the effectiveness
of the combination of the introduction of a tramway with introducing
a public facility for urban residents and implementing a policy to promote activeness around it, on urban sprawl. By using an agent-based
model (ABM), which was built for simulating urban structure changes
through autonomous behavior of urban residents, this research clarified
that, depend on the urban initial state, the combination of these policies
can lead the two different types of compact city: the polycentric-form
and the monocentric-form.

Keywords: Agent-based model · Urban design
Urban sprawl · Compact city · Land use

1 Introduction

1.1 Urban Sprawl Issues

The world population has rapidly increased during our current century along
with the previous century, and continued urbanization has taken place at various
places around the globe [13]. Many researchers and experts predict that this
unrelenting urbanization will not fade but continue to advance [26]. Under such
circumstances, urban sprawl has attracted much attention as one of the issues
that has been most widely discussed in the past few decades, coming under fire
as an unsustainable form of urbanization.

Urban sprawl is commonly defined by the following land-use characteristics
[10, 15, 21, 30]:

- Expansion of urban area in outer fringe (undeveloped) area
- Low-density development
- Scattered development (multi-direction)
- Leapfrog development (discontinuity)

© Springer Nature Switzerland AG 2018
T. Miller et al. (Eds.): PRIMA 2018, LNAI 11224, pp. 35–50, 2018.
https://doi.org/10.1007/978-3-030-03098-8_3

- Commercial strip development

Urban sprawl is often criticized because of its following negative impacts [10, 12, 21, 31]:

- Increase in traffic congestion and commuting time, air pollution, and increase in energy consumption
- Increase in infrastructure maintenance and operation cost
- Hollowing out in urban central area, economic disparity, employment imbalance, and loss of neighboring community
- Loss of agricultural and natural land

These negative impacts cannot be disregard, since urban sprawl causes greater environmental impacts than other land-uses [6].

In the future, Japan will definitely have a shrinking as well as ever-aging population. At the same time, the population has continued to concentrate in large city regions. These reasons have given rise especially to a concern about the serious negative impact caused by urban sprawl [2].

1.2 Shift into Compact City

Researchers and experts have studied a shift into "Compact City", as a countermeasure against urban sprawl [15, 19].

Compact city does not have a generally accepted definition. It is, however, commonly defined by the following characteristics [5, 8, 15, 33]:

- High-density
- Concentration of development
- Development in public transportation network

Two forms are found for city center:

- Monocentric-form
- Polycentric-form

It has been proved that compact city can overcome some of the negative impacts driven by urban sprawl. Many studies have also indicated that a compact city can enhance quality of life by offering a broad range of choices with regard to lifestyle and behavior including residences, travel, and shopping goods [8].

Considering the urban dynamics including sprawl as complex phenomena of mutual interactions of a wide variety of autonomous entities, such as individuals, households, and firms [7, 18, 24], however, highlights the difficulty in direct control of the urban dynamics.

1.3 Purpose of This Research

With these in mind, this research built an agent-based model (ABM) to simulate urban structure changes through the induction of autonomous daily travel and residential relocation of urban residents rather than the compulsion. And based on this ABM, this research verified the following points:

- The introduction of a tramway in the central urban area has been actively promoted in recent years. Is the combination of the introduction of a tramway with introducing a public facility for urban residents and implementing a policy to promote activeness around it effective in controlling urban sprawl?
- Is the combination of these policies also effective in improving existent urban sprawl?

2   Related Works and Position of this Research

To build the simulation model, this chapter referred to the findings of two research fields, agent-based land-use/transport interaction (LUTI) model and revitalization of urban central area.

2.1   Agent-Based LUTI Model

Urban sprawl is a special kind of land-use change, urban spatial expansion along a city boundary. Land-use changes come from its complex driving forces and their interactions [18,24]. Above all, the fundamental principle that land-use impacts transport and vice versa has been acknowledged by many scholars and supported by empirical findings [3]. These research efforts have culminated in the development of operational urban land-use/transport interaction (LUTI) models as decision support systems.

And recently, researchers have supported a concept to express the real-world complicated system including a city as a macro-level state that is generated by micro-level collective interactions of multiple autonomous agents [9]. The activity-based disaggregate modeling approach particularly emphasizes the point that each agent learns, modifies, and improves its own activities through interactions with the environment (including other agents) where the agent is located. Based on the above-mentioned concept of complexity science, this modeling approach is referred to as the agent-based model (ABM) [7,17,29].

The ABM initially applied to the land-use model as a spatially-explicit cellular automaton (CA) form. In the CA-based land-use models, which serve as a typical application in social science, the state of each individual cell in the model space indicates the specific land-use. Such models have subsequently continued to develop as hybrid agent-based urban models through relaxation of the basic assumptions. A series of these models have contributed to express complicated macro-level land-use patterns of cities including clusterization and sprawl as self-organization through micro-level adaptive behavior of agents. Such models have served to explore urban growth scenarios.

There have been, however, only a small number of applications of agent-based models to express agents spatially-explicitly both as households or firms relocating and as individuals using traffic networks in parallel. One such model to be called the seamless agent-based LUTI model is the bipolar formed urban dynamics simulation model by Taniguchi [32]. In this model, changes in distribution of residences emerge through the daily travel of individual residents (households) and their relocations which are spatially-explicitly expressed [32].

2.2 Revitalization of Urban Central Area

Recently, particularly in advanced nations, revitalization of urban central areas that hollowed out along with urban sprawl has become a critically important issue. Jacobs [20] has emphasized the attractiveness of a city as a lively and bustling place which has served as a market for exchange from the time before the establishment of the concept of nation or trading by using currency [20]. And researchers and experts have reevaluated the importance of informal public spaces for activities of local residents in the way of an antithesis to urban development on an inhuman scale as well as another way to regain people in urban central areas. The two factors are vital to forming such public space. First, such public space needs to serve as a hub for people in their daily lives so that they can visit there casually while they are out. Second, such public space needs to generate "street activeness" set in an open space, such as a street or a plaza, around the public space.

Library as an Urban Hub. As for urban hubs, public complexes based mainly on libraries have recently attracted much attention. The representative one is the series of Idea Store in London, U.K. [1]. Several pioneering libraries built and put into operation recently in Japan are also relevant to these cases[1]. These public libraries, while offering the library service as the core function, provide a wide variety of other services. These may include attached commercial facilities, such as cafes, and facilities that promote learning and civic activities. They also try to enhance convenience for visitors by various policies including the extension of opening time. By doing so, they aim to serve as a hub for local culture.

Street Activeness. Street activeness indicates a lively situation where individuals gather and stroll around downtown while enjoying exchanges, such as encountering various people, contacting various shopping goods, and experiencing other services [27]. Therefore, it can bring about not only usefulness or efficiency, but also creative, cultural, or recreational benefits. From an economic point of view, it has been long argued that the density of interactions by various people propels economic activity [25]. From a sociological point of view, the following positive feedback has been demonstrated empirically: the number of people that visited a certain place including their sojourn time they spent there can derive positive evaluations for the place, such as cheerful and lively atmosphere, and at the same time these positive evaluations attract further activities [22].

2.3 Position of This Research

By integrating the above-mentioned conceptual framework, Nagai [27] built the agent-based model (ABM) to consider qualitative benefit obtained by using infor-

---

[1] E.g., Musashino Place in Tokyo, Japan (2011), Takeo City Library in Saga, Japan (2013), Gifu Media Cosmos in Gifu, Japan (2015), Art Museum & Library, Ota in Gunma, Japan (2017).

mal public space and being in such a place, along with the daily travel of urban residents. And they clarified that the synergistic effects of some policies, such as locating of the public space and promoting activeness in such a place, are effective to maintain a compact urban structure [27]. On the other hand, an introduction of tramway is well known as one of the measures to reduce traffic congestion, save energy consumption, and reduce air pollution in urban area. In recent years momentum for introduction of tramway has also been raised in Japan [28]. Additionally, especially in Japan a large part of the land is mountainous, thus the area suitable for urbanization is relatively small [23]. And the population is also declining [2]. For these reasons, improvement of many cities that have already sprawled is considered to be more important. This research develops the conceptual framework introduced by Nagai [27] to verify whether the introduction of a tramway is effective in maintaining a compact urban structure, and whether it is also effective in improving an urban structure that has already sprawled.

3   Simulation Model

Based on Nagai [27], this research developed the experimental model in various factors including the change of the initial experimental state, the introduction of a tramway, and parameter refinement. The overview of the experimental model was described below according to the ODD (Overview, Design concepts, and Details) protocol.

3.1   Purpose

By modeling and running the ABM that abstracted a city and activities of the residents in the city, this research verified the effects of controlling the urban structure, which was planned according to the zoning with separation between residences and job locations, based on the combination of the introduction of a tramway with introducing a public facility for urban residents and implementing a policy to promote activeness around it. Additionally, this research verified the effects of improving the urban structure, which has already sprawled, based on the combination of them.

3.2   Entities and Scales

Entities are a planar urban schematic and household agents who act in the urban schematic. Both are spatially-explicit. Figure 1 shows the urban schematic. This is the abstraction of a part of typical regional cities in Japan, where a central business district (CBD) and bedroom towns connected by railway. They were planned according to the zoning with separation between residences and job locations. Therefore, they are also regarded as the polycentric-form compact city, which is composed of multiple hubs linked with traffic networks and sharing their own role [5, 33]. In the urban schematic, two domains are located: the residence district and the central business district (CBD). The residence district is the aggregation of residences, which are the starting point and the final destination of each household agent's daily travel which corresponds to commuting. CBD is the aggregation of job locations, which are also a halfway point of the travel. Two railway stations, the residence station and the central station, are located at the centers and they are connected by a railway. Additionally, a highway is located 500 m north of the railway. Furthermore, three tramway routes are radially installed around the central station as a hub (see next section for details). To simplify the simulation, uniform and high-density sidewalks and roads are located on this whole urban schematic. With the assumption, household agents can freely travel on this space on foot, by bicycle or private automobile.

In the residence district, as the initial location, residences of the same number as household agents, 1,000, are located randomly based on normal distribution centering on the residence stations. One household agent corresponds to 10 households in the real-world. Similarly, in CBD, job locations of the same number are also located. Additionally, one public facility such as a complex mentioned in the previous section: a public facility for stopping off (PFS), is located in the central area.

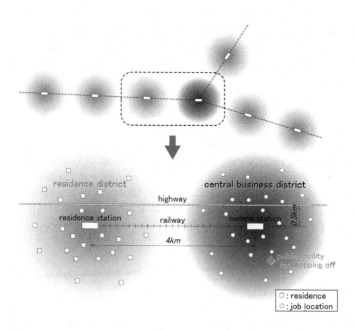

Fig. 1. Urban schematic

3.3 State Variables of Household Agent

State variables of household agent are as follows:

- Position of the residence
- Position of the job location
- Type of linked trip selected currently
- Value list of linked trips (updated based on daily travel cost)

In this research, the position of a job location corresponding to a certain household agent is always fixed. A linked trip indicates the series of travels of each household agent from the starting point to the destination.

3.4 Process Overview and Scheduling

Each household agent does daily travel based on the value list of linked trips, and fixes travel mode in one way through the learning period of repeating this daily travel 30 times. After that, for 1/10 of all household agents that are randomly chosen, relocate their residences. The change in land-use pattern is brought about through these residential relocations. In this research, after the loop process of residential relocation is repeated 20 times, the simulation stops processing.[2]

3.5 Sub-model of Daily Travel

Each household agent repeats daily travel according to the selected linked trip. The representative travel mode is either of the following: on foot, by bicycle, train, private automobile, or tramway. The initial representative travel mode of all household agents is train according to the original urban planning philosophy. Each household agent leaves the residence for the job location. And after all household agents arrive at each job location, they leave for PFS. After arriving and staying there, finally they return to the residence. When the household agents return to the residence, the total travel cost C is calculated according to the equation below.

$$C = w_t C_t + w_c C_c + w_f C_f - w_P P$$

C_t, C_c, C_f, and P indicate time cost, charge cost, fatigue cost, and activeness value. w_t, w_c, w_f, and w_P indicate each preference bias. The preference biases of all agents are assumed to be equal. According to this cost, the household agent updates the value V_i of the selected i-th linked trip, according to the equation below.

$$V_i \longleftarrow \alpha(-C) + (1 - \alpha)V_i$$

---

[2] This model assumes that 30 times of daily travels (a single loop process of residential relocation) represent two years in the real-world. Therefore, 20 loop processes of the residential relocation correspond to simulating 40 years of urban dynamics in the real-world.

The following travel of the household agent is done according to the linked trip selected by the ε-greedy method based on this value. And each household agent fixes their travel mode in one way through the learning period of repeating this daily travel 30 times. This setting is based on the findings that individuals choose travel modes and routes rather boundedly rationally and habitually [16].

Activeness Value. Regarding a 500 m radius around PFS as the zone of influence, the implementation of a policy to promote activeness is considered. Here, it is assumed that street activeness can be generated when household agents, which travel on foot or by bicycle within this range, interact face-to-face, namely when they agglomerate geographically. During this time, relevant household agents acquire benefit brought about by the street activeness, which is mentioned in the previous section, as activeness value P.

$$P = min(\eta_{ac}D_{ac}, P^{max})$$

$D_{ac}(agent)$ indicates the number of other household agents traveling on foot or by bicycle within r_{ac} meter radius centering on the relevant household agent. η_{ac} indicates coefficient of activeness. The total travel cost is reduced by the amount obtained by multiplying the activeness value P with preference bias w_P. The coefficient of activeness can be regarded as a level of effort to bring further street activeness within the relevant range according to the agglomeration of pedestrians. This coefficient is enhanced by projects such as arranging comfortable sidewalks and cycling roads, arranging attractive retail stores, or holding attractive events. Improvement in this coefficient enhances the benefit for travel on foot or by bicycle in the relevant range, increasing a balanced total travel cost. Therefore, this coefficient can be regarded as a coefficient of gain. Hereinafter, the policy that corresponds to improvement of this coefficient of activeness is referred to as the policy to promote activeness.

3.6 Sub-model of Residential Relocation

After all household agents fix their travel mode in one way through the learning period, 1/10 of all household agents that are randomly chosen relocate their residence. To the relevant household agents, 10 of candidate residences are presented randomly. The total living cost of these candidates is the sum of total travel cost and land rent. The total travel cost is calculated by conducting virtual daily travel from a candidate residence based on the travel mode fixed by the relevant household agent through learning. The land rent for the candidate residence increases corresponding to the agglomeration of neighboring residences and job locations. In other words, the local interactions between households, and between a household and an environment, also impact the change in land-use pattern through the change in land rent. Each household agents relocate to the candidate residence of which the total living cost C^l is the minimum out of 10 candidates.

3.7 Initialization and Input Data

Setting values of parameters of the urban schematic and household agent were set carefully based on the various mainly empirical materials, including socio-demographic and other statistical data published by public authorities e.g., the ministry of land, infrastructure and transport [2], and previous studies, while assuming a regional city in Japan.

3.8 Indicators to Estimate Experimental Result

By observing the result of each experimental scenario according to the indicators shown below, changes in the urban structure were evaluated.

- Percentage of each representative travel mode
- Total CO_2 emission (expressed as percentage relative to the scenario A)
- Average travel time
- Standard deviation of distribution of residences (the initial values are 8)
- Distribution map of residences.

4   Experiment 1 - Introduction of Tramway

This section verifies the change of the urban structure, which was formed according to the zoning with separation between residences and job locations, based on the combination of the introduction of tramway with introducing a public facility for urban residents and implementing a policy to promote activeness around it, described in Nagai [27].

4.1   Conditions of Experiment 1

The simulation here assumes that the urban schematic tramway routes imitate the "Karlsruhe Model" [11], where the routes are shared with ordinary railways. Therefore, three routes are radially installed centering on the central station as shown on Fig. 2, and the routes pass through CBD. Each route has tramway stops at 400 m intervals like ordinary tramway services in the real world. Along with this, residents can also choose the additional following four types of linked trips. The first two are by train and tramway in combination, and the other two are by tramway.

The experiments were conducted under the conditions of the following two types for the location of a public facility for stopping off (PFS).

- A : not introduced (no implementation of the policy to promote activeness)
- E : urban central area, 0.5 km south and 0.5 Km east from the central station

E was the most effective location to maintain compact urban structure in Nagai [27]. And the four types, 0, 10, 20, and 30, for coefficient of activeness. Hereinafter, each of these experiments is expressed e.g., scenario At, Et0 – 30,

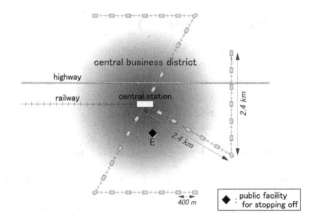

Fig. 2. Schematic of tramway routes

by combining the symbols of A and E indicating the location of PFS, the initial letter t for the word of tram, and the coefficient of activeness. Additionally, this section reproduces scenario A, where PFS was not introduced, and a policy to promote activeness around it was also not implemented, to compare with the new scenarios and validate the simulation model.

4.2   Results of Experiment 1

Table 1 shows the quantitative result of scenario A, At, and Et0 – 30. Figure 3 shows the final distributions of residences of the same scenarios.

The result of scenario At, when compared with scenario A, shows that the percentage of private automobile users decreased by close to 30 points, while the percentage of train (and tramway in combination) users increased accordingly. Along with this, the sprawl on the periphery of CBD was improved, and the total CO_2 emission also reduced considerably.

The results of scenario Et0 – 30 show that, in scenario Et0, the percentages of each travel mode and the sprawl level were almost the same as scenario At. As advancing the policy to promote activeness, however, the percentage of private automobile users got decreasing gradually. When the scenario reached Et30, the percentage of private automobile users decreased to less than 10%, and the percentage of train (and tramway in combination) users increased to more than 75%. Along with this, the cluster of residences of train users around the residence station was maintained quite clearly. Additionally, the percentage of tramway users increased to more than 15%. And the total CO_2 emission also reduced to less than 30%.

Table 1. Result of Experiment 1

Scenario	Percentage of representative travel modes						CO_2 emission	Travel time	Standard deviation	
	Walk	bicycle	Train	Automobile	train + Tram	Tram			x-cor	y-cor
A	1.3%	2.4%	7.3%	89.0%	0.0%	0.0%	100.0%	9.3 min	22.9	9.8
At	1.4%	2.6%	15.0%	49.7%	27.9%	3.5%	66.6%	20.6 min	17.0	8.4
Et0	1.1%	2.3%	14.4%	53.7%	25.3%	3.2%	91.1%	33.5 min	17.5	9.1
Et10	1.2%	1.5%	11.3%	21.6%	57.1%	7.4%	48.1%	39.4 min	13.9	7.8
Et20	1.2%	1.3%	9.5%	10.4%	65.7%	11.9%	32.9%	44.7 min	13.3	7.6
Et30	1.0%	1.1%	7.9%	7.1%	67.6%	15.3%	28.6%	47.6 min	13.7	8.0

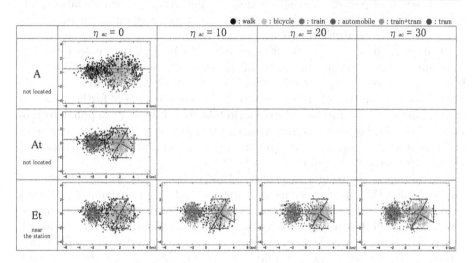

Fig. 3. Residences' final distribution of Experiment 1

5   Experiment 2 - Setting Urban Sprawl as Initial State

This section verifies the effect on improving the existent urban sprawl based on the implementation of the same policies including the introduction of tramway, described in the previous section.

5.1   Conditions of Experiment 2

This section sets the final state of scenario A as the experimental initial state. Most of the residences were distributed on the periphery of CBD as sprawl, and the percentage of private automobile users reached close to 90%. This shows the state after 20 loop processes of residential relocation (corresponding to 40 years) from the zoning with separation between residences and job locations. The edge routes of tramway also pass through the suburb area with sprawled residences.

The experiments were conducted under the conditions of the two types for the location of PFS and the four types for coefficient of activeness, like the previous section. Hereinafter, each of these experiments is expressed e.g., scenario SAt, SEt0 – 30, by combining the initial letter S for the word of sprawl, the symbols of A and E indicating the location of PFS, the initial letter t for the word of tram, and the coefficient of activeness. Additionally, scenario SEt30+, which was run for twice as long as SEt30, was executed.

5.2   Results of Experiment 2

Table 2 shows the quantitative result of scenario SAt, SEt0 – 30, and SEt30+. Figure 4 shows the final distributions of residences of the same scenarios.

The result of scenario SAt shows that the percentage of private automobile users increased further, and the sprawl of their residences on the periphery of CBD also advanced further, unlike scenario At.

The results of scenario SE0 – 30 also show that both the decrease in the private automobile users and the cluster of residences of train users around the residence station were not observed, unlike the series of Et. Particularly in scenario SEt0 – 20, the percentage of private automobile users increased further, and the sprawl also advanced further, like scenario SAt. In advancing the policy to promote activeness, however, the percentage of private automobile users decreased, and the percentage of tramway (and train in combination) users increased and reached close to 50% in total in scenario SEt30.

Furthermore, the results of scenario SEt30+, where scenario SEt30 was run further, shows that the percentage of tramway (and train in combination) users reached close to 90% in total. Along with this, the total CO_2 emission also reduced considerably, and the following two clusters of residences were formed. One is the cluster by residents commuting by train and tramway in combination (about 20%), on centering the residence station. The other is the cluster by residents commuting by tramway alone (about 70%), along tramway routes from the center to the periphery of CBD.

Table 2. Result of Experiment 2

Scenario	Percentage of representative travel modes						CO_2 emission	Travel time	Standard deviation	
	Walk	Bicycle	Train	Automobile	Train + tram	Tram			x-cor	y-cor
SAt	0.8%	1.3%	1.5%	93.4%	1.3%	1.7%	89.3%	7.5 min	27.3	11.7
SEt0	0.7%	0.9%	1.7%	94.1%	1.5%	1.2%	95.4%	20.9 min	21.6	14.2
SEt10	0.6%	0.6%	1.7%	94.5%	1.4%	1.2%	97.1%	21.1 min	21.9	14.2
SEt20	0.8%	0.7%	1.4%	91.8%	1.9%	3.3%	94.8%	21.3 min	21.9	14.3
SEt30	2.3%	0.9%	4.1%	44.9%	12.3%	35.6%	54.2%	37.4 min	22.5	14.2
SEt30+	0.8%	0.9%	1.4%	10.0%	19.4%	67.5%	20.6%	43.7 min	20.5	12.9

6   Discussion

6.1   Estimation of the Experimental Results

By combining the introduction of tramway with introducing a public facility for stopping off (PFS) and implementing a policy to promote activeness around it, the percentage of private automobile users decreased, when compared with

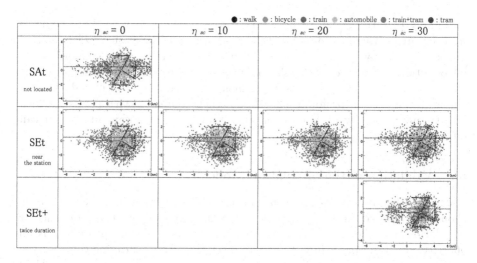

Fig. 4. Residences' final distribution of Experiment 5

the cases when no policies were implemented. And the percentage of train (and tramway in combination) users increased accordingly. Along with this, the total CO_2 emission reduced, and the compact urban structure, which was formed according to the zoning, was maintained. These suggest that the synergistic effects of the introduction of tramway, the proper location of the public facility for urban residents, and the policy to promote activeness around it, could impact positively on a both static and dynamic urban environment. This also seems to be because the policy to promote activeness, which is incentive to stroll about downtown, was effective to increase the percentage of tramway users, like the two transport policies in Nagai [27].

On the other hand, where the initial state was sprawl mainly with private automobiles, the introduction of tramway could not serve to control further sprawl and use of private automobiles. When combined with the introduction of the public facility and the implementation of the policy to promote activeness, however, most of the private automobile users switched to tramway use, although it took a long period. This suggests that once residents established the lifestyle of low-density residence in suburb and commuting by private automobile, that becomes robust, irreversible, and very difficult to be upset.

As for the residence distribution in the same scenario, most of the residences that are distributed along the tramway routes deviated from the initial polycentric-form compact city, which was planned according to the zoning with separation between residences and job locations. This, however, can gain the following positive evaluations of a monocentric-form compact city. First, the residents can establish a life where residences and job locations are nearby based mainly on use of public transportations, resulting in being free from traffic congestion and air pollution. Second, mixed land-use provides the residents with a broad range of social activities, while revitalizing the central urban area.

Simply put, the policy to promote activeness is a policy to lead people to walk by giving them incentives. On the other hand, many successful cases of introducing tramway in the real world are characterized with combining the introduction of tramway with other policies which serve as a benefit for people traveling on foot. That is, this experiment clarified that the introduction of tramway can exert a profound effect only when combined with policies, which lead tramway users' walk before and after they use a tramway, and how it can offer great benefits.

6.2   Validation of the Simulation Model

Because of the property of emergence in complex self-organizing systems, ABMs should be assessed based on validity rather than one-to-one correspondence or correlation measures [34]. Pattern-Oriented Modeling (POM) procedure is an effective validation procedure. In POM procedure, after identifying the observed patterns in the real-world characterizing the system to be modeled, the ABM is evaluated by whether the observed patterns are reproduced [29]. This section validated the simulation model according to the concept of POM.

In scenario A for the first experiment, the residence distribution significantly changed from separation between residences and job locations to sprawl where most of the residences on the periphery of CBD. This can be regarded as the reproduction of the growth process of a concentric low-density suburb based on the monocentric urban model which was proposed by Alonso [4] and subsequently supported by many related researches. This can be also regarded as the reproduction of the fact that many cities in Japan's urban areas have consistently expanded since the high economic growth period [14]. Furthermore, the travel mode used by most of the household agents living in suburb has switched from train to private automobiles. This can be also regarded as the reproduction of the fact that the main travel mode in commuting has switched from train to private automobiles, and the road traffic has reached saturation, especially in regional cities [2].

The purpose of the model is not to reproduce the real society precisely, but to analyze the mechanism of highly abstracted urban dynamics by a small number of elements and simple rules. Nevertheless, the simulation model reproduced the above multiple social phenomena which were not directly incorporated into the model. Therefore, these reproductions demonstrate that the simulation model can explain the real society to a certain level, and the experimental results of this research are valid.

7   Conclusion

The purpose of this research was to verify the effectiveness of the combination of the introduction of a tramway with introducing the public facility for urban residents and implementing the policy to promote activeness around it, on urban sprawl. So, this research built an agent-based model (ABM) for simulating urban structure changes through autonomous daily travel and residential relocations of urban residents. By using this model, the simulations were conducted based on the assumption of setting zoning with separation between residences and job locations as the initial state and combining these policies. These were followed by other simulations based on the assumption of setting urban sprawl as the initial state and combining these policies. As a result, these experiments clarified the following points and how they were.

- The synergistic effects of the introduction of a tramway, the proper location of a public facility for urban residents, and the policy to promote activeness around it, are effective in maintaining a polycentric-form compact urban structure in accordance with the initial plan.
- The introduction of a tramway targeting the urban sprawl can exert a profound effect only when combined with the above-mentioned policies, which lead tramway users' walk before and after using the tramway, although it takes a long period.
- A monocentric-form compact urban structure, which differs from the initial plan, is realized along with the above-mentioned point, improving the living environment for the residents and revitalizing the urban central area.

References

1. Idea store strategy. https://www.ideastore.co.uk
2. White paper on land, infrastructure and transport in 2016 - the ministry of land, infrastructure and transport. http://www.mlit.go.jp/hakusyo/mlit/h28/index.html
3. Acheampong, R.A., Silva, E.: Land use-transport interaction modeling: a review of the literature and future research directions. J. Transp. Land Use **8**(3), 11–38 (2015)
4. Alonso, W.: Location and Land Use. Toward a General Theory of Land Rent. Harvard University Press, Cambridge (1964)
5. Anderson, W.P., Kanaroglou, P.S., Miller, E.J.: Urban form, energy and the environment: a review of issues, evidence and policy. Urban Stud. **33**(1), 7–35 (1996)
6. Batisani, N., Yarnal, B.: Uncertainty awareness in urban sprawl simulations: lessons from a small US metropolitan region. Land Use Policy **26**(2), 178–185 (2009)
7. Batty, M.: Cities and Complexity: Understanding Cities with Cellular Automata, Agent-Based Models, and Fractals. The MIT press, Cambridge (2007)
8. Behan, K., Maoh, H., Kanaroglou, P.: Smart growth strategies, transportation and urban sprawl: simulated futures for hamilton, ontario. Can. Geogr./Le Géographe Can. **52**(3), 291–308 (2008)
9. Benenson, I.: Multi-agent simulations of residential dynamics in the city. Comput. Environ. Urban Syst. **22**(1), 25–42 (1998)
10. Brueckner, J.K., Mills, E., Kremer, M.: Urban sprawl: lessons from urban economics. Brookings-Wharton papers on urban affairs, pp. 65–97 (2001)
11. De Bruijn, H., Veeneman, W.: Decision-making for light rail. Transp. Res. Part A: Policy Pract. **43**(4), 349–359 (2009)
12. Deal, B., Schunk, D.: Spatial dynamic modeling and urban land use transformation: a simulation approach to assessing the costs of urban sprawl. Ecol. Econ. **51**(1), 79–95 (2004)

13. Desa, U.: World urbanization prospects, the 2011 revision. Final Report with Annex Tables. United Nations Department of Economic and Social Affairs, New York (2012)

14. Eaton, J., Eckstein, Z.: Cities and growth: theory and evidence from France and Japan. Reg. Sci. Urban Econ. **27**(4–5), 443–474 (1997)

15. Ewing, R.: Is Los Angeles-style sprawl desirable? J. Am. Planning Assoc. **63**(1), 107–126 (1997)

16. Fujii, S.: An empirical test of hypothesis on influence of travel behavior on residential choice behavior: a fundamental study on transportation measures for promoting compact cities. JSTE J. Traffic Eng

17. Gilbert, N.: Agent-Based Models. No. 153. Sage, Thousand Oaks (2008)

18. Gimblett, R., Daniel, T., Cherry, S., Meitner, M.J.: The simulation and visualization of complex human-environment interactions. Landscape Urban Planning **54**(1), 63–79 (2001)

19. Howley, P., Scott, M., Redmond, D.: An examination of residential preferences for less sustainable housing: exploring future mobility among dublin central city residents. Cities **26**(1), 1–8 (2009)

20. Jacobs, J.: The Economy of Cities. Vintage Books, New York City (1969)

21. Johnson, M.P.: Environmental impacts of urban sprawl: a survey of the literature and proposed research agenda. Environ. Planning A **33**(4), 717–735 (2001)

22. Kakoi, M., Nakamura, R., Saito, S.: Causal structure modeling of consumer's decision-making on selection of commercial facilities. Fukuoka Univ. Econ. Rev. **54**(3–4), 241–256 (2010)

23. Koike, H., Morimoto, A., Itoh, K.: A study on measures to promote bicycle usage in Japan. In: VeloMondial 2000-World Bicycle Conference, pp. 19–22. Citeseer (2000)

24. Ligtenberg, A., Bregt, A.K., Van Lammeren, R.: Multi-actor-based land use modelling: spatial planning using agents. Landscape Urban Planning **56**(1), 21–33 (2001)

25. Lucas, R.E.: On the mechanics of economic development. Econ. Soc. Monogr. **29**, 61–70 (1998)

26. Martine, G., Marshall, A., et al.: State of world population 2007: unleashing the potential of urban growth. UNFPA (2007)

27. Nagai, H., Kurahashi, S.: Bustle changes the city - facility for stopping off and modeling urban dynamics. Trans. Jpn. Soc. Artif. Intell. **32**(1), D-G26_1 (2017)

28. Nawrocki, J., Nakagawa, D., Matsunaka, R., Oba, T.: Measuring walkability and its effect on light rail usage: a comparative study of the usa and Japan. Urban Transp. XX **138**, 305 (2014)

29. Railsback, S.F., Grimm, V.: Agent-Based and Individual-Based Modeling: A Practical Introduction. Princeton University Press, Princeton (2011)

30. Schneider, A., Woodcock, C.E.: Compact, dispersed, fragmented, extensive? A comparison of urban growth in twenty-five global cities using remotely sensed data, pattern metrics and census information. Urban Stud. **45**(3), 659–692 (2008)

31. Scott, D.M., Kanaroglou, P.S., Anderson, W.P.: Impacts of commuting efficiency on congestion and emissions: case of the hamilton CMA, Canada. Transp. Res. Part D: Trans. Environ. **2**(4), 245–257 (1997)

32. Taniguchi, T., Takahashi, Y.: Multi-agent simulation about urban dynamics based on a hypothetical relationship between individuals' travel behavior and residential choice behavior. Trans. Soc. Instr. Control Eng. **47**(11), 571–580 (2011)

33. Tsai, Y.H.: Quantifying urban form: compactness versus' sprawl'. Urban Stud. **42**(1), 141–161 (2005)

34. Wu, F.: Calibration of stochastic cellular automata: the application to rural-urban land conversions. Int. J. Geograph. Inf. Sci. **16**(8), 795–818 (2002)

Application Domains for Multi-agent Systems

Multi Agent Flow Estimation Based on Bayesian Optimization with Time Delay and Low Dimensional Parameter Conversion

Hiroshi Kiyotake, Masahiro Kohjima, Tatsushi Matsubayashi[(✉)], and Hiroyuki Toda

NTT Service Evolution Laboratories, NTT Corporation, Kanagawa, Japan
{kiyotake.hiroshi,kohjima.masahiro,matsubayashi.tatsushi,
toda.hiroyuki}@lab.ntt.co.jp

Abstract. Forming comprehensive security plans is essential to ensure safety at large events. The Multi Agent Simulator (MAS) is widely used for preparing security plans that will guide responses to accidents at large events. For forming security plans, it is necessary that we simulate crowd behaviors that reflect real world observations. However, crowd behavior simulations require OD information (departure time, place of Origin, and Destination) of each agent. Moreover, from the viewpoint of protecting personal information, it is difficult to observe the complete and detailed trajectories of all pedestrians. Therefore, the OD information should be estimated from the data observed at several points, usually the number of people passing fixed points. In this paper, we propose an accurate method for estimating OD information; it has three features. First, by using Bayesian optimization (BO) which is widely used to find optimal hyper parameters in the machine learning fields, the OD information is efficiently and accurately estimated using fewer parameter searches. Second, by dividing the time window and ignoring the identity of the observed people, the parameter dimension of the OD information is reduced to yield a solvable search space. Third, by considering the time delay created by the physical separation of the observation points, we develop a more accurate objective function. Experiments evaluate the proposed method using the data collected at three events (University festival, projection-mapping event, and music live), and the accuracy with which reproduction MAS can reproduce the people flows is assessed. We also show an example of the MAS-based process used in making guidance plans to reduce crowd congestion.

Keywords: Multi-agent simulator · Bayesian optimization
Crowd behavior

1 Introduction

Large events such as music festivals and sports games can attract large crowds that can trigger crowd congestion. To ensure safe operation by avoiding con-

© Springer Nature Switzerland AG 2018
T. Miller et al. (Eds.): PRIMA 2018, LNAI 11224, pp. 53–69, 2018.
https://doi.org/10.1007/978-3-030-03098-8_4

gestion and accidents, effective plans (e.g. the placement of security guards, the guiding of participants toward common destinations) are critical. The Multi-Agent Simulation [3,5] (hereinafter abbreviated as MAS) approach has been widely used to realize effective planning [10,13]; MAS is used to generate a wide variety of security plans that are then compared. If the security plans are to be effective in the real world, MAS needs to reproduce reality. Therefore, it is necessary to determine the MAS parameters accurately. There are two types of MAS parameters. The first are micro parameters such as agent moving speed in the behavior model. There are many studies on the estimation of micro parameters, such as using MAS to reproduce the flow of people in a video [1,14]. The second are macro parameters, such as OD information (departure time, place of origin and destination), of the agents [8]. Although estimating macro parameters is important because they are dominant factors in determining congestion, few studies have tackled them. If trajectory information of all participants is available, these macro parameters can be obtained, but privacy concerns have made this unrealistic. One data source that can be observed practice is the number of pedestrians who pass one or more fixed points on a road; data can be gathered either by visual count or by video processing. The data contains information of crowd behavior but can not be used directly for estimating OD information of individuals.

For parameter estimation, we need to use a meta-heuristic approach that does not require an explicit function form such as a genetic algorithm [1,8]. This is because MAS is not represented by a combination of simple functions due to the interaction of many agents, and the output yielded by the input is not known until the run is completed. Figure 1 shows the process of estimating parameters by the meta-heuristic approach. In this method, at first, OD information is input to MAS. Next, MAS outputs the number of pedestrians observed at fixed points after completion. Then, based on past trial results, the candidate parameters that reduce the reproduction error are selected.

In this paper, we propose an efficient and highly accurate meta-heuristic estimation method. Figure 2 shows three key features of our method. These features allow it to estimate the parameters efficiently and accurately.

Bayesian optimization approach: For efficient estimation, we use Bayesian optimization (hereafter BO) which is widely used in the machine learning field to find optimal hyper parameters [9]. This method can efficiently estimate the input parameters since it predicts the reproduction error between the values observed in the real world and those output by MAS.

Parameter conversion technique: The estimation of OD information is difficult in practice because it involves a problem of high dimensionality. Therefore, we change the parameters of each agent to route-based parameters, i.e. the number of pedestrians moving on each route in each time window. This technique greatly reduces the dimensions of the parameters.

Design objective function: For accurate parameter estimation, it is necessary to consider that the same user or users may be observed in multiple time

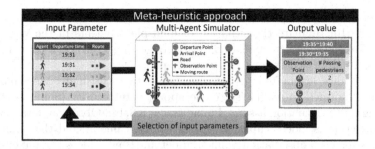

Fig. 1. Framework of our task

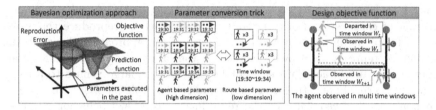

Fig. 2. Three key features of the proposed method

windows. Therefore, as the reproduction error to be optimized, we designed an objective function that uses observed values of multiple time windows in which agents are observed.

We conduct experiments to confirm the accuracy of our method in reproducing crowd behavior. The experiments validate the proposal using data collected at three large events, all of which attracted large crowds (several tens of thousands to several hundreds of thousands of people). The results show that the proposed method has higher accuracy than an existing method. We also analyze the effect of considering that the same agents are observed in multiple time windows. Finally, we will develop a guidance route that should be taken if an accident occurs in similar events in the future based on the crowd behaviors reproduced by our method.

The contributions of this paper are as follows.

1. Proposing MAS parameter estimation method based on BO.
2. Confirming that it can reproduce crowd behavior.
3. Verifying the effectiveness of the guidance created to ease a crowd congestion at actual events as reproduced by MAS.

2 Related Work

Several studies have simulated traffic accidents and disasters at large events, and verified the effectiveness of security plans prepared in advance [10,13]. Yamashita et al. [13] simulate a tsunami hitting a coastal area, and verify the evacuation time when guiding the pedestrians along evacuation routes as a security plan. Ueda et al. [10] simulate the situation of multiple accidents in the vicinity of the 2020 Tokyo Olympic venue, and verify congestion level when changing the movement route of pedestrians as a security plan.

Other studies attempted to use observed data to estimate MAS parameters that conformed to reality, since the appropriate security plan will change depending on the situation assumed in advance [1,8,14]. Observed data has various forms such as videos captured by fixed-point cameras and the number of people passing each observation point. Bera et al. [1] use videos from fixed-point cameras for estimating the RVO parameters (comfort speed, neighbor distance) of each agent, which are parameters commonly used in agent behavior models. Zhou et al. [14] also use video data for estimating the speed and the moving direction of each agent. Both methods were designed to reproduce the movement of people in an area covered by a camera. Their approach is, however, not suitable for reproducing crowd behavior in the large-scale venues that we are targeting, because video data can not be captured at large venues to assuage privacy concerns. Some studies use the number of people passing each observation point as observed data for the reproduction of crowd behavior [8]. They estimate the number of people on each moving route and the guidance pattern that was adopted on the day to prevent congestion. Their research has the same motivation as ours, and it is very similar to the task we address. However, their method requires more than a month to complete the estimations because they use the genetic algorithms shown below.

In estimating MAS parameters, the meta-heuristic optimization approach such as the genetic algorithm (GA) is often used [1,8]. In this approach, parameters are identified by running MAS repeatedly. To formulate a security plan for the next event at the venue, it is desirable to estimate parameters with as few trials as possible. For example, in order to update a security plan with popular artist's music live performance over several days, it is necessary that reproduction be completed within a few days. Therefore, as the GA-based approach requires a large number of MAS trials, it is not suitable for parameter estimation, since each large-scale MAS trial takes a long time to complete. In contrast, BO offers accurate estimation with just a few MAS trials. Therefore, the BO-based approach is suitable for parameter estimation of large-scale MAS.

The dimension of the parameters to be estimated, departure time and movement route for each agent, increases with the number of agents. Unfortunately, unlike GA, BO suffers the disadvantage that accuracy worsens as parameter dimensionality increases. BO for highly dimensional input parameters has been proposed mainly for two kinds of simple functions [4,12]. One is a low dimensional function buried in a high dimensional space [12] and the other is a high dimensional function expressed as the sum of low dimensional functions [4]. However, no BO proposal targets complicated high-dimensional functions such as MAS. We propose a key technique to convert high dimensional parameters into low dimension equivalents.

3   Proposed Method

3.1   Setting

The problem we address is OD estimation for each agent from observed data streams generated by counting the number of people passing fixed points. When the total number of people whose OD information should be estimated is U, the problem is recast as the optimization of parameter search in U-dimensional space.

The parameter set of departure time and route (the pair of Origin and Destination) of agent u is given as $\boldsymbol{\pi} = \{(t_u, r_u)\}_{u=1}^{U}$, where U is the number of agents passed to MAS. The objective function to be optimized, the error between the MAS output yielded by $\boldsymbol{\pi}$ and the observed data, is defined by $L(\boldsymbol{\pi})$, and the problem is expressed as follows,

$$\boldsymbol{\pi}^* = \arg \min_{\pi \in \mathcal{S}_\pi} L(\boldsymbol{\pi}), \tag{1}$$

where $\mathcal{S}_\pi$ is the U-dimensional search space for the OD parameters. With this problem setting, as the number of agents increases, the combination of parameters to be estimated increases exponentially. Therefore, it is necessary to realize a more practical setting.

Parameter conversion technique: Our key idea for avoiding the exponential increase in calculation cost is to avoid the parameter dimensionality curse of the OD information by using time window divisions and ignoring the identification of the observed people. The observed data $\boldsymbol{Y} \ (= \{y_{to}\}_{t,o}^{T,O} \in \mathbb{R}^{T \times O})$ is the number of people passing the o-th fixed point during $t \sim t + \Delta t$. To reproduce $\boldsymbol{Y}$ on MAS, identification of the people (agents) is not necessary to ensure the symmetry of the search space. Specifically, the objective function becomes same value if the two parameters $\boldsymbol{\pi}$ and $\boldsymbol{\pi}'$, indicating two agents that have the same departure time $(t_k = t_{k+1} = t^*)$ but different routes $(r_k \neq r_{k+1})$, are swapped. In short,

$$L(\boldsymbol{\pi}) = L(\boldsymbol{\pi}'), \quad \text{where} \quad \boldsymbol{\pi} = \{(t_1, r_1), \dots, (t^*, r_k), (t^*, r_{k+1}), \dots, (t_U, r_U)\}$$
$$\text{and} \quad \boldsymbol{\pi}' = \{(t_1, r_1), \dots, (t^*, r_{k+1}), (t^*, r_k), \dots, (t_U, r_U)\}. \tag{2}$$

Therefore, it is not necessary to estimate each agent's parameters for reproducing crowd behavior, since even if the departure time of an agent changes slightly the reproduction error does not change significantly. Therefore, agent's departure times in the same time window can be integrated to the route based parameter matrix $\boldsymbol{X} = \{x_{tr}\}_{t,r}^{T,R} \in \mathbb{R}^{T \times R}$, instead of the agent-based parameters $\boldsymbol{\pi}$. Where, x_{tr} is the number of pedestrians who move on route r and depart within the time window $W_t = [t, t + \Delta t)$ as follows,

$$x_{tr} = \# \text{ of } u \quad \text{s.t.} \quad t_u \in W_t \text{ and } r_u = r. \tag{3}$$

On the other hand, the inverse conversion from $\boldsymbol{X}$ to $\boldsymbol{\pi}$ cannot be determined strictly and uniquely. However, because of the above symmetry of the identification, small differences in the departure times of the agents generated from a uniform distribution within time window, W_t, yield minimal changes in the reproduction error. Therefore, π can be inversely converted from $\boldsymbol{X}$. The departure time of the u-th agent is given as $t_u \sim \mathcal{U}(W_t)$ and π is converted as follows:

$$\pi = \{\underbrace{(\mathcal{U}(W_1), 1), \cdots, (\mathcal{U}(W_1), R)}_{|\boldsymbol{x}_1|}, \cdots, \underbrace{(\mathcal{U}(W_T), 1), \cdots, (\mathcal{U}(W_T), R)}_{|\boldsymbol{x}_T|}\} \quad (4)$$

here $\boldsymbol{x}_t = \{x_{tr}\}_{r=1}^R$ is the total number of pedestrian vectors. By estimating $\boldsymbol{x}_t$ sequentially with t, the dimensionality of the parameter to be estimated becomes the number of routes, R ($R << U$). This means that rather than the original problem, we solve the following optimization problems for each time window,

$$\boldsymbol{x}_t^* = \arg \min_{\boldsymbol{x}_t \in \mathcal{S}_x} L(\boldsymbol{x}_t), \quad t = 1, \ldots, T, \quad (5)$$

where $\mathcal{S}_x$ is the positive real R-dimensional vector space, and T is the number of time windows. In the later experiment, whereas the dimensionality of the original problem is tens of thousands, the dimensionality after conversion ranges from 20 to 40. Called the *conversion technique*, it makes the original problem easy to solve.

Designing the objective function: To estimate $\boldsymbol{x}_t$ accurately, it is necessary to design an objective function that takes into consideration the time windows in which agents are observed. The relationship between the agent's departure time window and the observation time window is shown in Fig. 3. Agents departing at $W_{t-\omega}$ may be observed within W_t, where ω is the maximum window size in which the agent is observed. Therefore, the following relationship holds,

$$\hat{\boldsymbol{y}}_t = f(\boldsymbol{x}_{t-\omega}, \cdots, \boldsymbol{x}_t), \quad (6)$$

where f is a function that associates observation value $\hat{\boldsymbol{y}}_t$ at time window W_t on MAS executed with agent parameter π converted from $\boldsymbol{x}_{t-\omega}, \cdots, \boldsymbol{x}_t$. Also, the agents departing in time window W_t are observed in time window $W_{t'}(t' = t, \cdots, t + \omega)$. Thus, the objective function for estimating $\boldsymbol{x}_t$ is as follows,

$$L_\omega(\boldsymbol{x}_t) = \sum_{t'=t}^{t+\omega} \|\boldsymbol{y}_{t'} - \hat{\boldsymbol{y}}_{t'}\| = \sum_{t'=t}^{t+\omega} \|\boldsymbol{y}_{t'} - f(\boldsymbol{x}_{t'-\omega}, \cdots, \boldsymbol{x}_{t'})\|. \quad (7)$$

This objective function takes account of all the time windows observed until the agent arrives at the destination, and enables highly accurate estimation.

3.2   Multi Time Window Bayesian Optimization (MTWBO)

Our method (called **Multi Time Window Bayesian Optimization: MTWBO**) uses three features in estimating route-based parameters $\boldsymbol{x}_t$ for each time window W_t instead of agent-based parameters π. Figure 4 indicates the framework of our method.

First, the candidate route-based parameters, $\boldsymbol{x}_t$, that may reduce the reproduction error are selected using the BO approach based on past trial results of

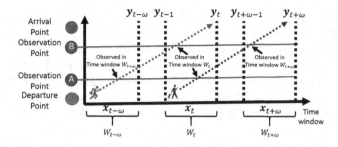

Fig. 3. Space-time map of departure time window and travel distance

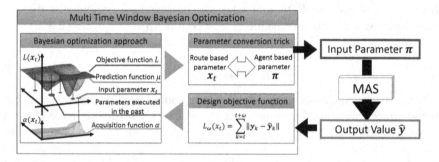

Fig. 4. Proposed method: outline

MAS. For parameter selection, the prediction function that predicts the reproduction error of any point is constructed based on the executed result of the parameter $\boldsymbol{x}_t^{(m)}$ $(m = 1, \ldots, M)$ randomly selected from parameter space $\mathcal{S}_x$. We denote the reproduction error of agent-based parameter $\boldsymbol{\pi}^{(m)}$ converted from $\boldsymbol{x}_t^{(m)}$ by the parameter conversion technique as $z_t^{(m)} = L_\omega(\boldsymbol{x}_t^{(m)})$, and past trial results as $D_t = \{(\boldsymbol{x}_t^{(m)}, z_t^{(m)}) \mid m = 1, \ldots, M\}$. Here, assuming that L_ω follows a Gaussian process [7], the reproduction error $z_t^{(m)} = L_\omega(\boldsymbol{x}_t^{(m)})$ at any point $\boldsymbol{x}_t^{(m)}$ follows a normal distribution with average $\mu(\boldsymbol{x}_t)$ and variance $\sigma(\boldsymbol{x}_t)$ as follows

$$z_t^{(m)} \sim \mathcal{N}(\mu(\boldsymbol{x}_t), \sigma(\boldsymbol{x}_t)), \tag{8}$$
$$\mu(\boldsymbol{x}_t; D_t) = \boldsymbol{k}^T(\boldsymbol{K} + \beta\boldsymbol{I})\boldsymbol{z}, \tag{9}$$
$$\sigma(\boldsymbol{x}_t; D_t) = k(\boldsymbol{x}_t, \boldsymbol{x}_t) - \boldsymbol{k}^T(\boldsymbol{K} + \beta\boldsymbol{I})^{-1}\boldsymbol{k}, \tag{10}$$

where $k : \mathcal{S}_x \times \mathcal{S}_x \to \mathbb{R}$ is a kernel function that measures the similarity between two parameters, $\boldsymbol{k} = (k(\boldsymbol{x}_t^{(m)}, \boldsymbol{x}_t))_{m=1}^M \in \mathbb{R}^M$, $\boldsymbol{K} = (k(\boldsymbol{x}_t^{(m)}, \boldsymbol{x}_t^{(m')}))_{m,m'=1}^M \in \mathbb{R}^{M \times M}$; β is a hyper-parameter, $\boldsymbol{I} \in \mathbb{R}^{M \times M}$ is an identity matrix, and $\boldsymbol{z} = (z_t^{(m)})_{m=1}^M \in \mathbb{R}^M$. In the later experiment, we use following commonly used Gaussian kernel,

$$k(\boldsymbol{x}_t^{(m_1)}, \boldsymbol{x}_t^{(m_2)}) = \exp(a\|\boldsymbol{x}_t^{(m_1)} - \boldsymbol{x}_t^{(m_2)}\|^2), \text{ and } a > 0. \tag{11}$$

Then, a parameter the has the highest possibility of updating the current best reproduction error is selected by utilizing the information of the prediction function. In the BO approach, we evaluate this possibility quantitatively using the acquisition function α. Parameters with low predicted reproduction error and parameters of unsearched areas take higher values in the acquisition function. In this paper, we use Expected Improvement (EI) [2,6,11] which is one of the most studied theoretical features for acquisition functions. EI is expressed as follows,

$$\alpha(\boldsymbol{x}_t; D_t) = (\mu(\boldsymbol{x}_t) - \tau)\Phi(\gamma(\boldsymbol{x}_t)) + \sigma(\boldsymbol{x}_t)\phi(\gamma(\boldsymbol{x}_t)), \quad \gamma(\boldsymbol{x}_t) = \frac{\mu(\boldsymbol{x}_t) - \tau}{\sigma(\boldsymbol{x}_t)}, (12)$$

where ϕ and Φ are the PDF and CDF of the standard normal distribution, respectively, and τ is the best value in trial results $z_t(m = 1, \ldots, M)$. We select the parameter that maximizes the acquisition function as the input of MAS.

$$\arg \max_{\boldsymbol{x}_t \in \mathcal{S}_x} \alpha(\boldsymbol{x}_t). \tag{13}$$

Next, the reproduction error of the chosen route-based parameter $\boldsymbol{x}_t$ is calculated. Since route-based parameters $\boldsymbol{x}_t$ cannot be input directly to MAS, they are converted into agent-based parameters $\boldsymbol{\pi}$ by using our parameter conversion technique. Then, the reproduction error for converted parameter $\boldsymbol{\pi}$ is calculated using the proposed objective function L_ω defined in Eq. (7). The pair of obtained parameter $\boldsymbol{x}_t$ and reproduction error $L_\omega(\boldsymbol{x}_t)$ is added to the past trial data, D_t, and then used to select a new input parameter of MAS.

Our algorithm estimates agent-based parameter $\boldsymbol{x}_t$ in each time window W_t in order. The value of the objective function depends on not only the previous time window parameter $\boldsymbol{x}'_t(t' = t - \omega, \ldots, t - 1)$, but also later time window parameter $\boldsymbol{x}'_t(t' = t + 1, \ldots, t + \omega)$ as shown Eq. (7). To allow the influence of subsequent parameters, it is necessary to estimate $\boldsymbol{x}_t$ again after estimating those time windows. That is, estimation from $\boldsymbol{x}_1$ to $\boldsymbol{x}_T$ is performed in multiple cycles. The estimation procedure is summarized as Algorithm 1.

4   Experiment

In this section, we confirm the effectiveness of the proposed method by using datasets gathered at multiple events. The two objectives of the experiment are as follows.

- Confirm that the proposal achieves higher estimation accuracy than existing methods and is more practical.
- Show how to determine window size, ω, for maximizing estimation accuracy.

4.1   Multi-agent Simulator

This paper uses a multi-lane graph-based MAS [10]. In MAS, each agent is directed to its destination along the shortest path considering the degree of

Algorithm 1. MTWBO

Input:
  L_ω : Objective function;
  $C \in \mathbb{N}^+$: Number of cycles;
  $T \in \mathbb{N}^+$: Number of time windows;
  $M \in \mathbb{N}^+$: Sample size in each Time window;
  $I \in \mathbb{N}^+$: Number of iterations in each Time window;
  $\omega \in \mathbb{N}^+$: Window size;
  $\mathcal{S}_x$: Parameter space;
1: Set x_t^* by random sampling from $\mathcal{S}_x$, $t = 1, \cdots T$
2: **for** $c = 1$ to C **do**
3:    **for** $t = 1$ to T **do**
4:        Collect $\{x_t^{(m)} | m = 1, \cdots, M\}$ by random sampling from $\mathcal{S}_x$
5:        Convert $x_t^{(m)}$ to $\pi^{(m)}$ by Eq.(4)
6:        **for** $m = 1$ to M **do**   //Running MAS
7:            $\hat{y}_{t'}^{(m)} = f(x_{t'-\omega}^*, \cdots, x_t^{(m)}, \cdots, x_{t'}^*)$ where $t' = t, \cdots t + \omega$
8:            $z_t^{(m)} = L_\omega(x_t^{(m)})$ by Eq. (7)
9:        **end for**
10:        $D_t = \{(x_t^{(m)}, z_t^{(m)}) | m = 1, \cdots, M\}$
11:        **for** $i = M + 1$ to $M + I$ **do**   //Input parameters selection
12:            Calculate $\mu(x_t)$, $\sigma(x_t)$ and $\alpha(x_t)$ on D_t following Eq. (9)(10)(11)
13:            $x_t^{(i)} = \mathrm{argmax}_{x_t \in \mathcal{S}} \alpha(x_t; D_t)$
14:            Convert $x_t^{(i)}$ to $\pi^{(i)}$ by Eq.(4)
15:            $\hat{y}_{t'}^{(i)} = f(x_{t'-\omega}^*, \cdots, x_t^{(i)}, \cdots, x_{t'}^*)$ where $t' = t, \cdots, t + \omega$
16:            $z_t^{(i)} = L_\omega(x_t^{(i)})$ following Eq. (7)
17:            $D_t = D_t \cup (x_t^{(i)}, z_t^{(i)})$
18:        **end for**
19:        $x_t^* \leftarrow \mathrm{argmin}_{x_t \in D_t} L_\omega(x_t)$
20:    **end for**
21: **end for**

congestion of the roads. The walking speed of pedestrians is reflected in the degree of congestion as follows,

$$
v = \begin{cases} v_{\max} & (\rho_c > \rho \geq 0) \\ 1.8/\rho - 0.3 & (6 > \rho \geq \rho_c) \\ 0.0 & (\rho \geq 6). \end{cases} \tag{14}
$$

Here, $\rho_c = 1.8/(v_{\max} + 0.3)$[persons/$m^2$] is the criterion for the degree of congestion. The maximum speed $v_{\max}$ is given a log normal distribution following $\ln \mathcal{N}(1.2$ [m/s], $0.12)$. MAS is written C-language and can control tens of thousands of agents within just a few seconds per 3600 steps.

4.2   Data Set

We collected the people flow data on the three venues by vision-based manual counts. Using the smartphone application that we made, the observers visually counted the people passing the observed points, shown by the red circled letters in Fig. 5(a). Departure points are indicated by blue circles and destinations by pink circles. Points that are both departure and destination are shown by green circles.

WASEDA: Waseda Festival[1] is one of the biggest school festivals in Japan. The central green shading on the map represents the university's premises; four stations lie on its borders. Participants move from the four stations towards the university's six gates when entering and move in the opposite directions when leaving. Also, a roughly 30 min parade is held during this event. The participants walked slowly with the parade. Therefore, they may be observed in multiple time windows.

YOYOGI: YOYOGI CANDLE 2020[2] is an event held in Yoyogi in Japan. The participants view a projection mapping display from above a bridge. In this event, we set the bridge itself as the destination in addition to the stations around the bridge.

LIVE: This event is a massive live music festival. We gathered data on the people leaving the event. Since it is a long distance from the hall to the station, many users were observed in multiple time windows. We set the route from the three exits to the station.

4.3 Estimation Accuracy

To evaluate estimation accuracy performance, we use the normalized absolute error. A lower value indicates that the method extracted the parameter that reproduced the agent's behavior more precisely. The normalized absolute error is defined as

$$\text{NAE} = \frac{\sum_t |\boldsymbol{y}_t - \hat{\boldsymbol{y}}_t|}{\sum_t |\boldsymbol{y}_t|},$$

We compare the proposed method with the following methods. (i) Random search (Random): Generate $\boldsymbol{x}$ randomly from parameter space $\mathcal{S}_x$. Then, we select the one with the highest estimation accuracy as the best parameter. (ii) Genetic Algorithm (GA): Search by combining values of input parameters using the genetic operators of selection, crossing, and mutation. The hyper parameters of each operator (crossing probability $c \in \{0.6, 0.7, 0.8, 0.9, 1.0\}$, mutation rate $m \in \{0.02, 0.04, 0.08\}$) are determined by grid search. Moreover, to investigate the effect of the proposed objective function L_ω, the time window size ω was set to 0 or the appropriate value explained later. Since the appropriate time window size ω is different for each data set, in the experimental results, it is shown as $\omega = *$. $\omega = 0$ means to consider the reproduction error for just a single time window. For fairness comparison, each method was restricted to the same number of MAS executions. Iterations of each time window are performed 120 times in 10 cycles for a total of 1200 iterations.

[1] http://www.wasedasai.net/2016/.
[2] http://www.ntt.co.jp/topics/pdf/topics_20171130.pdf.

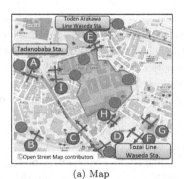

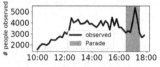

Observation Time	Measurement time interval
10:00~18:00	10
# Observation point	# Movement route
15	24

(b) Observation information

(a) Map

(c) The total number of people observed

WASEDA

Observation Time	Measurement time interval
18:00~21:30	1
# Observation point	# Movement route
26	30

(b) Observation information

(a) Map

(c) The total number of people observed

YOYOGI

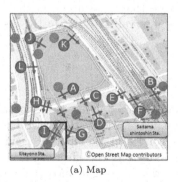

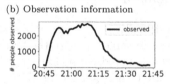

Observation Time	Measurement time interval
20:45~21:45	1
# Observation point	# Movement route
24	13

(b) Observation information

(a) Map

(c) The total number of people observed

LIVE

Fig. 5. Information from three events. (a) Map around the event venue and observation points. (b) Detailed observation information. (c) The total number of people observed during the event. (Color figure online)

4.4 Result

Quantitative evaluation of estimation performance: Figure 6(a) shows the estimation accuracy of each method for each data set. The result of GA is almost the same as random, because the number of trials is small and convergence was not achieved. In contrast, the proposed method had higher estimation accuracy than the existing methods. To investigate the estimation accuracy result in detail, NAE of the observation point near the departure point is shown in Fig. 6(b), and far from the departure point (i.e.: near to the destination) is shown in Fig. 6(c). As can be seen from Fig. 6(b), both MTWBO($\omega = 0$) and MTWBO($\omega = *$) yield highly accuracy estimations at observation points near the departure point. This is because MTWBO($\omega = 0$) can consider the values observed in a single time window. On the other hand, Fig. 6(c) shows that only MTWBO($\omega = *$) maintains high estimation accuracy for observation points far from the departure point. This is because only MTWBO($\omega = *$) can take into account observed values in multiple time windows. This confirms that designing the objective function properly enables highly accurate estimation.

Qualitative evaluation of estimation performance: Figure 7 shows the number of people passing through a far point by inputting the parameters estimated by each method. Closeness to the observed value (black line) indicates the realism of the simulation. This figure shows that MTWBO($\omega = *$) (blue line) can reproduce real observation values more accurately than the other methods. Note that YOYOGI results show only one hour flow including events, because of space constraints.

How to determine window size ω: We analyze how to determine window size ω for highly accurate estimation. Figure 8 shows the average travel time for 100 people moving on each route, and Fig. 9 shows the relationship between time window size ω and estimation accuracy. As these figures show, for highly precise estimation, it is sufficient to set the maximum value among the time window sizes necessary for transiting each route. Note that $\omega = 3$ can handle travel times of 30 min since the measurement time interval is 10 min in the result of WASEDA.

5 Application

This section forms a security plan as an example of applying the proposal. We verify the plan in three steps. In the first step, we reproduce the crowd behavior based on our estimated parameters. In the second step, we input an accident to MAS and cause congestion. In the third step, we verify the effect of the security plan prepared in advance. With regard to security plans, guidance to evacuation centers is often needed to handle sudden disasters. However, in the scenario of exiting an event venue, the destination has been decided, and changing the destination is not realistic. Therefore, we examine the congestion mitigation achieved by changing the movement route rather than the agent's destination. Accurate estimation of the number of people moving along each route by our method makes it possible to verify these plans.

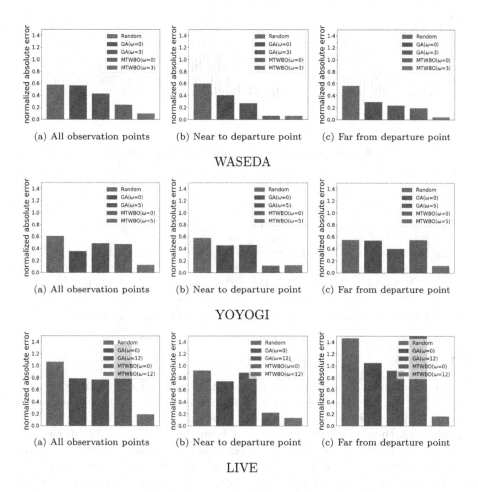

Fig. 6. Comparison of NAE of each method at (a) all observation points, (b) near to departure point, and (c) far from departure point. Lower values are better.

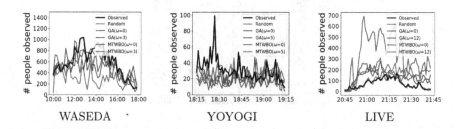

Fig. 7. Execution results of MAS using parameters estimated by each method. It shows the transitions in the number of people passing through observation points far from the departure point. (Color figure online)

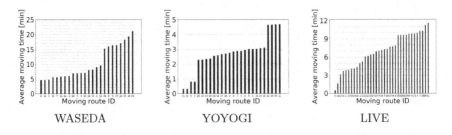

Fig. 8. Average travel time required to transit each route

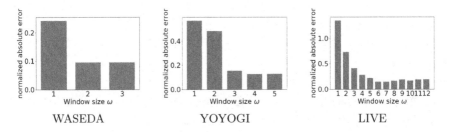

Fig. 9. Relation between time window size ω and estimation accuracy

5.1   Setting

Simulation case: We used the crowd movement of YOYOGI estimated by our method as the target. At this event, a maximum of about 500 people stayed on the bridge, which is the viewing area. The estimation result of our method showed that there many participants left from the left side of the bridge and went to the north station after the event. Therefore, we analyzed the crowd behavior assuming an accident closed the left end of the bridge. Because of the road closure, all the agents whose destination was a station had to leave from the right side of the bridge.

Fig. 10. Point of accident and guide route in each scenario (Color figure online)

Security plan scenario: Figure 10 shows where the accident occurred and each scenario. In this experiment, we compared (i) the naive scenario where all agents used the shortest path (orange) and (ii) the guidance scenario where all agents whose destination was a station were instructed to take the detour that used a wide road (green). Also, the shortest-path is a one-way road from north to south (blue).

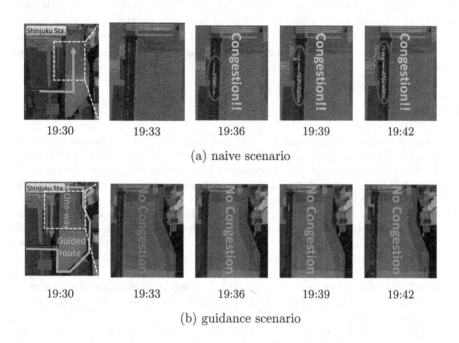

(a) naive scenario

(b) guidance scenario

Fig. 11. Crowd behavior with each scenario (Color figure online)

5.2   Results

We show the result of crowd behavior every three minutes from 19:30 at the end of the event following each scenario in Fig. 11. 3D city model data (©2017 ZENRIN CO.LTD) is used for visualization. Figure 11(a) shows that the crowd behavior created congestion when following the naive scenario. This is because people heading south from the station in addition to the people headed to the station used the same route (orange). Figure 11(b) shows the crowd behavior when following the guided scenario. People going south from the station and people heading from the bridge to the station took different routes. In this way, by using the estimation results provided by our method, we can assess how well guidance routes will reduce congestion without changing the destination.

6   Conclusion and Future Work

In this paper, to formulate MAS-based security plans for large-scale events that will generate heavy pedestrian flows, we showed how to accurately estimate the parameters that best reproduce crowd behavior. Our proposal, an estimation method with three key components, realizes efficient and highly accurate estimations. The estimation accuracy of the method was verified using data of crowd behavior gathered at three venues. Experiments showed that our method can efficiently output estimates that are highly accurate. In addition, as an application of the method, we also formed a security plan based on the estimation results provided by the method. In future work, we plan to study spatial parameter conversion techniques in order to accurately reproduce crowd behavior over wider areas.

References

1. Bera, A., Kim, S., Manocha, D.: Efficient trajectory extraction and parameter learning for data-driven crowd simulation. In: Proceedings of the 41st Graphics Interface Conference, pp. 65–72. Canadian Information Processing Society (2015)
2. Bull, A.D.: Convergence rates of efficient global optimization algorithms. J. Mach. Learn. Res. **12**(Oct), 2879–2904 (2011)
3. Castle, C.J.E., Waterson, N.P., Pellissier, E., Le Bail, S.: A comparison of grid-based and continuous space pedestrian modelling software: analysis of two UK train stations. In: Peacock, R., Kuligowski, E., Averill, J. (eds.) Pedestrian and Evacuation Dynamics, pp. 433–446. Springer, Boston (2011). https://doi.org/10.1007/978-1-4419-9725-8_39
4. Kandasamy, K., Schneider, J., Póczos, B.: High dimensional Bayesian optimisation and bandits via additive models. In: International Conference on Machine Learning, pp. 295–304 (2015)
5. Krajzewicz, D., Erdmann, J., Behrisch, M., Bieker, L.: Recent development and applications of SUMO-simulation of urban mobility. Int. J. Adv. Syst. Meas. **5**(3&4), 128–138 (2012)
6. Mockus, J.: Bayesian Approach to Global Optimization: Theory and Applications, vol. 37. Springer Science & Business Media, Berlin (2012)
7. Rasmussen, C.E., Williams, C.K.: Gaussian Process for Machine Learning. MIT Press, Cambridge (2006)
8. Shigenaka, S., Onishi, M., Yamashita, T., Noda, I.: Estimation of large-scale pedestrian movement using data assimilation. IEICE Inst. Electron. Inf. Commun. Eng. **101**(9), 1286–1294 (2018)
9. Snoek, J., Larochelle, H., Adams, R.P.: Practical Bayesian optimization of machine learning algorithms. In: Advances in Neural Information Processing Systems, pp. 2951–2959 (2012)
10. Ueda, N., Naya, F.: Spatio-temporal multidimensional collective data analysis for providing comfortable living anytime and anywhere. APSIPA Trans. Sign. Inf. Process. **7** (2018)
11. Vazquez, E., Bect, J.: Convergence properties of the expected improvement algorithm with fixed mean and covariance functions. J. Statist. Plann. Infer. **140**(11), 3088–3095 (2010)
12. Wang, Z., Hutter, F., Zoghi, M., Matheson, D., de Feitas, N.: Bayesian optimization in a billion dimensions via random embeddings. J. Artif. Intell. Res. **55**, 361–387 (2016)

13. Yamashita, T., Matsushima, H., Noda, I.: Exhaustive analysis with a pedestrian simulation environment for assistant of evacuation planning. Transp. Res. Procedia **2**, 264–272 (2014)
14. Zhou, B., Tang, X., Wang, X.: Learning collective crowd behaviors with dynamic pedestrian-agents. Int. J. Comput. Vis. **111**(1), 50–68 (2015)

Vector Representation Based Model Considering Randomness of User Mobility for Predicting Potential Users

Shaowen Peng[1], Xianzhong Xie[1(✉)], Tsunenori Mine[2(✉)], and Chang Su[1]

[1] College of Computer Science and Technology, Chongqing University of Posts and Telecommunications, Chongqing, China
swpeng95@gmail.com, {xiexzh,Changsu}@cqupt.edu.cn
[2] Department of Advanced Information Technology, Faculty of Information Science and Electrical Engineering, Kyushu University, Fukuoka, Japan
mine@ait.kyushu-u.ac.jp

Abstract. With increasing popularity of location-based social networks, POI recommendation has received much attention recently. Unlike most of the current studies which provide recommendations from perspective of users, in this paper, we focus on the perspective of Point-of-Interest (POI) for predicting potential users for a given POI. We propose a novel vector representation model for the prediction. Many current matrix factorization-based methods only pay attention to combining new information and basic matrix factorization, while in our model, we improve the matrix factorization model itself by replacing dot product with cosine similarity. We also address the problem of randomness of user's check-in behavior by applying deep neural network to modeling the relationships between the user's current check-in and context information of current check-in. Extensive experiments conducted on two real-world datasets demonstrate the superior performance of our proposed model and the effectiveness of the factors incorporated in our model.

Keywords: POI recommendation · Matrix factorization Location based social network · Vector representation

1 Introduction

With increasing popularity of location-based social networks (LBSNs), more people would like to post or share their locations in the real world to social network in the form of check-in, and users' mobility patterns could be modeled by analyzing these check-in data with algorithms. POI recommendation is such a study which provides users with recommendations of point-of-interests (POI) users will visit next based on the analysis of the check-in data. This study has received much attention due to its convenience to users and huge business opportunities it brings to advertisers.

A user's mobility pattern is influenced by many factors such as distance between user's current location and the location of POI, user's preference for the POI, and even

© Springer Nature Switzerland AG 2018
T. Miller et al. (Eds.): PRIMA 2018, LNAI 11224, pp. 70–85, 2018.
https://doi.org/10.1007/978-3-030-03098-8_5

the correlation with friends could influence the user's check-in behavior. Recently, context-aware recommendation has been extensively studied, many methods tries to incorporate new information to improve the performance of recommendation. POI2Vec (Feng et al. 2017) applies word2vec to modeling geographical influence and user preference for predicting future visitors. (Li et al. 2016) realizes the hardness to model user's POI decision making process, considers the information of friends and analyzes the correlation between the user and the friends to improve POI recommendation accuracy. CAPRF (Gao et al. 2015) models User Sentiment Indications based on the basic recommendation model, which reflect users' check-in experience. A positive tip the user leaves strengthens importance of this check-in, while a negative tip weakens its importance. However, all the above methods ignore randomness of the user's behavior (Song et al. 2010). Sometimes the user visits POIs for some personal reasons rather than the user's preference or geographical influence, thus it's hard to use these regular methods to predict their check-in behavior in these situations.

Many classic machine learning algorithms have been successfully applied to the POI recommendation tasks (Horozov et al. 2006, Zheng et al. 2010, Gambs et al. 2012). Matrix Factorization (Koren et al. 2009) is one of the most successful models among them. Many new methods have been proposed based on matrix factorization (Cheng et al. 2012, Lian et al. 2014) for POI recommendation tasks, while most of them try to incorporate new information like geographical influence and social influence into the matrix factorization model rather than improving matrix factorization itself. However, the disadvantage of matrix factorization (He et al. 2016) limits its performance. In our model, we attempt to address this problem.

Many of the POI recommendation methods provide recommendation from the perspective of users: given user historical check-in records, a list of POIs the user may visit in the future is provided. While in this paper, we focus on the perspective of POIs: given in one POI and check-in records, we predict potential users who will visit this POI. This research brings great values to the side of POI for digging potential customers.

In this paper, to improve performance of prediction, we try to explain the flaw of matrix factorization which uses dot product to capture the relationship between users and POIs. We conduct the experiments to prove that an angle between two vectors is more able to capture the relationship than dot product which cares about magnitude. In our model, information about users and POIs are all represented by k-dimensional vectors, and relationships between them are measured by cosine similarity. We incorporate three types of information for prediction: (1) User's preference for POIs: captured by a cosine similarity-based matrix factorization model. (2) Randomness of user's check-in behavior: as we discussed earlier, current methods fail to capture the randomness of the user's behavior which doesn't reflect his/her preference for POIs. To analyze the randomness, given one check-in, we treat the check-in records within a certain time period as context information for this check-in, then we apply deep neural network to modeling the relevance between context information and the check-in. (3) Geographical influence: user activity vector and POI influence vector are introduced for modeling the user's range of activity and the POI's influence on surrounding areas, we use cosine similarity of the two vectors to represent the willingness that user visits the POI from the perspective of geography.

The main contributions of this paper are summarized as follows:

- Unlike other matrix factorization-based models which only incorporate new information to the basic matrix factorization model, we improve the matrix factorization model itself by introducing cosine similarity to replace dot product which limits its performance.
- We propose a novel vector representation model for predicting potential users for POIs, which incorporate context information of check-in to capture the randomness of users' behavior, while other state-of-art methods fail to do.
- Results of experiments conducted on the real-world datasets show superior performance of our proposed model.

2   Related Works

Matrix factorization (MF) is one of the most popular methods in the fields of recommender systems and POI recommendation which was first used in the Netflix contest. Despite the great success of MF, the flaw that MF uses dot product to measure the relationships between the users and items can't be ignored. Many new methods have been proposed to improve the MF model. By pointing out that the relationship between users and items is non-linear, NeuMF (He et al. 2017) applies neural network to modeling the user-item relationships instead of the dot product used in the MF model and optimizes the model with a negative log-likelihood function. Based on the idea that the query and the documents are mapped into a lower semantic space with a non-linear projection used in DSSM (Huang et al. 2013), DMF (Xue et al. 2017) applies deep neural network to mapping user and item vectors into a latent structured space respectively and calculates the similarity between the two vectors as the output. A novel loss function is designed to incorporate the explicit ratings based on the binary cross-entropy loss function. Inspired by word embedding models, item embedding is proposed in (Liang et al. 2016) which factorizes an item co-occurrence matrix by calculating pointwise mutual information of item i and context j to explain item co-occurrence patterns.

Recently, POI recommendation task has received widespread attention; many new methods try to capture new features to improve results of recommendation. The model (Yuan et al. 2013) incorporates temporal influence into a user-based collaborative filtering method, which splits one day into equal time slots (by hour) and calculates similarity between users in terms of time slots instead of the whole check-in history, and spatial influence is also incorporated by modeling users' moving patterns based on a power law function. GeoMF (Lian et al. 2014) pays attention to geographical locations of POIs and reconstructs the User-POI matrix of geographical information. More specifically, the model divides the map into many grids with same sizes and introduces the user activity vector and the POI influence vector, and the influence of POIs to adjacent areas are modeled by a two-dimensional Gaussian function. The model (He et al. 2016) combines factorization models and Markov chain to generate transition tensor with each element representing the observed transition record of user u from location i to location j, while spatial influence and latent behavior patterns are also considered to predict users' next POIs. Recurrent Neural Networks (RNN) have been successfully applied to tasks for treating sequential data like natural language processing tasks; a novel model ST-RNN is proposed in (Liu et al. 2016), where temporal context and spatial context are represented as time-specific matrices and distance matrices for input elements to capture time interval and geographical distance information. In this paper, unlike most of the current studies which predict user's next check-in POI, we focus on a new perspective that predicts potential users given a specific POI at certain time.

3 Proposed Model

In this section, we first clarify the problem we try to figure out, then we explain the flaw of the MF model and introduce the detail of our proposed model. Finally, we present a unified model for predicting potential users.

3.1 Problem Definition

We denote a set of users as $U = \{u_1, u_2...u_m\}$, and POIs as $P = \{p_1, p_2...p_n\}$. Given a specific time slot t (in this paper, time is handled hourly), $C_{u,p,t}$ represents the rating of user u to POI p at time t from check-in datasets Ω, while rating is usually represented as implicit feedback in POI recommendation tasks:

$$C_{u,p,t} = \begin{cases} 1, & \textit{if u visted p at t} \\ 0, & \text{otherwise} \end{cases}$$

Given historical check-in records Ω of users and a POI p, our task is to predict potential users who will visit p at time t.

3.2 Vector Representation for User Preference

User preference measures users' interest for POIs. To predict potential users who may visit POIs, it's important to capture the degree of user interest in POIs. Matrix Factorization is a successful model for recommendation tasks. The basic idea of the MF model is to factorize User-POI visit matrix $C \in \mathbb{R}^{m \times n}$ to two low rank parameter matrices while each user and POI are represented by a latent space with dimension $k \ll \min(m, n)$, and user's preference for a POI is represented as dot product between user and item latent factors as:

$$\tilde{c}(p|u) = X_u^T Y_p = \sum_{f=0}^{k} X_{u,f} Y_{f,p} \tag{1}$$

However, dot product between two latent factors is unable to measure the relationship between them. Assume there are three vectors: a (1, 1), b (0.9, 0.9), c (0,2). Obviously, vector b is more similar to vector a than vector c. But according to the operation of dot product, similarity between vector a and c $a^T c > a^T b$ is larger. Dot product pays more attention to magnitude rather than angle between two vectors. Furthermore, for a User-POI interaction matrix shown in Fig. 1(a), we would like to calculate the similarity between users based on their preference to items, so we use Jaccard similarity as the ground truth similarity between users. Then we train a MF model based on the matrix of Fig. 1(a) and represent user latent factors in two-dimensional space as shown in Fig. 1(b). According to Jaccard similarity, the most similar user for u_4 and u_1 are u_2 and u_3, respectively, while the Fig. 1(b) shows wrong relationships between users, which means that dot product doesn't treat user and POI latent factors as vectors in k-dimensional space to consider their relationships. On the other hand, if we use Eq. (2), which calculates cosine similarity measuring the cosine value of the angle between two vectors, we can calculate the similarity more agree with the Jaccard similarity than dot product as shown in Fig. 1(c). Figure 1 (c) illustrates the user vectors after applying Eq. (2) to the MF model.

$$\tilde{c}(p|u) = \frac{X_u^T Y_p}{\| X_u \| \cdot \| Y_p \|} = \frac{\sum_{f=0}^{k} X_{u,f} Y_{f,p}}{\sqrt{\sum_{f=0}^{k} X_{u,f}^2} \cdot \sqrt{\sum_{f=0}^{k} Y_{p,f}^2}} \tag{2}$$

Furthermore, to evaluate the two MF models: dot product-based model (BasicMF) and cosine similarity-based model (VectorMF), we conducted preliminary experiments using a real-world data set. The results of the two models are shown in Fig. 1(d). We can see that the relationships obtained by the VectorMF model correspond to the true relationships, and the VectorMF model obviously outperforms the BasicMF model. This shows the necessity of using cosine similarity rather than dot product.

Similarly, we employ the cosine similarity-based MF model in our model to capture user preference for POIs. Each user and POI are associated with a vector in k-dimensional space, and willingness $S(p|u)$ that the user visit POIs is represented by cosine similarity between the user vector X_u and the POI vector Y_p.

$$S(p|u) = \frac{X_u^T Y_p}{\| X_u \| \cdot \| Y_p \|} \tag{3}$$

Larger of cosine similarity shows stronger interest of user u would like to visit POI p. In this paper, **we make a hypothesis to build our model that the angle between two vectors can measure relationships between them better than the magnitude.** Thus, information of users and POIs are represented by vectors in a geometric space, and relationships between vectors are calculated by cosine similarity.

3.3 Capturing Randomness of User's Behavior

User behavior pattern doesn't always reflect user preference. Sometimes user visits some POIs for personal reasons even though they aren't interested in those locations. So, it's hard to predict user's behavior by only considering their preference. Assuming that user's current behavior is related to his/her previous behaviors, given one check-in

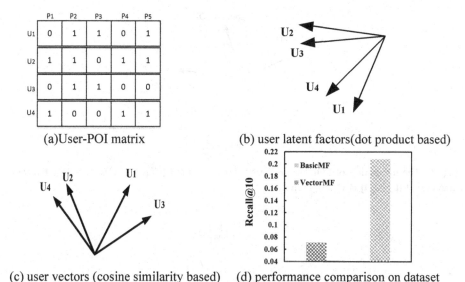

(a)User-POI matrix

(b) user latent factors(dot product based)

(c) user vectors (cosine similarity based)

(d) performance comparison on dataset

Fig. 1. An example for explaining the disadvantage of dot product used in MF model. (a): User-POI interaction matrix; (b): user latent factors (dot product based); (c): user vectors (cosine similarity based); (d): performance comparison between dot product based model and cosine similarity based model conducted on Gowalla (we will introduce later).

record $C_{u,p,t}$, we define the check-in records of user u within time periods μ as its context information $C(c_{u,p,t})$.

However, as shown in Fig. 2, users always visit different types of POIs. So, it's hard to find the relevance between current POI and context POIs by cosine similarity or other linear functions. Therefore, we apply deep neural network to mapping them into a latent structure space because of the great nonlinear mapping ability of neural network (Agrafiotis et al. 2000). Figure 3 illustrates detailed structure.

Current POI is represented as a high-dimensional vector which contains current POI's rating across all users. Context POIs are represented in the same way, but all of the vectors of context POIs are projected into a projection layer by averaging all of the context POIs as the structure in wrod2vec model (Mikolov et al. 2013). Then two vectors are mapped into latent spaces by neural network, where the mapping function $f(\cdot)$ is written as follows:

$$f_{cp}(x_{cp}) = R_n(\ldots R_2(R_1(x_{cp}^T W_{cp1})^T W_{cp2})\ldots)$$
$$f_p(x_p) = R_n(\ldots R_2(R_1(x_p^T W_{p1})^T W_{p2})\ldots)$$

(4)

$R(\cdot)$ is the ReLU activation function:

$$R(x) = max(0, x)$$

(5)

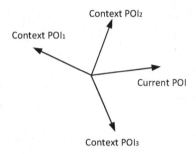

Fig. 2. The illustration of POI vectors user u visits at time t (Current POI) and visited within time period $[t - \mu, t]$ (Context POIs)

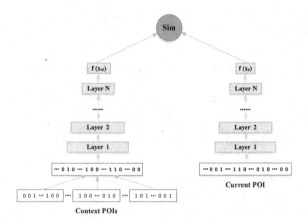

Fig. 3. The architecture for capturing randomness of user mobility

W_{cp1} and W_{p1} are weight matrices of the first layer for context POIs and current POI, respectively, W_{cp2} and W_{p2} are parameters of the second layer, and so on. Then after mapping the two input vectors to a latent space in which the relationship could be represented by a linear function, we use cosine similarity to measure their relationship.

$$S(p|C(c_{u,p,t})) = \frac{f_{cp}(x_{cp})^T f_p(x_p)}{\| f_{cp}(x_{cp}) \| \cdot \| f_p(x_p) \|} \tag{6}$$

3.4 Incorporating Geographical Influence

In the real world, a user's willingness to move from one place to another is associated with the distance between the two places. (Yuan et al. 2013) uses a power law function to model users' moving patterns. However, this model fails to capture the influence of POIs on adjacent areas. For example, a convenience store is visited by residents nearby, while people living several blocks away are unlikely to come. In contrast, the department store located in a central business district is always visited by people who live in every corner of the city. The difference between convenience stores and department stores are their influence on the surroundings; more famous POI brings larger influence on surrounding areas. In this section, our work is based on GeoMF (Lian et al. 2014) which employs Gaussian distribution to model the influence of POIs on surrounding area and works well. We divide the whole map into several grids with same size α, so that each POI could be assigned to one grid (area).

A user tends to visit areas with preferences, while the user hardly visits areas without interests. Since the whole map are consisted of some small areas, a user's preference for the areas could be represented by a vector called user activity vector A_u. The user activity vector could be either given in advance based on the user's check-in frequency to each area or learned in the training process. For convenience of computation, we give the user activity vector in advance in our codes.

Similarly, influence of a POI on surrounding areas could be represented by a POI influence vector I_p. How to model the influence on surrounding areas should be based on the following rules:

(1) The influence of the point of interest on the surrounding areas is decayed as the distance increases.
(2) Different POIs own different influences, more popular POI owns larger influence on surrounding areas.

In our model, we use two-dimensional Gaussian Function to model the POI influence:

$$I_{(x_0,y_0)to(x,y)} = K(x_0, y_0, x, y, \sigma^2)$$
$$K(\cdot) = \exp\left(-\tfrac{1}{2}\left(\tfrac{(x-x_0)^2}{\sigma^2} + \tfrac{(y-y_0)^2}{\sigma^2}\right)\right) \tag{7}$$

Each area can be represented by a two-dimensional coordinate. $I_{(x_0,y_0)to(x,y)}$ means influence from the area where the POI is located (x_0, y_0) to the target area (x, y). $K(\cdot)$ is the Gaussian Function, Variance σ^2 is associated with popularity of the POI.

So far, we have vectorized both the user's preference for areas and the POI's influence on surrounding areas. Given a user and a POI, the willingness $S(p|g_u^p)$ that the user visits the POI from geographical perspective (g_u^p) is calculated by cosine similarity between user activity vector A_u and POI influence vector I_p as follows.

$$S(p|g_u^p) = \frac{A_u^T I_p}{||A_u|| \cdot ||I_p||} \tag{8}$$

3.5 The Model for Predicting Potential Users

To predict potential users for a given POI, we need to capture users' check-in patterns precisely to measure each user's willingness to POIs. In our model, we first capture the user's preference for POIs based on the cosine similarity-based MF model; then given a check-in $C_{u,p,t}$, we define the check-in records in the time period $[t-\mu, t]$ as its context

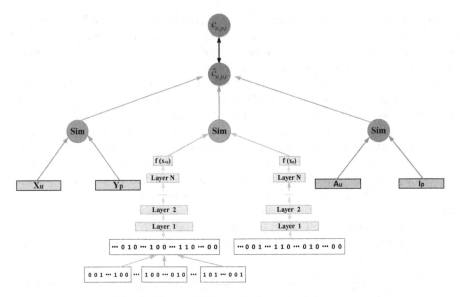

Fig. 4. The model for predicting potential users

information, apply deep neural network to modeling the relevance between context information and the check-in to capture randomness of the user's check-in behavior; in the meantime, we model the geographical influence on POIs and users by vectorizing the user's preference for areas and the POI's influence on surrounding areas. Based on the three factors incorporated in our model, users' willingness to POIs $\tilde{C}_{u,p,t}$ could be represented as Eq. (9), the unified model is shown in Fig. 4. We should notice that context information isn't considered for every check-in record. It depends on if there are check-in records in the time period [t-μ, t].

$$\tilde{c}_{u,p,t} = \begin{cases} S(p|u, C(c_{u,p,t}), g_u^p) & \text{if } C(c_{u,p,t}) \text{ exists} \\ S(p|u, g_u^p) & \text{otherwise} \end{cases} \tag{9}$$

For the convenience of expression, Eq. (9) could be rewritten as:

$$\tilde{c}_{u,p,t} = S(p|u) + i \cdot S(p|C(c_{u,p,t})) + S(p|g_u^p) \tag{10}$$

Here i is an indicator function, if context information exits, $i = 1$, otherwise $i = 0$. Given a POI p and time t, each user's willingness score to p is computed by Eq. (10). Then, we rank all users by their willingness scores $\tilde{C}_{u,p,t}$, and select top-N users as the potential users for the given POI.

3.6   Explicit Rating for Prediction

In our model, we treat users and POIs as vectors in k-dimensional space, and we only care about the angle between them which is calculated by cosine similarity. Therefore, the angle between vectors should be different according to users' preference for POIs. Implicit feedback is usually used in POI recommendation tasks, while in our model, we assume that the user's preference is reflected by the user's check-in frequency, so rating for POIs is represented as:

$$\bar{c}_{u,p_i,t} = \begin{cases} \dfrac{f_{p_i}}{\max\{f_{p_1}\cdots f_{p_i}\cdots f_{p_n}\}} & \text{if } u \text{ visited } p_i \text{ at } t \\ 0 & \text{otherwise} \end{cases}$$

f_{p_i} is the frequency of p_i that the user visited, $\{f_{p_1}\cdot\cdot f_{p_i}\cdot\cdot f_{p_n}\}$ is the set of frequencies of all POIs user u has visited. We assume the most visited POI as the user's favorite POI, cosine similarity between user vector and the user's favorite POI vector should be the largest, and ratings of other visited POIs are similarly determined by the user's check-in frequency. We randomly sample POIs which the user never visited at a certain rate as negative samples for training.

3.7 Parameter Inference

In this section, we introduce learning process of our model. Given a loss function which measures the loss between the model and the actual distribution of training data, we optimize parameter by minimizing the loss function.

$$L(\theta) = \sum_{\Omega^+ \cup \Omega^-} \left(\bar{c}_{u,p,t} - \frac{X_u^T Y_p}{\| X_u \| \cdot \| Y_p \|} - i \cdot \frac{f_{cp}(x_{cp})^T f_p(x_p)}{\| f_{cp}(x_{cp}) \| \cdot \| f_p(x_p) \|} - \frac{A_u^T I_p}{\|A_u\| \cdot \|I_p\|} \right)^2 + \lambda \| \theta \|^2 + \gamma \| A \| \tag{11}$$

Square loss function is chosen for training. Where $\theta = \{X, Y, W_{cp}, W_p, A\}$, W_p and W_{cp} contain several weight matrices which need to be optimized. We still give the learning process of user activity vector A_u which should be sparse and subjected to be greater than 0. λ and γ are parameters of L1 and L2 regularization.

We employ stochastic gradient descent (SGD) to estimate model parameters; to update the parameter, we need to calculate the derivatives of $L(\theta)$ with respect to the parameters. Let q be:

$$q = \bar{c}_{u,p,t} - \frac{X_u^T Y_p}{\| X_u \| \cdot \| Y_p \|} - i \cdot \frac{f_{cp}(x_{cp})^T f_p(x_p)}{\| f_{cp}(x_{xp}) \| \cdot \| f_p(x_p) \|} - \frac{A_u^T I_p}{\|A_u\| \cdot \|I_p\|}$$

Then derivatives could be calculated as follows.

$$\frac{\partial L}{\partial X_u} = \frac{q\left(X_u^T Y_p - 2 \| X_u \|^2 Y_p\right)}{\| Y_p \| \cdot \| X_u \|^3}$$

$$\frac{\partial L}{\partial Y_p} = \frac{q\left(X_u^T Y_p - 2 \| Y_p \|^2 X_u\right)}{\| X_u \| \cdot \| Y_p \|^3}$$

$$\frac{\partial L}{\partial A_u} = \frac{q\left(A_u^T I_p - 2 \parallel A_u \parallel^2 I_p\right)}{\parallel I_p \parallel \cdot \parallel A_u \parallel^3}$$

$$\frac{\partial L}{\partial W_{cp(i)}} = \frac{qi\left(f_{cp}(x_{cp})^T f_p(x_p) - 2 \parallel f_{cp}(x_{cp}) \parallel^2 f_p(x_p)\right)}{\parallel f_p(x_p) \parallel \cdot \parallel f_{cp}(x_{cp}) \parallel^3} \cdot a_{cp}^{i-1} \delta_{cp}^i$$

$$\frac{\partial L}{\partial W_{p(i)}} = \frac{qi\left(f_{cp}(x_{cp})^T f_p(x_p) - 2 \parallel f_p(x_p) \parallel^2 f_{cp}(x_{cp})\right)}{\parallel f_{cp}(x_{cp}) \parallel \cdot \parallel f_p(x_p) \parallel^3} \cdot a_p^{i-1} \delta_p^i$$

Where a^{i-1} is the output of layer $i - 1$ (or input of layer i), and $\delta^i = \frac{\partial f(x)}{\partial z^i} = \left(W_{i+1}^T \delta^{i+1}\right) \odot R'(z^i)$, z^i is the weighted input of layer i without activation, $\odot$ is the operation of elementwise multiplication. Lastly, the parameter could be updated as $w \leftarrow w - \eta \frac{\partial L}{\partial w}$. In the meanwhile, update of A_u should be $A_u \leftarrow max\left(0, A_u - \eta \frac{\partial L}{\partial w}\right)$ since user activity vectors are subjected to be greater than 0. The whole training procedure is shown in Algorithm 1.

Algorithm 1 Training Algorithm of Proposed Model

Input: check-in datasets Ω+, training iterations n,
　　　　learning rate η, parameters of regularization λ and γ,
　　　　context information is considered within time period μ,
　　　　the whole map is divided with size α, negative sampling rate ε,
Output: optimized parameter θ= {X, Y, A, W_cp, W_p},
1: Initialization:
2:　randomly initialize θ= {X, Y, A, W_cp, W_p};
3:　sample randomly at rate ε as negative samples Ω⁻, set Ω=Ω⁺∪Ω⁻;
4:　calculate POI influence matrix I;
5: Training:
6:　**for** iter from 1 to n **do**
7:　　**for** one_record in Ω **do**
8:　　　use equation(10) to calculate predicted scores;
9:　　　calculate loss function L(θ) according to equation(11);
10:　　**for** w in θ **do**
11:　　　**if** w in A **then**
12:　　　　$w \leftarrow max(0, w - \eta \frac{\partial L}{\partial w})$
13:　　　**else**
14:　　　　$w \leftarrow w - \eta \frac{\partial L}{\partial w}$
15:　　　**end if**
16:　　**end for**
17:　**end for**
18: **end for**

---

4 Experiments

In this section, first we introduce the datasets used in our experiments and what evaluation metrics we used to test the performance. Then, we evaluate the performance of our proposed model including: (1) effects of parameters, (2) comparison with other state-of-art models, (3) effectiveness of factors incorporated in our model.

4.1 Experimental Setup

We choose two real-world datasets to conduct experiments: Gowalla[1] within Chicago and Brightkite[2] within New York. We removed the users who checked in less than 10 times. The statistics of datasets are listed in Table 1.

Table 1. Statistics of datasets

Datasets	#User	#POI	#Check-in	#Density
Gowalla	1044	7502	49192	4.44×10^{-3}
Brightkite	1060	13985	80354	1.25×10^{-3}

We adopt Recall@N and Precision@N as evaluation metrics. Given a POI p, we rank all users by their predicted scores, then select TOP-N users as the prediction list R_p for this POI. A list of users who actually visited this POI are represented as S_p. the definitions of Recall@N and Precision@N are given below. We implemented our proposed model with PyTorch[3].

$$Recall@N = \frac{|R_p \cap S_p|}{|S_p|}$$
$$Precision@N = \frac{|R_p \cap S_p|}{|R_p|} \tag{12}$$

4.2 Effect of Parameters

The value of several parameters affects test performance of our model. First is the area size α that controls the dimension of user activity vectors and POI influence vectors. The effects of size α is shown in Fig. 5. We observe that there was no obvious rule to explain the relationships between α and the performance. Roughly speaking, the performance gets the best at $\alpha = 0.02$ which is about 1500 m on both of the datasets. Setting α too small means the map is divided into many small areas which makes the influence of POI decays quickly; while a too large α causes the slow decay rate which fails to model the influence of POI on surrounding areas. Based on the results shown in Fig. 5, we set $\alpha = 0.02$.

---

[1] http://snap.stanford.edu/data/loc-gowalla.html
[2] http://snap.stanford.edu/data/loc-brightkite.html
[3] https://pytorch.org/

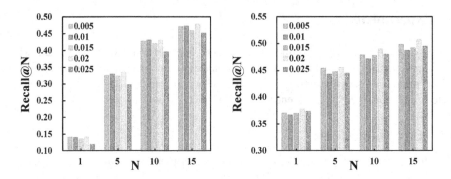

Fig. 5. Effect of area size α on Gowalla (left) and Brightkite (right)

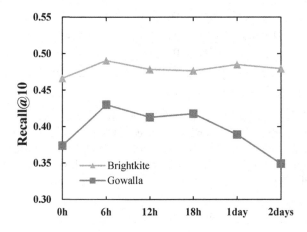

Fig. 6. Effect of time period μ

The second parameter is time period μ. From Fig. 6, it's clear that the performance increases as the length of time period increases and gets the best at 6 h, then it starts to get down. The performance on the Brightkite is less sensitive to the change on parameters; the reason may be the sparsity (compared with Gowalla) of the data that covers up the effect of parameters on results. For other parameters, learning rate η, weights of regularization λ and γ are set at 0.05, 0.0001, 0.0001, respectively.

4.3 Comparison

To evaluate the performance of our proposed model, we compare our method with the following baseline methods:

(1) **BasicMF:** Matrix Factorization (Koren et al. 2009), one of the most popular methods for recommendation tasks which consider user preference by calculating dot product of user latent factor and POI latent factor.

(2) **GeoMF:** modeling geographical influence on users and POIs based on MF model for POI Recommendation (Lian et al. 2014), which is a state-of-art method.
(3) **DMF:** Deep Matrix Factorization Models (Xue et al. 2017) combines deep neural network and Matrix Factorization for recommendation tasks.

Unlike the above baseline models, we replace dot product with cosine similarity to capture relationship between users and POIs, and incorporate three types of information in our model for prediction tasks. To evaluate the effectiveness of these factors incorporated into our model, we consider three approaches as: (4) **NonGeo:** Geographical influence is not considered for prediction. (5) **NonContext:** given one check-in record, we don't consider context information for capturing randomness. (6) **Dot-basedModel:** still incorporate three types of information, but instead of cosine similarity, we use dot product to capture relationships between users and POIs.

Table 2. Experimental results for predicting potential users

		recall@1	recall@5	recall@10	recall@15	pre@5	pre@10	pre@15
Gowalla	BasicMF	0.034	0.056	0.071	0.083	0.011	0.007	0.006
	GeoMF	0.040	0.104	0.152	0.192	0.021	0.015	0.013
	DMF	0.079	0.137	0.170	0.201	0.027	0.017	0.013
	Dot-based	0.034	0.116	0.177	0.238	0.023	0.018	0.016
	NonContext	0.085	0.180	0.222	0.251	0.036	0.022	0.017
	NonGeo	0.106	0.281	0.362	0.419	0.056	0.036	0.028
	Ours	**0.142**	**0.335**	**0.430**	**0.479**	**0.067**	**0.043**	**0.032**
Brightkite	BasicMF	0.217	0.308	0.328	0.344	0.062	0.033	0.023
	GeoMF	0.103	0.211	0.284	0.411	0.042	0.028	0.027
	DMF	0.292	0.335	0.358	0.378	0.067	0.036	0.025
	Dot-based	0.116	0.225	0.300	0.352	0.045	0.030	0.023
	NonContext	0.334	0.414	0.448	0.469	0.083	0.045	0.031
	NonGeo	0.343	0.407	0.432	0.450	0.081	0.043	0.030
	Ours	**0.347**	**0.456**	**0.491**	**0.508**	**0.091**	**0.049**	**0.034**

Table 2 shows the experimental results on two datasets. Our proposed model obviously outperforms the other state-of-arts methods. For example, compared with the DMF model which has the best performances among the baseline methods at Recall@5, our model outperforms DMF by 36% and 145% on Brightkite and Gowalla, respectively. Even the results on the NonGeo or NonContext are still better than the baseline methods.

Also, without the consideration of context information or geographical influence, the performance decreases to a great extent; while it declines the most when the cosine similarity is replaced by the dot product, which proves the effectiveness of these factors incorporated in our model, especially the necessity of vector representation.

5   Conclusion and Future Work

In this paper, we proposed a novel vector representation model to predict potential users for given POIs. We improved the matrix factorization model by replacing dot product with cosine similarity and applied the vector representation to our model. We modeled user's preference, randomness of the user's mobility pattern and geographical influence for prediction. Experimental results on two datasets showed superior performance of our proposed model compared to other state-of-art methods.

In future work, we will incorporate more new factors into our model for improving accuracy. Since cosine similarity isn't the only way to capture relationships between users and POIs, we will try to model the relationship by other ways.

Acknowledgement. This work is partially supported by JSPS KAKENHI Grant Number JP15H05708 and the Chongqing Nature Science Foundation under contract number cstc2016jcyjA0398.

References

Agrafiotis, D.K., Lobanov, V.S.: Nonlinear mapping networks. J. Chem. Inf. Comput. Sci. **40**(6), 1356–1362 (2000)

Cheng, C., Yang, H., King, I., et al.: Fused matrix factorization with geographical and social influence in location-based social networks. In: Aaai, vol. 12, pp. 17–23 (2012)

Feng, S., Cong, G., An, B., et al.: POI2Vec: geographical latent representation for predicting future visitors. In: AAAI, pp. 102–108 (2017)

Gambs, S., Killijian, M.O., del Prado Cortez, M.N.: Next place prediction using mobility markov chains. In: Proceedings of the First Workshop on Measurement, Privacy, and Mobility, ACM, vol. 3 (2012)

Gao, H., Tang, J., Hu, X., et al.: Content-aware point of interest recommendation on location-based social networks. In: AAAI, pp. 1721–1727 (2015)

He, J., Li, X., Liao, L., et al.: Inferring a personalized next point-of-interest recommendation model with latent behavior patterns. In: AAAI, pp. 137–143 (2016)

He, X., Liao, L., Zhang, H., et al.: Neural collaborative filtering. In: Proceedings of the 26th International Conference on World Wide Web. International World Wide Web Conferences Steering Committee, pp. 173–182 (2017)

Horozov, T., Narasimhan, N., Vasudevan, V.: Using location for personalized POI recommendations in mobile environments. In: 2006 International symposium on IEEE Applications and the Internet 2006 SAINT, pp. 6–129 (2006)

Huang, P.S., He, X., Gao, J., et al.: Learning deep structured semantic models for web search using clickthrough data. In: Proceedings of the 22nd ACM International Conference on Information and Knowledge Management, ACM, pp. 2333–2338 (2013)

Koren, Y., Bell, R., Volinsky, C.: Matrix factorization techniques for recommender systems. Computer **8**, 30–37 (2009)

Li, H., Ge, Y., Hong, R., et al.: Point-of-interest recommendations: learning potential check-ins from friends. In: Proceedings of the 22nd ACM SIGKDD International Conference on Knowledge Discovery and Data Mining, ACM, pp. 975–984 (2016)

Lian, D., Zhao, C., Xie, X., et al.: GeoMF: joint geographical modeling and matrix factorization for point-of-interest recommendation. In: Proceedings of the 20th ACM SIGKDD International Conference on Knowledge Discovery and Data Mining, ACM, pp. 831–840 (2014)

Liang, D., Altosaar, J., Charlin, L., et al.: Factorization meets the item embedding: regularizing matrix factorization with item co-occurrence. In: Proceedings of the 10th ACM Conference on Recommender Systems, ACM, pp. 59–66 (2016)

Liu, Q., Wu, S., Wang, L., et al.: Predicting the next location: a recurrent model with spatial and temporal contexts. In: AAAI, pp. 194–200 (2016)

Mikolov, T., Chen, K., Corrado, G., et al.: Efficient estimation of word representations in vector space (2013). arXiv preprint arXiv:1301.3781

Song, C., Qu, Z., Blumm, N., et al.: Limits of predictability in human mobility. Science **327** (5968), 1018–1021 (2010)

Xue, H.J., Dai, X., Zhang, J., et al.: Deep matrix factorization models for recommender systems. In: IJCAI, pp. 3203–3209 (2017)

Yuan, Q., Cong, G., Ma, Z., et al.: Time-aware point-of-interest recommendation. In: Proceedings of the 36th International ACM SIGIR Conference on Research and Development in Information Retrieval, ACM, pp. 363–372 (2013)

Zheng, V.W., Zheng, Y., Xie, X., et al.: Collaborative location and activity recommendations with GPS history data. In: Proceedings of the 19th International Conference on World Wide Web, ACM, pp. 1029–1038 (2010)

Collaboration and Coordination

Heterogeneous Teams for Homogeneous Performance

Ewa Andrejczuk[1]([✉]), Filippo Bistaffa[2], Christian Blum[2],
Juan A. Rodriguez-Aguilar[2], and Carles Sierra[2]

[1] ST Engineering - NTU Corporate Lab, School of Electrical and Electronic
Engineering (EEE-NTU), Nanyang Technological University, Singapore, Singapore
ewaa@ntu.edu.sg
[2] Artificial Intelligence Research Institute (IIIA-CSIC), Bellaterra, Spain
{filippo.bistaffa,christian.blum,jar,sierra}@iiia.csic.es

Abstract. Co-operative learning is used to refer to learning procedures for heterogeneous teams in which individuals and teamwork are organised to complete academic tasks. Key factors of team performance are competencies, personality and gender of team members. Here, we present a computational model that incorporates these key factors to form heterogeneous teams. In addition, we propose efficient algorithms to partition a classroom into teams of even size and homogeneous performance. The first algorithm is based on an ILP formulation. For small problem instances, this approach is appropriate. However, this is not the case for large problems for which we propose a heuristic algorithm. We study the computational properties of both algorithms when grouping students in a classroom into teams.

1 Introduction

Students learn best when they are actively engaged in the processing of information [24]. One way to involve students in active learning is to have them learn from one another within teams. Research shows that students working in teams tend to learn more and retain the knowledge longer than when the same content is presented by means of other instructional formats; they also appear more satisfied with their classes [6]. However, not just any team promotes learning. In order for learning to be productive, all teams in the classroom should be heterogeneous, that is, representative of the diversity of the whole class and balanced in size. Also, effective education must balance performance across teams, that is, performance should be as homogeneous as possible in the classroom: *No one should be left behind.*

Considerable work in fields such as organisational psychology, and industrial psychology has focused on various factors that influence team performance [5, 15,25,26]. [5,26] underline the importance of personality traits or *types* for team composition. Other studies have focused on how team members should differ or converge in their characteristics, such as personality, competencies, or gender, among others [15,25], in order to increase performance.

© Springer Nature Switzerland AG 2018
T. Miller et al. (Eds.): PRIMA 2018, LNAI 11224, pp. 89–105, 2018.
https://doi.org/10.1007/978-3-030-03098-8_6

Also in the area of multiagent systems, team composition has attracted much research. MAS research has widely acknowledged competencies as important to perform tasks of different nature [9,17,21]. However, the majority of approaches represent capabilities of agents in a Boolean way (i.e., an agent either has a required skill or not). This is a simplistic way to model an agent's set of capabilities since it ignores any skill degree. In real life, capabilities are not binary since every individual shows different performances for each competence. Additionally, the MAS literature has typically disregarded significant organizational psychology findings (with the exception of several recent, preliminary attempts like [11] or [3]). To the best of our knowledge, the current organizational psychology and MAS literature have not tackled how to compose teams taking into account the personality, gender and competencies of individuals.

Given this background, in this paper we address the following team composition problem commonly faced by educators. There is a *complex task that has to be solved by different teams of students of the same size* [1]. The task requires that each team has at least one student that shows a minimum level of competence for a given set of competencies. We have a pool of students with varying genders, personalities, and competencies' levels. The problem is how to partition students into teams that are balanced in size, competencies, personalities, and gender. We refer to these teams as *synergistic teams*.

This paper makes the following contributions. First, we identify and formalise a new type of real-world problem: the synergistic team composition problem (STCP), requiring *balanced* solutions in terms of team size and team value. Second, we propose two algorithms to solve STCP: an algorithm to optimally solve it that is very efficient for small instances, and an approximate algorithm that is effective for larger instances. And third, a computational comparison of both algorithms over realistic settings in an education context.

Outline. The remainder of this paper is structured as follows. Section 2 introduces basic definitions required by our team composition problem. Section 3 introduces the synergistic team composition problem. Section 4 details how to compute a team's synergistic value. Sections 5 and 6 describe how to optimally and approximately solve the synergistic team composition problem respectively. Then, Sect. 7 reports on our empirical analysis of both algorithms over artificially-generated instances of the synergistic team composition problem. Finally, Sect. 8 draws some conclusions and sets paths to future research.

2   Basic Definitions

We consider that each student has a gender, personality, and competencies.

First, to measure personality, we explore a novel method: the Post-Jungian Personality Theory [28], a modified version of the Myers-Briggs Type Indicator (MBTI) [8].[1] This questionnaire is short, contains only 20 quick questions (compared to the 93 MBTI questions). This is very convenient for both experts

---

[1] MBTI numerical values can be used with the same purpose.

designing teams and individuals doing the test since completing the test takes just a few minutes (for details of the questionnaire, see [28, p.21]). In contrast to the MBTI measure, which consists of four binary dimensions, the Post-Jungian Personality Theory uses the *numerical* data collected using the questionnaire [27]. The results of this method seem promising, since within a decade this novel approach has tripled the fraction of Stanford teams awarded US prizes by the Lincoln Foundation [27]. The test is based on the pioneering psychiatrist C. G. Jung's personality model [14]. It has two sets of variable pairs called psychological functions: (1) Sensing / Intuition (SN), and (2) Thinking/Feeling (TF) and two sets of attitudes: (3) Extroversion/Introversion (EI), and (4) Perception / Judgment (PJ).

Psychological functions and attitudes compose together a personality. The numerical values for each dimension of a personality (SN, TF, EI, PJ) are measured through a five multiple choice true/false questions. Thus,

Definition 1. *A* personality profile *is a tuple* $\langle sn, tf, ei, pj \rangle \in [-1,1]^4$, *where each of these four components represents one personality trait.*

Second, a competence integrates the knowledge, skills and attitudes that enable a student to act correctly in a job, task or situation [22]. Each student is assumed to possess a set of competencies with associated competence levels. Let $C = \{c_1, \ldots, c_k\}$ be the whole set of competencies, where each element $c_i \in C$ stands for a competence.

Definition 2. *A* student *is represented as a tuple* $\langle id, g, \mathbf{p}, l \rangle$ *such that: id is an identifier;* $g \in \{man, woman\}$ *is a gender;* $\mathbf{p} = \langle sn, tf, ei, pj \rangle$ *is a personality profile;* $l : C \rightarrow [0,1]$ *is a function that assigns the quality level of the outcome with respect to competence c.*[2]

Henceforth, we will note the set of students as $A = \{a_1, \ldots, a_n\}$. Moreover, we will use super-indexes to refer to students' attributes. For instance, given a student $a \in A$, id^a will refer to the *id* attribute of student a.

Definition 3 (Team). *A* team *is any subset of A with at least two students.*

We denote by $\mathcal{K}_A = (2^A \setminus \{\emptyset\}) \setminus \{\{a_i\} | a_i \in A\}$ the set of all possible teams in A.

Finally, a *team* is any subset of A with at least two students. We denote by $\mathcal{K}_A = (2^A \setminus \{\emptyset\}) \setminus \{\{a_i\} | a_i \in A\}$ the set of all possible teams in A.

3   The Synergistic Team Composition Problem

We can regard our team composition problem as a particular type of set partitioning. We will refer to any partition of A as a *team partition*. Since all teams should have an even size, we only consider team partitions whose teams are constrained by a given size.

---

[2] We assume that the competence level is zero when a student does not have a competence (or we do not know its value).

Definition 4. *Given a set of students A, we say that a team partition P_m of A is constrained by size m, $|A| \geq m \geq 2$, iff for every team $K \in P_m$, $m \leq |K| \leq m+1$.*

As $|K|/m$ is not necessarily a natural number, we may need to allow for some flexibility in team size within a partition. This is why we introduced above the condition $m \leq |K| \leq m + 1$. In practical terms, in a partition we want to have teams of sizes differing by at most one student. This is a common constraint when partitioning a classroom: we want teams to be balanced in size. We note by $\mathcal{P}_m(A)$ the set of all team partitions of A constrained by size m.

The question is: which partition to choose? We want to have teams that show a homogeneous behaviour so that there are no big differences in performance (i.e., we do not want partitions for which some teams perform well and some poorly; Remember, no one is to be left behind!). To do that, we first define the synergistic value of a team K, noted as $s(K)$, as an expectation of its performance. We present the formal definition of such a function in Sect. 4. Second, we define the overall performance of a partition as the Bernoulli-Nash product of individual teams' synergistic values, since this function evaluates better homogeneous ("fair") solutions [16] than other functions (e.g. the sum).

Definition 5. *Given a team partition P_m, the synergistic value of P_m is*

$$S(P_m) = \prod_{K \in P_m} s(K). \tag{1}$$

Thus, the STCP is solved by finding the partition with the highest synergistic value.

Definition 6. *Given a set of students A the* synergistic team composition problem (STCP) *is the problem of finding a team partition constrained by size m, $P_m^* \in \mathcal{P}_m(A)$, that maximises $S(P_m)$, namely:*

$$P_m^* = \underset{P_m \in \mathcal{P}_m(A)}{\arg\max} \; S(P_m)$$

3.1   Relation with the Coalition Formation Literature

The STCP is a particular case of a coalition generation problem [20]. Unfortunately, we cannot benefit from the algorithms in the literature. In particular, following [19], given a STCP we can identify a constrained coalition formation (CCF) game $\mathcal{G} = \langle A, \mathcal{P}_m(A), s \rangle$, where A is the set of students, $\mathcal{P}_m(A)$ is the set of feasible coalition structures (i.e. team partitions constrained by size m as per definition 4), and s is the characteristic function (synergistic value function) that assigns a real value to every coalition (team) that appears in some feasible coalition structure (team partition). Given the former CCF game, solving the STCP amounts to finding a coalition structure (team partition) with the highest total value. More precisely, the STCP poses a particular type of CCF game, a so-called *basic* CCF game [20]. Intuitively, the constraints in a basic CCF game are expressed in the form of: (1) sizes of coalitions that are allowed to form; and (2) subsets of students whose presence in any coalition is viewed as desirable/prohibited. On the one hand, a STCP naturally defines constraints on the size of coalitions. On the other hand, expressing a STCP as a CCF problem requires one positive constraint per feasible team (i.e., q positive constrains), while the set of negative constraints is empty. The number of positive constraints is so large for the problems we want to solve (i.e. >3000) that these problems are prohibitive for the algorithm in [19].

4 Computing Team Synergistic Values

A team K is effective solving a task when it is both *proficient* (covers the required competencies) and *congenial* (balances gender and psychological traits so that students work well together) [28]. We linearly combine these two aspects ($u_{prof}(K)$ and $u_{con}(K)$, respectively) into the synergistic value of K as follows:

Definition 7. *Given a team K, the synergistic value of team K is defined as:*

$$s(K) = \lambda \cdot u_{prof}(K) + (1 - \lambda) \cdot u_{con}(K) \tag{2}$$

$\lambda \in [0, 1]$ *is the relative importance of K being proficient.*

In general, the higher the value of λ, the higher the importance for the proficiency of a team. The setting of the value of λ depends on the task type. For instance, task types that are difficult and performed for the first time (no experts on that matter) require a high level of creativity and exchange of ideas, and hence, personality and gender balance (congeniality) should be more important than proficiency ($\lambda < 0.5$). However, for tasks where team members need to act fast (such as sport competitions or rescue teams) it is crucial for a team to be proficient ($\lambda > 0.5$). For creative task types that require certain levels of both proficiency and congeniality (such as creating a webpage) the value of λ should be set to 0.5 (so that congeniality and proficiency are equally important). The next subsections detail how to measure team proficiency and congeniality.

4.1 Evaluating Team Proficiency

Given a team and a task, we want to calculate the *degree of proficiency* of the team as a whole, noted u_{prof}. In other words, our aim is to match each competence with the student(s) whose personal competence level is closer to the task competence level requirement. With this we aim at avoiding both *under-proficient* and *over-proficient* allocations as both of those scenarios are ominous for team performance. In the first case, under-proficient students may get frustrated because they do not have enough knowledge to cope with the assigned competence requirements. In the second case, *over-proficient* students may get distracted and unmotivated because of the easiness of a job they are asked to do [7]).

In other words, given a team and a task, we want to measure how apt is the team to solve the task. We understand a task as a particular instance of a *task type* that specifies the competencies and competence levels required to solve it.

Definition 8. *A task type τ is defined as a tuple $\langle \lambda, \{(c_i, l_i, w_i)\}_{i \in I_\tau} \rangle$, where I_τ is the index set of the required competencies; $\lambda \in [0, 1]$ is the importance given to proficiency; $c_i \in C$ is a required competence; $l_i \in [0, 1]$ is the required competence level for c_i; $w_i \in [0, 1]$ is the importance of competence c_i; and $\sum_{i \in I_\tau} w_i = 1$.*

A task is an instance of a task type defined as:

Definition 9. *A task t is a tuple $\langle \tau, m \rangle$ such that τ is a task type and m is the required number of students, where $m \geq 2$.*

Henceforth, we denote by T the set of tasks and by $\mathcal{T}$ the set of task types. Moreover, we will note as $C_\tau = \{c_i | i \in I_\tau\}$ the set of competencies required by task type τ.

Students must feel both accountable and useful when working in a team [23]. Hence, each team member must be responsible for at least one competence; this is expressed as a *competence assignment* between competencies and students:

Definition 10. *Given task type τ and a team $K \in \mathcal{K}_\mathcal{A}$, a competence assignment is a function $\eta : K \to 2^{C_\tau}$ satisfying that $C_\tau = \bigcup_{a \in K} \eta(a)$. We note by Θ_τ^K the set of competence assignments for task type τ and team K.*

The degree of proficiency of a team will obviously depend on the particular student(s) assigned to each competence.

Definition 11. *Given task type τ, team K, and competence assignment η, the set $\delta(c_i) = \{a \in K | c_i \in \eta(a)\}$ stands for those students responsible of competence c_i.*

Informally, our aim is to match each competence c_i with the student(s) $\delta(c_i)$ whose personal competence level is closer to the task competence level requirement. With this we aim at avoiding both *under-proficient* (frustrated students because they cannot cope) and *over-proficient* (frustrated students because they get bored [7]) allocations.

Definition 12 *(Degree of under-proficiency).* *Given a task type τ, a team K, and an assignment η, we define the team's degree of under-proficiency for the task as:*

$$u(\eta) = \sum_{i \in I_\tau} w_i \cdot \frac{\sum_{a \in \delta(c_i)} |\min(l^a(c_i) - l_i, 0)|}{|\delta(c_i)| + 1}$$

Definition 13 *(Degree of over-proficiency).* *Given a task type τ, a team K, and an assignment η, we define the team's degree of over-proficiency for the task as:*

$$o(\eta) = \sum_{i \in I_\tau} w_i \cdot \frac{\sum_{a \in \delta(c_i)} \max(l^a(c_i) - l_i, 0)}{|\delta(c_i)| + 1}$$

Finally, we can calculate the team's proficiency degree to perform a task by combining its over-proficiency and under-proficiency as follows:

Definition 14. *Given a team K and a task of type τ, the proficiency degree of the team to perform an instance of τ is:*

$$u_{prof}(K) = \max_{\eta \in \Theta_\tau^K} (1 - (v \cdot u(\eta) + (1 - v) \cdot o(\eta)) \tag{3}$$

where $v \in [0, 1]$ is the penalty given to the under-proficiency of team K.

If we want to penalise teams that cannot cope with the competence requirements (i.e. they are under-competent) we need to choose a large value for v. And similarly a small v to penalise teams with members clearly over-competent. Although the exact value to choose will depend on the particular task type and student context, if the objective is to favour *effective* teams we should penalize more their under-proficiency and thus select a significantly large value for v. Given these definitions, $u_{prof}(K)$ is correctly defined for any team, task type and competence assignment:

Proposition 1. *For any task type τ, team K, and $\eta \in \Theta_\tau^K$, $u(\eta) + o(\eta) \in [0, 1)$ and $0 \le u_{prof}(K) < 1$.*

Proof. Soundness is straightforward as a student cannot be over- and under-proficient at the same time.

Computing $u_{prof}(K)$ is an optimisation problem: to have each competence assigned to at least one student and each student assigned to at least one competence so that the total *cost* of the assignment is minimal (in terms of under- and over-proficiency). Such optimisation problem can be cast and efficiently solved as a minimum cost flow problem [2]. The network model would contain $v = |K| + |C_\tau| + 2$ nodes and $e = |K| \cdot |C_\tau| + |K| + |C_\tau|$ edges. As discussed in [18], the minimum cost flow problem can be solved in $O(e \cdot log(v) \cdot (e + v \cdot log(v)))$ on a network with v nodes and e arcs.

4.2   Evaluating Team Congeniality

Given a team and a task, we also need to measure the *degree of congeniality* of the team, u_{con}, that is, how well do students work together in a creative and co-operative atmosphere. According to [10], the only truthful collaboration is the one containing tension, and disagreement as these improve the value of the ideas, expose the risks inherent in plan, and lead to enhanced trust among the team members. This conflict is generated by people having different views of the world (associated with opposing personality and gender), whereas harmony comes from agreement between people with similar personalities [28]. Based on these findings Douglas J. Wilde [27] compiled heuristics to successfully compose teams. According to Wilde's findings the most successful teams are: (i) teams whose SN and TF personality dimensions are as diverse as possible; (ii) teams with at least one student with positive EI and TF dimensions and negative PJ dimension, namely an extrovert, thinking and judging student (called ETJ personality); (iii) teams with at least one introvert student; and (iv) teams with gender balance. Hence, to define the *degree of congeniality* we get inspiration from [27] where D. J. Wilde uses psychological traits (see Sect. 2) to form successful teams. Formally, this can be captured by function:

$$u_{con}(K) = u_{SNTF}(K) + u_{ETJ}(K) + u_I(K) + u_{gender}(K),$$

with:

1. $u_{SNTF}(K) = \sigma(K, SN) \cdot \sigma(K, TF)$ measures the diversity in a team, where $\sigma(K, SN)$ and $\sigma(K, TF)$ stand for the standard deviations over the SN and TF personality traits of the members of team K. The larger the values of $\sigma(K, SN)$ and $\sigma(K, TF)$, the larger their product, and hence the larger the personality diversity along the SN and TF dimensions within a team.

2. $u_{ETJ}(K) = \max_{a \in K^{ETJ}} [\max(\boldsymbol{\alpha} \cdot \mathbf{p}, 0), 0]$ measures the utility of counting on ETJ personalities, being $K^{ETJ} = \{a \in K | tf^a > 0, ei^a > 0, pj^a > 0\}$ the set of students exhibiting ETJ personality, $\boldsymbol{\alpha} = (0, \alpha, \alpha, \alpha)$ is a vector, and α is the importance of counting on an extrovert, thinking, and judging student (ETJ personality).

3. $u_I(K) = \max_{a \in K} [\max(\boldsymbol{\beta} \cdot \mathbf{p}, 0), 0]$ is the utility of counting on an introvert student, $\boldsymbol{\beta} = (0, 0, -\beta, 0)$ is a vector and β is the importance of introvert students.

4. $u_{gender}(K) = \gamma \cdot \sin(\pi \cdot g(K))$ measures the importance of gender balance, where γ is a parameter to weigh the importance of gender balance, and $g(K) = \frac{w(K)}{w(K)+m(K)}$ calculates the ratio of women in a team ($w(K)$ and $m(K)$ are functions counting the number of women and men, respectively). A team K is perfectly gender-balanced iff $w(K) = m(K)$, and hence $\sin(\pi \cdot g(K)) = 1$.

5   Solving the STCP Optimally

Next we study how to optimally solve the STCP. We start by linearising the problem in Sect. 5.1. This allows us to solve the STCP with the aid of off-the-shelf solvers. Thereafter, in Sect. 5.2 we detail an optimal algorithm for the STCP.

5.1   Linearising the STCP

We denote by $n = |A|$ the number of students in A, by t a task of type $\langle \tau, m \rangle$, and by b the total number of teams, $b = \lfloor n/m \rfloor$. Note that depending on the cardinality of A and the desired team size, the number of students in each team may vary in size. For instance, if there are $n = 7$ students in A and we want to compose duets, we split students into two duets and one triplet. In general, whenever $n \geq m$: if $n \bmod m = 0$, each partition must contain b teams of size m; and if $n \bmod m \leq b$, each partition must contain $b - (n \bmod m)$ teams of size

m and n mod m teams of size $m + 1$.[3] Let $Q(n, m)$ be the quantity distribution of students in teams of sizes m and $m + 1$; these are called *feasible* teams.

Notice that the total number of feasible teams is $q = \binom{n}{m} + \min(n \bmod m, 1) \cdot \binom{n}{m+1}$. Therefore, let $K_1, \ldots, K_q$ denote the feasible teams in A, and $s(K_1), \ldots, s(K_q)$ their synergistic values concerning task t. Moreover, let b be the number of teams required to form a team partition. Finally, let C be a matrix of size $n \times q$ such that c_{ij} takes on value 1 if student a_i is part of team K_j, and 0 otherwise.

We shall consider the set of binary decision variables x_j, $1 \le j \le q$, to indicate whether team K_j is selected or not as part of the optimal solution of the STCP. Then, solving the STCP amounts to solving the following non-linear problem:

$$\max \prod_{j=1}^{q} s(K_j)^{x_j} \tag{4}$$

subject to:

$$\sum_{j=1}^{q} x_j = b \tag{5}$$

$$\sum_{j=1}^{b} c_{ij} \cdot x_j = 1 \quad \forall 1 \le i \le n \tag{6}$$

$$x_j \in \{0, 1\} \quad 1 \le j \le q \tag{7}$$

Notice that constraint 5 enforces that the number of teams in the team partition is b, whereas constraint 6 enforces that the selected teams form a partition by imposing that no student can belong to two selected teams at the same time. Now observe that Eq. 4 —the objective function— is non-linear. Nevertheless, it can be readily linearised if we consider the logarithm of $\prod_{j=1}^{q} s(K_j)^{x_j}$ as our objective function to maximise. Thus, solving the non-linear problem above is equivalent to solving the following binary linear program:

$$\max \sum_{j=1}^{q} x_j \cdot log(s(K_j)) \tag{8}$$

subject to: Eqs. 5, 6, and 7.

5.2 An Algorithm to Optimally Solve the STCP

Algorithm 1 shows the pseudocode of an optimal solver for the STCP. The algorithm starts by generating the input for an integer linear programming solver

---

[3] Beyond these cases, there is no way to compute a partition constrained by m (see def. 4). If so, $m' \le m$, $m' = \lfloor n/(b+1) \rfloor$ is the largest value smaller than m that can be used to compute partitions.

(lines 2 to 5). Line 2 generates all the possible teams of size m as dictated by the quantity distribution $Q(|A|, m)$. Thereafter, lines 3 and 4 compute the best synergistic value per team. That is, these lines compute (1) the competence assignment with the highest proficiency value. This amounts to solving an optimisation problem, as discussed at the end of subsection 4.1, and (2) the team's congenial value from the personalities and genders of the team members. Once all synergistic values are computed, we can generate an integer linear programming encoding of the problem like in Eq. 8 (line 5). The generated integer linear program (ILP) can be solved with the aid of an ILP solver (line 6) such as, for instance, CPLEX, Gurobi, or GLPK. Finally, the algorithm returns the team partition together with the competence assignments (line 7).

Algorithm 1. STCPSolver

Require: A ▷ The set of students
Require: $t = \langle \tau, m \rangle$ ▷ Task
Ensure: (P, η^*) ▷ Best partition found and best assignments
1: $P \leftarrow \emptyset$
2: $[K_1, \ldots, K_q] \leftarrow GenerateTeams(A, Q(|A|, m))$
3: **for** $i \in [1..q]$ **do**
4:     $(s(K_i), \eta_i^*) \leftarrow getBestSynergisticValue(K_i, t)$
5: $ILP \leftarrow generateILP([K_1, \ldots, K_q], [s(K_1), \ldots, s(K_q)], b)$
6: $P \leftarrow solve(ILP)$
7: **return** $(P, \{\eta_i^*\}_{K_i \in P})$

The cost of optimally solving an STCP can be split into: the cost of generating the ILP model, and the cost of solving it. As to the first cost, this comes from: (i) generating all the teams of sizes given by $Q(n, m)$ (line 2); (ii) computing the synergistic values of all teams (lines 3 and 4); (iii) generating a linear programming encoding (line 5). The cost of generating all teams is linear with the total number of teams, and hence $O(q)$. Note that the number of teams grows rapidly with increasing m and n. Moreover, the cost of computing the synergistic value for each team requires finding the optimal competence assignment. As discussed in Sec. 4.1, this can be cast as a minimum cost flow problem and solved in $O(m \cdot log(e) \cdot (m + e \cdot log(e)))$ time, where $e = m \cdot |C_\tau|$, being $|C_\tau|$ the number of competencies required by task type τ. Thus, generating the input to an ILP solver becomes increasingly costly as the number of students per team grows.

6   An Approximate Algorithm for the STCP

In this section we present an approximate algorithm — *SynTeam* (see Algorithm 2). *SynTeam* quickly finds an initial partition, to subsequently improve it by performing student swaps between teams. First, it randomly orders the list of students and assigns students to teams one by one from that list following

$Q(|A|, m)$ (see Sec. 5.1) to generate an initial solution $(P, S(P), \boldsymbol{\eta})$ (line 1). The assignment of students to competencies is solved as described in subsection 4.1.

Second, at each iteration, SynTeam generates a random neighbour of the current solution as follows (line 4). First, it randomly selects two teams from the current solution. Then, it computes the synergistic value of all partitions resulting from substituting the randomly selected teams by two new teams (and corresponding competence assignments. see Subsection 4.1) formed by reordering the students of the randomly selected teams in all possible ways. It stores the best option in $(P', S(P'), \boldsymbol{\eta}')$. In addition, if the current iteration is the n_l-th—not necessarily consecutive—non-improving iteration,[4] the following more fine-grained procedure is applied to $(P, \boldsymbol{\eta})$ (line 6). In the ascending order determined by team and student indexes it tries to swap two students from two different teams. The first improving solution found this way (if any) is stored in $(P', \boldsymbol{\eta}')$ and the c_l counter, for non-consecutive non-improving iterations, is re-initialized. Finally, the algorithm stops after n_r consecutive non-improving iterations.

Algorithm 2. SynTeam

Require: A ▷ The list of students
Require: n_r ▷ Max. # of consecutive non-impr. iterations
Require: n_l ▷ # of non-impr. iterations before student-swap
Ensure: $(P, \boldsymbol{\eta})$ ▷ Best partition found and best assignments
 1: $(P, S(P), \boldsymbol{\eta}) \leftarrow GenerateRandomSolution(A, Q(|A|, m))$
 2: $c_r \leftarrow 1,\ c_l \leftarrow 1$
 3: **while** $c_r \leq n_r$ **do**
 4:     $(P', S(P'), \boldsymbol{\eta}') \leftarrow GenerateRandomNeighbor(P, \boldsymbol{\eta})$
 5:     **if** $S(P') \leq S(P)$ and $c_l = n_l$ **then**
 6:         $(P', S(P'), \boldsymbol{\eta}') \leftarrow ApplyImprovingSwap(P, \boldsymbol{\eta})$
 7:         $c_l \leftarrow 1$
 8:     **if** $S(P') > S(P)$ **then**
 9:         $(P, S(P), \boldsymbol{\eta}) \leftarrow (P', S(P'), \boldsymbol{\eta}')$
10:         $c_r \leftarrow 1,\ c_l \leftarrow 1$
11:     **else**
12:         $c_r \leftarrow c_r + 1,\ c_l \leftarrow c_l + 1$
     return $(P, \boldsymbol{\eta})$

---

7 Experimental Results

In this section we compare our two STCP solvers: optimal (STCPSolver), and approximate (SynTeam). Our empirical evaluation compares: (1) their runtimes as team sizes and number of students increase; (2) the quality of SynTeam's approximate solutions; (3) the anytime performance of SynTeam with respect to STCPSolver.

---

[4] If the current solution is improved at an iteration, we refer to it as an improving iteration, a non-improving iteration otherwise.

7.1 Empirical Settings

Our empirical evaluation employs the following settings:

- **LP Solver.** We used CPLEX Optimization Studio v12.7.1 [13] for STCP-Solver.
- **Students.** We used actual-world data from 102 students, each one with an id, a gender, a personality profile, and seven competencies with varying competence levels.
- **Task type.** The task type used in our experiments here $\{(c_i, l_i, w_i)\}_{i \in [1,7]}$ was the same as the one used in our study involving real students [4]. It had seven equally important competencies, $w_i = 1/7$, with a maximally competence level requirement, $l_i = 1$, and the importance of proficiency set larger than congeniality, $\lambda = 0.8$. In an educational context, task types requiring more than seven competencies are rare and thus the task type used here is complex enough for our purposes [12].
- **Task.** Team size m ranged from 3 to 6. Larger team sizes were not considered because the generated STCPs were too costly for STCPSolver and rare in an education context.
- **Team proficiency.** As in this paper we are just interested in the computational properties of the algorithms, the concrete value for v is irrelevant. We used $v = 1$.
- **Team Congeniality.** We analytically assessed that to make each component of the personality requirements equally relevant, we must set importance values as follows: (1) $\alpha = 0.11$, (2) $\beta = 3 \cdot \alpha$, (3) $\gamma = 0.33$.
- **Number of iterations without improvement** (n_r). To give SynTeam a chance to visit all teams at least once without revisiting the same teams too many times, we decided to set n_r based on the value of b (number of teams in a partition). We experimentally observed how the quality of SynTeam solutions improved over time. Thus, setting n_r to $1.5 \cdot b$ offered a good compromise.
- **Frequency of local search** (n_l). We empirically observed that, after performing approximately $\frac{n_r}{6}$ random team re-compositions without improvement, the probability of finding an improvement was very low. Hence, we set n_l to $\frac{n_r}{6}$.

7.2 Computational Results

The experimental evaluation was performed on a cluster of PCs with Intel(R) Xeon(R) CPU 5670 CPUs of 12 nuclei of 2933 MHz and at least 40 Gigabytes of RAM. Moreover, we used IBM ILOG CPLEX v12.7.1 within both STCPSolver and SynTeam. Note that CPLEX is used within SynTeam in order to calculate, given a team, the optimal assignment of students to tasks. Moreover, note that CPLEX was run in one-threaded mode, in order to be able to perform a fair comparison.

Runtime Analysis. Figure 1 shows the performance, in terms of total running time, of SynTeam and STCPSolver for different teams as the number of students increases. We performed 20 runs for each configuration, and recorded the total run time average and standard deviation. As team size (m) increases, generating the input for STCPSolver becomes prohibitively costly. Therefore, for STCPSolver we were only able to do calculations for: 102 students for $m \in \{3, 4\}$, 60 students for $m = 5$, and 42 students for $m = 6$. For larger values of n and m, reading the problem was beyond CPLEX capabilities.[5] We observe that the runtime of STCPSolver dramatically increases with the number of students (n) and team size (m). Note that for team size $m = 6$ and $n = 42$ students, SynTeam is more than two orders of magnitude faster than STCPSolver.

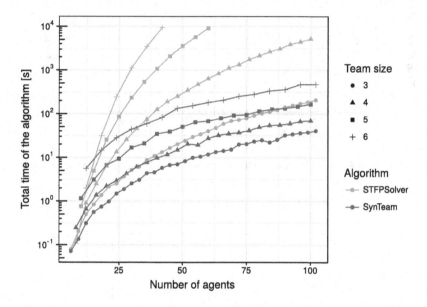

Fig. 1. SynTeam vs STCPSolver runtimes.

To better understand this result, we compared STCPSolver solving time (only CPLEX time) with SynTeam. That is, we disregard the time required by STCPSolver to generate the problem (lines 1–5 in Algorithm 1). Figure 2 shows this comparison. We observe that — even in this case — SynTeam is more efficient for larger instances (team sizes $m > 3$ and a growing number of students).

Quality Analysis. For each case we calculated the optimality ratio. Specifically, we divided the solution obtained by SynTeam by the optimal solution calculated by STCPSolver. Figure 4 illustrates this quality ratio with respect to the number of students and team sizes. The results show that the quality of approximate solutions slightly decreases with the number of students and team sizes but it always remains above approx. 95%.

---

[5] For instance, CPLEX must consider 12.271.512 binary variables for $n = 48$ and $m = 6$.

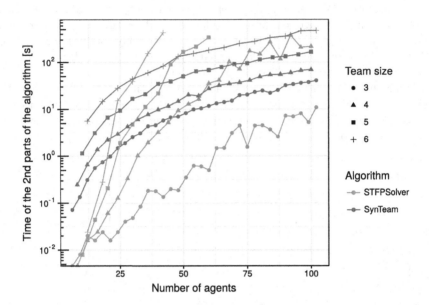

Fig. 2. SynTeam vs. STCPSolver solving times (disregarding problem generation time).

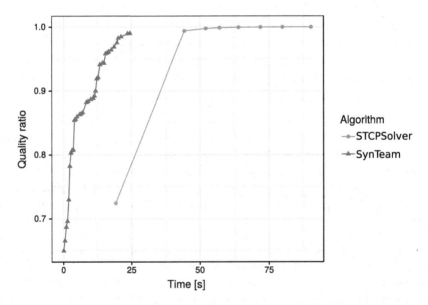

Fig. 3. Anytime performance (in quality ratio) of SynTeam vs. STCPSolver ($n = 45$, $m = 5$).

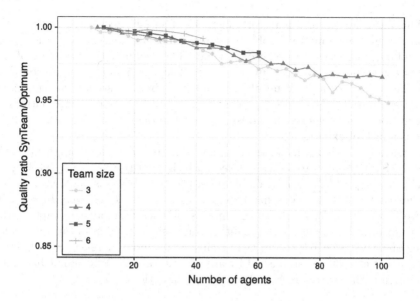

Fig. 4. SynTeam quality ratio.

Anytime performance. We chose the configuration with $n = 45$ students and team size $m = 5$, since it is still in the region of problems that STCPSolver could afford. Figure 3 shows the evolution of the best solutions found over time (divided by the optimal solution) for both algorithms. Note that the problem generation time required by STCPSolver is not included, and hence we only plot the CPLEX solving time. Observe that SynTeam provides very good solutions in approx. 15 s, while STCPSolver needs approximately 20 seconds (in addition to more than 1000 s of preprocessing time) to come up with a first, low-quality solution. To conclude, to reach optimality, STCPSolver requires nearly two orders of magnitude more time than the one required by SynTeam to obtain solutions very close to optimality.

8   Conclusions

In this paper, we considered the Synergistic Team Composition Problem (STCP) in the context of student team composition and proposed both an optimal and an approximate solution to this problem. First, we discussed an algorithm to optimally solve the STCP called STCPSolver. When we noticed that the algorithm is only effective for small instances of the problem, we developed SynTeam, a greedy algorithm for partitioning groups of humans into proficient, gender, psychologically and size balanced teams, which yields a good, but not necessarily optimum solution. Our computational evaluation shows that the larger the number of students and team sizes, the larger the benefits of SynTeam with respect to STCPSolver. Furthermore, SynTeam provides good quality approximate solutions (beyond 95% with respect to the optimal).

This paper identified a real-world instance of an interesting new type of constrained coalition formation problem requiring a *balanced* coalition structure in terms of coalition sizes and coalitional values. The computational analysis of our proposed algorithms gives the guidelines for their use by any organisation that faces the need to form problem solving teams (e.g. in a classroom, in a company, in a research unit). The algorithm composes teams in a purely automatic way without consulting experts, which is a huge advantage for environments where there is a lack of experts.

Finally, we have implemented a freely available web-based application to solve the STCP that automatically selects which algorithm to use depending on the size of the problem. It is available here: https://eduteams.iiia.csic.es.

This new problem, STCP, has potential to spur future research. In particular, we aim at considering richer and more sophisticated models to capture the various factors that influence the coalition composition process in the real world. For instance, we want to be able to add constraints and preferences coming from experts that cannot be established by any algorithm, e.g. Ana cannot be in the same team with José as they used to have a romantic relationship.

Acknowledgements. This work was supported by the CIMBVAL project (funded by MINECO, project number TIN2017-89758-R), 2017 SGR 172, the AppPhil project (funded by RecerCaixa 2017) and Collectiveware (TIN2015-66863-C2-1-R MINECO/FEDER). Bistaffa was supported by the H2020-MSCA-IF-2016 HPA4CF project. The research was partially supported by the ST Engineering - NTU corporate Lab through the NRF corporate lab@university scheme.

References

1. Acuña, S.T., Gómez, M., Juristo, N.: How do personality, team processes and task characteristics relate to job satisfaction and software quality? Inf. Softw. Technol. **51**(3), 627–639 (2009)
2. Ahuja, R.K., Magnanti, T.L., Orlin, J.B.: Network Flows: Theory, Algorithms, and Applications (1993)
3. Alberola, J.M., Del Val, E., Sanchez-Anguix, V., Palomares, A., Teruel, M.D.: An artificial intelligence tool for heterogeneous team formation in the classroom. Knowl.-Based Syst. **101**, 1–14 (2016)
4. Andrejczuk, E., Rodríguez-Aguilar, J.A., Roig, C., Sierra, C.: Synergistic team composition. In: Proceedings of the 16th Conference on Autonomous Agents and MultiAgent Systems, pp. 1463–1465, International Foundation for Autonomous Agents and Multiagent Systems (2017)
5. Arnold, J., Randall, R.: Work Psychology. Pearson Education Limited, Harlow (2010)
6. Barkley, E.F., Cross, K.P., Major, C.H.: Collaborative Learning Techniques: A Handbook for College Faculty. John Wiley & Sons, Hoboken (2014)
7. Bashshur, M.R., Hernández, A., Peiró, J.M.: The impact of underemployment on individual and team performance. In: Maynard, D., Feldman, D. (eds.) Underemployment, pp. 187–213. Springer, New York (2011). https://doi.org/10.1007/978-1-4419-9413-4_10

8. Briggs, I., Myers, P.B.: Gifts Differing: Understanding Personality Type. Davies-Black Publishing, Mountain View (1995)
9. Chen, B., Chen, X., Timsina, A., Soh, L.: Considering agent and task openness in ad hoc team formation. In: Proceedings of the 2015 International Conference on Autonomous Agents and Multiagent Systems, AAMAS 2015, Istanbul, Turkey, 4–8 May 2015, pp 1861–1862 (2015)
10. Davey, L.: If Your Team Agrees on Everything, Working Together is Pointless. Harvard Business Review, Boston (2017)
11. Farhangian, M., Purvis, M.K., Purvis, M., Savarimuthu, B.T.R.: Modeling the effects of personality on team formation in self-assembly teams. In: Chen, Q., Torroni, P., Villata, S., Hsu, J., Omicini, A. (eds.) PRIMA 2015. LNCS (LNAI), vol. 9387, pp. 538–546. Springer, Cham (2015). https://doi.org/10.1007/978-3-319-25524-8_36
12. Gardner, H.: The theory of multiple intelligences. Ann. Dyslexia **37**(1), 19–35 (1987)
13. IBM.: IBM ILOG CPLEX Optimization Studio (2017)
14. Jung, C.G.: Psychological Types. Princeton University Press, Princeton (1921)
15. Mount, M.K., Barrick, M.R., Stewart, G.L.: Five-factor model of personality and performance in jobs involving interpersonal interactions. Hum. perform. **11**(2–3), 145–165 (1998)
16. Nash, J.: The bargaining problem. Econometrica **18**(2), 155–162 (1950)
17. Okimoto, T., Schwind, N., Clement, M., Ribeiro, T., Inoue, K., Marquis, P.: How to form a task-oriented robust team. In: Proceedings of the 2015 International Conference on Autonomous Agents and Multiagent Systems, AAMAS 2015, pp. 395–403. International Foundation for Autonomous Agents and Multiagent Systems (2015)
18. Orlin, J.B.: A faster strongly polynomial minimum cost flow algorithm. Oper. Res. **41**(2), 338–350 (1993)
19. Rahwan, T., et al.: Constrained coalition formation. In: Burgard, W., Roth, D., (eds.) AAAI, AAAI Press (2011)
20. Rahwan, T., Michalak, T.P., Wooldridge, M., Jennings, N.R.: Coalition structure generation: a survey. Artif. Intell. **229**, 139–174 (2015)
21. Rangapuram, S.S., Bühler, T., Hein, M.: Towards realistic team formation in social networks based on densest subgraphs (2015). CoRR, abs/1505.06661
22. Roe, R.A.: Competences-a key towards the integration of theory and practice in work psychology. Gedrag en Organisatie **15**(4), 203–224 (2002)
23. Slavin, R.E.: Synthesis of research of cooperative learning. Educ. Leadersh. **48**(5), 71–82 (1991)
24. Vosniadou, S.: How Children Learn. Educational Practices Series. International Academy of Education (2001). https://books.google.com.sg/books?id=1gwmAQAAMAAJ
25. West, M.A.: Effective Teamwork: Practical Lessons Learned from Organizational Research. Wiley-Blackwell, West Sussex (2012)
26. White, K.B.: Mis project teams: an investigation of cognitive style implications. MIS Q. **8**(2), 95–101 (1984)
27. Wilde, D.J.: Teamology: The Construction and Organization of Effective Teams. Springer, London (2009)
28. Wilde, D.J.: Post-Jungian Personality Theory for Individuals and Teams. SYDROSE LP, (2013)

Solving Multiagent Constraint Optimization Problems on the Constraint Composite Graph

Ferdinando Fioretto[1]([⊠]), Hong Xu[2], Sven Koenig[2], and T. K. Satish Kumar[2]

[1] Georgia Institute of Technology, Atlanta, GA, USA
fioretto@gatech.edu
[2] University of Southern California, Los Angeles, CA, USA
{hongx,skoenig}@usc.edu,tkskwork@gmail.com

Abstract. We introduce the *Constraint Composite Graph* (CCG) for *Distributed Constraint Optimization Problems* (DCOPs), a popular paradigm used for the description and resolution of cooperative multiagent problems. The CCG is a novel graphical representation of DCOPs on which agents can coordinate their assignments to solve the distributed problem suboptimally. By leveraging this representation, agents are able to reduce the size of the problem. We propose a novel variant of Max-Sum—a popular DCOP incomplete algorithm—called *CCG-Max-Sum*, which is applied to CCGs, and demonstrate its efficiency and effectiveness on DCOP benchmarks based on several network topologies.

1 Introduction

In a cooperative *multiagent system*, multiple autonomous agents interact to pursue personal goals and to achieve shared objectives. The *Distributed Constraint Optimization Problem (DCOP)* model [6,17] is an elegant formalism to describe cooperative multiagent problems that are distributed in nature. In this model, a collection of agents coordinate a value assignment to the problem variables with the goal of optimizing a global objective within the confines of localized communication. DCOPs have been used to solve a variety of problems in the context of coordination and resource allocation [9,30], sensor networks [5], and device coordination in smart homes [8,22].

DCOP algorithms are either *complete* or *incomplete*. Complete algorithms find an optimal solution to the problem employing one of two broad modus operandi: distributed search-based techniques [17,26] or distributed inference-based techniques [20,24]. In search-based techniques, agents traverse the search

The research at the University of Southern California was supported by the National Science Foundation (NSF) under grant numbers 1724392, 1409987, and 1817189. The views and conclusions contained in this document are those of the authors and should not be interpreted as representing the official policies, either expressed or implied, of the sponsoring organizations, agencies or the U.S. government.

T. Miller et al. (Eds.): PRIMA 2018, LNAI 11224, pp. 106–122, 2018.
https://doi.org/10.1007/978-3-030-03098-8_7

space by selecting value assignments and communicating them to other agents. Inference-based techniques rely instead on the notion of agent belief, describing the best cost an agent can achieve for each value assignment to its variables. These beliefs drive the value-selection process of the agents to find an optimal solution to the problem. Since finding an optimal DCOP solution is NP-hard [17], optimally solving a DCOP requires exponential time or space in the worst case. Thus, there is growing interest in the development of incomplete algorithms, which trade off solution quality for better runtimes. Similar to complete algorithms, incomplete algorithms can be classified as local search-based [16,27] and inference-based [5]. Some incomplete algorithms have been used in different multiagent applications. For instance, Max-Sum [5] is an inference-based incomplete algorithm which has been successfully used to solve sensor networks problems [5] and smart home coordination problems [22].

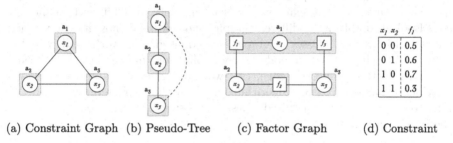

(a) Constraint Graph   (b) Pseudo-Tree   (c) Factor Graph   (d) Constraint

Fig. 1. DCOP constraint graph (a), pseudotree (b), factor graph (c), and a constraint (d).

In both complete and incomplete DCOP algorithms, the problem resolution process is characterized by the graphical representation of the problem. The three most important problem representations are the *constraint graph*, the *pseudo-tree*, and the *factor graph*. The first one represents a problem as a graph whose nodes describe the variables and whose edges describe the constraints. The second one is a rearrangement of the constraint graph, where a subset of edges forms a rooted tree and where two variables participating in the same constraint appear in the same branch of the tree. The third one represents the problem as a bipartite graph where nodes represent both variables and constraints, and edges link the constraint nodes to the variables participating in the associated constraint. In many local search algorithms, such as MGM [16], DSA [27], or the region-optimal algorithm family [19], agents operate directly on the constraint graph and perform distributed local searches by exchanging information with their neighbors in the constraint graph. In the main inference-based algorithms, the agents operate on either a pseudo-tree (e.g., P-DCOP [21]) or a factor graph (e.g., Max-Sum). In the former case, agents exchange messages following the structure of the pseudo-tree, typically alternating between a phase in which messages are propagated up from the leaf agents to the root agent of the pseudo-tree, and one in which information is propagated down. In the latter case, there are two types of entities, which represent variables and constraints. Both of them participate in the message-exchange process to solve the problem.

All these representations allow agents to exploit the graphical structure of the problem. However, they hide the numerical structure of the problem's constraints. Thus, in this paper, we introduce the *Constraint Composite Graph (CCG)* for DCOPs, a lifted graphical representation that provides a framework for exploiting simultaneously the graphical structure of the agent-coordination process as well as the numerical structure of the constraints involving the variables controlled by the agents. CCGs have recently been introduced in the context of *Weighted Constraint Satisfaction Problems (WCSPs)* [13,15], and shown to be highly effective in solving a wide range of problems [25]. We contribute to the development of inference-based DCOP algorithms by presenting a novel framework for solving DCOPs sub-optimally whose agent interactions are driven by the structure of the CCG representation. We analyze the behavior of our framework on federated social network problems (introduced in Sect. 5) and random Boolean problems on different graph topologies and show its effectiveness on several important classes of graphs, including grid networks and scale-free networks, which are used to model many applications in distributed settings.

To the best of our knowledge, this work describes the first proposal of a distributed message-passing algorithm based on the CCG representation. We refer to our algorithm as a "lifted" message passing algorithm since it works on the CCG representation of a DCOP.

2 Background

We now review the distributed constraint optimization framework, the graphical models commonly adopted to represent a DCOP, and the CCG model.

Distributed Constraint Optimization. A *Distributed Constraint Optimization Problem (DCOP)* is a tuple $P = \langle \mathbf{X}, \mathbf{D}, \mathbf{F}, \mathbf{A}, \alpha \rangle$, where: $\mathbf{X} = \{x_1, \ldots, x_n\}$ is a set of *variables*; $\mathbf{D} = \{D_{x_1}, \ldots, D_{x_n}\}$ is a set of finite *domains* for the variables in $\mathbf{X}$; $\mathbf{F} = \{f_1, \ldots, f_e\}$ is a set of *constraints* (also called *cost functions*), where $f : \prod_{x \in \mathbf{x}^f} D_x \to \mathbb{R}_+ \cup \{\infty\}$ and $\mathbf{x}^f \subseteq \mathbf{X}$ is the set of the variables (also called the *scope*) of f; $\mathbf{A} = \{a_1, \ldots, a_p\}$ is a set of *agents*; and $\alpha : \mathbf{X} \to \mathbf{A}$ is a function that maps each variable to one agent. Figure 1(d) shows an example constraint. It specifies the costs of all combinations of values for the variables x_1, x_2 in its scope. For a variable $x \in \mathbf{X}$, we use $\mathbf{f}^x$ to denote the set of constraints that involve x in their scopes.

A *partial assignment* σ_X is an assignment of values to a set of variables $X \subseteq \mathbf{X}$ that is consistent with their domains; i.e., it is a partial function $\theta : \mathbf{X} \to \cup_{i=1}^n D_{x_i}$ such that, for each $x_j \in \mathbf{X}$, if $\theta(x_j)$ is defined (i.e., $x_j \in X$), then $\theta(x_j) \in D_{x_j}$. For a set of variables $V = \{x_{i_1}, \ldots, x_{i_h}\} \subseteq X$, $\pi_V(\sigma_X) = \langle \theta(x_{i_1}), \ldots, \theta(x_{i_h}) \rangle$ is the *projection* of σ_X onto the variables in V, where $i_1 < \ldots < i_h$. When $V = \{x_i\}$ is a singleton, we write $\pi_{x_i}(\sigma_X)$ to denote the projection of σ_X onto x_i. The *cost* $\mathcal{F}(\sigma_X) = \sum_{f \in \mathbf{F}: \mathbf{x}^f \subseteq X} f(\pi_{\mathbf{x}^f}(\sigma_X))$ of an assignment σ_X is the sum of the evaluation of the constraints involving all variables in X. A *solution* is a partial assignment σ_X (written σ for shorthand) for all variables of the problem, i.e., with $X = \mathbf{X}$, whose cost is finite (i.e., $\mathcal{F}(\sigma) \neq \infty$). The goal is to find an optimal solution $\sigma^* = \mathrm{argmin}_\sigma \mathcal{F}(\sigma)$. In this paper, we restrict our attention to Boolean DCOPs (i.e., DCOPs where all domains are $\{0,1\}$). Despite our focus on Boolean DCOPs, the concepts introduced in the next sections are generalizable, as discussed in Sect. 6.

Given a DCOP P, its *constraint graph* is $G_P = (\mathbf{X}, E_C)$, where an undirected edge $\{x, y\} \in E_C$ exists if and only if there exists an $f \in \mathbf{F}$ such that $\{x, y\} \subseteq \mathbf{x}^f$. The constraint graph provides a standard representation of a DCOP instance. It highlights the locality of interactions among agents and therefore is commonly adopted by DCOP algorithms. Figure 1(a) shows an example constraint graph of a DCOP instance with three agents a_1, a_2, and a_3, each controlling one variable with domain $\{0,1\}$. There are three constraints: f_1 with scope $\mathbf{x}^{f_1} = \{x_1, x_2\}$, f_2 with scope $\mathbf{x}^{f_2} = \{x_2, x_3\}$, and f_3 with scope $\mathbf{x}^{f_3} = \{x_1, x_3\}$.

A *pseudo-tree* for P is a spanning tree $T_P = \langle \mathbf{X}, E_T \rangle$ of G_P, i.e., a connected subgraph of G_P that contains all nodes and is a rooted tree, with the following additional condition: for each $x, y \in \mathbf{X}$, if $\{x, y\} \subseteq \mathbf{x}^f$ for some $f \in \mathbf{F}$, then x and y appear in the same branch of T_P (i.e., x is an ancestor of y in T_P or vice versa). Figure 1(b) shows one possible pseudo-tree for our example DCOP, where the solid lines represent tree edges and the dotted line represents a *backedge* that connects an agent with one of its ancestors.

A factor graph [12] is a bipartite graph used to represent the factorization of a function. Given a DCOP instance P, the corresponding factor graph $F_P = \langle \mathbf{X}, \mathbf{F}, E_F \rangle$ is composed of variable nodes $x \in \mathbf{X}$, function nodes $f \in \mathbf{F}$, and edges E_F such that there is an undirected edge between function node f and variable node x if and only if $x \in \mathbf{x}^f$. Figure 1(c) illustrates the factor graph of our example DCOP instance, where each agent a_i controls its variable x_i and, in addition, a_1 controls the constraints f_1 and f_3, and a_2 controls the constraint f_2.

Max-Sum. Max-Sum [5] is a popular incomplete DCOP algorithm. Its agents operate on a factor graph F_P through a synchronous iterative process. Albeit the logic of each variable node and each function node is executed within an agent, to ease exposition, in what follows, we treat them as entities that are able to send and receive messages. In each iteration, each function node f exchanges messages with the nodes of variables in its scope $\mathbf{x}^f$, and each variable node x exchanges messages with the nodes of constraints which involve x in their scopes $\mathbf{f}^x$. Thus, each node exchanges messages with its neighbors in the factor graph.

The content of the messages sent by each function (variable) node is based exclusively on the information received from neighboring variable (function) nodes. The message $q_{x \to f}^i$ sent by a variable node x to a function node f in $\mathbf{f}^x$ in iteration i contains, for each value $d \in D_x$, the aggregated costs for d received from all neighboring function nodes in iteration $i - 1$, excluding f. It is defined as a function $q_{x \to f}^i : D_x \to \mathbb{R}_+ \cup \{\infty\}$, whose value is 0 for all $d \in D_x$ when $i = 0$ and

$$q^i_{x \to f}(d) = \alpha^i_{xf} + \sum_{f' \in \mathbf{f}^x \setminus \{f\}} r^{i-1}_{f' \to x}(d) \tag{1}$$

when $i > 0$. Here, $r^{i-1}_{f' \to x}$ is the message received by variable node x from function node f' in iteration $i-1$ and α^i_{xf} is a *normalizing* constant used to prevent the values of the transmitted messages from growing arbitrarily and chosen so that $\sum_{d \in D_x} q^i_{x \to f}(d) = 0$ holds. The message $r^i_{f \to x}$ sent by a function node f to a variable node $x \in \mathbf{x}^f$ in iteration i contains, for each $d \in D_x$, the minimum cost of any assignments of values to the variables in $\mathbf{x}^f$ in which x takes value d. It is defined as a function $r^i_{f \to x} : D_x \to \mathbb{R}_+ \cup \{\infty\}$, whose value is 0 when $i=0$ and

$$r^i_{f \to x}(d) = \min_{\sigma_{\mathbf{x}^f} : \pi_x(\sigma_{\mathbf{x}^f})=d} f(\sigma_{\mathbf{x}^f}) + \sum_{x' \in \mathbf{x}^f \setminus \{x\}} q^i_{x' \to f}(\pi_{x'}(\sigma_{\mathbf{x}^f})) \tag{2}$$

when $i > 0$. Here, $\sigma_{\mathbf{x}^f}$ is a possible assignment of values to all variables in the scope $\mathbf{x}^f$ of the constraint f, given that variable $x \in \mathbf{x}^f$ takes value d. The agent controlling a variable node x decides its value assignment at the end of each iteration $i > 0$ by computing its associated belief $b^i_x(d)$ for each $d \in D_x$: $b^i_x(d) = \sum_{f \in \mathbf{f}^x} r^{i-1}_{f \to x}(d)$ and choosing the assignment d^{*i} such that, $d^{*i} = \operatorname{argmin}_{d \in D_x} b^i_x(d)$. This form of message passing allows for an inference-based method: Max-Sum agents initialize all their messages to 0 and, in each iteration $i > 0$, retain only the most recent messages, overwriting the messages received in previous iterations.

Max-Sum is an incomplete DCOP algorithm. However, on acyclic problems, it is guaranteed to converge to an optimal solution [5].

3   The Constraint Composite Graph

We now describe the *constraint composite graph (CCG)*, a graphical structure that can be used to represent DCOPs. Its goal is to exploit simultaneously the graphical structure of the agent interactions as well as the numerical structure of the cost functions. It is a node-weighted tripartite graph $G_{\mathrm{CCG}} = \langle V = \mathbf{X} \cup \mathbf{Y} \cup \mathbf{Z}, E, w \rangle$, where $\mathbf{X}$, $\mathbf{Y}$, and $\mathbf{Z}$ are a partition of V. The nodes in $\mathbf{X}$ correspond to the DCOP variables, while the nodes in $\mathbf{Y}$ and $\mathbf{Z}$ correspond to auxiliary variables introduced to model a reformulation of the original problem into a *Minimum Weighted Vertex Cover (MWVC)*.

The concept of a CCG was first proposed by Kumar [13] as a combinatorial structure associated with a *Weighted Constraint Satisfaction Problem (WCSP)*. WCSPs are similar to DCOPs, except that all computations are centralized. In that proposal, it was shown that the task of solving a WCSP can be reformulated as the task of finding a MWVC on its associated CCG [13–15]. A desirable property of the CCG is that it can be constructed in polynomial time and is always tripartite [13–15]. CCGs also enable the use of *kernelization methods* for solving WCSPs [25], which are polynomial-time procedures that can simplify a problem to a smaller one, called the kernel. The *Nemhauser-Trotter reduction*

Algorithm 1: CCG-Max-Sum

```
// CCG Construction Phase
```
1 **foreach** $f_i \in \mathbf{F}_i$ **do**
2     $p_i \leftarrow$ *construct-polynomial*(f_i);
3     $G_{CCG_i} = \langle V_i = X_i \cup Y_i \cup Z_i, E_i, w_i \rangle \leftarrow$ *decompose-polynomial*(p_i) ;

4 **foreach** $f \in \mathbf{F}_{CCG_i}$ *involving variable* v_j *with* $\alpha(v_j) \neq a_i$ **do**
5   a_i sends f to $a_{\alpha(v_j)}$;

6 When agent a_i receives f involving $v_i \in \mathbf{X}_i$ from neighboring agent a_j:
   $f_{v_i}(1) \leftarrow f_{v_i}(1) + f(1)$;
```
// Message Passing Phase
```
7 $\mu_{v_i \to v_j} \leftarrow 0$ $(\forall v_i \in V_i, \forall v_j \in N(v_i))$;
8 **while** *termination condition is not met* **do**
9   Wait for all messages $\mu_{v_j \to v_i}$ from $v_j \in N(v_i)$ $(\forall v_i \in V_i)$;
10   **foreach** $v_i \in V_i$ **do**
11   Update $\mu_{v_i \to v_j}$ according to Eq. (5);

12 **for** $v_i \in \mathbf{X}_i$ **do**
13   **if** $w_{v_i} < \sum_{v_j \in N(v_i)} \mu_{v_j \to v_i}$ **then** $v_i \leftarrow 1$ **else** $v_i \leftarrow 0$;

(NT reduction) [2,18] is one such kernelization method and uses a maxflow procedure to find the kernel.

In the next section, we introduce an extension of the Max-Sum algorithm, called CCG-Max-Sum, which can be used directly on CCGs.

4 CCG-Max-Sum

CCG-Max-Sum is an incomplete, iterative DCOP algorithm which works in two phases, namely, the *CCG construction* and the *message passing*, which are executed sequentially and summarized in Algorithm 1. In the CCG construction phase, the agents coordinate in the construction of a CCG and take ownership of the auxiliary variables and constraints introduced by this lifted graphical representation. Afterwards, in the message passing phase, the agents execute the iterative synchronous process which extends the Max-Sum algorithm.

In what follows, we use $G_i = \langle \mathbf{X}_i, \mathbf{F}_i \rangle$ to denote the subgraph of the constraint graph controlled by agent a_i, where the sets $\mathbf{X}_i \subseteq \mathbf{X}$ form a partition of the set of variables $\mathbf{X}$, and the sets $\mathbf{F}_i \subseteq \mathbf{F}$ form a partition for the constraint set $\mathbf{F}$.

4.1 CCG Construction Phase

The CCG construction proceeds in 3 stages:

1. Expressing Constraints as Polynomials. In this stage, each agent a_i transforms the constraints $f_i \in \mathbf{F}_i$ it controls into polynomials p_i (line 2 of Algorithm 1) using standard Gaussian Elimination. We use $G_{CCG_i} = \langle V_i = X_i \cup Y_i \cup Z_i, E_i, w_i \rangle$

to denote the portion of the CCG obtained from constraint f_i. Consider the example constraint f_1 in Fig. 1(d), which involves the variables x_1 and x_2. It can be written as a polynomial $p_1(x_1, x_2)$ in x_1 and x_2 of degree 1 each: $p_1(x_1, x_2) = c_{00} + c_{01}x_1 + c_{10}x_2 + c_{11}x_1x_2$. The coefficients c_{00}, c_{01}, c_{10}, and c_{11} of the polynomial can be computed by solving a system of linear equations, where each equation corresponds to an entry in the constraint table, using standard Gaussian Elimination. In our example:

$$p_1(0,0) = 0.5 \qquad p_1(0,1) = 0.6 \qquad p_1(1,0) = 0.7 \qquad p_1(1,1) = 0.3$$
$$c_{00} = 0.5 \qquad c_{01} = 0.1 \qquad c_{10} = 0.2 \qquad c_{11} = -0.5.$$

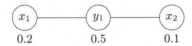

Fig. 2. The projection of an MWVC on the IS $\{x_1, x_2\}$ of this node-weighted undirected graph leads to Fig. 1(d). The weights on x_1, x_2, and y_1 are 0.2, 0.1, and 0.5, respectively. The entry 0.6 in cell ($x_1 = 0, x_2 = 1$) in Fig. 1(d), for example, indicates that, when x_1 is necessarily excluded from the MWVC but x_2 is necessarily included in it, then the weight of the MWVC $\{x_2, y_1\}$ is 0.6.

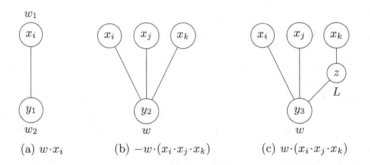

Fig. 3. The lifted graphical representation of terms in a polynomial for linear (a), negative nonlinear (b), and positive nonlinear (c) terms. We assume that $w > 0$ in (b) and (c) (but not in (a)). A node has a zero weight if no weight is shown. In (a), w_1 and w_2 satisfy $w_1 - w_2 = w$.

2. Decomposing the Terms of the Polynomials. In this stage, for each $f_i \in \mathbf{F}_i$, the agent that controls it constructs a subgraph G_{CCG_i} of the CCG (line 3 of Algorithm 1). At the end of this stage, each agent introduces new sets of auxiliary variables Y_i and Z_i and replaces its constraints with a new set $\mathbf{F}_{\text{CCG}_i}$ of

constraints that involve the decision variables and its newly introduced auxiliary variables. Before describing this procedure, we review the concept of the MWVC, a cornerstone concept for the notion of the CCG.

A *minimum node cover* of $G = \langle V, E \rangle$ is the smallest set of nodes $S \subseteq V$ such that every edge in E has at least one of its nodes in S. When G is node-weighted, (i.e., each node $v_i \in V$ has a non-negative weight w_i associated with it), its MWVC is defined as a node cover of minimum total weight of its nodes.

For a given graph G, one can project MWVCs on a given independent set (IS) $U \subseteq V$. (An IS is a set of nodes in which no two nodes are connected by an edge.) The input to such a projection is the graph G as well as an IS $U = \{u_1, u_2, \ldots, u_k\}$ on G. The output is a table of 2^k numbers. Each entry in this table corresponds to a k-bit vector. We say that a k-bit vector t imposes the following restrictions: **(a)** If the ith bit t_i is 0, then node u_i has to be excluded from the MWVC; and **(b)** if the ith bit t_i is 1, then the node u_i has to be included in the MWVC. The projection of an MWVC on the IS U is then defined to be a table with entries corresponding to each of the 2^k possible k-bit vectors $t^{(1)}, t^{(2)}, \ldots, t^{(2^k)}$. The value of the entry that corresponds to $t^{(j)}$ is the weight of the MWVC conditioned on the restrictions imposed by $t^{(j)}$.

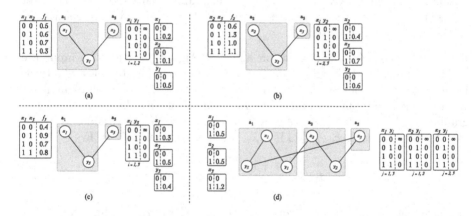

Fig. 4. (a)–(c): CCG gadget graph construction in the "Decomposing the Terms of Polynomials" stage for the example DCOP of Fig. 1. The original constraint, the associated CCG gadget, and the new constraint are shown on the left, middle, and right of each panel, respectively. (d): CCG construction in the "Merging Gadget Graphs into a CCG" stage for the example DCOP of Fig. 1. It is obtained by merging the CCG gadget graphs in (a)–(c).

Figure 2 illustrates this projection for the subgraph of our example DCOP problem of Fig. 1(a) that involves variables x_1 and x_2 and constraint f_1, whose costs are shown in Fig. 1(d).

The table produced by projecting an MWVC on the IS U can be viewed as a constraint over $|U|$ Boolean variables. Conversely, given a (Boolean) constraint, we can design a lifted representation for it so as to be able to view it as the projection of an MWVC on an IS for some intelligently constructed node-weighted undirected graph [13,14]. The lifted graphical representation of a constraint depends on the nature of the terms in the polynomial that describes the constraint. We distinguish three classes of terms: *linear terms*, *negative nonlinear terms*, and *positive nonlinear terms*. We can construct a lifted graphical representation, i.e., a *gadget graph*, for each term in the polynomial of each constraint as follows.

- **A linear term** is represented with the two-node graph shown in Fig. 3(a) by connecting the variable node with an auxiliary node.
- **A negative nonlinear term** is represented with the "flower" structure as depicted in Fig. 3(b). Consider the term $-w \cdot (x_i \cdot x_j \cdot x_k)$ where $w > 0$. Projecting an MWVC on the "flower" structure on the variable nodes represents $w - w \cdot (x_i \cdot x_j \cdot x_k)$. The constant term w does not affect the optimality of the solution.
- **A positive nonlinear term** is represented using the "flower+thorn" structure as depicted in Fig. 3(c). Consider the term $w \cdot (x_i \cdot x_j \cdot x_k)$ where $w > 0$. The projection of an MWVC on the "flower+thorn" structure on the variable nodes represents $L \cdot (1 - x_k) + w - w \cdot (x_i \cdot x_j \cdot (1 - x_k))$, where $L > w + 1$ is a large real number. By constructing gadget graphs that cancel out the lower order terms as shown before, we arrive at a lifted graphical representation of the positive nonlinear term.

Procedure *decompose-polynomial* on line 3 of Algorithm 1 takes as input the polynomial p_i associated with a constraint f_i, constructed in stage 1, and returns its lifted representation G_{CCG_i}, where $X_i = \mathbf{x}^{f_i}$, Y_i and Z_i are the set of auxiliary variables introduced by the procedure, E_i is the set of edges between the G_{CCG_i} graph nodes, and w_i is the set of weights associated with the variables in X_i, Y_i, and Z_i. For a variable $v_i \in X_i \cup Y_i \cup Z_i$, a unary constraint f_{v_i} in $\mathbf{F}_{\mathrm{CCG}_i}$ is

$$f_{v_i}(v_i) = \begin{cases} w_i, & \text{if } v_i = 1, \\ 0, & \text{if } v_i = 0. \end{cases} \tag{3}$$

For each edge $\{v_i, v_j\}$ in E_i, a constraint $f_{\{v_i, v_j\}}$ in $\mathbf{F}_{\mathrm{CCG}_i}$ is defined as

$$f_{\{v_i, v_j\}}(v_i, v_j) = \begin{cases} \infty, & \text{if } v_i = v_j = 0, \\ 0, & \text{otherwise.} \end{cases} \tag{4}$$

For a CCG gadget graph G_{CCG_i}, X_i contains nodes that correspond to decision variables, Z_i contains the nodes with weight L (if any), and Y_i contains the other nodes. At the end of this stage, each agent $a_i \in \mathbf{A}$ controls the set of decision variables in $\mathbf{X}_i$ and the set of auxiliary variables $\cup_{f_j \in \mathbf{F}_i}(Y_j \cup Z_j)$ for all constraints $f_j \in \mathbf{F}_i$ controlled by agent a_i.

3. Merging Gadget Graphs into a CCG. Finally, the CCG-Max-Sum agents construct the CCG by merging their gadget graphs G_{CCG_i}. This stage is done incrementally. Every time an agent builds a new gadget graph, it (1) updates its internal graphical representation to include the auxiliary variables introduced by the

construction, and (2) increases the weight associated with the agent's variables. Each agent a_i sends to its neighbor a_j all unary constraints in $\mathbf{F}_{\text{CCG}_i}$ involving variable v_j controlled by agent a_{j} (i.e., $\alpha(v_j) = a_j$) (lines 4–5). When an agent receives a new unary constraint f which involves one of its decision variables v_i, it increases the weight associated with the constraint ($f_{v_i}(v_i)$) by the value $f_{v_i}(1)$ (line 6). The communication structure of the underlying DCOP does not vary after the CCG construction. If an agent a_i is a neighbor of an agent a_j in the constraint graph of the original DCOP, then a_i is also a neighbor of a_j in the lifted DCOP representation.

Figure 4 shows the construction of the CCG associated with our example DCOP of Fig. 1. There are three unary and three binary constraints. Their lifted graphical representations are shown next to them. Every node in the CCG is given a weight equal to the sum of the individual weights of the nodes in the CCG gadget graphs. Computing the MWVC for the CCG yields an optimal solution for the DCOP: If variable $x_i \in \mathbf{X}$ is in the MWVC, then it is assigned the value 1 in the DCOP, otherwise it is assigned the value 0.

4.2   Message-Passing Phase

Once the CCG has been constructed, the agents start the message-passing phase to find a node cover with a small total weight. The message-passing scheme is similar to that of Max-Sum: During each iteration, each agent waits to receive all messages from its neighbors, updates the current values (beliefs) for the variables it controls, computes the messages to send to its neighbors based on its new beliefs, and sends these to all of its neighbors. Here, we adapt the algorithm presented in [25] (see Algorithm 1). Differently from Max-Sum, where each function node exchanges messages with its neighboring variable nodes, and each variable node exchanges messages with its neighboring function nodes, in CCG-Max-Sum, the messages are exchanged between (decision and auxiliary) variables nodes in the CCG. The message $\mu_{u \rightarrow v}$ sent by a variable u to a variable v in iteration i is:

$$\mu_{u \rightarrow v}^i = \max \left\{ w_u - \sum_{t \in N(u) \setminus \{v\}} \mu_{t \rightarrow u}^{i-1}, 0 \right\}, \tag{5}$$

where w_u is the weight associated with variable u, and $N(u)$ is the set of neighboring variables of variable u in the CCG. Equation (5) is derived from Eqs. (1) and (2) using an approach similar to that in [25]. These steps are shown on lines 7–11 of Algorithm 1. When the termination condition (e.g., a convergence criteria or a maximum number of iteration) is met, for a node v, if $w_v < \sum_{u \in N(v)} \mu_{u \rightarrow v}^i$, with i being the last iteration of the algorithm, then v is selected into the MWVC; otherwise it is not. A variable is assigned value 1 if its corresponding decision variable node in the CCG is selected into the MWVC; otherwise it is assigned value 0 (lines 12–13).

5   Experimental Evaluation

In this section, we compare the solution costs of CCG-Max-Sum, Max-Sum (executed on the factor graph), and DSA [27], a local search DCOP algorithm. DSA has been shown to outperform several other incomplete DCOP algorithms [3,10] and performs similarly to several Max-Sum variants, including Max-Sum_ADVP [29], which has been shown not to benefit from damping [3], where message values are modified to follow a weighted moving average process. We also analyze the effect of using the NT reduction [18], which solves a polynomial-time relaxation of the MWVC to expose optimal assignments to sets of variables, in conjunction with CCG-Max-Sum (denoted by CCG-Max-Sum-k). The NT reduction is executed as a preprocessing centralized step.[1] We use DSA-C with $p = 0.6$, where agents decide probabilistically if to select a local-non-worsening assignment, and adopt a damping strategy with weight 0.7 in all Max-Sum variants [3].

We evaluate all algorithms on *federated social network problems*—an application domain that we introduce below—and on random minimization Boolean DCOPs over three classical networks topologies [11]: *grid networks*, *scale-free networks*, and *random networks*, to cover both structured and unstructured problems. We implement all algorithms within an anytime framework, as proposed in [28], where the agents memorize the best solution found up to the current iteration. All results are averages of 30 runs.

Federated Social Networks. To address the privacy concerns raised in modern centralized social networks, open-source communities have developed decentralized social networks, such as *Diaspora*, *GNU Social*, and *pump.io* [23]. A *federated social network* (FSN) adopts a decentralized structure by allowing each user or group of users to maintain its server and communicating using a common inter-server protocol. In an FSN, multiple servers are used to store the information of the social network users. A server a_i fetches information from a server a_j if a user in a_i *follows* a user in a_j [23]. Qualitatively speaking, there are two fetching strategies: `freq-fetch`, that fetches frequently and caches less information, and `more-cache`, that fetches less frequently and caches more fetched information. Each strategy has its own advantages and disadvantages: `freq-fetch` incurs higher bandwidth costs but lower storage costs, while `more-cache` incurs lower bandwidth costs but higher storage costs. Since `freq-fetch` incurs bandwidth costs for both servers, this strategy takes effect between two servers only if both have the strategy `freq-fetch`.

We model the relationship between the costs and fetching strategies as a DCOP. The choice of strategy of each server a_i (which is modeled as an agent) is a variable x_i. $x_i = 1$ implies `freq-fetch`, and $x_i = 0$ implies `more-cache`.

The binary $f(x_i, x_j)$ cost functions capture the storage and bandwidth costs for servers a_i and a_j. A user in a_i following a user in a_j and a user in a_i and one

---

[1] Its runtime is comparable to that of one iteration of CCG-Max-Sum, which in turn takes 0.035 s on average in our experiments.

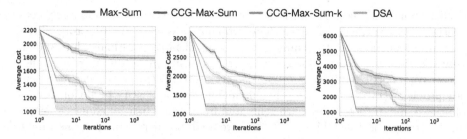

Fig. 5. FSN based on Twitter network data: 100 agents (left), 500 agents (center), and 1000 agents (right).

in a_j following each other are modeled, respectively, as

$$\begin{cases} \alpha_{ij}(c_i^b + c_j^b), & \text{if } x_i = x_j = 1 \\ \alpha_{ij}c_i^s, & \text{otherwise} \end{cases} \qquad \begin{cases} (\alpha_{ij} + \alpha_{ji})(c_i^b + c_j^b), & \text{if } x_i = x_j = 1 \\ \alpha_{ij}c_i^s + \alpha_{ji}c_j^s, & \text{otherwise,} \end{cases}$$

where c_i^b and c_i^s denote the unit bandwidth and unit storage costs of agent a_i, respectively, and α_{ij} is the amount of information that a_i fetches from a_j.

We model an FSN based on *Twitter network data* [4], which describe a graph whose nodes model Twitter users. There is a link between two nodes if at least one of the corresponding users follows the other one. The graph contains 456,626 nodes and 14,855,842 edges. We map the Twitter network to an FSN graph G. Its nodes represent the FSN servers and are constructed as follows. We first randomly assign one distinct Twitter user to each node in G. Then, we associate each remaining user u to a node of G with a probability proportional to the number of followers user u has in the corresponding server. We add an edge (a_i, a_j) to G if there exist a user in a_i and a user in a_j such that at least one of them follows the other one. The costs c_i^b and c_i^s are generated by sampling from the discrete uniform distribution $U(1, 10)$, and all weights α_{ij} are the number of users in a_i following users in a_j.

Figure 5 illustrates the anytime behavior of the algorithms on FSN problems with 100 (left), 500 (center), and 1000 (right) agents. The shaded region around each line describes the confidence interval of the solution costs reported by each algorithm. The plots use a log-10 scale for the x-axis. The algorithms in order of their solution costs (from highest to lowest) tend to be: Max-Sum, DSA, and both CCG-Max-Sum variants. In particular, CCG-Max-Sum-k dominates all other algorithms from the very first iteration.

Random DCOPs. We now discuss the solution cost of the algorithms on random minimization Boolean DCOPs. The costs of each assignment to the variables involved in a constraint are generated by sampling from the discrete uniform distribution $U(1, 100)$. For grid networks, we generate two-dimensional 10×10 grids and connect each node with its four nearest neighbors. For scale-free networks, we create an n-node network based on the Barabasi-Albert model [1]. Starting from a connected 2-node network, we repeatedly add a new node, randomly connecting it to two existing nodes. These two nodes are selected with probabilities that are proportional to the numbers of their incident edges. Finally, for random networks, we create an n-node network whose density p_1 produces $\lfloor n(n-1)p_1 \rfloor$ edges. We report experiments on low-density problems ($p_1 = 0.2$) and high density problems ($p_1 = 0.6$) and fix the maximum constraint arity to 4. Constraints of arity 4 and 3, respectively, are generated by merging first all cliques of size 4 and then those of size 3. The other edges are used to generate binary constraints. In each configuration, we verify that the resulting constraint graph is connected and set the number of agents to 100.

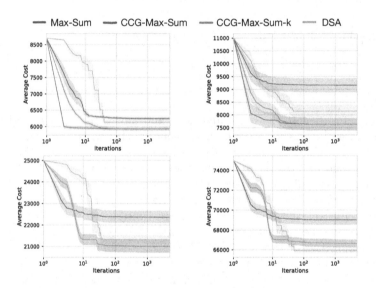

Fig. 6. Grid networks (top left), scale-free networks (top right), low-density random networks ($p_1 = 0.2$) (bottom left), and high-density random networks ($p_1 = 0.6$) (bottom right). The blue and red curves overlap in the last two plots.

The results are similar to the ones on FSN problems: The algorithms in order of their solution costs (from highest to lowest) tend to be: Max-Sum, DSA, and both CCG-Max-Sum variants, except on high-density random networks, where the solution costs of DSA are slightly lower than the ones of the CCG-Max-Sum variants. On grid, scale-free, and low-density random networks, CCG-Max-Sum-k dominates all other algorithms from the first ten iterations. On random networks (Fig. 6 (bottom)), the effect of kernelization is negligible and both CCG-Max-Sum variants are thus almost indistinguishable, meaning that both of them dominate all other algorithms on low-density random networks.

Thus, our experiments suggest that CCG-Max-Sum has strong advantages on grid and scale-free networks, which are important for a large variety of DCOP applications [5,8,22].

x_1	0	0	0	1	1	1
x_2	0	1	2	0	1	2
f_1	0.5	0.6	0.2	0.7	0.3	0.5

Fig. 7. A cost function with a non-Boolean variable. This cost function extends the Boolean cost function in Fig. 1(d) with x_2 being able to take 3 values 0, 1, and 2. The tuples highlighted in red are the parts additional to Fig. 1(d).

6   Discussion: Non-Boolean DCOPs

The construction of the CCG for CCG-Max-Sum can be extended to DCOPs with non-Boolean domains [14] as outlined in the following.

1. Expressing Constraints as Polynomials. For a cost function with non-Boolean variables, this step outputs polynomials of degrees at least 2 instead of polynomials of degree 1. The degree of each variable equals its domain size - 1. Figure 7 shows an example cost function. Similar to Boolean DCOPs, a polynomial of the following form can be used to characterize this cost function:

$$p_1(x_1, x_2) = c_{00} + c_{01}x_1 + c_{10}x_2 + c_{11}x_1x_2 + c_{20}x_2^2 + c_{21}x_1x_2^2.$$

Here, the coefficients $c_{00}, c_{01}, c_{10}, c_{11}, c_{20}$, and c_{21} can be computed by solving a system of linear equations, where each equation corresponds to an entry in the constraint table, using standard Gaussian Elimination. In our example:

$$p_1(0,0) = 0.5 \qquad p_1(0,1) = 0.6 \qquad p_1(0,2) = 0.2$$
$$p_1(1,0) = 0.7 \qquad p_1(1,1) = 0.3 \qquad p_1(1,2) = 0.5.$$

2. Decomposing the Terms of the Polynomials. The procedure to construct graph gadgets is similar to Boolean DCOPs, except that each variable x_i with domain $D_{x_i} = \{0, 1, \ldots, |D_{x_i}| - 1\}$ is now represented by $|D_{x_i}| - 1$ nodes in the gadget graph. The value of x_i in the to-be-determined optimal solution equals the number of nodes representing x_i in the computed MWVC. Figure 8 illustrates the lifted representation of linear terms, negative non-linear terms, and positive non-linear terms. It is not hard to verify that Fig. 8 (a-c) represent $w \cdot x_i$, $2w - w \cdot (x_i \cdot x_j)$ and $L \cdot (1 - x_j) + 2w - w \cdot (x_i \cdot (1 - x_j))$, respectively.

3. Merging Gadget Graphs into a CCG. Similar to Boolean DCOPs, a CCG can be constructed by merging all nodes corresponding to the same variable. The size of the CCG increases only polynomially in the domain sizes.

   Since the agents need to control the value of several CCG nodes, the local solving process, in which an agent decide the value assignments for each of the variables it controls, can be handled with a framework similar to that presented in [7], which was shown highly effective for solving multi-variable agent DCOPs.

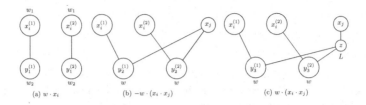

Fig. 8. The lifted graphical representation of terms in a polynomial for linear (a), negative nonlinear (b), and positive nonlinear (c) terms. Here, x_i and x_j have domain sizes 3 and 2, respectively. $x_i^{(1)}$ and $x_i^{(2)}$ are the two nodes representing x_i. We assume that $w > 0$ in (b) and (c). A node has a zero weight if no weight is shown. In (a), w_1 and w_2 satisfy $w_1 - w_2 = w$.

7   Conclusions

In this paper, we adapted the *Constraint Composite Graph (CCG)* graphical representation encoding for Distributed Constraint Optimization Problems (DCOPs). The CCG provides a framework for exploiting simultaneously the graphical structure of the agent interaction process as well as the numerical structure of the constraints of a DCOP instance. We use this representation to introduce CCG-Max-Sum, a novel incomplete DCOP algorithm which extends Max-Sum by executing the distributed message passing phase on the CCG.

Compared to a version of Max-Sum which is executed on factor graphs and other incomplete DCOP algorithms, CCG-Max-Sum finds solutions of better quality within fewer iterations on several DCOP benchmarks. While this paper introduced an inference-based algorithm operating on the CCG of a DCOP, we believe that CCGs can also be exploited with other classes of DCOP algorithms.

Future directions include extending the experiments evaluation to DCOPs with non-Boolean variables and applying CCG-Max-Sum to problems with hard constraints (e.g., constraints whose costs are either 0 or ∞), since many types of hard constraints can be simplified during the construction of the CCG, resulting in smaller problems.

References

1. Barabási, A.L., Albert, R.: Emergence of scaling in random networks. Science **286**(5439), 509–512 (1999)
2. Chlebík, M., Chlebíková, J.: Crown reductions for the minimum weighted vertex cover problem. Discret. Appl. Math. **156**(3), 292–312 (2008)
3. Cohen, L., Zivan, R.: Max-sum revisited: the real power of damping. In: Sukthankar, G., Rodriguez-Aguilar, J.A. (eds.) AAMAS 2017. LNCS (LNAI), vol. 10643, pp. 1505–1507. Springer, Cham (2017). https://doi.org/10.1007/978-3-319-71679-4_8
4. De Domenico, M., Lima, A., Mougel, P., Musolesi, M.: The anatomy of a scientific rumor. Sci. Rep. **3**, 2980 (2013)

5. Farinelli, A., Rogers, A., Petcu, A., Jennings, N.: Decentralised coordination of low-power embedded devices using the Max-sum algorithm. In: Proceedings of the International Conference on Autonomous Agents and Multiagent Systems (AAMAS), pp. 639–646 (2008)
6. Fioretto, F., Pontelli, E., Yeoh, W.: Distributed constraint optimization problems and applications: a survey. J. Artif. Intell. Res. **61**, 623–698 (2018)
7. Fioretto, F., Yeoh, W., Pontelli, E.: Multi-variable agents decomposition for DCOPs. In: Proceedings of the AAAI Conference on Artificial Intelligence (AAAI), pp. 2480–2486 (2016)
8. Fioretto, F., Yeoh, W., Pontelli, E.: A multiagent system approach to scheduling devices in smart homes. In: Proceedings of the International Conference on Autonomous Agents and Multiagent Systems (AAMAS), pp. 981–989 (2017)
9. Fioretto, F., Yeoh, W., Pontelli, E., Ma, Y., Ranade, S.: A DCOP approach to the economic dispatch with demand response. In: Proceedings of the International Conference on Autonomous Agents and Multiagent Systems (AAMAS), pp. 981–989 (2017)
10. Hoang, K.D., Fioretto, F., Yeoh, W., Pontelli, E., Zivan, R.: A large neighboring search schema for multi-agent optimization. In: Hooker, J. (ed.) CP 2018. LNCS, vol. 11008, pp. 688–706. Springer, Cham (2018). https://doi.org/10.1007/978-3-319-98334-9_44
11. Kiekintveld, C., Yin, Z., Kumar, A., Tambe, M.: Asynchronous algorithms for approximate distributed constraint optimization with quality bounds. In: Proceedings of the International Conference on Autonomous Agents and Multiagent Systems (AAMAS), pp. 133–140 (2010)
12. Kschischang, F.R., Frey, B.J., Loeliger, H.A.: Factor graphs and the sum-product algorithm. IEEE Trans. Inf. Theory **47**(2), 498–519 (2001)
13. Kumar, T.K.S.: A framework for hybrid tractability results in Boolean weighted constraint satisfaction problems. In: Stuckey, P.J. (ed.) CP 2008. LNCS, vol. 5202, pp. 282–297. Springer, Heidelberg (2008). https://doi.org/10.1007/978-3-540-85958-1_19
14. Kumar, T.K.S.: Lifting techniques for weighted constraint satisfaction problems. In: Proceedings of the International Symposium on Artificial Intelligence and Mathematics (ISAIM) (2008)
15. Kumar, T.K.S.: Kernelization, generation of bounds, and the scope of incremental computation for weighted constraint satisfaction problems. In: Proceedings of the International Symposium on Artificial Intelligence and Mathematics (ISAIM) (2016)
16. Maheswaran, R., Pearce, J., Tambe, M.: Distributed algorithms for DCOP: a graphical game-based approach. In: Proceedings of the Conference on Parallel and Distributed Computing Systems (PDCS), pp. 432–439 (2004)
17. Modi, P., Shen, W.M., Tambe, M., Yokoo, M.: ADOPT: asynchronous distributed constraint optimization with quality guarantees. Artif. Intell. **161**(1–2), 149–180 (2005)
18. Nemhauser, G.L., Trotter, L.E.: Vertex packings: structural properties and algorithms. Math. Program. **8**(1), 232–248 (1975)
19. Pearce, J., Tambe, M.: Quality guarantees on k-optimal solutions for distributed constraint optimization problems. In: Proceedings of the International Joint Conference on Artificial Intelligence (IJCAI), pp. 1446–1451 (2007)
20. Petcu, A., Faltings, B.: A scalable method for multiagent constraint optimization. In: Proceedings of the International Joint Conference on Artificial Intelligence (IJCAI), pp. 1413–1420 (2005)

21. Petcu, A., Faltings, B., Mailler, R.: PC-DPOP: a new partial centralization algorithm for distributed optimization. In: Proceedings of the International Joint Conference on Artificial Intelligence (IJCAI), pp. 167–172 (2007)
22. Rust, P., Picard, G., Ramparany, F.: Using message-passing DCOP algorithms to solve energy-efficient smart environment configuration problems. In: Proceedings of the International Joint Conference on Artificial Intelligence (IJCAI), pp. 468–474 (2016)
23. Silva, G., Reis, L., Terceiro, A., Meirelles, P., Kon, F.: Implementing federated social networking: report from the trenches. In: Proceedings of the International Symposium on Open Collaboration (OpenSym), pp. 8:1–8:10 (2017)
24. Vinyals, M., Rodríguez-Aguilar, J., Cerquides, J.: Constructing a unifying theory of dynamic programming DCOP algorithms via the generalized distributive law. J. Auton. Agents Multi-Agent Syst. 22(3), 439–464 (2011)
25. Xu, H., Satish Kumar, T.K., Koenig, S.: The Nemhauser-Trotter reduction and lifted message passing for the weighted CSP. In: Salvagnin, D., Lombardi, M. (eds.) CPAIOR 2017. LNCS, vol. 10335, pp. 387–402. Springer, Cham (2017). https://doi.org/10.1007/978-3-319-59776-8_31
26. Yeoh, W., Felner, A., Koenig, S.: BnB-ADOPT: an asynchronous branch-and-bound DCOP algorithm. J. Artif. Intell. Res. 38, 85–133 (2010)
27. Zhang, W., Wang, G., Xing, Z., Wittenberg, L.: Distributed stochastic search and distributed breakout: properties, comparison and applications to constraint optimization problems in sensor networks. Artif. Intell. 161(1–2), 55–87 (2005)
28. Zivan, R., Okamoto, S., Peled, H.: Explorative anytime local search for distributed constraint optimization. Artif. Intell. 212, 1–26 (2014)
29. Zivan, R., Parash, T., Naveh, Y.: Applying max-sum to asymmetric distributed constraint optimization. In: Proceedings of the International Joint Conference on Artificial Intelligence (IJCAI), pp. 432–439 (2015)
30. Zivan, R., Yedidsion, H., Okamoto, S., Glinton, R., Sycara, K.: Distributed constraint optimization for teams of mobile sensing agents. J. Auton. Agents Multi-Agent Syst. 29(3), 495–536 (2015)

Bounded Approximate Algorithm for Probabilistic Coalition Structure Generation

Kouki Matsumura[1], Tenda Okimoto[2(✉)], and Katsutoshi Hirayama[2]

[1] Graduate School of Information Science and Technology, Osaka University,
Osaka, Japan
matsumura@ai.sanken.osaka-u.ac.jp
[2] Faculty of Maritime Sciences, Kobe University, Kobe, Japan
{tenda,hirayama}@maritime.kobe-u.ac.jp

Abstract. How to form effective coalitions is an important issue in multi-agent systems. Coalition Structure Generation (CSG) is a fundamental problem that can formalize various applications related to multi-agent cooperation. CSG involves partitioning a set of agents into coalitions so that the social surplus (i.e. the sum of the values of all coalitions) is maximized. In the real world, it is natural to consider the uncertainty of agents' attendances, e.g., an agent is available only two or three days a week because of his/her own schedule. In other words, there is no guarantee to establish all coalitions. Probabilistic Coalition Structure Generation (PCSG) is the extension of CSG where the attendance type of each agent is considered. The aim of this problem is to find the optimal coalition structure which maximizes the sum of the expected values of all coalitions. In PCSG, since finding the optimal coalition structure becomes easily intractable, it is important to consider fast but approximate algorithms. In this paper, a formal framework for PCSG is introduced. An approximate algorithm for PCSG called Bounded Approximate Algorithm based on Attendance Types (BAAAT) is then presented. Also, we show that BAAAT can provide the theoretical bound of a solution a priori. In the experiments, BAAAT is evaluated on a number of benchmarks.

Keywords: Multi-agent Systems
Probabilistic Coalition Structure Generation

1 Introduction

Coalition Structure Generation (CSG) [1,16,20] is a key issue for various applications related to multi-agent cooperation, e.g., waste-water treatment system [6], distributed vehicle routing [22] and multi-sensor networks [4]. A CSG involves partitioning a set of agents into coalitions (where each coalition is a subset of the available set of agents) so that the social surplus is maximized. A partition

© Springer Nature Switzerland AG 2018
T. Miller et al. (Eds.): PRIMA 2018, LNAI 11224, pp. 123–139, 2018.
https://doi.org/10.1007/978-3-030-03098-8_8

is called a coalition structure. In CSG, the value of a coalition is assumed to be given by a black box function called a *characteristic function*, and the value of a coalition structure is provided by the sum of the values of all coalitions. It is well-known that CSG is equivalent to the *complete set partition problem* [26]. Various algorithms have been proposed for CSG problems, e.g., dynamic programming [26], anytime algorithms [19], and hybrid algorithms [12,17].

Let us consider the following scenario. There is a service company with three employees (*Ali*, *Bob* and *Chan*) dispatching interpreters. This company has received the requests of the simultaneous interpretation as shown in table 1: request 1 requires *Ali*, and the company gets $20 for it; request 2 pays $50 and needs *Bob*'s language skill; request 3 needs *Chan* and pays $10; request 4 pays $70 and needs *Ali* and *Bob*; request 5 pays $60 and needs *Ali* and *Chan*; request 6 needs *Bob* and *Chan* and pays $100; request 7 requires all three employees and pays $110. Assume that you are the manager of this service company and want to assign the employees to the job(s) so that the sum of the rewards is maximized. Then, this problem can be represented as a CSG problem. If you assign three employees *Ali*, *Bob* and *Chan* to the requests 1, 2 and 3 separately, i.e., the coalition structure $\{\{Ali\}, \{Bob\}, \{Chan\}\}$ is formed by singleton coalitions, the sum of the rewards obtained by this coalition structure is $20+$50+$10 = $80. When you assign *Ali* to the request 1, *Bob* and *Chan* to the request 6, the social surplus is maximized. In this case, the coalition structure is $\{\{Ali\}, \{Bob, Chan\}\}$ and the service company earns $20 + $100 = $120.

Table 1. Requests, coalitions, and rewards

Request	Coalition	Reward	Request	Coalition	Reward
1	$\{Ali\}$	$20	5	$\{Ali, Chan\}$	$60
2	$\{Bob\}$	$50	6	$\{Bob, Chan\}$	$100
3	$\{Chan\}$	$10	7	$\{Ali, Bob, Chan\}$	$110
4	$\{Ali, Bob\}$	$70	-	-	-

In the following, we are interested in the uncertainty of agents' attendances. In traditional CSG, it is guaranteed to establish all coalitions, that is, each agent joins any coalition with the probability 1.0. However, in the real world, it is natural to consider the uncertainty of agents' attendances, e.g., it might happen that an agent is available only two or three days a week because of his/her own schedule. In our example, it is natural that the manager of the service company asks three employs their schedules before assigning them to the jobs. In this paper, we assume that (i) each agent chooses, for instance, one of the following attendance types according to his/her own schedule[1], and (ii) the CSG maker (e.g. the manager) knows all information about the attendances.

---

[1] How to provide the participation rate of each agent is out of scope. Here, each agent chooses the attendance type including a given probability, e.g., {unsure (50%)}.

type 1 : {attend (90%)}, type 2 : {maybe attend (70%)}, type 3 : {unsure (50%)}, type 4 : {maybe not attend (30%)}, type 5 : {not attend (10%)}.

In this paper, the main focus is laid on the *Probabilistic Coalition Structure Generation* (PCSG) problem which is the extension of CSG where the attendance type of each agent is considered. First, a formal framework for PCSG is introduced where the aim is to find an optimal coalition structure which maximizes the sum of the expected values of all coalitions. In a PCSG problem, how to compute the expected value of a coalition is an important issue. In our framework, the expected value of a coalition is computed where any k agents might be absent. For instance, the expected value of the coalition $\{Ali, Chan\}$ for $k = 1$ (i.e. any one agent might be absent) is provided by the sum of the expected values in case (i) Ali and $Chan$ are attended, (ii) only Ali is attended, and (iii) only $Chan$ is attended.

Furthermore, an approximate algorithm for solving a PCSG problem called Bounded Approximate Algorithm based on Attendance Types (BAAAT) is presented. In PCSG problems, since finding the optimal coalition structure becomes easily intractable, it is important to consider fast but approximate algorithms. The basic idea of the proposed algorithm BAAAT is that for a given parameter $\tilde{p}$, (i) the singleton coalition is formed for an agent whose attendance type is below the parameter $\tilde{p}$, then (ii) an optimal coalition structure of the relaxed problem with the remaining agents is computed. Moreover, we show that BAAAT can provide the theoretical upper bound of the absolute errors of the solution, which can be obtained a priori, that is, the error bound is obtained before actually running the algorithm. In our experiments, the performances of BAAAT are evaluated on a number of benchmarks.

The rest of the paper is organized as follows. In Sect. 2, the framework for coalition structure generation (CSG) problem is provided. Section 3 introduces our framework for probabilistic coalition structure generation (PCSG) problem. The next section presents an approximate algorithm for PCSG problems, and the theoretical bound is provided. Afterward, some empirical results are presented. Just before the concluding section, some related works are discussed.

2   Coalition Structure Generation

In this section, the formalization of Coalition Structure Generation (CSG) problem is briefly described. CSG involves partitioning a set of agents into coalitions so that the social surplus (i.e. the sum of the values of all coalitions) is maximized.

Let us start with some preliminary definitions. Let $\mathcal{A} = \{a_1, a_2, \ldots, a_n\}$ be a finite set of agents. A coalition from $\mathcal{A}$, denoted as C, is a non-empty subset of $\mathcal{A}$. A coalition structure on $\mathcal{A}$, denoted as CS, is a partition on $\mathcal{A}$, i.e., a jointly exhaustive set of pairwise disjoint coalitions from $\mathcal{A}$. Formally, a coalition structure on $\mathcal{A}$ is a finite set of coalitions satisfying the following conditions:

$$\forall i, j \in \{1, 2, \ldots, m\}, \ i \neq j, \ C_i \cap C_j = \emptyset,$$

$$\bigcup_{C_i \in CS} C_i = \mathcal{A}.$$

In other words, each agent belongs to exactly one coalition, and some agents may be alone in their coalitions. In our running example for the service company dispatching interpreters with three agents *Ali*, *Bob* and *Chan*, there exist seven possible coalitions (i.e. $\{Ali\}$, $\{Bob\}$, $\{Chan\}$, $\{Ali, Bob\}$, $\{Ali, Chan\}$, $\{Bob, Chan\}$, $\{Ali, Bob, Chan\}$) and the following five coalition structures:

$$\{\{Ali\}, \{Bob\}, \{Chan\}\}, \{\{Ali\}, \{Bob, Chan\}\}, \{\{Bob\}, \{Ali, Chan\}\},$$
$$\{\{Chan\}, \{Ali, Bob\}\}, \{\{Ali, Bob, Chan\}\}.$$

Definition 1 (**CSG problem description**). A coalition structure generation problem description is defined by a pair $\mathsf{CSG} = \langle \mathcal{A}, v \rangle$ where $\mathcal{A} = \{a_1, a_2, \ldots, a_n\}$ is a set of agents and $v : 2^{\mathcal{A}} \to \mathbb{N}$ is a function called a characteristic function.

The value of a coalition C, denoted as $v(C)$, is given by the characteristic function v. The value of a coalition structure CS, denoted as $V(CS)$, is provided by the sum of the values of all coalitions, i.e.,

$$V(CS) = \sum_{C_i \in CS} v(C_i). \tag{1}$$

A coalition structure is said to be optimal, denoted as CS^*, if it maximizes the social surplus, that is, it satisfies the following condition:

$$\forall CS, \ V(CS) \leq V(CS^*).$$

Example 1 (CSG). Consider our running example of a service company with three employees *Ali*, *Bob* and *Chan*. This problem can be represented as a CSG: let $\mathsf{CSG} = \langle \mathcal{A}, v \rangle$ be a CSG problem description with $\mathcal{A} = \{Ali, Bob, Chan\}$, and the function v is characterized as follows:

$$v(\{Ali\}) = \$20, \ v(\{Bob\}) = \$50, \ v(\{Chan\}) = \$10,$$
$$v(\{Ali, Bob\}) = \$70, \ v(\{Ali, Chan\}) = \$60, \ v(\{Bob, Chan\}) = \$100,$$
$$v(\{Ali, Bob, Chan\}) = \$110.$$

The optimal coalition structure is $CS^* = \{\{Ali\}, \{Bob, Chan\}\}$, and the obtained value is $V(CS^*) = v(\{Ali\}) + v(\{Bob, Chan\}) = \$20 + \$100 = \$120$.

As illustrated on this running example, as stated otherwise, the characteristic function v is supposed to be represented extensively, as the set of pairs $\{(CS, v(CS)) \mid CS \subseteq \mathcal{A} \text{ and } CS \neq \emptyset\}$. The CSG problem is defined as follows:

Definition 2 (CSG problem).

- **Input:** A CSG problem description $CSG = \langle \mathcal{A}, v \rangle$,
- **Question:** Find an optimal coalition structure CS^* which maximizes the sum of the values of all coalitions.

A number of representation settings for characteristic functions have been pointed out in the literature, and some of them have been adapted to CSG and studied from the computational complexity viewpoint [14]. Among the representation frameworks which have been developed are marginal contribution nets (MC-nets) [8] and synergy coalition groups (SCGs) [3]. Contrastingly, some early works [21,22] assume that v is provided "fully extensionally" as an input of a CSG problem description, i.e., v is given as a table with $2^n - 1$ entries, associating with every coalition a number. Providing such an extensional representation of v makes the size of an input CSG to be exponential in the number of agents and maybe an unrealistic assumption for relatively large problems.

Yet there exist real applications involving only a dozen agents, for which an extensional representation of v is feasible. Thus, cooperative games can be used to analyze cost allocation problems, where the players are willing to form coalitions in order to get extra monetary savings as an effect of cooperation. For instance, in [6] the authors address the problem where nearby municipalities must take the decision on whether to cooperate in order to implement a Waste-water Treatment System (WTS). This type of problems can be represented formally as a CSG and it involves a few agents in essence, so that (i) considering a few numbers of agents for experimentations (as it is done in recent works on CSG experiments considering about 10–20 agents), and (ii) assuming an extensional representation of the characteristic function, can sometimes be considered as reasonable.

Lastly, let us focus on the specific cases for CSG problem where the characteristic function v is *subadditive* or *superadditive*. For a CSG problem description $CSG = \langle \mathcal{A}, v \rangle$, the characteristic function v is said to be subadditive if for any coalitions C_i and C_j with $C_i \cap C_j = \emptyset$, it holds $v(C_i) + v(C_j) \geq v(C_i \cup C_j)$, and it is called superadditive if it holds $v(C_i) + v(C_j) \leq v(C_i \cup C_j)$. It is well-known that in case the characteristic function is subadditive, the coalition structure formed by singleton coalitions is optimal, i.e., $CS^* = \{\{a_i\} | a_i \in \mathcal{A}\}$. For the superadditive case, the grand coalition, i.e., $CS^* = \{\mathcal{A}\}$, is an optimal one [21].

3   Probabilistic Coalition Structure Generation

In this section, a formal framework for Probabilistic Coalition Structure Generation (PCSG) problem is introduced where the aim is to find an optimal coalition structure which maximizes the sum of the expected values of all coalitions. In a PCSG problem, how to compute the expected value of a coalition is an important issue. In our framework, the expected value of a coalition is computed where any k agents might be absent.

Definition 3 (PCSG problem description). A probabilistic coalition struc-
ture generation problem description is defined by a tuple $\mathsf{PCSG} = \langle \mathcal{A}, v, f \rangle$ where
$\mathcal{A} = \{a_1, a_2, ..., a_n\}$ is a set of agents, $v : 2^{\mathcal{A}} \to \mathbb{N}$ is a characteristic function and
$f : \mathcal{A} \mapsto [0, 1]$ is a function that gives the attendance type/rate of each agent.

Here, we assume that the participation of each agent to join any coalition
is independent, that is, it has no influence on those of other agents. In the
following, the expected value of a coalition is computed where any k agents
might be absent. For a coalition C, let $\bar{a} \subseteq 2^C$ be a set of absent agents where
$|\bar{a}| = k$ and $0 \le k \le |C|$. For any $\bar{a}$, the remaining coalition by removing $\bar{a}$ from
a coalition C is denoted as $C \setminus \bar{a}$, and the value of this coalition is given by
$v(C \setminus \bar{a})$. The expected value of this coalition, denoted as $v_e(C, \bar{a})$, is defined by

$$v_e(C, \bar{a}) = v(C \setminus \bar{a}) \cdot \prod_{a \in C \setminus \bar{a}} f(a) \cdot \prod_{a' \in \bar{a}} (1 - f(a')). \tag{2}$$

The expected value of a coalition C, denoted as $v_{e,k}(C)$, is given by

$$v_{e,k}(C) = \sum_{\bar{a} \in 2^C} v_e(C, \bar{a}). \tag{3}$$

The expected value of a coalition structure CS, denoted as $V_e(CS)$, is computed
by the sum of the expected values of all coalitions as standard CSG, i.e.,

$$V_e(CS) = \sum_{C \in CS} v_{e,k}(C). \tag{4}$$

A coalition structure is said to be optimal, denoted as CS_e^*, if it maximizes the
sum of the expected values of all coalitions, i.e., it holds the following condition:

$$\forall CS, \ V_e(CS) \le V_e(CS_e^*).$$

The PCSG problem is defined as follows:

Definition 4 (PCSG problem).

- **Input:** A PCSG problem description $\mathsf{PCSG} = \langle \mathcal{A}, v, f \rangle$ and a non-negative
  integer k,
- **Question:** Find a coalition structure CS_e^* which maximizes the sum of the
  expected values of all coalitions.

Example 2 (PCSG). Consider our running example of a service company with
three employees. Assume that *Ali* reported the manager the type 1 (i.e. {attend
(90%)}), *Bob* chose the type 3 (i.e. {unsure (50%)}), and *Chan* selected the
type 4 (i.e. {maybe not attend (30%)}) for their attendance types. Moreover,
the manager sets the parameter $k = 1$, that is, he/she wants to maximize the
expected values of all coalitions where any one employee might be absent (e.g.

because of the illness or other unexpected matters). The expected value of each coalition is then computed by the Eqs. (2) and (3) as follows:

$$v_{e,k}(\{Ali\}) = 18, \ v_{e,k}(\{Bob\}) = 25, \ v_{e,k}(\{Chan\}) = 3,$$
$$v_{e,k}(\{Ali, Bob\}) = 43, \ v_{e,k}(\{Ali, Chan\}) = 29.1, \ v_{e,k}(\{Bob, Chan\}) = 34,$$
$$v_{e,k}(\{Ali, Bob, Chan\}) = 46.5.$$

For instance, consider the coalition formed by Ali and Bob (i.e. $\{Ali, Bob\}$). The expected value of this coalition is then computed as follows:

- Ali and Bob are attended : $v(\{Ali, Bob\}) \cdot f(Ali) \cdot f(Bob) = 70 \cdot (0.9 \cdot 0.5) = 31.5$.
- only Ali is attended : $v(\{Ali\}) \cdot f(Ali) \cdot (1 - f(Bob)) = 20 \cdot (0.9 \cdot 0.5) = 9$.
- only Bob is attended : $v(\{Bob\}) \cdot (1 - f(Ali)) \cdot f(Bob) = 50 \cdot (0.1 \cdot 0.5) = 2.5$.

The expected value of this coalition is given by $v_e(\{Ali, Bob\}) = 31.5 + 9 + 2.5 = 43$. Table 2 shows the expected values of all possible coalition structures. Compared to the optimal coalition structure in example 1, i.e., $CS^* = \{\{Ali\}, \{Bob, Chan\}\}$, the optimal coalition structure of this example is $CS_e^* = \{\{Bob\}, \{Ali, Chan\}\}$, and the expected value obtained by this coalition structure is $V_e(CS_e^*) = v_{e,k}(\{Bob\}) + v_{e,k}(\{Ali, Chan\}) = 25 + 29.1 = 54.1$.

Table 2. The expected values of all possible coalition structures

Coalition structure	Expected value
$\{\{Ali\}, \{Bob\}, \{Chan\}\}$	46
$\{\{Ali\}, \{Bob, Chan\}\}$	52
$\{\{Bob\}, \{Ali, Chan\}\}$	54.1
$\{\{Chan\}, \{Ali, Bob\}\}$	46
$\{\{Ali, Bob, Chan\}\}$	46.5

Let us now describe the specific cases for PCSG problem where the expected values of all coalitions satisfy the subadditivity or superadditivity. In those cases, the counterpart of the results in the standard CSG framework also hold in our PCSG framework, that is, in case it holds the subadditivity, the coalition structure formed by singleton coalitions is optimal (i.e. $CS_e^* = \{\{a_i\} | a_i \in \mathcal{A}\}$), and for the superadditivity case, the grand coalition is optimal (i.e. $CS_e^* = \{\mathcal{A}\}$).

Finally, let us introduce that a PCSG problem can be represented as a zero-one integer programming as a CSG problem. For the simplicity, we show the zero-one integer programming formulation of the Example 2 for PCSG problem.

The objective function and the constraints are formalized as follows:

$$max. \ 18 \cdot a_1 + 25 \cdot a_2 + 3 \cdot a_3 + 43 \cdot a_{12} + 29.1 \cdot a_{13} + 34 \cdot a_{23} + 46.5 \cdot a_{123}, \quad (5)$$

$$s.t \ \ a_1 + a_{12} + a_{13} + a_{123} = 1, \quad (6)$$

$$a_2 + a_{12} + a_{23} + a_{123} = 1, \quad (7)$$

$$a_3 + a_{13} + a_{23} + a_{123} = 1, \quad (8)$$

$$a_1, a_2, a_3, a_{12}, a_{13}, a_{23}, a_{123} \in \{0, 1\}. \quad (9)$$

Each variable $a_1, a_2, ..., a_{123}$ represents a coalition, e.g., a_1 is the coalition $\{Ali\}$ and a_{123} shows the grand coalition $\{\{Ali, Bob, Chan\}\}$, and it takes the value 0 or 1 (Eq. (9)). The Eq. (6) describes that Ali belongs to one of the coalitions $\{Ali\}, \{Ali, Bob\}, \{Ali, Chan\}, \{Ali, Bob, Chan\}$, and he cannot belong to different coalitions simultaneously. Similarly, the Eq. (7) shows the constraint for Bob and the Eq. (8) is for $Chan$. The Eq. (5) represents the objective function which maximizes the sum of the expected values of all coalitions, and each coefficient shows the expected value obtained by the corresponding coalition, e.g., 18 is for $\{Ali\}$ and 46.5 is for the grand coalition.

4   Bounded Approximate Algorithm

In this section, an approximate algorithm for PCSG problems called Bounded Approximate Algorithm based on Attendance Types (BAAAT) is presented. Furthermore, we show that BAAAT can provide the theoretical upper bound of the absolute errors of the solution, which can be obtained a priori.

4.1   Approximate Algorithm

The BAAAT has the following two phases :

Phase 1 : For a given parameter $\tilde{p}$ and the participation rate of an agent a (i.e. $f(a) = p$), form the singleton coalition for a if p is less than or equal to $\tilde{p}$.
Phase 2 : Find the optimal coalition structure of the relaxed PCSG problem with the remaining agents.

The basic idea of BAAAT is that for a given parameter $\tilde{p}$, the singleton coalition is formed for an agent who chooses the attendance type where the given probability is less than or equal to the parameter $\tilde{p}$. Then an optimal coalition structure of the relaxed problem with the remaining agents is computed.

We denote the coalition structure obtained in phase 2 as CS_e^- and the coalition structure provided by BAAAT as CS_e^+. Let us explain how BAAAT computes an approximate solution by using the Example 2. Given is the attendance type, i.e. the participation rate, $f(Ali) = 0.9$ (type1 : attend), $f(Bob) = 0.5$ (type 3 : unsure), $f(Chan) = 0.3$ (type 4 : maybe not attend), the parameter $k = 1$, and the following expected values of coalitions.

$$v_{e,k}(\{Ali\}) = 18, \ v_{e,k}(\{Bob\}) = 25, \ v_{e,k}(\{Chan\}) = 3,$$

$$v_{e,k}(\{Ali, Bob\}) = 43, \ v_{e,k}(\{Ali, Chan\}) = 29.1, \ v_{e,k}(\{Bob, Chan\}) = 34,$$

$$v_{e,k}(\{Ali, Bob, Chan\}) = 46.5.$$

Let be $\tilde{p} = 0.3$, i.e., the manager does not count on the agents who chose the attendance types 4 (i.e. may be not attend (30%)) and 5 (i.e. not attend (10%)). Since $Chan$ has reported the manager the attendance type 4, i.e., $f(Chan) = 0.3 = \tilde{p}$, the singleton coalition is formed for $Chan$ in phase 1. Then the relaxed PCSG problem with Ali and Bob is solved in phase 2, that is, the coalitions which includes $Chan$ can be ignored in the simplified problem as follows:

$$v_{e,k}(\{Ali\}) = 18, \ v_{e,k}(\{Bob\}) = 25, v_{e,k}(\{Ali, Bob\}) = 43.$$

Since the expected value of the coalition formed by Ali and Bob is equal to the sum of the expected values of singleton coalitions with Ali and Bob, i.e., $v_{e,k}(\{Ali, Bob\}) = 43 = v_{e,k}(\{Ali\}) + v_{e,k}(\{Bob\})$, the optimal coalition structures of the relaxed problem are $\{Ali, Bob\}$ and $\{\{Ali\}, \{Bob\}\}$. The solutions obtained by BAAAT are $CS_e^+ = \{\{Chan\}, \{Ali, Bob\}\}$ and $CS_e^+ = \{\{Ali\}, \{Bob\}, \{Chan\}\}$. In this problem, we have two solutions, but the expected values of these two coalition structures are same, i.e., $V_e(CS_e^+) = 46$.

4.2   Quality Guarantee

We show that BAAAT can provide the upper bound of the absolute errors of the solution, which can be obtained a priori, i.e., the error bound is obtained before actually running the algorithm. Let us denote by $\mathcal{C}_a$ the set of all coalitions that contain an agent a as a member, and let $\bar{A}$ be the set of agents whose probability is lower than or equal to a given parameter $\tilde{p}$ such that they form their own coalition in phase 1. Furthermore, let CS_e^- be the expected optimal coalition structure obtained by BAAAT in phase 2, and $r_a^{max} = max\{v_e(C) \mid C \in \mathcal{C}_a\}$, i.e., the maximal expected value of all coalitions which include agent a.

Lemma 1. Let $PCSG = \langle A, v, f \rangle$ be a probabilistic coalition structure generation problem description. For an optimal coalition structure CS_e^* and CS_e^-, the following inequality holds:

$$V_e(CS_e^*) - V_e(CS_e^-) \leq \sum_{\bar{a}_i \in \bar{A}} r_{\bar{a}_i}^{max} \tag{10}$$

Proof. We proof the claim by induction on the size of $\bar{A}$. In the base case, let us consider $\bar{A} = \emptyset$. Then, since no agents are selected/removed in phase 1 of BAAAT, the whole instance is solved to optimality in phase 2. This means that

$$V_e(CS_e^*) = V_e(CS_e^-).$$

On the other hand, $\sum_{\bar{a}_i \in \bar{A}} r_{\bar{a}_i}^{max} = 0$, so

$$V_e(CS_e^*) - V_e(CS_e^-) = 0 \leq 0 = \sum_{\bar{a}_i \in \bar{A}} r_{\bar{a}_i}^{max}$$

and the inequality (10) holds. Let us now assume that the inequality (10) holds for all $\bar{A}$ such that $|\bar{A}| = n$. More specifically, we assume that

$$V_e(CS_e^*) - V_e(CS_e^-) \le \sum_{i=1}^{n} r_{\bar{a}_i}^{max}, \quad \forall \bar{A}, \; |\bar{A}| = n. \tag{11}$$

Next, consider the case where $\bar{A} = \{\bar{a}_1, ..., \bar{a}_n, a_{n+1}^-\}$. We first observe the coalitions that form the expected optimal coalition structure CS_e^* and denote these by $CS_e^* = \{C_e^{*1}, ..., C_e^{*l}\}$. We also know that $\bar{a}_1$ must be in one of these coalitions $C_e^{*1}, ..., C_e^{*l}$ and without loss of generality we can assume that $C_e^{*1} = \{\bar{a}_1, b_1, ..., b_m\}$. It might happen that $b_i = \bar{a}_j$ for some $i \in [m]$, $j \in [n+1] \setminus \{1\}$ but this does not influence the following inequalities:

$$\begin{aligned}
V_e(CS_e^*) &= v_{e,k}(C_e^{*1}) + v_{e,k}(C_e^{*2}) + ... + v_{e,k}(C_e^{*l}) \\
&\le r_{\bar{a}_1}^{max} + v_{e,k}(C_e^{*2}) + ... + v_{e,k}(C_e^{*l}) \\
&\le r_{\bar{a}_1}^{max} + v_{e,k}(\{b_1\}) + ... + v_{e,k}(\{b_m\}) + v_{e,k}(C_e^{*2}) + ... + v_{e,k}(C_e^{*l}) \\
&\le r_{\bar{a}_1}^{max} + V_e(CS_e^{-\bar{a}_1}),
\end{aligned}$$

where $V_e(CS_e^{-\bar{a}_1})$ denotes the optimal expected coalition structure on the set of agents $\mathcal{A} \setminus \{\bar{a}_1\}$. The last inequality follows from the fact that $\{\{b_1\}, ..., \{b_m\}, C_e^{*2}, ..., C_e^{*l}\}$ is a coalition structure over the agents in $\mathcal{A} \setminus \{\bar{a}_1\}$ and $V_e(CS_e^{-\bar{a}_1})$ is the expected optimal such coalition structure. Now, we need to still remove agents $\bar{a}_2, ..., \bar{a}_n$ to reach phase 2 of BAAAT and to be able to compare $V_e(CS_e^*)$ with $V_e(CS_e^-)$. However, by the induction hypothesis (11) on $CS_e^{-\bar{a}_1}$, we have

$$V_e(CS_e^*) - V_e(CS_e^-) \le \sum_{i=2}^{n+1} r_{\bar{a}_i}^{max}$$

Thus, it holds

$$\begin{aligned}
V_e(CS_e^*) &\le r_{\bar{a}_1}^{max} + V_e(CS_e^{-\bar{a}_1}) \\
&\le r_{\bar{a}_1}^{max} + \sum_{i=2}^{n+1} r_{\bar{a}_i}^{max} + V_e(CS_e) \\
&\le \sum_{i=1}^{n+1} r_{\bar{a}_i}^{max} + V_e(CS_e^-)
\end{aligned}$$

Proposition 1. Let $\mathsf{PCSG} = \langle \mathcal{A}, v, f \rangle$ be a probabilistic coalition structure generation problem description. For an optimal coalition structure CS_e^* and the approximate coalition structure CS_e^+ obtained by BAAAT, the following holds:

$$V_e(CS_e^*) - V_e(CS_e^+) \le \sum_{\bar{a}_i \in \bar{A}} \{r_{\bar{a}_i}^{max} - v_{e,k}(\bar{a}_i)\} \tag{12}$$

Proof. By Lemma 1, it holds

$$V_e(CS_e^*) - V_e(CS_e^-) \leq \sum_{\bar{a}_i \in \bar{A}} r_{\bar{a}_i}^{max}$$

Now we subtract $\sum_{\bar{a}_i \in \bar{A}} v_e(\bar{a}_i)$ from the both sides, then we have

$$\{V_e(CS_e^*) - V_e(CS_e^-)\} - \sum_{\bar{a}_i \in \bar{A}} v_{e,k}(\bar{a}_i) \leq \sum_{\bar{a}_i \in \bar{A}} r_{\bar{a}_i}^{max} - \sum_{\bar{a}_i \in \bar{A}} v_{e,k}(\bar{a}_i)$$

$$V_e(CS_e^*) - \{V_e(CS_e^-) + \sum_{\bar{a}_i \in \bar{A}} v_{e,k}(\bar{a}_i)\} \leq \sum_{\bar{a}_i \in \bar{A}} \{r_{\bar{a}_i}^{max} - v_{e,k}(\bar{a}_i)\}$$

$$V_e(CS_e^*) - V_e(CS_e^+) \leq \sum_{\bar{a}_i \in \bar{A}} \{r_{\bar{a}_i}^{max} - v_{e,k}(\bar{a}_i)\}$$

Let us now focus on the specific case for PCSG problem.

Proposition 2. Let PCSG $= \langle A, v, f \rangle$ be a probabilistic coalition structure generation problem description. In case the expected values of all coalitions satisfy the subadditivity, the coalition structure CS_e^+ obtained by **BAAAT** is optimal, i.e., it holds

$$CS_e^* = CS_e^+ \tag{13}$$

Proof. (Sketch) In the subadditive case, the optimal coalition structure CS_e^* is formed by singleton coalitions. So, we just need to show that CS_e^+ has the form $CS_e^+ = \{\{a_i\} | a_i \in \mathcal{A}\}$. In phase 1 of **BAAAT**, the singleton coalition is always formed. In phase 2, since it holds the subadditivity, the optimal coalition structure CS_e^- of the relaxed problem is formed by singleton coalitions. Thus, the solution CS_e^+ obtained by **BAAAT** is formed by singleton coalitions.

5   Experimental Evaluation

In this section, BAAAT is evaluated on a number of benchmarks. As preliminary experiments, the influence of the value $k = |\bar{a}|$ (i.e. the number of agents who might be absent) is first investigated. Next, the performances of BAAAT are evaluated. In order to compute an optimal coalition structure, the CPLEX solver is used. The attendance type (i.e. participation rate) of each agent is randomly chosen from type 1 : {attend (90%)} to type 5 : {not attend (10%)}. For each setting, 100 problem instances are generated, and they are based on several probability distributions for the characteristic function v used in the literature:

- Uniform: $v(C) = Uniform(0, |C|)$ [11].
- Normal: $v(C) = Normal(\mu = 10 * |C|, \sigma^2 = 0.1)$ [18].
- Modified uniform: $v(C) = Uniform(0, 10 * |C|) + a$, where $a = Uniform(0, 50)$ with probability 0.2 and $a = 0$ otherwise [23].
- Modified normal: $v(C) = Normal(10 * |C|, 0.01) + a$ (a is as above) [17].
- Beta: $v(C) = |C| * Beta(\alpha = \beta = 0.5)$ [12].
- Gamma: $v(C) = |C| * Gamma(k = \theta = 2)$ [12].

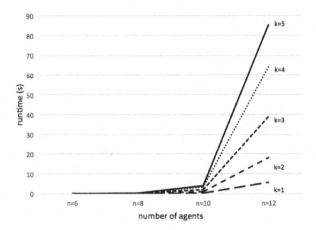

Fig. 1. The average runtime for different value of k.

5.1 Preliminary Experiments

The influence of the value $k = |\bar{a}|$ is investigated. Specifically, we compare the runtime for finding an optimal coalition structure by varying the value $k = |\bar{a}|$. Figure 1 represents the average runtime for different k for the uniform case[2]. When the number of agents is small, the influence of k on the runtime is small. However, the difference becomes larger when the number of agents increases, e.g., in case the number of agents is 12, the average runtime is 5.8 s. for $k = 1$ and it is 85.1 s. for $k = 5$. The experimental results revealed that the influence of k on the runtime becomes larger when the number of agents increases. This is because it requires to consider $\binom{n}{k}$ possible cases in the Eq. (3) in order to compute the expected value for each coalition. For instance, in our running example, when $k = 2$, it requires to consider $\binom{3}{0} + \binom{3}{1} + \binom{3}{2} = 7$ cases to compute the expected value for the coalition $\{Ali, Bob, Chan\}$, i.e., all employees attend, one of them might be absent, and two of them might be absent. However, in case the number of agents increases from 3 to 4 for $k = 2$, we need to consider $\binom{4}{0} + \binom{4}{1} + \binom{4}{2}$ $= 11$ possible cases for computing the expected value of this coalition. In the following experiments, we mostly use the setting in case $k = 1$.

5.2 Performance of **BAAAT**

The approximate algorithm BAAAT is evaluated on a number of benchmarks. In our experiments, BAAAT is implemented in Python and carried out all experiments on 6 core running at 3.3 GHz with 32GB of RAM. We set the parameter $\tilde{p}$ to 0.3, that is, we form the singleton coalition for an agent who reports the attendance type 4 : {maybe not attend (30%)} or type 5 : {not attend (10%)}. Figure 2 represents the average runtime of BAAAT in the uniform case. The x-axis shows the number of agents and the y-axis represents the average runtime.

---

[2] We observed the similar results as shown in Fig. 1 for other cases.

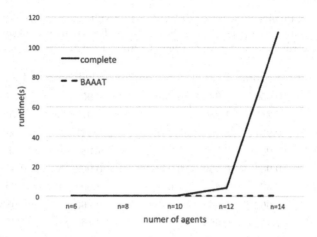

Fig. 2. The average runtime of the complete algorithm and BAAAT.

Table 3. The average runtime of the complete algorithm and BAAAT.

# Agents	Algorithms	Uniform	Normal	Mod. uniform	Mod. normal	Beta	Gamma
6	Complete	0.02	0.02	0.02	0.02	0.02	0.02
	BAAAT	0.01	0.01	0.01	0.01	0.01	0.01
8	Complete	0.07	0.07	0.07	0.07	0.07	0.06
	BAAAT	0.02	0.02	0.02	0.02	0.02	0.02
10	Complete	0.33	0.37	0.32	0.33	0.34	0.38
	BAAAT	0.04	0.04	0.04	0.04	0.04	0.03
12	Complete	5.82	5.82	5.62	5.72	5.70	5.46
	BAAAT	0.08	0.08	0.13	0.10	0.10	0.08
14	Complete	109.9	109.2	95.9	97.5	98.1	98.0
	BAAAT	0.52	0.54	0.61	0.40	0.86	0.72

The dotted line shows the results of BAAAT and the solid line is for the complete one. When the number of agents is small, both algorithms can solve the problems very quickly. However, in case the number of agents increases, the difference of the average runtime between the two algorithms becomes significant. When the number of agents is 14, the average runtime of BAAAT is 0.52 s, while it is 109.9 s. for the CPLEX solver. Table 3 shows the detailed results of runtime for all settings. In all cases, we observed similar results shown in Fig. 2.

Table 4 shows (a) the quality of an obtained solution by BAAAT (i.e., $V(CS_e^+)$ $/V(CS_e^*)$) and (b) the estimated quality of an optimal solution based on the absolute error bound for BAAAT (i.e., $(V_e(CS_e^+) + \sum_{\bar{a}_i \in \bar{A}} \{r_{\bar{a}_i}^{max} - v_{e,k}(\bar{a}_i)\})/V_e(CS_e^*)$). The results of (a) and (b) are normalized by the quality of an actual optimal solution, where (a) should be less than 1.0, and (b) should be more than 1.0. For all of them, a value closer to 1 is desirable. For the results of (a), we can see that the expected values obtained by BAAAT are more than

Table 4. Solution quality obtained by BAAAT. The results of (a) represent the quality of an obtained solution and (b) show the estimated quality of an optimal solution based on the absolute error bound. For all of them, a value closer to 1 is desirable.

# Agents	Quality	Uniform	Normal	Mod. uniform	Mod. normal	Beta	Gamma
6	(a)	0.950	0.999	0.939	0.954	0.972	0.976
	(b)	2.28	1.98	1.81	1.97	1.70	1.76
8	(a)	0.964	0.999	0.961	0.941	0.981	0.975
	(b)	2.08	2.06	1.98	1.98	1.69	1.79
10	(a)	0.963	0.999	0.954	0.968	0.981	0.969
	(b)	2.32	2.45	2.07	2.09	1.84	1.92
12	(a)	0.962	0.999	0.950	0.960	0.983	0.972
	(b)	2.49	2.58	2.15	2.16	1.85	1.99
14	(a)	0.965	0.994	0.956	0.956	0.981	0.973
	(b)	2.71	2.74	2.07	2.25	1.76	2.03

95% of the optimal values in most cases. For the results of (b), we can see that the value (i.e. a priori bound) increases slightly in all cases when the number of agents increases.

6   Related Work

In coalition formation including CSG, many works have been devoted so far to the uncertainty of forming a coalition. Chalkiadakis et al. [2] focused on the uncertainty of types (capabilities) of agents, and proposed a Bayesian reinforcement learning framework for repeated coalition formation under type uncertainty. In this framework, the agents maintain and update beliefs about the types of others through the experience gained by repeated interaction with others, and improve their ability to form useful coalitions. Compared to this work, we focus on the attendance type (i.e. the uncertainty of agents' attendances), while a type is considered as the capability of an agent. Also, the payoffs to coalitions depend on capabilities and actions in this work, but we compute them with the payoffs given by the characteristic function and the probability of the attendance type. Kraus et al. [10] worked on the coalition formation under coalitional value uncertainty. In this framework, a set of tasks is given, and each task is performed by a different agent. The agents may not know the value of a task to another agent or the cost of performing it, but they know the overall payoff associated with performing a set of tasks and the capabilities of the other agents. Faye et al. [7] worked on dynamic coalition formation in dynamic uncertain environments. This work investigates dynamic, uncertain environments in which tasks may evolve during execution, and agents and resource availability may vary rapidly and unpredictably. None of those works actually considers the attendance type of each agent for CSG, making them quite different from the present work.

Moreover, related to our work is team formation problems (TF) [13,25]. TF is the problem of forming the best possible team to perform some tasks of interest, given some limited resources. Nair et al. [13] worked on forming a team with the maximum expected value so that the team has all the required skills to accomplish the tasks of interest. Compared to the TF problem, CSG (and PCSG) is similar to the *complete set partition problem* [26], while TF is equivalent to the *set cover problem* [9]. Okimoto et al. [15] worked on the robustness issue in team formation problems. In this work, a set of agents and a set of tasks are given, and the aim is to form a team which is robust, i.e., which can achieve the given tasks even if some agents break down. Considering the value k (i.e. the number of agents who might be absent) is similar to the robustness defined in this work.

7   Conclusion

How to form a coalition is a major issue for many applications related to multi-agent cooperation. Coalition Structure Generation (CSG) involves partitioning a set of agents into coalitions so that the social surplus is maximized. Probabilistic Coalition Structure Generation (PCSG) is the extension of CSG where the aim is to find the optimal coalition structure which maximizes the sum of the expected values of all coalitions. The contributions of this paper are as follows:

- A formal framework for the Probabilistic Coalition Structure Generation (PCSG) is introduced where the attendance type of each agent is considered. Also, we provide the way how to compute the expected value of a coalition.
- An approximate algorithm for solving a PCSG problem called Bounded Approximate Algorithm based on Attendance Types (BAAAT) is presented. Furthermore, we show that our algorithm BAAAT can provide the upper bound of the absolute errors of the solution, which can be obtained a priori, that is, the error bound is obtained before actually running the algorithm.
- The performances of BAAAT is evaluated on the number of benchmarks. Our experimental results revealed that (i) it can solve PCSG problems very quickly, (ii) it provides high solution quality, and (iii) the estimated quality of an optimal solution (i.e. theoretical bound) increase slightly when the number of agents increases. Also, the influence of the value k is investigated.

As our future works, we would like to investigate the concise representation of the characteristic function in PCSG. In PCSG, since the number of coalitions is exponential in the number of agents, it is required to reduce the representation size of characteristic function which provides the value of each coalition. We will plan to apply the type based concise representation [24] in our framework. Furthermore, we will intend to apply our framework to real-world problems, e.g., multi-sensor networks [4] and distributed vehicle routing [22], and solve them by using our algorithm BAAAT. Lastly, we would like to extend our framework to a dynamic setting in which the set of agents $\mathcal{A}$ may change w.r.t. time with the objective to apply it to a distributed robot team reconfiguration problem [5].

References

1. Bachrach, Y., Kohli, P., Kolmogorov, V., Zadimoghaddam, M.: Optimal coalition structure generation in cooperative graph games. In: AAAI, pp. 81–87 (2013)
2. Chalkiadakis, G., Boutilier, C.: Sequentially optimal repeated coalition formation under uncertainty. Auton. Agents Multi-Agent Syst. **24**(3), 441–484 (2012)
3. Conitzer, V., Sandholm, T.: Complexity of constructing solutions in the core based on synergies among coalitions. Artif. Intell. **170**(6–7), 607–619 (2006)
4. Dang, V., Dash, R., Rogers, A., Jennings, N.: Overlapping coalition formation for efficient data fusion in multi- sensor networks. In: AAAI, pp. 635–640 (2006)
5. Dasgupta, P., Cheng, K.: Robust multi-robot team formations using weighted voting games. Distrib. Auton. Robot. Syst. **83**, 373–387 (2013)
6. Dinar, A., Moretti, S., Patrone, F., Zara, S.: Application of stochastic cooperative games in water resources. In: Goetz, R.U., Berga, D. (eds.) Frontiers in Water Resource Economics. Natural Resource Management and Policy, vol. 29. Springer, Boston (2006). https://doi.org/10.1007/0-387-30056-2_1
7. Faye, P., Aknine, S., Sene, M., Shehory, O.: Dynamic coalitions formation in dynamic uncertain environments. In: WI-IAT, vol. 2, pp. 273–276 (2015)
8. Ieong, S., Shoham, Y.: Marginal contribution nets: a compact representation scheme for coalitional games. In: ACM EC, pp. 193–202 (2005)
9. Karp, R.M.: Reducibility among combinatorial problems. In: Miller, R.E., Thatcher, J.W., Bohlinger, J.D. (eds.) Complexity of Computer Computations. The IBM Research Symposia Series. Springer, Boston (1972). https://doi.org/10.1007/978-1-4684-2001-2_9
10. Kraus, S., Shehory, O., Taase, G.: Coalition formation with uncertain heterogeneous information. In: AAMAS, pp. 1–8 (2003)
11. Larson, K., Sandholm, T.: Anytime coalition structure generation: an average case study. J. Exp. Theor. Artif. Intell. **12**(1), 23–42 (2000)
12. Michalak, T., Rahwan, T., Elkind, E., Wooldridge, M., Jennings, N.: A hybrid exact algorithm for complete set partitioning. J. Artif. Intell. **230**, 14–50 (2016)
13. Nair, R., Tambe, M.: Hybrid BDI-POMDP framework for multiagent teaming. J. Artif. Intell. Res. **23**, 367–420 (2005)
14. Ohta, N., Conitzer, V., Ichimura, R., Sakurai, Y., Iwasaki, A., Yokoo, M.: Coalition structure generation utilizing compact characteristic function representations. In: Gent, I.P. (ed.) CP 2009. LNCS, vol. 5732, pp. 623–638. Springer, Heidelberg (2009). https://doi.org/10.1007/978-3-642-04244-7_49
15. Okimoto, T., Schwind, N., Clement, M., Ribeiro, T., Inoue, K., Marquis, P.: How to form a task-oriented robust team. In: AAMAS, pp. 395–403 (2015)
16. Rahwan, T., Jennings, N.: Coalition structure generation: dynamic programming meets anytime optimization. In: AAAI, pp. 156–161 (2008)
17. Rahwan, T., Michalak, T., Jennings, N.: A hybrid algorithm for coalition structure generation. In: AAAI, pp. 1443–1449 (2012)
18. Rahwan, T., Ramchurn, S., Dang, V., Giovannucci, A., Jennings, N.: Anytime optimal coalition structure generation. In: AAAI, pp. 1184–1190 (2007)
19. Rahwan, T., Ramchurn, S., Jennings, N., Giovannucci, A.: An anytime algorithm for optimal coalition structure generation. J. Artif. Intell. Res. **34**, 521–567 (2009)
20. Sandholm, T.: An implementation of the contract net protocol based on marginal cost calculations. In: 11th National Conference on Artificial Intelligence, pp. 295–308 (1993)

21. Sandholm, T., Larson, K., Andersson, M., Shehory, O., Tohmé, F.: Coalition structure generation with worst case guarantees. Artif. Intell. **111**(1–2), 209–238 (1999)
22. Sandholm, T., Lesser, V.: Coalitions among computationally bounded agents. Artif. Intell. **94**(1–2), 99–137 (1997)
23. Service, T., Adams, J.: Approximate coalition structure generation. In: AAAI, pp. 854–859 (2010)
24. Ueda, S., Kitaki, M., Iwasaki, A., Yokoo, M.: Concise characteristic function representations in coalitional games based on agent types. In: IJCAI, pp. 393–399 (2011)
25. Vidal, J.: The effects of co-operation on multiagent search in task-oriented domains. J. Exp. Theor. Artif. Intell. **16**(1), 5–18 (2004)
26. Yeh, D.: A dynamic programming approach to the complete set partitioning problem. BIT Comput. Sci. Numer. Math. **26**(4), 467–474 (1986)

Robust Coalition Structure Generation

Tenda Okimoto[1]([⊠]), Nicolas Schwind[2], Emir Demirović[3], Katsumi Inoue[4],
and Pierre Marquis[5]

[1] Kobe University, Kobe, Japan
tenda@maritime.kobe-u.ac.jp
[2] National Institute of Advanced Industrial Science and Technology, Tokyo, Japan
[3] School of Computing and Information Systems, University of Melbourne,
Melbourne, Australia
[4] National Institute of Informatics, Tokyo Institute of Technology, Tokyo, Japan
[5] CRIL-CNRS, Université d'Artois, Institut Universitaire de France, Lens, France

Abstract. How to form effective coalitions is an important issue in multi-agent systems. Coalition Structure Generation (CSG) involves partitioning a set of agents into coalitions so that the social surplus (i.e. the sum of the rewards obtained by each coalition) is maximized. In many cases, one is interested in computing a partition of the set of agents which maximizes the social surplus, but is robust as well, which means that it is not required to recompute new coalitions if some agents break down. In this paper, the focus is laid on the Robust Coalition Structure Generation (RCSG) problem. A formal framework is defined and some decision and optimization problems for RCSG are pointed out. The computational complexity of RCSG is then identified. An algorithm for RCSG (called AmorCSG) is presented and evaluated on a number of benchmarks.

Keywords: Multi-agent system · Coalition structure generation
Robustness

1 Introduction

Coalition Structure Generation (CSG) [14,20] is a key issue for a number of applications related to multi-agent cooperation, e.g., waste-water treatment system [5], distributed vehicle routing [20] and multi-sensor networks [3]. CSG involves partitioning a set of agents into coalitions so that the sum of the values of all coalitions is maximized. In CSG, it is well-known that finding an optimal coalition structure which maximizes the social surplus is **NP**-hard. Indeed, the decision problem associated with CSG is equivalent to the *complete set partition problem* [23] which is **NP**-complete.

Robustness (i.e., it is not required to recompute new coalitions of CSG even if some agents break down) is an expected property of CSG. In this paper, the focus is laid on the Robust Coalition Structure Generation (RCSG) problem. A formal framework for the RCSG problem is presented and some decision and optimization problems for RCSG are pointed out. A coalition structure is viewed as

© Springer Nature Switzerland AG 2018
T. Miller et al. (Eds.): PRIMA 2018, LNAI 11224, pp. 140–157, 2018.
https://doi.org/10.1007/978-3-030-03098-8_9

k-robust (for a given non-negative integer k) if removing any subset of k agents from it leads the remaining coalitions to still be beneficial. The RCSG *decision* problem consists in determining whether there exists a u-beneficial and k-robust coalition structure, for a given reward threshold u and robustness threshold k. We identify the computational complexity of the RCSG decision problem. While the standard CSG problem is **NP**-complete, we show that the RCSG decision problem is inherently harder unless the polynomial hierarchy collapses (RCSG is Σ_2^p-complete). One of the *optimization* counterparts of this problem consists in fixing the robustness threshold k and finding one of the most beneficial coalition structures meeting the robustness requirement. Dually, one can also fix the reward threshold u and optimize the robustness of a u-beneficial coalition structure. Lastly, one can consider the *bi-objective optimization problem* where the aim is to optimize both the reward and the robustness of a coalition structure.

As an application domain, we believe that the vehicle routing problem [18] is promising area, which can be formalized as CSG, where geographically dispersed dispatch centers of several companies cooperate. When we consider both the effectiveness and robustness of the drivers' groups, this problem amounts to a robust CSG problem. Another application area is about the multi-sensor networks [3], which can be also formalized as CSG. Consider several sensors in an airport or in a shopping center where some sensors collaborate and observe a certain area for the security reason. Then, forming effective and robust groups of sensors, amounts to solving a RCSG problem.

Related to our work is the team formation problem (TF) [11,22]. Compared to the TF problem, CSG is similar to the *complete set partition problem* [23], while TF is equivalent to the *set cover problem* [7]. The robustness issue has recently been considered in TF [13]. Our approach of robustness in CSG is similar to the one developed in this work. However, this paper focuses on the robustness issue for CSG. Also, the significant difference between RCSG and robust TF lies in the complexity of each of the corresponding decision problems: RCSG is shown here to be Σ_2^p-complete, whereas robust TF is "only" **NP**-complete. To the best of our knowledge, the robustness issue for CSG have been left unaddressed so far in the literature.

2   Coalition Structure Generation

Let us start with some preliminary definitions. Let $A = \{a_1, a_2, \ldots, a_n\}$ be a finite set of agents. A coalition from A, denoted as C, is a non-empty subset of A. A coalition structure on A, denoted as CS, is a partition on A, i.e., a jointly exhaustive set of pairwise disjoint coalitions from A. Formally, a coalition structure CS (on A) is a set of coalitions $\{C_1, \ldots, C_m\}$ such that for each $i, j \in \{1, 2, \ldots, m\}$ such that $i \neq j$, we have that $C_i \cap C_j = \emptyset$ and $\bigcup_{C_i \in CS} C_i = A$.

Definition 1 (CSG problem description). A coalition structure generation problem description is defined by a pair $\mathsf{CSG} = \langle A, v \rangle$ where $A = \{a_1, a_2, \ldots, a_n\}$ is a set of agents and $v : 2^A \to \mathbb{N}$ is a function called a characteristic function.

The *value* of a coalition C, denoted as $v(C)$, is given by the characteristic function v. The value of a coalition structure CS, denoted as $V(CS)$, is the sum of the values of each coalition, i.e., $V(CS) = \sum_{C_i \in CS} v(C_i)$. A coalition structure is said to be optimal, denoted as CS^*, if CS^* satisfies the followings: $\forall CS, V(CS) \leq V(CS^*)$.

Example 1 (CSG). Let us consider the following scenario. The olympic games will be held in Tokyo and it requires some interpreters in different stadiums, e.g., athletics stadium, swimming stadium and basketball stadium etc. A service company dispatching interpreters with three employees (*Ana*, *Becky* and *Carol*) has received the requests of the simultaneous interpretation and send them employees to different stadiums: request 1 requires *Ana*, and the company gets \$20 for it; request 2 pays \$30 and needs *Becky*'s language skill; request 3 needs *Carol* and pays \$10; request 4 pays \$80 and needs *Ana* and *Becky*; request 5 pays \$90 and needs *Ana* and *Carol*; request 6 needs *Becky* and *Carol* and pays \$70; request 7 requires all employees and pays \$110. Assume that you are the manager of this service company and want to assign the employees to job(s) so that the sum of the rewards is maximized. Then, this problem can be represented as a CSG: let CSG $= \langle A, v \rangle$ be a CSG problem description with $A = \{Ana, Becky, Carol\}$, and the function v is characterized as follows:

$$v(\{Ana\}) = \$20, \quad v(\{Becky\}) = \$30, \quad v(\{Carol\}) = \$10,$$
$$v(\{Ana, Becky\}) = \$80, \quad v(\{Ana, Carol\}) = \$90, \quad v(\{Becky, Carol\}) = \$70,$$
$$v(\{Ana, Becky, Carol\}) = \$110.$$

The optimal coalition structure is $CS^* = \{\{Becky\}, \{Ana, Carol\}\}$, and the obtained value by CS^* is $V(CS^*) = v(\{Becky\}) + v(\{Ana, Carol\}) = \$30 + \$90 = \$120$.

An expected property for coalition structures is to ensure a given level of efficiency. Formally, this (quite standard) property can be stated as follows:

Definition 2 (Beneficialness). Let $CSG = \langle A, v \rangle$ be a CSG problem description. Given a coalition structure CS and a non-negative integer u, CS is said to be *u-beneficial* if the value of CS is larger than u: $V(CS) \geq u$.

Let us stress an important remark as to the representation of the characteristic function v in a CSG. In our running example about the service company dispatching interpreters, v is defined "implicitly", i.e., it is viewed as an oracle. One possible generalization of our example above to an arbitrary number n of agents would be to associate with every coalition C a number depending on the size of C only; in such a case, the corresponding characteristic function v can be represented with a size in $\mathcal{O}(n)$. A number of representation settings for characteristic functions have been pointed out in the literature, and some of them have been adapted to CSG and studied from the computational complexity viewpoint [12]. Among the representation frameworks which have been developed are marginal contribution nets (MC-nets) [6] and synergy coalition groups (SCGs) [2]. Contrastingly, some early work [19,20] assume that v is provided "fully extensionally" as an input of a CSG problem description, i.e., v is given as a table with $2^n - 1$ entries, associating with every coalition a number. Providing such an extensional representation of v makes the size of an input CSG to be exponential in the number of agents and may be an unrealistic assumption for relatively large problems. Yet there exist many real world applications involving only a dozen of agents (e.g. because of the limited resources), for which an extensional representation of v is feasible [3,9,18]. Thus, cooperative games can be used to analyze cost allocation problems, where the players are willing to form coalitions in order to get extra monetary savings as an effect of cooperation. For instance, in [5] the authors address the problem where nearby municipalities must take the decision on whether to cooperate in order to implement a Wastewater Treatment System (WTS). These types of problem can be represented formally as a CSG and it involves a few agents in essence, so that (i) considering a few number of agents for experimentations, and (ii) assuming an extensional representation of the characteristic function, can sometimes be considered as reasonable.

So both choices of representation for v (i.e., "implicit" vs. "extensional") have been considered in the literature. It turns out that for a number of implicit representations of v (including MC-nets and SCG, see [12]), the complexity of computing a beneficial coalition structure (cf. Definition 2) is **NP**-hard:

Definition 3 (DP-CSG)

- **Input:** A coalition structure generation problem description $CSG = \langle A, v \rangle$, and a non-negative integer u,
- **Question:** Does there exist a coalition structure CS such that CS is u-beneficial?

As mentioned above, the complexity of DP-CSG is **NP**-complete in general:

Theorem 1 ([19]). If the characteristic function v is computable in polynomial time, then DP-CSG is **NP**-complete.

In the next section, we will show that computing a "robust" coalition structure is an intrinsically harder problem than the traditional CSG problem.

3 Robust Coalition Structure Generation

In this section, a formal framework for Robust Coalition Structure Generation (RCSG) is defined. Furthermore, both the decision and optimization problems for RCSG are considered. Also, the computational complexity of RCSG is identified.

Let $A = \{a_1, \ldots, a_n\}$ be a set of agents and $A' \subseteq A$. The *restriction on A'* of a coalition C from A is defined as the set $C \cap A'$. We extend this notion of restriction on coalition structures as follows. The *restriction on A'* of a coalition structure $CS = \{C_1, \ldots, C_m\}$ on A is defined as the coalition structure $CS' = \{C'_1, \ldots, C'_m\} \setminus \{\emptyset\}$ on A', where for each $i \in \{1, \ldots, m\}$, C'_i is the restriction on A' of C_i. Consider the same coalition structure generation problem in our example of the service company dispatching interpreters. Let us consider the coalition structure $CS = \{\{Ana, Becky\}, \{Carol\}\}$ and $A' = \{Ana, Carol\}$. Then, the restriction on A' of CS is the coalition structure $\{\{Ana\}, \{Carol\}\}$. Robustness can now be defined in formal terms as follows:

Definition 4 (Robust Coalition Structure). Let $CSG = \langle A, v \rangle$ be a CSG problem description. For a given coalition structure CS on A and non-negative integers u and k, CS is said to be (u, k)-*robust* if for every $A' \subseteq A$, such that $|A'| \geq n - k$, the restriction on A' of CS is u-beneficial.

That is to say, a coalition structure is (u, k)-*robust* if whenever k agents are removed from it, the "remaining" coalition structure is u-beneficial. Obviously enough, robustness generalizes the usual notion of beneficialness in CSG. Indeed, we trivially have that for any non-negative integer u, a CSG is u-beneficial if and only if it is $(u, 0)$-robust.

Example 1 (continued). Let us consider the service company dispatching interpreters with three employees. The manager of this company planed to assign *Becky* to the request 2 and *Ana* and *Carol* to the request 5 so that he/she gets the maximal rewards. However, what's happen if one of them cannot work on the day because of the illness or other unexpected matters. For instance, let $u = \$70$ and $k = 1$, that is, the manager wants to have at least \$70 even if such an event would occur. In this example, the optimal coalition structure planed in advance is $CS^* = \{\{Becky\}, \{Ana, Carol\}\}$. To check whether CS^* is $(70, 1)$-robust, we check for each removed agent from CS^* whether the remaining coalition structure is 70-beneficial. We have that: $V(CS^* \setminus \{Ana\}) = v(\{Becky\}) + v(\{Carol\}) = \$40$, $V(CS^* \setminus \{Becky\}) = v(\{Ana, Carol\}) = \$90$, $V(CS^* \setminus \{Carol\}) = v(\{Ana\}) + v(\{Becky\}) = \$50$. When we remove *Ana* from CS^*, the remaining coalition structure is not 70-beneficial. Intuitively, this comes from the fact that it is not "safe" to form the coalition $\{Ana, Carol\}$ to get a reward of \$90, since the absence of *Ana* from this coalition would leave *Carol* alone, getting a reward of \$10. Thus, CS^* is not $(70, 1)$-robust. However, $CS = \{\{Ana, Becky, Carol\}\}$ is $(70, 1)$-robust, since all remaining coalition structures are 70-beneficial after we remove each agent from CS, i.e., $V(CS \setminus \{Ana\}) = \$70$, $V(CS \setminus \{Becky\}) = \$90$, and $V(CS \setminus \{Carol\}) = \$80$.

In the following, we assume that the characteristic function v of $CSG = \langle A, v \rangle$ satisfies the property of *monotonicity*, i.e., for all coalitions C, C', if $C \subseteq C'$ then $v(C) \leq v(C')$. This property requires that adding an agent to a given coalition is harmless, or stated otherwise, removing an agent from a coalition does not result in an increase of its value. This assumption is very natural when considering the robustness issue, as we are interested in dealing with the "damages" caused to a coalition structure when removing a number of agents from it.[1] Nonetheless,

---

[1] Note that the property of monotonicity differs from the super-additivity which requires that for all coalitions C, C', it holds $v(C) + v(C') \leq v(C \cup C')$ and is stronger than monotonicity.

this assumption does not affect the following complexity results, that is, it does not make the RCSG problem computationally easier.

Definition 5 (DP-RCSG)

- **Input:** A CSG problem description $CSG = \langle A, v \rangle$, with v computable in polynomial time, and two non-negative integers u and k,
- **Question:** Does there exist a coalition structure CS such that CS is (u, k)-robust?

In the general case, computing a robust coalition structure is a harder problem than computing a beneficial one (unless the polynomial hierarchy collapses):

Proposition 1. DP-RCSG is Σ_2^P-complete. Σ_2^P-hardness holds even if the characteristic function satisfies monotonicity.

Proof. Let us first prove that RCSG is in Σ_2^P. Let $CSG = \langle A, v \rangle$ be a CSG problem description such that $A = \{a_1, \ldots, a_n\}$, and u and k be two non-negative integers. Consider the following non-deterministic polynomial algorithm with **NP** oracle:

1. Guess a set $CS = \{C_1, \ldots, C_m\}$ of coalitions from A;
2. Check that CS is a coalition structure on A;
3. Check using an **NP** oracle that there does not exist a set of agents $A' \subseteq A$ such that $|A'| = n - k$ and such that the restriction of CS on A' is not u-beneficial.

This algorithm decides RCSG, showing that RCSG is in Σ_2^P.

We prove that Σ_2^P-hardness holds for RCSG by consider a reduction in polynomial time to the complementary problem of RCSG from the following Π_2^P-hard problem, that is, the validity problem for 3-CNF quantified boolean formulas (QBFs) of the form $\forall X \exists Y.\alpha$ where $X = \{x_1, \ldots, x_n\}$ and $Y = \{y_1, \ldots, y_n\}$ are two disjoint sets of propositional atoms and α is 3-CNF propositional formula such that $Var(\alpha) = X \cup Y$. Consider such a QBF $\forall X \exists Y.\alpha$, and let us associate with it an RCSG problem description $\langle A, v \rangle$, where A is the set of agents $A = \{a_1, \bar{a}_1, b_1, \bar{b}_1, \ldots, a_n, \bar{a}_n, b_n, \bar{b}_n\}$, and v is a characteristic function $v : 2^A \mapsto \mathbb{N}$ given as follows. Let us first define:

- the mapping x associating any literal over X with a pair of agents from A, defined for every (possibly negated) literal x_i as $x(x_i) = \{a_i, \bar{a}_i\}$ if x_i is a positive literal, otherwise $x(x_i) = \{b_i, \bar{b}_i\}$;
- the mapping y associating any literal over Y with a pair of agents from A, defined for every (possibly negated) literal y_i as $y(y_i) = \{a_i, b_i\}$ if y_i is a positive literal, otherwise $y(y_i) = \{\bar{a}_i, \bar{b}_i\}$.

Additionally, we assume that α is viewed as a set of clauses written as (l_i, l_j, l_k), where l_i, l_j, l_k are literals from $X \cup Y$, and such that the literals l_i, l_j, l_k are ordered in such a way that if $l_i \in Y$ (resp. $l_j \in Y$) then $l_j, l_k \in Y$ (resp.

$l_k \in Y$). Then a clause $(l_i, l_j, l_k) \in \alpha$ can be of the form (x_i, x_j, y_k), (x_i, y_j, y_k) or (y_i, y_j, y_k), since the presence of clauses of the form (x_i, x_j, x_k) make the QBF trivially not valid.

Then given the QBF $\forall X \exists Y.\alpha$, the characteristic function v is defined as follows. Consider the function p associating any literal p_q from $X \cup Y$ with a pair of agents from A, defined as $p(p_q) = x(x_l)$ if $p_q = x_l$, otherwise $p(p_q) = y(y_m)$ when $p_q = y_m$. For each coalition $C \subseteq A$, we set:

(i) $v(C) = 2n + 1$ if there exists $i \in \{1, \ldots, n\}$ such that $\{a_i, \bar{a}_i\} \subseteq C$ or $\{b_i, \bar{b}_i\} \subseteq C$;

(ii) $v(C) = n+1$ if there exists a clause (p_i, p_j, p_k) from α such that $p(p_q) \cap C \neq \emptyset$, for any $q \in \{i, j, k\}$;

(iii) $v(C) = 1$ in the remaining cases.

We often refer to these conditions as (i), (ii) and (iii) in the rest of the proof.

First, one can easily check that v satisfies (monotonicity). Indeed, one can see that for any coalition $C \subseteq A$, if C satisfies condition (i) (resp., condition (ii), (iii), (iv)), then any coalition C' such that $C \subseteq C'$ also satisfies condition (i) (resp., condition (ii), (iii), (iv)). Hence, for all coalitions $C, C' \subseteq A$, if $C \subseteq C'$ then $v(C) \leq v(C')$. Therefore, v satisfies (monotonicity).

We intend now to prove that the QBF $\forall X \exists Y.\alpha$ is valid if and only if there does not exist any coalition structure which is $(2n+1, 2n)$-robust, i.e., if and only if for every coalition structure CS on A, there exists a set $A' \subseteq A, |A'| = 2n$, such that the restriction on A' of CS is not $(2n+1)$-beneficial. This would show that the complementary problem of RCSG is $\mathbf{\Pi}_2^{\mathbf{P}}$-hard, thus that RCSG is $\mathbf{\Sigma}_2^{\mathbf{P}}$-hard.

(If part) We show the contrapositive of the claim. Assume that the QBF $\forall X \exists Y.\alpha$ is not valid, i.e., $\exists X \forall Y. \neg \alpha$ is satisfiable, and let us prove that there exists a coalition structure which is $(2n+1, 2n)$-robust. So let ω_X be an interpretation over X such that for any interpretation ω_Y over Y, one the clauses of α is not satisfied by $\omega_X \cup \omega_Y$. Define the coalition structure CS_r as $CS_r = \{C_r, C_r^1, \ldots, C_r^n\}$, where:

- $C_r = \{a_i, \bar{a}_i \mid i \in \{1, \ldots, n\}, \omega_X(x_i) = 0\} \cup \{b_i, \bar{b}_i \mid i \in \{1, \ldots, n\}, \omega_X(x_i) = 1\}$;
- for each $i \in \{1, \ldots, n\}$, $C_r^i = \{a_i, \bar{a}_i, b_i, \bar{b}_i\} \setminus C_r$.

Let us show that CS is $(2n, 2n + 1)$-robust, i.e., for any set $A' \subseteq A$ such that $|A'| = 2n$, the restriction on A' of CS is $(2n+1)$-beneficial. From condition (i), we know that for any coalition C, if there exists $i \in \{1, \ldots, n\}$ such that $\{a_i, \bar{a}_i\} \subseteq C$ or $\{b_i, \bar{b}_i\} \subseteq C$, then $v(C) = 2n + 1$, so that for any coalition structure CS containing such a coalition C we would get that $v(CS) \geq 2n + 1$. Yet by construction of our coalition structure $CS_r = \{C_r, C_r^1, \ldots, C_r^n\}$, for every $i \in \{1, \ldots, n\}$ we have that $\{a_i, \bar{a}_i\} \subseteq C$ for some coalition $C \in CS_r$ and $\{b_i, \bar{b}_i\} \subseteq C$ for some coalition $C \in CS_r$. And we have $4n$ elements in A, thus for any set $A' \subseteq A$ such that $|A'| = 2n$, in the case where $\{a_i, \bar{a}_i\} \subseteq A'$ or $\{b_i, \bar{b}_i\} \subseteq A'$ for some $i \in \{1, \ldots, n\}$, we get that $v(C \cap A') = 2n + 1$ for some coalition $C \in CS_r$ (cf. condition (i)), i.e., the restriction CS_r' on A' of CS_r satisfies $v(CS_r') \geq 2n + 1$, and thus CS_r' is $(2n + 1)$-beneficial, which makes

CS_r $(2n, 2n + 1)$-robust, that was to be shown. So consider the remaining cases and assume that A' is formed of exactly one element among $\{a_i, \bar{a}_i\}$ and exactly one element among $\{b_i, \bar{b}_i\}$, for each $i \in \{1, \ldots, n\}$. So now, for any coalition $C_r^i \in CS_r$ ($i \in \{1, \ldots, n\}$), it can be checked by definition of C_r^i that $C_r^i \cap A'$ contains exactly one element from A. This means that none of the conditions (i), (ii), (iii) are satisfied by $C \cap A'$, and thus $v(C \cap A') = 1$ (cf. condition (iv)). To sum up, we have that $v(C_r^i \cap A') = 1$ for each coalition $C_r^i \in CS_r$ ($i \in \{1, \ldots, n\}$), and we need to prove that the restriction CS_r' of CS_r on A' satisfies $v(CS_r') \geq 2n + 1$; yet $v(CS_r') = \sum_{C \in CS_r} v(C \cap A')$, so $v(CS_r') = \sum_{C_r^i \in CS_r, i \in \{1,\ldots,n\}} v(C_r^i \cap A') + v(C_r \cap A') = n + v(C_r \cap A')$. Then we need to prove that $v(C_r \cap A') \geq (2n + 1) - n$, i.e., we must prove that $v(C_r \cap A') \geq n + 1$. Let us show that $v(C_r \cap A') = n + 1$. This is enough to show that $C_r \cap A'$ satisfies condition (ii) or (iii). Let us associate with C_r and A' the interpretation ω_Y over Y defined as follows, for each $i \in \{1, \ldots, n\}$:

- in the case where $\{a_i, \bar{a}_i\} \subseteq C_r$, then: $\omega_Y(y_i) = 0$ if $a_i \in A'$, otherwise $\omega_Y(y_i) = 1$ (i.e., if $\bar{a}_i \in A'$);
- in the remaining case (i.e., $\{b_i, \bar{b}_i\} \subseteq C_r$) then: $\omega_Y(y_i) = 0$ if $b_i \in A'$, otherwise $\omega_Y(y_i) = 1$ (i.e., if $\bar{b}_i \in A'$);

We know that there is at least one clause c from α which is not satisfied by $\omega_X \cup \omega_Y$. Such a clause c is of the form (x_i, y_j, y_k) or (y_i, y_j, y_k), but in any of the two cases we have that none of the literals of the clause is satisfied by $\omega_X \cup \omega_Y$. It can be a literal from X (denoted x_i below) or from Y (denoted y_i below). Let us denote l this literal, we fall into one of the two following cases:

- l is a literal x_i. If x_i is a positive literal, then $\omega_X(x_i) = 0$. Yet we know by definition of the coalition $C_r \in CS_r$ that $\{a_i, \bar{a}_i\} \subseteq C_r$, and we already know that A' contains exactly one element from $\{a_i, \bar{a}_i\}$, thus we get that $\{a_i, \bar{a}_i\} \cap (C_r \cap A') \neq \emptyset$. If x_i is a negative literal, then $\omega_X(x_i) = 1$. By a similar reasoning, we get that $\{b_i, \bar{b}_i\} \cap (C_r \cap A') \neq \emptyset$. Stated otherwise, we get that $x(x_i) \cap (C_r \cap A') \neq \emptyset$.
- l is a literal y_i. If y_i is a positive literal, then $\omega_Y(y_i) = 0$. Yet we know by definition of ω_Y that we are in the case where ($\{a_i, \bar{a}_i\} \subseteq C_r$ and $a_i \in A'$) or ($\{b_i, \bar{b}_i\} \subseteq C_r$ and $b_i \in A'$). Thus $C_r \cap A' = \{a_i\}$ or $C_r \cap A' = \{b_i\}$. Hence, $\{a_i, b_i\} \cap (C_r \cap A') \neq \emptyset$. If x_i is a negative literal, then $\omega_Y(y_i) = 1$. Yet similarly by definition of ω_Y we are in the case where ($\{a_i, \bar{a}_i\} \subseteq C_r$ and $\bar{a}_i \in A'$) or ($\{b_i, \bar{b}_i\} \subseteq C_r$ and $\bar{b}_i \in A'$). Thus $C_r \cap A' = \{\bar{a}_i\}$ or $C_r \cap A' = \{\bar{b}_i\}$. Hence, $\{\bar{a}_i, \bar{b}_i\} \cap (C_r \cap A') \neq \emptyset$. Stated otherwise, we get that $y(y_i) \cap (C_r \cap A') \neq \emptyset$.

From these two points, we can claim for the clause c which is not satisfied by $\omega_X \cup \omega_Y$ that: if c is of the form (x_i, y_j, y_k), then $x(x_i) \cap (C_r \cap A') \neq \emptyset$, $y(y_j) \cap (C_r \cap A') \neq \emptyset$ and $y(y_k) \cap (C_r \cap A') \neq \emptyset$; and if c is of the form (y_i, y_j, y_k), then $y(y_i) \cap (C_r \cap A') \neq \emptyset$, $y(y_j) \cap (C_r \cap A') \neq \emptyset$ and $y(y_k) \cap (C_r \cap A') \neq \emptyset$. By definition of the characteristic function v (cf. conditions (ii) and (iii)), we get that $v(C_r \cap A') = n + 1$, that was left to be shown and concludes this part of the proof.

(Only if part) We show the contraposite of the claim. Assume that there exists a coalition structure which is $(2n+1, 2n)$-robust, and let us prove that the QBF $\forall X \exists Y.\alpha$ is not valid, i.e., $\exists X \forall Y.\neg\alpha$ is satisfiable.

Let us introduce a preliminary notion. For a given $q \in \{0, \ldots, n\}$, we say that a coalition structure CS is *q-normal* if $CS = \{A\}$ when $q = 0$, and if $CS = \{C, C^1, \ldots, C^q\}$ when $q \in \{1, \ldots, n\}$ such that:

- for all $i \in \{1, \ldots, q\}$, $C^i = \{a_i, \bar{a}_i\}$ or $C^i = \{b_i, \bar{b}_i\}$;
- $C = A \setminus \bigcup\{C^i \mid C^i \in CS, i \in \{1, \ldots, q\}\}$.

For instance, when $n = 4$, the coalition structure $CS = \{C, C^1, C^2, C^3\}$ defined such that $C^1 = \{a_1, \bar{a}_1\}$, $C^2 = \{b_2, \bar{b}_2\}$, $C^3 = \{b_3, \bar{b}_3\}$ and $C = \{b_1, \bar{b}_1, a_2, \bar{a}_2, a_3, \bar{a}_3, a_4, \bar{a}_4, b_4, \bar{b}_4\}$ is 3-normal.

What we first intend to prove is that there exists a coalition structure which is *n-normal* and $(2n+1, 2n)$-robust. Beforehand, we want to show that for each $q \in \{1, \ldots, n\}$, there exists a coalition structure CS which is *q-normal* and such that for any $A' \subseteq A$, $|A'| = 2n$, there exists a coalition $C' \in CS_{\downarrow A'}$ which satisfies condition (i), (ii) or (iii), where $CS_{\downarrow A'}$ denotes the restriction of CS on A' (for short, we say that CS is *(i)-(ii)-(iii)-consistent* in the following). So to recap, we want to show that for each $q \in \{1, \ldots, n\}$, there exists a coalition structure CS which is *q-normal* and (i)-(ii)-(iii)-consistent. We prove it by recursion on q:

- Base case ($q = 0$): since the only 0-normal coalition structure is defined as $CS^0 = \{A\}$, it is enough to show that CS^0 is (ii)-(iii)-consistent, i.e., that for every set $A' \subseteq A$ such that $|A'| = 2n$, $A \cap A'$ satisfies condition (ii) or (iii). Yet we know that there exists a coalition structure which is $(2n+1, 2n)$-robust, so let CS_r be such a coalition structure. So for every set $A' \subseteq A$ such that $|A'| = 2n$, the restriction of CS_r on A' is $(2n+1)$-beneficial. Let $A' \subseteq A$, $|A'| = 2n$, such that for each $i \in \{1, \ldots, n\}$, A' contains exactly one element among $\{a_i, \bar{a}_i\}$ and exactly one element among $\{b_i, \bar{b}_i\}$. We can see then that no coalition from $CS_{r \downarrow A'}$ satisfies condition (i). Let us prove there exists a coalition from $CS_{r \downarrow A'}$ satisfying condition (ii) or (iii). Toward a contradiction, assume that there is no such coalition. Then for every coalition $C \in CS_{r \downarrow A'}$, $v(C) = 1$ (cf. condition (iv)). Yet there are $2n$ elements in A', which means that $v(CS_{r \downarrow A'}) \leq 2n$ (we get that $v(CS_{r \downarrow A'}) = 2n$ in the case where each coalition from $CS_{r \downarrow A'}$ is a singleton set). And yet CS_r is $(2n+1, 2n)$-robust, so $CS_{r \downarrow A'}$ is $(2n+1)$-beneficial, which leads to a contradiction. Hence, there exists a coalition from $CS_{r \downarrow A'}$ satisfying condition (ii) or (iii); let C' be such a coalition. We know that C' is a coalition from $CS_{r \downarrow A'}$, so $C' \subseteq A'$. But we also have $C' \subseteq A$, thus $C' \subseteq A \cap A'$. Hence, since C' satisfies condition (ii) or (iii), it is easy to see that $A \cap A'$ satisfies condition (ii) or (iii) as well. Therefore, CS^0 is (i)-(ii)-(iii)-consistent.
- Recursion step: let $CS^q = \{C, C^1, \ldots, C^q\}$ be a *q-normal* coalition structure for some $q \in \{0, \ldots, n-1\}$ ($CS^0 = \{A\}$), and assume that CS^q is (i)-(ii)-(iii)-consistent. Let us prove that there exists a coalition structure CS^{q+1} which is $(q+1)$-normal and (i)-(ii)-(iii)-consistent. Let us associate with $CS^q = \{C, C^1, \ldots, C^q\}$ the coalition structure $CS_a^{q+1} = \{C_a, C^1, \ldots, C^q, C_a^{q+1}\}$

where $C_a = C \setminus \{a_{q+1}, a_{\overline{q+1}}\}$ and $C_a^{q+1} = \{a_{q+1}, a_{\overline{q+1}}\}$; similarly, we associate with $CS^q = \{C, C^1, \ldots, C^q\}$ the coalition structure $CS_b^{q+1} = \{C_b, C^1, \ldots, C^q, C_b^{q+1}\}$ where $C_b = C \setminus \{b_{q+1}, b_{\overline{q+1}}\}$ and $C_b^{q+1} = \{b_{q+1}, b_{\overline{q+1}}\}$. It is easy to verify that CS_a^{q+1} and CS_b^{q+1} are well-defined coalitions structures, and that both of them are $(q+1)$-normal. So this is enough to show that one of these coalitions is (i)-(ii)-(iii)-consistent. Since CS^q is either (i)-(ii)-(iii)-consistent, for any $A' \subseteq A$, $|A'| = 2n$, there exists a coalition $C' \in CS_{\downarrow A'}^q$ which satisfies condition (i), (ii) or (iii). So let $A' \subseteq A$, $|A'| = 2n$, and let $C' \in CS_{\downarrow A'}^q$, we know that C' satisfies condition (i), (ii) or (iii). Yet by construction of CS_a^{q+1} and CS_b^{q+1} it is easy to see that if C' satisfies condition (i) (resp. condition (ii)), then both $CS_{a\downarrow A'}^{q+1}$ and $CS_{b\downarrow A'}^{q+1}$ contain a coalition which satisfies condition (i) (resp. condition (ii)). So assume that C' does not satisfy condition (i) nor (ii), so that C' satisfies condition (iii). But then, it is easy to verify that one of the two following cases holds: (1) for every $A'' \subseteq A$, $|A''| = 2n$, $CS_{a\downarrow A''}^{q+1}$ contains a coalition which satisfies condition (iii), or (2) for every $A'' \subseteq A$, $|A''| = 2n$, $CS_{b\downarrow A''}^{q+1}$ contains a coalition which satisfies condition (iii). Overall, we have shown that either CS_a^{q+1} or CS_b^{q+1} is (i)-(ii)-(iii)-consistent.

We have now proved that there exists a coalition structure $CS = \{C, C^1, \ldots, C^n\}$ which is n-normal and such that for any $A' \subseteq A$, $|A'| = 2n$, there exists a coalition $C' \in CS_{\downarrow A'}$ which satisfies condition (i), (ii) or (iii). Let us show that such a coalition structure CS is $(2n, 2n + 1)$-robust. Let $A' \subseteq A$, $|A| = 2n$ and let us show that $CS_{\downarrow A'}$ is $(2n + 1)$-beneficial. Let $C' \in CS_{\downarrow A'}$. Assume first that C' satisfies condition (i), then one can see that $v(C') = 2n + 1$ and thus $CS_{\downarrow A'}$ is $(2n + 1)$-beneficial. So assume that C' does not satisfy condition (i), i.e., C' satisfies condition (ii) or (iii). Note that in this case (because C' does not satisfy condition (i)), we know that A' contains exactly one element from $\{a_i, \bar{a}_i\}$ and exactly one element from $\{b_i, \bar{b}_i\}$, for each $i \in \{1, \ldots, n\}$. Then for each coalition $C^i \in CS$, $i \in \{1, \ldots, n\}$, we get that $C^i \cap A'$ is a singleton set and C^i satisfies none of the conditions (ii) and (iii), and thus $v(C^i \cap A') = 1$ (condition (iv)). We have that $v(CS_{\downarrow A'}) = v(C \cap A') + v(C^1 \cap A') + \cdots + v(C^n \cap A') = v(C \cap A') + n = v(C') + n = (n + 1) + n = 2n + 1$. Hence, $CS_{\downarrow A'}$ is $(2n + 1)$-beneficial.

We have proved that there exists a coalition structure which is n-normal and $(2n, 2n + 1)$-robust, denote it $CS_r = \{C_r, C_r^1, \ldots, C_r^n\}$. Now, it remains to show that the QBF $\exists X \forall Y. \neg \alpha$ is valid. Let us associate with CS_r the interpretation ω_X over X defined for each $i \in \{1, \ldots, n\}$ as $\omega_X(x_i) = 0$ if $C_r^i = \{b_i, \bar{b}_i\}$, otherwise $\omega_X(x_i) = 1$ (in the remaining case where $C^i = \{a_i, \bar{a}_i\}$). Now, let ω_Y be any interpretation over Y. It remains to show that $\omega_X \cup \omega_Y$ does not satisfy α, i.e., there exists a clause from α which is not satisfied by $\omega_X \cup \omega_Y$. With ω_Y we associate the set $A' \subseteq A$ characterized as follows: for each $i \in \{1, \ldots, n\}$, $\{a_i, b_i\} \subseteq A'$ and $\{\bar{a}_i, \bar{b}_i\} \cap A' = \emptyset$ if $\omega_Y(y_i) = 0$, otherwise $\{\bar{a}_i, \bar{b}_i\} \subseteq A'$ and $\{a_i, b_i\} \cap A' = \emptyset$. Note that for each $i \in \{1, \ldots, n\}$, A' contains exactly one element among $\{a_i, \bar{a}_i\}$ and exactly one element among $\{b_i, \bar{b}_i\}$. This means that for each $i \in \{1, \ldots, n\}$, $C_r^i \cap A'$ is a singleton set and thus $v(C_r^i \cap A') = 1$

(condition (iv)). So $v(CS_{r\downarrow A'}) = v(C_r \cap A') + v(C_r^1 \cap A') + \cdots + v(C_r^n \cap A') = v(C_r \cap A') + n$. Yet CS_r is $(2n, 2n+1)$-robust, so that $v(CS_{r\downarrow A'}) \geq 2n+1$, and thus $v(C_r \cap A') \geq n+1$, which means that $C_r \cap A'$ satisfies condition (i), (ii) or (iii). But by construction of A', one can see that $C_r \cap A'$ does not satisfy condition (i), so it satisfies condition (ii). We will show that the clause that enables condition (ii) to be satisfied, is not satisfied by $\omega_X \cup \omega_Y$. Let p_q be a literal from a clause from condition (ii):

- Assume first that $p_q = x_l$ for some $l \in \{1, \ldots, n\}$.
    - If x_l is a positive literal, then we know that $p(p_q) = x(x_l) = \{a_l, \bar{a}_l\}$. Since $\{a_l, \bar{a}_l\} \cap C_r \cap A' \neq \emptyset$, it follows that $C_r^l = \{b_l, \bar{b}_l\}$. But then $\omega_X(x_l) = 0$.
    - If x_l is a negative literal, we analogously conclude that $\omega_X(x_l) = 1$.
  In both cases ω_X does not satisfy the clause when $p_q = x_l$ for some $l \in \{1, \ldots, n\}$.
- So assume now the remaining case holds, i.e., that $p_q = y_m$ for some $m \in \{1, \ldots, n\}$.
    - If y_m is a positive literal, then $p(p_q) = y(y_m) = \{a_m, b_m\}$. Since $\{a_m, b_m\} \cap C_r \cap A' \neq \emptyset$, we can conclude that $\{a_m, b_m\} \subseteq A'$ and thus $\omega_Y(y_m) = 0$.
    - If y_m is a negative literal, we analogously conclude that $\omega_Y(y_m) = 1$.
  In both cases ω_Y does not satisfy the clause when $p_q = y_m$ for some $m \in \{1, \ldots, n\}$.

We have just shown that the QBF $\exists X \forall Y. \neg \alpha$ is valid, which concludes this part of the proof.

We have shown that the QBF $\forall X \exists Y. \alpha$ is valid if and only if there does not exist a coalition structure CS which is $(2n+1, 2n)$-robust, which means that the complementary problem RCSG is $\mathbf{\Pi_2^p}$-hard. Therefore, RCSG is $\mathbf{\Sigma_2^p}$-hard. $\square$

Beyond the decision problem of RCSG, the following optimization problem could be considered: one sets a robustness threshold k and intend to optimize the beneficialness of the coalition structure; or one sets a beneficialness threshold u and intend to optimize the robustness of the coalition structure. We can also view the RCSG problem as a bi-objective constraint optimization problem, and be interested in computing Pareto optimal (i.e., non-dominated) coalition structures.

4   The AmorCSG Algorithm

We now describe AmorCSG, our complete algorithm to compute the coalition structure of maximum beneficialness. The algorithm is based on the integer-partitioning (IP) approach [10, 17]. We briefly describe the IP-approach and refer to the original works [10, 17] for more details. It starts by decomposing the search space into disjoint parts (*integer partitions*) and applies branch-and-bound to each subspace. Every integer partition of n (the number of agents) defines a subspace by associating the integers in the partition to the number of agents in each coalition (e.g. $1 + 3$ is a subspace with two coalitions with one and three agents). Note that the integer partitions generated by n are non-overlapping. The main advantage of the decomposition is that effective upper bounds can be calculated for partial solutions from a particular partition, which is an essential for pruning the search space in the branch-and-bound algorithm. Our algorithm follows the same structure as the IP algorithm, with the addition of the following important components: calculation of the robustness for coalitions and coalition structures, robust upper bounds, and our pruning technique for branch-and-bound. These are described in detail below. The pseudo-code of AmorCSG is given in Algorithm 1 and 2.

Algorithm 1. Branch-And-Bound Subspace Search

input: $CSG, I = [I_0, .., I_{m-1}], k$
output: CS in subspace I with the highest $r(CS, k)$

1 **begin**
2 | $CS^{best} \longleftarrow \emptyset; LB^{best} \longleftarrow -\infty; depth \longleftarrow 0$
3 | $CS \longleftarrow [C_0, C_1, .., C_{m-1}]$
4 | $C_i \longleftarrow \emptyset, \forall i$
5 | **while** $depth \geq 0$ **do**
6 | | **if** $depth = m$ **then**
7 | | | $depth \longleftarrow depth - 1$
8 | | | **if** $r(CS, k) > LB^{best}$ **then**
9 | | | | $LB^{best} \longleftarrow r(CS, k)$
10 | | | | $CS^{best} \longleftarrow CS$
11 | | **else**
12 | | | $C_{depth} \longleftarrow select\ next\ coalition\ not\ explored$
   | | | // if no new C_{depth} possible, backtrack
13 | | | **if** $C_{depth} = \emptyset$ **then**
14 | | | | $depth \longleftarrow depth - 1$
15 | | | | **continue**
16 | | | **if** $r(CS, k) + \sum_{depth < j < m} UB(I_j) > LB^{best}$ **then**
17 | | | | $depth \longleftarrow depth + 1$
18 | **return** CS^{best}

We considered extending other state-of-the-art CSG algorithms for RCSG namely ODP [10], ODP-IP [10], and inclusion-exclusion DP [1]. However, these approaches are not applicable to RCSG, as they are based on dynamic programming and the Bellman property does not hold for RCSG. Our method uses dynamic programming during its execution but the core part of the algorithm is branch-and-bound.

Definition 6. (Robustness of a Coalition (Structure)). Let $CSG = \langle A, v \rangle$ be a CSG problem description. For a given coalition structure CS on A and non-negative integer k, the *k-robustness* of CS, denoted $r(CS, k)$, is the maximal

---

Algorithm 2. AmorCSG Algorithm Outline

---

    input: $CSG = \langle A, v \rangle, k$
    output: $CS^* = argmax_{CS}(r(CS, k))$

1 **begin**
2     $IP \longleftarrow$ *generate integer partitions of* $|A|$
3     $UB^{rob} \longleftarrow$ *compute RobustUpperBounds(IP)* // Eq. 6
4     $LB^{best} \longleftarrow -\infty; CS^* \longleftarrow \emptyset$
5   **do**
6   **foreach** $I \in IP$ **do**
7   **if** $UB^{rob}(I) \leq LB^{best}$ **then**
8                 $IP \longleftarrow IP \setminus \{I\}$
9   **if** $IP = \emptyset$ **then**
10   **break**
11         $I_{next} \longleftarrow argmax\{UB^{rob}(I) : I \in IP\}$
12         $(val, CS) \longleftarrow searchSubspace(CSG, I, k)$ // Algorithm 1
13   **if** $val \geq LB^{best}$ **then**
14            $LB^{best} \longleftarrow val$
15            $CS^* \longleftarrow CS$
16   **while** $IP \neq \emptyset$
17   **return** CS^*

---

value u such that CS is (u, k)-robust. Similarly, the *k-robustness* of a coalition C, denoted $r(C, k)$, is the maximal value u if the coalition structure $\{\{C\}\}$ is (u, k)-robust.

Robustness Values for Each Coalition. For every coalition C we calculate $r(C, k')$ for each $k' \in [1, min(k, |C|)]$ as a preprocessing step, which represents the lowest beneficial value obtainable after removing k' agents from C. We compute $r(C, k')$ using a dynamic programming:

$$r(C, 0) = v(C), \tag{1}$$
$$r(C, k') = \min_{\substack{C' \subset C \\ |C'| = |C| - 1}} (r(C', k' - 1)), \forall k' \in [1, min(k, |C|)].$$

Robustness Values for a Particular Coalition Structure. For a given coalition structure CS we compute its robust value as $r(CS, k) = V(CS) - e(CS, k)$, where $e(CS, k)$ is defined as the optimal value of the following *multi-dimensional knapsack problem*:

$$e(CS, k) = \max \sum_{C \in CS} \sum_{j \in [1, |C|]} r(C, j) * x_{(C,j)} \tag{2}$$

$$\sum_{C \in CS} \sum_{j \in [1, |C|]} j * x_{(C,j)} \leq k \tag{3}$$

$$\sum_{j\in[1,|C|]} x_{(C,j)} \leq 1 \qquad \forall C \in CS \tag{4}$$

$$x_{(C,j)} \in \{0,1\} \qquad \forall C \in CS, j \in [1,|C|] \tag{5}$$

The value $e(CS,k)$ denotes the maximum penalty that can be achieved by removing k agents. The variables $x_{(C,j)}$ indicates if j agents are selected for removal from coalition C.

Robust Upper Bounds. For a given subspace generated by the partition $I = [I_0, I_1, \ldots, I_{m-1}]$ we compute the upper bound as:

$$UB^{rob}(I) = \max_{\substack{\sum_j v_j \leq k \\ v_j \in \mathbb{N}_0}} \left(\sum_{j\in[0,m)} (UB(max(0, I_j - y_j)))) \right) \tag{6}$$

In other words, we calculate maximum upper bound of all subspaces that can be generated by removing at most k agents from the subspace I. The upper bound of a partition I, $UB(I)$, is computed as in the integer-partition approach [10,17].

Branch-And-Bound Pruning. The partial solution CS can be pruned if it cannot be extended to a solution with a higher beneficial value than the best solution found so far (denoted LB^{best}). This is determined based on the upper bounds of the unassigned coalitions and LB^{best}:

$$r(CS,k) + \sum_{j\in[d+1,m)} (UB(I_i)) \leq LB^{best} \tag{7}$$

The solution CS can be pruned from the search if the above equation holds. Note that the (partial) solution CS has its first d coalitions assigned at search tree depth d.

4.1   Incremental Computation of R(CS, K)

The robust value $r(CS,k)$ is computed in each iteration incrementally using dynamic programming. Let c be the coalition that is added to the partial solution CS, we then have:

$$r(CS \cup c, k) = min\{r(CS, k-i) + r(c,i) | i \in [0,k]\} \tag{8}$$

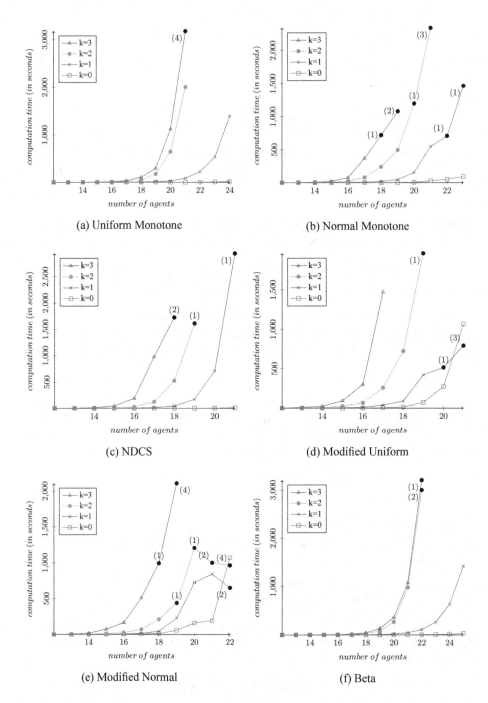

Fig. 1. Average runtime (five benchmarks for each n, the number of agents) on a variety of distributions with different values for k. Number of timeouts with a limit of 1 h shown in brackets.

5   Experimental Evaluation

We implemented AmorCSG and the integer-partition approach for CSG [10,17] in C++. The experiments were run on an Intel i7-7700HQ CPU @ 2.80 GHz with 32 GB of RAM. We experimented with instances based on several probability distributions for the characteristic function v used in the literature:

- Uniform: $v(C) = Uniform(0, |C|)$ [8].
- Normal: $v(C) = Normal(\mu = 10 * |C|, \sigma^2 = 0.1)$ [16].
- NDCS: $v(C) = Normal(\mu = |C|, \sigma^2 = \sqrt{|C|})$ [17].
- Modified uniform: $v(C) = Uniform(0, 10 * |C|) + a$, where $a = Uniform(0, 50)$ with probability 0.2 and $a = 0$ otherwise [21].
- Modified normal: $v(C) = Normal(10 * |C|, 0.01) + a$, where a is as above [15].
- Beta: $v(C) = |C| * Beta(\alpha = \beta = 0.5)$ [10].

The benchmarks were adjusted to ensure monotonicity. We compared the runtime for different values of n (number of agents) and $k \in [0, 3]$ (robustness parameter). Note that RCSG with $k = 0$ degenerates to CSG. The results are summarized in Fig. 1, averaged over five instances for each n.

The distribution used plays an important role in the execution time, more so than for standard CSG ($k = 0$). The main reason is that bounds on robustness cannot be approximated as accurately in general and this is further amplified for certain distributions. Furthermore, the strength of the robust bounds weakens with the increase in k. Hence, the algorithm must explicitly explore a large part of the search space, leading to higher run times when compared to CSG. In return, guarantees on robustness are provided.

6   Conclusion

In this paper, the robustness issue for CSG has been investigated. The contributions of this paper are as follows: A notion of robustness in the CSG framework has been formalized and shown useful. Furthermore, the corresponding decision and (bi-objective) optimization problems for RCSG have been studied and the computational complexity has been identified. Finally. a complete algorithm has been presented for solving a RCSG problem.

This work paves the way for a number of perspectives. Our complete algorithm (AmorCSG) can solve RCSG problem instances such as waste-water treatment system. For addressing large-scale RCSG instances, we plan to develop approximate algorithms. Another perspective will consist in considering the robustness issue in a *probabilistic* setting. In the framework presented in this paper, the robustness of a coalition structure is evaluated from the "worst-case" viewpoint. Another approach would be to consider each agent as "reliable" to a certain extent, e.g., by associating with each agent a_i a value $\alpha(a_i) \in [0, 1]$ standing for the probability that the agent may remain in its coalition at the next step. Obviously enough, this probabilistic setting departs from the one we proposed here. Lastly, we plan to extend our framework to a *dynamic* setting in which the set of agents A may change w.r.t. time, with the objective to apply it to a distributed robot team reconfiguration problem [4].

References

1. Björklund, A., Husfeldt, T., Koivisto, M.: Set partitioning via inclusion-exclusion. SIAM J. Comput. **39**(2), 546–563 (2009)
2. Conitzer, V., Sandholm, T.: Complexity of constructing solutions in the core based on synergies among coalitions. Artif. Intell. **170**(6–7), 607–619 (2006)
3. Dang, V., Dash, R., Rogers, A., Jennings, N.: Overlapping coalition formation for efficient data fusion in multi-sensor networks. In: AAAI, pp. 635–640 (2006)
4. Dasgupta, P., Cheng, K.: Robust multi-robot team formations using weighted voting games. In: Martinoli, A. (ed.) Distributed Autonomous Robotic Systems. STAR, vol. 83, pp. 373–387. Springer, Heidelberg (2013). https://doi.org/10.1007/978-3-642-32723-0_27
5. Dinar, A., Moretti, S., Patrone, F., Zara, S.: Application of stochastic cooperative games in water resources. In: Goetz, R.U., Berga, D. (eds.) Frontiers in Water Resource Economics. NRMP, vol. 29, pp. 1–20. Springer, Boston (2006). https://doi.org/10.1007/0-387-30056-2_1
6. Ieong, S., Shoham, Y.: Marginal contribution nets: a compact representation scheme for coalitional games. In: ACM EC, pp. 193–202 (2005)
7. Karp, R.M.: Reducibility among combinatorial problems. In: Miller, R.E., Thatcher, J.W., Bohlinger, J.D. (eds.) Complexity of Computer Computations. IRSS, pp. 85–103. Springer, Boston (1972). https://doi.org/10.1007/978-1-4684-2001-2_9
8. Larson, K., Sandholm, T.: Anytime coalition structure generation: an average case study. J. Exp. Theor. Artif. Intell. **12**(1), 23–42 (2000)
9. Lesser, V., Tambe, M., Ortiz, C. (eds.): Distributed Sensor Networks: A Multiagent Perspective. Kluwer Academic Publishers, Dordrecht (2003)
10. Michalak, T., Rahwan, T., Elkind, E., Wooldridge, M., Jennings, N.: A hybrid exact algorithm for complete set partitioning. J. Artif. Intell. **230**, 14–50 (2016)
11. Nair, R., Tambe, M.: Hybrid BDI-POMDP framework for multiagent teaming. J. Artif. Intell. Res. **23**, 367–420 (2005)
12. Ohta, N., Conitzer, V., Ichimura, R., Sakurai, Y., Iwasaki, A., Yokoo, M.: Coalition structure generation utilizing compact characteristic function representations. In: Gent, I.P. (ed.) CP 2009. LNCS, vol. 5732, pp. 623–638. Springer, Heidelberg (2009). https://doi.org/10.1007/978-3-642-04244-7_49
13. Okimoto, T., Schwind, N., Clement, M., Ribeiro, T., Inoue, K., Marquis, P.: How to form a task-oriented robust team. In: AAMAS, pp. 395–403 (2015)
14. Rahwan, T., Jennings, N.: Coalition structure generation: dynamic programming meets anytime optimization. In: AAAI, pp. 156–161 (2008)
15. Rahwan, T., Michalak, T., Jennings, N.: A hybrid algorithm for coalition structure generation. In: AAAI, pp. 1443–1449 (2012)
16. Rahwan, T., Ramchurn, S., Dang, V., Giovannucci, A., Jennings, N.: Anytime optimal coalition structure generation. In: AAAI, pp. 1184–1190 (2007)
17. Rahwan, T., Ramchurn, S., Jennings, N., Giovannucci, A.: An anytime algorithm for optimal coalition structure generation. J. Artif. Intell. Res. (JAIR) **34**, 521–567 (2009)
18. Sandholm, T.: An implementation of the contract net protocol based on marginal cost calculations. In: 11th National Conference on Artificial Intelligence, pp. 295–308 (1993)
19. Sandholm, T., Larson, K., Andersson, M., Shehory, O., Tohmé, F.: Coalition structure generation with worst case guarantees. Artif. Intell. **111**(1–2), 209–238 (1999)

20. Sandholm, T., Lesser, V.R.: Coalitions among computationally bounded agents. Artif. Intell. **94**(1–2), 99–137 (1997)
21. Service, T., Adams, J.: Approximate coalition structure generation. In: AAAI, pp. 854–859 (2010)
22. Vidal, J.: The effects of co-operation on multiagent search in task-oriented domains. J. Exp. Theor. Artif. Intell. **16**(1), 5–18 (2004)
23. Yeh, D.: A dynamic programming approach to the complete set partitioning problem. BIT Comput. Sci. Numer. Math. **26**(4), 467–474 (1986)

An Anytime Algorithm for Simultaneous Coalition Structure Generation and Assignment

Fredrik Präntare$^{(\boxtimes)}$ and Fredrik Heintz
{Fredrik.Prantare,Fredrik.Heintz}@liu.se

Linköping University, 581 83 Linköping, Sweden

Abstract. A fundamental problem in artificial intelligence is how to organize and coordinate agents to improve their performance and skills. In this paper, we consider simultaneously generating coalitions of agents and assigning the coalitions to independent tasks, and present an anytime algorithm for the *simultaneous coalition structure generation and assignment* problem. This optimization problem has many real-world applications, including forming goal-oriented teams of agents. To evaluate the algorithm's performance, we extend established methods for synthetic problem set generation, and benchmark the algorithm against *CPLEX* using randomized data sets of varying distribution and complexity. We also apply the algorithm to solve the problem of assigning agents to regions in a major commercial strategy game, and show that the algorithm can be utilized in game-playing to coordinate smaller sets of agents in real-time.

Keywords: Coalition structure generation · Assignment problem

1 Introduction

An important research challenge in the domain of artificial intelligence is to solve the problem of how to organize and coordinate multiple artificial entities (e.g. agents) to improve their performance, behaviour, and/or capabilities. There are many approaches to this, including *task allocation* [7], *assignment* algorithms [4,12,15,16,29], *multi-agent reinforcement learning* [14], and organizational paradigms [10].

Coalition formation [11,24] is a major coordination-paradigm and study of *coalitions* (flat goal-oriented organizations of agents) that has received extensive coverage in the literature over the past two decades [22]. This paradigm typically involves forming coalitions and allocating tasks, with applications in economics [30], planning [6], sensor fusion [5], wireless networks [9], and cell networks [32]. In cooperative games with transferable utility, coalition formation generally involves identifying *coalition structures* (sets of disjoint and exhaustive coalitions) that maximizes social welfare (utility) through *coalition structure*

© Springer Nature Switzerland AG 2018
T. Miller et al. (Eds.): PRIMA 2018, LNAI 11224, pp. 158–174, 2018.
https://doi.org/10.1007/978-3-030-03098-8_10

generation [20]. Coalition structure generation is NP-complete [23], and many algorithms have been presented that solves this problem, including algorithms based on dynamic programming [18,31], tree-search [21], constraint optimization [27], and hybrid techniques [19]—each with their own strengths and weaknesses, making them suitable for solving different types of problems. Variations on the coalition structure generation problem also exist, e.g. with overlapping coalitions—where agents have limited resources that they can use to partake in multiple coalitions at the same time [3,8].

Coalition structure generation and assignment (of coalitional goals) are two processes for coordination that are often treated separately—including the majority of the previous examples. This is because traditional algorithms for coalition structure generation have no notion of independent coalitional goals, even though coalitions are often described as goal-oriented organizational structures. In instances for which coordination of multiple coalitions is important, this may generate suboptimal teams for achieving and accomplishing the tasks and goals at hand, and would typically require two different utility functions: one for deciding on which coalitions to form, and one for assigning them to tasks/goals. This is potentially disadvantageous, since it is often complicated to create good utility functions (or to generate realistic performance measures), and it is not necessarily a simple task to predict how the two utility functions influence the quality of generated solutions. Also, there are many settings and scenarios in which the utility of a team not only depends on its members and the environment, but also on the task/goal it is assigned to. It would therefore be beneficial if algorithms for coalition structure generation could take advantage of goal-orientation.

To make this possible, and to address the aforementioned issues, we present an anytime algorithm that solves the *simultaneous coalition structure generation and assignment* problem by integrating coalition-to-task assignment into the formation of coalitions. We accomplish this by extending the coalition structure generation problem, and generating coalition structures for which each coalition is assigned to exactly one goal. Our algorithm can thus be used to create structured collaboration through explicit goal-orientation. Furthermore, our algorithm only requires one utility function, has the ability to prune large parts of the search space, can give worst-case guarantees on solutions, and always generates an optimal solution when run to completion.

To evaluate the algorithm's performance, we extend established methods for generating synthetic problem sets, and benchmark our algorithm against *CPLEX*—a commercial state-of-the-art optimization software. Our experiments are conducted to deduce whether the presented algorithm can handle difficult data sets efficiently. We also apply our algorithm to solve the problem of simultaneously forming and assigning groups of armies to regions in the commercial strategy game *Europa Universalis 4*, and empirically show that our algorithm can be used to optimally solve a difficult game-playing problem in real-time. Apart from being applied to strategy games, our algorithm can potentially be used to solve many important real-world problems. It could, for example, be used to form optimal cross-functional teams aimed at solving a set of problems, to assist in the organization and coordination of subsystems in an artificial entity (e.g. a robot), or to allocate tasks in multi-agent systems (e.g. multi-robot facilities). Since the algorithm is anytime and can return a valid solution even if it is interrupted prior to finishing a search, it can potentially be used in many real-world scenarios with real-time constraints as well, including time-critical systems for managing tactical decisions.

Note that this paper is the full-paper version of a previous extended abstract [17]. This version has been thoroughly revised and extended. The presented algorithm, its presentation, and the benchmarks herein, have all been significantly improved.

We begin by formalizing the problem that we solve in Sect. 2. Then, in Sect. 3, we describe our algorithm. In Sect. 4, we present the results from our experiments. Finally, in Sect. 5, we conclude with a summary.

2   Problem Formalization

The simultaneous coalition structure generation and assignment problem formalizes as:

Input: A set of agents $A = \{a_1, ..., a_n\}$, a list of tasks $T = \langle t_1, ..., t_m \rangle$, and the value $v(C, t) \mapsto \mathbb{R}$ for assigning any coalition $C \subseteq A$ to any task $t \in T$.

Output: A list of coalitions $\langle C_1, ..., C_m \rangle$ that maximizes $\sum_{i=1}^{m} v(C_i, t_i)$, where $C_i \subseteq A$ for $i = 1, ..., m$, $C_i \cap C_j = \emptyset$ for all $i \neq j$, and $\bigcup_{i=1}^{m} C_i = A$.

Note that we use the sum $V(S) = \sum_{i=1}^{m} v(C_i, t_i)$ to denote the value of a solution $S = \langle C_1, ..., C_m \rangle$ throughout this report. We also use the terms *agent* and *task* as abstractions (they can be substituted for any type of entities, e.g. resources, regions), and we use the conventions $n = |A|$ and $m = |T|$.

Now, with this in mind, and given the aforementioned input, we can also formalize this problem using a *binary integer programming* model:

$$\text{Maximize} \quad \sum_{j=0}^{2^n-1} \sum_{k=1}^{m} x_{jk} \cdot v(C^j, t_k)$$

$$\text{subject to} \quad \sum_{j=0}^{2^n-1} \sum_{k=1}^{m} x_{jk} \cdot y_{ij} = 1 \qquad i = 1, ..., n$$

$$\sum_{k=1}^{m} x_{jk} \leq 1 \qquad j = 1, ..., 2^n - 1$$

$$\sum_{j=0}^{2^n-1} x_{jk} = 1 \qquad k = 1, ..., m$$

$$x_{jk} \in \{0, 1\}$$

where $y_{ij} = 1$ if agent $a_i \in C^j$, $y_{ij} = 0$ if not, and C^j is a coalition defined through its *binary coalition-encoding* given by j over A (see Definition 1). Note that $x_{jk} = 1$ if and only if coalition C^j is to be assigned to task t_k, and that $C^0 = \emptyset$ is the only coalition that can be assigned to multiple tasks. The first constraint ensures disjoint and exhaustive coalitions, while the second and third constraints ensures coalition-to-task bijections.

Definition 1. *Binary coalition-encoding. Given a set of agents $A = \{a_1, ..., a_n\}$, and the non-negative integer $j < 2^n$ on binary form $j = b_1 2^0 + b_2 2^1 + ... + b_n 2^{(n-1)}$ with $b_i \in \{0, 1\}$ for all $i \in \mathbb{N}$, we say that the coalition $C^j \subseteq A$ has a binary coalition-encoding given by j over A if and only if $b_k = 1 \iff a_k \in C^j$ for $k = 1, ..., n$. For example, if the coalition C^j has a binary coalition-encoding given by j over $\{a_1, ..., a_n\}$, we have $C^0 = \emptyset$ for $j = 0$, $C^3 = \{a_1, a_2\}$ for $j = 3 = 11_2$, and $C^8 = \{a_4\}$ for $j = 8 = 1000_2$.*

3   Algorithm Description

To solve this optimization problem, we propose an anytime search algorithm that utilizes branch-and-bound and a search space representation based on multiset permutations of integer partitions. By doing so, our algorithm always generates optimal solutions when run to exhaustion, and solutions with worst-case guarantees when interrupted prior to finishing a search. The algorithm consists of the following major steps:

   I. Partitioning of the search space.
  II. Calculation of the bounds for partitions.
 III. Searching for solutions using branch-and-bound.

These steps are described in the following subsections.

3.1   Partitioning of the Search Space

To partition the search space, we use a search space representation that is based on *multiset permutations* (ordered arrangements) of *integer partitions* (see Definition 2). In this representation, a list of non-negative integers $\langle p_1, ..., p_m \rangle$ represents all solutions $\langle C_1, ..., C_m \rangle$ with $|C_i| = p_i$ for $i = 1, ..., m$. Note that this is, technically speaking, a *refinement* (or an extension) of Rahwan, Ramchurn, Jennings and Giovannucci's search space representation for conventional coalition structure generation [21].

Definition 2. *Integer partition. An integer partition of $y \in \mathbb{N}$ is a multiset of positive integers $\{x_1, ..., x_k\}$ such that:*

$$\sum_{i=1}^{k} x_i = y$$

For example, the multiset $\{1, 1, 2\}$ is an integer partition of 4 since $1 + 1 + 2 = 4$, and $\{1, 2, 12, 15\}$ is an integer partition of 30 since $1 + 2 + 12 + 15 = 30$.

In more detail, we generate all multiset permutations of m-sized non-negative integer partitions of n. We use the following three steps to do so:

1. First, generate the set M_1 of all integer partitions of n that has m or fewer elements. For example, if $n = 4$ and $m = 3$, then $M_1 = \{\{4\}, \{3, 1\}, \{2, 2\}, \{2, 1, 1\}\}$. Algorithms that can be used to generate these integer partitions already exist, e.g. [1, 25]. In our case, order is of no concern, and it is trivial to exclude integer partitions that have more than m elements, so any algorithm can potentially be used.
2. Generate M_2 by appending zeros to the integer partitions in M_1 (that we generated during *step 1*) until all of them have m elements. For example, if $n = 4$ and $m = 3$, then $M_2 = \{\{4, 0, 0\}, \{3, 1, 0\}, \{2, 2, 0\}, \{2, 1, 1\}\}$.
3. Now, let M_3 be the set of all multiset permutations of the multisets in M_2. For example, if $n = 4$ and $m = 3$, then $M_3 =$
   $\{\ \langle 4, 0, 0 \rangle, \langle 0, 4, 0 \rangle, \langle 0, 0, 4 \rangle, \langle 0, 2, 2 \rangle, \langle 2, 0, 2 \rangle, \langle 2, 2, 0 \rangle,$
   $\langle 3, 1, 0 \rangle, \langle 3, 0, 1 \rangle, \langle 0, 3, 1 \rangle, \langle 1, 3, 0 \rangle, \langle 1, 0, 3 \rangle, \langle 0, 1, 3 \rangle,$
   $\langle 2, 1, 1 \rangle, \langle 1, 2, 1 \rangle, \langle 1, 1, 2 \rangle\ \}$

   Each multiset permutation $\langle p_1, ..., p_m \rangle \in M_3$ represents the partition (subspace) that contains all solutions $\langle C_1, ..., C_m \rangle$ with $|C_i| = p_i$ and $C_i \subseteq A$ for $i = 1, ..., m$. For instance, if $n = 4$ and $m = 3$, the multiset permutation $\langle 3, 1, 0 \rangle$ then represents $\langle \{a_1, a_2, a_3\}, \{a_4\}, \emptyset \rangle$, $\langle \{a_1, a_2, a_4\}, \{a_3\}, \emptyset \rangle$, $\langle \{a_1, a_3, a_4\}, \{a_2\}, \emptyset \rangle$, and $\langle \{a_2, a_3, a_4\}, \{a_1\}, \emptyset \rangle$. Note that there exists several known algorithms that can generate these multiset permutations in $O(1)$ per permutation, e.g. [26, 28].

The reason that partitions represented by the multiset permutations in M_3 cover the whole search space, is the fact that every coalition structure that consists of k agents can be mapped to exactly one of the integer partitions of k (see [21] for proof). For example, the coalition structure $\{\{a_1, a_2\}, \{a_3\}\}$ can be mapped to $\{2, 1\}$, and $\{\{a_1, a_2, a_3\}\}$ to $\{3\}$. In *step 1*, we generate the partitions that correspond to these mappings. We then remove unnecessary coalition structures in *step 2*, so that we only look at coalition structures that can represent valid solutions (i.e. m-sized coalition structures). Finally, in *step 3*, we refine the representation of the search space that was generated in *step 2*, by taking advantage of the fact that we are only interested in coalition-to-task bijections.

Now, given any multiset permutation $P = \langle p_1, ..., p_m \rangle$ generated through this process, let $\mathbb{S}_P$ denote the set of all possible solutions $\langle C_1, ..., C_m \rangle$ with $|C_i| = p_i$ and $C_i \subseteq A$ for $i = 1, ..., m$. In other words, let $\mathbb{S}_P$ be the subspace of the search space that contains all solutions represented by the multiset permutation $P \in M_3$.

3.2   Calculation of the Bounds for Partitions

To establish bounds for partitions (subspaces), so that the algorithm can make more informed decisions during search, let $\mathbb{C}_p := \{X \subseteq A : |X| = p\}$, i.e. the set of all p-sized coalitions, and define:

- $M(p,t) := \max \{v(C,t) : C \in \mathbb{C}_p\}$
- $Avg(p,t) := \frac{1}{|\mathbb{C}_p|} \sum \{v(C,t) : C \in \mathbb{C}_p\}$

We can now establish an upper and a lower bound for the value of the best possible solution in $\mathbb{S}_P$ as the sums $\sum_{i=1}^m M(p_i, t_i)$ and $\sum_{i=1}^m Avg(p_i, t_i)$, respectively. For proofs, see Theorems 1 and 2. Note that this lower bound, that we base on the average values of coalitional values, is better than the one you would achieve by using the more straight-forward $\min \{v(C,t) : C \in \mathbb{C}_p\}$. A proof for this follows directly from the definition of $Avg(p,t)$.

Theorem 1. $u_P = \sum_{i=1}^m M(p_i, t_i)$ is an upper bound for the value of the best possible solution in the subspace $\mathbb{S}_P$ that is represented by $P = \langle p_1, ..., p_m \rangle$. In other words, $\sum_{i=1}^m v(C_i, t_i) \le u_P$ for all $\langle C_1, ..., C_m \rangle \in \mathbb{S}_P$.

Proof. If $\langle C_1, ..., C_m \rangle \in \mathbb{S}_P$, then $p_i = |C_i|$ for $i = 1, ..., m$. From this, it follows that:

$$M(p_i, t_i) = M(|C_i|, t_i) \tag{1}$$

Since $v(C_i, t_i) \le M(|C_i|, t_i)$ for $i = 1, ..., m$, we have:

$$\sum_{i=1}^m v(C_i, t_i) \le \sum_{i=1}^m M(|C_i|, t_i)$$

Based on this, and (1), we conclude that:

$$\sum_{i=1}^m v(C_i, t_i) \le \sum_{i=1}^m M(p_i, t_i)$$

$\square$

Theorem 2. $l_P = \sum_{i=1}^m Avg(p_i, t_i)$ is a lower bound for the value of the best possible solution in the subspace $\mathbb{S}_P$ that is represented by $P = \langle p_1, ..., p_m \rangle$. In other words:

$$l_P \le \max_{\langle C_1, ..., C_m \rangle \in \mathbb{S}_P} \{\sum_{i=1}^m v(C_i, t_i)\}$$

Proof. Recall that, for the arithmetic mean $\overline{y_1, ..., y_k}$ of a finite set $\{y_1, ..., y_k\} \subset \mathbb{R}$, the following holds:

$$\overline{y_1, ..., y_k} \le \max \{y_1, ..., y_k\} \tag{2}$$

Now, since there are $|\mathbb{C}_p|$ coalitions of size $p \in P$, we have:

$$|\mathbb{S}_P| = X_i \cdot |\mathbb{C}_{p_i}| \tag{3}$$

for some integer $X_i \in \mathbb{N}$ for $i = 1, ..., m$. This is because there are $|\mathbb{C}_{p_i}|$ different coalitions that can be assigned to task t_i, and for each coalition assigned to t_i, we have X_i ways of assigning coalitions to the other tasks $t_1, ..., t_{i-1}, t_{i+1}, ..., t_m$. Following this argument, there are exactly X_i solutions in $\mathbb{S}_P$ for which any coalition C with $|C| = p_i$ is the ith coalition. Based on this and (3), we can calculate the arithmetic mean of $\mathbb{V}_P := \{\sum_{i=1}^{m} v(C_i, t_i) : \langle C_1, ..., C_m \rangle \in \mathbb{S}_P\}$, i.e. the set of the values of the solutions in $\mathbb{S}_P$, as follows:

$$\overline{\mathbb{V}_P} = \frac{1}{|\mathbb{S}_P|} \sum_{i=1}^{m} \sum_{C \in \mathbb{C}_{p_i}} X_i \cdot v(C, t_i)$$

$$= \sum_{i=1}^{m} \sum_{C \in \mathbb{C}_{p_i}} \frac{X_i}{|\mathbb{S}_P|} \cdot v(C, t_i)$$

$$= \sum_{i=1}^{m} \sum_{C \in \mathbb{C}_{p_i}} \frac{1}{|\mathbb{C}_{p_i}|} \cdot v(C, t_i)$$

$$= \sum_{i=1}^{m} \frac{1}{|\mathbb{C}_{p_i}|} \sum_{C \in \mathbb{C}_{p_i}} v(C, t_i)$$

$$= \sum_{i=1}^{m} Avg(p_i, t_i)$$

From this and (2), we conclude:

$$\sum_{i=1}^{m} Avg(p_i, t_i) \leq \max_{\langle C_1, ..., C_m \rangle \in \mathbb{S}_P} \{\sum_{i=1}^{m} v(C_i, t_i)\}$$

□

Since the performance measure for each coalition-to-task assignment is assumed to be known, the bounds can, in practice, be calculated without having to enumerate or generate any solution. For instance, by enumerating all coalition-to-task values, the lower bounds can be calculated using a moving average.

3.3   Searching for Solutions Using Branch-and-Bound

We search for solutions by searching one partition (subspace) at a time, and discard partitions that only contain suboptimal solutions (i.e. a partition is discarded when its upper bound is lower than the value of the best solution found so far). With this in mind, consider the following observation: Finding a better solution than the best that we have found can potentially make it possible to discard (additional) partitions, and thus reduce execution time by decreasing the search space that we need to consider. To potentially take advantage of this observation, we design a mechanism, based on defining a precedence order that dictates the order for which we search partitions, that ultimately makes it possible to find better solutions more quickly, and use heuristics to guide search.

Note that the efficiency induced by any search order depends on the problem that is being solved. In our case, we assume that there exists no *a priori* knowledge in regards to the domain, except for the coalition-to-task utility function $v \mapsto \mathbb{R}$, and we instead have to take advantage of domain-independent information (e.g. partitions and their bounds). It is possible to utilize potential domain-specific information when it is available, which is likely a more efficient strategy for solving many real-world problems. In any case, the domain-independent order of precedence for searching partitions that we use is defined as follows:

$$P_1 \prec P_2 \quad \text{if} \quad u_{P_1} + l_{P_1} > u_{P_2} + l_{P_2}$$

where $P_1 \prec P_2$ denotes that the partition represented by the multiset permutation $P_1 \in M_3$ is searched before the partition represented by $P_2 \in M_3$. u_P and l_P are defined as in the previous subsection.

We use Algorithms 1 and 2 to search a subspace $\mathbb{S}_P$ (represented by the multiset permutation $P \in M_3$) for $\arg\max_{S \in \mathbb{S}_P} \boldsymbol{V}(S)$. If interrupted before termination, these algorithms return the best feasible solution found so far, denoted S'. Note that we use a notation based on brackets to indicate an element at a specific position of a list or a vector. For example, the notation $S[j]$ corresponds to the coalition $C_j \in S$, and the notation $A[i]$ corresponds to the agent $a_i \in A$.

Algorithm 1 . InitAndStartSearchSubspace(A, T, P, S', u_P)

Initializes and starts the search procedure defined in *Algorithm 2*, thus searching $\mathbb{S}_P$.

1: **if** S' is uninitialized **then**
2:      $S' \leftarrow \emptyset_{|T|}$ ▷ S' is initialized to a list of $m = |T|$ empty coalitions.
3: **end if**
4: **return** SearchSubspace($A, T, P, u_P, 1, \emptyset_{|T|}, 0.0, S'$)

To address the high memory requirements for generating and storing many multiset permutations (required for generating the precedence order), it is possible to generate and store multiset permutations in memory-bounded blocks (distinct sets of multiset permutations). These blocks can sequentially be generated and searched during partitioning. The more blocks we use, the less memory is required. In our case, we use each set $Q \in M_2$ generated in *step 2* during the partitioning phase (described in Subsection 3.1) to represent a block. In other words, each disjoint group of distinct multiset permutations *in which all multiset permutations have the same members* is searched in sequence according to some criterion. The particular criterion that we use is defined as:

$$Q_1 \prec Q_2 \quad \text{if} \quad w_{Q_1} + f_{Q_1} > w_{Q_2} + f_{Q_2}$$

Algorithm 2 . SearchSubspace(A, T, P, u, i, $\overrightarrow{S}$, $\overrightarrow{v}$, S')
Recursively searches the subspace $\mathbb{S}_P$ represented by the multiset permutation P.

1: **if** $i > |A|$ **then**   ▷ All agents have been assigned to a coalition in $\overrightarrow{S}$.
2:    **return** $\overrightarrow{S}$
3: **end if**
4: **for** $j = 1, ..., |T|$ **do**
5:    **if** $|\overrightarrow{S}[j]| \neq P[j]$ **then**
6:       $\overrightarrow{S}[j] \leftarrow \overrightarrow{S}[j] \cup \{A[i]\}$ ▷ Assign agent $A[i]$ to the coalition $\overrightarrow{S}[j]$.
7:       **if** $|\overrightarrow{S}[j]| = P[j]$ **then**   ▷ Update the intermediary values.
8:          $\overrightarrow{v} \leftarrow \overrightarrow{v} + \boldsymbol{v}(\overrightarrow{S}[j], T[j])$
9:          $u \leftarrow u - \boldsymbol{M}(P[j], T[j])$
10:       **end if**
11:       **if** $S' = \emptyset_{|T|}$ **or** $\overrightarrow{v} + u > \boldsymbol{V}(S')$ **then**   ▷ Check if a better solution is
    possible.
12:          $S'' \leftarrow$ SearchSubspace(A, T, P, u, $i+1$, $\overrightarrow{S}$, $\overrightarrow{v}$, S')
13:          **if** $S' = \emptyset_{|T|}$ **or** $\boldsymbol{V}(S'') > \boldsymbol{V}(S')$ **then**
14:             $S' \leftarrow S''$ ▷ Update the best solution found so far.
15:          **end if**
16:       **end if**
17:       **if** *interrupt* has been requested **then**
18:          **return** S'
19:       **end if**
20:       **if** $|\overrightarrow{S}[j]| = P[j]$ **then**   ▷ Reset the intermediary values.
21:          $\overrightarrow{v} \leftarrow \overrightarrow{v} - \boldsymbol{v}(\overrightarrow{S}[j], T[j])$
22:          $u \leftarrow u + \boldsymbol{M}(P[j], T[j])$
23:       **end if**
24:       $\overrightarrow{S}[j] \leftarrow \overrightarrow{S}[j] \setminus \{A[i]\}$ ▷ Remove agent $A[i]$ from the coalition $\overrightarrow{S}[j]$.
25:    **end if**
26: **end for**
27: **return** S'

---

where $Q_1 \prec Q_2$ denotes that the solutions represented by the group of multiset permutations consisting of the members $q_1, ..., q_m$ is searched before the solutions represented by the group of multiset permutations consisting of the members $p_1, ..., p_m$, where $\{q_1, ..., q_m\} = Q_1$ and $\{p_1, ..., p_m\} = Q_2$, with $Q_1 \in M_2$ and $Q_2 \in M_2$. w_Q and f_Q are defined (similarly to the partition bounds), for all $Q \in M_2$, as follows:

- $w_Q := \sum_{q \in Q} \{\max_{i=1,...,m} \boldsymbol{M}(q, t_i)\}$
- $f_Q := \sum_{q \in Q} \{\frac{1}{m} \sum_{i=1,...,m} \boldsymbol{Avg}(q, t_i)\}$

w_Q and f_Q can, similarly to partition bounds, be computed without having to enumerate or generate any solutions. Moreover, the algorithm can search these blocks in parallel using separate processes. Also, the blocks can be partitioned into several smaller parts to further decrease memory usage.

4 Evaluation and Results

A common approach to evaluating optimization algorithms is to use standardized problem instances for benchmarking. To our knowledge, no such instances exist for the simultaneous coalition structure generation and assignment problem. We therefore translate standardized problem instances from a similar domain. More specifically, we extend established methods for synthetic problem set generation used for benchmarking coalition structure generation algorithms. The extended methods are then used to generate difficult problem sets of varying distribution and complexity that we use to benchmark our algorithm against *IBM ILOG CPLEX Optimization Studio*—a commercial state-of-the-art optimization software.

Larson and Sandholm [13] provided standardized synthetic problem instances for the coalition structure generation problem by using normal and uniform probability distributions to generate randomized coalitional values. Following Rahwan et al. [21], we denote these distributions *NPD* and *UPD*, respectively. To benchmark our algorithm, we extend these distributions to our domain, so that we also take tasks into consideration. In addition to NPD and UPD, we also extend and use *NDCS*, a distribution that was proposed by Rahwan et al. [21] for benchmarking coalition structure generation algorithms. Our extensions of these probability distributions, to our task-dependent domain, are defined as follows:

- **UPD:** $v(C,t) \sim |C| \cdot \mathcal{U}(0,1)$
- **NPD:** $v(C,t) \sim |C| \cdot \mathcal{N}(1, 0.1^2)$
- **NDCS:** $v(C,t) \sim \mathcal{N}(|C|, |C|)$

where $\mathcal{N}(\sigma, \mu)$ and $\mathcal{U}(a, b)$ are the normal and uniform distributions, respectively, given a coalition $C \subseteq A$ and a task $t \in T$.

The results of our experiments that were based on these distributions, and from applying the algorithm to a commercial strategy game, are presented in Subsects. 4.2 and 4.3, respectively.

4.1 Implementation and Hardware

Our algorithm was implemented in *C++11*, and all synthetic problem sets were generated using the random number generators `normal_distribution` (for NDCS and NPD) and `uniform_real_distribution` (for UPD) from the *C++ Standard Library*. All tests were conducted using *Windows 10* (x64), an *Intel* 7700K 4200 MHz CPU, and 16 GB of 3000 MHz DDR4 memory.

4.2 Results of the Synthetic Experiments

The result of each experiment was produced by calculating the average of the resulting values (i.e. time measurements and numerical values of solution quality) from 50 generated problem sets per probability distribution and experiment.

Also, to compete on equal terms, both CPLEX and our algorithm were only allowed to use a single CPU thread during all tests (even though both approaches support parallel computing). Furthermore, the algorithms did not have any *a priori* knowledge of the problems that they were given to solve.

Note that we, throughout this section, use the abbreviation *MP* (short for multiset permutation) to denote our algorithm.

The execution time to find an optimal solution for 8 tasks is plotted using a logarithmic scale in Fig. 1, in which we benchmark MP against CPLEX with different numbers of agents, using problem sets generated with UPD, NPD and NDCS.

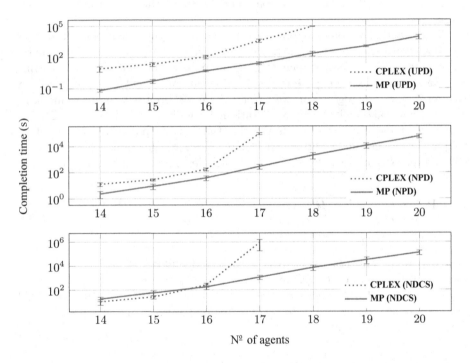

Fig. 1. Execution time for solving synthetic problems with 8 tasks. The values for the coalition-to-task assignments were generated using UPD (top), NPD (middle) and NDCS (bottom).

The results in these graphs show that our algorithm (MP) is considerably faster (by many orders of magnitude) than CPLEX for almost all distributions and problem sets. When there are more than 16 agents, CPLEX has difficulty finding optimal solutions within a reasonable time, especially for NPD and NDCS, as can be seen in the graphs above. MP, however, manages to find optimal solutions for all problems (at least up to 20 agents) within a reasonable time. In these logarithmic graphs, MP is clearly linear, while CPLEX is not. Furthermore, MP is clearly sensitive to the distribution of utility values. A potential reason for this is that the efficiency of MP depends on its ability to discard partitions. Naturally, this ability is affected by the distribution of the utility values in the problem being solved.

We plot the execution time to find an optimal solution for 16 agents in Fig. 2, and instead look at how the number of tasks (2 to 12) affect performance. We used 16 agents in these tests, since CPLEX didn't manage to find optimal solutions within a reasonable time for problems with more agents.

As can be seen in Fig. 2: CPLEX demonstrates inconsistent behaviour for problems when varying the number of tasks. This includes increased execution time in easier problems with few (2 to 4) tasks. With this in mind, our algorithm is considerably faster for most problem sets, except for those with many (8 to 12) tasks generated by NDCS. A reason could be that, when we increase the number of tasks, MP consequently generates larger integer partitions. As a consequence, the blocks generated by MP also becomes much larger, since the number of possible multiset permutations grows exponentially in the number of tasks. These multiset permutations take a considerable time to generate, even if (or when) MP discards the entire partitions that they represent.

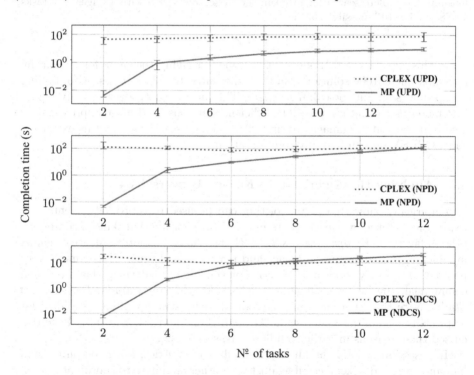

Fig. 2. Execution time to solve synthetic problems with 16 agents. Generated using UPD (top), NPD (middle) and NDCS (bottom).

In Fig. 3, we look at the quality of the anytime solutions generated by MP. We used 12 agents and 8 tasks for this purpose, and interrupted the algorithm during search by only allowing it to evaluate a fixed number of solutions. The total number of possible solutions for 12 agents and 8 tasks is $8^{12} \approx 7 \times 10^{10}$. We show the value $V_{anytime}$ of the best solution that our algorithm has found after a number of evaluated solutions, divided by the value V_{opt} of an optimal solution, on the y-axis. In this experiment, all utility values were generated using NDCS.

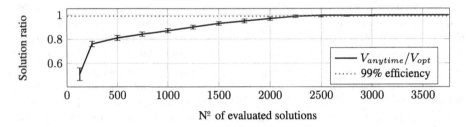

Fig. 3. The quality of anytime solutions when our algorithm is interrupted prior to finishing a complete search for problem sets based on NDCS with 12 agents, 8 tasks and $8^{12} \approx 7 \times 10^{10}$ possible solutions.

In this experiment, MP's execution time is roughly the same for evaluating any subsequent 1000 solutions, and was measured to 0.34 ± 0.27 s. Also, finding an optimal solution took 3.07 ± 1.75 s. This means that, after roughly 0.34 s, MP manages to find close to 90% efficient solutions, and after approximately 1 second, MP often manages to find 99% efficient solutions. For this execution time, CPLEX fails to find any solution at all.

4.3   Applying the Algorithm to Europa Universalis 4

To empirically show that the algorithm can be used to coordinate agents in a real-world scenario, we applied it to improve the coordination skills of computer-based players in *Europa Universalis 4* (EU4)—a very complex strategy game, in which agents are required to act and reason in real-time. This game is very popular, with many thousands of active players, and was developed and released commercially by the Swedish game development company *Paradox Development Studio*. Note that there are many reasons to why strategy games are ideal for empirically evaluating and testing AI algorithms, and other authors have discussed these reasons in earlier publications, see e.g. [2].

In a session of EU4, hundreds of simulated countries, both computer- and human-controlled alike, face off against each other, and have to coordinate themselves to defeat their opponents—they have to form alliances, coordinate armies, handle diplomacy, and wage war. To play this dynamic (and partially observable) game successfully, the players have to continuously solve simultaneous coalition structure generation and assignment problems by assigning their armies to different regions. Previously, the computer-based players in EU4 used an *ad hoc* anytime search algorithm to do so—a highly specialized algorithm designed for the context of EU4, inherently based on expert knowledge and heuristics.

In collaboration with the game's developers, we benchmarked our algorithm against theirs. To do so, we used the same problem sets (generated by the game) and utility function (based on expert knowledge and defined by the developers) for both algorithms. We ran both algorithms while the game was playing, measured the algorithms' execution time, and compared the values of the solutions that the two algorithms generated. The following constraints held for all EU4 problem sets: $n \in [1, 8]$ and $m \in [1, 35]$. However, there were at most $30^8 \approx 6.56 \cdot 10^{11}$ solutions for the largest problem sets that were generated by the game (i.e. problems with $n = 8$ armies and $m = 30$ regions).

The results from these experiments show that applying the algorithm to EU4 was a great success in terms of improving the computer-based players' performance (i.e. an increase of solution quality) and computational efficiency (i.e. reduction of execution time). In fact, our algorithm managed to find an optimal solution for all problems in less time than a game's frame (approximately $1/20 \approx 0.05\,\text{s}$)—and compared to the developer's algorithm, our algorithm decreased the execution time to, on average, 0.24% of theirs. Our algorithm also increased the numerical quality of solutions by, on average, 565% over theirs, and their algorithm seldom managed to find an optimal solution. These are the results from solving, in total, 13922 problem sets that were generated while playing the game during 3 separate simulated sessions. Note that these results are not only promising in terms of performance, but also on the basis of generalization: If the utility functions that are used in EU4 were to change (e.g. due to environment alterations), the *ad hoc* algorithm might have to be altered. This is not the case for our algorithm, since it does not make any assumptions on coalitions' utility functions, or the game's rules. Therefore, our algorithm is potentially cheaper and easier to maintain. Finally, note that EU4's environment is not superadditive: Adding an agent to a coalition does not necessarily increase its value, since the regions' have supply-based limitations that can reduce larger coalitions' values.

5   Conclusions

In this paper, we presented an anytime algorithm that solves the simultaneous coalition structure generation and assignment problem by integrating assignment into the formation of coalitions. We are, to the best of our knowledge, the first to study and solve this problem in a formal context.

Moreover, to benchmark the presented algorithm, we extended established methods for benchmarking coalition structure generation algorithms to our domain, and then used synthetic problem sets to empirically evaluate its performance. We benchmarked our algorithm against CPLEX, due to the lack of specialized algorithms for the simultaneous coalition structure generation and assignment problem.

Our results clearly demonstrate that our algorithm is superior to CPLEX in solving synthetic instances of the simultaneous coalition structure generation and assignment problem. Also, our algorithm does not have to search for very long before it can find high-quality solutions—even when interrupted prior to finishing a complete search. This is beneficial in many real-time systems (e.g. real-world multi-agent systems), in which feasible solutions must be available fast, but optimality is not necessarily required. Apart from these properties, our algorithm is able to give worst-case guarantees on solutions.

By using our algorithm to improve the coordination of computer-based players in Europa Universalis 4, we demonstrated that it can be used to solve a real-world simultaneous coalition structure generation and assignment problem more efficiently than previous algorithms.

For future work, it would be interesting to investigate other approaches to solving this problem, including dynamic programming and greedy algorithms. We also intend to analyze the algorithm's parallel computing performance, and look at the problem of simultaneous coalition structure generation and assignment with overlapping coalitions. Finally, it would be interesting to see if machine learning could be applied to solve large-scale simultaneous coalition structure generation and assignment problems, or increase our algorithm's performance by improving its search heuristics.

Acknowledgments. This work was partially supported by the Wallenberg AI, Autonomous Systems and Software Program (WASP) funded by the Knut and Alice Wallenberg Foundation.

References

1. Andrews, G., Eriksson, K.: Integer Partitions. Cambridge University Press, Cambridge (2004)
2. Buro, M.: Real-time strategy games: a new AI research challenge. In: International Joint Conference on Artificial Intelligence, pp. 1534–1535 (2003)
3. Chalkiadakis, G., Elkind, E., Markakis, E., Polukarov, M., Jennings, N.R.: Cooperative games with overlapping coalitions. J. Artif. Intell. Res. **39**, 179–216 (2010)
4. Chu, P.C., Beasley, J.E.: A genetic algorithm for the generalised assignment problem. Comput. Oper. Res. **24**(1), 17–23 (1997)
5. Dang, V.D., Dash, R.K., Rogers, A., Jennings, N.R.: Overlapping coalition formation for efficient data fusion in multi-sensor networks. In: AAAI, vol. 6, pp. 635–640 (2006)
6. Dukeman, A., Adams, J.A.: Hybrid mission planning with coalition formation. Auton. Agents Multi-Agent Syst. **31**(6), 1424–1466 (2017)
7. Gerkey, B.P., Matarić, M.J.: A formal analysis and taxonomy of task allocation in multi-robot systems. Int. J. Robot. Res. **23**(9), 939–954 (2004)
8. Habib, F.R., Polukarov, M., Gerding, E.H.: Optimising social welfare in multi-resource threshold task games. In: An, B., Bazzan, A., Leite, J., Villata, S., van der Torre, L. (eds.) PRIMA 2017. LNCS (LNAI), vol. 10621, pp. 110–126. Springer, Cham (2017). https://doi.org/10.1007/978-3-319-69131-2_7
9. Han, Z., Poor, H.V.: Coalition games with cooperative transmission: a cure for the curse of boundary nodes in selfish packet-forwarding wireless networks. IEEE Trans. Commun. **57**(1), 203–213 (2009)

10. Horling, B., Lesser, V.: A survey of multi-agent organizational paradigms. Knowl. Eng. Rev. **19**(4), 281–316 (2004)
11. Kelso, A.S., Crawford, V.P.: Job matching, coalition formation, and gross substitutes. Econometrica: J. Econ. Soc. 1483–1504 (1982)
12. Kuhn, H.W.: The hungarian method for the assignment problem. Nav. Res. Logist. (NRL) **2**(1–2), 83–97 (1955)
13. Larson, K.S., Sandholm, T.W.: Anytime coalition structure generation: an average case study. J. Exp. Theor. Artif. Intell. **12**(1), 23–42 (2000)
14. Leibo, J.Z., Zambaldi, V., Lanctot, M., Marecki, J., Graepel, T.: Multi-agent reinforcement learning in sequential social dilemmas. In: Proceedings of the 16th Conference on Autonomous Agents and MultiAgent Systems, pp. 464–473. International Foundation for Autonomous Agents and Multiagent Systems (2017)
15. Munkres, J.: Algorithms for the assignment and transportation problems. J. Soc. Ind. Appl. Math. **5**(1), 32–38 (1957)
16. Pentico, D.W.: Assignment problems: a golden anniversary survey. Eur. J. Oper. Res. **176**(2), 774–793 (2007)
17. Präntare, F., Ragnemalm, I., Heintz, F.: An algorithm for simultaneous coalition structure generation and task assignment. In: An, B., Bazzan, A., Leite, J., Villata, S., van der Torre, L. (eds.) PRIMA 2017. LNCS (LNAI), vol. 10621, pp. 514–522. Springer, Cham (2017). https://doi.org/10.1007/978-3-319-69131-2_34
18. Rahwan, T., Jennings, N.R.: An improved dynamic programming algorithm for coalition structure generation. In: Proceedings of the 7th International Joint Conference on Autonomous Agents and Multiagent Systems, vol. 3, pp. 1417–1420. International Foundation for Autonomous Agents and Multiagent Systems (2008)
19. Rahwan, T., Michalak, T.P., Jennings, N.R.: A hybrid algorithm for coalition structure generation. In: AAAI, pp. 1443–1449 (2012)
20. Rahwan, T., Michalak, T.P., Wooldridge, M., Jennings, N.R.: Coalition structure generation: a survey. Artif. Intell. **229**, 139–174 (2015)
21. Rahwan, T., Ramchurn, S.D., Jennings, N.R., Giovannucci, A.: An anytime algorithm for optimal coalition structure generation. J. Artif. Intell. Res. **34**, 521–567 (2009)
22. Ray, D., Vohra, R.: Coalition formation. In: Handbook of Game Theory with Economic Applications, vol. 4, pp. 239–326. Elsevier (2015)
23. Sandholm, T., Larson, K., Andersson, M., Shehory, O., Tohmé, F.: Coalition structure generation with worst case guarantees. Artif. Intell. **111**(1–2), 209–238 (1999)
24. Shehory, O., Kraus, S.: Methods for task allocation via agent coalition formation. Artif. Intell. **101**(1–2), 165–200 (1998)
25. Stojmenović, I., Zoghbi, A.: Fast algorithms for genegrating integer partitions. Int. J. Comput. Math. **70**(2), 319–332 (1998)
26. Takaoka, T.: An $O(1)$ time algorithm for generating multiset permutations. ISAAC 1999. LNCS, vol. 1741, pp. 237–246. Springer, Heidelberg (1999). https://doi.org/10.1007/3-540-46632-0_25
27. Ueda, S., Iwasaki, A., Yokoo, M., Silaghi, M.C., Hirayama, K., Matsui, T.: Coalition structure generation based on distributed constraint optimization. In: AAAI, vol. 10, pp. 197–203 (2010)
28. Williams, A.: Loopless generation of multiset permutations using a constant number of variables by prefix shifts. In: Proceedings of the Twentieth Annual ACM-SIAM Symposium on Discrete Algorithms, pp. 987–996. Society for Industrial and Applied Mathematics (2009)
29. Yamada, T., Nasu, Y.: Heuristic and exact algorithms for the simultaneous assignment problem. Eur. J. Oper. Res. **123**(3), 531–542 (2000)

30. Yamamoto, J., Sycara, K.: A stable and efficient buyer coalition formation scheme for e-marketplaces. In: Proceedings of the Fifth International Conference on Autonomous Agents, pp. 576–583. ACM (2001)
31. Yeh, D.Y.: A dynamic programming approach to the complete set partitioning problem. BIT Numer. Math. **26**(4), 467–474 (1986)
32. Zhang, Z., Song, L., Han, Z., Saad, W.: Coalitional games with overlapping coalitions for interference management in small cell networks. IEEE Trans. Wireless Commun. **13**(5), 2659–2669 (2014)

Economic Paradigms

Cost Sharing Security Information
with Minimal Release Delay

Mingyu Guo$^{(\boxtimes)}$, Yong Yang, and Muhammad Ali Babar

The University of Adelaide, Adelaide, Australia
{mingyu.guo,ali.babar}@adelaide.edu.au
yong.yang@student.adelaide.edu.au

Abstract. We study a cost sharing problem derived from bug bounty programs, where agents gain utility by the amount of time they get to enjoy the cost shared information. Once the information is provided to an agent, it cannot be retracted. The goal, instead of maximizing revenue, is to pick a time as early as possible, so that enough agents are willing to cost share the information and enjoy it for a premium time period, while other agents wait and enjoy the information for free after a certain amount of release delay. We design a series of mechanisms with the goal of minimizing the maximum delay and the total delay. Under prior-free settings, our final mechanism achieves a competitive ratio of 4 in terms of maximum delay, against an undominated mechanism. Finally, we assume some distributions of the agents' valuations, and investigate our mechanism's performance in terms of expected delays.

Keywords: Mechanism design · Cost sharing · Bug bounty

1 Introduction

The market for software vulnerabilities—also known as bugs—is a crowded one. For those holding a serious bug to sell, there are many kinds of interested customers: the software vendors themselves that can produce official patches, the anonymous buyers in the black markets that boast greater reward [1], and many others in between—such as the vulnerability brokers.

As defined by Böhme [3], by vulnerability brokers, we refer to organizations other than software vendors that purchase vulnerabilities and produce corresponding defense services (such as intrusion detection systems [8]) for their subscribers. Bug bounty programs offered by vulnerability brokers provide greater financial incentives for vulnerability sellers, as their customers could include large corporations and government agencies that have huge budgets for security [8]. One common problem these programs have is that their subscribers are usually charged an annual subscription fee [3], while they certainly don't produce a constant number of security updates every year, and each customer may not benefit equally with each update—for example, an update that helps prevent a bug in

© Springer Nature Switzerland AG 2018
T. Miller et al. (Eds.): PRIMA 2018, LNAI 11224, pp. 177–193, 2018.
https://doi.org/10.1007/978-3-030-03098-8_11

Windows operating system would be of little interest to customers that don't use Windows at all, though they still have to pay the fixed subscription fee.

While this inequality can be trivially solved by designing as many subscription levels as necessary, we are introducing a game-theoretical model for non-profit bug bounty programs that both solves this efficiency problem and promotes general software security.

Specifically, we study the mechanism design problem of selling one bug (information regarding it) to multiple agents. The goal is not to make a profit, but we need the mechanism to cover the cost of the bug. All agents receive the bug if enough payments can be collected to cover the cost. To incentivize payments, agents who do not pay receive the bug slightly delayed. Our goal is to maximize the social welfare by minimizing the maximum and the total delay. We end up with a mechanism that is 4-competitive against an undominated mechanism in terms of maximum delay, and for expected delay, we did some experiments under some assumptions on the distributions of the agents' valuations.

Although this problem we are studying is derived from bug bounty programs, it certainly could relate to other systems. So here we define the traits that characterize the problem. The service or good that is sold has unlimited supply once funded (zero marginal cost), and cannot be retracted once given to a user. The most common examples are information and digital goods. The agents have a valuation function that is non-decreasing in terms of time: the earlier the agent gets the information, the more utility she receives. And as we are designing non-profit systems, the mechanism should be budget balanced: we charge the agents exactly the amount needed to purchase the bug which the defense information is derived from. Finally, we want to incentivize enough payments with long premium time periods (periods exclusively enjoyed by the paying agents). But we also want the premium time periods to be as short as possible so that non-paying agents can receive the information sooner, as it leads to higher social welfare.

2   Related Research

With more and more critical software vulnerabilities catching the public's attention, there's an increasing amount of literature on the market for vulnerabilities. However, we failed to identify any research that shares the same problem structure or the same goal as ours, so the following work is mostly on understanding the vulnerability market, and inspirations for future work, rather than what our study is based on.

Regarding the vendor's possible reluctance to accept and fix reported vulnerabilities responsibly, Canfield et al. [4] made quite a few recommendations on ways to incentivize vendors to fix the software's vulnerabilities responsibly, and general improvement suggestions including allowing negotiations of the severity level of discovered vulnerabilities; on the subject of how and when should bugs be disclosed to the general public. Arora et al. [2] produced numerical simulations which suggested instant disclosure of vulnerabilities to be sub-optimal. Nizovtsev and Thursby [13], unlike others, used a game-theoretic approach to show that full disclosure can be an equilibrium strategy, and commented on the pressure of instant disclosure may put on vendors may have a long-term effect that improves software quality. Also, there had been discussions on the feasibility of introducing markets for trading bugs openly [11], with some going as far as designing revenue-maximizing mechanisms for them [5,6].

Then, when introducing new bug bounty programs, it's quite necessary to consider its effect outside the expected producer and consumer population. Maillart et al. [10] proved that each newly launched program has a negative effect on submissions to existing bug bounty programs, and they also analyzed the bounty hunters' expected gains and strategies in participating in bug bounty programs. Specifically for vulnerability brokers, Kannan et al. [9] emphasized a caveat that a vulnerability broker (which is called a market-based infomediary in their paper) always has incentive to leak the actual vulnerability, as "... This leakage exposes non-subscribers to attacks from the hacker. The leakage also serves to increase the users incentives to subscribe to the infomediary's service."

Finally, we found a sorely lacking amount of literature on existing vulnerability brokers and the actual sellers of vulnerabilities. Although a few papers on these topics were located [5,6,8], we did not find any detailed models or discussions, perhaps due to the secretive nature of the cybersecurity business.

3   Model Description

We study the problem of selling one bug (with a fixed cost) to n agents. Our goal is *not* to make a profit, but we need the mechanism to cover the cost of the bug. Without loss of generality, we assume the cost of the bug is 1.

Our mechanism would generally charge a total payment of 1 from the agents (or charge 0, in which case the bug is not sold). If the bug is sold, then we provide the bug to *all* agents, including those who pay very little or do not pay at all. There are a few reasons for this design decision:

- The main goal of this non-profit system is to promote general software security, so we would like to have as many people protected from the vulnerability as possible.
- Since no cost is incurred in distributing the bug once funded, the system and the agents don't lose anything by allowing the presence of free riders.
- In practise, providing free security information encourages more agents to join the system. Under our cost sharing mechanism, including more agents actually generally leads to less individual payment and increased utilities for everyone.

To incentivize payments, if an agent has a higher valuation (is willing to pay more), then our mechanism provides the bug information to this agent slightly earlier. For the free riders, they receive the bug for free, except that there is a bit of delay. Our aim is to minimize the delay (we cannot completely get rid of the delay as it is needed for collecting payments).

We assume the bug has a life cycle of $[0, 1]$. Time 0 is when the sale starts. Time 1 is when the bug reaches its end of life cycle (or when the bug becomes public knowledge).

We use v_i to denote agent i's type. If agent i receives the bug at time t, then her valuation equals $(1 - t)v_i$. That is, if she receives the bug at time 0, then her valuation is simply v_i. If she receives the bug at time 1, then her valuation is 0.

We use $t_i^M(v_i, v_{-i})$ and $p_i^M(v_i, v_{-i})$ to denote agent i's allocation time and payment, under mechanism M, when agent i reports v_i and the other agents report v_{-i}.[1] Agent i's utility $u_i^M(v_i, v_{-i})$ is $(1 - t_i^M(v_i, v_{-i}))v_i - p_i^M(v_i, v_{-i})$.

We enforce three mechanism constraints in this paper: *strategy-proofness*, *individual rationality*, and *ex post budget balance*. They are formally defined as follows:

- Strategy-proofness: for any v_i, v_i', v_{-i},

$$(1 - t_i^M(v_i, v_{-i}))v_i - p_i^M(v_i, v_{-i}) \geq (1 - t_i^M(v_i', v_{-i}))v_i - p_i^M(v_i', v_{-i})$$

- Individual Rationality: for any v_i, v_{-i},

$$(1 - t_i^M(v_i, v_{-i}))v_i - p_i^M(v_i, v_{-i}) \geq 0$$

- Ex post budget balance[2]:
  If the bug is sold, then we must have

$$\sum_i p_i^M(v_i, v_{-i}) = 1$$

  If the bug is not sold, then we must have that for all i

$$p_i^M(v_i, v_{-i}) = 0 \text{ and } t_i^M(v_i, v_{-i}) = 1$$

We study the minimization of two different mechanism design objectives. The MAX-DELAY and SUM-DELAY are defined as follows:

$$\text{MAX-DELAY: } \max_i t_i^M(v_i, v_{-i})$$

$$\text{SUM-DELAY: } \sum_i t_i^M(v_i, v_{-i})$$

Our setting is a single-parameter setting where Myerson's characterization applies.

Claim (Myerson's Characterization [12]*).* Let M be a strategy-proof and individually rational mechanism, we must have that

---

[1] For randomized mechanisms, the allocation times and payments are the expected values over the random bits.

[2] For randomized mechanisms, we require that for all realizations of the random bits, the constraint holds.

- For any i and v_{-i}, $t_i^M(v_i, v_{-i})$ is non-increasing in v_i. That is, by reporting higher, an agent's allocation time never becomes later.
- The agents' payments are completely characterized by the allocation times. That is, p_i^M is determined by t_i^M.

$$p_i^M(v_i, v_{-i}) = v_i(1 - t_i^M(v_i, v_{-i})) - \int_{z=0}^{v_i} (1 - t_i^M(z, v_{-i})) \, dz$$

The above payment characterization also implies that both the payment $p_i^M(v_i, v_{-i})$ and the utility $u_i^M(v_i, v_{-i})$ are non-decreasing in v_i.

4   Prior-Free Settings

In this section, we focus on problem settings where we do not have the prior distributions over the agents' types. For both MAX-DELAY and SUM-DELAY, the notion of optimal mechanism is not well-defined. Given two mechanisms A and B, mechanism A may outperform mechanism B under some type profiles, and vice versa for some other type profiles.

We adopt the following dominance relationships for comparing mechanisms.

Definition 1. *Mechanism A MAX-DELAY-DOMINATES mechanism B, if*

- *for every type profile, the MAX-DELAY under mechanism A is at most[3] that under mechanism B.*
- *for some type profiles, the MAX-DELAY under mechanism A is less than that under mechanism B.*

A mechanism is MAX-DELAY-UNDOMINATED, if it is not dominated by any strategy-proof and individually rational mechanisms.

Definition 2. *Mechanism A SUM-DELAY-DOMINATES mechanism B, if*

- *for every type profile, the SUM-DELAY under mechanism A is at most that under mechanism B.*
- *for some type profiles, the SUM-DELAY under mechanism A is less than that under mechanism B.*

A mechanism is SUM-DELAY-UNDOMINATED, if it is not dominated by any strategy-proof and individually rational mechanisms.

---

[3] Tie-breaking detail: given a type profile, if under A, the bug is not sold (max delay is 1), and under B, the bug is sold (the max delay happens to be also 1), then we interpret that the max delay under A is *not* at most that under B.

For our model, one trivial mechanism works as follows:

Cost Sharing (CS)

Strategy-proofness: Yes
Individual rationality: Yes
Ex post budget balance: Yes

- Consider the following set:
  $$K = \{k \mid k \text{ values among the } v_i \text{ are at least } 1/k, 1 \le k \le n\}$$

- If K is empty, then the bug is not sold. Every agent's allocation time is 1 and pays 0.
- If K is not empty, then the highest $k^* = \max K$ agents each pays $1/k^*$ and receives the bug at time 0. The other agents receive the bug at time 1 and each pays 0.

The above mechanism is strategy-proof, individually rational, and ex post budget balanced. Under the mechanism, k^* agents join in the cost sharing and their delays are 0s, but the remaining agents all have the maximum delay 1. Both the MAX-DELAY and the SUM-DELAY are bad when k^* is small. One natural improvement is as follows:

Cost Sharing with Deadline (CSD)

Strategy-proofness: Yes
Individual rationality: Yes
Ex post budget balance: No

- Set a constant deadline of $0 \le t_C \le 1$. Under the mechanism, an agent's allocation time is at most t_C.
- Consider the following set:
  $$K = \{k \mid k \text{ values among the } v_i \text{ are at least } \frac{1}{kt_C}, 1 \le k \le n\}$$

- If K is empty, then the bug is not sold. Every agent's allocation time is t_C and pays 0.
- If K is not empty, then the highest $k^* = \max K$ agents each pays $1/k^*$ and receives the bug at time 0. The other agents receive the bug at time t_C and each pays 0.

The idea essentially is that we run the trivial cost sharing (CS) mechanism on the time interval $[0, t_C]$, and every agent receives the time interval $[t_C, 1]$ *for free*. The mechanism remains strategy-proof and individually rational. Unfortunately, the mechanism is not ex post budget balanced—even if the cost sharing failed (*e.g.*, K is empty), we still need to reveal the bug to the agents at time t_C for free. If $t_C < 1$, we have to pay the seller without collecting back any payments.

The reason we describe the CSD mechanism is because our final mechanism uses it as a sub-component, and the way it is used fixes the budget balance issue.

Example 1. Let us consider the type profile (0.9, 0.8, 0.26, 0.26). We run the cost sharing with deadline (CSD) mechanism using different t_C values:

- If we set $t_C = 0.9$, then agent 1 and 2 would receive the bug at time 0 and each pays 0.5. Agent 3 and 4 pay nothing but they have to wait until time 0.9.
- If we set $t_C = 0.7$, then agent 1 and 2 would still receive the bug at time 0 and each pays 0.5. Agent 3 and 4 pay nothing but they only need to wait until 0.7. This is obviously better.
- If we set $t_C = 0.5$, then all agents pay 0 and only wait until 0.5. However, we run into budget issue in this scenario.

We need t_C to be small, in order to have shorter delays. However, if t_C is too small, we have budget issues. The optimal t_C value depends on the type profile. For the above type profile, the optimal $t_C = \frac{0.5}{0.8} = 0.625$. When $t_C = 0.625$, agent 2 is still willing to pay 0.5 for the time interval $[0, 0.625]$ as $0.8 \times 0.625 = 0.5$.

Definition 3. *Given a type profile* $(v_1, v_2, \ldots, v_n)$, *consider the following set:*

$$K(t_C) = \{k \mid k \text{ values among the } v_i \text{ are at least } \frac{1}{kt_C}, \ 1 \le k \le n\}$$

t_C *is between 0 and 1. As* t_C *becomes smaller, the set* $K(t_C)$ *also becomes smaller. Let* t_C^* *be the minimum value so that* $K(t_C^*)$ *is not empty. If such* t_C^* *does not exist* (*e.g.*, $K(1)$ *is empty*), *then we set* $t_C^* = 1$.
t_C^* *is called the* **optimal deadline** *for this type profile.*

Instead of using a constant deadline, we may pick the optimal deadline for every type profile.

Cost Sharing with Optimal Deadline (CSOD)

Strategy-proofness: No
Individual rationality: Yes
Ex post budget balance: Yes

- For every type profile, we calculate its optimal deadline.
- We run CSD using the optimal deadline.

CSOD is ex post budget balanced. If we cannot find k agents to pay $1/k$ each for any k, then the optimal deadline is 1 and the cost sharing failed. That is, we simply do not reveal the bug (choose not to buy the bug from the seller).

Unfortunately, we gained some and lost some. Due to changing deadlines, the mechanism is not strategy-proof.

Example 2. Let us re-consider the type profile (0.9, 0.8, 0.26, 0.26). The optimal deadline for this type profile is 0.625. By reporting truthfully, agent 2 receives the bug at time 0 and pays 0.5. However, she can lower her type to 0.26 (the optimal deadline is now slightly below 1). Agent 2 still receives the bug at time 0 but only pays 0.25.

Other than not being strategy-proof, under our prior-free settings, CSOD is optimal in the following senses:

Theorem 1. *Cost sharing with optimal deadline (CSOD) is both* Max-Delay-Undominated *and* Sum-Delay-Undominated.

Proof. We first focus on Max-Delay-Undominance. Let M be a strategy-proof and individually rational mechanism that Max-Delay-Dominates CSOD.

We will prove by contradiction that such a mechanism does not exist.

Let $(v_1, v_2, \ldots, v_n)$ be an arbitrary type profile. Without loss of generality, we assume $v_1 \geq v_2 \geq \ldots v_n$. We will show that M's allocations and payments must be identical to that of CSOD for this type profile. That is, M must be identical to CSOD, which results in a contradiction.

We first consider type profiles under which the bug is sold under CSOD. We still denote the type profile under discussion by $(v_1, v_2, \ldots, v_n)$. Let k^* be the number of agents who participate in the cost sharing under CSOD.

We construct the following type profile:

$$\underbrace{(1/k^*, \ldots, 1/k^*}_{k^*}, 0, \ldots, 0) \tag{1}$$

For the above type profile, under CSOD, the first k^* agents receive the bug at time 0 and each pays $1/k^*$. By dominance assumption (both Max-Delay-Dominance and Sum-Delay-Dominance), under M, the bug must also be sold. To collect 1, the first k^* agents must each pays $1/k^*$ and must receive the bug at time 0 due to individual rationality.

Let us then construct a slightly modified type profile:

$$(v_1, \underbrace{1/k^*, \ldots, 1/k^*}_{k^*-1}, 0, \ldots, 0) \tag{2}$$

Since $v_1 \geq 1/k^*$, under M, agent 1 must still receive the bug at time 0 due to the monotonicity constraint. Agent 1's payment must still be $1/k^*$. If the new payment is lower, then had agent 1's true type been $1/k^*$, it is beneficial to report v_1 instead. If the new payment is higher, then agent 1 benefits by reporting $1/k^*$ instead. Agent 2 to k^* still pay $1/k^*$ and receive the bug at time 0 due to individual rationality.

We repeat the above reasoning by constructing another slightly modified type profile:

$$(v_1, v_2, \underbrace{1/k^*, \ldots, 1/k^*}_{k^*-2}, 0, \ldots, 0) \tag{3}$$

Due to the monotonicity constraint, agent 2 still pays $1/k^*$ and receives the bug at time 0. Had agent 1 reported $1/k^*$, he would receive the bug at time 0 and pay $1/k^*$, so due to the monotonicity constraint, agent 1 still pays $1/k^*$ and receives the bug at time 0 under type profile (3). The rest of the agents must be responsible for the remaining $(k^* - 2)/k^*$, so they still each pays $1/k^*$ and receives the bug at time 0.

At the end, we can show that under M, for the following type profile, the first k^* agents each pays $1/k^*$ and must receive the bug at 0.

$$(v_1, v_2, \ldots, v_{k^*}, 0, \ldots, 0) \tag{4}$$

For the above type profile (4), there are $n - k^*$ agents reporting 0s. For such agents, their payments must be 0 due to individual rationality. Since M MAX-DELAY-DOMINATES[4] CSOD, these agents' allocation time must be at most $\frac{1}{k^* v_{k^*}}$, which is their allocation time under CSOD (this value is the optimal deadline). We show that they cannot receive the bug strictly earlier than $\frac{1}{k^* v_{k^*}}$ under M.

Let us consider the following type profile:

$$(v_1, v_2, \ldots, v_{k^*}, \frac{k^* v_{k^*}}{k^* + 1}, \ldots, 0) \tag{5}$$

For type profile (5), agent $k^* + 1$ must receive the bug at time 0 and pay $1/(k^* + 1)$. She can actually benefit by reporting 0 instead, if under type profile (4), agents reporting 0 receive the bug at $\frac{1}{k^* v_{k^*}}^* < \frac{1}{k^* v_{k^*}}$ for free.

utility for reporting truthfully $= \dfrac{k^* v_{k^*}}{k^* + 1} - \dfrac{1}{k^* + 1}$, utility for reporting 0 $=$

$$\dfrac{k^* v_{k^*}}{k^* + 1}(1 - \dfrac{1}{k^* v_{k^*}}^*) > \dfrac{k^* v_{k^*}}{k^* + 1}(1 - \dfrac{1}{k^* v_{k^*}}) = \dfrac{k^* v_{k^*}}{k^* + 1} - \dfrac{1}{k^* + 1}$$

Therefore, for type profile (4), all agents who report 0 must receive the bug at exactly $\frac{1}{k^* v_{k^*}}$. That is, for type profile (4), M and CSOD are equivalent.

---

[4] The claim remains true if we switch to SUM-DELAY-DOMINANCE.

Now let us construct yet another modified type profile:

$$(v_1, v_2, \ldots, v_{k^*}, v_{k^*+1}, 0, \ldots, 0) \tag{6}$$

Here, we must have $v_{k^*+1} < \frac{k^* v_{k^*}}{k^*+1}$. Otherwise, under the original type profile, we would have more than k^* agents who join the cost sharing. We assume under M, agent k^*+1 receives the bug at time t and pays p. t is at most $\frac{1}{k^* v_{k^*}}$ due to the monotonicity constraint. We have

utility when the true type is v_{k^*+1} and reporting truthfully $= v_{k^*+1}(1-t) - p$

utility when the true type is v_{k^*+1} and reporting $0 = v_{k^*+1}(1 - \frac{1}{k^* v_{k^*}})$

Therefore,

$$v_{k^*+1}(1-t) - p \geq v_{k^*+1}(1 - \frac{1}{k^* v_{k^*}}) \tag{7}$$

Had agent k^*+1's type been $\frac{k^* v_{k^*}}{k^*+1}$, her utility for reporting her true type must be at least her utility when reporting v_{k^*+1}. That is,

utility when the true type is $\frac{k^* v_{k^*}}{k^*+1}$ and reporting truthfully $= \frac{k^* v_{k^*}}{k^*+1} - \frac{1}{k^*+1}$

utility when the true type is $\frac{k^* v_{k^*}}{k^*+1}$ and reporting $v_{k^*+1} = \frac{k^* v_{k^*}}{k^*+1}(1-t) - p$

That is,

$$\frac{k^* v_{k^*}}{k^*+1} - \frac{1}{k^*+1} \geq \frac{k^* v_{k^*}}{k^*+1}(1-t) - p \tag{8}$$

Combine Eqs.(7), (8), $v_{k^*+1} < \frac{k^* v_{k^*}}{k^*+1}$, and $t \leq \frac{1}{k^* v_{k^*}}$, we have $p = 0$ and $t = \frac{1}{k^* v_{k^*}}$. That is, under type profile (6), agent k^*+1's allocation and payment remain the same whether she reports 0 or v_{k^*+1}.

Repeat the above steps, we can show that under the following arbitrary profile, agent k^*+2 to n's allocation and payment also remain the same as when they report 0.

$$(v_1, v_2, \ldots, v_{k^*}, v_{k^*+1}, v_{k^*+2}, \ldots, v_n) \tag{9}$$

That is, for type profiles where the bug is sold under CSOD, M and CSOD are equivalent.

We then consider an arbitrary type profile for which the bug is not sold under CSOD. Due to the monotonicity constraint, an agent's utility never decreases when her type increases. If any agent i receives the bug at time t that is strictly before 1 and pays p, then due to the individual rationality constraint, we have that $v_i(1-t) - p \geq 0$. v_i must be strictly below 1, otherwise the bug is sold under

CSOD. Had agent i's true type been higher but still below 1 (say, to $v_i + \epsilon$), her utility must be positive, because she can always report v_i even when her true type is $v_i + \epsilon$. But earlier we proved that had v_i's true type been 1, she would receive the bug at time 0 and pay 1. Her utility is 0 when her type is 1. This means her utility decreased if we change her true type from $v_i + \epsilon$ to 1, which is a contradiction. That is, all agents must receive the bug at time 1 (and must pay 0). Therefore, for an arbitrary type profile for which the bug is not sold under CSOD, M still behaves the same.

In the above proof, all places where we reference MAX-DELAY-DOMINANCE can be changed to SUM-DELAY-DOMINANCE. □

CSOD is both MAX-DELAY-UNDOMINATED and SUM-DELAY-UNDOMINATED, but it is not strategy-proof. We now propose our final mechanism in this section, which builds on CSOD. The new mechanism is strategy-proof and its delay is within a constant factor of CSOD.[5]

Group-Based Cost Sharing with Optimal Deadline (GCSOD)

Strategy-proofness: Yes
Individual rationality: Yes
Ex post budget balance: Yes

- For agent i, we flip a fair coin to randomly assign her to either the left group or the right group.
- We calculate the optimal deadlines of both groups.
- We run CSD on both groups.
- The left group uses the optimal deadline from the right group and vice versa.

Claim. Group-based cost sharing with optimal deadline (GCSOD) is strategy-proof, individually rational, and ex post budget balanced.

Proof. Every agent participates in a CSD so strategy-proofness and individual rationality hold. Let D_L and D_R be the optimal deadlines of the left and right groups, respectively. If $D_L < D_R$, then the left group will definitely succeed in the cost sharing, because its optimal deadline is D_L and now they face an extended deadline. The right group will definitely fail in the cost sharing, as they face a deadline that is earlier than the optimal one. At the end, some agents in the left group pay and receive the bug at 0, and the remaining agents in the left group receive the bug at time D_R for free. All agents in the right group receive the bug at time D_L for free. If $D_L > D_R$, the reasoning is the same. If $D_L = D_R < 1$, then we simply tie-break in favour of the left group. If $D_L = D_R = 1$, then potentially both groups fail in the cost sharing, in which case, we simply do not reveal the bug (do not buy it from the seller). □

---

[5] That is, we fixed the strategy-proofness issue at the cost of longer delays, but it is within a constant factor.

Definition 4. *Mechanism A is α-Max-Delay-Competitive against mechanism B if for every agent i, every type profile, we have that the max delay under A is at most α times the max delay under B.*

α-Sum-Delay-Competitive *is defined similarly.*

Theorem 2. GCSOD *is* 4-Max-Delay-Competitive *against* CSOD *under two technical assumptions:*

- *No agent's valuation for the bug exceeds the whole cost. That is, $v_i \leq 1$ for all i.*
- *At least one agent does not participate in the cost sharing under* CSOD.

There's no way to ensure that the first assumption always holds, but it can be argued that it at least holds in the scenarios of cost sharing serious bugs beyond any individual's purchasing power. The second assumption is needed only because in the single case of everyone joining the cost sharing under CSOD, the max delay is 0. While under GCSOD, the max delay is always greater than 0 so it would not be competitive in this case only. And for the other assumption, as our system would welcome as many agents as possible, it is expected that there are always agents who don't value a new bug very much so that they would prefer to be free riders instead of participating in the cost sharing under CSOD.

Proof. Let us consider an arbitrary type profile that satisfies both technical assumptions. We denote it by $(v_1, v_2, \ldots, v_n)$. Without loss of generality, we assume $v_1 \geq v_2 \geq \cdots \geq v_n$. Let k^* be the number of agents who join the cost sharing under CSOD. The optimal deadline under CSOD is then $D^* = \frac{1}{k^* v_{k^*}}$, which is exactly the max delay for this type profile.

Under a specific random grouping, for the set of agents from 1 to k^*, we assume k_L agents are assigned to the left group and $k_R = k^* - k_L$ agents are assigned to the right group.

For the left group, the optimal deadline is at most $\frac{1}{k_L v_{k^*}}$ if $k_L \geq 1$, which is at most $\frac{k^*}{k_L} D^*$. When $k_L = 0$, the optimal deadline is at most 1. Under CSOD, since all types are at most 1, the optimal deadline D^* is at least $1/k^*$. That is, if $k_L = 0$, the optimal deadline of the left group is at most $k^* D^*$.

In summary, the optimal deadline of the left group is at most $\frac{k^*}{k_L} D^*$ if $k_L \geq 1$ and $k^* D^*$ if $k_L = 0$. That is, the optimal deadline of the left group is at most $\frac{k^*}{\max\{1, k_L\}} D^*$

Similarly, the optimal deadline of the right group is at most $\frac{k^*}{\max\{1, k_R\}} D^*$

The max delay under GCSOD is at most the worse of these two deadlines. The ratio between the max delay under GCSOD and the max delay under CSOD is then at most $\frac{k^*}{\max\{1, \min\{k_L, k^* - k_L\}\}}$.

We use $\alpha(k)$ to denote the expected ratio (expectation with regard to the random groupings):

$$\alpha(k) = \sum_{k_L=0}^{k} \frac{1}{2^k} \binom{k}{k_L} \frac{k}{\max\{1, \min\{k_L, k - k_L\}\}} \tag{10}$$

We define $\beta(k) = \alpha(k)2^k$.

$$\beta(k) = \sum_{k_L=0}^{k} \binom{k}{k_L} \frac{k}{\max\{1, \min\{k_L, k - k_L\}\}} = \sum_{k_L=1}^{k-1} \binom{k}{k_L} \frac{k}{\min\{k_L, k - k_L\}} + 2k$$

If k is even and at least 50, then

$$\beta(k) = \sum_{k_L=1}^{k/2-1} \binom{k}{k_L} \frac{k}{\min\{k_L, k - k_L\}} + \sum_{k_L=k/2+1}^{k-1} \binom{k}{k_L} \frac{k}{\min\{k_L, k - k_L\}} + 2\binom{k}{k/2} + 2k$$

$$= 2 \sum_{k_L=1}^{k/2-1} \binom{k}{k_L} \frac{k}{k_L} + 2\binom{k}{k/2} + 2k$$

$$\beta(k) = 2 \sum_{k_L=1}^{k/2-1} \binom{k+1}{k_L+1} \frac{(k_L+1)k}{(k+1)k_L} + 2\binom{k}{k/2} + 2k$$

$$\le 4 \sum_{k_L=1}^{k/2-3} \binom{k+1}{k_L+1} + 2\binom{k+1}{k/2-1} \frac{(k/2-1)k}{(k+1)(k/2-2)}$$

$$+ 2\binom{k+1}{k/2} \frac{(k/2)k}{(k+1)(k/2-1)} + 2\binom{k+1}{k/2} + 2k$$

$$\le 4 \sum_{k_L=1}^{k/2-3} \binom{k+1}{k_L+1} + 2.1\binom{k+1}{k/2-1} + 4.1\binom{k+1}{k/2} + 2k$$

The ratio between $\binom{k+1}{k/2}$ and $\binom{k+1}{k/2-1}$ is at most 1.08 when k is at least 50.

$$\beta(k) \le 4 \sum_{k_L=1}^{k/2-3} \binom{k+1}{k_L+1} + 4\binom{k+1}{k/2-1} + 4\binom{k+1}{k/2} + 2k \le 4 \sum_{k_L=0}^{k/2-1} \binom{k+1}{k_L+1} \le 4 \times 2^k$$

We omit the similar proof when k is odd. In summary, we have $\alpha(k) \le 4$ when $k \ge 50$. For smaller k, we numerically calculated $\alpha(k)$. All values are below 4. $\square$

Corollary 1. GCSOD *is* 8-SUM-DELAY-COMPETITIVE *against* CSOD *under two technical assumptions:*

- *No agent's valuation for the bug exceeds the whole cost. That is, $v_i \le 1$ for all i.*
- *At least half of the agents do not participate in the cost sharing under CSOD.*

Proof. Let D^* and k^* be the optimal deadline and the number of agents who join the cost sharing under CSOD. The SUM-DELAY of the agents under CSOD is $(n - k^*)D^*$. Under GCSOD, the deadlines are at most $4D^*$ according to Theorem 2. The SUM-DELAY is then at most $4D^*n$. Therefore, the competitive ratio is $\frac{4n}{n - k^*}$, which is at least 8 if $k^* \leq n/2$.   □

5   Settings with Prior Distributions

In this section, we assume that there is a publicly known prior distribution over the agents' types. Specifically, we assume that every agent's type is drawn from an identical and independent distribution, whose support is $[0, U]$. We still enforce the same set of mechanism constraints as before, namely, strategy-proofness, individually rationality, and ex post budget balance. Our aim is to minimize the *expected* MAX-DELAY or the *expected* SUM-DELAY. Our main results are two linear programs for computing the lower bounds of *expected* MAX-DELAY and *expected* SUM-DELAY. We then compare the performance of CS and GCSOD against these lower bounds.

The key idea to obtain the lower bounds is to relax the ex post budget balance constraint to the following:

– With probability $\mathbb{C}$, the bug is not sold under the optimal mechanism. $\mathbb{C}$ depends on both the mechanism and the distribution.
– Every agent's expected payment is then $(1-\mathbb{C})/n$, as the agents' distributions are symmetric.[6]
– Every agent's expected allocation time is at least $\mathbb{C}$, as the allocation time is 1 with probability $\mathbb{C}$.

We divide the support of the type distribution $[0, D]$ into H equal segments. We use δ to denote D/H. The i-th segment is then $[(i-1)\delta, i\delta]$. Noting that the agents' distributions are symmetric, we do not need to differentiate the agents when we define the following notation. We use t_i to denote an agent's expected allocation time when her type is $i\delta$. That is, t_0 is an agent's expected allocation time when her type is 0, and t_H is her expected allocation time when her type is D. Similarly, we use p_i to denote an agent's expected payment when her type is $i\delta$. The t_i and the p_i are the variables in our linear programming models.

Due to Myerson's characterization, the t_H must be non-increasing. That is,

$$1 \geq t_0 \geq t_1 \geq \cdots \geq t_H \geq 0$$

---

[6] It is without loss of generality to assume that the optimal mechanism does not treat the agents differently based on their identities. Given a non-anonymous mechanism, we can trivially create an "average" version of it over all permutations of the identities [7]. The resulting mechanism is anonymous and has the same MAX-DELAY and SUM-DELAY.

We recall that strategy-proofness and individual rationality together imply that the agents' payments are completely characterized by the allocation times. Using notation from Sect. 3, we have

$$p_i^M(v_i, v_{-i}) = v_i(1 - t_i^M(v_i, v_{-i})) - \int_{z=0}^{v_i} (1 - t_i^M(z, v_{-i}))\, dz$$

Using notation from this section, that is

$$i\delta(1 - t_i) - \sum_{z=1}^{i}(1 - t_z)\delta \le p_i \le i\delta(1 - t_i) - \sum_{z=0}^{i-1}(1 - t_z)\delta$$

$\mathbb{C}$ is another variable in our linear programming model. We use $\mathbb{P}(i)$ to denote the probability that an agent's type falls inside the i-th interval $[(i-1)\delta, i\delta]$. Since every agent's expected payment is $(1 - \mathbb{C})/n$, we have

$$\sum_{z=1}^{H} \mathbb{P}(z)p_{z-1} \le (1 - \mathbb{C})/n \le \sum_{z=1}^{H} \mathbb{P}(z)p_z$$

Since an agent's expected allocation time is at least $\mathbb{C}$, we have

$$\sum_{z=1}^{H} \mathbb{P}(z)t_{z-1} \ge \mathbb{C}$$

The expected SUM-DELAY is at least $\sum_{z=1}^{H} \mathbb{P}(z)t_z$. We minimize it to compute a lower bound for the expected SUM-DELAY.

To compute a lower bound on the expected MAX-DELAY, we introduce a few more notations:

- Let $A(i)$ be the expected MAX-DELAY when all agents report higher than $i\delta$.
- Let $P^A(i)$ be the probability that all agents report higher than $i\delta$.
- Let $B(i)$ be the expected MAX-DELAY when at least one agent reports at most $i\delta$.
- Let $P^B(i)$ be the probability that at least one agent reports at most $i\delta$.
- Let $C(i)$ be an agent's expected delay when she reports at most $i\delta$.

The expected MAX-DELAY is at least the following for any i:

$$A(i) \times P^A(i) + B(i) \times P^B(i) \ge B(i) \times P^B(i) \ge C(i) \times P^B(i)$$

We minimize (11) to compute a lower bound on the expected MAX-DELAY.

$$C(i) \times P^B(i) \ge \frac{\sum_{z=1}^{i} t_z \mathbb{P}(z)}{\sum_{z=1}^{i} \mathbb{P}(z)} \times \left\{ 1 - \left(\sum_{z=i+1}^{H} \mathbb{P}(z) \right)^n \right\} \qquad (11)$$

We present the expected delays of CS and GCSOD under different distributions. $U(0,1)$ refers to the case where every agent's valuation is drawn from

	MAX-DELAY			SUM-DELAY		
	GCSOD	CS	Lower bound	GCSOD	CS	Lower bound
$U(0,1)$, $n = 1$	1.00	1.00	0.89	1.00	1.00	0.89
$U(0,1)$, $n = 2$	0.87	0.75	0.67	1.75	1.50	0.96
$U(0,1)$, $n = 5$	0.85	0.67	0.46	2.67	1.41	0.94
$U(0,1)$, $n = 10$	0.68	0.65	0.29	3.01	1.13	0.89
$N(0.5,0.2)$, $n = 1$	1.00	1.00	0.97	1.00	1.00	0.97
$N(0.5,0.2)$, $n = 2$	0.87	0.75	0.63	1.75	1.50	0.89
$N(0.5,0.2)$, $n = 5$	0.79	0.27	0.20	2.13	0.40	0.27
$N(0.5,0.2)$, $n = 10$	0.54	0.15	0.11	2.20	0.17	0.14
$N(0.5,0.4)$, $n = 1$	0.95	0.95	0.92	0.95	0.95	0.92
$N(0.5,0.4)$, $n = 2$	0.88	0.76	0.66	1.73	1.48	0.94
$N(0.5,0.4)$, $n = 5$	0.84	0.57	0.40	2.54	1.09	0.71
$N(0.5,0.4)$, $n = 10$	0.65	0.50	0.26	2.76	0.74	0.59

the uniform distribution from 0 to 1. $N(0.5, 0.2)$ refers to the case where every agent's valuation is drawn from the normal distribution with mean 0.5 and standard devastation 0.2, conditional on that the value is between 0 and 1.

CS outperforms GCSOD in terms of both MAX-DELAY and SUM-DELAY. This is not too surprising because GCSOD is designed for its competitive ratio in the worst case. Our derived lower bounds show that CS is fairly close to optimality in a lot of cases.

6   Conclusions and Future Work

We have come up with a mechanism with competitive ratios of 4 for max delay and 8 for sum delay under certain assumptions. As the problem setting is rather new, there are plenty of options to be explored when designing mechanisms with better performance. Possible solutions showing promise include, for exmaple, another method we considered but did not dedicate as much time into—scheduling fixed prices for different sections of time periods, regardless of the agents' submitted valuations. But such a mechanism will require extensive simulations and analyses to evaluate its performance. It should also be noted that the lack of data for such simulations is to be addressed.

While most of our result is presented under prior-free settings, we made a certain number of assumptions, some of which easily hold true for realistic applications—and therefore rather trivial—some of which less so. For example, there is an assumption that there is at least one agent not participating in the cost sharing in the benchmark function CSOD. This is necessary because we cannot evaluate any mechanism's resulting time against 0 and produce a valid competitive ratio, while this can also be easily satisfied by including free-riders who are determined not to contribute at all. But for the assumption that no agent's valuation exceeds the total required amount, although it is introduced because of similar reasons, we cannot expect it to hold true for every case. So either removing existing constraints to generalize the solution or adding more assumptions to yield better results would be reasonable as immediate future work.

References

1. Algarni, A., Malaiya, Y.: Software vulnerability markets: discoverers and buyers. Int. J. Comput. Inf. Sci. Eng. **8**(3), 482–484 (2014)
2. Arora, A., Telang, R., Xu, H.: Optimal policy for software vulnerability disclosure. Manage. Sci. **54**(4), 642–656 (2008)
3. Böhme, R.: A comparison of market approaches to software vulnerability disclosure. In: Müller, G. (ed.) ETRICS 2006. LNCS, vol. 3995, pp. 298–311. Springer, Heidelberg (2006). https://doi.org/10.1007/11766155_21
4. Canfield, C., Catota, F., Rajkarnikar, N.: A national cyber bug broker: retrofitting transparency (2015). https://www.andrew.cmu.edu/user/ccanfiel/National-Cyber-Bug-Broker_final.pdf
5. Guo, M., Hata, H., Babar, A.: Revenue maximizing markets for zero-day exploits. In: Baldoni, M., Chopra, A.K., Son, T.C., Hirayama, K., Torroni, P. (eds.) PRIMA 2016. LNCS (LNAI), vol. 9862, pp. 247–260. Springer, Cham (2016). https://doi.org/10.1007/978-3-319-44832-9_15
6. Guo, M., Hata, H., Babar, A.: Optimizing affine maximizer auctions via linear programming: an application to revenue maximizing mechanism design for zero-day exploits markets. In: An, B., Bazzan, A., Leite, J., Villata, S., van der Torre, L. (eds.) PRIMA 2017. LNCS (LNAI), vol. 10621, pp. 280–292. Springer, Cham (2017). https://doi.org/10.1007/978-3-319-69131-2_17
7. Guo, M., Markakis, E., Apt, K.R., Conitzer, V.: Undominated groves mechanisms. J. Artif. Intell. Res. **46**, 129–163 (2013)
8. Howard, R.: Cyber Fraud: Tactics, Techniques and Procedures. CRC Press, Boca Raton (2009)
9. Kannan, K., Telang, R.: Market for software vulnerabilities? Think again. Manage. Sci. **51**(5), 726–740 (2005)
10. Maillart, T., Zhao, M., Grossklags, J., Chuang, J.: Given enough eyeballs, all bugs are shallow? Revisiting eric raymond with bug bounty programs. J. Cybersecur. **3**(2), 81–90 (2017)
11. Miller, C.: The legitimate vulnerability market: inside the secretive world of 0-day exploit sales. In: Sixth Workshop on the Economics of Information Security (2007)
12. Myerson, R.B.: Optimal auction design. Math. Oper. Res. **6**(1), 58–73 (1981)
13. Nizovtsev, D., Thursby, M.: To disclose or not? An analysis of software user behavior. Inf. Econ. Policy **19**(1), 43–64 (2007)

Fast Algorithms for Computing Interim Allocations in Single-Parameter Environments

Amy Greenwald, Jasper Lee, and Takehiro Oyakawa$^{(\boxtimes)}$

Brown University, Providence, RI 02912, USA
{amy_greenwald,jasperchlee,takehiro_oyakawa}@brown.edu

Abstract. Myerson's seminal work characterized optimal auctions; applied naively, however, his approach yields exponential-time algorithms. Using Border's theorem, in contrast, one can solve mechanism design problems in polynomial time. This latter approach relies on linear programming machinery, the mechanics of which are significantly more complicated than Myerson's. Motivated by the simplicity and transparency of Myerson's analysis, we present fast algorithms for computing interim allocations in simple auction settings. These methods apply to both surplus and revenue maximization, and yield *ex-ante* symmetric solutions.

Keywords: Mechanism design · Auctions · Simple algorithms

1 Introduction

In a sealed-bid auction with bidders whose values are described by a single-parameter, Vickrey [10] showed that bidders can be incentivized to bid their true value by allocating to a highest bidder, and requiring winners to pay the second highest bid. Consequently, Vickrey auctions maximize surplus. Building on this idea, Myerson [8] showed that the auctioneer can maximize the total expected revenue by allocating to a bidder with the highest virtual value, and adding to this design a reserve price. In such auctions, one may naturally ask: what is the total expected surplus and revenue, what is the probability of a bidder being allocating, and how much should each bidder expect to pay?

Note that it is straightforward to estimate total expected surplus and revenue using Monte Carlo methods. But beyond these aggregate quantities, we are also interested in the details of the mechanism, namely the allocation probabilities and payments. To answer all three of the aforementioned questions, one could apply Vickrey's or Myerson's analyses in a straightforward manner, but this would yield an exponential time algorithm—exponential in the number of bidders.[1] Alternatively, using Border's theorem, one could instead compute

---

[1] In this work, we assume discrete value distributions. Assuming continuous value distributions, the mathematical program for the expected surplus or revenue-maximizing allocations and payments can be solved analytically.

© Springer Nature Switzerland AG 2018
T. Miller et al. (Eds.): PRIMA 2018, LNAI 11224, pp. 194–209, 2018.
https://doi.org/10.1007/978-3-030-03098-8_12

the quantities of interest in polynomial time (See, for example, Cai et al. [3]). This latter approach, however, which employs linear programming, buys us no understanding of the solution.[2] This lack of intuition is problematic for bidders who want to understand their probability of winning, and how much they should expect to pay. In sum, existing methods may not allow bidders to reason about an auction's outcome in sufficient detail without spending an exponential amount of time or implementing a linear program.

In this paper, we show that in certain sealed-bid auctions, assuming bidders values are described by a single parameter, one does not need to invoke such machinery. We put forth alternative solutions, which are both fast and intuitive, and avoid the black-box nature of linear programming. Our methods apply to the "standard" dominant-strategy incentive-compatible single-good, sealed-bid; k-Vickrey; and sponsored search auctions implied by Myerson's analysis.

These three auction formats are well-defined, up to tie-breaking. As many bidders would not be satisfied with a serially dictatorial allocation scheme (see, for example, [9]), we restrict our attention to *ex-ante* symmetric mechanisms— those in which the probability of winning for each of the highest bidders is $1/Z$, when Z bidders place the highest bid. Our methods are designed to preserve the interim allocations of *ex-ante* symmetric mechanisms.[3]

In each setting, we describe how to compute interim allocations in time polynomial in the number of bidders, while preserving symmetry. Further, our methods provide intuition that justifies the resulting allocations. As a byproduct of computing interim allocations, our algorithms also output total expected surplus and revenue. Specifically, we provide three methods. We express their complexities in terms of the number of bidders n and the size of the value space $\mathfrak{K}$:

1. We show that exact interim allocations can be computed in polynomial time when there are no ties, and we use perturbations to arrive at approximately-optimal interim allocations otherwise. Our method is simple to implement, and takes $O(n \log \mathfrak{K})$ time to compute an interim allocation.
2. We also show that by sampling tie-breaking rules, we can use dynamic programming to arrive at interim allocations with small errors. This method also takes $O(n^2 \log \mathfrak{K})$ time to compute an interim allocation in the single-good setting, but extends to cases in which there are k goods.
3. Finally, we show that by using dynamic programming, we can compute exact interim allocations. This method takes $O(n^3 \log \mathfrak{K})$ time in the single-good setting, but extends to cases in which there are k goods.

Related Work. In principle, revenue maximization for some mechanism design problems can be solved using Border's characterization of interim feasible outcomes [1] and an ellipsoid-style algorithm with a separation oracle [7]. See, for

---

[2] Analogously, one can use linear programming to solve the fractional knapsack problem. A greedy approach, which is also optimal, in effect explains the solution.

[3] That said, our randomized algorithms can be extended to work for any randomized tie-breaking scheme, because any randomized tie-breaking scheme can be expressed as a convex combination of deterministic tie-breaking schemes.

example, Cai et al. [2]. However, in practice, such mechanisms tend to be expensive and do not have the simplicity and elegance of the pointwise maximization procedure Myerson's analysis yields. Additionally, recent work by Gopalan et al. [5] describes limitations to using such methods, further motivating us to seek alternative methods of solving for expected surplus and revenue, interim allocations, and interim payments. We make use of perturbations for handling ties, as Hartline [6] did for revenue curves. Additionally, we assume value distributions are discrete with finite support, as was previously studied by Elkind [4].

2   Model and Background

An auctioneer would like to sell some set of goods or services to some subset of n bidders. Each bidder $i \in N = \{1, \ldots, n\}$ has a private value (or type) $0 \leq v_i \in T_i$ that is independently drawn from some discrete distribution F_i with finite support. Let $T = T_1 \times \cdots \times T_n$ be the set of all possible value vectors (profiles), and let $F = F_1 \times \cdots \times F_n$ be the distribution over value vectors $\mathbf{v} = (v_1, \ldots, v_n) \in T$. Let the cardinality of the largest type space be $\mathfrak{K} = \max_{i \in N} |T_i|$. Let $\mathbf{b} = (b_1, \ldots, b_n) \in \mathbb{R}^n$ be a vector of bids, where the ith entry b_i is bidder i's bid. For any vector $\mathbf{y} \in \mathbb{R}^n$, we use the notation $\mathbf{y} = (y_i, \mathbf{y}_{-i})$, where $\mathbf{y}_{-i} = (y_1, \ldots, y_{i-1}, y_{i+1}, \ldots, y_n)$. Similarly, $T_{-i} = \prod_{j \neq i} T_j$ and $F_{-i} = \prod_{j \neq i} F_j$.

Given a vector of reports $\mathbf{b}$, a mechanism determines an allocation rule $\mathbf{x}(\mathbf{b}) \in [0, 1]^n$, where bidder i's allocation probability is $x_i(b_i, \mathbf{b}_{-i})$, together with a payment rule $\mathbf{p}(\mathbf{b}) \in \mathbb{R}_{\geq 0}^n$, where bidder i's payment is $p_i(b_i, \mathbf{b}_{-i})$. We define bidder i's quasi-linear utility function as $= v_i x_i(b_i, \mathbf{b}_{-i}) - p_i(b_i, \mathbf{b}_{-i})$.

Next, we formalize the usual constraints imposed on optimal auction design. Because we restrict our attention to incentive compatible auctions, where it is optimal to bid truthfully, hereafter, we write $x_i(v_i, \mathbf{v}_{-i})$ instead of $x_i(b_i, \mathbf{b}_{-i})$, and $p_i(v_i, \mathbf{v}_{-i})$ instead of $p_i(b_i, \mathbf{b}_{-i})$. We introduce **interim allocation** and **interim payment** variables, respectively: $\hat{x}_i(v_i) = \mathbb{E}_{\mathbf{v}_{-i}}[x_i(v_i, \mathbf{v}_{-i})]$ and $\hat{p}_i(v_i) = \mathbb{E}_{\mathbf{v}_{-i}}[p_i(v_i, \mathbf{v}_{-i})]$. These variables comprise the interim allocation and payment rules, $\hat{\mathbf{x}}(\mathbf{v}) \in [0, 1]^n$ and $\hat{\mathbf{p}}(\mathbf{v}) \in \mathbb{R}_{\geq 0}^n$. We call a mechanism **(Bayesian) incentive compatible** (IC) if all bidders maximize their expected utility by reporting truthfully, assuming all other bidders are reporting truthfully: $\forall i \in N$ and $\forall v_i, w_i \in T_i$, $v_i \hat{x}_i(v_i) - \hat{p}_i(v_i) \geq v_i \hat{x}_i(w_i) - \hat{p}_i(w_i)$. We say a mechanism is **Individually rational** (IR) if it insists on non-negative expected utilities: $\forall i \in N$ and $\forall v_i \in T_i$, $v_i \hat{x}_i(v_i) - \hat{p}_i(v_i) \geq 0$. A mechanism is **ex-post feasible** (XP) if it never overallocates: $\forall \mathbf{v} \in T$, $\sum_{i=1}^n x_i(v_i, \mathbf{v}_{-i}) \leq 1$. Finally, we require that $0 \leq x_i(v_i, \mathbf{v}_{-i}), \hat{x}_i(v_i) \leq 1$, $\forall i \in N$, $\forall v_i \in T_i$ and $\forall \mathbf{v}_{-i} \in T_{-i}$.

Background. Myerson's first expressed his payment theorem [8] assuming bidders draw values from continuous distributions. Here, we apply his analysis to discrete values. Specifically, we assume the distribution of values is drawn from the discrete type space $T_i = \{z_{i,k} : 1 \leq k \leq M_i\}$, of cardinality $|T_i| = M_i$, where $z_{i,j} < z_{i,k}$ for $j < k$, and we let $z_{i,|T_i|+1} = z_{i,|T_i|}$. We also assume the probability of type $z_{i,k} \in T_i$ is given by cumulative distribution function $F_i(z_{i,k})$

and corresponding probability mass function $f_i(z_{i,k})$. In addition, $f_{-i}(\mathbf{v}_{-i})$ is the probability mass function of $\mathbf{v}_{-i} \in T_{-i}$.

Theorem 1 ([8]). *An optimal mechanism is IC and IR iff for all $i \in N$: the allocation rule $\hat{\mathbf{x}}$ is monotone, i.e., $\forall v_i \geq w_i \in T_i$, $\hat{x}_i(v_i) \geq \hat{x}_i(w_i)$; and interim payment is given by: $\forall z_{i,\ell} \in T_i$, $\hat{p}_i(z_{i,\ell}) = z_{i,1}\hat{x}_i(z_{i,1}) + \sum_{k=2}^{\ell} z_{i,k} (\hat{x}_i(z_{i,k}) - \hat{x}_i(z_{i,k-1}))$.*

Myerson also proved that expected revenue can be expressed as something called expected **virtual surplus**, which he defined in terms of virtual values. Using our notation, we define **virtual values** as follows: $\psi_i(z_{i,k}, z_{i,k+1}) = z_{i,k} - (z_{i,k+1} - z_{i,k}) \left(\frac{1 - F_i(z_{i,k})}{f_i(z_{i,k})} \right)$. We use the shorthand $\psi_i(v_i) \equiv \psi_i(z_{i,k}, z_{i,k+1})$, where $v_i = z_{i,k}$ for some $1 \leq k \leq |T_i|$. We assume our distributions are regular, as in [8], so that $\psi_i(z_{i,k+1}) > \psi_i(z_{i,k})$ whenever $z_{i,k+1} > z_{i,k}$. Using the discrete version of Myerson's payment formula (Theorem 1), and following a similar analysis to that of Myerson [8], we arrive at the following theorem:

Theorem 2 ([8]). *If a mechanism is IC and IR, then $\sum_{i \in N} \mathbb{E}_{z_{i,k} \sim F_i} [\hat{p}_i(z_{i,k})] = \sum_{i \in N} \mathbb{E}_{z_{i,k} \sim F_i} [\psi_i(z_{i,k}) \hat{x}_i(z_{i,k})]$.*

In maximizing total expected virtual surplus, bidders with negative virtual values will never be allocated. Since bidders must place a bid that maps to a non-negative virtual value in order to be allocated, each bidder i has a **reserve price**, $\psi_i^{-1}(0)$, which is the smallest bid she may place in order to possibly be allocated, and the smallest possible payment she must make when allocated.

Using Myerson's analysis, we can maximize either objective—total expected surplus, $\mathbb{E}_{\mathbf{v} \sim F}[\mathbf{v} \cdot \mathbf{x}(\mathbf{v})]$, or virtual surplus, $\mathbb{E}_{\mathbf{v} \sim F}[\psi(\mathbf{v}) \cdot \mathbf{x}(\mathbf{v})]$—by solving the problem pointwise, meaning solving for an optimal allocation for each $\mathbf{v}$ in turn, subject only to ex-post feasibility. This can be done (see Algorithm 2) while preserving *ex-ante* symmetry, without using a serially dictatorial allocation scheme. The ensuing interim allocations can then be supported with Myerson's payments, thereby ensuring IC and IR. However, this procedure is exponential in time, as it requires iterating over all $O(\mathfrak{K}^n)$ value vectors. We will present a scheme for computing *ex-ante* symmetric interim allocations in polynomial time.

3   Perturbing (Virtual) Values

In this section, we show how one can perturb (virtual) values and compute interim allocations in polynomial time. We first describe how, when all types are unique, interim allocations can be computed exactly in polynomial time. We then handle the general case, by making use of perturbed (virtual) values, and bounding the errors that may result from this method.

3.1   Special Case: No Ties

We describe how, in the single-good setting, the expected revenue from each bidder can be described by a partition of calculations in which at most one bidder can be allocated. This partitioning does not change the fact that calculating total expected revenue takes an exponential amount of time. However, in the very special case of no ties, this partitioning leads to a polynomial-time calculation.

Bidder i can only be allocated when the following criteria are met:

- i has placed a bid that meets i's reserve price: $\psi_i(v_i) \geq 0$, and
- i's virtual value is the highest: $\psi_i(v_i) \geq \max_{j \in N \setminus i} \psi_j(v_j)$.

Let $w(\mathbf{v})$ be the set of bidders that can potentially be allocated, i.e., $w(\mathbf{v}) = \{i : \psi_i(v_i) \geq 0, \psi_i(v_i) \geq \max_{j \in N \setminus i} \psi_j(v_j), \forall i \in N\}$. The ex-ante probability that a bidder is allocated depends on whether there are any ties or not, and is given by $x_i(v_i, \mathbf{v}_{-i}) = 1_{i \in w(\mathbf{v})} / |w(\mathbf{v})|^{-1}$ if $w(\mathbf{v})$ non-empty, and 0 otherwise. We know that i will not be allocated when she bids less than her reserve price; only values at least as large as the reserve price may be allocated. Let $\tau_i^{\geq 0}$ be the set of bidder i's values that at least match her reserve price: $\tau_i^{\geq 0} = \{z_{i,k} : \psi_i(z_{i,k}) \geq 0, \forall z_{i,k} \in T_i\}$. Similarly, we know that bidder i is guaranteed not to be allocated when there exists any other bidder with virtual value larger than i's. Specifically, in order for i to win with value $z_{i,k}$, the other bidders virtual values must be at most $\psi_i(z_{i,k})$. Let $\tau_{-i}^{\leq \psi_i(z_{i,k})}$ be the set of profiles other bidders may have where i's virtual value, $\psi_i(z_{i,k})$, is at least as large as any other: $\tau_{-i}^{\leq \psi_i(z_{i,k})} = \{\mathbf{v}_{-i} : \max_{j \in N \setminus i} \psi_j(v_j) \leq \psi_{i,k}(z_{i,k}), \forall \mathbf{v}_{-i} \in T_{-i}\}$. We can now express the interim allocation $\hat{x}_i(z_{i,k})$ as follows: $\hat{x}_i(z_{i,k}) = \sum \{x_i(z_{i,k}, \mathbf{v}_{-i}) f_{-i}(\mathbf{v}_{-i}) \mid \mathbf{v}_{-i} \in \tau_{-i}^{\leq \psi_i(z_{i,k})}\}$. Furthermore, we can partition the calculation of total expected revenue from bidder i as follows: $\sum_{1 \leq k \leq |T_i|} \psi_i(z_{i,k}) f_i(z_{i,k}) \hat{x}_i(z_{i,k}) = \sum_{z_{i,k} \in \tau_i^{\geq 0}} \psi_i(z_{i,k}) f_i(z_{i,k}) \hat{x}_i(z_{i,k})$. This total expected revenue formula involves only a subset of T. However, as indicated by our expression for total expected revenue this subset is still exponential in size. Next, we observe that when there are no ties, computing total expected revenue can be done in polynomial time.

Assuming no ties, when i wins, $x_i(v_i, \mathbf{v}_{-i}) = 1$. Let $\tau_{-i}^{< \psi_i(z_{i,k})}$ be the set of profiles other bidders may have where i's virtual value, $\psi_i(z_{i,k})$, is *strictly* larger than any other: $\tau_{-i}^{< \psi_i(z_{i,k})} = \{\mathbf{v}_{-i} : \max_{j \in N \setminus i} \psi_j(v_j) < \psi_{i,k}(z_{i,k}), \forall \mathbf{v}_{-i} \in T_{-i}\}$. In this strict case, the interim allocation is $\hat{x}_i(z_{i,k}) = \sum_{\mathbf{v}_{-i} \in \tau_{-i}^{< \psi_i(z_{i,k})}} f_{-i}(\mathbf{v}_{-i})$. Finally, since we are working with independently distributed random variables, the interim allocation calculation is no longer exponential: $\hat{x}_i(z_{i,k}) = \prod_{j \neq i} \Pr(\psi_i(z_{i,k}) > \psi_j(z_{j,\ell})) = \prod_{j \neq i} \sum_{z_{j,\ell} : \psi_i(z_{i,k}) > \psi_j(z_{j,\ell})} f_j(z_{j,\ell})$. In other words, assuming no ties, interim allocations can be computed in polynomial time. Consequently, we can also compute total expected revenue in polynomial time in this case.

We describe this procedure in Algorithm 1, where L_i denotes i's virtual value function. Algorithm 1 runs in polynomial time. For each bidder, setting $\hat{x}_i(z_{i,k})$ to 0 for all $z_{i,k} \in T_i \setminus \tau_{i,L_i}^{\geq 0}$ is $O(\mathfrak{K})$, while computing $\hat{x}_i(z_{i,k})$ is $O(n\mathfrak{K})$. We note that we can improve this run time by precomputing all the F_i, and then running binary search. In this way, an interim allocation can be found in $O(n \log \mathfrak{K})$ time. For any fixed bidder i, running the interim allocation computation for all

---

Algorithm 1. Optimized Pointwise Maximizer (No Ties)

1: **for all** $i \in N$ **do**
2:     **for all** $z_{i,k} \in T_i \setminus \tau_{i,L_i}^{\geq 0}$ **do** $\triangleright \, \tau_{i,L_i}^{\geq 0} = \{z_{i,k} : L_i(z_{i,k}) \geq 0, \forall z_{i,k} \in T_i\}$
3:        $\hat{x}_i(z_{i,k}) \leftarrow 0$
4:     **end for**
5:     **for all** $z_{i,k} \in \tau_{i,L_i}^{\geq 0}$ **do** $\triangleright$ Calculate interim allocations
6:        $\hat{x}_i(z_{i,k}) \leftarrow \prod_{j \neq i} \sum_{z_{j,\ell}:L_i(z_{i,k})>L_j(z_{j,\ell})} f_j(z_{j,\ell})$
7:     **end for**
8:     **for** $\ell = 1$ **to** $|T_i|$ **do** $\triangleright$ Calculate interim payments
9:        $\hat{p}_i(z_{i,\ell}) \leftarrow z_{i,1}\hat{x}_i(z_{i,1}) + \sum_{k=2}^{\ell} z_{i,k}(\hat{x}_i(z_{i,k}) - \hat{x}_i(z_{i,k-1}))$
10:    **end for**
11: **end for**
12: $S \leftarrow \sum_{i=1}^{n} \mathbb{E}_{z_{i,\ell}}[z_{i,\ell}\hat{x}_i(z_{i,\ell})]$ $\triangleright$ Total expected surplus
13: $R \leftarrow \sum_{i=1}^{n} \mathbb{E}_{z_{i,\ell}}[\hat{p}_i(z_{i,\ell})]$ $\triangleright$ Total expected revenue
14: **return** S, R, $\hat{\mathbf{x}}$, $\hat{\mathbf{p}}$

$z_{i,k} \in \tau_{i,L_i}^{\geq 0}$ is $O(n\mathfrak{K}^2)$, and computing every $\hat{p}_i(z_{i,\ell})$ is $O(\mathfrak{K})$, as we only require constant time to compute $\hat{p}_i(z_{i,\ell+1})$ using $\hat{p}_i(z_{i,\ell})$. Therefore, determining all interim allocations takes $O(n^2\mathfrak{K}^2)$, and determining all interim payments takes $O(n\mathfrak{K})$. Computing S takes $O(n\mathfrak{K})$. Computing R takes $O(n\mathfrak{K})$. Therefore, the complexity of Algorithm 1 is $O(n^2\mathfrak{K}^2)$, or $O(n^2\mathfrak{K}\log\mathfrak{K})$, if we precompute all the F_i.

Remark 1. When there are no ties, and L_i is the identity function, Algorithm 1 provides a way of maximizing total expected surplus in polynomial time.

Remark 2. Generalizing the interim allocation computation used in Algorithm 1 beyond the one-good setting may increase the complexity to undesirable levels. For example, consider the k-Vickrey auction, in which there are k identical goods for sale, and assume the bidders have unit demands. Those bidders who are not among the top k are not allocated. For $k > 1$, we need to consider all the ways in which i can be the $1 \leq \ell \leq k$-th highest bidder. For each type, this takes $O(n^k)$.

Next, we adapt Algorithm 1 to the general case when there are ties.

3.2 Breaking Ties with Perturbations

At this point, we have observed that one can calculate total expected revenue in polynomial-time when there are no ties. It remains, then, to show how ties can also be handled in polynomial-time. Here, we show how this can be done by *perturbing* (virtual) values.

Similar to Hartline's perturbation approach [6], our strategy for handling ties will be to transform any set of virtual values into one that is guaranteed to have no ties, without changing the allocation function too much. In this section, we show that we can modify virtual values slightly so that

- any virtual value larger (smaller) than any other virtual value continues to remain larger (smaller), and
- any virtual value above (below) the reserve price remains above (below) the reserve price.

This method will yield, in expectation, allocations described by a pointwise maximizer which preserves tie-breaking probabilities and does not employ a serially dictatorial allocation scheme. However, if one is interested in an outcome that uses a serially dictatorial allocation method, then the method described in this section can be adapted to do so.

More formally, our perturbations satisfy the following two lemmas.

Lemma 1. *There exists an $\epsilon_A \in \mathbb{R}_{>0}$ such that for all $r_{i,k} \in [0,1]$, if $\psi_i(z_{i,k}) > \psi_j(z_{j,\ell})$, then $\psi_i(z_{i,k}) + r_{i,k}\epsilon_A > \psi_j(z_{j,\ell}) + r_{j,\ell}\epsilon_A$, for all $i,j \in N$, $1 \leq k \leq |T_i|$, $1 \leq \ell \leq |T_j|$.*

Computing an ϵ_A can be done in polynomial time. Given unique virtual values, one can construct a set of absolute differences of all unique virtual values S, and then let $\epsilon_A = \min S/2$. If all virtual values are the same, then $\epsilon = 1$ suffices.

Lemma 2. *There exists an $\epsilon_B \in \mathbb{R}_{>0}$ such that for all $r_{i,k} \in [0,1]$, if $\psi_i(z_{i,k}) \geq 0$, then $\psi_i(z_{i,k}) + r_{i,k}\epsilon_B \geq 0$, and if $\psi_i(z_{i,k}) < 0$, then $\psi_i(z_{i,k}) + r_{i,k}\epsilon_B < 0$, for all $i,j \in N$, $1 \leq k \leq |T_i|$, $1 \leq \ell \leq |T_j|$.*

Computing an ϵ_B can be done in polynomial time. Given a set of non-zero virtual values S, one can set $\epsilon_B = \min|\psi|/2$, where ψ is the smallest absolute value of the elements in S.

We say that an ϵ is a **valid** ϵ if it satisfies the properties named in Lemmas 1 and 2 (and restated in Theorem 4.3). The existence of a valid ϵ is given by the following theorem:

Theorem 3. *There exists a valid $\epsilon \in \mathbb{R}_{>0}$ such that for all $r_{i,k} \in [0,1]$, the following properties hold:*

- *if $\psi_i(z_{i,k}) > \psi_j(z_{j,\ell})$, then $\psi_i(z_{i,k}) + r_{i,k}\epsilon > \psi_j(z_{j,\ell}) + r_{j,\ell}\epsilon$,*
- *if $\psi_i(z_{i,k}) \geq 0$, then $\psi_i(z_{i,k}) + r_{i,k}\epsilon \geq 0$, and*
- *if $\psi_i(z_{i,k}) < 0$, then $\psi_i(z_{i,k}) + r_{i,k}\epsilon < 0$,*

for all $i,j \in N$, $1 \leq k \leq |T_i|$, $1 \leq \ell \leq |T_j|$.

Theorem 3 tells us that unique virtual values may be changed without affecting their ordering among other virtual values, and non-negative (negative) virtual values can likewise be changed and remain non-negative (negative). Thus, perturbing a unique virtual value will not alter its corresponding allocation.

Even more interesting, any tied virtual values which are perturbed will no longer be so, provided that changes to virtual values are unique. We use this observation to compute total expected revenue in polynomial time.

Let the **perturbed virtual value function** $\tilde{\psi}_i : T_i \to \mathbb{R}$ be defined as $\tilde{\psi}_i(z_{i,k}) = \psi_i(z_{i,k}) + r_{i,k}\epsilon, \forall z_{i,k} \in T_i$, where all $r_{i,k}$ variables are drawn independently from a continuous uniform distribution. Since all $r_{i,k}$ variables are being drawn from a continuous distribution, the probability that $r_{i,k} = r_{j,\ell}$ is 0, so each bidder's perturbed virtual values should be unique.

Remark 3. Due to machine precision issues, non-unique $r_{i,k}$ terms may appear in an actual implementation of the perturbed virtual value function. To ensure correctness, a check may be implemented to see if this is ever the case, and a new set of $r_{i,k}$ values may be drawn if non-uniqueness is observed. Drawing $O(n\mathfrak{K})$ random numbers and checking for uniqueness is $O(n\mathfrak{K})$, so this should not greatly affect runtime. For example, one may check for uniqueness by inserting each $r_{i,k}$ into a hash table, keeping track of the number of times each $r_{i,k}$ is seen.

Notice that drawing $r_{i,k}$ from a $U(0,1)$ distribution is akin to picking a winner at random when there are ties. This means that we can compute total expected revenue without any error despite using perturbed virtual values when determining allocations, as computing interim allocations and interim payments can each be computed in polynomial time.

Theorem 4. *Total expected revenue can be computed in polynomial time using perturbed virtual value functions.*

Remark 4. Our choice of ϵ and $r_{i,k}$ ensures that virtual values are perturbed upwards. While it may be possible to perturb virtual values down with an appropriate choice of ϵ and values drawn from, say, a $U(-1,1)$ distribution, so that $\tilde{\psi}_i(z_{i,k}) < \psi_i(z_{i,k})$ is possible, any virtual value equal to zero may become negative. Our choice of ϵ and $U(0,1)$ was made to avoid this possibility, so that a bidder with a zero virtual value may be allocated.

The analysis and remark given is not specific to virtual values, and can be applied to values as well. We can construct a **perturbed value function**, $\tilde{v}_i : T \to \mathbb{R}$, where $\tilde{v}_i(z_{i,k}) = z_{i,k} + r_{i,k}\epsilon'$ for all $i \in N$, $\forall z_{i,k} \in T_i$, with a valid ϵ' computed using values instead of virtual values.

Corollary 1. *Total expected surplus can be computed in polynomial time using perturbed value functions.*

Perturbing (virtual) values once and running Algorithm 1 may not yield a good estimate of interim allocations. Next, we show that by running Algorithm 1 multiple times, the interim allocations we compute will be close to optimal.

3.3   Interim Allocations and Payments

Given that we can, in polynomial time, compute interim allocations, even in the presence of ties, we can now argue that multiple runs of Algorithm 1 allows us to obtain *ex-ante* symmetric interim allocations.

Let $\mathbf{v}$ be a bidder profile where multiple bidders have the highest virtual value. Ordinarily, each bidder $i \in w(\mathbf{v})$ has probability $p = |w(\mathbf{v})|^{-1}$ of being allocated: i.e., $x_i(v_i, \mathbf{v}_{-i}) = p$. However, by using perturbed virtual values, allocations $\tilde{x}_i(v_i, \mathbf{v}_{-i})$ are either 0 with probability $1 - p$, or 1 with probability p. This means $\mathbb{E}[\tilde{x}_i(v_i, \mathbf{v}_{-i})] = 1(p) + 0(1 - p) = p$. While $x_i(v_i, \mathbf{v}_{-i}) \neq \tilde{x}_i(v_i, \mathbf{v}_{-i})$, it holds that $x_i(v_i, \mathbf{v}_{-i}) = \mathbb{E}[\tilde{x}_i(v_i, \mathbf{v}_{-i})]$.

Observe that $\tilde{x}_i(v_i, \mathbf{v}_{-i})$ is a Bernoulli random variable with mean p and variance $p(1-p)$. Assuming multiple runs of Algorithm 1, let $\tilde{x}_i^d(v_i, \mathbf{v}_{-i})$ be an allocation of the dth run. Let $y_{i,D}(\mathbf{v}) = \frac{\sum_{d=1}^{D} \tilde{x}_i^d(\mathbf{v})}{D}$ be the estimate of $\tilde{x}_i(\mathbf{v})$ after D observations of vector $\mathbf{v}$. By Chebyshev's inequality, for a fixed $a > 0$, $\Pr(|y_{i,D}(\mathbf{v}) - x_i(\mathbf{v})| \geq a) \leq \frac{p(1-p)}{a^2 D}$. This suggests that for a fixed $\mathbf{v}$, we can recover a good estimate of the allocation $x_i(v_i, \mathbf{v}_{-i})$ with high probability after a few runs of Algorithm 1.

Interim allocations $\hat{x}_i(v_i)$ are dependent on the outcomes $x_i(v_i, \mathbf{v}_{-i})$ for every $\mathbf{v}_{-i} \in T_{-i}$. Let $\chi(v_i)$ be the set of $\mathbf{v}_{-i}$ in which i may win, but ties with at least one other bidder: $\chi(v_i) = \{\mathbf{v}_{-i} \in T_{-i} : |w(v_i, \mathbf{v}_{-i})| > 1, i \in w(v_i, \mathbf{v}_{-i})\}$. To obtain a good estimate of an interim allocation $\hat{x}_i(v_i)$, we can use a union bound to determine how many times we should run Algorithm 1:

$$\sum_{\mathbf{v}_{-i} \in \chi(v_i)} \Pr\left(|y_{i,D}(v_i, \mathbf{v}_{-i}) - x_i(v_i, \mathbf{v}_{-i})| \geq a\right) \leq \sum_{\mathbf{v}_{-i} \in \chi(v_i)} \frac{(1 - |w(v_i, \mathbf{v}_{-i})|^{-1})}{|w(v_i, \mathbf{v}_{-i})| a^2 D}.$$

In words, Chebyshev's inequality tells us that the number of times we should run Algorithm 1 is directly proportional to the number of ties there are. When there are no ties, only one run is sufficient. An exponential number of ties would require an exponential number of runs to recover a good estimate of interim allocations. With a good estimate of interim allocations, a good estimate of interim payments can then be computed using Myerson's payment formula.

Remark 5. Like Myerson [8], we assumed our distributions are regular, so that $\psi_i(z_{i,k+1}) > \psi_i(z_{i,k})$ whenever $z_{i,k+1} > z_{i,k}$. However, some works, such as [6], use regularity to describe distributions so that virtual values are not strictly increasing with respect to value. By adding small perturbations, we cannot guarantee that $\tilde{\psi}_i(z_{i,k+1}) \geq \tilde{\psi}_i(z_{i,k})$ whenever $\psi_i(z_{i,k+1}) = \psi_i(z_{i,k})$. In expectation, whenever $\psi_i(z_{i,k+1}) = \psi_i(z_{i,k})$, $\mathbb{E}\left[\tilde{\psi}_i(z_{i,k+1})\right] = \mathbb{E}\left[\tilde{\psi}_i(z_{i,k})\right]$, so averaging the result across multiple runs of Algorithm 1 preserves virtual value monotonicity, and hence allocation monotonicity, in expectation.

We next describe our second method of computing interim allocations, which involves sampling tie-breaking schemes, and extends to multiple goods.

4   Sampling Tie-Breaking Schemes

Our analysis of interim allocations thus far applies only in the case of a single good. We now present simple randomized algorithms that use dynamic programming to estimate interim allocations. These algorithms apply to the k-Vickrey auction and to sponsored search.

Recall that in a k-Vickrey auction, there are k identical goods, and they are allocated to the k highest bidders. As usual, we assume symmetric random tie-breaking. Equivalently, a random permutation of bidder priorities can be sampled before the auction, with ties then broken according to this permutation.

We characterize the k-Vickrey auction allocation process (from the perspective of bidder 1), assuming a deterministic tie-breaking permutation π, as:

1. Initialize counts L, which keeps track of the number of bids higher than bidder 1's, and R, which keeps track of the number of bids lower than bidder 1's, to 0.
2. For bidder i from 2 to n:
   (a) Case 1: $v_i > v_1$, then increment L.
   (b) Case 2: $v_i = v_1$ and $\pi(i) > \pi(1)$, then increment L.
   (c) Otherwise: increment R.
3. If $L \geq k$, then $x_1(v_1, \mathbf{v}_{-1}) = 0$, otherwise $x_1(v_1, \mathbf{v}_{-1}) = 1$.

From this, we can derive a dynamic programming algorithm for calculating the interim allocation of bidder 1 assuming the deterministic tie-breaking permutation π. We compute a table T, where $T(i, \ell)$ is the probability that the value of variable L is equal to ℓ after the ith iteration in the characterization, assuming that the bidder values $\mathbf{v}_{-1}$ are drawn from F_{-1}. Initialize all entries to be 0. Then set $T(i = 1, \ell = 0) = 1$. Now for $2 \leq i \leq n$ and $0 \leq \ell < n$, the table T satisfies the following recurrence:

$$- T(i, \ell) = \Pr_{v_i \sim F_i}(v_i \geq v_1) T(i-1, \ell-1) + \Pr_{v_i \sim F_i}(v_i < v_1) T(i-1, \ell).$$

With this table, the interim allocation of bidder 1 given value v_1 is $\sum_{\ell < k} T(n, \ell)$.

If we randomly sampled a uniform π, the expected value of the above dynamic program is the interim allocation we seek. This gives us a simple randomized framework for estimating the interim allocation of bidder 1 (and, in general, any bidder i) in the case of fair tie-breaking, given her value of v_1:

1. For m times:
   (a) Sample a uniformly random tie-breaking permutation π of bidders.
   (b) Compute the interim allocation of bidder 1 using π.
2. Return the average interim allocation.

Observe that interim allocations in these settings, using any tie-breaking permutation, are bounded in $[0, 1]$. Letting p_{v_1} be the probability that $\mathbf{v}_{-1}$ requires tie-breaking for the allocation of bidder 1, then the variance of the interim allocation of bidder 1 over the randomness of the permutation is bounded by $\Theta(p_{v_1})$. Thus, in order to achieve an estimation accuracy of $\epsilon' = \frac{\epsilon}{n}$ with probability $1 - \frac{\delta}{n\mathfrak{K}}$ in each of the interim allocations (per player and type), we can calculate a sufficient *sample complexity* m for the above algorithm using the tail bound of Bernstein's inequality, $\Pr_{X_i \text{ i.i.d.}}\left(|\bar{X} - \mathbb{E}[X_1]| > \epsilon'\right) \leq 2e^{-\frac{m\epsilon'^2}{2(\text{Var}[X_1] + \frac{1}{3}\epsilon')}}$, for X_i i.i.d. random variables bounded in $[0, 1]$, and $\bar{X} = \frac{\sum_{i=1}^m X_i}{m}$. So, $m = \Theta\left(\left(\frac{p_{v_1} n^2}{\epsilon^2} + \frac{1}{\epsilon}\right) \log \frac{n\mathfrak{K}}{\delta}\right)$ suffices. Note that for value distributions that do not concentrate around a few support elements, the probability p_{v_1} is going to be small.

To interpret the accuracy and failure probability we chose, n is the number of bidders and $\mathfrak{K}$ is the maximum cardinality of the type space of any bidder. Therefore, with probability $1 - \delta$, none of the interim allocations of any player and any type have estimates more than $\frac{\epsilon}{n}$ away from the truth. With these accuracy bounds, we can compute the interim payments per bidder per type to accuracy $\frac{\epsilon V}{n}$, where V is the maximum range of the type space of any bidder. Similarly, the expected payment per bidder, from the perspective of the mechanism designer, is estimated to within accuracy $\frac{\epsilon V}{n}$. The sum over bidders gives an estimate of the expected revenue to an additive error of ϵV.

Summarizing, the above algorithm estimates the expected revenue in an auction to an additive error of ϵV, with probability at least $1 - \delta$.

The time complexity for calculating an interim allocation is $\tilde{O}(mn^2)$, since the allocation process takes $O(n^2 \log \mathfrak{K})$ time to simulate. In the regime of constant ϵ and δ, the run time of this randomized algorithm scales in the worst case as $O(n^4 \log n\mathfrak{K})$, when the probability of ties is large, meaning a concentration of value probabilities. However, in practice, values are not often concentrated around discrete values, so the estimate should converge faster than $\tilde{O}(n^4)$ time.

This framework can be generalized to the setting of *sponsored search*. In this setting, there are k non-identical slots on a search webpage, with $\alpha_1 \geq \cdots \geq \alpha_k$ click-through rates, and $\alpha_i = 0$ for $i > k$. The allocation assigns the ith highest bidder to slot i for $i \leq k$. That is, $x_i(v_i, \mathbf{v}_{-i}) = \alpha_{\text{rank}(i)}$, where rank($i$) is the rank of b_i in the bid vector, again breaking ties randomly and symmetrically.

In order to estimate the interim allocations for sponsored search, we slightly modify the dynamic programming algorithm that was used to calculate interim allocations using a deterministic tie-breaking rule. We still compute the table T as described, but the returned answer is now $\sum_{\ell < k} T(n, \ell) \alpha_{\ell+1}$. The rest of the estimation algorithm, and the complexity analysis, are unchanged.

We have thus far presented two randomized methods of computing interim allocations. We next present our final method of computing interim allocations, which does not involve randomization and yields exact solutions.

5   Deterministic Algorithms for Interim Allocations

Above we presented randomized algorithms for estimating interim allocations in the single good, k-Vickrey, and sponsored search settings. We now present deterministic dynamic programs that compute these interim allocations exactly.

Single Good Auctions. The interim allocations in a single good auction can be calculated precisely, without randomization, even in the case of possible ties. The following characterization of the allocation process determines, given a bid vector, the allocation of bidder 1 with symmetric tie breaking:

1. Initialize a boolean variable B, which indicates if bidder 1 loses, to false, and a count E, which keeps track of the number of ties, to 0.
2. For bidder i from 2 to n:
   (a) If $v_i > v_1$, then set B to true.
   (b) If $v_i = v_1$, then increment E.
3. If B is true, then $x_1(v_1, \mathbf{v}_{-1}) = 0$, otherwise $x_1(v_1, \mathbf{v}_{-1}) = \frac{1}{E+1}$.

Using this characterization, we can compute the interim allocation of bidder 1, given her value v_1, by a dynamic programming algorithm. We compute a table T, where $T(i, b, e)$ is the probability that the values of variables B and E are equal respectively to b and e after the ith iteration in the characterization, assuming that the bidder values $\mathbf{v}_{-1}$ are drawn from F_{-1}. Initialize all entries to be 0. Then set $T(i = 1, b = \text{false}, e = 0) = 1$. For $2 \le i \le n$ and $0 \le e < n$, the table T satisfies the following recurrence:

- $T(i, \text{true}, e) = \text{Pr}_{v_i \sim F_i}(v_i > v_1)(T(i - 1, \text{true}, e) + T(i - 1, \text{false}, e)) + \text{Pr}_{v_i \sim F_i}(v_i = v_1)T(i - 1, \text{true}, e - 1) + \text{Pr}_{v_i \sim F_i}(v_i < v_1)T(i - 1, \text{true}, e)$
- $T(i, \text{false}, e) = \text{Pr}_{v_i \sim F_i}(v_i = v_1)T(i - 1, \text{false}, e - 1) + \text{Pr}_{v_i \sim F_i}(v_i < v_1)T(i - 1, \text{false}, e)$.

Then, the interim allocation of bidder 1 given value v_1 is $\sum_e \frac{T(n, \text{false}, e)}{e+1}$.

k-Vickrey Auctions and Sponsored Search. We generalize from single good auctions to k-Vickrey auctions, and present a polynomial time dynamic programming algorithm to compute the interim allocations, and hence also the interim payments and expected revenue.

We refine our characterization of the allocation process from the single good auction to the following:

1. Initialize counts L, which keeps track of the number of bids higher than bidder 1's, and E, which keeps track of the number of bids tied with bidder 1's, and R, which keeps track of the number of bids lower than bidder 1's, to 0.
2. For bidder i from 2 to n:
   (a) If $v_i > v_1$, then increment L, else if $v_i = v_1$, increment E, otherwise increment R.
3. If $L \ge k$, then $x_1(v_1, \mathbf{v}_{-1}) = 0$, otherwise $x_1(v_1, \mathbf{v}_{-1}) = \frac{1}{E+1}$.

Then, to calculate the interim allocation for bidder 1, we adapt the above dynamic programming algorithm to compute a new table T', where $T'(i, \ell, e)$ is the probability that the values of variables L and E are ℓ and e respectively after the ith iteration. Initialize all entries to be 0. Then set $T(i = 1, \ell = 0, e = 0) = 1$. For $2 \le i \le n$, $0 \le \ell < n$, and $0 \le e < n$, the adapted recurrence is as follows:

- $T'(i, \ell, e) = \text{Pr}_{v_i \sim F_i}(v_i > v_1)T'(i-1, \ell-1, e) + \text{Pr}_{v_i \sim F_i}(v_i = v_1)T'(i-1, \ell, e-1) + \text{Pr}_{v_i \sim F_i}(v_i < v_1)T'(i-1, \ell, e)$.

For the sponsored search setting, Bidder 1's interim allocation is instead $\sum_{(\ell < k, e)} T'(n, \ell, e)\frac{\sum_{i=\ell+1}^{\ell+e+1} \alpha_i}{e+1}$, where α_i is the allocation to the ith highest bidder.

The complexity of this algorithm is $O(n^3 \log \Re)$: the table is of $O(n^3)$ size and the probabilities in the recurrence can be computed in time logarithmic in the size of the type spaces. Such run time is no worse than the run time given in Sect. 4, for fixed ϵ and δ.

Comparing our last method to the earlier ones, we find that there is a tradeoff between accuracy and run time. Although this last method computes interim allocations exactly, depending on use case, a randomized algorithm that produces very accurate estimates may be more, or less, useful than an exact algorithm.

6 Conclusion

We show how to solve for the interim allocation function in a variety of single-parameter auction settings. In the classic single-good setting, we show how one can modify Myerson's exponential-time pointwise-maximization approach to compute interim allocations in polynomial time. We then show how one can use randomness to estimate the interim allocation function by perturbing (virtual) values. These methods enable fast computation of the interim quantities and estimation of total expected surplus and revenue in the single-good setting.

We then go on to show how one can use dynamic programming in the single-good setting, and beyond. We present both deterministic and randomized algorithms that compute interim allocations in the k-Vickrey and the sponsored-search settings. While the randomized methods provide a simple and intuitive way of estimating interim allocations, the deterministic methods are exact—and both preserve symmetry regardless of ties. All of our algorithms presented have a common theme: in order to accurately compute interim allocations, we must deal with the issue of *ties*. It is easy to claim victory over the lesser; much less so over equals. The combinatorial issues involving ties leads to multiple paths in understanding probabilities of winning. In the future, we plan to investigate the effect of ties in more complicated single-parameter auction settings, such as knapsack auctions.

Acknowledgments. This research was supported by NSF Grant #1217761.

Appendix

A Proofs

A.1 Proof of Lemma 1

Proof. Consider any set of virtual values $\psi_1 > \psi_2 > \psi_3$. For $c, d \in \{1, 2, 3\}$, let $\delta_{c,d} = (\psi_c - \psi_d)$ for $c < d$. Let r_c be any number in $[0, 1]$. The difference between any r_c and r_d cannot exceed 1, so $\delta_{c,d} = (\psi_c - \psi_d) \geq (r_d - r_c)\delta_{c,d}$. Let $0 < \epsilon_A < \epsilon_A^U = \min\{\delta_{c,d} : c, d \in \{1, 2, 3\}, c < d\}$. Then we have $(\psi_c - \psi_d) > (r_d - r_c)\epsilon_A$, so $\psi_c + r_c\epsilon_A > \psi_d + r_d\epsilon_A$. See Fig. 1.

Fig. 1. Graphical depiction of the proof of Lemma 1. Any change of the virtual values by ϵ_A preserves the ordering of virtual values.

A.2   Proof of Lemma 2

Proof. Let ϵ_B^U be the minimum of the absolute value of the set of all non-zero virtual values: $\epsilon_B^U = \min\{|\psi_i(z_{i,k})| : \psi_i(z_{i,k}) \neq 0, \forall i \in N, \forall z_{i,k} \in T_i\}$. Let $0 < \epsilon_B < \epsilon_B^U$. Any virtual value $\psi_i(z_{i,k}) \geq 0$ can have ϵ_B added to it and remain non-negative. Similarly, any virtual value $\psi_i(z_{i,k}) < 0$ can have ϵ_B added to it and remain negative, since $\epsilon_B < |\psi_i(z_{i,k})|$. See Fig. 2.

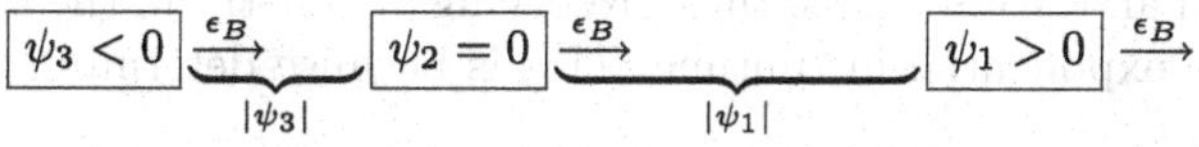

Fig. 2. Graphical depiction of the proof of Lemma 2. Any change of the virtual values by ϵ_B does not change whether virtual values are negative or not.

A.3   Proof of Theorem 3

Proof. Lemma 1 shows the existence of an ϵ_A which satisfies the first property, and Lemma 2 shows the existence of an ϵ_B which satisfies the latter properties. These values are not unique: for any ϵ_A, ϵ_B, we can construct an $\epsilon_A' < \epsilon_A$ and $\epsilon_B' < \epsilon_B$. Thus, the minimum of ϵ_A and ϵ_B satisfies all three properties of the theorem.

A.4   Proof of Theorem 4

Proof. For any value vector $\mathbf{v} \in T$, Algorithm 1 will allocate only to bidders with the highest non-negative virtual value. As defined earlier, let $w(\mathbf{v})$ be the set of bidders with the highest virtual value. Suppose instead of virtual values, we used perturbed virtual values. Let $\tilde{w}(\mathbf{v})$ be the set of bidders with the highest perturbed virtual values that have met their reserve price:

$$\tilde{w}(\mathbf{v}) = \left\{ i : \tilde{\psi}_i(v_i) \geq 0, \tilde{\psi}_i(v_i) \geq \max_{j \in N \setminus i} \tilde{\psi}_j(v_j), \forall i \in N \right\}.$$

Using a valid ϵ guarantees that the intersection of $w(\mathbf{v})$ and $\tilde{w}(\mathbf{v})$ is nonempty. If there are no ties, then $w(\mathbf{v}) = \tilde{w}(\mathbf{v})$.

The interesting case is when there are ties. Since all perturbed virtual values are unique, $|w(\mathbf{v}) \cap \tilde{w}(\mathbf{v})| = 1$, and the unique bidder $i^* \in w(\mathbf{v}) \cap \tilde{w}(\mathbf{v})$ contributes $\psi_{i^*}(v_{i^*})$ to the total expected virtual surplus. The probability that $i \in \tilde{w}(\mathbf{v})$ is allocated depends on the perturbations. Since perturbations are drawn independently and uniformly at random, the $r_{i,k}$ values act as tie-breaking rules, where the probability that any $j \in w(\mathbf{v})$ wins is uniform over the cardinality of $w(\mathbf{v})$, just as in Algorithm 2. The maximum virtual surplus attained from any convex combination of winners in $w(\mathbf{v})$ where $\sum_{j \in w(\mathbf{v})} x_j(v_j, \mathbf{v}_{-j}) = 1$ is $\sum_{j \in w(\mathbf{v})} \psi_j(v_j) x_j(v_j, \mathbf{v}_{-j}) = \max_{j \in w(\mathbf{v})} \psi_j(v_j)$, which is the outcome of Algorithm 2. In Algorithm 1, the virtual surplus given by $\mathbf{v}$ is $\psi_{i^*}(v_{i^*})$. Since $\max_{j \in w(\mathbf{v})} \psi_j(v_j) = \psi_{i^*}(v_{i^*})$, the contribution any $\mathbf{v} \in T$ has on total expected revenue is equivalent in both algorithms.

B   Algorithms

B.1   Pointwise Maximization

Algorithm 2 describes the pointwise approach in detail for the one-good setting, where, when maximizing total expected surplus is the objective, each L_i is the identity function. When maximizing total expected revenue, each L_i is the virtual value function. Further notice that Algorithm 2 preserves tie-breaking probabilities in allocation terms, thus preserving symmetry in the final outcome. Algorithm 2 is exponential in runtime. This is because determining the interim

---

Algorithm 2. Pointwise Maximizer

1: **for all** $\mathbf{v} \in T$ **do**   ▷ Find allocations
2:     $\mathbf{x}(\mathbf{v}) \leftarrow \mathbf{0}$
3:     **if** any of the $L_i(v_i)$'s are positive **then**
4:         $w \leftarrow \arg\max_i \{L_i(v_i)\}$
5:         **for all** $i^* \in w$ **do**
6:             $x_{i^*}(v_{i^*}, \mathbf{v}_{-i^*}) \leftarrow 1/|w|$
7:         **end for**
8:     **end if**
9: **end for**
10: **for all** $i \in N$ **do**   ▷ Compute interim quantities
11:     **for** $\ell = 1$ to $|T_i|$ **do**
12:         $\hat{x}_i(z_{i,\ell}) \leftarrow \mathbb{E}_{\mathbf{v}_{-i}}[x_i(z_{i,\ell}, \mathbf{v}_{-i})]$
13:         $\hat{p}_i(z_{i,\ell}) \leftarrow z_{i,1}\hat{x}_i(z_{i,1}) + \sum_{k=2}^{\ell} z_{i,k}\left(\hat{x}_i(z_{i,k}) - \hat{x}_i(z_{i,k-1})\right)$
14:     **end for**
15: **end for**
16: $S \leftarrow \sum_{i=1}^{n} \mathbb{E}_{z_{i,\ell}}[z_{i,\ell}\hat{x}_i(z_{i,\ell})]$ ▷ Total expected surplus
17: $R \leftarrow \sum_{i=1}^{n} \mathbb{E}_{z_{i,\ell}}[\hat{p}_i(z_{i,\ell})]$ ▷ Total expected revenue
18: **return** S, R, $\hat{\mathbf{x}}$, $\hat{\mathbf{p}}$

---

allocation takes exponential time. Indeed, if we are given interim allocations, we can solve for interim payments, total expected surplus, and total expected revenue in polynomial time. Thus, we see that the bottleneck is computing interim allocations, and is the main subject of this paper. We first analyze the one-good setting in detail, and then analyze other single-parameter settings. There are $O(\mathfrak{K}^n)$ value vectors in T. For each value vector, determining allocations is $O(n)$, so determining all allocations is $O(n\mathfrak{K}^n)$. Each $\hat{x}_i(z_{i,\ell})$ is computed in $O(\mathfrak{K}^{n-1})$, so determining all interim allocations takes $O(n\mathfrak{K}^n)$. Each $\hat{p}_i(z_{i,\ell})$ is computed in $O(\mathfrak{K})$, so determining all interim payments takes $O(n\mathfrak{K}^2)$. Computing S is done in $O(n\mathfrak{K})$. Computing R is done in $O(n\mathfrak{K})$. Therefore, the complexity of Algorithm 2 is $O(n\mathfrak{K}^n)$.

References

1. Border, K.C.: Implementation of reduced form auctions: a geometric approach. Econ. J. Econ. Soc. **59**, 1175–1187 (1991)
2. Cai, Y., Daskalakis, C., Weinberg, S.M.: Optimal multi-dimensional mechanism design: reducing revenue to welfare maximization. In: 2012 IEEE 53rd Annual Symposium on Foundations of Computer Science (FOCS), pp. 130–139. IEEE (2012)
3. Cai, Y., Daskalakis, C., Weinberg, S.M.: Understanding incentives: mechanism design becomes algorithm design. In: 2013 IEEE 54th Annual Symposium on Foundations of Computer Science (FOCS), pp. 618–627. IEEE (2013)
4. Elkind, E.: Designing and learning optimal finite support auctions. In: Proceedings of the Eighteenth Annual ACM-SIAM Symposium on Discrete Algorithms. Society for Industrial and Applied Mathematics, pp. 736–745 (2007)
5. Gopalan, P., Nisan, N., Roughgarden, T.: Public projects, Boolean functions and the borders of border's theorem. arXiv preprint arXiv:1504.07687 (2015)
6. Hartline, J.D.: Mechanism design and approximation (2013)
7. Khachiyan, L.: Polynomial algorithm in linear programming. In: Akademiia Nauk SSSR, Doklady, vol. 244, pp. 1093–1096 (1979)
8. Myerson, R.B.: Optimal auction design. Math. Oper. Res. **6**(1), 58–73 (1981)
9. Svensson, L.G.: Strategy-proof allocation of indivisible goods. Soc. Choice Welf. **16**(4), 557–567 (1999)
10. Vickrey, W.: Counterspeculation, auctions, and competitive sealed tenders. J. Financ. **16**(1), 8–37 (1961)

On Existence, Mixtures, Computation and Efficiency in Multi-objective Games

Anisse Ismaili[⊠]

RIKEN, Center for Advanced Intelligence Project AIP, Tokyo, Japan
anisse.ismaili@riken.jp

Abstract. In a multi-objective game, each individual's payoff is a *vector-valued* function of everyone's actions. Under such vectorial payoffs, Pareto-efficiency is used to formulate each individual's best-response condition, inducing Pareto-Nash equilibria as the fundamental solution concept. In this work, we follow a classical game-theoretic agenda to study equilibria. Firstly, we show in several ways that numerous pure-strategy Pareto-Nash equilibria exist. Secondly, we propose a more consistent extension to mixed-strategy equilibria. Thirdly, we introduce a measurement of the efficiency of multiple objectives games, which purpose is to keep the information on each objective: the multi-objective coordination ratio. Finally, we provide algorithms that compute Pareto-Nash equilibria and that compute or approximate the multi-objective coordination ratio.

Keywords: Multi-objective game · Pareto-nash equilibrium

1 Introduction

Game theory and microeconomics assume that individuals evaluate outcomes into scalars. However, bounded rationality can hardly be modeled consistently by agents simply comparing scalars: *"The classical theory does not tolerate the incomparability of oranges and apples"* [25]. Money is another case of scalarization of the values of outcomes. For instance, while 'making money' theoretically creates value [26], the tobacco industry making money and killing approximately six million people every year [31] is hardly a creation of value[1].

In this work, we assume that agents evaluate outcomes over a finite set of distinct objectives[2]; hence, agents have vectorial payoffs. For instance, in the case of tobacco consumers, this slightly more informative model would keep the information on these three objectives [4]: smoking pleasure, cigarette cost and consequences on life expectancy. In literature, this model was called games with vectorial payoffs, multi-objective games or multi-criteria games; and several applications were considered (see e.g. [30,32]). Indeed, behaviors are less assumptively

---

[1] Tobacco consumers are free to value and choose cigarettes how it pleases them. However, is value the same when they inhale, as when they die suffocating?

[2] It is a backtrack from the subjective theory of value, which typically aggregates values on each objective/commodity into a single scalar by using an utility function.

© Springer Nature Switzerland AG 2018
T. Miller et al. (Eds.): PRIMA 2018, LNAI 11224, pp. 210–225, 2018.
https://doi.org/10.1007/978-3-030-03098-8_13

modeled by a partial preference: the Pareto-dominance. Using Pareto-efficiency in place of best-response condition induces Pareto-Nash (PN) equilibria as the solution concept for stability, without even assuming that individuals combine the objectives in a precise manner. Pareto-Nash equilibria encompass the outcomes, even under unknown, uncertain or inconsistent preferences.

This paper more particularly addresses two unexplored issues. (1) The algorithmic aspects of multi-objective games have never been studied. (2) Also, the efficiency of Pareto-Nash equilibria has never been a concern.

Related Literature on Mixed-Strategies and Similar Strategy Spaces. Games with vectorial payoffs, or multi-objective games, were firstly introduced in the late fifties by Blackwell and Shapley [1,24]. The former shows the existence of a mixed-strategy Pareto-Nash equilibrium in finite two-player zero-sum multi-objective games. The later generalizes this existence result to finite multi-objective games. Both use a definition of mixed-strategy Pareto-Nash equilibria that suffers an inconsistency: pure-strategy Pareto-Nash equilibria are not included in the set of mixed-strategy Nash equilibria (see Sect. 4). Nonetheless, there is an established literature on games with vector payoffs that uses this definition. Deep formal works generalized known existence results [24] to individual action-sets being compact convex subsets of a normed space [29]. Weak Pareto-Nash equilibria can be approximated [16].

Works Related to Pure Strategies and Algorithms. [30] achieves to characterize the entire set of Pareto-Nash equilibria by mean of augmented Tchebycheff norms. However, the number of dimensions that parameterize these Tchebycheff norms is algorithmically prohibitive. [20] shows that a MO potential function guarantees that a Pareto-Nash equilibrium exists in finite MO games.

In Sect. 3, we show in three different settings that pure-strategy Pareto-Nash equilibria are guaranteed to exist, or very likely to be numerous. In Sect. 4, we show an inconsistency in the current concept of mixed-strategy PN equilibrium, and propose an extension to solve this flaw. In Sect. 5, in the fashion of the price of anarchy [14], we define a measurement of the worst-case efficiency of individualistic behaviors in games, compared to the optimum. In the multi-objective case, it is far from trivial, as worst-case equilibria and optima are not uniquely defined. In Sect. 6, we show how to compute the set of (worst) pure-strategy Pareto-Nash equilibria for several game structures, and provide algorithms to compute and approximate our multi-objective coordination ratio[3].

2   Preliminaries

Definition 1. A *multi-objective game* (MO game, or MOG) is defined by the following tuple $(N, \{A^i\}_{i \in N}, \mathcal{D}, \{\boldsymbol{u}^i\}_{i \in N})$:

– The agents set is $N = \{1, \ldots, n\}$. Agent i decides action a^i in action-set A^i.

---

[3] All the proofs are in the long paper on arxiv.

- The shared list of objectives is denoted by $\mathcal{D} = \{1,\ldots,d\}$ and every agent $i \in N$ gets her payoff from function $\boldsymbol{u}^i : A = A^1 \times \ldots \times A^n \to \mathbb{R}^d$ which maps every overall action to a *vector-valued* payoff; e.g., real $u_k^i(\boldsymbol{a})$ is the payoff of agent i on objective k for action-profile $\boldsymbol{a} = (a^1,\ldots,a^n)$.

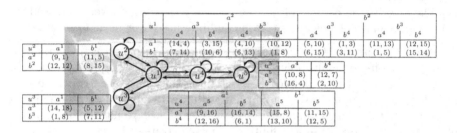

Fig. 1. Didactic toy example in Ocean Shores city.

In the subjective theory of value, every individual evaluates her endowment $(u_1^i,\ldots,u_d^i)$ however she wants based on an utility function $v^i : \mathbb{R}^d \to \mathbb{R}$. The theory of multi-objective games [1,24] aims at allowing for individuals that behave according to several unknown, uncertain, or inconsistent utility functions. These utility functions are reduced to their common denominator: the Pareto-dominance, as defined below. That vector $\boldsymbol{y} \in \mathbb{R}^d$ weakly-Pareto-dominates and respectively *Pareto-dominates* vector $\boldsymbol{x} \in \mathbb{R}^d$ is denoted and defined by:

$$\boldsymbol{y} \succsim \boldsymbol{x} \Leftrightarrow \forall k \in \mathcal{D}, \quad y_k \geq x_k,$$
$$\boldsymbol{y} \succ \boldsymbol{x} \Leftrightarrow \forall k \in \mathcal{D}, \quad y_k \geq x_k \text{ and } \exists k \in \mathcal{D}, y_k > x_k.$$

For the preferences of individuals, given an adversary action-profile $\boldsymbol{a}^{-i} = (a^j \mid j \neq i)$, this defines a partial rationality on set $\boldsymbol{u}^i(A^i, \boldsymbol{a}^{-i}) = \{\boldsymbol{u}^i(b^i, \boldsymbol{a}^{-i}) \mid b^i \in A^i\}$, which is less assumptive than complete orders, since it does not presume any individual utility function $v^i : \mathbb{R}^d \to \mathbb{R}$. Formally, given a finite set of vectors $X \subseteq \mathbb{R}^d$, the set of *Pareto-efficient* vectors is defined as the following set of non-Pareto-dominated vectors:

$$\text{EFF}[X] = \{\boldsymbol{y} \in X \mid \forall \boldsymbol{x} \in X, \text{ not } (\boldsymbol{x} \succ \boldsymbol{y})\}.$$

Since Pareto-dominance is a partial order, it induces a multiplicity of Pareto-efficient vectors. These are the best compromises between objectives. Similarly, let $\text{WST}[X] = \{\boldsymbol{y} \in X \mid \forall \boldsymbol{x} \in X, \text{not}(\boldsymbol{y} \succ \boldsymbol{x})\}$ denote the worst vectors.

In a multi-objective game, individuals behave according to the Pareto - dominance, inducing the solution concept *Pareto-Nash equilibrium* (PN), formally defined as any action-profile $\boldsymbol{a} \in A$ such that for every agent $i \in N$:

$$\boldsymbol{u}^i(a^i, \boldsymbol{a}^{-i}) \quad \in \quad \text{EFF}\big[\ \{\boldsymbol{u}^i(b^i, \boldsymbol{a}^{-i}) \mid b^i \in A^i\} \ \big].$$

We call these conditions *Pareto-efficient responses*. Let PN $\subseteq A$ denote the set of Pareto-Nash equilibria. For instance, in Fig. 1, action-profile $(b^1, b^2, a^3, b^4, b^5)$ is a PN equilibrium, since each action, given the adversary local action profile (column), is Pareto-efficient among the given agent's two actions (rows). In this example, there are 13 Pareto-Nash equilibria (depicted in Fig. 2).

Such an encompassing solution concept provides the first phase for bounding the efficiency of games. It is well-known that individualistic behaviors can be far from the optimum/maximum in terms of utilitarian evaluation $u(a) = \sum_{i \in N} u^i(a)$. In single-objective games[4], this inefficiency is measured by the *Coordination Ratio* $\mathrm{CR} = \frac{\min[u(PN)]}{\max[u(A)]}$ [14], which is more commonly known as the *Price of Anarchy* [23]. However, in the multi-objective case, the utilitarian social welfare $u(a) = \sum_{i \in N} u^i(a)$ is a vector-valued function $u : A \to \mathbb{R}^d$ with respect to d objectives. To study the efficiency of Pareto-Nash equilibria, we introduce:

- set of *equilibria outcomes* $\mathcal{E}$ = $u(\mathrm{PN})$ $(\subset \mathbb{R}^d)$,
- set of *efficient outcomes* $\mathcal{F}$ = $\mathrm{EFF}[u(A)]$ $(\subset \mathbb{R}^d)$.

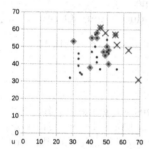

The utilitarian outcomes are a set of vectors, depicted above. Worst case equilibria and optima are not uniquely defined. The ratio of set of equilibria outcomes $\mathcal{E}$ ($\Diamond$) to set of efficient outcomes $\mathcal{F}$ ($\times$) would be a ratio of sets, which remains undefined. It would be crucial that such a definition keeps information for every objective. E.g., we want to remember that a car pollutes, or that a cigarette kills, not just that it makes some economic agents happy.

Fig. 2. Biobjective set of utilitarian outcomes $u(A) \subset \mathbb{R}^2$ in Ocean Shores.

3   Numerous Pure Strategy Pareto-Nash Equilibria Exist

This section demonstrates the existence of pure strategy Pareto-Nash equilibria. Firstly, we write how the existence results from single-objective (SO) games can be retrieved in MO games. Secondly, we generalize the equilibria existence results of single-objective potential games to multi-objective potential games. Thirdly, we show that on average, numerous Pareto-Nash equilibria exist.

---

[4] In the single-objective case, Pareto-Nash and Nash equilibria coincide.

3.1   Reductions from MO Games to SO Games

In the literature, most rationalities are constructed by means of a utility function $v^i : \mathbb{R}^d \to \mathbb{R}$, which is monotonic with respect to the Pareto-dominance, that is:

$$\boldsymbol{x} \succ \boldsymbol{y} \Rightarrow v^i(\boldsymbol{x}) > v^i(\boldsymbol{y})$$

Such functions are called *Pareto-monotonic*. For instance, these include positive weighted sums, Cobb-Douglas utilities, and utility functions in general as assumed by the Arrow-Debreu theorem.

A straightforward consequence is that the set of Pareto-efficient vectors contains the optima of any Pareto-monotonic utility function. Formally, given a MOG Γ, from Pareto-monotonic utility functions $V = (v^i : \mathbb{R}^d \to \mathbb{R} | i \in N)$ the single-objective game $V \circ \Gamma = (N, \{A^i\}_{i \in N}, \{v^i \circ \boldsymbol{u}^i\}_{i \in N})$ results from the given utilities, and one has: $\mathrm{PN}(V \circ \Gamma) \subseteq \mathrm{PN}(\Gamma)$. In other words, Pareto-Nash equilibria encompass the game's outcome, regardless of the unknown preferences.

Also, inclusion $\mathrm{PN}(V \circ \Gamma) \subseteq \mathrm{PN}(\Gamma)$ argues for the guaranteed existence of numerous PN equilibria in MO games, under the following assumptions:

1. the structure of the SO game on every objective is the same,
2. equilibria are guaranteed in that structure of SO game,
3. and a positive linear combination of the MO game induces that SO game.

This remark is the canonical argument used in previous results (e.g. [20,24]).

3.2   Multi-objective Potentials

We now explore potential games, as introduced for congestion games by Robert Rosenthal [15,22] and recently generalized to MO games [20]. The existence of an MO potential function guarantees that at least one Pareto-Nash equilibrium exists [20]. We go further and completely characterize the set of PN equilibria.

Definition 2. An MO game $\Gamma = (N, \{A^i\}_{i \in N}, \mathcal{D}, \{\boldsymbol{u}^i\}_{i \in N})$ admits *(exact)* potential function $\boldsymbol{\Phi} : A \to \mathbb{R}^d$ if and only if for every action-profile $\boldsymbol{a} \in A$, for every agent $i \in N$ and for every action $b^i \in A^i$, one has:

$$\forall k \in \mathcal{D}, \quad \Phi_k(b^i, \boldsymbol{a}^{-i}) - \Phi_k(\boldsymbol{a}) \;=\; u_k^i(b^i, \boldsymbol{a}^{-i}) - u_k^i(\boldsymbol{a}).$$

That is, function $\boldsymbol{\Phi}$ additively accumulates the vectorial values of each deviation.

Definition 3. Given a vector valued function $\boldsymbol{\Phi} : A \to \mathbb{R}^d$, let the set of *locally efficient* action-profiles $\mathrm{LOC}(\boldsymbol{\Phi})$ be the set of action-profiles $\boldsymbol{a} \in A$ such that:

$$\boldsymbol{\Phi}(\boldsymbol{a}) \in \mathrm{EFF}[\{\boldsymbol{\Phi}(b^i, \boldsymbol{a}^{-i}) \in \mathbb{R}^d \mid i \in N, b^i \in A^i\}].$$

Set $\mathrm{LOC}(\boldsymbol{\Phi})$ corresponds to a generalization of local optima for function $\boldsymbol{\Phi}$, and is non-empty if sets N, $\mathcal{D}$ and A are finite. Moreover, due to the loose requirement for local efficiency, set $\mathrm{LOC}(\boldsymbol{\Phi})$ is likely to contain numerous action-profiles.

Theorem 1. Let $\Gamma = (N, \{A^i\}_{i\in N}, \mathcal{D}, \{u^i\}_{i\in N})$ be a finite multi-objective game[5] that admits potential function Φ. Then, it holds that:

$$PN(\Gamma) = LOC(\Phi) \neq \emptyset.$$

This theorem completely characterizes the set of Pareto-Nash equilibria as the set of locally efficient action-profiles for function Φ, which is a non-empty set with numerous action-profiles. More generally, Theorem 1 also holds when sets N and $\mathcal{D}$ are finite and sets A^i are just compact.

3.3 Likelihood of Equilibrium in Random Games

Another manner to study whether a PN-equilibrium exists is to provide a probability distribution on a family of finite games and then discuss the probability of PN-equilibrium existence. A similar methodology was successfully applied [7,9,21] to SO games in several settings where every SO payoff $u^i(a)$ is independently and identically distributed by a uniform distribution on continuous intervals $[0, 1]$. At the heart of this subsection, let random variable Z denote the number of pure Nash-equilibria action-profiles in the game. In the SO case, there is almost surely only one best response. However, when considering MO games, a main technical difference lies in the average number of "best responses" (or here, Pareto-efficient responses), which in most cases exceeds 1, due to the surface-like shape of the Pareto-efficient set in $\mathbb{R}^d$, surface which is $(d-1)$ dimensional. Here, we assume a probability distribution $\mathbb{P}_{n,\alpha,\beta}$, that builds randomly the Pareto-efficient response tables of an n-agent normal form game with α actions-per-agent: for every agent i and every adversary action-profile $\boldsymbol{a}^{-i} \in \prod_{j\neq i} A^j$, there is a fixed number $\beta : 1 < \beta \leq \alpha$ of Pareto-efficient responses, for the sake of simplicity.

Theorem 2. Given numbers $n \geq 2$ of agents, $\alpha \geq 2$ of actions-per-agent and $\beta \leq \alpha$ of Pareto-efficient responses, based on probability distribution $\mathbb{P}_{n,\alpha,\beta}$, the number Z of Pareto-Nash equilibria satisfies $\mathbb{E}[Z] = \beta^n$ and:

$$\mathbb{P}\left((1-\gamma)\beta^n \leq Z \leq (1+\gamma)\beta^n\right) \geq 1 - \frac{1}{\gamma^2 \beta^n}, \quad \forall \gamma \in (0,1).$$

It argues for the existence of numerous Pareto-Nash equilibria when there are enough agents and efficient responses, and follows from the Bienaymé-Tchebychev inequality. For instance, (given $\gamma = 1/2$) the probability that the number of Pareto-Nash equilibria Z is between $(1/2)\beta^n$ and $(3/2)\beta^n$, is at least $1 - 4\beta^{-n}$, which for $\beta = 2$ efficient responses and $n = 5$ agents, gives $\mathbb{P}(16 \leq Z \leq 48) \geq 7/8$.

---

[5] In a finite multi-objective game, sets N, $\{A^i\}_{i\in N}$ and $\mathcal{D}$ are finite.

4   Consistent Extension to Mixed Strategies

To guarantee equilibrium existence by means of fixed-point theorems on compact sets [17,27], the finite action sets of every agent are expanded to include *mixed strategies*. That is: every agent i decides a probability distribution p^i in the set $\Delta(A^i)$ of probability distributions over his action-set A^i. Each payoff function $\boldsymbol{u}^i$ is redefined to be the expected utility

$$\boldsymbol{u}^i(\boldsymbol{p}) = \mathbb{E}_{a \sim p}[\boldsymbol{u}^i(\boldsymbol{a})],$$

under the mixed-strategy profile $\boldsymbol{p} = (p^1, \ldots, p^n) \in \prod_{i \in N} \Delta(A^i)$. This defines a mixed-extension of the original game. The stability concept induced is called a mixed-strategy Nash equilibrium.

In MOGs, Pareto-Nash equilibria based on their original definition by Blackwell [1] and Shapley [24] (below) are those usually considered [2,5,28,32].

Definition 4. Given finite MO game $\Gamma = (N, \{A^i\}_{i \in N}, \{\mathcal{D}\}, \{\boldsymbol{u}^i\}_{i \in N})$, a mixed-strategy profile $\boldsymbol{p} = (p^1, \ldots, p^n) \in \prod_{i \in N} \Delta(A^i)$ is a mixed-strategy Pareto-Nash equilibrium if and only if it satisfies for every agent i:

$$\boldsymbol{u}^i(p^i, \boldsymbol{p}^{-i}) \in \mathrm{EFF}\left[\{\boldsymbol{u}^i(q^i, \boldsymbol{p}^{-i}) \in \mathbb{R}^d \mid q^i \in \Delta(A^i)\}\right]$$

The rational behind this first definition is the following. For every agent i, mixed-strategy $p^i \in \Delta(A^i)$ acts as a convex-combination of set of vectorial payoffs $\boldsymbol{u}^i(A^i, \boldsymbol{p}^{-i})$ and the best-response condition is replaced by the fact that mixed-strategy p^i should have a Pareto-efficient evaluation $\boldsymbol{u}^i(p^i, \boldsymbol{p}^{-i})$ among the elements of this convex set of evaluations $\{\boldsymbol{u}^i(q^i, \boldsymbol{p}^{-i}) \in \mathbb{R}^d \mid q^i \in \Delta(A^i)\}$. That is, a mixed-strategy Pareto-Nash equilibrium is a pure-strategy Pareto-Nash equilibrium in finite game Γ's mixed extension. However, as depicted in Fig. 3, Definition 1 fails to fulfill two fundamental requirements:

1. Pure-strategy equilibria must be included in mixed-strategy equilibria.
2. Mixed-strategies also enable to model a risk-averse agent.

Proof. Figure 3 demonstrates these side effects.

To fulfill the two requirements, instead of efficient mixed actions, we consider mixtures of efficient pure-actions. As in Fig. 3, it corrects both side effects.

Definition 5. Given a finite multi-objective game $(N, \{A^i\}_{i \in N}, \{\mathcal{D}\}, \{\boldsymbol{u}^i\}_{i \in N})$, a mixed-strategy Pareto-Nash equilibrium is a mixed-strategy profile $\boldsymbol{p} = (p^1, \ldots, p^n) \in \prod_{i \in N} \Delta(A^i)$, such that for every agent i and action $a^i \in A^i$ if a^i is played with positive probability $p^i(a^i) > 0$, then it holds that

$$\boldsymbol{u}^i(a^i, \boldsymbol{p}^{-i}) \quad \in \quad \mathrm{EFF}\left[\boldsymbol{u}^i(A^i, \boldsymbol{p}^{-i})\right].$$

This generalized definition connects in the single-objective case to a less know definition of Nash-equilibria (see [18], p. 30, Theorem 2.1). In this alternative definition, each mixed strategy must be a mixture of pure-strategies that are best-responses. In other words, the support of each mixed strategy must be included in the set of pure-strategy best-responses. Furthermore, concerning existence, since this revised definition contains the former one, (which is guaranteed to exist) the new definition is guaranteed to exist too.

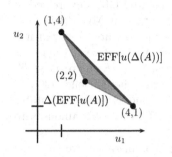

The three outcomes, $u(A) = \{(1,4),(2,2),(4,1)\}$, are depicted by black dots. With Def. 4, since the mixed outcomes are all convex-combinations of $\{(1,4),(2,2),(4,1)\}$, the Pareto-efficient mixed-strategies are here the convex-combinations of $\{(1,4),(4,1)\}$; and outcome $(2,2)$ is Pareto-dominated. Not every pure-strategy Pareto-Nash equilibrium is a mixed-strategy one, which is a severe inconsistency. Furthermore, since outcome $(2,2)$ is well balanced, it may also be decided with a non-null probability, e.g., if the agent's utility is concave [6], or if she is risk-averse [21]. Our *revised* definition considers instead all the convex-combinations of the Pareto-efficient pure actions $\{(1,4),(2,2),(4,1)\}$.

Fig. 3. Single-agent three-actions bi-objective game showing inconsistencies. (The coordinates correspond to the bi-objective valuation (u_1, u_2).)

5 Multi-objective Coordination Ratio

In the single-objective case, the coordination ratio measures the efficiency loss of equilibria compared to the optimum. In MO games, we claim that it is critical to study efficiency with respect to every objective. Even after the actions, the game analyst still has access to the vectorial payoffs. In this section, we follow the agenda outlined in the introduction, to define a *multi-objective coordination ratio* MO-CR$[\mathcal{E}, \mathcal{F}]$ of the set of equilibria outcomes $\mathcal{E}$ to the set of efficient outcomes $\mathcal{F}$, that fills the critical purpose to keep information on each objective.

First, we state the list of desirable properties that we want the ratio to satisfy. For the purpose of having meaningful divisions and ratios, some vectors are positive in this section. Given vectors $\rho, y \in \mathbb{R}^d$ and $z \in \mathbb{R}^d_+$, vector $\rho \star y \in \mathbb{R}^d$ is defined by $\forall k \in \mathcal{D}, (\rho \star y)_k = \rho_k y_k$. Vector $y/z \in \mathbb{R}^d$ is defined by $\forall k \in \mathcal{D}, (y/z)_k = y_k/z_k$. Given vector $r \in \mathbb{R}^d$ and set of vectors Y, set $r \star Y$ is defined by $\{r \star y \in \mathbb{R}^d_+ | y \in Y\}$ and for $r \in \mathbb{R}^d_+$, set Y/r is defined by $\{y/r \in \mathbb{R}^d | y \in Y\}$. Given $x \in \mathbb{R}^d$, cone $\mathcal{C}(x)$ denotes $\{y \in \mathbb{R}^d \mid x \succsim y\}$, and given $X \subset \mathbb{R}^d$, cone-union $\mathcal{C}(X)$ is defined by $\cup_{x \in X} \mathcal{C}(x)$. Vector $\mathbf{0}$ denotes a vector with d zeros, and $\mathbf{1}$ denotes a vector with d ones.

The first property that we require from MO-CR$[\mathcal{E}, \mathcal{F}]$ is to be on a *multi-objective ratio scale*. Given $\mathcal{E}, \mathcal{F} \subset \mathbb{R}^d_+$ and $r \in \mathbb{R}^d_+$, the following shall hold.

$$\text{MO-CR}[\mathcal{E}, \mathcal{F}] \quad \subseteq \mathbb{R}^d \tag{1}$$

$$\text{MO-CR}[\{\mathbf{0}\}, \mathcal{F}] \quad = \{\mathbf{0}\} \tag{2}$$

$$\text{MO-CR}[r \star \mathcal{E}, \mathcal{F}] \quad = r \star \text{MO-CR}[\mathcal{E}, \mathcal{F}] \tag{3}$$

$$\text{MO-CR}[\mathcal{E}, r \star \mathcal{F}] \quad = \text{MO-CR}[\mathcal{E}, \mathcal{F}]/r \tag{4}$$

$$\mathcal{E} \subseteq \mathcal{F} \quad \Leftrightarrow \mathbf{1} \in \text{MO-CR}[\mathcal{E}, \mathcal{F}] \tag{5}$$

To fix these ideas one can think of $d = 1$ and given two positive numbers e, f, to the properties of ratio e/f. Equation (1) states that MO-CR is expressed in a multi-objective space. Equations (2), (3) and (4) state that MO-CR is well-centered and sensitive on each objective to multiplications of outcomes, which is what we want. For instance, if $\mathcal{E}$ is three times better on objective k, then so is MO-CR. If there are two times more efficient opportunities in $\mathcal{F}$ on objective k', then MO-CR is one half on objective k'. In other words, the efficiency of each objective independently reflects on MO-CR in a ratio-scale. Equation (5) states that if all equilibria outcomes are efficient (i.e. $\mathcal{E} \subseteq \mathcal{F}$), then this amounts to $1 \in$ MO-CR$[\mathcal{E}, \mathcal{F}]$, i.e. the MO game is fully efficient.

These requirements rule out a set of first ideas. For instance, we can rule out comparisons of equilibria outcomes to ideal vector $\mathcal{I} = (\max_{z \in \mathcal{F}}\{z_k\} | k \in \mathcal{D})$ does not satisfy requirement (5) to have $1 \in$ MO-CR$[\mathcal{E}, \mathcal{F}]$ when $\mathcal{E} \subseteq \mathcal{F}$. By starting from a social welfare $f : \mathbb{R}_+^d \to \mathbb{R}_+$, taking ratio $\min f(\mathcal{E}) / \max f(\mathcal{F})$, induces the same problem.

This measurement should also be non-dictatorial, in the sense that no point of view should be imposed on what the overall efficiency is: no prior choice must be done on the set of efficient outcomes. Formally, if two sets of efficient outcomes $\mathcal{F}, \mathcal{F}' \subset \mathbb{R}_+^d$ differ even slightly, then this must reflect at least for some numerator set $\mathcal{E}$ onto ratio MO-CR$[\mathcal{E}, \mathcal{F}]$. This amounts to a disjunction on efficient outcomes. Finally MO-CR$[\mathcal{E}, \mathcal{F}]$ must provide guaranteed efficiency ratios that hold for every equilibrium outcome $y \in \mathcal{E}$, which amounts to a conjunction on equilibria outcomes. The definition below follows from these requirements.

Firstly, the efficiency of *one* equilibrium $y \in \mathcal{E}$ is quantified without prior choices on what efficient outcome should we compare it to, as required:

$$R[y, \mathcal{F}] \quad = \quad \bigcup_{z \in \mathcal{F}} C(y/z),$$

The idea is that we do not take sides with any efficient outcome. Instead, we define with flexibility and without a dictatorship a disjunctive set of guaranteed efficiency ratios, which lets the differences between two sets of efficient outcomes $\mathcal{F}, \mathcal{F}' \subset \mathbb{R}_+^d$ reflect onto ratio MO-CR$[\mathcal{E}, \mathcal{F}]$.

Secondly, in MOGs, on average, there are many Pareto-Nash equilibria. An efficiency *guarantee* $\rho \in \mathbb{R}^d$ should hold for every equilibrium outcome. It induces this conjunctive definition of the set of guaranteed vectorial ratios:

$$R[\mathcal{E}, \mathcal{F}] \quad = \quad \bigcap_{y \in \mathcal{E}} R[y, \mathcal{F}].$$

In fact, because of the conjunction on equilibria outcomes, the set $R[\mathcal{E}, \mathcal{F}]$ only depends on sets WST$[\mathcal{E}]$ (instead of set $\mathcal{E}$) and $\mathcal{F}$.

Finally, if two bounds on efficiencies ρ and ρ' are such that $\rho \succ \rho'$ (e.g. the former guarantees fraction $\rho = (0.75, 0.75)$ of efficiency and the later fraction $\rho' = (0.5, 0.5)$), then ρ' brings no more information; hence, MO-CR is defined using EFF on the guaranteed efficiency ratios $R[\text{WST}[\mathcal{E}], \mathcal{F}]$. These points are summed up in the following definition:

Definition 6 (MO-CR). Given an MO game, vector $\rho \in \mathbb{R}^d$ bounds its inefficiency (i.e. $\rho \in R[\mathcal{E}, \mathcal{F}]$) if and only if the following holds (see Fig. 4):

$$\forall y \in \mathcal{E}, \quad \exists z \in \mathcal{F}, \quad y/z \succsim \rho.$$

The multi-objective coordination ratio MO-CR$[\mathcal{E}, \mathcal{F}]$ is then defined as:

$$\text{MO-CR}[\mathcal{E}, \mathcal{F}] \quad = \quad \text{EFF}[R[\text{WST}[\mathcal{E}], \mathcal{F}]].$$

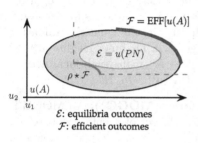

The multi-objective coordination ratio can be explained by the implications of a vectorial ratio $\rho \in$ MO-CR: for each vector $y \in \mathcal{E}$, an efficient outcome $z^{(y)} \in \mathcal{F}$ exists such that y Pareto-dominates vector $\rho \star z^{(y)}$. In other words, equilibria outcomes $\mathcal{E}$ are at least as good as set of vectors $\rho \star \mathcal{F}$: If $\rho \in R[\mathcal{E}, \mathcal{F}]$, then every equilibrium satisfies the ratio of efficiency ρ in an unspecified manner. In other words, the equilibria outcomes are contained in the "at least as good as $\rho \star \mathcal{F}$" cone-union, that is: $\mathcal{E} \subseteq (\rho \star \mathcal{F}) + \mathbb{R}^d_+$. Moreover, since ρ is tight, set $\mathcal{E}$ sticks to $\rho \star \mathcal{F}$.

Fig. 4. Didactic depiction of a guaranteed vectorial ratio ρ from MO-CR$[\mathcal{E}, \mathcal{F}]$.

The most famous results of the coordination ratio (or price of anarchy) are stated analytically on families of games, for instance on congestion games [3,23]. Such results would also be desirable in the multi-objective case. However, the underlying proofs do not survive this generalization: while best response inequalities can be summed in single-objective cases, here, non-Pareto-dominances cannot. This issue is independent of the chosen efficiency measurement and motivates numerical approaches, as proposed in the next section.

6   Computation

In this section, we provide algorithms for computing the set of pure-strategy Pareto-Nash equilibria and for computing the multi-objective coordination ratio.

6.1   Computing Pure-Strategy Pareto-Nash Equilibria

If the MO game is given in *normal form*, then it is made of the MO payoffs of every agent $i \in N$ on every action-profile $a \in A$. Since there are $n\alpha^n$ such vectors, where recall that n is the number of agents, α the number of actions per agent and d the number of objectives, the length of this input is $L(n) = n\alpha^n d$. Then, enumeration of the action-profiles works efficiently with respect to length function L, using a simple argument similar to [11].

Theorem 3. *Given a MO game in normal form, computing the set of the best (resp. worst) equilibria outcomes EFF[$\mathcal{E}$] (resp. WST[$\mathcal{E}$]) takes polynomial time*

$$O(n\alpha^{n+1}d + \alpha^{2n}d) \quad = \quad O(L^2).$$

Moreover, if $d = 2$, this complexity is lowered to quasi-linear-time

$$O(n\alpha^n \log_2(\alpha)) = O(L \log_2(\alpha)).$$

Graphical games provide compact representations of massive multi-agent games when the payoff functions of the agents only depend on a local subset of the agents [13]. Graphical games can be generalized in a straightforward manner to assuming vectorial payoffs. Formally, there is a support graph $G = (N, E)$ where each vertex represents an agent, and an agent i's evaluation function only depends on the actions of the agents in his inner-neighbourhood $\mathcal{N}(i) = \{j \in N | (j, i) \in E\}$. That is $u^i : A^{\mathcal{N}(i)} \to \mathbb{R}^d$ maps each local action-profile $a^{\mathcal{N}(i)} \in A^{\mathcal{N}(i)}$ to a multi-objective payoff $u^i(a^{\mathcal{N}(i)}) \in \mathbb{R}^d$.

Definition 7 (Multi-objective graphical game (MOGG)). An MOGG is a tuple $(G = (N, E), \{A^i\}_{i \in N}, \mathcal{D}, \{u^i\}_{i \in N})$. N is the set of agents. $\{A^i\}_{i \in N}$ are their individual action-sets. $\mathcal{D}$ is the set of all objectives. Every function $u^i : A^{\mathcal{N}(i)} \to \mathbb{R}^d$ is vector-valued, and its scope is vertex i's neighborhood.

Figure 1 pictures a didactic instance of an MOGG. In the same manner as computing equilibria in graphical games was reduced to junction-tree algorithms [6], it is also possible to exploit a generalized MO junction-tree algorithm [8,10]. However, even though this MO junction-tree algorithm is not in polynomial time (but rather pseudo-polynomial time), it still remains faster than browsing the Cartesian product of action-sets and is tractable on average, as experimented in the appendix. Symmetric games [12] can also be generalized to MOGs:

Definition 8. In a *multi-objective symmetric game*, individual payoffs are not impacted by the agents' identities. There is one sole action-set A^* for every agent i. So, when deciding action $a^* \in A^*$, the multi-objective reward only depends on the number of agents that decided every action. Consequently, the game is not specified for every action-profile $a \in A = \prod_{i \in N} A^*$ and every agent i, but rather for every action $a^* \in A^*$ and every *configuration* $c : A^* \to \mathbb{N}$, where number $c(a^*) \in \mathbb{N}$ indicates the number of agents deciding action a^*. Therefore, the utility is given by a function u^* such that $u^*(a^*, c) \in \mathbb{R}^d$ is the payoff for deciding action a^* when configuration c occurs.

There is a number $\binom{n+\alpha-1}{\alpha-1}$ of configurations[6] to which the MO symmetric game associates MO vectors. As a consequence, generalizing to vectorial payoffs, the representation length is $L = \alpha\binom{n+\alpha-1}{\alpha-1}d$, and when the numbers α and d are fixed constant, length is $L(n) \in \Theta(\alpha n^\alpha d)$. Quite simply, for computing $\mathcal{E}$, EFF[$\mathcal{E}$] and WST[$\mathcal{E}$], configurations enumeration already takes polynomial time.

---

[6] To enumerate the number of ways to distribute number n of symmetric agents into α parts, one enumerates the ways to choose $\alpha - 1$ "separators" in $n + \alpha - 1$ elements.

Theorem 4. *Given a multi-objective symmetric game with fixed α,*

- *computing PN and $\mathcal{E}$ takes time $O(n^\alpha \alpha^2 d) = O(L\alpha)$;*
- *computing EFF[$\mathcal{E}$] and WST[$\mathcal{E}$] takes time $O(n^{2\alpha} d) = O(L^2)$. If $d = 2$, this lowers to $O(L(\alpha + \log(L)))$.*

6.2 Computing MO-CR

In this subsection, we address the problem of computing the set MO-CR[$\mathcal{E}, \mathcal{F}$], given sets of worst equilibria outcomes WST[$\mathcal{E}$] and efficient outcomes $\mathcal{F}$. Algorithm 1 (below) computes such set. In the algorithm, set D^t denotes a set of vectors. Given two vectors, $x, y \in \mathbb{R}^d_+$, let $x \wedge y$ denote the vector defined by $\forall k \in \mathcal{D}$, $(x \wedge y)_k = \min\{x_k, y_k\}$, let $x^y \in \mathbb{R}^d_+$ be the vector defined by $\forall k \in \mathcal{D}, (x^y)_k = (x_k)^{y_k}$, and recall that $\forall k \in \mathcal{D}$, $(x/y)_k = x_k/y_k$.

Input: WST[$\mathcal{E}$] = $\{y^1, \ldots, y^q\}$ and $\mathcal{F} = \{z^1, \ldots, z^m\}$
Output: MO-CR = EFF[R[WST[$\mathcal{E}$], $\mathcal{F}$]]

create $D^1 \leftarrow \{y^1/z \in \mathbb{R}^d_+ \mid z \in \mathcal{F}\}$
for $t = 2, \ldots, q$ **do**
$\quad \mid \quad D^t \leftarrow$ EFF[$\{\rho \wedge (y^t/z) \mid \rho \in D^{t-1}, \ z \in \mathcal{F}\}$]
end
return D^q

Algorithm 1: Computing MO-CR in polynomial-time

Theorem 5. *Algorithm 1 outputs MO-CR[$\mathcal{E}, \mathcal{F}$] in poly-time $O((qm)^{2d-1}d)$, where $q = |WST[\mathcal{E}]|$ and $m = |\mathcal{F}|$ denote the size of the inputs, and d is fixed.*

Proof. Algorithm 1 calculates product $\cap_{y \in \text{WST}[\mathcal{E}]} \cup_{z \in \mathcal{F}} \mathcal{C}(y/z)$, where there could be m^q terms in the output. This set-algebra of cone-unions is compact.

A decisive corollary is that given an MO game with length L that satisfies $q = O(\text{poly}(L))$, $m = O(\text{poly}(L))$ and both sets WST[$\mathcal{E}$] and $\mathcal{F}$ are computable in time $O(\text{poly}(L))$, then one can compute MO-CR in polynomial time $O(\text{poly}(L))$. For instance, it is the case with MO normal forms or MO symmetric games. So this approach is not intractable in the most basic cases.

6.3 Approximation of the MO-CR for MO Compact Representations

Unfortunately, Algorithm 1 is not practical when the MO game has a compact form and cardinalities q, m are exponentials with respect to the compact size of the game's representation. For instance, this is the case for multi-objective graphical games. Theorem 6 below answers this issue by taking only a small and approximate representation of sets WST[$\mathcal{E}$] and $\mathcal{F}$, in order to output a guaranteed approximation of sets MO-CR or R[WST[$\mathcal{E}$], $\mathcal{F}$]. This suggests the following general method:

1. Given a compact MOG representation, compute quickly an approximation $E^{(\varepsilon)}$ of $\mathrm{WST}[\mathcal{E}]$ and an approximation $F^{(\varepsilon')}$ of $\mathcal{F}$.
2. Then, given $E^{(\varepsilon)}$ and $F^{(\varepsilon')}$, use Algorithm 1 to approximate the MO-CR.

For this general method to be implemented rigorously, we must specify the precise definitions of the two approximations required in input, for the desired output to be indeed some approximation of the MO-CR.

Firstly, let us specify the output. The ratios in $R[\mathrm{WST}[\mathcal{E}], \mathcal{F}]$ must be represented, even approximately, but only by using valid ratios of efficiency, as below.

Definition 9 $((1 + \varepsilon)$-covering). Given $R \subset \mathbb{R}_+^d$ and $\varepsilon > 0$, $R^{(\varepsilon)} \subset R$ is a $(1 + \varepsilon)$-covering of R, if and only if:

$$\forall \boldsymbol{\rho} \in R, \quad \exists \boldsymbol{\rho}' \in R^{(\varepsilon)} : \quad (1 + \varepsilon)\boldsymbol{\rho}' \succsim \boldsymbol{\rho}$$

For instance, $R[\mathrm{WST}[\mathcal{E}], \mathcal{F}]$ is $(1+0)$-covered by MO-CR $= \mathrm{EFF}[R[\mathrm{WST}[\mathcal{E}], \mathcal{F}]]$. Denote $\boldsymbol{\varphi} : \mathbb{R}_+^d \to \mathbb{N}^d$ the discretization into the $(1 + \varepsilon)$-logarithmic grid. Given a vector $\boldsymbol{x} \in \mathbb{R}_+^d$, $\boldsymbol{\varphi}(\boldsymbol{x})$ is defined by: $\forall k \in \mathcal{D}, \quad \varphi_k(\boldsymbol{x}) = \lfloor \log_{(1+\varepsilon)}(x_k) \rfloor$. A typical implementation of $(1 + \varepsilon)$-coverings are the logarithmic $(1 + \varepsilon)$-coverings, which consist in taking one vector of R in each reciprocal image of $\boldsymbol{\varphi}(R)$. That is, for each $\boldsymbol{l} \in \boldsymbol{\varphi}(R)$, take one $\boldsymbol{\rho}$ in $\boldsymbol{\varphi}^{-1}(\boldsymbol{l})$. The logarithmic grid is depicted in Fig. 5.

Now we must specify rigorously what approximate representations $E^{(\varepsilon_1)}$ of set $\mathrm{WST}[\mathcal{E}]$, and $F^{(\varepsilon_2)}$ of set $\mathcal{F}$ we should take in input, in order to guarantee that $R[E^{(\varepsilon_1)}, F^{(\varepsilon_2)}]$ is an $(1+\varepsilon)$-covering of $R[\mathrm{WST}[\mathcal{E}], \mathcal{F}]$. Definitions 10 and 11 come from the need of specific approximate representations that will carry the guarantees to the approximate final output $R[E^{(\varepsilon_1)}, F^{(\varepsilon_2)}]$.

Definition 10 $((1 + \varepsilon)$-under-covering). Given $\varepsilon > 0$, $E \subset \mathbb{R}_+^d$ and $E^{(\varepsilon)} \subset \mathbb{R}_+^d$, $E^{(\varepsilon)}$ $(1 + \varepsilon)$-under-covers E if and only if:

$$\forall \boldsymbol{y} \in E, \quad \exists \boldsymbol{y}' \in E^{(\varepsilon)} : \boldsymbol{y} \succsim \boldsymbol{y}'$$
$$\text{and} \quad \forall \boldsymbol{y}' \in E^{(\varepsilon)}, \quad \exists \boldsymbol{y} \in E : (1 + \varepsilon)\boldsymbol{y}' \succsim \boldsymbol{y}$$

The first condition states that $E^{(\varepsilon)}$ bounds E from below. The second condition states that this lower bound is precise within a multiplicative $(1+\varepsilon)$. Given E, one can implement Definition 10 by using the log-grid (see e.g. Fig. 5):

$$E^{(\varepsilon)} \leftarrow \mathrm{WST}\left[\ \{ \boldsymbol{e}^{\boldsymbol{l}} \in \mathbb{R}_+^d \mid \boldsymbol{l} \in \boldsymbol{\varphi}(\mathrm{WST}[\mathcal{E}]) \} \ \right]$$

where $\boldsymbol{\varphi}(\mathrm{WST}[\mathcal{E}]) = \{ \boldsymbol{\varphi}(\boldsymbol{y}) \in \mathbb{N}^d \mid \boldsymbol{y} \in \mathrm{WST}[\mathcal{E}] \}$, and given $\boldsymbol{l} \in \mathbb{N}^d$, the vector $\boldsymbol{e}^{\boldsymbol{l}}$ is defined by $(\boldsymbol{e}^{\boldsymbol{l}})_k = (1 + \varepsilon)^{l_k}$. Now let us state what approximation is required on the set of efficient outcomes $\mathcal{F}$.

Definition 11 $((1+\varepsilon)$-stick-covering). Given $\varepsilon > 0$, $F \subset \mathbb{R}_+^d$ and $F^{(\varepsilon)} \subset \mathbb{R}_+^d$, $F^{(\varepsilon)}$ $(1 + \varepsilon)$-stick-covers F if and only if:

$$\forall \boldsymbol{z}' \in F^{(\varepsilon)}, \quad \exists \boldsymbol{z} \in F : \boldsymbol{z}' \succsim \boldsymbol{z}$$
$$\text{and} \quad \forall \boldsymbol{z} \in F, \quad \exists \boldsymbol{z}' \in F^{(\varepsilon)} : (1 + \varepsilon)\boldsymbol{z} \succsim \boldsymbol{z}'$$

The first condition is easily satisfiable by $F^{(\varepsilon)} \subseteq F$. The second condition states that $F^{(\varepsilon)}$ sticks to F. Given F, one can implement Definition 11 as in Fig. 5: Take one element of $\mathcal{F}$ per cell of the logarithmic grid, and then take WST of this set of elements. Now we can state that with an approximate Phase 1, the precision transfers to Phase 2 in polynomial time, as follows.

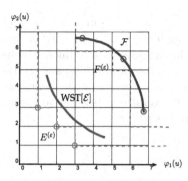

$E^{(\varepsilon)}$ (the green dots below WST$[\mathcal{E}]$) is a $(1 + \varepsilon)$-under-covering of set WST$[\mathcal{E}]$.

$F^{(\varepsilon)}$ (the three red dots in $\mathcal{F}$) is a $(1+\varepsilon)$-stick-covering of the dark-red set $\mathcal{F}$.

Fig. 5. MO approximations, depictions of under and stick coverings

Lemma 1. *Given* $\varepsilon_1, \varepsilon_2 > 0$ *and approximations* E *of* $\mathcal{E}$ *and* F *of* $\mathcal{F}$, *if*

$$\forall y \in \mathcal{E}, \exists y' \in E, \quad y \succsim y' \quad and \quad \forall y' \in E, \exists y \in \mathcal{E}, \quad (1 + \varepsilon_1)y' \succsim y \quad (6)$$

$$\forall z' \in F, \exists z \in \mathcal{F}, \quad z' \succsim z \quad and \quad \forall z \in \mathcal{F}, \exists z' \in F, \quad (1 + \varepsilon_2)z \succsim z' \quad (7)$$

holds, then it follows that $R[E, F] \subseteq R[\mathcal{E}, \mathcal{F}]$ *and:*

$$\forall \rho \in R[\mathcal{E}, \mathcal{F}], \quad \exists \rho' \in R[E, F], \quad (1 + \varepsilon_1)(1 + \varepsilon_2)\rho' \succsim \rho \quad (8)$$

Equations (6) and (7) state approximation bounds as in Definitions 10 and 11. Equations (6) state that $(1 + \varepsilon_1)^{-1}\mathcal{E}$ bounds below E which bounds below $\mathcal{E}$. Equations (7) state that $\mathcal{F}$ bounds below F which bounds below $(1 + \varepsilon_2)\mathcal{F}$. Crucially, whatever the sizes of $\mathcal{E}$ and $\mathcal{F}$, there exist such approximations E and F with respective sizes $O((1/\varepsilon_1)^{d-1})$ and $O((1/\varepsilon_2)^{d-1})$ [19], yielding the approximation scheme below.

Theorem 6 (Approximation Scheme for MO-CR). *Given a compact MOG of representation length* L, *precisions* $\varepsilon_1, \varepsilon_2 > 0$ *and two algorithms to compute approximations* E *of* $\mathcal{E}$ *and* F *of* $\mathcal{F}$ *in the sense of Eqs. (6) and (7) that take time* $\theta_{\mathcal{E}}(\varepsilon_1, L)$ *and* $\theta_{\mathcal{F}}(\varepsilon_2, L)$, *one can approximate* $R[\mathcal{E}, \mathcal{F}]$ *in the sense of Eq. (8) in time* $O\left(\theta_{\mathcal{E}}(\varepsilon_1, L) + \theta_{\mathcal{F}}(\varepsilon_2, L) + (\varepsilon_1\varepsilon_2)^{-(d-1)(2d-1)}\right)$.

For MO graphical games, Phase 1 could be instantiated with approximate junction-tree algorithms on MO graphical models [8]. For MO symmetric action-graph games, in the same fashion, one could generalize existing algorithms [12]. More generally, for the worst equilibria WST$[\mathcal{E}]$ and the efficient outcomes $\mathcal{F}$, one could also use meta-heuristics with experimental guarantees.

7   Conclusion: Discussion and Prospects

Along with equilibrium existence, potential functions also usually guarantee the convergence of best-response dynamics. This easily generalizes to dynamics where every deviation step is an individual Pareto-improvement. However, when studying a dynamics based on a refinement of the Pareto-dominance, convergence is not always guaranteed.

Pareto-Nash equilibria, which encompass the possible outcomes of MO games, very likely exist. The precision of PN-equilibria inevitably relies on the uncertainty on preferences. A promising research path would be to linearly constrain the utility functions of agents. This would induce a polytope and would boil down to another MO game where every objective corresponds to an extreme point of the induced polytope. The efficiency of several multi-objective games could be analyzed by using the contributions in this paper.

References

1. Blackwell, D., et al.: An analog of the minimax theorem for vector payoffs. Pac. J. Math. **6**(1), 1–8 (1956)
2. Borm, P., Tijs, S., van den Aarssen, J.: Pareto equilibria in multiobjective games. Methods Oper. Res. **60**, 303–312 (1988)
3. Christodoulou, G., Koutsoupias, E.: The price of anarchy of finite congestion games. In: Proceedings of the Thirty-seventh Annual ACM Symposium on Theory of Computing, pp. 67–73. ACM (2005)
4. Conover, C.: Is Smoking Irrational? Frobes/Healthcare, Fiscal, And Tax (2014)
5. Corley, H.: Games with vector payoffs. J. Optim. Theory an Appl. **47**(4), 491–498 (1985)
6. Daskalakis, C., Papadimitriou, C.: Computing pure Nash equilibria in graphical games via Markov random fields. In: ACM-EC, pp. 91–99 (2006)
7. Dresher, M.: Probability of a pure equilibrium point in n-person games. J. Combin. Theory **8**(1), 134–145 (1970)
8. Dubus, J.P., Gonzales, C., Perny, P.: Multiobjective optimization using GAI models. In: IJCAI, pp. 1902–1907 (2009)
9. Goldberg, K., Goldman, A., Newman, M.: The probability of an equilibrium point. J. Res. Nat. Bureau Stand. B. Math. Sci. **72**(2), 93–101 (1968)
10. Gonzales, C., Perny, P., Dubus, J.P.: Decision making with multiple objectives using GAI networks. Artif. Intell. **175**(7), 1153–1179 (2011)
11. Gottlob, G., Greco, G., Scarcello, F.: Pure Nash equilibria: hard and easy games. J. Artif. Intell. Res. **24**, 357–406 (2005)
12. Jiang, A.X., Leyton-Brown, K.: Computing pure Nash equilibria in symmetric action graph games. In: AAAI, vol. 1, pp. 79-85 (2007)
13. Kearns, M., Littman, M.L., Singh, S.: Graphical models for game theory. In: Proceedings of the Seventeenth Conference on Uncertainty in Artificial Intelligence, pp. 253–260. Morgan Kaufmann Publishers Inc. (2001)
14. Koutsoupias, E., Papadimitriou, C.: Worst-case equilibria. In: Meinel, C., Tison, S. (eds.) STACS 1999. LNCS, vol. 1563, pp. 404–413. Springer, Heidelberg (1999). https://doi.org/10.1007/3-540-49116-3_38

15. Monderer, D., Shapley, L.S.: Potential games. Games Econ. Behav. **14**(1), 124–143 (1996)
16. Morgan, J.: Approximations and well-posedness in multicriteria games. Ann. Oper. Res. **137**(1), 257–268 (2005)
17. Nash, J.: Equilibrium points in n-person games. Proc. Nat. Acad. Sci. **36**(1), 48–49 (1950)
18. Papadimitriou, C.: The complexity of finding Nash equilibria. Algorithmic Game Theory **2**, 30 (2007)
19. Papadimitriou, C.H., Yannakakis, M.: On the approximability of trade-offs and optimal access of web sources. In: Proceedings of the 41st Annual Symposium on Foundations of Computer Science, pp. 86–92. IEEE (2000)
20. Patrone, F., Pusillo, L., Tijs, S.: Multicriteria games and potentials. Top **15**(1), 138–145 (2007)
21. Rinott, Y., Scarsini, M.: On the number of pure strategy Nash equilibria in random games. Games Econ. Behav. **33**(2), 274–293 (2000)
22. Rosenthal, R.W.: A class of games possessing pure-strategy Nash equilibria. Int. J. Game Theory **2**(1), 65–67 (1973)
23. Roughgarden, T.: Intrinsic robustness of the price of anarchy. In: Proceedings of the Forty-First Annual ACM Symposium on Theory of Computing, pp. 513–522. ACM (2009)
24. Shapley, L.S.: Equilibrium points in games with vector payoffs. Naval Res. Logist. Q. **6**(1), 57–61 (1959)
25. Simon, H.A.: A behavioral model of rational choice. Q. J. Econ. **69**, 99–118 (1955)
26. Smith, A.: An Inquiry into the Nature and Causes of the Wealth of Nations. Edwin Cannan's annotated edition (1776)
27. Von Neumann, J., Morgenstern, O.: Theory of Games and Economic Behavior. Princeton University Press, Princeton (1944)
28. Voorneveld, M.: Potential games and interactive decisions with multiple criteria. Center for Economic Research, Tilburg University (1999)
29. Wang, S.: Existence of a Pareto equilibrium. J. Optim. Theory Appl. **79**(2), 373–384 (1993)
30. Wierzbicki, A.P.: Multiple criteria games - theory and applications. J. Syst. Eng. Electr. **6**(2), 65–81 (1995)
31. World-Health-Organization: WHO report on the global tobacco epidemic (2011)
32. Zeleny, M.: Games with multiple payoffs. Int. J. Game Theory **4**(4), 179–191 (1975)

Student-Project-Resource Allocation: Complexity of the Symmetric Case

Anisse Ismaili[1]([✉]), Tomoaki Yamaguchi[2], and Makoto Yokoo[1,2]

[1] RIKEN, Center for Advanced Intelligence Project AIP, Tokyo, Japan
anisse.ismaili@riken.jp
[2] Kyushu University, Fukuoka, Japan
yamaguchi@agent.inf.kyushu-u.ac.jp, yokoo@inf.kyushu-u.ac.jp

Abstract. In this paper, we consider a student-project-resource allocation problem, in which students and indivisible resources are allocated to every project. The allocated resources determine endogenously the student capacity of a project. Traditionally, this problem is divided in two: (I) resources are allocated to projects based on expected demands (resource allocation problem), and (II) students are matched with projects based on the capacity determined in the previous problem (many-to-one matching problem). Although both problems are well-understood, unless the expectations used in the first problem are correct, we obtain a suboptimal outcome. Thus, it is desirable to solve this problem as a whole, without dividing it. We start by introducing a compact representation that takes advantage of the symmetry of preferences. Then, we show that computing a nonwasteful matching is FP^{NP}-complete. Besides, a fair matching can be found in polynomial-time. Finally, deciding whether a stable (i.e. nonwasteful and fair) matching exists is NP^{NP}-complete.

Keywords: Matching · Resource allocation · Complexity

1 Introduction

In this work, we propose a simple but fundamental model, which we call a *student-project-resource* matching-allocation problem. From a first perspective, this problem can be seen as a two-sided, many-to-one matching problem (Roth and Sotomayor 1990), since students are matched to each project based on the preferences of students and projects. From a different perspective, this problem also contains discrete resource allocation problems (Korte and Vygen 2018), since resources are allocated to each project. However, unlike the standard setting of two-sided many-to-one matching, where the capacity of each project (or school) is exogenously determined, we assume it is endogenously determined by the allocated resources. A common practice is to determine the resource allocation part based on some expected demands or past data, and fix the capacities of projects. Then, the actual allocation of students to projects is determined by

© Springer Nature Switzerland AG 2018
T. Miller et al. (Eds.): PRIMA 2018, LNAI 11224, pp. 226–241, 2018.
https://doi.org/10.1007/978-3-030-03098-8_14

using some matching mechanism. In this approach, if the expectations used in the first problem are incorrect, we obtain a suboptimal outcome. To avoid such inefficiency, it is desirable to solve this problem as a whole without dividing it into a matching and a resource allocation problem. One real-life instance is the nursery school waiting list problem in Japan (Okumura 2017), with children (students), schools (projects) and nurses (resources). Children are matched to schools whose quotas are endogenously determined by the assignment of nurses to schools. In April 2017, a record breaking number of 47,700 children were wait-listed for daycare centers, urging for more efficient methods to allocate nurses to schools.

This paper follows a stream of works that deals with constrained matching. Two-sided matching has been attracting considerable attention from AI researchers (Aziz et al. 2017; Hamada et al. 2017b; Hosseini et al. 2015; Kawase and Iwasaki 2017; Kurata et al. 2017). A standard market deals with maximum quotas, i.e., capacity limits that cannot be exceeded. However, many real-world matching markets are subject to a variety of distributional constraints, including regional maximum quotas, which restrict the total number of students assigned to a set of schools (Kamada and Kojima 2015), minimum quotas, which guarantee that a certain number of students are assigned to each school (Fragiadakis et al. 2016; Goto et al. 2016; Hamada et al. 2017a; Sönmez and Switzer 2013; Sönmez 2013), and diversity constraints, which enforce that a school satisfies a balance between different types (e.g. socioeconomic status) of students (Ehlers et al. 2014; Hafalir et al. 2013; Kojima 2012; Kurata et al. 2017). Also, there exists a stream of works that examines the computational complexity for finding a matching that satisfies some desirable properties under distributional constraints (Biró et al. 2010; Fleiner and Kamiyama 2012; Hamada et al. 2014). Furthermore, Abraham *et al.* (2007) consider a (many-to-one) student-project-lecturer allocation problem, where every lecturer proposes a set of projects. Students have preferences on projects, and lecturers on students. Projects and lecturers have fixed exogenous capacities. Their student-proposing and lecturer-proposing algorithms both compute a stable matching. Chiarandini *et al.* (2017) consider the problem of allocating students to projects, by using linear programming, under various constraints, like envy-freeness.

In normal representations (where every student is represented explicitly), the large number of students is a first computational issue. In this work, we assume that large classes of students have the same preferences. The idea of grouping students with same preferences is related to "agent types" for coalition structure generation Ueda *et al.* (2011). It allows the introduction of a compact representation that deals with a large number of students. This also defines computational problems that we study in this paper[1]. We show the following:

---

[1] Two different representations result in two different computational problems with distinct intricacies. Here, our results on this compact representation have no implications on normal representations. Conversely, results on the normal representation would not imply theorems as strong as in the present article. (E.g. if the number of projects is a constant, the normal case is tractable, while here it is intractable.).

Theorem 1 Verifying whether a student-project matching is made feasible by some resource-project allocation is NP-complete, even in structured cases. However, if all resources have same capacity, this feasibility is in P.

Theorem 2 If resources are also partitioned into classes, feasibility is in FPT.

Theorem 3 Verifying whether a feasible matching is non-wasteful is coNP-complete.

Theorem 4 Finding a nonwasteful matching is FP^{NP}-complete.

Theorem 5 Given a fixed number of projects, there is an FPTAS for approximating a nonwasteful matching.

Theorem 6 A fair matching can be computed in polynomial time.

Theorem 7 A stable (i.e., nonwasteful and fair) matching may not exist.

Theorem 8 Verifying whether a matching is stable is coNP-complete.

Theorem 9 Deciding whether a stable matching exists is NP^{NP}-complete.

2 Preliminaries

In this section, we introduce our model, representation and complexity notions.

Definition 1 (Student-Project-Resource (SPR) Instance). An SPR instance is a tuple $\mathcal{I} = (S, P, R, X, \succ_S, \succsim_P, T_R, q_R)$, defined as follows.

- $S = \{s_1, \ldots, s_n\}$ is a set of students.
- $P = \{p_1, \ldots, p_m\}$ is a set of projects.
- $R = \{r_1, \ldots, r_k\}$ is a set of resources.
- $X \subseteq S \times P$ is a finite set of contracts between students and projects.
- $\succ_S = (\succ_s)_{s \in S}$ is a profile of students' preferences on projects and home ($\emptyset$).
- $\succsim_P = (\succsim_p)_{p \in P}$ is a profile of projects' preferences on (subsets of) students.
- In profile $T_R = (T_r)_{r \in R}$, resource r is compatible with projects $T_r \subseteq P$.
- In profile $q_R = (q_r)_{r \in R}$, integer $q_r \in \mathbb{N}_{>0}$ is the capacity of resource r.

A contract $x = (s, p) \in X$ means that student s is matched to project p. For each student $s \in S$, strict order $\succ_s$ represents her preference over set $P \cup \{\emptyset\}$. For each project $p \in P$, weak order $\succsim_p$ represents its preference over set $S \cup \{\emptyset\}$.

Contract (s, p) is acceptable for student s if $p \succ_s \emptyset$ holds, and acceptable for project p if $s \succsim_p \emptyset$ holds. Without loss of generality, we assume that X is the set of every contract (s, p) which is acceptable for student s and project p. □

One may extend preferences $\succsim_p$ to 2^S in a non-specified manner that satisfies both following properties: (i) responsiveness: for every pair of students $s, s' \in S$ and every subset $S' \subseteq S \setminus \{s, s'\}$, $s \succsim_p s' \Leftrightarrow S' \cup \{s\} \succsim_p S' \cup \{s'\}$, and (ii) separability: for every $s \in S$ and every $S' \subseteq S \setminus \{s\}$, $s \succsim_p \emptyset \Leftrightarrow S' \cup \{s\} \succsim_p S'$.

Given preference $\succsim_p$, let $\sim_p$ (resp. $\succ_p$) be its symmetric (resp. asymmetric) part. Given subset of contracts $Y \subseteq X$, student s and project p, set Y_s denotes contracts $\{(s, p) \in Y \mid p \in P\}$ and set Y_p denotes $\{(s, p) \in Y \mid s \in S\}$. Preferences naturally extend over contracts. When no misunderstanding is possible, we omit the subscript and just write $\succ$ or $\succsim$.

2.1   Solution Concepts

In this subsection, we define the solution concepts that are studied in this paper. Our main interest lies in stable (i.e., nonwasteful and fair) matchings.

Definition 2 (Matching). A (many students to one project) matching is a subset of contracts $Y \subseteq X$ such that for every student s, $|Y_s| \leq 1$. We can then abuse shorthand Y in a functional manner:

- Student s is mapped to project $Y(s) \in P \cup \{\emptyset\}$.
- Project p hires students $Y(p) \subseteq S$.

□

Definition 3 (Feasibility). Matching $Y \subseteq X$ is feasible if there exists an allocation function $\mu : R \to P$ that maps each resource r to a compatible project $\mu(r) \in T_r$, and that satisfies[2] for every project $p \in P$ that:

$$|Y_p| \leq \sum_{r \in \mu^{-1}(p)} q_r.$$

A feasible matching (Y, μ) is a couple of a matching and an allocation as above. Let $q_\mu(p) = \sum_{r \in \mu^{-1}(p)} q_r$ be the total of capacities allocated to project p.   □

Definition 4 (Nonwastefulness). For feasible matching (Y, μ), a contract $(s, p) \in X \setminus Y$ is a claiming pair if and only if:

1. student s has preference $p \succ_s Y(s)$,
2. project p has preference $s \succ_p \emptyset$,
3. and matching $(Y \setminus Y_s) \cup \{(s, p)\}$ is feasible.

A feasible matching (Y, μ) is nonwasteful if it admits no claiming pair.   □

   For instance, in Fig. 1, (s_2, p_1) is a claiming pair: by exchanging resources r_1 and r_2, project p_1 (resp p_2) gets capacity 2 (resp. 1), and the new matching is feasible.

Definition 5 (Fairness). For feasible matching (Y, μ), contract $(s, p) \in X \setminus Y$ is an envious pair if and only if:

1. student s has preference $p \succ_s Y(s)$,
2. there exists a student $s' \in Y(p)$ such that project p prefers $s \succ_p s'$,
3. and matching $Y \setminus (Y_s \cup Y_{s'}) \cup \{(s, p)\}$ is feasible.

(Since matching Y is feasible, matching $Y \setminus (Y_s \cup Y_{s'}) \cup \{(s, p)\}$ is feasible too.) A feasible matching (Y, μ) is fair if it has no envious pair.   □

Definition 6 (Stability). A feasible matching (Y, μ) is stable if it is nonwasteful and fair: it admits no claiming pair and no envious pair.   □

Definition 7 (Mechanism). A mechanism φ, given any SPR instance, outputs a feasible matching. If a mechanism always obtains a feasible matching that satisfies property A (e.g., fairness), we say this mechanism is A (e.g., fair).   □

---

[2] To handle the case where $p \in P \backslash \mu(R)$ and then $\mu^{-1}(p) = \emptyset$, we assume the standard convention that an empty sum equals zero.

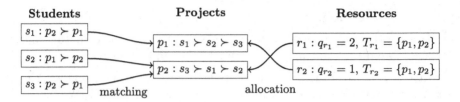

Fig. 1. Instance of student-project-resource allocation problem. The given matching is wasteful: (s_2, p_1) is a claiming pair; and it is unfair: s_1 envies s_2 on p_2.

2.2   Compact Representation Under Symmetry

A *normal* SPR instance is represented by the tuple in Definition 1; hence its length is polynomial in n, m and k, where the number of students n could be large. Instead, we propose a compact representation, tailored for instances with a large number of students. It takes advantage from the fact that numerous students can have the same preference, hence exponentially many students can be represented.

Definition 8 (Symmetric SPR Instance). In a symmetric SPR instance, set S is not fully represented, but is instead partitioned into student-classes $\{\sigma_1, \ldots, \sigma_\nu\}$. In every student class σ, students have the same preference over projects. Also, projects rank classes and are indifferent between students in the same class. For every student-class σ, we represent its number of students $\#\sigma$. Therefore, representation length is polynomial in ν, $\log(n)$, m and k. □

In this setting, at first, the representation of a matching as a map from S to P seems linear in n, hence non-compact w.r.t. $\log(n)$. To overcome this detail, a matching can also be represented compactly by $Y(\sigma, p) \in \mathbb{N}_{\geq 0}$ the number of students of each class mapped to each project.

2.3   Computational Problems

Computation times are always defined with respect to a representation length. We assume that the following concepts are common knowledge[3]: length function, decision problem, function problem, complexity classes P, FPT, NP, coNP, FP, FP^{NP}, NP^{NP}, $coNP^{NP}$, polynomial-time reduction, hardness and completeness (Papadimitriou 2003).

In this paper, we settle the computational complexity of the following problems. Our main interest lies in computing stable (i.e. nonwasteful and fair) matchings. While a nonwasteful matching (or a fair matching) always exists, we will show that a stable matching does not always exist. Hence, we address function problems for the formers, and a decision problem for the later.

---

[3] FP^{NP}: a solution can be found by calling polynomially many NP-oracles.
NP^{NP}: yes-instances can be solved in non deterministic polynomial-time by calling one NP-oracle.

Definition 9 (SPR Allocation Problems).

- Decision Problem SPR/SYM/FA:
  Given a symmetric SPR instance and a matching $Y \subseteq X$, is Y feasible?
- Decision Problem SPR/SYM/NW/VERIF:
  Given a sym. SPR instance and a feasible matching (Y, μ), is Y nonwasteful?
- Function Problem SPR/SYM/NW/FIND:
  Given a symmetric SPR instance, find a nonwasteful matching.
- Function Problem SPR/SYM/FAIR/FIND:
  Given a symmetric SPR instance, find a fair matching.
- Decision Problem SPR/SYM/NWFR/VERIF:
  Given a symmetric SPR instance and a feasible matching (Y, μ), is Y stable?
- Decision Problem SPR/SYM/NWFR/EXIST:
  Given a symmetric SPR instance, does a stable matching exist?

□

3   The Feasibility Problem

In this section, we study the problem of verifying whether a given matching Y is feasible. A simple tractable case is when all resources r have the same capacities $q_r = q$ and are compatible with every project $(T_r = P)$. Conversely, in the general case, we show completeness for class NP, even under strong assumptions.

Theorem 1. *Decision problem* SPR/SYM/FA *is NP-complete,*

1. *even when there are only two projects, two student-classes with only one acceptable project and $T_r = \{p_1, p_2\}$ for every resource r,*
2. *and even when for every resource r, capacity q_r is in $\{1, 3\}$.*

However, problem SPR/SYM/FA *is in class P when all resources r have the same capacity $q_r = q$, even if compatibilities $T_r \subseteq P$ vary between resources.*

Proof. Problem SPR/SYM/FA belongs to class NP: whether Y is feasible can be verified in polynomial time, when allocation μ is given as a certificate.   □

Proof (1.). Let any instance of PARTITION be defined by positive integer set $B = \{b_1, \ldots, b_k\}$. It asks whether there is a subset $B' \subseteq B$ s.t. $\sum_{b \in B'} b = \sum_{b \in B \setminus B'} b$.

We reduce it to an instance of SPR/SYM/FA. There are two projects. We identify resources R to integers B and the resources' capacities are $q_R = (b_1, \ldots, b_n)$. For every resource r, compatibilities $T_r = \{p_1, p_2\}$ hold. Let integer β be defined by $2\beta = \sum_{b \in B} b$. (The odd case is trivial.) There are two student classes of size β whose only acceptable project is p_1 (resp. p_2). In matching Y, the number of students assigned to projects is $|Y_{p_1}| = |Y_{p_2}| = \beta$.

One can identify subset $B' \subseteq B$ (resp. $B \setminus B'$) to resources set $\mu^{-1}(p_1)$ (resp. $\mu^{-1}(p_2)$), and weight $\sum_{b \in B'} b$ (resp. $\sum_{b \in B \setminus B'} b$) to project capacity $q_\mu(p_1) = \sum_{r \in \mu^{-1}(p_1)} q_r$ (resp. $q_\mu(p_2) = \sum_{r \in \mu^{-1}(p_2)} q_r$). The only way that $q_\mu(p_1) \geq \beta$ and $q_\mu(p_2) \geq \beta$ holds is when $q_\mu(p_1) = q_\mu(p_2) = \beta$. Consequently, there exists a subset $B' \subseteq B$ such that $\sum_{b \in B'} b = \sum_{b \in B \setminus B'} b$, if and only if there exists an allocation μ that makes Y feasible.   □

base set and 3-sets / resources

3-sets / projects	b1	b2	b3	⋯	b7	b8	b3k	C1	C2	⋯	Cm
3 students → C1	1	1	1					3			
3 students → C2			1		1	1			3		
3 students → C3					1	1	1			3	
3 students → C4		1	1	1						3	
3 students → C5			1		1	1				3	
3 students → Cm			1	1	1						3
3k students → p_{m+1}								3	3	3 3	3

Fig. 2. Reduction from problem X3C to SPR/SYM/FA, described in proof of Theorem 1.2. We depict X3C instance $\mathcal{C} = \{b_1b_2b_3,\ b_4b_6b_7,\ b_7b_8b_9,\ b_4b_5b_6,\ b_5b_8b_9,\ b_5b_6b_7\}$ on base $B = \{b_1, \ldots, b_9\}$. Each line represents a 3-set/project asking resources for three students, and the last line is a project asking for $3k$ resources. Each column represents a resource and the projects it is compatible with. In each square is the capacity of the resource (the same inside each column). Darker is a solution for X3C and SPR/SYM/FA; C_1, C_2, C_5 is an exact cover, and the allocation maps every resource to one project.

Proof (2.). Let any instance of X3C be defined by a set $B = \{b_1, \ldots, b_{3k}\}$ and a collection $\mathcal{C} = \{C_1, \ldots, C_m\}$ of 3-element subsets of B. It asks whether there exists a subcollection $\mathcal{C}' \subseteq \mathcal{C}$ such that every element of B occurs in exactly one member $C \in \mathcal{C}'$. We reduce it to an instance of SPR/SYM/FA (Fig. 2). Projects P are identified with collection $\mathcal{C}$ and a last element p_{m+1}. On every project $C \in P$, we define a subset S_C of three students wants to go, and on project p_{m+1}, a subset S_{m+1} of $3k$ students. Hence, the set of students is $S = S_{m+1} \cup \bigcup_{C \in P} S_C$, and total demand in resources is for $3m + 3k$ students. Resources R are identified with set $B \cup \mathcal{C}$. For every resource $b \in B$, we define $T_b = \{C \in \mathcal{C} \mid b \in C\}$ and capacity $q_b = 1$. For every resource $C \in \mathcal{C}$, we define $T_C = \{C, p_{m+1}\}$ and capacity $q_b = 3$. Hence, total offer in resources is $3k + 3m$, from $3k + m$ different resources.

(yes⇒yes.) Let subcollection $\mathcal{C}' \subseteq \mathcal{C}$ be an exact cover of B. Then one has feasible allocation $\mu : B \cup \mathcal{C} \to \mathcal{C} \cup \{p_{m+1}\}$ defined by:

- if $C \in \mathcal{C}'$, then $\mu(C) = p_{m+1}$ and $\forall b \in C, \mu(b) = C$;
- if $C \in \mathcal{C} \setminus \mathcal{C}'$, then $\mu(C) = C$.

Indeed, μ is a feasible allocation. It is a function (that maps every resource $b \in B$) because $\mathcal{C}'$ is an exact cover. If 3-set/project C is in the exact cover, since $|C| = 3$, it receives three resources. And, if a 3-set/project C is not in the exact cover, then it receives a resource of capacity three. The remaining resources (of remaining capacity $3k + 3m - 3m = 3k$) are mapped to project p_{m+1}, which then gets the allocated capacity $3k$ that it required.

(yes⇐yes.) Assuming feasibility by some $\mu : B \cup \mathcal{C} \to \mathcal{C} \cup \{p_{m+1}\}$, since total demand equates total offer $(3k + 3m)$, no project $p \in \{C_1, \ldots, C_m, p_{m+1}\}$ has excess resources, and only gets exactly the capacity it needs. Hence, if a resource C from $\mathcal{C}$ is allocated to p_{m+1}, then every resource $b \in C$ are allocated to project C. And, if a resource C from $\mathcal{C}$ is allocated to project C, no additional resources are allocated to project C. (It would contradict the tightness on capacities.) Therefore, subcollection $\mathcal{C}' = \mu^{-1}(p_{m+1})$ is an exact cover of B. Indeed, by definition of $\mathcal{C}'$, every element $b \in B$ is mapped to a 3-set in $\mathcal{C}'$ which receives exactly the right number (by tightness). □

Proof (However). If all resources r have the same capacity $q_r = q$, then the feasibility problem reduces to one where every project p asks for $\lceil \frac{|Y_p|}{q} \rceil$ resources, and all resources r have unitary capacity $q_r = 1$. Compatibilities $T_r \subseteq P$ are still combinatoric, but what remains of the problem boils down to a maximum flow problem that the Edmonds-Karp algorithm solves in polynomial-time Edmonds and Karp (1972).

This maximum flow problem is as follows. In the direction of flows, there is a super-source, the set of resources, the set of projects, and a super-sink. There are edges from the super-source to every resource, with edge-capacity one. Every resource r has edges going to compatible projects T_r and edge-capacity one. Every project has an edge to the super-sink, with edge-capacity $\lceil \frac{|Y_p|}{q} \rceil$. These later edges are all saturated in a maximum flow[4], if and only if, there is a feasible assignment of resources to projects. The assignment is given by the flow of resources to projects, due to the integral flow theorem. □

Theorem 2. *Assume that resource set $R = \{r_1, \ldots, r_k\}$ can be partitioned into κ resource-classes $\{\rho_1, \ldots, \rho_\kappa\}$ where inside every class ρ, resources have the same capacity, and assume that every resource is compatible with all projects.*

Then, for every class ρ, we only need to represent the number of resource $\#\rho$, and the representation length of the feasibility problem becomes $\Theta(m \log(n) + \kappa \log(k))$. Moreover, there is an $O(k^{2\kappa} m \log(n))$ algorithm addressing feasibility. Therefore, under this assumption, SPR/SYM/FA is in FPT w.r.t. (k, κ).

Proof. Given any integer $i \in \mathbb{N}_{\geq 0}$, let set $[i]$ be defined by $\{0, 1, \ldots, i\}$. Let integers $(x_1, \ldots, x_m) \in [n]^m$ be the capacities that must be achieved for the m projects. We proceed by dynamic programming on substructures $F_j(z_1, \ldots, z_\kappa) \in \mathbb{B}$, defined for every $0 \leq j \leq m$ and every $(z_1, \ldots, z_\kappa) \in [\#\rho_1] \times \ldots \times [\#\rho_\kappa]$, as *true* if and only if the capacities of projects $p_1, \ldots, p_j$ can be satisfied while still having $(z_1, \ldots, z_\kappa)$ resources unused. One can compute F_{j+1} as a function of F_j in time $O(k^\kappa \times k^\kappa)$. Indeed, there are at most k^κ entries in F_{j+1} and at most k^κ ways to satisfy capacity requirement $|Y_{p_{j+1}}|$ by using resources $(z_1, \ldots, z_\kappa)$. □

Since the number of resources k is an exponential of $\log(k)$ in the length, it is necessary to also include k as a parameter along κ, to formulate a FPT.

---

[4] That is, the maximum flow has the maximum possible value $\sum_{p \in P} \lceil \frac{|Y_p|}{q} \rceil$.

4   Computing a Nonwasteful Matching

In this section, we are interested in computing a nonwasteful matching. We start by showing that verifying whether a given feasible matching is nonwasteful is coNP-complete. Then, we adapt the Serial Dictatorship (SD) mechanism that was described in Goto *et al.* (2017), to our symmetric representation, and show that a nonwasteful mechanism can always be computed by $O(\nu m \log(n))$ queries to an oracle for verification problem SPR/SYM/NW/VERIF. Finally, we settle the complexity of computing a nonwasteful matching: SPR/SYM/NW/FIND is complete for FP^{NP} (to solve a polynomial number of queries to an NP-oracle). Also, we propose an FPTAS that assumes a bounded number of projects.

Theorem 3. *SPR/SYM/NW/VERIF is coNP-complete, even when there are only three projects, three student-classes with one acceptable projet, and every resource r is compatible with $T_r = \{p_1, p_2, p_3\}$. Besides, SPR/SYM/NW/VERIF can be decided by $O(\nu m)$ queries to an oracle for SPR/SYM/FA.*

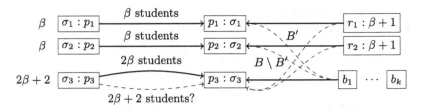

Fig. 3. Reduction from PARTITION to the complement of SPR/SYM/NW/VERIF. The thick (resp. dashed) arrows are the given matching (resp. a solution for PARTITION).

Proof. SPR/SYM/NW/VERIF is in coNP. Indeed, a claiming pair (s, p) along with the allocation μ' that makes $(Y \setminus Y_s) \cup \{(s, p)\}$ feasible are an easy certificate that matching Y is not nonwasteful.

(Hardness.) Let any instance of PARTITION be defined by positive integer set $B = \{b_1, \ldots, b_k\}$. It asks whether there exists a subset of integers $B' \subseteq B$ such that $\sum_{b \in B'} b = \sum_{b \in B \setminus B'} b$. We reduce the instance to the following instance of SPR/SYM/NW/VERIF, represented in Fig. 3. Let integer β be defined by $2\beta = \sum_{b \in B} b$. (The odd case is trivial.) There are three projects p_1, p_2, p_3 and three student classes $\sigma_1, \sigma_2, \sigma_3$ where p_i is the only acceptable project of students in class σ_i. The numbers of students in each class are $\sigma_1 = \beta, \sigma_2 = \beta, \sigma_3 = 2\beta+2$. There are $k+2$ resources. Resources r_1 and r_2 have capacities $\beta+1$. The other k resources are identified with set B and have capacities $q_{b_j} = b_j$. Every resource r has compatibilities $T_r = \{p_1, p_2, p_3\}$. In the given feasible matching (Y, μ), the allocation is $\mu(r_1) = p_1$, $\mu(r_2) = p_2$ and $\mu^{-1}(p_3) = B$. In Y, the β students from σ_1 (resp. σ_2) go to p_1 (resp. p_2), and only 2β students from σ_3 can be matched with p_3. (Two students from σ_3 stay home.) Hence the only possible claiming pairs are between σ_3 and p_3.

(yes⇒yes) If there exists a subset of integers $B' \subseteq B$ such that $\sum_{b \in B'} b = \sum_{b \in B \setminus B'} b = \beta$, then we can construct an allocation μ' defined by $\mu'^{-1}(p_1) = B'$, $\mu'^{-1}(p_2) = B \setminus B'$ and $\mu'^{-1}(p_3) = \{r_1, r_2\}$. Hence, $q_{\mu'}(p_1) = q_{\mu'}(p_2) = \beta$ and $q_{\mu'}(p_3) = 2\beta + 2$. Consequently, there are claiming pairs between σ_3 and p_3.

(yes⇐yes) Remark that the total excess of resources is two. If there is a claiming pair (between σ_3 and p_3), then p_1 or p_2 has an excess resource of zero, which cannot happen by using r_1 or r_2 who have capacity $\beta + 1$. Hence, $\mu'^{-1}(p_1)$ or $\mu'^{-1}(p_2)$ is a solution for PARTITION.   □

Theorem 4. *Concerning the computation of a nonwasteful matching:*

1. *There exists a non-wasteful mechanism for* SPR/SYM/NW/FIND. *Given a constant-time oracle for problem* SPR/SYM/FA, *it takes time* $O(\nu m \log(n))$. *(It requires to solve* $O(\nu m \log(n))$ *NP-complete problems* SPR/SYM/FA.)*
2. *Function problem* SPR/SYM/NW/FIND *is* FP^{NP}-*complete, even when there are only two projects, two student-classes (where students only have one acceptable project) and* $T_r = \{p_1, p_2\}$ *for every resource* r.

A positive corollary of 1. is that the tractable cases formulated in theorems 1 and 2 induce efficient algorithms for computing a non-wasteful mechanism. Conversely, 2. implies that in the general case, solving one SPR/SYM/NW/FIND instance is as hard as deciding a polynomial number of embedded SAT instances.

Proof (1.). We adapt Mechanism Serial Dictatorship (SD) [Goto et al. (2017)]. Their idea is to start from an empty matching Y, and to iterate serially on each student $s \in S$ by choosing contract $(s, p) \in X$ where (s, p) is the most preferred contract for s such that $Y \cup \{(s, p)\}$ is feasible (or by choosing no contract for s if no such contract exists). This mechanism is non-wasteful, because a claiming pair for Y would contradict that contract (s, p) is student s's top-preferred in what is still feasible. Also, it asks for feasibility at most $O(nm)$ times. (Besides, it is strategyproof.) For symmetric instances, here is an equivalent algorithm:

Definition 10 (Mechanism SD for Symmetric SPR Instances).
Let ℓ be an exogenous order on student-classes, where $\ell(i)$ is the i-th class in ℓ.

Initialization: Set matching Y to $\emptyset$.

For student-class σ in $\{\ell(1), \ldots, \ell(\nu)\}$: let integer θ be #σ
    For project p in order of preference $\succ_\sigma$ (and acceptable for σ):

1. Find the largest integer $\theta' \in [0, \theta]$ s.t. if $Y(\sigma, p)$ is set to $Y(\sigma, p) + \theta'$ then Y is still feasible, by mean of a dichotomy on θ' in $[0, \theta]$

2. Set $Y(\sigma, p)$ to $Y(\sigma, p) + \theta'$ and θ to $\theta - \theta'$. (If $\theta = 0$, go to next σ.)

The idea is to iterate on each student-class σ (instead of students) and on projects p, following σ's preference $\succ_\sigma$. Integer θ is the number of students in σ that remain to be matched. At each iteration, we determine maximal number θ' of remaining students $s \in \sigma$ who can get contract (s, p) while keeping Y feasible, by a dichotomy on $\theta' \in [0, \theta]$; hence in time $\log(n)$. The outcome is the same as if SD had been applied to each single student, hence both mechanisms are equivalent and satisfy the same properties. Therefore, SPR/SYM/NW/FIND is in class FP^{NP}. □

Proof (2.). Mechanism SD for the symmetric case shows that function problem SPR/SYM/NW/FIND is in class FP^{NP}. Let any instance of function problem MINPARTITION be defined by positive integer set $B = \{b_1, \ldots, b_m\}$. It requires to find a subset $B' \subseteq B$ that minimizes $|\sum_{b \in B'} b - \sum_{b \in B \setminus B'} b|$. It is FP^{NP}-complete (Gasarch et al. 1995, Theorem 3.6). We reduce this instance to the following SPR/SYM/NW/FIND instance, in the sense that finding a solution for the later, provides the optimum for the former. There are two projects p_1 and p_2. β students want to go to each project. Resources R are identified to multiset B in the sense that $q_{b_i} = b_i$ and $T_{b_i} = \{p_1, p_2\}$, for every resource/integer $b_i \in R \equiv B$.

The idea: nonwastefulness enforces balance between projects p_1 and p_2. Indeed, a nonwasteful matching (Y, μ) maximizes the least allocated project, otherwise this project has claiming pairs (while the other has an excess of resources). It follows that $B' = \mu^{-1}(p_1)$ minimizes $|\sum_{b \in B'} b - \sum_{b \in B \setminus B'} b|$. □

4.1   Computing an Approximately Nonwasteful Matching

In this subsection, we provide a positive result on the approximability of nonwasteful matchings, under the assumption that the number of projects is fixed. We start by defining what is meant here by approximately nonwasteful, and then expose our approximation theorem.

Definition 11 (Approximate Nonwastefulness). Given $\varepsilon \geq 0$ and feasible matching (Y, μ), a contract $(s, p) \in X \setminus Y$ is an $(1 + \varepsilon)$-claiming pair iff:

1. student s has preference $p \succ_s Y(s)$,
2. project p has preference $s \succ_p \emptyset$,
3. and considering matching $Y' = (Y \setminus Y_s) \cup \{(s, p)\}$, any matching with capacity requirements $(\lfloor (1 + \varepsilon)|Y'(p')| \rfloor \mid p' \in P)$ is feasible.

Given $\varepsilon \geq 0$, a feasible matching (Y, μ) is approximately $(1 + \varepsilon)$-nonwasteful if it admits no $(1 + \varepsilon)$-claiming pair as defined just above. □

This concept generalizes nonwasteful matchings (case $\varepsilon = 0$). It means that an approximately nonwasteful matching is a feasible matching that relaxes the notion of nonwastefulness. Indeed, $(1 + \varepsilon)$-claiming pairs are more demanding and fewer; it is then less demanding on a feasible matching to not admit $(1 + \varepsilon)$-claiming pairs. By definition, it guarantees that no (nonwasteful) matching can use $(1 + \varepsilon)$ times more seats than a $(1 + \varepsilon)$-nonwasteful matching.

Theorem 5. *For a fixed number of projects m and $\varepsilon > 0$, there is an FPTAS that computes a $(1+\varepsilon)$-nonwasteful matching in time $O\left(\nu m \ (\log(n) k (1/\varepsilon))^{m+1}\right)$.*

Proof. The idea is to run SD, but only checking an approximate feasibility that will answer no in a bounded set of cases where it should say yes-feasible. For this purpose, we use standard techniques from multi-objective approximation algorithms (see e.g. on the multi-objective knapsack problem (Erlebach et al. 2002, Sect. 4.2), which itself generalizes approximation algorithms in the fashion of Vazirani (2001, Chap. 8)).

Feasibility space $[1, n]^m$ is sliced geometrically on each project/dimension p by $F_p = \{1, (1 + \varepsilon)^{\frac{1}{k}}, (1 + \varepsilon)^{\frac{2}{k}}, \ldots, (1 + \varepsilon)^{\frac{u}{k}}\}$, where $u \geq k \log_{(1+\varepsilon)}(n) = O(k(1/\varepsilon) \log(n))$ fits the purpose. The discretized feasibility space is then $F = F_1 \times \ldots \times F_m$, which has size $O\left((k(1/\varepsilon) \log(n))^m\right)$. We then define a dynamic programming table $T_r : F \to \{\text{false}, \text{true}\}$ (for resources $r \in \{r_0\} \cup \{r_1, \ldots, r_k\}$) that maps every capacity vector $x \in F$ to true if and only if there exists an allocation satisfying it by using resources $\{r_1, \ldots, r\} \subseteq \{r_1, \ldots, r_k\}$. Dynamic programming is achieved by initializing table T_{r_0} to false, but $T_{r_0}(0)$ to true. Then, to compute $T_{r_{j+1}}$ from T_{r_j}, one adds resources one by one: For every entry x true in T_{r_j}, rounded entries corresponding to $x + e_i q_{r_{j+1}}$, $1 \leq i \leq m$ are set to true in $T_{r_{j+1}}$. The chain of errors is small enough to guarantee approximation ratio $(1 + \varepsilon)$ on every project/objective (Erlebach et al. 2002, Sect. 4.2). □

5 Computing a Fair Matching

The Artificial Cap Deferred Acceptance mechanism (ACDA), described in Goto *et al.* (2017), is as follows. Choose an arbitrary assignment μ that maps every resource to a compatible project. For each project p, set its maximum quota (capacity limit) $q_\mu(p)$ to $\sum_{r \in \mu^{-1}(p)} q_r$, and run the standard deferred acceptance mechanism (DA) from Gale and Shapley (1962). Goto *et al.* (2017) shows that ACDA is fair, strategyproof and that it is in polynomial-time. Mechanism ACDA adapts equivalently to symmetric instances:

Theorem 6. *Symmetric ACDA is fair and in polynomial-time $O(\nu \log(n) m)$.*

Proof (sketch). In the standard deferred acceptance mechanism, at each iteration, students apply to projects, and projects select their top-students who applied, constrained by the quota. Here, the idea is straightforward: instead of students, student-classes apply. □

6 Computing a Stable Matching

In this section, we try to satisfy both nonwastefulness and fairness requirements and show that a stable (i.e. nonwasteful and fair) matching may not exist. Furthermore, we settle the complexity of deciding whether a stable matching exists as complete for the second level of the polynomial hierarchy.

Theorem 7. *A stable (i.e. nonwasteful and fair) matching may not exist.*

Proof. The counter-example is the following. There are two students s_1, s_2 and two projects p_1, p_2. One resource r is available, with $q_r = 1$ and $T_r = \{p_1, p_2\}$. Preferences are:

$$s_1 : p_1 \succ p_2 \succ \emptyset \qquad p_1 : s_2 \succ s_1 \succ \emptyset$$
$$s_2 : p_2 \succ p_1 \succ \emptyset \qquad p_2 : s_1 \succ s_2 \succ \emptyset$$

Since only one resource is available, assuming non-wastefulness, only matchings of one student are possible, but all are blocked:

- If $Y(s_1) = p_1$, then (s_2, p_1) is an envious pair.
- If $Y(s_1) = p_2$, then (s_1, p_1) is a claiming pair.
- If $Y(s_2) = p_1$, then (s_2, p_2) is an claiming pair.
- If $Y(s_2) = p_2$, then (s_1, p_2) is an envious pair.

□

Theorem 8. *Decision problem* SPR/SYM/NwFR/VERIF *is coNP-complete.*

Proof. The same proof as for SPR/SYM/Nw/VERIF adapts: since projects are indifferent to their acceptable students, the concept of envious pair is empty. □

Theorem 9. *Decision problem* SPR/SYM/NwFR/EXIST *is* NP^{NP}*-complete, even when there are only six projects and six student-classes.*

Proof. SPR/SYM/NwFR/EXIST is in class NP^{NP}: for 'yes'-instances, a non-wasteful and fair matching (Y, μ) can be efficiently verified by an NP-oracle.

Let any instance of $\exists\forall$SUBSETSUM be defined by positive integer sets $A = \{a_1, \ldots, a_{|A|}\}$, $B = \{b_1, \ldots, b_{|B|}\}$ and target $\theta \in \mathbb{N}_{>0}$. It asks whether:

$$\exists A' \subseteq A, \quad \forall B' \subseteq B, \quad \sum_{a \in A'} a + \sum_{b \in B'} b \neq \theta. \tag{1}$$

Its complement $\forall\exists$SUBSETSUM asks $\forall A' \subseteq A, \exists B' \subseteq B, \sum_{a \in A'} a + \sum_{b \in B'} b = \theta$. $\exists\forall$SUBSETSUM is NP^{NP}-complete (Hamada et al. 2017b, Lemma 2). It holds even if $\sum_{a \in A} a \leq \theta \leq \sum_{b \in B} b$, since the other cases have trivial answers. We reduce the given instance to an SPR/SYM/NwFR/EXIST instance, that will ask whether:

$$\exists \text{ feasible matching}(Y, \mu), \quad \forall (s, p) \text{ it is not a claiming or envious pair} \tag{2}$$

Our construct is depicted in Fig. 4. There are six projects $p_A, p'_A, p_B, p'_B, p_1, p_2$ and six student-classes $\sigma_a, \sigma'_a, \sigma_b, \sigma'_b, s_1, s_2$, where the last two are just students. The preferences of students and projects are depicted in Fig. 4. Set of resources R^A (resp. R^B) is identified with set A (resp. B) which defines its capacities. For every resource $a_i \in R^A$ (resp. $b_j \in R^B$), compatibilities are $T_{a_i} = \{p_A, p'_A\}$ (resp. $T_{b_i} = \{p_B, p'_B\}$). Elements s_1, s_2, p_1, p_2, r_1 are as in Theorem 5.

(1)$\Rightarrow$(2). Assume $\exists A' \subseteq A, \forall B' \subseteq B, \sum_{a \in A'} a + \sum_{b \in B'} b \neq \theta$, and let us construct a stable matching. One has $\mu^{-1}(p_A) = A'$ and $\mu^{-1}(p'_A) = A \setminus A'$, and $Y(\sigma_A, p_A) = \sum_{a \in A'} a$ and $Y(\sigma'_A, p'_A) = \sum_{a \in A \setminus A'} a$. No claiming pair can occur with p_A or p'_A because more resource for one, is less resource for the other, and an envious pair is impossible by lack of student classes. Then, let us choose $\mu^{-1}(p_B) = B'$ (resp. $\mu^{-1}(p'_B) = B \setminus B'$) such that $\min\{q_\mu(p_B) - \#\sigma_B, q_\mu(p'_B) - \#\sigma'_B\}$ is maximized given A'. Both capacities miss their targets, because of the first assumption (one below, one above), and there is no other allocation that would make a claiming pair between σ_B and p_B, or σ'_B and p'_B. (Same reason as Theorem 3.2.) Then, we can allocate r_1 to p_B or p'_B, and by emptiness, no claiming/envious pair occurs between s_1, s_2, p_1, p_2.

not(1)$\Rightarrow$not(2). Assume $\forall A' \subseteq A, \exists B' \subseteq B, \sum_{a \in A'} a + \sum_{b \in B'} b = \theta$, and for the sake of contradiction, let us assume a stable matching (Y, μ). Every resource $a_i \in R^A$ must be used. Let $\mu^{-1}(p_A) = A'$ and $\mu^{-1}(p'_A) = A \setminus A'$. Moreover, $Y(\sigma_A, p_B) = \sum_{a \in A \setminus A'} a$ and $Y(\sigma'_A, p'_B) = \sum_{a \in A'} a$; hence $|Y(p_B)| = \theta - \sum_{a \in A'} a$ and $|Y(p'_B)| = \sum_{a \in A'} a + \sum_{b \in B} b - \theta$. Let B' fit A' in the first assumption, $\mu^{-1}(p_B) = B'$ and $\mu^{-1}(p'_B) = B \setminus B'$. Hence all the students in σ_B and σ'_B are matched with p_B and p'_B: Using r_1 on p_B or p'_B would be a waste. But then, a claiming or envious pair occurs between s_1, s_2, p_1, p_2 (Theorem 5). $\qquad\Box$

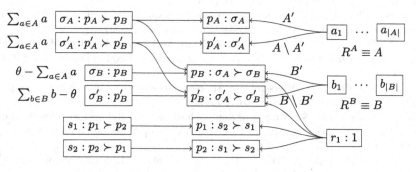

Fig. 4. Reduction from NP^{NP} problem $\exists\forall\textsc{SubsetSum}$ to SPR/Sym/NwFr/Exist. Left of students are the sizes of the classes. Arrows indicate acceptability/compatiblity.

7   Conclusion

In this paper, we proposed a compact representation for symmetric SPR instances. Then, we completely characterized the computational complexity of matching feasibility, nonwastefulness and stability: it is intractable to compute, but not under natural assumptions. Strikingly, only Theorem 9 involves students who consider more than two projects acceptable. It suggests that complexity does not come from the preferences of students, until Theorem 9.

Normal representations, where students are represented explicitly are a different representation, hence a different problem with distinct intricacies. An interesting prospect is to settle the complexity of the same problems for these non-compact representations. Besides, discovering more operational solutions like more tractable cases, MILP formulations, or approximation schemes, would be useful on the Student-Project-Resource Allocation problem.

Acknowledgement. This work was partially supported by JSPS KAKENHI (Grant Number 17H00761) and JST, Strategic International Collaborative Research Program, SICORP.

References

Abraham, D.J., Irving, R.W., Manlove, D.F.: Two algorithms for the student-project allocation problem. J. Discrete Algorithms **5**(1), 73–90 (2007)

Aziz, H., et al.: Stable matching with uncertain pairwise preferences. In: Proceedings of the 16th Conference on Autonomous Agents and MultiAgent Systems, AAMAS, pp. 344–352 (2017)

Biró, P., Fleiner, T., Irving, R.W., Manlove, D.F.: The college admissions problem with lower and common quotas. Theor. Comput. Sci. **411**(34–36), 3136–3153 (2010)

Chiarandini, M., Fagerberg, R., Gualandi, S.: Handling preferences in student-project allocation. Ann. Oper. Res. **270**, 1–14 (2017)

Edmonds, J., Karp, R.M.: Theoretical improvements in algorithmic efficiency for network flow problems. J. ACM (JACM) **19**(2), 248–264 (1972)

Ehlers, L., Hafalir, I.E., Yenmez, M.B., Yildirim, M.A.: School choice with controlled choice constraints: hard bounds versus soft bounds. J. Econ. Theory **153**, 648–683 (2014)

Erlebach, T., Kellerer, H., Pferschy, U.: Approximating multiobjective knapsack problems. Manage. Sci. **48**(12), 1603–1612 (2002)

Fleiner, T., Kamiyama, N.: A matroid approach to stable matchings with lower quotas. In: Proceedings of the 23rd Annual ACM-SIAM Symposium on Discrete Algorithms (SODA-12), pp. 135–142 (2012)

Fragiadakis, D., Iwasaki, A., Troyan, P., Ueda, S., Yokoo, M.: Strategyproof matching with minimum quotas. ACM Trans. Econ. Comput. **4**(1), 6:1–6:40 (2016)

Gale, D., Shapley, L.S., David Gale and Lloyd Stowell Shapley: College Admissions and the Stability of Marriage. Am. Math. Monthly **69**(1), 9–15 (1962)

Gasarch, W.I., Krentel, M.W., Rappoport, K.J.: OptP as the normal behavior of NP-complete problems. Math. Syst. Theory **28**(6), 487–514 (1995)

Goto, M., Iwasaki, A., Kawasaki, Y., Kurata, R., Yasuda, Y., Yokoo, M.: Strategyproof matching with regional minimum and maximum quotas. Artif. Intell. **235**, 40–57 (2016)

Goto, M., Kojima, F., Kurata, R., Tamura, A., Yokoo, M.: Designing matching mechanisms under general distributional constraints. Am. Econ. J.: Microecon. **9**(2), 226–62 (2017)

Hafalir, I.E., Yenmez, M.B., Yildirim, M.A.: Effective affirmative action in school choice. Theor. Econ. **8**(2), 325–363 (2013)

Hamada, K., Iwama, K., Miyazaki, S.: The hospitals/residents problem with lower quotas. Algorithmica **74**, 1–26 (2014)

Hamada, N., Hsu, C.-L., Kurata, R., Suzuki, T., Ueda, S., Yokoo, M.: Strategy-proof school choice mechanisms with minimum quotas and initial endowments. Artif. Intell. **249**, 47–71 (2017a)

Hamada, N., Ismaili, A., Suzuki, T., Yokoo, M.: Weighted matching markets with budget constraints. In: Proceedings of the 16th Conference on Autonomous Agents and MultiAgent Systems, AAMAS, pp. 317–325 (2017b)

Hosseini, H., Larson, K., Cohen, R.: On manipulablity of random serial dictatorship in sequential matching with dynamic preferences. In: Proceedings of the 29th Conference on Artificial Intelligence, AAAI, pp. 4168–4169 (2015)

Kamada, Y., Kojima, F.: Efficient matching under distributional constraints: theory and applications. Am. Econ. Rev. **105**(1), 67–99 (2015)

Kawase, Y., Iwasaki, A.: Near-feasible stable matchings with budget constraints. In: Proceedings of the 26th International Joint Conference on Artificial Intelligence, IJCAI, pp. 242–248 (2017)

Kojima, F.: School choice: impossibilities for affirmative action. Games Econ. Behav. **75**(2), 685–693 (2012)

Korte, B., Vygen, J.: Combinatorial Optimization: Theory and Algorithms. Springer, Heidelberg (2018)

Kurata, R., Hamada, N., Iwasaki, A., Yokoo, M.: Controlled school choice with soft bounds and overlapping types. J. Artif. Intell. Res. **58**, 153–184 (2017)

Okumura, Y.: School choice with general constraints: a market design approach for the nursery school waiting list problem in Japan. (2017). mimeo (https://www.academia.edu/19700640/)

Papadimitriou, C.H.: Computational Complexity. John Wiley and Sons Ltd., Hoboken (2003)

Roth, A.E., Sotomayor, M.A.O.: Two-Sided Matching: A Study in Game-Theoretic Modeling and Analysis (Econometric Society Monographs). Cambridge University Press, Cambridge (1990)

Sönmez, T., Switzer, T.B.: Matching with (branch-of-choice) contracts at the united states military academy. Econometrica **81**(2), 451–488 (2013)

Sönmez, T.: Bidding for army career specialties: improving the ROTC branching mechanism. J. Polit. Econ. **121**(1), 186–219 (2013)

Ueda, S., Kitaki, M., Iwasaki, A., Yokoo, M.: Concise characteristic function representations in coalitional games based on agent types. In: The 10th International Conference on Autonomous Agents and Multiagent Systems-Volume 3, pp. 1271–1272. International Foundation for Autonomous Agents and Multiagent Systems (2011)

Vazirani, V.V.: Approximation Algorithms. Springer, Heidelberg (2001)

Repeated Triangular Trade: Sustaining Circular Cooperation with Observation Errors

Kota Shigedomi[1](✉), Tadashi Sekiguchi[2], Atsushi Iwasaki[3], and Makoto Yokoo[1]

[1] Kyushu University, Motooka 744, Nishi-ku, Fukuoka, Japan
shigedomi@agent.inf.kyushu-u.ac.jp, yokoo@inf.kyushu-u.ac.jp
[2] Kyoto University, Yoshida-Honmachi, Sakyo-ku, Kyoto, Japan
sekiguchi@kier.kyoto-u.ac.jp
[3] University of Electro-Communications, Chofugaoka 1-5-1, Chofu, Tokyo, Japan
iwasaki@is.uec.ac.jp

Abstract. We introduce a new fundamental problem called *triangular trade*, which is a natural extension of the well-studied prisoner's dilemma for three (or more) players where a player cannot directly punish a seemingly defecting player. More specifically, this problem deals with a situation where the power/influence of players is one-way, players would be better off if they maintain circular cooperation, but each player has an incentive to defect. We analyze whether players can sustain such circular cooperation when they repeatedly play this game and each player observes the actions of another player with some observation errors (imperfect private monitoring). We confirm that no simple strategy can constitute an equilibrium within any reasonable parameter settings when there are only two actions: "Cooperate" and "Defect." Thus, we introduce two additional actions: "Whistle" and "Punish," which can be considered as a slight modification of "Cooperate." Then, players can achieve sustainable cooperation using a simple strategy called Remote Punishment strategy (RP), which constitutes an equilibrium for a wide range of parameters. Furthermore, we show the payoff obtained by a variant of RP is optimal within a very general class of strategies that covers virtually all meaningful strategies.

Keywords: Repeated games · Private monitoring
Belief-free equilibrium

1 Introduction

The prisoner's dilemma (PD) concisely represents a ubiquitous situation where the cooperation of two players is efficient, but each player has an incentive to defect. A repeated game, where players repeatedly play the same stage game (e.g., PD) over an infinite time horizon, is a formal model that can explain why cooperation arises in long-term relationships. In this paper, we introduce a new

© Springer Nature Switzerland AG 2018
T. Miller et al. (Eds.): PRIMA 2018, LNAI 11224, pp. 242–257, 2018.
https://doi.org/10.1007/978-3-030-03098-8_15

problem called *triangular trade*, which is similar to the PD, but a player cannot directly punish a player who has (seemingly) defected. In the real world, there exist many situations where the influence of players is not symmetric and can be considered as one-way (e.g., a teacher to a student/parent, a TV production company to a viewer). It is also common that such one-way relations create a cycle, e.g., a teacher affects a student/parent, the student/parent affects the school attended by the student, and the school affects the teacher, or a production company affects a viewer, the viewer affects a sponsor, and the sponsor affects the production company. In such situations, as in the PD, it is quite possible that the cooperation of all the players is efficient (e.g., the teacher gives a good lecture, the student/parent donate enough money, and the school supports the teacher), but each player has an incentive to defect. The triangular trade is a problem that concisely represents such a ubiquitous situation. Such a situation can occur in international trade among three countries, where the trade between two countries is strongly imbalanced [17]. Also, let us assume there exist a professor, a postdoctoral researcher, and a new Ph.D. student in a laboratory. Assume the professor can assist the postdoc to be a full-fledged researcher, the postdoc can give the student practical advice to start her research, and the student can bring some fresh ideas for the professor to explore a new research direction. Then, these players are in a triangular trade like situation. Since a player cannot directly punish a seemingly defecting player, obtaining sustainable cooperation appears difficult especially when a player can only imperfectly observe other players' actions. To the best of our knowledge, we are the first to analyze this problem in repeated games with imperfect private monitoring.

Repeated games have received considerable attention in the literature of AI, multi-agent systems, and economics. The case of perfect monitoring, where each player can observe other players' actions, is now well understood. There is also a large body of literature on the *imperfect monitoring* case, where players' actions are only imperfectly observed through some signals. Such imperfect monitoring cases are further classified into *public* and *private monitoring* cases. If *all* players observe the same set of signals that imperfectly indicate players' actions, we have an *imperfect public monitoring* case. An example is the PD game with action-errors, investigated by Nowak and Sigmund [20]. In contrast, suppose that each player observes her opponent's action with some observation errors. Assume that each player chooses "Cooperate" (C) or "Defect" (D), and a signal, which determines a player's outcome, can be either good (g) or bad (b). If the opponent plays C, a player usually observes g, but she may observe b with a small probability. An important feature of this model is that a player's observation is her private information (which is not known to the opponent). This is an example of *imperfect private monitoring*, where each player privately receives signals about the actions of other players. In private monitoring, verifying an equilibrium becomes hard since we need to check that no player has an incentive to deviate under any possible belief she might have on the past histories of other players. To overcome this difficulty, a special type of equilibrium called a *belief-free* equilibrium is identified, where checking whether a profile of strategies forms such an equilibrium becomes more tractable [9, 22]. Also, possible cooperative relations that are sustainable in the repeated PD are examined [8].

We first show that when there are only two actions C and D, there exists no profile of simple strategies that constitutes a belief-free equilibrium.[1] We confirm this fact by exhaustively enumerating all simple strategies. Thus, we consider adding new actions, which we call "Whistle" and "Punish." These actions are similar to C; they are dominated by D. Thus, adding them is irrelevant in a one-shot game, i.e., they do not affect the equilibria. Introducing such an action is not interesting with perfect or imperfect public monitoring, since it is well-known that cooperative relations are sustainable without introducing such an action due to the celebrated folk theorem [11, 12]. With imperfect private monitoring, introducing an action that can severely punish other players can be effective even if it is dominated by another action, i.e., the equilibria of a repeated game may significantly change if the added action changes the players' minimax values. Our argument is *not* based on this logic; these actions are mildly spiteful actions that do not change the minimax values.

To our surprise, it turns out that by adding these actions, players can achieve sustainable cooperation using a very simple strategy called Remote Punishment strategy (RP), which constitutes a belief-free equilibrium in a wide range of parameter settings. Since a belief-free equilibrium is a very strict requirement for an equilibrium, it is often the case that no strategies constitute a belief-free equilibrium. Even if one exists, it tends to be very complex and requires a sophisticated probabilistic state transition. Our RP is remarkable since it is a very simple deterministic strategy. We obtain a simple closed-form sufficient and necessary condition in which it constitutes a belief-free equilibrium. Furthermore, we show the payoff obtained by a variant of RP is optimal within a very general class of strategies that covers virtually all meaningful strategies.

2   Model

2.1   Repeated Triangular Trade

Let us describe the basic model of the triangular trade with three players. There are three players $N = \{0, 1, 2\}$. Each player $i \in N$ repeatedly plays the same stage game over an infinite horizon $t = 0, 1, 2, \ldots$. In each period, player i takes some action a_i from a finite set A. Assume an action profile in that period is $a = (a_0, a_1, a_2) \in A^3$. Then, her expected payoff in that period is given by stage game payoff function $u_i(a)$. In the triangular trade, we assume that the stage game payoff of player i depends only on her own action a_i and the action of player $i - 1$, i.e., a_{i-1}. In this paper, when we write player $i \pm k$ ($k \in \mathbb{N}$), it means player $i \pm k$ mod 3.[2]

---

[1] We say a strategy is simple when it is concisely represented by a finite-state automaton with a few states.

[2] The same applies to action $a_{i \pm k}$ or state $\theta_{i \pm k}$.

Table 1. Stage game payoff of player i (two actions)

$a_i \backslash a_{i-1}$	C	D
C	$1-c$	$-c$
D	1	0

In the basic model, we assume that actions $A = \{C, D\}$ and payoff u_i is given in Table 1, where $0 < c < 1$. In the triangular trade, player i makes a product and delivers it to player $i + 1$. Action C means that a player exerts adequate effort in the production (which incurs cost c), while action D means that a player exerts no effort at all (which incurs no cost). By receiving a product made with adequate effort, a player obtains benefit 1, while by receiving a product made with no effort, a player obtains no benefit. Note that this game has a similar characteristic as PD. Here, C is dominated by D. Thus, in the one-shot game, the dominant strategy equilibrium is that all players play D and their utilities are 0. However, if they play C, their utilities are $1 - c > 0$. The triangular trade can be considered as one natural extension of the PD for three (or more) players.[3] More specifically, a typical domain where a PD like situation would occur is *mutual aid*; each player has her own task, which can be done better with the help of another player, but a player obtains no merit by helping another. Assume a similar situation with three players, where each task requires at most two players, then a natural and efficient way is to maintain circular cooperation. This is exactly the same problem setting as the triangular trade.

Within each period, player i observes her private signal $\omega_i \in \Omega$ that is related to player $i - 1$'s action. Observations are $\Omega = \{g, b\}$. Observation g means that the delivered product from $i - 1$ has high quality and b means that it has low quality. Let $\boldsymbol{\omega} = (\omega_0, \omega_1, \omega_2) \in \Omega^3$ denote the profile of the private signals for all players. Let $o(\omega_i \mid a_{i-1})$ denote the marginal distribution of ω_i given player $i - 1$'s action a_{i-1}. The signals are independent, i.e., the probability that players receive the profile of private signals $\boldsymbol{\omega}$ when players take $\boldsymbol{a}$ is given as $o(\boldsymbol{\omega} \mid \boldsymbol{a}) = \prod_{i \in N} o(\omega_i \mid a_{i-1})$.

We assume *nearly-perfect* monitoring. When a player chooses C (or D), we assume that the "correct" signal is g (or b). We assume a player receives a correct signal with high probability q but she receives a wrong signal with small probability $1 - q$. Also, we assume no player can infer which action was taken (or not taken) by another player for sure; each signal $\omega_i \in \Omega$ occurs with a positive probability for any $a_{i-1} \in A$ (*full-support assumption*).

Player i's *realized* payoff, which is determined by her own action and signal, is denoted as $\pi_i(a_i, \omega_i)$. Hence, her expected payoff is given by $\sum_{\omega_i \in \Omega} \pi_i(a_i, \omega_i) \cdot o(\omega_i \mid a_{i-1})$. The product can occasionally have low (or high) quality even if the player exerts adequate effort (or no effort). It is natural to assume that

---

[3] There exist many other directions to extend the PD for three or more players, including the well-known public goods game [13]. Our extension is original, as it addresses the case where a player cannot directly punish a seemingly deviating player.

the benefit of the product is solely determined by its quality. We assume this expected value of the realized payoff is identical to stage game payoff $u_i(\boldsymbol{a})$. This formulation ensures that realized payoff π_i conveys no more information than a_i and ω_i. The particular values of the realized payoffs are not important for analyzing equilibria since their expected value, which is equal to $u_i(\boldsymbol{a})$, depends only on the action profile $\boldsymbol{a}$. Thus, in this paper, we do not specify the particular values of the realized payoffs. This model is standard in the literature of repeated games with private monitoring [18].

The stage game is repeatedly played over an infinite horizon. Player i's expected discounted payoff from a sequence of action profiles $\boldsymbol{a}^0, \boldsymbol{a}^1, \ldots$ is $\sum_{t=0}^{\infty} \delta^t u_i(\boldsymbol{a}^t)$, with discount factor $\delta \in (0, 1)$. The (expected) discounted *average payoff* (payoff per period) is defined as $(1 - \delta) \sum_{t=0}^{\infty} \delta^t u_i(\boldsymbol{a}^t)$. If a player obtains the same stage game payoff, say 1, for every period, the discounted average payoff becomes 1.

2.2 Strategy Representation and Equilibrium Concept

For player i, the set of her private histories in period t is $H_i^t := (A \times \Omega)^t$. Each element $h_i^t = (a_i^0, \omega_i^0, \ldots, a_i^{t-1}, \omega_i^{t-1}) \in H_i^t$ represents the sequence of her actions and observation profiles until the end of period $t - 1$. H_i^0 is interpreted as a singleton, which represents a (dummy) initial history. Let H_i denote all the possible histories of i, i.e., $\bigcup_{t \geq 0} H_i^t$. A (pure) strategy for player i is represented as function $s_i : H_i \rightarrow A$, which returns the action that player i chooses in period t given her history h_i^t. Let $\boldsymbol{s} = (s_i, \boldsymbol{s}_{-i})$ denote the profile of strategies, where s_i is i's strategy and $\boldsymbol{s}_{-i}$ is the profile of the strategies of the other players. Let $E_i(\boldsymbol{s})$ denote player i's discounted average payoff when all the players act based on strategy profile $\boldsymbol{s}$. We say s_i is a best response to $\boldsymbol{s}_{-i}$ if for any possible strategy s_i' of player i, $E_i((s_i, \boldsymbol{s}_{-i})) \geq E_i((s_i', \boldsymbol{s}_{-i}))$ holds.

A standard equilibrium concept in repeated games is a *sequential equilibrium*, which is a refinement of a subgame perfect equilibrium as well as a perfect Bayesian equilibrium [15]. In a private monitoring setting, profile of strategies $\boldsymbol{s}$ is a sequential equilibrium if for each $i \in N$, for any t, for any history $h_i^t \in H_i^t$, and a possible belief reached after observing h_i^t, acting according to s_i (for a given history h_i^t) is a best response under the belief.

A Finite-State Automaton (FSA) is a common approach for concisely representing a strategy in an infinitely repeated game. Player i's FSA M_i is defined by $\langle \Theta_i, \hat{\theta}_i, f_i, T_i \rangle$, where Θ_i is a set of states, $\hat{\theta}_i \in \Theta_i$ is an initial state, and $f_i : \Theta_i \rightarrow A$ determines the action choice in each state, and $T_i : \Theta_i \times \Omega \rightarrow \Theta_i$ specifies a deterministic state transition. Specifically, $T_i(\theta_i^t, \omega_i^t)$ returns next state θ_i^{t+1} when the current state is θ_i^t and player i's private signal is ω_i^t. For M_i and h_i^t, the action to choose in period t is defined as $f_i(\theta_i^t)$, where θ_i^t is the state reached after history h_i^t.

An FSA without specification of the initial state, i.e., $m_i = \langle \Theta_i, f_i, T_i \rangle$, is a *Finite-State preAutomaton* (pre-FSA). $(m_i, \hat{\theta}_i)$ denotes an FSA obtained by pre-FSA m_i, where the initial state is $\hat{\theta}_i$. Let $\boldsymbol{M} = (M_i)_{i \in N}$ denote a profile of

FSAs. Figure 1 shows an example of a pre-FSA (this pre-FSA is for the extended game with additional actions/observations introduced in the next section). Each node represents a state and a direct link represents a state transition according to an observation. For FSA M_i, let $\Theta_i^t \subseteq \Theta_i$ denote a set of states reachable in period t. By the full-support assumption, Θ_i^t is determined independently from the strategies of other players.

Now, we are ready to define a belief-free equilibrium, which is a special case of a sequential equilibrium.

Definition 1 (Belief-free equilibrium). *We say M is a belief-free equilibrium if for all t, for all $\boldsymbol{\theta} = (\theta_i)_{i \in N} \in \prod_{i \in N} \Theta_i^t$, and for all $i \in N$, (m_i, θ_i) is a best response when player $j \neq i$ is going to behave based on (m_j, θ_j).*

3   Game with Additional Actions and Observations

We exhaustively generated all small FSAs (each of which has at most three states) and confirmed that none of them constitutes a belief-free equilibrium under any reasonable parameter settings, except for a trivial strategy that simply plays D forever. More specifically, we checked parameter settings in which $0.1 \leq \delta \leq 0.9$ (in increments of 0.2), $0.55 \leq q \leq 0.95$ (in increments of 0.1), and $0.1 \leq c \leq 0.9$ (in increments of 0.1). Here, we restrict the number of states to three since the number of strategies grows quickly by increasing the number of states. The number of possible pre-FSAs with k states is given as $2^k \cdot k^{2^k}$ where the number of actions/observations is two. It is 5832 when $k = 3$, 2048576 when $k = 4$, and 312500000 when $k = 5$.

Consequently, we consider a slightly modified game with two additional actions and observations. Here, we assume that a player can slightly modify action C. More specifically, the player actually exerts adequate effort to produce a product, but she intentionally damages the product such that the benefit for the receiver is reduced and the receiver notices (with high probability) that the producer intentionally did so. There are two additional actions W ("Whistle") and P ("Punish"), and two associated observations w and p. The stage game payoff is given in Table 2. Here, doing W or P incurs cost c (as doing C). When player $i - 1$ plays W (or P), player i's benefit is reduced by y (or z) compared to the case where player $i - 1$ plays C. We assume $0 \leq y, z \leq 1$, i.e., P (or W) is a relatively mild spiteful action; it is weaker than (or at most equal to) making the product completely useless.

For actions C, D, W, and P, their "correct" signals are g, b, w, and p, respectively. Then, the observation probability $o(\omega_i \mid a_{i-1})$ is q when ω_i is the correct signal, and $e = (1 - q)/3$ when ω_i is an incorrect signal. We assume $1/4 < q < 1$, i.e., the correct signal is most likely.

4   Generalized Remote Punishment (GRP) Strategy

We first introduce a general class of strategies, which we call Generalized Remote Punishment (GRP). We say a strategy is an instance of GRP if it satisfies the following conditions.

Table 2. Stage game payoff (four actions)

$a_i \backslash a_{i-1}$	C	D	W	P
C	$1-c$	$-c$	$1-y-c$	$1-z-c$
D	1	0	$1-y$	$1-z$
W	$1-c$	$-c$	$1-y-c$	$1-z-c$
P	$1-c$	$-c$	$1-y-c$	$1-z-c$

- Each player's default action is C. As long as she observes g, she continues to play C.
- When a player observes b, with probability r, she takes particular action $\tilde{a}$, whose correct signal is $\tilde{\omega}$. Here, $\tilde{a}$ can be any action except C. We assume a player plays $\tilde{a}$ only when she observes b.
- If player i observes $\tilde{\omega}$, she starts punishing player $i+1$. The punishment can be arbitrary: it can be probabilistic and not necessarily by P, and can even be done over several periods.

Class GRP is very general and covers virtually all strategies in which we are interested. Since we are interested in sustainable cooperation, we can assume the default action is C without loss of generality. Also, since we are looking for an equilibrium strategy, the deviating action D must be punished somehow. In our setting, the only way to punish a seemingly defecting player is to ask the next player to do so. The following theorem illustrates the amount of inevitable loss due to imperfect monitoring.

Theorem 1. *If a strategy that is an instance of GRP constitutes a belief-free equilibrium, then a player's discounted average payoff is at most:*

$$(1-c) - \frac{ce}{(1-4e)} - \frac{ce}{(1-4e)^2}. \tag{1}$$

Proof. Let us examine the probability that when player i deviates to D at t, player $i+2$ receives $\tilde{\omega}$ at $t+1$. There are two cases: (i) no error occurs and $i+1$ plays $\tilde{a}$, and (ii) $i+1$ does not play $\tilde{a}$ (because she did not observe b due to an error, or she refrained from doing $\tilde{a}$ although she observed b), but $i+2$ receives $\tilde{\omega}$ due to an error. For (i), the probability is rq^2, and for (ii), the probability is $3e^2+(1-r)qe$. Thus, in total, it becomes $e+r-7re+12re^2$ (by using $q = 1-3e$).

On the other hand, even if player i plays C at t, there is a chance that player $i+2$ receives $\tilde{\omega}$ at $t+1$. There are two cases: (i) $i+1$ observes b due to an error, $i+1$ plays $\tilde{a}$, and no error occurs between $i+1$ and $i+2$, and (ii) $i+1$ does not play $\tilde{a}$ (because she did not observe b with or without an error, or she refrained from doing $\tilde{a}$ although she observed b), and $i+2$ observes $\tilde{\omega}$ due to an error. For (i), the probability is req, and for (ii), the probability is $(1-e)e + (1-r)e^2$. Thus, in total, it becomes $e + re - 4re^2$.

If a strategy constitutes a belief-free equilibrium, the current gain for deviating to D, i.e., c, must be offset by the future loss. Let F denote the impact of the punishment for player i's discounted expected payoff after $i+2$ observes $\tilde{\omega}$. Then, the following inequality must hold.

$$c \le \delta^2[(e+r-7re+12re^2)-(e+re-4re^2)]F$$
$$= \delta^2 r(1-4e)^2 F \tag{2}$$

Also, even if player i keeps on playing C, player $i+2$ observes $\tilde{\omega}$ with probability $e+re-4re^2$. Thus, the discounted average payoff is at most:

$$(1-\delta)[(1-c)+\delta(1-c)+\delta^2\{(1-c)-(e+re-4re^2)F\}$$
$$+\delta^3\{(1-c)-(e+re-4re^2)F\}+\ldots]$$
$$=(1-c)-\delta^2(e+re-4re^2)F.$$

From Inequality (2), we obtain it is at most:

$$(1-c)-\frac{ce}{(1-4e)}-\frac{ce}{r(1-4e)^2}.$$

This value is maximized at $r=1$, which is identical to (1).   □

5   Remote Punishment (RP) Strategy

We identify a very simple strategy that is an instance of GRP and can constitute a belief-free equilibrium with a wide range of parameter settings. We call it Remote Punishment strategy (RP). It is a kind of "reactive" (or one-memory [5]) strategy, in which the action in the current period is determined by the signal in the previous period. The signal-action mapping is given in Table 3. In plain words, as long as player i observes g, she plays C. When she observes b, i.e., player $i-1$ seems to play D, then she informs this fact to player $i+1$ by playing W. When she observes w, i.e., player $i-1$ seems to ask her to punish $i+1$, she plays P. Finally, when she observes p, i.e., player $i-1$ seems to punish her, she tolerates the punishment and plays C. The pre-FSA for RP is given in Fig. 1. There are three states S_C, S_W, S_P. In each state S_{a_i} (where $a_i \in \{C, W, P\}$), player i plays the specified action a_i. The initial state is S_C.

We illustrate in Fig. 2 how the action selection in period t of player i affects the possible states of players $i+1$, $i+2$, and i for periods $t+1$, $t+2$, and $t+3$, respectively. A thick arrow connects an action/state and its "correct" signal, which is observed with probability q. For example, when the action of player i in period t is C, the observation of player $i+1$ is g with probability q (and the probabilities of the other "wrong" signals are e). Thus, the state of player $i+1$ in period $t+1$ is S_c with probability $q+e=1-2e$, and the probabilities of the other states are e. Figure 2 illustrates that when the action of player i at t is either C, P, or W, the probability distribution of the state of player $i+2$ in period $t+2$ is the same (Lemma 1). More specifically, starting from C, P, or W and following thick arrows, we reach S_c in period $t+2$, which means that S_c is most likely and other states occur only by error. Also, the probability distribution of

Table 3. Signal-action mapping of RP

Previous signal	Current action
g	C
b	W
w	P
p	C

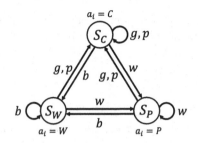

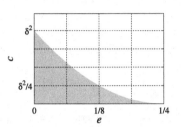

Fig. 1. Pre-FSA of RP

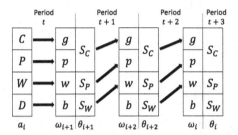

Fig. 2. Effect of action selection for probability distribution of states

Fig. 3. Parameter range where RP constitutes an equilibrium

the state of player i in period $t+3$ is the same regardless of the action of player i in period t (Lemma 3).

The following theorem characterizes the condition where RP constitutes a belief-free equilibrium.

Theorem 2. *The sufficient and necessary condition in which RP constitutes a belief-free equilibrium is:*

$$\delta^2(1-4e)^2 z \geq c. \tag{3}$$

This condition is intuitively natural; it says that sustainable cooperation is more likely to be established when (i) the cost of cooperation c is small, (ii) the players are patient (i.e., δ is large), (iii) the error probability e is small, and (iv) the punishment z is large. Figure 3 illustrates the range of e (x-axis) and c (y-axis) where this condition is satisfied assuming $z = 1$. When $e = 1/8$ (and q is $5/8$), then c must be at most $0.25\delta^2$, which is around 0.2 when δ is 0.9. Note that the value of y, i.e., the amount of reduced benefit for player i when player $i-1$ plays W, is irrelevant to this condition. Thus, it can be zero.

To prove this theorem, we need to show that player i has no incentive to deviate from RP regardless of the current states of the other players. Although there exist infinitely many possible deviations, by Proposition 12.2.3 in [18], it is sufficient to check a finite number of deviations, each of which chooses a different action only once, and immediately returns to the original strategy. This property is called one-shot deviation principle or one-deviation property [18].

Since all players use the same strategy, it is sufficient to check that there exists no profitable deviation for player 0. We utilize the following lemmas.

Lemma 1. *Let $\gamma_{i,t}$ (and $\gamma'_{i,t}$) denote the probability distribution of the state of player i in period t, i.e., it is a three element vector $\left(\gamma_{S_C} \; \gamma_{S_P} \; \gamma_{S_W}\right)$. Also, for given $\gamma_{i,t}$ (or $\gamma'_{i,t}$), let $\gamma_{i+k,t+k}$ (or $\gamma'_{i+k,t+k}$) denote the probability distribution of the state of player $i + k$ in period $t + k$ when all players follow RP. For all $k \geq 2$, for all $\gamma_{i,t}, \gamma'_{i,t}$, the following condition holds:*

$$\gamma_{i+k,t+k} = \gamma'_{i+k,t+k}.$$

In plain words, for $k \geq 2$, the probability distribution of player $i + k$'s state in period $t + k$ is identical regardless of the probability distribution of player i's state in period t.

Proof (Lemma 1). Let X denote the following matrix:

$$X = \begin{pmatrix} 1 - 2e & e & e \\ 1 - 2e & e & e \\ 2e & 1 - 3e & e \end{pmatrix},$$

i.e., it represents the transition probabilities from one state to another. Then, $\gamma_{i+1,t+1}$ is given by $\gamma_{i,t}X$, and $\gamma_{i+k,t+k}$ is given by $\gamma_{i,t}X^k$. X^2 is calculated as follows:

$$X^2 = \begin{pmatrix} 4e^2 - 3e + 1 & -4e^2 + 2e & e \\ 4e^2 - 3e + 1 & -4e^2 + 2e & e \\ 4e^2 - 3e + 1 & -4e^2 + 2e & e \end{pmatrix}.$$

Since all the row vectors in X^2 are identical, and for each row vector of X, the sum of its elements is 1, for any $k \geq 2$, all the row vectors in X^k are identical. Actually, for any $k \geq 2$, $X^k = X^2$ holds. Thus, for any $k \geq 2$, for all $\gamma_{i,t}$ and $\gamma'_{i,t}$, $\gamma_{i+k,t+k} = \gamma'_{i+k,t+k}$ holds. $\square$

Let V^θ denote the discounted average payoff of player 0 when all players follow RP and start from θ.

Lemma 2. *For all $\theta_1, \theta_2 \in \{S_C, S_W, S_P\}$, the following condition holds:*

$$V^{(S_C, \theta_1, \theta_2)} = V^{(S_W, \theta_1, \theta_2)} = V^{(S_P, \theta_1, \theta_2)}.$$

In plain words, the discounted average payoff of player 0 is identical regardless of her current state. This is a necessary condition for a belief-free equilibrium.

Proof (Lemma 2). Since all actions C, W, and P have the same cost, the cost of player 0 is identical as long as she plays RP. Thus, let us concentrate on her expected benefit, which is determined by player 2's action. The (discounted) expected benefit in period $t + \tau$ ($\tau \geq 0$) for player 0 is given as follows:

$$\delta^{t+\tau} \gamma_{2,t+\tau} \left(1 \; 1 - z \; 1 - y\right)^{\mathrm{T}}$$
$$= \delta^{t+\tau} \gamma_{2-\tau,t} X^\tau \left(1 \; 1 - z \; 1 - y\right)^{\mathrm{T}}.$$

In period t, i.e., $\tau = 0$, it depends only on $\gamma_{2,t}$. Therefore, it is identical regardless of $\gamma_{0,t}$. In period $t+1$, i.e., $\tau = 1$, it depends only on $\gamma_{1,t}$. Again, it is identical regardless of $\gamma_{0,t}$. In period $t + \tau$ with $\tau \geq 2$, from Lemma 1, the probability distribution of the state of player 2 must be identical for any $\gamma_{0,t}$. Thus, the expected benefit of player 0 is identical for any $\gamma_{0,t}$. Therefore, the expected discounted average payoff of player 0 is identical regardless of her current state.

$\square$

Lemma 3. *Assume player i plays action $a_i \in A$ (which might be different from the one specified by RP) at period t and acts according to RP thereafter. Then, for all $k \geq 3$, the conditional probability distributions of the states of player $i+k$ at period $t + k$ are identical regardless of a_i.*

Proof. Let $\gamma_C, \gamma_D, \gamma_W$, and γ_P denote the probability distributions of the states of player $i+1$ at period $t+1$, assuming player i plays C, D, W, and P at period t, respectively. Then, the probability distribution of player $i + k$ at period $t + k$, assuming player i plays C (or D, W, P) at period t, is given as $\gamma_C X^{k-1}$ (or $\gamma_D X^{k-1}, \gamma_W X^{k-1}, \gamma_P X^{k-1}$). From Lemma 1, these distributions are identical when $k - 1 \geq 2$. $\square$

Now, we are ready to prove Theorem 2.

Proof (Theorem 2). Assume player 0 deviates in period t (and returns to RP after $t + 1$). It is sufficient to compare the following two values: (i) the cost of player 0 at period t (which is determined by her chosen action a_0 in period t), and (ii) the benefit of player 0 at period $t+2$ (which is determined by a_2 in period $t + 2$). This is because, at period t, all the players except 0 follow the strategy. Thus, the benefit of player 0 is unchanged (only her cost can vary). At period $t + 1$, the action of player 2 is unchanged. At period $t + 2$, the benefit of player 0 is affected by the action of player 2. At and after period $t + 3$, the probability distributions of the states of the other players are the same (Lemma 3).

Let us compare these values for possible deviations. For any $(\theta_1, \theta_2) \in \Theta^2$, by the deviation from C to D at period t, the payoff increases by c since she exerts no effort. Let us examine the decreased amount of player 0's payoff at period $t + 2$. The probability distribution of player 2's states after two periods can be represented as follows: (i) $(1 - 2e\ e\ e) X$ when player 0 chooses C and (ii) $(2c\ c\ 1 - 3e) X$ when player 0 deviates to D. Then, the difference is given as:

$$\delta^2 \left(2e\ e\ 1 - 3e\right) X \left(1\ 1 - z\ 1 - y\right)^{\mathrm{T}}$$
$$- \delta^2 \left(1 - 2e\ e\ e\right) X \left(1\ 1 - z\ 1 - y\right)^{\mathrm{T}}$$
$$= \delta^2 \left(-(1 - 4e)\ 0\ 1 - 4e\right) X \left(1\ 1 - z\ 1 - y\right)^{\mathrm{T}}$$
$$= -\delta^2 (1 - 4e)^2 z.$$

Thus, the incentive constraint is given as Inequality (3). For the deviation from W or P to D, the results are the same as above. Also, from Lemma 2, there is no incentive for any deviation among C, P, and W. $\square$

Let us derive the discounted average payoff for RP.

Theorem 3. *When all players play RP, the discounted average payoff, i.e.,* $V^{(S_C,S_C,S_C)}$, *is given as follows:*

$$(1 - c) - \delta^2 e(1 - 4e)z - \delta ey - \delta ez. \tag{4}$$

Here, $(1 - c)$ is the ideal payoff when players keep on cooperating and no errors occur. Due to the errors, the discounted average payoff is reduced to some extent.

Proof (Theorem 3). As we showed in the proof of Lemma 1, for all $k \geq 2$, $X^k = X^2$ holds. The probability distribution of the states of player 2 at period t is given as follows (we assume X^0 is an identity matrix):

$$\begin{pmatrix} 1 & 0 & 0 \end{pmatrix} X^t.$$

As long as player 0 follows RP, the cost of her action is c. Also, the baseline benefit of player 0, which is determined by the action of player 2, is 1. Let us examine how the decreased amount of player 0's benefit affects her discounted average benefit. This amount is given as follows.

$$(1 - \delta) \sum_{t=0}^{\infty} \delta^t \begin{pmatrix} 1 & 0 & 0 \end{pmatrix} X^t \begin{pmatrix} 0 & z & y \end{pmatrix}^{\mathrm{T}}$$

$$= (1 - \delta)\delta \begin{pmatrix} 1 & 0 & 0 \end{pmatrix} X \begin{pmatrix} 0 & z & y \end{pmatrix}^{\mathrm{T}} + (1 - \delta) \sum_{t=2}^{\infty} \delta^t \begin{pmatrix} 1 & 0 & 0 \end{pmatrix} X^2 \begin{pmatrix} 0 & z & y \end{pmatrix}^{\mathrm{T}}$$

$$= (1 - \delta)\delta \begin{pmatrix} 1 - 2e & e & e \end{pmatrix} \begin{pmatrix} 0 & z & y \end{pmatrix}^{\mathrm{T}}$$

$$\quad + \delta^2 \begin{pmatrix} 4e^2 - 3e + 1 & -4e^2 + 2e & e \end{pmatrix} \begin{pmatrix} 0 & z & y \end{pmatrix}^{\mathrm{T}}$$

$$= \delta e(y + z) + \delta^2 e(1 - 4e)z$$

Thus, the discounted average payoff is given as Eq. (4).   □

6   Modification of RP (RP$^+$)

Let us consider a slightly modified version of RP, which we call RP$^+$. It achieves the upper bound of Condition (1). In RP, all players start from S_c at $t = 0$. A player has no incentive to deviate to W from C. Thus, if player i observes w at $t = 0$, it must be an observation error; punishing player $i + 1$ is meaningless. RP$^+$ avoids such futile punishments. The signal-action mapping of RP$^+$ and the pre-FSA are given in Table 4 and Fig. 4, respectively. The only change is that if a player observes w at $t = 0$, she plays C (instead of P) at $t = 1$.

The sufficient and necessary condition where RP$^+$ constitutes a belief-free equilibrium is identical to that of RP, i.e., Inequality (3). This is because a player has no incentive to deviate to W from C; the expected rewards in the current and future periods are identical.

Table 4. Signal-action mapping of RP$^+$

Previous signal	Current period	Current action
g		C
b		W
w	$t = 1$	C
	$t \geq 2$	P
p		C

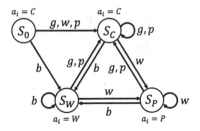

Fig. 4. Pre-FSA of RP$^+$

When all players play RP$^+$, the probability distribution of the state of player 1 at period 1 is $\gamma_{1,1} = (1 - e\ 0\ e)$. Therefore, in a similar way as Theorem 3, player 0's discounted average payoff is given as:

$$(1 - c) - (1 - \delta) \sum_{t=1}^{\infty} \delta^t \left(1 - e\ 0\ e\right) X^{t-1} \left(0\ z\ y\right)^{\mathrm{T}}$$
$$= (1 - c) - \delta e y - \delta^2 e(2 - 4e)z.$$

The payoff is improved by $\delta(1 - \delta)ez$.

Theorem 4. *The discounted average payoff of RP$^+$ becomes optimal within all strategies in GRP by appropriately choosing y and z.*

Proof. If we choose $y = 0$ and $z = \frac{c}{\delta^2(1-4e)^2}$, the discounted average payoff of RP$^+$, i.e., $(1 - c) - \delta e y - \delta^2 e(2 - 4e)z$, becomes identical to Condition (1). □

If players can appropriately choose the level of punishment z, Theorem 4 shows that RP$^+$ is optimal within GRP. If z is chosen exogenously such that it is strictly larger than $\frac{c}{\delta^2(1-4e)^2}$, RP$^+$ is no longer optimal. In such a case, we can slightly modify RP$^+$ so that when observing w, a player plays P with probability r' (and with probability $1 - r'$, she plays C), where $r' = \frac{c}{\delta^2(1-4e)^2 z}$. Then, this modified strategy becomes optimal within GRP and constitutes a belief-free equilibrium.

Extending RP and RP$^+$ for the case of four or more players (with more actions and observations) is straightforward. In general, an n-player case needs $n - 1$ additional actions/observations; one punishing action and $n - 2$ whistling actions. In the four-player case with two whistling actions W_1 and W_2, for instance, the idea is to choose W_1 if b is observed and to choose W_2 if a signal most likely under W_1 is observed. In this way, each player can ask the other players to punish an apparent deviator.

7   Discussions

7.1   Additional Actions/Observations

Let us argue whether the new actions we introduced (i.e., W and P) are available in real-life situations. First, y, i.e., the decreased amount of player $i + 1$'s benefit

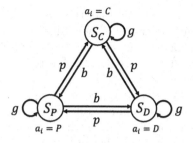

Fig. 5. Pre-FSA that constitutes a sequential equilibrium under $A = \{C, D, P\}$

when player i plays W, can be 0. Thus, W can be basically identical to C, but it must be distinguished from C with a high probability. Such a new action (and an observation) would be easy to implement (e.g., by cheap talk [10]). On the other hand, z, i.e., the decreased amount of the benefit for player $i + 1$ when player i plays P, must be large enough as shown in Theorem 2. However, within reasonable parameter settings, z can be smaller than 1. Thus, a relatively mild spiteful action, which decreases the value of the product, is sufficient.

The reason that we require *two* additional actions/observations is as follows. As discussed in Sect. 4, we need one action for punishment that can be distinguished from D in order to avoid the endless chain of punishment due to communication errors. Also, it is convenient to have another action for asking punishment. Actually, by adding just one action for punishment (i.e., without adding W), there exists an elaborated strategy that constitutes a sequential equilibrium in some parameter settings. However, it cannot constitute a belief-free equilibrium and its expected payoff is low compared to RP/RP$^+$. Figure 5 illustrates such an FSA. When all players follow this strategy, their default action is C. Assume player 0 observes b due to a communication error at period t. Also assume no error occurs afterward. Then, player 0 remains S_P for the next three periods. Player 1 moves to S_D in period $t+2$, then it moves to S_P in period $t+3$. Player 2 moves to S_P in period $t + 3$. Then, all players observe p and return to S_C in period $t + 4$. The case where player 0 observes p due to a communication error is symmetric to the above case; all players move to S_D, observe b, and return to S_C.

7.2   Related Literature

In the literature of AI and multi-agent systems, there are many streams associated with repeated games [4]: the complexity of equilibrium computation [1,3,16], multi-agent learning [2,6,24], repeated congestion games [25], partially observable stochastic games (POSGs) [7,14], etc.

The repeated PD with imperfect observability has been extensively studied, but most papers assume public monitoring. To the best of our knowledge, we are the first to introduce the idea of the triangular trade in repeated games with imperfect private monitoring. Also, the idea of adding a dominated and seemingly irrelevant action is new, whether the monitoring is public or private. A notable exception is Shigenaka et al. [23], who show that by adding a dominated action, sustainable cooperation can be achieved in the repeated PD and in a problem called a team production problem. In this paper, we deal with a different problem, i.e., the triangular trade.

In evolutionary biology, several types of "reciprocity," i.e., how altruistic behavior can evolve, have been examined [19]. Among these works, our triangular trade resembles indirect reciprocity [21], in which a pair is randomly chosen, and one player acts as a donor while the other player acts as a recipient. If the donor chooses "Cooperate," she pays cost c and the recipient receives benefit b. If the donor chooses "Defect," both receive 0. Our work is different from indirect reciprocity in the following points: (i) the same set of players repeatedly plays the game, and (ii) it deals with imperfect private monitoring and a belief-free equilibrium.

8   Conclusions and Future Works

In this paper, we proposed a new fundamental problem called triangular trade, which models a situation that is similar to the PD, i.e., the cooperation of players is efficient, but each player has an incentive to defect, while it is different from the PD since a player cannot directly punish a seemingly defecting player. We first showed that when there exist only two actions, no simple strategy constitutes a belief-free equilibrium. Then, we showed that by adding two additional actions (and associated observations), RP can constitute a belief-free equilibrium in a wide range of parameter settings. Furthermore, we showed the payoff obtained by a variant of RP (i.e., RP^+) is optimal within a very general class of strategies called GRP that covers virtually all meaningful strategies. Our future work includes examining the optimality of RP^+ in a more general setting (e.g., sequential equilibria).

Acknowledgements. This work was partially supported by JSPS KAKENHI (Grant Number 16KK0003, 17H00761, and 17H01787) and JST, Strategic International Collaborative Research Program, SICORP.

References

1. Andersen, G., Conitzer, V.: Fast equilibrium computation for infinitely repeated games. In: Proceedings of the 27th AAAI Conference on Artificial Intelligence, AAAI 2013, pp. 53–59 (2013)
2. Blum, A., Mansour, Y.: Learning, regret minimization, and equilibria. In: Nisan, N., Roughgarden, T., Tardos, E., Vazirani, V.V. (eds.) Algorithmic Game Theory, pp. 79–101. Cambridge University Press, Cambridge (2007)
3. Borgs, C., Chayes, J., Immorlica, N., Kalai, A.T., Mirrokni, V., Papadimitriou, C.: The myth of the folk theorem. Games Econ. Behav. **70**(1), 34–43 (2010)
4. Burkov, A., Chaib-draa, B.: Repeated games for multiagent systems: a survey. Knowl. Eng. Rev. **29**, 1–30 (2013)

5. Chen, L., Lin, F., Tang, P., Wang, K., Wang, R., Wang, S.: K-memory strategies in repeated games. In: Proceedings of the 16th Conference on Autonomous Agents and Multiagent Systems, AAMAS 2017, pp. 1493–1498 (2017)
6. Conitzer, V., Sandholm, T.: AWESOME: a general multiagent learning algorithm that converges in self-play and learns a best response against stationary opponents. Mach. Learn. **67**(1), 23–43 (2007)
7. Doshi, P., Gmytrasiewicz, P.J.: On the difficulty of achieving equilibrium in interactive POMDPs. In: Proceedings of the 21st National Conference on Artificial Intelligence, AAAI 2006, pp. 1131–1136 (2006)
8. Ely, J.C., Hörner, J., Olszewski, W.: Belief-free equilibria in repeated games. Econometrica **73**(2), 377–415 (2005)
9. Ely, J.C., Välimäki, J.: A robust folk theorem for the Prisoner's dilemma. J. Econ. Theory **102**(1), 84–105 (2002)
10. Farrell, J., Rabin, M.: Cheap talk. J. Econ. Perspect. **10**(3), 103–118 (1996)
11. Fudenberg, D., Levine, D., Maskin, E.: The folk theorem with imperfect public information. Econometrica **62**(5), 997–1039 (1994)
12. Fudenberg, D., Maskin, E.: The folk theorem in repeated games with discounting or with incomplete information. Econometrica **54**(3), 533–554 (1986)
13. Fudenberg, D., Tirole, J.: Game Theory. MIT Press, Cambridge (1991)
14. Hansen, E.A., Bernstein, D.S., Zilberstein, S.: Dynamic programming for partially observable stochastic games. In: Proceedings of the 19th National Conference on Artificial Intelligence, AAAI 2004, pp. 709–715 (2004)
15. Kreps, D.M., Wilson, R.: Sequential equilibria. Econometrica **50**(4), 863–894 (1982)
16. Littman, M.L., Stone, P.: A polynomial-time Nash equilibrium algorithm for repeated games. Decis. Support Syst. **39**(1), 55–66 (2005)
17. Maggi, G.: The role of multilateral institutions in international trade cooperation. Am. Econ. Rev. **89**(1), 190–214 (1999)
18. Mailath, G.J., Samuelson, L.: Repeated Games and Reputations. Oxford University Press, Oxford (2006)
19. Nowak, M.A.: Evolutionary Dynamics. Harvard University Press, Cambridge (2006)
20. Nowak, M.A., Sigmund, K.: A strategy of win-stay, lose-shift that outperforms tit-for-tat in Prisoner's dilemma. Nature **364**, 56–58 (1993)
21. Nowak, M.A., Sigmund, K.: Evolution of indirect reciprocity by image scoring. Nature **393**(6685), 573–577 (1998)
22. Piccione, M.: The repeated Prisoner's dilemma with imperfect private monitoring. J. Econ. Theory **102**(1), 70–83 (2002)
23. Shigenaka, F., Sekiguchi, T., Iwasaki, A., Yokoo, M.: Achieving sustainable cooperation in generalized Prisoner's dilemma with observation errors. In: Proceedings of the 31st AAAI Conference on Artificial Intelligence, AAAI 2017, pp. 677–683 (2017)
24. Shoham, Y., Leyton-Brown, K.: Learning and teaching. In: Multiagent Systems: Algorithmic, Game-Theoretic, and Logical Foundations, pp. 189–222. Cambridge University Press (2008)
25. Tennenholtz, M., Zohar, A.: Learning equilibria in repeated congestion games. In: Proceedings of the 8th International Joint Conference on Autonomous Agents and Multi-Agent System, AAMAS 2009, pp. 233–240 (2009)

Engineering Multi-agent Systems
and Human-Agent Interaction

Accountability and Responsibility
in Agent Organizations

Matteo Baldoni[1]([✉]) [iD], Cristina Baroglio[1] [iD], Olivier Boissier[2] [iD],
Katherine Marie May[1], Roberto Micalizio[1] [iD], and Stefano Tedeschi[1] [iD]

[1] Dipartimento di Informatica, Università degli Studi di Torino, Torino, Italy
{matteo.baldoni,cristina.baroglio,katherinemarie.may,roberto.micalizio,
stefano.tedeschi}@unito.it
[2] Laboratoire Hubert Curien UMR CNRS 5516, Institut Henri Fayol,
MINES Saint-Etienne, Saint-Etienne, France
Olivier.Boissier@emse.fr

Abstract. We discuss the limits of current agent organizations, and the
benefits of introducing an explicit account of responsibility and accountability. We, then, illustrate how through such notions it is possible to
design both organization specifications and organization entities, that
are guaranteed to properly distribute responsibilities, that is, not only
to own but also to connect the needed, distributed control over the goal
so as to enable its achievement.

Keywords: Accountability · Responsibility · Agent organizations

1 Introduction

Multiagent Systems (MAS) provide a programming paradigm for the development of complex systems, which are characterized by multiple autonomous
threads of execution that run in parallel, interact and coordinate with each
other. Several design methodologies and programming platforms that have been
proposed (e.g., [1]) are grounded on the metaphor of the *organization*. Such agent
organizations represent strategies decomposing complex organizational goals into
simpler sub-tasks and allocating them to roles. By adopting roles in the organization, agents acquire responsibilities and execute the corresponding tasks in a
distributed, coordinated and regulated fashion.

However, even if current models are targeting open systems by allocating
and enforcing rights and duties to agents about the tasks to realize, they lack
an explicit representation of the relationships between the agents, resulting in
the following limits: (*i*) difficulty for the agents to identify who should give resti-
tution to whom for a certain state of the organization, (*ii*) even if agents who
enter the organization are under the regulation of norms, that stipulate their
rights and duties, the organization has no guarantee that they will provide all
the accompanying proofs, that are induced by their responsibilities. We claim

T. Miller et al. (Eds.): PRIMA 2018, LNAI 11224, pp. 261–278, 2018.
https://doi.org/10.1007/978-3-030-03098-8_16

that the introduction of accountability relationships could enable a more fruitful participation of agents to the organization both from the agent and the organization perspectives. Accountability, indeed, is a fundamental concept that could help to overcome these limitations. However, this term is little understood and is often used to refer to answerability for one's actions or behavior. As [26] explains referring to Public Administrations, accountability plays a greater role in organizational processes than indicated by the idea of answerability. As underlined by the authors, accountability involves the *means* (i.e., the control on the necessary resources within and outside the organization) by which organizations and their members manage the expectations on fulfillment of their duties.

The objective of this paper is to introduce this broader perspective in agent organizations and demonstrate that it is an important ingredient that agent organizations should encompass. We propose thus to use accountabilities as explicitly taken social relationships, between an *account-giver* and an *account-taker* within an agent organization. Such relationships are mutually agreed by the parties and concern, in our proposal, roles, agents, goals (either complex or atomic). Accountability relationships are important in the design of agent organizations since, as we will explain, when they are properly defined the system properly distribute responsibilities, i.e., not only to own but also to "connect" the needed, distributed control over the goal so as to enable its achievement. In particular, we extend the specification of an organization in a way that enables the verification of the feasibility, for a group of agents, to incarnate the organizational roles properly, i.e., by respecting the accountabilities the agents can cooperate so as to achieve the organizational goal and discharge their responsibilities. The organizational model, thus, should no longer be a structure that distributes goals to its agents, but it should become *a way for coordinating responsibility assumption by the agents*.

The paper is so structured. Section 2 reviews the current existing agents organizational models and analyzes their current limitations w.r.t. accountability Sect. 3 proposes a formal definition of accountability and of the accompanying concept of responsibility. This proposal is then applied to agent organizations, defining accountability and responsibility relationships between roles and between agents. From these definitions, Sect. 4 shows how such relationships may help the design and enactment of agent organization definitions within open MAS. We illustrate this in the context of the $\mathcal{M}$OISE organization model which is part of the JaCaMo MAS-oriented programming platform [8]. The choice is representative of those approaches where the organization is described in terms of roles, goals and norms, and the organization issues obligations to push agents to pursue the assigned goals at the right moment.

2   Lack of Accountability in Agent Organizations

To face the inherent need of coordination among autonomous agents, the *organization* metaphor has been used for a long time in MAS. When looking back, a set of initial proposals [13,18] have defined an explicit structure of roles and relations, through which responsibilities of tasks are distributed by adoption of roles, among the agents participating in the organization. Such models are well adapted to "closed agent organization" where benevolent agents, always complying, coordinate with each other to achieve their responsibility assumptions (actions, goals or interactions). A second generation of organization models, following the electronic institution pioneering approaches [21], has introduced norms in the structure of roles and tasks, giving birth to *normative organization* [8,16,17,19,22]. These social coordination frameworks [1] are targeting "open socio-technical systems". Thanks to norms, the structures of distributed responsibilities among agents have been enriched with structures of *social expectations*: besides being the source of task responsibility assumption, roles have become the anchoring point of social expectations on the behavior of the agents who will play them in the organization. As for normative MAS [7], normative organizations are equipped with a set of mechanisms to publish, enact, adapt, monitor and enforce normative behaviors. Thus, once decided to adopt a role with the accompanying norms and thus participating to the organization, agents assume the responsibility of the targeted tasks. Moreover, they are expected by the organization to accomplish their duties. In case of violation, they are enforced to do so through sanctions.

However, while addressing the requirement of assigning duties and rights to agents, agent organizations are obfuscating accountability as pointed by [10,11]. Agent autonomy demands a different way of conceptualizing coordination by clearly constraining them in terms of responsibilities that are explicitly taken on by them, and by establishing a directed relationship from one agent to another, that reflects the legitimate expectations the second principal has of the first. Agent organizations have not established yet the foundational facts of accountability, i.e., following [6] who has control over the situation and who is responsible of acting (or not) in accordance with established expectations.

Lack of Control for the Agents. Current agent organizations are lacking an easy way, for the agents participating to them but also for the organization designers, to check who has control over the situation. That is to say, checking that the means to execute the expected tasks are properly provided to the agents who become in charge of them through their adopted roles, i.e., enabling agents to have control/power on resources, on other tasks, on other agents on which their duties depend. For instance, in an organization coordinating the building of a house, a bricklayer who depends on some other worker in charge of preparing the site does not have the means to ask about occurring delays. Not even the house owner has such means. Indeed, even if each co-worker, by reasoning on the organization specification, may know about the existence of others with whom it should coordinate, the co-worker has no explicit endorsement from the organization to do so. Assignment of roles to tasks in organization specifications and then roles to agents via their enactments are not sufficient to explain the control structure of the expected coordinated tasks in the organization.

Agents' Responsibility Is Not Well Captured. In most of the current normative organization approaches, when norms are enacted through adoption by agents of the role on which they bear, they are translated into deontic modalities or social commitments. Deontic modalities only constrain the agent who is in charge of fulfilling the norm. Targeting the control of its autonomy, they are lacking all what concerns the act of assuming responsibility in the broader context of the organization such as role adoption, detachment of duties. Social commitments [9,28] help to capture the deliberate act of the agent that takes on a duty by adopting the role, but still lack to capture the adoption of role itself, and the detachment. Moreover, besides detachment and adoption, there is a lack of an explicit social ground that clearly models in terms that are known and agreed upon by all agents participating in the organization, what duties an agent has accepted to bring about in interaction with others [15]. That is to say, when a failure occurs in the agent organization, it is not possible for an agent to attribute causal responsibilities nor to identify the causes of the failure.

In most of the approaches, then, it is assumed that the sanctions associated with the violation (or fulfillment) of an obligation are a sufficient tool for constraining agents' behaviors. However, in order to apply sanctions, there is a need to conduct an inquiry process, to investigate on the reasons of the failure or success in order to properly apply adequate and justified sanctions. Agents participating to the organization are thus also expected to provide proofs and explanations of their behaviors in the organization w.r.t. their responsibilities.

Organizations are dynamic structures with a life cycle chaining design, role adoption, execution with fulfillment and enforcement of corresponding social expectations. When tasks participating in the definition of social expectations, connected to roles, change, the organization is changed, restarting a new cycle of design, adoption and fulfillment. All current models in MAS are assuming such a life cycle. However, there is no explicit commitment that organizations will not change the tasks attached to social expectations during the time agents play the corresponding role. In case of malevolent organization, for instance, it may be possible that the organization dynamically changes the set of allocated tasks to roles, roles already adopted by agents. Thus when the normative organization issues an obligation towards an agent, that agent may not have the desire or a proper capability for satisfying that obligation (see [4,5] for instance). This short example demonstrates that currently social expectations are mainly directed from the organization to the agents, stating the expected agents' behaviors when adopting roles within the organization. The inverse relation, where the organization is engaging in expected behaviors with respect to the agents, does not exist.

3   Accountability in Agent Organizations

The accountability model that we will define aims at being used in the context of agent organizations. Before presenting this model, let's first introduce in Sect. 3.1, a definition of its components in the context of collective execution of plans, decomposition of tasks into subtasks with temporal relations as presented in Fig. 1. Based on this model, we will then define in Sect. 3.2, accountability relation in agent organizations.

3.1 Preliminary Definitions

As a first step, it is necessary to provide a language for expressing those conditions and behaviors to which accountabilities refer. To this aim, we rely upon *precedence logic* [29]. Precedence logic is an event-based linear temporal logic devised for modeling and reasoning about Web service composition. The interpretation of such a logic deals with occurrences of events along runs (i.e., sequence of instanced events). Event occurrences are assumed to be non-repeating and persistent: once an event has occurred, it has occurred forever. The logic has three primary operators: '$\lor$' (choice), '$\land$' (concurrence), and '$\cdot$' (before). The *before* operator allows constraining the order with which two events must occur, e.g., $a \cdot b$ means that a must occur before b, but the two events do not need to occur one immediately after the other. Such a language, thus, allows us to model complex expressions, whose execution needs to be coordinated as they are under the responsibility of different agents. Let e be an event. Then $\bar{e}$, the complement of e, is also an event. Initially, neither e nor $\bar{e}$ hold. On any run, either e or $\bar{e}$ may occur, not both. Intuitively, complementary events allow specifying situations in which an expected event e does not occur, either because of the occurrence of an opposite event, or because of the expiration of a time deadline.

Example 1 (Building a house). For the sake of explanation, we rely on the *building-a-house* example introduced in [8] for JaCaMo. We represent by means of precedence logic the functional specification of the organization:

- house_built $\doteq$ frame $\cdot$ (interior $\land$ exterior).
- frame $\doteq$ site_prepared $\cdot$ floors_laid $\cdot$ walls_built.
- interior $\doteq$ plumbing_installed $\cdot$ electrical_system_installed $\cdot$ (walls_painted $\lor$ wallpapered).
- exterior $\doteq$ roof_built $\cdot$ (windows_fitted $\land$ doors_fitted).

The main goal, house_built, requires the site to be prepared and then both the interior and exterior of the house to be built. The two activities can be performed in any order or even in parallel. All such sub-goals amount to complex processes. Most activities need to be carried out one after the other (e.g. site_prepared $\cdot$ floors_laid $\cdot$ walls_built) but concerning the walls, it will be up to the performer to decide whether to paint them or to lay paper on them. The decomposition of house_built is graphically shown by Fig. 1.

We also rely on the notion of *residuation*, inspired by [25,29]. Residuation allows tracking the progression of temporal logic expressions, hopefully arriving to their satisfaction, i.e., the completion of their execution. The *residual* of a temporal expression q with respect to an event e, denoted as q/e, is the remainder

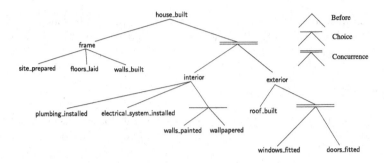

Fig. 1. The building-a-house goal's functional decomposition.

temporal expression that would be left over when e occurs, and whose satisfaction would guarantee the satisfaction of the original temporal expression q. Residual can be calculated by means of a set of rewrite rules. The following equations are due to Singh [25, 29]. Here, r is a sequence expression, and e is an event or $\top$. Below, Γ_u is the set of literals and their complements mentioned in u. Thus, for instance, $\Gamma_e = \{e, \overline{e}\} = \Gamma_{\overline{e}}$ and $\Gamma_{e \cdot f} = \{e, \overline{e}, f, \overline{f}\}$.

$$0/e \doteq 0 \qquad\qquad \top/e \doteq \top \qquad\qquad (r \wedge u)/e \doteq ((r/e) \wedge (u/e))$$
$$(r \vee u)/e \doteq ((r/e) \vee (u/e)) \quad (e \cdot r)/e \doteq r, \text{ if } e \notin \Gamma_r \quad r/e \doteq r, \text{ if } e \notin \Gamma_r$$
$$(e' \cdot r)/e \doteq 0, \text{ if } e \in \Gamma_r \quad (\overline{e} \cdot r)/e \doteq 0$$

Using the terminology in [3], we say that an event e is *relevant* to a temporal expression p if that event is involved in p, i.e. $p/e \not\equiv p$. Let us denote by $\boldsymbol{e}$ a sequence $e_1, e_2, \ldots, e_n$ of events. We extend the notion of residual of a temporal expression q to a sequence of events $\boldsymbol{e}$ as follows: $q/\boldsymbol{e} = (\ldots((q/e_1)/e_2)/\ldots)/e_n$. If $q/\boldsymbol{e} \equiv \top$ and all events in $\boldsymbol{e}$ are relevant to q, we say that the sequence $\boldsymbol{e}$ is an *actualization* of the temporal expression q (denoted by $\widehat{q}$).

Example 2. Let $(a \cdot b)/a$ be the temporal expression b, while $(a \cdot b)/\overline{a}$ and $(a \cdot b)/b$ cause the temporal expression to become false, in the first case because the opposite event of a occurs, in the second because event b occurs in the wrong order. Referring to Example 1, the residual of (plumbing_installed · electrical_system_installed· (walls_painted ∨ wallpapered))/plumbing_installed is electrical_system_installed · (walls_painted ∨ wallpapered). Instead, the residual of the latter temporal expression with respect to walls_painted would be false because the event occurrence disrupted the order, captured by the temporal expression. Finally, the residual of the temporal expression (plumbing_installed · electrical_system_installed· (walls_painted ∨ wallpapered)) with respect to the sequence {plumbing_installed, electrical_system_installed} is (walls_painted ∨ wallpapered).

3.2   Specifying Accountability in Agent Organizations

No unique and standard organization specification model exists yet to specify agent organization in the MAS domain. However, as pointed in [14], generally, their specifications are based on the concepts of *roles*, which have to be adopted by agents, *tasks* (e.g. actions, goals, interactions) assigned to roles through *norms*, usually expressed with deontic modalities. Agents' organizations' life cycle chains design, enactment (i.e., adoption of roles by agents, building what is usually called *organization entity*), execution (i.e., coordination of agents realizing their duties, monitoring, enforcement). The proposal that we explain fits equally well the specification of accountability in the context of organization specification and in the context of organization entity, i.e., accountability between roles at the specification level, and accountability between agents at the entity level. We let the structure of roles at the simplest expression (i.e., we won't consider groups or relations among roles).

In the following we use the notations $A(x, y, r, u)$ and $R(x, q)$ in order to explicitly represent accountabilities and responsibility assumptions respectively. By $A(x, y, r, u)$ we express that x, the account-giver, is accountable towards y, the account-taker, for the condition u when the condition r (*context*) holds. Both r and u are temporal expressions, given in precedence logic. If we think of a process being collectively executed, we can say that when the r part of the process is done, then x becomes accountable of the u part. When u is true, x is considered to have satisfied the expectation that was put on it by exercising its control, which means that it has built a proof that can be supplied to the account-taker. A proof here is intended as a set of recorded facts, that demonstrate the achievement of the specified condition. Indeed, the account-taker can ask at any time for a proof to the account-giver, provided that r is true (in this case the accountability is detached). Such a proof of the partial execution will amount to the set of facts collected that far. Along with the execution, expectation and control will evolve and will run out with the satisfaction of the accountability, and only the final proof will be left. When, instead, u is false, the expectation was violated, and x's control failed. When r is false, instead, the accountability expires. This means that those conditions, which subtend both the expectation about u and its control, do not hold anymore. Instead, by $R(x, q)$ we capture the responsibility assumption by x of the temporal expression q. When q is true the responsibility is fulfilled, when it is false, it is neglected.

We denote by **A** a set of accountabilities, calling it an *accountability specification*, and by **R** a *responsibility distribution*, that is a set of responsibility assumptions.

We use residuation to compute the progress of both accountabilities and responsibility assumptions: the idea is that, even though they are not temporal expressions, such relationships progress with the progress of their temporal expressions. $A(x, y, r/e, u/e)$ denotes the residual of $A(x, y, r, u)$ with respect to the sequence of events e. On the other hand, when $r/e \doteq 0$, we say that the accountability expires; when $r/e \doteq \top$ and $u/e \doteq 0$, the accountability is violated; when $u/e \doteq \top$ it is satisfied. Similarly, $R(x, q/e)$ denotes the residual of $R(x, q)$ with respect to the sequence of events e, while when $q/e \doteq \top$ the responsibility is fulfilled, and when $q/e \doteq 0$, it is neglected.

As explained since the introduction, $A(x, y, r, u)$ is grounded on *control* and *expectation*. While expectation is naturally conveyed with the accountability itself, the control needs to be recursively verified on the structure of u. In fact, x controls u either directly or indirectly by relying on accountabilities by other parties. In the following discussion we adopt the convention in [25] and limit sequences to just two events each. This is done to simplify the formalization and without loss of generality, because $e_1 \cdots e_n \equiv (e_1 \cdot e_2) \wedge \ldots \wedge (e_{n-1} \cdot e_n)$.

Definition 1 (Control). *Let A be an accountability specification, we denote by $\xi(x, r, u)$ the control in A of x over u in the context r ($\xi(x, r, u)$ in A holds). For control, the following rules hold:*

- *$\xi(x, r, u)$ in A if $u/r = \top$;*
- *$\xi(x, r, u' \wedge u'')$ in A if $\xi(x, r, u')$ in A and $\xi(x, r, u'')$ in A;*
- *$\xi(x, r, u' \vee u'')$ in A if $\xi(x, r, u')$ in A or $\xi(x, r, u'')$ in A;*
- *$\xi(x, r, u)$, where $u/r = u' \cdot u''$, in A if $\xi(x, r, r \cdot u')$ in A and $\xi(x, r \cdot u', r \cdot u' \cdot u'')$ in A;*
- *$\xi(x, r, u)$ in A if there exists $A(y, x, r', u) \in A$ such that $\xi(x, r, r')$ in $A - \{A(y, x, r', u)\}$.*

Notice that having control does not mean having the ability of making a temporal expression become true in any case, but that x has the possibility of realizing it. Moreover, the control relation on atomic temporal expressions cannot be checked from the specification only. The check depends on the responsibility assumption by the agent who has adopted the role.

Definition 2 (Accountability Closure). *Let A be an accountability specification, A is closed under control if for each $A(x, y, r, u) \in A$, such that u/r is not atomic, we have $\xi(x, r, u)$ in A.*

Residuation preserves control, indeed the following proposition holds.

Proposition 1. *Let A be an accountability specification that is closed under control, and let e be an event, then $A/e = \{A(x, y, r/e, u/e) | A(x, y, r, u) \in A\}$ is still closed under control.*

Proof. The proof proceeds by induction. To correctly define the base case, we select, at each inductive step, the subset A of the accountabilities that are relevant to a specific control expression. More precisely, given a control expression $\xi(x, r, u)$ in A, let us denote with $A|_{r,u}$ a set of accountabilities $\{A(z, w, p, q)\} \subseteq A$ such that either $p/r \not\equiv p$, $p/u \not\equiv p$, $q/r \not\equiv q$, or $q/u \not\equiv q$. Now, it is sufficient to assume that the control rules in Definition 1 hold in $A|_{r,u}$ (if this is true, they trivially hold in A, too).

Now let us show that A/e is closed under control if also A is closed under control. To demonstrate this, we show that the progression caused by an event e preserves control $\xi(x, r, u)$ in $A|_{r,u}$. By induction over the size of $A|_{r,u}$ and the length of u/r.

- Base case: $\xi(x, r, u)$ in $\mathbf{A}|_{r,u}$ holds and $u/r \equiv \top$, then it is obvious that also $\xi(x, r/e, u/e)$ holds in $\mathbf{A}$.
- Base case: $\xi(x, r, u)$ in $\mathbf{A}|_{r,u} = \{A(z, w, r', u')\}$ and $\xi(x, r, r')$ in $\{\}$ hold. Given the rules of control in Definition 1, it must be the case that $u \equiv u'$, $w \equiv x$. In addition, since $\xi(x, r, r')$ cannot base control upon another accountability relation, it must be the case that $r \equiv r'$ (falling in the previous base case). It follows that if $\xi(x, r, u)$ in $\mathbf{A}|_{r,u} = \{A(z, x, r', u)\}$ and $\xi(x, r, r)$ in $\{\}$ hold, also $\xi(x, r/e, u/e)$ in $(\mathbf{A}|_{r/e,u/e})/e = \{A(z, x, r'/e, u/e)\}$ and $\xi(x, r/e, r/e)$ in $\{\}/e$ hold.
- Inductive step, cases $\xi(x, r, u' \wedge u'')$ and $\xi(x, r, u' \vee u'')$ follow from definition of residuation, and from the rules of control.
- Inductive step, case $\xi(x, r, u)$, where $u/r = u' \cdot u''$. We have that $\xi(x, r, r \cdot u')$ in $\mathbf{A}|_{r,r \cdot u'}$ and $\xi(x, r \cdot u'/e, r \cdot u' \cdot u''/e)$ in $(\mathbf{A}|_{r \cdot u'/e, r \cdot u' \cdot u''/e})/e$ from the definition of control. Now, by inductive hypothesis, we have that $\xi(x, r/e, r \cdot u'/e)$ in $(\mathbf{A}|_{r/e, r \cdot u'/e})/e$ and $\xi(x, r \cdot u'/e, r \cdot u' \cdot u''/e)$ in $(\mathbf{A}|_{r \cdot u'/e, r \cdot u' \cdot u''/e})/e$. Thus, we conclude that $\xi(x, r/e, u/e)$ in $(\mathbf{A}|_{r/e, u/e})/e$. In fact if e is not relevant to r nor to u, than no change occurs, and control is trivially preserved. If e is relevant to both r and u, then e cannot be but the first element of r since otherwise it would progress the consequent condition to 0.
- We have $\xi(x, r, u)$ in $\mathbf{A}|_{r,u}$, then there is $A(y, x, r', u) \in \mathbf{A}|_{r,u}$ s.t. $\xi(x, r, r')$ in $(\mathbf{A}|_{r,u} - \{A(y, x, r', u)\})|_{r,r'}$. By inductive hypothesis, $\xi(x, r/e, r'/e)$ in $(\mathbf{A}|_{r,u} - \{A(y, x, r', u)\})|_{r,r'}/e$, that is $(\mathbf{A}|_{r/e,u/e} - \{A(y, x, r', u)\})|_{r,r'}$. Now, $\xi(x, r/e, r'/e)$ in $(\mathbf{A}|_{r/e,u/e} - \{A(y, x, r', u)\})$ because of the last set includes $\mathbf{A}|_{r/e,u/e} - \{A(y, x, r', u)\})|_{r,r'}$ and, for the same reason, $\xi(x, r'/e, r/e)$ in $\mathbf{A}|_{r/e,u/e}$ that proves the case. ∎

In words, this property means that the possibility of realizing a temporal expression is not disrupted by the occurrence of events, and that possibility remains step after step. Of course, agents, in their autonomy will maintain the decision about what to do (e.g., make an accountability expire) but this will remain in the proof.

We now show how accountabilities are complemented with responsibilities to the aim of developing full organization specifications and organization entities. In the following, we denote by $\mathbb{A}$ a set of accountability specifications $\mathbf{A}_i$, each of which is closed under control. Intuitively, each $\mathbf{A}_i$ in $\mathbb{A}$ represents a proper way to achieve the organizational goal. $\mathbb{A}$ is therefore the set of alternative solutions the organization designer considers as acceptable at runtime. In this paper, we assume that the designer has specified $\mathbb{A}$ in a way that complies with the design aims. In particular, we assume that for each $\mathbf{A}_i$ there is at least a sequence of events e that satisfies all the accountabilities in $\mathbf{A}_i$, allowing the achievement of the organizational goal. We denote by $[\![\mathbf{A}_i]\!]$ the set of event sequences that satisfy all the accountabilities in $\mathbf{A}_i$.

Any actual set of agents enacting roles within the organization, should therefore be such to satisfy at least one of the accountability specifications $\mathbf{A}_i$ in $\mathbb{A}$. To verify whether this occurs, we approach the problem in general terms by means of the responsibility characterization. Intuitively, assuming that agents are willing to take on a set of responsibilities, each declaring what is willing to bring about within the organization, the problem becomes to verify whether such a set of responsibility declarations fits at least one of the accountability specifications in $\mathbb{A}$. Part of such responsibilities will be due to the roles agents will enact, thus they can be considered as part of the specification of the organization (role responsibility), e.g., deduced from the definition of norms that connect roles to goals. Part of them may, instead, have as a source the agents themselves – constraints they pose on the organization for playing roles (agent responsibility). Depending on the source of responsibilities that is considered, thus, it will be possible either to check the consistency of the specification of the organization or to check the feasibility for a group of agents to incarnate the foreseen roles properly, i.e., respecting the accountabilities and preserving closure under control, which means that the agents can cooperate so as to achieve the organizational goal and discharge their responsibilities. The problem is formalized as follows.

Definition 3 (Accountability fitting). *Given a set of accountability specifications $\mathbb{A}$ and a responsibility distribution $\mathbf{R}$, we say that $\mathbf{R}$ fits $\mathbb{A}$, denoted by $\mathbf{R} \rightsquigarrow \mathbb{A}$, if there is $\mathbf{A} \in \mathbb{A}$ such that for each accountability $\mathsf{A}(x, y, r, u) \in \mathbf{A}$, there is a responsibility $\mathsf{R}(x, q) \in \mathbf{R}$ such that, for some actualization $\widehat{q}$, $(u/r)/\widehat{q} \equiv \top$.*

In particular, the following propositions hold.

Proposition 2. *Given a set of accountability specifications $\mathbb{A}$, and a responsibility distribution $\mathbf{R}$, such that $\mathbf{R} \rightsquigarrow \mathbb{A}$, let e be an event, then $\mathbf{R}/e \rightsquigarrow \mathbb{A}/e$.*

Proof. By Definition 3 (Accountability Fitting), we know that there exists in $\mathbb{A}$ at least one accountability specification $\mathbf{A}$ such that, for each $\mathsf{A}(x, y, r, u)$ there is one responsibility declaration $\mathsf{R}(x, q) \in \mathbf{R}$ such that $(u/r)/\widehat{q} \equiv \top$ some actualization $\widehat{q}$ of q. To show that $\mathbf{R}/e \rightsquigarrow \mathbb{A}/e$ we have just to show that $\mathbf{R}/e \rightsquigarrow \mathbf{A}/e$, for any possible event e. If e is irrelevant to $\mathbf{R}$, then $\mathbf{R}/e \equiv \mathbf{R}$, and hence the same actualizations that make $\mathbf{R}$ fit $\mathbf{A}$ are still possible in $\mathbf{R}/e$, and hence $\mathbf{R}/e \rightsquigarrow \mathbf{A}/e$. If e is relevant to some responsibility declaration $\mathsf{R}(x, q)$ in $\mathbf{R}$ we consider two cases:

- e is not relevant to $\mathbf{A}$, this happens when the responsibility taken on by x covers a wider set of events than actually required by $\mathbf{A}$. The actualizations of the residual expression q/e, thus, can still bring some accountabilities in $\mathbf{A}$ to satisfaction, namely for some $\mathsf{A}(x, y, r, u) \in \mathbf{A}$ it must happen $(u/r)/\widehat{q/e} \equiv \top$, and hence $\mathbf{R}/e \rightsquigarrow \mathbf{A}/e$.
- e is relevant to $\mathbf{A}$, that is, there exists at least one accountability $\mathsf{A}(x, y, r, u)$ such that e is relevant for r, u, or both. Since by hypothesis we know that $(u/r)/\widehat{q} \equiv \top$ holds, it must also hold that $((u/e)/(r/e))/\widehat{q/e} \equiv \top$, in fact the actualizations of the residual expression q/e are just suffixes of the actualizations of expression q.

Thus, since whichever event e occurs $\mathbf{R}/e \rightsquigarrow \mathbf{A}/e$, we conclude that $\mathbf{R}/e \rightsquigarrow \mathbb{A}/e$. ∎

Proposition 3. *Given a set of accountability specifications* $\mathbb{A}$*, and a responsibility distribution* $\mathbf{R}$ *such that* $\mathbf{R} \rightsquigarrow \mathbb{A}$*, then, there exists* e *such that: (1)* $e = \widehat{q}$ *where* $q = \bigwedge_{R(x,q_i) \in \mathbf{R}} q_i$ *(2)* $e \in [\![\mathbf{A}_i]\!]$*, for some* $\mathbf{A}_i$ *in* $\mathbb{A}$*.*

Proof. Let us assume, by absurd, that the sequence e does not exist. This means that for any sequence e we obtain by the actualizations of the responsibility declarations in $\mathbf{R}$, and for all accountability specification $\mathbf{A}_i \in \mathbb{A}$, there is at least one accountability $A(x, y, r, u) \in \mathbf{A}_i$, that does not progress to satisfaction when $A(x, y, r/e, u/e)$. That is to say, there is a gap in the responsibilities due to the fact that $R(x, p)$, such that $(u/r)/\widehat{p} \equiv \top$ is missing.

Of course, this is not possible as we are assuming by hypothesis that $\mathbf{R} \rightsquigarrow \mathbb{A}$ and hence, there must exist at least one accountability specification $\mathbf{A}$ in $\mathbb{A}$, such that, for accountability $A(x, y, r, u)$ in $\mathbf{A}$ there exists $R(x, p)$, such that $(u/r)/\widehat{p} \equiv \top$. It follows that, when a sequence e is an actualization of all the responsibilities in $\mathbf{R}$, it will also be an actualization of each accountability in at least one $\mathbf{A} \in \mathbb{A}$. ∎

Schlenker's well-known triangle model of responsibility [27] states that responsibility depends on three linkages called prescription-identity, identity-event, and event-prescription. Only when the three linkages are drawn will an individual feel responsible for something. We resort on this model to summarize what our proposal adds to organization specifications and organization entities.

Responsibility assumptions in $\mathbf{R}$ describe which duties agents take on when playing some roles inside an organization. From an organization designer's perspective, such duties would be captured in the simplest case through norm specification, or, in a richer form, norms would be complemented with requirements the agents have to comply with for adopting roles concerned by the norms. Still, this is on the organization side. On the agent side, obligations (per se) are received by fiat; following [20], they succeed in directing individual behavior only when they agree with the sensitivity of the individuals. Our proposal fills this design gap through explicitly declared/taken responsibility assumptions and accountability relationships, which give agents the means for reasoning about the implications of role enactment, and give designers the means for specifying organizations that show the good characteristics expressed by Proposition 3.

For a normative organization to function well, its agents should interiorize the norms in their behavior but when can this happen in open organizations? If the agent considers a norm (say, an obligation) as a prescription concerning one of its identities (i.e., one of the roles it plays in the organization having that norm) the norm would start being something more than "given by fiat". In our proposal this can be done because, even though here we do not focus on the process, $\mathbf{R}$ can be derived from the organization norms; in some case, the norm specification could even reduce to the specification of the responsibility distribution – which duties are up to which roles. That would not, however, be enough if the same agent cannot see the connection between the prescription and some events it concerns (in our setting, the prescription would apply in a context), and also between the event and the identified identity (the context as one in which the role has control over something). It is the co-presence of the three linkages (1) to create in the agent the urge to tackle that context, abiding by the prescription, by virtue of its role, should the prescription apply; (2) that helps the designer to create organizations where role specification and goal distribution combine well.

On the other hand, A is focused on accountability, basing it on the coordination aspect, and specifies alternative ways to be accountable in the achievement of the organizational goals. This separation of concerns encourages both modularity and reuse. In fact, the accountability specifications can be defined and verified w.r.t. responsibility concerning roles independently of the actual agents that will play roles in the organization itself. The separation of concerns is at two levels. First, the organization specification level: a same organization can be characterized by several accountability specifications and several responsibility distributions, that fit with each other. Second, the organization entity level. Here, the same set of agents can take responsibility and be accountable in different organizations specifications, as well as, different sets of agents could take responsibility and be accountable in the same organization specification. The proposed formalization enables the check that the responsibility, taken by agents according to the responsibility specification in the organization specification, fits the accountability in the organization entity, that is enacted from the accountability specification in the organization specification.

4   Example: Building a House

Let's consider Example 1, originally presented in [8], and relying on the three dimensions of the $\mathcal{M}$OISE organizational model [23]. The structural dimension specifies roles, groups and links between roles in the organization. The functional dimension is composed of one or more schemes that elicit how the global organizational goals are decomposed into subgoals and how these subgoals are grouped in coherent sets, called missions, to be distributed to roles in the normative dimension. This latter binds the two previous dimensions by specifying the roles' permissions and obligations for missions. While the model presented in the previous section is independent of a particular agent organization model, we demonstrate its use and interest, focusing on the roles, functional and normative dimensions of the $\mathcal{M}$OISE model.

As in the original *building-a-house* example, an agent wants to build a house on a plot. To achieve this goal the companies, he has contracted with, must coordinate and execute various tasks, part of which can be executed in parallel, while part depends on other tasks. The temporal order is specified by the functional specification of the process (cf. Fig. 1). Its translation in precedence logic is given in Example 1. The structural specification defines a group which includes the following roles: *House Owner (ho)*, *Boss (bo)*, *Frame Manager (fm)*, *Interior Exterior Manager (iem)*, *Site Prep Contractor (spc)*, *Bricklayer (bl)*, *Roofer (ro)*, *Fitter (ft)*, *Plumber (pl)*, *Electrician (el)*, *Painter (pa)*. The normative specification defining how each of the goals are allocated to roles will be described later when mapping it in terms of responsibilities.

The top-level organizational goal is house_built, of which bo should be in charge. On this basis, the designer can define the accountability relationship $A(bo, ho, \top, \text{frame} \cdot (\text{interior} \wedge \text{exterior}))$. Below, we report an example accountability specification $\mathbf{A}_1$ (see Fig. 2a) that includes the accountability of interest:

al$_1$. $A(bo, ho, \top, \text{frame} \cdot (\text{interior} \wedge \text{exterior}))$
al$_2$. $A(fm, bo, \top, \text{frame})$
al$_3$. $A(spc, fm, \top, \text{site\_prepared})$
al$_4$. $A(bl, fm, \text{site\_prepared}, \text{site\_prepared} \cdot \text{floors\_laid})$
al$_5$. $A(bl, fm, \text{site\_prepared} \cdot \text{floors\_laid}, \text{site\_prepared} \cdot \text{floors\_laid} \cdot \text{walls\_built})$
al$_6$. $A(iem, bo, \text{frame}, \text{frame} \cdot \text{interior})$
al$_7$. $A(iem, bo, \text{frame}, \text{frame} \cdot \text{exterior})$
al$_8$. $A(pl, iem, \text{frame}, \text{frame} \cdot \text{plumbing\_installed})$
al$_9$. $A(el, iem, \text{frame} \cdot \text{plumbing\_installed},$
        $\text{frame} \cdot \text{plumbing\_installed} \cdot \text{electrical\_system\_installed})$
al$_{10}$. $A(pa, iem, \text{frame} \cdot \text{plumbing\_installed} \cdot \text{electrical\_system\_installed},$
        $\text{frame} \cdot \text{plumbing\_installed} \cdot \text{electrical\_system\_installed} \cdot \text{walls\_painted})$
al$_{11}$. $A(ro, iem, \text{frame}, \text{frame} \cdot \text{roof\_built})$
al$_{12}$. $A(ft, iem, \text{frame} \cdot \text{roof\_built}, \text{frame} \cdot \text{roof\_built} \cdot \text{windows\_fitted})$
al$_{13}$. $A(ft, iem, \text{frame} \cdot \text{roof\_built}, \text{frame} \cdot \text{roof\_built} \cdot \text{doors\_fitted})$

It is easy to see that $\mathbf{A}_1$ is closed under control (see Definition 2). Let us start with al$_1$. We must verify if $\xi(bo, \top, \text{frame} \cdot (\text{interior} \wedge \text{exterior}))$ holds. To this aim, by Definition 1, we should have that $\xi(bo, \top, \text{frame})$ and $\xi(bo, \text{frame}, \text{frame} \cdot (\text{interior} \wedge \text{exterior}))$, which is true because of the accountabilities al$_2$, al$_6$, and al$_7$. Similarly for every relationship in $\mathbf{A}_1$. The choice walls_painted $\vee$ wallpapered in Example 1 enables an alternative accountability specification $\mathbf{A}_2$, by substituting al$_{10}$ with $A(pa, iem, \text{frame} \cdot \text{plumbing\_installed} \cdot \text{electrical\_system\_installed}, \text{frame} \cdot \text{plumbing\_installed} \cdot \text{electrical\_system\_installed} \cdot \text{wallpapered})$. We could, then, define $\mathbb{A}$ as the set $\{\mathbf{A}_1, \mathbf{A}_2\}$ if both are considered adequate by the designer.

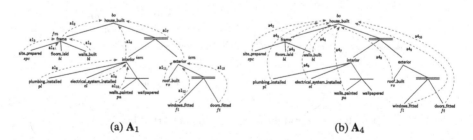

(a) $\mathbf{A}_1$ (b) $\mathbf{A}_4$

Fig. 2. Two accountability specifications for the building-a-house organization. Green arrows depict who is accountable towards whom. (Color figure online)

$\mathbf{A}_1$ and $\mathbf{A}_2$ rely on two managers, fm and iem, who act as intermediaries between their account-givers and bo: bo controls the overall process through the accountability relationships in which it is account-taker and the managers are account-givers. Accountability specification $\mathbf{A}_3$ shows a more substantial change. Here, fm is removed and spc and bl are directly accountable towards bo:

$a3_1$. $\mathsf{A}(spc, bo, \top, \mathsf{site\_prepared})$
$a3_2$. $\mathsf{A}(bl, bo, \mathsf{site\_prepared}, \mathsf{site\_prepared} \cdot \mathsf{floors\_laid})$
$a3_3$. $\mathsf{A}(bl, bo, \mathsf{site\_prepared} \cdot \mathsf{floors\_laid}, \mathsf{site\_prepared} \cdot \mathsf{floors\_laid} \cdot \mathsf{walls\_built})$

The extreme is when all accountabilities, though having the already seen shape, show bo as account-taker. This leads to $\mathbf{A}_4$ (see Fig. 2b) which includes:

$a4_1$. $\mathsf{A}(bo, ho, \top, \mathsf{frame} \cdot (\mathsf{interior} \wedge \mathsf{exterior}))$
$a4_2$. $\mathsf{A}(spc, bo, \top, \mathsf{site\_prepared})$
$a4_3$. $\mathsf{A}(bl, bo, \mathsf{site\_prepared}, \mathsf{site\_prepared} \cdot \mathsf{floors\_laid})$
$a4_4$. $\mathsf{A}(bl, bo, \mathsf{site\_prepared} \cdot \mathsf{floors\_laid}, \mathsf{site\_prepared} \cdot \mathsf{floors\_laid} \cdot \mathsf{walls\_built})$
$a4_5$. $\mathsf{A}(pl, bo, \mathsf{frame}, \mathsf{frame} \cdot \mathsf{plumbing\_installed})$
$a4_6$. *and so forth....*

Also $\mathbf{A}_3$ and $\mathbf{A}_4$, if deemed adequate, may be included in $\mathbb{A}$.

Finally, let us consider $\mathbf{A}_5$, which is similar to $\mathbf{A}_1$, but for $a1_3$, substituted by $a5_3$: $\mathsf{A}(spc, bo, \top, \mathsf{site\_prepared})$, and where $a1_8$ is not defined. Two main problems can be identified. First, for fm to have control over frame (i.e., $\mathsf{site\_prepared} \cdot \mathsf{floors\_laid} \cdot \mathsf{walls\_built}$), there should be three accountability relationships, one for each event, with fm as account-taker. In particular, spc should be accountable to fm rather than to bo (as, instead, encoded in $a5_3$) for $\mathsf{site\_prepared}$. Second, there is no accountability concerning $\mathsf{plumbing\_installed}$.

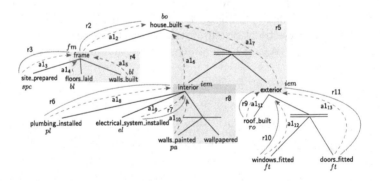

Fig. 3. Accountability specification $\mathbf{A}_1$ fitted by $\mathbf{R}$

Let us now consider the set of responsibility assumptions $\mathbf{R}$, depicted in Fig. 3:

r1. $R(bo, \text{frame} \cdot (\text{interior} \wedge \text{exterior}))$

r2. $R(fm, \text{frame})$

r3. $R(spc, \text{site\_prepared})$

r4. $R(bl, \text{floors\_laid} \cdot \text{walls\_built})$

r5. $R(iem, \text{interior} \wedge \text{exterior})$

r6. $R(pl, \text{plumbing\_installed})$

r7. $R(el, \text{electrical\_system\_installed})$

r8. $R(pa, \text{walls\_painted})$

r9. $R(ro, \text{roof\_built})$

r10. $R(ft, \text{windows\_fitted})$

r11. $R(ft, \text{doors\_fitted})$

This set of responsibilities can be deduced from the normative specification of the $\mathcal{M}$OISE organization specification that connects roles to goals of the functional specifications through missions. Thus, for instance, $R(bo, \text{frame} \cdot (\text{interior} \wedge \text{exterior}))$ is deduced from the norm stating that bo has the obligation of achieving interior $\wedge$ exterior after frame. Due to space limitations we cannot provide this normative specification.

It can easily be shown that **R** fits $\mathbb{A}$. Recalling Definition 3, there should be at least one $\mathbf{A}_i \in \mathbb{A}$ such that, for each accountability belonging to $\mathbf{A}_i$ there is a responsibility declaration belonging to **R** with an actualization that allows to satisfy the accountability, thus discharging the responsibility. This holds in particular with respect to $\mathbf{A}_1$. Indeed, let's consider, for instance, $a1_6$, $a1_7$ and r5. An actualization of interior is {plumbing_installed, electrical_system_installed, walls_painted}. Similarly, a possible actualization of exterior is {roof_built, windows_fitted, doors_fitted}. It's important to point out that these are not the only two allowed actualizations. Moreover, any interleaving which preserves the partial ordering of the two sequences is an actualization of interior $\wedge$ exterior. It is easy to show that such an actualization would bring both the consequents of $a1_6$, $a1_7$ (residuated w.r.t. the antecedent) to $\top$. The same holds for every accountability in $\mathbf{A}_1$. As a remark, it is important to highlight that the responsibility distribution **R** would fit $\mathbf{A}_4$, as well. However, the absence of the two managers in the accountability specification would make r2 and r5 unnecessary.

5   Conclusions and Future Work

In this paper we have proposed the foundational facts for specifying accountability within agent organizations. Such a specification complements the responsibility assumption, coming from the normative specification, which expresses social expectations on the rights and duties of the agents, participating to the organization. Based on precedence logic, this model of accountability involves roles in an organization specification, or agents in an organization entity. It is based on control relations and on social expectations about tasks contributing to the achievement of organizational goals. We have shown how it is possible to check that responsibility distribution in roles (or agents while playing roles) fits the accountability relationships coming from the accountability specification of the organization. As such, the proposal has many application fields, like software development, agent reasoning, organization management. Since the proposal relies on the constitutive elements of the approaches to agent organizations, i.e. roles, goals and norms, we could illustrate how this model can be used in the context of the $\mathcal{M}$OISE organization model, component of the JaCaMo platform. While here mainly demonstrated to support an organization designer–to check the coherence between an accountability specification and a responsibility distribution, the model could be used also at the agent level for providing agents with reasoning capabilities on those accountability relationships that come from the organizations to which they (may) participate.

Besides what already discussed, accountability relationships and responsibility, and in particular the presented proposal, will help to enrich the expression of social expectation by enlarging their scope and by introducing expectations from agents towards organization – thus turning organizations into structures of bilateral social expectations. The scope of social expectations are limited to the task to be executed. They are currently missing all what concerns the adoption of roles by agents. It is, usually, assumed that an agent who is going to adopt a role will necessarily have proper capabilities for each task it will ever receive. Organizations are trusting the agents for having the right capabilities for realizing what is expected from them when playing roles. There is no way of expressing social expectations on requirements for playing a role and of checking them. Few models have addressed this question by proposing modeling of contracts [12] or [2,24] involving agents and organization when adopting roles.

In the future, we intend to extend the proposal by including other forms of accountability relationships, such as the negative accountability, i.e., to capture that someone is expected not to impede social progress and negatively impact others. We will also study ways for leading agents to an agreement on a specific fitting of accountabilities when more than one exists.

References

1. Aldewereld, H., Boissier, O., Dignum, V., Noriega, P., Padget, J. (eds.): Social Coordination Frameworks for Social Technical Systems. LGTS, vol. 30. Springer, Cham (2016). https://doi.org/10.1007/978-3-319-33570-4
2. Aldewereld, H., Dignum, V., Jonker, C.M., van Riemsdijk, M.B.: Agreeing on role adoption in open organisations. KI-Künstliche Intelligenz **26**(1), 37–45 (2012)
3. Baldoni, M., Baroglio, C., Capuzzimati, F., Micalizio, R.: Type checking for protocol role enactments via commitments. J. Auton. Agents Multi-Agent Syst. **32**(3), 349–386 (2018)
4. Baldoni, M., Baroglio, C., May, K.M., Micalizio, R., Tedeschi, S.: Computational accountability in MAS organizations with ADOPT. J. Appl. Sci. **8**(4), 489 (2018). Special issue "Multi-Agent Systems"
5. Baldoni, M., Baroglio, C., May, K.M., Micalizio, R., Tedeschi, S.: ADOPT JaCaMo: accountability-driven organization programming technique for JaCaMo. In: An, B., Bazzan, A., Leite, J., Villata, S., van der Torre, L. (eds.) PRIMA 2017. LNCS, vol. 10621, pp. 295–312. Springer, Cham (2017). https://doi.org/10.1007/978-3-319-69131-2_18
6. Baldoni, M., Baroglio, C., May, K.M., Micalizio, R., Tedeschi, S.: An information model for computing accountabilities. In: Ghedini, C., Magnini, B., Passerini, A., Traverso, P. (eds.) Proceedings of 17th International Conference of the Italian Association for Artificial Intelligence, AI*IA 2018. LNAI, Trento, Italy. Springer (2018)

7. Boella, G., van der Torre, L.W.N., Verhagen, H.: Introduction to the special issue on normative multiagent systems. J. AAMAS **17**(1), 1–10 (2008)
8. Boissier, O., Bordini, R.H., Hübner, J.F., Ricci, A., Santi, A.: Multi-agent oriented programming with JaCaMo. Sci. Comput. Program. **78**(6), 747–761 (2013)
9. Castelfranchi, C.: Principles of individual social action. In: Contemporary Action Theory: Social Action, vol. 2, pp. 163–192. Kluwer, Dordrecht (1997)
10. Chopra, A.K., Dalpiaz, F., Aydemir, F.B., Giorgini, P., Mylopoulos, J., Singh, M.P.: Protos: foundations for engineering innovative sociotechnical systems. In: IEEE 22nd International Requirements Engineering Conference, pp. 53–62 (2014)
11. Chopra, A.K., Singh, M.P.: From social machines to social protocols: software engineering foundations for sociotechnical systems. In: Proceedings of the 25th International Conference on WWW (2016)
12. Colman, A., Han, J.: Operational management contracts for adaptive software organisation. In: Proceedings of the 2005 Australian Conference on Software Engineering, pp. 170–179. IEEE Computer Society (2005)
13. Corkill, D.D., Lesser, V.R.: The use of meta-level control for coordination in distributed problem solving network. In: Bundy, A. (ed.) Proceedings of the 8th International Joint Conference on Artificial Intelligence, IJCAI 1983, pp. 748–756. William Kaufmann, Los Altos (1983)
14. Coutinho, L.R., Sichman, J.S., Boissier, O.: Modelling dimensions for agent organizations. In: Handbook of Research on Multi-Agent Systems: Semantics and Dynamics of Organizational Models, pp. 18–50. IGI Global (2009)
15. da Rocha Costa, A.C.: Proposal for a notion of modularity in multiagent systems. In: Dalpiaz, F., Dix, J., van Riemsdijk, M.B. (eds.) Pre-proceedings of Engineering Multi-Agent Systems Workshop at AAMAS, Paris, pp. 21–40 (2014)
16. Dastani, M., Tinnemeier, N.A.M., Meyer, J.-J.C.: A programming language for normative multi-agent systems. In: Handbook of Research on Multi-Agent Systems: Semantics and Dynamics of Organizational Models, pp. 397–417. IGI Global (2009)
17. Dignum, V.: A model for organizational interaction: based on agents, founded in logic. Ph.D. thesis. Utrecht University (2004). Published by SIKS
18. Dignum, V.: Handbook of Research on Multi-Agent Systems: Semantics and Dynamics of Organizational Models. IGI Global, Hershey (2009)
19. Dignum, V., Vázquez-Salceda, J., Dignum, F.: OMNI: introducing social structure, norms and ontologies into agent organizations. In: Bordini, R.H., Dastani, M., Dix, J., El Fallah Seghrouchni, A. (eds.) ProMAS 2004. LNCS, vol. 3346, pp. 181–198. Springer, Heidelberg (2005). https://doi.org/10.1007/978-3-540-32260-3_10
20. Durkheim, E.: De la division du travail social. PUF, Paris (1893)
21. Esteva, M., Rodríguez-Aguilar, J.-A., Sierra, C., Garcia, P., Arcos, J.L.: On the formal specification of electronic institutions. In: Dignum, F., Sierra, C. (eds.) Agent Mediated Electronic Commerce. LNCS, vol. 1991, pp. 126–147. Springer, Heidelberg (2001). https://doi.org/10.1007/3-540-44682-6_8
22. Fornara, N., Viganò, F., Verdicchio, M., Colombetti, M.: Artificial institutions: a model of institutional reality for open multiagent systems. Artif. Intell. Law **16**(1), 89–105 (2008)
23. Hübner, J.F., Boissier, O., Kitio, R., Ricci, A.: Instrumenting multi-agent organisations with organisational artifacts and agents. Auton. Agents Multi-Agent Syst. **20**(3), 369–400 (2010)
24. Teussop, R.K.: Gestion de louverture au sein dorganisations multi-agents: une approche basée sur des artefacts organisationnels. Ph.D. thesis. EMSE, Saint-Etienne (2011)

25. Marengo, E., Baldoni, M., Baroglio, C., Chopra, A.K., Patti, V., Singh, M.P.: Commitments with regulations: reasoning about safety and control in REGULA. In: Proceedings of the 10th International Conference on Autonomous Agents and Multiagent Systems, AAMAS, vol. 2, pp. 467–474 (2011)
26. Romzek, B.S., Dubnick, M.J.: Accountability in the public sector: lessons from the challenger tragedy. Public Adm. Rev. **47**(3), 227–238 (1987)
27. Schlenker, B.R., Britt, T.W., Pennington, J., Rodolfo, M., Doherty, K.: The triangle model of responsibility. Psychol. Rev. **101**(4), 632–652 (1994)
28. Singh, M.P.: An ontology for commitments in multiagent systems. Artif. Intell. Law **7**(1), 97–113 (1999)
29. Singh, M.P.,: Distributed enactment of multiagent workflows: temporal logic for web service composition. In: Proceedings of the Second International Joint Conference on Autonomous Agents and Multiagent Systems, AAMAS 2003, Melbourne, Victoria, Australia, 14–18 July 2003, pp. 907–914. ACM (2003)

Runtime Norm Revision
Using Bayesian Networks

Davide Dell'Anna[✉], Mehdi Dastani, and Fabiano Dalpiaz

Utrecht University, Utrecht, The Netherlands
{d.dellanna,m.m.dastani,f.dalpiaz}@uu.nl

Abstract. To guarantee the overall intended objectives of a multiagent systems, the behavior of individual agents should be controlled and coordinated. Such coordination can be achieved, without limiting the agents' autonomy, via runtime norm enforcement. However, due to the dynamicity and uncertainty of the environment, the enforced norms can be ineffective. In this paper, we propose a runtime supervision mechanism that automatically revises norms when their enforcement appears to be ineffective. The decision to revise norms is taken based on a Bayesian Network that gives information about the likelihood of achieving the overall intended system objectives by enforcing the norms. Norms can be revised in three ways: relaxation, strengthening, and alteration. We evaluate the supervision mechanism on an urban smart traffic simulation.

Keywords: Norm revision · Multiagent systems · Bayesian networks

1 Introduction

A multiagent system consists of (heterogeneous) autonomous agents that coexist and interact in a shared open environment [1]. In order to guarantee the overall intended objectives of a multiagent system, the behavior of the autonomous agents should be coordinated [2]. In the multiagent systems literature, runtime norm enforcement is a widely studied mechanism for controlling and coordinating the runtime behavior of the agents without limiting their autonomy [3,4]. For example, a smart road populated by autonomous cars can control the cars' behavior by enforcing traffic rules, such as speed limitations, in order to improve throughput and safety of the road. In this paper, we do not focus on norm enforcement and assume that norms can be enforced on autonomous agents by means of, e.g., regimentation and sanctioning mechanisms.

However, due to the dynamicity and uncertainty involved in the agents' operating environments, such as sudden changes of weather conditions or accidents due to heavy traffic, enforcing the existing norms may not be sufficient to ensure the overall intended objectives [5]. For example, the enforcement of some speed norms may not improve traffic throughput or safety when the weather conditions change from extreme to normal (or vice versa). Given a set of norms and

© Springer Nature Switzerland AG 2018
T. Miller et al. (Eds.): PRIMA 2018, LNAI 11224, pp. 279–295, 2018.
https://doi.org/10.1007/978-3-030-03098-8_17

a set of environmental conditions, it is often hard—or practically impossible—to predict the effectiveness of enforcing specific norms in various environmental conditions [6]. This suggests that continuous evaluation of norm enforcement and dynamic revision of the norms at runtime are key factors to build an effective normative multiagent system capable of ensuring the overall system objectives within a dynamic and uncertain environment [7].

We introduce a runtime norm supervision mechanism that monitors the behavior of a multiagent system, evaluates the enforcement of the norms in terms of the overall system objectives, and, when needed, intervenes by revising the norms. For example, if the enforcement of adaptive traffic lights on a smart road significantly decreases the safety of cars in extreme weather conditions, our runtime norm supervision mechanism will suggest a revision of such norm proposing the enforcement of static traffic lights.

This paper focuses on the evaluation and revision of the norms enforced in the system. We describe three main types of norm revision (relaxation, strengthening and alteration) and provide two heuristic algorithms for suggesting norm revisions based on data that is collected and encoded into a Bayesian Network (called *Norm Bayesian Network*) at runtime. Such network is used to learn and reason about the correlation between norm satisfaction/violation and the overall system objectives achievement. The runtime norm supervision mechanism is implemented as an optimization process that uses a variation of the hill climbing optimization technique. Our revision algorithms are used in the optimization process to determine the next sets of norms to enforce in the system.

We report on an experimental evaluation of the supervision mechanism by applying it to an urban traffic simulation. Our implementation guarantees the identification of norm sets that ensure the overall system objectives. We compare the results obtained using hill climbing combined with and without our revision engine (i.e., Bayesian Network and revision strategies) and show that the proposed mechanism, using runtime information about norms effectiveness, allows to find optimal solutions with less revisions.

The paper is structured as follows. Section 2 describes a case study concerning urban traffic management. Section 3 presents the runtime supervision mechanism and the *Norm Bayesian Network*. Section 4 describes two algorithms for the suggestion of norms revision. Section 5 evaluates the effectiveness of the approach. Finally, Sects. 6 and 7 review related studies and conclude the paper.

2   Case Study: Norms for Urban Traffic Management

Consider a city where 10% of the cars are autonomous self-driving cars operating in a road network that is enriched with autonomous traffic controllers such as smart traffic lights and panels. The city council aims at improving the urban traffic by achieving two overall objectives: *minimize the average travel time* and *minimize the number of accidents*. To achieve such objectives, the city council plans to control and coordinate the traffic by enforcing traffic norms. To this end, the council is able to prescribe the self-driving cars to use a centralized navigation service (CNS) instead of their personal navigation system. The CNS can be either adaptive (able to autonomously change its own parameters at runtime) or static. The council may also prescribe the use of specific traffic controllers at road junctions. In particular, the council can enforce five possible obligation norms in the city:

- *every self-driving car is obliged to employ the routes suggested by an adaptive or static CNS* (denoted by $O(ans)$ and $O(sns)$).
- *every road junction is obliged to employ adaptive traffic lights* ($O(atl)$), *static traffic lights* ($O(stl)$), or *priority lines panels* ($O(pl)$).

Due to the highly dynamic nature of the city, drivers and cars can behave differently in different contexts (in this paper, we consider four contexts: *day* or *night*, *normal* or *extreme* weather). This makes it hard to determine in advance which set of norms will be the most effective in every context. For this reason, the city council aims at developing a traffic management system that starts with a set of norms, enforces the norms at run-time and monitors whether the enforcement of the norms is effective in the sense that they will guarantee the achievement of the overall objectives of minimizing travel time and accidents. In case norms are learned not to be effective, the traffic management system is expected to revise the norms accordingly.

Consider the norms $O(ans)$ and $O(sns)$ to be mutually exclusive, as well as the norms $O(atl), O(stl)$ and $O(pl)$. Based on these relationships, the city council disposes of a set $\mathcal{N}$ of 12 possible norm sets that could be enforced in the city: $\mathcal{N} = \{\{O(ans)\}, \{O(sns)\}, \{O(atl)\}, \{O(stl)\}, \{O(pl)\}, \{O(ans), O(atl)\}, \{O(ans), O(stl)\}, \{O(ans), O(pl)\}, \{O(sns), O(atl)\}, \{O(sns), O(stl)\}, \{O(sns), O(pl)\}, \emptyset\}$. When a navigation service is prescribed (e.g., in case of $\{O(ans)\}$) the routes suggested are followed by the self-driving cars in the 80% of the cases; when no navigation service is prescribed (e.g., in case of $\{O(pl)\}$) the self-driving cars use their own navigation system; finally when no junction management is prescribed (e.g., in case of $\{O(ans)\}$) the cars approaching the smart junctions follow the default priority-to-the-right rule.

In this paper norms are obligations expressed as propositional state formulae in conjunctive normal form and O denotes the obligation operator. Norms are considered here to be regimented, rather than enforced by means of sanctions. We leave sanction-based enforcement mechanism for future work; here, we study in detail the effect of imposing different norms on a multiagent system, their relationship with overall system objectives in different contexts and the possible strategies to revise norms when they are not effective.

3   Runtime Norm Supervision

We present the control loop performed by the runtime supervision mechanism (sketched in Fig. 1) to automatically evaluate and revise norms in order to achieve the overall objectives of a multiagent system.

Given a set $\mathcal{O}$ of boolean overall system objectives, a set $\mathcal{N}$ of all possible norm sets enforceable in the system and a set $\mathcal{C}$ of all possible contexts of the multiagent system, we call system *configuration* an assignment of a norm set $N \in \mathcal{N}$ to each possible context in $\mathcal{C}$. For example, given the four possible contexts $(day, normal)$, $(day, extreme)$, $(night, normal)$, $(night, extreme)$, and given the set $\mathcal{N}$ of possible norm sets defined in Sect. 2, an example of system configuration is $\{\langle(day, normal), \{O(p)\}\rangle, \langle(day, extreme), \{O(ans), O(p)\}\rangle, \langle(night, normal), \{O(sns)\}\rangle, \langle(night, extreme), \{O(atl), O(ans)\}\rangle\}$. A norm n is said to be *active* in a context c if $\langle c, N \rangle$ is in the system configuration and $n \in N$. Otherwise n is said *disabled*.

The control loop of the supervision mechanism starts with a *Norm Base* containing an initial system configuration. We assume a runtime *Monitoring* component that perfectly collects information about the satisfaction or violation of the norms in the contexts in which they are evaluated. Such component provides a boolean evaluation of the overall system objectives. This knowledge is used to learn, by means of a *Norm Bayesian Network* (described in Sect. 3.1), the dependencies between the satisfaction of the norms and the achievement of the objectives in the different contexts. A *Revision Trigger* component (described in Sect. 3.2) uses the learned knowledge to determine whether some norms should be revised. The norm revision process is executed by the *Revision Engine* component (described in Sect. 3.3) and generates as output a (possibly) new system configuration, replacing the current one in the *Norm base*.

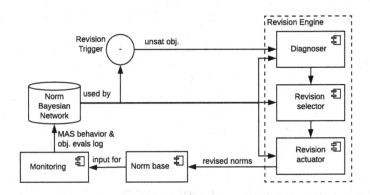

Fig. 1. The control loop of the runtime supervision mechanism.

We propose an implementation of the control loop above described as a variation of the hill climbing optimization technique. In particular, we consider the system configurations as possible solutions to explore in order to find an optimal one. The quality of a solution is determined, by means of runtime data, as the average probability of achievement of the overall objectives in all the contexts. Instead of terminating the exploration of the space when a local optimum is found, as in traditional hill climbing, we use as stopping criterion a constraint defined by the system designer that determines whether or not the current solution is acceptable (see Sect. 3.2). We use the *Revision Engine* to determine the next solution to try, when the current one is not acceptable.

Sections 3.1 and 4 describe the main components involved in the control loop. Section 5 provides an experimental evaluation of our implementation of the control loop. We compare the results that hill climbing can obtain by using our Revision Engine for the neighborhood definition with results that can be obtained by using heuristics that do not evaluate the effectiveness of the norms.

3.1   Norm Bayesian Network

Bayesian Networks have been widely used in many fields as knowledge representation structures for learning and reasoning about the inter-dependencies between their nodes [8]. We define a type of Bayesian Network called *Norm Bayesian Network* to represent and reason about norms and their relationship with overall objectives in different contexts. We call *contextual variables* monitorable environmental properties such as *Time* and *Weather*. Each of these variables is associated to a domain of values (e.g., *Time* can be either *day* or *night*, *Weather* can be either *normal* or *extreme*). Given a set of contextual variables we call *context* an assignment of a value to each contextual variable (e.g., given *Time* and *Weather* as above described, we have four possible contexts: (*day, normal*), (*day, extreme*), (*night, normal*), (*night, extreme*)).

A *Norm Bayesian Network* $\mathcal{NBN} = (\mathcal{X}, \mathcal{A}, \mathcal{P})$ is a Bayesian Network where:

- $\mathcal{X} = \mathbf{N} \cup \mathbf{O} \cup \mathbf{C}$ is a set of nodes, representing random variables in probability theory. The sets $\mathbf{N}$, $\mathbf{O}$ and $\mathbf{C}$ are disjoint. The set $\mathbf{N}$ consists of *norm nodes*; each node $N \in \mathbf{N}$ corresponds to one norm and has a discrete domain of 3 possible values: *obeyed*, *violated* and *disabled*. The set $\mathbf{O}$ consists of *objective nodes*; each node $O \in \mathbf{O}$ corresponds to a boolean objective and has a discrete domain of 2 values: *true* and *false*. Finally, the set $\mathbf{C}$ consists of *context nodes*; each node $C \in \mathbf{C}$ corresponds to a contextual variable and can have a discrete or continuous domain of values.
- $\mathcal{A} \subseteq (\mathbf{C} \times \mathbf{N}) \cup (\mathbf{C} \times \mathbf{O}) \cup (\mathbf{N} \times \mathbf{O})$ is the set of arrows connecting pairs of nodes. If there is an arrow from node X to node Y, X is called parent of Y.
- $\mathcal{P}$ is a set of conditional probability distributions, each one associated with a node in $\mathcal{X}$ and quantifying the effect of the parents on the node.

In the context of Bayesian Networks we use the following notation. $X, Y, \dots$ (italic uppercase) denotes random variables; $\mathbf{X}, \mathbf{Y}, \dots$ (bold uppercase) denotes sets of random variables; $v_1, v_2, \dots$ (italic lowercase) denotes values in the domain of a random variable; X_v denotes an assignment $(X = v)$ of value v to a random variable X; $\mathbf{x}$ (bold lowercase) denotes an assignment of values to a set of nodes $\mathbf{X}$; $\mathbf{X}_v$ denotes an assignment of value v to all nodes in $\mathbf{X}$; X_{act}

denotes the fact $\neg X_{dis} = \neg(X = disabled)$); $\neg\mathbf{x}_v^{\mathbf{X}}$ is equivalent to $\bigwedge_{X \in \mathbf{X}}(\neg X_v)$; $\mathbf{P}$ denotes a probability distribution; P denotes a single probability[1].

Figure 2 reports the *structure* $(\mathcal{X}, \mathcal{A})$ of an $\mathcal{NBN}$ for our case study. Notice the three types of nodes representing contextual variables, norms and overall objectives. Arrows connect each contextual variable to all norms and all objectives, and each norm to all the objectives. Nodes *Travel_Time* and *Accidents* correspond to the two overall objectives of minimizing travel time and accidents.

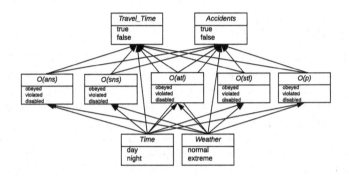

Fig. 2. The structure of the $\mathcal{NBN}$ for the case study of Sect. 2.

In Bayesian Networks, an evidence **e** is an observed assignment of values for some or all of the random variables in the network. An evidence **c** for all the context nodes **C** is an observation for a certain context (e.g., *Time* has value *day* and *Weather* has value *extreme*). For simplicity we use the term *context* also to refer to the associated evidence in the Bayesian Network. An evidence of value *obeyed* or *violated* for a norm node can be obtained when the corresponding norm is enforced in the multiagent system. When the norm is not enforced the only possible evidence for its corresponding node is *disabled*. Note that the evidence values are determined by the *Monitoring* component. Norms nodes, therefore, only collect statistical information about norm obedience in different contexts.

Note also that, for the sake of brevity, we omit a discussion about the learning technique (e.g., classical Bayesian learning) to train the network and we refer the reader to the existing literature (e.g., [8,9]). In the following, we assume that we dispose of a network trained with data produced by the *Monitoring* component.

3.2 Revision Trigger

Let e be an event denoting that changes in the probability distributions in the *Norm Bayesian Network* are not significant anymore (i.e., the variations in the distribution when a new sample is given are below a specified δ). Assuming

---

[1] When we refer to nodes of a specific type we use the corresponding notation convention, e.g., N refers to a node in **N**, **c** refers to an assignment of values to nodes in **C**, $\mathbf{N}_{viol}$ refers to an assignment of value *violated* to a set of norm nodes **N**, etc.

a population of agents that behaves consistently, such event will occur after some time. Let t_{oa} be a threshold defining the minimum average probability of achievement of the objectives desired by the system designer, and let c be the related constraint (e.g., $c = P(Travel\_Time_{true} \wedge Accidents_{true}) \geq 0.95$, with $t_{oa} = 0.95$). A revision (i.e., a new iteration of the hill climbing procedure) is triggered every time e occurs and c is not satisfied.

3.3   Revision Engine

Assume that the *Norm Bayesian Network* $\mathcal{NBN}$ of Fig. 2 is trained with data and that a norm revision is triggered by the *Revision Trigger*. We describe the three components of the *Revision Engine* shown in Fig. 1. Such components are used to determine the new norm set to enforce in the multiagent system.

Diagnoser. This component uses the $\mathcal{NBN}$ to generate an explanation for the objectives not being achieved. To do so, it first determines a context **mpc** that corresponds to the most problematic context in which the objectives are not achieved. $\mathbf{mpc} = argmax_{c \in all(c)} P(\mathbf{O}_{false} \mid \mathbf{c})$, where $all(\mathbf{c})$ is the set of all possible contexts (assignments of a value to each of the context nodes in $\mathcal{NBN}$).

Let $\mathcal{N}_{\mathbf{mpc}}$ be the set of norms currently active in the context corresponding to **mpc**, and $\mathbf{N}_a$ and $\mathbf{N}_d$ be the two disjoint sets of nodes in $\mathcal{NBN}$ that corresponds to the norms that are respectively active and disabled in the most problematic context. The Diagnoser determines the *most likely explanation* [10] $\mathbf{n}_e$ for $\mathbf{O}_{false}$ given **mpc**, in terms of satisfaction of the active norms in $\mathcal{N}_{\mathbf{mpc}}$.

$$\mathbf{n}_e = argmax_{\mathbf{n} \in \mathbf{n}_{\{ob,viol\}}^{\mathbf{N}_a}} P(\mathbf{n} \mid \mathbf{O}_{false} \wedge \mathbf{mpc} \wedge \mathbf{n}_{dis}^{\mathbf{N}_d} \wedge \neg \mathbf{n}_{dis}^{\mathbf{N}_a})$$

where $\mathbf{n}_{\{ob,viol\}}^{\mathbf{N}_a} = \{N_v \mid N \in \mathbf{N}_a, v \in \{ob, viol\}\}$ is the set of all the possible assignments of values (either *obeyed* or *violated*) to nodes $\mathbf{N}_a$.

Revision Selector. Given the most likely explanation $\mathbf{n}_e$, we aim to revise $\mathcal{N}_{\mathbf{mpc}}$ so to increase $P(\mathbf{O}_{true} \mid \mathbf{mpc})$ above the threshold t_{oa}. The Revision Selector determines the most adequate *type of revision* to perform.

We define three types of norm revision: *relaxation, strengthening, alteration*. Relaxing (strengthening) a propositional obligation norm $O(n)$ means replacing it with a new norm $O(n')$ such that n' is a less strict (stricter) formula than n (e.g., $O(ans \vee \perp)$ is a less strict obligation than $O(ans)$). A less strict (stricter) obligation makes the norm violated in fewer (more) situations, which means that more (less) behaviors are allowed. Any other revision of a norm $O(n)$ is an alteration. Relaxing (strengthening) a *set* of norms N means replacing it with a new norm set N' such that one or more norms in N' are a relaxation (strengthening) of norms in N and all the other norms are unchanged (e.g., $\{O(ans), O(atl)\}$ is a strenghtening of $\{O(atl)\}$). Any other revision of a set of norms N is an alteration of N (e.g., $\{O(ans)\}$ is an alteration of $\{O(sns)\}$).

The Revision Selector applies the following idea. To achieve the overall objectives in a certain context, some of the active norms are more useful if obeyed, others are more useful if violated, and the rest are always harmful (regardless of the fact that they are obeyed or violated). This information can be derived from the conditional probability distributions of nodes **N** as follows.

Consider the case of a single active norm N in $\mathcal{N}_{\mathbf{mpc}}$ ($\mathbf{N}_a = \{N\}$), a single boolean objective O, and a single context[2]. Figure 3a illustrates revision strategies based on the three types of relationships between N and O above described.

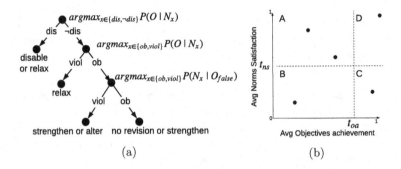

(a)   (b)

Fig. 3. (a) Decision tree for determining a suitable type of revision. (b) system configurations (points) in four states (A–D) w.r.t. the average satisfaction of the enforced norms and the average probability of achievement of the objectives.

The decision tree first determines whether the norm N is more useful for O when disabled or active. In the former case the norm is considered harmful, i.e., $N_{harm} \equiv (P(O_{true} \mid N_{dis}) > P(O_{true} \mid \neg N_{dis}))$. The most suitable strategy in this case is either to disable N or to relax N (relaxation is a "soft" kind of disabling, for it allow more behaviors). If N is not harmful, the decision tree compares the probabilities of N supporting O when obeyed and when violated.

If N is more useful for O when violated ($P(O_{true} \mid N_{viol}) > P(O_{true} \mid N_{ob}) \land \neg N_{harm}$), the suggested revision is to relax it, thereby turning some non-compliant (but useful to achieve O) behaviors into compliant ones. If N is more useful when obeyed (i.e., $P(O_{true} \mid N_{ob}) > P(O_{true} \mid N_{viol}) \land \neg N_{harm}$), the tree computes the most likely explanation for O not being achieved, between N being violated or obeyed. In the former case, the suggested revision is to strengthen N (restricting the allowed behaviors) or alter it (N is not effective). In the latter case, the suggestion is either to not revise (N may not be the cause of the problem) or to strengthen (N may not be strong enough to achieve O).

Section 4 presents two revision selection algorithms that apply the principle here described to the entire set of norms enforced in the system. The output of the Revision Selector is a set of norms annotated with suggested revisions (if any).

---

[2] In the following we omit the context from the conditional probabilities since implicit.

Revision Actuator. The task of this component is to determine the new norm set to enforce in the system. Given the set of norms annotated with suggested revisions (from the Revision Selector), and given a set of possible norm sets $\mathcal{N}$, the Revision Actuator selects a norm set $\mathcal{N}' \in \mathcal{N}$ that is as aligned as possible with the direction provided by the suggestions. For example, given the norm set $\{O(ans)\}$ and a suggestion of disabling norm $O(ans)$, the norm set in $\mathcal{N}$ that is the most aligned with the suggestion is the empty set $\{\}$. If multiple norm sets are available, different distance metrics can be defined, e.g., the similarity with the current norm set, or the sensitivity of the objectives to the change of the selected norms. In this paper, we use as distance metric the number of revision of norms needed to obtain $\mathcal{N}'$ from $\mathcal{N}$. For instance, two revisions are necessary to to obtain $\{O(ans), O(p)\}$ from $\{O(sns), O(atl)\}$: $O(sns)$ must be altered to $O(ans)$ and $O(atl)$ must be altered to $O(p)$. If there is no new norm set that is aligned with the provided suggestion (i.e., either the defined neighborhood of the current solution is empty or it contains only configurations that have already been tried) the Revision Actuator randomly selects a configuration never tried before, if any. Notice that this makes our implementation of hill climbing different from a traditional one and it guarantees to always converge to an optimal solution.

4   Revision Selection Algorithms

We present two algorithms for the Revision Selector component. The PUREBN algorithm enacts the decision tree of Fig. 3a for all the enforced norms. The STATEBASED algorithm takes also into account the overall status of the system in the current configuration. Both algorithms are invoked on the most problematic context defined in Sect. 3.3 and they both return a set of norms annotated with suggested revisions. Such set of norms is used as heuristic to determine the neighborhood of the current norm set in the hill climbing process.

4.1   PureBN

Algorithm 1 reports the PUREBN heuristic for the selection of norms revision. Line 2 determines, based on the top decision node of Fig. 3a, the norm set $\mathcal{N}'$ that has the highest probability to satisfy the objectives. If the current norm set has active norms, and there is some norm set that has not been attempted in the most problematic context yet (line 3), the most likely explanation n_e for not fulfilling the objectives is determined (line 4). Then, for each active norm in the new norm set $\mathcal{N}'$ (line 5), the algorithm determines the "desired" state, i.e., whether that norm helps better the satisfaction of the objectives when obeyed or violated (line 6). Finally, in line 7, the suggestion for the examined norm is determined based on the decision tree of Fig. 3a. If no norms are active or all possible norm sets have already been tried, PUREBN returns $\mathcal{N}'$: the best possible norm set for the most problematic context (skipping lines 4–7).

Algorithm 1. The PUREBN algorithm for revision selection

1: **function** PUREBN(**c**)
2:     $\mathcal{N}' \leftarrow$ GETBESTNORMSET(**c**)   ▷ obtain $\mathbf{N}'_a$ and $\mathbf{N}'_d$
3:     **if** $(|\mathbf{N}_a| > 0)$ && ¬ALLNORMSETTRIED(**c**) **then**
4:         $\mathbf{n}_e \leftarrow$ GETMLE($\mathbf{O}_{false}$, **c**)
5:         **for all** norms $N \in \mathbf{N}'_a$ **do**
6:             $n_{des} \leftarrow$ GETDESIREDVAL(N, **c**)
7:             SETSUGG($\{N\}$, GETSUGG(N, $\mathbf{n}_e$, n_{des}))
        return $\mathcal{N}'$

4.2   StateBased

While PUREBN provides a suggestion for each active norm, STATEBASED considers the average satisfaction of active norms and the average achievement of the overall objectives to suggest a specific type of revision per time.

Figure 3b plots system configurations in four states with respect to norms satisfaction and objectives achievement. The configurations in state A sufficiently satisfy the norms, but the objectives are not achieved to a sufficient extent. State B denotes insufficient norms satisfaction and objectives achievement. State C indicates that the objectives are achieved even though the norms are not satisfied. State D is the ideal area: the norms are satisfied and the objectives are achieved.

Assume we have, together with the threshold t_{oa}, an additional threshold t_{ns} that defines the desired probability of satisfaction of norms. STATEBASED first determines the average norms satisfaction and objectives achievement based on the evidence from the active norms in the most problematic context (lines 2). Like in PUREBN, the best possible norm set in the most problematic context is generated (line 3). If there are currently no active norms or $\mathcal{N}'$ contains at least one suggestion of type `disable`, the function returns immediately (line 4).

Three empty sets of norms are defined in line 5: obeyed norms that are better when violated *obbv*, violated norms that are better when violated *vabv*, and violated norms that are better when obeyed *vbbo*. After determining the most likely explanation $\mathbf{n}_e$ (line 6), the algorithm determines (line 7) the desired state (obeyed, violated) of all active norms of the new norm set. Using $\mathbf{n}_e$ (obeyed/violated) and the desired state (obeyed/violated), the norms are added to the corresponding sets *obbv*, *vavb*, and *vbbo* (line 8).

Lines 9–16 implement the idea visualized in Fig. 3b by comparing the state of the current norm set (*ns* and *oa*) against the thresholds t_{ns} and t_{oa}. If the configuration is in state A (lines 9–11), if *obbv* contains norms, the suggestion is to relax them; if *obbv* is empty, a suggestion to alter or strengthen is given for the active norms (the active norms behave as expected but the objectives are not achieved). In state B (lines 12–13), a relaxation of the norms that are better if violated is suggested, and an alteration or strengthening is suggested for the norms that are better if obeyed. In state C (lines 14–16), if there are violated norms that are better if violated, they are relaxed; if, instead, there are violated norms that are better if obeyed, the suggestion is to either alter or strengthen.

Algorithm 2. The STATEBASED algorithm for revision selection

1: **function** STATEBASED(**c**)
2:     $ns \leftarrow$ AVGNORMSAT($\mathbf{N}_a$, **c**); $oa \leftarrow$ AVGOBJACH($\mathbf{N}_a$, **c**)
3:     $\mathcal{N}' \leftarrow$ GETBESTNORMSET(**c**)   ▷ obtain $\mathbf{N}'_a$ and $\mathbf{N}'_d$
4:     **if** ($|\mathbf{N}_a| = 0$) || HASDIS($\mathcal{N}'$)) **then return** $\mathcal{N}'$
5:     $obbv \leftarrow vabv \leftarrow vbbo \leftarrow \{\}$
6:     $\mathbf{n}_e \leftarrow$ GETMLE($\mathbf{O}_{false}$, **c**)
7:     $\mathbf{n}_{des} \leftarrow$ GETDESIREDVAL($\mathbf{N}'_a$, **c**)
8:     DETERMINETYPE($\mathbf{N}'_a$, $\mathbf{n}_e$, $\mathbf{n}_{des}$, $obbv$, $vabv$, $vbbo$)
9:     **if** $ns \geq t_{ns}$ && $oa < t_{oa}$ **then**
10:        **if** $|obbv| > 0$ **then** SETSUGG($obbv$, relax)
11:        **else** SETSUGG($\mathbf{N}_a$, alter $\vee$ strengthen)
12:     **else if** $rs < t_{ns}$ && $ga < t_{oa}$ **then**
13:        SETSUGG($oobv \cup vabv$, relax); SETSUGG($vbbo$, alter $\vee$ strengthen)
14:     **else if** $rs < t_{ns}$ && $ga \geq t_{oa}$ **then**
15:        **if** $|vabv| > 0$ **then** SETSUGG($vabv$, relax)
16:        **else if** $|vbbo| > 0$ **then** SETSUGG($vbbo$, alter $\vee$ strengthen)
       return $\mathcal{N}'$

5 Evaluation

We conducted an experimental evaluation of our implementation of the runtime norm supervision mechanism in terms of *convergence speed* and *quality of the final solution*. We compare the results that can be obtained by using our *Revision Engine* with results that can be obtained with heuristics that do not evaluate the effectiveness of the norms.

We make use of a simulation of the scenario described in Sect. 2. We adopt the CrowdNav simulator from the self-adaptive systems literature [11]. CrowdNav consists of a number of cars traveling in a medium-size city (Eichstädt, Germany) with 450 streets and 1,200 intersections. Each car relies on a navigation service to receive a route. 90% of the cars use a default routing algorithm implemented in SUMO (the underlying traffic simulation engine), while the remaining 10% are smart cars that use a centralized navigation service. In CrowdNav such service is adaptive, i.e., it is able to autonomously adapt its parameters at runtime.

We extended CrowdNav to support, besides the adaptive service, also a static service, as well as different ways of managing junctions, in line with the norms described in Sect. 2. We use the two contextual properties *Time*, which can assume the values *day* (600 cars in the simulation) or *night* (300 cars), and *Weather*, which can be either *normal* or *extreme* (the maximum allowed speed is reduced by 25% in all the streets). We instrumented the extended CrowdNav to collect data about norm satisfaction and objectives achievement. The boolean value of the objective *Travel_Time* is obtained, every simulation-day, by determining whether, on average, the cars in the city took less than 2.5 times the optimal trip time[3] to reach their destination. The boolean value of the objective

---

[3] Actual trip time over the theoretical time w.r.t. to length and speed limits.

Accidents is obtained by determining whether there are less than 4 accidents per day.

5.1 Experiments

We implemented the runtime norm supervision mechanism as a modified version of hill climbing that accounts for t_{oa} as a stopping criterion: it stops only when either all the configurations have been tried or it finds a local optimum with an average objectives achievement probability higher than t_{oa}.

We used the algorithms PUREBN and STATEBASED of Sect. 4 as two possible heuristics for defining the neighborhood of a configuration: the neighborhood defined by PUREBN and STATEBASED is the set of all the configurations that satisfy their suggestions. We defined three additional configuration neighborhood metrics that do not take into account the acquired knowledge about the effectiveness of the enforced norms. (1) maximum distance 4 (MD4) includes in the neighbourhood all the configurations that are obtained by revising at most 4 norms[4]; (2) Maximum size 10 (NMS10) and (3) maximum size 20 (NMS20) define a neighborhood that includes the 10 and 20 closest configurations to the current one, respectively. We tested the hill climbing implementation with the 3 uninformed neighborhoods and we compared them with our proposals employing the PUREBN (HCPB) and the STATEBASED (HCSB) suggestion algorithms.

In order to determine the average quality in terms of objectives achievement, each algorithm has been executed starting from all of the possible configurations. The system has $12^4 = 20,736$ possible configurations (12 possible norm sets enforceable in any of the 4 contexts). Since in the worst case every algorithm may need to try all the configurations before stopping, to limit the experimentation time, we reduced the data set to 81 configurations via test case generation techniques[5]. We introduced then three additional configurations more distant from the others. Two of them are the best-scoring configurations. We defined experiments for three different thresholds t_{oa}, based on the distribution of values in the 84 tested configurations (see Fig. 4). T1 = 0.5, accepts as final configurations only the two best-scoring configurations in group A (2.4% of the total), which are significantly different (and therefore more distant) from the others; T2 = 0.4 accepts the configurations in groups A and B (9.5% of the total); and T3 − 0.37 acccpts configurations in groups A, B and C (17.8% of the total).

We compare the results in terms of (i) *convergence speed*: the number of steps attempted before stopping; and (ii) *solution quality*: the average objectives achievement probability of the final solution.

---

[4] Revising one norm leads to a distance of 2–3 from the original configuration, and each configuration has 10%–20% of all configurations in its neighborhood.

[5] We obtained 12 variants from *pairwise testing* with variables: time (day, night), weather (normal, extreme), CNS (none, adaptive, static), and junctions (none, adaptive lights, static lights, priority lanes). We grouped those variants in 4 groups (one per context) and we generated all their combinations to obtain 81 configurations.

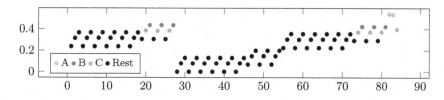

Fig. 4. Avg. probability of objectives achievement for the 84 tried configurations.

5.2 Analysis of the Results

Table 1 compares the 5 different tested algorithms. With threshold T1 ($t_{oa} = 0.5$), we tested a scenario where the (few) optimal configurations are slightly more distant from the others (while the median distance between the 82 suboptimal configurations is 6.3, the median distance with the remaining two is 7).

Table 1. Comparison of the algorithms with thresholds T1, T2 and T3. Values of Steps and Final columns are average values over the 84 different simulations.

Algo	T1 ($t_{ga} = 0.5$, 2 optimal conf.)			T2 ($t_{ga} = 0.4$, 8 optimal conf.)			T3 ($t_{ga} = 0.37$, 15 optimal conf.)		
	Steps (σ)	Final (σ)	Opt.	Steps (σ)	Final (σ)	Opt.	Steps (σ)	Final (σ)	Opt.
MD4	68.94 (21.47)	0.54 (0.00)	100%	24.48 (12.56)	0.45 (0.04)	100%	17.54 (9.56)	0.43 (0.05)	100%
ML10	88.54 (15.15)	0.54 (0.00)	100%	18.80 (10.62)	0.43 (0.02)	100%	11.15 (6.15)	0.40 (0.03)	100%
ML20	73.81 (17.93)	0.54 (0.00)	100%	23.80 (11.44)	0.44 (0.03)	100%	17.94 (9.08)	0.42 (0.04)	100%
HCPB	64.86 (27.48)	0.54 (0.00)	100%	11.90 (8.04)	0.43 (0.02)	100%	2.99 (3.03)	0.40 (0.03)	100%
HCSB	79.70 (22.05)	0.54 (0.00)	100%	5.10 (3.50)	0.43 (0.02)	100%	0.82 (0.39)	0.40 (0.03)	100%

In terms of convergence speed, with T1 our heuristics behave similarly to the others. On average, uninformed heuristics take around 77.08 steps, while HCPB and HCSB require 72.28 steps. Since all the algorithms give priority to the closest configurations in the neighborhood, they need to explore big part of the solution space before finding the 2 optimal configurations, which are more distant. HCPB slightly outperforms all the other heuristics. The reason is that its strategy is to suggest a revision for all the active norms in the current configuration. This strategy, compared to the others, accomodates the exploration of more diverse configurations (i.e., HCPB defines a more heterogeneous neighborhood), thereby favouring the discovery of the optimal ones.

With less demanding thresholds (T2 and T3), our algorithms significantly outperform the others. For T2, our heuristics HCPB and HCSB offer, on average, an improvement of $61.9\% = 1 - (8.5/22.36)$ over the tested uninformed heuristics in terms of convergence speed, while for T3 the efficiency gain is $87.7\% = 1 - (1.9/15.54)$. In particular, with T3, HCSB requires on average only 0.82 steps, i.e., it finds an optimal configuration after only one revision. Concerning solution quality, the results are comparable for all the algorithms in all the experiments.

These preliminary results, which shall be confirmed on other cases, support our hypothesis that heuristics that leverage knowledge about norm satisfaction

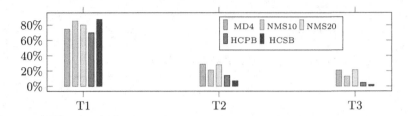

Fig. 5. Average percentage of explored configurations before finding an optimal one. 100% means trying, on average, all the 84 configurations.

allow efficient runtime norm revision, by altering a suboptimal norm set into an optimal one with only few revisions. Results concerning T1 suggest improvements of our algorithms in order to consider more exploration when a configuration is not found quickly. Figure 5 summarizes the convergence speed results.

It is finally worth to note that, in this paper, the selection of a norm set that satisfies the given suggestions depends on the number of available norm sets (only 12 in our experiments). However, thanks to the use of a Bayesian Network and to the concept of norm revision, the Revision Engine also provides information about the effectiveness of the norms w.r.t. the achievement of the overall objectives. Differently from classical search algorithms, therefore, our suggestion algorithms also provide direct information about how to revise the norms, supporting targeted human or automated intervention on the norms.

6   Related Work

Several papers have focused on deciding and proving the correctness of normative systems by model checking formulas describing desired properties such as liveness or safety properties [12–14]. Despite their elegance, these approaches do not fully cope with the dynamicity of today's complex systems. Recently, frameworks emerged to cope with norms dynamics and their impact on system specification.

Knobbout *et al.* [7] propose a dynamic logic to formally characterize the dynamics of state-based and action-based norms. Both in Knobbout's works [7,15] and in Alechina *et al.*'s [14], norm change is intended as norm addition. In this paper we investigated further types of norms revision that could be used to extend such framework for dynamic normative systems.

Aucher *et al.* [16] introduce a dynamic context logic to describe the operations of contraction and expansion of theories by introducing or removing new rules. Governatori *et al.* [17] investigate from a legal point of view the application of theory revision to reason about legal abrogations and annulments. The types of revision presented in this paper can be related to theory revision. However we have taken a multiagent systems standpoint, in which norm revision should be studied in terms of its impact on the overall system behavior. We leave for future work the study of the impact of a revision on the existing normative system.

Norms update has also been studied from the perspective of approximation [18], where an approximated version of a norm is obtained to cope with imperfect monitors for the original norm. The concept of approximation is similar to our notion of relaxation, however it is defined with respect to a specific monitor: an approximated norm is synthesized from the original one to maximize the violations detectable by the available imperfect monitor. In this paper we assumed perfect monitors and we focused instead on the effectiveness of norm enforcement to develop algorithms that suggest a norm revision when needed.

Cranefield *et al.* [19] present a Bayesian approach to norm identification. They show that agents can internalize norms that are already present in an environment, by learning from both norm compliant and norm violating behaviours. In this paper, instead of focusing on the agents, we used a Bayesian Network to collect information about norms effectiveness, regardless of their internalization in the agents. We used then the acquired knowledge to develop strategies for the suggestion of revisions of the norms that are enforced in the system.

7 Conclusion and Future Work

The complexity and unpredictability of modern multiagent systems allows only partial and incomplete domain knowledge at design-time. We proposed a runtime supervision mechanism to automatically revise the norms enforced in a multiagent system. The mechanism employs a Bayesian Network to collect data about norms satisfaction, and to learn their relationship with objectives achievement in different contexts. Informed by such data, the supervisor performs norm revision based on the revision suggested by the PUREBN and STATEBASED algorithms.

We implemented the supervision mechanism as a variant of the hill climbing optimization technique. Such variant always guarantees to find, if it exists, a norm set that ensures the overall system objectives. We evaluated our implementation in terms of convergence speed and quality of the final enforced norm set. We used an urban traffic simulation to compare the results that can be obtained by taking into account the knowledge learned at runtime about norms effectiveness, with results that can be obtained without such knowledge. The results show that the our heuristics outperform the tested uninformed ones by identifying the optimal solutions in significantly less number of revisions.

Future work will focus on four main directions. *Evaluation*: the scalability and computational complexity of the approach must be properly evaluated: the conditional probability tables of the objective nodes in the Bayesian Network grow exponentially with the number of norms. The structure of the *Norm Bayesian Network* does not leverage the conditional independence properties that may exist between different norms. In case of large sets of norms, the use of such network may become intractable. A solution is to use, when building the network, a model representing the hierarchy between norms (e.g., [20]). *Refined revision algorithms* shall be developed with a memory that provides information about the effectiveness of previous revisions; possible techniques include Q-Learning [21] and Dynamic Decision Networks [8]. Additional types of analysis of the Bayesian Network, such as sensitivity analysis [22], should be studied to help select a new norm set. It is possible to extend the current structure of the *Norm Bayesian Network* to support imperfect monitoring and uncertainty, through the introduction of an additional layer of nodes and a sensor model [8]. *Norm synthesis*, i.e., the automated generation of norms that can regulate the multiagent system by preventing harmful behaviors and by promoting useful behaviors, based on the revisions suggested and on agents preferences and their relationship with the system objectives. *Sanctions and their revision* can be studied as a way to influence the behavior of agents that goes beyond norm relaxation or strengthening.

References

1. Wooldridge, M.J.: An Introduction to MultiAgent Systems, 2nd edn. Wiley, Hoboken (2009)
2. Bulling, N., Dastani, M.: Norm-based mechanism design. Artif. Intell. **239**, 97–142 (2016)
3. Testerink, B., Dastani, M., Bulling, N.: Distributed controllers for norm enforcement. In: Proceedings of ECAI, pp. 751–759 (2016)
4. Alechina, N., Bulling, N., Dastani, M., Logan, B.: Practical run-time norm enforcement with bounded lookahead. In: Proceedings of AAMAS, pp. 443–451 (2015)
5. Letier, E., Van Lamsweerde, A.: Reasoning about partial goal satisfaction for requirements and design engineering. In: ACM SIGSOFT Software Engineering Notes, vol. 29, pp. 53–62. ACM (2004)
6. Ali, R., Dalpiaz, F., Giorgini, P., Souza, V.E.S.: Requirements evolution: from assumptions to reality. In: Halpin, T., et al. (eds.) BPMDS/EMMSAD. LNBIP, vol. 81, pp. 372–382. Springer, Heidelberg (2011). https://doi.org/10.1007/978-3-642-21759-3_27
7. Knobbout, M., Dastani, M., Meyer, J.C.: A dynamic logic of norm change. In: Proceedings of ECAI, pp. 886–894 (2016)
8. Russell, S.J., Norvig, P.: Artificial Intelligence - A Modern Approach, 3rd internat. edn. Pearson Education (2010)
9. Spiegelhalter, D.J., Dawid, A.P., Lauritzen, S.L., Cowell, R.G.: Bayesian analysis in expert systems. Stat. Sci. **8**(3), 219–247 (1993)
10. Kwisthout, J.: Most probable explanations in bayesian networks: complexity and tractability. Int. J. Approx. Reason. **52**(9), 1452–1469 (2011)
11. Schmid, S., Gerostathopoulos, I., Prehofer, C., Bures, T.: Self-adaptation based on big data analytics: a model problem and tool. In: Proceedings of SEAMS, pp. 102–108 (2017)
12. Dastani, M., Grossi, D., Meyer, J.-J.C., Tinnemeier, N.: Normative multi-agent programs and their logics. In: Meyer, J.-J.C., Broersen, J. (eds.) KRAMAS 2008. LNCS (LNAI), vol. 5605, pp. 16–31. Springer, Heidelberg (2009). https://doi.org/10.1007/978-3-642-05301-6_2
13. Knobbout, M., Dastani, M.: Reasoning under compliance assumptions in normative multiagent systems. In: Proceedings of AAMAS, pp. 331–340 (2012)
14. Alechina, N., Dastani, M., Logan, B.: Reasoning about normative update. In: Proceedings of IJCAI, pp. 20–26 (2013)
15. Knobbout, M., Dastani, M., Meyer, J.-J.C.: Reasoning about dynamic normative systems. In: Fermé, E., Leite, J. (eds.) JELIA 2014. LNCS (LNAI), vol. 8761, pp. 628–636. Springer, Cham (2014). https://doi.org/10.1007/978-3-319-11558-0_46

16. Aucher, G., Grossi, D., Herzig, A., Lorini, E.: Dynamic context logic. In: He, X., Horty, J., Pacuit, E. (eds.) LORI 2009. LNCS (LNAI), vol. 5834, pp. 15–26. Springer, Heidelberg (2009). https://doi.org/10.1007/978-3-642-04893-7_2
17. Governatori, G., Rotolo, A.: Changing legal systems: legal abrogations and annulments in defeasible logic. Log. J. IGPL **18**(1), 157–194 (2010)
18. Alechina, N., Dastani, M., Logan, B.: Norm approximation for imperfect monitors. In: Proceedings of AAMAS, pp. 117–124 (2014)
19. Cranefield, S., Meneguzzi, F., Oren, N., Savarimuthu, B.T.R.: A Bayesian approach to norm identification. In: Proceedings of ECAI, pp. 622–629 (2016)
20. Dell'Anna, D., Dalpiaz, F., Dastani, M.: Validating goal models via Bayesian networks. In: Proceedings of AIRE@RE (2018)
21. Rummery, G.A., Niranjan, M.: On-line Q-learning using connectionist systems. Technical report CUED/F-INFENG/TR-166, vol. 37. University of Cambridge, Cambridge (1994)
22. van der Gaag, L.C., Renooij, S., Coupé, V.M.: Sensitivity analysis of probabilistic networks. In: Lucas, P., Gámez, J.A., Salmerón, A. (eds.) Advances in Probabilistic Graphical Models. STUDFUZZ, pp. 103–124. Springer, Heidelberg (2007). https://doi.org/10.1007/978-3-540-68996-6_5

A Deep Reinforcement Learning Approach for Large-Scale Service Composition

Ahmed Moustafa$^{(\boxtimes)}$ and Takayuki Ito

Nagoya Instititute of Technology, Nagoya, Japan
{ahmed,ito.takayuki}@nitech.ac.jp

Abstract. As service-oriented environments become widespread, there exists a pressing need for service compositions to cope with the high scalability, complexity, heterogeneity and dynamicity features inherent in these environments. In this context, reinforcement learning has emerged as a powerful tool that empowers adaptive service composition in open and dynamic environments. However, most of the existing implementations of reinforcement learning algorithms for service compositions are inefficient and fail to handle large-scale service environments. Towards this end, this paper proposes a novel approach for adaptive service composition in dynamic and large-scale environments. The proposed approach employs deep reinforcement learning in order to address large-scale service environments with large number of service providers. Experimental results show the ability and efficiency of the proposed approach to provide successful service compositions in dynamic and large-scale service environments.

Keywords: Deep reinforcement learning · Service composition
Cloud computing

1 Introduction

The fundamental objective of service-oriented computing (SOC) is to enable the interoperability among different software and data applications running on a variety of platforms. Therefore, the full potential of service-oriented computing is realized only when there is an ecosystem of numerous service providers and service consumers collaborating with each other in order to attain certain business goals. Since one service cannot satisfy end-user requirements, there exists a need to combine component services into a composite service. In this regard, service composition becomes the most effective technology to implement a service-oriented architecture (SOA). A challenging issue towards this purpose is the selection of the best set of services that meet the quality of service (QoS) constraints, that are imposed by the consumer, from the set of

Supported by organization x.

T. Miller et al. (Eds.): PRIMA 2018, LNAI 11224, pp. 296–311, 2018.
https://doi.org/10.1007/978-3-030-03098-8_18

functionally equivalent concrete services, that is, QoS-aware service composition. QoS-aware service composition has been widely researched in the areas of service-oriented architecture and service-oriented computing [3,28]. However, most of the existing approaches for service composition are built on a deterministic view that fails when they face dynamic and continuously changing service environments. Therefore, due to the inherent dynamicity and complexity in service-oriented environments, a good service composition solution needs to adapt to the changes/fluctuations of these dynamic service environments. In addition, the explosive growth of the number of functionally-equivalent services puts a pressing need for efficient service composition algorithms that are able to deal with the combinatorial candidate service space in these large-scale service environments.

Reinforcement Learning (RL) is a strategy for sequential decision making processes in which an agent interacts with the environment in order to learn an optimal solution by trial and error. Reinforcement learning has been adopted in a wide range of fields including engineering, natural, and social sciences. Therefore, reinforcement learning has emerged as a powerful tool that promises to promote adaptive service composition in open and dynamic environments. Towards this end, RL adopts a learning scheme which learns by trial and error from the interaction with dynamic service environments. In this regard, RL has the capacity to optimize the service composition system to dynamically choose the best set of services without having a complete and full knowledge of the service environment. In recent years, adaptive service composition algorithms based on reinforcement learning have witnessed an increasing interest, especially those based on model-free online learning algorithms, such as Q-learning [13,22]. The basic idea behind these algorithms is modeling the service composition as a stochastic process in which an intelligent agent learns to select the set of Web services, with the highest QoS values, through sequential and iterative interactions with these services in a dynamic environment. These model-free online learning algorithms such as Q-learning are only appealing from a theoretical perspective. They proved their success when applied to small and medium-sized Web service environments. However, when deployed to large-scale service environments with large numbers of service providers, these algorithms fail to scale to high dimensional state and action spaces which affects the stability of the learning process.

The advent of deep learning has had a significant impact on many areas in artificial intelligence dramatically improving the state of the art in areas such as object detection, speech recognition, and language translation. Recently, deep convolutional neural networks have achieved unprecedented performance in several domains: for example, image classification [8], face recognition [9], and playing Atari games [12]. Towards this end, they use many layers of neurons, each arranged in overlapping tiles, in order to construct, increasingly abstract, localized representations of the data. In this paper, we employ deep learning in order to enable RL to scale to service environments that were previously intractable, i.e., service environments with high dimensional state and action spaces. To achieve this goal, we adopted a novel agent, a deep Q-network (DQN) [12], which is able to combine reinforcement learning with a class of artificial neural network [4] known as deep neural networks. In this regard, deep neural networks use hierarchical layers of tiled convolutional filters in order to progressively build up an accurate abstraction of large-scale service environments. We use these deep neural networks to reduce the effective depth and breadth of the search space by evaluating states using a value network, and sampling actions using a policy network [16]. The rest of this paper is organized as follows. The problem description and basic definitions are introduced in Sect. 2. Section 3 introduces a baseline model for reinforcement learning-based service composition in dynamic environments. Section 4 introduces a novel model for learning service composition in dynamic environments using deep reinforcement learning. In Sect. 5, the experimental results and discussions are presented for evaluating the proposed approach. Section 6 briefly reviews the related work. Finally, the paper is concluded and the future work is outlined in Sect. 7.

2   Preliminary

This section describes the process of service composition and presents the basic model related to the proposed algorithms. The proposed model employs Markov Decision Process (MDP) as a general scheme in order to describe the process of service composition and adaptation in dynamic environments. MDP is a discrete-time stochastic control process that is used to model sequential decision making in uncertain domains. The key components of MDP are formally defined as follows.

Definition 1 (Markov Decision Process (MDP)). An *MDP* is defined as a 5-tuple $MDP = <S, A, P, R, \gamma>$, where

- S is a finite set of states of the world;
- $A(s)$ is a finite set of actions depending on the current state $s \in S$;
- P is a probability value, i.e., when an action $a \in A$ is performed, the world makes a probabilistic transition from its current state s to a resulting state s' according to a probability distribution $P(s' \mid s, a)$; and
- R is a reward function. Similarly, when action a is performed, the world makes its transition from s to s', the composition receives a real-valued reward r, whose expected value is $r = R(s' \mid s, a)$.
- $\gamma \in [0, 1]$ is the discount factor that differentiates the importance of future rewards and immediate rewards.

The solution to MDP is a decision policy. In general, a decision policy π is a mapping from states to a probability distribution over actions. π is a mapping from states to actions, defined as $\pi : S \longrightarrow A$. If MDP is episodic, that is the state is reset after each episode of length t, then the sequence of states, actions and rewards in an episode constitutes a trajectory or rollout of the policy. Every rollout of the policy accumulates a reward from the environment that results in the return R. The goal of solution algorithm is to find an optimal policy which accumulates the maximum expected returns/rewards from all the states.

3   Reinforcement Learning for Service Composition

The purpose of RL is to design algorithms by which decision agents can learn to behave autonomously in some environment, from their interactions with this environment or from observations gathered from the environment. This environment is typically formulated as a Markov decision process (MDP). Unlike classical dynamic programming techniques, reinforcement learning algorithms do not need knowledge about the MDP and they target large MDPs where exact methods become infeasible. In this context, RL aims to determine an optimal control policy from their interactions with the environment. This policy can be achieved by approximating the so-called Q-function based on a set of four-tuples (s_t, a_t, r_t, s_{t+1}), where s_t denotes the environment state at time t, a_t the control action taken, r_t the instantaneous reward obtained, and s_{t+1} the successor state of the environment, and by determining the control policy from this Q-function [24].

The problem types that are best suited to RL are complex control problems, where there appears to be no obvious or easily programmable solution. For this reason, there exists a clear advantage of using RL for adaptive service composition in open and dynamic environments. Therefore, by using RL inside our composition model, it enables to learn the optimal service selection policy in an adaptive way. The key concepts used in the dynamic service composition based on MDP are formally defined as follows.

Definition 2 (A MDP-Based Web Service Composition (MDP-WSC)). An *MDP-WSC* is defined as a 6-tuple $MDP - WSC = <S^i, s_0^i, S_r^i, A_i(.), P^i, R^i>$, where

- S^i is a finite set of states/abstract services observed by agent i;
- $s_0^i \in S$ is the initial state and any execution of the service composition usually starts from this state;
- $S_r^i \subset S$ is the set of terminal states. Upon arriving at one of those states, an execution of the service composition terminates;
- $A^i(s)$ is the set of Web services that can be executed in state $s \in S^i$, a Web service ws belongs to A^i, only if some precondition ws^P is satisfied by s;
- P^i is the probability by which a Web service $ws \in A^i(s)$ can be invoked when agent i makes a transition from its current state s to a resulting state s'. For each state s, this transition occurs with a probability $P^i(s'|s, ws)$; and
- R^i is a reward function; when a Web service $ws \in A^i(s)$ is invoked, agent i makes a transition from s to s', the service consumer receives an immediate reward r^i, whose expected value is $R^i(s'|s, ws)$.

Considering the MDP-WSC model introduced previously, the task of the learning agent then becomes to distinguish the optimal workflow that offers the highest accumulated rewards. For each agent i, let W^i be the set of candidate workflows. Let R_{ws}^i be the reward associated with each Web service invocation ws_i for some workflow w. Let N be a fixed maximum number of invocations in each of the candidate workflows. The workflow w^*, that results in the maximum expected reward is called an optimal workflow.

This reward value can be calculated using the action value function [11, 26] as follows:

$$Q^i(s,a) \leftarrow Q^i(s,a) + \alpha[r + \gamma max_{a'} Q^i(s',a') - Q^i(s,a)], \tag{1}$$

where s represents the state space, i.e., abstract services, for all the possible workflows that agent i traverses in order to achieve a user's request, a is the action vector representing the available Web services, r is the reward given by selecting a particular service, α is the learning rate, which controls convergence and γ is the discount factor that reflects the learning policy. When agent i selects a Web service ws, agent i receives a reward which is an aggregate value for the QoS attributes of ws. This reward value can be calculated as follows:

$$r = \sum \omega \times \frac{Q_n - Q_n^{min}}{Q_n^{max} - Q_n^{min}}, \tag{2}$$

where Q_n represents the observed value of the nth quality attribute of Web service ws, Q_n^{max} and Q_n^{min} represent the maximum and the minimum values of the nth quality attribute of Web service ws, respectively. ω is a weighting factor.

In this model, an ϵ-greedy strategy is adopted to enable the learning agent to make a trade-off between selecting Web services that have been tried in the past, i.e., exploitation, and randomly selecting new Web services that may provide better results, i.e., exploration. For agent i, given a state s and a set of available Web services $A^i(s)$, agent i selects the next Web service a_j with a probability that can be calculated as follows:

$$P^i(a_j|s) = \begin{cases} (1 - \epsilon) \text{ if } a_j = argMax_a Q[s,a], \\ \epsilon \qquad \text{others}, \end{cases} \tag{3}$$

where ϵ is a probability distribution over individual Web services. Agent i chooses the best Web service according to its policy with probability $(1-\epsilon)$, and otherwise it selects a uniformly random Web service with probability ϵ.

4   Deep Reinforcement Learning for Service Composition

Deep learning is an area of machine learning algorithms that aim to learn multiple levels of representations and abstractions in order to help make sense of complex data such as images, sound, and text. Towards this end, deep learning adopts multiple layers of nonlinear processing units for feature extraction and transformation. Each successive layer uses the output of the previous layer as its own input. In fact, the word "deep" in "deep learning" refers to the number of layers through which the data is transformed. During the learning process, multiple levels of representations are constructed that correspond to different levels of abstractions. These levels of representations form a hierarchy of concepts. Deep learning architectures are often constructed on a layer by layer basis. In this regard, deep learning disengages several abstractions and chooses the most important features that are required in order to improve performance. Therefore, deep learning is suitable for both supervised and unsupervised learning tasks.

4.1 Deep Reinforcement Learning

The usage of deep learning algorithms within RL defines the field of deep reinforcement learning (DRL) [12,16]. Deep learning enables reinforcement learning to scale to problems that were previously intractable, i.e., problems with high dimensional state and action spaces, such as learning to play video games directly from the pixels [12]. In fact, large state and/or action spaces make it intractable to learn Q value estimates for each state and action pair independently. In order to solve this problem, deep reinforcement learning represents the various components of agents such as policies $\pi(s, a)$ and state/action spaces $Q(s, a)$ with deep neural networks. The parameters of these deep neural networks are trained using gradient descent in order to minimize some suitable loss function. In this context, the learning process proceeds as follows. First, the agent captures an observation from the environment and passes it as input to the deep neural network. The deep neural network, then, learns abstract representations from the high dimensional input/observation, then, it evaluates the action space and maps a suitable action according to the current observation. Finally, the environment responds to this action and makes a transition to the next observation. In this paper, a DRL-based approach is proposed in order to address the problem of service composition in large-scale environments.

4.2 Applying Deep Reinforcement Learning to Service Composition

In this section, a DRL-based approach is proposed in order to enable adaptive service composition in large-scale service environments. The proposed approach employs deep Q network (DQN) [12] as a baseline algorithm for learning adaptive compositions in large-scale service environments. In addition, the proposed approach is enhanced using a double Q learning technique in order to address the overestimation bias of Q-learning. In this regard, removing the overestimation bias of Q-learning is achieved by decoupling the selection step and the evaluation step of the bootstrap action. Moreover, a prioritized experience replay scheme is implemented that is able to improve data efficiency by replaying more often the transitions from which there is more to learn. Each of these enhancements promotes substantial performance improvements to the baseline learning algorithm. As a result, the adopted enhancements address several challenging issues. The proposed approach works as follows.

Deep Q Network. Deep neural networks and reinforcement learning are successfully combined in DQN [12] by using a convolutional neural network in order to approximate the action values of a given state S_t, which is fed as input to the neural network (in the form of a stack of raw pixel frames). At each step, based on the current state, the agent selects an action, ϵ-greedily, with respect to the action values and adds a transition to a replay memory buffer $(S_t, A_t, R_{t+1}, \gamma_{t+1}, S_{t+1})$. This replay memory buffer holds the last million transitions. Then, stochastic gradient descent is used in order to optimize the parameters of the neural network to minimize the loss as follows:

$$(R_{t+1} + \gamma_{t+1} \max_{\acute{a}} Q_{\bar{\theta}}(S_{t+1}, \acute{a}) - Q_{\theta}(S_t, A_t))^2 \tag{4}$$

where t is a time step that is randomly chosen from the replay memory. $\bar{\theta}$ represents the parameters of the target network. This target network is a periodic copy of the online network that is not directly optimized. θ represent the parameters of the online network where the gradient of the loss is only back-propagated to. This online network can be used in order to choose actions. The parameter optimization of this online network is performed using a variant algorithm of stochastic gradient descent [16]. The optimization process is conducted on mini-batches that are uniformly sampled from the experience replay. This means the time index represented as t in the loss above is a random time. This random time index is selected from the last million transitions rather than the current time. Therefore, a stable learning of Q values is enabled by the usage of target networks and experience replay. This stability, in turn, enabled superhuman performance in Atari games [12].

Double Q-learning. Due to the maximization step in Eq. 1, conventional Q learning is affected by overestimation bias. This overestimation bias, in its turns, leads to divergence and harms the stability of the learning process. In order to address this overestimation bias, the proposed algorithm employs a decoupling scheme [18] that aims to separate the selection of the action from the evaluation of this action. This separation happens in the maximization step that is performed for the bootstrap target. This decoupling scheme can be combined effectively with the deep Q network [19] using the loss as follows:

$$(R_{t+1} + \gamma_{t+1} Q_{\bar{\theta}}(S_{t+1}, argmax_{\acute{a}} Q_{\theta}(S_{t+1}, \acute{a})) - Q_{\theta}(S_t, A_t))^2 \tag{5}$$

This decoupling scheme has been proven to reduce the disadvantageous over-estimations that are present with DQN. This over-estimation reduction, in turn, improves the stability and performance of the learning process.

Prioritized Replay. The basic idea behind the experience replay step is to store the experiences of certain agent, and then, uniformly draw batches of these stored experiences in order to efficiently train the neural network. By keeping the experiences we draw random, the decision agent is able to learn more robustly in the task. However, in practice, the decision agent needs to sample more frequently from the experiences/transitions that have higher priority, i.e., the experiences from which there is more to learn. To achieve this goal, the proposed approach implements a prioritized experience replay scheme [15] that is able to sample transitions with probability p_t. This probability threshold p_t is relative to the last encountered absolute temporal difference error as follows:

$$p_t \propto |R_{t+1} + \gamma_{t+1} \max_{\acute{a}} Q_{\bar{\theta}}(S_{t+1}, \acute{a}) - Q_{\theta}(S_t, A_t)|^{\omega} \tag{6}$$

where ω is a hyper parameter that determines the shape of the distribution. Therefore, the prioritized replay scheme inserts new transitions into the experience memory/buffer with maximum priority. As a result, there exits a certain bias towards the recent transitions. In this regard, it is worth noting that stochastic transitions might also be favored, even though there is less experience to learn from them.

5 Experiments

Two simulation experiments have been conducted in order to evaluate the proposed learning approach from different perspectives. The first experiment studies the impact of the environment scale on the ability of the proposed approach to learn high quality service composition policies in large-scale service environments. The second experiment evaluates the performance of the proposed approach when operates in dynamic service environments and the impact of their inherent dynamicity on the learning process.

5.1 Experiment Setting

The proposed approach runs in successive iterations/episodes till reaching a convergence point. The learning agent converges to an optimal policy once it receives the same value of the accumulated rewards for a number of successive episodes. Those accumulated rewards are compared episode by episode and the difference is projected against a threshold. This threshold value is set to 0.001, and the number of successive episodes is set to 1000.

In the following experiments, three QoS attributes are considered, which are availability, reliability and response time, based on the QWS dataset [1]. The average accumulated reward r for each workflow is computed by aggregating the QoS vectors of its member Web services using Table 1 as follows:

Table 1. Aggregation functions

QoS parameter	Aggregation function
availability	$\sum_{i=1}^{n}(\log(availability(ws_i)))$
response time	$\sum_{i=1}^{n}(response\,time(ws_i))$
reliability	$\sum_{i=1}^{n}(\log(reliability(ws_i)))$

The following experiments compare the proposed prioritized double deep Q-learning approach (PDDQN) with the deep Q network approach (DQN) and the classic Q-learning based reinforcement learning approach (RL). The learning parameters are set up based on previous empirical simulations conducted by the authors in [13]. Those parameter settings are listed in Table 2. Also, all the simulation experiments are conducted on 3.2 GHz Intel Xeon 6 core iMac Pro with 32 GB of RAM and 8 MB of GPU.

Table 2. Parameter settings

Parameter	Meaning	Value
α	Learning rate	1
γ	Discount factor	0.8
ϵ	Exploration strategy	0.7
ν	Heuristic weighting factor	0.5
ω	QoS weighting factor	0.3

5.2   Experiment 1: Learning Quality

The purpose of this experiment is to study the ability of the proposed approach to find high quality service compositions in large-scale environments. The approach ability is measured in terms of the average accumulated rewards the learning agent receives when the solution converges to an optimal service selection policy. This reward value represents the aggregate QoS of the optimal workflow.

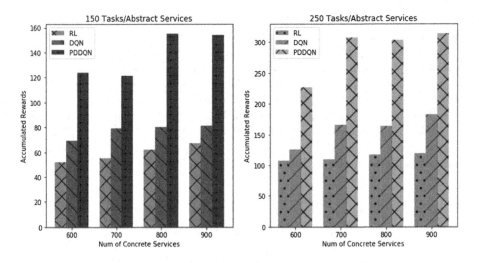

Fig. 1. The scalability of the proposed approach (number of tasks)

Totally two tests are carried out in this experiment. In Test 1, the scale of the service environment is represented by the number of concrete services assigned to each task/abstract service. Towards this end, we consider two workflows that consist of 150 tasks/abstract services and 250 tasks/abstract services, respectively. Then, we vary the number of available concrete Web services into a range of 600 to 900 per task. We run the proposed PDDQN approach under these environment scales and compare the average accumulated rewards obtained with their counterparts of the DQN and RL approaches.

As shown in Fig. 1, the proposed PDDQN approach outperforms both the DQN and RL approaches despite the environment scale. The PDDQN approach clearly gains higher accumulated rewards throughout the learning process, and thus, leads to higher quality solutions.

In Test 2, the scale of the service environment is represented by the number of tasks/abstract services used in each workflow. For this reason, we fix the number of concrete services to 700 and 900, and then vary the number of tasks/abstract services in a range from 100 to 250. The performance of the proposed PDDQN approach is also measured in terms of the average accumulated rewards that the learning agent receives when the solution converges to an optimal service composition policy. This reward value represents the aggregate QoS of the optimal workflow.

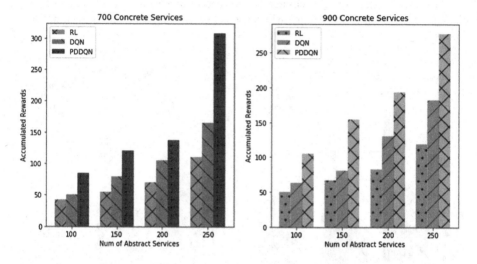

Fig. 2. The scalability of the proposed approach(number of concrete services)

Figure 2 depicts the relationship between the average accumulated rewards that are obtained by running the PDDQN approach and both the DQN and RL approaches multiple times with various number of tasks/abstract services per workflow. As shown in Fig. 2, the PDDQN service composition approach also outperforms both the DQN and RL approaches regardless of the number of tasks/abstract services per workflow. As the number of tasks/abstract services increases, the performance gap of these approaches increases in favor of the PDDQN service composition approach, which proves the scalability of the PDDQN approach and its ability to find high quality service compositions in large-scale environments.

5.3   Experiment 2: Dynamic Environment

The purpose of this experiment is to evaluate the ability of the proposed learning approach to find optimal service selection policies in dynamic service environments. The approach ability is measured by the accumulated rewards that the learning agent receives when it converges to the optimal service selection policy, in a dynamic service environment.

The dynamic changes in the service environment are expressed by the changes in the QoS values of the participant concrete services. These QoS values dynamically rise up or drop down for many reasons. Hence, affecting the reward values r which are received by the learning agent. The dynamic changes in the service environment are measured in this experiment by two factors. The first factor is the scale of change, which means how many concrete services in the running workflow are subject to QoS changes. The second factor is the frequency of this change, which means how frequently these concrete services experience new QoS values.

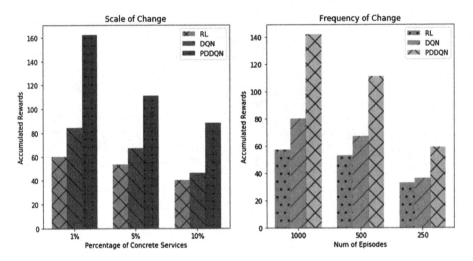

Fig. 3. Dynamic environment (a) scale of change (b) frequency of change

In order to experiment the first factor, i.e., the scale of change, we consider a workflow that consists of 200 tasks/abstract services and 700 concrete services per task. The QoS values of the participant concrete services are periodically varied with 1%, 5% and 10% respectively, every 500 episodes. Figure 3(a) depicts the impact of this change in the service environment on the performance of the proposed PDDQN approach. In Fig. 3(a), the x axis represents the percentage of change in the QoS values of the participant concrete services, and the y axis represents the average accumulated rewards that the learning agent receives when it converges to an optimal service selection policy. We can see from Fig. 3(a) that the proposed PDDQN approach accumulates 162 and 111 units of rewards, respectively, before it converges to an optimal policy in a service environment that experience 1% and 5% periodic changes in the QoS values of its participant concrete services. Compared to 84 and 67 units of rewards, and 60 and 53 units of rewards which are received by the DQN and RL approaches, respectively, under the same environment. These results show the efficiency of the proposed PDDQN approach in learning the optimal service selection policy in a complex and dynamic environment. These accumulated rewards drop to 88, 46 and 40 units of rewards for the PDDQN approach, the DQN approach and the RL approach, respectively, when considering a service environment that experience 10% periodic changes in the QoS values of its participant concrete services. These results are rational in such highly dynamic and fairly complex service environment.

In order to experiment the second factor, i.e., the frequency of change, we consider a workflow that consists of 200 tasks/abstract services and 700 concrete services per task. The QoS values of 5% of the participant concrete services are periodically varied every 250, 500 and 1000 episodes, in order.

Figure 3(b) depicts the impact of this change in the service environment on the performance of the proposed PDDQN approach. In Fig. 3(b), the x axis represents the frequency of change, i.e., the number of episodes the learning agent runs before the QoS values of the participant concrete services are varied according to a predefined percentage, and the y axis represents the average accumulated rewards that the learning agent receives before it converges to an optimal service selection policy. As shown in Fig. 3(b), the proposed PDDQN approach receives 142 and 111 units of rewards, before it converges to an optimal policy in a service environment that experience 5% periodic changes in the QoS values of its participant services every 1000 and 500 episodes, respectively. This is compared to the 80 and 67 units of rewards, and 57 and 53 units of rewards that are received by the DQN approach and RL approach, respectively, under the same service environment. Finally, the proposed PDDQN approach receives 59 units of accumulated rewards, compared to 36 and 33 unites of accumulated rewards received by the DQN and RL approaches, respectively, when considering a service environment that experience 5% change in its QoS values every 250 episodes. These results are reasonable in such a highly dynamic environment.

6   Related Work

Several approaches have been proposed in order to address adaptation in service oriented environments [2, 3, 28]. Wang *et al.* [23] proposed a two-phase approach for dynamic service composition and adaptation in which the service performance changes in different transactions. In the first phase, the uncertainty level is calculated by applying the cloud model proposed by Li *et al.* [10] in order to change the qualitative value of the QoS parameters to their quantitative equivalent. In the second phase, mixed integer programming (MIP) is used in order to select the proper services. In this context, service selection is determined by using a binary decision vector. Huang *et al.* [5] proposed a two-step procedure in order to satisfy the end users QoS requirements. In the first step, the proposed procedure attempts to select the set of single services that satisfy the first two types of the end users functional requirements, and eliminate the remaining requirements. In the second step, a virtual network of service providers is generated and modelled as a directed acyclic graph (DAG). It is then sufficient to apply an algorithm that determines the shortest path in this DAG in order to satisfy each users QoS requirements. A shortcoming of this procedure is that, for the two QoS parameters, the service selection problem is changed to a multi-constrained path problem when the constructing auxiliary graph is used. Ye *et al.* [27] proposed a model for QoS-aware service composition. In their model, the QoS parameters are divided into three groups, namely, ascending, descending, and equal QoS attributes. Then, a simple additive weighting method is employed in order to normalize the values of those QoS parameters. Finally, the authors applied a genetic algorithm where a roulette wheel service selection technique is used in order to excuse the crossover operation. Klein *et al.* [7] proposed an approach that separates the network and non-network QoS parameters of participant Web services. Towards this end, a QoS equation is introduced in order to calculate the network QoS, latency, and transfer rate among member Web services. In the last phase of the approach, a genetic-based selection algorithm is applied in order to generate composite services. However, the aforementioned techniques assume full and a priori knowledge of the service environment.

In order to solve this problem, RL has emerged as an effective and promising technique that promotes adaptive service composition in dynamic environments [13,17]. Towards this end, RL employs a trial and error exploration approach in order to discover an optimal policy and resolve incomplete information scenario. Early work to utilize reinforcement learning for service composition was proposed by Jureta *et al.* [6], where a multi-criteria driven reinforcement learning approach was introduced in order to ensure that the system is responsive to the changes in the availability of participant Web services. In their approach, the authors proposed a distributed architecture, which enabled single Web services to join and leave the composition at runtime. Then, a novel reinforcement learning based service provisioning algorithm was adopted in order to select and compose the participant Web services according to multiple quality attributes. A similar approach for dynamic service composition was proposed by Wang *et al.* [22]. In their approach, reinforcement learning was combined with preference logic in order to empower adaptive service provisioning. However, despite the effectiveness of these two approaches [6,22] in improving adaptability, their respective performance degraded when applied to complex and large-scale service environments. Moustafa and Zhang [14] proposed an approach that utilized multi-objective reinforcement learning in order to solve multi-criteria service composition problems. The proposed approach adopted a geometric operator, the convex hull, and a self organization mechanism, in order to facilitate service selection in dynamic and uncertain cloud environments. Although their approach achieved good results in comparison with the state-of-the-art, the efficiency of their approach also decreased when applied to large-scale service environments.

An early attempt to adopt the multi-agent reinforcement learning paradigm in dynamic service composition has been proposed by Wang and Wang [21]. However, their algorithm allows the learning agents to update the state-action only if the observed rewards/QoS values are higher than the previously recorded values. This might hinder learning and adaptation in dynamic service environments as only considering the higher QoS values will blind the learning agents to the drops in the QoS values and trap the agents into sub-optimal policies or policies that are no longer exist. In dynamic service environments, services are subject to rises and drops in their QoS values, and both cases should be treated equally. In addition, their algorithm does not take the potential collaboration between the multiple agents into consideration. Another multi-agent reinforcement learning model for service composition has been proposed by Xu et al. [25]. The proposed model uses multi-agent Q-learning with a hierarchical goal structure in order to accelerate the searching of candidate services during the learning process. However, this model fails to deal with complicated goals, with mutual dependencies among sub-goals, as the learning agents are fixed for certain service classes. A more mature and generic model has been proposed by Hong et al. [20] where team Markov Games are adopted in order to facilitate adaptive service composition in multiagent reinforcement learning scenarios. In their model, the coordination equilibrium and fictitious play process have been introduced in order to ensure that the agents converge to unique equilibrium when they face multiple equilibrium points. Then, a multi-agent Sarsa algorithm has been implemented in order to empower multi-agent service composition. However, in their current implementations, the aforementioned RL-based approaches do not perform well in large-scale service environments, as they suffer from the state-action space explosion.

7   Conclusion

This paper introduces a novel learning approach for adaptive service composition in large-scale environment. The proposed approach employs deep reinforcement learning in order to learn high quality service composition policies, while adapting to the changes in dynamic service environments efficiently. The experimental results reveal the ability of the proposed approach to combine deep learning and reinforcement learning in order to address large-scale service environments in an effective way. The future work is set to extend the proposed approach to multi-agent settings, and to study the trade-off between the number of learning agents and the scale of service environments.

References

1. Al-Masri, E., Mahmoud, Q.H.: Discovering the best web service. In: Proceedings of WWW, pp. 1257–1258 (2007)
2. Lee, C.-H., Hwang, S.-Y., Yen, I.-L.: A service pattern model for flexible service composition. In: Proceedings of IEEE ICWS, pp. 626–627, June 2012

3. Chiu, D., Agrawal, G.: Cost and accuracy aware scientific workflow composition for service-oriented environments. IEEE Trans. Serv. Comput. **4**(2), 140–152 (2012)
4. Gelly, S., Silver, D.: Combining online and offline knowledge in UCT. In: Proceedings of ICML, ICML 2007, pp. 273–280. ACM, New York (2007)
5. Huang, J., Liu, Y., Yu, R., Duan, Q., Tanaka, Y.: Modeling and algorithms for QoS-aware service composition in virtualization-based cloud computing. IEICE Trans. **96**–B(1), 10–19 (2013)
6. Jureta, I.J., Faulkner, S., Achbany, Y., Saerens, M.: Dynamic web service composition within a service-oriented architecture. In: IEEE International Conference on Web Services, ICWS 2007, pp. 304–311, July 2007
7. Klein, A., Ishikawa, F., Honiden, S.: SanGA: a self-adaptive network-aware approach to service composition. IEEE Trans. Serv. Comput. **7**(3), 452–464 (2014)
8. Krizhevsky, A., Sutskever, I., Hinton, G.E.: ImageNet classification with deep convolutional neural networks. In: Proceedings of NIPS, NIPS 2012, pp. 1097–1105. Curran Associates Inc. (2012)
9. Lawrence, S., Giles, C.L., Tsoi, A.C., Back, A.D.: Face recognition: a convolutional neural-network approach. IEEE Trans. Neural Netw. **8**(1), 98–113 (1997)
10. Li, D., Cheung, D., Shi, X., Ng, V.: Uncertainty reasoning based on cloud models in controllers. Comput. Math. Appl. **35**(3), 99–123 (1998)
11. Li, H., Dagli, C.H., Enke, D.: Short-term stock market timing prediction under reinforcement learning schemes. In: Proceedings of IEEE ADPRL, pp. 233–240 (2007)
12. Mnih, V.: Human-level control through deep reinforcement learning. Nature **518**(7540), 529–533 (2015)
13. Moustafa, A., Zhang, M.: Towards proactive web service adaptation. In: Ralyté, J., Franch, X., Brinkkemper, S., Wrycza, S. (eds.) CAiSE 2012. LNCS, vol. 7328, pp. 473–485. Springer, Heidelberg (2012). https://doi.org/10.1007/978-3-642-31095-9_31
14. Moustafa, A., Zhang, M.: Multi-objective service composition using reinforcement learning. In: Basu, S., Pautasso, C., Zhang, L., Fu, X. (eds.) ICSOC 2013. LNCS, vol. 8274, pp. 298–312. Springer, Heidelberg (2013). https://doi.org/10.1007/978-3-642-45005-1_21
15. Schaul, T., Quan, J., Antonoglou, I., Silver, D.: Prioritized experience replay. In: Proceedings of ICLR, Puerto Rico (2016)
16. Silver, D.: Mastering the game of go with deep neural networks and tree search. Nature **529**(7587), 484–489 (2016)
17. Tang, H., Liu, W., Zhou, L.: Web service composition method using hierarchical reinforcement learning. In: Yang, Y., Ma, M. (eds.) Green Communications and Networks. LNEE, vol. 113, pp. 1429–1438. Springer, Dordrecht (2012). https://doi.org/10.1007/978-94-007-2169-2_170
18. Van Hasselt, H.: Double q-learning. In: Proceedings of NIPS, pp. 2613–2621. Curran Associates Inc. (2010)
19. Van Hasselt, H., Guez, A., Silver, D.: Deep reinforcement learning with double q-learning. In: Proceedings of AAAI, AAAI 2016, pp. 2094–2100. AAAI Press (2016)
20. Wang, H., Chen, X., Wu, Q., Yu, Q., Zheng, Z., Bouguettaya, A.: Integrating on-policy reinforcement learning with multi-agent techniques for adaptive service composition. In: Franch, X., Ghose, A.K., Lewis, G.A., Bhiri, S. (eds.) ICSOC 2014. LNCS, vol. 8831, pp. 154–168. Springer, Heidelberg (2014). https://doi.org/10.1007/978-3-662-45391-9_11

21. Wang, H., Wang, X.: A novel approach to large-scale services composition. In: Ishikawa, Y., Li, J., Wang, W., Zhang, R., Zhang, W. (eds.) APWeb 2013. LNCS, vol. 7808, pp. 220–227. Springer, Heidelberg (2013). https://doi.org/10.1007/978-3-642-37401-2_23

22. Wang, H., Zhou, X., Zhou, X., Liu, W., Li, W., Bouguettaya, A.: Adaptive service composition based on reinforcement learning. In: Maglio, P.P., Weske, M., Yang, J., Fantinato, M. (eds.) ICSOC 2010. LNCS, vol. 6470, pp. 92–107. Springer, Heidelberg (2010). https://doi.org/10.1007/978-3-642-17358-5_7

23. Wang, S., Zheng, Z., Sun, Q., Zou, H., Yang, F.: Reliable web service selection via QoS uncertainty computing. Int. J. Web Grid Serv. **7**(4), 410–426 (2011)

24. Watkins, C.: Learning from delayed rewards. Ph.D. thesis, Cambridge University, England (1989)

25. Wenbo, X., Jian, C., Haiyan, Z., Lei, W.: A multi-agent learning model for service composition. In: Proceedings of APSCC, pp. 70–75, December 2012

26. Won Lee, J.: Stock price prediction using reinforcement learning. In: Proceedings of IEEE ISIE, vol. 1, pp. 690–695 (2001)

27. Ye, Z., Zhou, X., Bouguettaya, A.: Genetic algorithm based QoS-aware service compositions in cloud computing. In: Yu, J.X., Kim, M.H., Unland, R. (eds.) DASFAA 2011. LNCS, vol. 6588, pp. 321–334. Springer, Heidelberg (2011). https://doi.org/10.1007/978-3-642-20152-3_24

28. Zuohua, D., Mingyue, J., Kandel, A.: Port-based reliability computing for service composition. IEEE Trans. Serv. Comput. **5**(3), 422–436 (2012)

Narrowing Reinforcement Learning: Overcoming the Cold Start Problem for Personalized Health Interventions

Seyed Amin Tabatabaei$^{(\boxtimes)}$, Mark Hoogendoorn, and Aart van Halteren

Department of Computer Science, Vrije Universiteit Amsterdam, De Boelelaan 1081,
1081 HV Amsterdam, The Netherlands
{s.tabatabaei,m.hoogendoorn,a.t.van.halteren}@vu.nl

Abstract. Personalization of support in health and wellbeing settings is challenging. While personalization has shown to be highly beneficial to maximize the success of interventions, often only very limited experiences are available to personalize support strategies. Because of its focus on finding suitable actions/interventions that lead to long term rewards, reinforcement learning is very suitable for personalization but requires a substantial learning period. To overcome this so-called cold start problem, we propose a novel approach called narrowing reinforcement learning. The approach exploits experiences of the nearest neighbors around a user to generate a suitable policy, expressing which action to perform in what state. Using a narrowing function, the size of the neighborhood is reduced as more experiences are collected, allowing for the most personalized experience that is possible given the amount of collected experiences. An evaluation of the approach in a realistic simulator shows that it significantly outperforms the current state-of-the-art approaches for personalization in health and wellbeing using reinforcement learning.

Keywords: Reinforcement learning · Personalization
Health

1 Introduction

Rapid developments are seen in the domain of health and wellbeing, where managing one's health is becoming more and more supported by automated systems. These developments are fueled by the huge increase in data collected about people's health as well as an increased availability of sensor-enabled devices (e.g. smart phones, smart watches). Such devices can be used to provide assistance to people such that they make the right choices to improve or maintain their health. Over the last few years, a significant increase in the number of health related apps that can be downloaded on these devices is seen, totaling to nearly 100,000 health apps that are available for download in the iTunes store alone (cf. [2]). These apps include apps supporting physical activity (e.g. Nike+, Runkeeper,

© Springer Nature Switzerland AG 2018
T. Miller et al. (Eds.): PRIMA 2018, LNAI 11224, pp. 312–327, 2018.
https://doi.org/10.1007/978-3-030-03098-8_19

and Strava) as well as apps supporting mental health (e.g. Calm, HeadSpace, and MoodNotes).

While the current health apps are often downloaded, only a limited group of users find sustained benefits from using these apps. Personalization of such apps, where the app tailors its support strategies based on the user, is rarely seen (cf. [6]). Personalization can be established using more knowledge driven strategies (e.g. specify what message to send for different user profiles), but can also be performed in a data-driven way, thereby circumventing the need for a domain expert.

Reinforcement learning (see e.g. [7,9]) is a natural choice for personalization for health and wellbeing as it focuses on selecting the best actions with a more long term reward in mind. Here, the strategy defining which action to perform in what user state is referred to as a policy.

A problem that all data-driven approaches for personalization suffer from is the *cold start problem*: in the beginning, very few (or even no) experiences with the user are available, making it nearly impossible to provide a good level of personalization while this is precisely the period where the user should become engaged. For reinforcement learning, this problem is even more severe as it is known to require quite a few experiences with a user to be able to learn a good policy (see e.g. [11]). To remedy the cold start problem, one can exploit experiences obtained from other users. In recent work in the reinforcement learning domain, clustering of users has been proposed, showing promising results (cf. [4,11]). Users are clustered based on the data that is available about them (e.g. socio-demographic data, the experiences obtained thus far) and policies are created over all users within these clusters. While this is a good first step, there are a few downsides to this approach. First of all, the approach is not very flexible, as it always learns one policy over the entire cluster. Intuitively it makes more sense to start with exploiting a lot of users to generate policies, while making these policies more and more user specific when more experiences become available. Secondly, we suffer from the grey sheep problem (well known in collaborative filtering), where users can be atypical for their cluster, resulting in suboptimal personalization for both the grey sheep and the others in the cluster.

In this paper, we present an approach that overcomes the two disadvantages of cluster-based reinforcement learning. We call this approach *narrowing reinforcement learning*. The approach we propose considers a number of nearest neighbors around a user and exploits these nearest neighbors (combined with the user itself) for generating a policy for that specific user. Neighbors are defined based on a distance metric (such as dynamic time warping). This neighbor based approach guarantees that a policy for a user is based on users that are most alike, tackling the grey sheep problem. Secondly, the number of neighbors considered is reduced as we gain more experiences using a narrowing function. Hence, we use the most suitable number of neighbors in each part of the personalization process following the intuition we described before. We test the effectiveness of our approach compared to different benchmarks (including cluster-based reinforcement learning) in a simulator. The simulator encompasses agents that mimic human behavior by performing activities during a day and responding to support messages to improve their daily amount of physical activity.

This paper is organized as follows. First, we dive into the problem formulation and existing approaches. We then introduce our approach in Sect. 3. The experimental setup is described in Sect. 4, and Sect. 5 presents the results. Finally, Sect. 6 concludes the paper and provides avenues for future work.

2   Problem Formulation and Existing Approaches

As said, we want to create personalized interventions. We present our approach to improve the learning speed for reinforcement learning in this section. First, we describe the reinforcement learning problem we are facing in a generic way (cf. [4]), followed by a specification of the existing solutions to apply reinforcement learning for the problem at hand. This sets the stage for our novel approach.

2.1   Reinforcement Learning Problem Formulation

For specifying our reinforcement learning problem, we follow the approach put forward in [4]. A user is defined by means of u and the set of all users is identified by U, where $u \in U$. We see each user as a control problem that can be modeled as a Markov Decision Process [9]: $M_u = <S_u, A_u, T_a, R_a>$. In this formulation, S_u is a finite set of states of user u at any time point. A_u is the set of possible actions. In our problem, A_u shows the set of all possible interventions for that user. We assume that the set of possible actions and states are the same across the users. To model state transitions we use the probabilistic function $T :: S \times A \times S \to \mathbb{R}$. This function shows the probability to move from one state to another given a certain action that is performed. $R :: S \times A \to \mathbb{R}$ represents the reward given a state S and the action A performed to get to that state. In many reinforcement learning problems, it is not possible to observe all features related to the state of a user. In this case, a vector of features is observable, which is derived from the state s, $\phi(s) = <\phi_1(s), \phi_2(s), \ldots, \phi_n(s)>$. We can take $\phi(s)$ as a representation of the state s.

Assume that at time point t user u is in state s_u^t and $\phi(s_u^t)$ is the feature vector of this state. Based on a policy π the system selects and performs an action, a^t. In this case, $<\phi(s_u^t), a^t, r^t, \phi(s_u^{t+1})>$ shows the experience that by taking the action a^t the user state is changed to a state with the vector function of $\phi(s_u^{t+1})$, and r^t is received as reward of this transition.

All the past experiences of user u together form the trace for that user Σ_u:

$$\Sigma_u^t = <\phi(s_u^0), a^0, r^0, \phi(s_u^1), a^1, r^1, \ldots \phi(s_u^{t-1}), a^{t-1}, r^{t-1}, \phi(s_u^t)> \qquad (1)$$

Based on this formulation of the problem, the goal of the learning process is to learn the best policy π^* which specifies which action should be taken given a certain state $\pi :: S \rightarrow A$. The expected cumulative reward by doing an action a in state s is (given T as end time):

$$Q^\pi(s, a) = E_\pi\{\Sigma_t^T \gamma^t R(s_t, s_{t+1})|S^0 = s, a^0 = a\} \tag{2}$$

where at each time point action a is selected by policy, π ($a^t = \pi(s^t)$). And γ is a discount factor for future rewards ($0 \leqslant \gamma < 1$).

Learning algorithms try to find the optimum policy that maximizes the cumulative reward:

$$\pi^*(s) = argmax_a Q^{\pi^*}(s, a), \forall s \in S \tag{3}$$

Since we cannot be sure that the process satisfies the Markov property, we assume it is close enough that we can employ the standard reinforcement learning algorithms. With a Markovian state s, we can estimate the probability of transition to another state, s', and receiving reward r.

2.2 Existing Personalization Setups

Given our problem formulation, we can now formally describe what known algorithms do to develop personalized policies given the traces of users Σ_u we obtain (that are used to learn the policy). Here, we distinguish three approaches: separate, pooled, and clustered. We will briefly describe each one of them in more detail below.

Separated. The goal of this strategy is to learn a policy for each user u and only use the traces of that specific user. Hence, we use $\Sigma = \{\Sigma_u\}$ and do this for each user. This strategy learns a very personalized policy but is not able to learn a reasonable policy in a short term period.

Pooled. In this case, one policy is learned for all users, based on the experiences of all of them. To do that, we provide $\Sigma = \{\Sigma_u|u \in U\}$, and generate a single policy across all users. The advantage of this strategy is that learning can be done very fast, however it learns one policy for everybody, and there is no personalization.

Clustering. This strategy [4,11] is an intermediate approach and positioned between the two approaches that have just been explained. The aim is to make the reinforcement learning process more effective while still enabling a level of personalization. This strategy learns policies across groups (or clusters) of users that seem to be relatively alike. To learn a policy for one cluster of users the learning algorithm is fed with experiences of all members of that cluster C, $\Sigma = \{\Sigma_u|u \in C\}$. The clusters are made based on some distance metric between users and a clustering algorithm (e.g. k-means clustering). While this, of course, is a nice approach, it is not very flexible and even when enough experiences are available per individual user, still a cluster based policy is used.

3 Narrowing Reinforcement Learning

We propose a novel algorithm called *narrowing reinforcement learning, NRL.* This approach has a few ingredients that we will explain in more detail later. First, let us consider the basic idea. Narrowing reinforcement learning contains the following ingredients:

- At each learning step t (update of the policy) we learn a policy for each user u. To generate this policy we consider the traces of N_t users that are most like the user u, i.e. the nearest neighbors.
- To determine the nearest neighbors, a distance function $d :: U \times U \rightarrow \mathbb{R}$ is used.
- The number of users considered is changed over time using a *narrowing function.*

Algorithm 1 shows the connected steps in more detail, which follows the explanation above.

Algorithm 1. Narrowing Reinforcement Learning

```
 1  N = number-of-users;
 2  for  t = 1 : end-time do
 3      for current-user = 1 : number-of-users do
 4          similar-users = get-closest-users( user-id = current-user, size-of-group =
            N)
 5          Σ = get-experiences (list-of-users = similar-users)
 6          learned-policy = learn-policy ( learning-data = Σ) # reinforcement
            algorithms like Q-learning or LSPI
 7          selected-action = select-an-action (policy = learned-policy , state=
            current-state)
 8          do-action ( user = current-user, action = selected-action)
 9      end for
10      observe-and-collect-new-experiences();
11      N = determine-new-value(N) #N can be updated using an arbitrary regime
12  end for
```

The idea behind the approach is to learn individual policies per user but to use a variable additional amount of experiences from other users. Using the narrowing function, the amount of additional users from which data is used can be varied. Here, a typical narrowing function would use a large number of users in the beginning and reduce the number of neighbors over time. This allows for a quick generation of a policy in the beginning that is less tailored (because experiences from lots of users are used) while in later stages highly personalized policies can be generated. Since the nearest neighbors of that specific user are used, they are guaranteed to be the most like the current users (opposed to the cluster-based approach).

Let us now consider the ingredients in more detail, starting with the approach to find the nearest neighbors given a certain distance function. We then focus on example distance functions and end with the narrowing functions.

3.1 Defining the Nearest Neighbors

The idea of using the nearest neighbors is to learn one specific policy for each user, based on the data gathered from him and N most similar users to him (N nearest neighbors). Let us consider our distance function d again. We define the set of nearest neighbors of a user u as the set of users of size N out of the total set of users U that minimizes the distance to u:

$$nearest\_neighbors(u, N) = argmin_{U_s \subseteq (U-u): |U_s|=N} \sum_{\forall u_i \in U_s} d(u_i, u) \qquad (4)$$

Given a user u and a neighborhood size N we use the following traces:

$$\Sigma = \{\Sigma_n | n \in nearest\_neighbors(u, N)\} \cup \Sigma_u \qquad (5)$$

3.2 Distance Metric

As explained, we need to have a distance function d to estimate the similarity of pairs of users. There are multiple ways to do that. One approach would be to use socio-demographic data available right from the start. Alternatively, one could also use the experiences obtained by the users. While our idea is independent of the distance metric, we assume that only the experiences (traces) are used to determine the distance between users. Hence, we need to have these experiences to determine the distance. How we establish that is explained in the experimental setup. Given that we have some experiences, we use dynamic time warping (DTW) [1] to define the distance.

DTW is a technique to measure the distance of two time series (we can see traces as time series). This technique calculates the optimal match between them, and calculates the distance based on this optimum match. DTW not only allows for the traces that are shifted, but also takes into account that there might be a different speed between different traces. To calculate the distance of two traces, $dtw(\Sigma_{u_1}, \Sigma_{u_2})$ the DTW algorithm finds the best matching of the time points of two traces in a way that the sum of Euclidean distance of paired states is minimized. These pairs are ordered, which means pairing comes with the constraints that time order needs to be preserved (monotonically) [6]. Therefore, the first datapoint of traces has to be matched together, and the same goes for the last data points.

3.3 Narrowing Function

The last part includes the *narrowing function*, i.e. determining what value for N we should select in the different stages of the process. We can set this at a fixed value, where:

- $N = 0$: $\Sigma = \{\Sigma_u\}$: in this case the proposed strategy is the same as the separated strategy (fully personalization).
- $N = |U|$: $\Sigma = \{\Sigma_u | u \in U\}$: in this case, the proposed strategy is the same as pooled.

An important feature of the *narrowing reinforcement learning* is that the value of N can be dynamic during the time. To take advantage of a large number of users in the beginning (as data is limited in general), N should have a large value at the beginning. To take the advantage of the separated strategy later on, N should have a small value at the end. Therefore, it would be possible to initially have a large value for N, and decrease it over time. For this, we can apply various functions. In this case, we use two functions in the current paper, a linear function and an exponential function are used:

$$N_{t+1} = max(0, N_t - \alpha) \tag{6}$$
$$N_{t+1} = \beta N_t \tag{7}$$

If we select a positive value for α or a value for β such that $0 < \beta < 1$ we reduce the neighborhood size over time. By gradually decreasing the value of N, the shift from a pooled strategy to the separated strategy would be done smoothly, while being more flexible compared to using fixed clusters.

Figure 1 depicts our hypotheses of the performance of the various approaches, where the performance of the proposed method is the best of both worlds.

4   Experimental Setup

Evaluation of reinforcement learning algorithms is challenging, especially when dealing with people in a health setting. In order to perform a proper evaluation of algorithms that generate policies, it is required to either have a model of the world (being the human in this case) or to interact with humans directly. In this way, you can observe the states that result from selected actions as well as the rewards obtained. While studies with real humans are obviously the golden standard, studying a lot of different variants of algorithms (mainly to study the algorithmic improvements) will require a substantial number of experiments and human subjects, which is infeasible. We, therefore, opted for using a simulation environment which mimics realistic human behavior. The simulator is an open source simulator [4] that allows one to specify different profiles of users that drive the behavior. More details about the simulator are explained below as well as the experimental setup where we described how we use the simulator to evaluate the proposed approach.

4.1   Simulator

To do the required experiments, we used a simulator environment (cf. [4]) which generates realistic human behaviour. This simulator can be used to evaluate different strategies for motivating people to engage more in physical activity

Performance

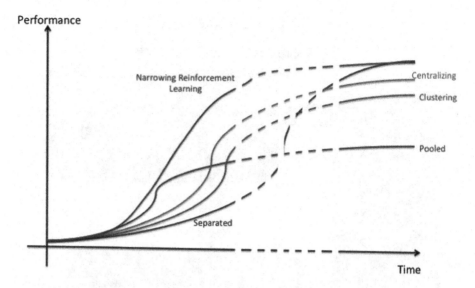

Fig. 1. Dynamics of performance of different strategies over time. The performance of the Pooled policy is very good at the beginning. The Separated policy is very slow, and its performance would be high after a long time, however its final performance would be the best. Narrowing Reinforcement Learning would have the benefits of both. It would be fast at the beginning and a high performance at the end.

(sports in this case). It encompasses a behavioral module that generates states for the users (represented by activities they perform during the day) as well as responses actions that are provided by the reinforcement learning algorithm. In this case, only two actions are available, namely to suggest the person to do sports, or not send a message. In addition, rewards are generated. The simulator has different components shown in Fig. 2.

Generate Agents: This component runs once at the beginning of the simulation and creates agents (representing real life users) based on pre-defined profiles. These profiles represent different lifestyles with different routines and habits. Essentially, the profiles indicate what activities people perform during a day, what the mean start time and duration of the activities as well as the standard deviation of both. Furthermore, the profiles express how users respond to interventions. Agents generated from the same profile have similarities in their life routines, but still each agent has its specific personality and properties.

To specify realistic profiles from which agents are spawned, we have used the dataset provided in [5]. This dataset contains information about what activities people have performed during one day. In addition, information is provided on job status. We have selected three groups of users (i.e. profiles) based on job status within this dataset and calculated the average start time and the average duration of each activity:

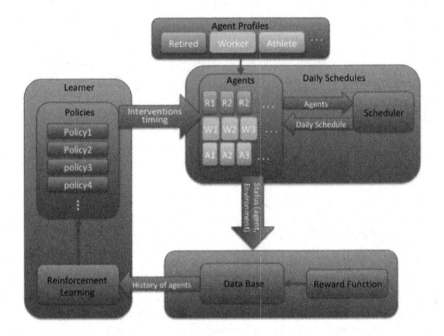

Fig. 2. Simulator environment

- "Retired" represents the daily schedule of elderly people who do not work. They have enough time to do some sport during the day, but they have preferences about the time for interventions (they do not like to be interrupted during a meal). To accept an intervention, the person will just look at his schedule, and will not accept if he has not enough time to do it during the next 3 h.
- "Worker" represents a person with a full-time job. A worker prefers to receive interventions during his lunch time. Although he checks his schedule for the next 24 h, because of his tight schedule it would be a difficult task to find some free time to work out.
- "Athletic" is the class of agents who love sports. An Athletic agent has a part time job, so his spare time is more than a worker, but less than a retired agent. He might even work out more than once on some days.

For each profile, the following activities are included: *sleep, breakfast, lunch, dinner, work.* The specification of the daily schedule for different profiles is presented in Table 1. In addition to the mentioned activities, by accepting the received interventions, an agent might do some workout.

In Table 1, the average of starting time and duration of each activity for different profiles are extracted from real dataset [5]. To make different agents from the same profile, for each new agent a random value from a normal distribution of $N(0, std_{activity})$ is added to the range of the start time (early start, late start) of each activity. As an example, "retired" agents are similar in the sense that

Table 1. Experimental setup: parameters of different profiles

Profile	Parameter	Activity				
		Sleep	Breakfast	Lunch	Dinner	Work
Worker	Early start	21:32	07:41	13:03	18:03	07:18
	Late start	22:32	08:44	13:51	20:03	09:48
	Std start	1.02	1.63	1.75	1.21	3.78
	Min duration	07:52	00:25	00:15	00:57	06:55
	Max duration	08:52	00:31	00:51	01:27	09:18
	Probability in weekdays	1, 1, 1, 1, 1, 1, 1	1, 1, 1, 1, 1, 1, 1	1, 1, 1, 1, 1, 1, 1	1, 1, 1, 1, 1, 1, 1	1, 1, 1, 1, 1, 0.5, 0.2
Athletic	Early start	21:18	08:06	12:38	18:21	09:15
	Late start	23:18	09:06	14:38	19:51	11:45
	Std start	1.06	1.43	1.77	1.55	3.84
	Min duration	08:35	00:15	00:21	00:17	05:37
	Max duration	09:35	00:30	00:51	00:47	06:07
	Probability in weekdays	1, 1, 1, 1, 1, 1, 1	1, 1, 1, 1, 1, 1, 1	1, 1, 1, 1, 1, 1, 1	1, 1, 1, 1, 1, 1, 1	1, 1, 1, 1, 1, 0, 0
Retired	Early start	21:19	06:36	12:54	17:50	08:00
	Late start	22:49	09:36	14:54	19:50	09:00
	Std start	1.08	1.40	1.86	1.23	00:00
	Min duration	07:55	01:18	0.23	00:18	08:00
	Max duration	09:55	01:30	00:47	00:54	08:00
	Probability in weekdays	1, 1, 1, 1, 1, 1, 1	1, 1, 1, 1, 1, 1, 1	1, 1, 1, 1, 1, 1, 1	1, 1, 1, 1, 1, 1, 1	0, 0, 0, 0, 0, 0, 0

they both do not work, while "Worker"s should work during working days. On the other hand, "retired" agents are not exactly the same because each has its own preferences for his daily schedule (e.g waking-up time, start time for eating breakfast, ...).

Create Daily Schedules: At the beginning of each day, a daily schedule is created for each agent based on his personal properties. The daily schedule of an agent is filled with start and end time of different activities (e.g. breakfast (start:8:10, end:8:43)), and he will be busy with this activities, or will be idle in the case of no activity is assigned for that specific moment. The daily schedule of an agent would not change during the day, except in the case that he receives and accepts an intervention which invites him to do some workout. In this case, the agent modifies his daily schedule and adds this new activity on it.

Following Daily Schedules: This component runs every second and for each agent checks if his current activity should stop or if he should start a new activity. Moreover, the current state of each agent is written in the database.

Reinforcement Learning: This component learns the best policy to send interventions based on the state of agents. This component runs at the beginning of each day. We deploy the methods we have explained throughout the paper here, we use feature-based least squares policy iteration (LSPI) [8]. The features of the state ($\phi(s)$) include (i) the current time (ii)the current weekday, (iii) whether the user already worked out in the current day (iv) fatigue level of the agent and (v) which activities are performed during the last hour.

Sending Interventions: At the beginning of each hour, for each agent this component applies the policy and decides to send an intervention[1] to him, or not.

Reward Function: In our experiments, the reward function, R_u, included both positive and negative rewards. Rewards are defined based on accepting/rejecting an intervention, doing the desired activity, and fatigue level of the agent. To be more precise, if the agent accepts an intervention a reward of $+1$ is given, and a negative reward of -1 in the case of rejection. Moreover, if the agent does some workout, the reward of $+10$ is given when he finishes this activity. The last type of reward is related to the fatigue level of the agent. If the agent becomes fatigue because of working out in several days in a row, a negative reward is given. The size of this negative reward is dependent on the number of days that the agent worked out (the more fatigue the agent is, the more negative rewards receive). The value of fatigue shows the number of times a user worked out during a couple of days in a row, without skipping working out for a day.

4.2   Experiments

Below, the experimental setup is described. First, we describe the setup of the learning algorithms followed by the way the experiments are run.

Learner: As the learning algorithm, we have used LSPI which is a good option when the state space is big and sparse (like our problem, especially during the first days). To learn a policy, at the beginning of each day, we apply LSPI and learn policies based on the selected traces that have been selected given the applied algorithm. For LSPI, we use an exploration rate of 0.05 (cf. [4]). it means that at 5% of hours, an action is selected by random.

Algorithms: We apply the separate, pooled and clustering schemes, and try different variants of the *narrowing reinforcement learning, NRL,* approach. For the latter, we apply different variants of the narrowing function. Both the linear and exponential *narrowing function* have hyperparameters. We did the experiment with different values for each, $(2, 3, 4, 5)$ for α and $(0.5, 0.75, 0.85, 0.90)$ for β. The results are reported in the next section. Note that for each experimental setting we performed five runs and averaged the rewards over those runs. We use 60 agents in our simulations (20 agents per profile).

Following the clustering approach, as we use traces of experiences to determine the distance between users we perform an initial "warmup" phase in which we apply a random policy for a number of days (we experiment with 1, 7 and 10 days) to gather initial traces on user experiences. Only after this part has been finished we start to learn policies.

---

[1] In our experiments, an intervention is just a message that would send to the agent and invite him to workout in that day. The agent can accept or reject it.

5   Results

Figure 3 shows the average and standard deviation of the accumulated reward of all agents over the different approaches. Before comparing the approaches, let us dive into the influence of the parameter setting upon the performance of the approach first. When it comes to the cluster-based approach, it shows that 7 days leads to the higher accumulated reward. For the *narrowing reinforcement learning* we consider the different settings of the narrowing function. Results show that the best results are achieved when $\alpha = 3$ for the linear narrowing function, or $\beta = 0.50$ for the exponential one.

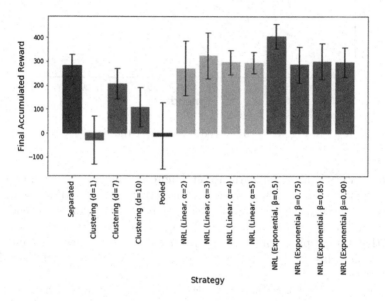

Fig. 3. Average of accumulated reward for different strategies

We have performed an unpaired Wilcoxon rank-sum test [10] to compare the final accumulated rewards of different runs of the best narrowing reinforcement learning (with exponential narrowing function, $\beta = 0.50$) and the separated approach (as the best strategy with highest average). The result of this test (p-$value = 0.0163$) reveals that the accumulated rewards of runs with *narrowing RL* strategy are significantly higher compared to the accumulated rewards of runs with separated strategy.

Figure 4 shows the average accumulated rewards over time for the different approaches (where we took the best performing parameter settings for the cluster-based and narrowing approaches). As can be seen, a few days after the beginning of the experiment, the pooled strategy has some downward trend. The reason is that at the beginning of the experiments the agents are not fatigued from working out. Because of that, the learner receives positive rewards for most

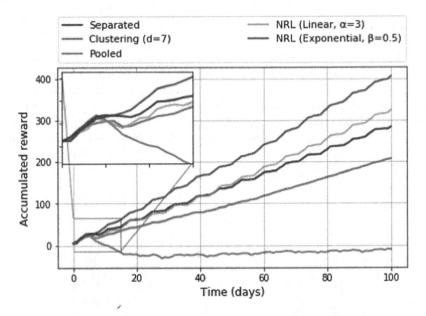

Fig. 4. Accumulated reward over the time

of the sent interventions and learns to send more and more interventions. Which makes fatigue many agents, and leads to negative rewards. After a few days, based on these negative rewards the learner updates the policy to send fewer interventions (it is explained more in Fig. 5). In all, even after this first days, we see that the graph of this strategy has a very limited upwards trend. The reason is that this strategy learns one policy for everybody, and there is no personalization.

Figures 5a and b show the daily reward received by agents from different profiles for two strategies, namely the narrowing reinforcement approach (with an exponential narrowing function, $\beta = 0.5$) and the results for the pooled approach. As can be seen, in both cases, the received rewards by Athletic agents is more than for the two other profiles. This is due to specific characteristics of these agents which are open to more workouts (and hence, can obtain a higher reward). Figure 5b shows that the learned policy with the pooled strategy receives a lot of rewards from Athletic agents, this leads to more and more interventions being sent as this agent type does not get tired easily and accepts all these workouts. However, since this strategy learns one policy for all agents, it will also send a lot of interventions to the retired and worker agents, causing negative rewards for these agents due to messages being rejected and fatigue building up. By receiving these new rewards, the number of actions will be reduced for all agents (Fig. 5d), which decrease the amount of negative rewards from retired and worker agents but also decrease the positive rewards from Athletic agents. This clearly shows the disadvantages of learning one policy for all agents. By looking at Fig. 5c, for the narrowing approach, we can see that at the beginning the number of

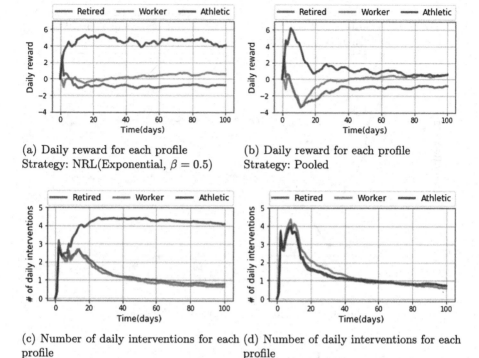

(a) Daily reward for each profile
Strategy: NRL(Exponential, $\beta = 0.5$)

(b) Daily reward for each profile
Strategy: Pooled

(c) Number of daily interventions for each profile
Strategy: NRL(Exponential, $\beta = 0.5$)

(d) Number of daily interventions for each profile
Strategy: Pooled

Fig. 5. Received reward and number of sent interventions for each profile. The results are shown for two strategies: NRL(a, c), Pooled(b, d)

interventions sent for different profiles are almost the same. But, after some time, the learned policies for athletic agents send more interventions in comparison to the learned policies for agents from other profiles. By narrowing the size of nearest neighbors, a higher level of personalization is achieved over time. Please note that in Fig. 5c, even though the number of sent interventions for the worker and retired agents is quite the same over days, the learned policies are different.

Figure 6 shows the average daily reward of runs with the different strategies. We have performed a paired Wilcoxon signed-rank to compare the average of daily rewards of different runs (5 runs for each) of narrowing reinforcement learning and separated. The result of this test ($p\text{-}value = 1.114e{-}14$) shows that the daily rewards of runs with the narrowing strategy are significantly higher than accumulated rewards of runs with separated strategy.

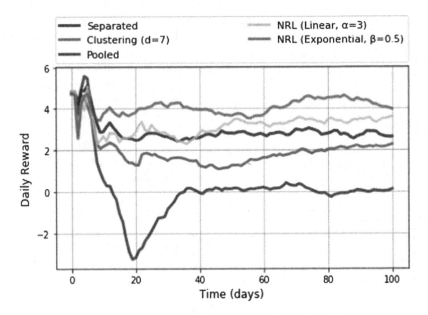

Fig. 6. Average of daily reward over the time

6   Conclusion and Future Work

Selecting the best technique to obtain personalization is highly dependent on the task at hand. Personalization in health and wellbeing domain is challenging since a sequence of actions should be selected, while the consequence of actions cannot be observed immediately. Reinforcement learning is a technique fits this setting very well [6]. However, reinforcement learning has its own drawbacks. The learning process needs quite a lot of experiences to learn a proper policy. As a result, learning a personalized policy based on the experiences of an individual would be very slow. Several approaches have been proposed before that try to overcome this problem.

Gonul *et al.* [3] adopted standard reinforcement learning methods to optimize the time of interventions. They use transfer learning for this purpose. To do that, the learned policy from other users is transferred to other users. This technique can solve the cold start problem (in [3] it is called a "jump start"). More specifically, transfer learning is used to learn the common patterns across individuals and that knowledge is used to achieve the "jump start" for new individuals. The approach does, however, assume initial users and data to be present, which is not a hard requirement in our case.

In [4,11] users are assigned to clusters based on the similarities in their behaviours. Then, one policy is learned for each cluster of users. Even though it is not a fully personalized technique, but there is a level of personalization in this technique and the technique outperforms a single policy across all users as well as one policy per user (but only in the beginning).

In this paper, we have presented an approach which we call *narrowing reinforcement learning* to remedy some of the shortcomings of current approaches to personalize interventions towards users. The proposed approach is general and independent to a specific domain. However, in this paper, we focus on the e-health domain and evaluate the approach by using a simulation environment in this domain. The approach significantly outperforms the other available approaches when we compare them in a realistic simulation environment.

As is clear, the function for decreasing the value of N has an important effect on the performance of the approach. In this paper, we tested two different functions, linear and exponential, and different values for their parameters. Results show that the exponential function for narrowing performs best.

An important question that can be the subject of further research is about the best strategy for decreasing the value of N. It should also be noted that it is not necessary to have one N for all agents. For each agent, we can have a separate N, which is updated at the beginning of each learning cycle.

References

1. Berndt, D.J., Clifford, J.: Using dynamic time warping to find patterns in time series. In: KDD Workshop, Seattle, WA, vol. 10, pp. 359–370 (1994)
2. Evans, K.: Heres to your (mobile) health: the number of iOS mobile health apps more than doubles. https://www.mobilestrategies360.com/2015/09/21/number-ios-mobile-health-apps-more-doubles. Accessed 30 Sept 2010
3. Gonul, S., Namli, T., Baskaya, M., Sinaci, A.A., Cosar, A., Toroslu, I.H.: Optimization of just-in-time adaptive interventions using reinforcement learning. In: Mouhoub, M., Sadaoui, S., Ait Mohamed, O., Ali, M. (eds.) IEA/AIE 2018. LNCS (LNAI), vol. 10868, pp. 334–341. Springer, Cham (2018). https://doi.org/10.1007/978-3-319-92058-0_32
4. El Hassouni, A., Hoogendoorn, M., van Otterlo, M., Barbaro, E.: Personalization of health interventions using cluster-based reinforcement learning. CoRR abs/1804.03592 (2018). http://arxiv.org/abs/1804.03592
5. Hofferth, S., Flood, S., Sobek, M.: American time use survey data extract builder: version 2.5 [dataset]. University of Maryland and Minneapolis, College Park, MD, University of Minnesota, MN, doi 10, D060 (2015)
6. Hoogendoorn, M., Funk, B.: Machine Learning for the Quantified Self: On the Art of Learning from Sensory Data. Springer, Cham (2017). https://doi.org/10.1007/978-3-319-66308-1
7. Sutton, R.S., Barto, A.G.: Reinforcement Learning: An Introduction, vol. 1. MIT Press, Cambridge (2018)
8. Watkins, C.J., Dayan, P.: Q-learning. Mach. Learn. 8(3–4), 279–292 (1992)
9. Wiering, M., Van Otterlo, M.: Reinforcement learning. Adapt. Learn. Optim. 12, 51 (2012)
10. Wilcoxon, F., Wilcox, R.A.: Some rapid approximate statistical procedures. Lederle Laboratories (1964)
11. Zhu, F., Guo, J., Xu, Z., Liao, P., Huang, J.: Group-driven reinforcement learning for personalized mHealth intervention. arXiv preprint arXiv:1708.04001 (2017)

Logic and Reasoning

Abstract Argumentation / Persuasion / Dynamics

Ryuta Arisaka$^{(\boxtimes)}$ and Ken Satoh

National Institute of Informatics, Chiyoda, Japan
ryutaarisaka@gmail.com, ksatoh@nii.ac.jp

Abstract. The act of persuasion, a key component in rhetoric argumentation, may be viewed as a dynamics modifier. We extend Dung's frameworks with acts of persuasion among agents, and consider interactions among attack, persuasion and defence that have been largely unheeded so far. We characterise basic notions of admissibilities in this framework, and show a way of enriching them through, effectively, CTL (computation tree logic) encoding, which also permits importation of the theoretical results known to the logic into our argumentation frameworks. Our aim is to complement the growing interest in coordination of static and dynamic argumentation.

1 Introduction

An interesting component of rhetoric argumentation is persuasion. We may code an act of it into $\boxed{\text{A:}a_1}$ $\dashrightarrow$ $\boxed{\text{B:}a_2}$ $^{a}\!\!-\!\!_b$ $\boxed{\text{B:}a_3}$ with the following intended meaning: some agent A's argument a_1 persuades an agent B into holding a_3; B, being persuaded, drops a_2. There can be various reasons for the persuasive act. It may be that A is a great teacher wanting to correct some inadvisable norm of B's, or perhaps A is a manipulator who benefits if a_2 is not present. Persuasion is popularly observed in social forums including YouTube and Twitter, and methods to represent it will help understand users' views on topics accurately. Another less pervasive form of persuasion is possible: $\boxed{\text{A:}a_1}$ $\multimap$ $\boxed{\text{B:}a_3}$ in which A persuades B with a_1 into expressing a_3 but without conversion. In either of the cases, persuasion acts as a dynamics modifier in rhetoric argumentation, allowing some argument to appear and disappear.

Of course - and this is one highlight of this paper - these acts will not be successful if a_1 is detected to be not a defensible argument: we may have $\boxed{\text{C:}a_3}$ $\rightarrow$ $\boxed{\text{A:}a_1}$ $\multimap$ $\boxed{\text{B:}a_2}$ where a_3 attacks a_1. Suppose now that B is aware of a_3, then B can defend against A's persuasion due to a_3's attack on a_1. B is not persuaded into holding a_2 in such a case. We will care for the interactions between attack, persuasion and defence.

While AGM-like argumentation framework revisions defining a class of argumentation frameworks to result from an initially given argumentation framework and an input (which could be argument(s), attack(s) or both), and persuasion

© Springer Nature Switzerland AG 2018
T. Miller et al. (Eds.): PRIMA 2018, LNAI 11224, pp. 331–343, 2018.
https://doi.org/10.1007/978-3-030-03098-8_20

in the context of (often two-parties) dialogue games, are being studied, there are very few studies in the literature that pursue coordination of statics and dynamics. One exception is the dynamic logic for programs adapted for argumentation by Doutre *et al.* [20,21], which is rich in expressiveness with non-deterministic operations, tests, sequential operations. Bridging dynamics and statics is important for detailed and more precise analysis of rhetoric argumentation. So far, however, the above-said interaction between attack, persuasion and defence has been largely unheeded. We first of all fill the gap by developing an abstract persuasion argumentation, an extension to Dung's argumentation theory [22]. We formulate the notion of static admissibility for our theory, and then show a way of diversifying it into other types of admissibilities through, effectively, CTL (computation tree logic) embedding.

1.1 Example Situations

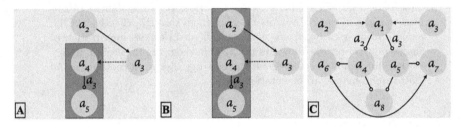

Defence and Reference Set. One aspect that has not been shed much light on in the literature of dynamic argumentation is defence against such persuasive acts (dynamic operations). Let us consider an example.

a_2 (Mr. X) Elma does not like the music.
a_3 (Mr. Z) We should get a piano.
a_4 (Mrs. Y) We can buy Elma a Hello Kitty shoulder bag.
a_5 (Mrs. Y) We will go to Yamaha Music Communications Co., Ltd. for a piano.

The relation among them is as shown in Figure $\boxed{\text{A}}$ ($\boxed{\text{B}}$): there is an attack from a_2 to a_3, and there is also a persuasion act by (Mr. Z holding) a_3 trying to convert a_4 into a_5. Suppose that a_5 is not initially on Mrs. Y's mind, that is, that it is not visible initially. If the persuasion by Mr. Z is successful, Mrs. Y changes her mind, dropping a_4 and gaining a_5. Otherwise, she holds onto a_4. In Dung theory, defence of an argument a_x is defined with respect to a set of arguments A. The reference set A defends a_x just when A's members attack all arguments attacking a_x. We see that this concept may be extended also to persuasion operations. For example, if, as marked with a rectangular box in Figure $\boxed{\text{A}}$, the reference set consists of a_4 and a_5 alone, it does not detect any flaw in a_3. Thus, the persuasion is successful with respect to the reference set. However, if it also contains a_2 attacking a_3 as in Figure $\boxed{\text{B}}$, it can prevent the persuasion from taking effect on a_4.

Multiple Persuasions. We have a kind of concurrency scenario when multiple persuasions act on an argument. Let us consider an example.

a_1 (Alice at London Bridge, having agreed to see Bob at 7 pm) I am going to have dinner with Bob. It is 7 pm now. He should be arriving soon.

a_2 (Tom, calling from Camden) Chris (Alice's brother) is looking for you. He is at Camden Bar. He says there is some urgent matter, can you please get to the bar as soon as possible?

a_3 (Katie, seeing Alice by chance) Hey Alice, you've left your laptop at King's library? You better go there now. Oh, and don't forget about your presentation tomorrow morning. Make sure you have slides ready!

Having been acquainted with Bob only recently, Alice is more inclined to getting to Camden Bar or to King's library. That is, a_4: I am going to Camden Bar, or a_5: I am going to King's library. She knows her brother is very stern. But the assignment of which Katie reminded Alice seems to be a thing that must be prioritised, too. Whichever option she is to go for, she must, thinks she, come up with excuses to justify her choice. Therefore:

a_6 (Alice's excuse) It is fine to skip dinner because I waited for Bob at London Bridge and he did not arrive in time. Besides, I suddenly have something urgent.

a_7 (Alice's excuse) I cannot see Chris. For my career, it is important that I perform well at presentation tomorrow. Chris will understand.

a_8 (Alice's excuse) I cannot go to King's library now, because it is always urgent when Chris calls me.

Figure [C] represents these arguments. Now, what we have is a potentially irreversible branching. If a_2 persuades a_1 into a_4, it is no longer possible for a_3 to persuade a_1, as a_1 will not be available for persuasion. If a_3 persuades a_1 into a_5, on the other hand, it is no longer possible that a_2 persuades a_1. A certain partial order may be defined among persuasion (as in preference-based argumentation), but the non-deterministic consideration leads to a more general theory (as in probabilistic argumentation) in which the actual behaviour of a system depends on run-time executions.

Just as in program analysis, however, it may be still possible to identify certain properties, whichever an actual path may be. In this particular example, (Alice holding) a_1 may be persuaded into holding a_4 or else a_5, and we cannot tell which with certainty. However, we can certainly predict a_8's emergence. Thus, by obtaining varieties in arguments admissibility by means of CTL, we can answer such a query as 'Is a_8 going to be an admissible argument in whatever order persuasive acts may take place?'.

2   Technical Backgrounds

Let $\mathcal{A}$ be a class of abstract entities which we understand as arguments. We denote any member of $\mathcal{A}$ by a with or without a subscript, and any finite subset of $\mathcal{A}$ by A with or without a subscript. An argumentation framework [22] is a tuple (A, R) where R is a binary relation over A. Let $F^{(A,R)}(A_1)$ denote $(A_1, R \cap (A_1 \times A_1))$, we denote by $2^{(A,R)}$ the following set: $\bigcup_{A_1 \subseteq A} F^{(A,R)}(A_1)$, i.e. all sub-argumentation frameworks of (A, R). When confusion is unlikely to occur, we abbreviate $F^{(A,R)}(A_1)$ for some A_1 by $F(A_1)$.

For any (A, R) an argument $a_1 \in A$ is said to attack $a_2 \in A$ if and only if, or iff, $(a_1, a_2) \in R$. A set of arguments $A_1 \subseteq A$ is said to defend $a_x \in A$ iff each $a_y \in A$ attacking a_x is attacked by at least one argument in A_1. A set of arguments $A_1 \subseteq A$ is said to be: conflict-free iff no member of A_1 attacks a member of A_1; admissible iff it is conflict-free and it defends all the members of A_1; complete iff it is admissible and includes any argument it defends; preferred iff it is a set-theoretically maximal admissible set; stable iff it is preferred and attacks every argument in $A \backslash A_1$; and grounded iff it is the set intersection of all complete sets of A.

3   Abstract Persuasion Argumentation

We define our Abstract Persuasion Argumentation (APA) framework to be a tuple $(A, R, R_{\mathbf{p}}, A_0, \hookrightarrow)$ for $A_0 \subseteq A$, for a ternary relation $R_{\mathbf{p}} : A \times (A \cup \{\epsilon\}) \times A$ and for another $\hookrightarrow : 2^A \times (2^{(A,R)} \times 2^{(A,R)})$. For $R_{\mathbf{p}}$, $(a_1, \epsilon, a_2) \in R_{\mathbf{p}}$ represents $a_1 \multimap a_2$ (passive persuasion or to induce), and $(a_1, a_2, a_3) \in R_{\mathbf{p}}$ represents $a_1 \dashrightarrow a_2 \overset{a}{\multimap} a_3$ (active persuasion or to convert). We refer to a subset of $R_{\mathbf{p}}$ by Γ with or without a subscript and/or a superscript.

APA is a dynamic argumentation framework where arguments can appear (go visible) or disappear (go invisible). As in a transition system, it comes with an initial state and a transition relation $\hookrightarrow$. For any APA framework $(A, R, R_{\mathbf{p}}, A_0, \hookrightarrow)$, we define a state to be a member $F(A_x)$ of $2^{(A,R)}$, and we say any argument that occurs in a state visible and any that does not occur in the state invisible, in each case at that particular state.[1] We define $F(A_0)$ to be the initial state.

Example 1. In Elma example, we assumed $A_0 = \{a_2, a_3, a_4\}$ and $F(A_0) = (A_0, \{(a_2, a_3)\})$. In Alice example, $A_0 = \{a_1, a_2, a_3\}$ and $F(A_0) = (A_0, \emptyset)$.

Definition 1 (Reachable states). *For APA $(A, R, R_{\mathbf{p}}, A_0, \hookrightarrow)$, for a set of arguments $A_x \subseteq A$, and for states $F(A_1)$ and $F(A_2)$, we say that there is a transition from $F(A_1)$ to $F(A_2)$ with respect to A_x iff it holds that $(A_x, (F(A_1), F(A_2))) \in \hookrightarrow$, which we alternatively state either as $(F(A_1), F(A_2)) \in \hookrightarrow^{A_x}$ or as $F(A_1) \hookrightarrow^{A_x} F(A_2)$. We say that a state $F(A_x)$ is reachable iff $F(A_x)$ either is the initial state or else is such that $F(A_0) \hookrightarrow^{A_{i_1}} \cdots \hookrightarrow^{A_{i_n}} F(A_x)$, $1 \leq n$.*

A reachable state is a static snapshot of an APA framework at one moment, which is a Dung argumentation framework. To enumerate all reachable states, it suffices to define $\hookrightarrow$ in specific detail. And this is where the notion of defence

---

[1] We assume the standard notion of occurrence.

against persuasive acts with respect to a reference set at a state - specifically visible arguments of the set at the state - comes into play:

Definition 2 (Possible persuasion acts). *For APA* $(A, R, R_{\mathbf{p}}, A_0, \hookrightarrow)$, *we say that a persuasion act* $(a_1, \alpha, a_2) \in R_{\mathbf{p}}$, $\alpha \in \{\epsilon\} \cup A$, *is possible with respect to: (i) a reference set* $A_x \subseteq A$; *and (ii) a state* $F(A_u)$ *iff* $a_1, \alpha \in A_u \cup \{\epsilon\}$ *and a_1 is not attacked by any member of $A_x \cap A_u$. We denote the set of all members of $R_{\mathbf{p}}$ that are possible with respect to a reference set $A_x \subseteq A$ and a state $F(A_u)$ by* $\Gamma_{F(A_u)}^{A_x}$.

Example 2 (Continued). In Elma example with $A_0 = \{a_2, a_3, a_4\}$, there is one argument, a_2, which is in A_0 (thus visible), and which attacks a_3, so $(a_2, a_3, a_4) \in R_{\mathbf{p}}$ is possible with respect to $A_x \subseteq A$ and $F(A_0)$ only if $a_2 \notin A_x$. $\Gamma_{F(A_0)}^{A_x}$ is: $\{(a_2, a_3, a_4)\}$ if $a_2 \notin A_x$; $\emptyset$, otherwise. In Alice example with $A_0 = \{a_1, a_2, a_3\}$, (a_2, a_1, a_4) and (a_3, a_1, a_5) are both possible with respect to any $A_x \subseteq A$ and $F(A_0)$, because for no $(a_x, \alpha, a_y) \in R_{\mathbf{p}}$ there is $(a_z, a_x) \in R$. $\Gamma_{F(A_0)}^{A_x} = \{(a_2, a_1, a_4), (a_3, a_1, a_5)\}$.

Since transition as we consider is non-deterministic, each persuasion act possible in a state may or may not execute for transition. Therefore, for any APA $(A, R, R_{\mathbf{p}}, A_0, \hookrightarrow)$, any reference set $A_x \subseteq A$ and any state $F(A_1)$, there are $2^{|\Gamma_{F(A_1)}^{A_x}|} - 1$ transitions, though some of them may be identical.

Definition 3 (Non-deterministic transition). *For APA* $(A, R, R_{\mathbf{p}}, A_0, \hookrightarrow)$, *for $A_1 \subseteq A$ and for $\Gamma \subseteq R_{\mathbf{p}}$, let* $neg^{A_1}(\Gamma)$ *be* $\{a_x \in A_1 \mid \exists a_1, a_2 \in A_1.(a_1, a_x, a_2) \in \Gamma\}$, *and let* $pos^{A_1}(\Gamma)$ *be* $\{a_2 \in A_1 \mid \exists a_1, \alpha \in A_1 \cup \{\epsilon\}.(a_1, \alpha, a_2) \in \Gamma\}$. *For $A_x \subseteq A$ and states $F(A_1)$ and $F(A_2)$, we define:* $F(A_1) \hookrightarrow^{A_x} F(A_2)$ *iff there is some* $\emptyset \subset \Gamma \subseteq \Gamma_{F(A_1)}^{A_x} \subseteq R_{\mathbf{p}}$ *such that* $A_2 = (A_1 \backslash neg^{A_1}(\Gamma)) \cup pos^{A_1}(\Gamma)$.

For $\Gamma \subseteq R_{\mathbf{p}}$, if $\Gamma \subseteq \Gamma_{F(A_1)}^{A_x}$, it is a (non-deterministically) chosen set of possible persuasion acts at $F(A_1)$. Thus, $neg^{A_1}(\Gamma)$ is the set of all visible arguments that are to be converted, and $pos^{A_1}(\Gamma)$ is that of all visible arguments that are to be generated, in the transition. As clear from this definition, while every member of $pos^{A_1}(\Gamma)$, if not visible in $F(A_1)$, will be visible in $F(A_2)$, not necessarily every member of $neg^{A_1}(\Gamma)$ will be invisible in $F(A_2)$ in case it also belongs to $pos^{A_1}(\Gamma)$, in which case the effect is offset.

Example 3. Consider the argumentation in the figures below, in each of which visible arguments are marked with a black border around the circle. Suppose $A_0 = \{a_1, a_2\}$ as in Figure $\boxed{D}$. At $F(A_0)$, there are more than one possible persuasion acts: $\Gamma_{F(A_0)}^{A_x} = \{(a_1, a_2, a_4), (a_2, a_1, a_3)\}$ for any reference set $A_x \subseteq A$. There are three transitions for $F(A_0)$, depending on which one(s) execute simultaneously. If just (a_1, a_2, a_4), a_2 will go invisible, while a_4 will be visible, so we have $F(A_0) \hookrightarrow^{A_x} F(A_1)$ (Figure $\boxed{E}$) for any A_x. If just (a_2, a_1, a_3), we have $F(A_0) \hookrightarrow^{A_y} F(A_2)$ (Figure $\boxed{F}$) for any A_y. Or both of them may execute at once, in which case both a_1 and a_2 will be invisible, and a_3 and a_4 meanwhile will be visible, so we have $F(A_0) \hookrightarrow^{A_z} F(A_3)$ (Figure $\boxed{G}$) for any A_z. Reasoning similarly for the new states, we eventually enumerate all reachable states and all transitions among them:

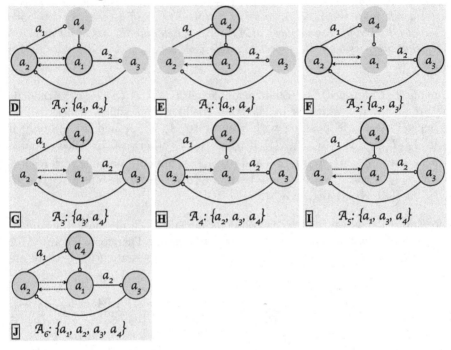

- $F(A_0) \hookrightarrow^{A_x} F(A_1)$, $F(A_0) \hookrightarrow^{A_y} F(A_2)$, $F(A_0) \hookrightarrow^{A_z} F(A_3)$.
- $F(A_1) \hookrightarrow^{A_u} F(A_1)$.
- $F(A_2) \hookrightarrow^{A_v} F(A_2)$.
- $F(A_3) \hookrightarrow^{A_p} F(A_4)$, $F(A_3) \hookrightarrow^{A_q} F(A_5)$, $F(A_3) \hookrightarrow^{A_r} F(A_6)$.
- $F(A_4) \hookrightarrow^{A_i} F(A_4)$, $F(A_4) \hookrightarrow^{A_j} F(A_6)$.
- $F(A_5) \hookrightarrow^{A_k} F(A_5)$, $F(A_5) \hookrightarrow^{A_c} F(A_6)$.
- $F(A_6) \hookrightarrow^{A_d} F(A_4)$, $F(A_6) \hookrightarrow^{A_f} F(A_5)$, $F(A_6) \hookrightarrow^{A_g} F(A_6)$.

The reference sets for the transitions are any subset of $\{a_1, a_2, a_3, a_4\}$. Notice, apart from the trivial self-transitions, states could oscillate infinitely between $F(A_4), F(A_5)$ and $F(A_6)$.

Proposition 1. *Suppose an APA framework δ with a finite number of arguments. It is necessary that the number of (reachable) states is finite. It is, however, not necessary that the number of transitions in δ is finite.*

3.1 Admissibilities

We now define the static notion of admissibility in APA frameworks, based on three criteria. For APA $(A, R, R_\mathbf{p}, A_0, \hookrightarrow)$,

Conflict-Freeness. We say that $A_1 \subseteq A$ is conflict-free in a (reachable) state $F(A_x)$ iff no member of $A_1 \cap A_x$ attacks a member of $A_1 \cap A_x$.

Defendedness. We say that a reference set $A_1 \subseteq A$ defends $a \in A$ in a state $F(A_x)$ iff either $a \notin A_x$ or else both of the conditions below hold.

1. Every $a_u \in A_x$ attacking a is attacked by at least one member of $A_x \cap A_1$ (counter-attack).
2. There is no state $F(A_y)$ such that both $F(A_x) \hookrightarrow^{A_1} F(A_y)$ and $a \notin A_y$ at once (no elimination).

We say that $A_1 \subseteq A$ is defended in a state $F(A_x)$ iff A_1 as a reference set defends every member of its in $F(A_x)$.

Properness. We say that $A_u \subseteq A$ is proper in a state $F(A_x)$ iff $A_u \subseteq A_x$.

Defendedness above extends Dung's defendedness naturally for $R_{\mathbf{p}}$. Properness ensures that we will not be talking of invisible arguments. With these properties, we say $A_u \subseteq A$ is: admissible in a state $F(A_1)$ iff A_u is conflict-free, defended and proper in $F(A_1)$; complete in a state $F(A_1)$ iff A_u is admissible in $F(A_1)$ and includes all arguments it defends; preferred iff no $A_v \subseteq A$ that is complete in a state $F(A_1)$ is a strict superset of A_u; stable iff it is preferred and attacks every member of $A_1 \backslash A_u$; and grounded in a state $F(A_1)$ iff it is the set intersection of all complete sets in $F(A_1)$. Since each state is a Dung argumentation framework, we have:

Proposition 2. *For APA* $(A, R, R_{\mathbf{p}}, A_0, \hookrightarrow)$, *for a state* $F(A_1)$ *and for* $A_x \subseteq A_1$: *if* A_x *is stable, then* A_x *is preferred; if* A_x *is preferred, then* A_x *is complete; if* A_x *is complete, then* A_x *is admissible; there exists at least one complete set; and there may not exist any stable set.*

For general admissibilities across transition, one way of describing more varieties is to embed this state-wise admissibility and transitions into computation tree logic (CTL) or other branching-time logic, by which model-theoretical results known to the logic become available to APA frameworks, too. We consider CTL with some path restrictions. Denote $\{\mathsf{ad}, \mathsf{co}, \mathsf{pr}, \mathsf{st}, \mathsf{gr}\}$ by Ω, and refer to a member of Ω by ω. Let the grammar of ϕ be:

$$\phi := \bot \mid \top \mid a \dot{\in}_\delta A_x \mid P_\delta(\omega, A_x) \mid \neg\phi \mid \phi \wedge \phi \mid \phi \vee \phi \mid \phi \supset \phi \mid \mathbf{AX}^\Sigma \phi \mid$$
$$\mathbf{EX}^\Sigma \phi \mid \mathbf{AF}^\Sigma \phi \mid \mathbf{EF}^\Sigma \phi \mid \mathbf{AG}^\Sigma \phi \mid \mathbf{EG}^\Sigma \phi \mid \mathbf{E}^\Sigma[\phi\mathbf{U}\phi] \mid \mathbf{A}^\Sigma[\phi\mathbf{U}\phi]$$

where both $a \dot{\in}_\delta A_x$ and $P_\delta(\omega, A_x)$ are atomic predicates for an APA framework $\delta := (A, R, R_{\mathbf{p}}, A_0, \hookrightarrow)$, with $A_x \subseteq A$, with $a \in A$ and with $\Sigma \subseteq 2^A$. $\mathbf{A}$ is 'in all branches', $\mathbf{E}$ is 'in some branch', $\mathbf{X}$ is 'next state', $\mathbf{F}$ is 'future state', $\mathbf{G}$ is 'all subsequent states', and $\mathbf{U}$ is 'until'. The superscripts restrict paths to only those reachable with member(s) of Σ as reference set(s). See below for the exact semantics. We denote the class of all atomic predicates for δ by $\mathcal{P}_\delta$. For semantics, let $L : \Omega \times 2^A \to 2^{\mathcal{P}_\delta}$ be a valuation function such that $L(\omega, A_x)$ is:

- $\{P_\delta(\mathsf{ad}, A_y) \in \mathcal{P}_\delta \mid A_y$ is admissible in $F(A_x)\}$ if $\omega = \mathsf{ad}$.

- $\{P_\delta(\mathsf{co}, A_y) \in \mathcal{P}_\delta \mid A_y \text{ is complete in } F(A_x)\}$ if $\omega = \mathsf{co}$.
- $\{P_\delta(\mathsf{pr}, A_y) \in \mathcal{P}_\delta \mid A_y \text{ is preferred in } F(A_x)\}$ if $\omega = \mathsf{pr}$.
- $\{P_\delta(\mathsf{st}, A_y) \in \mathcal{P}_\delta \mid A_y \text{ is stable in } F(A_x)\}$ if $\omega = \mathsf{st}$.
- $\{P_\delta(\mathsf{gr}, A_y) \in \mathcal{P}_\delta \mid A_y \text{ is grounded in } F(A_x)\}$ if $\omega = \mathsf{gr}$.

We define $\mathcal{M} := (\delta, L)$ to be a transition system with the following forcing relations.[2]

- $\mathcal{M}, A_1 \models \top$.
- $\mathcal{M}, A_1 \not\models \bot$.
- $\mathcal{M}, A_1 \models a \dot{\epsilon}_\delta A_x$ iff $a \in A_x$.
- $\mathcal{M}, A_1 \models P_\delta(\omega, A_x)$ iff $P_\delta(\omega, A_x) \in L(\omega, A_1)$ (in plain terms, this says A_x is admissible/complete/preferred/stable/grounded in a state $F(A_1)$).
- $\mathcal{M}, A_1 \models \neg\phi$ iff $\mathcal{M}, A_1 \not\models \phi$.
- $\mathcal{M}, A_1 \models \phi_1 \wedge \phi_2$ iff $\mathcal{M}, A_1 \models \phi_1$ and $\mathcal{M}, A_1 \models \phi_2$.
- $\mathcal{M}, A_1 \models \phi_1 \vee \phi_2$ iff $\mathcal{M}, A_1 \models \phi_1$ or $\mathcal{M}, A_1 \models \phi_2$.
- $\mathcal{M}, A_1 \models \phi_1 \supset \phi_2$ iff $\mathcal{M}, A_1 \not\models \phi_1$ or $\mathcal{M}, A_1 \models \phi_2$.
- $\mathcal{M}, A_1 \models \mathbf{AX}^\Sigma \phi$ iff $\mathcal{M}, A_2 \models \phi$ for each transition $F(A_1) \hookrightarrow^{A_x} F(A_2)$, $A_x \in \Sigma$.
- $\mathcal{M}, A_1 \models \mathbf{EX}^\Sigma \phi$ iff there is some transition $F(A_1) \hookrightarrow^{A_x} F(A_2)$, $A_x \in \Sigma$, such that $\mathcal{M}, A_2 \models \phi$.
- $\mathcal{M}, A_1 \models \mathbf{AF}^\Sigma \phi$ iff there is some $i \geq 0$ for each transition $F(A_1) \hookrightarrow^{A_{j1}} \cdots \hookrightarrow^{A_{ji}} F(A_{i+1})(\hookrightarrow^{A_x} \cdots)$, $A_{jk} \in \Sigma$ for $1 \leq k \leq i+1$, such that $\mathcal{M}, A_{i+1} \models \phi$.
- $\mathcal{M}, A_1 \models \mathbf{EF}^\Sigma \phi$ iff there are some $i \geq 1$ and a transition $F(A_1) \hookrightarrow^{A_{j1}} \cdots \hookrightarrow^{A_{ji}} F(A_{i+1})(\hookrightarrow^{A_x} \cdots)$, $A_{jk} \in \Sigma$ for $1 \leq k \leq i+1$, such that $\mathcal{M}, A_{i+1} \models \phi$.
- $\mathcal{M}, A_1 \models \mathbf{AG}^\Sigma \phi$ iff $\mathcal{M}, A_k \models \phi$ for each transition $F(A_1) \hookrightarrow^{A_{j1}} \cdots$, $A_{jn} \in \Sigma$ for $1 \leq n$, such that $F(A_k)$ occurs in the transition sequence.
- $\mathcal{M}, A_1 \models \mathbf{EG}^\Sigma \phi$ iff there is some transition $F(A_1) \hookrightarrow^{A_{j1}} \cdots$, $A_{jn} \in \Sigma$ for $1 \leq n$, such that $\mathcal{M}, A_k \models \phi$ and that $F(A_k)$ occurs in the transition sequence.
- $\mathcal{M}, A_1 \models \mathbf{A}^\Sigma[\phi_1 \mathbf{U} \phi_2]$ iff there exists some $i \geq 0$ for each transition $F(A_1) \hookrightarrow^{A_{j1}} \cdots \hookrightarrow^{A_{ji}} F(A_{i+1})(\hookrightarrow^{A_x} \cdots)$ such that $\mathcal{M}, A_{i+1} \models \phi_2$ and that $\mathcal{M}, A_k \models \phi_1$ for all $k < i+1$.
  $\mathcal{M}, A_1 \models \mathbf{E}^\Sigma[\phi_1 \mathbf{U} \phi_2]$ iff there exists some $i \geq 0$ and a transition $F(A_1) \hookrightarrow^{A_{j1}} \cdots \hookrightarrow^{A_{ji}} F(A_{i+1})(\hookrightarrow^{A_x} \cdots)$ such that $\mathcal{M}, A_{i+1} \models \phi_2$ and that $\mathcal{M}, A_k \models \phi_1$ for all $k < i+1$.

We say that ϕ is true (in δ) iff $(\delta, L), A_0 \models \phi$.

While this logic appears more graded than CTL for the superscripts Σ, there is an obvious encoding of it into the standard CTL with an additional atomic predicate in the grammar of ϕ that judges whether an argument is visible. That

---

[2] The liberty of allowing arguments into $\mathcal{M}$ causes no confusion, let alone issues. If one is so inclined, he/she may choose to consider that components of δ that appear in $\mathcal{M}$ are semantic counterparts of those that appear in the syntax of CTL with one-to-one correspondence between them.

is, we can for example replace $\mathbf{EX}^{\{A_x\}}\phi$ with $\mathbf{EX}(\phi_1 \wedge \phi) \vee \cdots \vee \mathbf{EX}(\phi_n \wedge \phi)$ if we can express by the expression that, for any transition $F(A_c) \hookrightarrow^{A_x} F(A_d)$ such that $F(A_c)$ is the state with respect to which the expression is evaluated, there exists some $1 \leq i \leq n$ such that ϕ_i holds good just when all and only members of A_d are visible, and that for every ϕ_i, $1 \leq i \leq n$, there exists some A_d such that $F(A_c) \hookrightarrow^{A_x} F(A_d)$ and that ϕ_i holds good just when all members of A_d are visible, which confirms that our logic is effectively CTL. It is straightforward to see the following well-known equivalences in our semantics:

Proposition 3 (De Morgan's Laws and Expansion Laws). $\neg \mathbf{AF}^{\Sigma}\phi \equiv \mathbf{EG}^{\Sigma}\neg\phi$, $\neg \mathbf{EF}^{\Sigma}\phi \equiv \mathbf{AG}^{\Sigma}\neg\phi$, $\neg \mathbf{AX}^{\Sigma}\phi \equiv \mathbf{EG}^{\Sigma}\neg\phi$ *(De Morgan's Laws)*, $\mathbf{AG}^{\Sigma}\phi \equiv \phi \wedge \mathbf{AX}^{\Sigma}\mathbf{AG}^{\Sigma}\phi$, $\mathbf{EG}^{\Sigma}\phi \equiv \phi \wedge \mathbf{EX}^{\Sigma}\mathbf{EG}^{\Sigma}\phi$, $\mathbf{AF}^{\Sigma}\phi \equiv \phi \vee \mathbf{AX}^{\Sigma}\mathbf{AF}^{\Sigma}\phi$, $\mathbf{EF}^{\Sigma}\phi \equiv \phi \vee \mathbf{EX}^{\Sigma}\mathbf{EF}^{\Sigma}\phi$, $\mathbf{A}^{\Sigma}[\phi_1 U \phi_2] \equiv \phi_2 \vee (\phi_1 \wedge \mathbf{AX}^{\Sigma}\mathbf{A}^{\Sigma}[\phi_1 U \phi_2])$, $\mathbf{E}^{\Sigma}[\phi_1 U \phi_2] \equiv \phi_2 \vee (\phi_1 \wedge \mathbf{EX}^{\Sigma}\mathbf{E}^{\Sigma}[\phi_1 U \phi_2])$ *(Expansion Laws)*.

Proof is by induction on the size (the number of symbols) of ϕ for each Σ. Other well-known general properties of CTL immediately hold true, such as existence of a sound and complete axiomatisation of CTL. Atomic entailments are decidable for any APA δ (with a finite number of arguments), since each state is a Dung argumentation framework.

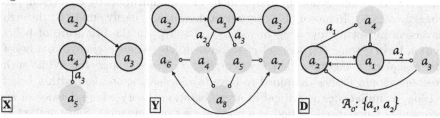

Example 4. For Elma example (re-listed above in Figure $\boxed{\text{X}}$ that marks initially visible arguments), recall $A_0 = \{a_2, a_3, a_4\}$. Denote the argumentation by δ. By stating that $(a_5 \dot{\in}_\delta A_1 \wedge \mathbf{EF}^{\{A_1\}} P_\delta(\mathsf{ad}, A_1)) \supset \neg a_2 \dot{\in}_\delta A_1$ is true, we have stated that if a_2 is a member of a reference set A_1, and if the same reference set is used for all transitions, A_1 that contains a_5 is never admissible.

For Alice example (re-listed above in Figure $\boxed{\text{Y}}$ that marks initially visible arguments), recall $A_0 = \{a_1, a_2, a_3\}$. Denote the argumentation by δ. By stating that $(\mathbf{AF}^{\{A_1\}}\mathbf{AG}^{\{A_1\}} P_\delta(\mathsf{co}, A_1)) \supset a_8 \dot{\in}_\delta A_1$ is true, we have stated that if a set of arguments A_1 is such that, in all branches with A_1 as the reference set, it will be permanently complete from some state on, then it must include a_8.

For the example in Figure $\boxed{\text{D}}$ (re-listed above), recall $A_0 = \{a_1, a_2\}$ within $A = \{a_1, a_2, a_3, a_4\}$. Assume: $\mathsf{Exct}(\{a_{i_1}, \ldots, a_{i_n}\}, A_2) \equiv ((a_{i_1} \dot{\in}_\delta A_2) \wedge \cdots \wedge (a_{i_n} \dot{\in}_\delta A_2)) \wedge (\neg a_{i_{n+1}} \dot{\in}_\delta A_2 \wedge \cdots \wedge \neg a_{i_m} \dot{\in}_\delta A_2)$ where $A_2 \subseteq A$ and where $\{a_{i_1}, \ldots, a_{i_m}\} \equiv \{a_1, \ldots, a_4\} \equiv A$. Assume also that $\Sigma = 2^A$.

$$\text{By } \mathsf{Exct}(\{a_2, a_3, a_4\}, A_4) \wedge \mathsf{Exct}(\{a_1, a_3, a_4\}, A_5) \wedge$$
$$\mathbf{AG}^{\Sigma}((P_\delta(\mathsf{ad}, A_4) \supset \mathbf{EF}^{\Sigma}(P_\delta(\mathsf{ad}, A_5) \wedge \neg P_\delta(\mathsf{ad}, A_4)))$$
$$\wedge (P_\delta(\mathsf{ad}, A_5) \supset \mathbf{EF}^{\Sigma}(P_\delta(\mathsf{ad}, A_4) \wedge \neg P_\delta(\mathsf{ad}, A_5)))),$$

We have described that when either of A_4 and A_5 is admissible in some reachable state, there is always a branch where the other becomes admissible and that becomes not admissible in some future state, that is to say, there can be an infinite number of oscillation among states that admit different sets of arguments.

Straightforwardly:

Proposition 4 (Non-monotonicity of admissibility). *Suppose APA* $(A, R, R_\mathbf{p}, A_0, \hookrightarrow)$, *and suppose that a set of arguments* $A_x \subseteq A$ *is admissible in a reachable state* $F(A_1)$. *It is not necessary that* A_x *be admissible in a state* $F(A_2)$ *which satisfies* $F(A_1) \hookrightarrow^{A_y} F(A_2)$ *for some* $A_y \subseteq A$.

4   Discussion and Related Work

For dynamics of argumentation, adaptation of the AGM-like belief revision [1, 28] to argumentation systems [9, 15, 16, 18, 19, 34] is popularly studied. In these studies, the focus is on restricting the class of resulting argumentation frameworks (post-states) by means of postulates for a given argumentation-framework (pre-state) and some action (add/remove an argument/attack/argumentation framework). In APA, generation by inducement and modification by conversion are primarily defined. Removal of an argument, however, is easily emulated through conversion by setting $a_1 = a_3$ in $(a_1, a_2, a_3) \in R_\mathbf{p}$. In the literature of belief revision theory, some consider selective revision [26], where a change to a belief set takes place *if the input that is attempting a change is accepted*. While such screening should be best assumed to have taken place beforehand within belief revision, a similar idea is critical in argumentation theory where defence of an argument is foundationally tied to a reference set of arguments. Since any set of arguments may be chosen to be a reference set, and since which arguments in the set are visible non-monotonically changes, it is not feasible to assume some persuasion acts successful and others not in all states.

Coordination of dynamics and statics is somehow under-investigated in the literature of argumentation theory. A kind for coalition profitability and formability semantics with what are termed conflict-eliminable sets of arguments [4] focuses on the interaction between sets of arguments before and after coalition formation. Doutre *et al.* show the use of propositional dynamic logic in program analysis/verification for encoding Dung theory and addition/removal of attacks and arguments [20, 21]. The logic comes with sequential operations, non-deterministic operations, tests. In comparison to their logic, our theory is an extension to Dung theory, which already provides a sound theoretical judgement for defence against attacks, which we extended also to persuasion acts. As far as we could fathom, such interaction between attack, persuasion, and defence has not been primarily studied in the literature. For another, a Dung-based theory has a certain appeal as a higher-level specification language. Consider the argumentation in Figure $\boxed{D}$. APA requires 4 arguments, its subset as the set of initially visible arguments, 2 inducements and 2 conversions for specification of the dynamic argumentation. By contrast, specification of a dynamic argumentation in the dynamic logic can be exponentially long as the number of non-deterministic branches increases; for the same dynamic argumentation in Figure $\boxed{D}$, it requires descriptions of all possible reachable states and transitions among them for the specification. We might take an analogy in chess here. While the number of branches in a chess game is astronomical, the game itself is specifiable in a small set of rules. For yet another, the dynamic logic facilitates dynamic changes to attacks in addition to arguments, which we did not study in this paper. The reason is mostly due to such consideration bound to lead to recursive persuasions and attacks (for recursive attacks/supports, see [3,6,8,14,24]) in our theory, which we believe will be better detailed in a separate paper for more formal interest.

Argumentation theories that accommodate aspects of persuasion have been noted across several papers. In [10], argumentation frameworks were augmented with values that controlled defeat judgement. Compared to their work, persuasion acts in APA are stand-alone relations which may be 'executed' non-deterministically and concurrently, may irreversibly modify visible arguments, and may produce loops. In most of argumentation papers on this topic, persuasion or negotiation is treated in a dialogue game [2,11,12,23,25,27,30–33] where proponent(s) and opponent(s) take turns to modify an argumentation framework. APA does not assume the turn-based nature. In real-time rhetoric argumentation, as also frequently seen in social forums, more than one dialogue or more than one line of persuasive act may be running simultaneously. In this work, we were more interested in modelling those situations. The various admissibility judgement enabled by (effectively) CTL (and other branching-time logic) should provide means of describing many types of argumentation queries.

Studies on temporal arguments include [5,7,13,29]. Most of these actually consider arguments that may be time-dependent. APA frameworks keep arguments abstract, and observe temporal progress through actual execution of persuasive acts. We use temporal logic for describing admissibilities rather than arguments (recall that $P_\delta(\omega, A_x)$ is a formula on admissibility, not an argument). In timed argumentation frameworks [13], arguments are available for set periods of time. Combined with APA, it should become possible to explain how and why arguments are available for the durations of time in the frameworks, the explanatory power incidentally having been the strength of argumentation theory.

5   Conclusion

We have shown a direction for abstract argumentation with dynamic operators extending Dung's theory. We set forth important properties and notions, and showed embedding of state-wise admissibility into CTL for various admissibilities across transitions. Many technical developments are expected to follow. Our contribution is promising for bringing together knowledge of abstract argumentation in AI and techniques and issues of concurrency in program analysis in a very near future. Cross-studies in the two domains are highly expected. Study in concurrent aspects of argumentation is important for evaluation of opinion transitions, which influences development of more effective sales approaches and better marketing in business, and consensus control tactics in politics. Harnessing our study with probabilistic methods is likely to form exciting research. For future work, we plan to: take into account nuances of persuasive acts such as pseudo-logic, scapegoating, threat, and half-truths [17]; and extend APA with multi-reference sets.

Acknowledgements. We thank anonymous reviewers for helpful comments. There was one suggestion concerning terms: to say to "convince" instead of "actively persuade" or "convert". We seriously contemplated the suggested modification, and only in the end chose to leave the text as it was.

References

1. Alchourrón, C.E., Makinson, D.: On the logic of theory change: safe contraction. Stud. Log. **44**, 405–422 (1985)
2. Amgoud, L., Parsons, S., Maudet, N.: Arguments, dialogue and negotiation. In: ECAI, pp. 338–342 (2000)
3. Arisaka, R., Satoh, K.: Voluntary manslaughter? A case study with meta-argumentation with supports. In: Kurahashi, S., Ohta, Y., Arai, S., Satoh, K., Bekki, D. (eds.) JSAI-isAI 2016. LNCS, vol. 10247, pp. 241–252. Springer, Cham (2017). https://doi.org/10.1007/978-3-319-61572-1_16
4. Arisaka, R., Satoh, K.: Coalition formability semantics with conflict-eliminable sets of arguments. In: AAMAS, pp. 1469–1471 (2017)
5. Augusto, J.C., Simari, G.R.: A temporal argumentative system. AI Commun. **12**(4), 237–257 (1999)
6. Baroni, P., Cerutti, F., Giacomin, M., Guida, G.: AFRA: argumentation framework with recursive attacks. Int. J. Approx. Reason. **52**, 19–37 (2011)
7. Barringer, H., Gabbay, D.M.: Modal and temporal argumentation networks. In: Manna, Z., Peled, D.A. (eds.) Time for Verification. LNCS, vol. 6200, pp. 1–25. Springer, Heidelberg (2010). https://doi.org/10.1007/978-3-642-13754-9_1
8. Barringer, H., Gabbay, D.M., Woods, J.: Temporal dynamics of argumentation networks. In: Mechanizing Mathematical Reasoning, pp. 59–98 (2005)
9. Baumann, R., Brewka, G.: AGM meets abstract argumentation: expansion and revision for dung frameworks. In: IJCAI, pp. 2734–2740 (2015)
10. Bench-Capon, T.J.M.: Persuasion in practial argument using value-based argumentation frameworks. J. Log. Comput. **13**(3), 429–448 (2003)
11. Bench-Capon, T.J.M., Doutre, S., Dunne, P.E.: Audiences in argumentation frameworks. Artif. Intell. **171**(1), 42–71 (2007)
12. Black, E., Hunter, A.: Reasons and options for updating an opponent model in persuasion dialogues. In: Black, E., Modgil, S., Oren, N. (eds.) TAFA 2015. LNCS, vol. 9524, pp. 21–39. Springer, Cham (2015). https://doi.org/10.1007/978-3-319-28460-6_2
13. Budán, M.C.D., Cobo, M.L., Martinez, D.C., Simari, G.R.: Bipolarity in temporal argumentation frameworks. Int. J. Approx. Reason. **84**, 1–22 (2017)
14. Cayrol, C., Fandinno, J., Fariñas del Cerro, L., Lagasquie-Schiex, M.-C.: Argumentation frameworks with recursive attacks and evidence-based supports. In: Ferrarotti, F., Woltran, S. (eds.) FoIKS 2018. LNCS, vol. 10833, pp. 150–169. Springer, Cham (2018). https://doi.org/10.1007/978-3-319-90050-6_9

15. Cayrol, C., de Saint-Cyr, F.D., Lagasquie-Schiex, M.-C.: Change in abstract argumentation frameworks: adding an argument. J. Artif. Intell. Res. **38**, 49–84 (2010)
16. Cayrol, C., Lagasquie-Schiex, M.-C.: Bipolarity in argumentation graphs: towards a better understanding. In: Benferhat, S., Grant, J. (eds.) SUM 2011. LNCS, vol. 6929, pp. 137–148. Springer, Heidelberg (2011). https://doi.org/10.1007/978-3-642-23963-2_12
17. Chomsky, N.: Hopes and Prospects. Haymarket Books, Chicago (2010)
18. Coste-Marquis, S., Konieczny, S., Mailly, J.-G., Marquis, P.: A translation-based approach for revision of argumentation frameworks. In: Fermé, E., Leite, J. (eds.) JELIA 2014. LNCS, vol. 8761, pp. 397–411. Springer, Cham (2014). https://doi.org/10.1007/978-3-319-11558-0_28
19. Coste-Marquis, S., Konieczny, S., Mailly, J.-G., Marquis, P.: On the revision of argumentation systems: minimal change of arguments statuses. In: KR (2014)
20. Doutre, S., Herzig, A., Perrussel, L.: A dynamic logic framework for abstract argumentation. In: KR (2014)
21. Doutre, S., Maffre, F., McBurney, P.: A dynamic logic framework for abstract argumentation: adding and removing arguments. In: Benferhat, S., Tabia, K., Ali, M. (eds.) IEA/AIE 2017. LNCS, vol. 10351, pp. 295–305. Springer, Cham (2017). https://doi.org/10.1007/978-3-319-60045-1_32
22. Dung, P.M.: On the acceptability of arguments and its fundamental role in non-monotonic reasoning, logic programming, and n-person games. Artif. Intell. **77**(2), 321–357 (1995)
23. Fan, X., Toni, F.: Assumption-based argumentation dialogues. In: IJCAI, pp. 198–203 (2011)
24. Gabbay, D.M.: Semantics for higher level attacks in extended argumentation frames part 1: overview. Stud. Log. **93**(2–3), 357–381 (2009)
25. Hadjinikolis, C., Siantos, Y., Modgil, S., Black, E., McBurney, P.: Opponent modelling in persuasion dialogues. In: IJCAI, pp. 164–170 (2013)
26. Hansson, S.O., Fermé, E.L., Cantwell, J., Falappa, M.A.: Credibility limited revision. J. Symb. Log. **66**(4), 1581–1596 (2001)
27. Hunter, A.: Modelling the persuadee in asymmetric argumentation dialogues for persuasion. In: IJCAI, pp. 3055–3061 (2015)
28. Katsuno, H., Mendelzon, A.O.: On the difference between updating a knowledge base and revising it. In: Belief Revision. Cambridge University Press (1992)
29. Mann, N., Hunter, A.: Argumentation using temporal knowledge. In: COMMA, pp. 204–215 (2008)
30. McBurney, P., van Eijk, R., Parsons, S., Amgoud, L.: A dialogue-game protocol for agent purchase negotiations. J. Auton. Agents Multi-Agent Syst. **7**, 235–273 (2003)
31. Prakken, H.: Coherence and flexibility in dialogue games for argumentation. J. Log. Comput. **15**(6), 1009–1040 (2005)
32. Prakken, H.: Formal systems for persuasion dialogue. Knowl. Eng. Rev. **21**(2), 163–188 (2006)
33. Rienstra, T., Thimm, M., Oren, N.: Opponent models with uncertainty for strategic argumentation. In: IJCAI, pp. 332–338 (2013)
34. Rotstein, N., Moguillansky, M.O., García, A.J., Simari, G.R.: An abstract argumentation framework for handling dynamics. In: Proceedings of the Argument, Dialogue and Decision Workshop in NMR 2008, pp. 131–139 (2008)

On Generating Explainable Plans with Assumption-Based Argumentation

Xiuyi Fan[✉]

Swansea University, Swansea, UK
xiuyi.fan@swansea.ac.uk

Abstract. Planning is a classic problem in Artificial Intelligence (AI). Recently, the need for creating "Explainable AI" has been recognised and voiced by many researchers. Leveraging on the strength of argumentation, in particular, the Related Admissible semantics for generating explanations, this work makes an initial step towards "explainable planning". We illustrate (1) how plan generation can be equated to constructing acceptable arguments and (2) how explanations for both "planning solutions" as well as "invalid plans" can be obtained by extracting information from an arguing process. We present an argumentation-based model which takes plans written in a STRIPS-like language as its inputs and returns Assumption-based Argumentation (ABA) frameworks as its outputs. The presented plan construction mapping is both sound and complete in that the planning problem has a solution if and only if its corresponding ABA framework has a set of Related Admissible arguments with the planning goal as its topic. We use the classic Tower of Hanoi puzzle as our case study and demonstrate how ABA can be used to solve this planning puzzle while giving explanations.

1 Introduction

Planning, known as the "reasoning side of acting" [17], has been long studied in artificial intelligence and seen its applications in many areas form robot navigation to manufacturing scheduling. Much research has been devoted to the development of expressive planning languages and efficient planners, e.g. [18,20]. Recently, we see that the need for developing transparent and explainable autonomous intelligent systems has been recognised and voiced by many researchers [6,21]. At the same time, argumentation [15], a knowledge representation and modelling technique in rapid development, for reasoning with incomplete and inconsistent information with its ability in explaining the results and processes of computation, has seen its use in many applications.

In this work, we present a study on modelling and solving planning problems with Assumption-based Argumentation (ABA) [5]. We establish the correspondence between ABA arguments and plans such that a planning problem has a solution (plan) if and only if the argument representing this solution is acceptable. On the front of plan explanation, we observe that a plan solution (1) meets

© Springer Nature Switzerland AG 2018
T. Miller et al. (Eds.): PRIMA 2018, LNAI 11224, pp. 344–361, 2018.
https://doi.org/10.1007/978-3-030-03098-8_21

all of its goals while (2) satisfying all pre-conditions of its actions. Thus, explanations for "successful" plans are focused on justifying these two criteria; and explanations for "failed" plans are focused on identifying unmet pre-conditions. The tasks of generating plans and explanations are unified under the computation of Related Admissible set of arguments using *dispute trees* [7].

To make our argumentation-based planning study concrete, we take a version of a classic planning puzzle, *Tower of Hanoi*, as a case study example. This example, though conceptually simple, exhibits typical planning characteristics and challenges. Roughly speaking, a *plan* takes a world containing multiple objects in the world's *initial state* to its *goal state* via a sequence of *actions* in discrete time steps. In each time step, multiple actions, subject to various *preconditions*, are possible to be performed. A search for suitable actions is needed to find solutions. By developing argumentation-based approaches to Tower of Hanoi, we establish the feasibility of using argumentation to plan and reveal the strength and potential future development for argumentation-based planning.

ABA is selected as the modelling and computation vehicle as it is a versatile structured argumentation framework with many successful applications, although similar results can be obtained with other structured argumentation frameworks, including ASPIC+ and DeLP [3]. Roughly, ABA assumptions represent actions (in the sense that we assume actions are valid unless its preconditions are not met), invalidity of world states (in the sense that we assume the environment is not in a specific state unless we prove it is in). Acceptable arguments correspond to planning solutions. We use well-defined argumentation semantics with sound computation tools to generate plans and explanations.

2 Background

Assumption-based Argumentation (ABA) frameworks are tuples $\langle \mathcal{L}, \mathcal{R}, \mathcal{A}, \mathcal{C} \rangle$, where

- $\langle \mathcal{L}, \mathcal{R} \rangle$ is a deductive system, with $\mathcal{L}$ the *language* and $\mathcal{R}$ a set of *rules* of the form $s_0 \leftarrow s_1, \ldots, s_m (m \geq 0, s_i \in \mathcal{L})$;
- $\mathcal{A} \subseteq \mathcal{L}$ is a (non-empty) set of *assumptions*;
- $\mathcal{C}$ is a total mapping from $\mathcal{A}$ into $2^{\mathcal{L}} - \{\{\}\}$, where each $s \in \mathcal{C}(a)$ is a *contrary* of a, for $a \in \mathcal{A}$.

Given $\rho = s_0 \leftarrow s_1, \ldots, s_m$, s_0 is referred to as the *head* and $s_1, \ldots, s_m$ as the *body*.

Arguments are deductions of claims using rules and supported by sets of assumptions; *Attacks* are *targeted* at the assumptions in the support of arguments:

- *an argument for (claim) $s \in \mathcal{L}$ supported by $\Delta \subseteq \mathcal{A}$ (denoted $\Delta \vdash s$) is a* finite tree with nodes labelled by sentences in $\mathcal{L}$ or by τ[1], the root labelled by s, leaves either τ or assumptions in Δ, and non-leaves s' with, as children, the elements of the body of some rule ρ with head s';

---

[1] $\tau \notin \mathcal{L}$ represents "true" and stands for the empty body of rules.

– *an argument* $A = \Delta_1 \vdash s_1$ attacks an argument $\Delta_2 \vdash s_2$ if and only if s_1 is a contrary of some assumption α in Δ_2, and we say A *targets at* α.

A *set of arguments As is admissible* if and only if As is *conflict-free* (i.e. no argument in As attacks any argument in As) and all arguments attacking some argument in As are counter attacked by arguments in As; an *argument is admissible* if and only if it belongs to an admissible set of arguments.

We will use the notion of *Related Admissible* and *Argument Explanation* introduced in [8] for some of our results, defined as follows. Given an ABA framework $F = \langle \mathcal{L}, \mathcal{R}, \mathcal{A}, \mathcal{C} \rangle$, $\mathbb{AG}^F$ denotes the set of all arguments in F. Let $X, Y \in \mathbb{AG}^F$. X *defends* Y if and only if: (1) $X = Y$; or (2) $\exists Z \in \mathbb{AG}^F$, such that X attacks Z and Z attacks Y; or (3) $\exists Z \in \mathbb{AG}^F$, such that X defends Z and Z defends Y. $S \subseteq \mathbb{AG}^F$ *defends* $X \in \mathbb{AG}^F$ if and only if $\forall Y \in S$: Y defends X. Let $s \in \mathcal{L}$ and $A, B \in \mathbb{AG}^F$, A *defends* s if and only if s is the claim of B and A defends B.

A *set of arguments As is Related Admissible* if and only if: (1) As is admissible, (2) there exists a *topic* sentence χ (of As), χ is the claim of some argument in As, such that for all $B \in As$, B defends χ. As is an *explanation* of χ.

We will use the *abstract dispute trees* of [7] to compute explanations for our plans. An *abstract dispute tree* for an argument A is a (possibly infinite) tree $\mathcal{T}^a$ such that:[2]

1. every node of $\mathcal{T}^a$ holds an argument B and is labelled by either *proponent* (**P**) or *opponent* (**O**), but not both, denoted by $L : B$, for $L \in \{P, O\}$; (a node labelled by **P**/**O** is called a **P**/**O** node, respectively);
2. the root of $\mathcal{T}^a$ is a **P** node holding A;
3. for every **P** node N holding an argument B, and for every argument C that attacks B, there exists a child of N, which is an **O** node holding C;
4. for every **O** node N holding an argument B, there exists *at most*[3] one child of N which is a **P** node holding an argument which targets some assumption α in the support of B; if N has a child attacking α, then α is said to be the *culprit* in B;
5. there are no other nodes in $\mathcal{T}^a$ except those given by 1–4 above.

The set of all assumptions in (the support of arguments held by) the **P** nodes in $\mathcal{T}^a$ is called the *defence set* of $\mathcal{T}^a$. In an abstract dispute tree $\mathcal{T}^a$, a **P** node N is *defeated* if and only if N is the root of a sub-tree in $\mathcal{T}^a$ such that the defence set of the sub-tree is not admissible. A *winning attacker* N' of N is a child node of N such that either (1) there is an **O** leaf node in the tree rooted at N' or (2) there is an argument held at both a **P** node in the tree rooted at N' and an **O** node in $\mathcal{T}^a$. Abstract dispute trees can be used to compute (related) admissibility semantics:

---

[2] Here, a stands for 'abstract'. Also, 'proponent' and 'opponent' should be seen as roles/fictitious participants in a debate rather than actual agents.

[3] In the original definition of abstract dispute tree [7], every **O** node is required to have *exactly* one child. We incorporate this requirement into the definition of *admissible* dispute tree given later, so that our notion of admissible abstract dispute tree and the admissible abstract dispute trees of [7] coincide.

- Let an abstract dispute tree $\mathcal{T}^a$ be *admissible* if and only if each **O** node has *exactly* one child and no culprit in the argument of an **O** node in $\mathcal{T}^a$ belongs to the defence set of $\mathcal{T}^a$. If a dispute tree is not admissible, it is *non-admissible*.
- The defence set of an admissible abstract dispute tree is admissible (Theorem 5.1 in [7]), and thus the root node of an admissible dispute tree is admissible.
- The defence set of an admissible abstract dispute tree is Related Admissible (Theorem 1 in [8]) with the claim of the argument held by the root of the tree being the topic sentence (Theorem 5 in [8]).

3   Planning Preliminaries

We consider an instance of the standard, also the most widely used, planning representation, STRIPS, as given in [17]. A planning problem $\mathcal{P}$ is a tuple $\mathcal{P} = (\Sigma, s_0, S_g)$; $\Sigma = (S, A, \gamma)$ is the planning domain, S the set of states, A the set of actions, γ the deterministic transition function, s_0 the initial state, and S_g the set of goal states. Each state in S is described by a set of predicates and each predicate is either a *flexible relation* or a *rigid relation*. The transition function γ is specified through a set of *planning operators*, each representing an *action*. A planning operator is given by *name*, *precond* and *effects*, where name is syntactically a predicate, precond and effects are sets of predicates, describing the pre-conditions and the effects of the action, respectively. A plan is a sequence of actions; and a solution to a planning problem is a plan from the initial state to the goal state.

We use the following classic *Tower of Hanoi* example to illustrate.

Example 1. As in a classic Tower of Hanoi game, we have three rods, r_1, r_2, r_3. To simplify the example, we use only two disks d_1 and d_2. The problem states S is described by two flexible relations `clear` and `on`, as well as a rigid relation `smaller`. The initial and the goal states are shown in Fig. 1. Specifically, the initial state s_0 is described with the following predicates:

$\text{clear}(r_2)$ $\quad\quad$ $\text{clear}(r_3)$ $\quad\quad$ $\text{clear}(d_1)$ $\quad\quad$ $\text{on}(d_1, d_2)$
$\text{on}(d_2, r_1)$ $\quad\quad$ $\text{smaller}(d_1, r_1)$ $\text{smaller}(d_1, r_2)$ $\text{smaller}(d_1, r_3)$
$\text{smaller}(d_2, r_1)$ $\text{smaller}(d_2, r_2)$ $\text{smaller}(d_2, r_3)$ $\text{smaller}(d_1, d_2)$

The goal state s_g is described by: $\text{on}(d_1, d_2)$ $\text{on}(d_2, r_3)$.

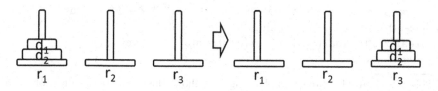

Fig. 1. A Tower of Hanoi game with two discs d_1 and d_2 and three rods r_1, r_2 and r_3. The initial state is shown on the left hand side and the goal state is shown on the right hand side.

There is a single planning operator:

> move(D, A, B)
>> precond : smaller(D, B), on(D, A), clear(D), clear(B)
>> effects : clear(A), on(D, B), ¬on(D, A), ¬clear(B)

The action sequence $(\text{move}(d_1, r_2), \text{move}(d_2, r_3), \text{move}(d_1, d_2))$ is a solution.

To model planning with argumentation, we take the *bounded planning approach* as in SAT based planners [17]. Namely, we focus on finding plans of some known length n for some fixed n. Each $i, 0 \leq i \leq n$ is a *step* of the planning problem, and *for each step k there is one and only one action taking place.*[4] Specifically,

- we denote each predicate with k variables representing a flexible relation as a new predicate with $k + 1$ variables, where the last variable is the step;
- we leave all predicates representing rigid relations unchanged;
- for each action taking place at step k, its pre-conditions are composed of predicates representing rigid relations and predicates representing flexible relations with their last variables k; effects of this action are composed of predicates representing flexible relations with their last variables $k + 1$.

Effectively, a bounded planning problem can be described with a tuple $\langle \mathbb{A}, s_0, s_g, \mathbb{F}, \mathbb{R}, \mathbb{K} \rangle$, a set of actions $\mathbb{A}$, the initial state s_0, the goal state s_g, a set of flexible relation $\mathbb{F}$, a set of rigid relation $\mathbb{R}$ and the step bound $\mathbb{K}$. The goal state is a set of *goals* denoted by flexible relations with their last variable (the step variable) specified as $\mathbb{K}$.

Given a plan $(m_1, \ldots, m_n)$ in a bounded planning problem, we say that a flexible relation $\text{FR}(\overline{A}, K)$[5] *holds* at step k if and only if either (1) $\text{FR}(\overline{A}, 0) \in s_0$, or (2) $\text{FR}(\overline{A}, i)$ in the effects of some action $m_i, i \leq k$ and $\neg\text{FR}(\overline{A}, j)$ is not in the effects of any action m_j for $i < j \leq k$.

For each action m in a plan P, we use $S(m)$ to denote the step of action m in P.

Example 2. (Example 1 continued.) With step introduced, the three predicates are:

clear(X, K), on(X, Y, K), smaller(X, Y).

The planning operator is:

> move(D, A, B, K)
>> precond : smaller(D, B), on(D, A, K), clear(D, K), clear(B, K)
>> effects : clear(A, K + 1), on(D, B, K + 1), ¬on(D, A, K + 1), ¬clear(B, K + 1)

Suppose that $\mathbb{K} = 3$, a plan taking the initial state

> clear(r_2, 0) clear(r_3, 0) clear(d_1, 0) on(d_1, d_2, 0) on(d_2, d_1, 0)

to the goal state

---

[4] This is a standard approach in planning as it allows the complete specification of the planning search space. Techniques have been developed to estimate the step bound, see e.g. [17].

[5] We use the convention that the over-line on A denotes that $\overline{A}$ represents a list of variables of unspecified length. Variables without over-lines are "normal" variables.

$on(d_1, d_2, 3)$ $on(d_2, d_1, 3)$
is the sequence $(move(d_1, d_2, r_2, 0),\ move(d_2, r_1, r_3, 1),\ move(d_1, r_2, d_2, 2))$. Clearly, this plan is a solution to this planning problem.

4 Plan Explanations

Given a bounded planning problem introduced in the previous section, we make the following observation:

A plan is a solution if the following two conditions hold:

C1. All pre-conditions hold for all actions in the plan.
C2. All goals in the goal state hold at the end of plan.

Thus, to "explain" why a plan is a solution, we want to show that both (**C1**) and (**C2**) are satisfied in the sense that an "explanation" should justify that all pre-conditions and goals are met at the right steps, formally:

Definition 1. *Given a bounded planing problem $\mathcal{P}$ with a solution P. An explanation for P being a solution to $\mathcal{P}$ is the set $S = s_g \cup \{C|C$ is a precondition for an action in $P\}$ such that every predicate in S holds at its respective step.*

We illustrate Definition 1 with the following example.

Example 3 (Example 2 continued). To simplify the illustration, we let the step bound $\mathbb{K} = 2$ and the goal state $s_g = \{on(d_1, r_2, 2), on(d_2, r_3, 2)\}$. To see that $(move(d_1, r_2, 0), move(d_2, r_3, 1))$ is a solution, we observe that[6]:

- all predicates in s_g hold at step 2; and
- all pre-conditions hold for $mv(d_1, d_2, r_2, 0)$ at step 0:
  $on(d_1, d_2, 0), sm(d_1, r_2), cl(d_1, 0), cl(r_2, 0)$
- all pre-conditions hold for $mv(d_2, r_1, r_3, 1)$ at step 1:
  $on(d_2, d_1, 1), sm(d_2, r_3), cl(d_2, 1), cl(r_3, 1)$

Definition 1 specifies explanations for solutions to planning problems. On the other hand, to explain "why a plan fails to be a solution", we introduce "invalidity" of plans by identifying actions not meeting their pre-conditions or occurred at the same step as other actions. These invalid actions "explain" the invalidity of a plan.

Definition 2. *Let $P = (m_1, \ldots, m_n)$ be a plan. An action m_i is invalid in P if either one of the following two conditions holds.*

1. *There exists a pre-condition C of m_i such that C does not hold at step $S(m_i)$. In this case, C is an* explanation *for the invalidity of m_i.*
2. *There exists an action m_j in P, $j < i$, such that $S(m_i) = S(m_j)$. In this case m_j is an* explanation *for the invalidity of m_i.*

If a plan P contains no invalid action, then P is valid; otherwise, P is invalid.

---

[6] mv, cl and sm are short-hands for move, clear and smaller, respectively.

We illustrate Definition 2 with the following example.

Example 4 (Example 2 continued.) With the Tower of Hanoi game as specified, let the step bound $\mathbb{K} = 2$. Given a plan $P = (\mathtt{move}(\mathtt{d_1}, \mathtt{d_2}, \mathtt{r_3}, 0)$, $\mathtt{move}(\mathtt{d_2}, \mathtt{r_1}, \mathtt{d_1}, 1))$, the action $\mathtt{move}(\mathtt{d_2}, \mathtt{r_1}, \mathtt{d_1}, 1)$ is invalid as $\mathtt{small}(\mathtt{d_2}, \mathtt{d_1})$, a pre-condition of $\mathtt{move}(\mathtt{d_2}, \mathtt{r_1}, \mathtt{d_1}, 1)$, does not hold at step 1. (Note that since $\mathtt{small}(\mathtt{A}, \mathtt{B})$ is a rigid relation, $\mathtt{small}(\mathtt{d_2}, \mathtt{d_1})$ never holds.) We thus have $\mathtt{small}(\mathtt{d_2}, \mathtt{d_1})$ as an explanation for $\mathtt{move}(\mathtt{d_2}, \mathtt{r_1}, \mathtt{d_1}, 1)$. Since P contains an invalid action, P is invalid.

For $P' = (\mathtt{move}(\mathtt{d_1}, \mathtt{d_2}, \mathtt{r_2}, 0), \mathtt{move}(\mathtt{d_1}, \mathtt{d_2}, \mathtt{r_3}, 0))$, the action $\mathtt{move}(\mathtt{d_1}, \mathtt{d_2}, \mathtt{r_3}, 0)$ is invalid, and its explanation is $\mathtt{move}(\mathtt{d_1}, \mathtt{d_2}, \mathtt{r_2}, 0)$. This is easy to see as both actions occur at step 0. As previously, P' is invalid.

5   Planning with ABA

Thus far, we have reviewed bounded planning problems and presented several definitions of explanations. We show how ABA can be used to solve bounded planning problems in this section and how explanations can be extracted from an arguing process in the next section. To model planning with ABA, the main task is to represent bounded planning problems with ABA frameworks. Formally,

Definition 3. *Given a bounded planning problem* $\mathcal{P} = \langle \mathbb{A}, s_0, s_g, \mathbb{F}, \mathbb{R}, \mathbb{K} \rangle$, *let the following denote a generic action in* $\mathbb{A}$,

   $\mathtt{act}(\overline{\mathtt{A}}, \mathtt{K})$
      $\mathtt{precond} : \mathtt{PreC_1}(\overline{\mathtt{C_1}}, \mathtt{K}), \ldots, \mathtt{PreC_w}(\overline{\mathtt{C_w}}, \mathtt{K})$
      $\mathtt{effects} : \mathtt{Ef_1}(\overline{\mathtt{E_1}}, \mathtt{K} + 1), \ldots, \mathtt{Ef_m}(\overline{\mathtt{E_m}}, \mathtt{K} + 1),$
then the ABA framework corresponding to $\mathcal{P}$ *is* $F = \langle \mathcal{L}, \mathcal{R}, \mathcal{A}, \mathcal{C} \rangle$, *in which*[7]

- $\mathcal{R}$ *is constructed as follows.*

   1. *Let* $s_g = \{\mathtt{g_1}, \ldots, \mathtt{g_n}\}$, *insert the rule:* $\mathtt{goal} \leftarrow \mathtt{g_1}, \ldots, \mathtt{g_n}$.
   2. *For each action in* $\mathbb{A}$, *insert rules:*
      $\mathtt{aE}(\mathtt{act}, \overline{\mathtt{A}}, \mathtt{K} + 1) \leftarrow \mathtt{act}(\overline{\mathtt{A}}, \mathtt{K}); \mathtt{hasAct}(\mathtt{K}) \leftarrow \mathtt{act}(\overline{\mathtt{A}}, \mathtt{K}).$
      $\mathtt{Ef_1}(\overline{\mathtt{E_1}}, \mathtt{K}) \leftarrow \mathtt{aE}(\mathtt{act}, \overline{\mathtt{A}}, \mathtt{K}); \ldots; \mathtt{Ef_m}(\overline{\mathtt{E_m}}, \mathtt{K}) \leftarrow \mathtt{aE}(\mathtt{act}, \overline{\mathtt{A}}, \mathtt{K}).$
   3. *For each flexible relation* $\mathtt{FR}(\overline{\mathtt{A}}, \mathtt{K})$ *in* $\mathbb{F}$, *insert a rule:*
      $\mathtt{FR}(\overline{\mathtt{A}}, \mathtt{K} + 1) \leftarrow \mathtt{FR}(\overline{\mathtt{A}}, \mathtt{K}), \mathtt{hasAct}(\mathtt{K}), \mathtt{df}(\mathtt{FR}, \overline{\mathtt{A}}, \mathtt{K} + 1).$
   4. *For each rigid relation* $\mathtt{RR}(\overline{\mathtt{A}})$ *in* $\mathbb{R}$, *insert the rule:* $\mathtt{RR}(\overline{\mathtt{A}}) \leftarrow$.
   5. *Let* $s_0 = \{\mathtt{P_1}(\overline{\mathtt{I_0}}, 0), \ldots, \mathtt{P_n}(\overline{\mathtt{I_n}}, 0)\}$, *insert rules* $\mathtt{P_1}(\overline{\mathtt{I_0}}, 0) \leftarrow; \ldots;$ $\mathtt{P_n}(\overline{\mathtt{I_n}}, 0) \leftarrow$.

- $\mathcal{A}$ *is constructed as follows.*

---

[7] When defining ABA frameworks, we omit to indicate the language component, as this can be easily inferred from the other components (being the set of all sentences occurring in rules, assumptions, and contraries). Also, we use rule schemata to simplify the notation. Each rule schema represents the set of grounded rules.

1. *For each action in* $\mathbb{A}$, *insert the following assumptions:*
   $\text{act}(\overline{A}, K), \text{not\_PreC}_1(\overline{C_1}, K), \ldots, \text{not\_PreC}_w(\overline{C_w}, K)$
2. *For each flexible relation* $\text{FR}(\overline{A}, K)$ *in* $\mathbb{F}$, *insert* $\text{df}(\text{FR}, \overline{A}, K)$ *to* $\mathcal{A}$.

- $\mathcal{C}$ *is such that:*

  1. *For each action let* act' *be the name of an action in* $\mathbb{A}$, *then*
     - $\mathcal{C}(\text{act}(\overline{A}, K)) = \{\text{act}'(\overline{B}, K) \, | \text{act}' \neq \text{act} \text{ or } \overline{B} \neq \overline{A}\} \cup$
       $\{\text{not\_PreC}_1(\overline{C_1}, K), \ldots, \text{not\_PreC}_w(\overline{C_w}, K)\};$
     - *for* $i = 1, \ldots, w$, $\mathcal{C}(\text{not\_PreC}_i(\overline{C_i}, K)) = \{\text{PreC}_i(\overline{C_i}, K)\}$.
  2. $\mathcal{C}(\text{df}(\text{FR}, \overline{A}, K)) = \{\neg\text{FR}(\overline{A}, K)\}$.

In Definition 3, reaching the goal state s_g is modelled with the rule

$$\text{goal} \leftarrow g_1, \ldots, g_n$$

such that to reach the goal state, we need to prove each of its goals in the goal set. Then, for each action $\text{act}(\overline{A}, K)$, taking a list of variables $\overline{A}$ at step K, we use the rule

$$\text{aE}(\text{act}, \overline{A}, K+1) \leftarrow \text{act}(\overline{A}, K);$$

to describe that effects of act can be realised by performing act. Note that act has step variable K whereas aE has step variable $K + 1$, indicating the advance in time. Rule

$$\text{hasAct}(K) \leftarrow \text{act}(\overline{A}, K)$$

states that there is an action taking place at step K if there is an action act at K. Rules

$$\text{Ef}_1(\overline{E_1}, K) \leftarrow \text{aE}(\text{act}, \overline{A}, K); \ldots; \text{Ef}_m(\overline{E_m}, K) \leftarrow \text{aE}(\text{act}, \overline{A}, K)$$

describe each and every predicate listed as an effect of act can be derived from aE, at the same time step as aE. Rule

$$\text{FR}(\overline{A}, K+1) \leftarrow \text{FR}(\overline{A}, K), \text{hasAct}(K), \text{df}(\text{FR}, \overline{A}, K+1)$$

describes that for every predicate FR describing a flexible relation, it is the case that if $\text{FR}(\overline{A})$ holds at step K, and there is some action taking place at step K, then it is assumed that, $\text{FR}(\overline{A})$ holds at step $K + 1$. The assumption $\text{df}(\text{FR}, \overline{A}, K+1)$ states that, by default, FR can be carried forward from K to $K + 1$. $\text{hasAct}(K)$ is introduced in the body of the rule to enforce that at least one action has taken place during this step. Rule

$$\text{RR}(\overline{A}) \leftarrow$$

specifies that all rigid relations RR hold at all steps. Rules

$$P_1(\overline{I_0}, 0) \leftarrow; \ldots; P_n(\overline{I_n}, 0) \leftarrow.$$

specify that all predicates in the initial state s_0 hold at step 0.

Assumptions and contraries are such that:

- all actions are assumptions with contraries being either
    1. any other action at the same step or
    2. failure of meeting pre-conditions of the action.

    We enforce that any two different actions are in conflict at the same step; and if any pre-condition does not meet for an action, then the action cannot be performed.
- $\mathcal{C}(\mathtt{not\_PreC_i}(\overline{C_i}, K)) = \{\mathtt{PreC_i}(\overline{C_i}, K)\}$ specifies that the contrary of not meeting a pre-condition is meeting it.
- $\mathcal{C}(\mathtt{df}(\mathtt{FR}, \overline{A}, K)) = \{\neg\mathtt{FR}(\overline{A}, K)\}$ specifies that the assumption $\mathtt{df}(\mathtt{FR}, \overline{A}, K)$ does not hold if it can be shown explicitly that $\mathtt{FR}(\overline{A}, K)$ does not hold, at step K.

Example 5 (Example 2 continued.) Let the step bound $\mathbb{K} = 3$. The ABA framework corresponding to this planning problem is $\langle \mathcal{L}, \mathcal{R}, \mathcal{A}, \mathcal{C} \rangle$, given as follows.[8]

- $\mathcal{R}$ is composed of the following rules.

    $\mathtt{goal} \leftarrow \mathtt{on}(d_1, d_2, 3), \mathtt{on}(d_2, r_3, 3);$

    $\mathtt{hA}(K) \leftarrow \mathtt{mv}(D, A, B, K);$ $\qquad$ $\mathtt{aE}(\mathtt{mv}, D, A, B, K) \leftarrow \mathtt{mv}(D, A, B, K);$

    $\mathtt{cl}(A, K+1) \leftarrow \mathtt{aE}(\mathtt{mv}, D, A, B, K);$ $\quad$ $\neg\mathtt{cl}(B, K+1) \leftarrow \mathtt{aE}(\mathtt{mv}, D, A, B, K);$

    $\mathtt{on}(D, B, K+1) \leftarrow \mathtt{aE}(\mathtt{mv}, D, A, B, K);$ $\neg\mathtt{on}(D, A, K+1) \leftarrow \mathtt{aE}(\mathtt{mv}, D, A, B, K);$

    $\mathtt{cl}(A, K+1) \leftarrow \mathtt{cl}(A, K), \mathtt{hA}(K), \mathtt{df}(\mathtt{cl}, A, K+1);$ $\qquad$ $\mathtt{sm}(d_1, d_2) \leftarrow;$

    $\mathtt{on}(D, A, K+1) \leftarrow \mathtt{on}(D, A, K), \mathtt{hA}(K), \mathtt{df}(\mathtt{on}, D, F, K+1);$ $\mathtt{sm}(d_2, r_3) \leftarrow;$

    $\mathtt{sm}(d_1, r_1) \leftarrow;$ $\mathtt{sm}(d_1, r_2) \leftarrow;$ $\mathtt{sm}(d_1, r_3) \leftarrow;$ $\mathtt{sm}(d_2, r_1) \leftarrow;$ $\quad$ $\mathtt{sm}(d_2, r_2) \leftarrow;$

    $\mathtt{cl}(r_2, 0) \leftarrow;$ $\quad$ $\mathtt{cl}(r_3, 0) \leftarrow;$ $\quad$ $\mathtt{cl}(d_1, 0) \leftarrow;$ $\quad$ $\mathtt{on}(d_1, d_2, 0) \leftarrow;$ $\mathtt{on}(d_2, r_1, 0) \leftarrow;$
- $\mathcal{A}$ is composed of the following assumptions.

    $\mathtt{mv}(D, A, B, K), \mathtt{df}(\mathtt{on}, D, F, K), \mathtt{df}(\mathtt{cl}, A, K), \mathtt{not\_on}(D, F, K), \mathtt{not\_cl}(A, K)$

- $\mathcal{C}$ is such that:

    $$\mathcal{C}(\mathtt{mv}(D, A, B, K)) = \{\mathtt{not\_sm}(D, B), \mathtt{not\_on}(D, A, K), \mathtt{not\_cl}(D, K), \mathtt{not\_cl}(B, K)\}$$
    $$\cup \{\mathtt{mv}(D', A', B', K) | \mathtt{mv}(D', A', B', K) \neq \mathtt{mv}(D, A, B, K)\}$$

    $$\mathcal{C}(\mathtt{df}(\mathtt{on}, D, F, K)) = \{\neg\mathtt{on}(D, F, K)\} \mathcal{C}(\mathtt{not\_on}(D, F, K)) = \{\mathtt{on}(D, F, K)\}$$
    $$\mathcal{C}(\mathtt{df}(\mathtt{cl}, A, K)) = \{\neg\mathtt{cl}(A, K)\} \mathcal{C}(\mathtt{not\_cl}(A, K)) = \{\mathtt{cl}(A, K)\}$$

Now we are ready to present our main results on the correspondence between planning problems and ABA frameworks, with the next two theorems.

Theorem 1. *Given a bounded planning problem $\mathcal{P}$ with a solution $S = (m_1, \ldots, m_n)$, let F be the ABA framework corresponding to $\mathcal{P}$. Then, there is a related admissible set of arguments RF in F with its topic sentence $\mathtt{goal}$ such that m_i in S are assumptions supporting arguments in RF.*

Proof. (Sketch.) We need to show that (1) RF is admissible, (2) all arguments in RF defend $\mathtt{goal}$. Note that each m_i in S is of the form $\mathtt{act}(\overline{A}, i)$. To show (1), we start by observing that since S is a solution, there is an argument $A = \{\mathtt{act}(\overline{A_n}, n), \ldots\} \vdash \mathtt{goal}$ in F. Arguments attacking A are in the following three forms:

---

[8] $\mathtt{hA}$ is shorthand for $\mathtt{hasAct}$.

1. $\{\mathtt{act}_i(\overline{A'_i}, \mathtt{n})\} \vdash \mathtt{act}_i(\overline{A'_i}, \mathtt{n})$, targeting at the assumption $\mathtt{act}(\overline{A}, \mathtt{n})$, representing alternative moves one can make at step $\mathtt{n}$,
2. $\{\mathtt{not\_PreC}_i(\overline{C_i}, \mathtt{n})\} \vdash \mathtt{not\_PreC}_i(\overline{C_i}, \mathtt{n})$, also targeting at $\mathtt{act}(\overline{A}, \mathtt{n})$, representing challenges to pre-conditions of the action at $\mathtt{n}$,
3. $\Delta' \vdash \neg\mathtt{FR}(\overline{A}, \mathtt{n})$, targeting at assumptions $\mathtt{df}(\mathtt{FR}, \overline{A}, \mathtt{n})$, representing challenges to flexible relations that they may not hold from one step to the next.

Attacking arguments in form (1) can be counterattacked by arguments $\{\mathtt{act}(\overline{A}, \mathtt{n})\} \vdash \mathtt{act}(\overline{A}, \mathtt{n})$ in RF. This can be read as, *although it is possible to make some other actions at step n, we can always choose to make action* $\mathtt{act}$. Attacking arguments in form (2) can be counterattacked by arguments $\Delta^* \vdash \mathtt{PreC}_i(\overline{C_i}, \mathtt{n})$ in RF. Since S is a solution, all pre-conditions at each step must be met. This can be read as, *each action at step* $\mathtt{n}$ *meets all of its pre-conditions*. Attacking arguments in form (3), if they exist, indicate that there is some other plan S' such that $\neg\mathtt{FR}(\overline{A}, \mathtt{n})$ is in the goal state of S' and S' is not part of S. Since S is a solution, all pre-conditions in all of its actions must hold, for any S' composed by actions $\mathtt{act}'(\overline{B}, L) \in \Delta'$ differ from the ones in S (up to step n), $\mathtt{act}'(\overline{B}, L)$ can be targeted by argument $\{\mathtt{act}(\overline{A}, L)\} \vdash \mathtt{act}(\overline{A}, L)$ in RF for $\mathtt{act}(\overline{A}, L)$ in S. This can be read as, *although there are some other plans S' such that S' invalidates some pre-condition of an action in S, S withstands such attacks as all of its actions meet their pre-conditions*. With this reasoning, we can see that all arguments in RF defend $\mathtt{goal}$, thus meeting the second condition.

Theorem 2. *Given a bounded planning problem $\mathcal{P}$ with its corresponding ABA framework F, let RA be a related admissible set of arguments with topic sentence* $\mathtt{goal}$, $S = \{\mathtt{act}(\overline{A}, K) | \mathtt{act}(\overline{A}, K)$ *is the name of an action in $\mathbb{A}$ and $\mathtt{act}(\overline{A}, K)$ is an assumption of an argument in $RA\}$, then the sequence $(m_1, \ldots, m_n)$, for which $\{m_1, \ldots, m_n\} = S$ and $S(m_i) < S(m_j)$ if and only if $i < j$ is a solution to $\mathcal{P}$.*

Proof. (Sketch.) From Definition 3 we can see that RF is related admissible only when there is a sequence of actions taking the initial state to the goal state. Thus, all actions in assumptions defending $\mathtt{goal}$ consist a solution.

Theorems 1 and 2 sanction that bounded planning problems can be modelled with ABA frameworks such that solutions correspond to related admissible arguments. We illustrate these results with the following example.

Example 6 (Example 5 continued.) An argument for $\mathtt{goal}$ is $A = \Delta \vdash \mathtt{goal}$ with $\Delta = \{\mathtt{mv}(d_1, r_2, d_2, 2), \mathtt{mv}(d_2, r_1, r_3, 1), \mathtt{df}(\mathtt{on}, d_2, r_3, 3)\}$ (see Fig. 2). Arguments targeting $\mathtt{mv}(d_1, r_2, d_2, 2)$ include

$B = \{\mathtt{mv}(d_1, r_2, r_1, 2)\} \vdash \mathtt{mv}(d_1, r_2, r_1, 2) \; C = \{\mathtt{mv}(d_2, r_3, r_1, 2)\} \vdash \mathtt{mv}(d_2, r_3, r_1, 2)$
$D = \{\mathtt{not\_on}(d_1, r_2, 2)\} \vdash \mathtt{not\_on}(d_1, r_2, 2) \; E = \{\mathtt{not\_cl}(d_1, 2)\} \vdash \mathtt{not\_cl}(d_1, 2)$
$F = \{\mathtt{not\_cl}(d_2, 2)\} \vdash \mathtt{not\_cl}(d_2, 2) \; G = \{\mathtt{not\_sm}(d_1, d_2)\} \vdash \mathtt{not\_sm}(d_1, d_2)$

Arguments B and C can be attacked by $H = \{\text{mv}(d_1, r_2, d_2, 2)\} \vdash$ $\text{mv}(d_1, r_2, d_2, 2)$.

Arguments D can be attacked by (Fig. 3)

$I = \{\text{mv}(d_1, d_2, r_2, 0), \text{mv}(d_2, r_1, r_3, 1), \text{df}(\text{on}, d_1, r_2, 2)\} \vdash \text{on}(d_1, r_2, 2)$

Arguments E can be attacked by (Fig. 4)

$J = \{\text{mv}(d_1, d_2, r_2, 0), \text{mv}(d_2, r_1, r_3, 1), \text{df}(\text{cl}, d_1, 2), \text{df}(\text{cl}, d_1, 1)\} \vdash \text{cl}(d_1, 2)$

Arguments F can be attacked by (Fig. 5)

$K = \{\text{mv}(d_1, d_2, r_2, 0), \text{mv}(d_2, r_1, r_3, 1), \text{df}(\text{cl}, d_2, 2)\} \vdash \text{cl}(d_2, 2)$

Arguments G can be attacked by $L = \{\} \vdash \text{sm}(d_1, d_2)$.

We can see that arguments H, I, J, K and L all defend A. Arguments targeting $\text{mv}(d_2, r_1, r_3, 1)$ and $\text{df}(\text{on}, d_2, r_3, 3)$ can be counter-attacked similarly. H, J, K can also be defended with arguments in similar patterns. Overall, A is in a related admissible set with its topic goal and assumptions in Δ form a solution to the planning problem.

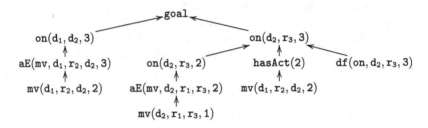

Fig. 2. An argument for goal in Example 6.

By Theorem 5 of [8], we know that assumptions in arguments held by proponent nodes of an admissible dispute tree are related admissible with the claim of the argument held by the root of the tree as the topic sentence. Thus, given Theorem 2, the following corollary holds.

Corollary 1. *Given a bounded planing problem* $\mathcal{P} = \langle \mathbb{A}, s_0, s_g, \mathbb{F}, \mathbb{R}, \mathbb{K} \rangle$ *with* F *the ABA framework corresponding to* $\mathcal{P}$*, if there is an admissible abstract dispute tree* T^a *for* goal*, then* $\{\text{act}(\overline{A}, K) | \text{act}(\overline{A}, K)$ *is a name of action in* $\mathbb{A}$ *and* $\mathbf{P} : \{\text{act}(\overline{A}, K), \dots\} \vdash \_ \text{ is in } T^a\}$ *is a solution to* $\mathcal{P}$*.*[9]

Proof. Follows directly from Theorem 5 of [8] and Theorem 2.

Corollary 1 sanctions that abstract dispute trees can be used to compute solutions for bounded planning problems. This is a useful result as it allows us to use a semantics computation tool to compute plan solutions.

---

[9] Throughout, $\_$ stands for an anonymous variable.

$\mathtt{on}(d_1, r_2, 2)$
$\mathtt{on}(d_1, r_2, 1)$
$\mathtt{hasAct}(1)$
$\mathtt{df}(\mathtt{on}, d_1, r_2, 2)$
$\mathtt{aE}(\mathtt{mv}, d_1, d_2, r_2, 1)$
$\mathtt{mv}(d_2, r_1, r_3, 1)$
$\mathtt{mv}(d_1, d_2, r_2, 0)$

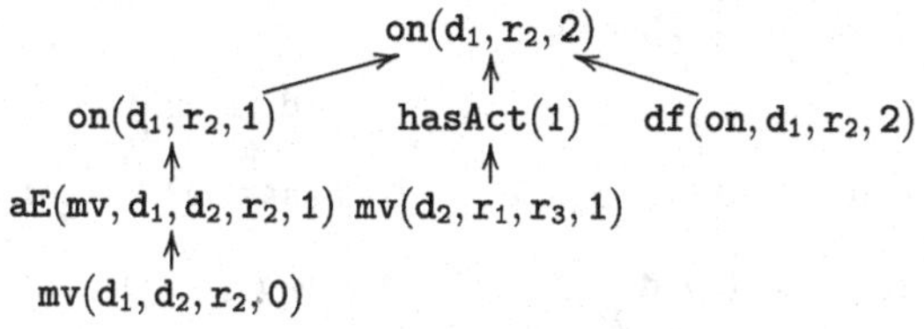

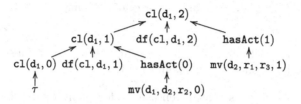

Fig. 3. An argument for $\mathtt{on}(d_1, r_2, 2)$ in Example 6.

$\mathtt{cl}(d_1, 2)$
$\mathtt{cl}(d_1, 1)$
$\mathtt{df}(\mathtt{cl}, d_1, 2)$
$\mathtt{hasAct}(1)$
$\mathtt{cl}(d_1, 0)$
$\mathtt{df}(\mathtt{cl}, d_1, 1)$
$\mathtt{hasAct}(0)$
$\mathtt{mv}(d_2, r_1, r_3, 1)$
$\top$
$\mathtt{mv}(d_1, d_2, r_2, 0)$

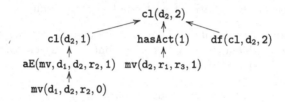

Fig. 4. An argument for $\mathtt{cl}(d_1, 2)$ in Example 6.

$\mathtt{cl}(d_2, 2)$
$\mathtt{cl}(d_2, 1)$
$\mathtt{hasAct}(1)$
$\mathtt{df}(\mathtt{cl}, d_2, 2)$
$\mathtt{aE}(\mathtt{mv}, d_1, d_2, r_2, 1)$
$\mathtt{mv}(d_2, r_1, r_3, 1)$
$\mathtt{mv}(d_1, d_2, r_2, 0)$

Fig. 5. An argument for $\mathtt{cl}(r_2, 2)$ in Example 6.

6 Extracting Explanations from ABA

In the previous section, we have shown how ABA can be used to compute solutions for bounded planning problems by identifying a related admissible set of arguments for the topic goal. Corollary 1 establishes the connection between solutions and abstract dispute trees. In this section, we focus on extracting explanations from dispute trees.

Proposition 1. *Given a bounded planning problem $\mathcal{P}$ with corresponding ABA framework F, let E be an explanation for* $_ \vdash \mathtt{goal}$ *in F. Then, $S = s_g \cup \{s | _ \vdash s \in E\}$ contains an explanation for a plan P being a solution to $\mathcal{P}$, where P consists of actions represented by action assumptions supporting arguments in E.*

Proof. (Sketch.) By Theorem 2, and the definition of explanations for argument in ABA frameworks (see the Background section), P is a solution to $\mathcal{P}$. Since P is a solution, all pre-conditions of all actions in P must hold at their respective steps. By Definition 3, each action in the plan is mapped to an assumption with contraries being assumptions $\mathtt{not_PreC_i}$ for all of its pre-conditions. Since the contrary of $\mathtt{not_PreC_i}$ is $\mathtt{PreC_i}$, there must be an admissible argument for each

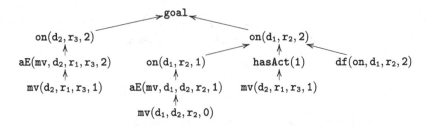

Fig. 6. An argument for `goal` in Example 7.

$\texttt{PreC}_i$. Thus, S by containing all goals in s_g and all pre-conditions of all actions, contains an explanation for P, by Definition 1.

Proposition 1 sanctions that, given a bounded planning problem $\mathcal{P}$ with its corresponding ABA framework F, by computing an explanation for the argument $_- \vdash$ `goal`, we not only compute a solution to $\mathcal{P}$, but also an explanation for this solution. We illustrate Proposition 1 with the following example.

Example 7 (Example 3 continued.) The ABA framework corresponding to this bounded planning problem (with $\mathbb{K} = 2$, $s_g = \{\texttt{on}(\texttt{d}_1, \texttt{r}_2, 2), \texttt{on}(\texttt{d}_2, \texttt{r}_3, 2)\}$) is the ABA framework shown in Example 5 with the rule

$$\texttt{goal} \leftarrow \texttt{on}(\texttt{d}_1, \texttt{d}_2, 3), \texttt{on}(\texttt{d}_2, \texttt{r}_3, 3)$$

replaced by

$$\texttt{goal} \leftarrow \texttt{on}(\texttt{d}_1, \texttt{r}_2, 2), \texttt{on}(\texttt{d}_2, \texttt{r}_3, 2)$$

and everything else unaltered. The argument A for `goal` is shown in Fig. 6. Arguments attacking A are summarised in Table 1. Argument B targets at assumption $\texttt{df}(\texttt{on}, \texttt{d}_1, \texttt{r}_2, 2)$. Arguments $C1$–$C5$ target at assumption $\texttt{mv}(\texttt{d}_1, \texttt{d}_2, \texttt{r}_2, 0)$. Arguments $D1$–$D5$ target at assumption $\texttt{mv}(\texttt{d}_2, \texttt{r}_1, \texttt{r}_3, 1)$. Note that $B, C1$ and $D1$ represent sets of arguments with A unified to different r_is and d_js.

Arguments attacking $B, C1$–$C5$ and $D1$–$D5$ are shown in Table 2. Here, X' attack X, for $X = B$, $C1$–$C5$, $D1$–$D5$. Arguments attacking B' and $D1'$ are $D1$–$D5$. Arguments attacking $C1'$ are $C1$–$C5$. Arguments attacking $D2'$ are: $C1$–$C5$ and $E = \{\texttt{mv}(\texttt{d}_2, \texttt{r}_1, \texttt{A}, 0)\} \vdash \neg\texttt{on}(\texttt{d}_2, \texttt{r}_1, 1)$. Arguments attacking $D3'$ are: $C1$–$C5$ and $F = \{\texttt{mv}(\texttt{A}, \texttt{B}, \texttt{d}_2, 0)\} \vdash \neg\texttt{cl}(\texttt{d}_2, 1)$. Arguments attacking $D4'$ are: $C1$–$C5$ and $G = \{\texttt{mv}(\texttt{A}, \texttt{B}, \texttt{d}_3, 0)\} \vdash \neg\texttt{cl}(\texttt{r}_3, 1)$. Argument $C1'$ attacks E, F and G. In summary, we can see that the related admissible set of arguments, which is the defence set of the tree, together with the goal set, contains explanations for the plan being a solution.

Proposition 2. *Given a bounded planning problem $\mathcal{P}$ with corresponding ABA framework F, let $P = (m_1, \ldots, m_n)$ be an invalid plan. If there is a non-admissible dispute tree $\mathcal{T}^a$ for $_- \vdash$ `goal` such that $m_1, \ldots, m_n$ support arguments*

Table 1. Arguments attacking A in Example 7.

$B = \{\mathtt{mv(d_1, r_2, A, 1)}\} \vdash \neg\mathtt{on(d_1, r_2, 2)}$

$C1 = \{\mathtt{mv(A, B, C, 0)}\} \vdash \mathtt{mv(A, B, C, 0)}$	$C2 = \{\mathtt{not\_on(d_1, d_2, 0)}\} \vdash \mathtt{not\_on(d_1, d_2, 0)}$
$C3 = \{\mathtt{not\_cl(d_1, 0)}\} \vdash \mathtt{not\_cl(d_1, 0)}$	$C4 = \{\mathtt{not\_cl(r_2, 0)}\} \vdash \mathtt{not\_cl(r_2, 0)}$
$C5 = \{\mathtt{not\_sm(d_1, r_2)}\} \vdash \mathtt{not\_sm(d_1, r_2)}$	$D1 = \{\mathtt{mv(A, B, C, 1)}\} \vdash \mathtt{mv(A, B, C, 1)}$
$D2 = \{\mathtt{not\_on(d_2, r_1, 1)}\} \vdash \mathtt{not\_on(d_2, r_1, 1)}$	$D3 = \{\mathtt{not\_cl(d_2, 1)}\} \vdash \mathtt{not\_cl(d_2, 1)}$
$D4 = \{\mathtt{not\_cl(r_3, 1)}\} \vdash \mathtt{not\_cl(r_3, 1)}$	$D5 = \{\mathtt{not\_sm(d_1, r_3)}\} \vdash \mathtt{not\_sm(d_1, r_3)}$

Table 2. Arguments attacking $B, C1$–$C5$ and $D1$–$D5$ in Example 7.

$B' = \{\mathtt{mv(d_2, r_1, r_3, 1)}\} \vdash \mathtt{mv(d_2, r_1, r_3, 1)}$	$C1' = \{\mathtt{mv(d_1, d_2, r_2, 0)}\} \vdash \mathtt{mv(d_1, d_2, r_2, 0)}$
$C2' = \{\} \vdash \mathtt{on(d_1, d_2, 0)}$	$C3' = \{\} \vdash \mathtt{cl(d_1, 0)}$
$C4' = \{\} \vdash \mathtt{cl(r_2, 0)}$	$C5' = \{\} \vdash \mathtt{sm(d_1, r_2)}$

$D1' = \{\mathtt{mv(d_2, r_1, r_3, 1)}\} \vdash \mathtt{mv(d_2, r_1, r_3, 1)}$

$D2' = \{\mathtt{mv(d_1, d_2, r_2, 0)}, \mathtt{df(on, d_2, r_1, 1)}\} \vdash \mathtt{on(d_2, r_1, 1)}$

$D3' = \{\mathtt{mv(d_1, d_2, r_2, 0)}, \mathtt{df(cl, d_2, 1)}\} \vdash \mathtt{cl(d_2, 1)}$

$D4' = \{\mathtt{mv(d_1, d_2, r_2, 0)}, \mathtt{df(cl, r_3, 1)}\} \vdash \mathtt{cl(r_3, 1)}$ $\qquad D5' = \{\} \vdash \mathtt{sm(d_2, r_3)}$

held by $\mathbf{P}$ nodes in $\mathcal{T}^a$. Then, if a node $N = \mathbf{P} : \{\mathtt{m_i}, \ldots\} \vdash \_$ is defeated and $A = \{\mathtt{not\_PreC_i(\overline{C_i}, K)}\} \vdash \mathtt{not\_PreC_i(\overline{C_i}, K)}$ held by N's winning attacker, then $\mathtt{PreC_i(\overline{C_i}, K)}$ is in an explanation for the invalidity of P.

Proof (Sketch.) By Definition 2, to show that $\mathtt{PreC_i(\overline{C_i}, K)}$ is in an explanation for the invalidity of P is to show that $\mathtt{PreC_i(\overline{C_i}, K)}$ is not held at K. This is achieved by showing that the argument A held in $\mathcal{T}^a$. Since A is held by a winning attacker of N, in $\mathcal{T}^a$, meaning that it cannot be disapproved, $\mathtt{PreC_i(\overline{C_i}, K)}$ cannot be held. Thus it is in an explanation for the invalidity of P.

Proposition 2 sanctions that to identify explanations for invalid actions, we can look at dispute trees and find non-admissible sub-trees and their successful attackers. We illustrate Proposition 2 with the following example.

Example 8 (Example 4 continued.) Let the goal state $s_g = \{\mathtt{on(d_1, r_3, 2)},$ $\mathtt{on(d_2, d_1, 2)}\}$. An argument for goal is $A = \Delta \vdash \mathtt{goal}$ with $\Delta = \{\mathtt{mv(d_1, d_2, r_3, 0)}, \mathtt{mv(d_2, r_1, d_1, 1)}, \mathtt{df(on, d_1, r_3, 2)}\}$. Arguments targeting at $\mathtt{mv(d_2, r_1, d_1, 1)}$ include the following:

$B = \{\mathtt{mv(d_2, r_1, r_2, 1)}\} \vdash \mathtt{mv(d_2, r_1, r_2, 1)}$,

$C = \{\mathtt{not\_on(d_2, r_1, 1)}\} \vdash \mathtt{not\_on(d_2, r_1, 1)}$,

$D = \{\mathtt{not\_cl(d_1, 1)}\} \vdash \mathtt{not\_cl(d_1, 1)}$,

$E = \{\mathtt{not\_cl(d_2, 1)}\} \vdash \mathtt{not\_cl(d_2, 1)}$,

$F = \{\mathtt{not\_sm(d_2, d_1)}\} \vdash \mathtt{not\_sm(d_2, d_1)}$.

$G = \{\mathtt{mv(d_2, r_1, d_1, 1)}\} \vdash \{\mathtt{mv(d_2, r_1, d_1, 1)}\}$ attacks B.

$H = \{\mathtt{mv(d_1, d_2, r_3, 0)}, \mathtt{df(on, d_2, r_1, 1)}\} \vdash \mathtt{on(d_2, r_1, 1)}$ attacks C.

$I = \{\mathtt{df(cl, d_1, 1)}, \mathtt{mv(d_1, d_2, r_3, 0)}\} \vdash \mathtt{cl(d_1, 1)}$ attacks D.

$J = \{\mathtt{mv(d_1, d_2, r_3, 0)}\} \vdash \mathtt{cl(d_2, 1)}$ attacks E.

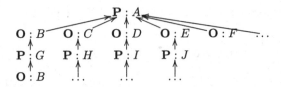

Fig. 7. An illustration of a fraction of the non-admissible dispute tree for $\Delta \vdash$ goal with $\Delta = \{\text{mv}(d_1, d_2, r_3, 0), \text{mv}(d_2, r_1, d_1, 1), \text{df}(\text{on}, d_1, r_3, 2)\}$ in Example 8. Since **O** : F has no **P** child, **O** : F is a winning attacker.

However, no argument can attack F as there is no argument for $\text{sm}(d_2, d_1)$. Thus, **O** : F is a winning attacker and **P** : A is defeated. A fraction of the abstract dispute tree for A is shown in Fig. 7. Thus, we conclude that the unmet precondition $\text{sm}(d_2, d_1)$ is in an explanation for the invalidity of the plan.

For simplicity, we only present results for plan invalidity due to unmet preconditions. In general, however, by Definition 2, a plan is invalid if there are multiple actions take place at the same time. It is easy to see that such invalidity can be easily captured in dispute trees as the contrary of an assumption representing an action includes all other actions taking place at the same step. Therefore, if a defeated node labelled by an argument supported by an action assumption and the winning attacker holds an argument with an action as its claim, then the action in the winning attacker is in an explanation.

7   Related Work

Very recently, [10] presented a study on "Explainable Planing". Not connected to argumentation, the authors proposed six questions to be answered by "explainable planners". That paper focuses on high level discussion with no theoretical result. The two forms of explanations presented in this work can be viewed as (at least partial) answers to three of their questions: **Q1:** *Why did you do that?* (because such moves are valid), **Q2** *Why didn't you do something else?* (because "something else" is not valid) and **Q4:** *Why can't you do that?* (because certain precondition does not meet), as our explanations justify actions in plans and identify invalid ones.

Argumentation has seen its use in planning since 1980s (see e.g. [12,14]), in the context of urban planning. Formal arguments are constructed to evaluate the pros and cons of urban plans. Our work differs from theirs as we view plans as sequences of actions and argumentation is used to generate these sequences.

Connection between planning and defeasible argumentation has been made in [11] with an application in [9]. Their works are based on DeLP where arguments are in the level of actions and a tailored algorithm has been developed for searching the suitable plans. Our work differs from theirs as we use ABA arguments to represent plans with existing argumentation semantics computing techniques so that explanations can be obtained along the course.

Conflict resolution in goal selection and planning has been studied by researchers in argumentation [1,13]. Our work differs from theirs as, in addition to using entirely different argumentation languages, we use argumentation as a modelling tool for solving planning problems and derive explanations from our solutions; whereas they use argumentation to model agent actions and desires so that more suitable actions can be selected.

In multi-agent negotiation, there are works on connecting argumentation with the classic planners [16,19]. There, argumentation-based negotiation is viewed as a planning problem with negotiation utterances being agents' actions. Under such modelling, negotiation is then solved with existing planner, e.g., HTN. Similarly, argumentation-based persuasion can be viewed as a planning problem and solved with existing planning techniques [4]. Our work is orthogonal to those as we use argumentation to plan instead of using planner to argue.

Agent planning has been studied in [2]. There, agents' beliefs and actions are analysed in a single argumentation framework, such that plans satisfying agents' desires can be directly generated. Our work differs from theirs as, instead of studying BDI agent planning in a specifically defined language, we present a generic representation for planning problems represented in STRIPS. Moreover, by explicity representing planning steps, our approach reasons with temporal information, which is not supported in [2]. Thus, a better generalisation and improved applicability have been achieved.

8 Conclusion

Empowering AI techniques with the ability of generating explanations is central to bringing trust to autonomous systems. In this paper, we have looked at how to use ABA to model planning problems and to generate explanations. The aim is to develop planning techniques which not only produce solutions, but also generate explanations for solutions (and non-solutions). Taking a generic planning problem represented in a standard STRIPS-like language, our model generates an "ABA counterpart" of the problem. The correspondence is realised such that plan solutions correspond to Related Admissible arguments with the topic being the goal state. The proposed plan construction method is both sound and complete in the sense that a solution exists if and only if the corresponding Related Admissible arguments exist.

To generate planning explanations, we again rely on the Related Admissible semantics and its computation means, dispute trees. We observe that a plan is a solution if and only if all goals are met at the end of the plan and there is no unmet pre-condition in any action in the plan. Related Admissible set of arguments computed with dispute trees contain justifications for all actions meeting their pre-conditions. Moreover, by looking at "defeated nodes" in non-admissible dispute trees, we identify unmet pre-conditions, which explain why some plans are not solutions.

In future, we will further explore argumentation-based explanations in planning. Namely, we would like to study explanations for questions such as "Why plan A is better than plan B?", "Why certain goal can never be reached by any plan?". We will also study argumentation-based dialectical explanation, which can be used in multi-agent planning. Moreover, we will look at mapping other planning languages with argumentation, e.g. support partial order planning and conditional-effects of actions.

References

1. Amgoud, L., Cayrol, C.: On the use of an ATMS for handling conflicting desires. In: Proceedings of KR, pp. 194–202 (2004)
2. Amgoud, L., Devred, C., Lagasquie-Schiex, M.: Generating possible intentions with constrained argumentation systems. IJAR **52**(9), 1363–1391 (2011)
3. Besnard, P., Garcia, A., Hunter, A., Modgil, S., Prakken, H., Simari, G., Toni, F.: Special issue: tutorials on structured argumentation. Argum. Comput. **5**(1) (2014)
4. Black, E., Coles, A.J., Hampson, C.: Planning for persuasion. In: Proceedings of AAMAS, pp. 933–942 (2017)
5. Čyras, K., Fan, X., Schulz, C., Toni, F.: Assumption-based argumentation: disputes, explanations, preferences. IfCoLog JLTA **4**(8) (2017)
6. Doran, D., Schulz, S., Besold, T.R.: What does explainable AI really mean? A new conceptualization of perspectives. CoRR, arXiv:abs/1710.00794 (2017)
7. Dung, P.M., Kowalski, R.A., Toni, F.: Dialectic proof procedures for assumption-based, admissible argumentation. AIJ **170**, 114–159 (2006)
8. Fan, X., Toni, F.: On computing explanations in argumentation. In: Proceedings of AAAI, pp. 1496–1502 (2015)
9. Ferrando, S.P., Onaindia, E.: Defeasible argumentation for multi-agent planning in ambient intelligence applications. In: Proceedings of AAMAS, pp. 509–516. IFAAMS, Richland (2012)
10. Fox, M., Long, D., Magazzeni, D.: Explainable planning. CoRR, arXiv:abs/1709.10256 (2017)
11. García, D.R., García, A.J., Simari, G.R.: Defeasible reasoning and partial order planning. In: Hartmann, S., Kern-Isberner, G. (eds.) FoIKS 2008. LNCS, vol. 4932, pp. 311–328. Springer, Heidelberg (2008). https://doi.org/10.1007/978-3-540-77684-0_21
12. Goldstein, H.A.: Planning as argumentation. Environ. Plan. B: Plan. Des. **11**(3), 297–312 (1984)
13. Hulstijn, J., van der Torre, L.W.N.: Combining goal generation and planning in an argumentation framework. In: Proceedings of NMR, pp. 212–218 (2004)
14. Lapintie, K.: Analysing and evaluating argumentation in planning. Environ. Plan. B: Plan. Des. **25**(2), 187–204 (1998)
15. Modgil, S.: The added value of argumentation. In: Ossowski, S. (ed.) Agreement Technologies, vol. 8, pp. 357–403. Springer, Heidelberg (2013). https://doi.org/10.1007/978-94-007-5583-3_21
16. Monteserin, A., Amandi, A.: Argumentation-based negotiation planning for autonomous agents. Decis. Support. Syst. **51**(3), 532–548 (2011)
17. Nau, D., Ghallab, M., Traverso, P.: Automated Planning: Theory & Practice. Morgan Kaufmann Publishers Inc., San Francisco (2004)
18. Nilsson, N.J.: Principles of Artificial Intelligence. Morgan Kaufmann Publishers Inc., San Francisco (1980)

19. Panisson, A.R., Farias, G., Fraitas, A., Meneguzzi, F., Vieira, R., Bordini, R.H.: Planning interactions for agents in argumentation-based negotiation. In: Proceedings of ArgMAS (2014)
20. Vallati, M., Chrpa, L., Grzes, M., McCluskey, T.L., Roberts, M., Sanner, S.: The 2014 international planning competition: progress and trends. AI Mag. **36**(3), 90–98 (2015)
21. Wachter, S., Mittelstadt, B., Floridi, L.: Transparent, explainable, and accountable AI for robotics. Sci. Robot. **2**(6) (2017)

A Temporal Planning Example with Assumption-Based Argumentation

Xiuyi Fan[✉]

Swansea University, Swansea, UK
xiuyi.fan@swansea.ac.uk

Abstract. Agent planning has attracted much research attention in recent years. In argumentation, agent planning has been studied by several researchers with significant contributions made in modelling agent goals, desires and actions. However, there is little work that connects argumentation semantics, plan construction and temporal information in a unified framework. In this work, we use a version of the classic *blocks world* planning problem as our case study and demonstrate how Assumption-based Argumentation can be used to tackle planning problems with explicit time step information. In our approach, the process of plan construction is equated to constructing acceptable arguments (with respect to an argumentation semantics) with temporal aspects taken into consideration.

1 Introduction

Agent planning has been studied with argumentation-based approaches by several researchers. Notably, Amgoud and her colleagues have studied joining *deliberation* and *means-ends reasoning* in a single unified argumentation system such that "[the] system combines option generation and checking the feasibility of options" [1,2]. In their work, argumentation has been used to identify agent intentions in a way that the resulting intentions satisfy the argumentation rationality postulates [2]. However, in their work, temporal reasoning has not been considered as agent goals are fulfilled by *sets* of actions instantaneously rather than through *a sequence* of actions over a course of plan execution. On the other hand, García et al. [4] have studied incorporating defeasible information in agent planning, as originally proposed by Pollock [6]. In García's work, argumentation has been introduced to model defeasibility in planning [4]. Their work is more inline with classic planning approaches (see e.g. [5]) in that their plans are sequences of actions with effects. Although temporal information has been considered in [4] with arguments modelling defeasibility, they have used a specifically designed search process to identify suitable plans. Thus their plans are not confirmed to argumentation rationality postulates in the same way as [2].

In this work, we study using Assumption-based Argumentation (ABA) [3] to solve planning problems. In the same spirit as [4], we consider plans consist sequences of actions and performing an action results changes to the "world

© Springer Nature Switzerland AG 2018
T. Miller et al. (Eds.): PRIMA 2018, LNAI 11224, pp. 362–370, 2018.
https://doi.org/10.1007/978-3-030-03098-8_22

state". Thus, the execution of a plan transfers the world from some "initial situation" to a "final situation". The designed transformation is carried out argumentatively so argumentation semantics can be used to validate plans. Unlike [4], where a dedicated algorithm was introduced to search for plan solutions, we equate plan solution construction with acceptable argument computation. In our work, actions are modelled with assumptions and the contrary of an assumption describe conditions for which an action cannot be performed; the efforts of an action describe changes to the world state, updating available actions. Overall, our work can be viewed as an illustration of an ABA instantiation of Pollock's idea on defeasible planning: "It is argued that the planning must instead be done defeasibly, making the default assumption that there are no threats and then modifying plans as threats are discovered" [6].

2   Background

Assumption-based Argumentation (ABA) frameworks are tuples $\langle \mathcal{L}, \mathcal{R}, \mathcal{A}, \mathcal{C} \rangle$,

- $\langle \mathcal{L}, \mathcal{R} \rangle$ is a deductive system, with $\mathcal{L}$ the *language* and $\mathcal{R}$ a set of *rules* of the form $s_0 \leftarrow s_1, \ldots, s_m (m \geq 0, s_i \in \mathcal{L})$;
- $\mathcal{A} \subseteq \mathcal{L}$ is a (non-empty) set of *assumptions*;
- $\mathcal{C}$ is a total mapping from $\mathcal{A}$ into $2^{\mathcal{L}} - \{\{\}\}$, where each $s \in \mathcal{C}(a)$ is a *contrary* of a, for $a \in \mathcal{A}$.

Given a rule $\rho = s_0 \leftarrow s_1, \ldots, s_m$, s_0 is referred to as the *head* and $s_1, \ldots, s_m$ as the *body*. A rule with an empty body is referred to as a *fact*.

Arguments are deductions of claims using rules and supported by sets of assumptions; *Attacks* are *targeted* at the assumptions in the support of arguments:

- an *argument for (claim)* $s \in \mathcal{L}$ supported by $\Delta \subseteq \mathcal{A}$ (denoted $\Delta \vdash s$) is a finite tree with nodes labelled by sentences in $\mathcal{L}$ or by τ[1], the root labelled by s, leaves either τ or assumptions in Δ, and non-leaves s' with, as children, the elements of the body of some rule ρ with head s';
- an *argument* $A = \Delta_1 \vdash s_1$ attacks an argument $\Delta_2 \vdash s_2$ iff s_1 is a contrary of some assumption α in Δ_2, and we say A *targets at* α.

A *set of arguments As is admissible* iff *As* is *conflict-free* (i.e. no argument in *As* attacks any argument in *As*) and all arguments attacking some argument in *As* are counter attacked by arguments in *As*; an *argument is admissible* iff it belongs to an admissible set of arguments.

3   Planning in Blocks World

A blocks world (Fig. 1) contains a set of "blocks" of different sizes and a set of "locations" where each block is at some location, and each location could have a

---

[1] $\tau \notin \mathcal{L}$ represents "true" and stands for the empty body of rules.

"block pile" such that if two blocks r, r' are in a pile then r is placed higher than r', iff r is smaller than r'. The initial and final situations are two placements of blocks. Two types of actions are possible to a block, (1) moving it from one location to another while satisfying the "smaller-block-placed-higher" constraint and (2) no-operation, i.e., not to move it. A plan is a sequence of actions which transfers the initial situation to the final one. Formally, we use the following four definitions.

Fig. 1. A blocks world with two blocks $r1$ and $r2$ and three locations a, b and c. The initial situation is shown on the left-hand side and the final situation is shown on the right-hand side.

Definition 1. *A* blocks world *is a tuple* $\langle R, L, < \rangle$ *in which* R *is a set of* blocks, L *is a set of* locations *and* $< \subseteq R \times R$ *is a total order such that for* $r_1, r_2 \in R$, $r_1 < r_2$ *iff* r_1 *is smaller than* r_2.

Definition 2. *A blocks world planning problem is a tuple* $\langle W, T, S_0, S_n \rangle$ *where*

- $W = \langle R, L, < \rangle$ *is a blocks world,*
- $T = \langle t_0, \ldots, t_n \rangle$ *is a time step sequence,*
- *a* situation S_i *(for a time step t_i in* T*) is a set* $\{at(r_1, l_1, t_i), \ldots, at(r_n, l_m, t_i)\}$ *specifying the location* $l_j \in L$ *for each block* $r_k \in R$. *For a situation* S_i, *there is no* $r_k \in R$ *such that* r_k *is not specified in* S_i. *Moreover,*
  - $S_0 = \{at(r_1, l_1, t_0), \ldots, at(r_n, l_m, t_0)\}$ *is the* initial situation, *and*
  - $S_n = \{at(r_1, l'_1, t_n), \ldots, at(r_n, l'_m, t_n)\}$ *is the* final situation.

Definition 3. *In a blocks world* $\langle R, L, < \rangle$, *the two* actions *are: (1)* $move(X, L, L', T)$, *move* $X \in R$ *from* $L \in L$ *to* $L' \in L$ *at time step* T, *and (2)* $noOp(X, L, T)$, *do nothing to* $X \in R$ *sitting at* $L \in L$ *at time* T.
  Given $S_i = \{at(r_1, l_1, t_i), \ldots, at(r_n, l_i, t_i)\}$, *then apply* $move(r_i, l, l', t_i)$ *to* S_i *yield* $(S_i \setminus \{at(r_i, l, t_i)\}) \cup \{at(r_i, l', t_{i+1})\}$; *apply* $noOp(r_i, l, t_i)$ *to* S_i *yield* $(S_i \setminus \{at(r_i, l, t_i)\}) \cup \{at(r_i, l, t_{i+1})\}$.
  $move(X, L, L', T)$ *is valid* iff *all of the following conditions hold (at time T):*

(C1) X sits at L;
(C2) there is no $X' \in R$ such that X' is at L and $X' < X$;
(C3) if there is a block at L', then let $X' \in R$ be the top block at L', $X < X'$;
(C4) X is not being moved to a different location $L' \in L$; and
(C5) there is no other block $X' \in R$ being moved to L.

Definition 4. *A plan for* $\langle W, \mathtt{T}, S_0, S_n \rangle$ *is a set*

$$\{P(r_1, t_0) \ldots P(r_m, t_0)\} \cup \ldots \cup \{P(r_1, t_n) \ldots P(r_m, t_n)\}$$

where each $P(r_i, t_j)$ *is either* $move(r_i, l, l', t_j)$ *or* $noOp(r_i, l, t_j)$ *such that* S_1 *is obtained by applying all* $P(r, 0)$ *to* S_0; S_{i+1} *is obtained by applying all* $P(r, t_i)$ *to* S_i; *and* S_n *is obtained by applying all* $P(r, t_{n-1})$ *to* S_{n-1}.

A plan P *is* valid *iff all actions in* P *are valid; otherwise,* P *is* invalid.

We illustrate Definition 2–4 with the following example.

Example 1. Given the blocks world shown in Fig. 1, we have blocks $\mathtt{R} = \{r_1, r_2\}$, locations $\mathtt{L} = \{a, b, c\}$ and time steps $\mathtt{T} = \langle t_0, t_1, t_2, t_3 \rangle$. Moreover, r_1 is smaller than r_2. The initial situation is $\{at(r_1, a, t_0), at(r_2, a, t_0)\}$ and the final situation is $\{at(r_1, c, t_3), at(r_2, c, t_3)\}$. It is easy to see that $\{move(r_1, a, b, t_0),$ $noOp(r_2, a, t_0),$ $noOp(r_1, b, t_1),$ $move(r_2, a, c, t_1),$ $move(r_1, b, c, t_2),$ $noOp(r_2, c, t_2)\}$ is a plan.

4 Planning in Blocks World with ABA

We take a two-step approach to model blocks world planning with ABA. Firstly, we define the *core framework* wrt a blocks world; then, for any given specific problem with a given time step sequence and initial, final situations, we define an *instantiated framework* (extending the core framework) to generate specific plans. Formally,

Definition 5. *Given a blocks world* $W = \langle \mathtt{R}, \mathtt{L}, < \rangle$, *the core framework corresponding to* W *is an ABA framework* $F_0 = \langle \mathcal{L}_0, \mathcal{R}_0, \mathcal{A}_0, \mathcal{C}_0 \rangle$ *such that:*[2]

– $\mathcal{R}_0$ *contains the following rules and nothing else.*

$$above(X, X', L, T) \leftarrow at(X, L, T), at(X', L, T), smaller(X, X') \tag{1}$$
$$at(X, L, T) \leftarrow at(X, L, T^-), noOp(X, L, T^-), succ(T, T^-) \tag{2}$$
$$at(X, L, T) \leftarrow at(X, L', T^-), move(X, L', L, T^-), succ(T, T^-) \tag{3}$$
$$occupied(X, L, T) \leftarrow at(X', L, T), smaller(X', X) \tag{4}$$
$$smaller(X, X') \leftarrow \tag{5}$$

– $\mathcal{A}_0$ *contains the following assumptions and nothing else.*

$$move(X, L', L, T) \qquad noOp(X, L, T) \qquad notAt(X, L, T)$$

– $\mathcal{C}_0$ *is such that:*

$$\mathcal{C}(move(X, L', L, T)) = \{noOp(X, L, T), move(X, L', L'', T),$$
$$move(X', L'', L, T), above(X', X, L, T),$$
$$occupied(X, L, T), notAt(X, L', T)\}$$
$$\mathcal{C}(noOp(X, L, T)) = \{move(X, L, L', T)\}$$
$$\mathcal{C}(notAt(X, L, T)) = \{at(X, L, T)\}$$

---

[2] We use rule and assumption schemata to simplify our notations. Specifically, in each of the rules, assumptions and contraries, we have $X, X' \in \mathtt{R}, X \neq X', L, L', L'' \in \mathtt{L}, L \neq L', L \neq L'', L' \neq L''$ and T, T^- in some time step sequence. In Rule 5, we also enforce that $X < X'$.

Table 1. Arguments attacking A in Example 2.

Arguments targeting at $move(r_1, a, b, t_0)$:
$B_1 = \{m(r_1, a, c, t_0)\} \vdash m(r_1, a, c, t_0), B_2 = \{m(r_2, a, b, t_0)\} \vdash m(r_2, a, b, t_0),$
$B_3 = \{m(r_2, c, b, t_0)\} \vdash m(r_2, c, b, t_0),\ B_4 = \{n(r_1, a, t_0)\} \vdash n(r_1, a, t_0),$
$B_5 = \{nA(r_1, a, t_0)\} \vdash nA(r_1, a, t_0)$
Arguments targeting at $n(r_2, a, t_0)$:
$C_1 = \{m(r_2, a, b, t_0)\} \vdash m(r_2, a, b, t_0), C_2 = \{m(r_2, a, c, t_0)\} \vdash m(r_2, a, c, t_0).$
Arguments targeting at $n(r_1, b, t_1)$:
$D_1 = \{m(r_1, b, a, t_1)\} \vdash m(r_2, b, a, t_1), D_2 = \{m(r_1, b, c, t_1)\} \vdash m(r_2, b, c, t_1).$
Arguments targeting at $m(r_2, a, c, t_1)$:
$E_1 = \{m(r_2, a, b, t_1)\} \vdash m(r_2, a, b, t_1), E_2 = \{m(r_1, a, c, t_1)\} \vdash m(r_1, a, c, t_1),$
$E_3 = \{m(r_1, b, c, t_1)\} \vdash m(r_1, b, c, t_1),\ E_4 = \{n(r_2, a, t_1)\} \vdash n(r_2, a, t_1),$
$E_5 = \{nA(r_2, a, t_1)\} \vdash nA(r_2, a, t_1),\quad E_7 = \{m(r_1, a, c, t_0)\} \vdash o(r_2, c, t_1),$
$E_6 = \{n(r_1, a, t_0), n(r_2, a, t_0)\} \vdash above(r_1, r_2, a, t_1).$
Arguments targeting at $m(r_1, b, c, t_2)$:
$F_1 = \{m(r_1, b, a, t_2)\} \vdash m(r_1, b, a, t_2), F_2 = \{m(r_2, a, c, t_2)\} \vdash m(r_2, a, c, t_2),$
$F_3 = \{m(r_2, b, c, t_2)\} \vdash m(r_2, b, c, t_2),\ F_4 = \{n(r_1, b, t_2)\} \vdash n(r_1, b, t_2),$
$F_5 = \{nA(r_1, b, t_2)\} \vdash nA(r_1, b, t_2)$
Arguments targeting at $n(r_2, c, t_2)$:
$G_1 = \{m(r_2, c, a, t_2)\} \vdash m(r_2, c, a, t_2), G_2 = \{m(r_2, c, b, t_2)\} \vdash m(r_2, c, b, t_2)$

Rule 1 states that a block X is above another block X' at time T if both X and X' are at the same location L at time T and X is smaller than X'. Rule 2 states that if a block X is at location L at t_i and it is not moved at t_i, then X is at L at time t_{i+1}. Rule 3 states that, at t_i, if a block X is at location L' and X is moved from L' to L, then X is at L at t_{i+1}. Rule 4 states that a location L is occupied wrt to a block X if there is another block X' at L such that X' is smaller than X. Rule 5 states that X is smaller than X' for all $X < X'$.

Assumptions $\mathcal{A}_0$ and their contraries $\mathcal{C}_0$ can be read as:

1. we move a block X from L' to L at time T unless (a) we do not move X, or (b) we move it to a different L'', or (c) some other block $X' \neq X$ is moved to L, or (d) some other block X' is on top of X, or (e) X is no smaller than the top of pile block at L, or (f) X is not at L'.
2. we do not move a block X unless we move it;
3. a block X is not at a location L unless it is at L.

Within a blocks world, a planning problem can be modelled with an instantiated framework, defined as follows.

Definition 6. *For a planning problem $\Pi = \langle W, \mathrm{T}, S_0, S_n \rangle$, let $\langle \mathcal{L}_0, \mathcal{R}_0, \mathcal{A}_0, \mathcal{C}_0 \rangle$ be the core framework for W, then the instantiated framework corresponding to Π is an ABA framework $F_I = \langle \mathcal{L}_I, \mathcal{R}_I, \mathcal{A}_I, \mathcal{C}_I \rangle$ such that:*

- $\mathcal{R}_I$ is $\mathcal{R}_0$ with the following additional rules:

$$goal \leftarrow s_1, \ldots, s_m, \text{ for } \{s_1, \ldots, s_m\} = S_n, \tag{1}$$
$$succ(T, T^-) \leftarrow, \text{ for all } T, T^- \in \mathbf{T} \text{ such that } T \text{ is the successor of } T^-, \tag{2}$$
$$s \leftarrow \text{ for each } s \in S_0; \tag{3}$$

- $\mathcal{A}_I = \mathcal{A}_0$, and for each $\alpha \in \mathcal{A}_I$, $\mathcal{C}_I(\alpha) = \mathcal{C}_0(\alpha)$.

The core framework corresponding to a blocks world W capturing generic information about W. The instantiated framework encodes information that is specific to a planning problem. Namely, $\mathcal{R}_I$ contains all rules in $\mathcal{R}_0$ and with an addition rule to describe what is to be achieved in the final situation (Rule 1), facts to describe the time step sequence (Rule 2), and facts to describe the initial situation (Rule 3). We illustrate Definitions 5 and 6 with the following example.

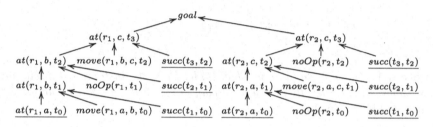

Fig. 2. An argument for *goal* in Example 2. To save space, all leaf nodes τ, as the child of underlined nodes, are omitted.

Example 2 (Example 1 continued.) As given in Definition 6, we introduce rules
$$goal \leftarrow at(r_1, c, t_3), at(r_2, c, t_3)$$
$$at(r_1, a, t_3) \leftarrow at(r_2, a, t_3) \leftarrow smaller(r_1, r_2) \leftarrow$$
in the instantiated framework. An admissible argument for *goal*, $A = \Delta \vdash goal$, is shown in Fig. 2 with $\Delta = \{move(r_1, a, b, t_0), noOp(r_2, a, t_0), noOp(r_1, b, t_1), move(r_2, a, c, t_1), move(r_1, b, c, t_2), noOp(r_2, c, t_2)\}$. Arguments attacking A are in Table 1.[3] Arguments attacking $B_1 \ldots G_2$ (thus defending A) are shown in Table 2 (B_1' attacks B_1, B_2' attacks B_2, etc.). We observe that all arguments in Table 2 are supported by assumptions in Δ except $B_3' = \{nA(r_2, c, t_0)\} \vdash nA(r_2, c, t_0)$, $E_2' = \{nA(r_1, a, t_1)\} \vdash nA(r_1, a, t_1)$ and $F_3' = \{nA(r_2, b, t_2)\} \vdash nA(r_2, b, t_2)$. Among these, B_3' is not attacked as there is no argument for $at(r_2, c, t_0)$. E_2' is attacked by $H = \{n(r_1, a, t_0)\} \vdash at(r_1, a, t_1)$ and F_3' is attacked by $I_1 = \{m(r_2, a, b, t_0), n(r_2, b, t_1)\} \vdash at(r_2, b, t_2)$, $I_2 = \{m(r_2, a, c, t_0), m(r_2, c, b, t_1)\} \vdash at(r_2, b, t_2)$, and argument $I_3 = \{n(r_2, a, t_0), m(r_2, a, b, t_1)\} \vdash at(r_2, b, t_2)$. However, H is attacked by B_1', I_1 and I_2 are attacked by B_2'. I_3 is attacked by E_1'. Thus, A is defended by arguments in Table 2.

---

[3] Here, m, n, nA and o are short-hands for *move, noOp, notAt* and *occupied*, respectively.

Table 2. Summary of arguments defending A in Example 2.

B_1' $\{m(r_1,a,b,t_0)\} \vdash m(r_1,a,b,t_0)$	B_2' $\{n(r_2,a,t_0)\} \vdash n(r_2,a,t_0)$
B_3' $\{nA(r_2,c,t_0)\} \vdash nA(r_2,c,t_0)$	B_4' $\{m(r_1,a,b,t_0)\} \vdash m(r_1,a,b,t_0)$
B_5' $\{\} \vdash at(r_1,a,t_0)$	
C_1' $\{n(r_2,a,t_0)\} \vdash n(r_2,a,t_0)$	C_2' $\{n(r_2,a,t_0)\} \vdash n(r_2,a,t_0)$
D_1' $\{n(r_1,b,t_1)\} \vdash n(r_1,b,t_1)$	D_2' $\{n(r_1,b,t_1)\} \vdash n(r_1,b,t_1)$
E_1' $\{m(r_2,a,c,t_1)\} \vdash m(r_2,a,c,t_1)$	E_2' $\{nA(r_1,a,t_1)\} \vdash nA(r_1,a,t_1)$
E_3' $\{n(r_1,b,t_1)\} \vdash n(r_1,b,t_1)$	E_4' $\{m(r_2,a,c,t_1)\} \vdash m(r_2,a,c,t_1)$
E_5' $\{n(r_2,a,t_0)\} \vdash at(r_2,a,t_1)$	E_6' $\{m(r_1,a,b,t_0)\} \vdash m(r_1,a,b,t_0)$
E_7' $\{m(r_1,a,b,t_0)\} \vdash m(r_1,a,b,t_0)$	
F_1' $\{m(r_1,b,c,t_2)\} \vdash m(r_1,b,c,t_2)$	F_2' $\{n(r_2,c,t_2)\} \vdash n(r_2,c,t_2)$
F_3' $\{nA(r_2,b,t_2)\} \vdash nA(r_2,b,t_2)$	F_4' $\{m(r_1,b,c,t_2)\} \vdash m(r_1,b,c,t_2)$
F_5' $\{m(r_1,a,b,t_0),n(r_1,b,t_1)\} \vdash at(r_1,b,t_2)$	
G_1' $\{n(r_2,c,t_2)\} \vdash n(r_2,c,t_2)$	G_2' $\{n(r_2,c,t_2)\} \vdash n(r_2,c,t_2)$

Theorem 1. *Given a planning problem Π, let F_I be the instantiated framework corresponding to Π, then there is a valid plan for Π iff there exists an admissible argument $\Delta \vdash goal$ in F_I.*

Proof (Sketch.) We first show that if a plan exists then an admissible argument $A = \Delta \vdash goal$. By Rule 1 in Definition 6, we know that to "prove" $goal$, we need to "prove" $at(X, L, t_n)$ for all blocks X, each at some location L. It is easy to see that using a combination of Rules 2 & 3 in Definition 5, all blocks can be placed to their specified locations (assuming t_n is large enough) so A can be constructed. To see that A is admissible, we make the following observations.

- Arguments targeting at $\alpha = noOp(\_,\_,\_)$ are of the form $\{move(\_,\_,\_,\_)\} \vdash move(\_,\_,\_,\_)$. These arguments can be counterattacked by $N = \{\alpha\} \vdash \alpha$. N does not attack A.
- Arguments targeting at $\alpha' = move(X, L, L', T)$ are of the following forms:
  (1) $\{noOp(X, L, T)\} \vdash noOp(X, L, T)$ (not to move X away from L at time T) and $\{move(X, L, L'', T)\} \vdash move(X, L, L'', T)$ (move X to a different location). These arguments can be counterattacked by $M = \{\alpha'\} \vdash \alpha'$. M does not attack A.
  (2) $\{move(X', L''', L', T)\} \vdash move(X, L'', L', T)$. These can be counterattacked by either $\{move(X', L''', L^*, T)\} \vdash move(X, L''', L^*, T)$ or $\{noOp(X', L''', T)\} \vdash noOp(X', L''', T)$ or $\{notAt(X', L''', T)\} \vdash notAt(X', L''', T)$. These arguments do not attack A.
  (3) $\_ \vdash above(X', X, L, T)$. By Rule 1 in Definition 5, to have arguments of this form, we need to have some block X' at the same location as X but smaller. Under such cases, X should not be moved thus no such $move(X, L, L', T)$ would be used to support A.
  (4) $\_ \vdash occupied(X', X, T)$. By Rule 4 in Definition 5, to have arguments of this form, we have some block smaller than X at the destination of the

Table 3. Arguments attacking A' in Example 3.

Arguments targeting at $move(r_1, a, c, t_0)$:
$B_1 = \{m(r_1, a, b, t_0)\} \vdash m(r_1, a, b, t_0)$ $B_2 = \{m(r_2, a, c, t_0)\} \vdash m(r_2, a, c, t_0)$
$B_3 = \{m(r_2, b, c, t_0)\} \vdash m(r_1, b, c, t_0)$ $B_4 = \{n(r_1, a, t_0)\} \vdash n(r_1, a, t_0)$
$B_5 = \{nA(r_1, a, t_0)\} \vdash nA(r_1, a, t_0)$
Arguments targeting at $noOp(r_2, a, t_0)$:
$C_1 = \{m(r_2, a, b, t_0)\} \vdash m(r_2, a, b, t_0)$ $C_2 = \{m(r_2, a, c, t_0)\} \vdash m(r_2, a, c, t_0)$
Arguments targeting at $noOp(r_1, c, t_1)$:
$D_1 = \{m(r_1, c, a, t_1)\} \vdash m(r_1, c, a, t_1)$ $D_2 = \{m(r_1, c, b, t_1)\} \vdash m(r_1, c, b, t_1)$
Arguments targeting at $move(r_2, a, c, t_1)$:
$E_1 = \{m(r_2, a, b, t_1)\} \vdash m(r_2, a, b, t_0)$ $E_2 = \{m(r_1, a, c, t_1)\} \vdash m(r_1, a, c, t_1)$
$E_3 = \{m(r_1, b, c, t_1)\} \vdash m(r_1, b, c, t_1)$ $E_4 = \{n(r_2, a, t_1)\} \vdash n(r_2, a, t_1)$
$E_5 = \{nA(r_2, a, t_1)\} \vdash nA(r_2, a, t_1)$ $E_6 = \{m(r_1, a, c, t_0)\} \vdash o(r_2, c, t_1)$
$E_7 = \{n(r_1, a, t_0), n(r_2, a, t_0)\} \vdash above(r_1, r_2, a, t_1)$

move. In such cases, X should not be moved to that destination so no such $move(X, L, L', T)$ would be used to support A.

Since a plan exists for this problem, a sequence of *moves* and *noOps*, which would not trigger indefensible attacks from $\Delta \vdash above(X', X, L, T)$ or $\Delta \vdash occupied(X', X, T)$ must exist. The other direction of this theorem is trivial as once an admissible A is found, assumptions from A consist a plan.   □

The following corollary follows trivially from Theorem 1.

Corollary 1 *Given a planning problem Π, let F_I be the instantiated framework corresponding to Π, if $\Delta \vdash goal$ is admissible in F_I, then Δ is a valid plan for Π.*[4]

Theorem 1 and Corollary 1 establish the connection between planning in blocks world and ABA frameworks. The admissibility of the argument A for *goal* can be viewed as a means to justify the "validity" of the plan as every assumption supporting the argument A is "defended". This can be read as every action in the plan is valid. Similarly, non-admissible arguments of the form $\Delta \vdash goal$ correspond to invalid plans, illustrated with the next example.

Example 3 Given the blocks world shown in Fig. 1, the plan

$$P = \{move(r_1, a, c, t_0), noOp(r_2, a, t_0), move(r_2, a, c, t_1), noOp(r_2, c, t_1)\}$$

is invalid as c is occupied by r_1 at t_1 and $r_1 < r_2$. So $move(r_2, a, c, t_1)$ is invalid and it is in an explanation for P. Let F_I be the instantiated framework.

$$A' = \{move(r_1, a, c, t_0), noOp(r_2, a, t_0), move(r_2, a, c, t_1), noOp(r_2, c, t_1)\} \vdash goal$$

---

[4] We abuse the notation Δ. Here and hereinafter, Δ is used to represent both a set of assumptions in the instantiated framework F_I and a plan containing a set of actions with syntactically identical names in the corresponding planning problem Π.

is not admissible in F_I. Arguments attacking A' are shown in Table 3. Using reasoning similar to Example 2, we see that A is able to defend all of its attackers except E_6 as E_6 is supported by a single assumption $m(r_1, a, c, t_0)$, which also supports A'. Thus, any argument B_i attacks E_6 must also attack A'. Any set of argument containing A', B_i cannot be conflict-free, therefore A' is not admissible.

5   Conclusion

In this paper, we studied how to use ABA to model planning problems in line with the *defeasible planning* proposal suggested by Pollock. Using blocks world as a case study, we demonstrated the feasibility of using ABA to plan. The two key ideas are (1) with actions modelled with assumptions, plan construction can be equated to the construction of ABA arguments and (2) by modelling action constraints as arguments attacking the plan, identifying valid plans can be equated to computing admissible ABA arguments. In future, we will generalise this work to create argumentation-based planning models, study its connection with situation calculus, SAT planning, or BDD-based symbolic planning and apply our work in some real-world practical planning applications.

References

1. Amgoud, L., Devred, C., Lagasquie-Schiex, M.: A constrained argumentation system for practical reasoning. In Proceedings of AAMAS, Richland, SC, pp. 429–436. International Foundation for Autonomous Agents and Multiagent Systems (2008)
2. Amgoud, L., Devred, C., Lagasquie-Schiex, M.: Generating possible intentions with constrained argumentation systems. IJAR **52**(9), 1363–1391 (2011)
3. Čyras, K., Fan, X., Schulz, C., Toni, F.: Assumption-based argumentation: disputes, explanations, preferences. J. Appl. Logics - IfCoLoG J. Logics Appl. **4**(8), 2407–2456 (2017)
4. García, D.R., García, A.J., Simari, G.R.: Defeasible reasoning and partial order planning. In: Hartmann, S., Kern-Isberner, G. (eds.) FoIKS 2008. LNCS, vol. 4932, pp. 311–328. Springer, Heidelberg (2008). https://doi.org/10.1007/978-3-540-77684-0_21
5. Nau, D., Ghallab, M., Traverso, P.: Automated Planning: Theory & Practice. Morgan Kaufmann Publishers Inc., San Francisco (2004)
6. Pollock, J.: Defeasible planning. In: Proceedings of AAAI Workshop, Integrating Planning, Scheduling and Execution in Dynamic and Uncertain Environments (1998)

Progressive Inference Algorithms for Probabilistic Argumentation

Nguyen Duy Hung$^{(\boxtimes)}$

Sirindhorn International Institute of Technology,
Pathum Thani, Thailand
hung.nd.siit@gmail.com

Abstract. We develop a progressive inference approach for Probabilistic Argumentation, and then implement obtained algorithms for three standard semantics: the credulous, the ideal, and the skeptical preferred semantics. Like their exact counterparts, these algorithms can be destined to compute the exact answers, however while doing so, they can output immediate answers increasingly close to the exact ones.

Keywords: Probabilistic argumentation · Approximate inference

1 Introduction

Probabilistic Argumentation (PA) aims at combining the strengths of argumentation theory and probability theory. Focusing on appropriate structures and semantics for PA, researchers in [6,9,14,17,22] have proposed different frameworks of PA. Others pay attention to computational issues, notably computing the probability that a given argument is acceptable under a certain semantics [10,11,21], or computing the probability that there exists an acceptable argument supporting a given proposition [12,13], among other issues [2,7,17]. Since the complexity of these algorithms, due to the nature of the problem, is not always bearable for applications, in this paper we are interested in their approximate counterparts. To this end, we can restrict ourselves to Probabilistic Assumption-based Argumentation (PABA [6] - a PA framework using Assumption-based Argumentation (ABA [1]) to structure arguments) without any loss of generality because, as shown in [13], many PA frameworks including [17,19] can be easily translated into PABA (see also Sect. 6). Let's illustrate our contributions using a sample PABA framework below[1], which is also used throughout the paper.

Example 1. Let $\mathcal{P} = (\mathcal{A}_p, \mathcal{N}, \mathcal{F})$ be a PABA framework where

- $\mathcal{F} = (\mathcal{R}, \mathcal{A}, \overline{})$ is an ABA framework with a set of (logical) assumptions $\mathcal{A} = \{not\ runaway, not\ bark, not\ alarm\}$ where the contrary $\overline{not\ x}$ of each assumption $not\ x$ is simply x, and $\mathcal{R}$ consists of inference rules for describing:

---

[1] PABA and ABA are formally defined in Sect. 2.

© Springer Nature Switzerland AG 2018
T. Miller et al. (Eds.): PRIMA 2018, LNAI 11224, pp. 371–386, 2018.
https://doi.org/10.1007/978-3-030-03098-8_23

- an alarm rings with different probabilities upon different events.
  $alarm \leftarrow burglary, earthquake, \boldsymbol{p1}\_alarm$
  $alarm \leftarrow burglary, \neg earthquake, \boldsymbol{p2}\_alarm$
  $alarm \leftarrow \neg burglary, earthquake, \boldsymbol{p3}\_alarm$
- a dog's behavior: it barks if there is a burglary, and runs away if there is an earthquake. If both events occur, it may do one or both actions.
  $bark \leftarrow burglary, not\ runaway \quad runaway \leftarrow earthquake, not\ bark$
- what a tenant might notice: $nothing \leftarrow not\ bark, not\ alarm$
- $\mathcal{A}_p$ is a set of probabilistic assumptions $\{b, e, p_1, p_2, p_3\}^2$ whose joint probability distribution is represented by a Bayesian network $\mathcal{N} = (G, \Theta)$ with structure G and probabilistic parameters Θ^3 below.

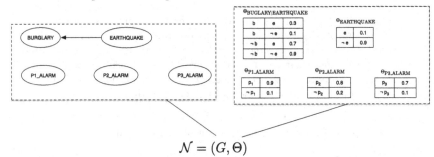

$$\mathcal{N} = (G, \Theta)$$

A **possible world** is a truth assignment to all probabilistic assumptions, and hence BN $\mathcal{N}$ can also be viewed as representing the probability distribution over the set of all possible worlds $\mathcal{W}$.

To compute the probability that there exists an acceptable argument for a given proposition q under a certain semantics sem, denoted $Pr_{sem}(q)$, a native approach is to follow the definition of $Pr_{sem}(q)$ (given in Sect. 2.4) directly, as follows: (1) iterate over the set of all possible worlds $\mathcal{W}$ to compute the subset $\mathcal{W}_q \subseteq \mathcal{W}$ in which there is an acceptable argument for q; and (2) compute the probability of each world $\omega \in \mathcal{W}_q$ and return their sum. For example, in computing $Pr_{cr}(bark)$ (the **credulous** semantics), the first step ends up with $\mathcal{W}_{bark} = \{\omega \in \mathcal{W} \mid \omega \supseteq \{b\}\}$, which intuitively says that the dog might bark whenever there is a burglary. However in computing $Pr_{sem}(bark)$ with $sem \in \{gr, id, sk\}$ (**grounded/ideal/skeptical** preferred), $\mathcal{W}_{bark} = \{\omega \in \mathcal{W} \mid \omega \supseteq \{b, \neg e\}\}$ since the dog surely barks only if there is no earthquake. Unfortunately this native approach *always* results in an exponential blowup since it iterates over as many as $2^{|\mathcal{A}_p|}$ possible worlds. An obvious way to address this problem, which is followed in [13], is to suppress this iteration. Concretely, the algorithms of [13] start from a given proposition q and characterizes the set of all possible worlds in which q is acceptable in terms of a DNF (Disjunctive Normal Form) formula whose each constituent disjunct describes a combination of probabilistic assumptions sufficient for the acceptability of q. Abstractly, this process can be seen as a

---

[2] Shorthands for $burglary, earthquake, \boldsymbol{p1}\_alarm, \boldsymbol{p2}\_alarm, \boldsymbol{p3}\_alarm$ respectively.
[3] The dependency of burglaries on earthquakes as well as parameter values are made up for the sake of illustrations.

translation $q \overset{sem}{\Longleftrightarrow} DNF_q$. For example, $bark \overset{cr}{\Longleftrightarrow} b$ while $bark \overset{sem}{\Longleftrightarrow} b \wedge \neg e$ for $sem \in \{gr, id, sk\}$. However, due to the complex nature of the problem, the complexity of these exact algorithms [13, 21] can be unbearable for many applications. Hence, in this paper we are interested in their approximate counterparts that can transparently substitute them. In particular, we show herein that the task can be solved increasingly well as time flies. As a result we obtain progressive algorithms, which can be destined to compute the exact answers and on the way doing so, can output immediate answers that are increasingly close to the exact ones. Figure 1(a) gives a visual illustration for what being said, while Fig. 1(b) offers an example: in computing $Pr_{sk}(bark)$, our progressive algorithms may return $Pr_{\mathcal{N}}(b \wedge \neg e)$ if they are destined to compute the exact answer or the given time budget is sufficient; otherwise may return an interval $[0, Pr_{\mathcal{N}}(b)]$.

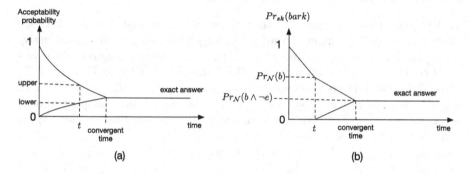

Fig. 1. Progressive inference

To the best of our knowledge, approximate inference has not been explored in the current PA literature, though approximate algorithms have been well developed and heavily used in related fields, like Probabilistic Graphical Models (see [16]) or Probabilistic Logic Programming (e.g. in Problog system [8]). The rest of this paper is structured as follows. Section 2 presents the background. Section 3 summarizes the exact approach in [13] and sets the stage for our approximate approach presented in Sect. 4. Section 5 materializes our approximate approach, presenting progressive algorithms in an abstract form and then in pseudo code. This section also demonstrates a Prolog-based implementation for three semantics: the credulous, the ideal, and the skeptical preferred (download link: http:// hung.network/prengine/2.0). Section 6 presents related work and concludes. Due to the lack of space, we omit the proofs of technical results.

2 Background

2.1 Abstract Argumentation

An AA framework [3] $\mathcal{F}$ is a pair (AR, Att) where AR is a set of arguments, $Att \subseteq AR \times AR$ and $(A, B) \in Att$ means that A attacks B. $S \subseteq AR$ attacks

$A \in AR$ iff $(B, A) \in Att$ for some $B \in S$. $A \in AR$ is acceptable wrt to S iff S attacks every argument attacking A. S is *conflict-free* iff S does not attack itself; *admissible* iff S is conflict-free and each argument in S is acceptable wrt S; *complete* iff S is admissible and contains every arguments acceptable wrt S; a *preferred* (credulous) extension iff S is a maximal (wrt set inclusion) complete set; the *grounded* extension iff S is the least complete set; the ideal extension iff it is the maximal admissible set contained in every preferred extension. An argument A is accepted under semantics $sem \in \{cr, gr, id\}^4$, denoted $\mathcal{F} \vdash_{sem} A$, iff A is in a sem extension. Finally A is **sk**eptically preferred accepted, denoted $\mathcal{F} \vdash_{sk} A$, if A is in each preferred extension. It is well-known that $\mathcal{F} \vdash_{gr} A \Longrightarrow \mathcal{F} \vdash_{sk} A \Longrightarrow \mathcal{F} \vdash_{id} A \Longrightarrow \mathcal{F} \vdash_{cr} A$ but the reverse may not hold.

2.2   Assumption-Based Argumentation

As AA ignores the internal structure of argument, an instance of AA called Assumption-Based Argumentation (ABA [4,5]) defines arguments by deductive proofs based on assumptions and inference rules. Assuming a language $\mathcal{L}$ consisting of countably many sentences, an ABA framework is a triple $\mathcal{F} = (\mathcal{R}, \mathcal{A}, \bar{\ })$ where $\mathcal{R}$ is a set of inference rules of the form $r : l_0 \leftarrow l_1, \ldots, l_n$ $(n \geq 0, l_i \in \mathcal{L})^5$, $\mathcal{A} \subseteq \mathcal{L}$ is a set of assumptions, and $\bar{\ }$ is a (total) one-to-one mapping from $\mathcal{A}$ into $\mathcal{L}$, where $\bar{x}$ is referred to as the *contrary* of x. Assumptions do not appear in the heads of inference rules.

A *(backward) deduction* of a conclusion q supported by a set of premises Q is a sequence of sets $S_1, S_2, \ldots, S_n$ where $S_i \subseteq \mathcal{L}$, $S_1 = \{q\}$, $S_n = Q$, and for every i, where σ is the selected proposition in S_i: $\sigma \notin Q$ and $S_{i+1} = S_i \setminus \{\sigma\} \cup body(r)$ for some inference rule $r \in \mathcal{R}$ with $head(r) = \sigma$.

An argument for $q \in \mathcal{L}$ supported by a set of assumptions Q is a deduction from q to Q and denoted by (Q, q). An argument (Q, q) attacks an argument (Q', q') if q is the contrary of some assumption in Q'.

A proposition q is said to be credulously/groundedly/ideally/skeptically accepted in ABA $\mathcal{F}$, denoted $\mathcal{F} \vdash_{sem} q$ (where $sem \in \{cr, gr, id, sk\}$) if in the AA framework consisting of above defined arguments and attacks, there is an argument for q accepted under the corresponding semantics of abstract argumentation. So the order of skepticism among ABA semantics is $\mathcal{F} \vdash_{gr} q \Longrightarrow \mathcal{F} \vdash_{sk} q \Longrightarrow \mathcal{F} \vdash_{id} q \Longrightarrow \mathcal{F} \vdash_{cr} q$. For a thorough tutorial of ABA, see [23].

2.3   AB-dispute Derivations

Different forms of dispute derivations have been developed to compute the semantics of ABA. To compute the credulous semantics of an ABA $\mathcal{F} = (\mathcal{R}, \mathcal{A}, \bar{\ })$, AB-dispute derivations simulate a dispute between two fictitious players: proponent and opponent. Formally, in [4,5] an AB-dispute derivation is defined as a sequence of tuples $\langle \mathcal{P}_0, \mathcal{O}_0, A_0, C_0 \rangle \ldots \langle \mathcal{P}_i, \mathcal{O}_i, A_i, C_i \rangle \ldots$, where A_i

---

[4] credulous/**gr**ounded/**id**eal semantics.
[5] For convenience, define $head(r) = l_0$ and $body(r) = \{l_1, \ldots l_n\}$.

is the set of defense assumptions (consisting of all assumptions occurring in the proponent's arguments) and C_i is the set of culprits (consisting of all opponent's assumptions that the proponent attacks). Multi-set $\mathcal{P}_i$ consists of propositions belonging to any of the proponent's potential arguments. Multi-set $\mathcal{O}_i$ consists of multi-sets of propositions representing the state of all of the opponent's potential arguments.

Definition 1. *1. An AB-dispute derivation using a selection strategy sl is a sequence $t_0, \ldots, t_i, t_{i+1}, \ldots$ where for each $i \geq 0$, two conditions below hold.*
   (a) t_i is a tuple $\langle \mathcal{P}_i, \mathcal{O}_i, A_i, C_i \rangle$ where $\mathcal{P}_i$ is a multi-set of propositions; $\mathcal{O}_i$ is a multi-set of finite multi-sets of propositions; A_i and C_i are sets of assumptions.
   (b) $t_{i+1} \in FollowAB_{\mathcal{F}}(t_i, sl)$ where $FollowAB_{\mathcal{F}}(t_i, sl)$ is defined by Definition 2.
*2. An AB-dispute derivation **for a proposition** π starts with $t_0 = \langle \{\pi\}, \emptyset, A \cap \{\pi\}, \emptyset \rangle$. It is said to be **successful** if it ends with t_n of the form $\langle \emptyset, \emptyset, \_, \_ \rangle$.*

Definition 2. *Given a tuple $t_i = \langle \mathcal{P}_i, \mathcal{O}_i, A_i, C_i \rangle$ and a selection function sl that selects: (1) a sentence $\sigma \in \mathcal{P}_i$, or (2) a sentence $\sigma \in S$ for some $S \in \mathcal{O}_i$, or (3) an empty set $\emptyset \in \mathcal{O}_i$; $FollowAB_{\mathcal{F}}(t_i, sl)$ is defined respectively as follows.*

1. If sl selects $\sigma \in \mathcal{P}_i$ then
   (a) if $\sigma \in A$ then $FollowAB_{\mathcal{F}}(t_i, sl) = \{\langle \mathcal{P}_i - \{\sigma\}, \mathcal{O}_i \cup \{\{\bar{\sigma}\}\}, A_i, C_i \rangle\}$.
   (b) otherwise, $FollowAB_{\mathcal{F}}(t_i, sl)$ consists of tuples $\langle \mathcal{P}_i \setminus \{\sigma\} \cup (Bd \setminus A_i), \mathcal{O}_i, A_i \cup (A \cap Bd), C_i \rangle$ for each rule $\sigma \leftarrow Bd$ in $\mathcal{R}$ such that $C_i \cap Bd = \emptyset$.
2. If sl selects $\sigma \in S$ for some $S \in \mathcal{O}_i$, then
   (a) If $\sigma \in A$, then
      i if $\sigma \in C_i$, then $FollowAB_{\mathcal{F}}(t_i, sl) = \{\langle \mathcal{P}_i, \mathcal{O}_i \setminus \{S\}, A_i, C_i \rangle\}$.
      ii otherwise,
         A. if $\sigma \in A_i$ then $FollowAB_{\mathcal{F}}(t_i, sl) = \{\langle \mathcal{P}_i, \mathcal{O}_i \setminus \{S\} \cup \{S \setminus \{\sigma\}\}, A_i, C_i \rangle\}$.
         B. otherwise, $FollowAB_{\mathcal{F}}(t_i, sl) = \{\langle \mathcal{P}_i \cup \{\bar{\sigma}\}, \mathcal{O} \setminus \{S\}, A_i, C_i \cup \{\sigma\} \rangle, \langle \mathcal{P}_i, \mathcal{O}_i \setminus \{S\} \cup \{S \setminus \{\sigma\}\}, A_i, C_i \rangle\}$.
   (b) otherwise, $FollowAB_{\mathcal{F}}(t_i, sl) = \{\langle \mathcal{P}_i, \mathcal{O}_i \setminus \{S\} \cup \{S \setminus \{\sigma\} \cup Bd \mid \sigma \leftarrow Bd \in \mathcal{R} \text{ and } Bd \cap C_i = \emptyset\}, A_i, C_i \rangle\}$.
3. If sl selects $\emptyset \in \mathcal{O}_i$ then $FollowAB_{\mathcal{F}}(t_i, sl) = \emptyset$.

Note that $FollowAB_{\mathcal{F}}(t_i, sl)$ is a singleton set except in two cases: 1.b and 2.a.ii.B. An example of successful AB-dispute derivations is given in Table 1.

The **soundness** and **completeness** of AB-dispute derivations for credulous acceptances have been proved in [5]. In particular: (1) Soundness: For any successful AB-dispute derivation $\langle \mathcal{P}_0, \mathcal{O}_0, A_0, C_0 \rangle, \ldots, \langle \mathcal{P}_n, \mathcal{O}_n, A_n, C_n \rangle$ for a proposition π, A_n is an admissible set of assumptions[6] and supports π; and (2) Completeness: In a positively acyclic and finitary ABA $\mathcal{F}$[7],

---

[6] Note that any admissible set of assumptions is a subset of some preferred set of assumptions; and any preferred set of assumptions is also admissible.

[7] An ABA $\mathcal{F}$ is finitary if for each node in the dependency graph of $\mathcal{F}$, there is a finite number of nodes reachable from it; and positively acyclic if in the dependency graph of $\mathcal{F}$, there is no infinite directed path consisting solely non-assumption nodes.

Table 1. A successful AB-dispute derivation for *bark* in ABA $\mathcal{F}'$ obtained from the ABA $\mathcal{F}$ in Example 1 by adding two facts: $e \leftarrow$ and $b \leftarrow$. Note that notation $\underline{x}$ means that x is selected by selection function sl.

	$\mathcal{P}_i$	$\mathcal{O}_i$	A_i	C_i	$FollowAB_{\mathcal{F}'}(t_i, sl)$
t_0	$\{\underline{bark}\}$	$\{\}$	$\{\}$	$\{\}$	$\{t_1\}$
t_1	$\{\underline{b}, not\ runaway\}$	$\{\}$	$\{not\ runaway\}$	$\{\}$	$\{t_2\}$
t_2	$\{\underline{not\ runaway}\}$	$\{\}$	$\{not\ runaway\}$	$\{\}$	$\{t_3\}$
t_3	$\{\}$	$\{\{\underline{runaway}\}\}$	$\{not\ runaway\}$	$\{\}$	$\{t_4\}$
t_4	$\{\}$	$\{\{\underline{e}, not\ bark\}\}$	$\{not\ runaway\}$	$\{\}$	$\{t_5\}$
t_5	$\{\}$	$\{\{\underline{not\ bark}\}\}$	$\{not\ runaway\}$	$\{\}$	$\{t_6\}$
t_6	$\{\underline{bark}\}$	$\{\}$	$\{not\ runaway\}$	$\{not\ bark\}$	$\{t_7\}$
t_7	$\{\underline{b}\}$	$\{\}$	$\{not\ runaway\}$	$\{not\ bark\}$	$\{t_8\}$
t_8	$\{\}$	$\{\}$	$\{not\ runaway\}$	$\{not\ bark\}$	undefined

- If π is supported by an admissible set S of assumptions, then for any selection strategy there is a successful AB-dispute derivation $\ldots, \langle \mathcal{P}_n, \mathcal{O}_n, A_n, C_n \rangle$ for π where $A_n \subseteq S$.
- There are no infinite AB-dispute derivations for any proposition.

2.4   Probabilistic Assumption-Based Argumentation

A PABA framework [6] represents a probability distribution of ABA frameworks. The focus of this paper is a subclass of PABA called Bayesian PABA [13] where the probabilistic information is represented by a Bayesian network.

Definition 3. *A (Bayesian) PABA framework $\mathcal{P}$ is a tuple $(\mathcal{A}_p, \mathcal{N}, \mathcal{F})$ where*

- $\mathcal{F} = (\mathcal{R}, \mathcal{A}, ^{\frown})$ *is an ABA framework with a set of (logical) assumptions $\mathcal{A}$ and a set of inference rules $\mathcal{R}$,*
- $\mathcal{A}_p = \{x_1, \ldots, x_m\}$ *is a set of so-called positive probabilistic assumptions and elements of $\neg \mathcal{A}_p = \{\neg x \mid x \in \mathcal{A}_p\}$ are called negative probabilistic assumptions[8], and*
- *No probabilistic assumption occurs in $\mathcal{A}$ or in the head of a rule in $\mathcal{R}$, and*
- $\mathcal{N} = (G, \Theta)$ *is a Bayesian network of Boolean variables such that for each (positive) probabilistic assumption $x_i \in \mathcal{A}_p$, $\mathcal{N}$ has a corresponding Boolean node X_i (with possible values $\{x_i, \neg x_i\}$) [9].*

The probability distribution induced by $\mathcal{N}$ is denoted by $Pr_{\mathcal{N}}(.)$. The semantics of PABA is defined as follows.

---

[8] A probabilistic assumption is an element of $\mathcal{A}_p \cup \neg \mathcal{A}_p$. A proposition not in $\mathcal{A}_p \cup \neg \mathcal{A}_p$ is called a non-probabilistic proposition.

[9] G is a directed acyclic graph over $\mathcal{X} = \{X_1, \ldots, X_m\}$ and Θ is a set of conditional probability tables (CPTs), one CPT $\Theta_{X|par(X)}$ for each $X \in \mathcal{X}$.

Definition 4. – *A **possible world** is a maximal (wrt set inclusion) consistent subset of $\mathcal{A}_p \cup \neg \mathcal{A}_p$.*
$\mathcal{W}$ denotes the set of all possible worlds, and for each $\omega \in \mathcal{W}$, $\mathcal{F}_\omega$ denotes the ABA framework $(\mathcal{R}_\omega, \mathcal{A}, \overline{})$ with $\mathcal{R}_\omega \triangleq \mathcal{R} \cup \{p \leftarrow | p \in \omega\}$.

– *The **acceptability probability of a proposition** q **under semantics** sem, denoted $Pr_{sem}(q)$, is the probability that there is an acceptable argument for q under sem, i.e. $Pr_{sem}(q) \triangleq \sum\limits_{\mathcal{F}_\omega \vdash_{sem} q}^{\omega \in \mathcal{W}} Pr_{\mathcal{N}}(\omega)$.*

Example 2 (Continue Example 1.) Table 2 shows the necessary and sufficient condition on a possible world $\omega \in \mathcal{W}$ for $\mathcal{F}_\omega \vdash_{sem} q$ (Note that $|\mathcal{W}| = 2^5$). For instance, the second rows says that for $sem \in \{id, sk, gr\}$, $\mathcal{F}_\omega \vdash_{sem} bark$ iff $\omega \supseteq \{b, \neg e\}$, thus $Pr_{sem}(bark) = \sum\limits_{\omega \supseteq \{b, \neg e\}}^{\omega \in \mathcal{W}} Pr_{\mathcal{N}}(\omega)$.

Table 2. Necessary and sufficient condition on ω for $\mathcal{F}_\omega \vdash_{sem} q$

q	$\mathcal{F}_\omega \vdash_{sem} q$ ($sem \in \{id, sk, gr\}$) iff	$\mathcal{F}_\omega \vdash_{cr} q$ iff
$bark$	$\omega \supseteq \{b, \neg e\}$	$\omega \supseteq \{b\}$
$runaway$	$\omega \supseteq \{\neg b, e\}$	$\omega \supseteq \{e\}$
$alarm$	$\omega \supseteq s_1 \vee \omega \supseteq s_2 \vee \omega \supseteq s_3$ where $s_1 = \{b, e, p_1\}, s_2 = \{b, \neg e, p_2\}, s_3 = \{\neg b, e, p_3\}$	$\omega \supseteq s_1 \vee \omega \supseteq s_2 \vee \omega \supseteq s_3$
$nothing$	$\omega \supseteq s_1' \vee \omega \supseteq s_2'$ where $s_1' = \{\neg b, \neg e\}, s_2' = \{\neg b, e, \neg p_3\}$	$\omega \supseteq s_1' \vee \omega \supseteq s_2' \vee \omega \supseteq s_3'$ where $s_3' = \{b, e, \neg p_1\}$

3   Exact Approach for PABA Inferences

From now on, we always refer to an arbitrary but fixed PABA framework $\mathcal{P} = (\mathcal{A}_p, \mathcal{N}, \mathcal{F})$ if not explicitly stated otherwise.

In this section we summarize the exact approach in [13] and set the stage for our approximate approach developed in the next section. As mentioned in the introduction, to compute $Pr_{sem}(q)$, q is first translated into a DNF formula DNF_q in such a way that each disjunct in DNF_q describes a combination of probabilistic assumptions sufficient for the acceptability of q. This DNF formula is represented by a set of subsets of possible worlds, called **frame**, as follows.

Definition 5. – *A **partial world** s is a subset (not necessarily proper) of a possible world and has probability $Pr_{\mathcal{N}}(s) = \sum\limits_{\omega \supseteq s}^{\omega \in \mathcal{W}} Pr_{\mathcal{N}}(\omega)$.*

– *A **frame** $\mathcal{S}$ is a set of partial worlds and has probability $Pr_{\mathcal{N}}(\mathcal{S}) = \sum\limits_{s \in \mathcal{S}} Pr_{\mathcal{N}}(s)$.*

Definition 6. *A partial world s is said to be **sufficient** for a proposition q under semantics sem (for short, **sem-sufficient** for q) if $\mathcal{F}_{s'} \vdash_{sem} q$ for any partial world $s' \supseteq s$.*[10]

Definition 7 *(**Exact Translations.**)*

- *A frame $\mathcal{S}$ is a frame **for a proposition** q **under a semantics** sem (for short, a **sem-frame** for q) if each partial world in $\mathcal{S}$ is sem-sufficient for q.*
- *A sem-frame $\mathcal{S}$ for a proposition q is said to be **complete** (written $q \stackrel{sem}{\Longleftrightarrow} \mathcal{S}$ and shortly read as "q is **translatable to** $\mathcal{S}$"), if for each possible world $\omega \in \mathcal{W}$ where $\mathcal{F}_\omega \vdash_{sem} q$, $\omega \supseteq s$ for some partial world $s \in \mathcal{S}$.*

Example 3 (Continue Example 2.) It is easy to verify the following translations (Table 3).

Table 3. Translating propositions into frames

Prop. q	Frame $\mathcal{S}$ where $q \stackrel{sem}{\Longleftrightarrow} \mathcal{S}$ for $sem \in \{id, sk, gr\}$	Frame $\mathcal{S}$ where $q \stackrel{cr}{\Longleftrightarrow} \mathcal{S}$
$alarm$	$\{\{b, e, p_1\}, \{b, \neg e, p_2\}, \{\neg b, e, p_3\}\}$	$\{\{b, e, p_1\}, \{b, \neg e, p_2\}, \{\neg b, e, p_3\}\}$
$bark$	$\{\{b, \neg e\}\}$	$\{\{b\}\}$
$runaway$	$\{\{\neg b, e\}\}$	$\{\{e\}\}$
$nothing$	$\{\{\neg b, \neg e\}, \{\neg b, e, \neg p_3\}\}$	$\{\{\neg b, \neg e\}, \{b, e, \neg p_1\}, \{\neg b, e, \neg p_3\}\}$

So to compute $Pr_{sem}(q)$, one can first translate $q \stackrel{sem}{\Longleftrightarrow} \mathcal{S}$, then compute $Pr_{\mathcal{N}}(\mathcal{S})$. The following theorem ensures the correctness of this approach.

Theorem 1. *1. If $q \stackrel{sem}{\Longleftrightarrow} \mathcal{S}$ then $Pr_{sem}(q) = Pr_{\mathcal{N}}(\mathcal{S})$.*
2. For any proposition q and semantics sem, $q \stackrel{sem}{\Longleftrightarrow} \mathcal{S}$ for some frame $\mathcal{S}$.

In [13], computing $Pr_{\mathcal{N}}(\mathcal{S})$ is done by Bayesian network algorithms thanks to the following lemma (See Example 4 below for an illustration).

Lemma 1. *Suppose that $\mathcal{S}$ is a frame in a PABA framework $(\mathcal{A}_p, \mathcal{N}, \mathcal{F})$ and $\mathcal{N}'$ is the Bayesian network obtained from $\mathcal{N}$ by adding: for each $s \in \mathcal{S}$, an AND gate representing the conjunction $\bigwedge s$; an OR gate representing the disjunction $\bigvee \mathcal{S}$. Then $Pr_{\mathcal{N}}(\mathcal{S}) = Pr_{\mathcal{N}'}(q)$, where q is the output of the OR gate.*

$Pr_{\mathcal{N}}(\mathcal{S})$ may also be computed by Probabilistic Logic Programming (PLP [8,18,20]), as follows.

Lemma 2. *Suppose that $\mathcal{S}$ is a frame in a PABA framework $(\mathcal{A}_p, \mathcal{N}, \mathcal{F})$ and R is the PLP program obtained from a PLP program representing $\mathcal{N}$ by adding a set of rules $\{q \leftarrow s \mid s \in \mathcal{S}\}$ where q is a new proposition not occurring in $\mathcal{P}$. Then $Pr_{\mathcal{N}}(\mathcal{S})$ coincides with the probability of q wrt R.*

---

[10] Note that $\mathcal{F}_{s'}$ is obtained from $\mathcal{F}$ by adding a set of facts $\{p \leftarrow \mid p \in s'\}$.

Example 4. $Pr_{sk}(nothing)$ can be computed by first translating $nothing \overset{sk}{\Leftrightarrow} S_{nothing} = \{\{\neg b, \neg e\}, \{\neg b, e, \neg p_3\}\}$, then computing $Pr_{\mathcal{N}}(S_{nothing})$ which can be done by querying $Pr_{\mathcal{N}'}(q)$ where $\mathcal{N}'$ is the following BN, or querying $Pr(q)$ wrt the following PLP program [11].

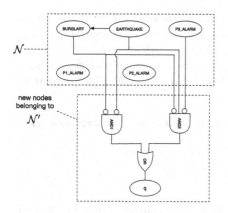

$\mathcal{N}$

new nodes
belonging to

$\mathcal{N}'$

Listing 1.1. A PLP program for solving PABA inference task

```
%% rules representing the original
%% BN network
0.1::e.
0.9::p1.
0.8::p2.
0.7::p3.
0.3:: p_b_given_e.
0.1:: p_b_given_no_e.
b :- e, p_b_given_e.
b :- not e, p_b_given_no_e.
%% added rules for solving inference task
q :- not b, not e.
q :- not b, e, not p3.
```

4   Approximate Approach

It is clear that $Pr_{sem}(q)$ can be approximately computed by either approximately translating $q \overset{sem}{\Longrightarrow} S$, or approximately answering $Pr_{\mathcal{N}}(S) = ?$. Given that algorithms for the second possibility have been well developed in the literature of Probabilistic Graphical Models [16] (furthermore, thanks to Lemma 2, existing approximate algorithms in Probabilistic Logic Programming can also be used), in this paper we focus on the first possibility. So the following definition lies at the heart of our approach. It introduces two kinds of approximate translations: $q \overset{sem}{\Longrightarrow} S$ and $q \overset{sem}{\Longleftarrow} S$, which can be seen as standing for $q \overset{sem}{\Longleftrightarrow} S' \Rightarrow S$ and $q \overset{sem}{\Longleftrightarrow} S' \Leftarrow S$ respectively. Concretely,

Definition 8 (*Approximate Translations*). *Wrt a semantics sem, we say that:*

1. *A proposition q is **under-translatable** to a frame S, written $q \overset{sem}{\Longrightarrow} S$, if q is translatable to a frame S' (i.e. $q \overset{sem}{\Longleftrightarrow} S'$) such that S' logically implies S.*
2. *A proposition q is **over-translatable** to a frame S, written $q \overset{sem}{\Longleftarrow} S$, if q is translatable to a frame S' such that S logically implies S'.*

Continue our running examples, some under-translations under $sem \in \{id, sk, gr\}$ are shown below.

---
[11] We use Problog [8] syntax.

$alarm \overset{sem}{\Longleftrightarrow} \{\{b,e,p_1\},\{b,\neg e,p_2\},\{\neg b,e,p_3\}\} \Rightarrow \{\emptyset\}$
$bark \overset{sem}{\Longleftrightarrow} \{\{b,\neg e\}\} \Rightarrow \{\{b\}\}$
$runaway \overset{sem}{\Longleftrightarrow} \{\{\neg b,e\}\} \Rightarrow \{\{e\}\}$
$nothing \overset{sem}{\Longleftrightarrow} \{\{\neg b,\neg e\},\{\neg b,e,\neg p_3\}\} \Rightarrow \{\{\neg b,\neg e\},\{b,e,\neg p_1\},\{\neg b,e,\neg p_3\}\}$

Note that an extreme case of over-translating q is $q \overset{sem}{\Longleftarrow} \{\}$, which turns q into an empty set of possible worlds. An extreme case of under-translating q is $q \overset{sem}{\Longrightarrow} \{\emptyset\}$, which turns q into the set of all possible worlds.

As stated in Theorem 2 below, approximate inferences using over-translations (resp. under-translations) result in probabilities that are smaller (resp. greater) than the exact ones.

Theorem 2. *Let q be a proposition, S be frame, and sem be an argumentation semantics.*

1. *If $q \overset{sem}{\Longleftarrow} S$ then $Pr_{sem}(q) \geq Pr_N(S)$.*
2. *If $q \overset{sem}{\Longrightarrow} S$ $Pr_{sem}(q) \leq Pr_N(S)$.*

The following lemma ensures that both kinds of approximate inferences shall converge to exact inferences.

Lemma 3. *$q \overset{sem}{\Longleftrightarrow} S$ if and only if $q \overset{sem}{\Longrightarrow} S$ and $q \overset{sem}{\Longleftarrow} S$.*

5   Progressive Algorithms

In this section, we materialize the approximate approach presented in the previous section, by presenting progressive algorithms first in an abstract form called *Translation schemes* (Subsect. 5.1) and then in pseudo code (Subsect. 5.2).

5.1   Translation Schemes

Intuitively, a Translation scheme for semantics *sem* controls the translation process defined in Definition 8. It is defined in terms of a set of states K and three helper functions γ, λ, δ. For example, a translation scheme for the credulous semantics is $\mathcal{M}_{cr} = \langle K, \gamma, \lambda, \delta \rangle$ where

1. K is the set of **states** of $\mathcal{M}_{cr}$. Concretely each state in K is a tuple of the form $\langle P, O, A, C \rangle$ as defined in Subsect. 2.3. A pair (k,s) of a state k and a partial world s is called a *configuration*.
2. γ, called the **acceptance function** of $\mathcal{M}_{cr}$, maps each state $k \in K$ to $\top$ or $\bot$ (true or false) where $\gamma(k) = \top$ iff k has the form $\langle \emptyset, \emptyset, \_, \_ \rangle$. A configuration (k,s) is called an *accepting configuration* if $\gamma(k) = \top$.
3. λ, called the **initialization function** of $\mathcal{M}_{cr}$, maps a given proposition q (which needs to be translated) to a singleton set $\lambda(q) = \{(\langle\{q\},\emptyset, A \cap \{q\},\emptyset\rangle,\emptyset)\}$ containing only one configuration $(\langle\{q\},\emptyset, A \cap \{q\},\emptyset\rangle,\emptyset)$.

4. δ, called the **transition function** of $\mathcal{M}_{cr}$, maps each pair (c, sl) where
   - $c = (k, s)$ is a non-accepting configuration, and
   - sl is a function that selects from $k = \langle \mathcal{P}, \mathcal{O}, A, C \rangle$ either (1) a sentence $\sigma \in \mathcal{P}$, or (2) a sentence $\sigma \in S$ for some $S \in \mathcal{O}$, or (3) an empty set $\emptyset \in \mathcal{O}$,

   into a set of configurations $\delta(c, sl)$ defined as follows.
   (a) If sl selects a sentence σ by case 1 or 2, and further σ is a probabilistic assumption not occurring in s, then $\delta(c, sl) = \{(k, s \cup \{\sigma\}), (k, s \cup \{\neg\sigma\})\}$.
   (b) Otherwise, $\delta(c, sl) = \{(k', s) \mid k' \in FollowAB_{\mathcal{F}_s}(k, sl)\}$.

In general, translation schemes have the following form.

Definition 9. *A Translation scheme is a tuple* $\mathcal{M} = \langle \mathcal{K}, \gamma, \lambda, \delta \rangle$ *where*

1. $\mathcal{K}$ *is a set of* ***states***. *A pair* (k, s) *of a state* k *and a partial world* s *is called a* ***configuration***.
2. γ, *an* ***acceptance function***, *maps each state* k *into a truth value where* $\gamma(k) = \top$ *(resp.* $\gamma(k) = \bot$*) means that* k *is an accepting state (resp. non-accepting state). An accepting (resp. non-accepting) configuration* (k, s) *is such that* $\gamma(k) = \top$ *(resp.* $\gamma(k) = \bot$*).*
3. λ, *an* ***initialization function***, *maps each proposition* q *into a set of configurations* $\lambda(q)$.
4. δ, *a* ***transition function***, *maps each pair* (c, sl) *where*
   - $c = (k, s)$ *is a non-accepting configuration, and*
   - sl *is a selection function whose only requirement is that* $sl(k)$ *is defined.*
   into a set of configurations $\delta(c, sl)$ *satisfying either conditions below.*
   (a) $\delta(c, sl) = \{(k, s \cup \{\sigma\}), (k, s \cup \{\neg\sigma\})\}$ *for some probabilistic assumption* σ *that does not occur in* s.
   (b) $\delta(c, sl) \subseteq \{(k', s) \mid k' \in \mathcal{K}\}$.

The following definition describes how a translation scheme runs in order translate a given proposition q.

Definition 10. *Wrt a Translation scheme* $\mathcal{M} = \langle \mathcal{K}, \gamma, \lambda, \delta \rangle$,

1. *A* ***frame derivation*** *for a sentence* q *using a selection strategy* sl *is a sequence of pairs* $(\mathcal{S}_0, \mathcal{T}_0) \ldots, (\mathcal{S}_i, \mathcal{T}_i) \ldots$ *where:*
   (a) $\mathcal{S}_i$ *is a set of partial worlds and* $\mathcal{T}_i$ *is a set of configurations. The first pair* $(\mathcal{S}_0, \mathcal{T}_0) = (\emptyset, \lambda(q))$.
   (b) *At each step* i, *sl selects a configuration* $c = (k, s)$ *from* $\mathcal{T}_i$, *and*
      i *If* c *is an accepting configuration, then* $\mathcal{T}_{i+1} = \mathcal{T}_i - \{c\}$ *and* $\mathcal{S}_{i+1} = \mathcal{S}_i \cup \{s\}$.
      ii. *Otherwise,* $\mathcal{T}_{i+1} = \mathcal{T}_i - \{c\} \cup \delta(c, sl)$ *and* $\mathcal{S}_{i+1} = \mathcal{S}_i$.
2. *A derivation* $(\mathcal{S}_0, \mathcal{T}_0), \ldots, (\mathcal{S}_n, \mathcal{T}_n)$ *is said to be* ***full*** *if* $\mathcal{T}_n = \emptyset$ *and in such a case* $\mathcal{S}_n$ *is called the* ***derived frame***.

We are interested in **sound** translation schemes, because they ensure that if $\mathcal{S}$ is a derived frame for proposition q, then q is translatable to $\mathcal{S}$. Concretely,

Definition 11. *Let* $\mathcal{M} = \langle \mathcal{K}, \gamma, \lambda, \delta \rangle$ *be a translation scheme and sem be an argumentation semantics. We say that* $\mathcal{M}$ *is* **sound** *under sem iff for any a full frame derivation* $(\mathcal{S}_0, \mathcal{T}_0), \ldots, (\mathcal{S}_n, \mathcal{T}_n)$ *of a proposition* q, $q \overset{sem}{\Longleftrightarrow} \mathcal{S}_n$.

For example, it turns out that:

Lemma 4. *The translation scheme* $\mathcal{M}_{cr}$ *(described at the beginning of this section) is sound under the credulous semantics[12].*

Finally, the following theorem says that full derivations of sound translation scheme perform exact translations, while partial derivations perform under-translations and over-translations at the same time.

Theorem 3. *Let* $\mathcal{M}$ *be a translation scheme, sem be an argumentation semantics and* q *be a proposition. If* $\mathcal{M}$ *is sound under sem, then for any full derivation* $(\mathcal{S}_0, \mathcal{T}_0), \ldots, (\mathcal{S}_n, \mathcal{T}_n)$ *of* q,

1. $q \overset{sem}{\Longleftrightarrow} \mathcal{S}_n$, *and*
2. *for any* $i < n$, $q \overset{sem}{\Longleftarrow} \mathcal{S}_i$ *and* $q \overset{sem}{\Longrightarrow} \mathcal{S}_i \cup \{s \mid (\_, s) \in \mathcal{T}_i\}$.

Data: A sentence q; a semantics *sem*; a non-negative integer *maxSteps*.
Result: An interval $[l, u]$ containing $Pr_{sem}(q)$

Function *ProgressiveInference(q, sem, maxSteps)*
  | $\mathcal{M} :=$ a sound translation scheme under *sem*;
  | $(\Pi, \Theta) :=$ a PLP program representing BN $\mathcal{N}$ of the underlying
  | PABA framework
  | $(\mathcal{S}, \mathcal{S}') := ProgressiveTranslation(q, maxSteps, \mathcal{M})$
  | **foreach** $s \in \mathcal{S}$ **do**
  | | $\Pi := \Pi \cup \{lower \leftarrow s\}$
  | **end**
  | **foreach** $s \in \mathcal{S}'$ **do**
  | | $\Pi := \Pi \cup \{upper \leftarrow s\}$
  | **end**
  | $l :=$ the probability of *lower* according to PLP program (Π, Θ)
  | $u :=$ the probability of *upper* according to PLP program (Π, Θ)
  | **return** $[l, u]$
  Algorithm 1: *ProgressiveInference(q, sem, maxSteps)*

5.2   Pseudo Code and Implementation

Now we are ready to give the pseudo codes for our progressive algorithms. The pseudo-code function *ProgressiveInference(q, sem, maxSteps)* given in Algorithm 1 combines progressive translation, which is performed by the pseudo-code function *ProgressiveTranslation(q, maxSteps, $\mathcal{M}$)* in Algorithm 2, and probabilistic query answering, which is done by PLP. Note that both functions receive a non-negative integer *maxSteps* as a proxy for time budget.

---

[12] We have developed sound translation schemes for the ideal semantics and skeptical preferred semantics. However they can not be presented here due to lack of space.

Data: A sentence q; a non-negative integer $maxSteps$; and a translation scheme $\mathcal{M} = \langle \_, \gamma, \lambda, \delta \rangle$ (the set of states $\mathcal{K}$ need not be passed in. This is important because $\mathcal{K}$ is often a big and even infinite set).

Result: A frame $\mathcal{S}$ such that $q \overset{sem}{\Longleftrightarrow} \mathcal{S}$ if given time budget is sufficient; otherwise a pair $(\mathcal{S}, \mathcal{S}')$ of frames such that $q \overset{sem}{\Longleftarrow} \mathcal{S}$ and $q \overset{sem}{\Longrightarrow} \mathcal{S}'$.

Function $ProgressiveTranslation(q, maxSteps, \mathcal{M})$

$(\mathcal{S}, \mathcal{T}) := (\emptyset, \lambda(q))$

$sl :=$ a selection strategy

Procedure $OneStepTranslation()$

  sl selects a configuration $c = (k, s)$ from $\mathcal{T}$

  $\mathcal{T} := \mathcal{T} - \{c\}$

  if $\gamma(k) = \top$ **then**

    $\mid \quad \mathcal{S} := \mathcal{S} \cup \{s\}$

  else

    $\mid \quad \mathcal{T} := \mathcal{T} \cup \delta(c, sl)$

  end

$stepCount := 0$

while $\mathcal{T} \neq \emptyset$ and $stepCount < maxSteps$ **do**

  $OneStepTranslation()$

  $stepCount := stepCount + 1$

end

if $\mathcal{T} = \emptyset$ **then**

  $\mid$ return $\mathcal{S}$;

else

  $\mid \quad \mathcal{S}' := \mathcal{S} \cup \{s \mid (\_, s) \in \mathcal{T}\}$

  $\mid$ return $(\mathcal{S}, \mathcal{S}')$;

end

Algorithm 2: $ProgressiveTranslation(q, maxSteps, \mathcal{M})$

The following theorem asserts the correctness of our progressive algorithms.

Theorem 4. *1. If $ProgressiveTranslation(q, maxSteps, \mathcal{M})$ returns a pair $(\mathcal{S}, \mathcal{S}')$ and the translation scheme $\mathcal{M}$ is sound under semantics sem, then $q \overset{sem}{\Longleftarrow} \mathcal{S}$ and $q \overset{sem}{\Longrightarrow} \mathcal{S}'$.*

2. If $ProgressiveInference(q, sem, maxSteps)$ returns an interval $[l, u]$ then $l \leq Pr_{sem}(q) \leq u$.

In the following, we demonstrate a Prolog-based implementation of the above algorithms. As illustrated by code listing 1.2, which specifies the PABA framework in Example 1, users specifies PABA frameworks using several predicates: iNas([...]) declares assumptions; contr(...) refers to the contrary of an assumption; iRule(..., [...]) declares an inference rule; iPas([...]) declares probabilistic assumptions; and iProblog(...) gives the file path of a Problog program encoding a Bayesian network, which is exemplified by Code listing 1.3. The screen shot in Fig. 2 shows how users call our progressive algorithms to compute $Pr_{sem}(nothing)$ using predicate prob. For example, the last call "prob(sk, nothing, Pr_sk_nothing, Frame, 50)" queries $Pr_{sk}(nothing)$ with $maxSteps = 50$. It turns out that this time budget is sufficient for producing the exact answer 0.831. In the call just before, we give $maxSteps = 40$ and receive a probability interval $[0.81, 0.834]$ instead of the exact probability.

Listing 1.2. The framework in Ex 1

```
%% Declare probabilistic assumptions
iPas([b, e, p1, p2, p3]).
%% Declare Bayesian network
iProblog("./BN.pl").
%% Declare logical assumptions
iNas([naf_runaway, naf_bark, naf_alarm]).
iRule(contr(naf_runaway),[runaway]).
iRule(contr(naf_bark),[bark]).
iRule(contr(naf_alarm),[alarm]).
%% Inference rules
iRule(bark,[b, naf_runaway]).
iRule(runaway,[e, naf_bark]).
iRule(alarm,[b, e, p1]).
iRule(alarm,[b, not(e), p2]).
iRule(alarm,[not(b), e, p3]).
iRule(nothing,[naf_bark, naf_alarm]).
```

Listing 1.3. Content of file BN.pl

```
0.1::e.
0.9::p1.
0.8::p2.
0.7::p3.
0.3:: p_b_given_e.
0.1:: p_b_given_no_e.
b :- e, p_b_given_e.
b :- not e, p_b_given_no_e.
```

```
● ● ●                     ▓ Prengine2.0 — Python • swipl — 92×24

?- prob(cr, nothing, Pr_cr_nothing).
Pr_cr_nothing = 0.834 .

?- prob(id, nothing, Pr_id_nothing).
Pr_id_nothing = 0.831 .

?- prob(sk, nothing, Pr_sk_nothing).
Pr_sk_nothing = 0.831 .

?- MaxSteps = 10, prob(sk, nothing, Pr_sk_nothing, Frame,MaxSteps).
MaxSteps = 10,
Pr_sk_nothing = [0, 0.834],
Frame = ([], [[not(p3), e, not(b)], [not(e), not(b)], [not(p1), e, b]]) .

?- prob(sk, nothing, Pr_sk_nothing, Frame, 40).
Pr_sk_nothing = [0.81, 0.834],
Frame = ([[not(e), not(b)]], [[not(e), not(b)], [not(p3), e, not(b)], [not(p1), e, b]]) .

?- prob(sk, nothing, Pr_sk_nothing, Frame, 50).
Pr_sk_nothing = 0.831,
Frame = [[not(p3), e, not(b)], [not(e), not(b)]] .

?- []
```

Fig. 2. Calling progressive algorithms

6   Conclusions and Related Work

We develop progressive inference algorithms for three PA semantics: the credulous, the ideal, and the skeptical preferred semantics. To the best of our knowledge, approximate inference has not been explored in the current literature of PA, though one might say that classical AA [3] has offered a somewhat crude way to this issue, namely that one can approximate one semantics by another that is more amenable to computation. For example, one may approximate the skeptical preferred semantics by the credulous semantics, getting false positives sometimes (since a credulously acceptable argument may not be skeptically-preferred acceptable). On the other hand, if willing to have false negatives, one can approximate the skeptical preferred semantics by the ideal semantics, which can be in turn approximated by the grounded semantics. Since PA subsumes AA, the approximate inference problem addressed in this paper is broader than the corresponding one in AA. It is worth noting that computing the semantics is just one (possibly the most important) among other computational problems studied in the PA literature. For example, in [17] Li et al. have used a Monte-Carlo simulation to approximate the probability of a set of arguments consistent with an argumentation semantics in their model of Probabilistic Abstract Argumentation (Li's PAA). The complexity of this problem is investigated in [7]. As briefly presented in the introduction, PABA and Li's PAA are just two PA models among many others [9,14,15,19,22] (for a recent review, see [15]). Though we restrict ourselves to PABA, our developed algorithms are directly applicable to, for example the PA models in [17,19], because, as shown in [13], these models can be translated easily to PABA. In general, this translation approach can be extended for any PA models adopting the distribution semantics, according to which a PA framework is viewed as a compact representation of a probability distribution of classical AA frameworks. Not in this line are the PA models in [9,14,15,22] whose semantics are defined in terms of some *rational conditions* on a function $f : AR \rightarrow [0,1]$, for $f(A)$ to represent the "value" of argument A, taking into account an attack relation $Att \subseteq AR \times AR$ between the arguments. Note that $f(A)$ has been given diverse interpretations, from the truth of A, the reliability of A, the probability of A being effective, the belief degree put into A by some agent [9]. It is interesting to explore progressive inference algorithms for computing such a value $f(A)$.

Acknowledgment. This work is supported by SIIT Young Researcher Grant, contract no SIIT 2017-YRG-NH02.

References

1. Bondarenko, A., Dung, P.M., Kowalski, R.A., Toni, F.: An abstract, argumentation-theoretic approach to default reasoning. Artif. Intell. **93**(1), 63–101 (1997)
2. Doder, D., Woltran, S.: Probabilistic argumentation frameworks – a logical approach. In: Straccia, U., Calì, A. (eds.) SUM 2014. LNCS (LNAI), vol. 8720, pp. 134–147. Springer, Cham (2014). https://doi.org/10.1007/978-3-319-11508-5_12
3. Dung, P.M.: On the acceptability of arguments and its fundamental role in nonmonotonic reasoning, logic programming and n-person games. Artif. Intell. **77**(2), 321–357 (1995)
4. Dung, P.M., Kowalski, R.A., Toni, F.: Dialectic proof procedures for assumption-based, admissible argumentation. Artif. Intell. **170**(2), 114–159 (2006)
5. Dung, P.M., Mancarella, P., Toni, F.: Computing ideal skeptical argumentation. Artif. Intell. **171**(10–15), 642–674 (2007)

6. Dung, P.M., Thang, P.M.: Towards (probabilistic) argumentation for jury-based dispute resolution. COMMA **2010**, 171–182 (2010)

7. Fazzinga, B., Flesca, S., Parisi, F.: On the complexity of probabilistic abstract argumentation frameworks. ACM Trans. Comput. Logic **16**(3), 22:1–22:39 (2015)

8. Fierens, D., et al.: Inference and learning in probabilistic logic programsx using weighted boolean formulas. Theory Pract. Log. Program. **15**(3), 358–401 (2015)

9. Gabbay, D.M., Rodrigues, O.: Probabilistic argumentation. An equational approach. CoRR (2015)

10. Hung, N.D.: The distribution semantics of extended argumentation. In: Chen, J., Theeramunkong, T., Supnithi, T., Tang, X. (eds.) KSS 2017. CCIS, vol. 780, pp. 197–211. Springer, Singapore (2017). https://doi.org/10.1007/978-981-10-6989-5_17

11. Hung, N.D.: A generalization of probabilistic argumentation with Dempster-Shafer Theory. In: Kern-Isberner, G., Fürnkranz, J., Thimm, M. (eds.) KI 2017. LNCS (LNAI), vol. 10505, pp. 155–169. Springer, Cham (2017). https://doi.org/10.1007/978-3-319-67190-1_12

12. Hung, N.D.: Inference and learning in probabilistic argumentation. In: Phon-Amnuaisuk, S., Ang, S.-P., Lee, S.-Y. (eds.) MIWAI 2017. LNCS (LNAI), vol. 10607, pp. 3–17. Springer, Cham (2017). https://doi.org/10.1007/978-3-319-69456-6_1

13. Hung, N.D.: Inference procedures and engine for probabilistic argumentation. Int. J. Approx. Reason. **90**, 163–191 (2017)

14. Hunter, A.: A probabilistic approach to modelling uncertain logical arguments. Int. J. Approx. Reason. **54**(1), 47–81 (2013)

15. Hunter, A., Thimm, M.: Probabilistic reasoning with abstract argumentation frameworks. J. Artif. Intell. Res. **59**, 565–611 (2017)

16. Koller, D., Friedman, N.: Probabilistic Graphical Models: Principles and Techniques. Adaptive Computation and Machine Learning. MIT Press, Cambridge (2009)

17. Li, H., Oren, N., Norman, T.J.: Probabilistic argumentation frameworks. In: Modgil, S., Oren, N., Toni, F. (eds.) TAFA 2011. LNCS (LNAI), vol. 7132, pp. 1–16. Springer, Heidelberg (2012). https://doi.org/10.1007/978-3-642-29184-5_1

18. Poole, D.: The independent choice logic and beyond. In: De Raedt, L., Frasconi, P., Kersting, K., Muggleton, S. (eds.) Probabilistic Inductive Logic Programming. LNCS (LNAI), vol. 4911, pp. 222–243. Springer, Heidelberg (2008). https://doi.org/10.1007/978-3-540-78652-8_8

19. Rienstra, T.: Towards a probabilistic dung-style argumentation system. In: AT, pp. 138–152. CEUR (2012)

20. Sato, T., Kameya, Y.: New advances in logic-based probabilistic modeling by PRISM. In: De Raedt, L., Frasconi, P., Kersting, K., Muggleton, S. (eds.) Probabilistic Inductive Logic Programming. LNCS (LNAI), vol. 4911, pp. 118–155. Springer, Heidelberg (2008). https://doi.org/10.1007/978-3-540-78652-8_5

21. Thang, P.M.: Dialectical proof procedures for probabilistic abstract argumentation. In: Baldoni, M., Chopra, A.K., Son, T.C., Hirayama, K., Torroni, P. (eds.) PRIMA 2016. LNCS (LNAI), vol. 9862, pp. 397–406. Springer, Cham (2016). https://doi.org/10.1007/978-3-319-44832-9_27

22. Thimm, M.: A probabilistic semantics for abstract argumentation. In: ECAI, vol. 242, pp. 750–755. ISO Press (2012)

23. Toni, F.: A tutorial on assumption-based argumentation. Argum. Comput. **5**(1), 89–117 (2014)

Computing Preferences in Abstract Argumentation

Quratul-ain Mahesar$^{(\boxtimes)}$, Nir Oren, and Wamberto W. Vasconcelos

Department of Computing Science, University of Aberdeen, Aberdeen, UK
{quratul-ain.mahesar,n.oren,w.w.vasconcelos}@abdn.ac.uk

Abstract. We present an extension-based approach for computing preferences in an abstract argumentation system. Although numerous argumentation semantics have been developed previously for identifying acceptable sets of arguments from an argumentation framework, there is a lack of justification behind their acceptability based on implicit argument preferences. This paper presents a novel algorithm for exhaustively computing and enumerating all possible sets of preferences for a conflict-free set of arguments in an abstract argumentation framework. We prove the soundness and completeness of the algorithm. The research establishes that preferences are determined using an extension-based approach after the evaluation phase (acceptability of arguments) rather than stated beforehand. We also present some novel insights by comparing the computed preferences for the extensions.

1 Introduction

Preferences play a central part in decision making and have been extensively studied in various disciplines such as economy, operations research, psychology and philosophy [21]. Preferences are used in many areas of artificial intelligence including planning, scheduling, multi-agent systems, combinatorial auctions and game playing [27]. Preference elicitation is a very difficult task and automating the process of preference extraction can be very difficult. The complexity of eliciting preferences and representational questions like dealing with uncertainty has remained a very active research area [18,22,27].

Argumentation has gained an increasing popularity in Artificial Intelligence (AI). It has been widely used for handling inconsistent knowledge bases [11,16,25], and dealing with uncertainty in decision making [6,12,20]. Logic-based abstract argumentation [15] provides a formal representation of preferences. An abstract argumentation framework is a directed graph consisting of nodes that represent unique atomic arguments and directed edges that represent an attack between two arguments. This visual representation of an argumentation framework as a directed graph is also known as an argumentation graph. Acceptable sets of arguments called extensions for an argumentation framework can be computed based on various acceptability semantics [15].

T. Miller et al. (Eds.): PRIMA 2018, LNAI 11224, pp. 387–402, 2018.
https://doi.org/10.1007/978-3-030-03098-8_24

Arguments can have different strengths, e.g., an argument relies on more certain or important information than another. This has led to the introduction of preference-based argumentation framework consisting of preference relations between arguments [1, 2, 4, 6, 19, 23]. Furthermore, preferences are taken into account in the evaluation of arguments at the semantic level, which is also known as preference-based acceptability [5]. The basic idea is to accept undefeated arguments and also arguments that are preferred to their attacking arguments, as these arguments can defend themselves against their attacking arguments.

Several variations of argumentation frameworks with preferences have been studied previously. Value-based argumentation framework (VAF) [9] extends a standard argumentation framework to take into account values promoted by arguments. Preferences over arguments are determined by the values the arguments promote or support. The idea is to accept undefeated arguments and also arguments who promote values that are more important or preferred to the values promoted by their attacking arguments. Furthermore, value-based argumentation frameworks (VAF) have been extended to take into account the possibility that arguments may support multiple values, and therefore, various types of preferences over values could be considered in order to deal with real world situations [17]. Another variation is an extended argumentation framework (EAF) [19] that considers the case where arguments can express preferences between other arguments.

Further studies on preference-based argumentation frameworks led to the observation that ignoring the attacks where the attacked argument is stronger than the attacking argument does not always give intuitive results [7, 19], since the resulting extension violates the basic condition imposed on acceptability semantics, which is the conflict-freeness of extensions, thus violating the rationality postulates given in [13]. This problem was later resolved in a new preference-based argumentation framework that guarantees conflict-free extensions with a symmetric conflict relation [3, 19]. The preference relation is then used to determine the direction of the defeat relation between the two arguments. Furthermore, preference relations have been used to refine the results of a framework by comparing its extensions [8].

Although a preference-based argumentation framework (PAF) has been previously studied to represent an abstract argumentation framework [17], there seems to be no previous work on automatically computing implicit argument preferences in an abstract argumentation framework using an extension-based approach. Furthermore, there have been no attempts to perform an exhaustive search for all possible preferences, and their explicit enumeration. The aim of our research is to exhaustively compute all possible sets of argument preferences that hold for a given set of conflict-free arguments in an abstract argumentation framework. We present a novel algorithm to perform this computation.

The remainder of this paper is structured as follows. In Sect. 2, we present the background on abstract argumentation framework and acceptability semantics for acceptable set of arguments also known as extensions which is followed by background on preference-based argumentation framework. In Sect. 3, we present an algorithm for computing all possible sets of preferences for a given extension and abstract argumentation framework, and we prove the soundness and completeness of the algorithm. In Sect. 4, we present the evaluation and results. Finally, we conclude and suggest future work in Sect. 5.

2   Background

An *argumentation framework* is simply a set of arguments and a binary attack relation among them. Given an argumentation framework, the aim of argumentation theory is to identify the sets of arguments that can survive the conflicts expressed in the framework. In this work, we only consider finite abstract argumentation frameworks.

Definition 1 *(Abstract Argumentation Framework [15]): An abstract argumentation framework (AAF) is a pair $AAF = (\mathcal{A}, \mathcal{R})$, where $\mathcal{A}$ is a set of arguments and $\mathcal{R}$ is an attack relation ($\mathcal{R} \subseteq \mathcal{A} \times \mathcal{A}$). The notation $(A, B) \in \mathcal{R}$ where $A, B \in \mathcal{A}$ denotes that A attacks B.*

Fig. 1. Example abstract argumentation framework AAF_1

An abstract argumentation framework is a directed graph where the arguments are represented as nodes and the attack relations as directed edges. An example abstract argumentation framework $(\mathcal{A}, \mathcal{R})$ is shown in Fig. 1, where $\mathcal{A} = \{A, B, C, D, E\}$ and $\mathcal{R} = \{(A, B), (C, B), (C, D), (D, C), (D, E)\}$, which means that A attacks B, C attacks both B and D, and D attacks both C and E.

Dung [15] originally introduced an extension approach to define the acceptability of arguments in an argumentation framework. An extension is a subset of $\mathcal{A}$ that represents the set of arguments that can be accepted together. Dung's semantics are based on a *conflict-free* set of arguments, i.e., a set should not be self-contradictory nor include arguments that attack each other. This is defined formally as follows.

Definition 2 *(Conflict-freeness): Let $(\mathcal{A}, \mathcal{R})$ be an argumentation framework. The set $\mathcal{E} \subseteq \mathcal{A}$ is conflict-free if and only if there are no $A, B \in \mathcal{E}$ such that $(A, B) \in \mathcal{R}$*

The minimal requirement for an extension to be acceptable is *conflict-freeness*. Many other acceptability semantics have been introduced in the literature, and from these the most common are given as follows.

Definition 3 *(Extensions): Let $AAF = (\mathcal{A}, \mathcal{R})$ be an argumentation framework, and set $\mathcal{E} \subseteq \mathcal{A}$ and $A, B, C \in \mathcal{A}$*

- *$\mathcal{E}$ is admissible iff it is conflict free and defends all its arguments. $\mathcal{E}$ defends A iff for every argument $B \in \mathcal{A}$, if we have $(B, A) \in \mathcal{R}$ then there exists $C \in \mathcal{E}$ such that $(C, B) \in \mathcal{R}$.*
- *$\mathcal{E}$ is a complete extension iff $\mathcal{E}$ is an admissible set which contains all the arguments it defends.*
- *$\mathcal{E}$ is a preferred extension iff it is a maximal (with respect to set inclusion) admissible set.*
- *$\mathcal{E}$ is a stable extension iff it is conflict-free and for all $A \in \mathcal{A} \setminus \mathcal{E}$, there exists an argument $B \in \mathcal{E}$ such that $(B, A) \in \mathcal{R}$.*
- *$\mathcal{E}$ is a grounded extension iff $\mathcal{E}$ is a minimal (for set inclusion) complete extension.*

Every argumentation framework has at least one admissible set (the empty set), exactly one grounded extension, one or more complete extensions, one or more preferred extensions, and zero or more stable extensions. The following example shows the extensions for the abstract argumentation framework of Fig. 1.

Example 1. Given the abstract argumentation framework of Fig. 1, then we compute its extensions as follows:

- Conflict free: $\{A, C, E\}, \{A, D\}, \{B, D\}, \{A, C\}, \{A, E\}, \{B, E\}, \{C, E\}, \{A\},$ $\{B\}, \{C\}, \{D\}, \{E\}, \emptyset$
- Admissible: $\{A, C, E\}, \{A, C\}, \{A, D\}, \{C, E\}, \{A\}, \{C\}, \{D\}, \emptyset$
- Complete: $\{A, C, E\}, \{A, D\}, \{A\}$
- Preferred: $\{A, C, E\}, \{A, D\}$
- Stable: $\{A, C, E\}, \{A, D\}$
- Grounded: $\{A\}$

While an abstract argumentation framework captures the basic interactions between arguments, it does not consider factors such as argument strength, i.e., arguments may not necessarily have the same strengths [10, 14, 25]. Consequently, preferences over arguments can be added to the argumentation framework and taken into account in order to evaluate arguments [2, 4, 6, 19, 23], which is demonstrated in the following example [5].

Example 2. Let $(\mathcal{A}, \mathcal{R})$ be an argumentation framework with $\mathcal{A} = \{A, B, C\}$ and $\mathcal{R} = \{(A, B), (B, C)\}$. The set of acceptable argument is $\{A, C\}$. However, suppose argument B is preferred to A and C. How can we combine the preference over arguments and the attack relation to decide which arguments are acceptable? We can say that, since B is preferred to A, it can defend itself from the attack of A. This would lead us to accepting B and rejecting C.

Dung's framework has been extended by introducing preference relations into argumentation systems, which is known as a preference-based argumentation framework (PAF) [1]. A PAF extends an abstract argumentation framework to account for preferences over arguments. The attack relation in a preference-based argumentation framework is called defeat, and is denoted by Def.

Definition 4 *(Preference-based Argumentation Framework (PAF) [1]). A preference-based argumentation framework is a triple $(\mathcal{A}, Def, \geq)$ where $\mathcal{A}$ is a set of arguments, Def is the defeat binary relation on $\mathcal{A}$, and $\geq$ is a (partial or total) pre-ordering defined on $\mathcal{A} \times \mathcal{A}$. The notation $(A, B) \in Def$ means that argument A defeats argument B.*

The notation $A \geq B$ means that argument A is at least as preferred as B and the relation $>$ is the strict counterpart of $\geq$.

Fig. 2. Example abstract argumentation framework AAF_2

Example 3. Let there be the argumentation framework of Fig. 2. Preferences could be applied in two ways [8]: one way is to apply preferences at the time of argument acceptability (semantic level); and second way is to compute all preferred extensions and filter them by the application of the preferences. By using the first method, if we assume $\{A > B, C > D\}$ is the set of preferences between arguments, then we get a single extension $\mathcal{E} = \{A, C\}$. Now, by using the second method, we first compute all preferred extensions $[\{A, C\}, \{B, D\}]$. These extensions could now be filtered by the application of the set of preferences $\{A > B, C > D\}$ which suggest $\{A, C\}$ to be better than $\{B, D\}$.

A preference-based argumentation framework can represent an abstract argumentation framework [17]:

Definition 5 *(PAF representing an AAF). A preference-based argumentation framework $(\mathcal{A}, Def, \geq)$ represents an abstract argumentation framework $(\mathcal{A}, \mathcal{R})$ iff $\forall A, B \in \mathcal{A}$, it is the case that $(A, B) \in \mathcal{R}$ iff $(A, B) \in Def$ and it is not the case that $B > A$*

3   An Extension-Based Approach for Computing Preferences

It has been previously shown that each preference-based argumentation framework represents one argumentation framework, however each argumentation framework can be represented by various preference-based argumentation frameworks [17]. Following this, we introduce an extension-based approach for computing sets of preferences for a subset of conflict-free arguments in an abstract argumentation framework. For any two arguments A and B in an argumentation framework, we use the strict preference relation $A > B$ to denote that A is strictly preferred to B, i.e., A is of greater strength than B, and we use the preference relation $A = B$ to denote that A and B are of equal strength or preference. Following are the three cases that we have identified for which the preferences are computed for a given conflict-free extension $\mathcal{E}$ in an abstract argumentation framework $AAF = \langle \mathcal{A}, \mathcal{R} \rangle$.

- **Case 1:** Suppose $\alpha, \beta \in \mathcal{A}$ and $\alpha \in \mathcal{E}$, $\beta \notin \mathcal{E}$ such that α are attacked by arguments β, and α are not defended by any other arguments (not equal to α) in the extension. We have the following preferences for all α and β: $\alpha > \beta$.
- **Case 2:** Suppose $\alpha, \beta \in \mathcal{A}$ and $\alpha \in \mathcal{E}$, $\beta \notin \mathcal{E}$, and suppose α attack arguments β and β do not attack α. We have the following preferences for all α and β: $\beta \not> \alpha$, i.e., $(\alpha > \beta) \vee (\alpha = \beta)$.
- **Case 3:** Suppose $\alpha, \beta, \gamma \in \mathcal{A}$ and $\alpha, \gamma \in \mathcal{E}$, $\beta \notin \mathcal{E}$ where α, β and γ are different arguments, such that, α are attacked by arguments β but defended by arguments γ in the extension, i.e., γ attack β. We have the following preferences for all α and β: $(\alpha > \beta) \vee (\alpha = \beta) \vee (\beta > \alpha)$.

A worked example of how preferences are computed using the above three cases is as follows.

Example 4. Let there be the abstract argumentation framework $(\mathcal{A}, \mathcal{R})$ of Fig. 1, where $\mathcal{A} = \{A, B, C, D, E\}$ and $\mathcal{R} = \{(A, B), (C, B), (C, D), (D, C), (D, E)\}$. We consider the conflict-free extensions $\mathcal{E}_1 = \{A, C, E\}$, $\mathcal{E}_2 = \{A, D\}$ for computing preferences. For the extension $\mathcal{E}_1 = \{A, C, E\}$, we have the following preferences for each case.

- **Case 1:** $(C > D)$
- **Case 2:** $((A > B) \vee (A = B)) \wedge ((C > B) \vee (C = B))$
- **Case 3:** $(E > D) \vee (E = D) \vee (D > E)$

  Combining the preferences from the three cases we get $(C > D) \wedge (((A > B) \vee (A = B)) \wedge ((C > B) \vee (C = B))) \wedge ((E > D) \vee (E = D) \vee (D > E))$, which gives us the following sets of preferences:

$$\{C > D, A > B, C > B, E > D\}$$
$$\{C > D, A > B, C > B, E = D\}$$
$$\{C > D, A > B, C > B, D > E\}$$
$$\{C > D, A > B, C = B, E > D\}$$
$$\{C > D, A > B, C = B, E = D\}$$
$$\{C > D, A > B, C = B, D > E\}$$
$$\{C > D, A = B, C > B, E > D\}$$
$$\{C > D, A = B, C > B, E = D\}$$
$$\{C > D, A = B, C > B, D > E\}$$
$$\{C > D, A = B, C = B, E > D\}$$

$$\{C > D, A = B, C = B, E = D\}$$
$$\{C > D, A = B, C = B, D > E\}$$

For the extension $\mathcal{E}_2 = \{A, D\}$, we have the following preferences for each case.

- **Case 1:** $(D > C)$
- **Case 2:** $((A > B) \vee (A = B)) \wedge ((D > E) \vee (D = E))$
- **Case 3:** $\emptyset$

Combining the preferences from the three cases we get $(D > C) \wedge (((A > B) \vee (A = B)) \wedge ((D > E) \vee (D = E))) \wedge \emptyset$, which gives us the following sets of preferences:

$$\{D > C, A > B, D > E\},$$
$$\{D > C, A > B, D = E\},$$
$$\{D > C, A = B, D > E\},$$
$$\{D > C, A = B, D = E\}$$

Algorithm 1 exhaustively computes all possible sets of preferences for a given input extension (consisting of conflict-free arguments) in an abstract argumentation framework (AAF) using the above three cases. The input of Algorithm 1 is a tuple $\langle AAF, \mathcal{E} \rangle$, where:

- Abstract argumentation framework $AAF = \langle \mathcal{A}, \mathcal{R} \rangle$, $\mathcal{A}$ denotes the set of all arguments in the AAF, and $\mathcal{R}$ denotes the attack relation between arguments.
- Extension $\mathcal{E}$ consists of a finite number of conflict-free arguments such that $\mathcal{E} \subseteq \mathcal{A}$.

The algorithm computes and outputs a set consisting of finite sets of preferences, where each set of preferences is represented as $Prefs = \{A > B, B = C, ...\}$ such that $\{A, B, C\} \subseteq \mathcal{A}$.

Algorithm 1. Compute all preferences

Require: AAF, an abstract argumentation framework
Require: $\mathcal{E}$, an extension consisting of conflict-free arguments
Ensure: $PrefSet$, the set of sets of all possible preferences
1: **function** COMPUTEALLPREFERENCES($AAF, \mathcal{E}$)
2:     $Prefs \leftarrow$ COMPUTEPREFERENCES$_1$($AAF, \mathcal{E}$)
3:     $PrefSet \leftarrow$ COMPUTEPREFERENCES$_2$($AAF, \mathcal{E}, Prefs$)
4:     $PrefSet \leftarrow$ COMPUTEPREFERENCES$_3$($AAF, \mathcal{E}, PrefSet$)
5:     **return** $PrefSet$
6: **end function**

We establish that our approach is sound (that is, all its outputs are correct) and complete (that is, it outputs all possible solutions). We start with its soundness:

Algorithm 2. Compute preferences (Case 1)

Require: AAF, an abstract argumentation framework
Require: $\mathcal{E}$, an extension consisting of conflict-free arguments
Ensure: $Prefs$, a set of preferences
1: **function** COMPUTEPREFERENCES$_1(AAF, \mathcal{E})$
2:     $Prefs \leftarrow \emptyset$
3:     **for all** $A \in \mathcal{E}$ **do**
4:         $Attackers \leftarrow \{B \mid (B, A) \in \mathcal{R}\}$ ▷ get all attackers of A
5:         **for all** $B \in Attackers$ **do**
6:             $Defenders \leftarrow \{C \mid C \neq A, C \in \mathcal{E}, (C, B) \in \mathcal{R}\}$ ▷ $C \neq A$ attacks B &
    defends A
7:             **if** $Defenders = \emptyset$ **then**   ▷ if B not attacked by any C
8:                 $Prefs \leftarrow Prefs \cup \{A > B\}$ ▷ add preference $A > B$
9:             **end if**
10:         **end for**
11:     **end for**
12:     **return** $Prefs$
13: **end function**

Theorem 1. *Algorithm 1 is sound in that given an abstract argumentation framework AAF and an extension $\mathcal{E}$ as input, every output preference set $Prefs \in PrefSet$, when applied to the AAF results in the input $\mathcal{E}$ (under a given semantics).*

Proof. We prove this by exploring all cases and how these are handled by Algorithms 2–4. Each set of preferences computed for each subset of arguments $\alpha, \beta, \gamma \subseteq \mathcal{A}$ is such that $\alpha, \gamma \subseteq \mathcal{E}, \beta \cap \mathcal{E} = \emptyset$. We proceed to show how each of the auxiliary Algorithms 2–4 help us achieve this.

Algorithm 2 computing each case 1 preference of the form $A > B, A \in \mathcal{E}, B \in \beta, (B, A) \in \mathcal{R}$ ensures that the following holds:

1. There is no $C \in \mathcal{E}, C \neq A$ such that $(C, B) \in \mathcal{R}$ (lines 6–7).
2. $A \in \mathcal{E}$ since A is preferred to its attacking argument B, which invalidates the attack $(B, A) \in \mathcal{R}$.
3. Since the input extension $\mathcal{E}$ consists of conflict free arguments, if $A \in \mathcal{E}$ then its attacking argument $B \notin \mathcal{E}$. This supports that $\beta \cap \mathcal{E} = \emptyset$.

Algorithm 3 computing each case 2 preferences of the form $A > B, A = B, A \in \mathcal{E}, B \in \beta, (A, B) \in \mathcal{R}, (B, A) \notin \mathcal{R}$ ensures the following holds:

1. Since A attacks B and B does not attack A, we have two different preferences between A and B, namely, $A > B, A = B$. Therefore $A \in \mathcal{E}$ with respect to each of these preferences.
2. Preferences $A > B, A = B$ will be in different preference sets, as per lines 8 and 9. We will have $Prefs_1 \leftarrow Prefs \cup \{A > B\}$ and $Prefs_2 \leftarrow Prefs \cup \{A = B\}$, where $Prefs$ consists of preferences of case 1.

Algorithm 4 computing each case 3 preferences of the form $A > B, A = B, B > A, A \in \alpha, B \in \beta, C \in \gamma, (B, A) \in \mathcal{R}, (C, B) \in \mathcal{R}$ ensures the following holds:

Algorithm 3. Compute preferences (Case 2)

Require: AAF, an abstract argumentation framework
Require: $\mathcal{E}$, an extension consisting of conflict free arguments
Require: $Prefs$, a set of preferences
Ensure: $PrefSet$, a set of sets of preferences

```
 1: function ComputePreferences₂(AAF, E, Prefs)
 2:     PrefSet ← {Prefs}
 3:     PrefSet' ← ∅
 4:     for all A ∈ E do
 5:         Attacked ← {B | (A, B) ∈ R ∧ (B, A) ∉ R}        ▷ get arguments A attacks
 6:         for all B ∈ Attacked do                          ▷ for all B attacked by A
 7:             for all Prefs ∈ PrefSet do            ▷ for all sets of preferences Prefs
 8:                 PrefSet' ← PrefSet' ∪ {Prefs ∪ {A > B}}      ▷ add Prefs ∪ {A > B}
 9:                 PrefSet' ← PrefSet' ∪ {Prefs ∪ {A = B}}      ▷ add Prefs ∪ {A = B}
10:             end for
11:             PrefSet ← PrefSet'
12:             PrefSet' ← ∅
13:         end for
14:     end for
15:     return PrefSet
16: end function
```

---

1. Since C defends A from the attack of B, we have three different preferences between A and B, namely, $A > B$, $A = B$ and $B > A$. Therefore $A \in \mathcal{E}$ with respect to each of these preferences.
2. Preferences $A > B, A = B, B > A$ will be in different preference sets, as per lines 9, 10 and 11. We will have $Prefs_1 \leftarrow Prefs \cup \{A > B\}$, $Prefs_2 \leftarrow Prefs \cup \{A = B\}$ and $Prefs_3 \leftarrow Prefs \cup \{B > A\}$, where $Prefs$ consists of preferences of cases 1 and 2.

$\square$

Theorem 2. *Algorithm 1 is complete in that given an abstract argumentation framework AAF and an extension $\mathcal{E}$ as input, if there is a preference set Prefs $\in$ PrefSet which when applied to the AAF results in the input $\mathcal{E}$ (under a given semantics), then Algorithm 1 will find it.*

Proof. Similar to above, we prove this by exploring all cases and how these are handled by Algorithms 2–4. We find all sets of preferences computed for each subset of arguments $\alpha, \beta, \gamma \subseteq \mathcal{A}, \alpha, \gamma \subseteq \mathcal{E}, \beta \cap \mathcal{E} = \emptyset$. We proceed to show how each of the auxiliary Algorithms 2–4 help us achieve this.

Algorithm 2 computes all case 1 preferences of the form $A > B, A \in \mathcal{E}, B \in \beta, (B, A) \in \mathcal{R}$. Lines 3-11 exhaustively search for $A \in \mathcal{E}$ for which there is an attacker B (not attacked by any $C \neq A$). If there are such $A, B \in \mathcal{A}$, the algorithm will find them and add $A > B$ to a set of preferences.

Algorithm 3 computes all case 2 preferences of the form $A > B, A = B, B \in \beta, A \in \mathcal{E}, (A, B) \in \mathcal{R}, (B, A) \notin \mathcal{R}$. Lines 4-14 exhaustively search for $A \in \mathcal{E}$ for

---

Algorithm 4. Compute preferences (Case 3)

Require: AAF, an abstract argumentation framework
Require: $\mathcal{E}$, an extension consisting of conflict free arguments
Require: $PrefSet$, a set of sets of preferences
Ensure: $PrefSet$, an updated set of sets of preferences
1: **function** COMPUTEPREFERENCES$_3(AAF, \mathcal{E}, PrefSet)$
2:      $PrefSet' \leftarrow \emptyset$
3:      **for all** $A \in \mathcal{E}$ **do**
4:          $Attackers \leftarrow \{B \mid (B, A) \in \mathcal{R}\}$ ▷ get all attackers of A
5:          **for all** $B \in Attackers$ **do**
6:              $Defenders \leftarrow \{C \mid C \neq A, C \in \mathcal{E}, (C, B) \in \mathcal{R}\}$ ▷ $C \neq A$ attacks B &
    defends A
7:              **if** $Defenders \neq \emptyset$ **then**
8:                  **for all** $Prefs \in PrefSet$ **do**   ▷ for all sets of preferences $Prefs$
9:                      $PrefSet' \leftarrow PrefSet' \cup \{Prefs \cup \{A > B\}\}$ ▷ add $Prefs \cup \{A > B\}$
10:                     $PrefSet' \leftarrow PrefSet' \cup \{Prefs \cup \{A = B\}\}$ ▷ add $Prefs \cup \{A = B\}$
11:                     $PrefSet' \leftarrow PrefSet' \cup \{Prefs \cup \{B > A\}\}$ ▷ add $Prefs \cup \{B > A\}$
12:                 **end for**
13:                 $PrefSet \leftarrow PrefSet'$
14:                 $PrefSet' \leftarrow \emptyset$
15:             **end if**
16:         **end for**
17:     **end for**
18:     **return** $PrefSet$
19: **end function**

---

which there is an attacked argument B and B does not attack A. If there are such $A, B \in \mathcal{A}$, the algorithm will find them and add each $A > B, A = B$ to a different set of preferences.

Algorithm 4 computes all case 3 preferences of the form $A > B, A = B, B > A, A \in \alpha, B \in \beta, C \in \gamma, (B, A) \in \mathcal{R}, (C, B) \in \mathcal{R}$. Lines 3–17 exhaustively search for $A \in \mathcal{E}$ for which there is an attacker B and there is a defender C that attacks B. If there are such $A, B, C \in \mathcal{A}$, the algorithm will find them and add each $A > B, A = B, B > A$ to a different set of preferences.   □

4   Evaluation and Results

In this section, we present an illustrative example to demonstrate and evaluate Algorithm 1. Suppose we have an input abstract argumentation framework $(\mathcal{A}, \mathcal{R})$ shown in Fig. 1, where $\mathcal{A} = \{A, B, C, D, E\}$ and $\mathcal{R} = \{(A, B), (C, B), (C, D), (D, C), (D, E)\}$. We consider the conflict-free extension $\mathcal{E}_1 = \{A, C, E\}$ for computing preferences. Table 1 shows the preferences computed at lines 2, 3 and 4 of Algorithm 1.

– At line 2, Algorithm 2 is called, which returns the set of case 1 preferences $\{C > D\}$.

Table 1. Computing preferences for extension $\{A, C, E\}$

Line no.	Preference sets
2	$\{C > D\}$
3	$\{C > D, A > B, C > B\}$
	$\{C > D, A > B, C = B\}$
	$\{C > D, A = B, C > B\}$
	$\{C > D, A = B, C = B\}$
4	$\{C > D, A > B, C > B, E > D\}$
	$\{C > D, A > B, C > B, E = D\}$
	$\{C > D, A > B, C > B, D > E\}$
	$\{C > D, A > B, C = B, E > D\}$
	$\{C > D, A > B, C = B, E = D\}$
	$\{C > D, A > B, C = B, D > E\}$
	$\{C > D, A = B, C > B, E > D\}$
	$\{C > D, A = B, C > B, E = D\}$
	$\{C > D, A = B, C > B, D > E\}$
	$\{C > D, A = B, C = B, E > D\}$
	$\{C > D, A = B, C = B, E = D\}$
	$\{C > D, A = B, C = B, D > E\}$

- At line 3, Algorithm 3 is called, which returns the sets of preferences (cases 1 and 2 combined together) $\{C > D, A > B, C > B\}$, $\{C > D, A > B, C = B\}$, $\{C > D, A = B, C > B\}$, $\{C > D, A = B, C = B\}$.
- Finally at line 4, Algorithm 4 is called, which returns the sets of preferences (cases 1, 2 and 3 combined together) $\{C > D, A > B, C > B, E > D\}$, $\{C > D, A > B, C > B, E = D\}$, $\{C > D, A > B, C > B, D > E\}$, $\{C > D, A > B, C = B, E > D\}$, $\{C > D, A > B, C = B, E = D\}$, $\{C > D, A > B, C = B, D > E\}$, $\{C > D, A = B, C > B, E > D\}$, $\{C > D, A = B, C > B, E = D\}$, $\{C > D, A = B, C > B, D > E\}$, $\{C > D, A = B, C = B, E > D\}$, $\{C > D, A = B, C = B, E = D\}$, $\{C > D, A = B, C = B, D > E\}$.

Table 2 presents the sets of preferences for the two preferred extensions $\{A, C, E\}$ and $\{A, D\}$ of the abstract argumentation framework given above and shown in Fig. 1. The sets of preferences for all conflict-free extensions for this example abstract argumentation framework are shown in Table 3 in the Appendix.

The unique preferences for an extension in comparison to another extension can be computed by Algorithm 5. By analysing the preference sets shown in Table 2, we can identify the unique preferences for extension $\{A, C, E\}$, which

Table 2. Preferences for the preferred extensions $\{A, C, E\}$ and $\{A, D\}$

Preferred extensions	Preference sets	Unique preferences	Common preferences
$\{A, C, E\}$	$\{C > D, A > B, C > B, E > D\}$	$C > D$	$A > B$
	$\{C > D, A > B, C > B, E = D\}$	$E > D$	$A = B$
	$\{C > D, A > B, C > B, D > E\}$	$C > B$	$D > E$
	$\{C > D, A > B, C = B, E > D\}$	$C = B$	$D = E$
	$\{C > D, A > B, C = B, E = D\}$		
	$\{C > D, A > B, C = B, D > E\}$		
	$\{C > D, A = B, C > B, E > D\}$		
	$\{C > D, A = B, C > B, E = D\}$		
	$\{C > D, A = B, C > B, D > E\}$		
	$\{C > D, A = B, C = B, E > D\}$		
	$\{C > D, A = B, C = B, E = D\}$		
	$\{C > D, A = B, C = B, D > E\}$		
$\{A, D\}$	$\{D > C, A > B, D > E\}$	$D > C$	
	$\{D > C, A > B, D = E\}$		
	$\{D > C, A = B, D > E\}$		
	$\{D > C, A = B, D = E\}$		

Algorithm 5. Algorithm for Computing Unique Preferences

Require: *PrefSet₁*, the set of sets of preferences for first extension.
Require: *PrefSet₂*, the set of sets of preferences for second extension.
Ensure: *UniquePrefs*, unique preferences for first extension.
1: **function** COMPUTEUNIQUEPREFERENCES(*PrefSet1*, *PrefSet2*)
2:     **for all** $Prefs_1 \in PrefSet_1$ **do**
3:         **for all** $p \in Prefs_1$ **do**
4:             **if** $\nexists Prefs_2 \in PrefSet_2$ s.t. $p \in Prefs_2$ **then**
5:                 $UniquePrefs \leftarrow UniquePrefs \cup p$
6:             **end if**
7:         **end for**
8:     **end for**
        return *UniquePrefs*
9: **end function**

---

are $C > D, E > D, C > B$ and $C = B$[1], and the unique preferences for extension $\{A, D\}$, which is $D > C$. Since, at least one unique preference for each extension is in its corresponding preference set, therefore it can be concluded that if we evaluate the example abstract argumentation framework given in Fig. 1 with a corresponding preference set of a given preferred extension, then the evaluation results in exactly the same preferred extension.

---

[1] This means it could be either $C > B$ or $C = B$.

Algorithm 6. Algorithm for Computing Common Preferences

Require: $PrefSet_1$, the set of sets of preferences for first extension.
Require: $PrefSet_2$, the set of sets of preferences for second extension.
Ensure: $CommonPrefs$, common preferences for both extensions.
 1: **function** COMPUTECOMMONPREFERENCES($PrefSet_1$, $PrefSet_2$)
 2:    **for all** $Prefs_1 \in PrefSet_1$ **do**
 3:      **for all** $p \in Prefs_1$ **do**
 4:        **if** $\exists Prefs_2 \in PrefSet_2$ s.t. $p \in Prefs_2$ **then**
 5:          $CommonPrefs \leftarrow CommonPrefs \cup p$
 6:        **end if**
 7:      **end for**
 8:    **end for**
      return $CommonPrefs$
 9: **end function**

Furthermore, we can identify preferences that are common to both extensions, which are $A > B$, $A = B$, $D > E$, $D = E^2$. The common preferences for any two extensions can be computed by Algorithm 6. It is interesting to note that, extension $\{A, C, E\}$ can have preferences $D > E$ and $D = E$, considering D is not present in the extension. It can be concluded that if we evaluate the example abstract argumentation framework given in Fig. 1, then we get both preferred extensions with the following preference sets: $\{A > B, D > E\}$, $\{A > B, D = E\}$, $\{A = B, D > E\}$ and $\{A = B, D = E\}$.

5   Conclusions and Future Work

In this paper we have described a novel extension-based approach to compute abstract argument preferences. We present an algorithm that takes an abstract argumentation framework and a set of conflict-free arguments (extension) as input and computes all possible sets of preferences that are valid for the acceptability of the arguments in the input extension. The main contributions of our work are as follows:

1. An extension-based approach is employed for computing argument preferences. Thus, preferences specifically justify the reasoning behind the acceptability of the arguments in an extension.
2. Preferences are computed at the end of the argumentation process and need not be stated in advance.
3. Exhaustive search is performed to compute all possible sets of preferences.
4. The approach operates on a conflict-free extension as input which is the minimal acceptability semantic, therefore, it can take as input most of the extensions given in the literature and stated in this paper.

As future work, we plan to investigate different ways to aggregate and assess the sets of preferences. Furthermore, we also plan to do an empirical evaluation

---

[2] This means it could be either $A > B$ or $A = B$, and similarly $D > E$ or $D = E$.

of our proposed work on concrete examples. This will allow us to filter sets of preferences, i.e., to accept or reject them; or to rank the sets of preferences by human participants. This work has applications in decision support systems [26] and recommender systems [24], where the resulting decision(s) or recommendation(s) can be justified by the preference set(s).

Acknowledgments. Financial support from The UK Engineering and Physical Sciences Research Council (EPSRC) for the grant (EP/P011829/1), *Supporting Security Policy with Effective Digital Intervention (SSPEDI)* is gratefully acknowledged.

Appendix

Table 3. Preference sets for all conflict-free extensions

Conflict-free extensions	Preference sets
$\{A, C, E\}$	$\{C > D, A > B, C > B, E > D\}$
	$\{C > D, A > B, C > B, E = D\}$
	$\{C > D, A > B, C > B, D > E\}$
	$\{C > D, A > B, C = B, E > D\}$
	$\{C > D, A > B, C = B, E = D\}$
	$\{C > D, A > B, C = B, D > E\}$
	$\{C > D, A = B, C > B, E > D\}$
	$\{C > D, A = B, C > B, E = D\}$
	$\{C > D, A = B, C > B, D > E\}$
	$\{C > D, A = B, C = B, E > D\}$
	$\{C > D, A = B, C = B, E = D\}$
	$\{C > D, A = B, C = B, D > E\}$
$\{A, D\}$	$\{D > C, A > B, D > E\}$
	$\{D > C, A > B, D = E\}$
	$\{D > C, A = B, D > E\}$
	$\{D > C, A = B, D = E\}$
$\{B, D\}$	$\{B > A, B > C, D > C, D > E\}$
	$\{B > A, B > C, D > C, D = E\}$
$\{A, C\}$	$\{C > D, A > B, C > B\}$
	$\{C > D, A > B, C = B\}$
	$\{C > D, A = B, C > B\}$
	$\{C > D, A = B, C = B\}$
$\{A, E\}$	$\{E > D, A > B\}$
	$\{E > D, A = B\}$
$\{B, E\}$	$\{B > A, B > C, E > D\}$
$\{C, E\}$	$\{C > D, C > B, E > D\}$
	$\{C > D, C > B, E = D\}$
	$\{C > D, C > B, D > E\}$
	$\{C > D, C = B, E > D\}$
	$\{C > D, C = B, E = D\}$
	$\{C > D, C = B, D > E\}$
$\{A\}$	$\{A > B\}$
	$\{A = B\}$
$\{B\}$	$\{B > A, B > C\}$
$\{C\}$	$\{C > D, C > B\}$
	$\{C > D, C = B\}$
$\{D\}$	$\{D > C, D > E\}$
	$\{D > C, D = E\}$
$\{E\}$	$\{E > D\}$
$\emptyset$	$\emptyset$

References

1. Amgoud, L., Cayrol, C.: On the acceptability of arguments in preference-based argumentation. In: Proceedings of the Fourteenth Conference on Uncertainty in Artificial Intelligence, UAI 1998, pp. 1–7. Morgan Kaufmann Publishers Inc., San Francisco (1998)
2. Amgoud, L., Cayrol, C., Berre, D.L.: Comparing arguments using preference orderings for argument-based reasoning. In: Proceedings Eighth IEEE International Conference on Tools with Artificial Intelligence, pp. 400–403 (1996)
3. Amgoud, L., Vesic, S.: A new approach for preference-based argumentation frameworks. Ann. Math. Artif. Intell. **63**(2), 149–183 (2011)
4. Amgoud, L., Cayrol, C.: Integrating preference orderings into argument-based reasoning. In: Gabbay, D.M., Kruse, R., Nonnengart, A., Ohlbach, H.J. (eds.) ECSQARU/FAPR -1997. LNCS, vol. 1244, pp. 159–170. Springer, Heidelberg (1997). https://doi.org/10.1007/BFb0035620
5. Amgoud, L., Cayrol, C.: A reasoning model based on the production of acceptable arguments. Ann. Math. Artif. Intell. **34**(1), 197–215 (2002)
6. Amgoud, L., Prade, H.: Using arguments for making and explaining decisions. Artif. Intell. **173**(3), 413–436 (2009)
7. Amgoud, L., Vesic, S.: Generalizing stable semantics by preferences. In: Proceedings of the 2010 Conference on Computational Models of Argument: Proceedings of COMMA 2010, pp. 39–50. IOS Press (2010)
8. Amgoud, L., Vesic, S.: Rich preference-based argumentation frameworks. Int. J. Approx. Reason. **55**(2), 585–606 (2014)
9. Bench-Capon, T.J.M.: Persuasion in practical argument using value-based argumentation frameworks. J. Log. Comput. **13**(3), 429–448 (2003)
10. Benferhat, S., Dubois, D., Prade, H.: Argumentative inference in uncertain and inconsistent knowledge bases. In: Heckerman, D., Mamdani, A. (eds.) Uncertainty in Artificial Intelligence, pp. 411–419. Morgan Kaufmann (1993)
11. Besnard, P., Hunter, A.: A logic-based theory of deductive arguments. Artif. Intell. **128**(1), 203–235 (2001)
12. Bonet, B., Geffner, H.: Arguing for decisions: a qualitative model of decision making. In: Proceedings of the Twelfth International Conference on Uncertainty in Artificial Intelligence, UAI 1996, pp. 98–105. Morgan Kaufmann Publishers Inc. (1996)
13. Caminada, M., Amgoud, L.: On the evaluation of argumentation formalisms. Artif. Intell. **171**(5), 286–310 (2007)
14. Cayrol, C., Royer, V., Saurel, C.: Management of preferences in assumption-based reasoning. In: Bouchon-Meunier, B., Valverde, L., Yager, R.R. (eds.) IPMU 1992. LNCS, vol. 682, pp. 13–22. Springer, Heidelberg (1993). https://doi.org/10.1007/3-540-56735-6_39
15. Dung, P.M.: On the acceptability of arguments and its fundamental role in non-monotonic reasoning, logic programming and n-person games. Artif. Intell. **77**, 321–357 (1995)
16. García, A.J., Simari, G.R.: Defeasible logic programming: an argumentative approach. Theory Pract. Log. Program. **4**(2), 95–138 (2004)
17. Kaci, S., van der Torre, L.: Preference-based argumentation: arguments supporting multiple values. Int. J. Approx. Reason. **48**(3), 730–751 (2008)
18. Konczak, K.: Voting procedures with incomplete preferences. In: Proceedings of IJCAI 2005 Multidisciplinary Workshop on Advances in Preference Handling (2005)

19. Modgil, S.: Reasoning about preferences in argumentation frameworks. Artif. Intell. **173**(9), 901–934 (2009)
20. Muller, J., Hunter, A.: An argumentation-based approach for decision making. In: Proceedings of the 2012 IEEE 24th International Conference on Tools with Artificial Intelligence, ICTAI 2012, vol. 01, pp. 564–571. IEEE Computer Society (2012)
21. Pigozzi, G., Tsoukiàs, A., Viappiani, P.: Preferences in artificial intelligence. Ann. Math. Artif. Intell. **77**(3), 361–401 (2016)
22. Pini, M., Rossi, F., Venable, K., Walsh, T.: Incompleteness and incomparability in preference aggregation: complexity results. Artif. Intell. **175**(7), 1272–1289 (2011)
23. Prakken, H., Sartor, G.: Argument-based extended logic programming with defeasible priorities. J. Appl. Non-Class. Log. **7**, 25–75 (1997)
24. Ricci, F., Rokach, L., Shapira, B., Kantor, P.B.: Recommender Systems Handbook, 1st edn. Springer, Heidelberg (2010). https://doi.org/10.1007/978-0-387-85820-3
25. Simari, G.R., Loui, R.P.: A mathematical treatment of defeasible reasoning and its implementation. Artif. Intell. **53**(2), 125–157 (1992)
26. Sprague, Jr., R.H., Watson, H.J. (eds.): Decision Support Systems, 3rd edn. Putting Theory into Practice. Prentice-Hall Inc., Upper Saddle River (1993)
27. Walsh, T.: Representing and reasoning with preferences. AI Mag. **28**(4), 59–70 (2007)

Notions of Instrumentality
in Agency Logic

Kees van Berkel$^{(\boxtimes)}$ and Matteo Pascucci$^{(\boxtimes)}$

Institute of Logic and Computation, TU Wien, Vienna, Austria
kees@logic.at, matteo.pascucci@tuwien.ac.at

Abstract. We present a logic of agency called *LAE* whose language includes propositional constants for actions and expectations. The logic is based on Von Wright's theory of agency in general and his analysis of instrumentality in particular. An axiomatization of the logic, including an independence of agents axiom, is provided and soundness and completeness are shown with respect to its intended class of frames. The framework of *LAE* will allow us to formally define a manifold of concepts involved in agency theories, including Von Wright's four elementary forms of action, the notion of forbearance and notions of instrumentality that make reference to an agent's expectations.

Keywords: Action logic · Agency · Expectations · Instrumentality

1 Introduction

What do we mean when we ascribe *agency* to a human being? We most likely assert that this person has the ability to perform an action. This answer highlights two key aspects of agency: *ability* and *action*. A third key aspect of agency is that actions can be seen in most cases as means to an end; that is, as *instruments*. The present work provides a logical framework to reason about the interplay of these three aspects of agency. While the notions of ability and action have been formally addressed for the past few decades, the notion of instrumentality seems to have received minor attention in the literature thus far. Philosophical analyses of instrumentality as such are scarce, although the concept of 'means to an end' is paramount to any theory of agency. Despite these limitations, we believe that logical investigations around instrumentality should be established on firm philosophical grounds. The present work aims at providing a formal account of instrumentality within a framework of agency logic and will be largely based on ideas presented by Georg Henrik von Wright [13–15], who can be regarded as one of the founding fathers of the logic of action [2].

Two prominent formal frameworks have been developed for the last few decades with respect to the logical treatment of agency: *stit-logic* [4,10] and *propositional dynamic logic* (PDL) [7,8]. The main difference between the two approaches can be pinpointed as follows: in stit-logic the focus has been largely

© Springer Nature Switzerland AG 2018
T. Miller et al. (Eds.): PRIMA 2018, LNAI 11224, pp. 403–419, 2018.
https://doi.org/10.1007/978-3-030-03098-8_25

put on the formal treatment of (explicit) agents on the basis of available choices, whereas in PDL the focus has been put on the formal analysis of (explicit) actions, regarded as transitions between states. In this article we reconstruct both frameworks within a logic including propositional constants for actions and expectations called *LAE* (*logic of actions and expectations*); our contribution is related to previous proposals that aim either at extending one framework to include the other, such as [16], or at defining one framework within the other, such as [9]. Our main purpose is to use *LAE* in order to provide a formal definition of various notions of instrumentality that rely on Von Wright's ideas. Special attention will be paid to how these notions interact with an agent's expectations. The article is divided as follows: in Sect. 2 we present and elaborate on Von Wright's ideas; in Sect. 3 we introduce the system *LAE* and prove its soundness and completeness. Finally, in Sect. 4, we formally specify the main notions of the theory of agency and instrumentality at issue.

2   A Theory of Agency and Instrumentality

2.1   Acting

To 'bring about something' and to 'prevent something' are essential characteristics of what it is to act. What is brought about is a *state of affairs* and, for that reason, to 'see to it that p' means that one acts "in such a manner that the state of affairs that p is the result of one's action" [13, p. 37]. From this account it follows that acting is strongly related to the *emergence* of a particular result (perhaps not always the desired one). An account of action, hence, heavily depends on the notion of change.

A change is a *transition* from an initial state to an end-state. These transitions can be triggered by events in which agents play no role (e.g., a moon eclipse); however, in many cases they are triggered by an agent's behaviour. In particular, an agent may decide to act or not to act in a certain way in a given circumstance and this behaviour may produce several different results (at least, in a non-deterministic world). For this reason, we say that an action triggers a set of possible transitions from an initial state to a set of end-states. To act, then, is to provoke a specific form of change: it is a change brought about by the interference of an agent with the "course of nature" [15, p. 36]; one can *a posteriori* say that if the agent had not acted, the course of history *would* have been different. This is what Von Wright calls the *counterfactual element* of action [13, p. 43].

In order to understand how a result p is related to an action, one also has to take into account whether p holds or not in the initial state. Indeed, an agent may bring about p in two ways: either the initial state is $\neg p$ and the agent's behaviour changes it to the result p, or the initial state is p and the agent prevents it from changing to $\neg p$ [15, p. 42]. Summing up, the analysis in this section provides us with three main characteristics of action: (i) the initial state, (ii) the result of the agent's behaviour (i.e., the end-state) and (iii) the counterfactual 'course of nature'. Taking into account also the difference between p and $\neg p$ as atomic results, Von Wright classifies *four elementary forms of agent behaviour*; the first two concern actions that 'bring about' something, the latter two are actions that 'prevent' something from happening [15, pp. 43–44]:

- *producing* p: constructively bringing p into 'existence' (Fig. 1a);[1]
- *destroying* p: without the agent's acting p would have 'prevailed' (Fig. 1b);
- *preserving* p: if the agent does not act, then p will 'perish' (Fig. 1c);
- *suppressing* p: if the agent does not act, then p will 'emerge' (Fig. 1d).

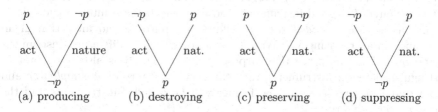

(a) producing   (b) destroying   (c) preserving   (d) suppressing

Fig. 1. Von Wright's four elementary types of action.

2.2   Actions

Up until now we have been talking about 'acts' without specification. Commonly, a distinction is made between two sorts of actions: actions described in an impersonal, generic way (e.g. 'writing') and concrete, individual instances of these generic actions, as performed by a particular agent at a particular time (e.g. 'I am currently writing'). The former are frequently called '*action-types*', whereas the latter can be named '*action-tokens*'. Following Von Wright, generic actions (i.e., types) can be regarded as 'categories' to which individual 'cases' (i.e., tokens) belong [15, p. 36].

Here we will generalize this account of actions by considering also *negative actions* and *complex actions*. This will enable us to speak of, for instance, the action-type 'not opening the door' and the action-type 'not opening the door or closing the window'. Negative actions are usually not expressible in the language of propositional dynamic logic, but they are taken into account in other formal approaches to agency which make explicit reference to actions, such as [2] and [3]. We will regard both action-types and action-tokens as essential to our logic of agency: As was pointed out in the previous section, an agent's behaviour at a particular state triggers a set of possible transitions and, therefore, represents an action-token. Moreover, as we will clarify in the next section, a proper notion of instrumentality makes reference to action-types; that is, in order to determine whether an action is a good instrument for a given purpose, one has to consider the outcomes of previous transitions triggered by actions of that type.

---

[1] The term used by Von Wright for this behaviour is 'doing p'. We avoid this expression because we reserve 'doing' for actions, and use 'producing' for results.

2.3 Instrumentality

Actions can be regarded as instrument serving a particular purpose; they are 'means to an end'. For instance, 'pressing Y on the keyboard' and 'pulling the handbrake of a car' are respectively instruments to 'confirm a procedure on a computer terminal' and to 'perform an emergency stop'. In this section several distinct forms of instrumentality will be presented that will be formally addressed in subsequent sections. As a philosophical basis, we will borrow from and extend Von Wright's analysis of instrumental goodness, as presented in [14, pp. 19–40]. To avoid ambiguity, the term 'proper instrument' is here regarded as an appropriate synonym for 'good instrument' and they will be used interchangeably.

Let us call an *intended* state of affairs ϕ a purpose and an action Δ an instrument. Paraphrasing Von Wright, an action Δ will qualify as a ϕ-instrument if and only if Δ can serve the purpose ϕ [14, p. 21]. It is also important to distinguish between instruments that can serve the purpose ϕ *simpliciter* and those that can serve ϕ *well*. The former will be called ϕ-instruments and the latter *proper* ϕ-instruments.

To qualify a particular instrument suitable for a particular purpose, we base our judgment on *past performance*; for example, with respect to questions of instrumentality we often make remarks such as 'it has worked before' and 'it has never disappointed me (thus far)'. In the first case, we recognize a weak criterion; that is, the instrument *has* served the purpose at least once and, for that reason, it *can* serve the purpose. In the latter case, we identify a stronger criterion for instrumentality; that is, there have been applications of the instrument and these applications *have always served* the purpose and, for that reason, the instrument serves the purpose *well*. Hence, notions of instrumentality are based on past experience. This experience, subsequently, can be either impersonal or personal (e.g., 'this machine has been tested' or 'I have used this tool before'). Thus far, we established two definitions of impersonal instrumentality:

(1) AGENT-INDEPENDENT BASIC INSTRUMENTALITY: action-type Δ is a basic ϕ-instrument if and only if Δ has served the purpose ϕ at least once in the past.

(2) AGENT-INDEPENDENT PROPER INSTRUMENTALITY: action-type Δ is a proper ϕ-instrument if and only if (i) Δ is a basic ϕ-instrument and (ii) Δ has always served the purpose ϕ in the past.

Hence, notions of instrumentality relate to both purpose and past performance. However, when we judge that 'these scissors are a proper instrument for me to cut this piece of paper', what do we mean? Von Wright briefly remarks that "judgments of instrumental goodness, usually, even if not necessarily, contain a conjectural element" [14, p. 27]. In other words, practical statements about instrumentality also contain reference to *expectations* about the instrument's future performance. Hence, agent-bound instrumentality is based on both (i) the past performance of particular action-tokens associated with a certain type and (ii) the expected continuation of this performance in the nearby future. In contrast to agent-independent statements of instrumentality, statements of this form will vary over agents. What is more, the conjectural element of expected performance does not guarantee any future result: the agent might simply be wrong [14, p. 27]. The fact that the instrument has served the purpose well in the past, does not guarantee that it will not fail in the future. In our formal framework we will strongly emphasize these fundamental aspects of agent-bound instrumentality by investigating different notions of instrumentality that are restricted by the agent's expectations.

Lastly, we emphasize that expectations must be regarded as those future moments which the agent considers *more likely to happen*. An agent's expectations about the nearby future are therefore a subset of all possible next moments. We will accordingly introduce a formal restriction on expectations in Sect. 3.[2]

From the above we derive two agent-bound definitions of instrumentality:

(3) AGENT-BOUND BASIC INSTRUMENTALITY: An instrument Δ is a basic ϕ-instrument for agent α at moment m if and only if (i) Δ is a basic ϕ-instrument and (ii) α expects that Δ will serve ϕ at m.

(4) AGENT-BOUND PROPER INSTRUMENTALITY: An instrument Δ is a proper ϕ-instrument for agent α at moment m if and only if (i) Δ is a proper ϕ-instrument and (ii) α expects that Δ will serve ϕ at m.

The agent-independent and agent-dependent notions of instrumentality (1)–(4) will be formally addressed in Sect. 4.

In passing, *ability* can be regarded as an abstract form of agentive instrumentality; namely, saying that 'an agent is able to behave in a certain way which guarantees a result' is an abstraction of saying that 'there exists an instrument (action) which the agent can successfully employ to obtain that result'. Moreover, saying that an agent α is able to obtain ϕ through an action Δ, given that Δ has always led α to ϕ in the past, is essentially the same as saying that α *excels* at performing Δ to obtain ϕ. In this sense, Von Wright's concept of ability, 'being good *at* something', is strongly related to our concept of agent-bound proper instrumentality (cf. the analysis of 'technical goodness' as ability and skill in [14, pp. 32–39]).

3   The System *LAE*

We start our formal presentation with a boolean algebra of actions and subsequently introduce the language of the logic *LAE*, in which the performance of an action by an agent will be represented by a formula. Let $Action = \{\delta_1, ..., \delta_n\}$ be a finite set of atomic action-types. The set $Action^*$ of complex action-types is defined by the following BNF:

$$\Delta ::= \delta_i | \Delta \cup \Delta | \overline{\Delta}$$

---

[2] We want to stress that the term 'expectation' must not be regarded as an epistemic notion, such as knowledge. Although an agent can have expectations about the future, the agent might still have imperfect knowledge of these expected future states.

where $\delta_i \in Action$. The operations $\cup$ and — are respectively used to form *disjunctions of action-types* (e.g., 'turning-left or turning-right') and *negations of action-types* (e.g., 'not turning-right'). If $Agent = \{\alpha_1, ..., \alpha_m\}$ is a finite set of agent constants, an *agent-bound action-type* is an expression of kind Δ^{α_i}, where $\Delta \in Action^*$ and $\alpha_i \in Agent$. Let $Var = \{p_1, p_2, p_3, ...\}$ be a countable set of propositional variables; furthermore, for any $\alpha_i \in Agent$, let $Wit^{\alpha_i} = \{\mathfrak{d}_1^{\alpha_i}, ..., \mathfrak{d}_n^{\alpha_i}\}$ be a set of propositional constants respectively witnessing the performance of the atomic action-types δ_1, ..., δ_n by α_i and let $\mathfrak{e}^{\alpha_i}$ be a propositional constant witnessing the compatibility of a state with α_i's expectations.[3] Notice that $|Wit^{\alpha_i}| = |Action| = n$. The set $\bigcup_{\alpha_i \in Agent} Wit^{\alpha_i}$ can be simply denoted by Wit. The language $\mathcal{L}$ is defined by the following BNF:

$$\phi ::= p_i \,|\, \mathfrak{e}^{\alpha_j} \,|\, \mathfrak{d}_i^{\alpha_j} \,|\, \neg\phi \,|\, \phi \rightarrow \phi \,|\, \Box\phi \,|\, N\phi$$

for any $p_i \in Var$, $\alpha_j \in Agent$ and $\mathfrak{d}_i^{\alpha_j} \in Wit$. We can read $\Box\phi$ as 'in all successor states ϕ is the case' and $N\phi$ as 'in the actual successor state ϕ is the case'. We use standard definitions for additional boolean and modal operators. For instance, $\Diamond\phi$ abbreviates $\neg\Box\neg\phi$ and means 'in some successor state ϕ is the case'. Expressions like $\mathfrak{e}^{\alpha_j}$ and $\mathfrak{d}_i^{\alpha_j}$ mean respectively 'the most recent expectations of agent α_j are met' and 'agent α_j has just performed action δ_i'. The set of atomic propositional symbols in $\mathcal{L}$ is $Atom = Var \cup Wit \cup \{\mathfrak{e}^{\alpha_j} : \alpha_j \in Agent\}$.

Let t be a translation function mapping agent-bound action-types to formulas of $\mathcal{L}$ as below:

- for any $\delta_i \in Action$ and $\alpha_j \in Agent$, $t(\delta_i^{\alpha_j}) = \mathfrak{d}_i^{\alpha_j}$,
- for any $\Delta \in Action^*$ and $\alpha_i \in Agent$, $t(\overline{\Delta}^{\alpha_i}) = \neg t(\Delta^{\alpha_i})$;
- for any $\Delta, \Gamma \in Action^*$ and $\alpha_i, \alpha_j \in Agent$, $t(\Delta^{\alpha_i} \cup \Gamma^{\alpha_j}) = t(\Delta^{\alpha_i}) \vee t(\Gamma^{\alpha_j})$.

Let LAE be the system specified below:

A0 if ϕ is a propositional tautology, then $\vdash_{LAE} \phi$;

R0 $\phi, \phi \rightarrow \psi \vdash_{LAE} \psi$;

A1 $\Box(\phi \rightarrow \psi) \rightarrow (\Box\phi \rightarrow \Box\psi)$;

R1 if $\vdash_{LAE} \phi$, then $\vdash_{LAE} \Box\phi$;

A2 $N(\phi \rightarrow \psi) \rightarrow (N\phi \rightarrow N\psi)$;

A3 $\neg N\phi \rightarrow N\neg\phi$;

A4 $\Box\phi \rightarrow N\phi$;

A5 for any list of (distinct) $\alpha_1, ..., \alpha_n \in Agent$ and list of (non-necessarily distinct) $\Delta_1, ..., \Delta_n \in Action^*$,
$(\Diamond t(\Delta_1^{\alpha_1}) \wedge ... \wedge \Diamond t(\Delta_n^{\alpha_n})) \rightarrow \Diamond(t(\Delta_1^{\alpha_1}) \wedge ... \wedge t(\Delta_n^{\alpha_n}))$;

A6 for any $\alpha_j \in Agent$, $\Diamond\mathfrak{e}^{\alpha_j} \rightarrow \Diamond\neg\mathfrak{e}^{\alpha_j}$.

The most relevant axioms of the system S are A3, which guarantees that every state has a unique successor, A4, which says that the actual successor of a state is within the set of its successors, A5, which represents the stit-logic principle known as *independence of agents*, and A6, which ensures that agents never expect

---

[3] The use of propositional constants in modal logic can be traced back at least to [1].

all possible future state-of-affairs to happen (if at a given state there are successor states satisfying an agent's expectations, then there are also successor states not satisfying the expectations).[4] The semantics for *LAE* will clarify that none of these axioms implies that a state has successors. Thus, the system can be used to reason about scenarios in which there are final possible states. Furthermore, it is noteworthy that the principle of 'independence of agents' is compatible with a scenario in which an agent ends in a state that does not meet that agent's (most recent) expectations.

We define the following additional operators:

E1 for any $\Delta \in Action^*$ and $\alpha_i \in Agent$,
$[\Delta^{\alpha_i}]^{would}\phi =_{def} \Box(t(\Delta^{\alpha_i}) \rightarrow \phi)$;

E2 for any $\Delta \in Action^*$ and $\alpha_i \in Agent$,
$[\Delta^{\alpha_i}]^{could}\phi =_{def} \Box(t(\Delta^{\alpha_i}) \rightarrow \phi) \wedge \Diamond t(\Delta^{\alpha_i})$;

E3 for any $\Delta \in Action^*$ and $\alpha_i \in Agent$,
$[\Delta^{\alpha_i}]^{will}\phi =_{def} \Box(t(\Delta^{\alpha_i}) \rightarrow \phi) \wedge \neg N \neg t(\Delta^{\alpha_i})$.

We can read the formula $[\Delta^{\alpha_i}]^{would}\phi$ as 'at the current state, by behaving in accordance with Δ, α_i would bring about ϕ'. (Notice that this does not ensure that α_i is currently able to behave in accordance with Δ.) The formula $[\Delta^{\alpha_i}]^{could}\phi$ means 'at the current state, by behaving in accordance with Δ, α_i would bring about ϕ and α_i could (i.e., is able to) behave in accordance with Δ'. Finally, the formula $[\Delta^{\alpha_i}]^{will}\phi$ means 'at the current state, by behaving in accordance with Δ, α_i would bring about ϕ and α_i will actually behave in accordance with Δ'.

A relational frame to interpret the language $\mathcal{L}$ is an ordered tuple $\mathfrak{F} = \langle W, \{W_{\mathfrak{d}_i^{\alpha_j}} : \mathfrak{d}_i^{\alpha_j} \in \mathcal{L}\}, \{W_{\mathfrak{e}^{\alpha_j}} : \mathfrak{e}^{\alpha_j} \in \mathcal{L}\}, R, R_N \rangle$, where $W = \{w_1, w_2, w_3, ...\}$ is a set of states, each $W_{\mathfrak{d}_i^{\alpha_j}}$ and each $W_{\mathfrak{e}^{\alpha_j}}$ is a subset of W and R and R_N are binary relations over W. The relation R captures the idea of a transition from a state to one of its immediate successors. As we pointed out in Sect. 2, a transition can be triggered by any event and so it does not require, in general, an active interference of an agent. The relation R_N represents transitions in the *course of events that can be considered actual with respect to a given state*; namely, we have $wR_N u$ only if u is an immediate successor of w and belongs to the actual future of w. Thus, the notion of actual future is *state-dependent*. This allows one to reason about the actual future of counterfactual states as well.[5]

---

[4] The 'independence of agents' axiom is central to stit-logic; it ensures that when choices are made *simultaneously*, an agent cannot *a priori* limit the choices available to the others; see e.g. [4, pp. 217–218]. Axiom A6 allows for the possibility that an agent has contradictory expectations about the future which cannot be realized.

[5] For instance, suppose that at w it started raining and I decided to take a walk without bringing an umbrella with me. Thus, I am in a state w' such that in the future of w' I will very likely get wet; however, had I decided to bring an umbrella with me at w, I would have ended in a state w'' such that in the future of w'' I would not have got wet. Therefore, one can also say that in the *actual future of the counterfactual state* w'' I would not have got wet.

A relational model to interpret $\mathcal{L}$ is an ordered tuple $\mathfrak{M} = \langle \mathfrak{F}, V \rangle$ where $\mathfrak{F}$ is a relational frame and V is a valuation function which maps atomic propositional symbols to sets of states and satisfies the following conditions:

- $V(\mathfrak{d}_i^{\alpha_j}) = W_{\mathfrak{d}_i^{\alpha_j}}$, for any $\mathfrak{d}_i^{\alpha_j} \in \mathcal{L}$;
- $V(\mathfrak{e}^{\alpha_j}) = W_{\mathfrak{e}^{\alpha_j}}$, for any $\mathfrak{e}^{\alpha_j} \in \mathcal{L}$.

Thus, propositional constants have the same interpretation in all models over a frame. Formulas of $\mathcal{L}$ are evaluated at a state of a model in the customary way. Truth-conditions are defined as follows:

- $\mathfrak{M}, w \vDash \chi$ iff $w \in V(\chi)$, for any $\chi \in Atom$;
- $\mathfrak{M}, w \vDash \neg\phi$ iff $\mathfrak{M}, w \nvDash \phi$;
- $\mathfrak{M}, w \vDash \phi \to \psi$ iff $\mathfrak{M}, w \nvDash \phi$ or $\mathfrak{M}, w \vDash \psi$;
- $\mathfrak{M}, w \vDash \Box\phi$ iff for all $v \in W$ s.t. wRv we have $\mathfrak{M}, v \vDash \phi$;
- $\mathfrak{M}, w \vDash N\phi$ iff for all $v \in W$ s.t. $wR_N v$, we have $\mathfrak{M}, v \vDash \phi$.

Let $\mathfrak{F}, w \vDash \phi$ mean that $\mathfrak{M}, w \vDash \phi$ for all models $\mathfrak{M}$ over the frame $\mathfrak{F}$. The notion of validity of a formula with respect to (w.r.t.) a model, a frame, a class of models and a class of frames is defined in the standard way. Finally, for a given formula $\phi \in \mathcal{L}$, let $||\phi||^{\mathfrak{M}} = \{w \in W : \mathfrak{M}, w \vDash \phi\}$ and $||\phi||^{\mathfrak{F}} = \{w \in W : \mathfrak{F}, w \vDash \phi\}$. Due to the fixed interpretation of propositional constants and the definition of the translation function t, we have that, given a frame $\mathfrak{F}$ and an arbitrary model $\mathfrak{M}$ over it:

- $||t(\Delta^{\alpha_i})||^{\mathfrak{F}} = ||t(\Delta^{\alpha_i})||^{\mathfrak{M}}$, for any $\Delta \in Action^*$ and any $\alpha_i \in Agent$.

Let C_f be the class of all frames satisfying the following properties:

p(A3) for all $w \in W$, if there is $u \in W$ s.t. $wR_N u$, then for all $v \in W$ s.t. $wR_N v$, we have $v = u$;

p(A4) for all $w, v \in W$, if $wR_N v$, then wRv;

p(A5) for all $w \in W$ and for all lists of distinct agents $\alpha_1, ..., \alpha_n$, if there are (non-necessarily distinct) action-types $\Delta_1, ..., \Delta_n$ s.t. for $1 \le i \le n$ there is $u_i \in W$ s.t. wRu_i and $u_i \in ||t(\Delta_i^{\alpha_i})||^{\mathfrak{F}}$, then there is $v \in W$ s.t. wRv and $v \in ||t(\Delta_1^{\alpha_1})||^{\mathfrak{F}} \cap ... \cap ||t(\Delta_n^{\alpha_n})||^{\mathfrak{F}}$;

p(A6) for all $w \in W$ and $\alpha_j \in Agent$, if there is $v \in W$ s.t. wRv and $v \in ||\mathfrak{e}^{\alpha_j}||^{\mathfrak{F}}$, then there is also $u \in W$ s.t. wRu and $u \notin ||\mathfrak{e}^{\alpha_j}||^{\mathfrak{F}}$.

The class C_f is non-empty. Indeed, the following is a very simple frame belonging to it: $\mathfrak{F} = \langle W, \{W_{\mathfrak{d}_i^{\alpha_j}} : \mathfrak{d}_i^{\alpha_j} \in \mathcal{L}\}, \{W_{\mathfrak{e}^{\alpha_j}} : \mathfrak{e}^{\alpha_j} \in \mathcal{L}\}, R, R_N \rangle$, where $W = \{w_1, w_2\}$, $W_{\mathfrak{d}_i^{\alpha_j}} = \{w_2\}$ for any $\mathfrak{d}_i^{\alpha_j} \in \mathcal{L}$, $W_{\mathfrak{e}^{\alpha_j}} = \emptyset$ for any $\mathfrak{e}^{\alpha_j} \in \mathcal{L}$ and $R = R_N = \{(w_1, w_2)\}$. It is straightforward to verify that p(A3)-p(A6) are satisfied by $\mathfrak{F}$.

Theorem 1. *The system LAE is sound w.r.t. the class C_f.*

Proof. Axioms A0, A1 and A2 are valid in all relational frames and rules R0 and R1 preserve validity in all relational frames. In the case of A3, take an arbitrary frame $\mathfrak{F} \in C_f$ and a model $\mathfrak{M}$ over it. Assume $\mathfrak{M}, w \vDash \neg N\phi$ for some $w \in W$;

from this we can infer that there is $v \in W$ s.t. $wR_N v$ and $\mathfrak{M}, v \vDash \neg\phi$; by p(A3), it follows that for all $u \in W$ s.t. $wR_N u$, $u = v$. Therefore, $\mathfrak{M}, w \vDash N\neg\phi$. In the case of A4, assume $\mathfrak{M}, w \vDash \Box\phi$; then, for all $v \in W$ s.t. wRv we have $\mathfrak{M}, v \vDash \phi$. By p(A4), we can infer that for all $u \in W$ s.t. $wR_N u$ we have $\mathfrak{M}, u \vDash \phi$. Hence, $\mathfrak{M}, w \vDash N\phi$. In the case of A5, let, for some distinct $\alpha_1, ..., \alpha_n \in Agent$ and some (non-necessarily distinct) $\Delta_1, ..., \Delta_n \in Action^*$, $\mathfrak{M}, w \vDash \Diamond t(\Delta_1^{\alpha_1}) \wedge ... \wedge \Diamond t(\Delta_n^{\alpha_n})$. From this we can infer that there are (non-necessarily distinct) $v_1, ..., v_n \in W$ s.t., for $1 \leq i \leq n$, wRv_i and $v_i \in ||t(\Delta_i^{\alpha_i})||^{\mathfrak{F}}$. By p(A5), we can infer that there is $u \in W$ s.t. wRu and $u \in ||t(\Delta_1^{\alpha_1})||^{\mathfrak{F}} \cap ... \cap ||t(\Delta_n^{\alpha_n})||^{\mathfrak{F}}$. Hence, $\mathfrak{M}, w \vDash \Diamond(t(\Delta_1^{\alpha_1}) \wedge ... \wedge t(\Delta_n^{\alpha_n}))$. In the case of A6, assume $\mathfrak{M}, w \vDash \Diamond e^{\alpha_j}$ for some $e^{\alpha_j} \in \mathcal{L}$. Then, there is $v \in W$ s.t. wRv and $\mathfrak{M}, v \vDash e^{\alpha_j}$. By p(A6), we can infer that there is $u \in W$ s.t. wRu and $\mathfrak{M}, u \vDash \neg e^{\alpha_j}$; hence, $\mathfrak{M}, w \vDash \Diamond \neg e^{\alpha_j}$.

Let $\mathfrak{F}^{LAE}$ be the canonical frame for LAE, defined as follows:

- W^{LAE} is the set of all maximally LAE-consistent sets of formulas;
- for any $w, v \in W^{LAE}$, $wR^{LAE}v$ iff $\{\phi : \Box\phi \in w\} \subseteq v$;
- for any $w, v \in W^{LAE}$, $wR_N^{LAE}v$ iff $\{\phi : N\phi \in w\} \subseteq v$;
- for any $\mathfrak{d}_i^{\alpha_j} \in \mathcal{L}$, $W_{\mathfrak{d}_i^{\alpha_j}}^{LAE} = \{w \in W^{LAE} : \mathfrak{d}_i^{\alpha_j} \in w\}$;
- for any $e^{\alpha_j} \in \mathcal{L}$, $W_{e^{\alpha_j}}^{LAE} = \{w \in W^{LAE} : e^{\alpha_j} \in w\}$.

The canonical model for LAE, denoted by $\mathfrak{M}^{LAE}$, is obtained by adding a valuation function V^{LAE} s.t.:

- for any $\chi \in Atom$, $V^{LAE}(\chi) = \{w \in W^{LAE} : \chi \in w\}$.

Any alternative valuation function V on the canonical frame must satisfy the aforementioned restrictions on propositional constants (namely, $V(\mathfrak{d}_i^{\alpha_j}) = W_{\mathfrak{d}_i^{\alpha_j}}^{LAE}$, etc.). By usual properties of canonical models, for any formula $\phi \in \mathcal{L}$ and any state $w \in W^{LAE}$, we have $\mathfrak{M}^{LAE}, w \vDash \phi$ iff $\phi \in w$.

The following theorem illustrates some properties of the frame $\mathfrak{F}^{LAE}$.

Theorem 2. Let $R_{\Delta^{\alpha_i}}^{LAE}$ be a binary relation over W^{LAE} s.t., for any $w, v \in W^{LAE}$, $wR_{\Delta^{\alpha_i}}^{LAE}v$ iff $\{\phi : [\Delta^{\alpha_i}]^{would}\phi \in w\} \subseteq v$; we show some of the properties of this relation:

(I) $R_{\Delta^{\alpha_i}}^{LAE} \subseteq R^{LAE}$;
(II) $R_{\Delta^{\alpha_i} \cup \Gamma^{\alpha_j}}^{LAE} = R_{\Delta^{\alpha_i}}^{LAE} \cup R_{\Gamma^{\alpha_j}}^{LAE}$;
(III) $R_{\overline{\Delta^{\alpha_i}}}^{LAE} = R^{LAE} \cap \overline{R_{\Delta^{\alpha_i}}^{LAE}}$.

Proof. Let w be an arbitrary world in the canonical model of LAE.
(I) Assume $wR_{\Delta^{\alpha_i}}^{LAE}v$; then, $\{\phi : [\Delta^{\alpha_i}]^{would}\phi \in w\} \subseteq v$. Furthermore, let $\neg(wR^{LAE}v)$; then there is $\Box\psi \in w$ s.t. $\psi \notin v$. From this and ordinary modal reasoning it follows that $\Box(t(\Delta^{\alpha_i}) \to \psi) \in w$ and $[\Delta^{\alpha_i}]^{would}\psi \in w$, so $\psi \in v$, which represents a contradiction.
(II) Assume $wR_{\Delta^{\alpha_i} \cup \Gamma^{\alpha_j}}^{LAE}v$. Then, $\{\phi : [\Delta^{\alpha_i} \cup \Gamma^{\alpha_j}]^{would}\phi \in w\} \subseteq v$, which entails $\{\phi : \Box((t(\Delta^{\alpha_i}) \vee t(\Gamma^{\alpha_j})) \to \phi) \in w\} \subseteq v$ and $\{\phi : \Box(t(\Delta^{\alpha_i}) \to \phi) \wedge \Box(t(\Gamma^{\alpha_j}) \to$

$\phi) \in w\} \subseteq v$, so $\{\phi : [\Delta^{\alpha_i}]^{would}\phi \wedge [\Gamma^{\alpha_j}]^{would}\phi) \in w\} \subseteq v$. Suppose $\neg(wR^{LAE}_{\Delta^{\alpha_i}} \cup R^{LAE}_{\Gamma^{\alpha_j}}v)$; then, there are $[\Delta^{\alpha_i}]^{would}\psi, [\Gamma^{\alpha_j}]^{would}\chi \in w$ s.t. $\psi, \chi \notin v$. From this it follows that $\Box(t(\Delta^{\alpha_i}) \to \psi), \Box(t(\Gamma^{\alpha_j}) \to \chi) \in w$. Since $\Box(t(\Delta^{\alpha_i}) \to (t(\Delta^{\alpha_i}) \vee t(\Gamma^{\alpha_j}))) \wedge \Box(t(\Gamma^{\alpha_j}) \to (t(\Delta^{\alpha_i}) \vee t(\Gamma^{\alpha_j}))) \in w$, then $t(\Delta^{\alpha_i}) \vee t(\Gamma^{\alpha_j}) \in v$, which means that either $t(\Delta^{\alpha_i}) \in v$ or $t(\Gamma^{\alpha_j}) \in v$. Since we know that $wR^{LAE}_{\Delta^{\alpha_i} \cup \Gamma^{\alpha_j}}v$ entails $wR^{LAE}v$, then $\{\phi : \Box\phi \in w\} \subseteq v$. This means that if $t(\Delta^{\alpha_i}) \in v$, then $\psi \in v$; if $t(\Gamma^{\alpha_j}) \in v$, then $\chi \in v$. A contradiction arises in both cases.

Assume $\neg(wR^{LAE}_{\Delta^{\alpha_i} \cup \Gamma^{\alpha_j}}v)$; then, there is $[\Delta^{\alpha_i} \cup \Gamma^{\alpha_j}]^{would}\psi \in w$ s.t. $\psi \notin v$. Therefore, $\Box((t(\Delta^{\alpha_i}) \vee t(\Gamma^{\alpha_j})) \to \psi) \in w$. Suppose $wR^{LAE}v$ (otherwise the intended result trivially follows); then, since $\Box(\neg\psi \to \neg(t(\Delta^{\alpha_i}) \vee t(\Gamma^{\alpha_j}))) \in w$, then $\neg(t(\Delta^{\alpha_i}) \vee t(\Gamma^{\alpha_j})) \in v$, whence $\neg t(\Delta^{\alpha_i}), \neg t(\Gamma^{\alpha_j}) \in v$, so $\{\phi : [\Delta^{\alpha_i}]^{would}\phi \in w\} \nsubseteq v$ and $\{\phi : [\Gamma^{\alpha_j}]^{would}\phi \in w\} \nsubseteq v$, hence $\neg(wR^{LAE}_{\Delta^{\alpha_i}} \cup R^{LAE}_{\Gamma^{\alpha_j}}v)$.

(III) Let $wR^{LAE}_{\Delta^{\alpha_i}}v$; then, $\{\phi : [\overline{\Delta^{\alpha_i}}]^{would}\phi \in w\} \subseteq v$; we know that from this it is possible to infer $wR^{LAE}v$. Since $[\Delta^{\alpha_i}]^{would}t(\Delta^{\alpha_i}), [\overline{\Delta^{\alpha_i}}]^{would}\neg t(\Delta^{\alpha_i}) \in w$, then $\neg t(\Delta^{\alpha_i}) \in v$ and $t(\Delta^{\alpha_i}) \notin v$, so $\neg(wR^{LAE}_{\Delta^{\alpha_i}}v)$, which is $wR^{\overline{LAE}}_{\Delta^{\alpha_i}}v$, and $wR^{LAE} \cap \overline{R^{LAE}_{\Delta^{\alpha_i}}}v$.

Let $\neg(wR^{LAE}_{\Delta^{\alpha_i}}v)$; then, there is $[\overline{\Delta^{\alpha_i}}]^{would}\psi \in w$ s.t. $\psi \notin v$. Assume $wR^{LAE}v$; since $\Box(\neg t(\Delta^{\alpha_i}) \to \psi) \in w$, then $\neg t(\Delta^{\alpha_i}) \to \psi \in v$, so $t(\Delta^{\alpha_i}) \in v$. Let $[\Delta^{\alpha_i}]^{would}\chi \in w$; then, $\Box(t(\Delta^{\alpha_i}) \to \chi) \in w$ and $\chi \in v$; thus, $\{\phi : [\Delta^{\alpha_i}]^{would}\phi \in w\} \subseteq v$, which means $wR^{LAE}_{\Delta^{\alpha_i}}v$ and $\neg(wR^{LAE} \cap \overline{R^{LAE}_{\Delta^{\alpha_i}}}v)$.

Theorem 3. *The frame $\mathfrak{F}^{LAE}$ belongs to the class C_f.*

Proof. We need to show that $\mathfrak{F}^{LAE}$ satisfies the properties p(A3)–p(A6). In the case of p(A3), suppose $wR^{LAE}_N v$, $wR^{LAE}_N u$ and $v \neq u$. Then, there is ϕ s.t. $\phi \in v$ and $\phi \notin u$. In the canonical model $\mathfrak{M}^{LAE}$ we have $\mathfrak{M}^{LAE}, v \vDash \phi$ and $\mathfrak{M}^{LAE}, u \vDash \neg\phi$, so $\mathfrak{M}^{LAE}, w \vDash \neg N\phi$ and, by A3, $\mathfrak{M}^{LAE}, w \vDash N\neg\phi$, which entails $\mathfrak{M}^{LAE}, v \vDash \neg\phi$, whence $\phi, \neg\phi \in v$: contradiction. In the case of p(A4), suppose that $wR^{LAE}_N v$ and $\neg wR^{LAE}v$. Then there is $\Box\phi \in w$ s.t. $\phi \notin v$; however, by A4, $N\phi \in w$ and this entails $\neg wR^{LAE}_N v$: contradiction. In the case of p(A5), suppose that for a list of distinct agents $\alpha_1, ..., \alpha_n$ and for a list of (non-necessarily distinct) action-types $\Delta_1, ..., \Delta_n$, we have that there are (non-necessarily distinct) worlds $u_1, ..., u_n$ s.t., for $1 \leq i \leq n$, $wR^{LAE}u_i$ and $u_i \in ||t(\Delta_i^{\alpha_i})||^{\mathfrak{F}}$. Then, $w \in ||\Diamond t(\Delta_1^{\alpha_1})||^{\mathfrak{F}} \cap ... \cap ||\Diamond t(\Delta_n^{\alpha_n})||^{\mathfrak{F}}$, which entails $\Diamond t(\Delta_1^{\alpha_1}) \wedge ... \wedge \Diamond t(\Delta_n^{\alpha_n}) \in w$ and, by A4, we get $\Diamond(t(\Delta_1^{\alpha_1}) \wedge ... \wedge t(\Delta_n^{\alpha_n})) \in w$. Assume that there is no maximally LAE-consistent set v s.t. $\{\phi : \Box\phi \in w\} \cup \{(t(\Delta_1^{\alpha_1}) \wedge ... \wedge t(\Delta_n^{\alpha_n}))\} \subseteq v$; then, $\vdash_{LAE} (\phi_1 \wedge ... \wedge \phi_m) \to \neg(t(\Delta_1^{\alpha_1}) \wedge ... \wedge t(\Delta_n^{\alpha_n}))$ for some $\phi_1, ..., \phi_m \in \{\phi : \Box\phi \in w\}$. From this one can infer $\vdash_{LAE} \Box(\phi_1 \wedge ... \wedge \phi_m) \to \Box\neg(t(\Delta_1^{\alpha_1}) \wedge ... \wedge t(\Delta_n^{\alpha_n}))$, so $\vdash_{LAE} (\Diamond t(\Delta_1^{\alpha_1}) \wedge ... \wedge \Diamond t(\Delta_n^{\alpha_n}) \wedge \Box(\phi_1 \wedge ... \wedge \phi_m)) \to \neg\Diamond(t(\Delta_1^{\alpha_1}) \wedge ... \wedge t(\Delta_n^{\alpha_n}))$; however, this is impossible since we know that $\vdash_{LAE} (\Diamond t(\Delta_1^{\alpha_1}) \wedge ... \wedge \Diamond t(\Delta_n^{\alpha_n})) \to \Diamond(t(\Delta_1^{\alpha_1}) \wedge ... \wedge t(\Delta_n^{\alpha_n}))$. Hence, we can conclude that there is a maximally LAE-consistent set v s.t. $wR^{LAE}v$ and $v \in ||(t(\Delta_1^{\alpha_1})||^{\mathfrak{F}} \cap ... \cap ||t(\Delta_n^{\alpha_n}))||^{\mathfrak{F}}$. In the case of p(A6), assume that $wR^{LAE}v$ and $v \in ||\mathfrak{e}^{\alpha_i}||^{\mathfrak{F}}$ for some $\mathfrak{e}^{\alpha_i} \in \mathcal{L}$; then, suppose that the set $\{\phi : \Box\phi \in w\} \cup \{\neg\mathfrak{e}^{\alpha_i}\}$ is not LAE-consistent. From this one can infer that $\vdash_{LAE} \Box(\phi_1 \wedge ... \wedge \phi_n) \to \neg\Diamond\neg\mathfrak{e}^{\alpha_i}$ for some $\phi_1, ..., \phi_n \in \{\phi : \Box\phi \in w\}$; hence, $\vdash_{LAE} (\Box(\phi_1 \wedge ... \wedge \phi_n) \wedge \Diamond\mathfrak{e}^{\alpha_i}) \to \neg\Diamond\neg\mathfrak{e}^{\alpha_i}$, which contradicts A6. Then, there is a maximally LAE-consistent set u s.t. $\{\phi : \Box\phi \in w\} \cup \{\neg\mathbf{e}^{\alpha_i}\} \subseteq u$, which means $u \in ||\neg\mathbf{e}^{\alpha_i}||^{\mathfrak{F}}$ and $wR^{LAE}u$.

An immediate consequence of Theorem 3 is that LAE is complete w.r.t. the class C_f; hence, together with Theorem 1, this entails that LAE is characterized by the class C_f. Furthermore, as a consequence of Theorem 2 and Theorem 3, the following schemata, which capture the properties of a boolean algebra of action-types, are provable in LAE:[6]

T1 $[\Delta^{\alpha_i} \cup \Gamma^{\alpha_j}]^{would}\phi \equiv [\Gamma^{\alpha_j} \cup \Delta^{\alpha_i}]^{would}\phi$;

T2 $[\Delta^{\alpha_i} \cup (\Gamma^{\alpha_j} \cup \Sigma^{\alpha_k})]^{would}\phi \equiv [(\Delta^{\alpha_i} \cup \Gamma^{\alpha_j}) \cup \Sigma^{\alpha_k}]^{would}\phi$;

T3 $[\overline{\overline{\Delta^{\alpha_i} \cup \Gamma^{\alpha_j}} \cup \overline{\Delta^{\alpha_i} \cup \Gamma^{\alpha_j}}}]^{would}\phi \equiv [\Delta^{\alpha_i}]^{would}\phi$.

We will now show that the system LAE is also characterized by a subclass of C_f that includes only tree-like frames which resemble more familiar structures used in the literature for logics of agency, in particular, diverse stit-logics (e.g. [4,6,10,16]). A *branching-time frame with immediate successors* is an ordered tuple $\mathfrak{F} = \langle T, \{T_{\mathfrak{d}_i^{\alpha_j}} : \mathfrak{d}_i^{\alpha_j} \in \mathcal{L}\}, \{T_{\mathbf{e}^{\alpha_j}} : \mathbf{e}^{\alpha_j} \in \mathcal{L}\}, < \rangle$ where $T = \{m_1, m_2, m_3, ...\}$ is a set of moments, each $T_{\mathfrak{d}_i^{\alpha_j}}$ and each $T_{\mathbf{e}^{\alpha_j}}$ is a subset of T and $<$ is a binary asymmetric, intransitive and backward linear relation over T, namely:

– $\forall m, m' \in T : (m < m' \rightarrow \neg(m' < m))$;
– $\forall m, m', m'' \in T : ((m < m' \land m' < m'') \rightarrow \neg(m < m''))$;
– $\forall m, m', m'' \in T : (m' < m \land m'' < m) \rightarrow m' = m''$.

We define the usual machinery related to branching-time frames. Let $\ll$ be the transitive closure of $<$; then, T is partially ordered by $\ll$ and any $\ll$-maximal chain of moments can be called a history. Let H be the set of histories in a given branching-time frame $\mathfrak{F}$ and $H_m = \{h \in H : m \in h\}$ the set of all histories in $\mathfrak{F}$ 'passing through' a moment m. A model over a branching-time frame with immediate successors is an ordered tuple $\mathfrak{M} = \langle \mathfrak{F}, V \rangle$, where $\mathfrak{F}$ is the underlying frame and V a valuation function mapping atomic propositional symbols to moments and satisfying the usual restrictions on propositional constants.[7] Formulas of $\mathcal{L}$ are in this case evaluated with reference to a moment/history pair in a model.[8] Let *actual* be a function which associates to a moment m the only successor of m (*if any*) which belongs to the actual future of m, then:[9]

---

[6] Future work can be devoted to extensions of the language of LAE including operators for concatenations and iterations of action-types, in the spirit of [7,8].

[7] In the context of 'next moment' agency logic there is no need to assign atomic symbols to moment/history pairs, as observed in [6].

[8] Reference to histories provides a general framework suitable to express more complex notions related to indeterminism; for instance, one could add to the language of LAE an operator saying that something will always hold in one history passing through a given moment. Such an operator is not definable in terms of $\Box$ in infinite trees.

[9] Notice that, by definition, *actual* can be a *partial* function (a moment may have no actual successor even if an agent expects it to have some) and has some remarkable difference with the 'thin red line' function of the stit-logic literature [4]; indeed,

- $\mathfrak{M}, (m/h) \vDash \chi$ iff $m \in V(\chi)$, for any $\chi \in Atom$;
- $\mathfrak{M}, (m/h) \vDash \neg\phi$ iff $\mathfrak{M}, (m/h) \nvDash \phi$;
- $\mathfrak{M}, (m/h) \vDash \phi \to \psi$ iff $\mathfrak{M}, (m/h) \nvDash \phi$ or $\mathfrak{M}, (m/h) \vDash \psi$;
- $\mathfrak{M}, (m/h) \vDash \Box\phi$ iff for all $m' \in T$ s.t. $m < m'$ and all $h' \in H_{m'}$ we have $\mathfrak{M}, (m'/h') \vDash \phi$;
- $\mathfrak{M}, (m/h) \vDash N\phi$ iff $\mathfrak{M}, (actual(m)/h') \vDash \phi$ for all $h' \in H_{actual(m)}$.

Notice that according to the definition of $actual(m)$, if m has no actual successor, then $\mathfrak{M}, (m/h) \vDash N\phi$ for every $\phi \in \mathcal{L}$. In order to formally specify a class of branching time frames with immediate successors contained in C_f, we define the relations R and R_N in terms of moment/history pairs and the relation $<$, as follows:

- $(m/h)R(m'/h')$ iff $m < m'$, $h \in H_m$ and $h' \in H_{m'}$;
- $(m/h)R_N(m'/h')$ iff $m' = actual(m)$, $h \in H_m$ and $h' \in H_{m'}$.

The last two semantic clauses are then respectively equivalent to:

- $\mathfrak{M}, (m/h) \vDash \Box\phi$ iff for all (m'/h') s.t. $(m/h)R(m'/h')$, $\mathfrak{M}, (m'/h') \vDash \phi$;
- $\mathfrak{M}, (m/h) \vDash N\phi$ iff for all (m'/h') s.t. $(m/h)R_N(m'/h')$, $\mathfrak{M}, (m'/h') \vDash \phi$.

Let us say that a branching-time frame with immediate successors is an *lae-frame* iff it satisfies the properties p(A3)-p(A6). The class of all lae-frames can be denoted by C_f^{lae}; clearly, $C_f^{lae} \subset C_f$. In order to claim that *LAE* is also characterized by C_f^{lae}, one needs to show that the additional properties of lae-frames cannot be forced by any formula of the language $\mathcal{L}$. But this follows from well-known results concerning the correspondence theory of propositional modal languages. We sketch the proof below, relying on notions illustrated in [5].

Theorem 4. *For any $\phi \in \mathcal{L}$, if $C_f^{lae} \vDash \phi$, then $C_f \vDash \phi$.*

Proof. By contraposition, assume that ϕ is not valid in some model $\mathfrak{M}$ over a frame $\mathfrak{F}$ in C_f. This means that for some world w^* in the domain of $\mathfrak{M}$, we have $\mathfrak{M}, w^* \vDash \neg\phi$. Let $\mathfrak{M}'$ be the submodel of $\mathfrak{M}$ generated by w^*; then $\mathfrak{M}', w^* \vDash \neg\phi$. $\mathfrak{M}'$ can be transformed into a model $\mathfrak{M}^t$ over an asymmetric, intransitive tree $\mathfrak{F}^t$ rooted in w^*, whose set of states W^t consists of the sequences $\langle w_1, ..., w_n \rangle$ s.t. $w_1, ..., w_n \in W'$, $w_1 = w^*$ and $w_1 R' w_2, ..., w_{n-1} R' w_n$ (W' and R' being respectively the domain and the accessibility relation associated with $\Box$ in $\mathfrak{M}'$) and whose relations R^t and R_N^t are defined as follows:

- for any $u, v \in W^t$, uR^tv iff $u = \langle w_1, ..., w_n \rangle$, $v = \langle w_1, ..., w_n, w_{n+1} \rangle$ and $w_n R' w_{n+1}$;

---

the thin red line function assigns to each moment m a unique history to which m belongs (the actual history w.r.t. m), whereas *actual* assigns to m only its actual successor, if the latter exists. This solves some objections raised in [4] against the use of functions to represent actuality in branching-time; for instance, while there are problems of 'thin red line inheritance' among states related by $<$, there is no problem of 'actual successor inheritance', since any two states related by $<$ have different actual successors (if any).

– for any $u, v \in W^t$, $uR^t_N v$ iff $u = \langle w_1, ..., w_n \rangle$, $v = \langle w_1, ..., w_n, w_{n+1} \rangle$ and $w_n R'_N w_{n+1}$.

Let Π be a function from W' to $\wp(W^t)$ s.t. $\Pi(u) = \{\langle w_1, ..., w_n \rangle : w_n = u\}$; then, for all $u \in W'$ and all $\psi \in \mathcal{L}$ we have $\mathfrak{M}', u \vDash \psi$ iff $\mathfrak{M}^t, x \vDash \psi$ for every $x \in \Pi(u)$. Therefore, since $\Pi(w^*) \supseteq \{w^*\}$, we get $\mathfrak{M}^t, w^* \vDash \neg\phi$. Finally, let H^t be the set of histories in $\mathfrak{M}^t$; transform $\mathfrak{M}^t$ into a model $\mathfrak{M}^{fin}$ obtained by replacing every state $u \in W^t$ with a state $u_\sim = \{(w/h) : u \in \Pi(w)$ and $h \in H^t_u\}$. Define a binary relation $<^{fin}$ over W^{fin} s.t. $u_\sim <^{fin} v_\sim$ iff $uR^t v$; it follows that, for all $u_\sim \in W^{fin}$, $H^{fin}_{u_\sim} = H^t_u$. Let R^{fin} and R^{fin}_N be defined in terms of $<^{fin}$ as in branching-time frames with immediate successors, where $actual(w_\sim) = w'_\sim$ iff $wR^t_N w'$. $\mathfrak{M}^{fin}$ is a model over an lae-frame by construction. It can be easily proved that for all $u \in W^t$ and all $\psi \in \mathcal{L}$, we have $\mathfrak{M}^t, u \vDash \psi$ iff $\mathfrak{M}^{fin}, (w/h) \vDash \psi$ for every $(w/h) \in u_\sim$ iff $\mathfrak{M}^{fin}, u_\sim \vDash \psi$, hence $\mathfrak{M}^{fin}, w^*_\sim \vDash \neg\phi$.

We conclude with some theorems of LAE involving the operators in $E1 - E3$:

T4 $([\Delta^{\alpha_1}_1]^{could}\phi_1 \wedge ... \wedge [\Delta^{\alpha_n}_n]^{could}\phi_n) \to [\Delta^{\alpha_1}_1 \cap ... \cap \Delta^{\alpha_n}_n]^{could}(\phi_1 \wedge ... \wedge \phi_n)$, where $\alpha_1, ..., \alpha_n$ are distinct;

T5 $[\Delta^{\alpha_i}]^{could}\phi \to \neg[\Delta^{\alpha_i}]^{could}\neg\phi$;

T6 $[\Delta^{\alpha_i}]^{will}\phi \to \neg[\Delta^{\alpha_i}]^{will}\neg\phi$;

T7 $[\Delta^{\alpha_i}]^{will}\phi \to [\Delta^{\alpha_i}]^{could}\phi$;

T8 $[\Delta^{\alpha_i}]^{could}\phi \to [\Delta^{\alpha_i}]^{would}\phi$.

T4 expresses the familiar 'independence of agents' principle in its agency appearance; T4 equivalents for 'will' and 'would' are also provable in LAE. T5 and T6 express that the defined operators for 'could' and 'will' behave in accordance with seriality. Clearly, we do not have a T5 equivalent for 'would'. T7 and T8 are bridge-theorems that express the relations between 'will', 'could' and 'would'. Finally, notice that the operators in E1-E3 can be modified by taking into account also agents' expectations, as illustrated below:

– $\mathfrak{M}, (m/h) \vDash [\Delta^{\alpha_i}]^{would}_{ex}\phi$ iff $\mathfrak{M}, (m/h) \vDash \Box((t(\Delta^{\alpha_i}) \wedge e^{\alpha_i}) \to \phi)$;

– $\mathfrak{M}, (m/h) \vDash [\Delta^{\alpha_i}]^{could}_{ex}\phi$ iff $\mathfrak{M}, (m/h) \vDash \Box((t(\Delta^{\alpha_i}) \wedge e^{\alpha_i}) \to \phi)$ and $\mathfrak{M}, (m/h) \vDash \Diamond(t(\Delta^{\alpha_i}) \wedge e^{\alpha_i})$;

– $\mathfrak{M}, (m/h) \vDash [\Delta^{\alpha_i}]^{will}_{ex}\phi$ iff $\mathfrak{M}, (m/h) \vDash \Box((t(\Delta^{\alpha_i}) \wedge e^{\alpha_i}) \to \phi)$ and $\mathfrak{M}, (actual(m)/h') \vDash t(\Delta^{\alpha_i}) \wedge e^{\alpha_i}$ for all $h' \in H_{actual(m)}$.

4   Discussion and Final Remarks

Performing Actions. Several concepts pertaining to the theory of agency introduced in this paper can be formally specified within the syntactical and semantic framework of the logic LAE. Recall (Sect. 2) that, by making reference to initial states, end-states, and counterfactual states, Von Wright derives four elementary forms of action: producing, destroying, preserving and suppressing. Although a formal approach to these terms is not new (cf. [2,11]), the logic LAE allows us to expand them to more complex notions interacting with actions, expectations, instrumentality and ability:

(a) $m/h \models [\Delta^{\alpha_i}]^{prod}p$ iff $m/h \models \neg p$ and $m/h \models [\Delta^{\alpha_i}]^{will}p$ and $\exists m', \exists h' \in H_{m'}$ s.t. $m < m'$ and $m'/h' \models \neg p$

(b) $m/h \models [\Delta^{\alpha_i}]^{destr}p$ iff $m/h \models p$ and $m/h \models [\Delta^{\alpha_i}]^{will}\neg p$ and $\exists m', \exists h' \in H_{m'}$ s.t. $m < m'$ and $m'/h' \models p$

(c) $m/h \models [\Delta^{\alpha_i}]^{pres}p$ iff $m/h \models p$ and $m/h \models [\Delta^{\alpha_i}]^{will}p$ and $\exists m', \exists h' \in H_{m'}$ s.t. $m < m'$ and $m'/h' \models \neg p$

(d) $m/h \models [\Delta^{\alpha_i}]^{supp}p$ iff $m/h \models \neg p$ and $m/h \models [\Delta^{\alpha_i}]^{will}\neg p$ and $\exists m', \exists h' \in H_{m'}$ s.t. $m < m'$ and $m'/h' \models p$

The above formulae allow us to make explicit reference to the instruments that lead to producing, destroying, preserving and suppressing p, respectively. (Notice that (a)–(d) refer to atomic results.) We provide the intuitive reading of (a), the others will be similar: 'at the current state, by behaving in accordance with Δ, α_i produces p' means that '(i) $\neg p$ is currently the case; (ii) α actually behaves in accordance with Δ; (iii) p will actually be the case immediately after and (iv) $\neg p$ could otherwise be the case immediately after'.

Von Wright's reading of the four actions is stronger than ours, since he represents them in a *binary setting*: through agent α's conduct p will be the case, whereas through α's not-acting $\neg p$ would be the case. We believe that this account is too strong: it gives the agent α complete power over the faith of p. Definitions (a)–(d), instead, exemplify that α has the capability of determining the faith of p with some behaviour Δ, but cannot determine the faith of p through not acting.

Furthermore, observe that in our framework we can also redefine these four elementary actions in terms of *could* and *would*, as well as with reference to an agent's expectations. For the sake of discussion, we only provide the definition of 'agent α could destroy p by behaving in accordance with Δ':

(-) $m/h \models [\Delta^{\alpha_i}]^{could}_{destr}p$ iff $m/h \models p$ and $m/h \models [\Delta^{\alpha_i}]^{could}\neg p$ and $\exists m', \exists h' \in H_{m'}$ s.t. $m < m'$ and $m'/h' \models p$

Definitions (a)–(d) entail that propositions true at every next state, can neither be brought about nor prevented by any agent. Such definitions can therefore be seen as strong notions of *deliberative* action (cf. 'dstit' in [10]). This result brings us to the concept of *forbearance* (omission). Following Von Wright [15, p. 45], to forbear is stronger than to merely not act. In fact, it presupposes the ability to perform what is forborne. We introduce the following definition:

(e) $m/h \models [\Delta^{\alpha_i}]^{forb}\top$ iff $m/h \models [\Delta^{\alpha_i}]^{could}\top$ and $m/h \models [\overline{\Delta^{\alpha_i}}]^{will}\top$

Forbearance explicitly refers to actions: the usage of $\top$ (i.e., 'tautology') in (e) refers to the possibility to behave in accordance with action Δ and is interpreted as 'agent α forbears to behave in accordance with Δ' if and only if 'α could behave in accordance with Δ, but will behave in accordance with $\overline{\Delta}$ instead'.

Definitions (a)–(e) can be easily extended to formal notions of forbearance relating to results. We only illustrate the notion of 'forbearing to destroy p':

(-) $m/h \models [\Delta^{\alpha_i}]^{forb}_{destr} p$ iff $m/h \models p$ and $m/h \models [\Delta^{\alpha_i}]^{could} \neg p$ and

$m/h \models [\overline{\Delta^{\alpha_i}}]^{will} \top$ and $\exists m'$, $\exists h' \in H_{m'}$ s.t.

$m < m'$ and $m'/h' \models p$

Instrumentality. In Sect. 2 we made a distinction between weak and strong concepts of instrumentality, as well as agent-independent and agent-bound concepts. We will now provide their formalizations in the framework of LAE:

basic instrumentality

(f) $m/h \models [\Delta]^{b-instr} \phi$ iff $\exists m'$ s.t. $m' < m$ and for some $\alpha_i \in Agent$ we have $m'/h \models [\Delta^{\alpha_i}]^{will} \phi$

proper instrumentality

(g) $m/h \models [\Delta]^{p-instr} \phi$ iff   (i) $m/h \models [\Delta]^{b-instr} \phi$ and (ii) $\forall m', \forall h'$ s.t. $m' < m$ and $h' \in H_{m'}$ and for all $\alpha_i \in Agent$ we have $m'/h' \models [\Delta^{\alpha_i}]^{would} \phi$

basic α-instrumentality

(h) $m/h \models [\Delta^{\alpha_i}]^{b-instr}_{ex} \phi$ iff   (i) $m/h \models [\Delta^{\alpha_i}]^{could} \phi$ and (ii) $\exists m'$ s.t. $m' < m$ and $m'/h \models [\Delta^{\alpha_i}]^{will} \phi$

proper α-instrumentality

(i) $m/h \models [\Delta^{\alpha_i}]^{p-instr}_{ex} \phi$ iff   (i) $m/h \models [\Delta^{\alpha_i}]^{b-instr}_{ex} \phi$ and (ii) $\forall m', \forall h'$ s.t. $m' < m$ and $h' \in H_{m'}$ we have $m'/h' \models [\Delta^{\alpha_i}]^{would} \phi$

Definitions (f) and (g) employ the *will*-operator to ensure that, in the past, ϕ has been the actual result of behaviour in accordance with Δ and not just the result of lucky coincidence. Furthermore, (f) and (g) express instrumentality independent of past expectations. Moreover, (g) requires that, everywhere in the past, behaviour in accordance with Δ would have led to ϕ.

Definitions (h) and (i), instead, introduce respectively weak and strong agent-bound notions of instrumentality, the difference with the former two is that (h) and (i) consist of both future expectations and past experience: the agent expects the *continuation* of the instrument's past performance. We don't limit past experience to past expectations since an agent might discover concrete rules of instrumentality through the experience of unexpected results and actions. Observe that agent-bound instrumentality is defined through *all* three terms 'could', 'will' and 'would', relating respectively to 'the present state', 'a past state' and 'all past states'. Lastly, we emphasize that all formal definitions (f)–(i) allow for the agent to be disenchanted; that is, even proper-instruments might presently fail to lead to the intended result and agents might end in a state in which their expectations are not met.

In conclusion, taking both agent-dependent expectations and actions as the basis of our logic of agency we were able to construct three different notions of agency: *would*, *could* and *will*, each with its corresponding expectation-variant.

Together, these concepts were sufficient to address several extensions of Von Wright's elementary actions, including forbearance, as well as several formal definitions of instrumentality. As a final remark, we mention that both the process of generalizing actions and deriving notions of instrumentality are associated with induction and, for that reason, with the problems that come with it. Here, we only accentuate that the above formalization is in line with Von Wright's division of the problem of induction into two distinct problems [12]. First, there is the problem of justifying whether generalized statements are true for all observed cases (i.e., with respect to the past). This part is formally represented by definition (g). Secondly, there is the problem of using these generalized statements for future predictions. Von Wright remarks that here we seem to be satisfied with something less stringent: "Scarcely anybody would pretend that predictions, even when based upon the safest inductions, might not fail sometimes" [12, p. 51]. The latter is captured through the formal behaviour of expectations in LAE and the first clauses of definitions (h) and (i).

Acknowledgements. This work was funded by the WWTF project MA16-28.

References

1. Anderson, A.R.: A reduction of deontic logic to alethic modal logic. Mind **67**(265), 100–103 (1958)
2. Åqvist, L.: Old foundations for the logic of agency and action. Studia Logica **72**(3), 313–338 (2002)
3. Bentzen, M.M.: Action type deontic logic. J. Log. Lang. Inf. **23**(4), 397–414 (2014)
4. Belnap, N., Perloff, M., Xu, M.: Facing the Future. Agents and Choices in our Indeterminist World. Oxford University Press, Oxford (2001)
5. Blackburn, P., de Rijke, M., Venema, Y.: Modal Logic. Cambridge University Press, Cambridge (2001)
6. Broersen, J.: A logical analysis of the interaction between 'Obligation-to-do' and 'Knowingly Doing'. In: van der Meyden, R., van der Torre, L. (eds.) DEON 2008. LNCS (LNAI), vol. 5076, pp. 140–154. Springer, Heidelberg (2008). https://doi.org/10.1007/978-3-540-70525-3_12
7. Fischer, M., Ladner, R.: Propositional dynamic logic of regular programs. J. Comput. Syst. Sci. **18**(2), 194–211 (1979)
8. Harel, D., Kozen, D., Tiuryn, J.: Dynamic Logic. Cambridge University Press, Cambridge (2000)
9. Herzig, A., Lorini, E.: A dynamic logic of agency I: STIT, capabilities and powers. J. Log. Lang. Inf. **19**(1), 89–121 (2010)
10. Horty, J.: Agency and Deontic Logic. Oxford University Press, Oxford (2001)
11. Segerberg, K.: Getting started: beginnings in the logic of action. Studia Logica **51**(3), 347–378 (1992)
12. von Wright, G.H.: The Logical Problem of Induction. Barnes & Noble, New York (1957)
13. von Wright, G.H.: An Essay in Deontic Logic and the General Theory of Action. North-Holland Publishing Company, Amsterdam (1968)
14. von Wright, G.H.: The Varieties of Goodness. Routledge & Kegan Paul, London and Henley (1972). Fourth impression

15. von Wright, G.H.: Norm and Action: A Logical Enquiry. Routledge & Kegan Paul, London and Henley (1977). Fourth impression
16. Xu, M.: Combinations of STIT and actions. J. Log. Lang. Inf. **19**(4), 485–503 (2010)

Short Papers

Augmented Reality for Multi-agent Simulation of Air Operations

Lyndon Benke[1,2], Michael Papasimeon[1,2(✉)], and Kevin McDonald[3]

[1] Defence Science and Technology Group, Melbourne, Australia
[2] School of Computing and Information Systems, The University of Melbourne, Melbourne, Australia
[3] STELaRLab, Lockheed Martin Australia, Melbourne, Australia

Abstract. This paper demonstrates the potential of augmented reality to enhance visualisation and facilitate interrogation of multi-agent simulations of military operations. It describes four use cases for augmented reality in the context of constructive and virtual simulation for operations research, and discusses work undertaken and proposed future projects in both small and large augmented environments. The prototypes developed are used to assess the feasibility and benefits of applying augmented reality to simulation visualisation, wargaming, and the explainability and interpretability of agent behaviour.

Keywords: Augmented reality · Visualisation · Multi-agent simulation

1 Introduction

Multi-agent simulation is used to model the behaviour of intelligent agents in complex environments in applications such as military operations, transport management and medical research. In the field of aerospace operations research, adversarial flight simulators are used by analysts to develop and assess tactics for domains such as air combat [6]. As new artificial intelligence techniques are employed to develop and optimise these tactical behaviours [11,12], the ability to efficiently understand and explain agent decision making has become as important as the effectiveness and efficiency of the behaviours themselves.

Although graphical visualisation has been used for many years as a tool for understanding the behaviour of agents in multi-agent flight simulations, the ability of these interfaces to effectively interrogate activity has frequently been limited [3,5,7]. Traditionally, analysts have interacted with simulations using a keyboard-video-mouse (KVM) interface, such as the display of aircraft traces shown in Fig. 1. However, the modelling of modern tactics, sensors and networks, and of the intricate agent decision-making generated by artificial intelligence techniques, has increased the complexity of these visualisations. This poses new challenges for usability and explainability, and existing methods for interacting with these simulations may no longer be sufficient.

© Springer Nature Switzerland AG 2018
T. Miller et al. (Eds.): PRIMA 2018, LNAI 11224, pp. 423–430, 2018.
https://doi.org/10.1007/978-3-030-03098-8_26

Augmented reality (AR) technologies have the potential to provide a more natural and collaborative interface to visualisations of agent behaviour, by providing more efficient interfaces for analysts, enabling shared visualisation between multiple users, and affording a mechanism for improved explainability of complex agent reasoning models. In the air combat domain, augmented reality may be used to provide visualisations of agent reasoning that are not possible using traditional methods, including the display of agents overlaid on real-world locations and the visualisation of complex geometries in three dimensions.

This paper presents four use cases chosen to demonstrate the potential of augmented reality as an interface to multi-agent simulations of air operations (Sect. 3), and describes work completed to date addressing these through the development of software prototypes (Sect. 4). The aim of this paper is to provide an initial assessment of the benefits provided by AR for the comprehension of multi-agent simulations of air operations, and to determine the limitations of current AR technology for use in the context of military operations analysis.

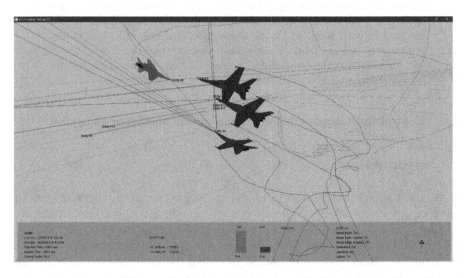

Fig. 1. Screenshot of XCombat, a desktop 3D visualisation application used to display the trajectories of agent-controlled aircraft in ACE [9], a constructive air combat simulator.

2   Related Work

The integration of agent technology with augmented reality is not a recent idea [4]. Military operations analysis, experimentation and wargaming have often been at the forefront of simulation and visualisation technologies; multi-agent simulations and virtual and augmented reality [3] technology are no exceptions. Hence, it is not surprising that AR has begun to play a role in visualising, exploring and interacting with multi-agent simulations of military operations [1]. In

2015, the US Army developed an AR research testbed called ARES [10] with goals to address training, mission command and operational decision making, while McDonald and Papasimeon [7] described an AR interface to an air combat multi-agent simulation (described in Sect. 4). More recently, the US Army explored AR technology to evaluate the simulation of a battlefield [5].

3   Use Cases

Four main use cases for interacting with multi-agent simulations of air operations in AR were identified: (a) visualisation of agent behaviour, (b) visualisation of agent decision making, (c) interactive agent-based simulation, and (d) distributed simulation-based wargaming. These use cases were chosen as being representative of common tasks conducted by operations analysts: defining multi-agent scenarios for study, interpreting the results of constructive simulations, and conducting wargaming exercises with subject matter experts. The high level architecture for each use case is provided in Fig. 2.

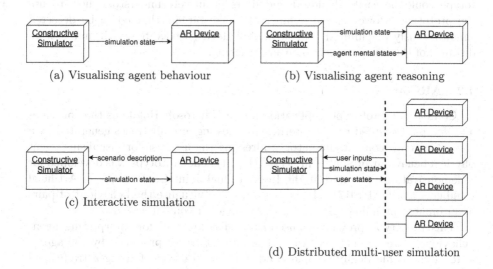

Fig. 2. High level architecture of the four representative use cases

4   Multi-agent Augmented Reality Prototypes

A number of prototype augmented reality applications were developed to explore the use cases presented in Sect. 3, described briefly below with an initial high-level assessment of the benefits and limitations of each prototype in the context of military operations analysis. Two approaches to AR were considered during this project. Prototype applications for hand-held devices were developed using the Vuforia Augmented Reality SDK [13] and Unity game engine [8], and tested on tablets, smart phones and laptops. Prototypes for wearable AR devices were developed using the Windows 10 SDK and Microsoft Mixed Reality Toolkit for Unity and tested on the Microsoft HoloLens head-mounted device [2].

4.1   AR Dice

AR Dice is an AR prototype for hand-held mobile devices that addresses the requirement for interactive simulation presented in Sect. 3 (Fig. 3). Described in detail by McDonald and Papasimeon [7], this prototype was developed with the aim of investigating the potential of AR as a two-way interface to multi-agent air combat constructive simulations. Printed image targets are used to position simulation entities on a physical tabletop. These targets are tracked by the application and used to initialise a constructive simulation, which when executed produces aircraft traces that are displayed on the mobile device.

The prototype encouraged multi-user participation by allowing several users to collaboratively define a scenario by moving their respective image targets around the table. The prevalence of mobile devices also meant that the prototype could be easily deployed and users intuitively understood how to use the prototype. However, the number of image targets that could be detected simultaneously was limited, and the mobile device needed to be within a certain distance of the image target to ensure tracking.

4.2   ARCombat

ARCombat is a prototype application for the Microsoft HoloLens that provides a tabletop augmented reality interface for viewing aircraft traces generated by a constructive air combat simulator, addressing the use case for visualising agent physical behaviour presented in Sect. 3 (Fig. 4). The prototype was developed for a demonstration presented at the International Joint Conferences on Artificial Intelligence (IJCAI 2017) [11], and was used to visualise the behaviour of pairs of automated planning agents in a close-range air combat scenario.

This prototype provided a useful visualisation tool for interpreting agent behaviour in air combat scenarios. The aircraft traces produced by the agents were often geometrically complex and difficult to interpret using a traditional KVM interface; the tabletop display provided depth and enabled users to move naturally around the augmented display to improve their points of view. However, the novelty of the AR interface competed with the demonstration of the automated planner; users were often so caught up in the experience of trying a wearable AR device that they were distracted from the content.

4.3   HoloHUD

HoloHUD is a prototype air traffic control tool for the Microsoft HoloLens that displays live and simulated aircraft at their real-world positions using target indicators overlaid on the user's visual field (Fig. 5). Unlike the table-top visualisation provided by ARCombat (Sect. 4.2), this prototype addresses the use

Fig. 3. AR Dice, a prototype AR interface for mobile devices.

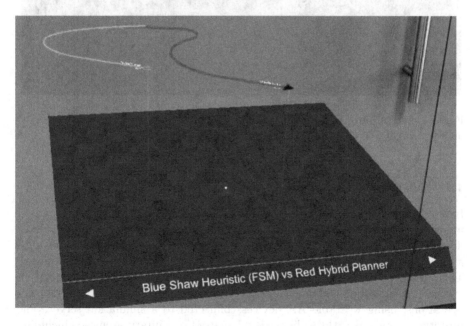

Fig. 4. ARCombat, a prototype AR application for visualising agent behaviour.

case for visualising agent physical behaviour presented in Sect. 3 by providing the user with a first-person view of the agents at world scale. Figure 6 describes the high-level architecture of the application. Live entity data such as position and heading are retrieved directly from aircraft in the local area using a low-cost software defined radio and an open source ADSB decoder. Synthetic aircraft in the scenario are implemented as agents in a real-time simulator.

This prototype demonstrated a key benefit of wearable AR for world-scale visualisation of agent behaviour: users could determine the real-world locations of the agents quickly and intuitively, avoiding the traditional mental translation from a two-dimensional monitor. However, the limited field of view of the device resulted in users needing to scan the sky for aircraft indicators (this can be partially mitigated by adding visual cues).

Fig. 5. HoloHUD, an AR prototype for visualising live and constructive entities. VA140 indicates a real aircraft while Agent-1 is a simulated agent.

4.4   Battlespace Management Tool

In a collaborative project with the Royal Australian Air Force (RAAF) and an industry partner, a prototype battlespace management and wargaming tool was developed to explore how AR technology could provide air force planners with a more natural and collaborative interface to simulations of military scenarios. This prototype addressed the requirement for distributed multi-user simulation (Sect. 3) by providing a shared interface to a multi-agent simulation of military operations, using wearable AR devices connected to a simulation server. The prototype provided a three-dimensional map of a military scenario, including interactive military units.

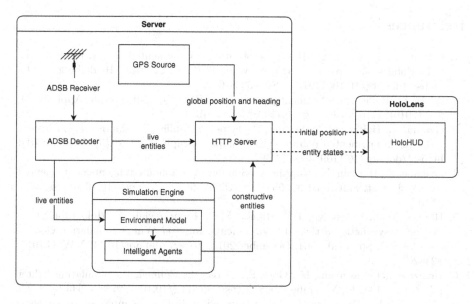

Fig. 6. HoloHUD high level architecture

The prototype successfully demonstrated the potential for AR to provide a more natural and collaborative interface to simulation-based wargaming. However, the limited field of view, weight, and placement of the head-mounted display caused discomfort and control difficulties for a number of participants, while battery life limited the duration of exercises. It was assessed that while the wearable AR interface was valuable as a demonstration of the potential of AR technology, it was not yet suitable for use in operational wargaming.

5   Conclusions

This paper has demonstrated the potential for augmented reality technology to enhance the visualisation and interrogation of multi-agent simulations of military operations. Four representative use cases were presented along with a number of prototypes exploring real-world applications of this technology.

Limitations of current hardware, such as tracking and immersion issues with hand-held AR technologies, and field-of-view, battery life, comfort and control issues with wearable devices, mean that while current AR technology is as an effective research tool for analysts interrogating agent behaviour, further advances are required before it can be used for wargaming in operational environments. It was observed during a number of demonstrations of the AR prototypes that the novelty of the AR interface itself often overshadowed the information being conveyed; users became so focused on the experience of trying and learning to use the AR devices that they were distracted from the content. This effect will lessen over time as AR technology becomes more widespread and familiar, but remains a consideration when using AR technology to convey information.

References

1. Livingston, M.A., et al.: Military applications of augmented reality. In: Furht, B. (ed.) Handbook of Augmented Reality, pp. 671–706. Springer, Heidelberg (2011). https://doi.org/10.1007/978-1-4614-0064-6_31
2. Avila, L., Bailey, M.: Augment your reality. IEEE Comput. Graph. Appl. **36**(1), 6–7 (2016). https://doi.org/10.1109/MCG.2016.17
3. Azuma, R., Baillot, Y., Behringer, R., Feiner, S., Julier, S., MacIntyre, B.: Recent advances in augmented reality. IEEE Comput. Graph. Appl. **21**(6), 34–47 (2001). https://doi.org/10.1109/38.963459
4. Gelenbe, E., Hussain, K., Kaptan, V.: Simulating autonomous agents in augmented reality. J. Syst. Softw. **74**(3), 255–268 (2005). https://doi.org/10.1016/j.jss.2004.01.016
5. Haynes, M.B., Etheredge, T.P., Rigney, M.C., Fronckowiak, T.: Holographic simulation of synthetic battlefield environments. In: 2017 Winter Simulation Conference (WSC), pp. 4560–4561, December 2017. https://doi.org/10.1109/WSC.2017.8248204
6. Heinze, C., Papasimeon, M., Goss, S., Cross, M., Connell, R.: Simulating fighter pilots, pp. 113–130, November 2008. https://doi.org/10.1007/978-3-7643-8571-2_7
7. Mcdonald, K., Papasimeon, M.: Augmented reality as an interface to air combat multi-agent simulation. In: Proceedings of the 2015 Australasian Simulation Technology Conference (SimTecT 2015) (2015)
8. Messaoudi, F., Simon, G., Ksentini, A.: Dissecting games engines: the case of Unity3D. In: 2015 International Workshop on Network and Systems Support for Games (NetGames), pp. 1–6, December 2015. https://doi.org/10.1109/NetGames.2015.7382990
9. Papasimeon, M., Benke, L., Brain, R., Finkelstein, L.: Multiagent simulation of adversarial socio-technical systems. In: Proceedings of the Seventeenth International Conference on Autonomous Agents and Multiagent Systems, AAMAS 2018 (2018)
10. Amburn, C.R., Vey, N., Boyce, M., Mize, M.: The Augmented REality Sandtable (ARES). Technical Report ARL-SR-0340, US Army Research Laboratory (ARL), October 2015. https://doi.org/10.13140/RG.2.1.2685.0006
11. Ramirez, M., Papasimeon, M., Benke, L., Lipovetzky, N., Miller, T., Pearce, A.R.: Real-Time UAV maneuvering via automated planning in simulations. In: International Joint Conferences on Artificial Intelligence Organization, pp. 5243–5245, August 2017. https://doi.org/10.24963/ijcai.2017/778
12. Ramirez, M., et al.: Integrated hybrid planning and programmed control for real-time UAV maneuvering. In: Proceedings of the Seventeenth International Conference on Autonomous Agents and Multiagent Systems, AAMAS 2018, July 2018
13. Santos, A.B.D., Dourado, J.B., Bezerra, A.: ARToolkit and Qualcomm Vuforia: an analytical collation. In: 2016 XVIII Symposium on Virtual and Augmented Reality (SVR), pp. 229–233, June 2016. https://doi.org/10.1109/SVR.2016.46

Abstracting Reinforcement Learning Agents with Prior Knowledge

Nicolas Bougie[1,2]([⊠]) and Ryutaro Ichise[2]

[1] Sokendai, The Graduate University for Advanced Studies, Tokyo, Japan
[2] National Institute of Informatics, Tokyo, Japan
{nicolas-bougie,ichise}@nii.ac.jp

Abstract. Recent breakthroughs in reinforcement learning have enabled the creation of learning agents for solving a wide variety of sequential decision problems. However, these methods require a large number of iterations in complex environments. A standard paradigm to tackle this challenge is to extend reinforcement learning to handle function approximation with deep learning. Lack of interpretability and impossibility to introduce background knowledge limits their usability in many safety-critical real-world scenarios. In this paper, we propose a new agent architecture to combine reinforcement learning and external knowledge. We derive a rule-based variant version of the Sarsa(λ) algorithm, which we call Sarsa-rb(λ), that augments data with complex knowledge and exploits similarities among states. We apply our method to a trading task from the stock market environment. We show that the resulting agent leads to much better performance but also improves training speed compared to the Deep Q-learning (DQN) algorithm and the Deep Deterministic Policy Gradients (DDPG) algorithm.

Keywords: Reinforcement learning · Learning agent
Symbolic reinforcement learning · Reasoning about knowledge
Agent architecture

1 Introduction

In the last few years, we have seen an increasing interest on the study of learning agents. The reinforcement learning approach has drawn the attention of researchers in artificial intelligence and multi-agent systems. They have made significant progress to learn good policies in many domains. Well-known temporal difference (TD) methods such as Sarsa [19] or Q-learning [21] learn to predict the best action to take by step-wise interactions with the environment. In particular, Q-learning has been shown to be effective in solving the traveling salesman problem [7] or learning to drive a bicycle [15]. However large or continuous state spaces limit their application to simple environments.

Recently, deep reinforcement learning wherein a deep neural network is combined with reinforcement learning has proved to be very successful in mastering

© Springer Nature Switzerland AG 2018
T. Miller et al. (Eds.): PRIMA 2018, LNAI 11224, pp. 431–439, 2018.
https://doi.org/10.1007/978-3-030-03098-8_27

complex tasks. A significant example is the combination of neural networks and Q-learning, resulting in "Deep Q-Learning" (DQN) [12], able to achieve human performance on many tasks including Atari video games [2].

Learning from scratch and lack of interpretability impose some problems on deep reinforcement learning methods. The impossibility to explain and understand the reason for a decision also restricts their use to non-safety critical domains, excluding, for example, medicine or law. Combining simple reinforcement learning techniques and external knowledge [4] aims to address these challenges.

An approach to introduce external knowledge, *Symbolic Reinforcement Learning* [5], combines a system that learns an abstracted representation of the environment and high-order reasoning. However, it cannot support ongoing adaptation to a new environment. Compact state representation [16] focuses on creating an abstracted representation of the states [6]. It can enable a faster learning than training the agent on the raw data without facing the drawbacks of deep learning. Andre et al. [1] hierarchically abstract the states by decomposing the states into subroutines but has been limited to simple domains. Other attempts [3] don't take advantage of state similarities [17] or produce non-interpretable states [14]. All the previously cited approaches suffer from lack of interpretation reducing their usage in critical applications such as autonomous driving.

This paper demonstrates that abstracting a reinforcement learning agent with prior knowledge can overcome these challenges to learn control policies. We seek to address these shortcomings by proposing a new variant of the Sarsa(λ) algorithm [18] which represents the states as understandable rules. Rules transform raw data into a compressed and symbolic representation, reducing the state space size. To deal with the problem of training speed and highly fluctuating environments, we propose a sub-states mechanism which exploits similarities among rules. Sub-states allow a more frequent update of the Q-values thereby smooth and speed-up the learning. Furthermore, we adapted eligibility traces, which turned out to be critical in guiding the algorithm to solve tasks. Finally, our agent learns effective policies in a small number of iterations and exhibits higher performance than the best generally-applicable reinforcement learning methods.

2   Reinforcement Learning

Reinforcement learning consists of an agent learning a policy π by interacting with an environment. At each time-step the agent receives an observation s_t and chooses an action a_t. The agent gets a feedback from the environment called a reward r_t. Given this reward and the observation, the agent can update its policy to improve the future rewards.

Given a discount factor γ, the future discounted rewards, called return R_t, is defined as follows:

$$R_t = \sum_{t'=t}^{T} \gamma^{t'-t} r_{t'} \tag{1}$$

where T is the time-step at which the epoch terminates.

The goal of reinforcement learning is to learn to select the action with the maximum return R_t achievable for a given observation [20]. From Eq. (1), we can define the action value $Q^{\pi}(s, a)$ at a time t as the expected reward for selecting an action a for a given state s_t and following a policy π.

$$Q^{\pi}(s, a) = \mathbb{E}\left[R_t \mid s_t = s, a \right] \tag{2}$$

The optimal policy π^* is defined as selecting the action with the optimal Q-value, the highest expected return, followed by an optimal sequence of actions. This obeys the Bellman optimality equation:

$$Q^*(s, a) = \mathbb{E}\left[r + \gamma \max_{a'} Q^*(s', a') \mid s, a \right] \tag{3}$$

In temporal difference (TD) learning methods such as Q-learning or Sarsa, the Q-values are updated after each time-step instead of updating the values after each epoch, as happens in Monte Carlo learning.

2.1   Sarsa Algorithm

Sarsa [19] is a common TD control technique to approximate $\pi \approx \pi^*$. The estimation of the action value function is iteratively performed by updating $Q(s, a)$. This algorithm is considered as an on-policy method since the update rule is related to the policy that is learned, as follows:

$$Q(s_t, a_t) \leftarrow Q(s_t, a_t) + \alpha[r_{t+1} + \gamma Q(s_{t+1}, a_{t+1}) - Q(s_t, a_t)] \tag{4}$$

The choice of the action follows a policy derived from Q. The most common policy called ϵ-greedy policy trade-off the exploration/exploitation dilemma. In case of exploration, a random action is sampled whereas exploitation selects the action with the highest estimated return. In order to converge to a stable policy, the probability of exploitation must increase over time.

2.2   Eligibility Traces

Since it takes time to back-propagate the rewards to the previous Q-values, the above model suffers from slow training in sparse reward environments. Eligibility traces is a mechanism to handle the problem of delayed rewards. Many temporal-difference (TD) methods including Sarsa or Q-learning can use eligibility traces. In popular Sarsa(λ) or Q-learning(λ), λ refers to eligibility traces or n-steps returns. In case of Sarsa(λ), this leads to the following update rule:

$$Q_{t+1}(s, a) = Q_t(s, a) + \alpha \left[r_{t+1} + \gamma Q_t(s_{t+1}, a_{t+1}) - Q_t(s_t, a_t) \right] e_t(s, a) \; \forall s, a \tag{5}$$

where

$$e_t(s, a) = \begin{cases} \lambda e_{t-1}(s, a) + 1, & \text{if } s = s_t \text{ and } a = a_t \\ \lambda e_{t-1}(s, a) & \text{otherwise} \end{cases} \tag{6}$$

The temporal difference error for a state is estimated in a bootstrapping process. Instead of looking only at the current reward, in Monte Carlo methods the prediction is made based on the successive states.

3   Rule-Based Sarsa(λ)

We propose a simple method, rule-based Sarsa (Sarsa-rb), to enable Sarsa in continuous spaces by injecting external knowledge. Besides the general idea that the state representation has the role of encoding and compressing essential information about the task while discarding irrelevant states, it enables to inject prior knowledge. In Sarsa-rb, external knowledge is jointly used to enhance states representation and to efficiently initialize the Q-values. As in Sarsa, the agent estimates the Q-values. However, each state is represented by a rule. There are various advantages of representing the states by rules. Their compositional structure makes possible to combine and recombine the rules and interpret them. Furthermore, the present architecture maps high-dimensional raw input into a lower-dimensional rule space which reduces the number of Q-values to estimate.

While Sarsa-rb provides some advantages over Sarsa in terms of quality of policy, we can significantly improve their training time with a sub-states mechanism. This enables to exploit similarities among rules to maximize the benefit of past experience to face new similar situations. Instead of updating one Q-value at each iteration, our model updates several Q-values which share similar information with the current state, leading to a significant speed-up. Finally, we adapt the eligibility trace λ technique to take advantage of the sub-states, rule-based Sarsa(λ) (Sarsa-rb(λ)).

3.1   Rule-Based Sarsa (Sarsa-rb)

The Sarsa algorithm maintains a parametrized Q-function which maps the state representations to their Q-values. Instead of using the state space or a discretization of it, our representation relies on rules. States are replaced by a set of rules, R, each Q-value is mapped to a rule. A rule associates a pattern to an action. Patterns define whether a Q-value is active or not and the recommended actions to improve the Q-value initialization.

A pattern is an arbitrarily complex conjunction of variables. The variables represent significant events in the task. Finally, a rule links a pattern to action. Given an observation obs_t, the active state is the state for which its associated pattern is satisfied, in other words, all its variables are active. Since no pattern is always satisfied, we added an "empty" state. This is the default state, active regardless of the input.

In Sarsa, the Q-values are uniformly initialized. We take advantage of prior knowledge by initializing the Q-values according to the recommended actions of the rules:

$$Q(s_{t=0}, a_{t=0}) = \begin{cases} \mathcal{N}(\mu, \sigma^2), & \text{if } rule_{action} = a \\ 0 & \text{otherwise} \end{cases} \tag{7}$$

with μ the mean and σ^2 the variance. For a state s, the initialization of the Q-value with the action recommended by the rule follows a normal distribution centered around μ, greater than 0. The other Q-values are initialized to 0.

This rule-based representation can now be used to learn an effective policy in large state space domains. Our contribution here is to propose a technique to jointly use background knowledge and reinforcement learning to decrease training time of the agent (rule-based representation) and avoid learning from scratch (Q-value initialization).

3.2 Prior Knowledge for Rule Generation

Rules are created according to our knowledge about the task. The technique retrieves patterns from external sources of data. This idea can be extended to other domains, for example visual, by adapting the symbolic representation methods [8] or more sophisticated methods [11].

An intuitive approach to create the rules relies on human or background knowledge about domains. For example, if the task involves driving a car, background knowledge can be extracted from highway rules. The action associated with a pattern can be let empty if it cannot be predicted without much affecting the quality of the agent.

We can use our expertise about time-series and stock markets. To deal with that, the rules can be based on candlestick patterns [13]. This stock-market analysis technique estimates the trend of the share price by identifying patterns into time series.

3.3 Sub-states

In TD methods without eligibility traces, only one Q-value is updated at each iteration. In TD methods with eligibility traces, the reward is propagated to the previous states. Instead, we propose an approach to update the similar states while back-propagating the reward to the previous states. We refer to this mechanism as *sub-states*. The goal is to get most of the benefits of the shared information among the rules while keeping the rest of the Sarsa algorithm intact and efficient. The sub-states are constructed by augmenting each Q-value with an ensemble of sub-states, $sub_s(s, a)$. Since each state is represented by a pattern, we define the sub-states as its sub-patterns, the combinations of the variables. To avoid a too large number of sub-states, we limit the size of the sub-rules to conjunctions of at least 3 variables.

We provide modifications to the estimation and update of the Q-values inspired by Sarsa to incorporate sub-states. The estimation of a Q-value $Q'(s,a)$ takes into account the Q-value itself $Q(s,a)$ and the value of the sub-states $Q(s',a)$. This process is now guided by the previously obtained rewards of the similar states and sub-states:

$$Q'(s,a) = Q(s,a) + \sum_{s' \in sub_s(s,a)} Q(s',a) \tag{8}$$

with $sub_s(s,a)$ the sub-states of a state (s,a). $Q(s',a)$ refers to the estimation of the value of the sub-state s' given the action a. Adding this term grounds the values of the unvisited states, and makes the value induced by the values of the similar visited states. Note that we limit the weight of the term $Q(s',a)$ in the $Q'(s,a)$ estimation such as $Q(s',a) << Q(s,a)$ to ensure convergence towards an optimal policy. We achieved this mechanism during the update step.

3.4   Eligibility Traces

Directly implementing Sarsa-rb proved to be slow to learn in environments with sparse rewards. Our method, Sarsa-rb(λ), is derived from Sarsa(λ). Adding n-steps returns helps to propagate the current reward r_t to the earlier states. We allow a propagation of r_t to the earlier sub-states by changing their eligibility traces. The idea behind is that a sub-state similar to the current state is likely to get a similar reward by following the same action. The update of the current state s remains unchanged from Sarsa(λ):

$$\begin{cases} E(s,a) = E(s,a) + 1 \\ E(y,a) = E(y,a) + e^{-sim(y,s)}, & \text{if y is a sub-states of s} \\ E(y,a) = E(y,a) + \dfrac{e^{-sim(y,s)^2}}{K}, & \text{otherwise} \end{cases} \tag{9}$$

$E(s,a)$ denotes the eligibility trace of the state s and $E(y,a)$ the eligibility trace of the sub-state y for a given action a. We refer to $sim(y,s)$ as the similarity between the sub-state y and the state s. We compute the similarity score as the number of different variables between a sub-state y and a state s, $sim(y,s) = |y \cup s| - |y \cap s|$. We bounded the score between 0 (identical) and 1.

Since sub-states are often updated, we avoid exploding eligibility trace values by adding an exponential decay and a constant K. Updates performed in this manner allow to estimate more accurately Q-values.

4   Experiments

We evaluated our agent, Sarsa-rb(λ), on the OpenAI trading environment, a complex and fluctuating simulation from real stock market data. The agent observes the last stock price described by the open price, the close price, and the highest/lowest price during a one minute interval. We limit the possible actions to *Buy*, *Hold* and *Sell*. Each episode was played until the training data are consumed, approximatively 10^5 iterations. In total, we used 4 datasets with a duration varying between 2 years and 5 years. We trained the model on one stock index and we used the three other datasets as external sources of knowledge to generate the rules. Among the training examples, 80% are randomly selected for training the model and the remaining for the evaluation. We found that μ the mean equals to 0.25 and σ equals to 0.2 were the best parameters to initialize the Q-values. We use $K = 100$ as decay factor of eligibility traces. To create the rules, we first compute the percentage increase in the share price 14 days later and then estimate an optimal action associated with each pattern. In total, we took into account 40 candlestick patterns.

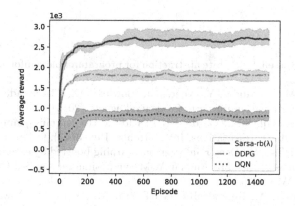

Fig. 1. Performance curves for a selection of algorithms: original deep Q-learning algorithm (red), deep deterministic policy gradients algorithm (green) and Sarsa-rb(λ) (blue). (Color figure online)

We evaluated Sarsa-rb(λ) trained with the sub-states mechanism. We used a deep recurrent Q-learning model [9] and a DDPG model [10] as baselines. For this evaluation, we individually tuned the hyper-parameters of each model. We decreased the learning rate from $\alpha = 0.3$ to $\alpha = 0.0001$, we increased the eligibility trace from $\lambda = 0.9$ to $\lambda = 0.995$, and then used $\epsilon = 0.01$, $\lambda = 0.9405$ and $K = 100$. The plots are averaged over 5 runs. Finally, we used the external knowledge based rules as the states of Sarsa-rb(λ). We report the learning curve on the testing dataset in Fig. 1. Sarsa-rb(λ) always achieve a score higher than DQN and DDPG. As shown in Fig. 1, Sarsa-rb(λ) clearly improves over DQN, we obtained an average reward after converging around 3.3 times higher. DDPG appears less fluctuating than Sarsa-rb(λ) but also less effective. We conclude that our model learns a better policy than a neural network based approach in a similar number of training steps.

5   Conclusion

This paper introduced a new model of learning agents to combine reinforcement learning and external knowledge. We demonstrated its ability to solve complex and highly fluctuating tasks, trading in stock market. Additionally, this algorithm is fully interpretable and understandable. Our central thesis is to enhance state representation of Sarsa(λ) with background knowledge and speed up learning with a sub-states mechanism. Further benefits stem from efficiently updating eligibility traces and improving the learning rate decay. Moreover, our approach can be easily adapted to solve new tasks with a very limited amount of human work. We have demonstrated the effectiveness of our algorithm to decrease the training time and to learn a better and more efficient policy.

References

1. Andre, D., Russell, S.J.: State abstraction for programmable reinforcement learning agents (2002)
2. Bellemare, M.G., Naddaf, Y., Veness, J., Bowling, M.: The arcade learning environment: an evaluation platform for general agents (2013)
3. Boots, B., Siddiqi, S.M., Gordon, G.J.: Closing the learning-planning loop with predictive state representations. Int. J. Robot. Res. **30**(7), 954–966 (2011)
4. Bougie, N., Ichise, R.: Deep reinforcement learning boosted by external knowledge. In: Proceedings of the 33rd Annual ACM Symposium on Applied Computing, pp. 331–338. ACM (2018)
5. d'Avila Garcez, A., Resende Riquetti Dutra, A., Alonso, E.: Towards Symbolic Reinforcement Learning with Common Sense. ArXiv e-prints, April 2018
6. Džeroski, S., De Raedt, L., Driessens, K.: Relational reinforcement learning. Mach. Learn. **43**(1–2), 7–52 (2001)
7. Gambardella, L.M., Dorigo, M.: Ant-Q: a reinforcement learning approach to the traveling salesman problem. In: Machine Learning Proceedings 1995, pp. 252–260. Elsevier (1995)
8. Garnelo, M., Arulkumaran, K., Shanahan, M.: Towards deep symbolic reinforcement learning. In: Abbeel, P., Chen, P., Silver, D., Singh, S. (eds.) NIPS. Neural Information Processing Systems Foundation, La Jolla, California (2016)
9. Hausknecht, M., Stone, P.: Deep recurrent Q-learning for partially observable MDPs (2015)
10. Lillicrap, T.P., et al.: Continuous control with deep reinforcement learning. arXiv preprint arXiv:1509.02971 (2015)
11. Mashayekhi, M., Gras, R.: Rule extraction from random forest: the RF+HC methods. In: Barbosa, D., Milios, E. (eds.) CANADIAN AI 2015. LNCS (LNAI), vol. 9091, pp. 223–237. Springer, Cham (2015). https://doi.org/10.1007/978-3-319-18356-5_20
12. Mnih, V., et al.: Playing Atari with deep reinforcement learning. arXiv preprint arXiv:1312.5602 (2013)
13. Nison, S.: Japanese Candlestick Charting Techniques: A Contemporary Guide to the Ancient Investment Techniques of the Far East. Penguin, London (2001)
14. Papudesi, V., Huber, M.: Learning behaviorally grounded state representations for reinforcement learning agents (2006)

15. Randløv, J., Alstrøm, P.: Learning to drive a bicycle using reinforcement learning and shaping. Proc. ICML **98**, 463–471 (1998)
16. Rosencrantz, M., Gordon, G., Thrun, S.: Learning low dimensional predictive representations. In: Proceedings of the Twenty-First ICML. ACM (2004)
17. Singh, S.P., Jaakkola, T., Jordan, M.I.: Reinforcement learning with soft state aggregation. In: Proceedings of NIPS, pp. 361–368 (1995)
18. Singh, S.P., Sutton, R.S.: Reinforcement learning with replacing eligibility traces. Mach. Learn. **22**(1–3), 123–158 (1996)
19. Sutton, R.S.: Generalization in reinforcement learning: successful examples using sparse coarse coding. In: Proceedings of NIPS, pp. 1038–1044 (1996)
20. Sutton, R.S., Barto, A.G.: Reinforcement Learning: An Introduction. MIT Press, Cambridge (1998)
21. Watkins, C.J., Dayan, P.: Q-learning. Mach. Learn. **8**(3–4), 279–292 (1992)

A Multi-modal Urban Traffic Agent-Based Framework to Study Individual Response to Catastrophic Events

Kevin Chapuis[1,4]([⊠]), Patrick Taillandier[2], Benoit Gaudou[1,3,4],
Alexis Drogoul[1,4], and Eric Daudé[5]

[1] Sorbonne University, IRD, UMMISCO, 93143 Bondy, France
kevin.chapuis@gmail.com
[2] MIAT, University of Toulouse, INRA, Castanet-Tolosan, France
[3] University Toulouse Capitole, IRIT, Toulouse, France
[4] USTH - AVAST, ICTLab, Hanoi, Vietnam
[5] CNRS, Rouen University, UMR IDEES, Rouen, France

Abstract. Urban traffic is made of a variety of mobility modes that have to be taken into account to explore the impact of catastrophic event. From individual mobility behaviors to macroscopic traffic dynamics, agent-based modeling provides an interesting conceptual framework to study this question. Unfortunately, most proposals in the domain do not provide any simple way to model these multi-modal trajectories, and thus fell short at simulating in a credible way the outcomes of a catastrophic event, like natural or industrial hazards. This paper presents an agent-based framework implemented with the GAMA modeling platform that aims at overcoming this lack. An application of this model for the study of flood crisis in a district of Hanoi (Vietnam) is presented.

1 Introduction

The Agent-Based Modeling paradigm has been used for several decades to model urban traffic. This well-established field of research has seen many frameworks populating the scientific landscape such as MATSim [13], SUMO [14] or SimMobility [2] to name only a few. Those generic toolkits make it possible to build a traffic model to study several phenomena from nanoscopic – *e.g.* lane change and cross section – to macroscopic dynamic – *e.g.* mass congestion and residential relocation. Thanks to the agent paradigm, it is possible to explicitly represent the decision making process and action of heterogeneous actors, including transportation providers, political institutions or end users like pedestrians and drivers.

However, most of the influential proposals in the domain focus on demand, supply and control of traffic transportation system [3]. While this covers almost all urban planners' concerns about problems such as how to design, maintain and expand traffic systems, they are not suitable for studying the outcomes of

© Springer Nature Switzerland AG 2018
T. Miller et al. (Eds.): PRIMA 2018, LNAI 11224, pp. 440–448, 2018.
https://doi.org/10.1007/978-3-030-03098-8_28

uncommon and/or extreme event [7,11]. Indeed, mobility in a crisis context is radically different from mobility in a normal situation: individuals can change destination goals and/or modes of transport very quickly; they may adopt a specific attitude, for example nervousness, fear, impatience; finally, the transport networks can themselves be affected either by the hazard directly (flood or earthquake) or indirectly (traffic lights interruption). Unfortunately, adapting generic toolkits to this type of context requires to build extensions using a generic programming language like C++ or JAVA, which is out of reach of most modelers. The framework presented in this paper aims at being able to simulate this type of situation with easy to use modeling tools.

The paper is structured as follows: Sect. 2 discusses about the other agent-based models and frameworks proposed in recent years. The model we proposed is presented in Sect. 3. Section 4 illustrates the use of the framework by presenting the case of the evacuation of a district of Hanoi, Vietnam. Finally, Sect. 5 serves as conclusion.

2   Agent-Based Model and Simulation of Urban Traffic in Crisis Situation

2.1   Agent-Based Urban Traffic Framework

The most important multi-agent traffic frameworks like MATSim, SUMO and SimMobility are based on highly efficient multi-modal traffic model to study demand, supply and control of traffic systems. Several extensions of these platforms have been proposed in order to investigate the impact of catastrophic event on transportation system. However, those proposal exhibit two drawbacks for our concern: they are either based on the O-D paradigm or use very simple model of pedestrian mobility. For example, [15] propose a mass evacuation model based on MATSim that requires to use pre-calculated evacuation trips, hence failing to capture individual response; [8] design a SUMO extension (VEBEN++) to study individual response to catastrophic event where pedestrian follow a path on a network without any direct interaction with other road users (including other pedestrians), which does not reflect actual people movement in crisis situation [4].

In order to tackle this issue, a solution consists in using a generic agent-based modeling platform. Among the existing open-source generic platforms such as Mason, Netlogo or Cormas, one of the most suitable for traffic simulation is GAMA [10]. Indeed GAMA provides modelers a complete modeling language (GAML: GAma Modeling Language) and different features that can be used by modelers to develop traffic models [20]. It has already been used for several traffic models such as the ones proposed by [7,16].

2.2   Crisis Event in Urban Traffic Agent-Based Model

While aforementioned frameworks make it possible to model regular urban traffic, most of them do not propose extended features to study the disruption induced by crisis events [7]. On the other hand, even if there are several agent-based models that study evacuation model, there is no dedicated framework to the best of our knowledge [11]. Netlogo is still widely used but does not provide native features to handle large scale traffic models [17]. Furthermore, agent based traffic model that study crisis situation and evacuation do not incorporate complex transportation system often [21]. Those multi-agent evacuation models usually come with limitations, such as a narrowed area – *e.g.* buildings [5] – or a limited number or only one mode of transportation – *e.g.* pedestrian in a crowd [18].

GAMA has been recently used to study evacuation and traffic under catastrophic event [1,7] as an alternative to Netlogo. The platform has several well suited features such as GIS native integration and simple and efficient primitives for car as well as pedestrian mobility over network and continuous topography. In the next section we describe the tools we developed to further enhance GAMA accuracy to model large-scale traffic and evacuation during catastrophic event.

3   An ABMS Framework of Multi-modal Urban Mobility in Crisis Events

Our proposal is an attempt to bring easy to use, flexible and scalable modeling features to study multi-modal traffic systems during crisis events. An example of implementation and an instance on a real case study (described in Sect. 4) are implemented using the GAMA platform [10].

3.1   Proposal - Desiderata

The key agent type of our framework is the human being. The main corollary and our main contribution is that the human agent will always be an entity distinct from its vehicle. Hence, we need to distinguish the decision-maker human agent and its various mobility ways all over the simulation. To this end, we designed our template for the human agent to have full autonomy on the strategical and tactical level of mobility decision process. The activity paradigm provide enough flexibility to cope with immediate danger (*e.g.* stop the current activity to go to a safe place) but agents also have the capacity to define how they should go to their destination, including the ability to adapt their current course of action to the uncommon circumstances (*e.g.* to continue evacuating at foot considering a mass car congestion).

3.2   The Environment

The environment is composed of the spatial and physical entities that drive, support or constrain the human mobility. The studied system must be made of two main entities that are buildings and mobility environment (e.g. road network and walking area), but can optionally be made up of non buildings areas like park, parking, water, etc. Our framework provides a complete adapter for

OpenStreetMap (OSM) data, meaning that any case study road network, buildings and walking area can be easily setup using raw OSM data. Alternatively, modelers can setup the environment using classical shapefile that will required several mandatory attributes for buildings and roads to be define within file.

The Buildings. The buildings are related to human activity, so they can drive agent mobility: go to the workplace, go home, go to shopping center, etc. Each building is made of a localized shape and should at least have a building type (the human activity), like dwelling, amenity, school or office. Building can have model related feature, like being a shelter or the number of floors, that can be used to shape agent response to catastrophic event.

Mobility Environment. We design mobility environment to be adapted to each mobility modes: pedestrians, cars, bikes or trains can obviously not move on the same support. However these supports are not always mutually exclusive as roads can be used by pedestrians, cars or bus. Hence, we organize mobility environment in two different topology: a two-dimensions continuous walking area and a roads network. The former is exclusive to pedestrian while the later can be used by every vehicle and pedestrian.

Road Network. The roads are considered to be one-dimension spatial entities (*i.e.* polyline) organized as a graph. Each road has a speed limit and a number of lanes while intersection manage traffic light and priority. There are both agent so they can have pro-active behavior, e.g. deterioration due to a catastrophic event.

Walking Area. Pedestrian area mixes all walkable space, such as parks, public places or parking. Those spaces can have a great impact on the traffic during catastrophic event: parks can turn into safe area during earthquake, near river or seaside can become dangerous area during flood event, etc. Opposite to the road network, the walking area is made of two-dimensions geometrical shape. We provide with the framework tools to compute and generate this walking area from available data (more details can be found in the next Section).

3.3 Mobile Entities: People and Vehicle Agents

People. Realistic traffic simulations need statistically realistic population of agents. To this purpose, we use an open source synthetic population generator called Gen* [6] that will initialize agents demographic attributes like age and gender. This generation also provide agent with the mandatory location for home place and optional other places like school or workplace.

Meso-Traffic Related Features. Every agent must be provided with an agenda in the form of a list of localized activities associated with an appointment and a desired mobility mode. During simulation, activities will trigger agent mobility:

the time of departure is calculated based on expected travel time and time of appointment considering walking and motorized movement with constant speed. The path and modes to use are computed using behavioral rules and shortest path algorithm: agent will choose the most efficient mode in term of time, while computing shortest path using NBA* algorithm [19]. On the tactical level, each agent is able to update its path when changes in the environment does not let them move to their current destination, including the ability to change the mode of transportation. Triggering event, like congestion, overwhelming travel time or impracticable street, are flexible and must be stated by the modelers.

Micro-Traffic Related Features. Agent are able to walk on a continuous space, while following the shortest path on a virtual pedestrian network. Thus, the mobility support is made of the defined walking area minus all obstacles, like building and water body, the virtual network being build automatically from it: we design an algorithm using Delaunay's triangulation to scattered the walking area and connect triangle to each other to build the network. Regarding pedestrian movement, we design an algorithm inspired by the social force model [12]. It define how people move on the continuous space, avoiding collision and adapting direction and speed to other pedestrian.

Vehicles. They are the mean by which people agents will move on the road network. The driving capacities are handled by vehicles although adjusted by people agent attributes: *e.g.* the tendency to overstep speed limit depends on people agent attributes. Hence, a vehicle needs a driver people agent to define destination and to adapt its behavior, while it can also contain some other people agents that will only be passengers. Vehicle operational level rely on the GAMA advanced driving skill, which consists in attributes and methods dedicated to the driving behavior of agent. [20] proposal provides more details about additions brought by the advanced driving skill.

3.4 Catastrophic Event

At the moment, the integration of hazard event modeling is under active development and already provide static and basic dynamic models of catastrophic event. The static approach is the most simple and consists in defining the central localization of the event and a radius. To further enhance realism, modelers can import GIS data to characterize the spatial spread of the event over time. Alternatively, modelers can use a cellular automata diffusion dynamic to mimic the dispersion of the zone impacted by the event. The algorithm has already been used to simulate flood and fire spread [1,9], and can be initialized using input data.

4   Case Study: Multi-modal Evacuation in a Ward of Hanoi

Authorities of the Vietnam city capital have launched in 2018 a large project to mitigate risks that could potentially result from natural as well as industrial disasters for Hanoi. Management and control of such extreme events in large urban area is a huge challenge [11]. In this paper we consider the ward of Phuc Xa, located between the dyke and the Red River, in the North of the Old Quarter of Hanoi.

4.1   Input Data and Parameters

For GIS data we had to transpose *cadastre* image to vector-based road network and buildings. School, university, market and hospital were extracted from OSM data, but because of lack of data, we assume amenities (like shops or workplace) to be uniformly distributed among building with a high probability.

To illustrate the use of our framework we design a proof of concept experiment. The generated population is a simplification of the actual one with 15 767 agents with a probability of 0.15 to be under 18, and a probability of 0.52 to be a woman. To locate them, we used an uniform spatial distribution. Agents are also bound with a workplace or school depending on age, respectively between 18 and 65 years old and under or equal to 17 years old. Each people under 18 is considered as having a motorbike.

Fig. 1. Simulation snapshot: the green triangles represent the people agents, and the blue rectangles the motorbikes (Color figure online)

We built three types of agenda according to age: one for scholarship, active people and retired. The first two ones are made of a main activity every day week – respectively school or work – and the last template is made of wandering activities in the morning and the afternoon. All the three end the day after the last activity in the afternoon with the return to the home place.

4.2   Simulation of Multi-modal Traffic and Evacuation Model

The normal course of the simulation is a work day of the week, agent following their agenda. Each step of the simulation represents 1 s in real life (86400 simulation cycles for a whole day) because micro-traffic dynamic needs to keep simulated time in a short scale: indeed, the time frame for human and vehicle agent to avoid obstacle and other agents must remain credible in terms of distance and speed because they act sequentially. Moreover, we know that individual behavior during a catastrophic event can change rapidly according to the local context and behaviors of the neighbors.

In order to test the capacity of our framework to simulate a complete evacuation of the area, we triggered a signal for the people agents to evacuate the simulated area at 8am. We defined all three exits of the quarter to be at the opposite of the Red River. For the choose of mode to evacuate, agent will choose the less time consuming mode, meaning at foot if there are close to exit or using motorbike if there expects to get to exist quicker.

The batch simulation took less than 44 min (average duration of a simulation cycle: 0.35 s on a personal computer) on the computer used for the experiment. This computation time is acceptable, especially as there are many possibilities to decrease it, in particular by using parallel computing.

5   Conclusion and Perspectives

Our framework gathers tools to model multi-modal urban traffic and individual response to catastrophic event with Gama. In this proposition, we detailed some of the new built-in features we bring to the platform to ease the design of realistic pedestrian and vehicle behavior. Furthermore we incorporated additional tools to add catastrophic event and model agent response within traffic simulation. We applied the framework to a case study mixing pedestrian and motorcycle mode for evacuation of a dense urban area.

To further refine our proposal, we plan to add a richer cognitive architecture to human agents coupling BDI classical mechanics with emotions and social norms to help modeling traffic rules and transgression during egress. Finally, we plan to apply our framework to case study involving public transport in day-to-day mobility as well as special freight for evacuation purpose.

Acknowledgment. This work is supported by the ANR ESCAPE project, grant ANR-16-CE39-0011-01 of the French Agence Nationale de la Recherche.

References

1. Adam, C., Gaudou, B.: Modelling human behaviours in disasters from interviews: application to melbourne bushfires. JASSS **20**(3), 12 (2017)
2. Adnan, M., et al.: Simmobility: a multi-scale integrated agent-based simulation platform. In: 95th Annual Meeting of the Transportation Research Board Forthcoming in Transportation Research Record (2016)

3. Bazzan, A.L., Klügl, F.: A review on agent-based technology for traffic and transportation. Knowl. Eng. Rev. **29**(3), 375–403 (2014)
4. Beck, E., Dugdale, J., Van Truong, H., Adam, C., Colbeau-Justin, L.: Crisis mobility of pedestrians: from survey to modelling, lessons from Lebanon and Argentina. In: Hanachi, C., Bénaben, F., Charoy, F. (eds.) ISCRAM-med 2014. LNBIP, vol. 196, pp. 57–70. Springer, Cham (2014). https://doi.org/10.1007/978-3-319-11818-5_6
5. Bo, Y., Cheng, W., Hua, H., Lijun, L.: A multi-agent and PSO based simulation for human behavior in emergency evacuation, pp. 296–300. IEEE, December 2007
6. Chapuis, K., Taillandier, P., Misslin, R., Drogoul, A.: Gen*: a generic toolkit to generate spatially explicit synthetic populations. Int. J. Geograph. Inf. Sci. **32**(6), 1194–1210 (2018)
7. Czura, G., Taillandier, P., Tranouez, P., Daudé, É.: MOSAIIC: city-level agent-based traffic simulation adapted to emergency situations. In: Takayasu, H., Ito, N., Noda, I., Takayasu, M. (eds.) Proceedings of the International Conference on Social Modeling and Simulation, plus Econophysics Colloquium 2014. SPC, pp. 265–274. Springer, Cham (2015). https://doi.org/10.1007/978-3-319-20591-5_24
8. Flötteröd, Y.P., Erdmann, J.: Dynamic reroute modeling for emergency evacuation: case study of Brunswick City. Germany. Int. J. Mech. Aerosp. Indus. Mechatron. Manuf. Eng. **12**(4), 99–109 (2018)
9. Gasmi, N., et al.: Reproducing and exploring past events using agent-based geo-historical models. In: Grimaldo, F., Norling, E. (eds.) MABS 2014. LNCS (LNAI), vol. 9002, pp. 151–163. Springer, Cham (2015). https://doi.org/10.1007/978-3-319-14627-0_11
10. Grignard, A., Taillandier, P., Gaudou, B., Vo, D.A., Huynh, N.Q., Drogoul, A.: GAMA 1.6: advancing the art of complex agent-based modeling and simulation. In: Boella, G., Elkind, E., Savarimuthu, B.T.R., Dignum, F., Purvis, M.K. (eds.) PRIMA 2013. LNCS (LNAI), vol. 8291, pp. 117–131. Springer, Heidelberg (2013). https://doi.org/10.1007/978-3-642-44927-7_9
11. Hawe, G.I., Coates, G., Wilson, D.T., Crouch, R.S.: Agent-based simulation for large-scale emergency response: a survey of usage and implementation. ACM Comput. Surv. **45**(1), 1–51 (2012)
12. Helbing, D., Molnar, P.: Social force model for pedestrian dynamics. Phys. Rev. E **51**(5), 4282–4286 (1995)
13. Horni, A., Nagel, K., Axhausen, K.W.: The Multi-Agent Transport Simulation MATSim. Ubiquity Press, London (2016)
14. Krajzewicz, D., Erdmann, J., Behrisch, M., Bieker, L.: Recent development and applications of SUMO - simulation of urban MObility. Int. J. Adv. Syst. Meas. **5**(3&4), 128–138 (2012)
15. Lämmel, G., Klügl, F., Nagel, K.: The MATSim network flow model for traffic simulation adapted to large-scale emergency egress and an application to the evacuation of the Indonesian City of Padang in case of a Tsunami warning. In: Timmermans, H. (ed.) Pedestrian Behavior: Models, Data Collection and Applications. Emerald (2009)
16. Lucien, L., Lang, C., Marilleau, N., Philippe, L.: Multiagent hybrid architecture for collaborative exchanges between communicating vehicles in an urban context. Procedia Comput. Sci. **83**, 695–699 (2016)
17. Mayrhofer, C.: Performance, scale and time in agent-based traffic modelling with NetLogo. GI_ Forum **2015**, 567–570 (2015)

18. Mordvintsev, A.S., Krzhizhanovskaya, V.V., Lees, M.H., Sloot, P.M.A.: Simulation of city evacuation coupled to flood dynamics. In: Weidmann, U., Kirsch, U., Schreckenberg, M. (eds.) Pedestrian and Evacuation Dynamics 2012, pp. 485–499. Springer, Cham (2014). https://doi.org/10.1007/978-3-319-02447-9_40
19. Pijls, W., Post, H.: Yet another bidirectional algorithm for shortest paths, p. 9 (2009)
20. Taillandier, P.: Traffic simulation with the GAMA platform. In: International Workshop on Agents in Traffic and Transportation, p. 8, May 2014
21. Wang, H., Mostafizi, A., Cramer, L.A., Cox, D., Park, H.: An agent-based model of a multimodal near-field tsunami evacuation: decision-making and life safety. Transp. Res. Part C: Emerg. Technol. **64**, 86–100 (2016)

Dialogue Games for Enforcement
of Argument Acceptance and Rejection
via Attack Removal

Jérémie Dauphin[1(✉)] and Ken Satoh[2]

[1] CSC, University of Luxembourg, Esch-sur-Alzette, Luxembourg
jeremie.dauphin@uni.lu
[2] National Institute of Informatics, Tokyo, Japan

Abstract. Argumentation is dynamic in nature and most commonly exists in dialogical form between different agents trying to convince each other. While abstract argumentation framework are mostly static, many studies have focused on dynamical aspects and changes to these static frameworks. An important problem is the one of *argument enforcement*, modifying an argumentation framework in order to ensure that a certain argument is accepted. In this paper, we use *dialogue games* to provide an exhaustive list of minimal sets of attacks such that when removed, a given argument is credulously accepted with respect to preferred semantics. We then extend the method to enforce other acceptability statuses and cope with sets of arguments.

Keywords: Abstract argumentation · Dialogue games
Argument enforcement · Attack removal · Dynamical argumentation

1 Introduction

Argumentation is a dynamic process where one party attempts to convince another, or itself, of the validity of some statement. This process involves both parties putting arguments in favor or against the validity of said statement in turns, until one party has been convinced by running out of counter-arguments.

Abstract argumentation [6] provides a static approach where all arguments and their interactions are given from the beginning in what is called an argumentation framework, and the acceptability of the arguments is determined based on the entire state of the framework. While the dialogical nature might appear to be missing at first, dialogue games can be extracted from such a framework where one focuses on the acceptability status of a single argument with a process very similar to the one described in the earlier paragraph.

When focusing on adding a dynamic aspect to abstract argumentation, one common problem is the problem of argument enforcement: given a particular

J. Dauphin–The work of Jérémie Dauphin was supported by the H2020 Marie Skłodowska-Curie grant number 690974 for the project MIREL.

© Springer Nature Switzerland AG 2018
T. Miller et al. (Eds.): PRIMA 2018, LNAI 11224, pp. 449–457, 2018.
https://doi.org/10.1007/978-3-030-03098-8_29

argument in a framework, what changes are required in order to change the status of the argument from rejected to accepted or vice-versa? This problem is tightly linked to persuasion [8], as the goal of an agent there is for the other agent to accept or perhaps reject a given argument of interest, and hence the question of what the best approach is for this goal. There is also an element of strategy, as the other party might have an objective of their own, perhaps wanting to conserve their beliefs about certain arguments more than about others.

There has been much work already on the problem of argument enforcement. In his paper, Baumann [2] studies the minimal necessary additions, in terms of arguments and attacks, one needs to perform in order to enforce the acceptability of a given argument. Coste-Marquis et al. [5] examine the enforcement issue from the point of view of belief revision by allowing only for change in the attacks.

On another side, there also exists studies on the effects of argumentation framework manipulation. In their paper, Cayrol et al. [4] study the possible repercussions that the addition of an argument might have on the framework. Another study by Boella et al. [3] focuses on the effects that removing arguments and attacks in an argumentation framework have on the grounded extension. Liao et al. [9] propose a partitioning method to efficiently compute the repercussions of changes in an abstract argumentation framework.

In this paper, we provide an algorithm to compute an exhaustive list of sets of attacks, which, when removed, toggle the acceptance status of an argument, as well as a formal framework to ensure the well behavior of the algorithm. In practice, the operation of removing an attack could for example be performed by arguing for the preference of the attacked argument over its attacker, or by reformulating the argument so that it still reaches the same conclusion but from different, less vulnerable premises. Since operations of this kind come with a cost, we wish to minimize these costs, but since these costs might differ between the different attacks, we also wish to provide an exhaustive list of solutions.

In Sect. 2, we provide preliminary definitions of abstract argumentation upon which we build our results. In Sect. 3, we delve into the problem of enforcing the credulous acceptance of an argument with respect to the preferred semantics. We finish in Sect. 4 with a conclusion and discussion of potential future work.

2   Preliminaries

In this section we provide definitions of existing notions of abstract argumentation and dialogue games which will be used later on.

An argumentation framework [6] (AF) is a pair $\langle A, R \rangle$ where A is a finite set of atomic entities called *arguments*, and $R \subseteq A \times A$ is a relation of *attack*.

Definition 1. *Let $F = \langle A, R \rangle$ be an AF and $S \subseteq A$ a set of arguments. We say that S is:* conflict-free *iff there exist no $a, b \in S$ such that a attacks b;* admissible *iff it is conflict-free and for all $a \in S$, $b \in A$ such that b attacks a, there exists $c \in S$ such that c attacks b; and a* preferred extension *iff it is a $\subseteq$-maximal admissible set.*

The preferred semantics is the function which returns all preferred extensions of a given AF. Since it may return more than one extension, we also define different degrees of acceptance.

Definition 2. *Let $F = \langle A, R \rangle$ be an AF, $a \in A$ an argument. We say that a is: credulously accepted iff for some preferred extensions E, $a \in E$; rejected iff for all preferred extensions E, $a \notin E$.*

Dialogue games [7, 10, 12] provide a proof theory to test the acceptability of a given argument in a fixed AF. The games involve two players, the *proponent* and the *opponent*, where moves are of the form a_p with a an argument and $p \in \{\mathsf{pro}, \mathsf{opp}\}$ a player. The game starts with a_{pro}, where a is the argument to be tested. The opponent then moves forward an argument to attack it, attempting to undermine its acceptability. A *legal move function* is a function from sequences of moves to sets of moves which, given a sequence of moves, dictates which moves could possibly be put forward next by the opposing player. We also define a *dispute* on an argument a as a finite sequence of moves $a_{\mathsf{pro}} \leftarrow b_{\mathsf{opp}} \leftarrow \ldots$ starting with a_{pro}, such that every move is a legal move with respect to the earlier part of the dispute according to a set legal move function. If a dispute has no more legal moves, we say that the dispute is *final* and that the player who put forward the last move is the *winner* of the dispute.

Definition 3. *Let $F = \langle A, R \rangle$ be an argumentation framework and d a dispute in F with last move a_p. The legal move function f_{pref} for the preferred semantics is defined as follows:*

1. *if $p = \mathsf{pro}$, then $f_{pref}(d) = \{b_{\mathsf{opp}} \mid (b, a) \in R, \nexists b_{\mathsf{opp}} \in d\}$;*
2. *otherwise, $f_{pref}(d) = \{b_{\mathsf{pro}} \mid (b, a) \in R\}$.*

The acceptability of an argument is then determined by whether or not the proponent has a *strategy* to win the dialogue game. This is a conditional plan which is formally represented by a set of disputes including a dispute for each possible move of the opponent. The definition makes use of the notion of *sub-dispute*, which is a sub-sequence of a dispute with the same initial argument.

Definition 4. *Let $F = \langle A, R \rangle$ be an argumentation framework, $a \in A$ an argument and f a legal move function. A defending strategy for a in F with respect to f is a non-empty set of disputes T such that:*

1. *each dispute in T has initial argument a and is won by pro;*
2. *for each $d \in T$ and for each sub-dispute d' of d, if the last move in d' is an argument b moved by pro, then for any $c \in f(d')$, there exists a $d'' \in T$ such that $d \leftarrow c$ is a sub-dispute of d'';*
3. *there is no $d, d' \in T, b \in A$ such that $b_{\mathsf{pro}} \in d$ and $b_{\mathsf{opp}} \in d'$.*

The last item represents the requirement that the strategy must be conflict-free, since the goal is to construct an admissible set. Note that these are usually called winning strategies in the literature, however since we will later define strategies for the victory of the opponent, we prefer using the term *defending*.

The existence of a defending strategy for a given argument is equivalent to its credulous acceptability [10].

Theorem 1. *Let $F = \langle A, R \rangle$ be an argumentation framework and $a \in A$ an argument. a is credulously accepted in F with respect to the preferred semantics iff there is a defending strategy for a in F with respect to f_{pref}.*

3   Enforcing Credulous Acceptance for Preferred Semantics

In this section, we first provide a few new definitions and associated results for dialogue games, and then use these to provide a procedure for identifying minimal sets of attacks to be removed in order to enforce credulous acceptability of a given argument with respect to the preferred semantics. We start by defining a counterpart to the defending strategies, i.e. a notion of strategy for the opponent to win the dispute.

Definition 5. *Let $F = \langle A, R \rangle$ be an argumentation framework, $a \in A$ an argument and f a legal move function. An* opposing strategy *for a in F with respect to f is a non-empty set of disputes T such that:*

1. *each dispute in T has initial argument a and either is won by opp, or contains a move b_{pro} such that there exists $d' \in T$ with $b_{opp} \in d'$;*
2. *for each $d \in T$ and for each sub-dispute d' of d, if the last move in d' is an argument b moved by opp, then for any c that pro can legally move against b, there exists a $d'' \in T$ such that $d \leftarrow c_{opp}$ is a sub-dispute of d''.*

The opponent's goal is to prevent the proponent from successfully defending the argument in focus and thus construct an admissible set containing it. The opponent does this by providing a set of argument attacks from which the proponent cannot fully defend, and thus shows no admissible set containing the argument in focus can be constructed.

Theorem 2. *Let $F = \langle A, R \rangle$ be an argumentation framework and $a \in A$ an argument. There exists a defending strategy for a in F with respect to f_{pref} iff there does not exist an opposing strategy for a in F with respect to f_{pref}.*

Proof sketch. This follows from Zermelo's Theorem [13].   □

Corollary 1. *Let $F = \langle A, R \rangle$ be an argumentation framework and $a \in A$ an argument. a is rejected in F with respect to the preferred semantics iff there is an opposing strategy for a in F with respect to f_{pref}.*

We have now laid down the foundations for dialogue games, in which we can identify whether an argument is accepted or rejected by providing defending strategies, respectively opposing strategies for said argument. In order to alter that argument's acceptance status, we can use this information in order to pinpoint minimal sets of attacks which, when removed, guarantee that the argument's status is changed. For this, we first have to be able to retrieve the attacks which correspond to each player's moves in a particular strategy.

Definition 6. *Let $F = \langle A, R \rangle$ be an AF and d a dispute. We define the attacking set of d to be $\mathcal{A}(d) = \{(a, b) \mid$ for some dispute $d', d' \leftarrow b_{pro} \leftarrow a_{opp}$ is a sub-dispute of $d\}$. We define the defending set of d to be $\mathcal{D}(d) = \{(a, b) \mid$ for some dispute $d', d' \leftarrow b_{opp} \leftarrow a_{pro}$ is a sub-dispute of $d\}$.*

For a set of disputes D, we write $\mathcal{A}(D)$ for $\bigcup_{d \in D} \mathcal{A}(d)$, and similarly, $\mathcal{D}(D)$ for $\bigcup_{d \in D} \mathcal{D}(d)$.

We wish to disrupt all winning strategies of a given player, which will hence give his counter-part a strategy to win. We do this by removing one of the player's possible moves from each winning strategy in the form of attack removal. To identify these attacks, since we want to work with minimal changes to the framework, we use *minimal hitting sets*.

Definition 7. *Let E be a set and S a set of subsets of E. We define the set of hitting sets of S to be $\mathcal{HS}(S) = \{s \subseteq E \mid \forall s' \in S, s \cap s' \neq \emptyset\}$. We also define the set of minimal hitting sets of S to be $\mathcal{MHS}(S) = \{s \in \mathcal{HS}(S) \mid \nexists s' \in \mathcal{HS}(S)$ such that $s' \subset s\}$.*

The enumeration of all minimal hitting sets can be efficiently done using for example the algorithm described by Satoh et al. [11].

Example 1. Let $S = \{\{(a, b), (c, d)\}, \{(c, d), (e, f)\}\}$. Then, the minimal hitting sets of S are $\mathcal{MHS}(S) = \{\{(a, b), (e, f)\}, \{(c, d)\}\}$.

If an argument is rejected, we can enumerate all the opposing strategies for it. We then identify candidate sets of attacks to be removed by computing the minimal hitting sets of the attacking sets in the opposing strategies.

Definition 8. *Let $F = \langle A, R \rangle$ and S a set of strategies in F. We define the set of critical attack sets of S to be $\mathcal{CA}(S) = \mathcal{MHS}(\{\mathcal{A}(T) \mid T \in S\})$. We also define the set of critical defense sets of S to be $\mathcal{CD}(S) = \mathcal{MHS}(\{\mathcal{D}(T) \mid T \in S\})$.*

Our first result with regard to argument status enforcement is that entirely removing at least one of these sets of attacks is required in order to enforce the acceptance of the argument of interest.

Lemma 1. *Let $F = \langle A, R \rangle$ be an AF where some argument $a \in A$ is rejected with respect to preferred semantics and S the set of opposing strategies for a with respect to f_{pref}. For all $R' \subseteq R$, if there is no $s \in \mathcal{CA}(S)$ such that $s \subseteq (R \setminus R')$, then a is rejected in $F' = \langle A, R' \rangle$.*

Proof sketch. There exists at least one opposing strategy which is still viable in F', otherwise there would be a critical attack set which has been fully removed. Hence, a is still rejected in F'. $\qquad\square$

This lemma shows that fully removing some of the critical attacks of S is a necessary condition to enforce the acceptability of the argument of interest a. Now the question is whether this is a sufficient condition to ensure it. An issue could arise when removing a *controversial* attack with respect to a, i.e. an attack which appears in $\mathcal{A}(d)$ and $\mathcal{D}(d')$ for two disputes d and d' with initial argument a. Deleting such an attack might also hinder some of the proponent's potential new defending strategies and give rise to new opposing strategies. Hence, when removing such an attack, one might need to iterate the argument enforcement procedure.

Algorithm 1. Enumeration of solutions for enforcement of credulous acceptance with respect to preferred semantics

---

Input: $\langle A, R \rangle$ is an AF with $a \in A$, $Except \subseteq R$ is a set of attacks.
Output: $sols$ is the exhaustive set of minimal solutions to the enforcement problem.
1: **procedure** ENUMATKSACC($\langle A, R \rangle, a, Except$)   ▷ Enumerate all solutions
2:      $S \leftarrow$ OPPSTRATS(F, a)
3:      **if** $S = \emptyset$ **then return** $\{\emptyset\}$ ▷ If already accepted, solution is no change
4:      **end if**
5:      $sols := \emptyset$
6:      $C \leftarrow$ CA(S)
7:      **for** every $s \in C$ such that $\nexists e \in Except$ with $e \subseteq s$ **do**
8:          **if** $\exists r \in s$ such that r is controversial **then**
9:              $E := Except \cup (C \setminus \{s\})$
10:             $sols := sols \cup \{s \cup s' \mid s' \in$ ENUMATKSACC($\langle A, R \setminus s \rangle, a, E$)$\}$
11:         **else**
12:             $sols := sols \cup \{s\}$
13:         **end if**
14:     **end for**
15:     **return** $sols$
16: **end procedure**

Algorithm 1 provides the details of how to compute the exhaustive list of minimal sets of attack to be removed in order to enforce the acceptance of an argument a in a framework F. The algorithm relies on a function OPPSTRATS which computes and returns all opposing strategies for a given argument in a given framework, and a function CA which computes the set of critical attack sets of a given set of strategies. Note that the procedure ENUMATKSACC should initially be called with an empty set of exceptions, however if some sets of attacks in the framework are already determined to be jointly crucial and impossible to remove, one can add them to the initial set of exceptions. This set of exceptions is mainly used in order to prevent the iterated procedure called in line 10 to consider removing attacks which could already have been selected at an earlier stage and hence ensure the minimality of the output. If the set of exceptions is initially too restrictive, it is possible that no solution is returned.

Example 2. Consider the argumentation framework $F_2 = \langle A_2, R_2 \rangle$ and final disputes for the argument a depicted in Fig. 1. In this framework, there are two opposing strategies: $T_1 = \{d_1\}$ and $T_2 = \{d_4\}$. We get that $\mathcal{C}\mathcal{A}(T_1 \cup T_2) = \{S_1, S_2, S_3, S_4\}$, where $S_1 = \{(b, a), (e, a)\}$, $S_2 = \{(j, h), (k, i)\}$,

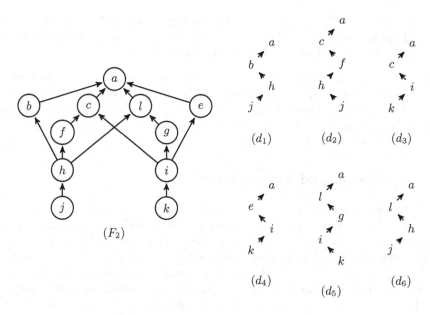

Fig. 1. Example argumentation framework F_2 and all final disputes for a in F_2.

$S_3 = \{(e,a), (j,h)\}$ and $S_4 = \{(b,a), (k,i)\}$. Since S_1 contains no controversial attacks, it is directly listed as a solution. On the other hand, both (j,h) and (k,i) are controversial since (j,h) also appears in $\mathcal{D}(d_2)$ and (k,i) also appears in $\mathcal{D}(d_5)$. However, it turns out that a is accepted in $\langle A_2, R_2 \setminus S_2 \rangle$ and hence $\{(j,h), (k,i)\}$ is a solution. Next, we consider S_3. This one contains a controversial attack as well, so we have to compute the solutions for enforcing a in $\langle A_2, R_2 \setminus S_3 \rangle$, which gives us three solutions: $\{(c,a)\}$, $\{(h,f)\}$ and $\{(k,i)\}$. Since $\{(k,i), (j,h)\}$ is already a solution, we only take $\{(c,a)\}$ and $\{(h,f)\}$, giving us two new solutions in F: $\{(j,h), (e,a), (c,a)\}$ and $\{(j,h), (e,a), (h,f)\}$. Lastly, S_4 also contains a controversial attack, so we once again iterate the procedure in $\langle A_2, R_2 \setminus S_4 \rangle$, giving us three solutions: $\{(l,a)\}$, $\{(i,g)\}$ and $\{(j,h)\}$, of which we ignore $\{(j,h)\}$. In the end, we have 6 solutions:

1. $\{(e,a), (b,a)\}$ 3. $\{(e,a), (j,h), (c,a)\}$ 5. $\{(b,a), (k,i), (l,a)\}$
2. $\{(j,h), (k,i)\}$ 4. $\{(e,a), (j,h), (h,f)\}$ 6. $\{(b,a), (k,i), (i,g)\}$

Theorem 3. *Let $F = \langle A, R \rangle$ where $a \in A$ is rejected with respect to preferred semantics, and sols the set returned by calling* $\text{ENUMATKSACC}(F, a, \emptyset)$. *For all $s \in$ sols, a is credulously accepted in $\langle A, R \setminus s \rangle$ with respect to the preferred semantics, and for all R' such that $(R \setminus s) \subset R' \subseteq R$, a is rejected with respect to preferred semantics in $\langle A, R' \rangle$.*

Proof sketch. The minimality result follows from Lemma 1. Similarly, the correctness of the solutions follows from Theorem 2. In the cases of controversial attack removals, Lemma 1 might need to be applied multiple times while Theorem 2 applies only on the final framework. Note that since the initial set of attacks is finite, the algorithm is guaranteed to terminate.   □

Algorithm 1 can be adapted to work for the enforcement of argument rejection by retrieving defending strategies in line 2 and computing critical defense sets in line 6 instead. This modified algorithm will then disrupt defending strategies in a similar way and thus give rise to at least one opposing strategy, ensuring the rejection of the argument in question.

4   Conclusion and Future Work

In this paper, we have described results in dialogue games for abstract argumentation frameworks which have allowed us to provide an algorithm for the computation of minimal sets of attacks which, when removed from the framework, enforce the credulous acceptability of a given argument with respect to preferred semantics, which can be easily modified to enforce rejection instead.

Future work could include similar procedures for other semantics, such as stable, semi-stable and ideal, of which the dialogue games have been briefly discussed by Modgil et al. [10], but also for semantics such as stage2 or cf2 [1]. One could also use the results in this paper to focus on the removal of arguments instead of attacks, or a mixture of both.

References

1. Baroni, P., Giacomin, M., Guida, G.: SCC-recursiveness: a general schema for argumentation semantics. Artif. Intell. **168**, 162–210 (2005)
2. Baumann, R.: What does it take to enforce an argument? Minimal change in abstract argumentation. ECAI **12**, 127–132 (2012)
3. Boella, G., Kaci, S., van der Torre, L.: Dynamics in argumentation with single extensions: abstraction principles and the grounded extension. In: Sossai, C., Chemello, G. (eds.) ECSQARU 2009. LNCS (LNAI), vol. 5590, pp. 107–118. Springer, Heidelberg (2009). https://doi.org/10.1007/978-3-642-02906-6_11
4. Cayrol, C., Dupin de Saint-Cyr, F., Lagasquie-Schiex, M.-C.: Change in abstract argumentation frameworks: adding an argument. J. Artif. Intell. Res. **38**, 49–84 (2010)
5. Coste-Marquis, S., Konieczny, S., Mailly, J.-G., Marquis, P.: On the revision of argumentation systems: minimal change of arguments statuses. KR **14**, 52–61 (2014)
6. Phan Minh Dung: On the acceptability of arguments and its fundamental role in nonmonotonic reasoning, logic programming and n-person games. Artif. Intell. **77**(2), 321–357 (1995)
7. Dunne, P.E., Bench-Capon, T.J.M.: Two party immediate response disputes: properties and efficiency. Artif. Intell. **149**(2), 221–250 (2003)
8. Gabbriellini, S., Torroni, P.: A new framework for ABMs based on argumentative reasoning. In: Kamiński, B., Koloch, G. (eds.) Advances in Social Simulation. Advances in Intelligent Systems and Computing, vol. 229, pp. 25–36. Springer, Heidelberg (2014). https://doi.org/10.1007/978-3-642-39829-2_3

9. Liao, B., Jin, L., Koons, R.C.: Dynamics of argumentation systems: a division-based method. Artif. Intell. **175**(11), 1790–1814 (2011)
10. Modgil, S., Caminada, M.: Proof theories and algorithms for abstract argumentation frameworks. In: Simari, G., Rahwan, I. (eds.) Argumentation in Artificial Intelligence, pp. 105–129. Springer, Boston (2009). https://doi.org/10.1007/978-0-387-98197-0_6
11. Satoh, K., Uno, T.: Enumerating maximal frequent sets using irredundant dualization. In: Grieser, G., Tanaka, Y., Yamamoto, A. (eds.) DS 2003. LNCS (LNAI), vol. 2843, pp. 256–268. Springer, Heidelberg (2003). https://doi.org/10.1007/978-3-540-39644-4_22
12. Vreeswik, G.A.W., Prakken, H.: Credulous and sceptical argument games for preferred semantics. In: Ojeda-Aciego, M., de Guzmán, I.P., Brewka, G., Moniz Pereira, L. (eds.) JELIA 2000. LNCS (LNAI), vol. 1919, pp. 239–253. Springer, Heidelberg (2000). https://doi.org/10.1007/3-540-40006-0_17
13. Zermelo, E.: Über eine Anwendung der Mengenlehre auf die Theorie des Schachspiels. In: Proceedings of the Fifth International Congress of Mathematicians, vol. 2, pp. 501–504. II, Cambridge UP, Cambridge (1913)

Learning Strategic Group Formation for Coordinated Behavior in Adversarial Multi-Agent with Double DQN

Elhadji Amadou Oury Diallo[(⊠)] and Toshiharu Sugawara

Department of Computer Science and Communications Engineering,
Waseda University, 3-4-1 Okubo, Shinjuku-ku, Tokyo 169-8555, Japan
diallo.oury@fuji.waseda.jp, sugawara@waseda.jp

Abstract. We examine whether a team of agents can learn geometric and strategic group formations by using deep reinforcement learning in adversarial multi-agent systems. This is a significant point underlying the control and coordination of multiple autonomous and intelligent agents. While there are many possible approaches to solve this problem, we are interested in fully end-to-end learning method where agents do not have any prior knowledge of the environment and its dynamics. In this paper, we propose a scalable and distributed double DQN framework to train adversarial multi-agent systems. We show that a large number of agents can learn to cooperatively move, attack and defend themselves in various geometric formations and battle tactics like encirclement, guerrilla warfare, frontal attack, flanking maneuver, and so on. We finally show that agents create an emergent and collective flocking behaviors by using local views from the environment only.

Keywords: Multi-agent systems
Deep reinforcement learning · Collective intelligence
Coordination · Cooperation

1 Introduction

Multi-agent systems (MAS) [12] are systems where agents in the same environment collectively solve a problem that is very difficult and complex to solve by a single agent [3]. To achieve such collective behavior, intelligent agents are often implemented on the basis of some behaviors from nature and society such as flocking [9] and group formation [4]. For instance, in an adversarial environment, agents learn how to minimize their encounters with opponents by strategically forming a group and by combining their knowledge of the environment to maximize the probability of avoiding opponents and obstacles. This behavior is very important in an adversarial environment with a large number of agents with limited field of views. This can be seen as the same strategy used by a group

This work is partly supported by JSPS KAKENHI Grant Number 17KT0044.

© Springer Nature Switzerland AG 2018
T. Miller et al. (Eds.): PRIMA 2018, LNAI 11224, pp. 458–466, 2018.
https://doi.org/10.1007/978-3-030-03098-8_30

of humans or animals in real life. They coordinate between them and generate collective behaviors which can be seen as intelligent because the knowledge or behavior of an isolated individual agent is not enough to learn anything useful from the environment.

In general, policies are goal-directed and can last for a relatively long time. These policies might just cease to exist when the goal no longer exists or agents have already achieved their predefined goal. Even if the agents do not generally have a global view of their environment, the local behavior of an individual agent affects other agents' behavior, thereby resulting in very complex global behaviors of the team. In addition, scalability is a very important issue [8], particularly in learning systems where the environment is non-stationary because the dynamics change frequently and agents have to adapt their behaviors accordingly [5]. Furthermore, if we have a leader or decision-maker agent that decides which action should be taken by agents, the performance of the system might slow down.

We address the fundamental question: can deep reinforcement learning agents find the strategic group formation by combining the local views of individual agents in a multi-agent context and adapt to the change of opponent strategies in an adversarial environment. When we apply deep reinforcement learning techniques in MAS, we always ask what will happen when the number of agents drastically increases. Will the network converge? Will the agents be able to learn interesting strategies or policies that help them to achieve their goal or sub-goal? These are very important questions because the dimensionality of the tasks grows exponentially with the number of agents.

2   Related Work

Balch et al. [1] presented a behavior-based multi-robot team formation and formation-keeping. They demonstrated that robots could form teams to reach navigational goals, avoid hazards and simultaneously remain in formation. Desai et al. [4] proposed a graph theoretical method of modeling a formation of non-holonomic mobile robots and developed a framework for transitioning from one formation to another. They dealt with situations where agents have to briefly cease their formation to avoid obstacles. Barfoot et al. [2] studied the motion planning for formations of mobile robots, where the robots used predetermined geometrical constraints throughout their travel. Nathan and Barbosa [7] studied the emergence of V-like formations during bird flight by introducing a distributes positioning rules to guide agents' movements. They also try to find the basic behavior that generates a flock and collective behavior strategies using mathematical framework.

One drawback of these methods is that the strategies are always given. In other words, the agents cannot generally discover a set of new strategies. Unfortunately, defining such behaviors manually is tedious and complex. In the aforementioned papers, some parts of the process were hand-designed. They generally calculate the expected outcome that could be derived if a group or flock was formed. Then, they select the optimal groups to form after estimating all possible outcomes. And finally, they divide the set of agents into exhaustive and disjoint groups. One drawback of this method is that the system becomes very complex as the number of agents increases. In addition, we cannot always design and predict all possible and useful formations in a complex environment.

3   Problem

3.1   Multi-agent Reinforcement Learning

A Multi-agent Markov game is defined as $\langle N, S, A, R, T \rangle$, where $N = \{1, \ldots, n\}$ is a set of n agents, S a finite state space, $A = A^1 \times \cdots \times A^n$ is a joint action space of agents (where A_i is the action space of agent i), $R : S \times A \to \mathbb{R}$ is the common expected reward function; and $T : S \times A \times S \to [0, 1]$ is a probabilistic transition function. At each timestep t, agent i takes action a_t^i sampled from the policy π_t^i in state $s_t \in S$, where $\pi^i : S \times A^i$ and $s_t = \left(s_t^1, \ldots, s_t^n\right)$. When a joint action $a_t = \left(a_t^1, \ldots a_t^n\right)$ is executed, the environment transits from s_t to s_{t+1} with a probability $p(s_{t+1}|s_t, a_t) \in T$ and agent i receives a reward $r_t^i = R(s_{t+1}|s_t^i, a_t^i)$. The goal of the agents is to find a deterministic joint policy $\pi = \left(\pi^1, \ldots \pi^n\right)$ so as to maximize the sum of their individual reward $r_t = \sum_{i=1}^n r_t^i$.

3.2   Adversarial MAS Environment

In this paper, we used a well-known adversarial multi-agent domain, the so-called "Battle game" [10], in which two teams of many agents are fighting against each other. Agents of the same team cooperate with their teammates to find some strategies in order to defeat the opponent team. The main goal is to kill as much opponents as possible by invading the neighbor territories and by using some warfare strategies. Our environment operates on two (2) teams of n agents and runs from some initial positioning of the agents inside a square in two-dimensional space for each team.

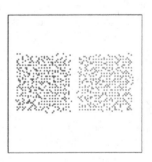

Fig. 1. Initial state

An agent can take up to 7 actions: going up, going down, going left, going right, turning left, turning right and shooting. An agent is dead after being attacked three (3) times. An episode ends when all agents on one team have been killed or after $1,000$ timesteps. The winning team is the one who has the highest number of alive agents.

3.3   Reward Scheme

Each agent receives a reward of -0.01 after each step. An agent gets $+5$ when it kills an opponent, and receives -5 when the agent is killed by an opponent. An agent receives a small negative reward of -0.01 whenever it attacks an empty position. An agent receives $+1$ for attacking an opponent, and -1 if it is being attacked. The global reward of each team is the sum of all the rewards received by agents of the same time at any timestep t, $r_t = \sum_{i=1}^{n} r_t^i$.

4 Method

4.1 Proposed Learning Framework

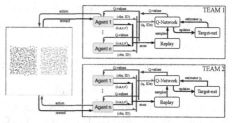

We proposed a distributed learning framework for training adversarial multi-agent systems with a large number of agents (Fig. 2). In our framework, each agent has its own local view s_t^i, its own action space a_t^i and its own reward r_t^i. At every timestep t, an individual agent observes its local environment, takes an action, and receives a local scalar reward. Agents only know their own individual action and they do not observe each other's action.

Fig. 2. Scalable adversarial MAS architecture. The environment constitutes of two teams of n agents ($n = 100, 200, 300, 400$) each at the beginning of each episode.

In this model, all members of the same team use the same neural network. The deep Q network of each team receives a "tensorized" observation at time t (see Sect. 4.2). Each agent asynchronously infers its action from the output of the network which contains the Q-values of every possible action for all agents.

4.2 Observation

The main environment is represented as a square grid. The image is converted into grayscale. And then every agent uses a filtering method to delimit its local view controlled by the parameter k (Fig. 3). The input of each network is a tensorized stack of all local views of agents at any given

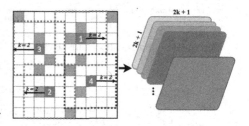

Fig. 3. 3D Tensor observation.

timestep. Each agent senses distances to neighboring agents within a radius k from its current position. Each channel represents the local view s_t^i of each individual agent of the same team. Using only this information, a network can learn a policy that is able to establish and maintain a certain group formation and to cooperatively locate and eliminate the opponents. This representation can be thought of as an aggregation of all inputs from different sensors of many robots. In our implementation, the local view s_t^i of a dead agent is $s_t^i = \mathbf{1}_{(2k+1, 2k+1)}$, an identity matrix of size $(2k + 1, 2k + 1)$ whose entries are 1. This practically means that the local views of a dead agent is white as is the background.

5   Results

5.1   Experimental Settings

We use the following parameters for all our experiments: learning rate $\alpha = 0.00025$, discount factor $\gamma = 0.99$. We update the target network every $10,000$ timesteps. To stabilize learning, we feed the network with medium size mini-batches of 250 samples. The double DQN [11] network structure is similar to the one from [6]. The experimental results in the following sections describe the average values of ten (10) experimental runs with different random seeds.

5.2   Convergence and Improvement of Group Behaviors

Figure 4 represents the training performance of our baseline implementation where we have 100 agents per team with a narrow local field of view ($k = 3$). The average error of each team is shown in Fig. 4a. In the beginning, the losses were high because of the high values of $\varepsilon(t)$. After more or less than $1,000$ episodes and smaller values of $\varepsilon(t)$, each network's training loss converges to a very low value close to null.

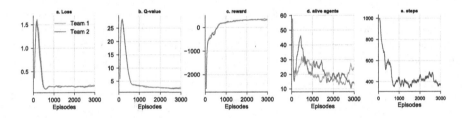

Fig. 4. Training result of our adversarial multi-agent with $n = 100$ and $k = 3$.

By using double DQN [11], we make sure that the networks do not over-estimate the Q-values, and consequently, the action-state values will converge to the actual Q-values. The average Q-values of each team is shown in Fig. 4b. Agents were taking random actions by sampling from high values of $\varepsilon(t)$ in the beginning. After training sufficiently enough, agents started to take good actions based on their near-optimal policies.

Figure 4c shows the average reward per episode for each team during training time. We see that both networks tend to have approximately the same reward. Our reward scheme could make a group of agents learn how to efficiently form various strategic group formations based on their opponents' strategies.

Figure 4d shows the number of alive agents at the end of each episode for each team. This helps us evaluate how often each team wins and to know exactly how many agents are still alive at the end of an episode. First, the team with the largest number of agents at time t uses some tactics to eliminate as many opponents as possible in a very short time before the opponents' counter-attack.

Then, both teams reach a kind of equilibrium in which they use similar group formation strategies. And finally, agents periodically update their strategies to effectively defend themselves against the opponents.

5.3   Scalability

The input of each network is smaller when k is smaller because the input shape is $(n, (2k + 1), (2k + 1))$. That mainly justified why we observed low loss values for $k = 3, 4$ (Figs. 4a, 5a, f and k). Moreover, all networks started to use their optimal policies after $1,000$ episodes. No matter what the values of k are, all networks converge to the same Q-values soon or late (Figs. 5b, g and l). As the number of agents increases, the networks converge to the actual Q-values independently to their local field of views.

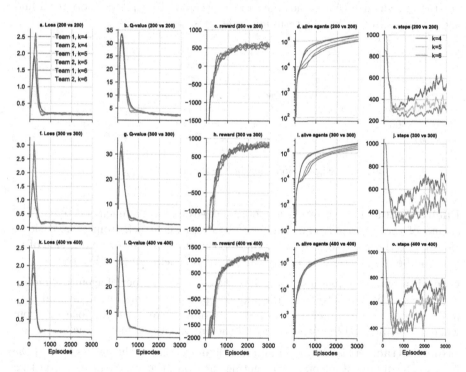

Fig. 5. Training performance of our adversarial multi-agent with different number of agents ($n = 200, 300, 400$) and field of view ranges ($k = 4, 5, 6$). (d), (i), and (n) show the cumulative number of alive agents.

Despite the fact that all settings did converge, we can see that the agents with $k = 3$ take much longer to learn a new strategy or to adapt their behaviors. This can be explained by the fact that with a small field of views, agents cannot see the surrounding opponents, hence their lack of good defense strategies. After

$1,000$ episodes, both teams started to learn not only how to attack but how to defend themselves for a relatively longer period. A larger field of view ($k = 5, 6$) helps agents to simultaneously learn good attack and defense strategies.

While with large k, both teams learn the same strategies and they can kill approximately the same number of opponents, they also rapidly co-adapt themselves based on the opponents' behaviors by finding some good defense strategies. We can conclude that our proposed learning framework is scalable in nonstationary and adversarial learning environments with a large number of agents.

5.4   Learned Team Strategies

In the following, we describe the most common observed strategic group formations learned by agents. It seems like most of the following strategies always appeared in all experiments. As we train agents, we might observe slightly variant tactics which do have the same roots. Agents often prefer short-term and aggressive strategies to long-term and safe ones.

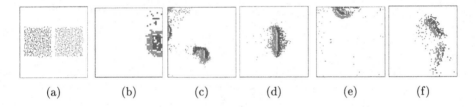

(a)   (b)   (c)   (d)   (e)   (f)

Fig. 6. Some learned team strategies.

Encirclement. This situation is highly dangerous for the encircled team. The agents of the encircled team can be subject to an attack from several sides. However, if there are some obstacles inside the environment or on one side of it, it would be much harder to achieve a full encirclement attack. (Fig. 6b)

Guerrilla warfare. It is a strategy in which a small number of agent use mobility tactics to fight a larger and less-mobile opponent team. The main goal is to inflict damage on a target and immediately move away from the location from where the attack did happened to avoid the opponents' counter-attack (Fig. 6c).

Frontal attack. This is a direct and hostile movement of the agents toward the front of the opponent agents. By targeting the front, the attackers are subjecting themselves to the maximum defensive power of the enemy (Fig. 6d).

Flanking maneuver. This consists of a movement of agents of the same team around a flank to achieve an advantageous position over enemies. Agents easily form echelons in which they are diagonally aligned. However, this strategy is not always safe when the team is outnumbered. (Fig. 6e)

Pincer movement. Similarly to the flanking maneuver, this is a tactic in which agents of the same team simultaneously attack both flanks of the opponent team. This generally leads to a frontal attack on each flank (Fig. 6f).

5.5 Discussion

Our reward structure appears to make this domain a negative-sum game as points are lost for time and scores are balanced for attacks and kills only during the beginning of the training. In other words, the positive and negative rewards of all agents will add up to less than zero only during the first episodes when the values of ε are high. Then, the environment becomes a zero-sum game before generating positive-sum outcomes in which the sum of positive and negative rewards is greater than zero.

In our framework, each agent has its own Q-values and they simultaneously act in a decentralized manner. Therefore, the problem is much more complex than having centralized learning, where two agents compete with each other in a grid world. One of the main advantages of our method is that we do not necessarily need to retrain the network from scratch for a different number of agents. Even though our agents are homogeneous, it is easy to see that our agents can adapt their strategies against the change of opponents' strategies.

6   Conclusion

We demonstrated that agents keep forming groups whenever new ones are necessary. Also, the formations are dissolved whenever it is beneficial to do so. The networks have learned how to effectively position and move agents for the emergence of group formation during and after training. This proves that grouping provides greater protection against opponents. We confirmed that local behavior of an individual can conspire to determine very complex global behaviors of multi-agent systems.

References

1. Balch, T., Arkin, R.C.: Behavior-based formation control for multirobot teams. IEEE Trans. Robot. Autom. **14**(6), 926–939 (1998)
2. Barfoot, T.D., Clark, C.M.: Motion planning for formations of mobile robots. Robot. Autonom. Syst. **46**(2), 65–78 (2004)
3. Buşoniu, L., Babuška, R., De Schutter, B.: Multi-agent reinforcement learning: an overview. In: Srinivasan, D., Jain L.C. (eds) Innovations in Multi-Agent Systems and Applications - 1, Studies in Computational Intelligence, vol 310, Springer, Heidelberg (2010). https://doi.org/10.1007/978-3-642-14435-6_7
4. Desai, J.P., Ostrowski, J., Kumar, V.: Controlling formations of multiple mobile robots. In: Proceedings 1998 IEEE International Conference on Robotics and Automation (Cat. No.98CH36146), vol. 4, pp. 2864–2869. May 1998
5. Diallo, E.A.O., Sugiyama, A., Sugawara, T.: Learning to coordinate with deep reinforcement learning in doubles pong game. In: 16th IEEE International Conference on Machine Learning and Applications (ICMLA), pp. 14–19. Dec 2017
6. Mnih, V., et al.: Human-level control through deep reinforcement learning. Nature **518**(7540), 529 (2015)
7. Nathan, A., Barbosa, V.C.: V-like formations in flocks of artificial birds. CoRR abs/cs/0611032 (2006). http://arxiv.org/abs/cs/0611032

8. Rana, O.F., Stout, K.: What is scalability in multi-agent systems? In: Proceedings of the Fourth International Conference on Autonomous Agents, pp. 56–63. AGENTS 2000, ACM, New York (2000)
9. Reynolds, C.W.: Flocks, herds and schools: a distributed behavioral model. In: ACM SIGGRAPH Computer Graphics, vol. 21, pp. 25–34. ACM (1987)
10. Sukhbaatar, S., Szlam, A., Fergus, R.: Learning multiagent communication with backpropagation. In: NIPS (2016)
11. Van Hasselt, H., Guez, A., Silver, D.: Deep reinforcement learning with double Q-learning. AAAI **16**, 2094–2100 (2016)
12. Wooldridge, M.: An Introduction to Multiagent Systems. John Wiley & Sons, Hoboken (2009)

Personalization of Health Interventions Using Cluster-Based Reinforcement Learning

Ali el Hassouni[1(✉)], Mark Hoogendoorn[1], Martijn van Otterlo[2], and Eduardo Barbaro[3]

[1] Department of Computer Science, Vrije Universiteit Amsterdam, Amsterdam, The Netherlands
{a.el.hassouni,m.hoogendoorn}@vu.nl
[2] Department of Artificial Intelligence, Tilburg University, Tilburg, The Netherlands
m.vanotterlo@uvt.nl
[3] Mobiquity Inc., Amsterdam, The Netherlands
ebarbaro@mobiquityinc.com

Abstract. Research has shown that personalization of health interventions can contribute to an improved effectiveness. Reinforcement learning algorithms can be used to perform such tailoring. In this paper, we present a cluster-based reinforcement learning approach which learns optimal policies for groups of users. Such an approach can speed up the learning process while still giving a level of personalization. We apply both online and batch learning to learn policies over the clusters and introduce a publicly available simulator which we have developed to evaluate the approach. The results show batch learning significantly outperforms online learning. Furthermore, near-optimal clustering is found which proves to be beneficial in learning significantly better policies compared to learning per user and learning across all users.

Keywords: Reinforcement learning · Personalization · m-Health

1 Introduction

Within the health domain, an ever increasing amount of data originating from a variety of sources is being collected about people's health state and behavior. Smart devices not only allow for the collection of data, but can also be used to provide interventions to users directly. One-size-fits-all solutions, where each user gets the same intervention, have been shown less effective compared to more personalized approaches that tailor interventions to (groups of) users (see e.g. [3]). The data collected from the users can help to establish this personalization.

A challenging aspect of intervention personalization is that success is often not immediately clear and that interventions are composed of *sequences* of actions that should act in harmony, and thus reinforcement learning (RL) (see

© Springer Nature Switzerland AG 2018
T. Miller et al. (Eds.): PRIMA 2018, LNAI 11224, pp. 467–475, 2018.
https://doi.org/10.1007/978-3-030-03098-8_31

e.g. [9]) arises as a very natural solution (cf. [2]). RL typically requires a substantial learning period before a suitable policy is found. In our setting, we do not have a sufficiently long learning period per user. Hence, there is a need to substantially shorten the learning period. To establish this, we can either: (1) start with an existing model (transfer learning, see e.g. [7]) or (2) pool data from multiple users who are, in some way, similar to learn policies (cf. [10]).

In this paper, we present a cluster-based RL algorithm which builds on top of the work done by [10] and test it for a complex health setting using a dedicated simulator we have built. We use K-Medoids clustering with Dynamic Time Warping (DTW) [1] as the distance function to find suitable clusters. We learn policies over the clusters using both an online RL algorithm (Q-learning, cf. [8]) and a batch-algorithm (LSPI. cf. [4]). We compare the cluster-based approach to learning a single policy across all users and learning completely individualized policies. The aforementioned simulation environment generates realistic user data for a health setting. Here, the aim is to coach users towards a more active lifestyle. In comparison with [10], our approach relies on a more sophisticated and complex simulation environment where several types of users are simulated with each their own behavioral profile and personal preferences which allows for highly personalized policies. Furthermore, we apply clustering using a state-of-the-art distance metric to learn optimal policies for clusters of users. Also, the stochasticity in the behavior of users makes the simulation environment a very robust testbed for RL algorithms.

2   Approach

Generally, we want to learn an *intervention strategy* for many types of *users*, without knowing beforehand which types of users exist, how they differ behaviorally, and how they react differently to interventions. We employ RL to optimize our system by *experimenting* with different intervention strategies.

Users and Interventions. Let U be the set of *users*. We see each user $u \in U$ as a *control problem* modeled as a *Markov decision process* [9] $M_u = \langle S_u, I, T_u, R_u \rangle$, where S_u is a finite set of *states* the user u can be in, I is the set of possible interventions (*actions*) for u, $T_u :: S_u \times I \times S_u \to [0,1]$ is a probabilistic *transition function* over u's states S_u, and $R_u :: S_u \times I \to \mathbb{R}$ is a *reward function* assigning reward $r = R_u(s_u, i)$ to each state $s_u \in S_u$ and action $i \in I$.

The user's state set S_u consists of the *observable* features of the user state. In general, we cannot observe *all* relevant features of the true underlying user state s_{true} and S_u is therefore restricted to measurable aspects, modeled through a set of *basis functions* over a state $s_u \in S_u$. That is, we use the feature vector representation $\phi(s_u) = \langle \phi_1(s_u), \phi_2(s_u), \ldots, \phi_n(s_u) \rangle^\top$ of the state $s_u \in S$ of user u as representation. If there is no confusion we will use s_u instead of $\phi(s_u)$. The transition function T_u, which determines how a user $u \in U$ moves from state $s_u \in S_u$ to $s'_u \in S_u$ due to action $i \in I$, is not accessible from the viewpoint of the RL algorithm, a natural assumption when dealing with real human users. In

Sect. 3, we do show how we have implemented it for the artificial users in our simulator. The granularity of modeling T_u can be set based on the case at hand, ranging from seconds to hours, denoted by Δt. Finally, the reward function R_u determines the goal of optimization and is explained in more detail in 4.

Every time point a user u is in some state $s_u \in S$, the system chooses an intervention $i \in I$, upon which the user enters a new state s'_u, receiving a reward r. Note that for both the transition and reward function it is unknown whether they can be considered *Markov*, and thus whether the user can be controlled as an MDP. Nevertheless, we assume it is close enough such that we can employ standard RL algorithms. With a state that is Markov we can make predictions of future states using only the current state. Note also that all users share the same state representation, but can differ in R_u and T_u. An alternative strategy would be to *learn* the dynamics of T_u and R_u from experience as in *model-based* RL (e.g. see [6]), but here we focus on learning them *implicitly* by clustering users who are similar in their behavior (and thus T_u and R_u).

Evaluating and Learning Interventions. The goal is to learn intervention strategies, or *policies*, for all users. For any user $u \in U$, $\pi :: S_u \to I$ specifies the intervention for user u in state s_u. The intervention $i = \pi(s_u)$ will cause user u to transition to a new state s'_u and a reward $r = R_u(s_u, i)$ is obtained, resulting in the *experience* $\langle s_u, i, r, s'_u \rangle$. A sequence of experiences for user u can be compactly represented as $\langle s_u, i, r, s'_u, i', r', s''_u, i'', r'', \ldots \rangle$ and is called a *trace* for user u. For the sake of simplicity we will drop the user subscript if possible. To compare policies, we look at the *expected reward* they receive in the long run, represented by so-called Q-functions. For Q-learning, we optimize the policy using the standard formulation of a Q-learning approach (see e.g. [6]). Note that for all users U together one Q-function is learned. In addition, we use variants of *experience replay* [5] which amounts to performing additional updates by "replaying" experienced traces backwards to propagate rewards quicker. In our setting, we sample the experience pairs in chronological order instead of random. Using disjoint experience pairs would have been the better alternative if the set of traces we learn from was larger.

In our second method, LSPI, we employ the basis function representation $\phi(s)$ of a state and compute a *linear function approximation* of the Q-function, $\hat{Q} = \sum_{j=1}^{k} \phi(s) w_k$, from a batch of experiences E. Here, $\boldsymbol{w} = \langle w_1, \ldots, w_k \rangle$ consists of tunable *weights*. LSPI implements an approximate version of standard *policy iteration* (cf. [6]) by alternating a *policy evaluation step* and a *policy improvement step*. However, due to the linear approximation, the evaluation step can be computed by representing the batch of experiences in matrix form and using them to find an optimal weight vector $\boldsymbol{w}$.

Two Learning Phases. For any given set of users we define two optimization phases. In the first phase (*warm-up*) we employ a default policy π_{def} (see the experimental section for details) to generate traces for each user, and use all experiences of all users to compute $Q^{\pi_{\text{def}}}$. By maximization we obtain a better policy π' that is used at the start of the second phase (*learning*). During this phase we iteratively apply the policy to obtain experiences and update our Q-function (and policy) using either Q-learning or LSPI. In this phase some exploration is used, reducing the amount of exploration ϵ over time.

Cluster-Based Policy Improvement. So far, we have assumed all users belong to one group. Our main hypothesis is that since users have different (but unknown) transition and reward functions, learning one general policy for all users will not be optimal. To remedy this, we add a clustering step after the warm-up phase. We employ K-Medoids clustering and by employing DTW instead of a default Euclidean distance, we can also measure similarity when two users are out of phase. The traces that are used here contain the states and rewards. Matching two traces needs to satisfy constraints: (1) every data point from the trace of the first user has to be matched with at least one data point from the trace of the second user and vice versa, (2) the first (and last) data point from the trace of the first user has to be matched with that of the second user, and (3) the mapping of the data points from the trace of the first user to those of the second user must increase monotonically. We split user traces by day and deploy DTW to calculate the optimal match.

Let U be the set of users targeted in the warm-up phase, and Σ^U the set of all traces generated. Let $\Sigma^{u_i,m}$ be user i's experiences during day m, excluding the interventions. The similarity between users u_1 and u_2 is defined:

$$S_{DTW}(u_1, u_2) = \sum_{m=0}^{M} DTW(\Sigma^{u_1,m}, \Sigma^{u_2,m}) \tag{1}$$

Let the number of resulting clusters be k and $\Sigma_1^U, \ldots, \Sigma_k^U$ be the partitioning of Σ^U, and let $U_1, \ldots U_k$ be the partitioning of U. Instead of utilizing all experiences of U for one Q-function, we now induce a separate Q-function $Q_{\Sigma_i^U}$ (and corresponding policy $\pi_{\Sigma_i^U}$) for each user set U_i based on the traces in Σ_i^U and continue with learning and performance phases for each subgroup individually.

3   Simulator

In our health setting applying RL directly to real users would be prohibited by the number of interaction samples required to learn good strategies. We therefore built a simulator to experiment with algorithmic settings first.

3.1   Schedules

We assume that we have n users in our simulator: $\{u_1, \ldots, u_n\}$, originating from the set U as defined before. Each of these users can conduct one of m activities at each time point ($\{\varphi_1, \ldots, \varphi_m\}$). Time points in our simulator have a discrete step size δt. Let Φ denote the possible values of the activity. Example activities are working, sleeping, working out, and eating breakfast. Each user has a unique activity that is being conducted at a time point $t \in T$ ($activity : A \times T \rightarrow \Phi$). Note that this activity can also be *none*. For each user, a *template* schedule can be specified, which expresses for each activity φ_i: (i) an early and late start time ($early\_start(\varphi_i)$ and $late\_start(\varphi_i)$), (ii) a minimum and maximum duration of the activity ($min\_duration(\varphi_i)$ and $max\_duration(\varphi_i)$), (iii) a standard deviation of the duration of the activity ($sd\_duration(\varphi_i)$), (iv) a probability per day of performing the activity ($p(\varphi_i, day)$), and (v) priorities of other activities over this activity. Using these template schedules, a complete schedule is derived which instantiates activities at each time point, on a per day basis.

3.2 Interventions and Rewards

Besides performing activities during a day, interventions can also be sent to users. In our system, the set of interventions I contains a binary action as $\{yes, no\}$, representing at each decision moment whether the system sends an intervention or not. Acceptance of a message is determined by conditions in the user's profile. If a message is sent at the right time and a gap in the schedule is between t_{plan_min} and $t_{plan\_min} + t_{plan\_duration}$ from the time the message is sent, the activity will be performed. These parameters define a time window in the schedule into which the users will try to fit the desired activity.

4 Experimental Setup

As said, we focus on a health setting where learning a policy as fast as possible (i.e. based on limited experiences) is essential. Within this paper, we aim to answer the following questions: **RQ1** *How do batch and online learning in our simulator setting differ, and how can generalization be employed to speed up learning?*, **RQ2** *Can a cluster-based RL algorithm learn faster compared to (1) learning per individual user or (2) learning across all users at once?*, and **RQ3** *Can we effectively cluster users based on traces of their states and rewards?*

Simulator Setup. In our simulator setup, we aim to improve the amount of physical activity of users. We include several types of users. More specifically, we employ three *prototypical users*, referred to as the *workaholic*, the *sporter* (an avid athlete), and the *retiree*. The simulator itself runs on a fine-grained time scale (δt is one second) while we model T_u at a coarser granularity (Δt is one hour). We include the following activities: *sleep, breakfast, lunch, dinner, work, workout*. We use three profiles with $n = 33$ agents each from which daily activities are spawned with some level of variability per agent.

The goal of the scenario is to make sure the total work out time meets the guideline for the amount of daily physical activity (30 min per day). Messages can be sent to the user to start working out. The acceptance of the message is dependent on the planning horizon of the user and whether it fits into the schedule where the workaholic needs to know long in advance, the retiree works with a short advance notice and the sporter is right in the middle. In addition, acceptance windows are defined (during lunch for workers (with probability 0.7), outside of lunch for retiree (0.5) and anytime for sporters (0.9)). How long the workout activity will be performed is defined in the profile of the user *Fatigue* plays a role here. Fatigue can build up when working out across multiple days. The value of fatigue is the number of times a user worked out in total during a consecutive number of days where at least one workout per day occurred.

Algorithm Setup. As features for the state (i.e. $\phi(s_u)$) we use: (i) the current time (hours), (ii) the current week day (0-6), (iii) whether the user has already worked out today (binary), (iv) fatigue level (numerical), and (v) which activities were performed in the last hour (six binary features). All these features are realistically observable through sensor information, or inferable.

The reward function R_u consists of three components. If an intervention is sent and the user accepts it, the immediate reward is $+1$ (otherwise -1). A second reward component is obtained while the user is exercising, where the exact reward value is scaled relative to the length of the exercise ($+0$ per Δt) and when the user finishes exercising ($+10$). A third component is related to the fatigue level of the agent at each hour of the day: higher levels result in a small negative reward (-0.1 per unit of fatigue per hour) which *shape* the intervention strategy such that it does not overstimulate the user with exercises.

The first part of a simulation run is a *warm-up* phase of seven days where interventions are driven by a *default policy* which sends one intervention per day to each user at random between 9:00 h and 21:00 h. This allows us to perform exploration and to generate traces for clustering.

The second part of a simulation run is the *learning phase* that lasts for 100 days. Immediately after the start of this phase we update the Q-table and learn LSPI policies using the traces generated during the warm-up phase. During the *learning phase* we perform updates to Q-table once every hour and update the LSPI policies at the end of each day. For Q learning and LSPI we use $\gamma = 0.95$, and $\epsilon = 0.05$ and 0.01 resp. and the learning rate α for Q-learning decreases from an initial 0.2 with 1% every day. These parameters have been set using grid search for γ between 0.85 and 0.95 with step size 0.05, ϵ between 0 and 0.05 with step size 0.05 and α was fixed at 0.2 with a 1% decrease rate every day. For LSPI the maximum number of iterations was set at 20 with a threshold of the change in policy weights as a stopping criterion of 0.00001 and we use a *first win* tie breaking strategy. We initialize the Q-values with a random value between 0 and 1 if the action of the state-action pair is 0 otherwise we initialize the Q-values with a random number between -1 and 0, all to encourage exploration. To speed up the learning we use experience replay. We store the last 250 experiences and use these to update the Q-values.

Setup of Runs. To answer our research questions, we run several simulations. First, we vary the type of RL algorithm: online (Q-learning) and batch learning

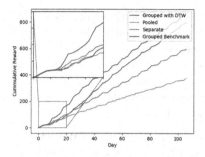

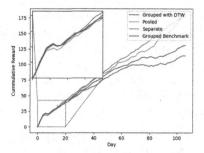

Fig. 1. Cumulative reward LSPI   **Fig. 2.** Cumulative reward Q Learning

(LSPI); this enables us to answer *RQ1*. For each type of algorithm, we compare runs where we learn a single policy across all users (*pooled approach*) to a *cluster-based* approach and learning a completely individualized policy for each user (*separate approach*). This variation reflects *RQ2*. For each algorithm we do two simulation runs for the cluster-based approach; one simulation run using K-Medoids clustering with the DTW distance (*cluster-based approach*) and a second simulation run using three homogeneous clusters, one for each type of agent (*grouped benchmark approach*). The latter provides us with a benchmark to evaluate the cluster quality (i.e. *RQ3*). Hence, in total we perform eight runs.

5 Results

Batch versus Online Learning: Figures 1 and 2 demonstrate that LSPI significantly outperforms Q-learning when we compare the average daily reward over the 100 days. Significance has been tested using a Wilcoxon Signed-Rank test with a significance level of 0.05. The Q-learning experiments show that online (table-based) learning without generalizing over states is not capable of learning reasonable policies in a period of 100 days. LSPI on the other hand, generalizes over states and utilizes the relatively short amount of interaction much better. This is not a surprise, but it does confirm that generalization – over the experiences of multiple agents, but also over states – is needed to obtain reasonable policies in "human-scale" interaction time (and thus answers RQ1).

Different Learning Approaches: The grouped benchmark approach with LSPI provided us with a policy that outperformed all other policies in this setting. The grouped approach using clustering with DTW was the second best performing approach. The separate approach has the ability to match the performance of the grouped benchmark approach given enough time to learn. At the same time the grouped approach clearly outperformed the pooled approach which indicates that clustering helps us learn better policies in a shorter amount of time, by generalizing over the *groups* of agents. With the cluster-based approach we are able to speed up the learning time in comparison with the pooled approach to potentially reach better policies. The policies that were produced by

Q-learning show little variation in terms of performance resulting from the different learning approaches. On the contrary, LSPI produces policies learned using the same approaches that are significantly different among each other (Wilcoxon Signed-Rank test, 0.05 significance). Although Q-learning shows little differences across the setups, an interesting observation is that clustering using knowledge about the profiles of the users performs slightly worse in terms of average daily reward than the remaining approach while using Q-learning.

Clustering: Clustering with the K-Medoids algorithm and the DTW distance metric for LSPI is clearly near-optimal. Two users of the type *retiree* were confused as the type *sporter* and one *sporter* was put together with the *workaholics* in the same cluster. For the Q-learning case similar patterns were observed.

6   Discussion

In this paper, we have introduced steps towards a cluster-based RL approach for personalization of health interventions. Based on the results we can say that: **RQ1:** RL with batch learning and function approximation outperforms table-based RL using online learning in a significant way, thereby disqualifying the latter when interaction time is short. **RQ2:** A cluster-based RL can learn a significantly better policy within 100 days compared to learning per user and learning across all users, provided that a suitable clustering is found. **RQ3:** Learning suitable clusters using the Dynamic Time Warping distance function and K-Medoids clustering based on traces of states and rewards over 7 days shows to be very feasible, resulting in a near perfect clustering. While our simulator exhibits realistic behavior, we plan on moving more and more to a setting where the actual user is in the loop. Furthermore, from a methodological side, we aim to experiment with more powerful RL techniques, and we want to explore different clustering algorithms and more distance metrics to improve the clustering itself.

References

1. Berndt, D.J., Clifford, J.: Using dynamic time warping to find patterns in time series. In: Proceedings of the 3rd International Conference on Knowledge Discovery and Data Mining, pp. 359–370 (1994)
2. Hoogendoorn, M., Funk, B.: Machine Learning for the Quantified Self: On the Art of Learning from Sensory Data. Springer, New York City (2017). https://doi.org/10.1007/978-3-319-66308-1
3. Kranzler, H.R., McKay, J.R.: Personalized treatment of alcohol dependence. Curr. Psychiatry Rep. **14**(5), 486–493 (2012)
4. Lagoudakis, M.G., Parr, R.: Least-squares policy iteration. J. Mach. Learn. Res. **4**(Dec), 1107–1149 (2003)
5. Lin, L.J.: Self-improving reactive agents based on reinforcement learning, planning and teaching. Mach. Learn. **8**(3–4), 293–321 (1992)
6. Sutton, R.S., Barto, A.G.: Reinforcement Learning: An Introduction, 2nd edn. MIT press, Cambridge (2017). in progress

7. Taylor, M.E., Stone, P.: Transfer learning for reinforcement learning domains: a survey. J. Mach. Learn. Res. **10**(Jul), 1633–1685 (2009)
8. Watkins, C.J., Dayan, P.: Q-learning. Mach. learn. **8**(3–4), 279–292 (1992)
9. Wiering, M., van Otterlo, M.: Reinforcement Learning: State of the Art. Springer, Heidelberg (2012). https://doi.org/10.1007/978-3-642-27645-3
10. Zhu, F., Guo, J., Xu, Z., Liao, P., Huang, J.: Group-driven reinforcement learning for personalized mHealth intervention (2017). arXiv preprint arXiv:1708.04001

Using Generative Adversarial Networks to Develop a Realistic Human Behavior Simulator

Ali el Hassouni[1]([✉]), Mark Hoogendoorn[1], and Vesa Muhonen[2]

[1] Department of Computer Science, Vrije Universiteit Amsterdam,
Amsterdam, The Netherlands
{a.el.hassouni,m.hoogendoorn}@vu.nl
[2] Mobiquity Inc., Amsterdam, The Netherlands
vmuhonen@mobiquityinc.com

Abstract. Simulation environments have proven to be very useful as testbeds for reinforcement learning (RL) algorithms. For settings where an actual human user is involved, these simulation environments allow one to test out the suitability of new RL approaches without having to include real users at first. It obviously does require the simulator to have a certain degree of realism, however, realistic simulators for the behavior of humans in the health domain are rarely seen. To generate realistic behavior, the simulator could be driven by data from real users, but this might lead to privacy issues. In this paper, we propose to use Generative Adversarial Networks (GANs) for generating realistic simulation environments. In this first step, we use an existing simulator that simulates daily activities of users and the GANs are used to generate realistic sensory data that accompanies such activities. After training, the original (potentially privacy sensitive) data can be thrown away and the simulator can simply be driven by the GAN models. Results show that a model trained on real data shows similar performance on the data artificially generated by the GAN.

Keywords: Simulation · Generative adversarial networks
Reinforcement learning · Deep learning · e-Health

1 Introduction

Applications of RL rely on the notion of sequential decision making [2]. The goal is to learn optimal policies for selecting actions that maximize long-term reward. Consequently, the effectiveness of such learned policies only become apparent in the long run. Hence, lengthy experiments are needed to generate suitable policies. Simulation environments give researchers the ability to develop and rigorously test novel RL algorithms and methods and generate policies before applying them in a real-world setting. Recent developments in RL rely heavily on simulation environments as testbeds for the algorithms [12].

© Springer Nature Switzerland AG 2018
T. Miller et al. (Eds.): PRIMA 2018, LNAI 11224, pp. 476–483, 2018.
https://doi.org/10.1007/978-3-030-03098-8_32

In the domain of e-Health, the focus of this paper, RL algorithms are the appropriate choice for solving sequential decision problems such as sending interventions to improve the health state of users. The application of RL algorithms in e-Health has been limited by data availability, data reliability, and privacy constraints. It could clearly benefit from a suitable simulation environment. Currently, however, none are available that include a realistic simulation of human behavior. Due to discrepancies between the simulation environments and the real world, the newly developed algorithms shown to work well in simulation, or even policies learned in such simulations, can perform poorly in real-life settings [4]. On that account, simulation environments should be based on actual data to minimize the gap between simulation and reality. However, sharing this data might lead to privacy issues if the environment is to be made available to the community, which clearly is highly desirable.

In this paper, we propose to exploit GANs to develop behavioral models that mimic human behavior as an approach to take simulation environments for e-Health to the next level. This paper presents a first step in this endeavor: we focus on GANs that are able to generate sensory values that mimic those of real humans. We show that we can employ these techniques to develop models that learn from real-world sensory data to synthesize realistic sensory data for human behavior, a crucial first step in the development of a simulation environment for this domain as e-Health applications are often driven by sensory data of users. The approach can also help to remedy privacy issues: we use privacy-sensitive data in a secure environment once to generate the GAN models, and can then share the resulting model with the community as it no longer contains the real users' data. We embed the GANs into an existing simulation environment (cf. [7]) that we extend and make more mature. This simulator focuses on a health setting where users conduct certain activities and adapt their activities based on interventions. To evaluate the performance of our generative models and show that we meet the required level of realism, we use an activity recognition model that can classify human activity from raw sensory input, which is known to be highly accurate (cf. [3]) and observe the difference in performance on the real and artificially generated data. All the above-mentioned models make use of the Long Short-Term Memory networks (LSTMs) [8] or variations thereof.

This paper is organized as follows. In Sect. 2 we present related work, while Sect. 3 explains our simulation environment. Section 4 details how we use GANs to generate behavior in the simulation environment. Section 5 describes the experimental setup, and the results are presented in Sect. 6. Finally, we present our conclusions.

2   Related Work

Limited work has been done in relation to generating realistic data related to human behavior for simulation environments using GANs. [11] argues that access to sensory data can be very beneficial in the area of e-Health for tasks such as health monitoring and activity recognition. They also argue that this type of data is very sensitive and contains information that needs to be protected. They propose an approach using a replacement autoencoder along with a GAN to remedy this. With the approach, they preserve the privacy of the data while simultaneously allowing for the usage of realistic sensory data. Alzantot *et al.* [1] used GANs to synthesize accelerometer data from mobile phones. They showed that realistic accelerometer data can be generated using LSTM and Mixture Density networks. The results presented by this work are promising and shows that these methods can be very effective given a large set of training data. Tseng *et al.* [13] use RL in combination with a simulation in the health domain using GANs. They used deep RL techniques to develop automated radiation protocols for patients with lung cancer. Historical treatment plans where used to learn these protocols. They use a GAN to learn the characteristics of the patients from a relatively small dataset and use it to generate more data. This is required to make learning with deep RL viable. Secondly, they use a deep neural network to reconstruct an artificial environment for radiotherapy. They do this using both the original data as well as the synthetic data.

3   Simulation Environment

Generally, we want to simulate the real-world process of artificial people (users) performing activities over time. These users generate experiences that can be used by an RL driven agent to learn optimal policies. These policies are used to make decisions at fixed points in time. The decisions that have to be made are related to sending a specific intervention to a certain user. In this paper, we further develop upon an earlier version of the simulation environment [7]. Figure 1 provides an illustration of this system. The environment API is a communication layer that allows the learning agents to send interventions to the users and observe data about these users (i.e. the state). This observed data is used to learn optimal policies and use these policies to make decisions.

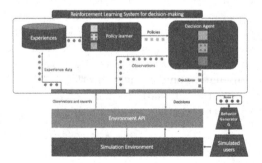

Fig. 1. Simulation environment for RL algorithms in the e-Health domain.

Let us turn a bit more formal. We define U as the set of *users* and assume we have n users in our simulation environment: $\{u_1, \ldots, u_n\}$. Each user can perform an activity out of a set of m activities Φ ($\Phi = \{\varphi_1, \ldots, \varphi_m\}$). Examples of activities are sleeping, eating, working and working out. The simulation environment runs in ticks, these are discrete steps of size δt. Users perform one unique activity at any certain time point t of a simulation run ($activity : A \times T \rightarrow \Phi$). When a user is not performing an activity (idle) we denote the activity with (*none*). In short, a simulation run is a sequence of unique mappings of the activities space onto time points in T. Users generate sequences of experiences $\langle s_u, i, r, s'_u, i', r', \dots \rangle$ where at every time point δt, the observable state of user $u \in U$ is denoted by $s_u \in S$, the intervention by $i \in I$ and the observed scalar reward drawn from the reward function R_u by r.

In parallel, a learning and decision-making system is ticking along with the simulation environment. The learning and decision making system interacts with the simulation environment and has partial observability of the states. Furthermore, this system can influence the environment through interventions that are sent to users in the simulation environment. The learning system uses the observed experiences to learn optimal policies. Furthermore, it uses the observations to make decisions about intervening using the learned policies and models.

User schedules are based on generic profiles that specify what activities users perform, including a certain variability. Furthermore, user schedules are adjusted based on the current schedule and responses of the user to an intervention. For each user, a template schedule is created at the start of each day. This schedule denotes the different activities the user will perform during that day. For each activity φ_i, several parameter values are specified, see [7] for more details.

Once activities are generated in the simulator, it is possible to generate the proper observations for the RL algorithm (i.e. the observable state of the user s_u). In this case, we assume that we cannot directly observe the activities, but only their accompanying sensor values. As mentioned in the beginning, we use GANs to generate appropriate values for these activities. How we do this will be explained in the next section, which is the main contribution of this paper. The rewards can be defined based on these observations.

4   Using GANs to Generate Sensor Data

Generative Adversarial Networks. GANs [6] are a class of algorithms with two neural networks, a generator, and a discriminator, that are competing in a zero-sum game. The generator, denoted by G, generates samples $x = G(z; \Theta^{(G)})$. Here z denotes random noise and $\Theta^{(G)}$ the weights of the network. The adversary of the generator, the discriminator D, has the task of distinguishing between sequences sampled from the training data and sequences generated by the generative network. The discriminator generates a probability, denoted by $D(x; \Theta^{(D)})$, indicating whether the sequence is a real example drawn from the training data or whether it is a sequence generated by the generator network.

Long-Short Term Memory Networks. We employ GANs to generate sequences of accelerometer data. Gated Recurrent neural networks are the most effective sequence models used in practical applications of deep learning techniques [5]. Given that the sequences of sensory data are of highly temporal nature we deploy LSTM networks, a type of network falling under the Gated Recurrent Neural Networks category.

Dataset. To develop a GAN that generates realistic sensory data, we need a realistic dataset. We use the WISDM dataset [10] for this purpose. This data is known as the Wireless Sensor Data Mining dataset and consists of labeled 3D accelerometer data (x, y, and z) from real people captured while they performed several activities humans engage in on a daily basis. There are 6 activities included in this dataset and these are climbing stairs (upstairs and downstairs), jogging, sitting, standing and walking.

5   Experiments

The main goal of this paper is to show that we can generate realistic human data using GANs. In our experiments, we focus on evaluating to what extent the data that is generated differs from real data. This is our performance criterion: that an independent model is not able to distinguish between the real and generated data. Below, we detail how each of the components is set up.

5.1   Activity Classifier Setup

As a first step, we started out with the development of a classifier for daily human activities which acts as the aforementioned independent model. The sequence length is 160 data points which amount to 8 s worth of data. As a preprocessing step, segments of length 160 data points were created with a shifting window of 20 data points. The segments were labeled with the activities that occurred at that moment. 80% of the WISDM data was randomly selected for training and 20% of the data was used for testing. An LSTM network with 2 hidden layers was used. Each hidden layer has 64 hidden units. ReLu activation was used along with a forget bias of 1 for the hidden layer. For the output layer, Softmax activation was chosen along with a forget bias of 1. Softmax cross entropy with logits with L2 regularization of 0.0015 was used as the cost function. Adam optimizer with a learning rate of 0.0025 was selected. The batch size during training is 1024. The choice of algorithm, network architecture and parameters selected were based on [3] and [9].

5.2   Generative Adversarial Network Setup

For training the GAN, we use the Adam optimizer with a learning rate of 0.1 with a learning rate decay of 1e-10, a clip value of 1, β_1 of 0.5 and β_2 of 0.55. We use a batch size of 24 for the real data and 1 for the synthetic data. Binary cross entropy is used as the loss function and the accuracy is used as the metric of choice. We describe further details about the generator and the discriminator in the next two sections. The parameters selection and network architectures were chosen based on inspiration from different existing work in the area of generative adversarial networks [1,11]. During initial experiments, we employed a grid search between different optimizers (SGD, Adam, and RMSprop) and activation functions (tanh, sigmoid, linear and ReLu). The best performing combinations were selected and are described below.

Generator. For the generator, we use a deep neural network that contains 1 hidden layer and one output layer. The hidden layer is an LSTM layer with 64 hidden units. We use a dropout rate of 0.5 for this layer along with a tanh activation function and hard-sigmoid as the recurrent activation function. The output layer is a fully connected layer with 3 output neurons (x, y, and z). The activation function is the linear activation function. The Adam optimizer with identical parameters to the ones selected for the GAN is used.

Discriminator. The discriminator is a deep neural network of 2 hidden layers and 1 output layer. The first hidden layer is an LSTM layer with 32 hidden units, a dropout rate of 0.5 along with a tanh activation function and hard sigmoid as the recurrent activation function. The second hidden layer is a fully connected layer of 16 hidden neurons with a linear activation function and a dropout rate of 0.5. The output layer is a fully connected layer with one neuron and the tanh activation function. We use SGD as the optimizer with a learning rate of 0.01, a learning rate decay of 1e-6, a momentum of 0.8 and Nesterov accelerated gradient descent. Binary cross entropy was selected as the loss function and the accuracy is used as the metric for tracking the accuracy of the model.

6   Results

6.1   Activity Classifier

Our results demonstrate that we can classify daily human activities with an accuracy of 97.33% on the test set when using the independent classifier. These results show that the training accuracy is slightly higher than the test accuracy while the training loss is slightly lower than the test loss. The model stabilizes after 40 epochs. The results also show that the algorithm misclassified a relatively large number of samples from the activities Downstairs as Upstairs and vice versa and Sitting as Standing. The activities Jogging, Standing, and Walking have the highest accuracies.

6.2   Generative Adversarial Networks

To validate the performance of the generated sequences for the activities, we rely on the independent activity classifier we developed earlier. Figure 2 shows the probabilities that the generated sequences belong to any of the 6 activities over time. The classifier classifies the generated Jogging sequences from the beginning as either Walking or Jogging. Downstairs and Upstairs also occur with relatively smaller probabilities. The probabilities for Standing and Sitting are low in comparison with all other activities.

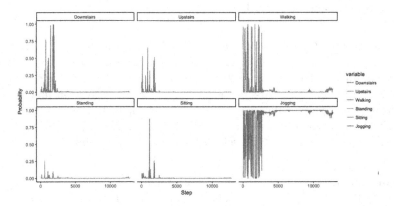

Fig. 2. Validating the generated data using the activity recognition classifier.

Table 1 presents for each activity the iteration at which the GAN could be considered as converged and the average classification accuracy for 500 iterations after convergence using the independent classifier. The activities Jogging, Walking and Downstairs are classified by the classifier with the highest average accuracies. Upstairs, Standing and Sitting have significantly lower accuracies but are higher than random classification.

Table 1. Overview of the performance of the generator for different activities.

	Jogging	Walking	Downstairs	Upstairs	Standing	Sitting
Convergence iteration	3000	3200	7800	15475	2000	1180
Average prob classification	0.97	0.85	0.89	0.20	0.07	0.21

7   Conclusion

In this paper, we have introduced the first steps towards a realistic simulator for health settings. Realistic simulators are needed as testbeds for RL algorithms because of lack of data and inability to experiment extensively with real users during the development phase of the algorithms. We present an approach whereby existing data generated by real users is used to develop a GAN for synthesizing human behavior. GANs allows us to solve data privacy issues as well. In this first case, the generative model generates sensory data belonging to activities a simulated user is performing at a certain point in time. Our results show that we can employ GANs to develop generative models that learn from actual data to generate sensory data belonging to behaviors of users. We validate our approach using an activity recognition classifier that was trained and tested on a real dataset. The number of training iterations and training samples needed to develop an accurate generative model prove to be in the magnitude of a few thousand to a few ten thousands.

References

1. Alzantot, M., Chakraborty, S., Srivastava, M.B.: SenseGen: a deep learning architecture for synthetic sensor data generation. In: 2017 IEEE International Conference on Pervasive Computing and Communications Workshops (PerCom Workshops), pp. 188–193 (2017)
2. Barto, A.G., Sutton, R.S., Watkins, C.J.C.H.: Learning and sequential decision making. In: Learning and Computational Neuroscience, pp. 539–602. MIT Press (1989)
3. Chevalier, G.: LSTM human activity recognition (2017). https://github.com/guillaume-chevalier/LSTM-Human-Activity-Recognition
4. Christiano, P.F., et al.: Transfer from simulation to real world through learning deep inverse dynamics model. CoRR abs/1610.03518 (2016). http://arxiv.org/abs/1610.03518
5. Goodfellow, I., Bengio, Y., Courville, A.: Deep Learning. The MIT Press, Cambridge (2016)
6. Goodfellow, I., et al.: Generative adversarial nets. In: Advances in Neural Information Processing Systems, pp. 2672–2680 (2014)
7. El Hassouni, A., Hoogendoorn, M., van Otterlo, M., Barbaro, E.: Personalization of health interventions using cluster-based reinforcement learning. CoRR abs/1804.03592 (2018). http://arxiv.org/abs/1804.03592
8. Hochreiter, S., Schmidhuber, J.: Long short-term memory. Neural Comput. **9**(8), 1735–1780 (1997). https://doi.org/10.1162/neco.1997.9.8.1735
9. Hoogendoorn, M., Funk, B.: Machine Learning for the Quantified Self: On the Art of Learning from Sensory Data. Springer, Heidelberg (2017). https://doi.org/10.1007/978-3-319-66308-1
10. Kwapisz, J.R., Weiss, G.M., Moore, S.A.: Activity recognition using cell phone accelerometers. SIGKDD Explor. Newsl. **12**(2), 74–82 (2011). https://doi.org/10.1145/1964897.1964918
11. Malekzadeh, M., Clegg, R.G., Haddadi, H.: Replacement AutoEncoder: a privacy-preserving algorithm for sensory data analysis. In: 2018 IEEE/ACM Third International Conference on Internet-of-Things Design and Implementation (IoTDI), pp. 165–176, April 2018. https://doi.org/10.1109/IoTDI.2018.00025
12. Sutton, R.S., Barto, A.G.: Reinforcement Learning: An Introduction, vol. 1. MIT press, Cambridge (2018)
13. Tseng, H.H., Luo, Y., Cui, S., Chien, J.T., Ten Haken, R.K., Naqa, I.E.: Deep reinforcement learning for automated radiation adaptation in lung cancer. Med. Phys. **44**(12), 6690–6705 (2017)

A Deontic Argumentation Framework Based on Deontic Defeasible Logic

Guido Governatori[1(✉)], Antonino Rotolo[2(✉)], and Régis Riveret[1(✉)]

[1] Data61, CSIRO, Brisbane, Australia
{guido.governatori,regis.riveret}@csiro.au
[2] CIRSFID, University of Bologna, Bologna, Italy
antonino.rotolo@unibo.it

Abstract. Deontic Defeasible Logic (DDL) is a simple and computationally efficient approach for the representation of normative reasoning. Traditionally defeasible logics are defined proof theoretically based on the proof conditions for the logic. In this paper we present an argumentation system that corresponds to a variant of DDL. The resulting machinery is able to grasp in a natural way intuitions behind deontic reasoning with conditional norms featuring obligations, prohibitions, and (strong or weak) permissions.

Keywords: Argumentation · Deontic argumentation
Deontic Defeasible Logic

1 Introduction

Computational models of argument address defeasible claims raised on the basis of partial, uncertain and possibly conflicting pieces of information. Argumentation is pervasive in artificial intelligence, with many application domains [2].

Normative systems, and in particular legal systems, constitute a rich test bed and a major application domain for formal models of argument [13]. There, models of argument have applications ranging from case-based reasoning [14] to strategic studies in legal interactions [16, 17].

When representing and reasoning upon norms, deontic concepts such as obligation, prohibition and permission play a crucial role; and there exist some studies of deontic reasoning with formal models of argument, and a few argument-based models focus on (conditional) norms, deontic operators and their interplay [3, 4].

Besides these undertakings in deontic argumentation, many deontic formalisms have been previously designed [6]. Amongst formalisms with practical applications, DDL has been perhaps the most developed to represent and reason upon norms [8–10]. Moreover and interestingly, Defeasible Logic (DL) has possible interpretations in terms of arguments [7, 12, 15], but its deontic variants have received little or no consideration to construct argument-based frameworks

© Springer Nature Switzerland AG 2018
T. Miller et al. (Eds.): PRIMA 2018, LNAI 11224, pp. 484–492, 2018.
https://doi.org/10.1007/978-3-030-03098-8_33

for deontic reasoning. In this paper, we consider constructs from DDL to build a deontic argumentation system.

Contribution. Following the approach in DDL, we offer a rich formalism able to express relevant aspects of deontic reasoning, such as contrary-to-duty obligations and preferences about permissions. The deontic argumentation framework is described in the remainder of the paper.

2   Deontic Argumentation System

This section presents the deontic argumentation system. We first specify its language, then arguments are constructed. Eventually, the justification and rejection of arguments are defined.

2.1   Language

The following definitions provide the building blocks of our formalism:

- literals and modalities ;
- preference operators for obligations and permissions.
- constitutive and deontic rules.

The attention is restricted to a simple propositional language with atomic negation and supplemented with a set of deontic operators $\{O, P\}$ where O indicates an obligation, and P a permission.

Definition 1. *A literal is a **plain literal** iff it is an atomic proposition p or the negation of an atomic proposition, i.e., $\neg p$. A literal is a **deontic literal** iff it has either the form Ol or Pl or $\neg Ol$ or $\neg Pl$ where l is a plain literal. A literal is either a plain literal or a deontic literal.*

Notation 1. *Given a set of literals $\mathcal{L}$, the set of plain literals in $\mathcal{L}$ is denoted as $\mathrm{Lit}_{\mathcal{L}}$ and the set of modal literals as $\mathrm{ModLit}_{\mathcal{L}}$. However, in the remainder, the set of literals may be left implicit, and we may omit the subscript $\mathcal{L}$.*

We introduce two preference operators, $\otimes$ for obligations and $\odot$ for permissions. These operators are used to build chains of preferences, called $\otimes$- and $\odot$-expressions. Intuitively, an $\otimes$-expression such as $l_1 \otimes l_2 \otimes \ldots \otimes l_n$ indicates that the obligation that l_1 is preferred to the one that l_2, which is preferred to l_3 etc.

Definition 2. *Let $\oslash \in \{\otimes, \odot\}$. An $\oslash$-**expression** is defined as follows:*

1. *every literal $l \in \mathrm{Lit}$ is an $\oslash$-expression;*
2. *if A is an $\oslash$-expression and $c_1, \ldots, c_k \in \mathrm{Lit}$, then $A \oslash c_1 \oslash \cdots \oslash c_k$ is an $\oslash$-expression;*
3. *nothing else is an $\oslash$-expression.*

Notation 2. *Given a set of literals $\mathcal{L}$, the set of $\oslash$-expressions defined by $\mathcal{L}$ is denoted* $\mathrm{Pref}_{\oslash,\mathcal{L}}$ *or simply* $\mathrm{Pref}_{\oslash}$ *if $\mathcal{L}$ is left implicit.*

Definition 3. *Let Lbl be a set of arbitrary labels. A set of rules Rul is a **well-formed set of rules** over a set of literals $\mathcal{L}$ iff:*

$$Rul \subseteq (Rul_{\mathsf{d}}^{\mathsf{O}} \cup Rul_{\mathsf{d}}^{\mathsf{O}} \cup Rul_{\mathsf{d}}^{c}) \cup (Rul_{\mathsf{dft}}^{\mathsf{O}} \cup Rul_{\mathsf{dft}}^{c})$$

such that

$Rul_{\mathsf{d}}^{\mathsf{O}} = \{r : a_1, \dots, a_n \Rightarrow_{\mathsf{O}} b \mid r \in \mathrm{Lbl}, \{a_1, \dots, a_n\} \subseteq \mathrm{Lit} \cup \mathrm{ModLit}, b \in \mathrm{Pref}_{\otimes}\}$
$Rul_{\mathsf{d}}^{\mathsf{P}} = \{r : a_1, \dots, a_n \Rightarrow_{\mathsf{P}} b \mid r \in \mathrm{Lbl}, \{a_1, \dots, a_n\} \subseteq \mathrm{Lit} \cup \mathrm{ModLit}, b \in \mathrm{Pref}_{\odot}\}$
$Rul_{\mathsf{d}}^{c} = \{r : a_1, \dots, a_n \Rightarrow_{c} b \mid r \in \mathrm{Lbl}, \{a_1, \dots, a_n\} \subseteq \mathrm{Lit}, b \in \mathrm{Lit}\}$
$Rul_{\mathsf{dft}}^{\mathsf{O}} = \{r : a_1, \dots, a_n \rightsquigarrow_{\mathsf{O}} b \mid r \in \mathrm{Lbl}, \{a_1, \dots, a_n\} \subseteq \mathrm{Lit} \cup \mathrm{ModLit}, b \in \mathrm{Lit}\}$
$Rul_{\mathsf{dft}}^{c} = \{r : a_1, \dots, a_n \rightsquigarrow_{c} b \mid r \in \mathrm{Lbl}, \{a_1, \dots, a_n\} \subseteq \mathrm{Lit}, b \in \mathrm{Lit}\}.$

Rules with an arrow $\Rightarrow$ are defeasible rules, while rules with an arrow $\rightsquigarrow$ are so-called defeaters which are essentially used to specify exceptions to defeasible rules. A defeasible rule can be used to support its consequent, whereas a defeater does not support its consequent.

Notation 3. *The set of antecedents of a rule r is denoted* $\mathrm{A}(r)$, *and* $\mathrm{C}(r)$ *denotes its consequent. Other abbreviations are, for example,* $Rul^{\mathsf{O}} = Rul_{\mathsf{d}}^{\mathsf{O}} \cup Rul_{\mathsf{dft}}^{\mathsf{O}}$, *and* $Rul[b]$ *to denote the set of rules whose consequent is b, and* $Rul_{\mathsf{d}}[b]$ *the set of defeasible rules whose consequent is b.*

Consequents of rules can be incompatible, and such incompatibilities are captured though complementary literals.

Notation 4. *The complementary of a literal q is denoted by $\sim q$; if q is a positive literal p, then $\sim q$ is $\neg p$, and if q is a negative literal $\neg p$, then $\sim q$ is p.*

Definition 4. *Let $l \in \mathrm{Lit} \cup \mathrm{ModLit}$ denote a literal. A set of literals is a set of **complementary literals** of l, denoted $\mathrm{Compl}(l)$, iff:*

- *if $l = p \in \mathrm{Lit}$ then $\mathrm{Compl}(l) = \{\sim l\}$;*
- $\mathrm{Compl}(\mathsf{O}l) = \{\neg\mathsf{O}l, \mathsf{O}\sim l, \neg\mathsf{P}l, \mathsf{P}\sim l\}$, $\mathrm{Compl}(\neg\mathsf{O}l) = \{\mathsf{O}l, \neg\mathsf{P}l\}$,
  $\mathrm{Compl}(\mathsf{P}l) = \{\mathsf{O}\sim l, \neg\mathsf{P}l\}$, $\mathrm{Compl}(\neg\mathsf{P}l) = \{\neg\mathsf{O}\sim l, \mathsf{P}l, \neg\mathsf{P}\sim l\}$.

As usual, we can define a *superiority relation* between rules to determine their relative strength in case of conflict. As shown in [1], we can disregard the superiority relation in the discussion, since modular transformations exist that empty this relation while maintaining the same conclusions in the language [8]. This result holds both for ambiguity blocking and ambiguity propagating DL [7]. It also applies to deontic extensions of DL (including the one with $\otimes$ and $\odot$ operators), by means of the notion of inferiorly defeated rules [11].

2.2   Arguments and Attacks

Defining the notion of argument in the current context is not obvious. The complexity mainly resides in the richness of the language (especially the presence of the operators $\otimes$ and $\odot$) and in the constructive nature of the introduction of modalities. The derivation of a modal literal such as Ob depends on the constructive provability of b using rules such as $a_1, \ldots, a_n \Rightarrow_O b$, and the derivation of $\neg Ob$ depends on showing that there is no proof for Ob. We propose thus the following definition of arguments.

Definition 5. *An **argument** A **for a conclusion** p generated from a set of rules Rul is a (possibly infinite) tree where*

1. *the root node is labelled by literal p;*
2. *any node is labelled by either a literal $h \in \mathrm{Lit} \cup \mathrm{ModLit}$ or no literals;*

and such that:

1. *if the node labelled by h has children $h_1, \ldots, h_n$ $(n > 0)$, then all arcs connecting $h_1, \ldots h_n$ to h are labelled by exactly one rule $r \in \mathrm{Rul}$ with $A(r) = \{b_1, \ldots, b_n\}$ such that $h_1 = b_1, \ldots, h_n = b_n$, and either*
   - *(a) if $r \in \mathrm{Rul}_d^O$ and $C(r) = c_1 \otimes \cdots \otimes c_m$ then $h = Oc_k$ $(1 \leq k \leq m)$;*
   - *(b) if $r \in \mathrm{Rul}_d^P$ and $C(r) = c_1 \odot \cdots \odot c_m$ then $h = Pc_k$ $(1 \leq k \leq m)$;*
   - *(c) if $r \in \mathrm{Rul}_d^C$ then $h = C(r)$;*
   - *(d) if $r \in \mathrm{Rul}_{dft}^O$ then $h = p = \neg OC(r)$ is the root of the argument;*
   - *(e) if $r \in \mathrm{Rul}_{dft}^C$ then $h = p = C(r)$ is the root of the argument;*
2. *if the node labelled by h has no children (i.e. h is a leaf node), then either*
   - *(a) h is labelled by no literals;*
   - *(b) $h = \neg \Box l$ $(\Box \in \mathrm{Mod})$;*
   - *(c) $h = Pl$.*

The interpretation of item (d) is as follows. First of all, notice that we have to do with a case where a defeater is considered. A defeater for O with head p does not positively prove anything, but it can attack any obligation rule $a_1, \ldots a_n \Rightarrow_O \neg p$ supporting $\neg p$ (i.e., proving $O\neg p$). Conceptually, this means that the defeater can be a reason for stating that p is not obligatory, i.e., that $\neg Op$ is the case. Notice, also, that such a defeater—as any defeater here, and as done in standard argumentation semantics for DL [7]—can only label arcs leading to a root. In the modal case, this makes the interaction among arguments simple, as the concept of derivation for a negative modal literal depends on the relation between the argument considered and other arguments attacking the former one. Hence—as we will see—that $\neg Op$ is justified depends on the absence of successful arguments whose conclusion is $O\neg p$.

Remark 1. Item (b) of the last condition where the modality $\Box$ is a permission P captures the case where the conclusion l as strong permission—i.e. a permission derived from a rule with $\Rightarrow_P$—is defeated (as we will see later). If the modality $\Box$ is an obligation O, then it captures the case where a weak permission is put forward. Similarly, the last item (c) of condition (2) captures the case where a weak permission is assumed. In both cases, such a weak permission is not directly expressed in a specific deontic rule and cannot be constructively reflected in the tree-structure. In this sense, such nodes can only be leaf nodes.

Example 1. Suppose we have the following rule set:

$$\{r_1 : \;\; \Rightarrow_O c_1 \otimes c_2, \qquad\qquad r_2 : Oc_1, \neg Op \Rightarrow_P q\}.$$

Then, we can build an argument as in Fig. 1.   □

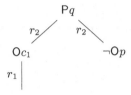

Fig. 1. An argument.

We may employ some auxiliary terminology.

- A *supportive argument* is a finite argument in which no defeaters are used.
- An argument is *positive* iff no defeater is used in it.
- A *constitutive argument* is an argument where all rules are constitutive rules.
- Any literal/modal literal labelling any node of an argument A is *a conclusion* of A.

Definition 6. *Let A denote any argument with height $j \geq 1$ for any literal p.[1] The **top subargument** of A, denoted A^t, is the top subargument of A with height 1. Let us use $R(A^t)$ to denote the rule associated with the arcs arriving at the root of A^t.*

On the basis of arguments, we provide the core notion of the approach —*argument agglomeration set*— which gathers all arguments that are strictly needed to accept an argument. Such agglomeration set caters for two cases:

- when nodes are labelled by rule conclusions, in case of $\otimes$- or $\odot$-expressions in the head of rules such as $a \otimes b$ and $p \odot q$, the fact that Ob or Pq label nodes means that a and $O\neg p$ have been concluded;
- when leaf nodes are labelled modal literals such as $\neg Op$ we fall in the case discussed in Remark 1; even here, conditions external to the single argument at stake must be checked, which is required to verify that such an argument is justified.

Definition 7. *Let $A \in Args$ be an argument such that for every node h of A labelled by a modal literal $\neg Ol$, $\neg Pl$, Ol or Pl, the arcs leading to h are labelled by*

---

[1] As usual, the height of an argument is the number of edges on the longest path between the root and a leaf node.

- *(for literals such as Ol) $r : b_1, \ldots, b_n \Rightarrow c_1 \otimes \cdots \otimes c_m$ and $l = c_k$ ($1 \le k \le m$),* and
- *(for literals such as Pl) $r : b_1, \ldots, b_n \Rightarrow d_1 \odot \cdots \odot d_m$ and $l = d_k$ ($1 \le k \le m$).*

*An **argument agglomeration set** $\mathrm{Aggl}(A) \subseteq Args$ w.r.t. A is a smallest set of arguments such that $A \in \mathrm{Aggl}(A)$ and:*

- *for each (leaf) node labelled $\neg Ol$ or $\neg Pl$,*
  - *there is an argument $B \in \mathrm{Aggl}(A)$ whose conclusion is $p \in \mathrm{Compl}(Ol)$;*
  - *$\mathrm{Aggl}(B) \subseteq \mathrm{Aggl}(A)$;*
- *for each node labelled c_j ($1 \le j < k$),*
  - *there is an argument $C \in \mathrm{Aggl}(A)$ whose conclusion is $\neg c_j \in \mathrm{Compl}(c_j)$;*
  - *$\mathrm{Aggl}(C) \subseteq \mathrm{Aggl}(A)$;*
- *for each node labelled d_j ($1 \le j < k$),*
  - *there is an argument $D \in \mathrm{Aggl}(A)$ whose conclusion is $q \in \mathrm{Compl}(Pd_j)$;*
  - *$\mathrm{Aggl}(D) \subseteq \mathrm{Aggl}(A)$.*

Remark 2. The agglomeration set of any argument A gathers all arguments that are strictly needed to accept the construction of A. Thus, the agglomeration set of A can be viewed as a single argument where special arcs connect nodes in A labelled by modal literals obtained by rules supporting $\oslash$-expressions.

Example 2. Suppose the following rules:

$$\{\, r_1 : \ \Rightarrow_c \neg c_1, \qquad r_3 : \ \Rightarrow_O c_1 \otimes c_2,$$
$$r_2 : \ \leadsto_O \neg p, \qquad r_4 : Oc_2, \neg Op \Rightarrow_P d_1 \odot d_2 \,\}.$$

Then, we can build the following arguments[2]:

A : $\quad \Rightarrow Oc_2, \neg Op \Rightarrow Pd1,$ B : $\quad \Rightarrow \neg c_1,$ C : $\quad \leadsto_O \neg p$

which agglomerate as illustrated in Fig. 2.

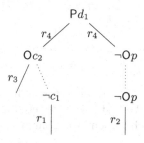

Fig. 2. An argument agglomeration set, where the dotted arc represent the relation between arguments in the agglomeration.

---

[2] Arrows indicate the type of rule used.

Eventually, arguments supporting complementary literals attack each other.

Definition 8. *An argument A* **attacks** *an argument B iff*

1. *there exists a node of B labelled by m, and*
2. *there exists a node of A labelled by l ∈ Compl(m).*

A set of arguments S attacks an argument B iff there is an argument A in S that attacks B.

2.3   Justified and Rejected Arguments

The justification of arguments has been thoroughly studied in the literature, and multiple semantics have been proposed. As we are dealing with DL, we resort to the argumentation semantics for variants of DL as presented in [7].

The usual definition of accepted arguments is slightly adapted to embrace argument agglomeration sets.

Definition 9. *An argument A is an* **accepted argument** *w.r.t a set of arguments S iff A is finite, and every argument attacking any argument in any Aggl(A) is attacked by S.*

From accepted arguments, and similarly as [5], we can define justified arguments using a 'characteristic function'.

Definition 10. *Let Args be a set of arguments. The* **deontic justification characteristic function** *of Args is a function* $J_i : \mathrm{pow}(Args) \to \mathrm{pow}(Args)$ *such that:*

- $J_0 = \emptyset$, *and*
- $J_{i+1} = \{A \in Args \mid A \text{ is accepted w.r.t. } J_i\}.$

Definition 11. *Let Args be a set of arguments. The* **set of justified arguments** *of Args is* $JArgs = \bigcup_{i=1}^{\infty} J_i$.

Definition 12. *Let Args be a set of arguments. A literal is a* **justified literal** *if it is a conclusion of a supportive argument in JArgs.*

Once justified arguments and literals are established, rejected arguments and literals can be determined. We first define rejected arguments with respect to a generic set of arguments which is then instantiated as a set of justified arguments.

Definition 13. *An argument A is a* **rejected argument** *by a set of arguments S iff either*

1. *a proper subargument B of A is in S, or*
2. *B is attacked by a finite argument.*

Definition 14. *Let T be a set of arguments. The* **deontic rejection characteristic function** *of Args is a function $R_i(T) : \mathrm{pow}(Args) \to \mathrm{pow}(Args)$ such that*

- $R_0(T) = \emptyset$, *and*
- $R_{i+1}(T) = \{A \in Args \mid A$ *is rejected by* $R_i(T)$ *and* $T\}$.

Definition 15. *The* **set of rejected arguments** *w.r.t. T is $RArgs = \bigcup_{i=1}^{\infty} R_i(T)$. An argument is rejected if it is rejected w.r.t. JArgs.*

From justified and rejected arguments with respect to justified arguments, we define rejected literals.

Definition 16. *A literal l is a* **rejected literal** *by T iff there is no supportive argument for l in $Args - RArgs(T)$. A literal l is rejected if it is rejected by JArgs.*

In reference to the above definition, we can note that the set of justified arguments $JArgs$ is included in $Args - RArgs(JArgs)$. Furthermore, some arguments in $Args - RArgs(T)$ may be neither justified nor rejected. Consequently, a literal may be neither justified nor rejected. In this case, we may say that the status of the literal is undetermined.

Example 3. Let us suppose two arguments A and B attacking each other. Argument A supports literal a, while argument B supports literal $\neg a$. The set of justified arguments is empty, and thus the set of rejected arguments is empty. Consequently, literals a and $\neg a$ are neither justified nor rejected. Their status is undetermined. □

3 Conclusion

A deontic rule-based argumentation framework has been devised to capture normative knowledge and reasoning upon it. To do so, we have been inspired by works in DDL and extended the argumentation machinery developed in [7].

The main source of difficulties resided in the introduction of modal and deontic-preference operators. In particular, the introduction of modalities required to significantly modify the concept of argument and the basic system of [7]. Indeed, the derivation of a modal literal such as Ob depends on the constructive provability of b using rules such as $a_1, \ldots, a_n \Rightarrow_O b$, and the derivation of $\neg Ob$ requires that there is no proof for Ob. We have thus devised argument agglomeration sets which, to the best of our knowledge, have no counterparts in the argumentation literature.

References

1. Antoniou, G., Billington, D., Governatori, G., Maher, M.J.: Representation results for defeasible logic. ACM Trans. Comput. Logic **2**, 255–287 (2001)
2. Atkinson, K., et al.: Towards artificial argumentation. AI Mag. **38**(3), 25–36 (2017)
3. Beirlaen, M., Heyninck, J., Straßer, C.: Structured argumentation with prioritized conditional obligations and permissions. J. Log. Comput., exy005 (2018)
4. Beirlaen, M., Straßer, C.: A structured argumentation framework for detaching conditional obligations. CoRR abs/1606.00339 (2016)
5. Dung, P.M.: On the acceptability of arguments and its fundamental role in non-monotonic reasoning, logic programming and n-person games. Artif. Intell. **77**(2), 321–358 (1995)
6. Gabbay, D., Horty, J., Parent, X., van der Meyden, R., van der Torre, L. (eds.): Handbook of Deontic Logic and Normative Systems. College Publications, London (2013)
7. Governatori, G., Maher, M.J., Antoniou, G., Billington, D.: Argumentation semantics for defeasible logic. J. Log. Comput. **14**(5), 675–702 (2004)
8. Governatori, G., Rotolo, A.: BIO logical agents: norms, beliefs, intentions in defeasible logic. Auton. Agents Multi-Agent Syst. **17**(1), 36–69 (2008)
9. Governatori, G., Rotolo, A., Calardo, E.: Possible world semantics for defeasible deontic logic. In: Ågotnes, T., Broersen, J., Elgesem, D. (eds.) DEON 2012. LNCS (LNAI), vol. 7393, pp. 46–60. Springer, Heidelberg (2012). https://doi.org/10.1007/978-3-642-31570-1_4
10. Governatori, G., Rotolo, A., Sartor, G.: Temporalised normative positions in defeasible logic. In: Proceedings of the 10th International Conference on Artificial Intelligence and Law, pp. 25–34. ACM (2005)
11. Lam, H.-P., Governatori, G.: What are the necessity rules in defeasible reasoning? In: Delgrande, J.P., Faber, W. (eds.) LPNMR 2011. LNCS (LNAI), vol. 6645, pp. 187–192. Springer, Heidelberg (2011). https://doi.org/10.1007/978-3-642-20895-9_17
12. Lam, H.P., Governatori, G., Riveret, R.: On ASPIC$^+$ and defeasible logic. In: Baroni, P. (ed.) Proceedings of 6th International Conference on Computational Models of Argument. IOS Press, Amsterdam (2016)
13. Prakken, H., Sartor, G.: Law and logic: a review from an argumentation perspective. Artif. Intell. **227**, 214–245 (2015)
14. Prakken, H., Wyner, A.Z., Bench-Capon, T.J.M., Atkinson, K.: A formalization of argumentation schemes for legal case-based reasoning in ASPIC$^+$. J. Log. Comput. **25**(5), 1141–1166 (2015)
15. Riveret, R., Governatori, G., Rotolo, A.: Argumentation semantics for temporal defeasible logic. In: Proceedings of the 3rd Starting AI Researchers' Symposium, pp. 267–268. IOS Press (2006)
16. Riveret, R., Prakken, H., Rotolo, A., Sartor, G.: Heuristics in argumentation: a game-theoretical investigation. In: Proceedings of the 2nd International Conference on Computational Models of Argument, pp. 324–335. IOS Press (2008)
17. Sartor, G., Rudnianski, M., Rotolo, A., Riveret, R., Mayor, E.: Why lawyers are nice (or nasty): a game-theoretical argumentation exercise. In: Proceedings of the 12th International Conference on Artificial Intelligence and Law, pp. 108–117. ACM (2009)

Simulations vs. Human Playing
in Repeated Prisoner's Dilemma

Yao Zhang[(⊠)], He Wang[(⊠)], Jingxian Huang[(⊠)], and Dengji Zhao[(⊠)]

School of Information Science and Technology,
ShanghaiTech University, Shanghai, China
{zhangyao1,wanghe,huangjx,zhaodj}@shanghaitech.edu.cn

Abstract. The repeated prisoner's dilemma is an essential game model
which is widely applied in real-world economic situations such as price
competition between similar products. Studies of the game have focused
on the equilibrium strategies for rational players in simplified settings,
which do not necessarily reflect the complexity of real-world applications. Therefore, this paper proposes an advanced model that mimics the
real-world dynamics of the game, and uses both simulations and human-
playing to study the robustness and applicability of different strategies in
the game. The result indeed discovers certain weaknesses of the classical
strategies. It further shows that well-known dominant strategies such as
tit-for-tat are rarely played by human players (less than 5% of the participants played dominant strategies) and instead they tend to use more
involved strategies, which again demonstrates their bounded rationality.
Our model also plays a crucial role in analyzing real-world multi-agent
systems involving human players.

1 Introduction

The prisoner's dilemma is the best-known game in social cooperation [8]. A rich
literature on game theory has focused on the conflict and cooperation models of
the prisoner's dilemma. For instance, Andreoni and Miller [3] designed experiments to let people compete against each other and sometimes let computers to
play the prisoner's dilemma game. They showed that players tend to cooperate
in the repeated prisoner's dilemma game.

However, most of the literature is based on theoretical deduction and only
focuses on unitary strategy in simple settings. For example, Press *et al.* [9]
showed that there exist strategies that one player can enforce a unilateral claim to
an unfair share of rewards. However, in practice, such strategies can hardly occur
due to their high computational costs. Hence, we want to study the repeated
prisoner's dilemma from a more practical perspective. Based on the work of evolutionary game [9,10] and repeated game [2,5], we propose a novel game model
to mimic real-world environments. Our goal is to understand the survivability
of a strategy when it has to face multiple agents with different strategies in the
repeated game. We run simulations to test classical and new defined strategies

© Springer Nature Switzerland AG 2018
T. Miller et al. (Eds.): PRIMA 2018, LNAI 11224, pp. 493–501, 2018.
https://doi.org/10.1007/978-3-030-03098-8_34

under our model. Besides, we also want to understand how people will play in the real world applications. The work done by Mao *et al.* [7] inspired us that it is a good way to study human's behaviour via web experiments, thus we have designed a web game for human players and collected their behaviours.

By analyzing the simulations, we found that tit-for-tat (TFT) [4] strategy still maintains its advantages and survives in most of the games, although it is not always dominant. However, in the human-playing games, we found that most people didn't choose the strategies like TFT that perform better in the simulations. One reason is that TFT cannot get benefits when the opponents always choose cooperation. This weakness of TFT can be easily discovered in our model. Another important reason is that people may not be rational during the games. Actually, according to our observations, people prefer to use simple strategies, since simple strategies can be chosen with less efforts [1]. Our results show that in the real-world multi-agent systems involving human players, the analysis combining predictable irrationality is very important, but it has not been well-studied in the literature.

2   The Model

We consider a repeated prisoner's dilemma game with n agents/players denoted by a set $N = \{1, 2, ..., n\}$. Each agent $i \in N$ has two private elements: utility p_i and strategy s_i, where $p_i \in \mathbb{R}$ is i's total utility in the present time (all players' utilities are zero before the game starts) and s_i is a function of type $e^k \mapsto a^k$. $a^k \in \{\mathcal{C}, \mathcal{D}\}$ is the action of i in the kth round of the game, where $\mathcal{C}$ denotes cooperates and $\mathcal{D}$ denotes defects. e^k is the game state for i in the kth round and specifically, it is the form of (p_i, a_i^{k-1}, j), where j is i's opponent in the kth round. j will be randomly selected among other agents. Unlike traditional settings, where one agent only plays with one another agent with the same strategy until the end, we let each agent play with all other agents (who may use different strategies) with the same probability. Therefore, each agent's opponent may vary between rounds, but she remembers the action history of all her opponents when they meet again. Given i and j's actions a_i^k and a_j^k in round k, i's utility of the stage game is denoted by p_i^k. Therefore, after the kth round, p_i for each agent i is $\sum_{l=1}^{k} p_i^l$, where we do not involve artificial discount factors for simplicity and also in reality the life-time of the repeated game is limited due to the swift change of environments. We assume that the game lasts for $T > 1$ rounds.

Our goal is to study the repeated prisoner's dilemma from a new perspective: to understand the survivability of a strategy when it has to face multiple agents with different strategies in the repeated game. The types of strategies involved in our model will be defined in Sect. 2.1. The concept of survivability is defined as follows.

Definition 1 ((p, ϵ)-survivable). *Given two strategy types A and B, for all agents $i \in N$, $s_i \in \{A, B\}$ and the proportion of agents with type A is $p \in (0, 1)$, we say A is (p, ϵ)-survivable over B if in the end of the game (i.e. after T*

rounds), the average utility of type A agents is not less than ϵ times of the average utility of type B agents, where $\epsilon \in (0, 1]$.

Intuitively, A is (p, ϵ)-survivable over B means that when agents with only type A and B compete in the game, if the proportion of type A agents is $p \in (0, 1)$, then the agents with strategy A achieve an average utility that is not less than the average utility of agents with strategy B times a discount factor ϵ.

Definition 2 (p-dominant). *Given strategy types A, B and C, for two different game settings:*

1. *$\forall$ agents $i \in N$, $s_i \in \{A, C\}$ and the proportion of agents with type A is p,*
2. *$\forall$ agents $i \in N$, $s_i \in \{B, C\}$ and the proportion of agents with type B is p,*

*we say A is p-**dominant** B **over** C if the average utility of type A agents in setting 1 is not less than the average utility of type B agents in setting 2.*

Intuitively, A is p-dominant B over C means that in a setting consisting of agents with only types B and C and the proportion of type B agents is p, if we just replace strategy B by A, then the average utility of type B agents is non-decreasing after the replacement.

2.1   Strategy Types

In the following, we define all the strategy types studied in the paper.

Type 1 (Constant(p)). *Constant(p) is a strategy with a probability p to cooperate and a probability $(1 - p)$ to defect. Specifically, when $p = 0.5$, we call it a **Random**.*

Type 2 (Action-Based). *Action-Based is a strategy that the probability of cooperation p is increased by $\Delta p = k \times p$ if the opponent chooses defect, otherwise decreases Δp. In this paper, we set $k = 0.02$ and the initial p to be 1.*

Type 3 (TFT(k)). *TFT(k) is a strategy that if the opponent chooses defect k times in succession, then it chooses defect in the next round, otherwise, it chooses cooperation. Specifically, when $k = 1$ and $k = 2$, **TFT**(1) is called **TFT** (as known as tit-for-tat) and **TFT**(2) is called **Co-TFT**.*

Type 4 (Revenger(k, r)). *Revenger (as known as grim trigger strategy) is a non-forgiving strategy that cooperates initially, but keeps defecting after being defected [6]. We introduce strategy **Revenger**(k) that initially cooperates and defects forever when the opponent defects $k \geq 1$ times in succession. We also define **Revenger**(k, r) such that it initially cooperates and when the opponent defects $k \geq 1$ times in succession it defects until the opponent cooperates $r \geq 1$ times in succession.*

Type 5 (Bayesian). *Bayesian is a strategy that can learn the probability distribution of the opponent's action in a long run. In each round k, when i plays with j, it calculates the probability p_i^k to for i to cooperate as the following.*

$$\begin{bmatrix} b_{11} & b_{12} \\ b_{21} & b_{22} \end{bmatrix} \begin{bmatrix} p_i^{k-1} \\ 1 - p_i^{k-1} \end{bmatrix} = \begin{bmatrix} p_i^k \\ 1 - p_i^k \end{bmatrix}$$

where b_{11}, b_{12}, b_{21} and b_{22} are estimators of $Pr(a_j = C \mid a_i = C)$, $Pr(a_j = C \mid a_i = D)$, $Pr(a_j = D \mid a_i = C)$ and $Pr(a_j = D \mid a_i = D)$ respectively. These values will be estimated by the games' results before k^{th} round. Intuitively, if the opponent has a fixed probability distribution on actions, Bayesian can converge to the same distribution. Hence Bayesian strategy can be considered as a generalized TFT, which tries to imitate the opponent's behaviour.

2.2 Strategy Evaluation Settings

To evaluate all the strategies defined above, we conducted both agent-based simulations and designed a web-game involving human-players. For each stage game of the repeated prisoner's dilemma game, we apply the payoff matrix given by Table 1.

Table 1. Payoff matrix of the stage game.

Player 2 \ Player 1	C	D
C	2\2	-1\3
D	3\-1	0\0

3   Simulations

We first introduce our simulations, where we test the survivability of all the strategies defined above under our model.

3.1 Settings

We ran the simulations between each pair of all types defined above. For each pair, we simulated the condition that one of the pair has a proportion p from 0.1 to 0.9 with p changing by 0.1 each time and each simulation has 12 agents ($n = 12$) and runs 80 rounds ($T = 80$). We recorded the utilities of each simulation between every two types in the range of all possible proportions of p. Figure 1 shows the results when TFT plays against Constant(0) at $p = 0.1$ and 0.5 respectively.

Furthermore, for each pair of types (A and B), we checked that at which proportion p, A is (p, ϵ)-survivable over B and also checked that at which proportion p, A is p-dominant B over Random. We set $\epsilon = 0.8$, because it is hard to define whether they can survive or not when their average utility is just less than their adversary a little. We recorded all possible proportions p which can ensure their survivability. Some results are shown in Tables 2 and 3. Table 2 shows the results of p-dominant and Table 3 shows the results of $(p, 0.8)$-survivable. In each table, the tuple (x, y) means that the type of agents in the row can survive when their proportion is from $x/10$ to $y/10$ against with the type in the column.

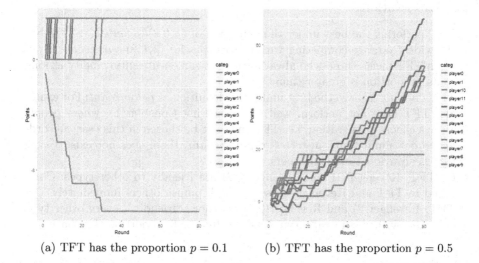

(a) TFT has the proportion $p = 0.1$ (b) TFT has the proportion $p = 0.5$

Fig. 1. The simulation results of TFT vs. Constant(0), where the players with smaller ids are of type TFT.

Table 2. *p-dominant* (Compared to random type)

	Const(0)	Const(.3)	Const(1)	AB	TFT	Co-TFT	Revenger	Revenger(2)	Revenger(2,2)	Bayesian
Action based	(4, 9)	(6, 9)	(3, 4)	NULL	(1, 7)	(2, 3)	(1, 9)	(8, 9)	(7, 8)	(4, 9)
TFT	(1, 9)	(1, 9)	(8, 9)	(1, 8)	NULL	(8, 9)	(1, 9)	(2, 4)	(7, 8)	(2, 9)
Co-TFT	(1, 9)	(9, 9)	(5, 7)	(1, 4)	(1, 9)	NULL	(1, 9)	(5, 9)	(4, 5)	(0, 0)
Revenger	(1, 9)	(1, 9)	(2, 5)	(1, 5)	(1, 7)	(6, 7)	NULL	(5, 8)	(4, 6)	(1, 9)
Revenger(2)	(1, 9)	(9, 9)	(2, 9)	(1, 9)	(1, 9)	(6, 7)	(1, 9)	NULL	(1, 3)	(0, 0)
Revenger(2,2)	(1, 9)	(0, 0)	(2, 3)	(1, 7)	(1, 9)	(2, 4)	(1, 9)	(3, 6)	NULL	(0, 0)
Bayesian	(1, 9)	(6, 9)	(1, 9)	(7, 9)	(1, 2)	(1, 9)	(0, 0)	(1, 9)	(1, 9)	NULL
Const(0)	NULL	NULL	NULL	(4, 9)	(7, 8)	(1, 9)	(7, 9)	(1, 9)	(1, 9)	(1, 9)
Const(.3)	NULL	NULL	NULL	(5, 9)	(8, 9)	(1, 9)	(0, 0)	(1, 9)	(1, 9)	(1, 9)
Const(1)	NULL	NULL	NULL	(1, 5))	(1, 5)	(6, 8)	(1, 9)	(9, 9)	(5, 6)	(0, 0)

Table 3. $(p, 0.8)$-*survivable*

	Const(0)	Const(.5)	Const(1)	AB	TFT	Co-TFT	Revenger	Revenger(2)	Revenger(2,2)	Bayesian
Action based	(7, 9)	(3, 9)	(1, 9)	NULL	(1, 9)	(1, 9)	(1, 9)	(1, 9)	(1, 9)	(1, 9)
TFT	(3, 9)	(1, 9)	(1, 9)	(1, 9)	NULL	(1, 9)	(1, 9)	(1, 9)	(1, 9)	(1, 9)
Co-TFT	(8, 9)	(0, 0)	(1, 9)	(1, 9)	(1, 9)	NULL	(1, 9)	(1, 9)	(1, 9)	(5, 9)
Revenger	(3, 9)	(1, 9)	(1, 9)	(1, 9)	(1, 9)	(1, 9)	NULL	(1, 9)	(1, 9)	(1, 9)
Revenger(2)	(9, 9)	(8, 9)	(1, 9)	(1, 9)	(1, 9)	(1, 9)	(1, 9)	NULL	(1, 9)	(5, 9)
Revenger(2,2)	(8, 9)	(7, 8)	(1, 9)	(1, 9)	(1, 9)	(1, 9)	(1, 9)	(1, 9)	NULL	(6, 9)
Bayesian	(0, 0)	(1, 9)	(1, 9)	(1, 9)	(6, 9)	(1, 9)	(0, 0)	(1, 9)	(1, 9)	NULL
Const(0)	NULL	NULL	NULL	(4, 9)	(8, 9)	(1, 9)	(7, 9)	(1, 9)	(1, 9)	(1, 9)
Const(.5)	NULL	NULL	NULL	(1, 9)	(5, 9)	(1, 9)	(9, 9)	(1, 9)	(1, 9)	(3, 8)
Const(1)	NULL	NULL	NULL	(1, 9)	(1, 9)	(1, 9)	(1, 9)	(1, 9)	(1, 9)	(0, 0)

3.2 Observations

1. TFT performs the best under the definition of $(p, 0.8)$-*survivable*: TFT has the widest p-range competing with other types for $(p, 0.8)$-*survivable*. Even when TFT meets those who always defect, it can ensure survivability as long as its proportion is greater than 30%.
2. TFT does not behave the best under the definition of p-*dominant*: For example, TFT does not perform well when meeting Constant(1), where people always choose cooperation, i.e. TFT may not be chosen in this case. According to our simulations, in terms of p-*dominant*, there does not exist a type that is always better than others.
3. Co-TFT, Revenger(2) and Revenger(2,2) are friendly to other types: Compared to TFT and Revenger those who will punish others immediately, Co-TFT, Revenger(2) and Revenger(2,2) are more "friendly": every other type competes with them can "survive" no matter what proportion they have.

3.3 Summary

By analysing the simulations results, we can see that traditional strategies like TFT and Revenger are still effective under our setting. However, in games where the other agents always tend to cooperate, TFT cannot get benefits by taking the advantage of defect since TFT will always choose cooperate as well. Thus the performance of TFT under the definition of p-*dominant* is not dominant since some other types can get very high score by defecting agents who always choose cooperation. Because of this, people may not choose TFT-like strategies in practice.

4 Human Players vs. Agents

To investigate how human players behave in the repeated prisoner's dilemma game, we designed a web game which also contains multiple computer-controlled-agents. A human player is asked to play with one of the agents for many rounds. Meanwhile, other agents are playing the game at the same time with other human players. The goal of the human player is to get the highest utility among all the players, both human players and agents.

We released two versions of the game. In the first version, players can easily get the highest score because agents have a high possibility of using simple strategies such as Constant, while in the second version, we removed those too simple strategies and only choose four strategies: Bayesian, Random, Revenger and TFT. There were 194 people joined the first version which was available from December 26th, 2017 to December 28th, 2017. For the second version, 121 people joined from December 29th, 2017 to December 31st, 2017.

4.1   Observations

In the first version, when getting a high score is easy, many people just choose *simple* strategies. We say a player plays a simple strategy if her actions are just repeating a certain pattern, as shown in Fig. 2(a). In Figs. 2(a) and (b), the *x*-axis refers to the round of the game between a human player and a computer-simulated agent while the *y*-axis refers to their actions. Here, 0 means cooperation and 1 means defect. The title of the figure indicates the strategy chosen by the computer-simulated agent. In the second version, when getting a high score becomes harder, more people started to try complex strategies to adapt to the agents' strategies, as shown in Fig. 2(b).

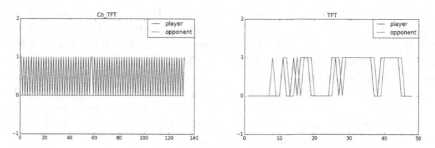

(a) Human players play simple patterns   (b) Human players play complex strategies

Fig. 2. Examples of human players playing simple and non-simple strategies.

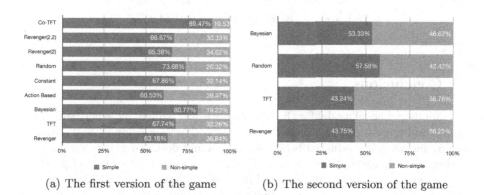

(a) The first version of the game   (b) The second version of the game

Fig. 3. The proportion of human players playing simple strategies vs. non-simple ones.

Figures 3(a) and (b) show the proportion of people who use simple and non-simple strategies. In the figures, *y*-axis is the strategy chosen by our computer agents. For each type of computer agents, we collected all the actions of human players and counted the number of players who played simple strategy. The longer the left part of the bar is, the more likely human players will choose a simple strategy. We noticed that in the second version, the proportion of those who only use simple strategies decreases sharply. This indicates that when the environment becomes harder to survive, people tend to adopt more involved strategies.

4.2 Compared with Simulations

According to the simulations shown in Sect. 3, the TFT strategy and Revenger strategy have the best performance in terms of survivability. However, in the real-world games with human players, we found that very few people used TFT or Revenger. As shown in Table 4, in the first version less than 5% of the players played TFT-like or Revenger-like strategies. In the second version, although people tended to use more involved strategies, the number of people who used TFT-like or Revenger-like does not increase. This shows that most people in the real-world game have irrational behaviours. This is irrational because this does not give them better utility, but it is also an expected behaviour since people tend to choose strategies which need less efforts [1]. On the other hand, in terms of p-dominant, TFT does not maintain its advantages. This indicates the importance of the analysis combining predictable irrationality in the game, which has not been well studied in the literature.

Table 4. TFT-like, Revenger-like

	The 1st version	The 2nd version
Revenger-like	6/194 (3.09%)	4/121 (3.31%)
TFT-like	8/194 (4.12%)	6/121 (4.96%)

5 Conclusions

We proposed a novel model for the repeated prisoner's dilemma, where simulated agents and human players compete with each other in a complex and dynamic environments. We conducted both simulations and designed games with human players to evaluate the survivability of various strategies in theory and practice. In the simulations, our studies showed that classical strategies such as tit-for-tat, are not always good when we evaluate them by comparing to other strategies under our definition of p-dominant. In human-involved experiments, our studies showed that most people are irrational when they play the game. Most of them choose simpler strategies, even though they know there exist better strategies such as TFT and Revenger. Furthermore, people are willing to adopt more complex strategies when the games become harder for them to survive.

The novel game model proposed in the paper can be applied to the study of social evolution and other economic settings such as commercial trading and marketing. The work is also valuable for studying the relationships between agents, e.g. friendship and adversarial relationship, which have different levels of tolerance. Furthermore, we haven't touched the memoryless effects, which worth further investigations with more involved strategies.

References

1. Ariely, D., Holzwarth, A.: The choice architecture of privacy decision-making. Health Technol. **7**(1), 1–8 (2017)
2. Abreu, D.: On the theory of infinitely repeated games with discounting. Econometrica **56**(2), 383–396 (1988)
3. Andreoni, J., Miller, J.H.: Rational cooperation in the finitely repeated prisoners' dilemma: experimental evidence. Econ. J. **103**, 570–585 (1993)
4. Axelrod, R.: The Evolution of Cooperation. Basic Books, Inc., New York (1984)
5. Benoit, J.P., Krishna, V.: Finitely repeated games. Econometrica **53**, 905–922 (1985)
6. Friedman, J.W.: A non-cooperative equilibrium for supergames. Rev. Econ. Stud. **38**(1), 1–12 (1971)
7. Mao, A., Dworkin, L., Suri, S., Watts, D.J.: Resilient cooperators stabilize long-run cooperation in the finitely repeated prisoner's dilemma. Nature Commun. **8** (2017). Article No. 13800
8. Newman, P.: The New Palgrave Dictionary of Economics and the Law. Palgrave Macmillan, Basingstoke, UK (1998). https://books.google.com/books?id=k3KuCwAAQBAJ
9. Press, W.H., Dyson, F.J.: Iterated prisoner's dilemma contains strategies that dominate any evolutionary opponent. Proc. Nat. Acad. Sci. **109**(26), 10409–10413 (2012)
10. Sigmund, K., Nowak, M.A.: Evolutionary game theory. Curr. Biol. **9**(14), R503–R505 (1999)

Adaptive Budget Allocation for Sequential Tasks in Crowdsourcing

Yuya Itoh and Shigeo Matsubara[✉]

Kyoto University, Kyoto 606-8501, Japan
y-itoh@ai.soc.i.kyoto-u.ac.jp, matsubara@i.kyoto-u.ac.jp

Abstract. This paper proposes a new budget allocation method for crowdsourced sequential tasks. Sequential tasks mean that an output of a task becomes an input to another task, and the quality of the final artifact depends on the qualities of the preceding tasks. In crowdsourcing, the abilities of workers are often difficult to learn in advance. Thus, the fixed budget allocation to the component tasks cannot respond to the realized situation. Also, the requester is often difficult to evaluate the quality of intermediate artifacts accurately, which results in misallocating the budget and wasting a budget. To overcome these difficulties, we have developed a contingent budget allocation method, i.e., generating a conditional plan given uncertainty about the intermediate states and action effects, by formalized a problem as POMDP and introducing a quality evaluation action. The experimental results show that the proposed method can find a solution in a reasonable time and improve the quality of the final artifact.

Keywords: Cooperation · Budget allocation · POMDP Crowdsourcing

1 Introduction

In crowdsourcing, a complicated task is often divided into more than one simple subtasks, and then the requester asks workers to solve these subtasks [2]. Although there are several ways of task decomposition, this study focuses sequential tasks. Sequential tasks mean that an output of a subtask becomes an input of another subtask, and the quality of the final artifact depends on the quality of preceding artifacts. For example, a Find-Fix-Verify workflow was proposed for English proofreading tasks [2]. Specifically, in Find tasks, workers are asked to identify the patches that need proofreading throughout the whole article. In Fix tasks, workers are recruited to correct the errors in all patches as many as they can. In Verify tasks, all the corrections made in the Fix stage are verified by other workers. Here, if the workers of the Find task fail to find the patches to be fixed, workers of the Fix and Verify tasks cannot recover such failure.

Here, a challenge is how to allocate the budget into subtasks under the budget constraint. This problem has been studied in [4,5]. Their method, however, can

© Springer Nature Switzerland AG 2018
T. Miller et al. (Eds.): PRIMA 2018, LNAI 11224, pp. 502–509, 2018.
https://doi.org/10.1007/978-3-030-03098-8_35

be viewed as static in that the budget allocation is determined in advance, and it does not respond to any events occurred during the execution process. Such fixed budget allocation may result in wasting the budget and deficit or missing the opportunity to save the budget. For example, assume that an allocation plan specifies that the first subtask is allocated to three workers. If the quality of the artifact submitted by the first worker is very high, allocating the same subtask to additional two workers is redundant. In such a case, it is better to re-allocate the budget to the succeeding subtasks.

On the other hand, a dynamic workflow control has been studied in [3]. Their method enables the requester to respond to the events during the execution. However, they do not explicitly consider the budget constraint, i.e., a state is characterized only by the qualities of the artifacts. This may cause a deficit in executing the remaining plan. Also, incorporating the budget constraint may make the computation intractable. Thus, developing a method for dynamic workflow control under the budget constraint in crowdsourcing is new as long as the authors' knowledge.

Another issue in controlling the crowd is that accurately evaluating the quality of intermediate artifacts is often difficult for the requester. In crowdsourcing, the requester can publish an evaluation task that asks other workers to evaluate the quality of artifacts. However, it needs to determine when the requester should publish evaluation tasks. The payment for crowdsourced tasks is often cheap but publishing evaluation tasks at every time incurs high costs.

To solve this problem, we provide a model of adaptive budget allocation problem based on Partially-Observable Markov Decision Process (POMDP). There are related studies that apply POMDP to crowdsourcing workflow control [3], but, as mentioned above, their research does not consider the budget constraint explicitly, i.e., there is no discussion of how to incorporate the budget constraint into the model. A simple introduction of the budget constraint brings the explosion of the problem space, which makes the computation intractable. We formalize a problem as POMDP with quality evaluation actions and discretize the problem space regarding the budget constraint. The experimental results show that the proposed method outperforms the baseline methods.

The contribution of this paper is summarized as follows.

- First, we propose a formalization of the workflow control problem as POMDP. In this formalization, we introduce quality evaluation actions. By designing an appropriate reward function, we succeeded to obtain the desirable control policy.
- Second, we show the effectiveness of our method in a simulation. In the simulation, we introduced discretization to reduce the computational complexity. We verified that desirable control is attained.

The rest of the paper is organized as follows. In Sect. 2, we explain a budget allocation problem for sequential tasks, and in Sect. 3, we formalize the problem as POMDP. In Sect. 4, we evaluate the proposed method, and Sect. 5 concludes the discussions.

2   Budget Allocation Problem

This section provides a model of budget allocation problems for sequential tasks. A task is divided into $N(>1)$ subtasks. The i-th subtask is called as subtask i. Different subtasks are carried out by the different workers, and workers execute at most one subtask. The difficulty of subtask i is designated as $d_i \in [0,1]$.

A worker is characterized by its type j who has the ability level of $a_{i,j}$ for subtask i. The higher ability level a worker has, the higher quality of the artifact can be produced.

The quality of the artifact is determined by the quality function whose inputs are the worker's ability and the quality of the preceding task. If q_{i-1} represents the quality for subtask i, we assume $q_i = f(a_{i,j}, q_{i-1})$. The ability distribution of workers choosing subtask i depends on the payment w_i for subtask i. We do not consider the existence of high-ability but lazy workers.

The requester's utility is defined by the quality of the final artifact. The requester has a budget constraint on the task. If the expense does not exceed the budget, the remaining amount does not affect the requester's utility.

The requester has the budget of B and sets the payment for each subtask (HITs) so that the total amount of payment does not exceed the budget. Here, HIT means a minimum unit of tasks in crowdsourcing. The requester can publish the same subtask more than one times to increase the quality of artifact. We assume that the payment w_i ($w_i \leq B$) is the same for HITs for subtask i. Here, a budget allocation problem can be formalized as the optimization problem of finding the payment w_i ($w_i \leq B$) that maximizes the quality, q_N, of the final artifact.

3   Problem Formalization as POMDP

This section formalizes a budget allocation problem as a Partially-Observable Markov Decision Process (POMDP). POMDP is a tuple of $< S, A, T, O, Z, R >$, i.e., the set of states, the set of actions, the transition function, the set of observations, the observation function, and the reward.

Definition 1. *A budget allocation problem is represented by a tuple of* $< S, A, T, O, Z, R >$, *where*

- $S = \{s_i = (i, q_i, B_i, q_{i-1}) \mid i \in 1, \cdots N\}$, *the index i represents the subtask in question, q_i represents the quality of an artifact for subtask i, B_i represents the remaining budget, q_{i-1} represents the quality of the artifact for the preceding subtask $i-1$.*
- $A = \{CURRENT(w_i), NEXT(w_{i+1}), EVAL(w_{\mathrm{EVAL}}) \mid w \in [0, B]\}$, w_i, w_{i+1}, *and w_{EVAL} represent the payments for workers completing subtask i, subtask $i+1$, and an evaluation task, respectively. The set of actions consists of the Cartesian product of the type of actions and the payment of the subtask.*

- T: The quality of artifact in the next state is determined by the quality function described in Sect. 2, where the inputs are the worker's ability $a_{i,j} \in [0,1]$ the payment w_i, and the quality for the preceding subtask. $a_{i,j}$ is drawn from the distribution function of $F(a_{i,j})$. The budget in the next state is equal to the difference between the current budget and w_i. If $CURRENT$ is chosen, $q_i = \max\{q_i, q_i'\}$, where q_i is the quality of the owned result and q_i' is the quality of the newly obtained result. If $NEXT$ is chosen, the number of subtask i is incremented by one.
- $O = \{o \mid o \in [0,1]\}$, o represents the quality of the artifact given through the evaluation task.
- $Z = \{P(o \mid q_i, w_{\text{EVAL}}) = N(q_i, \sigma^2)\}$
- $R = \{R(q_N) \mid R(q_N) \in \mathbb{R}\}$, the reward is given by the reward function R.

The requester agent cannot directly observe the quality of an artifact but can indirectly observe the quality of an artifact by publishing an evaluation task. The agent recognizes the outcome of the evaluation task as observation o. We assume the followings. When the requester agent publishes the evaluation task in state s_i, the probability of getting o as an observation follows the normal distribution $N(q_i, \sigma^2)$, where q_i represents the true value of the quality in state s_i.

Rewards are not payments to workers but are received by the requester agent, which can be classified into the following three cases.

- If all subtasks are completed, the agent obtains the following reward $R(q_N)$ that corresponds to the quality q_N of the final subtask.

$$R(q_N) = \begin{cases} 0 & (q_N < q_\theta) \\ 1000 \frac{(e^{q_N} - 1)}{(e-1)} & (q_N \geq q_\theta) \end{cases}$$

Here, q_θ represents the minimum requirement for the quality, and if the final quality is less than the minimum requirement q_θ, the agent gets nothing.
- If the budget runs out before completing all the subtasks, the agent gets some penalty, i.e., the negative reward.
- In the intermediate states except the above two cases, the agent gets the reward of zero.

The reason for introducing this minimum requirement is as follows. As using a reward function having a gentle slope, we could not obtain the desirable policy in the experiments. To overcome this difficulty, we introduced the minimum requirement in the reward function. We assume that the human requester enjoys the artifact if the quality is larger than zero, but we can use an arbitrary reward function for the requester agent (computer) to obtain a desirable policy.

4   Evaluations

We evaluated the adaptive budget allocation method proposed in Sect. 3 by using simulations.

4.1   Experimental Settings

Quality of Artifacts. To run a simulation, we need to give a concrete form of the quality function. As a quality function that satisfies assumptions, we assume that the quality $q_i \in [0,1]$ for subtask i is defined as $q_i = f(a_{i,j}, q_{i-1}) = (1 - d_i)^{1/\alpha_i a_{i,j}} \cdot q_{i-1}$. Here, d_i, $\alpha_i (> 0)$, $a_{i,j}$, and q_{i-1} represent the difficulty of subtask i, the weight on subtask i, the worker's ability, and the quality of the preceding subtask $i-1$, respectively. The worker's ability $a_{i,j}$ is drawn from the probability density function $g_0(a_{i,j})$ with the support $[a_L, a_H]$ for a unit payment, and $g(a_{i,j}) = g_0(a_{i,j}/w_i)/w_i$ with the support $[w_i a_L, w_i a_H]$ for a payment w_i. We assume that $q_0 = 1$, since the first subtask does not have any preceding subtask. If the total number of subtasks is N, the final quality of the task, q^*, is given by the following expression.

$$q^* = q_N = \prod_{i=1}^{N} (1 - d_i)^{1/\alpha_i a_{i,j}}$$

Distribution of Workers' Abilities. The set of workers accepting the task depends on the payment. We examine the following two cases, although we assume that all the component subtasks have the same distribution of workers' abilities.

(a) Convex Distribution: There are two peaks in the distribution, each of which corresponds to high-ability workers and low-ability workers. There are few workers having the median ability.
(b) Concave Distribution: There is a single peak in the distribution, i.e., many workers have the median ability.

Discretization of the Problem Space. We set the upper bound of the payment W and the number of ability level L. If W and L are set to the larger values, more elaborated control of budget allocation becomes possible. On the other hand, it increases the computational cost of solving POMDPs. By balancing the tractability with the feasibility of dealing with actual tasks, we use the settings of $W = 8$ and $L = 3$.

Task Decomposition. A task is decomposed into more than one subtasks. There are several ways of decomposing a task. For example, a task is decomposed into three subtasks in the Find-Fix-Verify workflow [2]. We examine the case that a task is decomposed into three subtasks, i.e., $N = 3$.

Combinations of the Difficulties of Subtasks. The objective of task decomposition is to reduce the difficulty of completing the task. There exist various cases in the difficulties of subtasks. For example, in the study of collaborative workflow, a translation task is decomposed into three subtasks [1], where it is

Table 1. Workers' ability distribution

	(a) Convex	(b) Concave
$a_{i,j} = 0.2$	0.45	0.20
$a_{i,j} = 0.6$	0.10	0.60
$a_{i,j} = 1.0$	0.45	0.20

Table 2. Task difficulties

	(1) Increasing	(2) Decreasing
d_1	0.3	0.7
d_2	0.5	0.5
d_3	0.7	0.3

considered that the third subtask (target synthesis) is easiest and the second subtask (assistive translation) is the most difficult. However, a way of decomposition is not limited to such one. We examine the following two cases.

(1) Increasing difficulties: The difficulty of the succeeding subtask is higher than that of the preceding subtask.
(2) Decreasing difficulties: The difficulty of the succeeding subtask is lower than that of the preceding subtask.

Methods to Be Compared. To evaluate the performance of the proposed method, we compare it with two static methods that determine the budget allocation and the number of publishing each subtask in advance.

Equal-division agent (E-Agent)
   Allocate the budget on subtasks equally, and further divide equally the allocated budget into the HITs included in each subtask.
Difficulty-based agent (D-Agent)
   Allocate the budget on subtasks in proportional to the difficulties of the subtasks.

Here, it is assumed that E-Agent and D-Agent repeatedly publish the same number of HITs for each subtask. We will compare the proposed agent called P-Agent with E-Agent and D-Agent.

   D-Agent can be viewed as the existing methods for budget allocation because the existing method by Tran-Thanh [4,5] cannot respond to the events during the execution. Their method is more elaborated in that they created the accuracy models of a Find-Fix-Verify workflow. Thus, their method may perform better than D-Agent, but obtaining the accuracy model for different task domains itself is often costly.

4.2   Simulation

We examined the four cases by combining the two cases of workers' ability distribution, (a) convex, (b) concave, and the two cases of task difficulties, (1) increasing difficulties, (2) decreasing difficulties. By using (a-1), we represent the case of combining (a) convex distribution with (1) increasing difficulties. We examined the four cases, (a-1), (a-2), (b-1), and (b-2). Tables 1 and 2 show the details of the ability distributions for a unit payment and the task difficulties, respectively.

We assume that the requester agent has the budget of $B = 40$. For the payment for a *CURRENT* action and a *NEXT* action, we set $w_i = 1, \cdots, 7$, while for the payment for an *EVAL* action, we set $w_{EVAL} = 1$. This is because the evaluation task is, in general, easier than the creation tasks such as finding patches to be fixed.

In the experiment, we ran the simulation twenty times for each case and calculated the average value of the quality of the final artifact. To remove the effect of the randomness on workers' abilities, we first create the queue of workers whose abilities are drawn from the specified distributions and simulate the workers appear according to the queue, which enables us to fairly compare the three methods with each other.

4.3   Simulation Results

Figure 1 shows the simulation results of the four cases. In these graphs, the horizontal axis represents the index of subtasks, while the vertical axis represents the ratio of the obtained quality to that in the optimal budget allocation. The optimal budget allocation is calculated by assuming that the requester can observe the order of the workers' arrival as well as the abilities of all workers in advance,

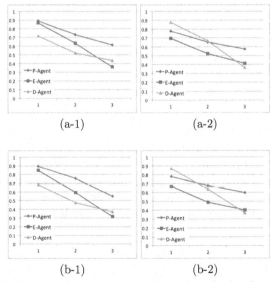

In each graph, the horizontal axis represents the index of subtasks, while the vertical axis represents the ratio of the obtained quality to that in the optimal budget allocation.

Fig. 1. Comparison of P-Agent with E-Agent and D-Agent

although achieving such qualities is virtually impossible. These graphs elucidate that P-Agent can achieve the highest quality for all the four cases.

For the cases of the decreasing difficulties, i.e., (a-2) and (b-2), D-Agent achieves the higher quality of an artifact for the first subtask, compared to P-Agent. This is because the first subtask is most difficult than others and D-Agent tries to pay more for the first subtask compared to P-Agent. However, P-Agent finally becomes superior to D-Agent at the last subtask. Also, for the final quality, D-Agent outperforms E-Agent in the case of increasing difficulties, i.e., (a-1) and (b-1), while E-Agent outperforms D-Agent in the case of decreasing difficulties, i.e., (a-2) and (b-2).

5   Conclusions

We have developed an adaptive budget allocation method for crowdsourced sequential tasks. Sequential tasks mean that an output of a task becomes an input to another task, and the quality of the final artifact depends on the qualities of the preceding tasks. Our method enables the requester to adaptively control the workflow, considering the budget constraint simultaneously. The simulation results showed that our method outperforms the baseline methods. A limitation of this study is that we assume that the quality function and the distribution of workers' ability are known. Incorporating multi-armed bandits to overcome the limitation is included in our future work.

Acknowledgments. This research was partially supported by a Grant-in-Aid for Scientific Research (A) (17H00759, 2017-2020) from Japan Society for the Promotion of Science (JSPS).

References

1. Ambati, V., Vogel, S., Carbonell, J.: Collaborative workflow for crowdsourcing translation. In: Proceedings of the ACM 2012 Conference on Computer Supported Cooperative Work, CSCW 2012, pp. 1191–1194 (2012)
2. Bernstein, M.S., et al.: Soylent: a word processor with a crowd inside. In: Proceedings of the 23rd Annual ACM Symposium on User Interface Software and Technology, UIST 2010, pp. 313–322 (2010)
3. Dai, P., Lin, C.H., Weld, D.S.: Pomdp-based control of workflows for crowdsourcing. Artif. Intell. **202**, 52–85 (2013)
4. Tran-Thanh, L., Huynh, T.D., Rosenfeld, A., Ramchurn, S.D., Jennings, N.R.: Budgetfix: budget limited crowdsourcing for interdependent task allocation with quality guarantees. In: Proceedings of the 2014 International Conference on Autonomous Agents and Multi-agent Systems, AAMAS 2014, pp. 477–484 (2014)
5. Tran-Thanh, L., Huynh, T.D., Rosenfeld, A., Ramchurn, S.D., Jennings, N.R.: Crowdsourcing complex workflows under budget constraints. In: Proceedings of the Twenty-Ninth AAAI Conference on Artificial Intelligence, AAAI 2015, pp. 1298–1304 (2015)

Helping Forensic Analysts to Attribute Cyber-Attacks: An Argumentation-Based Reasoner

Erisa Karafili[1]([⊠]), Linna Wang[1], Antonis C. Kakas[2], and Emil Lupu[1]

[1] Department of Computing, Imperial College London, London, UK
{e.karafili,linna.wang15,e.c.lupu}@imperial.ac.uk
[2] Department of Computer Science, University of Cyprus, Nicosia, Cyprus
antonis@ucy.ac.cy

Abstract. Discovering who performed a cyber-attack or from where it originated is essential in order to determine an appropriate response and future risk mitigation measures. In this work, we propose a novel argumentation-based reasoner for analyzing and attributing cyber-attacks that combines both technical and social evidence. Our reasoner helps the digital forensics analyst during the analysis of the forensic evidence by providing to the analyst the possible culprits of the attack, new derived evidence, hints about missing evidence, and insights about other paths of investigation. The proposed reasoner is flexible, deals with conflicting and incomplete evidence, and was tested on real cyber-attacks cases.

1 Introduction

We are currently facing an escalation of cyber-attacks [10] and an aggravation of their effects [3]. The expected exponential increase of the use of IoT and other smart connected devices, together with the growing dependabilities the users have on these devices, make the users more vulnerable and exposed to cyber threats. General preventive and mitigative measures are not sufficient, as there is a need to enforce protective measures that are specific to the attacker (group of attackers) that is performing the attack. Attacker-specific countermeasures would be highly effective and would contain the attack damage. These targeted measures require to discover the entity performing/related to the attack. Identifying who performed the attack would help to bring the culprits of the attack into justice.

Attribution is the process of assigning an action of a cyber-attack to a particular actor. The attribution problem is not trivial as attackers often use deceptive and anti-forensics techniques [4]. Currently, the attribution process is mainly human-based, hence easily biased and error prone, and labour intensive as it involves skilled human resources to analyze enormous amounts of low format data [2]. Digital forensics helps during the attribution process, as it collects, examines, and reports the forensic evidence [9]. Nevertheless, digital forensics

© Springer Nature Switzerland AG 2018
T. Miller et al. (Eds.): PRIMA 2018, LNAI 11224, pp. 510–518, 2018.
https://doi.org/10.1007/978-3-030-03098-8_36

techniques suffer from the limitations derived from the big amount of data to be collected (where there is a need for efficient evidence collection) and analyzed [1,7], and from the fact that it considers only the technical aspects of an attack, without examining the social/geopolitical/economical aspects where the attack took place. A major challenge of digital forensics techniques is that they cannot work with contradictory pieces of evidence or incomplete information.

In this work, we propose an argumentation-based reasoner (ABR) to help the forensic analysts during the analysis and attribution of cyber-attacks. Given different pieces of digital forensics and social evidence, our reasoner derives new information, such as, the potential identity of the attacker, together with an explanation of how the reasoner arrived to its conclusion, and proposes to the user new investigation paths. ABR was based on preliminary results of a decision process framework introduced in [8], and is able to work with incomplete and conflicting evidence, provided by the user, whom we expect to be the forensic analyst. To the best of our knowledge, this is the first reasoner that combines technical and social evidence during the analysis and attribution process of cyber-attacks.

ABR consists of two main components: a set of reasoning rules, called *core rules*, and the *background knowledge*. The core rules model the reasoning used by the forensic analysts during the analysis and attribution of real cyber-attacks. The background knowledge is formed of common knowledge usually used by the analyst, e.g., countries characteristics, prominent cyber groups, past attacks. The core rules use the pieces of evidence given by the user together with the background knowledge to derive a conclusion. The reasoning behind ABR is unbiased and its combination with expert knowledge provides an efficient and accurate analysis and attribution.

We based our reasoner on the Q-Model [13], a social science attribution model, in order to include the social evidence in our reasoning, alongside technical indications. This model describes the procedure of putting together technical and social evidence, followed by the forensic analysts during the attribution of cyber-attacks. The use of the Q-Model enables ABR to structure the reasoning rules and the evidence in three different layers: technical, operational, and strategic, and to work with social and technical pieces of evidence.

We decided to use argumentation reasoning for our reasoner as it allows to capture the knowledge in the same natural and direct form as the human forensic analysts. The use of preference-based argumentation [5,6], permits ABR to deal with conflicting pieces of information, by introducing preferences between rules. We use Gorgias [5], a preference-based argumentation reasoning tool that uses abduction, to construct ABR. The ability to work with incomplete information makes *abduction* suitable to use in the attribution process, as it fills the *knowledge gaps* in our reasoning, and gives to the analyst potential leads to follow and carry out further investigations.

Prior to our work argumentation has been applied to attribution in [11,14], where a probabilistic model is introduced. However, the framework introduced in [11,14] does not use any social evidence or background knowledge that are useful in detecting motives, capabilities, and potential culprits.

The goal of our reasoner is *not to* substitute the forensic analyst but rather to provide a supporting tool to help with the analysis and attribution of cyber-attacks. Therefore, when ABR gives an output to the user, e.g., who is the culprit, or new insights, it provides also an explanation of the given result, allowing the user to adjust and refine the reasoning used by ABR.

In Sect. 2 we introduce the argumentation framework used by ABR. We present ABR and its main components in Sect. 3. We conclude in Sect. 4 and propose some future research directions.

2   Preference-Based Argumentation Framework

The proposed reasoner is based on preference-based argumentation [5,12], as we believe it is best suited for interacting with an analyst during the analysis and attribution of cyber-attacks. In particular, we use the framework proposed in [5, 6] that represents multi-agent application problems via argumentation reasoning. This framework permits us to work with conflicting pieces of evidence, or pieces of evidence that derive conflicting conclusions by introducing preference rules. Preference-based argumentation allows us to handle *non-monotonic reasoning* in attribution, where the introduction of new evidence might change the result of the attribution (due to conflicting arguments). For example, given the argument pair $(T, P)^1$ extracted from the core rules of ABR:

$$T = \{ \ r_1 : attackOrig(X, Attack) \leftarrow \ ipGeoloc(X, IP), attackSourceIP(IP, Attack),$$
$$r_2 : \neg attackOrig(X, Attack) \leftarrow ipGeoloc(X, IP), attackSourceIP(IP, Attack),$$
$$spoofedIP(IP)\}$$
$$P = \{ \ pref_1 : r_2 > r_1\}$$

where rule r_1 states that *Attack* originates from X, $(attackOrig(X, Attack))$, if the source IP of the attack is geolocated in X, while r_2 states that *Attack* does not originate from X, if the source IP of the attack is geolocated in X and the IP is spoofed. If we have the following pieces of evidence:

$$E = \{attackSourceIP(ip1, attack1), ipGeoloc(countryC, ip1)\}$$

we get $attackOrig(countryC, attack1)$ as the conclusion of the argument. However, if we have the evidence:

$$E = \{attackSourceIP(ip2, attack2), ipGeoloc(countryC, ip2), spoofedIP(ip2)\}$$

then the conclusion is $\neg attackOrig(countryC, attack2)$, thus $attack2$ was not originated from $countryC$, as according to the preference rule $pref_1$, we prefer rule r_2 over rule r_1.

---

[1] T represents the argument rules, while P represents the preference rules.

3 Argumentation-Based Reasoner

Our argumentation based reasoner, *ABR*, is based on two main components, the *core rules* and the *background knowledge*, see Fig. 1. The core rules use the pieces of evidence of an observed cyber-attack, which are given as input by the user, together with the background knowledge and give as output the answer as to who/where the observed attack can be attributed to. As the main goal of *ABR* is to help the analyst to gain new insights, it is crucial that *ABR* provides explainable and transparent results to the user. Therefore, *ABR* outputs the result as well as its associated score and the used derivations together with their supporting and/or conflicting rules, and the corresponding graphical representations. The score represents the confidence *ABR* has in the result, and is used to order multiple results. Furthermore, *ABR* provides hints about other investigation paths, by giving a list of missing pieces of evidence that, if provided, can bring into new conclusions. The suggested hints permit the analyst to put in act an efficient prioritized evidence collection. *ABR* models the iterative and incremental nature of the attribution process, where it provides an answer with new information to the analyst, and can integrate additional input from the analyst, which makes *ABR* suitable to be used in conjunction with human experts.

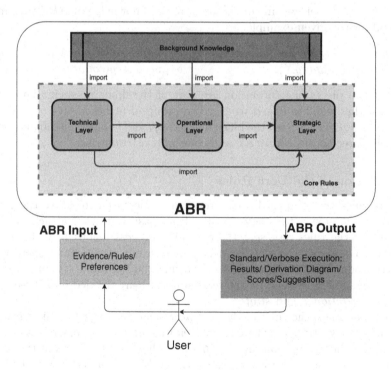

Fig. 1. *ABR* Overview

Let us now introduce an example, where, for the sake of understandability, we simplify the representation of rules and pieces of evidence.

Example 1. Suppose an attack a has occurred, and the analyst is able to recover the IP's from where the attack came from, geolocate them, and check if they can be used or not for the analysis process by checking if they are spoofed or not. An analysis of the attack states that it was performed using malware m and that m shares code with another known malware $mal2$. We represent below the pieces of evidence that the analyst provides to ABR, denoted by $caseE_i$.

$caseE_1 : attackSourceIP(ip1, a),$ $caseE_2 : attackSourceIP(ip2, a),$
$caseE_3 : ipGeoloc(ip1, countryX),$ $caseE_4 : ipGeoloc(ip2, countryY),$
$caseE_5 : spoofedIP(ip2),$ $caseE_6 : hasMotive(countryY, a),$
$caseE_7 : malwareUsed(m, a),$ $caseE_8 : sharedCode(m, mal2).$

The first five focus on technical evidence related to the IP's from where the attack originates, $ip1$, $ip2$, and their geolocation, correspondingly in $countryX$ and $countryY$. $ip2$ is found to be spoofed. Evidence $caseE_6$ provides ABR with some social information related to the attack, stating that $countryY$ has motives to perform a. The last two pieces of evidence, deal with the type of attack, stating that malware m was used in a, and it shares code with $mal2$.

We introduce below some of the background knowledge of ABR that might be useful for the given example.

$bg_1 : malwareLinkedTo(mal2, aGroup),$ $bg_2 : notFromBlackMarket(mal2),$
$bg_3 : country(countryX),$ $bg_4 : country(countryY).$

The first two pieces of information are part of the domain specific knowledge. bg_1 states that $mal2$ is linked to a known group of attackers $aGroup$, and bg_2 states that $mal2$ is not from the black market. bg_3 and bg_4 are general knowledge, where ABR recognises $countryX$ and $countryY$ as countries.   □

3.1   Division of the Core Rules

The core rules are composed of the reasoning rules used to derive the various conclusions. We extracted the core rules from past real cyber-attacks' attributions, where the rules represent the reasoning process followed by the forensic analysts. To deal with the social evidence, we base our reasoner on a social model for attribution, called *Q-Model* [13]. Following the Q-Model, the pieces of evidence (given and derived), and the reasoning rules are divided into three layers: *technical, operational,* and *strategic.*

In our reasoner, the rules of the *technical layer* deal with technical evidence of the attack, e.g., IP from where the attack was originated, time of attack, logs. The rules of the *operational layer* deal with other social aspects of the attack, e.g., the motives of the attack, the needed capabilities to perform it. The rules of the *strategic layer* deal with who might have done the attack, or who is taking advantage from it. Depending on the layer a rule/evidence is part of, we call it a technical, operational, or strategic rule/evidence.

Let us show through an example, how these layers are connected to each other and what type of evidence and rules goes to which layer. One of the rules of the strategic layer is the following[2]:

$$s_1 : isCulprit(X, A) \leftarrow hasMotive(X, A), hasCapability(X, A).$$

saying that entity X is the culprit of attack A, if it has the motivations to perform the attack $hasMotive(X, A)$ and it has the capability to conduct it $hasCapability(X, A)$. The evidence used in the above rule is given by the user or is derived using rules of the technical and operational layer. In particular, the evidence $hasCapability$ depends on the type of attack.

$$o_1 : hasCapability(X, A) \leftarrow requireHighResource(A), hasResource(X).$$

The above rule is an operational layer rule and states that X has the capability to perform attack A, in case A requires high resources $requireHighResource(A)$ and X has these resources $hasResource(X)$. The rule below, which is part of the technical layer, derives the $requireHighResource(A)$ evidence from the skill level needed by the attacker to perform A.

$$t_1 : requireHighResource(A) \leftarrow highLevelSkill(A).$$

The $highLevelSkill(A)$ evidence is derived using the technical layer rule below:

$$t_2 : highLevelSkill(A) \leftarrow malwareUsed(M, A), usesZeroDayVuln(M).$$

where the used pieces of evidence are technical ones. The above rule states that A is a high level skill attack, if the used malware, $malwareUsed(M, A)$, exploits zero day vulnerabilities, $usesZeroDayVuln(M)$.

Example 2. Following from Example 1, reasoning rules can be used to derive the results. For example, we show below a strategic reasoning rule used by ABR to derive that $aGroup$ might be the culprit of the attack.

$$\begin{aligned} s_2 : isCulprit(X, A) \leftarrow\ & malwareUsed(M1, A), similar(M1, M2), \\ & notFromBlackMarket(M1), \\ & notFromBlackMarket(M2), \\ & malwareLinkedTo(M2, X). \end{aligned}$$

The rule states that a certain entity X is the attacker, if the malware used $M1$ is similar to malware $M2$ that is linked to entity X. The $similar(M1, M2)$ evidence can be derived using a technical rule, such as:

$$t_3 : similar(M1, M2) \leftarrow sharedCode(M1, M2).$$

which considers that two malwares are similar if they share a significant part of their code, $sharedCode(M1, M2)$. □

---

[2] The rule's name represents the layer of the rule, i.e., the rules' names of the technical, operational, and strategic layer start correspondingly with t, o, and s.

3.2   *ABR* execution

Given the pieces of evidence to *ABR*, the user can execute *ABR* in two modes. In *standard mode*, it gives as result the answers to the queries, e.g., wether a particular entity performed the attack. In *verbose mode*, it gives as result hints of what other pieces of evidence are required to reach a specific conclusion, given the evidence found so far. We tested *ABR* with real cyber-attacks cases, taken from public reports, and artifacted examples. *ABR* was able to correctly identify the culprits given the appropriate pieces of evidence. In verbose mode, *ABR*'s results include the missing evidence (when some pieces of evidence were omitted) or suggest appropriate investigation paths to be followed by the analyst.

Standard Mode. The standard execution is called after providing to *ABR* the pieces of evidence and making a query. This mode gives as result the answer of the query, e.g., if an entity is the culprit or not of the attack, if there are other attacks similar to the exiting one, from where the attack originated, or all the entities that might be the culprits of the examined cyber-attack. For every given answer, *ABR* provides the derivations rules and pieces of evidence used to arrive at the conclusion, together with a graphical representation of the derivation, and a score of the result, based on a scoring system. It also provides an argumentation tree of the used reasoning rules that shows how the different conflicting arguments supporting/attacking the various possibilities of attribution are considered.

Example 3. Going back to Example 1, when *ABR* is given the pieces of evidence and is asked "who is the culprit" it gives the following output:

$$aGroup, \ countryX, \ countryY.$$

ABR gives three different answers as it is able to prove for each of them that they might be the culprit. Thus, it provides all the above answers together with their explanations.   □

Verbose Mode. The verbose mode is usually used when there are not enough pieces of evidence to support a conclusion, or when the user wants to know other paths of investigation. Given the pieces of evidence *ABR*'s verbose execution identifies the *missing pieces of evidence* necessary to reach other or more precise conclusions. The list suggests to the user other pieces of evidence to be collected, and hints to other investigation paths.

Example 4. Some of the results of executing *ABR* in verbose mode given the pieces of evidence of Example 1 are shown below:

$$hasMotive(countryX, a), \ target(X, a), \ hasMotive(countryZ, a).$$

The first suggestion asks if *countryX* has motive to perform the attack, in order to make the attribution more precise. The second one, $target(X, a)$, asks which were the targets of a. The last suggestion, asks if the user can provide evidence ($hasMotive$) for another country, $countryZ$, as this country is linked with a prominent group of attackers that is able to perform this type of attack, and it usually performs attacks for $countryZ$.   □

4   Conclusions and Future Works

A correct and swift attribution of cyber-attacks permits to put in place adequate mitigative and preventive measures. Attributing cyber-attacks is a delicate and difficult task, due to the large amount of often conflicting evidence that needs to be analysed and the fact that attackers use deceptive and anti-forensics techniques. In this work we proposed a reasoner (ABR), based on a preference-based argumentation that helps the forensic analyst during the analysis of forensic evidence of an observed cyber-attack and its attribution. ABR provides the analyst with an answer as of where the observed attack originated and to who it can be attributed. The proposed reasoner automates the attribution process and is fully flexible, as it allows and supports the analyst to introduce new evidence, rules, and preferences.

As future work, we plan to increase ABR reasoning capabilities by adding new reasoning rules, and background knowledge. In order to fully automate the attribution process, we intend to enrich ABR with an automatic evidence extraction/collection, by integrating ABR with digital forensics tools and data mining techniques.

Acknowledgments. Erisa Karafili was supported by the European Union's H2020 research and innovation programme under the Marie Skłodowska-Curie grant agreement No. 746667.

References

1. Carrier, B.: Defining digital forensic examination and analysis tools using abstraction layers. Int. J. Digit. Evid. **1**(4), 1–12 (2003)
2. da Cruz Nassif, L.F., Hruschka, E.R.: Document clustering for forensic analysis: an approach for improving computer inspection. IEEE Trans. Inf. Forensic Secur. **8**(1), 46–54 (2013)
3. DCMS: Cyber security breaches survey 2018 (2018). https://www.gov.uk/government/statistics/cyber-security-breaches-survey-2018
4. Goutam, R.K.: The problem of attribution in cyber security. Int. J. Comput. Appl. Found. Comput. Sci. **131**(7), 34–36 (2015)
5. Kakas, A., Moraitis, P.: Argumentation based decision making for autonomous agents. In: AAMAS 2003, pp. 883–890 (2003)
6. Kakas, A.C., Mancarella, P., Dung, P.M.: The acceptability semantics for logic programs. In: International Conference on Logic Programming, pp. 504–519 (1994)
7. Karafili, E., Cristani, M., Viganò, L.: A formal approach to analyzing cyber-forensics evidence. In: Lopez, J., Zhou, J., Soriano, M. (eds.) ESORICS 2018. LNCS, vol. 11098, pp. 281–301. Springer, Cham (2018). https://doi.org/10.1007/978-3-319-99073-6_14

8. Karafili, E., Kakas, A.C., Spanoudakis, N.I., Lupu, E.C.: Argumentation-based Security for Social Good. In: AAAI Fall Symposium Series (2017)

9. Kent, K., Chevalier, S., Grance, T., Dang, H.: SP 800–86. Guide to Integrating Forensic Techniques into Incident Response. Technical report, NIST (2006)

10. Newman, L.H.: The Biggest Cybersecurity Disasters of 2017 So Far (2017). https://www.wired.com/story/2017-biggest-hacks-so-far/

11. Nunes, E., Shakarian, P., Simari, G.I.: Toward argumentation-based cyber attribution. In: AAAI Workshops (2016)

12. Prakken, H., Sartor, G.: Argument-based extended logic programming with defeasible priorities. J. Appl. Non-Class. Log. **7**(1), 25–75 (1997)

13. Rid, T., Buchanan, B.: Attributing cyber attacks. J. Strat. Stud. **38**(1–2), 4–37 (2015)

14. Shakarian, P., Simari, G.I., Moores, G., Parsons, S.: Cyber attribution: an argumentation-based approach. In: Jajodia, S., Shakarian, P., Subrahmanian, V.S., Swarup, V., Wang, C. (eds.) Cyber Warfare. AIS, vol. 56, pp. 151–171. Springer, Cham (2015). https://doi.org/10.1007/978-3-319-14039-1_8

Agent33: An Automated Negotiator with Heuristic Method for Searching Bids Around Nash Bargaining Solution

Shan Liu$^{(\boxtimes)}$, Ahmed Moustafa, and Takayuki Ito

Nagoya Institute of Technology, Nagoya, Japan
liu.shan@itolab.nitech.ac.jp, {ahmed,ito.takayuki}@nitech.ac.jp

Abstract. The international Automated Negotiating Agents Competition (ANAC) is being held annually since 2010 in order to bring together the researchers from the multi-agent negotiation community. In this regard, the Repeated Multilateral Negotiation League (RMNL), one of the four negotiation research challenges in ANAC 2018, requires participants to design and implement an intelligent negotiating agent, that is able to negotiate with two other opponents and that is able to learn from its previous negotiation experiences. In this context, in this paper, we design a negotiating agent that focuses on searching the space of suitable bids that provide high utilities for both sides near the Nash Bargaining Solution (NBS) using a novel heuristic method. The proposed agent has participated in the ANAC competition successfully and finished in the second place in the social welfare category.

Keywords: Automated negotiation · Heuristic method
Bid searching · Nash bargaining solution

1 Introduction

In this paper, we present Agent33, an intelligent agent negotiation strategy that was designed and implemented in order to participate in the ANAC RMNL 2018. ANAC 2018 [1] includes four different negotiation research challenges. One of these challenges, i.e., RMNL, promotes the researchers to develop successful automated negotiators for scenarios where there is incomplete information about their opponents. In order to achieve this goal, it allows a set of automated negotiating agents to compete against each other, in a closed trilateral multi issue setting using Stacked Alternating Offers Protocol (SAOP) [2].

A review of several strategies that were adopted by many agents from the past competitions reveals the introduction of plenty of algorithms for bid searching, such as Simulated Annealing (SA) [3], the Bids Replacement by the Agreement and Reject (A/R) [4], the Combination of *the Best Bid, the Best Offered Bid* and *the Frequency Bid* [5]. However, a number of limitations exist in these algorithms. In order to solve these problems, this paper introduces Agent33. Agent33 is an

© Springer Nature Switzerland AG 2018
T. Miller et al. (Eds.): PRIMA 2018, LNAI 11224, pp. 519–526, 2018.
https://doi.org/10.1007/978-3-030-03098-8_37

intelligent negotiating agent that aims to solve these problems by employing an effective bid search strategy and a successful bid acceptance strategy.

The rest of this paper is organized as follows. Section 2 describes the negotiation environment in ANAC 2018. Section 3 introduces the proposed negotiation strategy. Section 4 presents the ANAC 2018 competition results, along with their evaluation and discussion. Section 5 analyzes the proposed negotiating strategy and discusses the evaluation results. Section 6 briefly presents the related work. Section 7 summarizes the conclusion and outlines the future work.

2   The Negotiation Environment

This section describes the negotiation environment where the participant agents competed during the ANAC 2018. The description of the negotiation environment consists of the following parts as follows.

2.1   Competition Setup

The chosen competition is a multi-party closed negotiation among three agents, without any knowledge of the preferences and strategies of the opponent agents, where the negotiating agents used the Stacked Alternating Offers Protocol (SAOP). In this context, each agent has three minutes to deliberate. In addition, a reservation value is allowed to be held in certain scenarios. Each negotiation round is repeated five times. Also, the utility functions are linear and the participant agents are able to negotiate about a large set of previously unknown preferences.

2.2   General Environment for Negotiation with Intelligent Multi-purpose Usage Simulation (GENIUS)

GENIUS [6] is a negotiation environment that implements an open architecture for heterogeneous negotiating agents. It provides a testbed for negotiating agents that includes a set of negotiation problems for benchmarking these agents, a library of negotiation strategies, and a set of analytical tools in order to evaluate the performance of the participant agents.

2.3   Preferences of the Negotiation Parties

The preferences for each agent in all domains are given by a weighted sum utility function. In this regard, each agent has its own utility function. This utility function is expressed as follows:

$$u_a(b) = \sum_{j \in I} V_a(b_j) \cdot w_{a,j} \tag{1}$$

where each issue $j \in I$ can take a value v_j from a predefined set of valid values for that issue which is denoted by D_j (i.e., $v_j \in D_j$), where each agent can access this domain information. In addition, a bid $b = (b_1,...,b_{|I|})$ is an assignment of values to all issues where $b_1 \in D_1$. $V_a(b_j)$ denotes Agent a valuation of the value for the issue j in the bid b. $w_{a,j}$ denotes Agent a the weight of its issue j.

2.4   Time Constraints

There are three important factors that are defined in order to increase the degree of complication of the negotiation and make it similar to real life scenarios. These factors are deadline, discount factor and reservation value. During each negotiation round, bid offers are exchanged in real time with a deadline set after specific minutes, which is three minutes in the ANAC 2018. If the participant agents cannot reach an agreement by the deadline, their utility values are set to the reservation value. In addition, this agreement prospect decreases over time according to a certain discount factor, which means the more time an agreement takes, the lower utilities the participant agents receive. As a result, reservation value is set equal to disagreement point. An example of discount factor [7] is presented in Fig. 1.

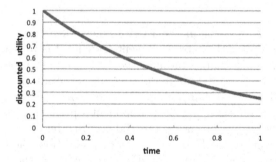

Fig. 1. An example of discount factor

3   Description of the Proposed Agent

The majority of the participant agents in the ANAC competitions are implemented in the BOA framework [8]. In this regard, a negotiating agent in the BOA framework, called a BOA agent, consists of four components as follows:

Bidding Strategy. A *bidding strategy* is a mapping which maps a negotiation trace to a bid. The bidding strategy is able to interact with the opponent model by communicating with it.

Opponent Model. An *opponent model* in the BOA framework is a learning technique that constructs a model of the preference profile of this opponent.

Opponent Model Strategy. An *opponent model strategy* specifies how the opponent model is used in order to select a bid for the opponent, and if that opponent model could be updated in a specific turn.

Acceptance Strategy. The *acceptance strategy* determines whether the opponent's bid is acceptable and is considered enough decide to end the negotiation prematurely.

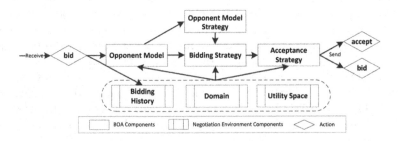

Fig. 2. The BOA framework architecture

The lifecycle of an agent in the BOA framework architecture is shown in Fig. 2. The main idea of the proposed agent (Agent33) is to search an approximate scope of the bids that lie around the NBS, and then, offer one of these bids that yields high utility for all participant negotiators. In other words, there is no need to build complete preference profiles for opponent negotiators, instead, focus on searching these opponent's preference issues. Therefore, this work focuses on implementing the Bidding Strategy and the Acceptance Strategy components of the BOA Framework. In addition, the Domain and the Negotiation Status are also implemented as components of the negotiation environment. We will discuss the Bidding Strategy and the Bid Acceptance Strategy in the following two subsections.

3.1   Bidding Strategy: A Heuristic Method for Searching a Nash Bargaining Solution (NBS)

The proposed agent (Agent33) works as follows. The Bidding Strategy aims to propose bids around the NBS [9] because these bids are expected to posses higher values of the joint utility. However, it is difficult to find the NBS with an incomplete utility values. Therefore, Agent33 uses a novel heuristic method in order to find the promising bids around the NBS. In other words, Agent33 only searches for the promising bids in a small scope around the NBS. In order to achieve this goal, the proposed heuristic method aims to construct a list of the opponents prior issues, which is incrementally updated throughout the negotiation process.

The process to find the opponents prior issues consists of two steps. The first step calculates the standard deviation of each value's frequency in each issue and names the result as Value Standard Deviation. While the second step calculates the standard deviation of each issue's Value Standard Deviation and names the result as Issue Standard Deviation. In this context, if a certain negotiator has large Issue Standard Deviation, it means this negotiator has an obvious preference of the prior issues. The issues with high Value Standard Deviation are the prior issues of this negotiator and the values with high frequency are the prior values of these prior issues. These prior issues and their prior values are set in a pair that is called Prior Pair. In other words, we believe that the issues whose values are frequently changed by opponent negotiators are not crucial for them.

Using the aforementioned concepts, the proposed agent (Agent33) constructs a bid by combining the opponent's Prior Pair with its own Prior Pair, and then chooses the values of other issues randomly. However, during the negotiation process, if opponent negotiators compromise at an early stage, or if they do not have any prior issues, Agent33 might return errors. In addition, if a conflict is found among the prior issues, Agent33 then uses the Prior Pair of the opponent negotiators as priority. It is important to note that the repetition of negotiation helps to improve the accuracy of prediction. From above, it is presumed that the proposed heuristic method is able to reduce the bid searching scope and to find promising bids around the NBS, which improves the probability to find a suitable bid. The comparison of the bid searching scope is presented in Fig. 3. A simple example is presented in Fig. 4.

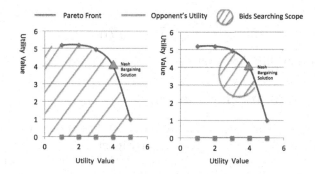

Fig. 3. The bid searching scope without our method (right) and with our method (left)

3.2 Bid Acceptance Strategy

In this subsection, we present the bid acceptance strategy. If the utility of a certain bid is greater than a preset threshold value, then the proposed agent accepts this bid. This threshold value is decreasing as time passes. In addition, this threshold value is calculated using the following equation.

$$Threshold = \max\{(1 - (1 - df) \cdot \log(e - 1.9 + (e - 1)^{\alpha}) \cdot t), emax\} \quad (2)$$

```
e.g.: A scenario which has three issues, a, b, c is given. Each issue has three
values, as a1,a2,a3. Assuming that Agent1 participates the negotiation and
provides bids as follows:


Agent1:            RESULT:
a1, b1, c2         Value Standard Deviation  a: 4.90, b: 2.83, c: 0.0
a1, b1, c1         Issue Standard Deviation: 3.48 > 0.0
a1, b1, c3         Order of values by comparing standard deviation: a, b, c
a1, b1, c1         Prior issues of Agent1 : a, b
a1, b2, c2         Prior values of Agent1 : a1, b1
a1, b2, c3
...
```

Fig. 4. A simple example of the bidding strategy

where df represents a discount factor. α is a parameter which we set as 4.5 optionally. t represents the current time. $emax$ means the estimated maximum which is calculated using the following equation.

$$emax(t) = \mu(t) + (1 - \mu(t)) \cdot d(t) \tag{3}$$

where $\mu(t)$ is the utility mean of the opponent's offers in the agent's utility space. $d(t)$ [4] is a function for estimating the utility width of the opponent offers in this agent utility space which is given by Farma Agent in the ANAC 2016 competition as follow:

$$d(t) = \frac{\sqrt{3}\sigma(t)}{\sqrt{\mu(t)(1 - \mu(t))}} \tag{4}$$

where σ is the standard deviation.

4   The Results and Evaluation

There are 21 participant agents who represent ten institutions from eight countries in the ANAC RMNL 2018. The 21 participant agents are divided by three pools randomly. Through the qualifying round, the top three performing agents in each pool can proceed to the final round.

The ANAC RMNL 2018 competition has two categories: the individual category, in which the participant agents are ranked according to the individual utility they have obtained, and the social welfare category in which the participant agents are ranked by the social utility, which is the sum of these agent's individual utilities and their opponents' utilities. The final round has been run among nine finalists in each category with four selected scenarios submitted by the participants. For each scenario, 2520 negotiations were run. The results of the qualifying round of the social welfare category is presented in Fig. 5. The proposed agent (Agent33) won the second place in the final round of the social welfare category as shown in Fig. 6 which demonstrated its efficiency by wining the second place in this competitive environment.

Qualify Round Result (Pool C)

Agent Name	Individual Utility	Social Welfare
AgentNP1	0.512177707	1.52976242
GroupY	0.485323479	1.33874982
ATeamAgent	0.345297603	0.980979189
Sontag	0.484535782	1.515047114
Agent33	0.428666974	1.419233621
Agent_Hama	0.469592183	1.393009022
Exp-Rubick	-	-

Overall Ranking (Social welfare)

Fig. 5. The qualify round results of the social welfare category (Pool C)

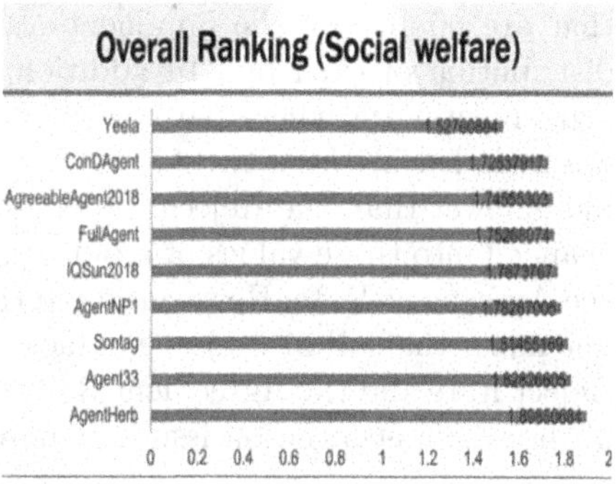

Fig. 6. The final round results of the social welfare category

5 Discussion

In the proposed negotiation strategy, the negotiating agent (Agent33) compares among the different negotiation issues by the standard deviation of their values, and then, chooses the issues with the highest standard deviation values as prior issues. In this regard, the most frequent values of each prior issue are considered as prior values. Therefore, instead of modeling the opponents' utility distribution, the proposed agent focuses on searching the scope of the bids that are able to return high utilities for all participant agents.

At the current stage, the proposed agent does not focus on the acceptance strategy, therefore, the proposed agent performed weakly in the individual category. In order to solve this problem, the proposed agent needs to consider the existing threshold calculation strategies, and the necessary techniques needed to combine these strategies with the proposed bid searching strategy.

6 Related Work

In AgentM [5], which is the champion in both the individual category and the social welfare category in the ANAC 2014, Niimi et al. proposed a bids combination strategy which offers a combined bid that consists of *the Best Bid*, *the Best Offered Bid*, and *the Frequency Bid*. This agent used *the Best Bid* as a base bid, and replaced two issues' values of *the Best Bid* randomly with a random issue value of *the Best Offered Bid* and a random issue value of *the Frequency Bid*, respectively. In order to generate *the Frequency Bid*, they counted up the number of all issue values and chose the most frequent value for each issue. The same consideration is also used in Agent Farma and Agent Terra in the ANAC 2016. However, all of the three agents did not consider the importance level of each issue.

In Agent Farma17 [10], the Agreement and Reject (A/R) idea is used for offering a more acceptable bid. This agent focused on the frequency of bids that are offered by the opponents, and calculated the cumulative probability distribution of each bid. In addition, this agent set up a Reject Rate and an Agreement Rate where part of the bids that are accepted from the opponents are included in these two types. If the cumulative probability of the accepted bid is lower than the Reject Rate, the values of certain issues will be randomly changed into those values of a bid which has higher cumulative probability than the Agreement Rate. However, a bid that has higher cumulative probability does not mean that all of its issue values are acceptable. Instead of focusing on the Reject Rate and the Agreement Rate of the bids, considering an Agreement Rate of the whole negotiation issues is more suitable.

7   Conclusion

In this paper, we proposed an intelligent negotiation agent that utilizes the previous bids of its opponents in order to search for the successful bids around Nash Bargaining Solution. The final round results of the ANAC RNML 2018 competition demonstrated that the proposed agent is able to search the suitable bids scope around Nash Bargaining Solution and succeeded to lead other participant agents where the proposed agent achieved higher social utilities. Future work is set to study the necessary improvements that are needed to achieve a high individual utility and to reduce the scope of bid searching.

References

1. ANAC 2018. http://web.tuat.ac.jp/~katfuji/ANAC2018/
2. Slides of repeated multilateral negotiation league results. In: ANAC 2018. http://web.tuat.ac.jp/~katfuji/ANAC2018/Results_Genius.pdf
3. Du, K.-L., Swamy, M.N.S.: Simulated annealing. Search and Optimization by Metaheuristics, pp. 29–36. Springer, Cham (2016). https://doi.org/10.1007/978-3-319-41192-7_2
4. Toyama, T., Ito, T.: Concession based on maximum utilities estimated by a divided uniform distribution. In: The Seventh International Automated Negotiating Agents Competition (ANAC 2016) (2016)
5. Niimi, M., Ito, T.: AgentM. In: Fukuta, N., Ito, T., Zhang, M., Fujita, K., Robu, V. (eds.) Recent Advances in Agent-based Complex Automated Negotiation. SCI, vol. 638, pp. 235–240. Springer, Cham (2016). https://doi.org/10.1007/978-3-319-30307-9_15
6. GENIUS. http://ii.tudelft.nl/genius/
7. Morii, S., Kawaguchi, S., Ito, T.: Analysis of agent strategy based on discount utility in Automated negotiating agents competition (ANAC 2012). In: JAWS 2012 (2012)
8. Baarslag, T., Pasman, W., Hindriks, K., Tykhonov, D.: Using the genius framework for running autonomous negotiating agents (2018)
9. Cho, I., Matsui, A.: Search theory, competitive equilibrium, and the Nash bargaining solution. J. Econ. Theory **148**(4), 1659–1688 (2013). Pavan, A., Ortoleva, P., Siniscalchi, M., Veldkamp, L., Vives, X. (eds.)
10. ANAC 2017. http://web.tuat.ac.jp/~katfuji/ANAC2017/

Effect of Viewing Directions on Deep Reinforcement Learning in 3D Virtual Environment *Minecraft*

Taiju Matsui[1(✉)], Satoshi Oyama[1,2], and Masahito Kurihara[1]

[1] Graduate School of Information Science and Technology, Hokkaido University,
Kita 14, Nishi 9, Kita-ku, Sapporo, Hokkaido 060-0814, Japan
`matsui-t@complex.ist.hokudai.ac.jp`
[2] Global Institution for Collaborative Research and Education, Hokkaido University,
Kita 14, Nishi 9, Kita-ku, Sapporo, Hokkaido 060-0814, Japan

Abstract. Deep reinforcement learning, which has recently attracted
the interest of AI researchers, combines deep neural networks (DNNs)
and reinforcement learning (RL). By approximating a function in RL
with a DNN, it enables an agent to learn in a complex environment represented by low-level features such as the pixels used in a 3D video game.
However, learning from low-level features is sometimes problematic. For
example, a small difference in input pixels results in completely different
behaviors of an agent. In this study, as an example of such problems, we
focus on the viewing directions of an agent in a 3D virtual environment
(*Minecraft*) and analyze their effect on the efficiency of deep reinforcement learning.

1 Introduction

Recent developments in deep neural networks (DNNs) have enhanced the capability of DNNs to process high-dimensional data and to serve as vision in
autonomous agents. This progress has made it possible for artificial intelligence
(AI) to learn behaviors in video games directly from the screen images, which
is called visual learning. In particular, Deep Q-Network (DQN) [3,4], an algorithm proposed by DeepMind for Google, outperformed a human expert player
in Atari 2600 games with 2D image data. In 2016, Google DeepMind proposed
an asynchronous method [2]. One of the algorithms based on this method, called
asynchronous advantage actor-critic (A3C), has surpassed all existing methods
in efficiency and gain score.

Deep reinforcement learning (DRL) algorithms combine deep learning (DL)
and reinforcement learning (RL). In DL, image data is used to define the representation of states, while RL is used for approximating the outputs of the DNN
to outputs of RL. But image data are too complex to use as a representation. For
example, image data expressed using RGB has a $\langle \text{height} \rangle \times \langle \text{width} \rangle \times \langle 3(\text{RGB}) \rangle$
$\times \langle 256(0{\sim}255) \rangle$ pattern. However, in most RL environments, visual information

© Springer Nature Switzerland AG 2018
T. Miller et al. (Eds.): PRIMA 2018, LNAI 11224, pp. 527–534, 2018.
https://doi.org/10.1007/978-3-030-03098-8_38

available to agents is restricted, which very much complicates the process of representation learning. In the case of learning from first-person view image data in a 3D virtual environment, agents have limited information about the environment and sometimes misunderstand their states. Furthermore, when pixels change color due to a change in the sight direction, learning from such image data becomes unstable. In order to acquire best action from the first-person views in a 3D environment, an algorithm that can handle this complexity is needed. In this study, as a preparation for developing such algorithm, we investigate differences in learning processes and acquired behavior in relation to the elevation angle of the agent's view when playing *Minecraft*.

The viewing direction is deeply related to the important psychological state of humans and animals such as attention and curiosity. It is also an important means of communication among them. We think controlling the viewing direction is an essential element to build autonomous agents and multiagent systems that operate in complex environments.

2   Related Work

This section describes the research related to deep reinforcement learning and the environment of *Minecraft*.

2.1   Deep Reinforcement Learning

Deep reinforcement learning algorithms approximate policy $\pi(s, a; \theta)$, value function $V(s; \theta)$, $Q(s, a; \theta)$, or both of them with the outputs of deep learning, where s, a, and θ represent state, action, and DNN parameters, respectively. These algorithms combine deep learning and reinforcement learning and use image data for learning specific actions. However, using non-linear approximators such as neural networks decreases the robustness of reinforcement learning. It is well known that loss of robustness is caused by the correlation between data sorted by a time series and a policy or a value function. Two DRL methods, DQN and A3C, solve this problem in their own way.

Deep Q-Network. DQNs use two methods for stability. One of them is called experience replay in which tuples, sets of [state, action, reward, next state], are saved to experience replay memory for the last T steps of exploration. The algorithm then learns by mini batches randomly sampled from the experience replay memory every few explorations. Although this method reduces correlations, it has two weak points. One is that the on-policy algorithms are not applicable because the data from exploration is based on a previous policy. The other is that the size of the experience replay memory tends to be large.

The second method is called fixed target network. In DQNs, there is a learning phase after every few explorations. During that phase, a little changes in value functions update the policy greatly, causing loss of robustness of the algorithm. To avoid this problem, the DNN parameters θ are fixed to θ^- during the learning phase. This contrivance is called fixed target network.

Asynchronous Advantage Actor-Critic. In A3C, the algorithm contains parallel threads for collecting data by exploration to reduce correlation, and the threads run asynchronously. Since asynchronous threads run apart from each other, the collected data is the same as the randomly sampled data. Each threads computes in the following order.

1. Copy from global network parameter θ to thread's own local network parameter θ^-.
2. Explore the learning environment based on own parameter, and compute the gradient $d\theta$ from the loss function $L(\theta)$. $L(\theta)$ is computed from temporal difference error.
3. After several explorations, send gradient $d\theta$ to global network and update parameter by gradient decent.
4. Return to step 1. and repeat the process until T_{max}.

Here, copying parameter at 1 has the same effect as the fixed-target network of the DQN. These parameters are optimized by gradient decent of the REINFORCE algorithm [6] and use Advantage function for estimating a current state value in this time. Advantage function is as follows:

$$A_t = \sum_{i=0}^{k-1} \gamma^i r_{t+1} + \gamma^k V(s_{t+k}; \theta_v) - V(s_t; \theta_v) \tag{1}$$

Owning Advantage function, the algorithm could use more future data than temporal difference error calculated by Bellman equation. Using Advantage function, the gradient of parameters are calculated by the following formula.

$$d\theta \leftarrow d\theta + \alpha \nabla_\theta \log \pi(s_t, a_t; \theta) A_t + \beta \nabla_\theta H(\pi(s_t; \theta)) \tag{2}$$
$$d\theta_v \leftarrow d\theta_v + \alpha \nabla_{\theta_v} A_t^2 \tag{3}$$

Here, third term of (2) is the entropy term for stochastic normalization.

2.2   Minecraft (Project Malmo)

Minecraft is a videogame sold by Microsoft in a genre called sandbox. Sandbox games have no forced mission, so the playing styles and the environment are flexible. In *Minecraft*, the environment is made of various cubes, but is similar to the real world we live in. The environment has the following features.

- Agents are affected by gravity, but cubes placed in the environment are not, with some exception.
- Enemies are spawned under certain circumstances.
- There is a concept of time. Time affects Brightness of the environment.
- There is a concept of biome and different terrains; various blocks and creatures are existed in each biome.

The agents can perform the following actions.

- Destroy and get almost all blocks by continuous attack. Some blocks require a special tool for destroying.
- Relocate the conquered blocks to the adjacent spaces.
- Combine blocks or items and create new blocks or items, called crafting.
- Use the newly crafted items.

Microsoft Research released a platform called *Project Malmo* [1] at GitHub in 2016. It's aim is to provide a testbed/sandbox for developing AI agents within *Minecraft*. This release provides a framework for interactions between the agent and the environment and facilitates the development of the *Minecraft* experimental environment.

3   Experiment in Minecraft

3.1   Purpose of the Experiment

The purpose of the experiment is to investigate the differences in the learning process and acquired behavior in relation to the elevation angle of the agent's view in *Minecraft*.

3.2   Configuration of Learning Task

Here, we describe the configuration of the task using Project Malmo. The outline of the learning task is to "advance without falling down the road and without branching", as a simple problem is preferred for investigating the effect of changes in the elevation angle. An episode ends when the agent reaches the goal (the end of the road), or falls down the road, or when time is up. The score is calculated and recorded by the advantage function. The environment is composed of a road having several corners, and the agent gets RGB images ($84 \times 84 \times 3$) as a representation of the current state (Fig. 1). The agent can take actions that combine "advance, turn left, turn right" with the exception of taking no action. The reward for the agent is designed as $+1.0$ when the goal is reached, -1.0 when the agent falls down the road or when time is up, and $+0.1$ when the agent proceeds down the road for 1 block in *Minecraft* in order to avoid acquiring the behavior of the agent turning in the same spot. In the experiment, we set the elevation angle of the agents' view to $0°$, $-30°$, and $-45°$, then learn during 2 million steps (a step is about 0.1 s) (Fig. 2). Because the information about the road is different from each angle, it is expected that the results of the experiment will also be different.

3.3   Experimental Results

Difference in Learning Process. Figure 3 shows the average score of every 10,000 steps in the learning process of 2 million steps. It indicates that the more information about the road is caught in the agent's view, the earlier the agent acquires suitable behavior.

Bird's - eye view of the environment   **Agent's view**

Fig. 1. Environment using for learning

angle 0°   **angle −30°**   **angle −45°**

Fig. 2. Each agent's view at different elevation angles

Difference in Acquired Behavior. After the learning process, we collect the data on the average scores, average advanced degrees and the goal arrival rates from 1,000 episodes. The results are presented in Fig. 4. It also shows the significance of the information about the road in the agent's view. These results are similar to the results of the previous experiments Sect. 3.3.

The Points of Falling down. The points where the agents fall down are shown in Fig. 5. The agents with a view of 0° fall down at the beginning of the road, in its straight part, because the agent cannot obtain useful information enough to pass. On the contrary, the agents with a view of −30° and −45° can obtain information that helps them reach the goal. However, they also fall down at a certain point. This is because the actions are discrete and binarized to "do" or "not do", which sometimes cause the agents to lose sight at the corners of the road.

3.4   Discussion

In the experiment of learning process, the learning process is affected by the agents' view during the time required for learning. In the experiment Sect. 3.3, the acquired behavior is also affected by the view. This proves that the amount of information necessary to achieve the learning task is extremely important for exploration in a 3D virtual environment by the first-person view. Furthermore, in the experiment Sect. 3.3, it is necessary not only to give the appropriate view but also to make the actions continuous. Therefore, we consider that the control of the agents' view is an important issue for exploration in a 3D virtual environment by the first-person view.

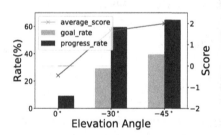

Fig. 3. Average score every 10,000 steps during learning process

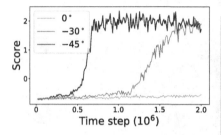

Fig. 4. Average score, progress rate, and goal rate by 1,000 episodes

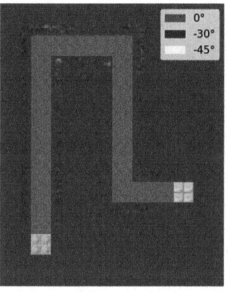

Fig. 5. Difference in falling position

4   Additional Experiment

We prepared a more difficult task for evaluating the difficulty of learning the control of agent's view direction. In this new task, the basic rules are the same as in the previous task, but the road is randomly generated with a fixed length. The road does not have any branches or loops, and its terminus is a tower of specific blocks. Figure 6 is an example of the generated road of such environment. We compared the learning process and acquired behavior with the agent controlling the view direction (the sight-controlling agent), in addition to the agents with fixed angles in our previous experiment.

Fig. 6. Environment for additional experiment

4.1 Result of Additional Experiment

We compared difference in learning process and acquired behavior. Figure 7 shows the average scores of the learning process and Fig. 8 shows the evaluations of each agent. Both of them indicate the difficulty of controlling agent's sight direction. In Fig. 7, the sight-controlling agent could not outperform other agents even if it was trained for longer than the others. In Fig. 8, the sight-controlling agent shows the results similar to the agent with a view of 0° and it indicates the training was not successful.

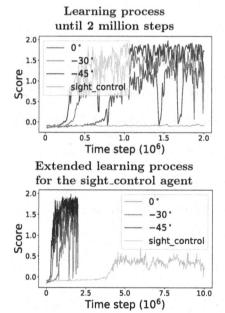

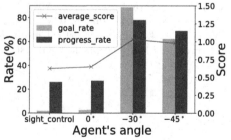

Fig. 7. Average score every 10,000 steps during learning process in additional experiment

Fig. 8. Average score, progress rate, and goal rate by 1,000 episodes in additional experiment

4.2   Discussion on Additional Experiment

In the additional experiment, the difficulty of controlling agent's sight direction was indicated. It might be caused by vast and discrete action space. The sight-controlling agent has 17 patterns of actions, which are about 3 times as many as the actions of other agents. It can affect the results as the curse of dimensionality. Hence, to learn complex behavior to control site direction, we improve the learning algorithm so that it can solve the problem of the large actions space.

5   Conclusion and Future Work

In this paper, we explained the methods of Deep Reinforcement Learning, then investigated the effects of directions of agents' view in 3D virtual environment for the task acquiring behavior using one of the methods, A3C.

As a future work, we suggested controlling agents' view direction and presented the results of the preliminary experiment. Since A3C was proposed in 2016, the methods with various additions to A3C is proposed. One of these methods [5] used curiosity by self-supervised prediction. It calculates internal reward from input images apart from external reward given as reply of action by the environment. We consider concept of internal reward is useful for exploration in 3D virtual environment by first person view. Therefore, we set a goal for proposing an algorithm to control agent's view direction.

References

1. Johnson, M., Hofmann, K., Hutton, T., Bignell, D.: The Malmo platform for artificial intelligence experimentation. In: IJCAI, pp. 4246–4247 (2016)
2. Mnih, V., et al.: Asynchronous methods for deep reinforcement learning. In: ICML, pp. 1928–1937 (2016)
3. Mnih, V., et al.: Playing atari with deep reinforcement learning. In: NIPS Deep Learning Workshop (2013)
4. Mnih, V., et al.: Human-level control through deep reinforcement learning. Nature **518**, 529–533 (2015)
5. Pathak, D., Agrawal, P., Efros, A.A., Darrell, T.: Curiosity-driven exploration by self-supervised prediction. In: ICML, pp. 2778–2787 (2017)
6. Williams, R.J.: Simple statistical gradient-following algorithms for connectionist reinforcement learning. Mach. Learn. **8**(3), 229–256 (1992)

A Study of Relaxation Approaches for Asymmetric Constraint Optimization Problems

Toshihiro Matsui[✉] and Hiroshi Matsuo

Nagoya Institute of Technology, Gokiso-cho, Show-ku, Nagoya, Aichi 466-8555, Japan
{matsui.t,matsuo}@nitch.ac.jp

Abstract. The Distributed Constraint Optimization Problem (DCOP) has been studied as a fundamental optimization problem that represents various problems on multiagent systems. We focus on the asymmetric DCOPs where each objective function is differently defined as an evaluation of an agent. This class of problems is studied as a multi-objective problem for the preferences of individual agents. In this work, we investigate the possibility of a solution framework based on relaxation methods as a scalable and inexact solution approach for this class of problems. We address a bottleneck problem that minimizes the worst-case cost value. As the first study, we apply a penalty method to the minimization problems of the maximum cost values.

Keywords: Distributed Constraint Optimization
Asymmetric problem · Bottleneck · Relaxation · Penalty method

1 Introduction

The Distributed Constraint Optimization Problem (DCOP) [2] has been studied as a fundamental optimization problem that represents various problems on multiagent systems. With DCOPs, multiagent cooperation problems, including the distributed task allocation of meeting scheduling, smart grids and emergency responses, are formalized. A DCOP consists of variables and objective functions that represent the states of agents and the relationship among agents. In the original DCOP, the objective functions are commonly defined for related agents. In recent studies, asymmetric multi-objective problems where the objective functions are differently defined for individual agents are addressed [1,6,7]. These classes of problems represent several practical cases that optimize multiple objectives for preferences of individual agents.

There are several approaches of solution methods for DCOPs including stochastic local search, tree-search, dynamic programming, belief propagation and relaxation approaches. Those approaches can also be applied to asymmetric problems with several modifications. Most studies of asymmetric problems with preferences of agents address exact solution methods or those variations. While

© Springer Nature Switzerland AG 2018
T. Miller et al. (Eds.): PRIMA 2018, LNAI 11224, pp. 535–543, 2018.
https://doi.org/10.1007/978-3-030-03098-8_39

the relaxation methods [4,8] are proposed as a relatively scalable and inexact approach for DCOPs, the opportunities to apply those methods to asymmetric problems have not been well addressed.

In this work, we investigate the relaxation approaches for asymmetric constraint optimization problems. As the first study, we apply a penalty method to the minimization problems of the maximum cost values. The effects of the proposed methods are experimentally evaluated.

2   Preliminary

2.1   Distributed Constraint Optimization Problem

The Distributed Constraint Optimization Problem (DCOP) [2] is a combinational optimization problem on multiagent systems and defined by (A, X, D, F), where A is a set of agents, X is a set of variables, D is a set of domains of variables, and F is a set of cost functions. Variable $x_i \in X$ represents the state or decision of agent $i \in A$. For simplicity, we assume that an agent has a single variable. The variable x_i takes a value in a set of discrete values $D_i \in D$. Cost function $f_{i,j}(x_i, x_j) \in F$ defines the cost values for assignments to the pair of variables x_i and x_j. We also assume that each cost function $f_{i,j}$ is defined as a binary function: $f_{i,j} : D_i \times D_j \to \mathbb{N}_0$. The goal is to find the assignments to the variables that minimize the global cost function $\sum_{f_{i,j} \in F} f_{i,j}$ in a decentralized manner.

2.2   Optimization of Bottlenecks in Asymmetric Multi-objective Problems

The situations where each agent has different evaluations for the assignments to variables are represented with an Asymmetric DCOP [3] which is defined by (A, X, D, F). Here, A, X and D are the same as the DCOP. F is a set of asymmetric cost functions. An asymmetric cost function $f_{i,j}(x_i, x_j) \in F$ defines the evaluation of agent i. For simplicity, we assume that $f_{i,j}$ and $f_{j,i}$ are defined as a pair of functions. In particular, we focus on the Asymmetric Multi-Objective DCOP (AMODCOP) [6] where each agent locally aggregates its related cost functions. The local cost f_i of agent i is defined as the summation of the functions related to i: $f_i = \sum_k f_{i,k}$. f_i is considered as the objective of agent i. Namely the problem is a multiple objective problem where each agent i has its own objective f_i. We denote by $F_i \subseteq F$ a set of all functions $f_{i,k}$.

To evaluate multiple objectives, we employ scalarization functions [5]. A traditional scalarization is the summation of cost values $\sum_i f_i$. While the minimization of the summation is Pareto optimal, it does not consider inequality among agents. A different basic scalarization is the maximum cost value $\max_i f_i$, which is also called the Tchebycheff function. While the minimization of the maximum cost value improves the worst-case cost for all agents, it is not Pareto optimal. The Tchebycheff function is improved with the summation. Augmented weighted Tchebycheff function is approximately defined with a small value a: $\max_i f_i + a \sum_i f_i$. The optimization with this scalarization is Pareto optimal and improves the worst-case and the total cost values. The goal is to find the solution that minimizes scalarized values. We mainly focus on the bottlenecks (i.e. worst-case cost values).

2.3   Solution Methods Using Relaxation

Several solution methods are based on the relaxation of DCOPs [4,8]. In [4], the original DCOP is represented with a quadratic encoding. The problem is relaxed as a Lagrangian relaxation problem. Then, the relaxed problem and corresponding dual problem are repeatedly optimized with a decentralized solution method. See the literature for details of the method. In the following sections, we employ a similar encoding approach, while it is a simple penalty method.

3   Applying Relaxation Methods to Asymmetric Problems

3.1   Basic Scheme

For AMODCOPs, we investigate solution methods with relaxation approaches. As the basic scheme, we employ simple relaxation problems and solution methods. For the minimization of the summation, we employ the following original problem.

$$\text{minimize} \sum_{i \in A} \sum_{f_{i,j} \in F_i} \boldsymbol{\alpha}_i^{i,j\,\mathrm{T}} \boldsymbol{F}_{i,j} \boldsymbol{\alpha}_j^{i,j} \tag{1}$$

$$\text{subject to } \boldsymbol{x}_i = \boldsymbol{\alpha}_i^{i,j}, \ \boldsymbol{x}_j = \boldsymbol{\alpha}_j^{i,j}, \ \forall f_{i,j} \in F. \tag{2}$$

Here, $\boldsymbol{x}_k$ and $\boldsymbol{\alpha}_k^{i,j}$ take a $|D_k|$ dimensional vector from $\{[1, 0, \cdots, 0]^{\mathrm{T}} \cdots [0, \cdots, 0, 1]^{\mathrm{T}}\}$. If the original x_k takes its l-th value, $\boldsymbol{x}_k$ corresponding to x_k takes a vector whose l-th dimension value is one. Here, we do not explicitly write the constraint conditions of the domain of the vectors. Moreover, we also omit the above constraint conditions of $\boldsymbol{x}_k$ and $\boldsymbol{\alpha}_k^{i,j}$ due to space limits in the following. $\boldsymbol{F}_{i,j}$ is a matrix that represents the values of asymmetric function $f_{i,j}$.

For simplicity, we employ average vector $\overline{\boldsymbol{x}}_i$ for all $\boldsymbol{\alpha}_i^{i,j}$ and $\boldsymbol{\alpha}_i^{j,i}$ instead of $\boldsymbol{x}_i$. In addition, we also add linear and quadratic penalty terms with parameters $\boldsymbol{\mu}_i^{i,j}$, $\boldsymbol{\mu}_j^{i,j}$ and λ. With these modifications, the relaxation problem is represented as follows.

$$\text{minimize} \sum_{i \in A} \left(\sum_{f_{i,j} \in F_i} \boldsymbol{\alpha}_i^{i,j\,\mathrm{T}} \boldsymbol{F}_{i,j} \boldsymbol{\alpha}_j^{i,j} + \right. \tag{3}$$

$$\left. \sum_{f_{i,j} \in F_i} \boldsymbol{\mu}_i^{i,j} (\overline{\boldsymbol{x}}_i - \boldsymbol{\alpha}_i^{i,j}) + \lambda ||\overline{\boldsymbol{x}}_i - \boldsymbol{\alpha}_i^{i,j}||_2^2 + \sum_{f_{i,j} \in F_i} \boldsymbol{\mu}_j^{i,j} (\overline{\boldsymbol{x}}_j - \boldsymbol{\alpha}_j^{i,j}) + \lambda ||\overline{\boldsymbol{x}}_j - \boldsymbol{\alpha}_j^{i,j}||_2^2 \right).$$

Here, we do not relax the domain of vectors for simplicity. Since $\overline{x}_i$, $\alpha_i^{i,j}$ and $\alpha_i^{j,i}$ are not easily determined simultaneously, $\overline{x}_i$ is approximately updated in each iterative optimization process. To determine an assignment to original variable x_i from average vector $\overline{x}_i$, we simply select a dimension with the largest element value.

Based on the problem shown above, we basically employ the following update rule at each time step t.

$$\text{minimize} \sum_{i \in A} \left(\sum_{f_{i,j} \in F_i} \alpha_i^{i,j\,T}(t) F_{i,j} \alpha_j^{i,j}(t) + \right. \tag{4}$$

$$\sum_{f_{i,j} \in F_i} \mu_i^{i,j}(t)(\overline{x}_i(t) - \alpha_i^{i,j}(t)) + \lambda ||\overline{x}_i(t) - \alpha_i^{i,j}(t)||_2^2 +$$

$$\left. \sum_{f_{i,j} \in F_i} \mu_j^{i,j}(t)(\overline{x}_j(t) - \alpha_j^{i,j}(t)) + \lambda ||\overline{x}_j(t) - \alpha_j^{i,j}(t)||_2^2 \right),$$

$$\overline{x}_i(t+1) = \frac{1}{m_i} \sum_{f_{i,j}, f_{j,i} \in F} (\alpha_i^{i,j}(t) + \alpha_i^{j,i}(t)), \ \forall i \in A, \tag{5}$$

$$\mu_i^{i,j}(t+1) = \mu_i^{i,j}(t) + \pi(\overline{x}_i(t+1) - \alpha_i^{i,j}(t)), \ \forall f_{i,j} \in F, \tag{6}$$

$$\mu_j^{i,j}(t+1) = \mu_j^{i,j}(t) + \pi(\overline{x}_j(t+1) - \alpha_j^{i,j}(t)), \ \forall f_{i,j} \in F. \tag{7}$$

Here, m_i is the number of functions such that $f_{i,j}, f_{j,i} \in F$. π is an update parameter.

The variables and parameters of the above rule can be distributed among agents. Agent i has the following elements: (1) all $f_{i,j} \in F_i$, (2) $\alpha_i^{i,j}$ and $\alpha_i^{i,j}$ for all $f_{i,j} \in F_i$, (3) $\mu_i^{i,j}$ and $\mu_j^{i,j}$ for all $f_{i,j} \in F_i$, and 4) λ and π. On the other hand, average vector $\overline{x}_i$ must be shared by all related agents. Therefore, corresponding agents aggregate $\overline{x}_i$. Agent i has $\overline{x}_k^i$ for each x_k related to $f_{i,j}$ in F_i. Each $\overline{x}_k^i$ is aggregated for agent i and all neighborhood agents j, which are related to i with $f_{i,j}$.

The computation of aggregation consists of two synchronized phases as follows: (1) Each agent i aggregates its own $\alpha_i^{i,j}$. In addition, agent i also collects $\alpha_i^{j,i}$ from all neighborhood agents. As a result, the summation vector of all $\alpha_i^{k,l}$ for i is computed. The summation vector can be averaged by the number of aggregated copy $2|F_i|$. (2) Each agent i collects the aggregated vectors from all neighborhood agents.

The local problem of agent i is represented as follows.

$$\text{minimize} \sum_{f_{i,j} \in F_i} \left(\alpha_i^{i,j\,T} F_{i,j} \alpha_j^{i,j} + \right. \tag{8}$$

$$\left. \mu_i^{i,j}(\overline{x}_i^i - \alpha_i^{i,j}) + \lambda ||\overline{x}_i^i - \alpha_i^{i,j}||_2^2 + \mu_j^{i,j}(\overline{x}_j^i - \alpha_j^{i,j}) + \lambda ||\overline{x}_j^i - \alpha_j^{i,j}||_2^2 \right).$$

The procedure of agent i in each time step is as follows: (1) In the initial time step, reset all $\mu_i^{i,j}$ and $\mu_j^{i,j}$ to zero. (2) Under all $\mu_i^{i,j}$, $\mu_j^{i,j}$ and $\overline{x}_i^i$, find the assignment to all $\alpha_i^{i,j}$ and $\alpha_j^{i,j}$ that minimizes i's local problem. (3) Aggregate $\bar{x}_k^i$ from related neighborhood agents. (4) Update all $\mu_i^{i,j}$ and $\mu_j^{i,j}$ based on their corresponding gaps. (5) Repeat the processing from step (2) until the cut-off time step. Here, the processes of all agents are synchronized at each interaction.

Note that the relaxed problem is not a lower bound problem due to discrete variables. In addition, the convergence is not assured due to non-convex functions in general cases. As in the first study, we mainly focus on the perturbation of the solution method. We assume a distributed snapshot algorithm to commit with a best solution.

3.2   Modifications with Threshold Value for Bottleneck Problems

Next, we apply the above scheme to the case of the mini-max problem. Here, we introduce a scalar threshold value β, which is considered as the objective. Since we assume that each $f_{i,j}$ takes non-negative integer values, β also takes similar values. We assume that the range of β is known. β is related to each aggregation of local cost functions of an agent with a constraint condition.

$$\text{minimize } \beta \tag{9}$$
$$\text{subject to } \Big(\sum_{f_{i,j} \in F_i} \alpha_i^{i,j\,T} F_{i,j} \alpha_j^{i,j} \Big) \le \beta, \ \forall i \in A.$$

Similar to the case of the minimization of the summation shown in Eq. (3), an approximate relaxation problem can be represented. In this case, the additional constraint conditions for β and the aggregations of local functions are relaxed with non-negative scalar multipliers μ^{F_i}. However, there are several problems in this formalization as follows: (1) There are different types of constraint conditions whose relaxations might differently affect the solution. (2) While β is an objective value, it relates with other functions as a threshold value. (3) β is shared by all agents. For these problems, we investigate several heuristic approaches below.

3.3   Priority of Penalty Terms

To represent the priority of different constraint conditions, we employ different scales of the update parameters for the multipliers of relaxed conditions. In the above case, $\pi^{\mu^{F_i}}$ and $\pi^{\mu^{i,j}}$ are employed for two types constraints instead of π in Sect. 3.1. λ is also replaced to different parameters for corresponding constraints. The different weight values will emphasize the priority of constraint conditions.

3.4   Aggregation and Search of Threshold Value

To investigate the methods to determine the value of β, we first employ a dedicated central agent, while such an agent will be a bottleneck of communication. Basically, the central agent maintains the value of β. On the other hand, the β should be agreed on by all agents. To represent this situation, a copy β_i of β is introduced for each agent i, similar to $\boldsymbol{x}_i$ and $\boldsymbol{\alpha}_i^{i,j}$. With β and β_i, the problem and its relaxation can be represented as follows.

$$\text{minimize } \beta \tag{10}$$
$$\text{subject to } \beta_i = \beta \,, \; \forall i \in A \,,$$
$$\left(\sum_{f_{i,j} \in F_i} \boldsymbol{\alpha}_i^{i,j\,T} \boldsymbol{F}_{i,j} \boldsymbol{\alpha}_j^{i,j} \right) \leq \beta_i \,, \; \forall i \in A \,.$$

$$\text{minimize } \beta + \sum_{i \in A} \left(\mu^{\beta_i} (\beta - \beta_i) + \lambda^{\beta_i} ||\beta - \beta_i||_2^2 + \right. \tag{11}$$
$$\mu^{F_i} \left(\left(\sum_{f_{i,j} \in F_i} \boldsymbol{\alpha}_i^{i,j\,T} \boldsymbol{F}_{i,j} \boldsymbol{\alpha}_j^{i,j} \right) - \beta_i \right) + \lambda^{F_i} || \max(0, \left(\sum_{f_{i,j} \in F_i} \boldsymbol{\alpha}_i^{i,j\,T} \boldsymbol{F}_{i,j} \boldsymbol{\alpha}_j^{i,j} \right) - \beta_i) ||_2^2 +$$
$$\left. \sum_{f_{i,j} \in F_i} \mu_i^{i,j} (\overline{\boldsymbol{x}}_i - \boldsymbol{\alpha}_i^{i,j}) + \lambda^{i,j} ||\overline{\boldsymbol{x}}_i - \boldsymbol{\alpha}_i^{i,j}||_2^2 + \sum_{f_{i,j} \in F_i} \mu_j^{i,j} (\overline{\boldsymbol{x}}_j - \boldsymbol{\alpha}_j^{i,j}) + \lambda^{i,j} ||\overline{\boldsymbol{x}}_j - \boldsymbol{\alpha}_j^{i,j}||_2^2 \right).$$

The local problem of i is represented as follows.

$$\text{minimize } \mu^{\beta_i'} (\beta - \beta_i) + \lambda^{\beta_i'} ||\beta - \beta_i||_2^2 + \tag{12}$$
$$\mu^{F_i} \left(\left(\sum_{f_{i,j} \in F_i} \boldsymbol{\alpha}_i^{i,j\,T} \boldsymbol{F}_{i,j} \boldsymbol{\alpha}_j^{i,j} \right) - \beta_i \right) + \lambda^{F_i} || \max(0, \left(\sum_{f_{i,j} \in F_i} \boldsymbol{\alpha}_i^{i,j\,T} \boldsymbol{F}_{i,j} \boldsymbol{\alpha}_j^{i,j} \right) - \beta_i) ||_2^2 +$$
$$\sum_{f_{i,j} \in F_i} \mu_i^{i,j} (\overline{\boldsymbol{x}}_i - \boldsymbol{\alpha}_i^{i,j}) + \lambda^{i,j} ||\overline{\boldsymbol{x}}_i - \boldsymbol{\alpha}_i^{i,j}||_2^2 + \sum_{f_{i,j} \in F_i} \mu_j^{i,j} (\overline{\boldsymbol{x}}_j - \boldsymbol{\alpha}_j^{i,j}) + \lambda^{i,j} ||\overline{\boldsymbol{x}}_j - \boldsymbol{\alpha}_j^{i,j}||_2^2 \,.$$

The local problem of the central agent is represented as follows.

$$\text{minimize } \beta + \sum_{i \in A} \left(\mu^{\beta_i''} (\beta - \beta_i) + \lambda^{\beta_i''} ||\beta - \beta_i||_2^2 \right). \tag{13}$$

Since β and β_i are shared among agents, those values cannot be simultaneously determined. As an approximation method, previous value $\beta_i(t-1)$ of current $\beta_i(t)$ is employed in each time step t. The procedure for the central agent in each time step is as follows: (1) In the initial time step, collect initial β_i from all agents. Reset all $\mu^{\beta_i''}$ of the central agent to zero. (2) Under all $\mu^{\beta_i''}$, find the assignment to β that minimizes the local problem. (3) Notify all agents of the current β. (4) After the update of β_i in all agents i, collect current β_i. (5) Update all $\mu^{\beta_i''}$ based on their corresponding gaps. (6) Repeat the processing from step 2) until the cut-off time step. The procedure for each agent i resembles that shown in Sect. 3.1, while it contains additional steps to exchange β and β_i. Here, $\overline{\boldsymbol{x}}_k^i$ are aggregated by neighboring agents as shown in Sect. 3.1.

Now we address another approach without the central agent. Instead of β in the central agent, similar to Eq. (13), each agent i approximately optimizes the threshold $\tilde{\beta}^i$ under the constraints for its own β_i and each β_j of agent j in a range. On the other hand, the local problem of each agent i resembles one shown in Eq. (12), except β is replaced by $\tilde{\beta}^i$. To collect more information, agent i can collect β_k from agents k within a diameter r from the agent i with some communication trade-off. Here, we assume $r = 2$ that is the same as the aggregation of $\overline{x}_k^i$.

3.5   Augmented Weighted Tchebycheff Function

Here, we also investigate the case where the objective is defined with the augmented weighted Tchebycheff function. The objective function is as follows: minimize $\beta + a \sum_{f_{i,j} \in F_i} \alpha_i^{i,j\,T} F_{i,j} \alpha_j^{i,j}$. The relaxed problem also resembles the case of the minimization of the maximum cost. Since the relaxed problem already contains the term of the total cost as shown in Eq. (11), the coefficient μ^{F_i} of the term is replaced by $(\mu^{F_i} + a)$.

4   Evaluation

We experimentally evaluated the proposed approach using asymmetric DCOPs with fifty ternary variables, which take one of three values, and 120 constraints. The maximum degree of variables on constraint graphs is six. Following cost functions $f_{i,j}$ are evaluated. **u1_100**: random integer values in $[1, 100]$ with uniform distribution. **g9_2**: rounded random integer values based on gamma distribution with $(\alpha, \beta) = (9, 2)$.

Following methods are compared. **sum.**: the minimization of the summation cost value. Parameter π is set to 1. **max. dst. fpx/eql**: the minimization of the maximum cost value. Here, only the version without the central agent is shown, since we found that the results resemble the cases with the central agent. Paramters $(\pi^{\mu^{i,j}}, \pi^{\mu^{F_i}}, \pi^{\mu^{\beta_i'}}, \pi^{\mu^{\beta_i''}})$ for Eqs. (12) and (13) are set to $(1, 10, 5, 1)$ for fpx and $(1, 1, 1, 1)$ for eql, respectively. In the case of fpx, the penalty terms of the threshold value are emphasized. **awt. 1e-3/1e-9**: the minimization of the augmented weighted Tchebycheff function. The methods with parameters 1e-3 and 1e-9 (i.e. 10^{-3} and 10^{-9}) for a are evaluated. The paramters $(\pi^{\mu^{i,j}}, \pi^{\mu^{F_i}}, \pi^{\mu^{\beta_i'}}, \pi^{\mu^{\beta_i''}})$ are set to $(1, 10, 5, 1)$.

Each λ^* is set to $\pi^*/2$ similar to the extended Lagrangian method. For local problems of agents, we employed an exact solution method based on a tree search and did not relax the discrete values of variables. We employed a synchronized simulator with cut-off time step $t = 200$. Results are averaged over ten problem instances.

Tables 1 and 2 show the best upper bound value of the objective function, the best summation/maximum cost value, and the summation/maximum cost value that is averaged over an execution. Here, we computed the upper bound from feasible solutions that are collected as snapshots of the system. The averaged summation/maximum cost value represents the perturbation of the solution method. In the case of u1_100, the best cost values relatively correspond to the objectives to be minimized. The minimization of summation/maximization found the smallest summation/maximum value in average. In the case of 'max. dst.', fbx found relateively smaller maximum values than eql. That reveals the

Table 1. Solution qualities: u1_100

opt.	Best			avg.	
	ub.	sum.	max.	sum.	max.
sum.	9303.7	9303.7	296.0	10269.3	362.0
max. dst. fbx	256.3	9648.9	256.3	9962.2	290.9
max. dst. eql	258.9	9564.6	258.9	10166.2	311.1
awt. 1e-3	260.2	9525.8	250.6	9768.6	279.9
awt. 1e-9	252.6	9516.4	252.6	9769.6	284.4

Table 2. Solution qualities: g9_2

opt.	Best			avg.	
	ub.	sum.	max.	sum.	max.
sum.	3709.9	3709.9	97.2	3923.3	114.0
max. dst. fbx	95.9	3957.4	95.9	3979.4	97.9
max. dst. eql	95.2	3782.7	95.2	3940.8	109.9
awt. 1e-3	99.0	3875.4	95.1	3929.7	98.2
awt. 1e-9	95.1	3875.4	95.1	3929.7	98.2

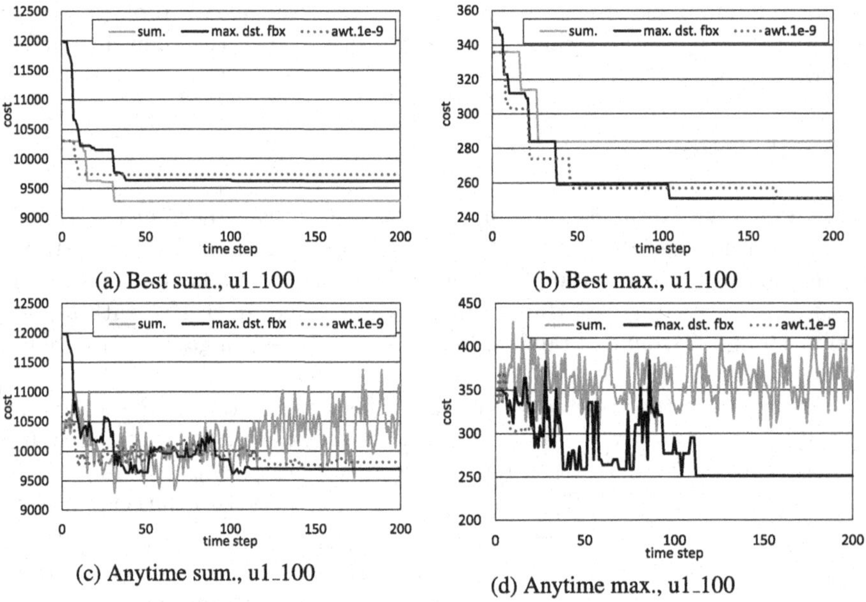

(a) Best sum., u1_100

(b) Best max., u1_100

(c) Anytime sum., u1_100

(d) Anytime max., u1_100

Fig. 1. Best and anytime cost values

effect of tuning the weight parameters of penalty terms. While the summation cost values by 'awt.' is rather smaller than 'max. dst.', 'awt.' also reduced the maximum cost value in several cases. This can be considered that the minimization of summation cost values causes additional perturbations to escape from local optimal solutions. Two parameters of 'awt.' slightly affected the solutions. In the case of g9_2, the effect of 'max. dst.' was not so well. The non-uniform distributions and relatively narrow range of objective functions affected the local search. In our environment, for the case of u1_100, the total usage time for all agents was 50.3, 79.9, and 77.7 ms for 'sum.', 'max. dst. fbx' and 'awt. 1e-9', respectively.

Figure 1 shows a set of examples of each best/anytime cost value. In the anytime curve, the minimization of the maximum cost value often converges rather than the summation. The threshold value β performs as a temperature parameter.

5   Conclusion

In this work, we investigated relaxation approaches for asymmetric multi-objective constraint optimization problems. As the first study, we applied a penalty method to the minimization problems of the maximum cost values. The results show the proposed approaches work reasonably well, and a benefit of the relaxation method is their perturbations. Future works will include improvement of the relaxation method to ensure good lower bounds and convergence, detailed theoretical analysis, comparison with related solution methods, and evaluation with practical problems.

Acknowledgement. This work was supported in part by JSPS KAKENHI Grant Number JP16K00301 and Tatematsu Zaidan.

References

1. Netzer, A., Meisels, A.: Distributed envy minimization for resource allocation. In: 5th International Conference on Agents and Artificial Intelligence, vol. 1, pp. 15–24 (2013)
2. Fioretto, F., Pontelli, E., Yeoh, W.: Distributed constraint optimization problems and applications: a survey. J. Artif. Intell. Res. **61**, 623–698 (2018)
3. Grinshpoun, T., Grubshtein, A., Zivan, R., Netzer, A., Meisels, A.: Asymmetric distributed constraint optimization problems. J. Artif. Intell. Res. **47**, 613–647 (2013)
4. Hatano, D., Hirayama, K.: DeQED: an efficient divide-and-coordinate algorithm for DCOP. In: IJCAI 2013, Proceedings of the 23rd International Joint Conference on Artificial Intelligence, Beijing, China, 3–9 August 2013, pp. 566–572 (2013)
5. Marler, R.T., Arora, J.S.: Survey of multi-objective optimization methods for engineering. Struct. Multidiscip. Optim. **26**, 369–395 (2004)
6. Matsui, T., Matsuo, H., Silaghi, M., Hirayama, K., Yokoo, M.: Leximin asymmetric multiple objective distributed constraint optimization problem. Comput. Intell. **34**(1), 49–84 (2018)
7. Netzer, A., Meisels, A.: SOCIAL DCOP - social choice in distributed constraints optimization. In: Brazier, F.M.T., Nieuwenhuis, K., Pavlin, G., Warnier, M., Badica, C. (eds.) 5th International Symposium on Intelligent Distributed Computing, vol. 382, pp. 35–47. Springer, Heidelberg (2011). https://doi.org/10.1007/978-3-642-24013-3_5
8. Vinyals, M., Pujol, M., Rodriguez-Aguilar, J.A., Cerquides, J.: Divide-and-coordinate: DCOPs by agreement. In: 9th International Conference on Autonomous Agents and Multiagent Systems, pp. 149–156 (2010)

Sensor Placement for Plan Monitoring Using Genetic Programming

Felipe Meneguzzi[1]([✉]), Ramon Fraga Pereira[1], and Nir Oren[2]

[1] Pontifical Catholic University of Rio Grande do Sul, Porto Alegre, Brazil
`felipe.meneguzzi@pucrs.br`
`ramon.pereira@acad.pucrs.br`
[2] University of Aberdeen, Aberdeen, Scotland, UK
`n.oren@abdn.ac.uk`

Abstract. Monitoring plan execution is useful in various multi-agent applications, from agent cooperation to norm enforcement. Realistic environments often impose constraints on the capabilities of such monitoring, limiting the amount and coverage of available sensors. In this paper, we consider the problem of sensor placement within an environment to determine whether some behaviour has occurred. Our model is based on the semantics of planning, and we provide a simple formalism for describing sensors and behaviours in such a model. Given the computational complexity of the sensor placement problem, we investigate heuristic techniques for performing sensor placement, demonstrating that such techniques perform well even in complex domains.

1 Introduction

Norms are commonly used to obtain desirable behaviour within an open multi-agent system. Such norms specify obligations, permissions, and prohibitions on individual behaviour, preventing actions or states of affairs that an agent might find beneficial, but which will have a negative effect on others or the system environment as a whole [7]. Given a normative multi-agent system, the question arises as to how to ensure that agents comply with the norms. While it is possible to sometimes design the system so that violating a norm is irrational [11], or design the agents so that they are incapable of violating norms [2], doing so within an open system is often difficult or impossible. Instead, sanctioning mechanisms are normally introduced to punish, and therefore disincentivise norm violation [7]. Recent work has developed an approach to define how norms should be modified to be monitorable given an available set of imperfect monitors [1], and the problem we address here is the dual of such work. In turn, we consider a further problem, namely how to combine a set of so-called *primitive sensors*—available within the environment—to form a new sensor that will be able to detect whether some state of affairs does, or does not hold.

R. Fraga Pereira—This study was financed in part by the Coordenação de Aperfeiçoamento de Pessoal de Nivel Superior – Brasil (CAPES).

ⓒ Springer Nature Switzerland AG 2018
T. Miller et al. (Eds.): PRIMA 2018, LNAI 11224, pp. 544–551, 2018.
https://doi.org/10.1007/978-3-030-03098-8_40

We consider an abstract form of the problem, seeking to identify whether—with no prior knowledge on agent preferences—some behaviour can be detected by combining the primitive sensors. For example, consider two cameras overlooking different portions of a highway, and assume that each camera can uniquely identify individual cars. In such a system, the two cameras (i.e., the sensors) can be combined (synthesised) to form a new sensor which can detect a vehicle's average speed (i.e., a behaviour or state-of-affairs) over the stretch of highway. We refer to this problem as the *plan monitoring* problem.

We formally describe our primitive sensors and the behaviour we wish to detect as formulae within a simple logic. Synthesising a new sensor then involves creating a new formula by joining a subset of the primitive sensor formulae with operators from the logic. If this new formula is equivalent to the formula encoding the behaviour we wish to detect, then we are able to form a sensor for monitoring the behaviour. Since this is clearly a computationally hard problem, in this paper we consider a heuristic approach for the synthesis of our sensors using genetic programming.

2   Plan Monitoring

We formalise logic formulas over states in Definition 1—these are basically propositional-logic formulas to be evaluated in individual states.

Definition 1 (State Formula). *Let $\mathcal{F}$ be a set of fluents[1]. If $\varphi \in \mathcal{F}$ then φ is a state formula[2]. If φ and ψ are state formula, then $\varphi \wedge \psi$, $\varphi \vee \psi$, and $\neg\varphi$ are state formulas. Nothing else is a state formula. State formulas are evaluated according to a valuation function $V : S \to \mathcal{F}$, which returns a set of fluents that hold at state $s \in S$ (set of possible states). We write $s \models \phi$ (s is a model of ϕ) if $\phi \in V(s)$; $s \models \phi \wedge \psi$ iff $s \models \psi$ and $s \models \phi$; and $s \models \phi \vee \psi$ iff $s \models \psi$ or $s \models \phi$; and $s \models \neg\phi$ iff $s \not\models \phi$.*

To formalise plan monitoring tasks, we must express constraints over entire plans, made up of traces or sequences of states which occur (Definition 2).

Definition 2 (Path Formula). *If φ is a state formula, then φ is a path formula. If φ and ψ are path formulas, then $\varphi[Y]\psi$ and $\neg\varphi$ are path formulas. Let t_π be a trace and φ and $\varphi[Y]\psi$ be path formulas. Y represents the number of steps between state formulas. We write $t_\pi \models \varphi$ (t_π is model for φ) iff any state $s_i \in t_\pi \models \varphi$, and $t_\pi \models \varphi[Y]\psi$ iff $s_i, s_k \in t_\pi$; $s_i \models \varphi$; $s_{i+k} \models \psi$; and $Y \geq k$. We write $t_\pi \models \neg\varphi$ iff it is not the case that $t_\pi \models \varphi$.*

Path formulas can only be evaluated over plan traces (i.e., sequences of states), so a path formula $\varphi[Y]\psi$ is in a trace if φ holds in any state of the

---

[1] Fluents are ground logical predicates, which can either be positive or negated, and include constants for truth ($\top$) and falsehood ($\bot$).

[2] A state formula is comprised of a finite set fluents that represent logical values according to some interpretation.

trace, and ψ holds in any state within Y steps or less of when φ held. It should be noted that conjunctions over path formulae can be captured using $\varphi[0]\psi$. Together with negation, this provides us with disjunctions over path formulae.

Example 1. Consider the domain model illustrated in Fig. 1, and a trace $t_{b,a} = \langle [q], [p], [p, q] \rangle$ for a plan $\langle b, a \rangle$. Formula $q[2](p \wedge q)$ is true for this trace, whereas formula $q[1](p \wedge q)$ is not.

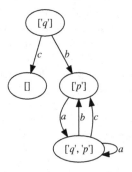

Fig. 1. Propositional domain example.

A sensor is a mechanism that evaluates path formulas over traces, and represents a concrete and indivisible (atomic) capability to evaluate path formulas on plan traces, following Definition 3.

Definition 3 (Sensor). *Let φ be a path formula and t_π be a trace, we say φ is a sensor for t_π iff $t_\pi \models \varphi$.*

Sensors can be aggregated to form monitors to detect specific desirable formulas, following Definition 4.

Definition 4 (Monitor). *Let $S = \{\varphi_1, \ldots \varphi_n\}$ be a set of sensors. A monitor M is a sensor obtained by combining a subset of S using path operations. M is a monitor for a trace t_π iff $t_\pi \models M$.*

We note that this formalisation of sensors and monitors provides a simple mechanism to describe partially observable monitoring problems. For example, in Fig. 1, if no available sensor has formulas referring to p, then a monitoring problem for this example is partially observable with respect to p. Algorithm 1 describes a simple function to compute whether a sensor is *sensitive* to a trace, returning a set of models for a given sensor, a trace, a state, and a set of actions.

Algorithm 1. Computation of the $\models$ relation.

Input: A sensor σ, a trace t_π, a state S, and a set of actions A.
Output: A set of models ($\models$) relation.

```
1:  function MODELS(σ, tπ, S, A)
2:      if σ is an atom then
3:          return σ = ⊤ or σ ∈ S
4:      else if σ = ¬φ then
5:          return ¬MODELS(φ, tπ, S, A)
6:      else                                                    ▷ σ is not an atom.
7:          (lhs, *, rhs) ← σ
8:          if * = ∧ then
9:              return MODELS(lhs, tπ, S, A) and MODELS(rhs, tπ, S, A)
10:         else if * = ∨ then
11:             return MODELS(lhs, tπ, S, A) or MODELS(rhs, tπ, S, A)
12:         else if * = [k] then
13:             if k = 0 then
14:                 return MODELS(lhs, tπ, S, A) and MODELS(rhs, tπ, S, A)
15:             else
16:                 a ← first action of tπ
17:                 t'π ← remainder tπ
18:                 S' ← γ(S, a)
19:                 if MODELS(lhs, tπ, S, A) then
20:                     if not MODELS(rhs, tπ, S, A) then
21:                         return MODELS(⊤ [k − 1] rhs, t'π, S', A)
22:                     else
23:                         return ⊤
24:                 else                      ▷ Did not apply to first state, need to check next.
25:                     return MODELS(σ, t'π, S', A)
```

2.1 Decision Problems

So far, we have defined individual sensors and described how these can be aggregated into more complex sensors, which we call monitors. We use these to represent imperfect sensing capabilities which, much like the real world, may not be capable of fully distinguishing the states and traces of interest. Thus, we need to be able to quantify the extent to which the resulting monitors can capture such traces. Building on the definition of sensors and monitors, we can now formally define the notions of sensitivity and specificity of a sensor with regards to a set of traces. More specifically, a sensor is sensitive to a set of traces if the formula of the sensor is true for each trace (Definition 5).

Definition 5 (Sensitive Sensor). *Let φ be an arbitrary sensor and $T_\Pi = \{t_{\pi_1}, \ldots t_{\pi_n}\}$ be a set of plan traces (i.e., the sequences of states induced by plans $\pi \in \Pi$) within a planning domain Π. φ is sensitive for the traces in T_Π iff $\forall_{t_\pi \in T_\Pi}(t_\pi \models \varphi)$, i.e., φ is a sensor for all traces in T_Π.*

Conversely, we want to be able to detect when specific plans *do not* trigger a sensor, leading to the notion of a specific sensor (Definition 6).

Definition 6 (Specific Sensor). *Let* φ *be an arbitrary sensor and* $T_\Pi = \{t_{\pi_1}, \ldots t_{\pi_n}\}$ *and* $T'_\Pi = \{t_{\pi_m}, \ldots t_{\pi_k}\}$ *be two sets of plan traces (i.e., the sequences of states induced by plans* $\pi \in \Pi$) *within a planning domain* Π *such that* $T_\Pi \cap T'_\Pi = \emptyset$ *and* $T_\Pi \cup T'_\Pi = \Pi$ *(i.e.,* T'_Π *consists of all the plans not in* T_Π). φ *is specific for the traces in* T_Π *iff* $\forall_{t_\pi \in T'_\Pi}(t_\pi \not\models \varphi)$, *i.e., that* φ *is not a sensor for any of the traces not in* T_Π.

Now that we can specify sets of traces for which a sensor is sensitive and specific to, we can proceed to defining the problem of generating a monitor that approximates the sensing capabilities of an intended sensor. That is, given a specific desired sensing capability, which we call an *intended sensor*, we want to be able to synthesise a sensor from a set of *actual* available sensors that covers as much of the model sensor's traces as possible. Thus, we define the problem of synthesising a sensor to agree with a model sensor as follows (Definition 7).

Definition 7 (Monitor Synthesis). *Let* $\Phi = \{\varphi_1, \ldots, \varphi_n\}$ *be a set of available sensors,* T_Π *and* T'_Π *be two set of traces such that* σ *is sensitive to* T_Π *and specific to* T'_Π, *and* σ *be an* intended sensor *formula such that no available sensor captures exactly the traces of the intended sensor, that is:* $\forall_{\varphi \in \Phi}\exists_{t_\pi \in T_\Pi}(t_\pi \models \sigma) \wedge (t_\pi \not\models \varphi)$, *i.e., no sensor in* Φ *is sensitive to the same traces as* σ; *or* $\forall_{\varphi \in \Phi}\forall_{t_\pi \in T'_\Pi}(t_\pi \not\models \sigma) \wedge (t_\pi \models \varphi)$, *i.e., no sensor in* Φ *is specific to the same traces as* σ.

The problem of synthesising a monitor for an *intended sensor* σ consists of creating a monitor $M_{\langle \varphi_j, \ldots, \varphi_j \rangle}$ such that $\{\varphi_j, \ldots, \varphi_j\} \subseteq \Phi$; $\forall_{t_\pi \in T_\Pi}(t_\pi \models M_{\langle \varphi_j, \ldots, \varphi_j \rangle})$ iff $(t_\pi \models \sigma)$; and $\forall_{t_\pi \in T'_\Pi}(t_\pi \not\models M_{\langle \varphi_j, \ldots, \varphi_j \rangle})$ iff $(t_\pi \not\models \sigma)$; i.e., the monitor agrees with the intended sensor for all traces. Synthesising an intended sensor may not be possible, given restrictions on the actual sensors available.

Since many plan monitoring applications rely on the ability to detect the execution of specific actions in an environment, we need to define sensors capable of detecting them. Definition 8 formally describes how such intended sensors can be built from the action specification.

Definition 8 (Sensor for Action). *Let* a *be an action of the form* $\langle pre(a), eff^+(a), eff^-(a) \rangle$. *We say a sensor built to detect formula:*

$$\left(\left(\bigwedge_{\phi \in pre(a)} \phi \right) [1] \left(\bigwedge_{\psi \in eff^+(a)} \psi \wedge \bigwedge_{\psi \in eff^-(a)} \neg\psi \right) \right)$$

is a sensor for a.

3 Synthesising Monitors Using Genetic Programming

We are now in a position to develop our approach to synthesising monitors using genetic programming. Consider a desired sensor F, and a set of traces T. We can partition this set of traces into two mutually exclusive sets, namely T^t where for any $t \in T^t$, $t \models F$, and T^f where for any $t \in T^f$, $t \not\models F$. Now given some other set of primitive sensors $\{k_1, \ldots, k_n\}$, we seek to find a formula containing these primitive sensors which partitions the traces in the same way. To generate such a formula—a candidate sensor—we must perform a search over the space of all possible sensors that can be constructed from our primitive sensors. One approach that has proven successful for performing a search over such a symbolic space is genetic programming [6], a form of evolutionary computing.

To describe the space of possible individuals within a genetic program, we must identify the terminal (leaf) nodes, as well as the form that non-terminal nodes can take. Now within the plan monitoring domain, we consider a set of *primitive sensors* consisting of formulae in the language described in Sect. 2. Our goal is to combine these primitive sensors in such a way so as to obtain the same inferences as some other formula, the *goal sensor*. The primitive sensors thus comprise one class of terminal nodes.

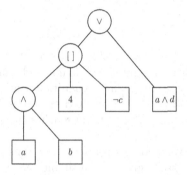

Fig. 2. An individual genetic program for the formula $((a \wedge b)[4]\neg c) \vee (a \wedge d)$ with primitive sensors a, b, $\neg c$ and $a \wedge d$.

Our logic consists of four operators—negation, conjunction, disjunction, and the path operator. Each of these forms a potential non-terminal node. We note that the path operator is a ternary operator which takes in two formulae as well as an integer. Therefore, the set of integers consists of another class of terminal nodes available within the genetic program, though this latter class of terminal nodes can only be used within a path operator. Figure 2 illustrates how the formula $((a \wedge b)[4]\neg c) \vee (a \wedge d)$ is represented as a genetic program, where a, b, $\neg c$ and $a \wedge d$ are primitive sensors.

Given an individual sensor, a set of traces, and a formula representing a target sensor, we can specify the fitness of the individual by evaluating the traces over the individual, and the target sensor, summing up the number of true positive and negative classifications of traces, and subtracting the false positive and negative trace classifications. For example, if the target sensor returns *true* for traces t_1, t_3 and t_4, and *false* for traces t_2 and t_5, while the individual returns true for t_1, t_2, t_3 and t_4 (and false for t_5), the individual's fitness would be 1. We then select fit individuals reproduce them (using copy, mutation and cross-over operations [6]) to create a new generation of individuals. This process repeats until a sufficiently fit individual is found encoding the synthesised sensor.

To define the quality of a synthesised sensor, we formally define a *monitor fitness* as an *F1-Score*[3] between the traces of the intended sensor and the invisible traces, following Definition 9.

Definition 9 (Monitor Fitness). *Let $\Phi = \{\varphi_1, \ldots, \varphi_n\}$ be a set of available sensors, $\mathcal{T}_\Pi$ and $\mathcal{T}'_\Pi$ be two set of traces, and σ be an intended sensor formula such that $\mathcal{T}_\Pi \models \sigma$, $\mathcal{T}'_\Pi \not\models \sigma$. We define quality in terms of the Precision and Recall of a monitor, where Precision is $Pr = \frac{|\{t_\pi \in \mathcal{T}_\Pi | \mathcal{M}_{\Phi'} \models t_\pi\}|}{|\mathcal{T}_\Pi| + |\mathcal{T}'_\Pi|}$, and Recall is $Re = \frac{|\{t_\pi \in \mathcal{T}_\Pi | \mathcal{M}_{\Phi'} \models t_\pi\}|}{|\mathcal{T}_\Pi|}$. The quality of an arbitrary monitor $\mathcal{M}_{\Phi'}$ such that $\Phi' \in \mathcal{P}(\Phi)$ (i.e., Φ' is an element of the power set of the available sensors) is the harmonic mean between Precision and Recall, F1-Score, which is quality $Q(\mathcal{M}_{\Phi'}, \mathcal{T}_\Pi, \mathcal{T}'_\Pi) = 2 \cdot \frac{Pr + Re}{Pr * Re}$.*

4   Related Work

A related approach to ours is the work of Keren et al. [4]. In this work, the authors introduce the problem of re-designing a domain model in order to facilitate (or improve) the process of goal and plan recognition, and such problem is called goal recognition *design* [4]. Goal recognition design aims to optimize the domain design so that goal and plan recognition approaches can provide inferences with as few observations as possible [5].

Alechina et al. [1] developed an approach that considers how norms should be modified to be monitorable given an available set of imperfect monitors. In this work, the authors define that a monitor is imperfect for a norm if it does not have sufficient observational capabilities to determine if an execution trace of a multi-agent system complies with or violates a given norm.

5   Conclusions and Future Work

In this work, we have demonstrated that a genetic programming based approach to sensor synthesis can create useful sensors for detecting the execution of actions and the occurrence of specific states within planning domains.

We are currently investigating several applications and future extensions of our work. First, the output of our approach can serve as input to Bayesian goal and plan recognition algorithms [10], with the quality of the synthesised sensor serving as a prior probability for the action having taken place. Second, we can apply our work to normative domains, determining the likelihood that some obliged or prohibited state of affairs did, or did not take place. Apart from these applications, we are also investigating more complex forms of the sensor

---

[3] *F1-Score* is the harmonic mean between *Precision* (i.e., positive predictive value) and *Recall* (i.e., true positive rate).

synthesis problem including creating sensors given some fixed budget. We also aim to use the notion of planning landmarks [3] (fluents or actions that cannot be avoided to achieve a goal from an initial state) in our approach for monitoring particular states (landmarks), since it has been done successfully for recognizing goals and detecting commitment abandonment [8,9].

References

1. Alechina, N., Dastani, M., Logan, B.: Norm approximation for imperfect monitors. In: Proceedings of the 13th International Conference on Autonomous Agents and MultiAgent Systems, AAMAS, pp. 117–124 (2014)
2. Grossi, D., Aldewereld, H., Dignum, F.: *Ubi Lex, Ibi Poena*: designing norm enforcement in e-institutions. In: Noriega, P., et al. (eds.) COIN -2006. LNCS, vol. 4386, pp. 101–114. Springer, Heidelberg (2007). https://doi.org/10.1007/978-3-540-74459-7_7
3. Hoffmann, J., Porteous, J., Sebastia, L.: Landmarks in Planning. J. Artif. Intell. Res. **22**(1), 215–278 (2004)
4. Keren, S., Gal, A., Karpas, E.: Goal recognition design. In: International Conference on Automated Planning and Scheduling, ICAPS (2014)
5. Keren, S., Gal, A., Karpas, E.: Goal recognition design with non-observable actions. In: Proceedings of the 31st AAAI Conference on Artificial Intelligence (2016)
6. Koza, J.R.: Genetic Programming: On the Programming of Computers by Means of Natural Selection. MIT Press, Cambridge (1992)
7. Luck, M., et al.: Normative agents. In: Ossowski, S. (ed.) Agreement Technologies. LGTS, vol. 8, pp. 209–220. Springer, Dordrecht (2013). https://doi.org/10.1007/978-94-007-5583-3_14
8. Pereira, R.F., Oren, N., Meneguzzi, F.: Detecting commitment abandonment by monitoring sub-optimal steps during plan execution. In: Proceedings of the 16th International Conference on Autonomous Agents and MultiAgent Systems, AAMAS, pp. 1685–1687 (2017)
9. Pereira, R.F., Oren, N., Meneguzzi, F.: Landmark-based heuristics for goal recognition. In: Proc. of the 32nd AAAI Conference on Artificial Intelligence (2017)
10. Ramírez, M., Geffner, H.: Probabilistic plan recognition using off-the-shelf classical planners. In: Proceedings of the 24th AAAI Conference on Artificial Intelligence (2010)
11. Shoham, Y., Tennenholtz, M.: On social laws for artificial agent societies: off-line design. Artif. Intell. **73**(1–2), 231–252 (1995)

Qualitative-Based Possibilistic $\mathcal{EL}$ Ontology

Rym Mohamed[1(✉)], Zied Loukil[1], and Zied Bouraoui[2]

[1] MIRACL Laboratory, ISIMS, Sfax, Tunisia
rymmohammed2@gmail.com, zied.loukil@isims.usf.tn
[2] CRIL CNRS & Univ Artois, Lens, France
bouraoui@cril.fr

Abstract. In different situations, information coming from different sources are often affected with uncertainty and imprecision. Representing such information generally gives rise to a prioritized (i.e. stratified) knowledge base. To reason with such prioritized knowledge in a principled way, we propose an extension of $\mathcal{EL}$ description logics within possibility theory, which provides a very natural framework to deal with ordinal, qualitative uncertainty, preferences and priorities. We first introduce the syntax and semantics of possibilistic $\mathcal{EL}$, and then provide the main related reasoning tasks. We show in particular that these tasks remain tractable in possibilistic $\mathcal{EL}$.

Keywords: Uncertainty handling · Possibility theory · EL ontology
Description logics

1 Introduction

Structured knowledge about concepts and relations between objects plays an important role in many applications such as information retrieval, natural language processing and bio-informatics. Ontologies offer a powerful framework to encode such structured knowledge. They are typically expressed using description logics (DLs for short) [1], and stored in two parts: a part that contains generic knowledge, i.e. semantic relationships between concepts and relations, and another part that contains data, i.e. information about which entities belong (resp. related) to what concepts (resp. relations). DLs provide the foundations of the Web Ontology Language $OWL2$[1], and its profiles $OWL2$-QL, $OWL2$-EL and $OWL2$-RL.

Recent years have witnessed an increasing interest in the use of $OWL2$-EL, which is based on a family of lightweight DLs called $\mathcal{EL}$ [2,5]). $\mathcal{EL}$ offers a good expressiveness in expressing ontological knowledge and guarantee the tractability of reasoning process especially for instance and subsumption checking.

---

[1] https://www.w3.org/TR/owl2-overview/.

© Springer Nature Switzerland AG 2018
T. Miller et al. (Eds.): PRIMA 2018, LNAI 11224, pp. 552–559, 2018.
https://doi.org/10.1007/978-3-030-03098-8_41

In different situations, especially in a Web setting, information are provided with uncertainty. Within the broad aim of uncertainty management in ontologies, several works have been proposed to extend DL within probabilistic (e.g. [12,13]) and non-probabilistic (e.g. [7,9,10,14]) uncertainty frameworks.

This paper focuses on qualitative uncertainty, which for instance holds when the information are provided by several sources where there exists a total pre-ordering between them reflecting their reliability, or when there exists a preference ranking between the provided information according to their level of priority [8]. Representing such information generally gives rise to prioritized or stratified knowledge base. To reason with such prioritized knowledge in a principled way, we focus in this paper on methods from possibility theory [11]. This theory offers a natural framework to deal with ordinal, qualitative uncertainty, preferences and priorities. This is often the case in applications where not enough data is available to estimate a meaningful probabilistic representation.

2   Preliminaries

In this section, we recall $\mathcal{EL}$ description logic considered in this paper, and then introduce the main notions of possibility theory rephrased within a description logic setting.

2.1   Recall on $\mathcal{EL}$ Family of Description Logics

Syntax. Let N_C, N_R, N_I be three pairwise disjoint sets where N_C denotes a set of atomic concept, N_R denotes a set of atomic role and N_I denotes a set individuals. The $\mathcal{EL}$ concept expressions are built according to the following syntax:

$$C, D \;\rightarrow\; \top \mid A \mid C \sqcap D \mid \exists r.C$$

where $A \in N_C$, $r \in N_R$.

An $\mathcal{EL}$ ontology (or knowledge base) consists of a set of general concept inclusion (GCI) axioms of the form $C \sqsubseteq D$, meaning that C is more specific than D or simply C is subsumed by D, a set of equivalence axioms of the form $C \equiv D$, which is the abbreviation of the two general concept inclusions $C \sqsubseteq D$ and $D \sqsubseteq C$, a set of concept assertions of the form $C(a)$, and a set of role assertions of the form $r(a, b)$.

Several extensions of $\mathcal{EL}$ have been considered. For example, $\mathcal{EL}^+$ extends $\mathcal{EL}$ with role inclusion axioms of the form $s \sqsubseteq r$ and role composition axioms of the form $r_1 \circ \ldots \circ r_n \sqsubseteq s$ where $r \circ s$ is the role composition expression. The logic $\mathcal{EL}^+_\bot$ extends $\mathcal{EL}^+$ by allowing the use of $\bot$ concept in concept expression. In this paper, we focus on $\mathcal{EL}^+_\bot$ as it is the main block of *OWL-EL*, for more detail about $\mathcal{EL}$ and its extensions, we refer to [3,4,6].

Semantics. The semantics is given in terms of interpretations $\mathcal{I} = (\Delta^\mathcal{I}, \cdot^\mathcal{I})$ which consist of a non-empty interpretation domain $\Delta^\mathcal{I}$ and an interpretation function $\cdot^\mathcal{I}$ that maps each individual $a^\mathcal{I} \in N_I$ to an element $a^\mathcal{I} \in \Delta^\mathcal{I}$, each concept $A \in N_C$ to a subset $A^{\mathcal{I}} \subseteq \Delta^{\mathcal{I}}$ and each role $r \in N_R$ to a subset $r^{\mathcal{I}} \subseteq \Delta^{\mathcal{I}} \times \Delta^{\mathcal{I}}$. Furthermore, the function $.^{\mathcal{I}}$ is extended in a straightforward way for concept and role expressions as depicted in Table 1.

Table 1. Syntax and Semantics of concept and role expressions.

	Syntax	Semantics
Atomic concept	A	$A^{\mathcal{I}} \subseteq \Delta^{\mathcal{I}}$
Atomic role	r	$r^{\mathcal{I}} \subseteq \Delta^{\mathcal{I}} \times \Delta^{\mathcal{I}}$
Individual	a	$a^{\mathcal{I}} \subseteq \Delta^{\mathcal{I}}$
Top	$\top$	$\Delta^{\mathcal{I}}$
Bottom	$\bot$	$\emptyset$
Conjunction	$C \sqcap D$	$C^{\mathcal{I}} \cap D^{\mathcal{I}}$
Existential restriction	$\exists r.C$	$\{x \subseteq \Delta^{\mathcal{I}} \mid \exists y \subseteq \Delta^{\mathcal{I}} \text{ s.t } (x,y) \subseteq r^{\mathcal{I}} \text{ and } y \subseteq C^{\mathcal{I}}\}$
Nominal	$\{a\}$	$\{a^{\mathcal{I}}\}$
Role chain	$r \circ s$	$\{\langle x,y \rangle \mid \exists z \subseteq \Delta^{\mathcal{I}} \text{ s.t } \langle x,z \rangle \in r^{\mathcal{I}} \text{ and } \langle z,y \rangle \in s^{\mathcal{I}}\}$

An interpretation $\mathcal{I}$ is said to be a model of (or satisfies) a GCI (resp. role inclusion, role composition) axiom, denoted by $\mathcal{I} \models C \sqsubseteq D$ (resp. $\mathcal{I} \models r \sqsubseteq s$, $\mathcal{I} \models r_1 \circ r_2 \sqsubseteq s$), if $C^{\mathcal{I}} \subseteq D^{\mathcal{I}}$ (resp. $r^{\mathcal{I}} \subseteq s^{\mathcal{I}}$, $(r_1 \circ r_2)^{\mathcal{I}} \subseteq s^{\mathcal{I}}$). Similarly, $\mathcal{I}$ satisfies a concept (resp. role) assertions, denoted $\mathcal{I} \models C(a)$ (resp. $\mathcal{I} \models r(a,b)$), if $a^{\mathcal{I}} \in C^{\mathcal{I}}$ (resp. $(a^{\mathcal{I}}, b^{\mathcal{I}}) \in r^{\mathcal{I}}$). An interpretation $\mathcal{I}$ is a model of an ontology $\mathcal{O}$ if it satisfies all the axioms of $\mathcal{O}$. An ontology is said to be consistent if it has a model. Otherwise, it is inconsistent. An axiom ϕ is entailed by an ontology, denoted by $\mathcal{O} \models \phi$, if ϕ is satisfied by every model of $\mathcal{O}$. We say that C is subsumed by D w.r.t an ontology $\mathcal{O}$ iff $\mathcal{O} \models C \sqsubseteq D$. Similarly, we say that a is an instance of C w.r.t $\mathcal{O}$ iff $\mathcal{O} \models C(a)$. A concept C is said to be in unsatisfiable w.r.t. $\mathcal{O}$ iff $\mathcal{O} \models C \sqsubseteq \bot$, otherwise C is said to be satisfiable.

In this paper, we will consider assertion free $\mathcal{EL}_{\bot}^{+}$, i.e $\mathcal{EL}_{\bot}^{+}$ without concept assertions $C(a)$ and role assertions $R(a,b)$. The main reasoning task that we consider is classification. It consists in computing all the entailed subsumption (and equivalences) that hold between atomic concepts of an ontology $\mathcal{O}$, or the $\top$ or $\bot$ concepts. We follow the procedure given in [3,4]. Let $\mathcal{O}$ be an $\mathcal{EL}_{\bot}^{+}$ ontology, the first step of reasoning consists in transforming the ontology $\mathcal{O}$ into normal form using a set of rules. We recall that $\mathcal{O}$ is said to be in normal form if each of its axioms has one of the following forms:

$$A \sqsubseteq B, A_1 \sqcap ... \sqcap A_n \sqsubseteq B, A \sqsubseteq \exists r.B, \exists r.A \sqsubseteq B, r \sqsubseteq s \text{ and } r_1 \circ r_2 \sqsubseteq s$$

where $A, B \in N_C \cup \{\top, \bot\}$ and $A_i \in N_C$.

Once the ontology is in normal form, reasoning is performed using the set of inference rules [3,4].

2.2 Possibility Theory

Let $\mathcal{L}$ be a description language and Ω be a universe of discourse on a set of DL interpretations, i.e. $\mathcal{I} = (\Delta^{\mathcal{I}}, \cdot^{\mathcal{I}}) \in \Omega$. We introduce the semantics of possibility theory over DL interpretations.

Possibility Distribution. A possibility distribution, denoted by π, is the main block of the possibility theory. A possibility distribution is a mapping from Ω to the unit interval $[0, 1]$ [2] that assigns to each interpretation $\mathcal{I} \in \Omega$ a possibility degree $\pi(\mathcal{I}) \in [0, 1]$ reflecting its compatibility or consistency w.r.t available knowledge. The weights could be interpreted in two ways, a numerical interpretation when values have a real sense, and an ordinal interpretation when values only reflect a total pre-order between the different states of the world. In this paper, we consider the latter interpretation, i.e. qualitative setting. We say that $\mathcal{I}$ is totally possible (i.e. fully consistent with available knowledge) when $\pi(\mathcal{I}) = 1$ and is impossible (i.e. fully inconsistent) when $\pi(\mathcal{I}) = 0$. Finally, given two interpretations $\mathcal{I}$ and $\mathcal{I}'$, we say that $\mathcal{I}$ is more consistent or more compatible than $\mathcal{I}'$ if $\pi(\mathcal{I}) > \pi(\mathcal{I}')$.

Possibility and Necessity Measures. Given a possibility distribution π, standard possibility theory offers two measures from 2^{Ω} to the interval $[0, 1]$ which discriminate between the plausibility and the certainty regarding an event $M \subseteq \Omega$. A possibility measure $\Pi(M) = \sup\{\pi(\mathcal{I}) : \mathcal{I} \in M\}$ evaluates to what extent M is compatible or plausible w.r.t available knowledge encoded by π. A necessity measure $N(M) = 1 - \Pi(\bar{M})$, which is a dual function to Π, evaluates to what extent M is certainty entailed from available knowledge encoded by π. When $N(M) = 1$, we say that M is certain. When $N(M) \in]0, 1[$, we say that M is somewhat certain. When $N(M) = 0$ and $N(\bar{M}) = 0$, we say that there is a total ignorance about M.

Let ϕ be an $\mathcal{EL}^+_{\bot}$ axiom and $Mod(\phi)$ be the set of models of ϕ. The possibility measure and necessity measure associated to ϕ are defined respectively as follows:
$$\Pi(Mod(\phi)) = \sup_{\mathcal{I} \in \Omega}\{\pi(\mathcal{I}) : \mathcal{I} \models \phi\}, \text{ and } N(Mod(\phi)) = 1 - \sup_{\mathcal{I} \in \Omega}\{\pi(\mathcal{I}) : \mathcal{I} \not\models \phi\}.$$
where $\mathcal{I} \models \phi$ is the satisfaction relation defined in Sect. 2.

3   Min-Based Possibilistic $\mathcal{EL}^+_{\bot}$

In the following, we introduce the syntax and semantics of the possibilistic extension of $\mathcal{EL}^+_{\bot}$ denoted by $\pi\text{-}\mathcal{EL}^+_{\bot}$.

Syntax. Let $\mathcal{O} = \{\phi_i : i = 1, \ldots, n\}$ be an $\mathcal{EL}^+_{\bot}$ ontology composed of a finite set of axioms as presented in Sect. 2. A possibilistic $\mathcal{EL}^+_{\bot}$ ontology, denoted by $\mathcal{O}_{\pi} = \{(\phi_i, \alpha_i) : i = 1, \ldots, n\}$, consists of a finite set of possibilistic axioms of the form (ϕ_i, α_i) where ϕ_i is a standard $\mathcal{EL}^+_{\bot}$ formula and α_i is its certainty

---

[2] In fact, it is a mapping from Ω to a totally ordered scale O. This scale may often be a finite set of integers or the unit interval $[0, 1]$ and encodes our knowledge on the real world. In general, one considers the interval $[0, 1]$.

degree, meaning that $N(\phi_i) \geq \alpha_i$. Note that the higher the degree α the more ϕ is certain. Note that the axioms with α_i's equal to '0' are not explicitly represented in the ontology. Moreover, when all the degrees are equal to 1, $\mathcal{O}_\pi$ coincides with a standard $\mathcal{EL}_\perp^+$ ontology $\mathcal{O}$. In a possibilistic ontology, the necessity degree attached with an axiom reflects its confidence degree.

Semantics. The semantics of possibilistic $\mathcal{EL}_\perp^+$ ontology $\mathcal{O}_\pi$ is given by a possibility distribution, denoted by $\pi_\mathcal{O}$, defined over the set of DL interpretations as presented in Sect. 2.2, namely $\Omega = \{\mathcal{I}_1, \ldots, \mathcal{I}_n\}$. The possibility distribution assigns to each interpretation $\mathcal{I} \in \Omega$ a possibility degree $\pi(\mathcal{I}) \in]0,1]$ reflecting to what extent this latter satisfies (see Sect. 2) the axioms of the ontology. More formally,

Definition 1. *The possibility distribution $\pi_\mathcal{O}$ associated with $\mathcal{EL}_\perp^+$ ontology $\mathcal{O}_\pi$ is defined as follows:*

$$\forall \mathcal{I} \in \Omega, \pi(\mathcal{I}) = \begin{cases} 1 & \text{if } \forall (\phi_i, \alpha_i) \in \mathcal{O}_\pi, \mathcal{I} \models \phi_i \\ 1 - max\{\alpha_i : (\phi_i, \alpha_i) \in \mathcal{O}_\pi, \mathcal{I} \not\models \phi\} & \text{otherwise.} \end{cases}$$

An important advantage of using possibilistic logic is that it can naturally deal with inconsistency, based on the notion of inconsistency degree. Therefore, one can associate to a $\mathcal{EL}_\perp^+$ ontology a degree of inconsistency (which usually ranges between 0 and 1 if we use the unit interval $]0,1]$ to encode certainty degrees).

An interpretation $\mathcal{I}$ is a model of $\mathcal{O}_\pi$ if it satisfies all the axioms of the ontology. In this case $\pi(\mathcal{I}) = 1$, which collapse with the standard definition of ontology model. This also means that the possibility distribution $\pi_\mathcal{O}$ is normalized. Otherwise, if $\mathcal{I}$ is not a model of $\mathcal{O}_\pi$, then the possibility degree $\pi(\mathcal{I})$ depends on the axiom having the maximum weight which is non satisfied (falsified) by the interpretation, namely $\pi(I) = 1 - max\{\alpha_i : (\phi_i, \alpha_i) \in \mathcal{O}_\pi, \mathcal{I} \not\models \phi_i\}$. In this case, the ontology is inconsistent and its inconsistency degree is $\forall \mathcal{I}, Inc(\mathcal{O}_\pi) = 1 - max(\pi(\mathcal{I}))$.

Definition 2. *Let $\mathcal{O}_\pi$ be a $\pi\text{-}\mathcal{EL}_\perp^+$ ontology, we define possibilistic entailment as follows:*

- *An axiom ϕ is entailed from $\mathcal{O}_\pi$, denoted by $\pi \models \phi$ if and only if $N(\phi) > 0$ where $N(\phi)$ is the necessity degree of ϕ computed from π.*
- *An axiom ϕ is entailed from $\mathcal{O}_\pi$ with a certainty degree α, denoted by $\pi \models (\phi, \alpha)$ if and only if $N(\phi) \geq \alpha > 0$ where $N(\phi)$ is the necessity degree of ϕ computed from π.*

In the following, we study reasoning in $\pi\text{-}\mathcal{EL}_\perp^+$ by given algorithms that compute the possibilistic entailment given in Definition 2. We focus on the subsumption problem in $\pi\text{-}\mathcal{EL}_\perp^+$ as possibilistic entailment, i.e., we study the problem of deciding whether $\mathcal{O}_\pi \models (A \sqsubseteq B, \alpha)$, where $A, B \in N_C \cup \{\top, \perp\}$. Notice that $\mathcal{O}_\pi \models (A \sqsubseteq B, \alpha)$ iff $\mathcal{O}_\pi \cup \{(C \sqsubseteq A, 1), (B \sqsubseteq D, 1)\} \models (C \sqsubseteq D, \alpha)$, where C, D are new atomic concepts. Similarly to standard $\mathcal{EL}_\perp^+$, we first provide in Table 2 the normalization rules needed to transform a $\pi\text{-}\mathcal{EL}_\perp^+$ ontology into normal form, and then we give in Table 3 the inference rules needed to compute entailment.

Table 2. Possibilistic normalization rules.

$$(\text{PNR}_0) \quad \frac{(C_1 \sqcap \top \sqcap C_2 \sqsubseteq D, \alpha)}{(C_1 \sqcap C_2 \sqsubseteq D, \alpha)}$$

$$(\text{PNR}_1) \quad \frac{(C_1 \sqcap \bot \sqcap C_2 \sqsubseteq D, \alpha)}{(\bot \sqsubseteq D, \alpha)} :$$

$$(\text{PNR}_2) \quad \frac{(C \sqsubseteq D_1 \sqcap D_2, \alpha)}{(C \sqsubseteq D_1, \alpha) \quad (C \sqsubseteq D_2, \alpha)}$$

$$(\text{PNR}_3) \quad \frac{(\exists r.C \sqsubseteq D, \alpha)}{(C \sqsubseteq A, 1) \quad (\exists r.A \sqsubseteq D, \alpha)} : C \notin N_c, A \text{ is a new concept}$$

$$(\text{PNR}_4) \quad \frac{(C \sqsubseteq D, \alpha)}{(C \sqsubseteq A, 1) \quad (A \sqsubseteq D, \alpha)} : C, D \notin N_c \cup \{\bot, \top\}, A \text{ is a new concept}$$

$$(\text{PNR}_5) \quad \frac{(B \sqsubseteq \exists r.C, \alpha)}{(B \sqsubseteq \exists r.A, 1) \quad (A \sqsubseteq C, \alpha)} : C \notin N_c, A \text{ is a new concept}$$

$$(\text{PNR}_6) \quad \frac{(C_1 \sqcap C \sqcap C_2 \sqsubseteq D, \alpha)}{(C \sqsubseteq A, 1) \quad (C_1 \sqcap A \sqcap C_2 \sqsubseteq D, \alpha)} : C \notin N_c \cup \{\bot, \top\}, A \text{ is a new concept}$$

Table 3. Possibilistic inference rules.

$$(\text{PIR}_0) \quad \frac{}{(A \sqsubseteq A, 1)} : A \in N_c \cup \{\bot, \top\}$$

$$(\text{PIR}_1) \quad \frac{}{(C \sqsubseteq \top, 1)} : C \sqsubseteq \top$$

$$(\text{PIR}_2) \quad \frac{}{(r, 1)} : r \in \mathcal{O}$$

$$(\text{PIR}_3) \quad \frac{(C \sqsubseteq D', \alpha_1) \quad (D' \sqsubseteq D, \alpha_2)}{(C \sqsubseteq D, \min(\alpha_1, \alpha_2))}$$

$$(\text{PIR}_4) \quad \frac{(A \sqsubseteq B_1 ... A \sqsubseteq B_n, \alpha_1) \quad (B_1 \sqcap ... \sqcap B_n \sqsubseteq B, \alpha_2)}{(A \sqsubseteq B, \min(\alpha_1, \alpha_2))} : A, B, B_i \in N_c \cup \{\bot, \top\}$$

$$(\text{PIR}_5) \quad \frac{(A \sqsubseteq \exists r.B, \alpha_1) \quad (B \sqsubseteq C, \alpha_2)}{(A \sqsubseteq \exists r.C, \min(\alpha_1, \alpha_2))} : A, B, C \in N_c \cup \{\bot, \top\}, C \neq \bot$$

$$(\text{PIR}_6) \quad \frac{(A \sqsubseteq \exists r.B, \alpha) \quad (B \sqsubseteq \bot, 1)}{(A \sqsubseteq \bot, \alpha)} : A, B \in N_c \cup \{\bot, \top\}$$

$$(\text{PIR}_7) \quad \frac{(A \sqsubseteq \exists r.B, \alpha_1) \quad (r \sqsubseteq s, \alpha_2)}{(A \sqsubseteq \exists s.B, \min(\alpha_1, \alpha_2))}$$

$$(\text{PIR}_8) \quad \frac{(r_1 \sqsubseteq r_2, \alpha_1) \quad (r_2 \sqsubseteq r_3, \alpha_2)}{(r_1 \sqsubseteq r_3, \min(\alpha_1, \alpha_2))}$$

$$(\text{PIR}_9) \quad \frac{(A \sqsubseteq \exists r_1.B, \alpha_1) \quad (B \sqsubseteq \exists r_2.A_2, \alpha_2) \quad (r_1 \circ r_2 \sqsubseteq s, \alpha_3)}{(A_1 \sqsubseteq \exists s.A_2, \min(\alpha_1, \alpha_2, \alpha_3))} : A_1, r_1, A_2 \in N_c \cup \{\bot, \top\}$$

To obtain these rules, we first introduce the following Lemma.

Lemma 1. *Let $\mathcal{O}_\pi$ be a possibilistic $\mathcal{EL}^+$ ontology that contains two axioms (ϕ, α_1) and (ϕ, α_2) then $\mathcal{O}_\pi$ and $\mathcal{O}'_\pi = \{\mathcal{O}_\pi \backslash \{(\phi, \alpha_1), (\phi, \alpha_2)\}\} \cup \{(\phi, \max(\alpha_1, \alpha_2))\}$ are equivalent in the sense that $\forall \mathcal{I} \in \Omega, \pi_{\mathcal{O}}(\mathcal{I}) = \pi_{\mathcal{O}'}(\mathcal{I})$. Namely, $\mathcal{O}_\pi$ and $\mathcal{O}'_\pi$ induce the same possibility distribution.*

Using this lemma, we have the following propositions.

Proposition 1. *Let $\mathcal{O}_\pi$ be a possibilistic $\mathcal{EL}^+_\perp$ ontology and let $\mathcal{O}^N_\pi$ be the ontology obtained from $\mathcal{O}_\pi$ by applying the normalization rules given in Table 2. Then $\mathcal{O}_\pi$ and $\mathcal{O}^N_\pi$ induce the same possibility distribution.*

Let us now study the inference rules and let $cl(\mathcal{O}_\pi)$ be the closure of the possibilistic $\mathcal{EL}^+_\perp$ ontology $\mathcal{O}_\pi$ obtained by applying the rules given in Tables 2 and 3. The following proposition holds.

Proposition 2. *Let $\mathcal{O}_\pi$ be an $\mathcal{EL}^+_\perp$ ontology and $cl(\mathcal{O}_\pi)$ be its closure under the rules depicted in Tables 2 and 3. Then $\mathcal{O}_\pi$ and $cl(\mathcal{O}_\pi)$ induce the same possibility distribution.*

The following proposition formalizes possibilistic entailment (Definition 2). It is given for subsumption relation as is the main task in $\mathcal{EL}$. However, it can be generalized to any axiom ϕ.

Proposition 3. *Let $cl(\mathcal{O}_\pi)$ be the closure of $\mathcal{O}_\pi$ a possibilistic $\mathcal{EL}^+_\perp$ ontology. Let $A, B \in N_c$ two concept of the ontology. Then $\mathcal{O}_\pi \models (A \sqsubseteq B, \alpha)$ if*

- $(A \sqsubseteq B, \beta) \in cl(\mathcal{O}_\pi)$ *with* $\beta \geq \alpha$
- $(A \sqsubseteq \perp, \beta) \in cl(\mathcal{O}_\pi)$ *with* $\beta \geq \alpha$.

Proposition 4. *Let $cl(\mathcal{O}_\pi)$ be the closure of $\mathcal{O}_\pi$ a possibilistic $\mathcal{EL}^+_\perp$ ontology obtained by applying the normalization rules and inference rules given respectively in Table 2 and 3. Then $cl(\mathcal{O}_\pi)$ is computed in polynomial time w.r.t the size of the ontology $|\mathcal{O}_\pi|$.*

4   Conclusion

In this paper, we investigated uncertainty-based extension of $\mathcal{EL}^+_\perp$ using possibility theory. We introduced the syntax and the semantics of this extension $\mathcal{EL}^+_\perp$, and then studied min-based reasoning to deal with qualitative uncertainty attached to the axioms of the ontology. An important result shown in this paper is that the computational complexity of subsumption remains polynomial.

As future work, we will broaden this work by adding nominal, concrete domain and range in order to propose a *possibilistic OWL2-EL*. We also plan to study a qualitative extension of $\mathcal{EL}$.

Acknowledgments. This work is supported by the European project H2020 Marie Sklodowska-Curie Actions (MSCA) research and Innovation Staff Exchange (RISE): AniAge (High Dimensional Heterogeneous Data based Animation Techniques for Southeast Asian Intangible Cultural Heritage.

References

1. Baader, F.: The Description Logic Handbook: Theory, Implementation and Applications. Cambridge University Press, Cambridge (2003)
2. Baader, F., Brandt, S., Lutz, C.: Pushing the EL envelope. In: Proceedings of the Nineteenth International Joint Conference on Artificial Intelligence, IJCAI 2005, Edinburgh, Scotland, UK, 30 July–5 August 2005, pp. 364–369 (2005)
3. Baader, F., Brandt, S., Lutz, C.: Pushing the EL envelope. In: IJCAI, vol. 5, pp. 364–369 (2005)
4. Baader, F., Brandt, S., Lutz, C.: Pushing the EL envelope further (2008)
5. Baader, F., Lutz, C., Brandt, S.: Pushing the EL envelope further. In: Proceedings of the Fourth OWLED Workshop on OWL: Experiences and Directions, Washington, DC, USA, 1–2 April 2008 (2008)
6. Baader, F., Lutz, C., Suntisrivaraporn, B.: Is tractable reasoning in extensions of the description logic EL useful in practice. In: Proceedings of the 2005 International Workshop on Methods for Modalities, M4M 2005, vol. 450. Citeseer (2005)
7. Benferhat, S., Bouraoui, Z.: Min-based possibilistic DL-Lite. J. Log. Comput. **27**(1), 261–297 (2017)
8. Benferhat, S., Bouraoui, Z., Tabia, K.: How to select one preferred assertional-based repair from inconsistent and prioritized DL-Lite knowledge bases? In: Proceedings of the Twenty-Fourth International Joint Conference on Artificial Intelligence, IJCAI 2015, Buenos Aires, Argentina, 25–31 July 2015, pp. 1450–1456 (2015)
9. Bobillo, F., Straccia, U.: Generalized fuzzy rough description logics. Inf. Sci. **189**, 43–62 (2012)
10. Boutouhami, K., Benferhat, S., Khellaf, F., Nouioua, F.: Uncertain lightweight ontologies in a product-based possibility theory framework. Int. J. Approx. Reason. **88**, 237–258 (2017)
11. Dubois, D., Prade, H.: Possibility theory. In: Computational Complexity, pp. 2240–2252. Springer, New York (2012). https://doi.org/10.1007/978-1-4614-1800-9
12. Lukasiewicz, T., Martinez, M.V., Orsi, G., Simari, G.I.: Heuristic ranking in tightly coupled probabilistic description logics. In: Proceedings of the Twenty-Eighth Conference on Uncertainty in Artificial Intelligence, Catalina Island, CA, USA, 14–18 August 2012, pp. 554–563 (2012)
13. Lukasiewicz, T., Straccia, U.: Managing uncertainty and vagueness in description logics for the semantic web. J. Web Semant. **6**(4), 291–308 (2008)
14. Straccia, U.: Description logics with fuzzy concrete domains. arXiv preprint arXiv:1207.1410 (2012)

FastVOI: Efficient Utility Elicitation During Negotiations

Yasser Mohammad[1,2(✉)] [iD] and Shinji Nakadai[1,3] [iD]

[1] AIST, Tokyo, Japan
{y.mohammad,s-nakadai}@aist.go.jp
[2] Assiut University, Asyut, Egypt
[3] NEC Datascience Research Laboratories, Tokyo, Japan

Abstract. Autonomous Negotiation is a promising technology that allows individuals and institutions to reduce the burden and cost of negotiating win-win agreements. A common challenge in practical applications is the inability or high cost of finding the utility value for each possible outcome of the negotiation before it even starts. Earlier work on utility elicitation during negotiations tried to avoid the need of full revelation of the utility function to the agent by interleaving elicitation and negotiation actions. This paper proposes an efficient elicitation algorithm that allows the agent to achieve similar utility at orders of magnitude higher speed compared with the state-of-the-art algorithm.

Keywords: Autonomous negotiation · Utility elicitation

1 Introduction

Automatic negotiation is attracting more attention from the research community in recent years especially given the rise of AI, machine learning systems and the Internet of Things (IoT) that promise to automate most repetitive aspects of our lives. Recent applications of automatic negotiation include permission management in IoT systems, Wi-Fi channel assignment [5], agriculture supply chain support, and providing feedback for student negotiation skills [8].

Most of this work assumes that the negotiation agent has perfect knowledge of the utility function of the person/entity it is representing during the negotiation. While this can be the case in some limited situations, in many real-world scenarios; it is not possible to have perfect apriori knowledge of this utility function.

Utility elicitation was studied extensively in the decision support community [6]. Most of this work focuses on the problem of eliciting the utility function of an actor for several possible outcomes of the decision process. Negotiation adds a new complexity to this problem because during negotiation it is not enough to know the utility value of some outcome for the user in order to propose/accept it but it is also essential to judge the probability that this outcome/offer is also acceptable by the partner(s) in the negotiation.

© Springer Nature Switzerland AG 2018
T. Miller et al. (Eds.): PRIMA 2018, LNAI 11224, pp. 560–567, 2018.
https://doi.org/10.1007/978-3-030-03098-8_42

More recently, few works have reported systems for utility elicitation *during* negotiation [2,3,10]. These systems build upon earlier work in *preference elicitation* in the decision support domain [4] while taking into account the specific features of negotiation.

The *optimal elicitation algorithm* [2] assumes that the actor (user) can be queried to provide *exact* utility values for different outcomes. This can be achieved using several possible elicitation strategies that does not require actual assignment of a numeric value to any outcome by the user so it is not restrictive. Nevertheless, this form of *deep* elicitation for each outcome considered is time-consuming and would lead to high levels of elicitation bother to the user that can sometimes be avoided. A *shallow* version of this algorithm was recently proposed that also uses a heuristic to manage avoid offering outcomes that turn out to have low utilities in the beginning of the negotiation [10].

The *Optimal Query Agent (OQA)* [3] avoids the problem of deep elicitation by assuming that a predefined set of possible queries are available that can reduce the uncertainty in the probability distribution of utility values for a given outcome. The system selects the optimal query at each point as the one maximizing the value of information which is the difference between the *expected expected utility* if the answer to the query is known compared with it if the answer is not known. The main disadvantage of this approach is its high computational cost which increases linearly with both the outcome space size and the number of available queries.

This paper proposes an efficient value of information based algorithm (FastVOI) that is shown to achieve the same utilities as OQA and provide a performance on-bar with an ideal agent with full knowledge of the utility function while reducing the complexity to $O(n \log n)$ where n is the number of outcomes.

2   Problem Setting

A negotiation session is conducted between multiple agents representing self-interested actors over a set of issues. Issues can have discrete or continuous values. Every possible assignment of a value to each issue is called an *outcome* and during negotiation it may also be called an *offer*. Ω denotes the – possibly uncountable – set of all outcomes and ω_i indicates a member of this set. If an agreement is reached, the agreed upon outcome is called a *contract* (ω_c). Each actor a is assumed to be self-interested with some internal *utility function* $\tilde{U}_a : \Omega \to [0,1]$ that assigns a numeric value (assumed to be normalized to the range 0 to 1 in this work) to every possible outcome.

The actor wishes to maximize the utility she receives from the negotiation through the behavior of its representing agent. Every actor also has a predefined *reserved value* (R_a) that she receives if the negotiation was broken either due to timing out or explicitly by one of the agents.

Negotiation sessions are conducted in *rounds* in which different outcomes are offered/judged by the agents according to some negotiation *protocol*. Negotiation protocols can be moderated with a moderator-agent that have a special role or unmoderated with all agents having similar roles. Several negotiation protocols have been proposed over the years. They can either be mediated [7] or un-mediated [1]. This work utilizes the Stacked Alternating Offers Protocol (SOAP) [1] but is not limited to it.

To provide an incentive for the agents to concede from the outcome with maximum utility, a time-limit is usually applied to the negotiation and the session is broken (times-out) automatically if no agreement is reached within a predefined real-time (T) or number of rounds limit (K). A constant cost δ_a is incurred by every agent at the end of each negotiation round to encourage early agreement. Moreover, any other costs incurred by the agent during the negotiation (e.g. bother cost to the actor) (C_a) is always subtracted from its final utility.

For the rest of this paper, k represents the round number, $t \equiv k/K$ is the relative time, and $n \equiv |\Omega|$ is the total number of outcomes. Superscripts represent round number. The proposed system can trivially be applied to cases with any combinations of real-time and round-limit constraints as well as to cases with constant or discounted negotiation cost.

The SOAP protocol works as follows: An ordering of the agents is defined. We assume—without loss of generality—that it is the same as the agent index a.

The first agent starts the negotiation by *offering* an outcome ω^0 which is visible to all other agents. The next agent either *accepts* the offer, ends the negotiation, or proposes a new offer.

This process is continued until one of the following stopping criteria is met:

- **Agreement:** An offer ω_c is accepted by all agents which is declared as the *contract*. Each agent a receives a utility of $\tilde{U}_a(\omega_c) - k \times \delta_a - C_a$.
- **Timeout:** A predefined number of offer exchanges/rounds (K) or a predefined number of seconds T has passed since the beginning of the negotiation. Each agent a receives a utility of $R_a - K\delta_a - C_a$.
- **Failure:** Some agent ends the negotiation when it has the chance to respond to some offer. Each agent a receives a utility of $R_a - k\delta_a - C_a$.

The agent a representing actor a is not assumed to have access to $\tilde{U}_a$ but have access to a joint probability distribution over possible outcome-utility values $\hat{U}_a^0 : [0, 1]^{|\Omega|} \rightarrow [0, 1]$. Hereafter, when the agent considered is clear from the context, the subscript a will be dropped.

In utility elicitation scenarios, the agent has the ability to *ask* the actor questions that would reduce this source of uncertainty. A reply from the actor can in general be modeled as a mapping from some joint probability distribution over outcome utilities to a new one with smaller spread of values (e.g. variance).

More formally, a negotiation scenario with elicitation adds a set of queries $Q^k \equiv \{q_l^k\}$ where each query q_l^k is defined as a set of tuples (r_{li}, p_{li}, c_{li}) and r_{li} is answer i for query l, p_{li} is the probability of getting this answer, and c_{li} is the cost of getting it (e.g. bother cost to the actor in utility units). In most cases the cost is the same for all answers and $c_{li} = c_{lj} = c_l \; \forall i, j$. Hereafter, m is the number of queries $|Q|$.

An answer r_{li} can generally be modeled as a function that receives a joint utility distribution $\hat{U}^k$ and returns another utility distribution $\hat{U}^{k+1}$ which has total lower spread/variance signaling a reduction of uncertainty. Elicitation during round k is the process of selecting one query q_l^k from Q^k, presenting it to the actor a, receiving a reply $r^k \in \{r_{li}\}$ then applying the transformation defined by that reply to the joint utility distribution: $\hat{U}^k \leftarrow r^k \left[\hat{U}^{k-1} \right]$.

3   VOI Elicitation Algorithm: Optimal Query Agent

The Value-of-information (VOI) based algorithm for preference elicitation was first proposed by Chajewska [4] in the context of decision theory. A related algorithm explicitly designed for elicitation during negotiations was recently proposed by Baarslag and Kaisars [3]. Our proposed variant is based on this algorithm. This section provides a brief description of it.

All VOI variants assume that of an acceptance model $\mathcal{M} : \Omega \to [0, 1]$ is available to the agent. We use the same subscript/superscript rules defined in Sect. 2 with the acceptance model.

A policy $\Psi \equiv \langle \omega_j | \omega_j \in \Omega \rangle$ of length D is an ordered sequence of outcomes (Ψ_i is the outcome at index i in Ψ).

Given an elicitation scenario and an acceptance model $\mathcal{M}$, the expected utility of following a policy Ψ will be:

$$EU\left(\Psi | \mathcal{M}, \tilde{U}\right) = \sum_{k=1}^{|\Psi|} \mathcal{M}\left(\Psi_k\right) \tilde{U}\left(\Psi_k\right) \prod_{j=1}^{k-1} \left(1 - \mathcal{M}\left(\Psi_j\right)\right). \tag{1}$$

Given that the agent has no access to the true utility of the actor $\tilde{U}$, it can only calculate the expectation of EU which is known as the expected expected utility [3]:

$$EEU\left(\Psi | \mathcal{M}, \hat{U}\right) = \sum_{k=1}^{|\Psi|} \mathbb{E}\left[\hat{U}_{\Psi_k}\right] \mathcal{M}\left(\Psi_k\right) \prod_{j=1}^{k-1} \left(1 - \mathcal{M}\left(\Psi_j\right)\right), \tag{2}$$

where, $\mathbb{E}[x]$ is the expected value of x.

An optimal policy π is a policy that maximizes EEU with respect to a given acceptance model and utility distribution:

$$\pi_{\mathcal{M}, \hat{U}} \equiv \operatorname*{argmax}_{\Psi} EEU\left(\Psi | \mathcal{M}, \hat{U}\right) \tag{3}$$

Baarslag and Kaisars [3] provided an efficient greedy algorithm for calculating $\pi_{\mathcal{M}, \hat{U}}$ that can calculate the optimal policy of length l given the one of length $l - 1$ by extending it with ω_* where:

$$\omega_* \equiv \operatorname*{argmax}_{\omega} \mathbb{E}\left[\hat{U}_\omega\right] \mathcal{M}\left(\omega\right).$$

Given $\mathcal{M}, \hat{U}$, the elicitation process of the Optimal Query Agent (OQA) [3] proceeds by calculating the optimal policy π with the expected expected utility under this policy (eeu^*), then for each question $q \in Q$, an *optimal alternative policy* π_{qr} for each possible answer r is calculated with the associated eeu_{qr} as:

$$\pi_{qr} = \underset{\Psi}{\operatorname{argmax}} EEU\left(\Psi | \mathcal{M}, r(\hat{U})\right). \tag{4}$$

The EEU of that question is then calculated as the weighted average of EEU of following the optimal policy after getting each answer with the associated cost subtracted. The VOI algorithm asks the question q^* that maximizes eeu_q as long as $eeu_{q^*} > eeu^*$ which means that asking this question would entail a positive value of information.

This approach to elicitation is promising as it puts few limitations on the kinds of questions being asked and provides a provably optimal solution under the aforementioned assumptions. Its main limitation is the high computational cost. Using the greedy algorithm for optimal policy calculation, the complexity of OQA is $O(nm)$. In general, the number of available queries will increase— at least—linearly with the number of outcomes because adding a new possible outcome will entail adding at least one relevant query about its utility if it is not already known. This leads to a quadratic complexity $O(n^2)$.

4   Proposed Algorithm

The main bottleneck in OQA calculations is finding the optimal policy associated with each answer. As this process is repeated for each answer of each query, it is beneficial to optimize it.

The process proposed by Barslaag et al. [3] detailed in Sect. 3 can find the optimal policy from scratch in $O(n)$ operations. We use a small variant of this process to find the optimal policy for the current distribution $\hat{U}$ keeping some extra information to speedup later calculations. Nevertheless, we propose an update process that can find the optimal policy associated with each answer in $O(\log n)$ given this modified initialization step.

To make it possible to update the EEU value associated with each question in $O(\log n)$ operations, the optimal policy is not stored as a list but as a sorted list implemented using a TREAP data structure. A TREAP data structure combines a tree and a heap leading to logarithmic search and access times by ensuring that the tree is balanced due to the randomization of the priority used to order it.

For each outcome ω, we can calculate the corresponding sorting key as:

$$eu_\omega = \mathbb{E}\left[\hat{U}_\omega\right]. \tag{5}$$

An *inverse* TREAP that uses the outcome as key and the corresponding expected utility (eu) as value is also initialized to speedup localization of outcomes within the first TREAP.

To simplify the notation, we define the cummulative sum and product at element i in Eq. 2 as:

$$P_i \equiv \prod_{j=1}^{i-1} 1 - \mathcal{M}(\pi_j), \tag{6}$$

$$S_i \equiv \sum_{k=1}^{i} \mathcal{M}(\omega_k) \mathbb{E}\left[\hat{U}_k\right] \prod_{j=1}^{k-1} 1 - \mathcal{M}(\pi_j) = \sum_{k=1}^{i} M_k eu_k P_k, \tag{7}$$

where $M_k \equiv \mathcal{M}(\pi_k)$, and $S_0 = 0$ and P is defined up to and including P_{n+1}.

Given these definitions, it is clear that $EEU = S_m$ (see Eqs. 2, 7). It can be shown that the policy calculated in this manner is actually optimal.

Given that we have the initialized optimal policy, if the expected utility of outcome π_k changed from eu_k to eu'_k without a change to the acceptance model, it can be shown that the new expected expected utility can be found as:

$$EEU' = \begin{cases} EEU - M_k eu_k + M_k eu'_k & j = k \\ EEU - S_k + S_{j-1} + M_k eu'_k P_j + (S_{k-1} - S_{j-1})(1 - M_k) & j < k \\ EEU - S_j + S_{k-1} + \frac{S_j - S_k}{1 - M_k} + \frac{M_k u'_k P_{j+1}}{1 - M_k} & j > k \end{cases} \tag{8}$$

where j is the new location of π_k in the optimal policy after the change. The case when the opponent model changes is slightly more involved and will not be presented here to simplify the presentation as it does not occur during utility elicitation because replies to questions from the user can only alter the expected utility of some outcomes but we assume that the user has no knowledge about the opponent to change the acceptance model beyond whatever it was initialized to be.

Once we have the optimal policy π and associated EEU value, we can find the optimal policy associated with any answer π_{qr} by deleting the node containing that outcome from the optimal policy then re-inserting it with the new eu value as calculated from Eq. 5 after replacing $\hat{U}_\omega$ with $r\left(\hat{U}_\omega\right)$. Both of these operations take logarithmic time. Moreover, the EEU value can be updated using Eq. 8 in constant time. This means that updating the optimal policies associated with each response for all queries requires $O(m \log n)$.

The elicitation process requires one application of optimal policy initialization routine which takes $O(n \log n)$ operations. After that, whenever acceptance probability $\mathcal{M}(\omega)$ or utility distribution $\hat{U}_\omega$ is changed for some outcome, only the associated value needs to be corrected and the optimal policy can then be updated in $O(\log n)$ operations. This process though, does not update the S_k and P_k values. This update can be done after applying this process in linear time. Note that we do not need to update the S_k and P_k values while calculating eeu_q values.

To find the best query to ask, we simply have to loop over all queries and for each answer apply the aforementioned update process once to find the associated optimal policy ($O(\log n)$). This means that the total complexity of the process of finding the best query with its associated EEU value is $O(m \log n)$.

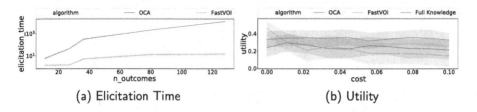

(a) Elicitation Time   (b) Utility

Fig. 1. The performance of different elicitation algorithms.

5   Evaluation

The main goal of this evaluation is to demonstrate the speed advantage of the proposed FastVOI algorithm. This section compares three agents: The OQA agent [3] representing state-of-the-art, the proposed FastVOI agent (Sect. 4), and a *Full Knowledge* agent that shared the same structure as the three other agents but had access to the real utility function of its actor.

The set of scenarios that we used for comparison are taken from the ANAC competition [9] which started in 2010 and is still running annually. We used five bilateral negotiation scenarios from 2012 and 2013 competitions, namely: *Fifty-fifty* (a zero-sum scenario with 11 outcomes), *Laptop* (high number of win-win outcomes with 27 outcomes), *Flight-booking* (An integrative scenario having both good and bad possibilities with 36 outcomes), *Barter* with 80 outcomes, and *Outfit* with 128 outcomes.

Each scenario was run 10 times with the negotiation agent assigned to one of the two sides randomly for 10 different elicitation costs from 0 to 0.1. The initial utility distributions for all outcomes were uniform over the total utility range (0 to 1). The other agent accepted any of the outcomes in the top 25% of its own utility value with a probability equal to that utility after normalization. The elicitation agent did not know this information but had an acceptance model that assigned a probability of acceptance equaling the utility of the opponent. This simplified opponent and opponent model were chosen following [3] to focus the analysis on the elicitation process.

Figure 1 shows the results of this experiment. At zero elicitation cost, all algorithms behaved similarly, nevertheless, with increased cost, all eliciting algorithms started to get less utility (Fig. 1b). The differences between OQA and FastVOI were solely due to rounding errors and tie breaking with equal expected utilities and led to no statistically significant difference (t-test $t = 0.163$, $p = 0.871$). Considering execution time (Fig. 1a), FastVOI was 3.61 times faster than OCA at 11 outcomes and 5947.6 times faster at 120 outcomes. These results support the theoretical analysis of Sect. 4. Due to lack of space more detailed experiments with randomly generated scenarios will not be reported.

One limitation of the work presented in this paper—and almost all elicitation during negotiation in the literature [2, 3, 10]—is the inability to use the internal structure of the utility function to guide the elicitation process. Utilizing the structure of the utility function will be one of our future research directions.

Another issue with all algorithms based on expected expected utility calculations is that they run the risk of offering some outcome early in the negotiation that leads to a very low utility specially in highly competitive scenarios (e.g. the Fifty-Fifty scenario). A reliance on minimizing maximum regret or a variant of the heuristic introduced in [10] for a simpler system may resolve this issue. Analyzing the effect of using an adaptive acceptance model is another direction of future research.

6   Conclusions

This paper presents an efficient algorithm for utility elicitation during negotiation based on rigorous analysis of the value of information provided with all possible queries. The proposed method achieves the same utility as the state-of-the-art algorithm while reducing the computational cost by a factor of $\frac{n}{\log n}$ which allows it to run orders of magnitude faster even for moderately sized problems. The proposed method was evaluated on realistic negotiation scenarios.

References

1. Aydoğan, R., Festen, D., Hindriks, K.V., Jonker, C.M.: Alternating offers protocols for multilateral negotiation. In: Fujita, K., et al. (eds.) Modern Approaches to Agent-based Complex Automated Negotiation. SCI, vol. 674, pp. 153–167. Springer, Cham (2017). https://doi.org/10.1007/978-3-319-51563-2_10
2. Baarslag, T., Gerding, E.H.: Optimal incremental preference elicitation during negotiation. In: IJCAI, pp. 3–9 (2015)
3. Baarslag, T., Kaisers, M.: The value of information in automated negotiation: a decision model for eliciting user preferences. In: Proceedings of the 16th Conference on Autonomous Agents and MultiAgent Systems, pp. 391–400 (2017)
4. Chajewska, U., Koller, D., Parr, R.: Making rational decisions using adaptive utility elicitation. In: AAAI/IAAI, pp. 363–369 (2000)
5. De La Hoz, E., Marsa-Maestre, I., Gimenez-Guzman, J.M., Orden, D., Klein, M.: Multi-agent nonlinear negotiation for Wi-Fi channel assignment. In: Proceedings of the 16th Conference on Autonomous Agents and MultiAgent Systems, pp. 1035–1043 (2017)
6. Ha, V., Haddawy, P.: Problem-focused incremental elicitation of multi-attribute tility models. In: Proceedings of the Thirteenth Conference on Uncertainty in Artificial Intelligence, pp. 215–222. Morgan Kaufmann Publishers Inc. (1997)
7. Ito, T., Hattori, H., Klein, M.: Multi-issue negotiation protocol for agents: exploring nonlinear utility spaces. In: IJCAI, vol. 7, pp. 1347–1352 (2007)
8. Johnson, E., Gratch, J., DeVault, D.: Towards an autonomous agent that provides automated feedback on students' negotiation skills. In: Proceedings of the 16th Conference on Autonomous Agents and MultiAgent Systems, pp. 410–418 (2017)
9. Jonker, C.M., Aydogan, R., Baarslag, T., Fujita, K., Ito, T., Hindriks, K.V.: Automated negotiating agents competition (anac). In: AAAI, pp. 5070–5072 (2017)
10. Mohammad, Y., Nakadai, S.: Utility elicitation during negotiation with practical elicitation strategies. In: IEEE SMC (2018)

An Agent-Based Approach to Simulate Post-earthquake Indoor Crowd Evacuation

Lin Ni[1], Vicente Gonzalez[1](✉)(iD), Jiamou Liu[1](iD), Anass Rahouti[2], Libo Zhang[3], and Bun Por Taing[1]

[1] The University of Auckland, Auckland, New Zealand
v.gonzalez@auckland.ac.nz
[2] The University of Mons, Mons, Belgium
[3] College of Computer and Information Science,
Southwest University, Chongqing, China

Abstract. This work employs an agent-based approach to model indoor post-earthquake evacuations. The model incorporates heterogeneous agents with a dynamic physical indoor environment that is damaged by the earthquake. To realistically recreate the decision making process of building occupants, we use a dual-graph model which combines a navigation mesh to support agents' physical movement and a perception graph to model cognition of the agents.

Keywords: Agent-based model · Earthquake evacuation
Simulation · Building information model

1 Introduction

One of the most important tasks involved in mitigating earthquake hazard is to evaluate indoor safety by developing an understanding of how people respond to the disaster and interact with their indoor environment [3]. Traditional methods such as questionnaires and drills posed many limitations and are not sufficient to assess the outcomes of evacuation within such a complex situation [7,15]. This calls for smart simulation approaches to predict evacuation behaviors. A suitable simulation solution would truthfully represent the physical area while taking into account the dynamic nature of the earthquake; it should also model individual differences and create a diverse evacuee population who perform complex cognition and decision making tasks.

The paper presents a new agent-based model for indoor post-earthquake evacuation. (a) We developed a prototype of a new simulation tool for indoor evacuation where agents navigate within a 3D domain towards a place of safety and perform a range of tasks along the way. (b) The model implements a new dual-layer data structure which combines a continuous physical layer and a discrete perception layer. (c) To evaluate our prototype, we build two case studies

© Springer Nature Switzerland AG 2018
T. Miller et al. (Eds.): PRIMA 2018, LNAI 11224, pp. 568–575, 2018.
https://doi.org/10.1007/978-3-030-03098-8_43

where the 3D domains are constructed using real-life building information. In each case study we deploy multiple agents and assess the effect of different human behaviors on evacuation.

Related Work. The recent decades have seen the development of many simulation methods for emergency evacuations. In particular, an *agent-based model* [5] represents the evacuees as a collection of autonomous and intelligent agents. It has the potential to describe individual behaviors and delivers a high level of realism for heterogeneous situations and bridges the micro/macro scopes. Research on agent-based emergency and egress models has concentrated so far on (1) outdoor evacuation for disasters such as earthquakes, tsunamis, and bush fires where focus is put on pedestrian or traffic flow, road congestions and optimal paths [1,13], and (2) indoor evacuation in the event of fire or a generic setting where the building is static [4,10,12,15].

We focus on post-earthquake indoor evacuation, which deviates from the situations above. Firstly, indoor evacuation presents a distinct set of challenges altogether as the indoor spaces are much more limited than outdoor while items tend to obstruct views of the evacuees. Secondly, an earthquake may change the accessible areas in a building and hence the floor layout. Thirdly, during earthquake evacuation, some common behavioral assumptions no longer hold true. For example, as opposed to in fire incidents, many governments demand building occupants not to evacuate immediately when an earthquake strikes, but rather, they should adopt a drop-cover-hold position until the shake completely stops before trying to move out of the building [8].

2   Model Description

The modeling phase contains two parts. The first is to create a 3D environment of the building interior and the second is to generate a population of agents.

For the 3D environment, the system develops the physical scene using building information modeling (BIM). A detailed 3D geometrical representation of the building interior is crafted using Autodesk Revit, a BIM software used by architects worldwide[1]. The BIM model is then imported to Unity3D as an environment for the agent-based simulations.

For the agents, the Belief-Desire-Intention (BDI) framework facilitates the description of how individuals make decisions in disasters [10,11,14]. A BDI agent implements 3 modules: a perception module, an interpreter module, and an intention module. We propose a BDI model that is embedded within the Unity3D game engine. This model is implemented as a new plug-in.

The system places a number of agents at random locations in the indoor environment. Each agent is specified a *movement speed* which is randomly generated from the general walking speed of $[1.42, 2.56]$ m/s [9]. Each agent is designed using a dual-layer behavioral model, which consists of a *physical layer* and a *perception layer*. The physical layer defines the continuous space in which the agents

---

[1] https://www.autodesk.com/solutions/bim.

move and interact; this is common to all agents. The perception layer represents the discrete knowledge of the agents, and is different for different agents. The mapping from the perception layer to the physical layer enables path finding and other behaviors of the agents. In particular, the decision making process is implemented consistently with the BDI framework as shown in Fig. 1.

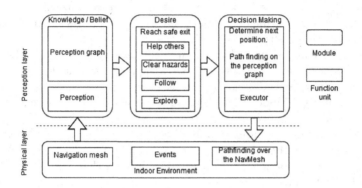

Fig. 1. The agent model

The physical layer represents the geometry of the indoor environment and agents physical movements within it. This layer consists of a continuous space. Each agent is represented by a cylindrical shape with a radius of 0.3 m and a collision radius of 0.5m. When traveling with an injured person, the combined collision radius becomes 1m [2]. The algorithm in the A* Pathfinding Project is called to realise pathfinding tasks of the agents[2].

The perception layer maintains a discrete *perception graph* which consists of *location nodes* which are positions in the 3D environment, and *edges* between close-by nodes. The entire building has a *global perception graph* $H = (V, E)$ which covers all closed regions of the building interior. At any time, any agent a will maintain a *local perception graph* $G_a = (V_a, E_a)$ that represents its own belief and knowledge. The set V_a of location nodes in G_a may be a subset of V which indicates that agent a may have partial knowledge of the 3D environment. For each agent, we generate an initial position, which is one of the location nodes in H. We then assign an initial knowledge percentage to the agent which could be 1 which denotes that the agent has full knowledge of the domain, 0 which denotes that the agent has zero knowledge, or any percentage $p \in (0, 1)$ which denotes partial knowledge. The initial knowledge graph G_a of agent a will then contain nodes that are within a certain distance from a and make up p portion of the entire node set V.

After the earthquake, a randomly selected set of edges in H will be removed denoting blocking caused by damage to the building. Thus, E_a may contain edges that are not in H. The agent may only update this knowledge when it perceives such a change in the environment during the evacuation.

---

[2] https://arongranberg.com/astar/.

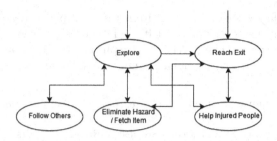

Fig. 2. The goal and subgoals of the agent

We elaborate on the decision making process performed by an agent during evacuation. We organize goals and subgoals into the structure as in Fig. 2.

- If the local perception graph G_a contains an exit, agent a would compute a shortest path in G_a from its current location to the closest exit, and move along this path.
- If G_a does not contain any exit, then agent a has an "explore" sub-goal which means that it is looking for an exit. Once the agent reaches the new location node, it may see more locations that are not in the current local perception graph G_a, and thus G_a is updated to reflect this new knowledge.
- An agent may follow another during the evacuation. In the scenarios of simulations undertaken, there was either none of the population or 10% of the population able to exhibit following behaviors [6].
- The proportions of injured agents range between 0%, 2.5% and 20%. Note that only seriously injured agents were integrated into our simulation, where they would not move unless if an uninjured helper agent was able to help.
- Each agent either had a belonging to take, or none to be collected. With methods on where the belongings would be placed were uncertain, the belongings were spread evenly throughout the environment, to be collected.

3   Evaluation

We carry out two case studies on real-world buildings of different types and run agent-based evacuation simulations on these buildings. We populated the virtual environment of each case study with 63 agents.

Case Study I. The Auckland City Hospital was chosen to be the modelled physical environment[3]. The visitor's area of a floor in the main building is modeled due to its multi-functional area. See Fig. 3.

Case Study II. We also simulate a 3-storey university building which includes multiple classrooms, corridors, stairs, etc. The layout of this building is significantly simpler than the hospital building, yet it covers a much larger area and

---

[3] https://www.naturalhazards.org.nz/NHRP/Hazard-themes/Societal-Resilience/
NHRP-Partner-led-Soc/Building-Quake-People.

the complexity for evacuation comes from the multiple storeys and the patio. Figure 3 shows the navigation mesh (left) and the perception graph (right) of the university environment. The perception graph has 342 location nodes. Table 1 summarises the characteristics of each simulated structure.

Table 1. Statistics about the two real-world building environments.

Scene	Length (m)	Width (m)	Stories	# Rooms	# Exits	# Local nodes
Hospital	78	54	1	~10	6	127
University	63	54	3	54	3	342

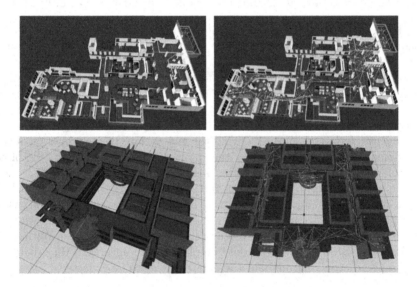

Fig. 3. The hospital navigation mesh (top-left) and the global perception graph (top-right). The university navigation mesh (bottom-left) and the global perception graph (bottom-right). Nodes are colored red and edges are green. (Color figure online)

We design several test scenarios for each scene by combining 16 parameters in 5 variables. (1) Firstly we use a variable 'Injured' to indicate the percentage of agents who have been seriously injured during the earthquake, and cannot move at all by themselves. (2) We then use a variable 'item' to denote the percentage of agents who will pick up valuable items along the way. (3) Thirdly, we vary the initial knowledge level of the agents. The test scenarios assume either that all agents have an initial knowledge of 3%, or 30%, or half of the agents have knowledge level 3% where the other half have 30%. (4) We then use a variable 'follow' to represent the action of the agents to follow other agents in case they do not know the way to any exit. (5) Last, we use a variable to denote the damage caused by the earthquake. In the hospital scene, we randomly put obstacles which blocks doorways and corridors. The number of obstacles range between 4 and 8. In the university building, we randomly put 10 obstacles which mostly concentrated on the staircase.

4 Results

For each test scenario, we run 10 times and use the average data result. We collect data about the evacuation time of each agent, the pass frequency of each knowledge node and exits, and the number of the injured agents and potential safety risks left behind after all the healthy agents get out.

Node Visitation Frequency. Most agents in all scenarios are able to successfully evacuate. However, the frequency of exits that the agents adopt are vastly different, as shown in Fig. 4 (left). We then extract the frequencies in which the agents visit the other location nodes. The ranked frequency is displayed in Fig. 4 (right) which indicates an exponential decrease.

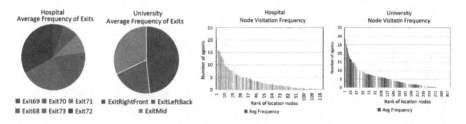

Fig. 4. The frequency of exits adopted by the agents (above) and the average node visitation frequency from the most frequently visited location node to the least for the hospital (bottom-left) and university (bottom-right) environment.

Evacuation Time. The evacuation time of an agent is the time taken it to go from its initial location to a place of safety (e.g. an exit). We measure the average evacuation time of all agents among 10 executions of our model. See Figs. 5 and 6. The generic scenario for the hospital is when 20% agents are injured, 35% are picking up items, half of the agents have initial knowledge 3% and the other half have 30%, and there are 4 edges that are blocked due to the earthquake. The generic scenario for the university is similar, except 10 edges are blocked due to the earthquake. The comparisons are made by changing one of the variables while fixing the other as above. Some consistent patterns emerge between the results from the two cases. In particular, the agents' initial knowledge is a significant factor for their effective evacuation as higher initial knowledge generally leads to a faster evacuation time. The behavior of picking up item also impacts evacuation time with the higher number of evacuees performing this action leading to in general slower evacuation time.

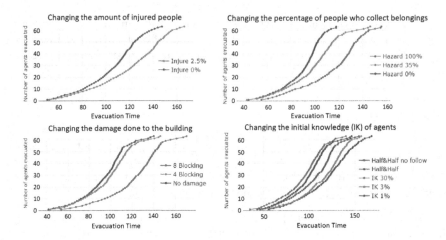

Fig. 5. The average number of agents evacuated after the quake for the hospital environment. Evacuation times are measured in seconds.

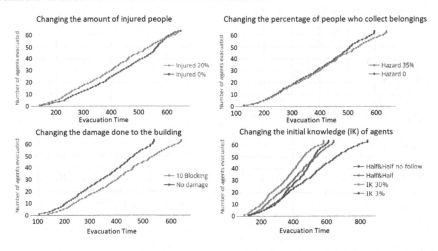

Fig. 6. The average number of agents evacuated after the quake for the university environment. Evacuation times are measured in seconds.

5   Conclusion and Future Work

This paper presents a prototyped agent-based model and simulation platform for indoor post-earthquake evacuation. Using two case studies, we show that our model is able to identify significant impact factors on the agent evacuation times. Future developments must include further behaviors and agent attributes that may affect the evacuation time such as 'hearing' capabilities, sign recognition, the initial spatial distribution of agents, and the evacuation time delay agents would experience when they help other agents.

References

1. Aguilar, L., Lalith, M., Ichimura, T., Hori, M.: Automatic evacuation management using a multi agent system and parallel meta-heuristic search. In: Baldoni, M., Chopra, A.K., Son, T.C., Hirayama, K., Torroni, P. (eds.) PRIMA 2016. LNCS (LNAI), vol. 9862, pp. 387–396. Springer, Cham (2016). https://doi.org/10.1007/978-3-319-44832-9_26
2. Elaine, N., Marieb, H., Katja, N.: Human Anatomy and Physiology with Mastering A&P. Pearson Education Ltd. (2016)
3. Ko, S., Spearpoint, M., Teo, A.: Trial evacuation of an industrial premises and evacuation model comparison. Fire Saf. J. **42**(2), 91–105 (2007)
4. Korhonen, T., Hostikka, S., Heliövaara, S., Ehtamo, H.: FDS+Evac: an agent based fire evacuation model. In: Klingsch, W., Rogsch, C., Schadschneider, A., Schreckenberg, M. (eds.) Pedestrian and Evacuation Dynamics, pp. 109–120. Springer, Heidelberg (2010). https://doi.org/10.1007/978-3-642-04504-2_8
5. Liu, S., Lo, S., Ma, J., Wang, W.: An agent-based microscopic pedestrian flow simulation model for pedestrian traffic problems. IEEE Trans. Intell. Transp. Syst. **15**(3), 992–1001 (2014)
6. Liu, Z., Jacques, C., Szyniszewski, S., Guest, J., Schafer, B., Igusa, T., Mitrani-Reiser, J.: Agent-based simulation of building evacuation after an earthquake: coupling human behavior with structural response. Nat. Hazards Rev. **17**(1), 04015019 (2015)
7. Lovreglio, R., et al.: The need for enhancing earthquake evacuee safety by using virtual reality serious games. In: Proceedings of the Lean and Computing in Construction Congress, Crete, Greece, pp. 4–12 (2017)
8. Ministry of Civil Defense and Emergency Management. Working from the same page: consistent messages for CDEM. Part B: Earthquakes (2015)
9. Mohler, B.J., Thompson, W.B., Creem-Regehr, S.H., Pick, H.L., Warren, W.H.: Visual flow influences gait transition speed and preferred walking speed. Exp. Brain Res. **181**(2), 221–228 (2007)
10. Okaya, M., Takahashi, T.: BDI agent model based evacuation simulation. In: AAMAS 2011, pp. 1297–1298 (2011)
11. Shendarkar, A., Vasudevan, K., Lee, S., Son, Y.-J.: Crowd simulation for emergency response using BDI agent based on virtual reality. In: Proceedings of WSC 2006, pp. 545–553. IEEE (2006)
12. Shi, J., Ren, A., Chen, C.: Agent-based evacuation model of large public buildings under fire conditions. Automat Constr. **18**(3), 338–347 (2009)
13. Singh, D., Padgham, L.: Community evacuation planning for bushfires using agent-based simulation. In: AAMAS 2015, pp. 1903–1904 (2015)
14. Singh, D., Padgham, L., Logan, B.: Integrating BDI agents with agent-based simulation platforms. Auton. Agents Multi Agent Syst. **30**(6), 1050–1071 (2016)
15. Tsai, J., et al.: ESCAPES: evacuation simulation with children, authorities, parents, emotions, and social comparison. In: AAMAS 2011, pp. 457–464 (2011)

A Template System for Modeling and Verifying Agent Behaviors

Shinpei Ogata[1(✉)], Yoshitaka Aoki[2], Hiroyuki Nakagawa[3],
and Kazuki Kobayashi[1]

[1] Shinshu University, 4-17-1, Wakasato, Nagano 380-8553, Japan
ogata@cs.shinshu-u.ac.jp, kby@shinshu-u.ac.jp
[2] Nihon Unisys, Ltd., 1-1-1 Toyosu, Koto-ku, Tokyo 135-8560, Japan
yoshitaka.aoki@unisys.co.jp
[3] Osaka University, 1-5, Yamadaoka, Suita, Osaka 565-0871, Japan
nakagawa@ist.osaka-u.ac.jp

Abstract. The spread of Cyber-Physical Systems (CPSs) leads developers to embed various agents in a large system. It is a complicated and difficult task to analyze and design such systems from comprehensive specifications such as an architecture document because many behaviors of many components including agents must be dealt with. In such a system, the appropriateness of interactions between components should be ensured. However, no method to efficiently define and verify behaviors in such interactions from such specifications taking into consideration the characteristics of CPSs has been proposed. To improve this situation, this paper preliminarily proposes a stepwise method to define and verify behaviors in interactions between CPS components. More specifically, a template system to stepwise define behaviors from an abstract level to a concrete level is presented based on an existing architecture modeling method. Furthermore, a model transformation tool for verifying such behavior definitions by using the model checking tool NuSMV is introduced.

Keywords: Architectural model · Cyber-Physical System
Model checking · Model transformation · Analysis and design
Behavior specification

1 Introduction

CPSs (Cyber-Physical Systems) such as IoT (Internet of Things) have become wide spread in recent years. Agents may numerously appear as CPSs' components since various components have to properly act and react to various environments such as natural environments. When developers analyze and design such CPSs, it is not easy to grasp the architecture because of the many components. According to existing research [1,2,13] on CPS development, reference architectures have been considered but such reference architectures are different from

© Springer Nature Switzerland AG 2018
T. Miller et al. (Eds.): PRIMA 2018, LNAI 11224, pp. 576–584, 2018.
https://doi.org/10.1007/978-3-030-03098-8_44

each other. In addition, no method combining approaches to flexibly document and efficiently verify architectures has been proposed. We [12] have proposed a method and tool to model the architectures of CPSs and verify it using the logic programming language Prolog, for early documentation and verification of the architecture of large CPSs. This method called TORTE can flexibly deal with differences between reference architectures because the method enables developers to easily extend kinds of relationships and the corresponding description spaces called layers into the model.

However, TORTE has not been suitable for handling agents' behaviors yet since it only models and verifies architectural, i.e. structural, aspects. Therefore, we propose a method to define behaviors of architectural components based on architecture models in TORTE (hereafter called TORTE architecture models). As a main research problem, it is evident that many complicated behaviors need to be defined for representing large CPSs. To facilitate such behavior definition, we propose a template system that helps developers stepwise define behaviors from an abstract level to a concrete level. Those behavior definitions are represented in the UML (Unified Modeling Language) state machine diagram notation which is familiar to embedded system development. In addition, we also newly propose a way of transforming behavior definitions into a model that can be checked by the model checking tool NuSMV [5] for assisting formal verification.

2   TORTE Architecture Model

We [12] have proposed a method of modeling and checking a CPS architecture from only a structural aspect. This method aims to assist analysis of a CPS architecture at an early stage of development in the twin peaks model [11]. TORTE architecture models are represented using UML class diagrams slightly extended, and consists of nodes as typed entities (Table 1) and directed edges as typed relationships (Table 2).

Figure 1 in which the result of merging four layers (i.e. `control`, `request`, `transmit-data` and `transmit-energy`) is shown shows a small example of a TORTE architecture model for explaining the process of the proposed method. For instance, `AgentC` controls `AgentA`, transmits energy to `AgentA`, requests data from `ObjectB`, and receives data from `ObjectB` and energy from `AgentD` or `AgentE`. The order of performing these behaviors is not required since this model only shows static relationships. The shapes of stick-men and rectangles represent agents and objects respectively, and have the detail types (e.g. `service` and `device`) specified by developers. Entities include both agents and objects in this paper because actual CPSs such as [7] do not consist of either agents or objects.

3   Proposed Method: A Template System for Modeling and Verifying Agent Behaviors

Agent designers should define the interactions among agents or at least anticipate what interactions happen even if the agents behave autonomously. Various Web

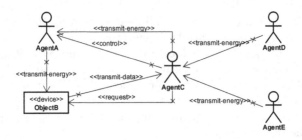

Fig. 1. Small example of a TORTE architecture model

Table 1. Types of entities

Type	Description
user	Users using or maintaining other entities
service	Services provided for other entities and deployed in cyberspace
edge	Edges constructing networks and deployed in physical space
device	Devices controlling or monitoring other entities and deployed in physical space
energy	Energy suppliers transmitting energy for other entities and deployed in physical space
environment	Natural environment stimulating other entities or monitoring them

Table 2. Types of architectural relationships

Type	Description
use	An entity uses a beneficial service of another entity
request	An entity requires data from another entity
control	An entity changes or maintains behaviors of another entity
monitor	An entity monitors another entity without requiring a response
transmit-data	An entity transmits data to another entity
transmit-energy	An entity transmits energy to another entity

services, devices, robots, etc. are agents which have the respective behaviors for the interactions with others. Consequently, such definition and anticipation are time-consuming tasks since many kinds of agents interact with each other in large CPSs. However, it is expected that such interactions are almost the same among various agents at a proper abstract level because their interactions are often constructed based on some existing protocols. Therefore, the proposed method aims to define agent behaviors in interactions from an abstract level to a concrete level in incremental steps so that agent designers can easily reuse abstract interaction definitions to efficiently define concrete behaviors.

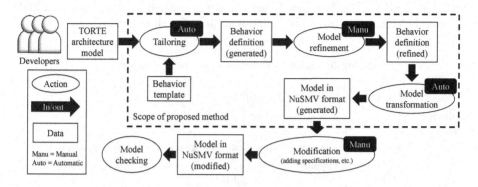

Fig. 2. Overview of the proposed method

Figure 2 shows an overview of the proposed method. The `Auto` actions are automatically performed using a tool for model transformation. The tool was prototyped in Java. Each of the actions and data in the scope of the proposed method is explained in detail in the corresponding subsequent section.

3.1   Behavior Template

A behavior template defines abstracted interactions among entities or entity-self behaviors, and is represented as a state machine diagram. The abstraction is realized by introducing variables referring a collection of entities as shown in Table 3. The common relationships and/or behaviors among entities can be defined into templates by properly using these variables.

Figure 3 shows examples of behavior templates for all pairs of entities that have a `transmit-energy` relationship. For instance, the diagram's name have two variables (i.e. `<all>` and `<everyone>`). The former and latter positions of the variables correspond to the `First` and `Second` parameters respectively in Table 3. Furthermore, variables used to represent communications among templates are provided for diagram element's properties, i.e. the trigger or guard of a transition. The `Both` parameter means that variables can be handled as the `First` or `Second` parameters.

For instance, the trigger `<this>.transmit-energy.passive.<another>` `== Transmitted_Energy` means that the transition to `Transmitting_Energy` from `Ready` is executed if `another` entity (excluding the `target` entity) transmits energy to `this` entity. Before writing each diagram, developers should pre-define all types of states, e.g. `Ready` and `Transmitting_Energy`, that is, like the terminology in DSL (Domain Specific Language).

The logic of interactions is often controlled by an entity's internal behaviors. The proposed method deals with such internal behaviors by introducing a behavior template named using the suffix `.self`. For instance, `<all>.self` is one of the ways of representing templates for internal behaviors. We do not focus on internal behaviors because the commonality between entities may be lower than interactions. We, however, believe that the separation of interactions and internal behaviors enhances the maintainability of each entity.

Table 3. Variables in behavior template (excerpt)

Context	Parameter	Variable	Description
Diagram name	First	`all`	All entities
	Second	`everyone`	All opposite entities on a specified relationship
		`anyone`	One of all opposite entities on a specified relationship
Diagram element property	Both	`this`	The entity represented at the first parameter in the name of the diagram containing this element
		`target`	The entity represented at the second parameter in the name of the diagram contains this element
		`other`	All entities relating with **this** entity on a specified relationship and excluding **target** entity
		`another`	One of all entities relating with **this** entity on a specified relationship and excluding **target** entity

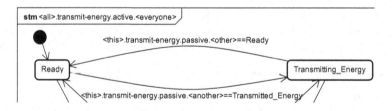

Fig. 3. Example of behavior template (excerpt)

3.2 Tailoring and Behavior Definition

The tailoring action instantiates behavior definitions from behavior templates by merging a TORTE architecture model with the templates. In other words,

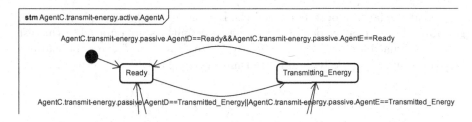

Fig. 4. Example of behavior definition (excerpt)

this process make abstract behaviors concrete. Figure 4 shows an example of the behavior definitions tailored using Figs. 1 and 3.

Behavior definitions are created for each pair of values derived from the first, e.g. .<all>, and second, e.g. .<everyone>, variables of the behavior template's name. In this example, the first value in a pair is derived from the range (i.e. AgentA to AgentE) referred by the **all** variable. The other value is derived from the range (e.g. AgentA) referred by the **everyone** variable. The latter range is determined by the value of the first parameter. For instance, the pair (*first, second*) can take (AgentC, AgentA) but not (AgentC, ObjectB) on the **transmit-energy** relationship.

Similarly, transition's properties using variables are tailored as well as behavior template's name. If **other** or **another** variable refers to multiple values, they are expanded into logical AND (i.e. &&) or logical OR (i.e. ||) operators respectively. For instance, AgentC receives energy from AgentD or AgentE. Therefore, <this>.transmit-energy.passive.<other> == Ready was replaced with AgentC.transmit-energy.passive.AgentD == Ready && AgentC.transmit-energy.passive.AgentE == Ready in Fig. 4.

3.3 Model Refinement

The model refinement action deals with special cases of behavior definitions manually. The behaviors of entities are normally different from each other even if the common behaviors can be extracted as templates. Therefore, multiple behavior definitions may need to be customized after the tailoring. Behavior definitions do not contain any variables in Table 3, so developers can intuitively edit them comparing them with behavior templates.

3.4 Model Transformation and Model in NuSMV Format

The model transformation action generates an artifact to formally check behavior definitions. Here, the artifact means a model in the NuSMV format, and excludes any specifications. Behavior definitions are familiar to such a model because both are written in state-transition-based notation. Table 4 summarizes the rules to relate behavior definitions with a model. The JUSTICE running keyword is given to each MODULE context because CPSs usually have control loops [9] which may break the fairness of state transitions. Listing 1 shows an example of a model generated from behavior definitions. A lot of definitions are omitted in this list because of space limitations, and the words "tea" and "tep" are abbreviations for "transmit_energy_active" and "transmit_energy_passive" respectively.

Table 4. Rules to relate behavior definition with NuSMV model

Behavior definition	NuSMV model
The name of an entity	The name of a MODULE context
State variables of other entities used in transitions	The parameters of a MODULE context
States in behavior definitions for one entity	State variables in a VAR context
The initial state indicated by the initial pseudo-state	The **init** functions in an ASSIGN context
Transitions including triggers and guards	The **next** functions in an ASSIGN context

```
1   MODULE agentc(agentd_tea_agentc,...)
2   VAR
3     agentc_tea_agenta:{Ready,Transmitting_Energy,...};
4   ASSIGN
5     init(agentc_tea_agenta):=Ready;
6     next(agentc_tea_agenta):=case
7       agentc_tea_agenta=Transmitting_Energy & (
            agentc_tep_agentd=Ready & ... ):Ready;
8     esac;
9   JUSTICE running
10  MODULE main
11  VAR
12    agentc: process agentc(agentd_tea_agentc,...);
```

Listing 1. Generated model in NuSMV format (excerpt)

4   Related Work

Several studies in the agent community are recently focusing on constructing CPSs based on agent technologies. Floretto et al. [6] have proposed a multi-agent system approach to scheduling devices in smart homes. This approach formalizes the device scheduling and coordination problem across multiple smart homes as a distributed multi-agent system. Nascimento [10] has proposed a preliminary agent-based mechanism that can adjust and reconfigure CPSs in accordance with environmental variants. Our study aims to aid construction of an adequate system architecture for multi-agent systems based on CPS.

Numerous studies focus on the verification of agent behaviors. In recent studies, Belardinelli et al. [3] have proposed a mechanism to verify agent abilities in the context of imperfect information. This mechanism gives a verification of ATL (alternating-time temporal logic) specifications. Boureanu et al. [4] proposed a method of verifying whether security protocols underlying CPSs are correct in a provable way. While these studies generally focus on verifying the correctness of agent's behaviors or interactions, our study uses a model checker to find omissions of interactions that cause potential failures of the system.

5   Conclusion

This paper preliminarily proposed a stepwise method to define and verify entities' behaviors including agents' behaviors. This method provides a feature of behavioral modeling based on a comprehensive TORTE architecture model with less effort than before, and model transformation from behavior templates to behavior definitions and from behavior definitions to the corresponding model in the NuSMV format. In future work, we plan to enhance a way of defining specifications used in model checking and visualizing the result of model checking, and then to conduct experiments in which various developers use the proposed method for various systems.

Acknowledgment. This work was supported by JSPS KAKENHI Grant Number JP17KT0043 and JP16K16043.

References

1. Industrial internet reference architecture version 1.7 (2015). http://www. iiconsortium.org/IIRA-1-7-ajs.pdf. Accessed 27 July 2016
2. Atzori, L., Iera, A., Morabito, G.: The Internet of Things: a survey. Comput. Netw. **54**(15), 2787–2805 (2010)
3. Belardinelli, F., Lomuscio, A.: Agent-based abstractions for verifying alternating-time temporal logic with imperfect information. In: Larson, et al. [3], pp. 1259–1267
4. Boureanu, I., Kouvaros, P., Lomuscio, A.: Verifying security properties in unbounded multiagent systems. In: Jonker, C.M., Marsella, S., Thangarajah, J., Tuyls, K. (eds.) Proceedings of the 2016 International Conference on Autonomous Agents & Multiagent Systems, Singapore, 9–13 May 2016, pp. 1209–1217. ACM (2016)
5. Cimatti, A., et al.: NuSMV 2: an OpenSource tool for symbolic model checking. In: Brinksma, E., Larsen, K.G. (eds.) CAV 2002. LNCS, vol. 2404, pp. 359–364. Springer, Heidelberg (2002). https://doi.org/10.1007/3-540-45657-0_29
6. Fioretto, F., Yeoh, W., Pontelli, E.: A multiagent system approach to scheduling devices in smart homes. In: Larson, et al. [8], pp. 981–989
7. Kobayashi, K., Fujikawa, Y., Saito, Y.: Monorail-based monitoring system for multipoint field observation. In: Proceedings of the 2014 International Workshop on Web Intelligence and Smart Sensing, pp. 8:1–8:2 (2014)

8. Larson, K., Winikoff, M., Das, S., Durfee, E.H. (eds.): Proceedings of the 16th Conference on Autonomous Agents and MultiAgent Systems, AAMAS 2017, São Paulo, Brazil, 8–12 May 2017. ACM (2017)

9. Leveson, N.: Engineering a Safer World: Systems Thinking Applied to Safety. Engineering Systems. MIT Press, Cambridge (2011)

10. Nascimento, N.: A self-configurable IoT agent system based on environmental variability. In: Proceedings of the 17th International Conference on Autonomous Agents and MultiAgent Systems, AAMAS 2018, pp. 1761–1763. International Foundation for Autonomous Agents and Multiagent Systems, Richland (2018)

11. Nuseibeh, B.: Weaving together requirements and architectures. Computer **34**(3), 115–117 (2001)

12. Ogata, S., Nakagawa, H., Aoki, Y., Kobayashi, K., Fukushima, Y.: A tool to edit and verify IoT system architecture model. In: MODELS (Satellite Events). CEUR Workshop Proceedings, vol. 2019, pp. 571–575. CEUR-WS.org (2017)

13. Patel, P., Morin, B., Chaudhary, S.: A model-driven development framework for developing sense-compute-control applications. In: Proceedings of the 1st International Workshop on Modern Software Engineering Methods for Industrial Automation, pp. 52–61 (2014)

Meta-Argumentation Frameworks
for Multi-party Dialogues

Gideon Ogunniye[1], Alice Toniolo[2], and Nir Oren[1(✉)]

[1] Department of Computing Science, University of Aberdeen, Scotland, UK
n.oren@abdn.ac.uk
[2] School of Computer Science, University of St Andrews, Scotland, UK

Abstract. The conclusions drawn from a dialogue depend both on the
content of the arguments, and the level of trust placed in the arguments
and the entity advancing them. In this paper, we describe a framework
for dialogue where such trust forms the basis for expressing preferences
between arguments, and in turn, for computing conclusions of the dialogue. Our framework contains object and meta-level arguments, and
uses ASPIC+ to represent arguments, while argument schemes capture
meta-level arguments about trust and preferences.

1 Introduction

In human dialogue, conclusions are drawn not only based on argument interactions, but also by considering the level of trust or confidence placed in the
arguments and those presenting them. Critically, as the dialogue progresses,
additional utterances can cause these levels of trust to change, and capturing
such changes is therefore important.

Since we consider the arguments advanced during the dialogue, as well
as argument about those arguments, our approach builds on Muller's meta-
argumentation system [7]. Here, *object-level* arguments are advanced which deal
with the topic of the dialogue. *Meta-level* arguments then describe arguments
about arguments, including whether an argument attacks another; what counts
as an argument; and whether an argument is preferred over another. Our focus
in this paper involves arguments which relate to trust between arguments, and
we consider several such classes of argument, described through argumentation
schemes. As the dialogue progresses, arguments attacking and supporting these
arguments can be introduced, causing shifts in trust over time, in contrast to
systems such as [2,3,11], where preferences and trust in arguments are fixed.

Our work combines several existing frameworks and techniques, and in the
next section, we provide the background necessary to our approach. In Sect. 3,
we introduce our dialogue model and the argument schemes used within our
meta-argumentation framework. Section 4 discusses an example of our work and
we conclude in Sect. 5.

© Springer Nature Switzerland AG 2018
T. Miller et al. (Eds.): PRIMA 2018, LNAI 11224, pp. 585–593, 2018.
https://doi.org/10.1007/978-3-030-03098-8_45

2   Background

Our work builds on a fragment of ASPIC+ [6], which uses abstract argumentation [4] to identify justified conclusions. We therefore begin by briefly discussing
these.

Definition 1. *An* argument framework *(AF) is a pair* $\langle \mathcal{A}, \mathcal{D} \rangle$ *where* $\mathcal{A}$ *is a set
of arguments and* $\mathcal{D} \subseteq \mathcal{A} \times \mathcal{A}$ *is a binary defeat relation. Given* $AF = \langle \mathcal{A}, \mathcal{D} \rangle$,
and $\mathcal{E} \subseteq \mathcal{A}$,

- $\mathcal{E}$ *is conflict-free iff there are no* $\phi_1, \phi_2 \in \mathcal{E}$ *s.t.* $(\phi_1, \phi_2) \in \mathcal{D}$.
- $\mathcal{E}$ *defends* ϕ_1 *iff for every* $(\phi_2, \phi_1) \in \mathcal{D}$, *there exist a* $\phi_3 \in \mathcal{E}$ *s.t.* $(\phi_3, \phi_2) \in \mathcal{D}$.
- $\mathcal{E}$ *is an admissible set iff* $\mathcal{E}$ *is conflict free and defends all its elements.*
- $\mathcal{E}$ *is a complete extension iff there are no other elements which it defends.*
- $\mathcal{E}$ *is a preferred extension iff it is a maximal complete extension.*

An extension identifies a consistent set of arguments and conclusions. While
many different classes of extensions have been defined, we focus on preferred
extensions here. It should be noted that an AF can have multiple different preferred extensions. An argument present in all extensions is *sceptically* justified;
if it is present in at least one extension, it is *credulously* justified.

AFs as described above are abstract and lack structure. Given a knowledge
base, we must be able to determine which arguments can be constructed, and
for this purpose, we make use of a fragment the popular ASPIC+ framework
[6]. ASPIC+ defines an *argumentation system* built from an (unspecified) logical language $\mathcal{L}$ which is closed under negation ($\neg$). Arguments are then formed
by repeatedly applying strict (elements of R_s) or defeasible (R_d) inference rules
to elements from a knowledge base $\mathcal{K}$. The argumentation system contains a
function $n : R_d \rightarrow \mathcal{K}$, associating defeasible rules with entities in the knowledge base. Arguments in ASPIC+ attack each other when inconsistencies exist
between them. ASPIC+ describes how preferences between arguments can be
obtained from preferences between rules and elements in the knowledge base
determining successful attacks; i.e. defeats. The resultant structure is referred
to as an *argumentation theory*, corresponding to an argumentation framework
as per Definition 1. In our approach, we consider only defeasible rules, no preferences, and assume that all elements in a knowledge base can be attacked.

Definition 2. *(Argument and Attack) [6]. An argument A on the basis of a
knowledge base $\mathcal{K}$ in argumentation system* $(\mathcal{L}, \neg, \mathcal{R}_d, n)$ *is*

1. μ *if* $\mu \in \mathcal{K}$ *with:* $Prem(A) = \{\mu\}$, $Conc(A) = \{\mu\}$, $Sub(A) = \{\mu\}$.
2. $A_1, \ldots, A_n \rightarrow / \Rightarrow \psi$ *if* $A_1, \ldots, A_n$ *are arguments such that there exists
   a defeasible rule* $Conc(A_1), \ldots, Conc(A_n) \Rightarrow \psi$ *in* $\mathcal{R}_d$ *with* $Prem(A) =
   Prem(A_1) \cup \ldots \cup Prem(A_n)$, $Conc(A) = \{\mu\}$, $Sub(A) = Sub(A_1) \cup \ldots \cup
   Sub(A_n) \cup \{A\}$.
3. A *attacks* B *iff* A *undercuts, rebuts or undermines* B, *where* A *undercuts* B
   (on B') *iff* $Conc(A) = \neg n(r)$ *for some* $B' \in Sub(B)$. A *rebuts* B *(on* B')
   iff $Conc(A) = \neg \mu$ *for some* $B' \in Sub(B)$ *of the form* $B_1'', \ldots, B_n'' \Rightarrow \mu$. A
   undermines B *(on* μ) *iff* $Conc(A) = \neg \mu$ *for a premise* μ *of* B *for an ordinary
   premise* μ *of* B.

3   Hierarchical Systems of Arguments and Dialogues

Our approach uses meta-level arguments about trust. These refer to object-level arguments about the original dialogue topic. We build on the ideas of Wooldridge [14], who suggested that arguments and dialogue are inherently meta-logical processes. Thus, arguments advanced in a dialogue are not restricted to asserting the truth or falsity of statements, but include arguments about arguments; taking a hierarchical view, arguments at level n of the hierarchy may refer to the same or lower levels in the hierarchy. In our work, we consider a hierarchy with 3 levels, labelled $l_0, \ldots l_2$. The object level (l_0) contains arguments and attacks related to the domain of discourse. Arguments at level l_1 support arguments at the object level and indirectly attack them by attacking other arguments within l_1. These capture the trust placed in object level arguments and attacks. Similarly, arguments at l_2 attack others in this level, as well as at level l_1, and capture trust in sources of object-level arguments. All of these arguments and the interactions between them are encoded in a *bimodal argument graph*.

3.1   Bimodal Argument Graphs

A bimodal argument graph is a hierarchical structure capturing object and meta-level arguments, and the attacks and supports between them.

Definition 3. *A* Bimodal Argument Graph *for a reasoner* Ag_I *is a tuple* $BAG_I = \langle \mathcal{A}_O, \mathcal{A}_{M_I}, \mathcal{D}_O, \mathcal{D}_{M_I}, \mathcal{S}_{MO_I}, \mathcal{S}_{MA_I} \rangle$ *where*

- $\mathcal{A}_O$ *and* $\mathcal{A}_{M_I}$ *are object-level and meta-level arguments respectively such that* $\mathcal{A}_O \cap \mathcal{A}_{M_I} = \emptyset$.
- $\mathcal{D}_O \subseteq \mathcal{A}_O \times \mathcal{A}_O$ *and* $\mathcal{D}_{M_I} \subseteq \mathcal{A}_{M_I} \times \mathcal{A}_{M_I}$ *are defeat relations for the object and meta-levels respectively.*
- $\mathcal{S}_{MO_I} \subseteq \mathcal{A}_{M_I} \times \mathcal{A}_O$, *is a support relation from meta-level to object-level arguments.*
- $\mathcal{S}_{MA_I} \subseteq \mathcal{A}_{M_I} \times \mathcal{R}_O$, *is a support relation from meta-level to object-level attacks.*

Bimodal argument graphs constrain arguments, requiring that for all $\phi \in \mathcal{A}_O$ *and* $(a, b) \in \mathcal{R}_O$ *there exists a* $\beta, \gamma \in \mathcal{A}_{M_I}$ *such that* $(\beta, \phi) \in \mathcal{S}_{MO_I}$ *and* $(\gamma, (a, b)) \in \mathcal{S}_{MA_I}$. *If* $(\beta, \phi) \in \mathcal{S}_{MO_I}$, *then* β *is said to support* ϕ.

Extensions within a bimodal argument graph (according to some semantics) are computed from the highest meta-level down to the object level. More specifically, the extension of the highest level is computed, and the subset of arguments at the next level down supported by arguments within the extension are used to form a sub-framework over which extensions are again computed. This process repeats itself until an extension at the object level can be computed.

3.2   The Object Level (l_0)

Our focus revolves around arguments obtained from a dialogue—a sequence of moves $D = [M_1, \ldots, M_x]$. We do not specify the protocol used to create this dialogue, but assume that each participant has a *commitment store* representing those arguments they are publicly committed to. Arguments can be *added* or *retracted* from each participant's commitment store. Furthermore, we assume that a participant is only committed to arguments that they have introduced. We denote the commitment store of participant Ag_i as CS_{Ag_i}, and call $\cup_{Ag_i} CS_{Ag_i}$ the *universal commitment store*, $\mathcal{UCS}$. The $\mathcal{UCS}$ corresponds to the set of arguments at the object level $\mathcal{A}_O$ in Definition 3. Both the individual and universal commitment stores are updated at each move of the dialogue.

After introducing an argument at the object level, additional arguments are added to the meta-levels monotonically. Let $\varphi(\cdot)$ indicate that an element should be trusted. At the meta-levels, every argument $a \in \mathcal{A}_O$ is supported by an argument α asserting that a should be trusted ($\varphi(a)$), every defeat $(a, b) \in \mathcal{D}_O$ should also be trusted ($\varphi(a, b)$), and that utterances by an agent Ag_i should be trusted ($\varphi(Ag_i)$). Additional arguments are instantiated via trust-related argument schemes.

We map arguments and attacks in our hierarchical system to arguments and defeats in a bimodal argument graph [7] by stating that argument a defeats argument b iff a attacks b and there are some meta-arguments α, β such that α supports a and β supports b and α attacks β. Properties of the argument framework at the object level is encoded using a fragment of ASPIC+. We assume that $\mathcal{L}$ is a predicate-based language with a finite number of constant symbols, and which can therefore (formally) be mapped to a propositional language.

Agents build meta-arguments about object-level arguments, attacks, and sources of argument by applying a set of defeasible rules which we define as argument schemes (and critical questions). At the meta-level, we do not consider preferences between arguments, meaning that attacks and defeats are equivalent here.

3.3   The First Meta-level (l_1)

The first meta-level contains facts and associated rules from which arguments can be formed regarding the object level arguments. Table 1 summarises the predicates which can appear at the meta-level, and describes the condition under which these are added. As individual utterances are made within the dialogue, additional predicates and arguments are monotonically added to the meta-level. The arguments are obtained from a set of trust specific argument schemes. These schemes describe inference rules from which arguments can be created, as well as critical questions which allow attacks against the arguments to occur. We detail these schemes in the remainder of this section[1].

---

[1] Due to lack of space, we formalise only some of the schemes and critical questions.

Table 1. Predicates for Trust Properties

Property	Definition
$defeats(a, b)$	argument a defeats argument b (i.e., $a, b \in \mathcal{A}$ and $(a, b) \in \mathcal{D}$)
$unattacked(a)$	argument a is unattacked (i.e., $a \in \mathcal{A}$ and $(b, a) \notin \mathcal{D}$)
$preferred(a, b)$	argument a is preferred to argument b (i.e., $a, b \in \mathcal{A}$, $(a, b) \lor (b, a) \in \mathcal{D}$ and a defeats b via meta-level arguments
$unattacked(a, b)$	$defeat(a, b)$ is unattacked (i.e., $a, b \in \mathcal{A}$, $(a, b) \in \mathcal{D}$ and $(c, a) \notin \mathcal{D}$)
$defended(a, b)$	$defeat(a, b)$ is defended (i.e., $a, b, c, d \in \mathcal{A}$, $(a, b) \in \mathcal{D}$, $(c, a) \in \mathcal{D}$ and there is $(d, c) \in \mathcal{D}$)
$conflict\_free(CS_{Ag_i})$	the commitment store CS_{Ag_i} is conflict-free (i.e., there exist no $\phi_1, \phi_2 \in CS_{Ag_i}$ such that $(\phi_1, \phi_2) \in \mathcal{D}$)
$retracted(a, CS_{Ag_i})$	argument a is retracted from CS_{Ag_i} (i.e., $CS_{Ag_i} = CS_{Ag_i} \cup b$ and $(b, a) \in \mathcal{D}$)

Argument from Lack of Justification (Arg_{LJ}). If a dialogue participant cannot justify their arguments, then these arguments should not be trusted. More formally, if a is in Ag_i's commitment store, and b (in the universal commitment store) defeats a, then a is not (skeptically) justified. In turn, this means that the argument and dialogue participant should not be trusted. Formally, we have the following defeasible inferences.

$$r_{SLJ} : a \in CS_{Ag_i}, b \in UCS, defeats(b, a) \Rightarrow \neg\varphi(a)/\neg\varphi Ag_i$$

A defeater to b serves as a critical question to prevent the application of the scheme.

$$r_{CQLJ} : \exists c \in UCS, defeats(c, b) \Rightarrow \varphi(a)/\varphi(Ag_i)$$

Argument from Void Precedence (Arg_{VP}). This scheme is adapted from the void precedence property of ranking based semantics [1], and states that a non-attacked argument is accepted, and should therefore be considered trusted. We omit its formalisation due triviality and lack of space.

Argument from Defence Precedence (Arg_{DP}). This scheme is also adapted from ranking based semantics [1], and states that an argument defended against its attackers by more preferred argument(s) should be trusted.

$$r_{SDP} : a, b, c \in UCS, defeats(b, a), defeats(c, b) \Rightarrow \varphi(a)$$

At the same time, d defeating c would undercut this scheme, and serves as a critical question (not formalised due to space constraints).

Argument from Preference Precedence (Arg_{PP}). This scheme specifies how attacks between conflicting object-level arguments are resolved with preferences. In effect, an (otherwise defeated) argument which is preferred remains trusted as long as it is justified. Again, another defeater of the argument would render this scheme invalid.

$$r_{SPP} : a, b \in UCS, defeats(a, b), preferred(b, a) \Rightarrow \varphi(b)$$

Trust can be placed not only in arguments and speakers, but also in defeats. If we have $\{(a, b), (c, a)\} \subseteq \mathcal{D}$, then (c, a) attacks (a, b). An argument (d, c) would defend (a, b) in this case. A defeat is then trusted if it is unattacked, defended, or originates from a justified argument, and is untrusted otherwise. This intuition is also captured in extended argument frameworks with second (or higher) order attacks [5]. It should be noted that a defeat may be trusted when both arguments it refers to are untrusted. Argument schemes for reasoning about trust in defeats are defined as follows.

Argument from Justified Defeat (Arg_{JD}). A defeat is trusted if it originates from a justified argument.

$$r_{SJD} = a, b \in UCS, defeats(a, b) \Rightarrow \varphi(a, b)$$

As elsewhere, the presence of a defeater of a serves to undercut this scheme.

$$r_{CQJD} : c \in UCS, defeats(c, a) \Rightarrow \neg\varphi(a, b)$$

Argument from Unattacked Defeat (Arg_{UD}) A defeat is trusted if it is unattacked.

Argument from Defended Defeat (Arg_{DD}). A defeat is trusted if it is defended. This scheme is undercut if the defeat that the defender attacks is preferred to the defender.

3.4   The Second Meta-level (l_2)

In this level we consider properties that can be inferred to establish meta-arguments about trust in the sources of arguments at l_0. These meta-arguments indirectly attack or support arguments at level l_0 by attacking or supporting arguments at level l_1. For example, the assertion $\neg\varphi(Ag_i)$ (i.e., the source Ag_i of an argument a should not be trusted), attacks all meta-arguments at level l_1 which support arguments advanced by Ag_i at level l_0. Argument schemes here include the following.

Argument from Self Contradiction (Arg_{SC}). This scheme is adapted from Walton's argument from inconsistent commitment [12], and states that an agent committed to two arguments which attack each other should not be trusted.

$$r_{SSC} : a, b \in CS_{Ag_i}, defeats(a, b) \vee defeats(b, a) \Rightarrow \neg\varphi(Ag_i)$$

A closely related argument scheme is *Argument from Consistency* (Arg_{CN}) stating that if all an agent's commitments are conflict free, then the agent should be trusted.

Argument from Retraction (Arg_{RN}). Retracting a commitment results in a loss of trust. When performing such a retraction, some premises or warrants are also typically retracted [13]. This means that a retraction should cause trust to be lost not only for the retraction itself, but also for other arguments which are defended by the retracted argument (unless these latter arguments are defended by other unretracted arguments). This leads to the following scheme.

$$r_{SRN} : a, b \in CS_{Ag_i}, c \in UCS, defeats(c, a), defeats(b, c), retracted(b) \Rightarrow \neg\varphi(Ag_i)$$

We have described how meta-arguments about trust at different levels can attack each other and support lower level arguments. In our approach, each dialogue participant Ag_I has an associated BAG_I, whose object level is built from the dialogue and their commitment stores. Meta-levels components are constructed subjectively from a private knowledge base of preferences and properties observed at the object level. The maximal set of arguments appearing in the extensions of all participant's BAGs is the set of trusted arguments within the dialogue.

4   Example

Consider a long running dialogue between three agents (Ag_1, Ag_3, Ag_3) about the death penalty. At the object level, the following arguments are advanced.

- Ag_1: The death penalty is a legitimate form of punishment. (a)
- Ag_2: God does not want us to kill. (b)
- Ag_3: God does not exist. (c)
- Ag_1: Some people believe in God. (d)
- Ag_2: The state has no right to put its subjects to death. (e)
- Ag_3: The legal status of the death penalty should not depend on beliefs. (f)
- Ag_1: All religions should have a say over public law. (g)
- Ag_2: Majorities in some democratic countries favour death penalty. (h).
- Ag_3: Even if God exists, religion should stop at the door of the temple. (i)

Note that Ag_2 has potentially contradicted themselves in arguments e and h. Instantiating Arg_{SC}, we have an argument at the second meta-level for $\neg\varphi(Ag_2)$, which attacks $\varphi(e)$, $\varphi(h)$ and any other arguments advanced by Ag_2 in the dialogue. While argument h is undefeated, and supports argument a, yielding $\varphi(a)$ using Arg_{DP}, the fact that we had obtained $\neg\varphi(Ag_2)$ means that this support is attacked. Figure 1 provides the full bimodal argument graph obtained from this dialogue, where meta-arguments are represented by their conclusions.

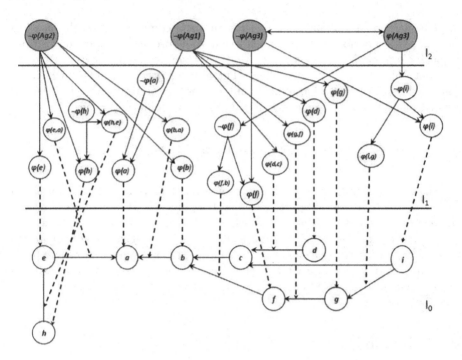

Fig. 1. Bimodal Graph for object and meta-level argumentation

5   Discussion and Conclusions

This paper presents an approach for reasoning about trust in dialogues that combines three of the most popular mechanisms used within computational modelling of argumentation: ASPIC+ [10], argument schemes [12] and meta-argumentation [7,11].

Unlike the systems described in [2,3] where preferences are given and fixed, our argument scheme based approach models how trust can be used as a rational basis for expressing preferences between arguments, determining successive attacks and for computing extensions. The systems in [8,11] compute argument acceptability on the basis of the trustworthiness of their sources and the feedback that the final quality of arguments provide on the source evaluation. Unlike our approach, these approaches do not consider how trust in arguments and their sources change dynamically within a dialogue. Also the work presented in [9] has considered different argument schemes for reasoning about trust in an individual. However, these rely on extra-dialogical properties, while our focus is on how utterances affect trust during a dialogue.

We are pursuing several avenues of future work. First, we seek to link our system with graded and numerical semantics. Second, we recognise that the argument schemes we describe are not exhaustive, and believe that additional argument schemes for trust can be identified. Finally, we must demonstrate that the manner in which our system computes trust is consistent with human intuitions, and that it satisfies certain desirable properties. If divergences between these exists, then the framework could serve as a useful foundation for describing and studying paradoxes in human-based trust.

References

1. Amgoud, L., Ben-Naim, J.: Ranking-based semantics for argumentation frameworks. In: Liu, W., Subrahmanian, V.S., Wijsen, J. (eds.) SUM 2013. LNCS (LNAI), vol. 8078, pp. 134–147. Springer, Heidelberg (2013). https://doi.org/10.1007/978-3-642-40381-1_11
2. Amgoud, L., Vesic, S.: Rich preference-based argumentation frameworks. Int. J. Approx. Reason. **55**(2), 585–606 (2014)
3. Bench-Capon, T.J.: Persuasion in practical argument using value-based argumentation frameworks. J. Logic Comput. **13**(3), 429–448 (2003)
4. Dung, P.M.: On the acceptability of arguments and its fundamental role in nonmonotonic reasoning, logic programming and n-person games. Artif. Intell. **77**(2), 321–357 (1995)
5. Modgil, S., Bench-Capon, T.: Integrating object and meta-level value based argumentation. Comput. Models Argument **172**, 240–251 (2008)
6. Modgil, S., Prakken, H.: The ASPIC+ framework for structured argumentation: a tutorial. Argument Comput. **5**(1), 31–62 (2014)
7. Müller, J., Hunter, A., Taylor, P.: Meta-level argumentation with argument schemes. In: Liu, W., Subrahmanian, V.S., Wijsen, J. (eds.) SUM 2013. LNCS (LNAI), vol. 8078, pp. 92–105. Springer, Heidelberg (2013). https://doi.org/10.1007/978-3-642-40381-1_8
8. Paglieri, F.: Trusting the messenger because of the message. Comput. Math. Organ. Theory **20**(2), 176–194 (2014)
9. Parsons, S.: Argument schemes for reasoning about trust. Argument Comput. **5**(2–3), 160–190 (2014)
10. Prakken, H.: An abstract framework for argumentation with structured arguments. Argument Comput. **1**(2), 93–124 (2010)
11. Villata, S., Boella, G., Gabbay, D.M., Van Der Torre, L.: A socio-cognitive model of trust using argumentation theory. Int. J. Approx. Reason. **54**(4), 541–559 (2013)
12. Walton, D., Reed, C., Macagno, F.: Argumentation Schemes. Cambridge University Press, Cambridge (2008)
13. Walton, D., Krabbe, E.C.: Commitment in dialogue: basic concepts of interpersonal reasoning. SUNY press, Albany (1995)
14. Wooldridge, M., McBurney, P., Parsons, S.: On the meta-logic of arguments. In: Proceedings of the 4th International Conference on Autonomous Agents and Multiagent Systems, pp. 560–567 (2005)

Resource-Driven Substructural Defeasible Logic

Francesco Olivieri[1]([✉]), Guido Governatori[1], Matteo Cristani[2], Nick van Beest[1], and Silvano Colombo-Tosatto[1]

[1] Data61, CSIRO, Dutton Park, Australia
francesco.olivieri@data61.csiro.au
[2] University of Verona, Verona, Italy

Abstract. Linear Logic and Defeasible Logic have been adopted to formalise different features relevant to agents: consumption of resources, and reasoning with exceptions. We propose a framework to combine substructural features, corresponding to the consumption of resources, with defeasibility aspects, and we discuss the design choices for the framework.

1 Introduction

Many logic-based approaches have been proposed to account for the rational behaviour of an agent. For example, in the well known BDI architecture (and architectures inspired by it), agents first deliberate about the goals to achieve and, based on such goals, they select the plans to implement from their plan libraries. Finally, during or after the execution of the plans, the agents receive feedback from the environment, which can trigger the so-called *reconsideration*: the activity to determine whether the intended goals are still achievable with the selected plan and the current state of execution.

Most of the logic-based approaches take an idealised representation: the agents have unlimited reasoning power, complete knowledge of the environment and their capabilities, and unlimited resources. Over the years, a few approaches (using different logics) have been advanced to overcome some of these ideal (unrealistic) assumptions.

In [8,13,14], the authors propose the use of Linear Logic to model the notion of resource utilisation, and to generate which plans the agent adopts to achieve its goals. In the same spirit, the authors of [5,6] address the problem of agents being able to take decisions from partial, incomplete, and possibly inconsistent knowledge bases, using (extensions of) Defeasible Logic (a computational and proof theoretic approach) to non-monotonic reasoning and reasoning with exceptions. While these last two approaches seem very far apart, they are both based on proof theory (where the key notion is on the idea of (logical) derivation), and both logics (for different reasons and different techniques) have been used for modelling business processes [1,3,7,10,12,15,16].

Formally, a business process can be understood as a compact representation of a set of traces, where a trace is a sequence of tasks. A business process is

© Springer Nature Switzerland AG 2018
T. Miller et al. (Eds.): PRIMA 2018, LNAI 11224, pp. 594–602, 2018.
https://doi.org/10.1007/978-3-030-03098-8_46

hence equivalent to a set of plans with possible choices. The idea behind the work mentioned above is to allow agents to use their deliberation phase to determine the business processes (instead of the plans) to execute.

This paper discusses the motivational ideas of a much deeper investigation, which will lead to the full formalisation of a foundational framework to model agents that create their plans during the deliberation phase, taking into account the utilisation of resources and possible exceptions. We highlight some design choices about the combination of linear logic (or more in general, *substructural logic*) and a computationally oriented non-monotonic formalism, but, due to the strict space limitations, we leave the technical implementation details for future works. The interested reader is referred to [11] for an up to date version of our work.

Logic is often described as the "art" of reasoning: a deductive system allows users to derive conclusions from given premises via the usage of (inference) rules. Under this prospective we can distinguish rules (or sequents, or instances of a consequence relation) and inference (or derivation) rules. A rule specifies that some consequences follow from some premises, while a derivation rule provides a recipe to determine the valid steps in a proof or derivation. A classical example of a derivation rule is Modus Ponens (i.e., from '$\Gamma \rightarrow \Theta$' and Γ to derive Θ, where Γ and Θ are sets of formulas).

If the formulas denote activities (or tasks) and resources, then the consequent is a sequence of tasks describing the activities to be done (and the order in which they have to be executed) to produce an outcome (and also, what resources are needed). Thus, we can use the rules to model transformation in a business process, and derivations as the traces of the process (or the ways in which the process can be executed or the runs of system).

A formalism that properly models processes should feature some key characteristics, and one of the most important ones is to identify which resources are *consumed* after a task has finished its execution. Consider the notorious vending machine scenario, where the dollar resource is spent to *produce* the can of cola. Trivially, once we get the cola, the dollar resource is no longer spendable (unless it can be, somehow, *replenished*).

(Standard) Defeasible Logic (SDL) [9] is a non-monotonic rule based formalism, that has been used to model exceptions and processes. The starting point being that, while rules define a relation between premises and conclusion, DL takes the stance that multiple relations are possible, and it focuses on the "strength" of the relationships. Three relationships, and a relation called *superiority* or *preference*, are identified: *strict rules* specifying that every time the antecedent holds so does the consequent; *defeasible rules* represent the non-monotonic part of the logic, when the antecedent holds then we can typically deduce the consequent as well, unless there is evidence supporting the contrary; and *defeaters*, when the antecedent holds the opposite of the consequent might not hold (defeaters are special rules whose only purpose is to prevent to draw opposite conclusions); finally, the superiority relation is the mechanism to solve conflicts, and allows us to derive conclusions when there are rules for conflicting conclusions. An example of rules with a baseline condition and exception is the scenario of inserting a dollar coin in a vending machine, and the outcome is that we get a cola unless the machine is out of order, or the machine is switched off. We can thus represent this scenario with the rules[1]:

$$r_1 : 1\$ \Rightarrow cola \quad r_2 : OutOfOrder \rightsquigarrow \neg cola \quad r_3 : Off \rightsquigarrow \neg cola.$$

Note that both r_2 and r_3 use defeaters instead of defeasible rules. This is because we do not want to obtain the resource *"notCola"* (of dubious meaning), but only to prevent to obtain the resource *cola* in case the machine is out of order or switched off.

Based on the discussion so far, the motivation of our research is that we want to combine, from a logic perspective, the mechanisms of defeasibility with mechanisms from substructural logic (to capture the order of resources, and the consumption of resources). It is clear that the resulting combination of logical machinery could provide a much better formalism for the representation of processes.

The remainder of this paper is structured as follows. Section 2 describes the features we want our logics to be equipped with. Section 3 concludes our work by presenting some related literature, and outlining current, and future, research.

2   Desired Properties

We dedicate this section to detailing which new features our logic needs to implement and, for each of them, to justify their importance with respect to real life problems.

Ordered List of Antecedents
Given the rule '$r : A, B \Rightarrow C$', the order in which we derive A and B is typically irrelevant for the derivation of C. As such, r may indistinctively assume the form '$B, A \Rightarrow C$'. Consider a login procedure which requires a username and password. Whether we insert one credential before the other does not affect a successful login.

Nonetheless, sometimes it is meaningful to consider an *ordered* sequence of atoms in the head of a rule, instead of an *unordered* set of antecedents. Suppose we have the two activities '*Check Creditworthiness*' and '*Approve Loan*'. Neither of them depends on the other. However, performing one activity before the other may affect the final result: if we approve the loan before creditworthiness has been checked and approved, then a loan may potentially be provided to someone who is not able to repay.

This allows us to capture the fact that some resources may be *independent* of each other from the derivational viewpoint (one does not *derive* the other), but are *dependent* from a temporal perspective (one must be *obtained* before the

---

[1] r_i is the name of rule i, symbol $\Rightarrow$ (resp. $\rightsquigarrow$) denotes defeasible rules (resp. defeaters).

other). Naturally, in the same set/list of antecedents, combinations of unordered and ordered sequences of literals is possible. For instance,

$$r : A; B; (C, D); E \Rightarrow F$$

represents a situation where, in order to obtain F, we need to first obtain A, then B, then either C or D in any order, and lastly, only after both C and D are obtained, we need to obtain E. The notation ';' is used as a separator between elements in an ordered sequence, while ',' separates unordered sets. In the rest of the paper, unless otherwise specified, every time we use the word "sequence", we intend that the literals are *ordered*; symmetrically, with the word "set", we intend that there is no order among the literals.

Multi-occurrence/Repetitions of Literals
From these ideas, it follows that some literals may appear in multiple instances, and that two rules such as

$$r : A; A; B \Rightarrow C \qquad \text{and} \qquad s : A; B; A \Rightarrow C$$

are semantically different. For instance, rule r may describe a scenario where the order of a product may require two deposit payments followed by a full payment prior to delivery. Regarding s, consider that A is now 'Add a tablespoon of ice sugar' and B is 'Stir for 1 min'. A perfect frosting requires many repetitions of A after B after A, for a specific number of repetitions.

Resources Consumption
Assume we have two rules,

$$r : A, B \Rightarrow D \qquad \text{and} \qquad s : A, C \Rightarrow E.$$

If we are able to derive A, B and C, then D and E are subsequently obtained. Deducing both D and E is a typical problem of *resource consumption*.

Given the financial state of a customer (i.e., their pay cheque and their monthly spending), a finance approval is sent to the customer for the requested loan. However, that finance approval can only be used once, given the financial situation of that customer. That is, they cannot obtain another loan with the same finance approval. If the customer wants to apply for another loan, they are required to obtain a new finance approval first.

This example indicates that some literals represent resources that are *consumed* during the derivation process: if they appear in the antecedent of a rule, and such a rule produces its conclusion, then the other rules with the same literals in their antecedent can no longer fire (unless there are multiple occurrences).

Conversely, some resources are *not* consumed once used. For instance, a policy at a bank may dictate that a customer has to be below 65 years old to be eligible for a mortgage. A similar requirement may hold for a car loan. However, a customer may apply for both a mortgage and a car loan, as neither of these applications invalidate the fact that the customer is younger than 65 years old. That is, the information regarding the customers' age is not consumed when used.

The discussion of when a resource has to be considered consumable/non-consumable is outside the scope of this paper. It is a duty of the knowledge engineer to decide whether to tag a resource as consumable, or non-consumable. For the remainder of this paper, we assume all literals to be consumable. The treatment/derivation of non-consumable literals is the same as in SDL, and thus something well known in the literature of SDL.

Concurrent Production
Symmetrically, we consider two distinct rules having the same conclusion:

$$r : A \Rightarrow C \qquad \text{and} \qquad s : B \Rightarrow C.$$

It now seems reasonable that, if both A and B are derived, then we conclude two instances of C (whereas in classical logics we only know that C holds true). For example, consider a family where it is tradition to have pizza on Friday evening. Last Friday, the parents were unable to communicate with each other during the day, and one baked the pizza while the other bought take-away on the way home.

However, there exists consistent cases where multiple rules for the same literal produce only *one* instance of the literal (even if they all fire). For example, both a digital or handwritten signature would provide permission to proceed with a request. The same request does not require permission twice: either it is permitted, or it is not.

Resource Consumption: A Team Defeater Perspective
Sceptical logics provide means to decide which conclusion to draw in case of contradicting information. Typically, a superiority relation is given among rules for contrary conclusions: it is possible to derive a conclusion only if there exists a *single* rule stronger than *all* the rules for the opposite literal.

Defeasible Logic handles conflicts differently, and the idea here is that of *team defeater*. We do not look at whether there is a single rule prevailing over all the other rules, but rather whether there exists a *team* of rules which can jointly defeat the rules for the contrary conclusion. That is, suppose rules r', r'' and r''' all conclude P, whilst s' and s'' are for $\neg P$. If $r' > s'$ and $r'' > s''$, then the team defeater made of $\{r', r''\}$ is sufficient to prove P.

The focus remains on resource consumption and production. As such, the questions we need to answer are, again, which resources are consumed, and how many instances of the conclusion are derived. We start by distinguishing the two scenarios where: (a) neither of the teams prevail, (b) one team wins. Consider

$$r' : A \Rightarrow P, \quad r'' : B \Rightarrow P, \quad r''' : C \Rightarrow P, \quad s' : D \Rightarrow \neg P, \quad s'' : E \Rightarrow \neg P.$$

In case (a), e.g., when no superiority is given, we cannot conclude for either conclusion. Hence, the question is "Will any of the resources be consumed?". In case (b), we assume $r' > s'$ and $r'' > s''$, and we conclude that P. How many instances of P are produced? One solution is to produce three instances of P and, accordingly, A, B and C are all consumed. We can instead consistently assume that we produce P twice, through the two winning rules r'' and r''' only, but not via r'; we thus consume B and C, but *not* A.

Lastly, on the perspective of the *defeated* rules another relevant question is: Are D and E ever consumed? As clear, there is no unique answer. There are consistent scenarios where the literals in the *defeated* rules are consumed, and other cases where they are not.

Consider the process of writing a scientific publication for a conference. If the paper is accepted, the *manuscript* resource is consumed, since it cannot be submitted again. On the contrary, if the paper is rejected, the *manuscript* resource is *not* consumed since it can be submitted again to other venues.

Multiple Conclusions and Resource Preservation

Consider internet shopping. As soon as we pay for our online order, the bank account balance decreases, the seller's account increases. Both the seller and the web site have the shipping address and, possibly, the credit card number.

The conclusion of a rule is usually a single literal. The above example suggests that a single rule may produce more than one conclusion, which cannot be represented by multiple rules with the same set of antecedents. For example, consider the rules

$$r : A, B \Rightarrow C \qquad \text{and} \qquad s : A, B \Rightarrow D.$$

In a propositional calculus, once the system derives A and B, by Modus Ponens, we obtain both C and D. However, when we consider resource consumption, then it is clear that only one rule can produce its conclusion, whilst the other cannot. We tackle this problem by allowing rules to have multiple conclusions. Thus, r and s can be merged into the single rule

$$r' : A, B \Rightarrow C, D.$$

Similar to our discussion on the ordering of antecedents, we may have any combination of ordered/unordered literals in the conclusion. In the previous example, only after we have provided the credit card credentials, our bank account decreases, whilst we can provide the shipping address before the credit card credentials, or the other way around.

The notion of multiple conclusions, along with the discussion on team defeaters, leads to another problem. Consider the two rules

$$r : A \Rightarrow B; C; D \qquad \text{and} \qquad s : E \Rightarrow \neg C,$$

where no superiority is given. Do we conclude that B or D? Moreover, what happens if now we have '$r : A \Rightarrow B, C, D$' and we establish that s is stronger then r? Do we conclude that B and D (meaning that only the derivation of C has been blocked by s), or will the production of B and D be affected also?

Loops

The importance of being able to properly handle loops is evident: loops play a fundamental role in many real life applications, from business processes to manufacturing. Back to the login procedure, if one of the credentials is wrong, the process loops back to a previous state, for instance, by asking the user to re-enter both credentials.

Naturally, a system is able to properly handle loops when it can handle/recognise the so-called *exit conditions*, to prevent infinite repetition of the same set of events. For example, after three wrong login attempts, the login procedure may prevent the user from further attempts and require them to undergo a *retrieve credential* procedure.

3   Conclusions, Related and Further Work

This work presented our recents investigations in combining sub-structural and non-monotonic features within the same logical framework; such a logical apparatus will be able to model agent planning while taking into account features such as resource consumption, order in which resources are taken into account, loops, *etc.* This is a complete novelty in the community of computational logic and knowledge representation.

Variants of SDL have been investigated so far as a means for devising business process traces [3,10,12]. While the idea is closely related to outline in the *Introduction* that a derivation corresponds to a trace in a process, the approach based on variants of SDL are not able to handle loops and, in general, repetitions of tasks. These aspects are elegantly captured by the sub-structural aspects presented in the paper.

Studies on light linear logic versions, with specific aspects of linearity related to resource consumption have been devised such as *light* and *soft linear logic* [2,4].

Applications of linear logic to problems indirectly related to business processes such as Petri Nets can be found in [7] and in [1,16]. However, such approaches are not able to handle in a natural fashion the aspect of exceptions. The representation of exception would require complex rules and encyclopaedic knowledge of the scenarios described by the processes encoded by rules/sequents.

The framework we have developed so far is already rather rich [11]. We are able to represent the following cases: 1. ordered sequences of literals in the antecedent with a single conclusion, 2.-(3.) ordered sequences (and unordered sets) of literals in the antecedent with multiple ordered conclusions, 4.-(5.) ordered sequences (and unordered sets) of literals in the antecedent with multiple unordered conclusions.

As discussed in *Resource Consumption* and *Multiple Conclusions and Resource Preservation*, things get even more complicated when we want to represent various nuances of resource consumption and dealing with team defeaters at the same time. So far we have developed proof conditions to describe two specific scenarios: (i) all, and only, the rules in the winning team defeater consume the resources[2] and we derive as many instances of the conclusion(s) as the

---

[2] Meaning that the rules in the losing team defeater *do not* consume any resource.

number of active rules in the winning team defeater, (ii) only some of the rules in the winning team defeater consume resources and, consequently, conclude their conclusion. We also formalised few different cases of when to stop the derivation in case of conflicting rules and multiple conclusions.

We are aware that combinations of the previous cases are of interest, and that other new cases are as well. This is part of our current research. The other part is, naturally, in proving the formal properties of our framework. We are proving that RSDL is semi-decidable, and even decidable when the theory is acyclic. We think that the problem of computing the extension of a theory[3] is likely to be decidable for larger classes that pure acyclic theories.

More research is required to determine the correct boundary between decidable and undecidable problems for these types of hybrid combinations and to provide a full map of the computational complexity analysis of the various options. However, the outline we discussed in this section seems to indicate that this is not a straightforward task. In this paper, we did not address the issue of how to model the motivational attitudes of the agents, we left the investigation of how to extend the framework to integrate with the framework of [5,6]. Related to this, we shall look at the problem of Business Process Compliance, in order to determine how to employ RSDL for marking up traces of processes corresponding to the execution of the a theory.

References

1. Engberg, U., Winskel, G.: Completeness results for linear logic on Petri nets. Ann. Pure Appl. Log. **86**(2), 101–135 (1997)
2. Gaboardi, M., Marion, J.Y., Della Rocca, S.R.: Soft linear logic and polynomial complexity classes. Electron. Not. Theoret. Comput. Sci. **205**(C), 67–87 (2008)
3. Ghooshchi, N.G., van Beest, N., Governatori, G., Olivieri, F., Sattar, A.: Visualisation of compliant declarative business processes. In: EDOC 2017, pp. 89–94. IEEE Computer Society (2017)
4. Girard, J.Y.: Light linear logic. Inf. Comput. **143**(2), 175–204 (1998)
5. Governatori, G., Olivieri, F., Scannapieco, S., Rotolo, A., Cristani, M.: The rational behind the concept of goal. Theory Pract. Log. Program. **16**(3), 296–324 (2016)
6. Governatori, G., Rotolo, A.: BIO logical agents: norms, beliefs, intentions in defeasible logic. J. Auton. Agents Multi Agent Syst. **17**(1), 36–69 (2008)
7. Kanovich, M., Ito, T.: Temporal linear logic specifications for concurrent processes. In: LICS 1997, pp. 48–57. IEEE Computer Society (1997)
8. Küngas, P., Matskin, M.: Linear logic, partial deduction and cooperative problem solving. In: Leite, J., Omicini, A., Sterling, L., Torroni, P. (eds.) DALT 2003. LNCS, vol. 2990, pp. 263–279. Springer, Heidelberg (2004). https://doi.org/10.1007/978-3-540-25932-9_14

---

[3] The extension of a defeasible theory is what we can prove (such literals belongs to the *positive extension*) and reject (such literals belongs to the *negative extension*). Roughly, given a defeasible theory D and a literal p, if $D \vdash +\Delta(\partial)p$ then p belongs to the positive extension of D; symmetrically, if $D \vdash -\Delta(\partial)p$ then p belongs to the negative extension.

9. Nute, D.: Defeasible logic. In: Handbook of Logic in Artificial Intelligence and Logic Programming, vol. 3. Oxford University Press (1987)

10. Olivieri, F., Cristani, M., Governatori, G.: Compliant business processes with exclusive choices from agent specification. In: Chen, Q., Torroni, P., Villata, S., Hsu, J., Omicini, A. (eds.) PRIMA 2015. LNCS, vol. 9387, pp. 603–612. Springer, Cham (2015). https://doi.org/10.1007/978-3-319-25524-8_43

11. Olivieri, F., Governatori, G., Cristani, M., van Beest, N., Colombo-Tosatto, S.: Resource-driven substructural defeasible logic. CoRR abs/1809.03656 (2018). https://arxiv.org/abs/1809.03656

12. Olivieri, F., Governatori, G., Scannapieco, S., Cristani, M.: Compliant business process design by declarative specifications. In: Boella, G., Elkind, E., Savarimuthu, B.T.R., Dignum, F., Purvis, M.K. (eds.) PRIMA 2013. LNCS, vol. 8291, pp. 213–228. Springer, Heidelberg (2013). https://doi.org/10.1007/978-3-642-44927-7_15

13. Pham, D.Q., Harland, J.: Temporal linear logic as a basis for flexible agent interactions. In: AAMAS 2007, pp. 28:1–28:8. ACM (2007)

14. Pham, D.Q., Harland, J., Winikoff, M.: Modeling agents' choices in temporal linear logic. In: Baldoni, M., Son, T.C., van Riemsdijk, M.B., Winikoff, M. (eds.) DALT 2007. LNCS, vol. 4897, pp. 140–157. Springer, Heidelberg (2008). https://doi.org/10.1007/978-3-540-77564-5_9

15. Rao, J., Küngas, P., Matskin, M.: Composition of semantic web services using linear logic theorem proving. Inf. Syst. **31**(4–5), 340–360 (2006)

16. Tanabe, M.: Timed Petri nets and temporal linear logic. In: Azéma, P., Balbo, G. (eds.) ICATPN 1997. LNCS, vol. 1248, pp. 156–174. Springer, Heidelberg (1997). https://doi.org/10.1007/3-540-63139-9_35

Decentralized Multi-agent Patrolling Strategies Using Global Idleness Estimation

Mehdi Othmani-Guibourg[1,2]($\boxtimes$), Amal El Fallah-Seghrouchni[2], and Jean-Loup Farges[1]

[1] ONERA, Toulouse, France
{mehdi.othmani-guibourg,jean-loup.farges}@onera.fr
[2] Sorbonne Université - Faculté des Sciences, CNRS, UMR 7606, LIP6, 75005 Paris, France
{mehdi.othmani,amal.elfallah}@lip6.fr

Abstract. This paper presents preliminary results in the challenge of developing decentralised strategies approaching the performances of centralised ones. Indeed, the latter is better than the former due to centralisation of information. The approach studied here involves the estimation of real node idlenesses (as known by the coordinator) from the individual ones retained by each agent. This relation between real and individual idlenesses is learnt using traces of execution of a centralised strategy by optimising an error criterion. The strategy thereupon, uses online the learnt relation and is assessed according to certain evaluation criteria. The results indicate that such a relation between perceived and real idlenesses is not a function, leading to large values of the fitting criterion. Finally, the assessment of the strategy shows that performances are good in terms of mean interval but unsatisfactory in terms of quadratic mean interval.

Keywords: Multi-agent systems · Multi-agent patrolling Artificial Neural Networks

1 Introduction

The patrol task is well-suited for being shared in space and time by several agents. There are a wide variety of problems that may be reformulated as a particular multi-agent patrol task. As a concrete example, the monitoring of an area by a swarm of drones does face the problem of coordinating them to patrol that area in order to detect certain events. A feature of multi-agent patrolling (MAP) is the difficulty to derive analytic results from its equations. Thereby it appears that the only method enabling to predict its behaviour is to simulate the local interactions of its components. Thus, the quality of a patrolling strategy is evaluated in simulation and it is consensual that a good strategy is one that minimises the time lag between two passages on the same place and for all places.

© Springer Nature Switzerland AG 2018
T. Miller et al. (Eds.): PRIMA 2018, LNAI 11224, pp. 603–611, 2018.
https://doi.org/10.1007/978-3-030-03098-8_47

Different types of strategies were proposed, however, few works concentrate on the problematic of using Artificial Neural Networks (ANN) for the MAP [2,4,7]. *We propose and evaluate new strategies using not only machine learning models, in particular an ANN based on the rectifier linear ReLU, but also a multi-dimensional linear model. In this way, new strategies embedding these models are introduced.*

The Sect. 2 presents the background useful to understand proposed developments: the MAP and ANN types used by the strategies. Then, Sect. 3 describes new strategies based on idleness estimation by ANN. In Sect. 4 these strategies are analysed. Finally, Sect. 5 draws some conclusions and indicates directions for further works.

2   Background

2.1   Multi-agent Patrolling

The MAP model consists of a society of agents noted $\mathbf{A}$, able to move in a graph noted $\mathbf{G} = (\mathbf{V}, \mathbf{E})$ representing a discretisation of the area to patrol. $\mathbf{V} = \{1, .., N\}$ is the set of nodes standing for the places to visit, and $\mathbf{E}$ is the set of edges connecting them. At each edge corresponds a *transit time* representing its travel time. At each node is associated a dynamic variable named *idleness*, indicating the time elapsed since it has not been visited by any agent [3]. The vector of idlenesses of all nodes at time t is noted $I_t(v)$ and the idleness of a node v, $I_t(v)$. At the beginning of a patrolling, agents are positioned on nodes and all idlenesses are set to 0. Finally, each time an agent arrives at a node v, it shall decide, among the edges connecting v, the next edge to travel.

A *strategy* of agent is an information processing method allowing each agent to take a decision each time it arrives at a node. Whatever the strategy considered, each agent intends actions based on its knowledge regarding idlenesses of nodes. Indeed, agents make idleness estimates that can be produced assuming different hypotheses:

- *individual idleness*: each agent considers only its own visits to update its estimated node idleness. It corresponds to the case where communication between agents is not possible. In the case of a mission with only one agent, *individual idleness* corresponds to *real idleness*, also called *global idleness*.
- *shared idleness*: all agents consider visits of all agents to reset estimated node idleness. In the case of perfect instantaneous communication between agents, or a mission with only one agent, *shared idleness* corresponds to *real idleness*, also called *global idleness*.

Among the wide family of strategies [1], two regarded as representative strategies are relevant here: *Conscientious Reactive* (CR) and *Heuristic Pathfinder Cognitive Coordinated* (HPCC). CR selects the next node to visit as the one with the highest individual idleness in its neighbourhood. HPCC is based on a perfect communication between agents: shared idlenesses are estimated by a coordinator on the basis of all paths of agents. Two methods are used: the first one called *Heuristic* selects the next node to visit, and the second one called *Pathfinder* chooses the path to go there [1,5].

Evaluation criteria relevant to establish aggregation measures based on *interval between visits* for a node are the *Mean Interval* (MI) and the *Quadratic Mean Interval* (QMI). In order to better evaluate the contribution of each agent when the population size varies, these criteria are normalised by multiplying values by the number of agents.

2.2 Artificial Neural Networks

ANNs are a special kind of *machine learning* models. Among the large variety of ANN, single layer and **multi-layer perceptrons** [6,8] are composed with one or several stacked layers of *neurons*, each one corresponding to a function that maps the outputs of the previous layer with the output of the current layer. Several kinds of functions are used. For example, the *identity*, the *logistic sigmoid* and the *linear rectifier* (ReLU), $f(z) = max(0, z)$. Each neuron computes a weighted and biased sum of the previous layer's outputs, which is finally passed through its function, making up thereby the neuron's output. When the functions are non-linear, they provide a basis for developing an approximation of the function to be learned.

Networks are generally optimised using *gradient-descent-based methods* by minimising a *cost function* representing the difference between the output of the network and its desired value [6,8]. A quite common cost is the *Mean Squared Error* (MSE).

3 Strategies Based on Idleness Estimation

This section presents the design of the three strategies using an idleness estimation called *Heuristic Pathfinder Mean Predictor* (HPMP), *Heuristic Pathfinder Linear Predictor* (HPLP) and *Heuristic Pathfinder ReLU Predictor* (HPRP).

3.1 Formal Definition

Estimator-Based Strategies. The three strategies use an estimator based on a trained statistical model noted $m(.,.)$: the decision-making process is carried out first by computing an estimate of the *global idleness* from the trained model, then by making the decision regarding the next node to visit with respect to this estimate. In our context, a temporal series representing the successive idlenesses each time an agent stands upon a node, the latter will be called an *idleness flow*.

Let I_t^a and $\hat{I}_t$ being the vectors of individual idlenesses of the agent a and the corresponding estimated global idlenesses, respectively, at the time t. Then, given that $\forall t \in \mathbf{T}, \forall a \in \mathbf{A}, \forall I_t^a \in \mathbb{R}^N$, $\hat{I}_t$ is defined such as:

$$\hat{I}_t = \min(\ \max(m(I_t^a, \boldsymbol{\theta}), 0),\ I_t^a\ ) \tag{1}$$

where $\boldsymbol{\theta}$ is the set of the statistical model's parameters, and min and max are component-wise functions ensuring that whatever the output of the model, the estimation of global idleness is positive and lower than the individual idleness.

For any agent, such an estimator will output estimates of the global idlenesses, called *estimated idlenesses*, from the current individual idlenesses fed as input. All the agents embed the same estimator, i.e. the same trained model. This strategy can be thought of as a reactive strategy using an artefact for estimating missing information regarding the area to patrol, and taking into account the idleness of nodes and thereby implicitly the agents' positions.

For a given scenario, the model learns to predict the global idleness vector corresponding to a current agent's individual idleness vector. Then, agents applies to the estimated global idlenesses the two methods described in the Sect. 2, namely the Heuristic method to select the next node to visit and the Pathfinder method to choose the path to go there.

However, the relation between individual idlenesses and global idlenesses may not be a function. The following theorem presents conditions under which this relation is not a function.

Theorem 1. *Let* $\mathbf{G} = (\mathbf{V}, \mathbf{E})$ *be a graph, let* $\mathbf{A}$ *be a society of agents and consider two runs of a given strategy, arbitrarily named first and second run. If:*

- *in initial state, a node* $u \in \mathbf{V}$ *is occupied with an agent* $a_1 \in \mathbf{A}$ *for the first run and with an agent* $a_2 \in \mathbf{A}$ *for the second run,* a_1 *and* a_2 *may have the same agent identifier, and*
- *a next node* $v \in \mathbf{V}$ *is selected by the strategy for the agent* a_1 *in the first run and for the agent* a_2 *in the second run and*
- *for the first run, it exist* $w \in \mathbf{V}, w \neq v$ *that is occupied by an agent* $a_3 \in A, a_3 \neq a_1, a_3 \neq a_2$ *or which has already been reached by* a_3 *when, at time* t, a_1 *arrives at* v *and*
- *for the second run, no agent has reached* w, *when at time* t, a_2 *arrives at* v,

then the relation between, the individual idleness I_t^a *and the global idleness* I_t *is not a function.*

Proof. At time t, the individual idlenesses for a_1 in the first run and for a_2 in the second run are equal: both have $I_t^a(j) = t, \forall j \neq v$ and $I_t^a(v) = 0$. For the first run $I_t(w)$, the global idleness of w, is equal to 0 if a_3 occupies it, or equal to $t - \tau < t$, where $\tau > 0$ is the travel time of agent a_3 from its initial position to w, otherwise. For the second run $I_t(w) = t$. Thus, to the same individual idleness corresponds two different values of the global idleness. Hence, the relation between the individual idleness I_t^a and the global idleness I_t is not a function.

Models. As indicated by the Eq. 1, for all the models studied here, the input and output both of dimension N, stand for the vector of individual idlenesses and the vector of estimated idlenesses, respectively.

First, the *mean model* consists of a model which estimates for each node, the global idleness as being the average of all global idlenesses of this node over all the global idleness flows. With such a model noted $Mean$, an agent $a \in \mathbf{A}$ carries out the estimation of the global idlenesses at $t \in \mathbf{T}$ as following:

$$\exists \boldsymbol{\theta} = \{B \in \mathcal{M}_{N \times 1}(\mathbb{R})\} : m(I_t^a, \boldsymbol{\theta}) = Mean(I_t^a, \boldsymbol{\theta}) = B \tag{2}$$

When such a model is used as global idleness estimator, the corresponding strategy is called Heuristic Pathfinder Mean Predictor (HPMP).

When the estimator corresponds to a linear model noted Lin or $Linear$, the strategy is termed Heuristic Pathfinder Linear Predictor HPLP. With such a model an agent $a \in \mathbf{A}$ carries out the estimation of the global idlenesses at $t \in \mathbf{T}$ as follows:

$$\exists \boldsymbol{\theta} = \{W \in \mathcal{M}_N(\mathbb{R})\} : m(I_t^a, \boldsymbol{\theta}) = Lin(I_t^a, \boldsymbol{\theta}) = W \cdot I_t^a \tag{3}$$

with W being the model's weight matrix. Training such a model corresponds to figure out the W minimising a certain distance between $m(I_t^a, \boldsymbol{\theta})$ and I_t.

Finally, an MLP composed with H hidden ReLU layers as described in the Sect. 2, is termed *ReLU model*, while its corresponding strategy is called Heuristic Pathfinder ReLU Predictor (HPLP). With such a model noted MLP_{ReLU}^H, an agent $a \in \mathbf{A}$ carries out the estimation of the global idlenesses at $t \in \mathbf{T}$ as following:

$$\begin{aligned}
\exists \boldsymbol{\theta} = \{W_h, W_{out} \in \mathcal{M}_N(\mathbb{R}) \ : h \in [|1, H|]\} : \\
m(I_t^a, \boldsymbol{\theta}) = MLP_{ReLU}^H(I_t^a, \boldsymbol{\theta}) \\
= W_{out} \cdot ReLU(\ W_H \cdot ReLU(\ W_{H-1} \cdot ReLU(\dots \\
W_2 \cdot ReLU(\ W_1 \cdot I_t^a\ )\ )\ ) \dots)\ )\ )
\end{aligned} \tag{4}$$

with $ReLU$ being the element-wise ReLU activation, and $\forall h \in [|0, H|]$, W_h the weight matrix of the layer h.

4 Experiments and Results

4.1 Scenarios and Training

Three different graphs were selected to evaluate the strategies: the maps *Islands*, *Grid* and A, as shown in the Fig. 1 [5]. For each map we tested the strategies CR, HPCC and the idleness-predictor-based strategies were trained from HPCC's simulation and tested. The tests were performed over population sizes of 5, 10, 15 and 25 agents and for each size we selected 100 *random starts*, also called *runs*. For each start, each strategy was tested over 3000 periods and, in average, an agent visits 650 nodes during one execution of 3000 periods. In doing so, the sequences used to train the models have approximately a length of 650 idleness vectors. For each scenario we trained 8 statistical models by minimising the MSE: a mean-based model, a linear model, three Multi-layer Perceptron (MLP) with sigmoid units and three different artificial neural networks with rectifier linear units (ReLU): an architecture with only one ReLU layer simply termed *ReLU*, another one with one hidden ReLU layer and the output layer being also a ReLU layer, termed *ReLU Output* (ReLUO), and finally an MLP with ReLU activation termed *ReLU MLP*. The data base was divided into a training base and a validation base with 80% of data in the training base. The training results indicates that the lowest MSE are obtained for a single layer of linear or ReLU neurons. Strategies based both on these networks and on the mean were selected for assessment.

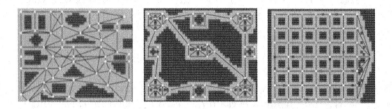

Fig. 1. Graphs used during assessment.

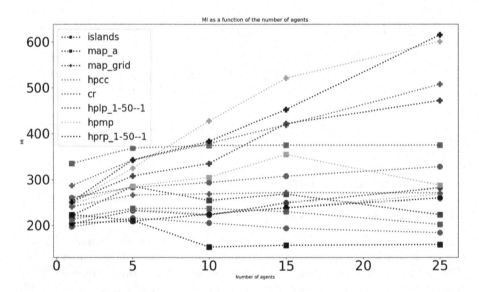

Fig. 2. Normalised QMI of the evaluated strategies in ordinate for the three maps w.r.t. the population sizes of agents in abscissa.

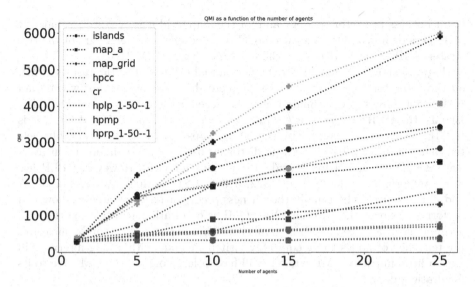

Fig. 3. Normalised MI of the evaluated strategies in ordinate for the three maps w.r.t. the population sizes of agents in abscissa.

4.2   Performance Results

To evaluate their performances, the studied strategies were tested and compared with CR and HPCC using normalised *MI* and *QMI* as evaluation criteria.

Figure 2 show all the results for the topologies Islands, A and Grid for the normalised MI. Not surprisingly, HPCC always outperformed all the others strategies on all the maps and for all the population sizes of agents. First, except for the map Grid, HPLP overwhelmingly outperforms the reactive strategy CR, while on the map Grid it is slightly better than CR. Unlike the others maps, this little difference can be explained in considering that, Grid being a topology where the nodes are uniformly distributed, the strategy CR is well adapted. However, HPLP remains better than CR on this map, except for the population size of 15 agents where they are approximately equal. Then, except for the map Islands, HPLP has always better performances over this criterion than HPMP. On that map, the performances of HPLP are approximately equal to the ones of HPMP for 5 and 10 agents. However, for 15 and 25 agents the former is worse than the latter. Results on Islands for 15 and 25 agents, on A for 5 and 15 agents and Grid for all the population sizes, seem to show that agents do not benefit from the presence of each other. Indeed, unlike HPCC which has a decreasing or stable normalised MI, it increases for HPLP. For the map Islands, HPRP is the best idleness predictor strategy over the normalised MI, except for 10 agents where it is approximately equal to HPLP and HPMP. On that map, it is also slightly better than HPCC for 5 agents. For the map A, HPRP is by far the best strategy. In average it is better than HPCC of 74 periods. Finally, as previously stated while comparing HPLP and HPRP to it, HPMP is most of the time the worst idleness predictor strategy and for the map Grid it is even worse than CR of 39 periods in average. The two models trained and used as a part of the two strategies HPLP and HPRP are thereby better than HPMP.

Figure 3 shows the results for the normalised QMI. Unlike the results of MI, on the three topologies the idleness predictor-based strategies are worst than HPCC and CR, the coordinated and the decentralised ones, respectively. For Islands, the HPRP is the worst strategy, while for the maps A and Grid, it is HPMP, which is the worst. For the latter maps, HPLP is incomparably better than the other two idleness predictor strategies with a difference in average with HPRP of 574 for A and 1161 periods for Grid. However, HPLP has worse performances than CR of 1522, 310 and 211 periods on the Islands, A and Grid, respectively. Finally the idleness predictor-based strategies show bad performances over the criterion QMI. QMI as quadratic mean takes better into account the difference of time intervals between the nodes and thereby measures the tendency of nodes to be equitably visited. A node with a long interval will have a little impact on MI, while it will have a large one on the QMI due to its quadratic growth.

Thereupon, the results show that good performances in average i.e. over MI are balanced by the ones of QMI. These results show the tendency of idleness predictor agents to visit a particular inferred set of nodes at the expense of the other ones.

5   Conclusion and Perspectives

We proposed and evaluated new strategies for the MAP. Those strategies are based on learning the relation between individual and global idlenesses. The assessment of selected strategies based on estimations of global idlenesses using learned model indicates good results in terms of MI, but also unsatisfactory results in terms of QMI.

Theorem 1 indicates that there may be no significant expectation for approximation improvement. Data analysis methods should be applied in order to check the presence of conditions implying that the relation between individual and global idlenesses is not a function. Other future research will aim at modifying the strategies in order to improve their performance in terms of QMI. One track is to consider some randomisation process when exploiting the estimation of global idlenesses by the model. For example, defining a probability distribution with $\hat{I}_t$ as a mean and the strategy could sample in this distribution, idlenesses' estimate. The global idleness approximation problem could be further investigated with other structures of ANN and better learning algorithms. Finally, it should be noted that there is a large set of possibilities for using ANN to try to learn some information from centralised strategies that is useful for decentralised strategies. For example, nodes sequences of centralised strategies could be learned using Long Short-Term Memory ANN architectures and directly used in a decentralised strategy. This kind of approach could be compared to the approach proposed here.

References

1. Almeida A., Castro, P.M., Menezes, T.R., Ramalho, G.L.: Combining idleness and distance to design heuristic agents for the patrolling task. In: II Brazilian Workshop in Games and Digital Entertainment, pp. 33–40 (2003)
2. D'Ambrosio, D.B., Goodell, S., Lehman, J., Risi, S., Stanley, K.O.: Multirobot behavior synchronization through direct neural network communication. In: Su, C.-Y., Rakheja, S., Liu, H. (eds.) ICIRA 2012. LNCS (LNAI), vol. 7507, pp. 603–614. Springer, Heidelberg (2012). https://doi.org/10.1007/978-3-642-33515-0_59
3. Chevaleyre, Y.: Theoretical analysis of the multi-agent patrolling problem. In: Proceedings of the International Conference On Intelligent Agent Technology, Beijing, China, pp. 302–308 (2004)
4. Guo, Y., Parker, L., Madhavan, R.: Collaborative robots for infrastructure security applications. In: Nedjah, N., Coelho, L.S., Mourelle, L.M. (eds.) Mobile Robots: The Evolutionary Approach. SCI, vol. 50, pp. 185–200. Springer, Heidelberg (2007). https://doi.org/10.1007/978-3-540-49720-2_9
5. Othmani-Guibourg, M., El Fallah-Seghrouchni, A., Farges, J.-L., Potop-Butucaru, M.: Multi-agent patrolling in dynamic environments. In: 2017 IEEE International Conference on Agents (ICA) (2017)
6. Rumelhart, D.E., Hinton, G.E., Williams, R.J.: Learning representations by back-propagating errors. Nature **323**, 533–536 (1986)
7. Sales, D.O., Feitosa, D., Osorio, F.S., Wolf, D.F.: Multi-agent autonomous patrolling system using ANN and FSM control. In: 2012 Second Brazilian Conference on Critical Embedded Systems, Campinas, pp. 48–53 (2012)
8. Werbos, P.: Beyond regression: new tools for prediction and analysis in the behavioral sciences. Ph.D. thesis, Harvard University (1974)

A Multi-agent Simulator Environment Based on the Robot Operating System for Human-Robot Interaction Applications

Poom Pianpak[✉], Tran Cao Son, and Phoebe O. Toups Dugas

Computer Science Department, New Mexico State University, Las Cruces, USA
ppianpak@nmsu.edu phoebe.toups.dugas@acm.org

Abstract. This paper describes a simulator environment for humans to direct a team of independent drones by allowing humans to issue high-level goals to the teams or drones. Given a goal, the environment will generate plans for the drones and monitor their execution while attending to humans requests (e.g., aborting a goal, introducing a new goal). For this reason, the environment includes two specific modules, a planning module and an execution and monitoring module, besides the modules for simulation and control of drones. The environment is implemented on the Robot Operating System (ROS), a well-known framework for the development of robotic applications, that facilitates the communication between its components. Experiments are included to highlight the applicability of the environment.

1 Introduction

Human-robot interaction (HRI) is highly studied [7,10,15], but existing work has primarily focused on interacting with a single robot. Interacting with a *team* of robots has just been explored [3–5,11,13,17]. This issue is exacerbated by the advent of low-cost and more capable drones[1]. We expect to see teams of drones working with minimal human supervision in the near future, greatly augmenting human capabilities [3,11,13,17]. These teams can be made maximally efficient if a lone human operator can direct them through well-designed two-way communication and appropriate control algorithms that abstract and simplify control. While control of singular drone is well-studied, the ability to control a drone team by a single human is limited.

The present research is developed in the context of supporting future human-drone team scenarios [1,2]. The research works from the vision that, in the near future, semi-autonomous drone teams can be directed by a single operator in the field. Such an operator needs to maintain situation awareness [8], that is, s/he must be safe in an unsafe environment and have a clear understanding of what is happening nearby.

---

[1] We use the term "drones" in a generic sense to refer to unmanned robotic systems.

© Springer Nature Switzerland AG 2018
T. Miller et al. (Eds.): PRIMA 2018, LNAI 11224, pp. 612–620, 2018.
https://doi.org/10.1007/978-3-030-03098-8_48

In this paper, we present a preliminary design and implementation of a simulated environment for a human operator to interact with a team of drones. The environment for Controlling Teams of Drones (eCTD), is a part of a larger project aimed at addressing issues arose from hybrid human-drone team coordination and planning. For this purpose, eCTD also includes a planning module and an execution monitoring module that enable human operators to issue high-level commands to the drones. eCTD is implemented on the Robot Operating System (ROS) [18], and the drones are simulated using the high-fidelity robot simulator Gazebo [12]. Our system uses the hector_quadrotor package [14] for the modeling, controlling, and simulation of the drones. The interaction between the system and humans (via wearable devices) is implemented over WebSockets. Our implementation is modular and can be extended or easily adapted to other packages available to ROS. For example, the hector_quadrotor package could be changed if the system is to be used with other robots; the planner used in the planning module could be replaced by any planning system that uses the Planning Domain Description Language (PDDL) as input language.

The paper is organized as follows. Section 2 reviews the basic of the Robot Operating System (ROS) and basic terminologies in planning. Section 3 describes in detail the design and implementation of eCTD, including the ins and outs between the system and the clients. Section 4 shows an example scenario that demonstrates the ability of eCTD to control and coordinate multiple drones. Section 5 summarizes the current state of eCTD and suggests the future work.

2   Background

2.1   Robot Operating System (ROS)

The Robot Operating System (ROS) is an open-source framework designed for writing robotics software [18]; it is considered to be the *de facto* standard for robot programming [16]. ROS uses a distributed, peer-to-peer architecture, where the components are built and run by a number of small tools [18].

Figure 1 shows a simple ROS setup with one *master*. A ROS Master provides registration and lookup services for ROS *nodes*, enabling them to locate each other. It hosts a *parameter server*, a shared dictionary that provides run-time parameter settings. It is a part of *roscore*, which is a set of prerequisites to run a ROS-based system.

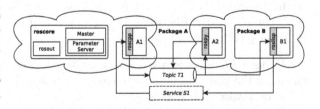

Fig. 1. Conceptual overview of ROS

A *ROS node* (A1, A2, and B1 in Fig. 1) is a process that performs computation. ROS nodes can locate a ROS Master, but they are generally unaware of each other's existence. They rely on *client library*[2] to communicate with the ROS Master and other nodes. A collection of nodes is organized in a *package*. A package is the most atomic unit for building and releasing software in ROS. In Fig. 1, nodes A1 and A2 are in package A while node B1 is in package B. Notice that even nodes in the same package could be run on different networks.

ROS provides two methods for nodes to communicate with each other directly (except for some negotiation with the ROS Master): *topic* and *service*. Topic could be viewed as a message bus. Nodes that publish data to a topic are called *publishers* and nodes that subscribe to receive messages from a topic are called *subscribers*. Each node can be a publisher and/or a subscriber to multiple topics. In Fig. 1, node A1 publishes, node A2 both publishes and subscribes, and node B1 subscribes to the topic named T1. Service could be viewed as a remote procedure call (RPC) request/response interaction. A node that provides a service is called a *service server*, and a node that makes a request to a service is called a *service client*. Service is different from topic is that there could only be a single service server for a given service. In Fig. 1, node A1 is a service server, while node B1 is a service client for the service named S1.

2.2   Planning Engine and Planning Domain Description

The planning engine employed in this project is CpA [19], one of the state-of-the-art conformant planning system. It is responsible for generating plans for drones given the high-level goals from a human. CpA uses the Planning Domain Definition Language (PDDL) [9] to encode its inputs, i.e., planning problems.

There are two main parts in a planning problem: a domain definition and a problem definition. The domain definition specifies a set of fluents that encode the state of the world and a set of actions that the drones can execute. For example, the fluent $TookOff(D)$ denotes that the drone D has been taken off. The set of actions that the drones can execute describe their effects (e.g., changing location of a drone, whether a drone is in the *flying* mode, etc.). In our experiments in Sect. 4, the following actions have been used:

- $AddLocation(L)$: Specify a location L and set it as unoccupied
- $FlyTo(D, L_1, L_2)$: Fly drone D from location L_1 to location L_2
- $TakeOff(D)$: Take off drone D

A *fluent literal* is either a fluent or its negation. A *state* is a collection of fluents of the planning domain. Given a state s and a fluent f, f is true in s if $f \in s$; otherwise, f is false in s.

The problem definition specifies the initial state of the world (e.g., the locations of the drones, the active regions, etc.) and the goals (e.g., D_1 needs to be at a location L_1 specified by the coordinates (x_1, y_1, z_1)). In the current implementation, the initial state is given by a set of fluents and a goal is given by a conjunction of fluent literals.

---

[2] The list of ROS client libraries: http://wiki.ros.org/Client%20Libraries.

3   eCTD: **Design and Implementation**

A detailed overview of eCTD is shown in Fig. 2. We have introduced several services (the boxes with dashed-line boundaries inside ROS), topics (the horizontal cylinders), a drone action server (the box with blue background), a drone controller (the box with orange background), and a high-level planning and execution monitoring component (the big green-dashed box) which consists of a planner, an

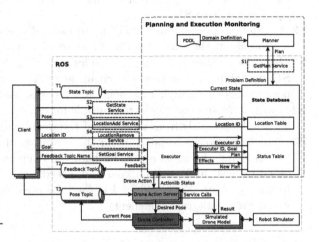

Fig. 2. Detailed overview of eCTD

executor, and a state database (or **SD**, for short).

Section 3.1 describes the clients of our system and the means for their interaction with other components. Section 3.2 explains how the state of the world is managed in our system, and how it is used to form a problem definition for a planner. Section 3.3 explains what happens when a goal request is received from a client, how a plan is made, and what feedback is returned to the client. Section 3.4 explains how drone actions are managed and executed.

3.1   Clients, Services, and Topics

Clients: In top-level view, the diagram in Fig. 2 consists of two parts: one that is inside ROS, and the other that is outside (the clients and the planner). Communication between systems inside and outside of ROS is facilitated by rosbridge_suite[3] [6] which enables the implementation of components inside ROS to stay unchanged. Those components could communicate with non-ROS components via WebSocket as if they were inside ROS. As a result, the clients of our system could be anything that can communicate via WebSocket. For our final project, the clients will be wearable devices and a game engine.

Services: In Fig. 2, the dashed boxes marked with **S1** to **S5** inside ROS are services implemented using ROS Service. They act as an interface between ROS and non-ROS systems. The description of each service is as follows:

S1 *GetPlan Service* is responsible for generating a plan for the drones given the current state of the world and the goals from the client. It takes the problem

---

[3]   https://github.com/RobotWebTools/rosbridge_suite.

description generated as a string from **SD** and sends to the planner. It then receives a plan (a sequence of actions) as an array of strings from the planner, and returns it to **SD**.

S2 *GetState Service* allows the clients to manually ask **SD** to publish the information about the current state of the world on the *State Topic* (see below).

S3 *LocationAdd Service* is responsible for updating the location table, a part of **SD**, by taking a pose from the client, generates a unique location ID for the pose, stores the mapping of them, and returns the ID to the client.

S4 *LocationRemove Service* is responsible for removing all objects associated to a given location ID from the state of the world and the location table.

S5 *SetGoal Service* is responsible for the execution of requests from clients, i.e., for achieving the goals issued by humans. It creates an executor thread for every request, and passes a goal and a feedback topic name from the client to the executor thread. Thread is used for possible concurrent execution of various requests from the clients.

Topics: ROS Topics are provided for the clients to track the activities of the system in almost real-time. eCTD includes three topics which are marked with **T1** (*State*), **T2** (*Feedback*), and **T3** (*Pose*) in Fig. 2.

T1 The *State Topic* contains the state published by **SD**. The published state consists of a set of fluents described by the planning domain and a map of location IDs used in the fluents to real poses.

T2 The *Feedback Topic* contains the feedback from an executor. Different executors could publish feedback to different feedback topics depending on the feedback topic name provided by the clients. Details of the feedback will be explained in Sect. 3.3.

T3 The *Pose Topic* contains the current pose of a drone. The pose consists of a position and an orientation. Each drone controller publishes the pose to its own pose topic.

3.2   The State Database and the Planning System

The state database (**SD**) and the planning system in Fig. 2 use the planning domain described in Subsect. 2.2 to generate plans for drones given goals from the clients. The main purpose of **SD** is to maintain the information about the current goals (from potentially different clients) and the current state of the world (see Subsect. 2.2).

SD has two important structures: the *location table* and the *status table*. The location table abbreviates poses to location IDs which we use in our fluents and is implemented as a map between location IDs and poses. The status table stores the goals from the clients and for each goal, a plan and the progress of the execution of the plan. The status table helps deciding whether re-planning is necessary and is implemented as a map between executor IDs and triples of goals, plans, and their execution progresses. Because our system needs to support concurrent executions, the implementation of the maps has to be thread-safe. The current system uses `libcuckoo`[4] to provide lock-free and thread-safe maps.

SD could be updated by an executor and a request from *LocationRemove* or *LocationAdd* services as described in Subsect. 3.1. Once **SD** has been updated, the content of **SD** will then be published to the *State* topic and the re-planning procedure will start if necessary.

Any planner using PDDL as its input can be used in our system. For language independence, the planner is placed outside of ROS. The communication between it and **SD**, which is inside ROS, is facilitated by `rosbridge_suite`. Our current system has been integrated with CPA planner [19].

When a goal is issued by a client, a problem definition is generated from **SD** and the goal. Most of the implementation to create the problem definition involve string manipulation and is omitted for brevity.

3.3   Execution Monitoring

The executor is in the center between the client, **SD**, and the drone action server. The main responsibility of the executor is to monitor the execution of the plan and send feedback updates to the client. When it is first created, it will ask for a unique ID from the status table. After it receives its own ID, it will request for a plan from **SD** by sending its ID and the goal to **SD**. The executor ID is used by the *status table*, as described in Subsect. 3.2. After the executor gets the plan, it will execute the actions sequentially. While the actions are being executed, the executor will periodically check with **SD** if the plan for its goal has been changed (e.g., human decides to cancel the mission, some action fails). If the plan has been changed, it will abort the current plan execution, ask for a new plan, and execute the new plan. If a drone action needs to be executed, it will be sent to the drone action server for execution (see Subsect. 3.4).

The feedback message published to the client through *Feedback Topic* contains the information pertaining to the execution status of a certain action and the executor ID. There are a total of seven statuses: three being intermediate statuses and four being terminal statuses. The state machine showing the transitions of the feedback statuses is shown in Fig. 3. The white boxes represent the intermediate statuses while the blue boxes represent the terminal statuses.

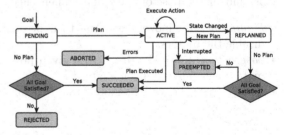

Fig. 3. Feedback status state machine

---

[4] https://github.com/efficient/libcuckoo.

The description of each status is as follows:

- STATUS_PENDING: The plan has not yet been made.
- STATUS_ACTIVE: The plan is being executed. The detail of the action being executed is supplied in the message.
- STATUS_REPLANNED: The plan has been changed.
- STATUS_REJECTED: The plan for the given goal could not be made. No action has been executed.
- STATUS_PREEMPTED: The action executed was interrupted by other plan execution.
- STATUS_ABORTED: Some errors have occurred while the plan was being executed. A description is supplied in the message.
- STATUS_SUCCEEDED: The goals have been satisfied.

3.4 Drone Control and Simulation

This section describes the *Drone Action Server*, *Drone Controller*, *Simulated Drone Model*, and *Robot Simulator* components shown in Fig. 2. Together, they are responsible for low-level drone operations. For each drone in the system, an instance of the drone action server, drone controller, and simulated drone model is created. We use `hector_quadrotor` package for the simulated drone model and `Gazebo` for the robot simulator. We implemented a simple PID control for the drone controller.

The drone action server is implemented using `actionlib`[5]. It enables the executor to monitor the execution of an individual action, whether the action has been executed successfully, has errors, or has been interrupted.

Currently, our drone action server provides three actions: landing, pose, and takeoff. All of the drone actions are parameterized with the drone ID, the locations, and/or the pose or the height. Their effects are as follows:

- *landing action*: move the drone to a predefined height above ground and disable the motors.
- *pose action*: move the drone to a given pose. This action assumes that the motors have already been enabled.
- *takeoff action*: enable the motors and take off the drone to a predefined height above ground.

4 Experiments

Due to space limitation, the detail of the experiments could be found in https://www.cs.nmsu.edu/~ppianpak/2018-PRIMA/full.pdf.

---

[5] https://github.com/ros/actionlib.

5   Conclusion and Future Work

In this paper, we described an environment for humans to direct a team of independent drones by providing the means for humans to communicate with the drones: humans can (*i*) issue high-level goals to the drones and (*ii*) receive feedbacks from the drones (e.g., the goal is not attainable or has been successfully achieved, etc.). The environment is implemented on the Robot Operating System with components specifically developed for planning and execution monitoring. It can handle multiple requests concurrently. We included experiments highlighting the capability of the environment in these aspects.

eCTD will be employed as the base for our quest in the design and development of wearable devices that allows a single human to control multiple drones at the same time. This will be our focus in the immediate future.

References

1. Alharthi, S.A., et al.: Practical insights into the design of future disaster response training simulations. In: Proceedings of the 15th ISCRAM Conference, pp. 818–830 (2018)
2. Alharthi, S.A., Sharma, H.N., Sunka, S., Dolgov, I., Toups Dugas, P.O.: Designing future disaster response team wearables from a grounding in practice. In: Proceedings of the Technology, Mind, and Society, TechMindSociety 2018, pp. 1:1–1:6. ACM (2018)
3. Brambilla, M., Ferrante, E., Birattari, M., Dorigo, M.: Swarm robotics: a review from the swarm engineering perspective. Swarm Intell. **7**(1), 1–41 (2013)
4. Chen, J., Barnes, M.: Supervisory control of multiple robots: effects of imperfect automation and individual differences. Hum. Factors **54**(2), 157–174 (2012)
5. Chien, S.Y., Wang, H., Lewis, M.: Human vs. algorithmic path planning for search and rescue by robot teams. In: Proceedings of the Human Factors and Ergonomics Society Annual Meeting, vol. 54, no. 4, pp. 379–383 (2010)
6. Crick, C., Jay, G., Osentoski, S., Pitzer, B., Jenkins, O.C.: Rosbridge: ROS for non-ROS users. In: Christensen, H.I., Khatib, O. (eds.) Robotics Research. STAR, vol. 100, pp. 493–504. Springer, Cham (2017). https://doi.org/10.1007/978-3-319-29363-9_28
7. Dautenhahn, K.: Methodology and themes of human-robot interaction: a growing research field. Int. J. Adv. Robot. Syst. **4**(1), 103–108 (2007)
8. Endsley, M.R.: Toward a theory of situation awareness in dynamic systems. Hum. Factors **37**(1), 32–64 (1995)
9. Ghallab, M., et al.: PDDL: the planning domain definition language, Version 1.2. Technical report, Yale (1998)
10. Goodrich, M., Schultz, A.: Human-robot interaction: a survey. Found. Trends Hum.-Comput. Interact. **1**(3), 203–275 (2007)
11. Kira, Z., Potter, M.: Exerting human control over decentralized robot swarms. In: ICARA 2009, pp. 566–571 (2009)
12. Koenig, N., Howard, A.: Design and use paradigms for Gazebo, an open-source multi-robot simulator. In: IROS, vol. 3, pp. 2149–2154. IEEE (2004)
13. Kolling, A., Nunnally, S., Lewis, M.: Towards human control of robot swarms. In: HRI, New York, NY, USA, pp. 89–96. ACM (2012)

14. Meyer, J., Sendobry, A., Kohlbrecher, S., Klingauf, U., Stryk, O.V.: Comprehensive simulation of quadrotor UAVs using ROS and Gazebo. In: SIMPAR (2012)
15. Murphy, R.: Humans, robots, rubble, and research. Interactions **12**(2), 37–39 (2005)
16. O'Kane, J.M.: A Gentle Introduction to ROS (2014)
17. Penders, J.: A robot swarm assisting a human fire-fighter. Adv. Robot. **25**(1–2), 93–117 (2011)
18. Quigley, M., et al.: ROS: an open-source robot operating system. In: ICRA workshop on open source software, Kobe, Japan, vol. 3, p. 5 (2009)
19. Tran, V., Nguyen, K., Son, T.C., Pontelli, E.: A conformant planner based on approximation: CpA(H). ACM TIST **4**(2), 36 (2013)

Agent Based Simulation for Evaluation of Signage System Considering Expression Form in Airport Passenger Terminals and Other Large Facilities

Eriko Shimada[1], Shohei Yamane[2], Kotaro Ohori[2], Hiroaki Yamada[2], and Shingo Takahashi[1(✉)]

[1] Waseda University, 3-4-1 Okubo, Shinjuku, Tokyo, Japan
shingo@waseda.jp
[2] Fujitsu Laboratories LTD., 4-1-1 Kamiodanaka, Nakahara, Kawasaki, Kanagawa, Japan

Abstract. Signage systems are installed in large facilities, such as airport passenger terminals, to help users easily move through the facility. Simulation systems for evaluating signage systems proposed so far could evaluate only information message and location arrangement from the three essential components of signage system design, which are information message, location arrangement, and expression form. We created a model to represent the sign selection and information acquisition behavior of pedestrian agents by introducing the concept of attractiveness, which can describe expression form. This simulation makes it possible to more clearly discern the effectiveness of signage system designs.

Keywords: Signage system design · Expression form
Agent-based simulation · Large facility

1 Introduction

A signage system is defined as a whole system of various signs and the content of the signs mutually connected in a unified way to systematically provide useful information about the facility [1]. The evaluation of a signage system is very critical for the design, but it has been evaluated only from a qualitative point of view, mainly using a checklist concerning the requirements for the signage system [2]. Since it is usually difficult to revise a signage system after its installation, a simulation model to dynamically and quantitatively evaluate the flow of pedestrian traffic and the overall signage system before installation is needed [3–6].

A pedestrian agent simulation is considered to be effective for designing pleasant walking spaces in commercial facilities or bustling spaces, including large facilities [7]. Wayfinding plays a key role in the pedestrian agent model. The previous related researches on wayfinding [8, 9] have shown that "attention" and "interest" of users are essentially related to pedestrian route selection behavior.

© Springer Nature Switzerland AG 2018
T. Miller et al. (Eds.): PRIMA 2018, LNAI 11224, pp. 621–629, 2018.
https://doi.org/10.1007/978-3-030-03098-8_49

The important attributes for developing and evaluating a signage system are information message, expression form, and location arrangement [1]. By combining these three attributes, facility managers can change the degree of attention or interest, depending on the pedestrian types and behavior history. It is important to consider also the concepts of simplicity, clarity, consistency, continuity, and systemicity in the expression form of a signage system [1]. According to public transport passenger facility guidelines [10], so far they have only focused on the simplicity and clarity as the elements of expression form. Airport users with different attributes probably want information different from that wanted by other users and probably perceive this information in a different way.

The purpose of this study is to develop a simulation system to evaluate signage system design quantitatively from a pedestrian's dynamical point of view before installation and to support decision-making for design and implementation of signage system using the three attributes mentioned above. The simulation system developed so far [11, 12] considered only information message and location arrangement. In this study, especially by considering expression form, as well as information content and location, we developed a model to represent the behavior by which pedestrian agents choose one sign among multiple signs and conduct scenario analyses to evaluate the model. To model the expression form, this paper introduces the concept of sign "attractiveness," which to our knowledge has not previously been incorporated into such a model.

2 Model

2.1 Environmental Model

The environmental model is composed of cells that pedestrian agents move through, nodes that are destinations of moving agents, and edges that are paths connecting the nodes. Figure 1 provides an example of an environmental model. Each cell has Node Type as a parameter as shown in Table 1.

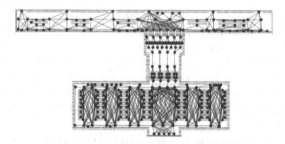

Fig. 1. Environmental model: points represent nodes and lines represent edges.

In this model, we define a connection between nodes as an edge, which represents a route. Each pedestrian agent follows routes to move between facilities.

Table 1. Node types

Node type	Description
Waypoint	Passage point on the route for agents to avoid obstacles
Procedural facility	Facility that agents must use before boarding in the environmental model
Commercial facility	Facility that each agent uses according to his or her purpose in the environmental model
Goal point	Point at which an agent disappears
Starting point	Point at which an agent appears

2.2 Sign Model

The sign model consists of coordinate as sign(x, y, floor), sign number as signFid, display orientation as signDirection(sightx, sighty), range of angle as signTheta, distance to convey information as signR, attributes of expression form as signPropertyset and signType. SignFid is divided into two types: areaSign and facilitySign. Each sign has an information message, which has the following five features: category information, area information, steps to need, route to a destination and facility information.

2.3 Pedestrian Agent Model

Pedestrian Agent Model's Attribute. The pedestrian agent model is composed of a coordinate of agent, the area of coordinate, the angle from signs, the distance from signs, a list of steps and facilities, the probability recalling each category as a destination, and the set of categories of facilities the agent wants to go to before boarding. In order for the agent to obtain information from the signs and select a facility as the next destination, 11 variables are required to express goal category, properties' weights, attractiveness set, area information, goal area, route information, facility information, facility list, facility utility, facility preference and goal facility.

Setup of Pedestrian Agent Model. The pedestrian agent model is set up in four steps. Step 1: an agent determines the flight to board. Step 2: the airport arrival time, check-in time, security check/departure inspection time, and flight time are registered in the schedule list. Step 3: based on the recall probability of each category, facilities to be used before flight departure are registered. Step 4: the attractiveness of each sign is calculated from the attribute related to the expression form of the sign and the degree of preference of the agent with respect to the attributes and times registered in the list.

Acquiring Information. The agent can probabilistically read the sign depending on the sign's attractiveness, if a sign is located inside the pedestrian agent's field of view and the agent is inside the sign's information delivery range (Fig. 2).

Attractiveness. We introduce the concept of sign attractiveness to the pedestrian agent model in this paper. Attractiveness represents the degree to which any sign attracts an agent. There are two purposes for introducing attractiveness.

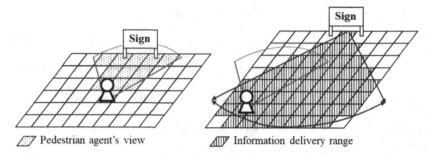

Fig. 2. Agent's visual recognition range and sign's information delivery area

The first is to augment expression form, which is one of the three essential components of the signage system design. Attractiveness is perceived more uniquely by each pedestrian agent making a decision based on the expression form and his or her state. Attractiveness expresses several attributes related to the expression form and the relationship between these attributes. This relationship, even if the expression form changes from sign to sign, helps maintain continuity throughout the signage system, and agents can take consistent actions using attractiveness cues. For example, suppose that a pedestrian agent transfers to domestic flights at the airport, follows red markings, and sees some changes in the expression form other than color, such as a decrease in character size or a decrease in sign clarity. The agent can continue to take consistent actions because the color provides continuity in the signage system.

The second purpose is to express the sign selection behavior according to the characteristics of agents' response to the expression form. Previous decision making models did not account for the difference in pedestrian agent characteristics with respect to expression form. In these models, agents who see the same sign obtain the same information, so the behavior of the agents with regard to the expression form is similar. We can express different pedestrian behavior depending on agent characteristics by introducing attractiveness. For example, it is possible to express agent behavior where agents cannot acquire information because multilingual notation is lacking in a sign and agents are more likely to approach signs having a format that they saw before.

Attractiveness is calculated as the selection probability of the agent's behavior with the multinomial logit model. In introducing attractiveness, the sign selection behavior consists of two steps. First, for each sign, the utility for the sign is calculated based on the respective sign parameters and agent parameters. Next, based on the calculated utility, the selection probability of the sign, which defines attractiveness, is calculated. The selection probability that information can be acquired from the sign and the amount of information an agent can obtain varies according to the attractiveness. The attractiveness model allows us to evaluate policies that consider differences in the characteristics of agents concerning the expression form. To construct the attractiveness model, we first select the attributes that represent the expression form. These attributes are specified according to the purpose of establishing a signage system by facility managers.

Pedestrian Agent Decision-Making. When selecting a commercial facility, an agent makes a decision in multiple stages (Fig. 3). First, the agent selects a category by choosing one category randomly from its category recall set, and the selected category is assigned to the goal category. Second, the agent selects an area by choosing one area randomly from the acquired area information that satisfies the goal category. Third, the agent selects a commercial facility. Then, the total steps spent at a facility and steps needed to move from the current position to the commercial facility are estimated and compared to the steps remaining until the scheduled time of arrival at the procedural facility. If the agent has the facility information that satisfies the goal category in the goal area, and sufficient steps are available, the procedural facility is registered in the facility recall set. The utility value (U) for each facility included in the facility recall set is calculated by the expression: $U_s = \gamma_{ns} + \delta \ time_{ns}$, using the preference for the facility and the transit time from the current position to the facility. Then a commercial facility as a destination is selected from the facility recall set using the multinomial logit model.

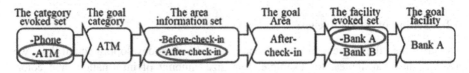

Fig. 3. Steps for selecting commercial facility destinations

Pedestrian Agent Walking Behavior. The walking behavior of the agent changes depending on the presence or absence of route information, the presence or absence of the target facility, and the current position. The target node is determined depending on the type of walking behavior: walking according to the route information, walking with no purpose, and random walking in a specific area or in general. A pedestrian agent searches the eight cells adjacent to its current position and enters the cell that is along the shortest route to the destination node. Then the agent updates its coordinates to match the new cell.

3   Simulation Experiment

3.1   Experimental Condition

We refer to the location arrangement of the signs at the Haneda Airport International Passenger Terminal (Fig. 4) as a prototype of the model.

The environmental model represents a virtual airport passenger terminal 255×570 cells (where each cell is 0.5 m $\times$ 0.5 m), divided into five areas: before-check-in area, after-check-in area, security-inspection/departure-examination area, after-departure right area and after-departure left area. In this experiment, a signage system is placed in two areas, before-departure and departure-floor. Signs 1 through 5 have only area information and indicate the direction to each area. Signs 6 through 9 have information on the area and facilities and describe the routes to destination facilities.

Fig. 4. Location arrangement of signs at an airport terminal.

The model has 18 commercial facilities, which are divided into eight categories such as restaurant, phone, exchange, ATM, and so on. The pedestrian agent population is 5,000, divided into five agent types representing different responses to the sign expression form. The pedestrian agents are generated based on the flight schedules of Haneda International Airport from 8 a.m. to 12 a.m., which is one of the busiest periods of the day. We conducted about 20,000 execution steps in each simulation, corresponding to 5.5 h in real time.

3.2   Setting of Attractiveness

To verify the effectiveness of attractiveness model before developing actual data, we assumed three attributes, for example, font size, amount of information, and color. First, with Eq. (1), we calculate the utility of the sign (sign$_i$) to the pedestrian agent (agent$_n$):

$$A_{in} = \beta_{1n} x_{1i} + \beta_{2n} x_{2i} + \beta_{3n} x_{3i} + \alpha_{in}, \tag{1}$$

where β_{kn} are the importance of each factor k for an agent, x_{ki} is the sign's ki attribute value, and α_{in} is the sign's error term for agent$_n$. Then we simulated selection behavior by classifying the utility of each agent in five typical types, as shown in Table 2.

Table 2. Agent utility types and values

Type	Utilities set for pedestrian agents		
	β1	β2	β3
A	Normal random number $-N$ $(0.2, 0.5^2)$	Normal random number $- N$ $(0.1, 0.75^2)$	Normal random number $- N$ $(0.1, 0.25^2)$
B	Normal random number $- N$ $(0.2, 0.5^2)$	Normal random number $- N$ $(0.1, 0.25^2)$	Normal random number $- N$ $(0.1, 0.75^2)$
C	1	1	0
D	0	0	1

Agents of each type react in a different way from other different type agents. Using scenarios, we can see how facility user types react. The uneven setting of types C and D can be expected to reveal more clearly the effectiveness of the attractiveness model.

3.3 Scenario Analyses for Variation in Expression Form

We generated agents of each type and verified four scenarios for sign expression form by setting the values of the three attributes representing expression form (Table 3).

Table 3. Values of each sign attributes for each scenario

Scenario	Sign 1			Sign 2			Sign 3			Sign 4			Sign 5		
	x1	x2	x3	x1	x2	x3	x1	x2	x3	x1	x2	x3	x1	x2	x3
1	0.33	0.33	0.33	0.33	0.33	0.33	0.33	0.33	0.33	0.33	0.33	0.33	0.33	0.33	0.33
2	0	0	1	0	0	1	0	0	1	0	1	0	0	1	0
3	0	1	0	0	0	1	0	1	0	0	0	1	0	1	0
4	10	10	0	10	10	0	10	10	0	10	10	0	10	10	0

Scenario	Sign 6			Sign 7			Sign 8			Sign 9		
	x1	x2	x3	x1	x2	x3	x1	x2	x3	x1	x2	x3
1	0.33	0.33	0.33	0.33	0.33	0.33	0.33	0.33	0.33	0.33	0.33	0.33
2	0.5	0	0.5	0.5	0	0.5	0.5	0	0.5	0.5	0.5	0
3	0.5	0.5	0	0.5	0	0.5	0.5	0.5	0	0.5	0	0.5
4	5	10	10	5	10	10	5	10	10	5	10	10

Facility signs in scenario 2 had more attributes of expression form than area signs. Since agents easily acquire information in areas that match their own characteristics, they will not get lost before arriving at the destination facility. In scenario 3, even after getting information from a sign, an agent might forget information while walking and be unable to follow signs continuously because it encounters a sign with low utility, and they cannot acquire information. We conducted 10 trails for each scenario and analyzed relationships between the amount of information acquired and signs in each scenario. Each dot on each graph expresses one execution result. The simulation results show how the signage system can work for each type of agents to reflect the information acquired based on attractiveness (Fig. 5).

By comparing the walking paths of the agents (Fig. 6), we see that type C and D agents took different routes. This shows that attractiveness changes by devising different expression forms, and this influences the paths taken by the agents.

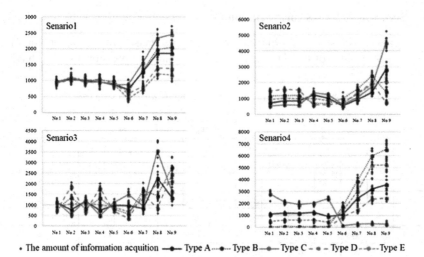

Fig. 5. Amount of information acquired

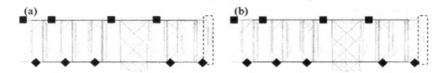

Fig. 6. Heat maps of agent walking routes: (a) type C and (b) type D.

4 Conclusion

In this paper, we proposed an agent based model for designing signage systems that considers the expression form of signs, and developed an agent based simulation tool for a large facility to quantitatively evaluate a signage system before its installation in a specific facility. We modeled the expression form by introducing an attractiveness index that represents the probability of users selecting a specific sign and obtaining useful information from it. Then, we verified its effectiveness of the attractiveness model by scenario analyses with four typical agent types applied to a virtual airport terminal. In order to apply the proposed model to a specific real-world situation, it is necessary to collect behavior data for sign use and facility selection by pedestrian agents in an actual large facility and estimate the parameters for each attribute of attractiveness.

References

1. Akase, T.: Sign System Planning: Public Space and System of Sign. Kajima Institute Publishing, Tokyo (2013)
2. Centre for Excellence in Universal Design: Building for everyone: a universal design approach, Internal environment and services, Booklet 4, Dublin, 30 May 2018
3. Alt, F., Schneegaß, S., Schmidt, A., Müller, J., Memarovic, N.: How to evaluate public displays. In: Proceedings of the 2012 International Symposium on Pervasive Displays, Article 17 (2012)
4. Müller, J., et al.: Display blindness: the effect of expectations on attention towards digital signage. In: Tokuda, H., Beigl, M., Friday, A., Brush, A.J.B., Tobe, Y. (eds.) Pervasive 2009. LNCS, vol. 5538, pp. 1–8. Springer, Heidelberg (2009). https://doi.org/10.1007/978-3-642-01516-8_1
5. Huang, Elaine M., Koster, A., Borchers, J.: Overcoming assumptions and uncovering practices: when does the public really look at public displays? In: Indulska, J., Patterson, Donald J., Rodden, T., Ott, M. (eds.) Pervasive 2008. LNCS, vol. 5013, pp. 228–243. Springer, Heidelberg (2008). https://doi.org/10.1007/978-3-540-79576-6_14
6. Müller, J., Exeler, J., Buzeck, M., Krüger, A.: ReflectiveSigns: digital signs that adapt to audience attention. In: Tokuda, H., Beigl, M., Friday, A., Brush, A.J.B., Tobe, Y. (eds.) Pervasive 2009. LNCS, vol. 5538, pp. 17–24. Springer, Heidelberg (2009). https://doi.org/10.1007/978-3-642-01516-8_3
7. Kaneda, T.: Pedestrian Agent Simulation Start With ArtiSoc. Kozo Keikaku Engineering Inc., Tokyo (2010)
8. Helmut, S.F., Martin, S., Georg, R., Johann, S., Volker, S.: Using cognitive agent-based simulation for the evaluation of indoor wayfinding systems. In: Proceedings of the 13th International Conference on Design & Decision Support Systems in Architecture and Urban Planning (2016)
9. Kielar, P.M., Borrmann, A.: Modeling pedestrians' interest in locations: a concept to improve simulations of pedestrian destination choice. Simul. Model. Pract. Theory **61**, 47–62 (2016)
10. Foundation for Promoting Personal Mobility and Ecological Transportation: Public transport Passenger Facility Sign System Guidebook, Taisei-Shuppan Co., Ltd., Tokyo (2002)
11. Ohori, K., Yamane, S., Anai, H., Utsumi, S., Takahashi, S.: An agent-based analysis of the effectiveness of signage system in a large-scale facility. In: Social Simulation Conference (2016)
12. Shimada, E., Yamane, S., Ohori, K., Yamada, H., Takahashi, S.: Evaluation of signage system in large public facility using agent's view. In: International Workshop: Artificial Intelligence of and for Business (2017)

Improving Route Traffic Estimation by Considering Staying Population

Hitoshi Shimizu[1]([⊠]), Tatsushi Matsubayashi[2], Yusuke Tanaka[2],
Tomoharu Iwata[1], Naonori Ueda[1], and Hiroshi Sawada[1,2]

[1] NTT Communication Science Laboratories, Kyoto, Japan
{shimizu.hitoshi,iwata.tomoharu,ueda.naonori,sawada.hiroshi}@lab.ntt.co.jp
[2] NTT Service Evolution Laboratories, Kanagawa, Japan
{matsubayashi.tatsushi,t.yusuke}@lab.ntt.co.jp

Abstract. Estimating the number of people who travel by a particular route (route traffic) is an important task for multi-agent simulations in the transportation field. Previous studies have used the traffic count to estimate the route traffic. We propose a new method that utilizes the staying population (stay count) in addition to the traffic count. With experiments using synthetic data, we demonstrate that the proposed method achieves a 19.85% smaller error rate than the conventional method when the traffic count's observation is incomplete. In addition, we analyze real-world data.

Keywords: Traffic estimation · Crowd simulator
Crowd measurement

1 Introduction

Multi-agent simulations have been widely used for studying traffic congestion and crowd security. For example, Helbing et al. simulated panic situations to understand human behavior during evacuations in crowd disasters [3]. As another example, Yamashita et al. used a crowd simulator to make a pedestrian guidance plan for a fireworks festival [9].

The results of a simulation depend heavily on its parameters. Determining such parameters as time, origins, and destinations of agent movements has a critical influence on whether the road will become congested. After estimating the number of people who are traveling by a particular *route* (route traffic), it can be used as the parameters of crowd simulations. So we estimate the route traffic from observations.

To estimate the route traffic, previous studies (e.g., [8]) used the observation values of the number of people who are passing through a particular *directed border* (traffic count). In this research, we propose a method that estimates the route traffic using both the number of people who stay at a particular *area* (stay count) and the traffic count. The traffic count can be measured by video recordings [6], IC cards at the ticket gates of stations, or infrared sensor data

© Springer Nature Switzerland AG 2018
T. Miller et al. (Eds.): PRIMA 2018, LNAI 11224, pp. 630–637, 2018.
https://doi.org/10.1007/978-3-030-03098-8_50

at the entrance of shops. On the other hand, the stay count can be measured by fixed-point cameras or by the operational data of mobile phones [7]. Since the traffic count might be more difficult to obtain in some places, our method is effective because it can handle multimodal data. Our proposed method uses the relationship between the route traffic and the stay count at the origin and destination areas of the route and estimates the route traffic that matches both the observed traffic and stay counts. Since solution constraints are added, the estimation accuracy is expected to improve.

2   Preliminaries

Road Network and Route. We represent a road network with *areas* and *directed borders*. Two adjacent areas share one border. The m-th area is denoted as v_m with $m \in \{1, \cdots , M\}$, and the ℓ-th directed border is denoted as e_ℓ with $\ell \in \{1, \cdots , L\}$. Note that one border has two directions for each side of the areas. Consider N people who move from one area to another. Let the number of people who passed directed border e_ℓ during the time period between $t - 1$ and t be $X_{t,\ell}$ (traffic count) with $t \in \{1, \cdots , T\}$, and let the number of people who are staying at area v_m at time t be $S_{t,m}$ (stay count) with $t \in \{0, \cdots , T\}$. The road network we used in this paper is illustrated in Fig. 1.

Let the i-th route be r_i with $i \in \{1, \cdots , I\}$. The k-th element of r_i is represented as area $r_i(k)$, where $k \in \{1, \cdots , K_i\}$. Then let the n-th person's trajectory be f_n with $n \in \{1, \cdots , N\}$. The t-th element of f_n is represented as route $f_n(t)$ by which she moves during the time period between $t - 1$ and t. Because moving takes time, the desired trajectory may be divided into many routes of multiple time periods. If she does not move by any route, $f_n(t) = \emptyset$. Finally, let the number of people whose trajectory $f_n(t) = r_i$ be route traffic $Y_{t,i}$. In this research, we estimate route traffic $\{Y_{t,i}\}_{t,i}$ with $t \in \{1, \cdots , T\}$, given $\{X_{t,\ell}\}_{t,\ell}$ and $\{S_{t,m}\}_{t,m}$.

Relationship Between Traffic and Stay Counts. Traffic count $X_{t,\ell}$ is observed for a specific time period, and stay count $S_{t,m}$ is observed at a specific time. For a correspondence between both observations, we use the change in stay count $D_{t,m} = S_{t,m} - S_{t-1,m}$. If we can observe the traffic count through all the directed borders connected to area v_m, the stay count will be identical as the difference between *the number of people who flow into the area* and *the number of people who flow out of it*. Since no information is added based on observations of the stay count, the estimation accuracy will not improve. Therefore, we improve the accuracy using the stay count under a situation where observation of the traffic count is incomplete. The relationship between these variables is illustrated in Fig. 2.

3   Conventional Method

In the communication field, a method has been developed for route traffic estimation [10,11], which approximates the amount of communication between every

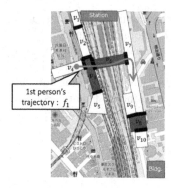

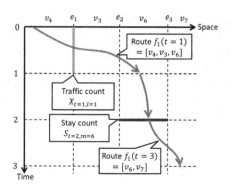

Fig. 1. Pedestrian road network: white and green squares represent areas. Green squares indicate areas where we observed the stay count. Red bars indicate directed borders where we observed the traffic count. An arrow indicates an example of a person's trajectory. The map [5] shows positions of the road network. "Station" denotes JR Shinjuku Station, and "Bldg." is the NTT Docomo Yoyogi Building. Projection mapping was performed on this building, and people viewed it from areas v_3, v_6, and v_8. (Color figure online)

Fig. 2. Example of a person's movement in a spatiotemporal graph. Vertical axis represents time and horizontal axis represents space. Arrows indicate elements of a person's trajectory shown in Fig. 1. Traffic count equals number of trajectories that cross the corresponding directed border (red line). Stay count equals number of trajectories that cross the corresponding area (green line). (Color figure online)

pair of nodes from the link traffic. Below we explain the conventional method based on a work [8] that applied this technology to the transportation field.

In each time period, the traffic count of one directed border is the sum of the route traffic that is passing through it. That is, using route $r_i (i : e_\ell \in r_i)$ that passes through directed border e_ℓ, the following is satisfied:

$$X_{t,\ell} \simeq \sum_{i:e_\ell \in r_i} Y_{t,i}. \tag{1}$$

We introduce integer matrix $A \in \mathbb{Z}^{L \times I}$ and describe the relationship of X and Y as $X \simeq AY$, where $A_{\ell,i} = 1$ if $e_\ell \in r_i$ and $A_{\ell,i} = 0$ otherwise. A is a routing matrix [10]. To estimate route traffic Y, we minimize the following objective function (2) to satisfy Eq. (1) as much as possible when traffic count X is given in each time period:

$$\sum_{\ell=1}^{L} \left| \sum_{i=1}^{I} A_{\ell,i} Y_{t,i} - X_{t,\ell} \right|^2 + \lambda_1 \left| \sum_{i=1}^{I} Y_{t,i} \right|^2. \tag{2}$$

The second term, which is added to reduce the number of people who are present, excludes trivial solutions where all people move only on a short route from immediately before each observed directed border to immediately afterwards. By adding this term, we can obtain a stable solution.

4   Proposed Method

In this research, we extend the conventional method to use the stay count observations. Stay count $S_{t,m}$ increases or decreases by the difference between the number of people arriving at v_m and departing from v_m. But if v_m appears in the middle (not at the origin or the destination) of route r_i, it does not affect the stay count because it flows into and out of the area. Therefore, with route r_i that contains v_m at the origin or the destination, the following is satisfied:

$$D_{t,m} \simeq \sum_{i:v_m=r_i(K_i)} Y_{t,i} - \sum_{i:v_m=r_i(1)} Y_{t,i}. \tag{3}$$

We next introduce integer matrix $B \in \mathbb{Z}^{M \times I}$ and describe the relationship of D and Y as $D \simeq BY$, where $B_{m,i} = 1$ if $r_{K_i} = v_m$, $B_{m,i} = -1$ if $r_1 = v_m$ and $B_{m,i} = 0$ otherwise. B is a staying matrix. When traffic count X and the change of stay count D are given in each time period, we need a solution that satisfies both Eqs. (1) and (3) as much as possible. For that purpose, we estimate route traffic Y by minimizing the following objective function (4) instead of (2):

$$\sum_{\ell=1}^{L} \left| \sum_{i=1}^{I} A_{\ell,i} Y_{t,i} - X_{t,\ell} \right|^2 + \lambda_1 \left| \sum_{i=1}^{I} Y_{t,i} \right|^2 + \lambda_2 \sum_{m=1}^{M} \left| \sum_{i=1}^{I} B_{m,i} Y_{t,i} - D_{t,m} \right|^2 . \tag{4}$$

We set hyperparameters $\lambda_1 = 10^{-2}, \lambda_2 = 10^3$, which minimized the observation errors in preliminary experiments.

5   Experiments

Road Networks. We evaluated our proposed method using data on the "YOYOGI CANDLE 2020" event, which was held at Shinjuku Station. We measured the traffic and stay counts on a road network around the event venue where thousands of pedestrians gathered. The road network consisted of 10 areas and 18 directed borders (Fig. 1), and the traffic counts were observed at all the directed borders. We enumerated the routes between every pair of areas. Because route r_i has no cycle and is uniquely determined by the origin and destination areas, $Y_{t,i}$ corresponds to the origin-destination (OD) traffic volume. In this setting, $L = 18, M = 3, I = 90$.

Synthetic Traffic Data. Since we did not observe the route traffic at this event, we generated synthetic data to validate the proposed method. The number of time periods T was 42, and 500 people moved in each time period. The selection probability of the origin and the destination followed multinomial distributions. Both multinomial distributions were generated based on a Dirichlet distribution with $\alpha = 0.8$. The people's origin and destination to be generated were determined based on the selection probability. But when the origin and destination areas were identical, the origin and destination selections were redone. After we generated route traffic Y in the above procedure, traffic count X and the change in stay count D were calculated by formulas (1) and (3). We created 100 data sets with different random seeds.

Real-World Data. We measured the traffic count of all the directed borders on the road network at one-minute intervals. We also measured the stay count of the three areas (the event's watching area) at five-minute intervals. Both counts were observed by human eyes and hands from 18:00 to 21:30 on November 29, 2017. To align the intervals of the traffic and stay counts, we aggregated the traffic count at five-minute intervals. In this setting, $T = 42$.

Results of Synthetic Traffic Data. We evaluated the estimation accuracy of the route traffic by synthetic data and used the Normalized Absolute Error (NAE) as an evaluation index: $\mathrm{NAE}_Y = \frac{\sum_t \sum_i |\hat{Y}_{t,i} - Y_{t,i}|}{\sum_t \sum_i |Y_{t,i}|}$, where $\hat{Y}_{t,i}$ is an estimated value for $Y_{t,i}$. We changed the number of observed directed borders of the traffic count from 1 to 18 and randomly selected directed borders that were observed for it. The number of stay count observations was three, and the observed areas were identical as the real-world data. Figure 3 shows NAE_Y in this experiment. When all 18 directed borders were observed, both methods had similar error rates. On the other hand, when one or more traffic count observations were missing, our proposed method's error rate was 19.85%

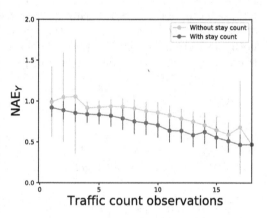

Fig. 3. Relationship between observation of traffic count and estimation error. Horizontal axis is number of directed borders to be observed for traffic count. Vertical axis shows error NAE_Y. Blue and green show conventional and proposed methods. Mean value was plotted for 100 data sets. Error bars indicate standard deviation. (Color figure online)

smaller on average than the conventional method. When the traffic count's observation is incomplete, the estimation accuracy of the route traffic was improved by solving it to match the stay count's observation. However, even when the traffic count's observation was perfect, the error was about 0.5, which doesn't seem sufficiently small. Such error is inevitable because the problem setting is ill-posed and the number of constraints is less than the number of unknown

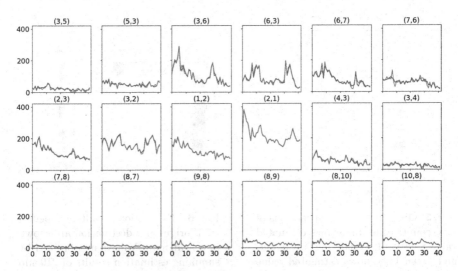

Fig. 4. Observation and estimations of traffic count: Blue line shows estimated value $\hat{X}$ without considering stay count, and green line shows estimated value $\hat{X}$ considering stay count. Observed value X almost completely matches estimated value without stay count. Above each figure, pairs of area IDs indicate the observed directed borders. (Color figure online)

Table 1. Estimation error of real-world data. NAE_X is error of traffic count. NAE_D is error of stay count.

Method	NAE_X	NAE_D	$\mathrm{NAE}_X + \mathrm{NAE}_D$
Conventional method	0.013	0.550	0.563
Proposed method	0.066	0.000	0.066

variables. If we added constraint conditions by observing the number of departing or arriving people at any area, we could further reduce the error.

Results of Real-World Data. We applied the proposed method to real-world data to obtain route traffic $\hat{Y}$. We calculated the traffic count ($\hat{X} = A\hat{Y}$), the change of the stay count ($\hat{D} = B\hat{Y}$), and stay count $\hat{S}_{t,m} = S_{0,m} + \sum_{t'=1}^{t} \hat{D}_{t',m}$. As a result, we confirmed that the estimation is almost consistent with the observations (Figs. 4 and 5). On the other hand, in the conventional method, although the estimation result agrees with the traffic count's observation, it is inconsistent with the stay count's observation. We defined NAE_X and NAE_D in a similar way as NAE_Y: $\mathrm{NAE}_X = \frac{\sum_t \sum_\ell |\hat{X}_{t,\ell} - X_{t,\ell}|}{\sum_t \sum_\ell |X_{t,\ell}|}$, $\mathrm{NAE}_D = \frac{\sum_t \sum_m |\hat{D}_{t,m} - D_{t,m}|}{\sum_t \sum_m |D_{t,m}|}$. By using $\mathrm{NAE}_X + \mathrm{NAE}_D$ as an evaluation measure based on observations, we confirmed that our proposed method is much more accurate than the conventional method (Table 1).

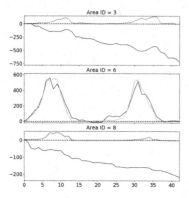

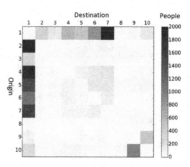

Fig. 5. Observation and estimations of stay count: Blue line shows estimated value $\hat{S}$ without considering stay count, and green line shows estimated value $\hat{S}$ considering stay count. Observed value S (red line) almost completely matches stay count estimation. Above each figure, area IDs indicate observed areas. (Color figure online)

Fig. 6. Estimation results of pedestrian origin and destination are shown in a heat map. Values are obtained by summing estimation results of 210 min for each route.

Figure 6 shows the result of aggregating the route traffic estimated by the proposed method at the origins and destinations. More than 30% of the pedestrians started at areas v_1 or v_7, and over 60% headed to areas v_1 or v_7. Since these areas are near Shinjuku Station where many station users were observed, we obtained a reasonable result that is consistent with our intuition.

6   Related Work

Since traffic simulators often need OD matrices as inputs, various techniques for OD estimation have been developed. For example, Abe et al. developed a technique to estimate the OD matrix using a simulator as an internal model [1]. However, since this method needs to repeatedly execute the simulator, it requires high computational cost. Another approach for OD matrix estimation is the four step model [4], which utilizes population distribution. But population distribution is not very accurate because it is derived from periodic censuses. Therefore this model is not suitable for traffic simulation with short-term fluctuations. Calabrese et al. developed a method of observing the stay count from mobile phone data and estimating traffic volume [2]. Although their method estimates the dynamic OD traffic volume, our method also simultaneously estimates the route traffic.

7   Conclusion

We addressed the problem of estimating route traffic from traffic and stay counts. With an experiment that used synthetic data, we improved the estimation accuracy utilizing the stay count with a staying matrix when the traffic count's observation is incomplete. In addition, we analyzed the human flows by estimating the route traffic from real-world data during a popular event. Although our data were observed by human eyes, the proposed method can be applied to data measured by camera. A future task will execute a crowd simulator using the estimated route traffic as input to reproduce the real world.

Acknowledgements. The authors thank Satoshi Oda and Yoshiyuki Okada of NTT Docomo, INC. for their cooperation with the measurement of the traffic and stay counts at the "YOYOGI CANDLE 2020" event.

References

1. Abe, K., Fujii, H., Yoshimura, S.: Inverse analysis of origin-destination matrix for microscopic traffic simulator. Comput. Model. Eng. Sci. **113**(1), 68–85 (2017)
2. Calabrese, F., Di Lorenzo, G., Liu, L., Ratti, C.: Estimating origin-destination flows using opportunistically collected mobile phone location data from one million users in Boston metropolitan area. IEEE Pervasive Comput. **10**(4), 36–44 (2011)
3. Helbing, D., Farkas, I.J., Molnar, P., Vicsek, T.: Simulation of pedestrian crowds in normal and evacuation situations. Pedestr. Evacuation Dyn. **21**(2), 21–58 (2002)
4. McNally, M.G.: The four-step model. In: Handbook of Transport Modelling, 2nd edn, pp. 35–53. Emerald Group Publishing Limited (2007)
5. OSM: Openstreetmap. https://openstreetmap.jp/
6. Savrasovs, M., Pticina, I.: Methodology of OD matrix estimation based on video recordings and traffic counts. Procedia Eng. **178**, 289–297 (2017). RelStat-2016: Proceedings of the 16th International Scientific Conference Reliability and Statistics in Transportation and Communication, Transport and Telecommunication Institute, Riga, Latvia, 19–22 October 2016
7. Sekimoto, Y., Shibasaki, R., Kanasugi, H., Usui, T., Shimazaki, Y.: PFlow: Reconstructing people flow recycling large-scale social survey data. IEEE Pervasive Comput. **10**(4), 27–35 (2011)
8. Shimizu, H., Otsuka, T., Iwata, T., Sawada, H., Ueda, N.: Estimation of agent parameters in crowd simulation. In: The 20th Information-Based Induction Sciences Workshop (IBIS), pp. d2–50 (2017). (in Japanese)
9. Yamashita, T., Okada, T., Noda, I.: Implementation of simulation environment for exhaustive analysis of huge-scale pedestrian flow. SICE J. Control. Meas. Syst. Integr. **6**(2), 137–146 (2013)
10. Zhang, Y., Roughan, M., Duffield, N., Greenberg, A.: Fast accurate computation of large-scale IP traffic matrices from link loads. In: ACM SIGMETRICS Performance Evaluation Review. vol. 31, pp. 206–217. ACM (2003)
11. Zhang, Y., Roughan, M., Lund, C., Donoho, D.: An information-theoretic approach to traffic matrix estimation. In: Proceedings of the 2003 Conference on Applications, Technologies, Architectures, and Protocols for Computer Communications, SIGCOMM 2003, pp. 301–312. ACM, New York (2003)

Proposal of Detour Path Suppression Method in PS Reinforcement Learning and Its Application to Altruistic Multi-agent Environment

Daisuke Shiraishi[1], Kazuteru Miyazaki[2(✉)], and Hiroaki Kobayashi[1]

[1] Meiji University, 1-1-1 HigashiMita, Tama, Kawasaki, Kanagawa 214-8571, Japan
{ce172038,kobayasi}@meiji.ac.jp
[2] National Institution for Academic Degrees and Quality Enhancement of Higher Education, 1-29-1 Gakuen-nishimachi, Kodaira, Tokyo 187-8587, Japan
teru@niad.ac.jp

Abstract. Profit Sharing is well known as a kind of reinforcement learning. In PS method, a reward is generally distributed with a geometrically decreasing function, and the common ratio of the function is called a discount rate. A large discount rate increases the learning speed, but a non-optimal policy may be learned. On the other hand, a small discount rate improves the performance of the policy, but the learning may not proceed smoothly due to the shallow learning depth. In this paper, in order to cope with these problems, we propose a method that reinforces detour paths and a non-detour path with different discount rates, respectively. Finally, this method is applied to an altruistic multi-agent environment to confirm its effectiveness.

Keywords: Reinforcement learning · Profit sharing · Detour path

1 Introduction

Reinforcement learning (RL) is a method for the robot to adapt to the environment. RL is a type of machine learning that adapts to the environment through trial and error searches. RL is a method to acquire an appropriate policy with a reward. Q-Learning (QL), Sarsa and Profit Sharing (PS) [3] are representative RL methods. QL can acquire the optimal policy in Markov decision processes (MDPs), but it cannot in non-Markovian environment. On the other hand, PS is one of exploitation-oriented learning methods and aims to learn not an optimal but a rational policy by strongly enhancing their experience. PS has some rationality even in a kind of non-Markovian environment [3].

In PS method, generally, the learning process progresses by distributing rewards using a geometrically decreasing function. The common ratio of this function is called a discount rate. A large discount rate increase learning speed but unsuitable rules may be learned. On the other hand, a small discount rate

© Springer Nature Switzerland AG 2018
T. Miller et al. (Eds.): PRIMA 2018, LNAI 11224, pp. 638–645, 2018.
https://doi.org/10.1007/978-3-030-03098-8_51

does not cause the above problem, but often decreases the learning speed because distributed rewards decrease too rapidly so that the learning does not progress in a long episode.

In this paper, in order to solve the problem, a new reward distribution method is proposed. In this method, first, we judge whether there are any detour paths in the episode or not, and then we distribute the reward to detour paths and the non-detour path, separately, to suppress the reinforcement of detour paths and prioritize the reinforcement of the non-detour path.

2 Reinforcement Learning

2.1 Environment in Reinforcement Learning

Let's consider an agent in an unknown environment. After perceiving sensory input from the environment, the agent selects and executes an action. Time is discretized by one input-action cycle called *a step*. The agent perceives the state input s_t from the environment as the observation o_t at the time t. If there is no restriction on the observability of the agent, i.e., $s_t = o_t$, the environment is called *a complete perception environment*. On the other hand, if there is some restriction, i.e., $s_t \neq o_t$, the environment is called *an incomplete perception environment*. In this paper, we assume that the environment is a complete perception environment.

The agent decides the action a_t based on the state s_t and the evaluation value (defined later). The pair of a state s_t and an action a_t selected in the state is called *a rule* and described as $rule(s_t, a_t)$, or simply (s_t, a_t). The agent changes the state s_t to the next state s_{t+1} by applying the rule. If the agent receives a (positive or negative) reward r_t at the state s_{t+1}, then the evaluation value is updated with the reward. If the probability of the state transition in the environment depends only on the state and the action, this state transition has Markov property and the process is called *a Markov Decision Processes* (MDP). A function that maps states to actions is called *a policy*. If the reward acquisition expectation value of a policy is positive, the policy is called *a rational policy*. *The optimal policy* is a policy that can maximize the amount of rewards. Reinforcement learning aims to acquire a policy that gives the maximum rewards with the least actions.

A series of rules that begins from a reward state or an initial state and ends with the next reward state is called *an episode*. If an episode contains rules of the same state but paired with different actions, the partial series from the state to the next is called *a detour path* and a rule in a detour path is called *a detour rule*. A rule always existing in a detour path is called *an ineffective rule*, and otherwise called *an effective rule*. Note that a detour rule is not always an ineffective rule, but an ineffective rule is always a detour rule.

2.2 Rationality Theorem [3] and Extended Rationality Theorem [4]

PS learns a rational policy by propagating a reward backward in an episode when a reward is given. Assume that a reward R is given at time $N + 1$ and the corresponding episode is $\{(s_1, a_1), (s_2, a_2), \cdots, (s_t, a_t), \cdots, (s_N, a_N)\}$, then the amount of rewards (the evaluation value) of the rule (s_t, a_t), $Q(s_t, a_t)$, is updated as follows:

$$Q(s_t, a_t) \leftarrow Q(s_t, a_t) + f(N - t), \quad t = N, N - 1, ..., 0. \tag{1}$$

The function $f(\cdot)$ is known as *a reinforcement function*. In this paper, we use a geometrically decreasing function:

$$f(i) = \lambda^i R, \tag{2}$$

where λ $(0 < \lambda < 1)$ is *the discount rate*.

In the case where there are ineffective and effective rules in the same state, the ineffective rules should be suppressed and the effective rules should be preferentially enhanced. The rationality theorem [3] gives a sufficient condition for a reinforcement function to suppress reinforcement of ineffective rules. One example of such functions is a geometrically decreasing function

$$f(i) = \lambda f(i - 1), \quad (\forall i = 1, 2, ..., W), \tag{3}$$

where $\lambda \leq 1/(L+1)$, W is the maximum episode length, and L is the maximum number of rules available in each state minus 1. The Eq. (2) is the simplest and representative geometrically decreasing function.

The extended rationality theorem [4] suppresses detour rules. Note that detour rules can be judged from one episode and if we suppress detour rules, the ineffective rule suppression will be performed efficiently, because ineffective rules are contained in detour rules. An example of functions satisfying the extended rationality theorem is given as follows:

$$\begin{cases} f(i) = \lambda f(i - 1), & \text{if the rule is a detour rule,} \\ f(i) \leq f(i - 1), & \text{if the rule is not a detour rule,} \end{cases} \quad \forall i = 1, 2, ..., W. \tag{4}$$

3   Proposal of Detour Paths Suppression Method

3.1   Detour Path Suppression Method (DPSM)

In this paper, we suppress detour rules similarly to the extended rationality theorem. But we separate detour rules from the non-detour rules in an episode explicitly. We show an example of reward distribution in Fig. 1.

We classify rules in the episode (the fist law of Fig. 1) into detour rules (the third law) and other rules (the second law) before reward distribution. The latter rules contain no detour rule, therefore, no ineffective rule. Hence, an arbitrary no-monotonically-increasing function can be used as the reinforcement function. Here, the discount rate of this function is called *a non-detour discount rate* and expressed as λ_0. For example, the reward R is distributed to non-detour rules $\{S1, S2, S3, S4, S5\}$ with the discount rate λ_0. In principle, λ_0 is required to be $0 < \lambda_0 \leq 1$, but it is desirable to take a value near to one in order to increase the learning horizon.

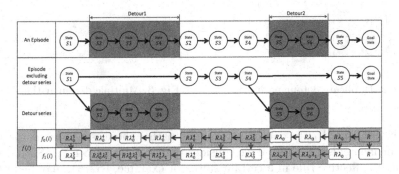

Fig. 1. Proposed method

For detour rules, the reward allotted to the rule immediately after the detour path is distributed to the rules in the detour path using a reinforcement function that satisfies the rationality theorem. The discount rate of this function will be called *a detour discount rate* and represented by λ_1. For example, for the detour rules $\{S2, S3, S4\}$, the rule immediately after the detour path is $S2$ and the allotted reward $\lambda_0^4 R$ is distributed to the rules $\{S2, S3, S4\}$ with the discount rate λ_1. Distributing rewards with this method, we can suppress the reward given to the detour paths and acquire a rational policy preferentially.

3.2 Detour Paths Discrimination Procedure (DPDP)

To apply the above method, first of all, we have to find out detour paths in an episode. Here, we describe a method to discriminant detour paths in an episode. From the definition of the detour path, a detour rule in an episode can be discriminated by the following algorithm:

1. $i = 1, j = N, d(k) = 0, (k = 1, 2, ..., N)$, where N is the episode length.
2. if $s_i = s_j$ and $a_i \neq a_j$ then go to 4.
3. $j-=1$. if $j > i$ then to 2 else then go to 5.
4. $d(k) = 1(k = i, i+1, ..., j-1)$.
5. $i+=1, j = N$. if $i > W$ then go to 2, else end loop.

This algorithm can discriminate whether the i th rule is in the detour path or not. If $d(i) = 1$, the ith rule is a detour rule, and if $d(i) = 0$, it is a non-detour rule. However, this algorithm cannot work when there are multiple detour paths and they overlap one another. We consider the problem in the next section.

Consideration of Duplicate Detour Paths. Figure 2 shows an example in which there are two detour paths $\{(S2, \gamma), (S3, \alpha), (S4, \beta)\}$ and $\{(S4, \beta), (S2, \beta)\}$ and they overlap each other. If the above detour paths discrimination algorithm is used, all the rules of both detour paths are judged as detour rules. However, if all these rules are discarded, no rule chain exists from $(S1, \alpha)$ to $(S4, \gamma)$. Note

Fig. 2. Duplicate detour paths   **Fig. 3.** Multiple detour paths

that if we discard only one of two detour paths, there is no detour path in the remained episode. First, if we consider the later path $\{(S4, \beta), (S2, \beta)\}$ as a detour, an effective rule in a certain state, for example, $(S2, \gamma)$, may be farther from the target state than a detour rule competing with it, for example, $(S2, \beta)$. Depending on the value of the discount rate, the reward value distributed to the detour rule may be larger than the reward value distributed to the effective rule. Therefore, this procedure is not suitable for learning. Next, if we consider the earlier path $\{(S2, \gamma), (S3, \alpha), (S4, \beta)\}$ as a detour, no effective rule in a certain state is farther from the target state than a detour rule competing with it and this procedure is suitable for learning. Therefore, in this paper, we discriminate only the earliest detour path among duplicate ones as a detour path.

Consideration of Multiple Detour Paths. We show an example in Fig. 3 where there are two detour path and they are multiple. Even in this case, both are a detour path by definition. Now, a detour path included in another is called as *a multiple detour path*. If a larger detour path is discriminated, a multiple detour path contained in it is also done. At first glance, this seems to be reasonable. However, in an environment with autoregressive rules it arouses a problem. A simple example of an environment with an autoregressive rule is shown in Fig. 4. In this environment, if the episode shown in Fig. 5 is given, the autoregressive rule of $S3$ will be enhances very strongly, because rewards will be added to the rule many times repeatedly. Note that consecutive selection of an autoregressive rule forms a multiple detour path. It is highly probable that the rules in the multiple detour path are rules that do not contribute to reward acquisition. Therefore, the rules in multiple detour paths are not distributed any rewards.

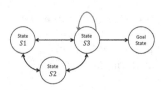

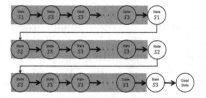

Fig. 4. Environment with recursive rule   **Fig. 5.** Rule selection

3.3   Extended Detour Paths Discrimination Procedure (E-DPDP)

Thus, in this paper we use the following algorithm as the detour path discrimination method. The difference from the above algorithm is discrimination of detour paths in a episode with duplicate and/or multiple detour paths.

1. $i = 1, j = N, d(k) = 0$ $(k = 1, 2, ..., N)$, where N is the episode length.
2. if $d(i) > 1$ then go to 6.
3. if $s_i = s_j$ and $a_i \neq a_j$ then go to 5.
4. $j- = 1$.if $j > i$ then to 3,else then go to 6.
5. $d(k)+ = 1(k = i, i + 1, ..., j - 1)$.
   (a) $l = i, m = j - 1, N' = j - 1$.
   (b) if $s_l = s_m$ and $a_l \neq a_m$ then go to (d).
   (c) $m- = 1$.if $m > l$ then to (b),else then go to (e).
   (d) $d(n)+ = 1(n = l, l + 1, ..., m - 1)$.
   (e) $l+ = 1, m = N'$.if $l < N'$ then to (b),else then go to 6.
6. $i+ = 1, j = N$.if $i < N$ then 3 else end loop.

This algorithm allows to determine if the i th rule is in the detour path or not. That is, the i th rule is a non-detour rule if $d(i) = 0$, a detour rule if $d(i) = 1$, and the multiple detour rule if $d(i) \geq 2$, respectively. We do not distribute any rewards to multiple detour rules.

4   Evaluation of DPSM Under Altruistic Multi-agent Environment

4.1   Setting

We use the environment used in the paper [2] to verify the effectiveness of DPSM under multi-agent environment. The agents aim to obtain rewards as uniformly as possible in the environment where more than one agent performs learning at the same time. DPSM is compared with the proposed method in the paper [2] by using the environment as shown in Fig. 6. Figure 6 are corresponds to the case of three agents in environments, respectively. Each agent is located in one of the squares, and can perceive vertically and horizontally neighboring squares on the agent. Thick line is a wall that prevents the perception of the square of the other side of the wall. As a result, an agent at hatched squares perceives the same input. The perception is one of {there is nothing, there are other agents, there is a wall} on each square. The agent cannot distinguish each agent form others. Each agent $(i = 1, 2, 3)$ is located in S_i at the time of starting the learning. The agent selects an action from {up, down, left, right} movement after obtaining the sensory input. Transition to the wall is not allowed, and the agent remains in the original square. Multiple agents can occupy the same square. Each agent $(i = 1, 2, 3)$ aims to move to the target state G_i, respectively. If an agent i transits to the target state G_i, a reward is given to all agents and the agent is returned to the square of the initial position S_i. As an action selection method, we use the ϵ-roulette strategy where the upper limit of the number of action selection times is decided.

Table 1. Results on 3 agents.

		$R = 10^2$	$R = 10^3$	$R = 10^4$	$R = 10^5$	$R = 10^6$
Paper [2]	A1	1074.8 (190.2)	1007.4 (222.7)	1007.4 (222.7)	2462.5 (790.7)	2722.8 (802.8)
	A2	174.3 (78.4)	709.5 (369.4)	709.5 (369.4)	2440.8 (835.2)	2714.4 (820.7)
	A3	182.8 (80.8)	709.5 (368.9)	709.5 (368.9)	2440.5 (835.2)	2714.1 (820.6)
$\lambda_0 = 0.3$	A1	923.5 (143.9)	934.5 (295.9)	1058.0 (439.1)	1045.2 (453.1)	1105.4 (486.6)
	A2	286.6 (122.7)	811.3 (390.8)	980.1 (509.4)	943.5 (536.5)	1041.8 (539.8)
	A3	287.9 (122.7)	811.1 (390.8)	980.0 (509.4)	943.3 (536.4)	1041.7 (539.8)
$\lambda_0 = 0.5$	A1	1076.6 (299.8)	1554.8 (404.1)	1605.2 (387.8)	1591.1 (375.4)	1659.9 (384.9)
	A2	1067.8 (308.6)	1554.2 (404.1)	1604.5 (375.4)	1590.4 (384.9)	1659.3 (384.9)
	A3	1067.6 (308.6)	1553.9 (404.1)	1604.3 (387.9)	1590.2 (375.5)	1659.0 (384.8)
$\lambda_0 = 0.7$	A1	1555.5 (162.7)	1676.5 (149.4)	1714.8 (161.0)	1751.0 (195.3)	1739.7 (183.4)
	A2	1554.9 (162.7)	1676.0 (149.5)	1714.2 (161.0)	1750.4 (195.3)	1739.1 (183.4)
	A3	1554.6 (162.7)	1675.7 (149.4)	1714.0 (160.9)	1750.2 (195.3)	1738.9 (183.4)
$\lambda_0 = 0.9$	A1	1222.5 (51.8)	1232.4 (61.1)	1244.6 (54.7)	1248.1 (65.5)	1232.9 (62.0)
	A2	1222.1 (51.8)	1231.9 (61.1)	1244.1 (54.8)	1247.6 (65.6)	1232.4 (62.0)
	A3	1221.8 (51.7)	1231.6 (61.1)	1243.8 (54.7)	1247.3 (65.5)	1232.1 (62.1)

The upper limit of the number of times is 100,000 in this paper. After ϵ values was calculated by $\epsilon = 1.0 - \frac{The\ number\ of\ selected\ action}{50000.0}$, generating a random number between 0.0 to 1.0. If the value of ϵ is zero or less, we set $\epsilon = 0.0$. If the value of ϵ is larger than the random number, we use roulette selection using evaluation values,

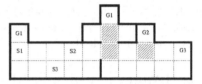

Fig. 6. Three agents environment

otherwise, we use random selection for the action selection. For this ϵ, ratio of roulette selection and random selection will reverse after 50,000 actions. If there is only one agent in Fig. 6, the perceptual aliasing problem [1] will be occurred since an agent at the hatched squares perceives the same sensory input. On the other hand, in a multi-agent learning, it may be possible to reduce the perceptual aliasing problem if the other agent moves properly. Such the behavior is likely to be derived by *an indirect reward*, and the method using an indirect reward has been proposed in the paper [2]. In this paper, we evaluate the performance of DPSM for this method.

4.2 Results and Discussion

The results of the method proposed in the paper [2] are shown in the first row of Table 1 for the reward value R from 10^2 to 10^6. The results of the case of three agents is shown in Table 1. The experiment was carried out 100 times by changing random seeds. These tables show the average value of the reward acquisition number of times and the standard deviation (in parentheses).

It can be seen that the performance of the paper [2] is greatly different depending on the reward value R. The method of the paper [2] uses PS as a basic learning method. When the reward value is low, learning at the start point of the episode does not progress easily, in general, since the reward is distributed by a discount rate of $\frac{1}{4}$. Then, we think that the desired behavior could not be obtained with a low reward value. Therefore, an experiment was conducted in which PS in the method of the paper [2] was changed to DPSM. In DPSM, the performance may change depending on the value of non-detour discount rate (λ_0). Therefore, an experiment was conducted in which λ_0 was varied from 0.3 to 0.9 in increments of 0.2, while λ_1 is kept to be $\frac{1}{4}$. Results are shown in the second and subsequent rows in the Table 1.

The method combined with DPSM, compared with the case of PS, obtains behaviors in which the reward acquisition frequency of each agent is close, and also S.D. is small, for each λ. In addition, the difference due to the reward value seen by the method of the case of PS is reduced. This is considered to be the result that the speed of learning of DPSM worked effectively in multi-agent learning. There are cases where the method of the case of PS is larger if simply looking at the reward acquisition times. Remark that we are aiming for the difference in the number of rewards acquisition times for each agent to be close, so we should not pay attention only to the magnitude of the reward acquisition times.

5   Conclusions

In this paper, in order to improve learning speed while satisfying rationality, we proposed a distribution method to suppress detour rules. In addition, we also considered detour paths in case of duplication. Furthermore, by adopting the concept of multiple detour paths, we made it a more robust discrimination method. We showed the discrimination algorithm that can discriminate detour path from one episode. In order to compare the proposed method with the conventional method, numerical experiments were conducted and effectiveness of the proposed method were shown. By using the proposed method, the learning efficiency was improved compared with the conventional method. Also we can confirm the effectiveness in an altruistic multi-agent environment. In the future, we aim to combine DPSM with deep learning. We will also apply our method to multi-agent environments such that control for a team of quadrotors, Keepaway task, and so on.

References

1. Chrisman, L.: Reinforcement learning with perceptual aliasing: the perceptual distinctions approach. In: Proceedings of the 10th National Conference on Artificial Intelligence, pp. 183–188 (1992)
2. Miyazaki, K.: A study of an indirect reward on multi-agent environments. Procedia Comput. Sci. **88**, 94–101 (2016)
3. Miyazaki, K., Yamamura, M., Kobayashi, S.: A theory of profit sharing in reinforcement learning. Trans. Jpn. Soc. Artif. Intell. **9**(4), 580–587 (1994). (in Japanese)
4. Uemura, W., Tatsumi, S.: About the reinforcement function for profit sharing. Trans. Jpn. Soc. Artif. Intell. **19**(4), 197–203 (2004). (in Japanese)

An Environment for Combinatorial Experiments in a Multi-agent Simulation for Disaster Response

Shunki Takami[1,2](✉) ⬤, Masaki Onishi[2]⬤, Kazunori Iwata[3]⬤, Nobuhiro Ito[4]⬤, Yohsuke Murase[5]⬤, and Takeshi Uchitane[6]

[1] Graduate School of Systems and Information Engineering, University of Tsukuba, Tsukuba, Japan
s-takami@aist.go.jp
[2] Artificial Intelligence Research Center, National Institute of Advanced Industrial Science and Technology (AIST), Tokyo, Japan
onishi@ni.aist.go.jp
[3] Department of Business Administration, Aichi University, Nagoya, Japan
kazunori@vega.aichi-u.ac.jp
[4] Department of Information Science, Aichi Institute of Technology, Toyota, Japan
n-ito@aitech.ac.jp
[5] RIKEN Advanced Institute for Computational Science, Kobe, Japan
yohsuke.murase@riken.jp
[6] Research Institute for Economics and Business Administration, Kobe University, Kobe, Japan
uchitane@rieb.kobe-u.ac.jp

Abstract. We present a research environment for combinatorial experiments for the RoboCupRescue Simulation, which is a platform for the study of disaster-relief strategies using multi-agent simulations. To simulate the agents in disaster-relief situations in the RoboCupRescue Simulation, it is necessary to implement a wide variety of algorithms for tasks such as such as group formation, path planning, and task allocation. Recently, we proposed a modular framework, the Agent Development Framework, that enables researchers to implement, study, and test each algorithm independently. Because the algorithms developed in this framework are mutually replaceable, it is possible to combine algorithms developed by different researchers. In this study, we further propose an experimental environment to efficiently handle the experiments of a huge number of possible combinations of the algorithms. As a demonstration, we test various combinations of the algorithms developed by the participants of RoboCup 2017 and show that there indeed exists a set of the algorithms that is superior to the original ones developed by each team.

Keywords: Experimental environment · Combinatorial experiment
Multi-agent system · RoboCupRescue Simulation

© Springer Nature Switzerland AG 2018
T. Miller et al. (Eds.): PRIMA 2018, LNAI 11224, pp. 646–654, 2018.
https://doi.org/10.1007/978-3-030-03098-8_52

1   Introduction

The annual RoboCup international robotics competition has hosted the Robo-CupRescue Simulation (RRS) project to confront large-scale natural disasters [4, 7]. In particular, the agent competition is a platform for studying disaster-rescue agents and simulations. The project's aim is to contribute to society by publishing the results for this project.

However, to solve the disaster-relief problem targeted by the RRS, it is necessary to implement a combination of multiple algorithms to solve tasks such as path planning, information sharing, and resource allocation [10]. In response to this situation, the Agent Development Framework (ADF) was proposed in recent years [11]. The ADF enables an algorithm to implement the modularity necessary for the operation of the agent by defining the basic structure of the agent program in the RRS. Researchers can easily use some modules developed by other researchers and substitute their modules for other researchers' modules. However, it is necessary to simulate all combinations to find the best one. This leads to a problem known as combinatorial explosion because the number of trials increases exponentially [3]. Therefore, it is difficult to manage the experiments manually.

In this paper, we propose an environment for combinatorial experiments with ADF modules in the RRS to promote the research of multi-agent systems. Further, actual combinatorial experiments confirm the effectiveness of the environment and show that it can contribute to future research in multi-agent simulations.

2   Research and Development in the RRS

2.1   Overview of the RRS

The RRS is a research platform that simulates disaster situations and disaster-relief activities on a computer. Figure 1 shows the activities of agents in the RRS. In the disaster-relief activities, researchers control six types of agents, namely the AmbulanceTeam, FireBrigade, and PoliceForce, as well as the headquarters of each unit. The AmbulanceTeam and AmbulanceCentre rescue other agents that cannot move by themselves. The FireBrigade and FireStation extinguish fires in buildings. The PoliceForce and PoliceOffice clear road blockages. In addition, there are other agents to simulate disaster situations, namely Civilian agents. The activities of these agents are evaluated by the city value score, which adopts a point-deduction scoring system [5].

Using the RRS, it is possible to research the application of artificial intelligence and information science to natural-disaster rescue problems. In the RRS project, five tasks are particularly advocated: Group Formation, Path Planning, Search, Multi-Task Allocation, and Communication [9]. Every year, competitions using agent programs are held for the purpose of technical exchange.

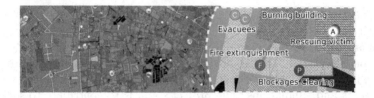

Fig. 1. (Left) part of the screen on which the simulation is running. (Right) view focusing on the activities of each disaster rescue agent.

2.2 Agent Development in the RRS

The disaster-relief problem handled by the RRS is a complex problem because the disaster conditions such as fire, building collapse, and the availability of wireless communication change from moment to moment in afflicted areas. These changes are addressed by the disaster-relief strategies of teams of disaster-relief robots, which differ according to the disaster situation. To construct a disaster-relief strategy, it is necessary to prepare all the algorithms for tasks such as route searching, information sharing, and resource allocation in the disaster environment.

The ADF was proposed to address such situations. The ADF defines the modularity necessary for the operation of an agent by defining the basic structure of the agent program in the RRS.

In the RRS project, five research tasks, Group Formation, Path Planning, Search, Multi-Task Allocation, and Communication, are proposed. In the present ADF, these tasks can be implemented separately, as shown in Fig. 2. Note that the ADF has been the standard framework of the RRS project from 2017 [13]. Therefore, the algorithms implemented by RRS researchers are interchangeable.

2.3 Experiments in the RRS

To develop and evaluate the RRS agents, it is necessary to conduct experiments on multiple disaster areas while considering various conditions such as the locations of fires, the rate at which buildings collapse, and communication situations.

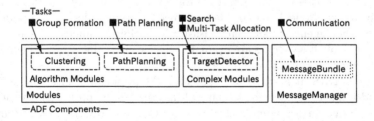

Fig. 2. ADF architecture. The upper black filled squares are the five tasks proposed by the RRS project. The lower dashed boxes are modules in the ADF. The arrows indicate relationships between the RRS tasks and ADF modules.

The parameters of an agent may also be set for each of these situations. Therefore, numerous simulations are required to obtain findings.

In the RRS, each simulation takes around 20 min to execute. Moreover, the agent calculations require sufficient memory capacity. The agent calculation processes are distributed to multiple computers and executed there.

In general, researchers have manually operated these experimental processes. The ADF enables combinatorial experiments of the algorithm modules to be easily conducted. However, the number of combinations increases exponentially with the number of modules. It is hence difficult to manage such experiments manually.

2.4   Related Work and Our Contribution

OACIS. OACIS is a simulation-execution management framework developed by the discrete-event simulation research team of the RIKEN Advanced Institute for Computational Science [8]. This software has the function of managing jobs. In particular, it has a job-management function that specializes in the execution of a simulation and a management function for experimental results. OACIS supports numerous simulations and performs analysis under various conditions by managing the experimental parameters and the results automatically.

However, complicated operations are required to execute the RRS simulations using OACIS because it is a general-purpose system for various types of simulation software. The creation of simulation scripts, agent programs, and disaster scenario files must be managed outside OACIS.

Our Contribution. In this paper, we propose an environment to manage combinatorial experiments in the RRS to support RSS research in which the ADF is used. Combinatorial experiments are an effective approach for developing and evaluating various algorithms and protocols in multi-agent systems. Our environment helps facilitate research on multi-agent systems. The environment is constructed using OACIS.

3   Design and Implementation

3.1   Design of Environment to Manage Experiments

Figure 3 shows the experimental processes of OACIS and our proposed environment, which is called RRS-OACIS in this paper. The RRS requires many manual operations, as indicated by the black dots in the figure. The operations specify various agents' parameters, control computer clusters, and collect numerous simulation results. RRS-OACIS can automate the operations shown in the shaded area in the figure. Moreover, automating the operations makes it easier to repeat experiments. The implementation of RRS-OACIS was carefully designed to ensure maintainability. RRS-OACIS does not modify the OACIS code because all control runs through application programming interfaces.

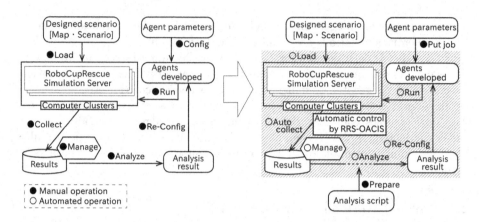

Fig. 3. OACIS and RRS-OACIS. (Left) OACIS operations before the integration of RRS-OACIS experimental management. (Right) OACIS operations after its integration.

We explain the parts that are implemented in RRS-OACIS. In other words, OACIS lacks some functionalities that RRS-OACIS provides.

- **Agent management**
  Although OACIS can manage simulators and experimental parameters, it cannot manage agent program files. RRS-OACIS provides a function to manage agent programs.
- **Map and scenario management**
  OACIS cannot deal with files related to maps and disaster scenarios. RRS-OACIS implements a function to manage these files.
- **Computer cluster management**
  In the RRS, one simulation is executed in a computer cluster consisting of many computers. Although OACIS can activate most simulations within a computer cluster, it cannot directly run the RRS. RRS-OACIS has a function that bridges the activation processes between OACIS and the RRS.
- **Simulation script**
  OACIS cannot deal with complex processes combined with multiple operations using multiple computers in a simulation. Therefore, it is necessary to prepare a script that describes a series of operations in a simulation. This script loads agent programs, map files, and scenario files. It then connects to each computer in the computer cluster and executes the simulation. The script creates an experiment as a single job in OACIS that OACIS can manage.
- **Simulator management**
  OACIS treats a simulation script and a set of parameters as a part of a simulator. In other words, the script and parameters are embedded into a simulator. Parameters differ depending on a purpose of an experiment, modules, and parameters of the algorithms. RRS-OACIS implements a mechanism that

automatically uses the appropriate scripts and parameters for the simulator according to the purpose of the simulation.

4   Combinatorial Experiment Example

4.1   Purpose of the Experiment

We present an example of combinatorial experiments to demonstrate the efficient features of our environment. In this example, the most effective combination was found through a large number of combinatorial experiments that changed many parameters such as the algorithm modules of the rescue agents. Finally, we developed rescue agents based on the result of those experiments. We evaluated their effectiveness.

4.2   Experimental Approach

The experiment was divided into three phases because there are a huge number of possible combinations for the experiments. First, we selected the target teams. All the teams of RoboCup 2017 ran on RRS-OACIS. The target teams are the top five performing teams in the experiment: MRL, Aura, RoboAKUT, LarvicSaurus, and CSU_Yunlu [1,2,6,12,14].

Second, we divided the combination patterns and select partial module combinations. The modules of each target team are used with the other modules that are necessary for experimenting with the combination pattern. In this paper, these modules are collectively called the base team. The combinations use the pattern, P_a, P_b, and P_c, as defined below.

P_a: BuildingDetector, RoadDetector, and HumanDetector;
P_b: the search module for each agent;
P_c: ActionFireFighting, ActionExtClear, ActionTransport, ActionExtMove, and the corresponding PathPlanning modules.

Finally, the best combination was selected by conducting an experiment to evaluate the top combinations for each base team that were selected in the second phase.

Only the San Francisco 3 (SF3) map in RoboCup 2017 was used because of the enormous number of combinations. All of the combination experiments were repeated three times to obtain the mean value of the scores. Therefore, the final number of simulations is 13,500. We conducted this experiment using 14 sets of clusters consisting of four computers (a total of 54 computers).

4.3   Results and Discussion

In this paper, we mention only the final combination result. Table 1 shows the result of a series of experiments; in other words, the best combination of algorithm modules. Table 2 compares the score of the designed agent with those of

Table 1. All adopted modules

Module type	Team	PathPlanning's team
BuildingDetector	LarvicSaurus	-
RoadDetector	MRL	-
HumanDetector	MRL	-
Search (FireBrigade)	CSU_Yunlu	-
Search (PoliceForce)	CSU_Yunlu	-
Search (AmbulanceTeam)	Aura	-
ActionFireFighting	LarvicSaurus	LarvicSaurus
ActionExtClear	MRL	MRL
ActionTransport	Aura	Aura
ActionExtMove	RoboAKUT	RoboAKUT

Table 2. SF3 scores of the base teams and designed agent

MRL	Aura	RoboAKUT	LarvicSaurus	CSU_Yunlu	Configured
56.83	46.90	44.42	49.46	52.47	63.51

some original agents of RoboCup2017. These results confirm that the designed agent is effective.

The experiments ran automatically and finished in nine days without any trouble. These results demonstrate that our environment is an effective approach for developing and evaluating the algorithms of multi-agent systems. To evaluate ideas for multi-agent systems, we need an evaluation framework to evaluate its effectiveness. Hence, our system is expected to contribute to the multi-agent and rescue engineering research community in this respect.

5   Conclusion

In this paper, we have proposed RRS-OACIS, that which is an environment for combinational combinatorial experiments of algorithm modules of for rescue agents in the RRS. To Its aim is to promote researches in multi-agent systems. The examples of a set of combinatorial combinational experiments have shown demonstrates the effectiveness of the environment. The proposed environment could provides an efficient simulation management system for multi-agent systems in the RRS. We Our aim is to give make the research results obtained in the RRS project back available to society by clarifying disaster-relief problems and proposing algorithms that are applicable to effective for disaster relief. Therefore, our environment can contribute to the multi-agent systems and rescue engineering research communities. We will improve the environment continuously while providing it to the RRS community.

Acknowledgment. This work was supported by JSPS KAKENHI Grant Number JP16K00310 and JP17K00317. This work was partially supported by MEXT Post-K project "Studies of multi-level spatiotemporal simulation of socioeconomic phenomena". We thank Kimberly Moravec, PhD, from Edanz Group (www.edanzediting.com/ac) for editing a draft of this manuscript.

References

1. Akın, H.L., Aşık, O.: RoboCup 2017 rescue simulation league team description RoboAKUT (Turkey) (2017). https://www.robocup2017.org/file/symposium/rescue_sim3/RCRS_2017_paper_13.pdf
2. Ardestani, P., Taherian, M., MohammadAliZadeh, P., Nikoo, E.J.: RoboCup rescue 2017- agent simulation League team description paper MRL (Iran) (2017). https://www.robocup2017.org/file/symposium/rescue_sim3/RCRS_2017_paper_7.pdf
3. Butterfield, A., Ngondi, G.E., Kerr, A.: Combinatorial explosion. In: A Dictionary of Computer Science. Oxford University Press (2016)
4. Committee, R.S.L.: RoboCuprescue simulation. http://rescuesim.robocup.org/
5. Faraji, F., Nardin, L.G., Modaresi, A., Helal, D., Iwata, K., Ito, N.: RoboCup rescue simulation league agent 2017 competition rules and setup. http://roborescue.sourceforge.net/web/2017/downloads/rules2017.pdf
6. Ghahramanpour, M., Absalan, A., Kandeh, A.: RoboCup 2017 rescue simulation league team description aura (Iran) (2017). https://www.robocup2017.org/file/symposium/rescue_sim3/RCRS_2017_paper_1.pdf
7. Kitano, H., Tadokoro, S.: RoboCup rescue: a grand challenge for multiagent and intelligent systems. AI Mag. **22**(1), 39 (2001)
8. Murase, Y., Uchitane, T., Ito, N.: A tool for parameter-space explorations. Physics Procedia **57**, 73–76 (2014). https://doi.org/10.1016/j.phpro.2014.08.134. Proceedings of the 27th Workshop on Computer Simulation Studies in Condensed Matter Physics (CSP2014)
9. Skinner, C., Ramchurn, S.: The robocup rescue simulation platform. In: Proceedings of the 9th International Conference on Autonomous Agents and Multiagent Systems: Volume 1 - Volume 1, International Foundation for Autonomous Agents and Multiagent Systems, Richland, SC, pp. 1647–1648. AAMAS 2010 (2010). http://dl.acm.org/citation.cfm?id=1838206.1838523
10. Takahashi, T., Takeuchi, I., Koto, T., Tadokoro, S., Noda, I.: *RoboCup-Rescue* disaster simulator architecture. In: Stone, P., Balch, T., Kraetzschmar, G. (eds.) RoboCup 2000. LNCS (LNAI), vol. 2019, pp. 379–384. Springer, Heidelberg (2001). https://doi.org/10.1007/3-540-45324-5_42. http://dl.acm.org/citation.cfm?id=646585.698826
11. Takami, S., Takayanagi, K., Jaishy, S., Ito, N., Iwata, K.: Agent-development framework based on modular structure to research disaster-relief activities. Int. J. Softw. Innov. (IJSI) **6**(4), 1–15 (2018). https://doi.org/10.4018/IJSI.2018100101. ID 210451
12. Tejada-Begazo, M., Rodríguez-Siu, K., Bernedo-Flores, L.: RoboCup 2017 rescue simulation league team description larvicsaurus (Perú) (2017). https://www.robocup2017.org/file/symposium/rescue_sim3/RCRS_2017_paper_5.pdf

13. Visser, A., Ito, N., Kleiner, A.: RoboCup rescue simulation innovation strategy. In: Bianchi, R.A.C., Akin, H.L., Ramamoorthy, S., Sugiura, K. (eds.) RoboCup 2014. LNCS (LNAI), vol. 8992, pp. 661–672. Springer, Cham (2015). https://doi.org/10. 1007/978-3-319-18615-3_54
14. Zhang, P., Kang, T., Jiang, F., Peng, J., Zhang, X.: RoboCup 2017 rescue simulation league team description CSU_yunlu (China) (2017). https://www. robocup2017.org/file/symposium/rescue_sim3/RCRS_2017_paper_4.pdf

Time-Series Predictions for People-Flow with Simulation Data

Hengjin Tang$^{(\boxtimes)}$, Tatsushi Matsubayashi, Daisuke Sato, and Hiroyuki Toda

NTT Service Evolution Lab., Hikarinooka 1-1, Yokosuka City, Japan
{tang.hengjin,matsubayashi.tatsushi,sato.daisuke,
toda.hiroyuki}@lab.ntt.co.jp

Abstract. In order to prevent accidents, it is important that the administrators of large-scale facilities or event organizers be able to analyze and predict human flow. Time series prediction is generally used for such situations. However, some cases have no historical data available such as the construction of new stadium. In such cases, the multi-agent simulator (MAS) is useful for generating sufficient simulation data to support the assessment of navigation plans, and predictions can be made more accurate by comparing simulation results to monitored data. In this paper, to predict the number of passengers at the multiple observation points, we use simulation data (generated by MAS) as a learning dataset for long short-term memory (LSTM). To compare the prediction accuracy of the proposed approach, we use the real world data collected at the music live events. In addition, for the comparison, we use the nearest neighbor approach that searches the most similar result from the pre-simulated results and predicts the human flow.

Keywords: Time series analysis · Deep learning
Multi-agent simulation

1 Introduction

The key tasks for the administrators of large-scale events include preventing accidents, alleviating congestion, and making evacuation plans. These are serious goals as the 31,674 concerts held in Japan in 2017 attracted nearly 48 million people [1]. From the point of safety, it is necessary to understand the potential human flows, beforehand, during, and after the event, where the spatial extent includes the facilities of the venue and its surroundings (stations, restaurants, etc.). Time series prediction [2] is generally used in such situations. The predictions of passengers at the multiple observations points are discussed in this paper.

In practical applications, two cases are considered for time-series analysis of human flows. One is that we have historical data around the target area. For example, if measurements have been made under the same or similar conditions in advance, it is possible to use the data for identifying the most appropriate

© Springer Nature Switzerland AG 2018
T. Miller et al. (Eds.): PRIMA 2018, LNAI 11224, pp. 655–662, 2018.
https://doi.org/10.1007/978-3-030-03098-8_53

parameters of multi-agent simulator. The second case denies the existence of historical data as the site, say a stadium, has not been built yet. In that case, MAS is widely used to understand the people flow [3]. It can be used to predict the flow patterns to a shopping mall that is under construction, and estimating the change in human flow when a new store opens inside a train station.

This paper mainly focuses on the second situation. By using a multi-agent simulator (MAS), we generate simulated human flow data as a learning data set for prediction models. We then use long short-term memory (LSTM [4]) to predict future flows as real data is acquired.

2   Related Works and Problem Settings

In this section, we explain the related works and define the problem settings. Previous research related to human navigation at large facilities was done by Yamashita et al. [5]. They constructed the multi-agent simulator (MAS) and made navigation scenarios for large facilities. They used historical data to search and evaluate the navigation scenarios created by using MAS. This paper differs in that it attempts to achieve accurate predictions with no measured data. Our approach is to use MAS to generate simulated data in order to make a prediction model.

There are many algorithms for time-series analysis. Vector Autoregression (VAR) [2] and Spatio-Temporal Kriging [6] can deal with both spatial and temporal effects. Those methods assume that the system can be modelled as second order stationary, so mean and variance are constant. Given two different observed values $x_{i,t}$ (observation point: i, time: t) and $x_{j,t+\tau}$ (observation point: j, time: $t+\tau$), the relationship of $x_{i,t}$ and $x_{j,t+\tau}$ is determined by the distance $d(i,j)$ and time difference τ in VAR and Spatio-Temporal Kriging. LSTM [4] is also used for dealing with spatio-temporal problems. As LSTM can deal with both short-term and long-term effects, we use LSTM instead of VAR or Spatio-Temporal Kriging; our expectation is that it can learn the spatio-temporal relationships between the observation points.

The following details the problem setting of our research.

Time, Computational Resources. First, we consider that the time and computational resources are sufficient for learning prediction models, and that the prediction results (lead times of several minutes to hours) should be output within few seconds. This assumption means we consider the cases like scheduled events (music concerts, fireworks, etc.), planned construction and store openings. In such cases, it is not a problem if we spend several hours or days in an advance examination, and there is sufficient time to learn the models.

Methods for Measuring Human Flows. In predicting human flows, there are two types of data that can be used either beforehand or in real time predictions. The first type is human trajectory data that can be obtained from GPS, position sensors etc. Obtaining all or almost all of the trajectories in the area of interest is beneficial for improving the accuracy of time-series predictions. Unfortunately, it is not realistic to assume that everyone will carry such sensors or release the data due to privacy concerns. While we might be able to secure some trajectories by getting approval beforehand, it is difficult to ensure that the characteristics of the people (observed trajectories) are not biased as regards the target. The second type of data is the number of people at specific points or areas as acquired by cameras and sensors, etc. It is relatively easy to get such data, and privacy concerns are not significant. Accordingly, this paper uses this type of data.

3   Proposed Approach

In our approach, learning data is generated by performing MAS runs on the area to predict the people flow. Then using the data to learn LSTM [4], and predict people flow with the support of online observations of people flow (real). Input X (the vector describes the number of observations at each point) to LSTM, and output the people flows at multiple observation points with the predicted time. Input and the initial values are as follows:

K The number of observation points. Different directions at the same point or area are counted as different observation points.

T The total observation time.

t The observation time, t is calculted by separating T at an uniform interval.

t_w The time window for learning data.

X The number of passengers at each observation point. $X = \{x_{k,t} \mid k = 1, \ldots, K, t = 1, \ldots, T\}$ where $x_{k,t}$ is the number of pedestrians at the k-th observation point at time t. $X_t = [x_{1,t}, \ldots, x_{K,t}]$ is a K dimensional vector. X^S, X^R and $\hat{X}$ mean the simulation data by MAS, real data, and predicted values by our model, respectively.

In the learning phase, our model uses simulation data $(X^S_{t-t_w+1}, \ldots, X^S_t)$ and X^S_{t+1} as an input-output pair, and trains the prediction model by backpropagation through time (BPTT) [7]. In the prediction phase, our model uses observed online real data $(X^R_{t-t_w+1}, \ldots, X^R_t)$ as an input for predicting 1-step ahead, and outputs the prediction values of $\hat{X}_{t+1}$, the number of people passing the K points at time $t+1$ in all the directions specified by the $[K]$ observation points. For predicting 2-step ahead or much later, we use the combinations of real data and predicted values by our model. For example, we use $(X^R_{t-t_w+2}, \ldots, X^R_t, \hat{X}_{t+1})$ as an input for predicting $\hat{X}_{t+2}$, and $(X^R_{t-t_w+3}, \ldots, X^R_t, \hat{X}_{t+1}, \hat{X}_{t+2})$ as an input for predicting $\hat{X}_{t+3}$.

Figure 1 shows a framework and a network architecture of our proposed approach, FC means fully connected layer (100 dimensions).

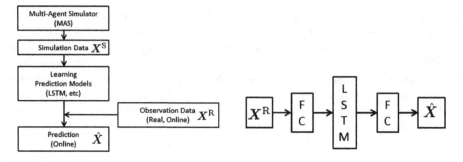

Fig. 1. Framework (left) and network architecture (right) of our proposed approach

4 Experiments

4.1 Data

In this paper, we use two types of data related to live music events.

Real data X^R: gathered on the days of the concerts (4 days)
Simulated data X^S: generated by MAS beforehand (400,000 trials)

Both real and simulated data are related to the situations of exiting from the stadium after concerts are finish. There are $K = 17$ observation points around the stadium (stadium gates, stations etc. see Fig. 2). There are two train lines serving the stadium (the nearest stations are Sta. A and B). The concert participants mainly used Sta. A, and few people used Sta. B. The total observation time is about 60 min ($T \approx 60$). The time width of each observation is 1 minute ($t = 1, \ldots, T$). Both simulation data and real data use the same observation points, time width, and total observation time. The number of people at each point (real data) was manually counted.

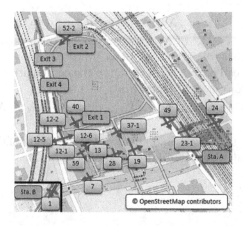

Fig. 2. The observation points

The simulated data was generated using the following parameters.

1. **The combination of exit gates {2}:** (Exit 1, 2, 3) and (Exit 1, 2, 3, 4).
2. **Number of people (total) {1}:** Fixed with $N = 22,000$.
3. **Train frequency {2}:** normal and irregular.
4. **Weather {2}:** fine and rainy.
5. **The number of moving paths {50,000}:** each pattern is generated by multiplying following 4 elements.
   5-1. **Start time {25}**
   5-2. **Peak flow $\{5^3\}$:** 5 volumes of flows from 3 exit gates (Exit 1, 2, 3).
   5-3. **Branch flow ratio $\{2^2\}$:** each agent choises the routes at the two intersection by the given probabilities.
   5-4. **Destination {4}:** 2 stations, 1 shopping mall, and 1 restaurant area.

Therefore, a total of $400,000$ ($2 \times 1 \times 2 \times 2 \times 50,000$) simulation patterns were used. "Start time" and "Peak flow" determine the flow distribution for each path. "Destination" determines where the people move after the concert finishes. In the experiments, both simulated and real data were normalized in a pre-processing step (before learning and prediction phases). All the data is normalized for each observation points $x_{k,t}, t = \{1, \ldots, T\}$.

4.2 Evaluation

We use the experiments to compare three approaches in terms of prediction accuracy: long short-term memory learned by simulated data (LSTM-S, learning data: 400,000), long short-term memory learned by real data (LSTM-R, learning data: 3 (days)), and nearest neighbor search using simulated data (NN-S). In the prediction phase of the three approaches, real data of one day is used (not used in the learning phase of LSTM-R). Figure 3 shows frameworks of LSTM-R and NN-S.

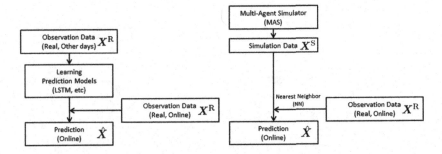

Fig. 3. Frameworks, left: LSTM-R and right: NN-S

The evaluation criterion is normalized absolute error (NAE),

$$NAE = \frac{\sum_{t=1}^{T} \sum_{k=1}^{K} \mid x_{k,t} - \hat{x}_{k,t} \mid}{\sum_{t=1}^{T} \sum_{k=1}^{K} x_{k,t}}, \tag{1}$$

and NAE for each time (NAE(t))

$$NAE(t) = \frac{\sum_{k=1}^{K} | x_{k,t} - \hat{x}_{k,t} |}{\sum_{k=1}^{K} x_{k,t}}, \qquad (2)$$

where $x_{k,t}$ means the sum of the observed values at point k from time $t-5$ to t (calculating the sum of the last 5 min passengers at every 1 min), and $\hat{x}_{k,t}$ means the predicted values corresponding to $x_{k,t}$ by NN-S, LSTM-S, or LSTM-R. The number of epochs in LSTM (real, sim) is 200. The calculating time for learning LSTM-R is 5 min (loading data: less than 1 s + learning model: 5 min) with 1 GPU, while that of learning LSTM-S is 45 min (loading data: 20 min + learning model: 25 min) with 32 GPUs. The prediction values are output immediately.

4.3   Results and Discussions

Figure 4 shows the observed values (true) and predicted values (LSTM, NN) at several points, "LSTM 5 m" and "sim 5 m" mean predictions with 5 min lead time output by LSTM-S and NN-S, respectively. Table 1 means average NAE at each observation point, compares prediction accuracy of LSTM-S and NN-S for 5, 10, 20, 30 min ahead, and the column NN-S, 0 min is calculated by the nearest values of simulation data to the real data (not for prediction). According to Fig. 4 and Table 1, prediction accuracy is poor at loc. 12-1 (a branching point) and loc. 52-2 (an exit gate).

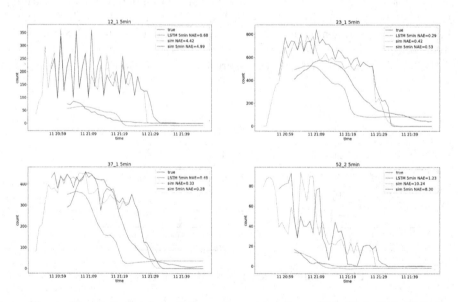

Fig. 4. Observation and prediction values at locations: 12-1, 23-1, 37-1, 52-2

Since loc. 12-1, 12-2, 12-5, and 12-6 are the intersection point and people would choose multiple destinations (to Sta. A, B, restaurants area, etc.), it is difficult to predict the exact values of human flow. The observation points near the exit gates are also difficult to predict. The number of human flow is largely depend on the navigation inside the statidum, and we cannot observe it.

Accuracy is better at loc. 23-1 (a point around a station) and loc. 37-1. The event participants left the stadium from several exit gates, and the most of the participants (approximately 80–90%) moved to Sta. A. The passengers counted at loc. 23-1 and 37-1 are assumed to be observed at other observation points (like exit gates at loc. 40, 52-2) before. Therefore, if the prediciton model can learn the relationships of each observation points well, the prediction accuracy at those points gain the benefits. According to our experiments, it seems LSTM's prediction model have a positive effects for this aspect.

Table 1. Average NAE at each observation point

Loc	LSTM-S				NN-S				
	5 min	10 min	20 min	30 min	0 min	5 min	10 min	20 min	30 min
12-1	0.676	0.977	4.30	11.3	4.42	4.99	4.46	7.94	1.00
23-1	0.292	0.477	0.613	0.343	0.422	0.532	0.488	0.444	0.932
37-1	0.452	0.669	0.823	0.867	0.325	0.285	0.307	0.439	1.00
52-2	1.23	4.01	28.2	26.8	10.2	8.30	8.44	2.17	1.00

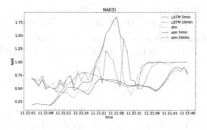

Fig. 5. NAE(t)

According to Fig. 5, LSTM seems more stable than NN. Table 2 provides a comparison of the three approaches by using average NAE (average among all the observation points). LSTM-S offers lower prediction accuracy than LSTM-R for lead times of 5 min and 10 min, but better accuracy than NN-S.

Table 2. Average NAE

Approach	5 min	10 min	30 min
LSTM-R	0.350	0.480	1.77
LSTM-S	0.412	0.576	0.534
NN-S	0.744	0.702	0.948

5   Conclusion

We constructed a multi-agent simulator and generated simulated data of people flows around a large facility. By using the simulated data as LSTM input, we learned a time-series prediction model. In addition, we verified the prediction accuracy of LSTM and nearest neighbor search for real data and simulated data.

As shown in the experiments, the difference in prediction accuracy is not small between using simulation data (LSTM-S, NN-S) and real data (LSTM-R), and the accuracy in LSTM-S and NN-S depends on the quality of simulation data generated by MAS. If the simulation data become much closer to the actual behaviors of human flow, the prediction by using simulation data would be more closer to the real observations. Therefore, improving the methods of searching parameters to generate simulation data in MAS is what we aim to do in the future work. Additionally, we also plan to consider the cases that have few pre-measurement data. In such cases, we assume both simulation and real data are used as the dataset in the learning phase. The approach can be considered as semi-supervised learning [8] and this will help us to improve the prediction accuracy.

References

1. All Japan Concert & Live Entertainment Promoters Conference (A.C.P.C.). http:// www.acpc.or.jp/marketing/. Accessed 14 June 2018
2. Hamilton, J.D.: Time Series Analysis. Princeton University Press, Princeton (1994)
3. Ueda, N., Naya, F.: Spatio-temporal multidimensional collective data analysis for providing comfortable living anytime and anywhere. APSIPA Trans. Sign. Inf. Process. **7**, 1–17 (2018)
4. Hochreiter, S., Schmidhuber, J.: Long short-term memory. Neural Comput. **9**(8), 1735–1780 (1997)
5. Yamashita, T., Okada, T., Noda, I.: Implementation of simulation environment for exhaustive analysis. SICE J. Control Meas. Syst. Integr. **6**(2), 137–146 (2013)
6. Cressie, N., Wikle, C.K.: Statistics for Spatio-Temporal Data. Wiley, Hoboken (2011)
7. Werbos, P.J.: Backpropagation through time: what it does and how to do it. Proc. IEEE **78**(10), 1550–1560 (1990)
8. Chapelle, O., Scholkopf, B., Zien, A.: Semi-supervised Learning. The MIT Press, Cambridge (2010)

Strategy for Learning Cooperative Behavior with Local Information for Multi-agent Systems

Fumito Uwano[✉] and Keiki Takadama

The University of Electro-Communications, W6-309, 1-5-1, Chofugaoka, Chofu-shi, Tokyo, Japan
{uwano@cas.lab,keiki@inf}.uec.ac.jp
http://www.cas.hc.uec.ac.jp/

Abstract. Toward learning cooperative behavior for any number of agents, this paper proposes a multi-agent reinforcement learning method without communication, called PMRL-based Learning for Any number of Agents (PLAA). PLAA prevents from agents reaching the purpose for spending too many times, and to promote the local multi-agent cooperation without communication by PMRL as a previous method. To guarantee the effectiveness of PLAA, this paper compares PLAA with Q-learning, and two previous methods in 10 kinds of the maze for the 2 and 3 agents. From the experimental result, we revealed those things: (a) PLAA is the most effective method for cooperation among 2 and 3 agents; (b) PLAA enable the agents to cooperate with each other in small iterations.

1 Introduction

Multi-agent system becomes an effective model to simulate human society, and solves the problem in this society by agents' cooperation. Iwashita et al. aim to give support to make a security plan by solving a urban road network security problem which guards and criminals are modeled with agents [2]. Multi-agent reinforcement learning (MARL) is a reinforcement learning technique to solve the problems of multi-agent system. The agents generally utilize information of other agents to cooperate with each other. Tan explored what kinds of information of other agents contribute to increasing the performance of multi-agent system [6]. However, it is hard for agents (i) to handle the information required to cooperate with each other as the number of agents increases and (ii) to acquire the current information of all other agents without delay or noise as the field of agents becomes large or the number of the relay agents increases. From this fact, it is important to explore methods without communication. However, this is very difficult because the agents do not know how they cooperate with each other [1,3]. Sen firstly addressed it and showed the possibility of reinforcement

This work was supported by JSPS KAKENHI Grant Number JP17J08724.

© Springer Nature Switzerland AG 2018
T. Miller et al. (Eds.): PRIMA 2018, LNAI 11224, pp. 663–670, 2018.
https://doi.org/10.1007/978-3-030-03098-8_54

learning which enables agents to cooperate with each other without communication [4]. After that, such an approach is improved from the theoretical and the efficient viewpoints. As the theoretical viewpoint, Profit Minimizing Reinforcement Learning (PMRL) [7] was proposed to theoretically guarantee the multi-agent cooperation under the condition of no random actions of agents. As the efficient viewpoint, on the other hand, Yielding Action Reinforcement Learning (YARL) [7] was proposed to decrease the number of learning iterations for the multi-agent cooperation. Both methods are useful to enable agents to cooperate with each other without communication. However, PMRL cannot guarantee the multi-agent cooperation when the number of agents is larger than two, while YARL cannot always derive the multi-agent cooperation. In addition, YARL might not perform well in situations of any number of agents because YARL is not theoretical method. To overcome these problems, this paper proposes PMRL-based Learning for Any number of Agents (PLAA) which two or more agents can cooperate with each other with maintaining the guarantee of PMRL and decreases the number of learning iterations.

2   Background

2.1   Q-Learning

Reinforcement Learning (RL) [5] is a try-and-error method which aims at maximizing an acquired reward per a unit time. As its general framework, an RL agent interacts with an environment: it observes a state from the environment, selects an action, receives a reward from the environment as the result of that action, and then learns from the reward. Note that this cycle from the observation to the next observation is called "step" in this paper. Among many RL methods, Q-learning [8] is a very popular RL method for a single-agent task. A Q-learning agent estimates state-action values (called Q-value) for the possible state-action pairs in the environment, $i.e.$, the agent estimates an discounted expected reward that it will receive when its action a is executed in its state s. The agent learns to acquire a policy $\pi(s, a)$ to decide which action should be executed to maximize a received reward. To maximize a received reward, $Q(s, a)$ is updated as follows.

$$Q(s, a) \leftarrow Q(s, a) + \alpha[r + \gamma \max_{a' \in A} Q(s', a') - Q(s, a)], \qquad (1)$$

where s' is the next-state when a is executed in s, a' is the next-action executed in the state s', r is the reward received from the environment, $\max Q(s', a')$ is the largest Q-value when executing the action $a' \in A$ in the state s'. In addition to these variables, α is the learning rate, while γ is the discount factor. Precisely, α is the real number from 0 to 1 which indicates the learning speed, while γ is the real number from 0 to 1 which indicates how much the future rewards should be considered as important.

2.2 Profit Minimizing Reinforcement Learning (PMRL)

To learn multi-agent cooperation without communication, Uwano et al. proposed Profit Minimizing Reinforcement Learning (PMRL) [7]. This method employs internal rewards to control the agents' learning. Each agent has the own internal rewards for any purposes, and calculate them from (external) rewards from the environment. The agent updates Q-value from the internal rewards. PMRL achieves multi-agent cooperation from three equations below. Equations (2) and (3) update priority of each purpose of the agent and the internal reward for one agent, respectively. In Eq. (2), bid_g is called goal value of the certain purpose g and a value indicating the priority of the purpose, $n_{achieve}$ is how much times the agent achieves this purpose, t_g is a minimum number of steps to achieve each purpose g, and $\phi(m)$ is a function indicating whether the agent achieve this purpose faster than any other agents or not. If the agent achieves this purpose fastest of all, $\phi(m) = 1$; otherwise, $\phi(m) = 0$. In Eq. (3), ir_g is the internal reward for each purpose g, and δ is a positive constant value. g' is the certain purpose without g, and G is a set including all purposes. PMRL can establish the cooperation even if δ is any value. The agent updates Q-values from the internal reward as the external reward.

$$bid_g = \frac{1}{n_{achieve}} \sum_{m=0}^{n_{achieve}} t_g \phi(m) \tag{2}$$

$$ir_g = \max_{g' \in G, g' \neq g} r\gamma^{t_{g'} - t_g} + \delta \tag{3}$$

In PMRL, the agent calculates the priorities and sets the internal reward every acquiring the reward. In addition, PMRL is a theoretical method, and two agents can always cooperate with each other in cooperation task.

3 Maze Problem and Dilemma

We employ a maze problem to validate whether the agent can change the behavior through its learning or not. The maze has several number of states, starts, and goals. The agents depart from the start and keep observing the states until they reach the goal. If the agents are on the goal, they can acquire the reward. During this cycle, the agents learn to reach the goal to acquire maximum gain par a unit time. In this paper, a cycle from its departing to reaching the goal is called "iteration". Since there are several number of agents in one maze, the agents cannot learn completely. This paper calls this situation "conflict", and the several agents have to yield this goal for other agents to solve the conflict. This situation is "dilemma", and this strategy changing is called "cooperation". Concretely, the cooperation is a policy that all agents can acquire the rewards for shortest step.

4   PMRL-based Learning for Any Number of Agents (PLAA)

The agent has Q-values, minimum number of steps, goal range, and goal values to learn cooperative behaviors. The goal range is a number to manage goals where the agent can reach.

4.1   Mechanisms

In PLAA, the agent learns for one iteration, and evaluates the iteration. PLAA employs ϵ-greedy selection in the learning phase, while it employs the greedy selection in the evaluation phase. From the evaluation, it stores the information including the minimum number of the steps and the number of other agents in the same state. After that, it calculates the goal values and sets the internal rewards. These processes are same as those of PMRL. However, if the current iteration becomes the several times of the threshold, it changes the goal range; otherwise, it returns to next iteration in PLAA. Note that the threshold is a positive integer from 0 to the maximum number of the iterations. The process of changing the goal range is a main point of PLAA.

Goal Range Determination Mechanism. The goal range is a positive integer to prevent from the agent reaching the goals: the agent can reach the several goals in order from the nearest goal, and the goal range is the number of the reachable goals. The goal range is initialized to 1. Since all agents have the goal ranges 1, the certain agents might have a conflict in one goal. If the number of the agents is two, they change the goal values to 2 as this number and learn to reach next nearest goal in order to resolve the conflict. If there are not any conflicts, this process is finished. If there are other conflicts in this situation, the agents making the conflicts change the goal ranges to the number of the agents. This is a goal range determination mechanism. Note that the conflict is determined whenever the agents reach the same goal for 4000 times in 5000 iterations. There are parameters $Cycle$ and $ProbConflict$ to determine the conflict. $Cycle$ is the iterations, and $ProbConflict$ is the probability to determine the times (4000 is calculated by $Cycle \times ProbConflict = 4000$ in above sentence).

Goal Value Calculation Mechanism. In the process of the calculating the goal values, the agents utilize Eq. (4) instead of Eq. (2). Equation (2) is easy to convergence the goal value, and not easy to be influenced from the minimum number of the steps acquired in the current iteration. Since PLAA has to find appropriate goal values whenever the goal range is changed, the goal value has to be calculated with putting emphasis on the new information. Equation (4) becomes easy to be influenced the newly added $t_g\phi(m)$ by changing the denominator from $n_{achieve}$ to constant value ξ.

$$bid_g = 1/\xi \sum_{m=0}^{n_{achieve}} ((\xi - 1)/\xi)^{n_{achieve}-m} \, t_g\phi(m) \qquad (4)$$

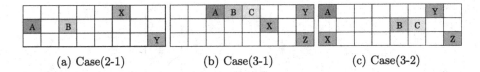

(a) Case(2-1)   (b) Case(3-1)   (c) Case(3-2)

Fig. 1. Examples of each case

5 Experiment

5.1 Experimental Design and Setting

To investigate the effectiveness of PLAA, we compare PLAA with three methods, Q-learning, PMRL, and YARL, in 3×8 grid mazes. There are three cases as follows, Case (2-1) for two agents, and Cases (3-1) and (3-2) for three agents. All agents have to cooperate with each others in Cases (2-1) and (3-1). In Case (3-2), only two agents have to cooperate with each other. There are 10 kinds of mazes which start and goal positions are different among all mazes in each case. Figure 1 shows examples of each case. In these mazes, A, B and C indicate start positions of agents, respectively. X, Y and Z indicate goal positions. Note that this paper identificates the agents and the goals with A, B, C, X, Y, and Z of each maze, respectively.

Evaluation Criterion and Parameters. This paper evaluates steps spent until all agents reach goals. The total number of experiments is determined by the number of trials (*e.g.*, 300 trials with 30 different seeds in 10 kinds of mazes for each case.) Learning iterations and steps are limited to 50000 and 100 as the threshold, respectively. Q-values of all states are initialized to 0. α and γ are set to 0.1 and 0.9, respectively. All methods employ ϵ-greedy selection in the learning phase, while they employ the greedy selection in the evaluation phase. Concretely, the agents select their actions according to the ϵ-greedy selection method with $\epsilon = 0.7$, and evaluate the learning result according to the greedy selection. We set $\epsilon = 0.7$ to find the minimum number of the steps from the start to all goals. An ordinary (external) reward is set to 10. δ is set to 10. A learning cycle $Cycle$ is set to 5000, threshold $ProbConflict$ is set to 0.8, and constant ξ is set to 500 in PLAA.

5.2 Experimental Result

Overall Result. Figure 2 shows the steps until the agents reach the goal in the mazes of Fig. 1 as the typical one of 10 results in each case. The vertical axis indicates the number of steps spent until all agents reach goals, while the horizontal axis indicates the learning iteration. The four lines in Fig. 2 indicate the results of Q-learning (blue lines), PMRL (orange lines), YARL (green lines), and PLAA (red lines), respectively. If the agents cannot cooperate with each other, the number of the steps become 100. In Fig. 2a, the line of Q-learning is

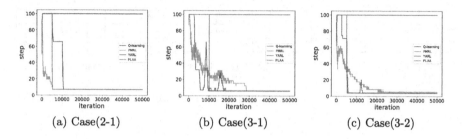

(a) Case(2-1)   (b) Case(3-1)   (c) Case(3-2)

Fig. 2. Result in sample maze of each case (Color figure online)

100 for almost all iterations, while those of PMRL, YARL, and PLAA become
the minimum number of the steps. Figures 2b and c indicate the results of Cases
(3-1) and (3-2). In Fig. 2c, the line of Q-learning indicates 100, those of YARL
and PLAA converge to the minimum number of the steps, and that of PMRL
becomes low but over the minimum number of the steps. Although Fig. 2b is
similar to Fig. 2c, the only line of PMRL do not converge to the minimum number
of the steps in Fig. 2c. Table 1 shows the results of three methods in all mazes.
In this table, "O" and "X" indicate the situations which the number of the steps
is minimum and not minimum in all seeds, respectively. "△" indicates that the
number of the steps is minimum in several seeds. From the Table 1, the agents
with PMRL can cooperate with each other in almost all mazes of Case (2-1), but
cannot in other cases. The agents with YARL can cooperate with each other in
almost all cases, but cannot in three mazes (maze 8 of Case (2-1), mazes 7 and 8
of Case (3-2)). The agents with PLAA can cooperate with each other, excluding
maze 6 of Case (3-1).

5.3   Discussion

From the results, PLAA is most effective method for each case. The agents
can learn to reach the goals with the cooperation for minimum steps. In the
following sentence, we compare and analyze the results of PLAA, PMRL, and
YARL. Figure 3 shows the maze 7 in Case (3-2). In this maze, Agent A, Agent
B, and Agent C indicate the start positions of the agents, while Goal X, Goal
Y, and Goal Z indicate the goal positions. In this maze, the number of the steps
in PMRL and PLAA is average of 5, 8, 9, and 100, while that in YARL is 8.
Since the minimum number of the steps is 5, YARL cannot find the minimum
number of the steps, while PMRL and PLAA can find that in certain seeds.
Concretely, the agents A and B have a conflict in the goal X, then both agents
update the goal ranges from 1 to 2. After that, the agent B and C have a
conflict in the goal Z, then the agent C update the goal ranges from 1 to 2. From
this mechanism, PLAA enable the agents to learn to reach the goals with the
minimum number of the steps. However, there is a case which PLAA performs
optimally. The case is that the minimum number of the steps in certain goal is
same as those in other goals. Since the agent can select both combinations of

Table 1. Overall result in all cases

PMRL										
	maze1	maze2	maze3	maze4	maze5	maze6	maze7	maze8	maze9	maze10
Case (2-1)	O	O	O	O	△	O	O	O	O	O
Case (3-1)	△	△	△	△	△	X	△	O	△	O
Case (3-2)	△	△	△	△	△	△	△	△	△	X

YARL										
	maze1	maze2	maze3	maze4	maze5	maze6	maze7	maze8	maze9	maze10
Case (2-1)	O	O	O	O	O	O	O	X	O	O
Case (3-3)	O	O	O	O	O	O	O	O	O	O
Case (3-2)	O	O	O	O	O	O	X	X	O	O

PLAA										
	maze1	maze2	maze3	maze4	maze5	maze6	maze7	maze8	maze9	maze10
Case (2-1)	O	O	O	O	O	O	O	O	O	O
Case (3-3)	O	O	O	O	O	X	O	O	O	O
Case (3-2)	O	O	O	O	O	O	△	O	O	O

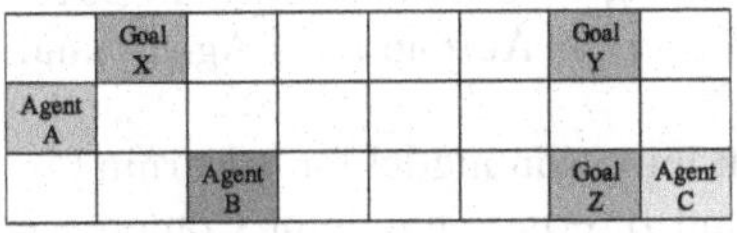

Fig. 3. maze 7 in Case (3-2)

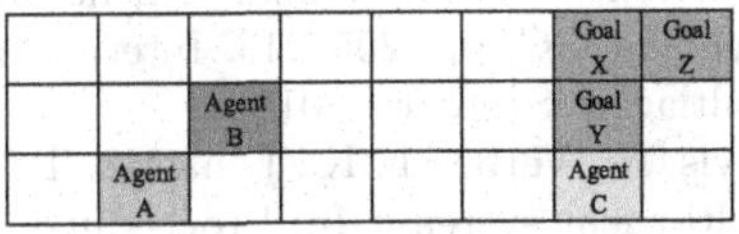

Fig. 4. maze 6 in Case (3-3)

the goals, and the goal range cannot perform well. Figure 4 shows the maze 6 in Case (3-1). The numbers of the steps in PLAA and PMRL are 9, while that in YARL is 7. In YARL, all agents have a conflict in the goal Y, then the agent B and C learns to reach the goal X and Z, respectively. The agents can reach the goals for the minimum number of the steps. In PLAA, all agent have a conflict in the goal Y, then all agents update the goal ranges from 1 to 3. From this mechanism, the agents can learn to reach the goals for very low steps but over the minimum number of the steps. To solve this issue, the agent C's the goal range should be 2.

6   Conclusion

This paper proposes reinforcement learning method for multi-agent cooperation without communication (PMAL-based Learning for Any number of Agents: PLAA). Concretely, PLAA is an extension of PMRL which changes the external reward to the internal reward for the cooperation. PLAA sets the goal range to prevent from the agents reaching the farthest goal: the agent can reach the several goals in order from the nearest goal, and the goal range is the number of the reachable goals. If the agents have a conflict, they change the goal range to the number of the agents. This paper compares PLAA with Q-learning, PMRL,

YARL in 10 kinds of the maze for the 2 and 3 agents. From the experimental result, we revealed those things: (a) PLAA is the most effective method for cooperation among 2 and 3 agents; and (b) PLAA enable the agents to cooperate with each other in small iterations.

PLAA can make cooperation in almost all situations. We would propose a new goal range setting strategy for all situations. Concretely, the PLAA agents update the goal range gradually. From the results of this research, since the optimal goal range for each agent always exists in each maze, it can be suggested that to extend PLAA contributes the multi-agent learning for several number of agents.

References

1. de Cote, E.M., Lazaric, A., Restelli, M.: Learning to cooperate in multi-agent social dilemmas. In: AAMAS, pp. 783–785, May 2006
2. Iwashita, H., Ohori, K., Anai, H., Iwasaki, A.: Simplifying urban network security games with cut-based graph contraction. In: Proceedings of the 2016 International Conference on Autonomous Agents and #38; Multiagent Systems, AAMAS 2016, Richland, SC, pp. 205–213. International Foundation for Autonomous Agents and Multiagent Systems (2016)
3. Tuyls, K., Verbeeck, K., Lenaerts, T.: A selection-mutation model for q-learning in multi-agent systems. In: Proceedings of the Second International Joint Conference on Autonomous Agents and Multiagent Systems, pp. 693–700. ACM, July 2003
4. Sen, S., Sekaran, M., Hale, J., et al.: Learning to coordinate without sharing information. In: AAAI, pp. 426–431 (1994)
5. Sutton, R.S., Barto, A.G.: Introduction to Reinforcement Learning, 1st edn. MIT Press, Cambridge (1998)
6. Tan, M.: Multi-agent reinforcement learning: independent vs. cooperative agents. In: Proceedings of the Tenth International Conference on Machine Learning, pp. 330–337. Morgan Kaufmann (1993)
7. Uwano, F., Takadama, K.: Comparison between reinforcement learning methods with different goal selections in multi-agent cooperation (special issue on cutting edge of reinforcement learning and its applications). J. Adv. Comput. Intell. Intell. Inf. **21**(5), 917–929 (2017)
8. Watkins, C.J.C.H.: Learning from Delayed Rewards. Ph.D. thesis, King's College (1989)

Better Collective Learning
with Consistency Guarantees

Lise-Marie Veillon[1,4], Gauvain Bourgne[2], and Henry Soldano[1,3(✉)]

[1] Université Paris 13, Sorbonne Paris Cité, L.I.P.N UMR-CNRS 7030,
Villetaneuse, France
{Veillon,Henry.Soldano}@lipn.univ-paris13.fr
[2] CNRS and Sorbonne Universités, LIP6 UMR 7606, Paris, France
Gauvain.Bourgne@lip6.fr
[3] Atelier de BioInformatique, ISYEB - UMR 7205 CNRS MNHN UPMC EPHE,
Museum National d'Histoire Naturelle, Paris, France
[4] Normandie Univ, UNICAEN, ENSICAEN, CNRS UMR6072, GREYC,
Caen, France

Abstract. We address two major issues of Waves, a collective learning protocol that has been recently proposed. The protocol aims at enhancing individual agent learning in an agent society organized in a network in which agents may interact with their neighbors. When considering a turn-based setting, Waves guarantees that at the end of a turn each agent has a model *consistent* with all observations present within the society. This guarantee is obtained thanks to exchange of observations and hypotheses between neighbors. All interactions are performed in parallel and the protocol may lead to redundancies and some lack of diversity in the hypotheses revised by the agents. The first issue concerns the redundancy that follows from the generation and transmission by agents of hypotheses equivalent to hypotheses previously encountered. The second issue is the lack of diversity that may result in losing the accuracy increase, with respect to an isolated agent, observed whenever all agents freely interact with each other.

1 Introduction

While artificial intelligence at the individual level remains an important area which recently made impressive progress, in particular regarding learning and adaptation, there is a clear need to study learning phenomena at the collective level, to observe efficiency of collective learning mechanism and to propose new interaction protocols with as much as possible theoretical guarantees.

In the setting we investigate, we consider a community of agents each individually needing to learn some model by accessing over time observations from its environment. The community has no shared memory while agents are nodes of a communication network and may communicate with their neighbors. The community is considered as *uniform* as agents are autonomous and have the same abilities and no predefined role. The agents have each the ability to repair

© Springer Nature Switzerland AG 2018
T. Miller et al. (Eds.): PRIMA 2018, LNAI 11224, pp. 671–679, 2018.
https://doi.org/10.1007/978-3-030-03098-8_55

their current model when confronted to observations that contradict this model. More precisely, an agent has to maintain the adequacy (we call that the *consistency*) of the model with the observations it has collected. As, at some moment, an agent has been confronted to a limited number of observations, a model only built from these observations would then not be accurate enough. However, as far as the agent benefits from the observations collected by the whole community, it could build a much better model in terms of *predictive accuracy*, i.e. in terms of consistency with respect to further observations. The first purpose of collective learning is then to allow agents to each have as good a model as if they had access to all the observations in the community, while satisfying the pre-requisite mentioned above: no shared memory, communications restricted to neighbors, and autonomy. Such pre-requisite corresponds to many practical situations, and are close to settings found in two other domains, namely *distributed systems with error correcting abilities* [2] and *swarm intelligence* [3]. A second purpose of collective learning is concerned with homogeneity of the models built within the community: the interaction between agents should not be limited to exchange of observations, but also allow the agents to confront their models thus resulting in a more homogeneous state of knowledge within the community.

Our contributions concern a recent collective learning protocol, named Waves [4] in which interactions are performed in parallel in an agent network and guarantees, at convergence, the consistency of a limited set of hypotheses selected according to the observations in the community. The propositions, presented Sect. 3, are twofold. Firstly, we address Sect. 3.1 computational redundancies by *avoiding useless critics* and *merging equivalent hypotheses*. Secondly, in Sect. 3.2 we focus on *restoring the accuracy increase with respect to a single agent* which is lost when Waves does not always provide a sufficient diversity on the hypotheses the agent revises. The resulting improvements of Waves are experimented Sect. 4.

2   Collective Learning in a Society of Agents

In a collective learning setting, a structured society of agents, represented as a graph where nodes are agents and edges are communicational links, performs a supervised learning task using the examples gathered by the members of the society in their respective example memories E_i. We consider a turn-based setting, with two phases. During the *information gathering phase*, each agent accesses its information source, possibly getting one or more new examples. Then, in the *collective learning phase*, which is our focus here, agents collaboratively build *hypotheses* based on their information and feedback from other agents. We focus on a simple learning task: concept learning of boolean formulae. At the end of this phase, we typically want to ensure *MAS-consistency*, meaning that the hypothesis of each agent is consistent with the set of all examples in the system (i.e. it classifies them correctly). A weaker requirement, *group-consistency*, only demands that each agent has a hypothesis consistent with the set of examples possessed by itself and its direct neighbors.

In previous work [1], collective learning has been studied in the context of a fully connected society of agents. The resulting generic protocol SMILE ensures MAS-consistency at the end of the collective learning phase. It is based on a *learner-critic* principle, where an agent which revises its hypothesis, thus taking a *learner* role, proposes the revised hypothesis to the other agents, that act as *critics*. As a critic, an agent either provides a counter-example or accepts the proposed hypothesis when it does not have such a counter-example. In the former case, the learner agent revises its hypothesis to take into account this counter-example, and the process is iterated with this revised hypothesis until the learner produces a MAS-consistent hypothesis that is then adopted by all agents. Experimental evaluations confirmed that SMILE learns hypotheses that are at least as accurate as the one formed by a single agent possessing all the examples in the society. Moreover, in complex boolean problem, it has shown a significant improvement in accuracy compared to such a single agent. This *accuracy increase* may however be lost if the example memories of the agents become too similar [1].

This paper builds upon the turn-based Waves protocol [4] which focuses on the autonomous and parallel behaviors of agents that communicate with their neighbors in a network. After the information gathering phase, each Waves agent confront the MAS-consistent hypotheses it kept from the previous turn with its new examples. If a hypothesis is contradicted, it revises it and proposes this revision around, initiating an interaction with its neighbors to reach group-consistency. Then, each of the neighbors, when notified of the group-consistency of some hypothesis h_L, is tasked with propagating h_L to its own neighbors by *checking* it: it will temporarily adopt it, starting new local interactions to validate the group consistency of h_L or revise it into a group consistent hypothesis h'_L. In the last case, h'_L is marked as a revision of h_L, so that other agents can infer that h_L was contradicted when receiving it.

Each agent a_i is equipped with a *working hypotheses memory*, defined as a tuple $\langle \theta_i, W_i, C_i, R_i \rangle$, where θ_i is the current hypothesis, which the agent is currently using in a local revision, if any. W_i is the waiting list of hypotheses, which the agent has no yet checked but intends to. C_i is the set of checked candidate hypotheses, which are the hypotheses that the agent already checked, which are known to be group-consistent (and might be MAS-consistent). R_i is the set of rejected hypotheses. It is a set of identifiers indicating the hypotheses that have been proved not to be MAS-consistent. *Waves-Hypothesis H* are represented as tuples $\langle id, date, h, Anc \rangle$ where id is a unique identifier of the hypothesis, $date$ indicates when (the turn) it was produced, h is its logical form, and Anc is the set of ancestors of H, that is, the identifier of the hypothesis h' of which it is a revision (if any) together with the ancestors of h'. The protocol unfolds as follows:

1. *Initial verification.* After the information gathering phase, each agent that received new examples confront them to C_i. If some $H \in C_i$ is contradicted, the agent revises it with example memory and takes the result as its new

current hypothesis θ_i, triggering the protocol with a local revision. It becomes *active* and resets C_i, R_i and W_i to $\emptyset$. Otherwise, the agent stays *passive*.

2. *Local revisions.* All active agents a_i are involved as *learner* in a local protocol with their neighbors (involved as *critics*) to check the group-consistency of their current hypothesis θ_i, revising it until it is ensured.

3. *Ending a local revision.* When an active agent a_i finishes a local revision, it updates θ_i and R_i if θ_i was revised during the interaction (adding its initial identifier to its ancestors and R_i and generating a new one) before sending valid(θ_i) to all its neighbors. If W_i is not empty, a_i chooses a new working hypothesis in W_i and triggers a new local protocol with it, otherwise it becomes passive.

4. *Managing hypotheses.* When receiving valid(H), agent a_i must deal with the underlying request to check it with its own neighbors. The process is in three steps:

   (a) *Initial reset.* First, if H is the first hypothesis that a_i would have to check in this turn (if its date is more recent than those of C_i or θ_i), C_i, R_i and W_i are set to $\emptyset$, and θ_i is set to H. a_i becomes active, starting a local protocol to check its new θ_i.

   (b) *Filtering.* Otherwise, the agent determines if it has already encountered H, as it should only check it once. If H itself is in $W_i \cup C_i \cup \{\theta_i\}$ or $H.id \in R_i$, H is already taken into account and not added anywhere, otherwise, H is added to W_i.

   (c) *Update from ancestors.* At last, the ancestors of H are added to R_i and any hypothesis in W_i or C_i that belongs to $H.Anc$ is removed. If θ_i is in $H.Anc$, then a_i gets in *cancelling* state and will stop its current revision as soon as it has finished receiving answers for its last propose. It will then pick a new current hypothesis in W_i and start the next check (or become passive if W_i is empty).

5. *End of phase.* The protocol ends when all agents are passive. Each agent then selects one of the shortest $H \in C_i$ (lesser number of terms) as its personal hypothesis h_i.

This protocol ensures that each turn terminates and that MAS-consistency is reached for all agents upon termination. However two issues appeared when analyzing the experimental results. Firstly, average accuracy of agents hypotheses do not always benefit from the accuracy increase observed in SMILE. Secondly, some network structures are too costly as computational power is spent on many redundant computations. We will see in next section how these issues can be mitigated to improve Waves performance.

3   Improving Waves

As agents process and spread information independently and in parallel, a number of redundancies appears in Waves. First, it may have, as a critic, to examine the consistency of the same logical hypothesis, either when different neighbors consecutively propose it the same Waves-hypothesis or when two different Waves-hypotheses with the same logical form are produced concurrently. We propose in Sect. 3.1 ways to reduce each of these redundancies. Second, agents' example memories also suffer from redundancy. With more hypotheses in the network there are more revisions and thus examples are more widely spread across the network leading to a loss in hypotheses diversity and causing the loss in accuracy increase mentioned above. This is the case in particular when many cycles and long distances between agents impose a lot of examples exchanges. With such a high memory redundancy, the agents tend to revise hypotheses in a same way, leading to a poor exploration of the hypothesis space. We thus propose in Sect. 3.2 some mechanisms to reduce this redundancy.

3.1 Reducing Computational Redundancies

Avoiding Useless Critics. Here, we are concerned with reducing the number of times a given hypothesis is proposed to the same critic agent by different learners. To prevent a given hypothesis from being proposed to the same critic agent by many different learners, we attach to each Waves-hypothesis H a set of agent identifiers $H.Crit$. When checking H, a learner agent will only **propose** it to neighbors that are not in $H.Crit$. Then, when ending a local revision (step 3), the learner a_i update $\theta_i.Crit$ with its neighbors. Note that all neighbors are then notified of group-consistency even if they did not participate as critics. Moreover, when receiving **valid**(H) where H is in W_i, agents will compare the received version of H with the stored one to update the critics of the stored one if needed. We call this process *critics recording*.

Merging Equivalent Hypotheses. In some settings, Waves generate a lot of logically equivalent hypotheses. Since, when keeping track of hypotheses, Waves agents are only concerned with their identifiers, such hypotheses will be propagated and checked independently. To avoid that, equivalent hypotheses should be grouped, but careful handling is needed to preserve Waves theoretical guarantees. The termination and MAS-consistency properties of Waves rely on the fact that any hypothesis that is formed will either (i) reach all agents in the system if it is MAS-consistent, or else (ii) generates at least one MAS-consistent descendant. This ensures both that C_i is not empty and that it does not contain any non MAS-consistent hypothesis. As, due to local revisions, a hypothesis can be revised to a logical equivalent of one of its ancestor, rejecting all hypotheses equivalent to a rejected one might remove all hypotheses from C_i.

Thus, when merging hypotheses, we must ensure that each unique identifier stays associated with its ancestors and is fully propagated. We do so by using *passports*, defined as a couple (id, Anc) where id is an identifier and Anc is its ancestors' set: passports are created with each hypothesis and never modified afterward. Equivalent hypotheses can thus be grouped in an equivalence class of Waves hypothesis, which will be called a *Waves eq-hypothesis* and defined as a tuple $\langle Pass, date, h[, Crit] \rangle$ where $Pass$ is the set of passports of the hypotheses that belong to this logical equivalence class; $date$ represents the turn in which all hypotheses of this class were produced (we only consider merging for hypotheses generated during the current turn); h is the logical form of the formula, common (modulo equivalence) to all hypotheses of this class; and $Crit$, if critics recording is used, is the set of agents that accepted a hypothesis of this class. Since critics focus on the logical content, this list can be shared by the class. Given $H_1 = \langle Pass_1, d_1, h_1[, Crit_1]\rangle$ and $H_1 = \langle Pass_2, d_2, h_2[, Crit_2]\rangle$ where $d_1 = d_2 = d$ and $h_1 \equiv h_2$ we can define the merging of these two eq-hypotheses as $Merge(H_1, H_2) = \langle Pass_1 \cup Pass_2, d, h_1[, Crit_1 \cup Crit_2]\rangle$.

Waves protocol then need some adaptation to deal with eq-Hypotheses. First, θ_i, W_i and C_i now stores Waves eq-hypotheses (R_i remains a set of ids). Hypothesis management phase (step 4 in Sect. 2) now has to deal with these equivalence classes while still ensuring full propagation of each individual identifier. This does not affect *Initial reset* (4.a), but *Filtering* step (4.b) must be thoroughly changed, as potential merging should be checked and passports updated in consequence. First the passport of the new eq-hypothesis is pruned of already rejected instances of the class (passports whose identifier is in R_i), before checking whether any of the passports is really new (meaning that its identifier has never been seen before by the agent). If not, the hypothesis management phase can be directly finished, otherwise, at least one identifier is new, but we must still check whether the logical content itself is new. The new hypotheses is thus compared in turn with θ_i, then W_i and C_i, replacing the stored eq-hypothesis by its merging with the new one if an equivalence is found. If the merging happens in C_i, a new `valid(H)` message has to be send to the neighbors to ensure propagation of the new identifiers. Then, if no merging is found with stored hypotheses, the new hypothesis is put in W_i or θ_i. The last step of hypothesis management, *Update from ancestors* (4.c) is also modified: eq-hypotheses are only removed when all their passports have been rejected. At last, we also need to check for potential merging when the agent has formed a new hypothesis at the end of a revision process.

3.2   Using Forgetness in Waves

Forgetness [1] is a mechanism used in SMILE to suppress redundancies in the example memories of the agents. When combined with broadcast in a complete graph, it improves performances both in term of efficiency and accuracy. When faced with long cycles or multiple examples by turn, Waves produces more hypotheses which provokes more examples sharing, causing a loss of the agents average accuracy. We could have each Wave-agent forget all its external examples (examples received from the other agents) at the end of each turn. But, when an example is spread far away, it is likely to be important and full forgetness will thus be prohibitively costly as such examples need to be repeatedly propagated from scratch. We propose then to select the external examples that should be forgotten at the end of the turn. For that purpose we shall take into account the *distance traveled* by examples to reach each agent. We define two criterion: (i) *Forgetting close examples*, that is, forgetting only examples that traveled less than a given distance k, i.e. examples whose distance tag is in $\{1, \ldots, k\}$;

(ii) *Forgetting odd distances*, that is, forgetting all external examples who traveled an odd number of steps. The idea here is that instead of trying to keep examples that traveled far in one's memory, it is enough to just ensure that at least one close agent keeps it: along the path of such an example, each agent will either keep it or have a neighbor that does so.

4 Experimentation

An experiment is typically composed of 100 runs, each one corresponding to a sequence of examples incrementally sent to random agents in the MAS. Experiments are performed on a node with 48 cores, considering system of 40 agents so that each agent can use its own core. Agents are tasked with learning a difficult boolean problem: the 11-multiplexer (M11). We study different layouts of the network of agents taken from [4] and covering various situations: Clique (fully-connected graph) gives an unconstrained case where all reference protocols are applicable; Tree5 (regular tree with five sons) is an acyclic graph with short path length representative of hierarchical structures; Wheel (one central node is connected to every other one, the others forming a circle) has lots of short cycles; SmW4p05 (Small-World built with Watts-Strogatz algorithm [5] with mean degree 4 and reconnection probability 0.5) is a structure commonly found in self organized networks such as peer-to-peer or social networks; Line and Circle (regular graph of degree 2) represent worst case scenario.

Critics Recording and Hypotheses Merging. We study the influence of both improvements on the whole process of learning and compare its cost at the end of learning which can be reached in M11 problem after around 300 examples. Figure 1 shows execution time for the different improvements considered. We focus first on comparing original Waves (1st bar in red) with its version with critics recording (Waves critMin, 2nd bar in blue). We can see that, even on the layout that benefits less from it (Tree5), critics recording is always beneficial: avoiding the critic of the agent who sent the hypothesis is enough to compensate the simple additional processing involved. Graphs like Clique and Wheel that contains many triangles show the biggest improvements. We focus, on a second time, on comparing the same original Waves with it's version with hypotheses merging (Waves merge, 3rd bar in pink). The benefit of merging hypotheses is clear in networks where the presence of cycles put it at a disadvantage against sequential protocols [4]. It also improves long distances propagation. In a cycle, a hypothesis can be criticized by the same agent on each side with the same counter-example so it's more likely that the revised hypotheses on each side are similar and benefit from being merged. Even in cases where the benefit is minimal, despite the increased complexity of eq-Waves hypotheses, execution time is not increased. At last, merging hypotheses and recording critics do not have the same influence and can be cumulated for greater benefit (Waves merge CritMin last bar in violet), especially in graphs with long paths and cycles where, while the main improvement comes from hypotheses merging, critics recording further enhance it. Both of these modifications have benefits on communicational and computational loads without any significant influence on accuracy.

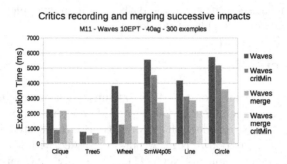

Fig. 1. Comparison of execution time for the improvements of Waves in different networks. (Color figure online)

Forgetness. Given the combined benefits of merging hypotheses and critics recording and their lack of influence on accuracy, we built upon these two improvements to study forgetness, which implies a trade-off between accuracy and execution time. We study two kinds of partial forgetness: *close examples* with $k = 2$ (Dist 1-2) and *odd distances* (Odd-Dist). Their execution time and average accuracy is compared in Fig. 2 to extreme cases of forgetting all external examples (All-ext) or none (none).

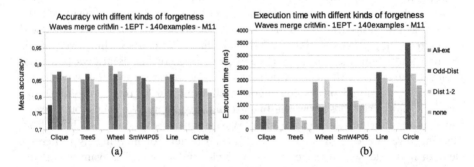

Fig. 2. Four kinds of partial forgetness from none to all external examples and their impact on (a) accuracy and (b) execution time in various 40 agents networks (results of `All-ext` from the last 3 graphs, omitted for scaling reason, are resp. 7600 ms, 25000 ms and 36000 ms).

We first observe that forgetting all external examples can get very costly in time when MAS have sparse structures with long distances. Partial forgetness can keep the learning computation time much lower. Both variants tend to improve accuracy at some time expense. Forgetting close examples is very layout dependent. If its threshold k is close to or greater than the network diameter, the protocol will behave like one forgetting of all external examples, time consuming but accurate. However a small k in networks with high diameter may have little difference with forgetting nothing. We can see these two cases with the networks Wheel and Line. When forgetting odd-distance examples, accuracy varies less between layouts since every example learned once is kept in the immediate neighborhood independently of the diameter. Accuracy results of this criterion are among the best while the time cost remains much more reasonable.

5   Conclusion

In this article we have provided and experimented improvements of the collective learning protocol Waves. Two major issues have been addressed. Firstly, by associating to each hypothesis information about its trajectory and merging equivalent hypotheses we avoid useless processing. Secondly, we have shown that the eventual lack of diversity in the agent memories may be tackled by allowing agents to forget part of the observations they have memorized. We provided a reliable scheme for such a forgetting process, and the emerging accuracy increase observed in previous protocols is then preserved with little additional cost. Still, there is lot to do to obtain a protocol that may be applied to more realistic problems. A collective learning approach with autonomous agents interacting with their neighbors is prominently interesting when the community is composed of many agents. Then, fully preserving the MAS-consistency guarantees leads to exchanging a lot of hypotheses and observations and there is a clear need to find a trade-off between (i) the proportion of observations present in the whole community with which an agent hypothesis is consistent and (ii) the cost of maintaining such a consistency guarantee. In a further work we will investigate this in large communities.

References

1. Bourgne, G., Soldano, H., El Fallah Seghrouchni, A.: Learning better together. In: Coelho, H., Studer, R., Wooldridge, M. (eds.) Proceedings of ECAI, vol. 215, pp. 85–90. IOS Press (2010)
2. Dolev, S.: Self-Stabilization. MIT Press, Cambridge (2000)
3. Eberhart, R., Shi, Y., Kennedy, J.: Swarm Intelligence. The Morgan Kaufmann Series in Artificial Intelligence. Elsevier Science, Elsevier (2001)
4. Veillon, L.M., Bourgne, G., Soldano, H.: Waves: a model of collective learning. In: IEEE/WIC/ACM International Conference on Web Intelligence, pp. 314–321. IEEE Press (2017)
5. Watts, D.J., Strogatz, S.H.: Collective dynamics of 'small-world' networks. Nature 393(6684), 440–442 (1998)

Author Index

Printed in the United States
by Baker & Taylor Publisher Services